Twentieth-Century Literary Criticism

Guide to Gale Literary Criticism Series

When you need to review criticism of literary works, these are the Gale series to use:

If the author's death date is:	You should turn to:
After Dec. 31, 1959 (or author is still living)	*CONTEMPORARY LITERARY CRITICISM* for example: Jorge Luis Borges, Anthony Burgess, William Faulkner, Mary Gordon, Ernest Hemingway, Iris Murdoch
1900 through 1959	***TWENTIETH-CENTURY LITERARY CRITICISM*** for example: Willa Cather, F. Scott Fitzgerald, Henry James, Mark Twain, Virginia Woolf
1800 through 1899	***NINETEENTH-CENTURY LITERATURE CRITICISM*** for example: Fedor Dostoevski, George Sand, Gerard Manley Hopkins, Emily Dickinson
1400 through 1799	***LITERATURE CRITICISM FROM 1400 TO 1800 (excluding Shakespeare)*** for example: Anne Bradstreet, Pierre Corneille, Daniel Defoe, Alexander Pope, Jonathan Swift, Phillis Wheatley
	SHAKESPEAREAN CRITICISM Shakespeare's plays and poetry
Antiquity through 1399	***CLASSICAL AND MEDIEVAL LITERATURE CRITICISM*** for example: Dante, Homer, Plato, Sophocles, Vergil, the Beowulf poet *(Volume 1 forthcoming)*

Gale also publishes related criticism series:

CHILDREN'S LITERATURE REVIEW

This ongoing series covers authors of all eras. Presents criticism on authors and author/illustrators who write for the preschool to junior-high audience.

CONTEMPORARY ISSUES CRITICISM

This two-volume set presents criticism on contemporary authors writing on current issues. Topics covered include the social sciences, philosophy, economics, natural science, law, and related areas.

ISSN 0276-8178

Volume 18

Twentieth-Century Literary Criticism

Excerpts from Criticism of the Works of Novelists, Poets, Playwrights, Short Story Writers, and Other Creative Writers Who Died between 1900 and 1960, from the First Published Critical Appraisals to Current Evaluations

Dennis Poupard
James E. Person, Jr.
Editors

Marie Lazzari
Thomas Ligotti
Associate Editors

Gale Research Company
Book Tower
Detroit, Michigan 48226

STAFF

Library of Congress Catalog Card Number 76-46132
ISBN 0-8103-2400-8
ISSN 0276-8178

Computerized photocomposition by
Typographics, Incorporated
Kansas City, Missouri

Printed in the United States

Contents

Preface

It is impossible to overvalue the importance of literature in the intellectual, emotional, and spiritual evolution of humanity. Literature is that which both lifts us out of everyday life and helps us to better understand it. Through the fictive lives of such characters as Anna Karenina, Jay Gatsby, or Leopold Bloom, our perceptions of the human condition are enlarged, and we are enriched.

Literary criticism can also give us insight into the human condition, as well as into the specific moral and intellectual atmosphere of an era, for the criteria by which a work of art is judged reflects contemporary philosophical and social attitudes. Literary criticism takes many forms: the traditional essay, the book or play review, even the parodic poem. Criticism can also be of several types: normative, descriptive, interpretive, textual, appreciative, generic. Collectively, the range of critical response helps us to understand a work of art, an author, an era.

Scope of the Series

Twentieth-Century Literary Criticism (TCLC) is designed to serve as an introduction for the student of twentieth-century literature to the authors of the period 1900 to 1960 and to the most significant commentators on these authors. The great poets, novelists, short story writers, playwrights, and philosophers of this period are by far the most popular writers for study in high school and college literature courses. Since a vast amount of relevant critical material confronts the student, *TCLC* presents significant passages from the most important published criticism to aid students in the location and selection of criticism on authors who died between 1900 and 1960.

The need for *TCLC* was suggested by the usefulness of the Gale series *Contemporary Literary Criticism (CLC),* which excerpts criticism on current writing. Because of the difference in time span under consideration *(CLC* considers authors who were still living after 1959), there is no duplication of material between *CLC* and *TCLC.* For further information about *CLC* and Gale's other criticism series, users should consult the Guide to Gale Literary Criticism Series preceding the title page in this volume.

Each volume of *TCLC* is carefully compiled to include authors who represent a variety of genres and nationalities and who are currently regarded as the most important writers of this era. In addition to major authors, *TCLC* also presents criticism on lesser-known writers whose significant contributions to literary history are important to the study of twentieth-century literature.

Each author entry in *TCLC* is intended to provide an overview of major criticism on an author. Therefore, the editors include approximately twenty authors in each 600-page volume (compared with approximately fifty authors in a *CLC* volume of similar size) so that more attention may be given to an author. Each author entry represents a historical survey of the critical response to that author's work: some early criticism is presented to indicate initial reactions, later criticism is selected to represent any rise or decline in the author's reputation, and current retrospective analyses provide students with a modern view. The length of an author entry is intended to reflect the amount of critical attention the author has received from critics writing in English, and from foreign criticism in translation. Critical articles and books that have not been translated into English are excluded. Every attempt has been made to identify and include excerpts from the seminal essays on each author's work. Additionally, as space permits, especially insightful essays of a more limited scope are included.

An author may appear more than once in the series because of the great quantity of critical material available, or because of a resurgence of criticism generated by events such as an author's centennial or anniversary celebration, the republication of an author's works, or the publication of a newly translated work or volume of letters. Generally, a few author entries in each volume of *TCLC* feature criticism on single works by major authors who have appeared previously in the series. Only those individual works that have been the subjects of vast amounts of criticism and are widely studied in literature classes are selected for this in-depth treatment. Thomas Hardy's *Tess of the d'Urbervilles* is the subject of such an entry in *TCLC,* Volume 18.

Organization of the Book

An author entry consists of the following elements: author heading, biographical and critical introduction, principal works, excerpts of criticism (each followed by a bibliographical citation), and an additional bibliography for further reading.

- The *author heading* consists of the author's full name, followed by birth and death dates. The unbracketed portion of the name denotes the form under which the author most commonly wrote. If an author wrote consistently under a pseudonym, the pseudonym will be listed in the author heading and the real name given in parentheses on the first line of the biographical and critical introduction. Also located at the beginning of the introduction to the author entry are any name variations under which an author wrote, including transliterated forms for authors whose languages use nonroman alphabets. Uncertainty as to a birth or death date is indicated by a question mark.

- The *biographical and critical introduction* contains background information designed to introduce the reader to an author and to the critical debate surrounding his or her work. Parenthetical material following many of the introductions provides references to biographical and critical reference series published by Gale, including *Children's Literature Review, Contemporary Authors, Dictionary of Literary Biography, Something about the Author,* and past volumes of *TCLC.*

- Most *TCLC* entries include *portraits* of the author. Many entries also contain illustrations of materials pertinent to an author's career, including holographs of manuscript pages, title pages, dust jackets, letters, or representations of important people, places, and events in an author's life.

- The *list of principal works* is chronological by date of first book publication and identifies the genre of each work. In the case of foreign authors where there are both foreign language publications and English translations, the title and date of the first English-language edition are given in brackets. Unless otherwise indicated, dramas are dated by first performance, not first publication.

- *Criticism* is arranged chronologically in each author entry to provide a useful perspective on changes in critical evaluation over the years. All titles by the author featured in the critical entry are printed in boldface type to enable the user to ascertain without difficulty the works being discussed. Also for purposes of easier identification, the critic's name and the publication date of the essay are given at the beginning of each piece of criticism. Unsigned criticism is preceded by the title of the journal in which it appeared. When an anonymous essay is later attributed to a critic, the critic's name appears in brackets at the beginning of the excerpt and in the bibliographical citation.

- Critical essays are prefaced by *explanatory notes* as an additional aid to students using *TCLC.* The explanatory notes provide several types of useful information, including: the reputation of a critic; the importance of a work of criticism; the specific type of criticism (biographical, psychoanalytic, structuralist, etc.); a synopsis of the criticism; and the growth of critical controversy or changes in critical trends regarding an author's work. In many cases, these notes cross-reference the work of critics who agree or disagree with each other. Dates in parentheses within the explanatory notes refer to a book publication date when they follow a book title and to an essay date when they follow a critic's name.

- A complete *bibliographical citation* designed to facilitate location of the original essay or book by the interested reader follows each piece of criticism. An asterisk (*) at the end of a citation indicates that the essay is on more than one author.

- The *additional bibliography* appearing at the end of each author entry suggests further reading on the author. In some cases it includes essays for which the editors could not obtain reprint rights. An asterisk (*) at the end of a citation indicates that the essay is on more than one author.

An appendix lists the sources from which material in each volume has been reprinted. It does not, however, list every book or periodical consulted in the preparation of the volume.

Cumulative Indexes

Each volume of *TCLC* includes a cumulative index to authors listing all the authors who have appeared in *Contemporary Literary Criticism, Twentieth-Century Literary Criticism, Nineteenth-Century Literature Criticism,* and *Literature Criticism from 1400 to 1800,* along with cross-references to the Gale series *Children's Literature Review, Authors in the News, Contemporary Authors, Contemporary Authors Autobiography Series, Dictionary of Literary Biography, Something about the Author,* and *Yesterday's Authors of Books for Children.* Users will welcome this cumulated author index as a useful tool for locating an author within the various series. The index, which lists birth and death dates when available, will be particularly valuable for those authors who are identified with a certain period but whose death date causes them to be placed in another, or for those authors whose careers span two periods. For example, F. Scott Fitzgerald is found in *TCLC,* yet a writer often associated with him, Ernest Hemingway, is found in *CLC.*

Each volume of *TCLC* also includes a cumulative nationality index. Author names are arranged alphabetically under their respective nationalities and followed by the volume numbers in which they appear.

A cumulative index to critics is another useful feature in *TCLC*. Under each critic's name are listed the authors on whom the critic has written and the volume and page where the criticism may be found.

Acknowledgments

No work of this scope can be accomplished without the cooperation of many people. The editors especially wish to thank the copyright holders of the excerpted criticism included in this volume, the permissions managers of many book and magazine publishing companies for assisting us in securing reprint rights, and Anthony Bogucki for assistance with copyright research. We are also grateful to the staffs of the Detroit Public Library, the Library of Congress, University of Detroit Library, University of Michigan Library, and Wayne State University Library for making their resources available to us.

Suggestions Are Welcome

In response to various suggestions, several features have been added to *TCLC* since the series began, including: explanatory notes to excerpted criticism that provide important information regarding critics and their work; a cumulative author index listing authors in all Gale literary criticism series; entries devoted to criticism on a single work by a major author; and more extensive illustrations.

Readers who wish to suggest authors to appear in future volumes, or who have other suggestions, are cordially invited to write the editors.

Authors to Be Featured in *TCLC,* Volumes 19 and 20

James Agee (American novelist and journalist)—Agee's *Let Us Now Praise Famous Men* and *A Death in the Family* are harshly realistic treatments of the moral crises and moral triumphs of mid-twentieth-century America. In addition, Agee's film criticism is recognized as the first serious consideration in English of film as a modern art form.

Arnold Bennett (English novelist)—Bennett is credited with introducing techniques of European Naturalism to the English novel. Set in the manufacturing district of the author's native Staffordshire, Bennett's novels tell of the thwarted ambitions of those who endure a dull, provincial existence.

Hermann Broch (Austrian novelist, poet, and essayist)—Broch was a philosophical novelist whose works are considered profound reflections upon the social and moral disintegration of modern Europe. His major works, which include his masterpiece *The Sleepwalkers,* have been compared to James Joyce's *Ulysses* and *Finnegans Wake* for their contribution to the Modernist exploration of language.

Jacques Futrelle (American novelist and short story writer)—Futrelle was the author of detective stories featuring Professor S. F. X. Van Dusen, also known as the Thinking Machine. A detective who utilized the classic deductive method pioneered by Arthur Conan Doyle's legendary detective Sherlock Holmes, the Thinking Machine is considered one of the most brilliant and bizarre heroes in the field of detective fiction.

Robert Cunninghame Graham (Scottish fiction writer, travel writer, and historian)—Called "the most singular of English writers" by the novelist W. H. Hudson, Cunninghame Graham was a world traveler, a socialist member of Parliament, and a friend of such authors as Joseph Conrad and George Bernard Shaw. Cunninghame Graham's works, both fiction and nonfiction, are based on the often dramatic experiences of his life.

John Gray (English poet and fiction writer)—Reputed to be the model for the title character of Oscar Wilde's *The Picture of Dorian Gray,* Gray is best known for his poetry collection *Silverpoints,* which is often considered one of the high-points of Decadent verse during the 1890s. His futuristic novel *Park: A Fantastic Story* has recently been reissued.

O. Henry (American short story writer)—O. Henry (William Sydney Porter) was one of America's most popular short story writers. His stories, known for their inventiveness and characteristic surprise endings, are widely anthologized and often compared to the works of Guy de Maupassant.

Julia Ward Howe (American poet and biographer)—A famous suffragette and social reformer, Howe was also a popular poet who is best known as the composer of "The Battle Hymn of the Republic."

T. E. Hulme (English poet)—A major influence on the work of T. S. Eliot, Ezra Pound, and other important twentieth-century poets, Hulme was the chief theorist of Imagism and Modernism in English poetry.

James Weldon Johnson (American novelist and poet)—One of the most prominent black public figures of his time, Johnson is also regarded as the principal forerunner of the Harlem Renaissance. His novel *The Autobiography of an Ex-Colored Man* was one of the first works of fiction to explore the complexity of race relations in America and profoundly influenced such writers as Ralph Ellison and Richard Wright.

Lionel Johnson (English poet and critic)—Johnson is considered one of the most important figures associated with the Decadent and Aesthetic movements of the 1890s. Like many of his contemporaries, he lived an eccentric life and died young, producing a small but distinguished body of works that reflect his most personal preoccupations while also representing many of the typical concerns of his generation.

Sheila Kaye-Smith (English novelist)—Kaye-Smith is best known for her novels of the Sussex countryside. Often compared to Thomas Hardy's Wessex novels, the works of Kaye-Smith also portray strong-willed male and female characters who demonstrate the natural vitality of an agrarian way of life.

Ludwig Lewisohn (American novelist and critic)—An important man of letters during the first quarter of the twentieth century, Lewisohn made a notable contribution to modern literature through his critical writings and his translations from German and French literature. Many of Lewisohn's later works of fiction and nonfiction reflect his concern for the plight of European Jews during the 1930s and 1940s.

Horacio Quiroga (Uruguayan short story writer)—Represented in English translation by the recently published *Decapitated Chicken, and Other Stories,* Quiroga's tales of death and madness in the jungles of South America reflect the influence of Edgar Allan Poe as well as the sensational tragedies of Quiroga's own life.

Rainer Maria Rilke (German poet and novelist)—Rilke's *The Notebooks of Malte Laurids Brigge,* a loosely autobiographical novel that explores the angst-ridden life of a hypersensitive man in Paris, is considered the author's most accomplished prose work. To mark a new translation of this novel, *TCLC* will devote an entire entry to critical discussion of this important work.

Jacques Roumain (Haitian novelist, poet, and essayist)—One of the most militant and influential Haitian intellectuals of this century, Roumain was the author of the novel *Masters of the Dew,* which was widely praised for its haunting stylistic beauty as well as its powerful social message.

Raymond Roussel (French novelist and dramatist)—Roussel was a wealthy eccentric who staged expensive but entirely unsuccessful productions of his own plays and published elaborate but ignored editions of his novels. He was claimed as a forerunner by the Surrealists for the extravagant and often shocking imagination demonstrated in his works and is today recognized as one of the oddest and most ingenious authors in modern literature.

John Ruskin (English critic)—Most renowned for his critical writings on art and architecture, particularly *Stones of Venice* and the five-volume series *Modern Painters*, Ruskin was also an important social critic. His advocacy of various reforms and his association with the Pre-Raphaelite circle of artists, writers, and thinkers place him at the intellectual and cultural center of Victorian England.

Lincoln Steffens (American journalist and autobiographer)—Steffens was one of a group of writers in the early twentieth century who were described as "muckrakers" by President Theodore Roosevelt. Steffens's call for radical reforms in American government and society forms the substance of his best works, including *The Shame of the Cities* and *The Struggle for Self Government*, and serves as the background to his highly readable *Autobiography*.

Mark Twain (American novelist)—Twain is considered by many to be the father of modern American literature. Breaking with the genteel literary conventions of the nineteenth century, Twain endowed his characters and narratives with the natural speech patterns of the common person and wrote about subjects hitherto believed beneath the consideration of serious art. He is renowned throughout the world for his greatest novel, *Huckleberry Finn*. *TCLC* will devote an entry solely to critical discussion of that controversial work. Included will be works of criticism written from the late nineteenth century through 1985, the centenary year of *Huckleberry Finn's* American publication and the one hundred-fiftieth anniversary of Twain's birth.

Beatrice and Sydney James Webb (English social writers)—Prominent members of the progressive Fabian society, the Webbs wrote sociological works significant to the advent of socialist reform in England and influenced the work of several major authors, including H. G. Wells and George Bernard Shaw.

H. G. Wells (English novelist)—Wells is best known today as one of the forerunners of modern science fiction and as a utopian idealist who foretold an era of chemical warfare, atomic weaponry, and world wars. *The Time Machine*, *The Invisible Man*, *The War of the Worlds*, *The Island of Doctor Moreau*, and several other works among Wells's canon are considered classics in the genres of science fiction and science fantasy. *TCLC* will devote an entire entry to Wells's accomplishments as a science fiction writer.

Owen Wister (American novelist)—Considered the founder of modern fiction about the Old West, Wister is best known as the author of *The Virginian*, a novel that established the basic character types, settings, and plots of the Western genre.

Virginia Woolf (English novelist)—Woolf is one of the most important English novelists of the twentieth century. *Mrs. Dalloway* is perhaps the most frequently studied of her novels and a landmark work in the history of modern fiction for its use of the literary device known as stream of consciousness. *TCLC* will devote an entire entry to this important work.

Emile Zola (French novelist, dramatist, and critic)—Zola was the founder and principal theorist of Naturalism, perhaps the most influential literary movement in modern literature. His twenty-volume series *Les Rougon-Macquart* is one of the monuments of Naturalist fiction, and served as a model for late nineteenth-century novelists seeking a more candid and accurate representation of human life.

Additional Authors to Appear in Future Volumes

Abbey, Henry 1842-1911
Abercrombie, Lascelles 1881-1938
Adamic, Louis 1898-1951
Ade, George 1866-1944
Agustini, Delmira 1886-1914
Akers, Elizabeth Chase 1832-1911
Akiko, Yosano 1878-1942
Aldanov, Mark 1886-1957
Aldrich, Thomas Bailey 1836-1907
Aliyu, Dan Sidi 1902-1920
Allen, Hervey 1889-1949
Archer, William 1856-1924
Arlen, Michael 1895-1956
Austin, Alfred 1835-1913
Austin, Mary 1868-1934
Bahr, Hermann 1863-1934
Bailey, Philip James 1816-1902
Barbour, Ralph Henry 1870-1944
Barreto, Lima 1881-1922
Benét, William Rose 1886-1950
Benjamin, Walter 1892-1940
Bennett, James Gordon, Jr. 1841-1918
Benson, E(dward) F(rederic) 1867-1940
Berdyaev, Nikolai Aleksandrovich 1874-1948
Beresford, J(ohn) D(avys) 1873-1947
Bergson, Henri 1859-1941
Binyon, Laurence 1869-1943
Bishop, John Peale 1892-1944
Blackmore, R(ichard) D(oddridge) 1825-1900
Blake, Lillie Devereux 1835-1913
Blum, Leon 1872-1950
Bodenheim, Maxwell 1892-1954
Bosschere, Jean de 1878-1953
Bowen, Marjorie 1886-1952
Byrne, Donn 1889-1928
Caine, Hall 1853-1931
Campana, Dino 1885-1932
Cannan, Gilbert 1884-1955
Chand, Prem 1880-1936
Churchill, Winston 1871-1947
Coppée, Francois 1842-1908
Corelli, Marie 1855-1924
Croce, Benedetto 1866-1952
Crofts, Freeman Wills 1879-1957
Crothers, Rachel 1878-1958
Cruze, James (Jens Cruz Bosen) 1884-1942
Curros, Enriquez Manuel 1851-1908
Dall, Caroline Wells (Healy) 1822-1912
Daudet, Leon 1867-1942
Davidson, John 1857-1909
Day, Clarence 1874-1935
Delafield, E.M. (Edme Elizabeth Monica de la Pasture) 1890-1943
Deneson, Jacob 1836-1919
DeVoto, Bernard 1897-1955
Douglas, (George) Norman 1868-1952
Douglas, Lloyd C(assel) 1877-1951
Dovzhenko, Alexander 1894-1956
Drinkwater, John 1882-1937
Drummond, W.H. 1854-1907
Durkheim, Emile 1858-1917
Duun, Olav 1876-1939
Eaton, Walter Prichard 1878-1957
Eggleston, Edward 1837-1902
Erskine, John 1879-1951
Fadeyev, Alexander 1901-1956
Ferland, Albert 1872-1943
Feydeau, Georges 1862-1921
Field, Rachel 1894-1924
Flecker, James Elroy 1884-1915
Fletcher, John Gould 1886-1950
Fogazzaro, Antonio 1842-1911
Francos, Karl Emil 1848-1904
Frank, Bruno 1886-1945
Frazer, (Sir) George 1854-1941
Freeman, R. Austin 1862-1943
Freud, Sigmund 1853-1939
Froding, Gustaf 1860-1911
Fuller, Henry Blake 1857-1929
Futabatei, Shimei 1864-1909
Gladkov, Fydor Vasilyevich 1883-1958
Glaspell, Susan 1876-1948
Glyn, Elinor 1864-1943
Golding, Louis 1895-1958
Gosse, Edmund 1849-1928
Gould, Gerald 1885-1936
Guest, Edgar 1881-1959
Gumilyov, Nikolay 1886-1921
Gyulai, Pal 1826-1909
Hale, Edward Everett 1822-1909
Hall, James 1887-1951
Harris, Frank 1856-1931
Hawthorne, Julian 1846-1934
Hernandez, Miguel 1910-1942
Hewlett, Maurice 1861-1923
Heyward, DuBose 1885-1940
Hilton, James 1900-1954
Hope, Anthony 1863-1933
Hudson, W(illiam) H(enry) 1841-1922
Huidobro, Vincente 1893-1948
Hviezdoslav (Pavol Orszagh) 1849-1921
Ilyas, Abu Shabaka 1903-1947
Imbs, Bravig 1904-1946
Ivanov, Vyacheslav Ivanovich 1866-1949
Jacobs, W(illiam) W(ymark) 1863-1943
James, Will 1892-1942
Jammes, Francis 1868-1938
Jerome, Jerome K(lapka) 1859-1927
Johnson, Fenton 1888-1958
Johnston, Mary 1870-1936
Jorgensen, Johannes 1866-1956
Khlebnikov, Victor 1885-1922
King, Grace 1851-1932
Kirby, William 1817-1906
Kline, Otis Albert 1891-1946
Kohut, Adolph 1848-1916
Korolenko, Vladimir 1853-1921
Kuzmin, Mikhail Alexseyevich 1875-1936
Lamm, Martin 1880-1950
Lawson, Henry 1867-1922
Ledwidge, Francis 1887-1917
Leipoldt, C. Louis 1880-1947
Lemonnier, Camille 1844-1913
Lima, Jorge De 1895-1953
Locke, Alain 1886-1954
Long, Frank Belknap 1903-1959
Louys, Pierre 1870-1925
Lucas, E(dward) V(errall) 1868-1938
Lyall, Edna 1857-1903
Maghar, Josef Suatopluk 1864-1945
Manning, Frederic 1887-1935
Maragall, Joan 1860-1911
Marais, Eugene 1871-1936
Martin du Gard, Roger 1881-1958
Masaryk, Tomas 1850-1939
McClellan, George Marion 1860-1934
McCoy, Horace 1897-1955
Meyrink, Gustave 1868-1932
Mirbeau, Octave 1850-1917
Mistral, Frederic 1830-1914
Molnar, Ferenc 1878-1952
Monro, Harold 1879-1932
Moore, Thomas Sturge 1870-1944
Morley, Christopher 1890-1957
Morley, S. Griswold 1883-1948
Mqhayi, S.E.K. 1875-1945
Murray, (George) Gilbert 1866-1957
Nansen, Peter 1861-1918
Nobre, Antonio 1867-1900
Nordhoff, Charles 1887-1947
Norris, Frank 1870-1902
Obstfelder, Sigborn 1866-1900
O'Dowd, Bernard 1866-1959
Ophuls, Max 1902-1957
Orczy, Baroness 1865-1947
Owen, Seaman 1861-1936
Page, Thomas Nelson 1853-1922
Papini, Giovanni 1881-1956
Parrington, Vernon L. 1871-1929
Peck, George W. 1840-1916
Péret, Benjamin 1899-1959
Phillips, Ulrich B. 1877-1934
Pickthall, Marjorie 1883-1922

Pinero, Arthur Wing 1855-1934
Pontoppidan, Henrik 1857-1943
Prem Chand, Mushi 1880-1936
Prévost, Marcel 1862-1941
Quiller-Couch, Arthur 1863-1944
Randall, James G. 1881-1953
Rappoport, Solomon 1863-1944
Read, Opie 1852-1939
Reisen (Reizen), Abraham 1875-1953
Remington, Frederic 1861-1909
Riley, James Whitcomb 1849-1916
Rinehart, Mary Roberts 1876-1958
Ring, Max 1817-1901
Rohmer, Sax 1883-1959
Rolland, Romain 1866-1944
Rozanov, Vasily Vasilyevich 1856-1919
Saar, Ferdinand von 1833-1906
Sabatini, Rafael 1875-1950
Saintsbury, George 1845-1933
Sakutaro, Hagiwara 1886-1942
Sanborn, Franklin Benjamin 1831-1917
Santayana, George 1863-1952
Sardou, Victorien 1831-1908
Schickele, René 1885-1940
Schwob, Marcel 1867-1905
Seabrook, William 1886-1945
Seton, Ernest Thompson 1860-1946
Shestov, Lev 1866-1938
Shiels, George 1886-1949
Skram, Bertha Amalie 1847-1905
Smith, Pauline 1883-1959
Sodergran, Edith Irene 1892-1923
Solovyov, Vladimir 1853-1900
Sorel, Georges 1847-1922
Spector, Mordechai 1859-1922
Spengler, Oswald 1880-1936
Squire, J(ohn) C(ollings) 1884-1958
Stavenhagen, Fritz 1876-1906
Stockton, Frank R. 1834-1902
Subrahmanya Bharati, C. 1882-1921
Sully-Prudhomme, Rene 1839-1907
Talev, Dimituv 1898-1966
Thoma, Ludwig 1867-1927
Trotsky, Leon 1870-1940
Tuchmann, Jules 1830-1901
Turner, W(alter) J(ames) R(edfern) 1889-1946
Vachell, Horace Annesley 1861-1955
Van Dine, S.S. (William H. Wright) 1888-1939
Van Dyke, Henry 1852-1933
Vazov, Ivan Minchov 1850-1921
Veblen, Thorstein 1857-1929
Villaespesa, Francisco 1877-1936
Wallace, Edgar 1874-1932
Wallace, Lewis 1827-1905
Walsh, Ernest 1895-1926
Webb, Mary 1881-1927
Webster, Jean 1876-1916
Whitlock, Brand 1869-1927
Wilson, Harry Leon 1867-1939
Wolf, Emma 1865-1932
Wood, Clement 1888-1950
Wren, P(ercival) C(hristopher) 1885-1941
Yonge, Charlotte Mary 1823-1901
Zecca, Ferdinand 1864-1947
Zeromski, Stefan 1864-1925

Readers are cordially invited to suggest additional authors to the editors.

(Joseph) Hilaire (Pierre Sébastien Réné Swanton) Belloc

1870-1953

French-born English poet, essayist, travel writer, biographer, critic, historian, journalist, and novelist.

The Granger Collection, New York

Belloc is considered one of the most controversial and accomplished men of letters of early twentieth-century England. An author whose writings continue to draw either the deep admiration or bitter contempt of readers, he was an outspoken proponent of radical social and economic reforms, all grounded in his vision of Europe as a "Catholic society." Although many critics have attacked Belloc's prescriptive polemical works for their tone of truculence and intolerance—and, especially, for recurrent elements of anti-Semitism—they have also joined in praise of his humor and poetic skill, hailing Belloc as the greatest English writer of light verse since Lewis Carroll and Edward Lear.

The son of a wealthy French father and English mother, Belloc was born in La Celle St. Cloud, France, a few days before the Franco-Prussian War broke out. The family fled to England at the news of the French army's collapse, returning after the war's end to discover that the Belloc home had been looted and vandalized by Prussian soldiers. Although the estate was eventually restored and made habitable, the evidence of destruction witnessed by Belloc's parents and later recounted to their children made a deep impression on Hilaire; throughout his life and through the two world wars, he habitually referred to Germany as "Prussia" and considered the "Prussians" a barbaric people worthy only of utter contempt. After the death of Belloc's father in 1872, the family again took up residence in England, where Belloc was raised and received a Catholic education, notably at Cardinal John Henry Newman's Oratory School near Birmingham, where he won many academic prizes and came to the attention of Newman himself. From his numerous travels between England and France, Belloc acquired a deep interest in history, polemics, and world literature. After serving for a year in a French artillery unit (he retained his French citizenship until 1902), Belloc continued his studies at Balliol College, Oxford, where he gained a reputation as a brilliant student, a skilled debater, and an aggressively outspoken champion of Roman Catholicism. Prejudice against Belloc's Catholicism led to his being rejected in his bid for a history fellowship, an experience that intensely embittered him. Through this rejection Belloc came to hate university dons in general, later directing many satiric attacks against them, portraying them as the smug, pretentious defenders of privilege. Years after his disappointment at Oxford, at the age of sixty-six Belloc wrote: "Oxford is for me a shrine, a memory, a tomb, and a poignant possessing grief. All would have been well if they would have received me."

By the mid-1890s Belloc had married and, through the influence of his sister Marie Belloc Lowndes, begun writing for various London newspapers and magazines. His first book, *Verses and Sonnets,* appeared in 1896, followed by *The Bad Child's Book of Beasts,* which satirized moralistic verse for children and proved immensely popular. Illustrated with superb complementary effect by Belloc's friend Basil T. Blackwood, *The Bad Child's Book of Beasts,* according to critics, contains much of the author's best light verse, as do such later collections as *More Beasts (for Worse Children), The Modern Traveller,* and *Cautionary Tales for Children.* An impulsive man who seldom lived in any one place for more than a few weeks and whose frequent trips to the continent proved a constant drain on his financial resources, Belloc welcomed the popular success of his verse collections. But, embracing Cardinal Edward Henry Manning's dictum that "all human conflict is ultimately theological," he perceived his primary role as that of polemicist and reformer, whose every work must reflect his desire for Europe's spiritual, social, and political return to its monarchist, Catholic heritage. Belloc's career as an advocate of Catholicism first attracted wide public attention in 1902 with *The Path to Rome,* perhaps his most famous single book, in which he recorded the thoughts and impressions that came to him during a walking trip through France and Italy to Rome. In addition to its infusion of Catholic thought, the work contains what later became acknowledged as typically Bellocian elements: rich, earthy humor; an eye for natural beauty; and a meditative spirit—all of which appear in the author's later travel books, which include *Esto Perpetua, The Four Men,* and *The Cruise of the "Nona."*

The period between the century's turn and the mid-1920s was the time of Belloc's widest fame and influence. Throughout these years Belloc's name and reputation were frequently linked in the public mind with G. K. Chesterton, whom Belloc had met around 1900 when each was a contributor to the radical journal the *Speaker*. In Chesterton, Belloc found a talented illustrator of his books, a friend, and a man who shared and publicly advocated many of his own religious and political views. Anti-industrial and antimodern in much of their advocacy, the two were jointly caricatured in print by George Bernard Shaw as "the Chesterbelloc," an absurd pantomime beast of elephantine appearance and outmoded beliefs. Both, according to Shaw and other adverse critics, had a passion for lost causes. Belloc and Chesterton were "Little Englanders"—opposed to British colonialism and imperialism—whose essays in the *Speaker* had infuriated many Londoners by the authors' opposition to Britain's imperial designs on South Africa and the nation's participation in the Boer War. Each looked to the Middle Ages as an era of spiritual and material fulfillment when Europe was united in Catholicism and small landowners worked their own, Church-allotted parcels of property, providing for their own individual needs, free from both the wage-slavery that later developed under capitalism and the confiscatory taxation and collectivist policies of state socialism. (Belloc in particular, after serving for several years as a Liberal M.P. in the House of Commons, held a cynical view of the modern British political system, seeing little difference in the methods of the government's Liberal and Conservative ministers, who were often, to his disgust, fellow clubmen and the closest of friends outside the halls of Parliament.) As an alternative both to capitalism and to the Fabian socialism advanced by such contemporaries as Shaw, H. G. Wells, and Beatrice and Sidney Webb, Belloc propounded an economic and political program called Distributism, a system of small landholding which harks back to Europe's pre-Reformation history. This system was outlined in the 1891 Papal Encyclical *Rerum Novarum,* and is fully described in Belloc's controversial essay *The Servile State,* published in 1912. In this work, which attacks both capitalism (which produces the "servile state" of wage-slavery) and socialism, Belloc called for a return to familial self-sufficiency through the widespread restoration of private property; according to his prescription, which has been described by many critics as at best quaint, and at worst ridiculously impractical, every family should own three acres and a cow. "The fundamental position of *The Servile State,*" A. N. Wilson has explained, "is this; that an Irish peasant who earns almost no money but owns his own land, burns his own peat, grows his own potatoes and milks his own cow is a freer creature than a clerk or factory hand who might earn ten times more money, but is compelled to work for someone else, and to live in a rented or leased house, and to be dependent on shopkeepers for his sustenance."

The Chesterbelloc's political ideas were also expounded in the *Eye Witness,* a weekly political and literary journal edited by Belloc, which became one of the most widely read periodicals in pre-war England. Belloc attracted as contributors such distinguished authors as Shaw, Wells, Maurice Baring, and Sir Arthur Quiller-Couch. In addition, he and his subeditor, Cecil Chesterton, involved the *Eye Witness* in a political uproar in 1912 when they uncovered the Marconi Scandal, in which several prominent government officials used confidential information concerning impending international business contracts in order to speculate in the stock of the Marconi Wireless Telegraph Company. Although Belloc continued to contribute articles and occasionally edit the periodical, the *Eye Witness* eventually passed to Cecil Chesterton's editorship as the *New Witness,* which, after Cecil's death in World War I, came under his brother's supervision, becoming in 1925 *G. K.'s Weekly,* the principal organ of the Distributist League. By then, Belloc had established himself as a polemicist who could write forceful and convincing essays on nearly any subject, in a prose style marked by clarity and wit. His reputation as a polemicist reached its zenith in 1926 when, in *A Companion to Mr. Wells's "Outline of History,"* he attacked his longtime opponent's popular book as a simpleminded, nonscientific, anti-Catholic document. A war of mutual refutation ensued, fought by both writers in the pages of several books and essays. Ironically, although much of the scientific community now affirms Wells's biological theses as presented in the *Outline,* during the 1920s the preponderance of evidence supported the findings of Belloc, who, in the minds of some observers, bested Wells in their exchange of polemical broadsides.

But his exchange with Wells was Belloc's last major triumph as a man of letters, as throughout the 1920s and 1930s his own ideas were increasingly brushed aside by a public uninterested in seeing Britain return to Catholic values and medieval social structures. Further, in light of the rise to power of Adolf Hitler and Benito Mussolini in Europe, a growing number of readers were offended by Belloc's casual use of anti-Semitic remarks in his works and his view of Mussolini as one of Europe's great warrior-kings reborn. In 1936, with Chesterton ill and near death and with Belloc performing much of the editorial work for *G. K.'s Weekly,* the periodical became one of the very few English journals of opinion to applaud Fascist Italy's one-sided military victory over Abyssinia (Ethiopia)—an editorial position which further tarred Belloc's reputation. Embittered that his opinions were no longer taken seriously and that his creative gifts were diminishing, Belloc spent the last years of his career writing histories and biographies, which have been described by Wilfrid Sheed as "a ream of unsound, unresearched history books blatantly taking the Catholic side of everything." In the early 1940s, after authoring over 150 books, Belloc was forced into retirement by age and a series of strokes. He spent the last ten years of his life in quiet retirement at his longtime home in rural Sussex, King's Land, dying in 1953.

Recent biographical and critical studies have revealed Belloc to be a much more complex and intriguing figure than the predictable, anti-Semitic crank portrayed by critics during his lifetime and the years immediately following. As a man, and particularly as a polemicist, he fought tenaciously to uphold his own conceptions of truth; as Michael H. Markel has described Belloc and his polemical style: "He was never modulated, restrained and understated. When he chose an enemy, he fought completely, with all the weapons he could find. Until the enemy was not only disarmed but conquered, Belloc pressed the attack." He held strong passions and strong hatreds, being at once a monarchist and an ardent admirer of the French Revolution in all its excesses, an insistent Catholic apologist and a man who could refer to Jesus as "a milksop" and the Bible as "a pack of lies," a man who expressed sympathy for Europe's Jews and outrage over the Holocaust, yet sprinkled his correspondence and published works with derisive references to "the Yids." As for this last matter, Belloc's reputation as an anti-Semitic hatemonger rests largely upon his book *The Jews,* published in 1922. In this work, Belloc warned that there existed in post-World War I Europe a "Jewish problem"—tension and mistrust between the Jewish minority and the suspicious, predominantly Gentile population—and that to ignore this tension would lead to an anti-Semitic persecution such as the world had never seen. But to even acknowledge that such tensions existed was itself considered an act of bigotry, and *The Jews,* then as now, went largely unread, being generally perceived as an anti-Semitic work. Although he admired Mussolini, Belloc detested Hitler, particularly the German's anti-Jewish ravings, and he was outspoken with anger and pity when his prophecy from *The Jews* began to come true within his lifetime. But even though he condemned persecution of Jews, he remained to the last a man who considered Jews "Christ-killers" and shylocks. To Belloc, Jews were altogether too prominent in the world of international finance, maintaining capitalism and industrialism through loans and investments, and thereby extending the "servile state." Capitalism was, to Belloc, itself an outgrowth of Protestantism, which had originated in "Prussia," usurped Church authority during the Middle Ages, given the peasants' Church-allocated land to the wealthy aristocracy, and driven the peasants themselves off the land and into wage-slavery under their new, rich rulers. Among the most scurrilous of Britain's Protestants were university dons, who, according to Belloc, trained the young to embrace the capitalist system, with its inherent need for cheap labor and easily obtained raw materials (hence its need for imperialistic colonialism), the success of which further enriched and entrenched the Jews in their positions of financial power. To replace capitalism and restore the power of Rome as the guiding force in Europe was Belloc's dream, for, as he wrote in his *Europe and the Faith,* "Europe will return to the Faith or she will perish. The Faith is Europe. And Europe is the Faith." A. N. Wilson has written of Belloc: "All his political standpoints sprang from his conviction that the Incarnate Christ had founded a Church, and that it was by divine providence that this Church had been established in the heart of the old Roman Empire. 'The Faith is Europe and Europe is the Faith.' From this conviction sprang, on the one hand his incredibly *naif* notion that Mussolini was a model of ancient imperial virtues; on the other, his detestation of the materialism of capitalists and bolsheviks, and his yearning for a political system in which the dignity of the poor was recognised; in which they were neither as children in a socialist nursery, nor as cogs in a capitalist machine; but as souls made in God's image and likeness, who in a sane world would lead free and independent lives with property of their own."

While Belloc's political and social views have proven unpopular, critics have highly praised the author's light verse, with W. H. Auden going so far as to state of Belloc that "as a writer of Light Verse, he has few equals and no superiors." In his widely known cautionary verse for children, Belloc assumed the perspective of a ridiculously stuffy and pedantic adult lecturing children on the inevitable catastrophes that result from improper behavior. Among his outstanding verses of this type are "Maria Who Made Faces and a Deplorable Marriage," "Godolphin Horne, Who Was Cursed with the Sin of Pride, and Became a Bootblack," and "Algernon, Who Played with a Loaded Gun, and, on Missing his Sister, Was Reprimanded by His Father." "Unlike Lear and Carroll, whose strategy was to bridge the gulf between adults and children," Markel has written, "Belloc startled his readers by exaggerating that gulf. Belloc's view of children did not look backward to the Victorian nonsense poets, but forward to the films of W. C. Fields." Like his children's verse, Belloc's satiric and noncautionary light verse is characterized by its jaunty, heavily rhythmic cadences and by the author's keen sense of the absurd, as reflected in "East and West" and in "Lines to a Don," which skewers a "Remote and ineffectual Don / That dared attack my Chesterton." Garry Wills has written that Belloc's comic verse "is as good as Swift's, as disciplined and as savage, fueled with scorn and hatred for human pettiness, compromise, betrayal." In addition to writing light verse, Belloc also wrote many serious poems and sonnets, which are commonly concerned with the human struggle against the idea of mortality. Of these, "Heroic Song in Praise of Wine" and "The Prophet Lost in the Hills at Evening" are among the most acclaimed of his poems. "His themes," according to Evelyn Waugh, "are the stuff of common life as he knew it in a warmer age; strenuous male companionship, romantic love of woman, the sea, the seasons, the transience of earthly beauty, the unremitting benevolent watchfulness of Our Lady and the angels, the innocence of childhood, the absurdity of pedantry and ambition, the wickedness and stark danger of power. His diction and prosody are the fruit of classical schooling. He was a Christian Shropshire Lad and, by that enrichment, immeasurably [A. E.] Housman's superior."

Belloc wrote in every genre except drama, but, according to critics, achieved wide success in but two: poetry and the personal essay. While his novels and polemical writings are considered too tightly bound to obscure issues of the early twentieth century and are little read, his poetry, as well as *The Path to Rome* and *The Four Men,* continue to attract the interest of readers and critics. In addition, Belloc's small corpus of literary criticism is considered highly insightful. But overshadowing his literary accomplishments is the common perception of Belloc as a loud, intolerant bull of a writer whose strongly stated opinions not only tainted the thought of the otherwise genial G. K. Chesterton, but also contributed to the atmosphere of anti-Jewish hatred that culminated in the Holocaust. Some critics have noted the odd fact that while all of Belloc's writings are frequently examined for evidence of anti-Semitism, the works of Shaw, who praised Joseph Stalin's policies during the great purges of the 1930s, and Wells, who in *Anticipations* (1902) flatly proposed the extermination of any race or group that dared oppose the coming omnicompetent utopian technocracy, are read and critically treated without reference to their authors' excesses. Several critics have explained this discrepancy by pointing out that, in light of the Holocaust, many people today consider anti-Semitism an unforgiveable attitude, and that while many moderns have seen newsreel films of Nazi concentration camps, no one has seen so much as a photograph of a Soviet gulag. "Given Belloc's abrasive manner and peculiarities of thought," Robert Royal has concluded, "it is not surprising that he has failed to attract a larger audience. But many other authors of the same period—Shaw, for example—are still read in spite of their eccentricities. Belloc has clearly been neglected because of his sharp opposition to almost everything that has become part of the liberal modern world. The world will not care to read Belloc, but those who pick up his best books to savor his historical imagination, the overall keenness of his mind, and the simple force of his prose will need no other reason to return to him again and again."

(See also *TCLC,* Vol. 7; *Contemporary Authors,* Vol. 106; *Yesterday's Authors of Books for Children,* Vol. 1; and *Dictionary of Literary Biography,* Vol. 19: *British Poets, 1880-1914.*)

PRINCIPAL WORKS

The Bad Child's Book of Beasts (verse) 1896
Verses and Sonnets (poetry and verse) 1896
More Beasts—For Worse Children (verse) 1897
The Modern Traveller (verse) 1898
Danton (biography) 1899
Lambkin's Remains (fictional biography) 1900
Robespierre (biography) 1901

The Path to Rome (travel sketches) 1902
Caliban's Guide to Letters (essays) 1903
Avril (criticism) 1904
Emmanuel Burden (novel) 1904
Esto Perpetua (travel sketches) 1906
Hills and the Sea (travel sketches) 1906
Cautionary Tales for Children (verse) 1907
On Nothing (essays) 1908
Marie Antoinette (biography) 1909
On Everything (essays) 1909
Verses (poetry and verse) 1910
The French Revolution (history) 1911
More Peers (verse) 1911
The Four Men: A Farrago (travel sketches) 1912
The Servile State (essay) 1912
The Free Press (essay) 1918
Europe and the Faith (history) 1920
The Jews (essay) 1922
Sonnets and Verse (poetry and verse) 1923
The Cruise of the "Nona" (travel sketches) 1925
A Companion to Mr. Wells's "Outline of History" (essay) 1926
Mr. Belloc Still Objects to Mr. Wells's "Outline of History" (essay) 1926
Many Cities (travel sketches) 1928
Survivals and New Arrivals (essay) 1929
New Cautionary Tales (verse) 1930
Charles the First: King of England (biography) 1933
Milton (biography) 1935
The Battleground: Syria and Palestine, the Seedbed of Religion (history) 1936; also published as *The Battle Ground,* 1936
The Hedge and the Horse (novel) 1936
Selected Essays (essays) 1936
The Crisis of Civilization (essays) 1937; also published as *The Crisis of Our Civilization,* 1937
Cautionary Verses (verse) 1939
Elizabethan Commentary (history) 1942
The Verse of Hilaire Belloc (verse) 1954

THE SPECTATOR (essay date 1896)

[*In the following excerpt, an anonymous critic highly praises* The Bad Child's Book of Beasts.]

A very clever little book of rhymes and pictures professes to be **"The Bad Child's Book of Beasts,"** and comes nearer to Lear's wonderful nonsense pictures and verses than anything we have seen since, though it is not quite so gleefully extravagant, and the humour is of a rather different kind. But the idea of the book is evidently that a "so-called" bad child needs nothing but a little fun to make him "unnaturally good,"—which means, we take it, that the bad child and the good child are deviations from the happy mean to much the same extent, and that the bad child needs laughing into the happy mean as much as the good child needs laughing out of that severe and priggish moderation which used to be held up to the earlier generations of this century as a model for their imitation in such books as "Sanford and Merton." The anonymous author of **"The Bad Child's Book of Beasts"** professes,—

The moral of this priceless work,
  If rightly understood,
Will make you—from a little Turk
  Unnaturally good.

That is, it will take the bad child through the other extreme before it brings him to the *juste milieu.* And we infer that the unnaturally good child will need to undergo a similar discipline to make him aware of "the falsehood of extremes" by betraying him into the wild and wayward demeanour which seems to find its climax in the supreme vice of never brushing his hair:—

Do not as evil children do
Who on the slightest grounds
Will imitate the Kangaroo
With wild unmeaning bounds.

Who take their manners from the Ape
  Their habits from the Bear,
Indulge the loud unseemly jape,
  And never brush their hair.

The bad child, therefore, is made to appreciate carefully those habits and manners in the world of beasts which are hardly fit for juvenile imitation or aspiration. . . . The only beast which comes in for any warm praise is the yak, which is set up as an example of benignant docility to the wild little boys who "will not brush their hair." The yak is tame, the yak is laborious, the yak will allow itself to be led about by a string, which is not true of any wild little boy, and the yak has a placid face and long silky hair. What could be a better companion for a mischievous little boy than this Harry Sandford among the beasts? Surely, too, the yak might be made a warning to the good little boy of what he may come to if he is too tame and teachable, as Harry Sandford has long been a warning to the children of the Edgeworthian régime. We see no reason at all why **"The Bad Child's Book of Beasts"** should not be "The Good Child's Book of Beasts" too. Only the bright example for the bad child should be the serious warning for the good child against being too tame and too amenable. (pp. 931-32)

And the child who is full of the self-importance of knowing rather more, and learning rather more rapidly, than his schoolfellows, is far more easily laughed out of his conceit than he could ever be argued out of it. Good fun is a remedy for foibles, and at least a danger-signal against deeper evil. The child or man who feels that good fun has a reproach and a sting for him, is well aware that he has wandered from the straight way. (p. 932)

"Fun as a Medicine," in The Spectator, *Vol. 77, No. 3574, December 26, 1896, pp. 391-92.*

FRANCIS THOMPSON (essay date 1899)

[*Thompson was one of the most important poets of the Catholic Revival in nineteenth-century English literature. Often compared to the seventeenth-century metaphysical poets, especially Richard Crashaw, he is best known for his poem* "The Hound of Heaven" *(1893), which displays Thompson's characteristic themes of spiritual struggle, redemption, and transcendent love. Like other writers of the fin de siècle period, Thompson wrote poetry and prose noted for rich verbal effects and a devotion to the values of aestheticism. In the following excerpt from an essay originally pub-*

lished in 1899, Thompson favorably reviews Belloc's Danton, *comparing it with another, concurrently published biography of the French revolutionist Georges Danton.*]

There was a real need for an account of the great Revolutionary which should be based on the most modern investigations, and, therefore, neither [Hilaire Belloc's ***Danton*** nor A. H. Beesly's ***Life of Danton***] is in itself superfluous. But it must be said that their combination is unfortunate for the reader, as it certainly is for the author and publishers concerned. The simultaneous appearance of two volumes, covering the same ground, from the same standpoint, with the same aim, relying more or less on the same new investigations, affects us with the sense of too much Danton. Of the two biographers, Mr. Belloc (whom we take to be of French extraction) is the more pictorial, and gives us a clearer *coup d'oeil*. Mr. Beesly, on the other hand, affords us more detail, and, on the whole, more precision of narrative. Both are uncompromising admirers of Danton, and in full sympathy with the Revolution. They have done undoubted good work by clearing away the garbled view of Danton with which Englishmen are familiar. But we must needs say that their advocacy is liable to become special pleading. Mr. Beesly, in particular, indulges in an audacious latitude of hypothesis when he desires to turn the flank of a story adverse to his hero, which can only be paralleled by Macaulay's explaining away of the charge against Addison that he arrested Steele for debt. Nevertheless, in this respect we prefer Mr. Beesly to his rival; for he squarely faces the music, so that we can judge for ourselves the validity of his conclusions. Mr. Belloc is apt to keep the hostile evidence out of court, and state only his results. It must not be understood, however, that there are not numerous cases where he directly proves his defence. He does so in regard to the charge that Danton acquired houses and property in the names of others in order to disguise his unrepublican wealth. In this and other ways the two books do, for some part, usefully complement each other; however, from a publishing standpoint, their simultaneous explosion upon the public must be adjudged unlucky and ill-considered. And in their common endeavour to overset the traditional conception of Danton they must be pronounced largely successful. "White-washed," perhaps, he is not—except in the eyes of such as accept unshrinkingly the entire revolutionary formula. But no one can read these volumes without feeling it necessary to revise much in his previous ideas of the Samson who pulled down the walls of the French monarchy. (pp. 387-88)

Francis Thompson, "French Literature and Frenchmen: 'Danton'," in his Literary Criticisms, *edited by Rev. Terence L. Connolly, S. J., E. P. Dutton and Company Inc., 1948, pp. 387-92.*

Cardinal Edward Henry Manning, a major influence upon Belloc. BBC Hulton Picture Library.

H. G. WELLS (essay date 1908)

[*Wells is best known today as one of the forerunners of modern science fiction and as a utopian idealist who foretold an era of chemical warfare, atomic weaponry, and world wars. His writing was shaped by the influence of Arnold Bennett, Frank Harris, Joseph Conrad, and other contemporaries with whom he exchanged criticism and opinions on the art of writing. Throughout much of his career, Wells wrote and lectured on the betterment of society through education and the advance of scientific innovation. A Fabian socialist and student of zoologist T. H. Huxley, Wells was, until his last bitter years, a believer in the gradual, inevitable moral and intellectual ascent of humanity. Much of his literary criticism was written during the 1890s at* The Saturday Review *under the direction of Harris. In the following excerpt from an essay originally published in 1908 in A. R. Orage's influential periodical* The New Age, *Wells compares his own social and political thought with that of Belloc and G. K. Chesterton, finding that the three share many common values: that when the supernaturalist element is removed from Chesterton's and Belloc's thought, there is left a socialist ethic similar to his own. A month after Wells's article appeared in* The New Age, *Bernard Shaw contributed an essay to the same journal, in which he gently chided Wells for being too shallow in his approach to Chesterton and Belloc, whom he then pilloried as "the Chesterbelloc" (see* TCLC, *Vol. 7). For further discussion of the socio-political ideas shared by Chesterton and Belloc, see the excerpts by Dwight Macdonald (1946) and Jay P. Corrin (1981).*]

It has been one of the less possible dreams of my life to be a painted Pagan God and live upon a ceiling. I crown myself becomingly in stars or tendrils or with electric coruscations (as the mood takes me), and wear an easy costume free from complications and appropriate to the climate of those agreeable spaces. The company about me on the clouds varies greatly with the mood of the vision, but always it is in some way, if not always a very obvious way, beautiful. One frequent presence is G. K. Chesterton, a joyous whirl of brushwork, appropriately garmented and crowned. When he is there, I remark, the whole ceiling is by a sort of radiation convivial. We drink limitless old October from handsome flagons, and we argue mightily about Pride (his weak point) and the nature of Deity. . . . Chesterton often—but never by any chance Belloc. Belloc I admire beyond measure, but there is a sort of partisan viciousness about Belloc that bars him from my celestial dreams. He never figures, no, not even in the remotest corner, on my ceiling. And yet the divine artist, by some strange skill that my ignorance of his technique saves me from the presumption of explaining, does indicate exactly where Belloc is. A little quiver of the paint, a faint aura, about the spectacular masses of Chesterton? I am not certain. But no intelligent beholder can look up and miss the remarkable fact that Belloc exists—and that he is away, safely away, away in his heaven, which is, of course, the Park Lane Imperialist's hell. There he presides. . . . (pp. 175-76)

In many ways we three are closely akin; we diverge not by necessity but accident, because we speak in different dialects and have divergent metaphysics. All that I can I shall persuade to my way of thinking about thought and to the use of words in my loose, expressive manner, but Belloc and Chesterton and I are too grown and set to change our languages now and learn new ones; we are on different roads, and so we must needs shout to one another across intervening abysses. These two say Socialism is a thing they do not want for men. We shall go on saying that now to the end of our days. But what we do all three want is something very alike. Our different roads are parallel. I aim at a growing collective life, a perpetually enhanced inheritance for our race, through the fullest, freest development of the individual life. What they aim at ultimately I do not understand, but it is manifest that its immediate form is the fullest and freest development of the individual life. We all three hate equally and sympathetically the spectacle of human beings blown up with windy wealth and irresponsible power as cruelly and absurdly as boys blow up frogs; we all three detest the complex causes that dwarf and cripple lives from the moment of birth and starve and debase great masses of mankind. We want as universally as possible the jolly life, men and women warm-blooded and well-aired, acting freely and joyously, gathering life as children gather corn-cockles in corn. We all three want people to have property of a real and personal sort, to have the son, as Chesterton put it, bringing up the port his father laid down, and pride in the pears one has grown in one's own garden. (pp. 176-77)

Chesterton and Belloc agree with the Socialist that the present world does not give at all what they want. They agree that it fails to do so through a wild derangement of our property relations. They are in agreement with the common contemporary man (whose creed is stated, I think, not unfairly, but with the omission of certain important articles by Chesterton), that the derangements of our property relations are to be remedied by concerted action and in part by altered laws. The land and all sorts of great common interests must be, if not owned, then at least controlled, managed, checked, redistributed by the State. Our real difference is only about a little more or a little less owning. I do not see how Belloc and Chesterton can stand for anything but a strong State as against those wild monsters of property, the strong, big private owners. The State must be complex and powerful enough to prevent them. State or plutocrat, there is really no other practical alternative before the world at the present time. Either we have to let the big financial adventurers, the aggregating capitalist and his Press, in a loose, informal combination, rule the earth, either we have got to stand aside from preventive legislation and leave things to work out on their present lines, or we have to construct a collective organization sufficiently strong for the protection of the liberties of the some-day-to-be-jolly common man. So far we go in common. If Belloc and Chesterston are not Socialists, they are at any rate not anti-Socialists. If they say they want an organized Christian State (which involves practically seven-tenths of the Socialist desire), then, in the face of our big common enemies, of adventurous capital, of alien Imperialism, base ambition, base intelligence, and common prejudice and ignorance, I do not mean to quarrel with them politically, so long as they force no quarrel on me. Their organised Christian State is nearer the organised State I want than our present plutocracy. Our ideals will fight some day, and it will be, I know, a first-rate fight, but to fight now is to let the enemy in. When we have got all we want in common, then and only then can we afford to differ. (pp. 178-79)

Differ as we may, Belloc and Chesterton are with all Socialists in being on the same side of the great political and social cleavage that opens at the present time. We and they are with the interests of the mass of common men as against that growing organisation of great owners who have common interests directly antagonistic to those of the community and State. We Socialists are only secondarily politicians. Our primary business is not to impose upon, but to ram right into the substance of that object of Chesterton's solicitude, the circle of ideas of the common man, the idea of the State as his own, as a thing he serves and is served by. We want to add to his sense of property rather than offend it. If I had my way I would do that at the street corners and on the trams. I would take down that alien-looking and detestable inscription "L.C.C.," and put up, "This Tram, this Street, belongs to the People of London." Would Chesterton or Belloc quarrel with that? Suppose that Chesterton is right, and that there are incurable things in the mind of the common man flatly hostile to our ideals; so much of our ideals will fail. But we are doing our best by our lights, and all we can. What are Chesterton and Belloc doing? If our ideal is partly right and partly wrong, are they trying to build up a better ideal? Will they state a Utopia and how they propose it shall be managed? If they lend their weight only to such fine old propositions as that a man wants freedom, that he has a right to do as he likes with his own, and so on, they won't help the common man much. All that fine talk, without some further exposition, goes to sustain Mr. Rockefeller's simple human love of property, and the woman and child sweating manufacturer in his fight for the inspector-free home industry. I bought on a bookstall the other day a pamphlet full of misrepresentation and bad argument against Socialism by an Australian Jew, published by the Single-Tax people apparently in a disinterested attempt to free the land from the landowner by the simple expedient of abusing anyone else who wanted to do as much but did not hold Henry George to be God and Lord; and I know Socialists who will protest with tears in their eyes against association with any human being who sings any song but the "Red Flag" and doubts whether Marx had much experience of affairs. Well, there is no reason why Chesterton and Belloc should at their level do the same sort of thing. When we talk on a ceiling or at a dinner-party with any touch of the celestial in its composition, Chesterton and I, Belloc and I, are antagonists with an undying feud, but in the fight against human selfishness and narrowness and for a finer, juster law, we are brothers—at the remotest, half-brothers. (pp. 180-81)

H. G. Wells, "About Chesterton and Belloc," in his An Englishman Looks at the World, *Cassell and Company, Ltd., 1914, pp. 175-82.**

C. S. LEWIS (letter date 1918)

[Lewis is considered one of the foremost Christian and mythopoeic authors of the twentieth century. Indebted principally to George

MacDonald, G. K. Chesterton, Charles Williams, and the writers of ancient Norse myths, he is regarded as a formidable logician and Christian polemicist, a perceptive literary critic, and—most highly—as a writer of fantasy literature. Lewis also held instructoral posts at Oxford and Cambridge, where he was an acknowledged authority on medieval and Renaissance literature. A traditionalist in his approach to life and art, he opposed the modern movement in literary criticism toward biographical and psychological interpretation. In place of this, Lewis practiced and propounded a theory of criticism that stressed the importance of the author's intent, rather than the reader's presuppositions and prejudices. In the following excerpt from a letter written at age nineteen and shortly before the publication of his first book, Lewis records his favorable first impression of Belloc's The Four Men.]

I have just finished reading a very pleasant book called **'The Four Men'**, by Hilaire Belloc. I always imagined that his books were of a very different kind but this is rather in the style of [George Borrow's] 'Lavengro,' only, it seems to me, more homely and humorous: in one or two places where the four wanderers sit in a little forest hut smoking and telling tales it rather reminds me of [James Stephens's] 'Crock of Gold'. (p. 229)

C. S. Lewis, in a letter to Arthur Greeves on August 31, 1918, in They Stand Together: The Letters of C. S. Lewis to Arthur Greeves (1914-1963), *edited by Walter Hooper, Macmillan Publishing Co., Inc., 1979, pp. 228-30.*

BERNARD SHAW (essay date 1918)

[*Shaw is generally considered the greatest and best-known dramatist to write in the English language since Shakespeare. Following the example of Henrik Ibsen, he succeeded in revolutionizing the English stage, disposing of the romantic conventions and devices of the "well-made play," and instituting the theater of ideas, grounded in realism. During the late nineteenth century, Shaw was also a prominent literary, art, and music critic. In 1895 he became the drama critic for* The Saturday Review, *and his reviews therein became known for their biting wit and brilliance. During his three years at* The Saturday Review, *Shaw determined that the theater was meant to be a "moral institution" and "elucidator of social conduct." The standards he applied to drama were quite simple: Is the play like real life? Does it convey sensible, socially progressive ideas? Because most of the drama produced during the 1890s failed to approach these ideals, Shaw usually assumed a severely critical and satirical attitude toward his subjects. Although he later wrote criticism of poetry and fiction—much of it collected in* Pen Portraits and Reviews *(1932)—Shaw was out of sympathy with both of these genres. He had little use for poetry, believing it poorly suited for the expression of ideas, and in his criticism of fiction he rarely got beyond the search for ideology. As Samuel Hynes has noted, Shaw was driven by a rage to better the world. A Fabian socialist, he wrote criticism that was often concerned with the humanitarian and politicial intent of the work under discussion. Shaw and Belloc disagreed on numerous matters of politics, economics, and religion, with Shaw giving Belloc and G. K. Chesterton the mocking joint-sobriquet "the Chesterbelloc" in a 1908 essay in* The New Age *(see* TCLC, *Vol. 7). In the following excerpt from an essay originally published in 1918, Shaw offers a generally favorable review of* The Free Press, *then proceeds to twit Belloc and the Chesterton brothers for their concept of, and approach to, coterie journalism.*]

"To release the truth against whatever odds, even if so doing can no longer help the Commonwealth, is a necessity for the soul," says Mr Belloc [in ***The Free Press***]. And again, "Those who prefer to sell themselves or to be cowed, gain as a rule, not even that ephemeral security for which they betrayed their fellows; meanwhile they leave to us [journalists] the only permanent form of power, which is the gift of mastery through persuasion."

Now it is more than forty years since my first contribution to the press appeared in print; and I am not sure that this necessity of the soul to which Mr Belloc testifies, thereby echoing Jeremiah (a Jew, I regret to say) who declared that the word was in his heart as a burning fire shut up in his bones, and he was weary with forbearing and could not stay, is really a necessity of *the* soul. I must ask whose soul? Certainly not that of your average journalist or of the man who swallows his articles as soothing syrup. The first necessity of such souls when truth is about, as it always is, is camouflage, or better still, complete cover. I, like Mr Belloc, and those heroes of the free press whom he celebrates in this book: Mr Orage, the Chestertons, and himself, have conducted truth raids, and seen all England rush to the cellars every time. It takes a very hardy constitution to stand the truth. Is an evening with Ibsen as popular as an evening with Mary Pickford at the movies? A simple No is hardly emphatic enough. One feels the need of the French *Point!* so useful in similar emergencies to Molière.

Before I forget it—for I am going to wander considerably—let me say that Mr Belloc's pamphlet is true enough within its own express limitations. It serves the press right, the parliament right, and our plutocratic humbugs right. But I think he lets the public off too easily; and as for the free press, by which he means specifically ***The New Age, The New Witness,*** and in general the coterie press, he is a bit of a flatterer. An amiable weakness; but still, a weakness.

The coterie press is no doubt a free press in a sense; and I have often availed myself of its freedom to say things I should not have been allowed to say elsewhere. When I want somebody to throw a stone at the Lord Mayor, or the Lord Chamberlain, or any other panjandrum, I do not offer six-and-eightpence to my solicitor to do it: I offer a shilling to a tramp. The tramp is free to throw the stone: the respectable solicitor is not. Similarly, when the missile is a literary one, I do not send it to ***The Times,*** I offer it to a coterie editor. He has the tramp's freedom. He is not afraid of the advertisers, because he has no advertisements. He is not afraid of the plutocrats, because he has no rich backers. He is not afraid of the lawyers, because he is not worth powder and shot. He is not afraid of losing his social position, because he is not in smart society, and would rather die than get into it. Sometimes he is not afraid of anything, because he has no sense.

In short, Mr Belloc will say with some impatience, the coterie editor is free; and I do not alter that fact by explaining why he is free. *Parfaitement, cher Hilaire* (which I may translate as "Who deniges of it, Betsy?"); but does this freedom, this irresponsibility, carry with it any guarantee of liberality or veracity? Clearly not: all that it does is, within certain limits, to allow the coterie paper to be liberal and veracious if it likes. But if you come to that, do not Lord Northcliffe's millions set him free to attack and destroy people who could crush a coterie paper by a libel action or by setting Dora at it, if Lord Northcliffe liked? Let us not deceive ourselves: we are between the nether millstone of the press that is too poor to tell the truth and the upper one of the press that is too rich. Mr Belloc says that the falsehood of the press operates more by suppression of truth than assertion of lies. Well, I am prepared to maintain that every coterie editor in the world suppresses more truth, according to his lights, than Lord Northcliffe. He perceives more. (pp. 35-7)

I have belonged to too many coteries to have any illusions on this point. My correspondents frequently appeal to me to intervene in some public question on the ground that I am a fearless champion of the truth and have never hesitated to say what I think. I reply always, "Heaven save your innocence! If you only knew all the things I think and dare not say!" (p. 38)

Mr Belloc is a good hater: the proof is that though he is a humorist, there is not in this little book of his, launched as a torpedo at poor Northcliffe, a single conscious joke. There are two unconscious ones. He speaks of "two dots arranged in a spiral" (let him arrange two dots in a spiral if he can); and he says that a newspaper report is less truthful than the thousand tongues of rumor because it tells the same thing simultaneously to a million people in the same words. And this is not a joke at all, because when all the witnesses tell the story in the same words, the case is sure to be a conspiracy. (pp. 39-40)

Mr Belloc himself has [with ***The New Witness***] achieved the astounding and hardly sane feat of establishing, with other people's capital, a press organ of the Holy Roman Empire in London in the twentieth century. He is driven to conclude that the able-minded editor with convictions will finally beat the whole field, and destroy the forces that now make his strife so inhumanly hazardous.

My own most polemical writings are to be found in the files of ***The Times, The Morning Post, The Daily Express, The World,*** and ***The Saturday Review.*** I found out early in my career that a Conservative paper may steal a horse when a Radical paper dare not look over a hedge, and that the rich, though very determined that the poor shall read nothing unconventional, are equally determined to be preached at themselves. In short, I found that only for the classes would I be allowed, and indeed tacitly required, to write on revolutionary assumptions. I filled their columns with sedition; and they filled my pockets (not very deep ones then) with money. In the press as in other departments the greatest freedom may be found where there is least talk about it. (p. 43)

Bernard Shaw, "How Free Is the Press? (Hilaire Belloc)," in his Pen Portraits and Reviews by Bernard Shaw, *revised edition, Constable and Company Limited, 1932, pp. 35-43.*

T. S. ELIOT (essay date 1927)

[*Perhaps the most influential poet and critic of the first half of the twentieth century, Eliot is closely identified with many of the qualities denoted by the term Modernism: experimentation, formal complexity, artistic and intellectual eclecticism, and a classicist view of the artist working at an emotional distance from his or her creation. He introduced a number of terms and concepts that strongly affected critical thought in his lifetime, among them the idea that poets must be conscious of the living tradition of literature in order for their work to have artistic and spiritual validity. In general, Eliot upheld values of traditionalism and discipline, and in 1928 he annexed Christian theology to his overall conservative world view. Of his criticism, he stated: "It is a by-product of my private poetry-workshop: or a prolongation of the thinking that went into the formation of my verse." In the following excerpt from a review of* A Companion to Mr. Wells's "Outline of History," *H. G. Wells's* Mr. Belloc Objects to Mr. Wells's "Outline of History," *and Belloc's* Mr. Belloc Still Objects to Mr. Wells's "Outline of History," *Eliot provides an overview of the Wells-Belloc debate, describing it as a see-sawing confrontation between two evenly matched champions whose arguments tend to merely convince the already convinced.*]

This is sometimes called the age of the specialist; it is also the age of the brilliant and voluble amateur. In some sciences, as mathematics and physics, the specialist is highly respected; in some, as in anthropology, it is difficult for the outsider always to distinguish between the specialist and the brilliant amateur; in others, such as history and theology, which have fallen into a certain decline, the amateur has it almost all his own way; and is judged, even from his lack of credentials, to speak with more authority than the specialist. An examination of the books under review will justify this assertion; a comparison of their sales would probably prove it.

The debate between Mr. Belloc and Mr. Wells is properly a theological debate, but, as is natural, our interest and amusement at the spectacle of these two highly paid pugilists is likely to eclipse our interest in the points at issue. Two black men, in a controversy, will sometimes taunt each other with being 'niggers'; Mr. Wells and Mr. Belloc undertake to show each other up in their knowledge of sciences in which both are amateurs. Both seem to the uninstructed reader to have succeeded. Towards the end (if it is the end) Mr. Wells gains a tactical advantage. We observe that in the ***Companion*** Mr. Belloc attacks him on a number of points of ancient and modern history. Mr. Wells has not an historical mind; he has a prodigious gift of historical imagination, which is comparable to Carlyle's, but this is quite a different gift from the understanding of history. *That* demands a degree of culture, civilization and maturity which Mr. Wells does not possess. I observe that he does not answer Mr. Belloc's objections to his account of history, and restricts the debate, on his side, to questions of comparative anatomy and pre-history. In this field he is much more competent, and here his peculiar imaginative gifts flourish. Mr. Belloc accordingly follows him on to this ground. He holds his own pretty well; but we feel that there is justice in Mr. Wells's complaint that he has not made any clearer the real position of the Catholic Church concerning evolution theories. We distrust them both; we agree with them both. But journalism begets journalism; only journalism can triumph over journalism. In such a debate as this; the reader is only convinced of what he believed already.

Mr. Belloc says that Mr. Wells has never learned to think. He is probably quite right. Whether he has himself learned to think is not conclusively proved by the present discussion, for in such a discussion the processes of thinking play very little part; the form of assertion is everything; and the faculty which is chiefly exercised by the kind of activities in which Mr. Belloc and Mr. Wells engage is the faculty of bluff. Still, Mr. Belloc was educated in a tradition formed by men who think, and is therefore able to 'place' Mr. Wells rather better than Mr. Wells places him. Neither Mr. Wells nor Mr. Belloc could be called a philosopher, and neither seems to have a very firm grasp of metaphysical essentials, but when Mr. Belloc attempts to describe the *tone* of Mr. Wells's utterances we find ourselves in agreement with him. Whether we accept or reject Mr. Belloc's own religious beliefs, we must accept the following paragraph:

'The reason, for instance, that you do not have mawkish religious sentiment hanging about such minds as, in Catholic countries, have lost the Faith, is that those minds are founded upon Intelligence and despise muddle-headed emotionalism. They admit their loss of doctrine, and they are not afraid to face the consequence of what they conceive to be the truth. But in nations not of Catholic culture it is the other way about. Men like Mr. Wells, who have ceased to believe that Our Blessed Lord was God, or even that He had Divine authority, cling desperately to the emotions which the old belief aroused—because they find those emotions pleasant. That is a piece of intellectual weakness for which corresponding men, atheists of the Catholic culture, very properly feel a hearty contempt.'

That is well said, and it applies to many persons in England besides Mr. Wells. (pp. 253-54)

T. S. Eliot, in a review of "A Companion to Mr. Wells's 'Outline of History,'' and "Mr. Belloc Still Objects," in The Monthly Criterion, *Vol. V. No. II, May, 1927, pp. 253-54.*

G. K. CHESTERTON (essay date 1933)

[Regarded as one of England's premier men of letters during the first half of the twentieth century, Chesterton is best known today as a colorful bon vivant, a witty essayist, and creator of the Father Brown mysteries and the fantasy The Man Who Was Thursday *(1908). Much of Chesterton's work reveals his childlike joie de vivre and reflects his pronounced Anglican and, later, Roman Catholic beliefs. His essays are characterized by their humor, frequent use of paradox, and chatty, rambling style. Chesterton and Belloc were longtime friends and collaborators, sharing many ideas on history, economics, and Catholicism, and jointly earning Bernard Shaw's wry sobriquet of the "Chesterbelloc." Frequently attacked during their era as the hapless champions of lost causes by other writers of more modern beliefs, the two often defended each other and their ideas in print and on the debating platform. In the following excerpt from a favorable review of* Charles the First: King of England, *Chesterton spiritedly refutes the common position that Belloc was a predictably partisan defender of old-fashioned ideas and a writer of uniformly prejudiced "Popish pamphlets."]*

I have decided, after some hesitation, to protest against what I consider a very bad case of not knowing how to read books—a case that may seem personal and even controversial, though it has really nothing to do with controversy. It has to do with how to read books.

I have before me a few books on Cavaliers and Roundheads, and I shall begin with Mr. Belloc's book on ***Charles the First, King of England,*** because it is a perfect example of what I mean. English people are not getting the good out of Mr. Belloc's books as books, because there is a stupid journalistic legend that he is a partisan. It is totally untrue. There are things on which Mr. Belloc disagrees with his countrymen; but he is most emphatically not a man repeating the views of his party and insisting on your agreeing with them; he is a man advancing very original views entirely his own and you are perfectly free to disagree with them. Many of his party do disagree with them; but you might as well read them and realise that they are new.

We hear a good deal nowadays about resistance to new ideas. It seems to mean entirely certain negative and sceptical ideas that are not new at all. A man who disbelieves in God, a man who disbelieves in marriage, or disbelieves in the duty of fighting for his country, may be right or wrong, but he is not new. All the arguments against Providence are in the Book of Job, all the arguments against immortality are in St. Thomas Aquinas, satires against marriage, and denunciations of war can be found in the most ancient pagan literature. What we commonly call modern ideas are all very ancient ideas; but if you want one or two new ideas you will find them in certain books, incidentally Mr. Belloc's book, and you can accept them or not as you choose. But they are not the stock-in-trade of a party. Mr. Belloc is opposed to Socialism, but his 'Servile State' is not an attack on Socialism or any sort of State tyranny; it is an entirely original economic theory, by which our social reforms tend, not to Socialism, but actually to the ancient status of masters and slaves. Mr. Belloc is a Catholic, but most Catholic writers, for instance, have described Queen Elizabeth as a tyrant. Mr. Belloc's whole point is that Queen Elizabeth was not a tyrant, but a victim of tyranny. Or again, Mr. Belloc does dislike Prussia, and, naturally, prefers France; but the friends and foes of Prussia would alike say that Bismarck's triumph was that he achieved the union of the German people. Mr. Belloc insists that Bismarck's triumph was that he prevented the union of the German people. If all the Germans had united, it would have been under Austria; Bismarck made sure that his Empire should be not large enough, but small enough, to leave the leadership to Prussia.

Now, all those are ideas to be judged in themselves, in books that you should read for yourselves. And it is not reading a book for yourself to open it with a newspaper prejudice that the writer writes nothing but Popish pamphlets when, in fact, he does nothing of the sort. So it is with this book on Charles I. It is not new to be on the side of Charles I, for Charles I himself, at least, remained loyally on the side of Charles I. It is not new to be on the side of Cromwell, for Cromwell was very much on the side of Cromwell. But nearly everybody will look at this book to see whether Mr. Belloc is a Cavalier or a Roundhead, instead of reading the book to agree or disagree with certain rather new and interesting views on history. What he suggests, for instance, substantially is this. The worst that can be said of Charles I is that he stood for modern ideas; the best that can be said for the Parliament is that it stood for old ideas. Now that point will probably be missed, not because it is partisan—I know of no party that has supported it—but simply because it is unfamiliar. It will take a long time to get people, I do not say to agree with it, but even to disagree with it.

In short, Mr. Belloc is not a partisan of the old Cavalier party, but he does doubtless dislike the fanaticism of the extreme Calvinist Party which led it to butcher prisoners and women and children. Does anybody like it very much? But anyhow his allusions to such things are quite brief and incidental; yet he devotes pages and pages to a perfectly fair and full statement of the case for Hampden and the refusal of Ship Money. It was quite a good case, but what was the case? It was that hitherto in history heavy taxation had been rare, and Parliament as a mediaeval institution accepted it with reluctance. Mediaeval men were not taxed all the time and to any extent, as we happy modern men are today. The King paid for everything out of his own large revenue, and seldom asked for more; but Charles I asked for more—and why? Why, because he was more like a modern statesman building the strong modern State, with its vast expenditure, its centralised power of police, its general claim to be what we call a great Power in Europe. If the Parliament was right, it was right for preserving an antiquated mediaeval thrift; if the King was wrong, he was wrong for introducing the great services and taxes of the modern world.

Now you will not find it easy to get that idea into some people's heads, because it is a new idea. Not because it is a Popish idea; on the contrary, if it praises the King, it only praises a Protestant King for waging a war on behalf of Protestants. That, by the way, is a big fact that is often forgotten. It is very doubtful whether Queen Elizabeth was really a champion of Protestantism in Europe, but is certain that Charles I was a

Belloc with Bernard Shaw and G. K. Chesterton. P. A. Reuter Features Ltd.

champion of Protestantism in Europe. He actually wanted the ship money to build ships in order to rescue the Huguenots, the French Protestants, from being besieged by a Cardinal and a Catholic King. Surely it is not Popery that makes Mr. Belloc support the King in that. The truth is that the King was a practical Protestant, and the Puritans were unpractical or impracticable Protestants. While they were talking nonsense or calling poor old Laud a Papist for wearing the plain surplice that all Anglican parsons now wear, he was conducting a crusade to defend Protestant Rochelle against Papistical Paris. . . .

Mr. Belloc, in his book, is not merely a Cavalier, he is a great many other things, including a man with a theory of his own, which you can throw away if you like, but which is not merely the old Cavalier theory or the old Catholic theory.

G. K. Chesterton, "Cavaliers and Roundheads," in The Listener, *Vol. X, No. 253, November 15, 1933, p. 765.**

REINHOLD NIEBUHR (essay date 1936)

[Niebuhr is considered one of the most important and influential Protestant theologians in twentieth-century America. The author of such works as The Children of Light and the Children of Darkness *(1944) and* Christian Realism and Political Problems *(1953), he persistently stressed the reality of original sin and emphasized the tragic condition of fallen humanity, opposing the secular and liberal Christian tendency toward discounting sin in favor of economic and political explanations of human misery. Niebuhr saw the problem of modern humanity as one in which an overwhelming sense of confusion and meaninglessness have been brought on by technocracy and the resulting rush for power. He saw the task of modern Christianity to be that of ministering to both the worldly as well as the spiritual needs of humankind. In the following excerpt, Niebuhr reviews* The Battleground: Syria and Palestine, the Seedbed of Religion, *identifying the book as a useful introduction to the history of Syria and Palestine.]*

Hilaire Belloc, whose vigorous pen has intrigued the interest of readers on many varied subjects, has hit upon the novel idea of using the study of Palestine as an occasion for the review of world history. The incidental relation of the little land of Syria to the great Oriental empires of early civilization, Assyria-Babylon, Egypt and Persia, gives him [in ***The Battleground***] the opportunity to present their histories in popular form, from the vantage point of their relation to the land of Palestine. The ascendency of the Alexandrine empire offers him the occasion to trace the rise of Greek civilization and then to portray the Maccabean revolt against this Greek dominion. Roman civilization is introduced as a kind of prelude to the beginning of Christian history. In the chapters devoted to the rise and development of Christianity, popular history is combined with fiction by the introduction of non-historical characters who are allowed to give their impressions of Jesus. These chapters are as a consequence least valuable and convincing. Literature is too full of imaginative elaborations of the life of Christ, good, bad and indifferent. This particular effort is too casual to be valuable.

The triumph of Christianity in Europe presents the opportunity to survey European civilization from the same vantage point of the Palestinian beginnings of a religion which was to be infused into that civilization. Mohammedanism comes into the picture as a kind of Christian heresy which seeks to strip historic Christianity of its elaborations and confine it again to the desert. Here the device of the author becomes somewhat strained and the Christian roots of Moslem faith are overstressed. The Crusades are related to the general theme as the final effort of a Christian civilization to reclaim the land of its birth and bring it into the orbit of its culture, an effort which ended in failure. The pattern which determines the author's work hardly allows him to do justice to the multifarious forces which played into that curious period of the Crusades and determined the combination of childish romance, religious fanaticism and political lust for power by which it is characterized.

A rather inadequate epilogue deals with the contemporary effort of Zionists to reclaim Palestine as a Jewish homeland. The author's chief interest in this chapter seems to center upon the relation of the Palestinian experiment to British foreign policy.

Naturally such a book rides rather lightly over many important critical and historical problems and abounds in dogmatic presuppositions which many readers will not be able to share. But it serves it own purpose admirably and furnishes the reader with entertaining historical instruction.

Reinhold Niebuhr, "Hilaire Belloc Looks at Zion," in New York Herald Tribune Books, *April 5, 1936, p. 3.*

E. C. BENTLEY (essay date 1936)

[Bentley is chiefly remembered today as the father of the modern detective novel. Although he was also a successful journalist, and famous in his native England for inventing a form of humorous verse known as the "clerihew," it was as the author of the murder mystery classic Trent's Last Case *(1913) that Bentley achieved international recognition. In this work, he disregarded or ironically reversed many of the conventions commonly associated with the detective genre, such as the infallibility of the detective and the ultimate triumph of reason, and in so doing he introduced an element of wit and realism into mystery fiction that it had previously lacked. He was chief literary critic of the London* Daily Telegraph *during World War II, and a contributor of political articles, literary criticism, and light verse to various English periodicals throughout his career. In the following excerpt, he favorably reviews* The Hedge and the Horse, *Belloc's last book containing illustrations by the critic's lifelong friend, G. K. Chesterton.]*

[***The Hedge and The Horse***] is the last of the fruits of a literary partnership that began over thirty years ago, when Mr. Belloc's ***Emmanuel Burden*** was published. It was then that the working of a new and rich vein of social satire was begun; then that Bellocian prose and Chestertonian drawing came together in that rarest of alliances, a complete and cordial and unbroken understanding between author and illustrator. (p. 86)

[***The Hedge and the Horse***] is a study in the injustice of Fate; "one man may steal a horse and another mayn't look over the hedge." One man can do anything and get away with it; and for every such man there are a hundred who, if they ever dared to try anything on, would be pounced upon instantly. Wilfred Straddle belonged to "the Hedge Club"; so that when it got about that, instead of being heir to millions, he had not a bean or the prospect of any, the social atmosphere dropped to zero wherever he showed his face. Bill Robinson was a very different creature. He was of "the Horse Club". He had never had any money, and everybody knew it. No one had a notion who his father was. Yet Bill lived among the Right People just like one of themselves. He was on the best of terms with all of them, and lived at their expense, in spite of the fact that they never thought of him as anything but a cad. (pp. 86-7)

Connoisseurs will agree with me (I hope) in setting down Bill as one of the most luscious of Mr. Belloc's innumerable creations, and Wilfred as one of the most sympathetic and touching of his various mugs. As for the plot of the novel, you will hear nothing of that from me, but that it is excellent. Being in the business in a small way myself, who knows better how maddening it is when some ass of a reviewer spoils the fun by giving away the guts of the story? (p. 87)

E. C. Bentley, "The Last Chesterbelloc," in G. K.'s Weekly, *Vol. XXIV, No. 604, October 8, 1936, pp. 86-7.*

ALFRED KAZIN (essay date 1936)

[A highly respected American literary critic, Kazin is best known for his essay collections The Inmost Leaf *(1955) and* Contemporaries *(1962), and particularly for* On Native Grounds *(1942), a study of American prose writing since the era of William Dean Howells. Having studied the works of "the critics who were the best writers—from Sainte-Beuve and Matthew Arnold to Edmund Wilson and Van Wyck Brooks" as an aid to his own critical understanding, Kazin has found that "criticism focussed many—if by no means all—of my own urges as a writer: to show literature as a deed in human history, and to find in each writer the uniqueness of the gift, of the essential vision, through which I hoped to penetrate into the mystery and sacredness of the individual soul." In the following excerpt from an essay written early in his career, Kazin offers lukewarm praise for Belloc's* Selected Essays, *a collection edited by John Edward Dineen, and concludes by sourly appraising Belloc's overall skill as an essayist.]*

Mr. Belloc appears here [in his **"Selected Essays"**] in a wee and unaccustomed rôle and bereft of most of his thunder. . . . [We] find Mr. Belloc in **"Conversation With a Cat,"** Mr. Belloc **"On a Lost Manuscript," "On the Tears of the Great," "On Inns," "On Rest," "On Lying,"** which is not the Belloc we know, but may be one easier to follow. But where is the great warrior for the church? Where is Mr. Chesterton's artillery? Where is the Democratic Royalist? . . .

I am glad . . . that Mr. Dineen included the section on Milton's sonnets from the biography of the poet. It was the best thing in that book, and here puts a little starch into a collection so touched with lavender. Tearing into Milton the poet, instead of waylaying him as a Protestant, Mr. Belloc wrote a keen and rather just study, together with some notes on how bad a great poet can be. **"Talking (And Singing) of the Nordic Man"** is a little heavy, but Mr. Belloc's laughter at the **"Great Aryan Myth"** is loud and unmistakable. But save for the lecture **"On Translation,"** which says nothing new, but is useful, Mr. Belloc is represented by small pieces on small topics.

The "informal essay," I think, demands more than whimsy, and when Mr. Belloc is not whimsical, he is rigid. There is something strained about his very lightness of touch, like an enormous windup brought to bear on a slow ball. As a result Mr. Belloc seems a little too heavy for his rôle. The belligerency and the fire are sometimes omitted, it is true, but though he tries to contain himself within a single frame, he never quite succeeds in being a miniaturist. There is melancholy in these pages, good feeling, now and then, and understanding that is so decisive as to appear authoritative; but the melancholy never strikes a single note, the good feeling is either reduced to a sigh or delivered as a curt affirmation. Mr. Belloc, I am afraid, has an extraordinary knack for making the trivial sound ponderous.

When he speaks in his usual tones, as in the piece on Milton, Mr. Belloc has an advantage over most critics: he has the grand manner, even if it is not entirely deserved. He is not, as Mr. Dineen reminds us, a Tory; merely "anti-Whig." With a thousand years of Christendom at his back, nevertheless, and the most powerful church in the world to defend, Mr. Belloc can afford his trenchant dignity, and we can only applaud the use he makes of it. I like him as the Defender of the Faith and I admire the courage with which, almost single-handed, he has fought the Reformation all over again. There is a touch of Old English grandeur about him, and as much stubbornness as bigotry. For our day he has been at once a Saintsbury and a Carlyle, while never being half as good as either. It is always significant when one reads a writer with as much pleasure as disagreement. But here, for once, there is only disagreement.

Alfred Kazin, "An Unaccustomed View of Mr. Belloc," in The New York Times Book Review, *November 29, 1936, p. 8.*

CHARLES WILLIAMS (essay date 1942)

[*Williams was a writer of supernatural fiction, a poet whose best works treat the legends of Logres (Arthurian Britain), and one of the central figures among the literary group known as the Oxford Christians or "Inklings." The religious, the magical, and the mythical are recurrent concerns in his works, reflecting his devout Anglicanism and lifelong interest in all aspects of the preternatural. Although his works are not today as well known as those of his fellow-Inklings C. S. Lewis and J. R. R. Tolkien, Williams was an important source of encouragement and influence among the group. Strongly partisan to the Church of England, Williams was irritated by Belloc's frequent polemical slaps at Anglicanism, writing on one occasion that "if the duel were still possible, and if I could hope to manage a sword, I should certainly before now have taken care to insult Mr. Belloc publicly on behalf of the Church of England, or of John Milton, or even of Queen Elizabeth." But in such books as* The Last Rally *and* Elizabethan Commentaries, *works published late in Belloc's career, Williams perceived more toleration and fair-mindedness in Belloc's work. In the following excerpt, he warmly praises* Elizabethan Commentaries.]

The central figure of Mr. Belloc's book [***Elizabethan Commentary***] is Elizabeth; but the chief interest for his readers is the sympathy with which he treats her. He has renewed his youth; in those days of his early career ("career" is the right word) he could not only see both sides but (almost) speak both sides, however much he might support one. That very remarkable realism of his underwent a kind of hardening. He did the historical work he had to do, but (though all his statistics may have been accurate) his style was unfair. His vaulting anger o'erleapt itself, and sometimes he did not even antagonize; he only annoyed. It is with very great delight that one finds now his passion real, but purified. He is almost stupendously fair to the Queen—in his insistence, for example, unlike some writers, that her terrible death "should be cited, not in Elizabeth's accusation, but in truth of our own mortal weakness. I say again it might happen to any of us". He adds that it was the last phase of "the abandonment of certitude and of the search for certitude".

The book, however, is not directly a life of the Queen. It deals with many subjects, and it deals with them—most of them—generously and wisely. . . .

It may seem absurd to claim Mr Belloc as an exponent of the classical spirit. He has been often romantic; too often, pseudo-romantic. But he has, in his greater passages, and they are not far from truly great, always meant that pure conclusion of romanticism which is the classic. He says of the Liturgy of the Church of England (even while declaring that it "achieved the separation between the older England . . . and the new England"): "The English Liturgy had appeared without generation, like a god. They are to be excused who profess towards it a sort of idolatry. . . . (It) . . . takes its permanent monumental place in the story of Europe." It is this sense of the power of the word which Mr. Belloc has exercised on us; he has written some things which stand in the next order to that Liturgy, and it is those things which continue to have power on us, and promulgate among us the ideas to which they belong.

Charles Williams, "More Power to Mr. Belloc," in Time & Tide, *Vol. 23, No. 19, May 9, 1942, p. 390.*

DWIGHT MACDONALD (essay date 1946)

[*An American essayist and critic, Macdonald was a noted proponent of various radical causes from the mid-1930s until his death in 1982. Founder of the journal* Politics *(1944-49), which welcomed "all varieties of radical thought," he pursued Trotskyism, anarchism, pacifism, and anti-communism before eventually settling on "conservative anarchism"—a humanistic libertarian ethic of which Thoreauesque civil disobediance is a part—as his personal ethic. In the following excerpt, Macdonald discusses* The Servile State, *dismissing it as a stylistically slick essay that is both dishonest in its purportedly neutral stance and wrong-headed in its central thesis.*]

[In ***The Servile State***] Belloc excoriates capitalism with Marxian vigor and in surprisingly Marxian terms. In addition, his nostalgia for the Middle Ages made him see what few Marxists of that time saw: that industrial progress and collectivism were, in fact, not leading toward socialism but toward something very different; and that decentralization was a major requirement of advance toward a better society. A remark like the following seems acute in the light of the present nationalization program in England: "Who can imagine that if, say, two of our great industries, coal and railways, were handed over to the state tomorrow, the armies of men organized therein would find any change of character of their lives, save in some increase of security and possibly in a very slight increase of earnings?"

The more one reads in the book, however, the more one realizes that Belloc's central thesis is spectacularly unsound; and since the book is no more than a scholastic elaboration of this thesis, there is nothing much left once it collapses. Belloc states his thesis in one sentence on page 101: "The capitalist state breeds a collectivist theory which *in action* produces something utterly different from collectivism: to wit, the servile state." This might appear unexceptionable enough, in the light of the Russian experience, except that Belloc's definition of the "servile state" is not what one might expect. Taking the instability and non-viability of capitalism for granted, Belloc outlines three possible future solutions:

> (a) Collectivism, or the placing of the means of production in the hands of the political officers of the community.
>
> (b) Property, or the reestablishment of a distributive state, in which the mass of citizens should severally own the means of production.
>
> (c) Slavery, or a servile state, in which those who do not own the means of production shall be legally compelled to work for those who do, and shall receive in exchange a security of livelihood.

Although he affects a "hard-boiled" scientific neutrality, Belloc's personal choice is clearly for the second alternative: a society of small farmers, merchants, and artisans owning their own means of production and exchanging their products on a free market—something like Jefferson's ideas, or Proudhon's. But he rightly points out that although this solution is logically conceivable, it seems historically unlikely, since the trend of capitalism is toward centralization. The main argument of his book is that this trend will result not in collectivism, as the Socialists expect, but in the "servile state." By this striking phrase Belloc does *not* mean—as the jacket blurb states and as Mr. Gauss's rather woolly introduction seems to imply—what critics of socialism from Herbert Spencer on have meant: regimentation by a state bureaucracy, which replaces the private capitalist as owner and exploiter. Rather does he mean, as he is at pains to repeat several dozen times in the course of a short book—his style, like Stalin's, has the repetitious, catechism quality of the theological seminary—a society in which small number of private capitalists force the non-owning masses to work for them by direct legal compulsion. Now it must be clear to a child—to write like the author—that just the opposite has happened. We have the state everywhere taking from private capitalism. Even in this country the state is more powerful economically and private business less so than they were twenty years ago. Throughout Europe basic industries are being nationalized, the bourgeoisie is vanishing as a significant social force, and while there are plenty of indications of the growth of servile relations, they are not arising on Belloc's basis. ("That state is not servile in which *all* citizens . . . must labor at the discretion of state officials.") The nationalization of industry which he proves in detail cannot ever take place in England is now coming about. As for Russia: in the preface to the 1927 edition Belloc writes, "I have not modified the sentence in which I say that state collectivism can show no working example, for the Russian Revolution . . . has *not* produced a collectivist state; on the contrary, it has produced a state the vast bulk of which—some nine-tenths—have, by it, been confirmed as peasant-holders." It was a brave bit of cauistry, with just enough truth to be effective. The Old Guard dies but never surrenders. And death came a few years later when Stalin put through the forced-collectivization program.

How did Belloc come to adopt such a fantastically wrong-headed thesis, and to stick to it as late as 1927? That he is a superficial thinker is clear from the false-lucid rhetoric of his style: baby-talk for the intelligentsia. That he is a doctrinaire of the most irresponsible kind, handling ideas and data with the fine free sweep of an undergraduate debater, appears in the forty-page "historical digression" in which he traces the social and economic history of Europe from the Roman Empire to the Industrial Revolution, showing how everything good flowed from the Catholic church and everything bad from the pagan centuries before its rise and the Protestant centuries after its decline. As a doctrinaire, he saw private property as an eternal principle, for good or ill; and the superficiality of his intelligence enables him to stick to this in the face of all evidence. His book might still be of value had he not adopted an "objective" pose throughout, insisting that he is not using the term "servile" pejoratively, and that he is not concerned with inquiring as to "which form of society might reasonably be preferred." This pseudoneutrality—for such it is, whether in Belloc or in Burnham—is a cheap rhetorical trick designed to persuade a scientific-minded audience. But once the thesis to be advanced thereby has been outmoded, very little is left. Had Belloc frankly tried to show the virtues of his "distributive" society and why it should "reasonably be preferred" to other societies, his book might still be to the point today. As it is, it would seem he outsmarted himself. (pp. 665-66)

Dwight Macdonald, "Slaves and a Sophist," in The Nation, *Vol. 163, No. 23, December 7, 1946, pp. 664-66.*

DESMOND MACCARTHY (essay date 1950)

[MacCarthy was one of the foremost English literary and dramatic critics of the twentieth century. He served for many years on the staff of the New Statesman *and edited* Life and Letters. *Among his many essay collections,* The Court Theatre 1904-1907: A Commentary and a Criticism *(1907)—a detailed account of three seasons during which the Court Theatre was dominated by Harley Granville-Barker and Bernard Shaw—is especially valued. According to his critics, MacCarthy brought to his work a wide range of reading, serious and sensitive judgment, an interest in the works of new writers, and high critical standards. In the following excerpt from a tribute to Belloc broadcast over the BBC Home Service on the occasion of the author's eightieth birthday, MacCarthy offers a laudatory overview of Belloc's long career, praising in particular his poetry and verse.]*

On July 27 Hilaire Belloc will be eighty years old. I do not suppose he will be greatly interested himself in that anniversary, but some of his friends are sure to drink a glass of good wine with him, and many absent ones will think of him on that occasion. . . .

I certainly cannot think of any other writer who has excelled, or expressed himself, in quite as many directions: drama is the only form he has never attempted. . . .

I have visited libraries where the works of Hilaire Belloc occupy several long shelves, but I doubt if even his ardent admirers possess them all. He has written innumerable essays—descriptive, critical, meditative and fantastic; books of travel on sea and land; vigorous controversial books on politics, religion, modern thought, racial problems, economics. He has written several political satires in the form of fiction like ***Mr. Clutterbuck's Election,*** and satires on university pendants like ***The Green Overcoat*** or ***Lambkin's Remains.*** (Do get hold of those, they will amuse you immensely.) He has written two of the best guidebooks—one to Paris, one to the Pyrenees. He has written one historical novel ***The Girondin,*** and one half-mocking stately romance called ***Belinda,*** and a volume of short period stories from Saxon days to the French Revolution called ***The Eye Witness,*** which clamours to be reprinted. He is an authority on famous battles from Hastings downwards. He has written on Napoleon's and Marlborough's campaigns and the Crusades. He has written a short history of England and lives of Cramer, Richelieu, Napoleon, Wolsey, Joan of Arc, Charles I, William the Conqueror, Cromwell, Milton, James II—and that list is not complete! Some of these are highly controversial, James II in particular. As an historian and biographer he interprets the Reformation, the Cromwellian rebellion and the revolution of 1688 from a Catholic point of view. He cannot be reckoned among the impartial historians, but his own bias constantly makes us aware of the bias in judgments which we regard as impartial simply because they are so familiar. His imaginative conception of the past and of character is extremely vivid.

In youth he wrote the lives of Marie Antoninette, Robespierre and Danton: still reckoned among the good English books about the French Revolution. He has written about sailing and rivers, and on that long Roman Road, 'Stane Street'; about his travels in Europe and North Africa and his rambles and rides up and down his beloved Sussex. He has written books discussing trenchantly the fundamental principles of government—of which ***The Servile State*** is to the point today, and examined English Party Government—perhaps with too French an eye. He has written the most amusing and widely read children's verses; vigorous satirical verse—as a scoffer few have matched him—*and* lyric poetry of so fine quality that his name will be remembered if only for that. Yet if Borrow's books have survived, why should not such a personal spirited book of travel and mental adventure as ***The Path To Rome*** also survive? Why not, indeed!

Readers of Mr. Belloc's prose know well how it rises into grander rhythms at moments of emotion or in describing something which has had for him a 'sacramental' or representative value—representative of the life of man. Before the first world war there was an 'Album of Opinions' in circulation—a sort of aesthetic questionnaire—I think drawn up by Robert Ross, art critic and wit—in which people asked their friends to record their answers to such questions as, 'Who do you think the best of living prose-writers? Who do you think the worst painter?' and so forth. Whenever this album was presented to me I used to write opposite the question 'Who do you think the most *underated* poet alive today?' 'Hilaire Belloc'. Sometimes the owner of the Album would say indulgently, 'Oh, that *is* interesting'—but she more often read my answer with bored contempt. Today that answer would not provoke astonishment. Among contemporary additions to Everyman's Library is a selection form his prose and verse, with a preface by A. G. Macdonell proclaiming his pre-eminence in both. But, if Mr. Macdonell and I are right that Hilaire Belloc is among the handful of contemporary poets whose work is good enough to last, why does general recognition still lag behind its merits?

It is not the small quantity of his verse; that was no bar to the wide recognition of Housman. Again, I think his versatility has something to do with it. In his collection of ***Sonnets and Verse,*** although that volume is far from bulky, the ironic, the rollicking, the romantic, the classical modes are all represented; and in each of these different spheres he has won attention so effectively that different readers are apt to judge him by one of them alone. Often when I have tried to drag others up to my own estimate of Belloc the poet, I have encountered—what shall I call it?—a censorious partiality for *one* department of his work. When I have praised him as a serious poet, I have been countered with the admission that his ***Bad Child's Book of Beasts*** is of course a masterpiece in nonsense. When I have urged his merits as an essayist saying, 'Do read ***Hills and the Sea***', I have been met with the admission that he is a first-rate satirist. When I have said, 'Look at his books of travel, his ***Path to Rome,*** and ***Esto Perpetua***' then I have been met with the admission that he has written first-rate accounts of battles and historical scenes; and when I have praised his ***Cranmer, Richelieu*** or ***Danton*** I have been fobbed off with 'Well, I grant you he has written a few good poems'. No writer has (for the time being) competed more disastrously with himself.

Of course I cannot remind you—*now*—how right these readers are in their several judgments, yet how wrong in their total estimates—time does not permit that. But not a few will recall, as I speak, portraits of absurd prigs, peers and imposters in his humorous verse.

His ***Cautionary Tales*** and ***More Peers*** hold a high place in comic English verse. And in his serious verse, when sweetness appears, it is 'honey from the lion's mouth', while in other poems he roars gloriously, defiantly. Then, together with A. E. Housman (who unfortunately seldom exercised that gift) he is the modern master of epigram. While the fighting mood, the mood of religious rest and moods of humility, despondency and defiance have found their appropriate exaltations in his lyric poems. I love the astringent *joy* in his poems. If ever my ear has caught the ring of that poetry which cannot be written by taking pains, yet cannot be perfected without them, I have heard it in Belloc's verse. (p. 119)

I remember once quoting [**'The Statue'**] and being met with the bored comment: 'Ah, yes, Landorian! *But Landor is a lasting poet!*' Yet observe, the Landorian note is only *one* on *this* poet's instrument, and recall that when Landor attempts to be light he is only monumentally skittish. But what gay enormity of relief is expressed in Belloc's epigram called **'The Telephone'.**

And what could be more successful than [his] satiric epigram **'On a Great Election'** that huge liberal rockover which in 1906 swept the Liberal Party into power and incidentally Mr. Belloc himself into the Parliament. . . .

What variety there is in that short book called ***Verses and Sonnets!*** There are not many pretty lamenting songs in English literature better than **'Ha'nacker Mill'**. . . . And finally, . . . [there is] his latest, longest, and—in passages—his greatest poem, **'In Praise of Wine'**. . . . I think we can afford to ignore any illiterate paper-tigers who try to tear that poet to pieces. Such poetry, I grant you, is traditional; I grant you it is not modern—but remember only a tiny portion of the world's *good* poetry can ever be—in any age, 'modern'. I grant you anybody capable of feeling understands such poetry at once. But perhaps that's an advantage. I grant you there is a distinction between rhetoric and poetry, but there is a noble eloquence which *is* poetry. What then shall we say of it in conclusion? The words of another great poet occur to me:

> The varying verse, the full resounding line,
> The long majestic march and energy divine.

(p. 120)

Desmond MacCarthy, "'Most Various of Living Authors'," in The Listener, *Vol. XLIV, No. 1122, July 27, 1950, pp. 119-20.*

EVELYN WAUGH (essay date 1954)

[From the publication in 1928 of his novel Decline and Fall *until his death in 1966, Waugh was England's leading satirical novelist. In such works as* Vile Bodies *(1930),* Scoop *(1938), and* The Loved One *(1948), he skewered such targets as the bored*

young sophisticates of the 1920s, the questionable values of the British press, and the American commercial trivialization of death. Considered a major Catholic author after his conversion in 1930, Waugh is best known today for his novel Brideshead Revisited *(1945), which examines the lives of the members of a wealthy Catholic family. Much of Waugh's post-conversion writings reflect the author's often-maligned Tory values of the preeminence of wealth, privilege, and proper insouciance. Waugh and Belloc were friends, and as such they have been occasionally likened to each other by critics for their militant Catholicism, sharp satiric skill, and bumptious personalities. In the following excerpt from a review written less than a year after Belloc's death, Waugh recalls his friend's funeral mass and the various sorts and classes of people who attended, likening the great diversity of this congregation to the diversity of Belloc's interests, many of which were reflected in* The Verse of Hilaire Belloc, *an omnibus collection which Waugh highly praises.*]

Hilaire Belloc's death last summer came at the end of nearly fifteen years during which he had written nothing and made no public appearance. Most of his books were out of print. The weekly paper to which he had devoted himself so prodigally had ceased publication. And yet at his Requiem Mass the great nave of Westminster Cathedral was thronged and by a congregation the greater part of whom, it seemed to one observer, were drawn by Belloc's fame rather than by personal acquaintance. It was not a literary occasion. Belloc was strictly, perhaps even ruthlessly, professional as a writer, but he made his life among men of action and women of society. Younger writers were often disconcerted when they discerned behind his massive courtesy an absolute ignorance of who they were and what they had written. There were friends in plenty in the Cathedral that August morning, men and women whose wide variety gave witness of the fullness of the man they were commemorating. (Belloc has been spoken of as a bigot and it is worth noting that of his close friends not more than half shared his religious faith and very few, if any, his political opinions.) But mingling with them and outnumbering them were people of all kinds and ages who may never have set eyes on Belloc but loved him in his work.

Those are Belloc's prime characters as a man and as a writer, his breadth of scope and the love he inspires. His poetry is quintessential of him. He himself recognized this fact most clearly. His prose works are copious, always lucid, often rising to fine passages of rhetoric, often memorable in their sharp definition of word, but they are for the most part the work of a craftsman, often a craftsman hired for an imposed task. His poetry is his art, something he kept quite distinct from literary commerce, to which he gave his full concentrated attention, into which he distilled all the noble essences which made him unique as a man, in which he confided as his warranty of lasting fame. Most of it was written before 1914, none after 1939. But in his years of leisure and rumination he never undertook the task of collection and collation. That, he was confident, would come later and here, very punctually, we have it [in ***The Verse of Hilaire Belloc***], a most welcome and worthy book. (p. 456)

There are more than 370 items in the collection, ranging in size and dignity from:

> I said to Heart, 'How goes it?' Heart replied:
> 'Right as a Ribstone Pippin!' But it lied.

to the sonorous ode on wine. The children's rhymes, almost every syllable of them a familiar quotation, are here reprinted without the illustrations which seemed an inalienable part of them. It is remarkable how well they stand alone. The order

Belloc in his later years. Courtesy of the Oxford Union Society.

of the original books of verses has been broken and the various poems felicitously regrouped under their forms as sonnets, songs, epigrams, ballades and so on. There are eleven items never before printed, thirteen that were privately printed, and forty-six that have not appeared in any previous collection. Now that all is gathered in, it can be seen how small a part of Belloc's work was 'Bellocian' in the vulgar usage.

> May all good fellows that here agree
> Drink Audit Ale in heaven with me,
> And may all my enemies go to hell!
> Noël! Noël! Noël! Noël!

Early lines, interpolations in a prose fantasy, far from typical, but meat for the parodist; the ebullience of a brief mood. Belloc's verse is by turn humorous, comic, tender, witty, angry, melancholy, formal; very seldom jolly. It is in large the complete expression of a man's soul—and a great soul. His themes are the stuff of common life as he knew it in a warmer age; strenuous male companionship, romantic love of woman, the sea, the seasons, the transience of earthly beauty, the unremitting benevolent watchfulness of Our Lady and the angels, the innocence of childhood, the absurdity of pedantry and ambition, the wickedness and stark danger of power. His diction and prosody are the fruit of classical schooling. He was a Christian Shropshire Lad and, by that enrichment, immeasurably Housman's superior. He needs no critical interpretation. He is here to be enjoyed. For that reason there were few articles about him in the literary reviews and many mourners at his obsequies.

He had an idiosyncratic conspectus, formed early, which seemed not to vary from 1912 until the day of his death. In his opinions, he was a traditionalist and a revolutionary. It will be the gracious task of Mr Robert Speaight, his biographer, to count the components of his intellectual structure and trace the origins of those seemingly discordant convictions which coexisted harmoniously in him. The reviewer of his ***Verses*** [sic] has an easier task, to express wonder at their variety and richness. (pp. 457-58)

Lines of Belloc's sing a multitude of memories. The wonder is, in finding them all collected, how profuse and how pure a genius is here displayed. (p. 458)

Evelyn Waugh, "Here's Richness," in his The Essays, Articles and Reviews of Evelyn Waugh, *edited by Donat Gallagher, Little, Brown and Company, 1984, pp. 456-58.*

RUSSELL KIRK (essay date 1954)

[*An American historian, political theorist, novelist, journalist, and lecturer, Kirk is one of America's most eminent conservative intellectuals. His works have provided a major impetus to the conservative revival that has developed since the 1950s.* The Conservative Mind *(1953), one of Kirk's early books, describes conservativism as a living body of ideas "struggling toward ascendancy in the United States"; in it Kirk traces the roots and canons of modern conservative thought to such important predecessors as Edmund Burke, John Adams, and Alexis de Tocqueville. Kirk has also been a trenchant critic of the decline of academic standards in American universities:* Decadence and Renewal in the Higher Learning *(1978), in particular, is a forceful denunciation of the "academic barbarism" which he states has replaced the traditional goals of higher education—wisdom and virtue—with the fallacious ones of "utilitarian efficiency," relaxed admissions, and innovative forms of education. The result, in Kirk's view, is that "the higher learning in America is a disgrace." Kirk's detractors have sometimes been skeptical of the charges he levels against liberal ideas and programs, accusing him of a simplistic, one-sided partisanship. His admirers, on the other hand, point to the alleged failure of liberal precepts—in particular those applied in the universities—as evidence of the incisiveness of Kirk's ideas and criticism. In the following excerpt from a review of Frederick Wilhelmsen's study* Hilaire Belloc: No Alienated Man *and a reprint edition of* The Path to Rome, *Kirk addresses Belloc's hatred, holding that it was directed solely at such targets as sham and pretension: legitimate targets for a Christian humanist. For an opposing view of Belloc's hatred, see the excerpt by David Lodge (1971).*]

"They will never love where they ought to love who do not hate where they ought to hate," Edmund Burke says in the fourth letter of the *Regicide Peace*. Hilaire Belloc . . . knew how to love and how to hate. We become the thing we hate, if we hate without understanding; but Belloc hated with discernment, and so is lovable as only a good, discerning hater is lovable. He hated all the shams and deceptions of his age, and "scourged the naked follies of the time." Possessed of the higher imagination, he detested the complacent pedant, and in a passage in that delightful book of travel and reflection, ***The Path to Rome,*** he struck home:

> Would you like to know why universities suffer from this curse of nervous disease? Why the greatest personages stammer or have St. Vitus' dance, or jabber at the lips, or hop in their walk, or have their heads screwed round, or tremble in their fingers, or go through life with great goggles like a motor car? Eh? I will tell you. It is the punishment of their *intellectual pride,* than which no sin is more offensive to the angels.

Now Belloc never was afflicted with intellectual pride, any more than Don Quixote, whom he much resembled in character; in this, as in other things, he did not come to incarnate the thing he hated; and therefore one does not resent even his worst inconsistencies, like his simultaneous affection for English monarchy and French republicanism, or his adulation of the Jacobins in despite of his yearnings after the mind of the Middle Ages. One even indulges him in his notion that the presidency of the United States is the finest modern example of true monarchy, "symbolizing a people and its traditions, exercising personal authority, responsible before the law, a public sacrifice to the land" (Mr. [Frederick] Wilhelmsen's words). With Belloc, as with Don Quixote, one can pardon a great deal of eccentricity for the sake of the transcendent vision which inspired his life and work. (pp. 483-84)

Against [the] degradation of the modern imagination, Belloc contended furiously, hating things that every lover of traditional human nature ought to hate. I do not think he is going to be forgotten; certainly the American publication of his ***Path to Rome,*** half a century after it first appeared in England, suggests that much of his work has taken on increased significance. The countries through which he walks on his way southward from the Moselle to Latium, the people with whom he talks, have a curiously antique flavor; he might almost have been walking and writing in the seventeenth century, instead of the last years of the nineteenth century; the automobile, mass-communication, and mass-production had not yet done their work in Germany, France, Switzerland, and Italy. The folk he admired along the way, like Belloc himself, were not alienated men; a subtle continuity linked them with their ancestors and with one another.

These people were not lost in the Lonely Crowd; and if we are to find our way out of mass loneliness, the anonymity of collectivism, we will need such truly human persons as Belloc. Mr. Wilhelmsen describes Hilaire Belloc as poet, or the dreamer of dreams; as sailor, or adventurer; as grizzlebeard, or the guardian of tradition. (These symbols are drawn from Belloc's book ***The Four Men.***) Poet and Sailor and Grizzlebeard are rare birds in the twentieth century; but if we deny them, then we will be saddled with the Barbarian; and that will be no pleasant servitude. Belloc himself knew the Barbarian for the nihilist of modern times that he is:

> We sit by and watch the Barbarian, we tolerate him; in the long stretches of peace we are not afraid.
>
> We are tickled by his irreverence, his comic inversion of our old certitudes and our fixed creeds refreshes us; we laugh. But as we laugh, we are watched by large and awful faces from beyond: and on those faces there is no smile.

(pp. 484-85)

Russell Kirk, in a review of "Hilaire Belloc: No Alienated Man" and "The Path to Rome," in The Western Political Quarterly, *Vol. VII, No. 3, September, 1954, pp. 483-85.*

ROBERT A. KANTRA (essay date 1965)

[*In the following excerpt, Kantra examines* The Path to Rome, The Four Men, *and several other of Belloc's works to elucidate the author's theory and use of irony.*]

The Path to Rome has many of the characteristics of ***The Four Men***, which Belloc subtitled "a farrago." Perhaps a polemic in disguise as George Shuster has called it, it is in any case an expressly literary pilgrimage as well as an actual travel record. The Catholic Church though geographically centered in Rome is the object of a kind of loyalty which transcends considerations of time and place. The path to Rome, like the walk through Sussex, has a literary significance which defies geographic and chronological identification. That is, the ambivalent devices of fantasy and morality and the conventions of autobiographic confession suggest that they both are a kind of fiction which, in Northrop Frye's schema, is called Menippean satire. The name of the literary form applies also to an attitude of mind.

The Path to Rome is in effect a sustained devotion like the Corpus Christi processional or the Stations of the Cross. This is not to deny that there is much humor in the book. Though not an account of a sentimental journey, it is full of Shandian tricks: a foolish Preface; word puns; ellipses, brackets, italics, and other peculiarities of punctuation; illustrations; nonsensical and irrelevant breaks ("So to make a long story short, as the publisher said when he published the popular edition of 'Pamela' . . ."); cataloging and dialoging. Belloc offers an explanation—by way of humorous anecdote—of "why a pilgrimage, an adventure so naturally full of great, wonderful, far-off and holy things should breed such fantastic nonsense as all this."

Yet, above all, the book is a first-person account of Belloc's "enchanted pilgrimage" or "great march" to a Church Triumphant rather than in behalf of a Church Militant. The description of the mountainous passages is more visionary than visual, what Frye calls free play of intellectual fancy, a vision of the world in terms of a single intellectual pattern: "When I call up for myself this great march I see it all mapped out in landscapes, each of which I caught from some mountain, and each of which joins to that before and to that after it, till I can piece together the whole road. The view here from the Hill of Archettes, the view from Ballon d'Alsace, from Glovelier Hill, from the Weissenstein . . . They unroll themselves all in their order till I can see Europe, and Rome shining at the end." Two Inner Voices, not people but rather attitudinal personae, constantly interrupt in order to clarify what Belloc has to say for himself to the reader. . . . Belloc throughout, in a kind of internal colloquy, entertains "a puzzling thought, very proper to a pilgrimage, which was: 'What do men mean by the desire to be dissolved and to enjoy the spirit free and without attachments?'" (pp. 131-32)

Belloc upon his arrival in Rome in 1901.

The Four Men: A Farrago is a satire by Belloc on appearances similar enough to ***The Path to Rome*** to invite comparison. A eulogy in praise of his native Sussex, the book was ordered by an American publisher but refused because of its "religious tone," a fact which I interpret as a symptom of its ambivalent nature. Like ***Path to Rome*** it too is a kind of pilgrimage, but even more full of "such fantastic nonsense," more sustained in its formal awareness or literary depiction of "dual destiny," more demonstrative of how "laughers have a gross cousinship with the most high" in prolonged "contrast and perpetual quarrel." The narrator "I" or "Myself" is less Belloc himself, for example, than is the narrator in ***Path to Rome***; "Myself" is less confessional in the autobiographic sense of personal revelation. He is less "real" as a person; he *is* indeed the other three personae: the Poet, the Sailor, and Grizzlebeard the philosopher; and the book he writes is, to use Frye's definition of confession, a sustained revelation of character and incident by a stream-of-consciousness technique. In ***Path to Rome*** Belloc is three men: I, Lector, and Auctor, the first only occasionally interrupted by the other two. In ***Four Men*** Belloc is Myself, Poet, Sailor, and Grizzlebeard in sustained colloquy. And the plot and scene as well as the narrator are subordinate to the purpose to which they are directed, and less directly identified with that purpose. The book is a travel fantasy: the personae represent no individual, real persons; and the locale though real enough is completely transformed in a dream sequence. This transformation is apparent from the beginning of the book: the frontispiece, for example, is a straightforward landscape painting of Sussex, while the first illustration (there are many, as in ***Path to Rome***) following the preface depicts a fanciful, utopian "Regni Regnorum cui vulgo Sussex nomen est." The time is "nine years ago" from October 29 to November 2, 1902—that is, Halloween, Feast of All Saints, and the Day of the Dead.

On a pilgrimage to "the land they know" (which is "really" Sussex in the dream of Myself), the four men (who are all "really" Belloc) sing Varronian songs on various heresies and religious abuses. The Sailor sings of Pelagius and a fictional "Bishop of Old Auxerre." . . . The Sailor tells the crowd listening that "every word of what we have just delivered to you is Government business." Nonsense, of course. So too the symbolism "when the Poet threw beer at a philosopher to baptise him and wake him into a new world." And the Man in the chair at the inn of Steyning, the "Hideous Being" (H. B.?), gives them a calling card bearing the fantastic name "Mr. Deusipsenotavit." All this no doubt has got a "religious tone" as the wary American publisher did fear. I submit that it is generically religious in its forcing a consideration of the differences between this world and an other world by way of an imaginative and necessarily nonsensical identification or confusion of them. This farrago has the effect of satire to the extent that the values of a real and imaginary world—the world of Government say, and a new world—are perceived as mixed or scrambled and, therefore, ridiculous.

Arguing the case for Belloc's "integrated Christian humanism," Frederick Wilhelmsen has asserted that "to grasp the essence of Belloc's integrated humanism is to possess the key to understanding his position as a satirist and controversialist" [see Additional Bibliography]. In his view, Belloc is no alienated man insofar as he neither "situates his destiny in this world" nor, despising the limits of the horizons, solely "contemplates the world beyond." Wilhelmsen calls ***Four Men*** "the most articulate and symbolic statement of the natural humanism underlying Belloc's militant Catholicism." He goes on to say that if Belloc is almost incomprehensible to the post-war intellectual (even the post-war Catholic intellectual), the lack of understanding can be traced to the amazing personal integration of the man and to the lack of comparable integration on the part of those most representative of the modern spirit. This may be pressing the case too much. Though Belloc is, no doubt, with Chesterton, Shaw, and Wells, among the Big Four of Edwardian Letters, and himself is Britain's foremost Catholic apologist in the twentieth century, it occurs to me that he is not much read. If such be the case, it may be beside the point to insist that he is incomprehensible. But the notion of an integrated Christian humanism does point to the kind of interest in two worlds which is, it seems to me, an unmistakable part of the form of religious satire: other-worldly commitment in constant interplay with this-worldly fact. The satire depends on or exists because of this juxtaposition. And secondly, it points willy-nilly to the relative nature of any definition of satire and the precariousness of "success" of any such satire. In a literary context of questionable viability and appeal, the integration of two kinds of value will be an attempt rather than an achievement. Religious satire, regarded as an attitude of mind as well as a literary form, will always be difficult to define or to find an audience for. Among literary historians, the Humanist-Christian antithesis is one of the most persistent, and slippery, commonplaces. And, as Robert C. Elliott has demonstrated, both a satirist's work and his status with respect to society are necessarily problematic; the power of satire is a mysterious and magical thing.

The *Mythos* of Winter, in Frye's literary theory, includes both irony and satire, the chief distinction being that irony is a lesser satire, satire a more militant irony. In terms of this theory, and considering the setting and time of ***Four Men***, I would say that Belloc's satire is autumnal rather than wintery, ironic rather than satiric. Considering the difference between irony and satire to be one of degree rather than kind, I would say that in Belloc's literary work the most "militant irony" is to be found in his political and economic satire: ***Emmanuel Burden, Mr. Clutterbuck's Election***, or ***A Change in the Cabinet***. His militant religious defenses more usually take the form of history, which is mostly what Belloc wrote (or, as his detractors would say, tried to write). His religious satire is both less frequent and less militantly ironic. As a series of literary skits, ***Caliban's Guide to Letters*** for example does not produce the artistic effect which Chesterton approbatively called blasphemy. It has nothing of the tragedy or tragic irony leading to the large visions of evil in a personal form, as they are created by many other religious satirists: Chesterton's Lord Ivywood in *The Flying Inn*, Benson's Julian Felsenburgh in *Lord of the World*, Firbank's eccentric and epicene Cardinal Pirelli, Huxley's Mustapha Mond in *Brave New World*, C. S. Lewis' disembodied Devil in *That Hideous Strength*, or Bertrand Russell's incarnate Inca in *Zahatapolk*. Belloc's Thomas Caliban, Doctor of Divinity and practicing journalist, solemnly asserts that "Whosoever works for Humanity works, whether he knows it or not, for himself as well." As a Comtean caricature, Caliban is effective enough, but surely not vicious. The "I" of the ***Guide*** is Caliban's literary executor, a punning word in the context; but his portrait of Caliban is, despite either of the nametags, pathetic rather than cruel. ***Lambkin's Remains*** is more biting, but again, for a work by a prolific apologist, remarkably gentle as religious satire. The butt of the joke, Lambkin, is a clerical don, but his portrait is, as Robert Speaight says, immortal in a minor way because of the infusion of satire with affection. Lambkin (a diminutive Lamb of God?) is no ogre, and in his portrait we scarcely begin to see the gentlemanly Prince of Darkness bottom side up. (pp. 132-35)

Irony may be a lesser satire. Still, according to my interest in Belloc's religious satire apart from his other genres, and insisting that it *is* religious in a way which goes beyond the obvious fact of its subject—namely, its religious intention and its effect depending at least on the recognition of that intention—I call to mind Belloc's essay **"On Irony"** as a statement of his intention. Irony is a sword, Belloc says, which must be *used* as a sword, but "which like some faery sword . . . cannot be used with any propriety save in God's purpose." It may be treated angrily where men love ease, he says, and be merely ignored when men have lost a sense of justice. And to many—the young, the pure, the ingenuous—irony must always "appear to have in it a quality of something evil, and so it has, for . . . it is a sword to wound." The intention of irony is to wound, and in the wounding to effect "the curing and preserving of morals." In Belloc's view, "irony is in touch with the divine and is a minister to truth"; and in the perception as well as in the literary creation of irony "there is nothing less than the power by which truth is of such effect among men. No man possessed of irony and using it has lived happily; nor has any man possessing it and using it died without having done great good to his fellows and secured a singular advantage to his own soul." It is a faery sword that the literary "executor" uses on Caliban. If a reader shares Belloc's view, the mutual assumption about irony is that even if it is "lesser satire" its effect is yet pain rather than pleasure, the intention of the writer and the reader alike being a kind of religious purgation. (pp. 135-36)

Robert A. Kantra, "Irony in Belloc," in Renascence, *Vol. XVII, No. 3, Spring, 1965, pp. 131-36.*

GARRY WILLS (essay date 1970)

[Wills is a syndicated American columnist and the author of books on such widely diverse subjects as Jack Ruby, race relations in America, and G. K. Chesterton. He is probably best known for his incisive political commentaries, especially as they appear in such books as Nixon Agonistes: The Crisis of a Self-Made Man *(1970)* and Confessions of a Conservative *(1979). A critic of both the American liberal and conservative establishments, Wills has been described by one critic as "an undogmatic conservative who is ready to let his experiences influence his conclusions" and who is "cheerfully resigned to being a singular conservative, a renegade in the eyes of others who crowd under that rubric." In the following excerpt, Wills surveys the various genres in which Bel-*

loc worked, finding the latter's strengths to lie in his poetry, literary criticism, and personal essays.]

Belloc, who had enough bad luck and then manufactured more, underwent the special trial of being best-known for what he did worst. In all his many roles, there is an exact gradation—the more it fit his known pose and persona, the less did it express his true gifts and genius. We need only list in order the principal claims on his contemporaries' attention to see how this fatal law worked:

1) *Historian.* He had prepared for an academic career as an historian, and did the bulk of his work in this field. His broad judgments and basic instincts corrected some errors of the time, and would have made one good book of wicked destruction. But he never filled in details, improved his vision, or grew as an historian. He lived off those first corrective exaggerations and punched out book after book by sheer stylistic bravado. He wrote ambitious biographies on cruises, in private homes, without libraries or sources, filling the books out with his vague impressive rhetoric, a *tour-de-force* of sorts, but one that spread and cheapened his gifts of eloquence.

Most of his historical work was done in the popular vein of "readable biography," yet he was not a portraitist. One rarely gets a sense of the individual. Belloc could not cast himself outside his own preoccupations, so what we get are portentous glimpses of cloudy battle—huge forces clashing, Faith, Europe, Reason, the West—always the same, whether the book be about Cranmer, Napoleon or Cromwell. When he ran out of particulars and could say nothing new, he trotted out the great Abstractions and made them stalk about his narrow stage like melodrama ghosts.

2) *War Commentator.* Belloc reached his largest popular audience, in both World Wars, as a newspaper analyst of Allied strategy. War fascinated him, in history and biography, and he loved to describe battles. But he liked them for the wrong reason. He thought them instances of human control, of the mind shaping events. He never learned Kutuzov's lesson about "the logic of battle," and he invariably simplified. This made his running commentary and prediction, in wartime, disastrously wrong.

3) *Catholic Apologist.* Because Belloc was always talking of "the Faith," of its destiny and historical fortunes, he is considered a theological propagandist. But what he usually meant was Christendom, the historical body of the faithful. About religious truths he read little and wrote less. The one most embarrassing moment in all his books comes when he tries to offer a logical proof for the existence of God. Belloc praised rigorous thinking, and his favorite stylists were those who could convey an impression of such rigor—Gibbon, Swift, Dr. Johnson. But it was all a matter of bracing literary *atmosphere.* Those without the style bored him (e.g., St. Thomas). Those with a more romantic style repelled him (e.g., St. Augustine—along with his official friend, and secret rival, Chesterton). Belloc was incapable of logic.

4) *Political Analyst.* Lacking rigor, he was prey to unchecked emotional prejudices, and these made his political views a crazyquilt. He was a monarchist who admired the French Revolution, a man of eighteenth-century taste who praised medieval institutions—once again, it is *style* that confuses his head by commanding his heart. Modern parliamentary politicians were not so much wicked or wrong as colorless. The overrated "predictions" of ***The Servile State***, falsified by events, have been exploited by people excerpting bits and tags to support the most disparate views.

5) *Novelist.* His contemporaries read the novels for contemporary (if veiled) reference and satire. But the wit is clogged and weighed down by the plotting and conventions of the novel form.

6) *Poet.* Things are getting better—it is emotion we must go to Belloc for, not thought. He felt he should have been a poet, and labored at it more than he would admit. His small body of work is full of haunting lines, but he could not sustain a single vision throughout a poem. Separate beauties detach themselves and drift, while all the rest sinks. The epigram is the only distance he can go, with any regularity, in serious verse.

7) *Literary Critic.* He did little of this, but it is all excellent. In fact, ***Avril*** is that rare thing, a perfect book—short, shaped, precise, a masterpiece itself, illuminating other masterpieces. Even when he treats literature just in passing, he does it with great feeling and insight—e.g., discussing the style of Cranmer or of Calvin. In fact, the only thing that could "explain" so obvious yet subtle a poem as Catullus 3 is Belloc's play with, and expansion of, its tone in *On a Lost Manuscript.*

Belloc's ***Milton***, too, is a better introduction to the poet than C. S. Lewis' better-known and widely used little book. Belloc begins with the main thing, a realization that Milton is not austere but intensely sensuous. In verbal witchery and sheer outpour of gorgeous sound he easily outdid Hopkins and Swinburne. Belloc offers the best approach to Milton's thought, such as it was—*trust the music.* What the music says, matters. What it doesn't, doesn't.

8) *Satirist.* Here he takes command. His comic verse is as good as Swift's, as disciplined and as savage, fueled with scorn and hatred for human pettiness, compromise, betrayal.

9) *Personal Essayist.* The sway of his emotions, the tug of contradictory loves and loyalties, all the things that mar his other work and thinking, here become sources of strength. He had few thoughts, but a thousand moods, and they play beautifully through the rainbow-prose of the essays, which are alternately (sometimes simultaneously) mournful and playful, frothy and meditative. The language runs free, not forced as in the histories and "big books," obeying his moods as it never did his mind. So much is this his medium, mastered by him, that he could extend the tone of personal essay to book length, in ***The Path to Rome*** or ***The Four Men***.

Even the good parts of his other books are often personal essays pushing up through the barren surface of narrative. Even a stray successful poem—like the one ending "On with my overcoat, and out into the night"—works because it uses the whimsy of his essay-style. His longer letters belong to the same genre, and make his output of essays staggering in size as well as quality. They are his best work, and he will live in them. (pp. 1218, 1221)

Garry Wills, "His Own Worst Critic," in National Review, *Vol. XXII, No. 45, November 17, 1970, pp. 1218, 1221.*

DAVID LODGE (essay date 1971)

[*Lodge is an English novelist, critic, and editor. The author of novels that reflect his Catholic background, he has also written book-length studies on the works of his co-religionists Graham*

Greene and Evelyn Waugh. In the following excerpt, Lodge examines the anti-Semitic element in Belloc's writings, finding that Belloc—and to a lesser extent, his friend G. K. Chesterton—contributed to Europe's atmosphere of anti-Jewish hatred which culminated in the Holocaust.]

[G. K. Chesterton and Hilaire Belloc] have suffered a steep decline in popularity over the last three decades. Chesterton is read more and more selectively by fewer and fewer people; and Belloc is in almost total eclipse. The world-famous partnership that George Bernard Shaw dubbed 'the Chesterbelloc' has had a great fall, and few seem interested in putting it together again.

There are many reasons for this. The Modern Movement in literature, which Chesterton and Belloc either opposed or ignored, has become classical for our culture, and their own work looks thin and faded in comparison. The form to which they devoted so much of their time and energy—the whimsical, ruminative essay—is dead and unmourned. Their intellectual amateurism is unfashionable. And the ideas for which they stood have largely lost their relevance.

Those ideas were always controversial, but they once commanded considerable respect, and the support of a large Christian, specifically Catholic, reading public. The Chesterbelloc's brand of Catholicism however—triumphalist, proselytizing, theologically conservative, Europe-orientated—is hardly congenial to the mood of the Church since Pope John XXIII and the Second Vatican Council. Chesterton and Belloc were the propagandists and cheer-leaders of the Catholic ghetto, dedicated to proving that it was really the City of God. Belloc described their strategy in a revealing letter:

> Threaten we cannot, because we are nobody, all the temporal power is on the other side. But we *can* spread the mood that we are the bosses and the *chic* and that a man who does not accept the Faith writes himself down as suburban. Upon these amiable lines do I proceed.

There is a certain irony in associating Chesterton and Belloc with the Catholic 'ghetto', because one of the major factors in the decline of their popularity is that they have the reputation of being anti-semitic. For liberal, non-Catholics this was always an objection to their work. . . . It is since the last World War, since 'Hitler's persecution' that the anti-Jewish sentiment in these two Catholic writers has become an embarrassment to their co-religionists. As Belloc's biographer, Robert Speaight, says of the repulsive Jewish financier, Mr. Barnett, portrayed in Belloc's first novel, 'too much has happened to the Jews since ***Emmanuel Burden*** was written for Mr. Barnett to make comfortable reading today'. (pp. 145-46)

The alleged anti-semitism of these two writers is not perhaps a purely literary question; but they were not purely literary writers. The charge has undoubtedly affected the reception of their work, yet it has never, as far as I know, been properly documented by their accusers, or honestly investigated by their defenders. It seems worthwhile, therefore, to try and establish exactly what the Chesterbelloc's attitude to the Jews was, how it fitted into the total structure of the two men's ideas, and how it related to attitudes and events in society at large.

Anti-semitism is only one form of a persistent and deplorable tendency of human beings, individually and collectively, to relieve feelings of fear and frustration by projecting them on to others. (p. 146)

In the days of the Early Church, Christianity was regarded as a Jewish sect, and Christians were as concerned to dissociate themselves from the Jews as from pagans. The effect of this acrimony can be seen in St John's use of the blanket term 'the Jews', where the earlier evangelists Matthew, Mark and Luke had used the more specific terms scribes, pharisees, elders, etc., to describe the opponents of Christ. In this way the idea developed that it was not mankind that had crucified Christ, but 'the Jews', a cursed race who were punished for their deicide by the Dispersion, but unrepentantly retained a spirit of revengeful malice, like the Devil himself. (p. 147)

Modern anti-semitism, however, also has other origins. It seems to begin with the attempt of a few clerical writers, early in the nineteenth century, to blame the French Revolution on a Jewish-Masonic conspiracy. This preposterous theory did not really catch on, but it was significant because, as Cohn points out, the eruption of anti-semitism later in the century was especially contagious among the people who felt most threatened by the changes in society that the Revolution had ushered in: democracy, industrialization, secularization.

The Jews themselves had benefited from those changes in Western Europe. Granted full civil rights, they came out of the ghettos and began to play a full part in society, their tradition and history fitting them for success in modern urban professions such as banking, commerce, journalism and the arts. This success, however, only produced envy and fear which could be exploited by fanatics and politicians. The Dreyfus case was a classic example: conservative and patriotic Frenchmen, demoralized by defeat in the Franco-Prussian war, found a perfect scapegoat in the notion of a Jewish spy who had infiltrated the top levels of military command. In Russia, the tottering Czarist regime sought to divert the unrest and frustration of its ill-governed people against the Jewish settlements in a series of organized pogroms. And it was the Czarist secret service which forged the notorious *Protocols of the Elders of Zion* some time in the late 1890s. (pp. 147-48)

Hilaire Belloc and G. K. Chesterton both denied, on many occasions, that they were anti-semites; and it is true that neither of them manifested this kind of prejudice in its most violent and extreme form. They both roundly condemned persecution and attempted extermination of Jews, and they dissociated themselves from race-hatred and the wilder fantasies about a Jewish conspiracy to dominate the world. Both were able to invoke the 'Some of my best friends . . .' argument. But they were, for various reasons, receptive to the two strains of anti-semitism summarily described above. Although they denied that there was a religious element in their feelings about the Jews, for Belloc at least the old idea of deicide was a reality, as this gruesomely arch comment in a letter reveals:

> The poor darlings, I'm awfully fond of them, and I'm awfully sorry for them, but it's their own silly fault—they ought to have left God alone.

The Christianity of both men was of a romantically conservative character, yearning back to a somewhat idealized medieval Christendom—the period when the demonology of anti-semitism was fully developed. (pp. 148-49)

Both Chesterton and Belloc were intensely critical of industrial capitalism. So, perhaps, were most enlightened men of their time; but whereas the latter tended to espouse some form of socialism as the solution, Chesterton and Belloc saw this as only promising a different kind of political and economic slavery. Their own political programme of Distributism (i.e. sharing out land in small parcels among the people) cut right across the conventional political spectrum. It was a quite impracticable policy, which led both men ultimately into frustration and a flirtation with fascism; but it provided the base from which they launched their critique of capitalism, in which usury was a key concept. (p. 149)

To Chesterton and Belloc, nineteenth-century capitalism was essentially usury, and the fact that Jews (most notably the Rothschild family) were prominent in the field of high finance was evidence that capitalism was essentially alien to Christian culture. Much (though not all) of their 'anti-semitism' consisted of identifying Jewry with the evils of modern capitalism. . . . In a letter, Belloc described parliamentary democracy in Europe as a sham: 'It means in practice government by a few rich men with an absurd preponderance of financial banking and largely Jaewish power.'

This kind of statement is not really falsifiable. That modern capitalism is a Jewish invention, or monopoly, is demonstrably untrue. But who can say whether Jews have exercised disproportionate or exceptionally unscrupulous control over it? It seems likely that, allowing for the fact that Jews have been channelled into commerce by their history, there has not been a more than average number of Jewish millionaires and Jewish swindlers; but how could you ever demonstrate this statistically? The position adopted by Chesterton and Belloc was of the kind which is not open to negative evidence, and for which positive evidence, in the nature of things, must inevitably be forthcoming. This is why their attitude sometimes appears uncomfortably like the paranoia of the fanatical anti-semite.

Their critique of British Imperialism in its late phase was often morally justified, but was unbalanced by their exaggeration of the part played by Jewish finance in imperialistic adventures. They claimed that the Boer War was engineered by Jewish millionaires with investments in South African mines. No doubt this *was* a factor, and Belloc's scathing **'Verses to a Lord who, in the House of Lords, said that those who opposed the South African Adventure confused Soldiers with Money-Grubbers'** makes the point forcefully. But many other people besides Jews had investments of either money or patriotic emotion in the war, without which it could not have been conducted.

The Lord addressed by Belloc would have been a businessman of Jewish extraction who had gone into politics and been rewarded with a peerage for his services and financial contributions to one of the parties. This was a common occurrence, and one that goaded the Chesterbelloc to fury. In their view such men were aliens who, under assumed names, had infiltrated the already corrupt British political system, and were using the privileges of power to further their own interests and those of the international Jewish business community, disregarding the interests of their adopted country. Belloc's early satirical novels were dedicated to exposing this type, especially in the character who appears in ***Emmanuel Burden*** . . . as Mr Barnett (not of course his real name) and reappears in [***Mr Clutterbuck's Election, A Change in the Cabinet,*** and ***Pongo and the Bull***] . . . , acquiring the titles of Lord Lambeth and the Duke of Battersea as he climbs the ladder of power. Barnett is the stock type of the odious Jewish financier: he is physically repulsive, with hooked nose, thick lips, gross body and greasy curls (Chesterton's illustrations to ***Emmanuel Burden*** enforce the point); he lacks refinement of manners, speaks with a lisp in broken syntax, and betrays his origins (the Frankfurt ghetto) with every gesture. Having survived the bankruptcy of his first

Caricature of Belloc by Richard Willson. Reproduced by permission of Richard Willson.

shady business enterprise, he makes his fortune in foreign speculations conducted under the respectable cover of imperialist expansion, manipulating the market and public opinion through a network of contacts and hirelings in politics and journalism.

These novels tend to follow a standard formula. There is a decent but stupid British merchant who becomes the tool of a Jewish-controlled ring of politicians and financiers, which is in turn opposed by a bluff, honest Englishman. ***Mr Clutterbuck's Election*** is particularly interesting because of the character of the bluff honest Englishman, Mr Bailey. For Mr Bailey is an avowed anti-semite:

> He had gone mad upon the Hebrew race. He saw Jews everywhere: he not only saw them everywhere, but he saw them in conspiracy. . . .According to him Lombroso was a Jew, Mr Roosevelt's friends and supporters the Belmonts were Jews, half the moneyed backers of Roosevelt were Jews, the famous critic Brandes was a Jew, Zola was a Jew, Nordau was a Jew, Witte was a Jew—or in some mysterious way connected with the Jews. . . . The disease advanced with his advancing age; soon all the great family of Arnold were Jews; half the aristocracy had Jewish blood; for a little he would have accused the Pope of Rome or the Royal Family itself; and I need hardly say that every widespread influence, from Freemasonry to the international finance of Europe, was Israelite in his eyes. . . .

At first sight this looks like a caricature of the anti-semite, put in to counterbalance, for the sake of fairness, the portrait of Barnett. The list of Jews and Jewish influences (which I have much reduced) seems intentionally preposterous. The narrator of this novel, however, is unreliable, and the truth is usually the reverse of what he appears to say. According to the logic of the book's rhetoric, therefore, the prejudices recorded in this passage are well-founded, and in fact the story confirms them: Mr. Bailey *does* uncover Jewish-inspired corruption and intrigue everywhere he goes. No doubt Belloc protected himself by throwing in a few patent absurdities—like the Pope and the Royal Family, but there is little doubt, on internal and external evidence, that Belloc presents Bailey as a man who erred, if he erred at all, on the side of truth.

Belloc was always the more violently anti-Jewish half of the Chesterbelloc, partly because he was more of a natural hater, a hard and aggressive man compared to the genial and much-loved Chesterton; and partly because of his origins and upbringing. (pp. 149-52)

[Although] both men were too humane and too intelligent to indulge in the hateful and irrational kind of anti-semitism which prepared the way for Hitler's policy of genocide, they often seem to be either unconsciously or irresponsibly flirting with it.

A crucial document here is Belloc's book, ***The Jews***. . . . In the course of it, he exposes the contradictions of extreme anti-semitism, and declares (he was of course writing after *The Times*'s exposure of the *Protocols*), 'the conception of a vast, age-long plot culminating in the contemporary Russian affair will not hold water.' . . . But he does say that 'the Anti-Semitic movement is essentially a reaction against the abnormal growth in Jewish power, and the new strength of Anti-Semitism is largely due to the Jews themselves.' . . . He does say that 'the Bolshevist Movement was *a* Jewish Movement.' . . . He does say that 'the Jew has *collectively* a power today, in the white world, altogether excessive.' . . . Again and again in this book, his most serious and responsible statement on the subject, Belloc uses the existence of anti-semitism as evidence that a 'problem' exists, never perceiving that anti-semitism itself might be the problem.

'It is the thesis of this book', Belloc begins, 'that the continued presence of the Jewish nation intermixed with other nations alien to it presents a permanent problem of the gravest character.' . . . Once you begin talking about 'problems' (it was Hitler's favourite diplomatic ploy), you imply the need for a solution, and the only solution in this case was Hitler's 'Final Solution'. Belloc claimed that there was an alternative—not 'elimination' but 'segregation' or, as he preferred to term it, 'recognition'. Considering the length of the book, Belloc is suspiciously vague about what this would entail, but it seems to mean some surrender of civil rights by the Jews in exchange for certain privileges—a return in fact to something like the medieval ghetto. . . . Belloc said that 'recognition' should be mutually agreed, but added darkly that if the Jew refused to co-operate, 'then the community will be compelled to legislate in spite of him.' . . . This all has an ominously prophetic note in view of the Nazis' initial legislative persecution of the Jews in the 'thirties. (pp. 154-55)

Is it fair to read such statements in the light of tragic later events? Certainly it is important to recognize that the kind of prejudice Chesterton and Belloc displayed was by no means uncommon in their time. When Belloc visited the United States in 1923, he was almost embarrassed by the violence of the anti-semitism he encountered. 'The Jew Question is a frightful bore here,' he wrote in a letter. 'People talk of it morning, noon and night. Those who know I have written a book on it take it for granted that I am in approval of a general massacre.'

The clichés of anti-Jewish prejudice litter the pages of twentieth-century literature up to the last War. T. S. Eliot and Ezra Pound are notorious in this respect. Their right-wing politics and (in Eliot's case) militant Christian orthodoxy made them sympathetic to the proto-fascist *Action Française* group led by Charles Maurras, which was a hotbed of anti-semitism. But writers of every ideological shade and level of brow were apt to exploit the stock response in portraying Jews. Wells and Arnold Bennett were guilty on occasion. 'An hotel full of Jews of the wrong, rich sort', sounds like a line from John Buchan, but is in fact from a story by D. H. Lawrence ('The Captain's Doll'). (p. 155)

[But like Wells, Lawrence, and the others, Chesterton and Belloc] were playing with fire; fire that (though the possibility never crossed their minds and would have shocked and horrified them had it done so) eventually burned in the oven of Auschwitz.

Basically, theirs was a failure of imagination. Celebrated for wit, humour, irony and paradox, they never seem to have turned these liberating modes of perception upon their own assumptions and prejudices. Belloc simply does not see that when (in ***The Jews***) he solemnly states with the air of uncovering a sinister secret, that Matthew Arnold, Charles Kingsley, 'General' Moss-Booth (founder of the Salvation Army) and Robert Browning had Jewish blood, he is making nonsense of his own argument that Jews are not assimilable into other societies—for it would be difficult to choose a more quintessentially English quartet of Eminent Victorians. He does not see that his own sense of nationality, so clearly divided between France and England, was precisely parallel to the dual nationality with which he taxed European Jews. Most glaringly of all, neither Chesterton nor Belloc perceived how vulnerable they were as members of the Catholic Church in a Protestant-secular state, to the criticisms they themselves made of the Jews. As Robert Speaight observes: 'Here, too, was a society highly, though less secretly organized, and in a measure set apart; conscious of its superiority, alien to some extent to all that stood outside it; international and in certain matters of moral consequence challenging civic authority; persecuted and perpetually resurgent.' In fact anti-Catholic prejudice tends to follow much the same pattern as anti-semitism, and Jesuits have, in their time, been accused of the same crimes, from poisoning wells to global conspiracy, as Rabbis. (pp. 156-57)

David Lodge, "The Chesterbelloc and the Jews," in his The Novelist at the Crossroads and Other Essays on Fiction and Criticism, *Cornell University Press, 1971, pp. 145-58.**

JAY P. CORRIN (essay date 1981)

[Corrin is an American educator. In the following excerpt from his study G. K. Chesterton and Hilaire Belloc: The Battle against Modernity, *he discusses the background and aim of Distributism, closely delineating the social and political views shared by Chesterton and Belloc.]*

The memorable Chesterbelloc partnership was a natural arrangement which grew out of a mutual distaste for imperialism and the philosophical anarchy of the *fin de siècle*. Despite the initial meaning of Shaw's portmanteau, the Chesterbelloc came to signify in the popular mind a particular Catholic approach to the social and political problems of modern Britain. At the base of their views was a strong belief in democracy and the common man and an appreciation of the social importance of private ownership and family life. These two men of enormous literary talent mounted a vigorous journalistic crusade and political movement that sought to beckon a decadent nation back to the fixed standards of an essentially Christian way of life.

The socio-political ideas propounded by Chesterton and Belloc, which came to be called Distributism, merit scholarly attention for a variety of reasons. Most importantly, Distributism was not an incidental phase of Chesterton's and Belloc's literary careers. Rather, it was the all-consuming passion which formed the basis of their philosophical assult on the evils of capitalist-industrial society, and indeed on the whole process of modernization itself. Unlike many modern English writers, who gave only superficial attention to politics, Chesterton and Belloc considered the exposition of the Distributist critique their most important moral duty. Distributist ideas color virtually all of their writings, and are therefore essential to a proper appreciation of the literary careers of Chesterton and Belloc.

Distributism is also of interest as intellectual history, for it constituted a revolutionary response to the conformity of the modern industrial age, and had a momentous impact on an entire generation of Catholic writers, not to mention those on the political left, such as G.D.H. Cole, R. H. Tawney, and the guild socialists. The Chesterbelloc's critique of collectivism tore gaping holes in Fabian philosophy and many people were drawn away from Fabianism because of it. In retrospect, Distributism seems to have been a generation or two in advance of the practical world. Indeed, one could argue that the Chesterbelloc's ideas have an even greater relevance to the problems of post-industrial than of industrial society. There is abundant evidence to suggest that contemporaries are now moving in many of the same directions prescribed by the Chesterbelloc. (pp. 201-02)

[The] present trend back to the basics of simple living and the new assaults on the dehumanizing technology of industrial capitalism demonstrated in the works of E. F. Schumacher, Paul Goodman, Ivan Illich, Jacques Ellul, and Michael Harrington, among others, and the increasing popularity of ecologically-minded, back-to-the-land periodicals such as Britian's *Resurgence* and the *Country Journal* in New England, attest to the current relevance of Distributist social and economic objectives.

In the beginning, the Chesterbelloc felt that social and political reform might be achieved through parliamentary politics. However, Belloc's personal encounter with what he called the "party system" convinced him that constructive change could come about only if the public were made to realize the insidious power of money, which, in his view, completely controlled parliamentary government. Hence, in 1911 he and Cecil Chesterton launched the *Eye-Witness*, a journalistic venture which aimed to convince the public that the nation's political system was riddled with corruption. The *Eye* and *New Witness* were not polite papers: they were intended to shock readers by laying bare the rottenness of British politics. The literary partnership of Hilaire Belloc and Cecil Chesterton, two controversialists with enormous capacities for hate, resulted in some rather rancorous journalism. Their potential for careless extremism was certainly manifested in the Marconi affair (an incident which served to alienate Belloc and both Chestertons from mainstream politics), and by the end of World War I the *New Witness* had earned a reputation for being not quite balanced on the subject of Prussians and Jews.

Belloc had an answer for what he felt was the deterioration of British politics and a bungled peace. According to his analysis, the old British aristocracy had been replaced by a clique of vulgar plutocrats who danced to the whims of financiers. To remedy this ill, he and Cecil Chesterton had called for some sweeping parliamentary changes and restoration of monarchical prerogative. (pp. 203-04)

Distributism and indeed the Chesterbelloc's whole approach to life were firmly rooted in the tradition of the Roman Church. This factor in itself made it inevitable that their political movement would function outside the normal paths of British politics. The fact that Chesterton and Belloc perpetually emphasized their ties with Rome undoubtedly prejudiced their case with the public, for Britain was steeped in an almost unbroken anti-Catholic tradition. In addition, the strong Whig-Protestant bias in British intellectual circles forced the Chesterbelloc to indulge in unusually tendentious historical polemics. Belloc, in particular, appears to have exaggerated his ideas just to get a public hearing. This only served to highlight the Chesterbelloc's public image as unrespectable political extremists. (pp. 204-05)

On the whole, the ideas of Chesterton and Belloc were not taken seriously by the political and religious establishment. There was good reason for this: if carried to its logical conclusion, Distributism would have led to revolution and anarchy. Like the Levellers of old, the Chesterbelloc fully intended to turn the world upside-down. Although Chesterton and Belloc had a negligible impact on mainstream politics, their perceptive judgment of industrial society and parliamentary government gained them an enthusiastic following amongst those who were upset at what they perceived as Britain's aimless drift into the twentieth century. Those who considered themselves part of the Distributist circle also approached politics and social issues from fundamentally Catholic assumptions. Opposed to the socialist complexion of the Labour movement as well as to the capitalist sympathies of the Tory Party, the Chesterbelloc alliance asserted that modern man needed the determinate standards of a hierarchical society, the security of private ownership, and a healthy family life in order to exercise the Christian ideal of freedom.

G. K.'s Weekly and the Distributist League were the major vehicles for bringing about the kinds of changes the Chesterbelloc felt necessary for Britain. (p. 205)

[They] were to show man the beauty and adventure of owning property. Ultimately, the success of Distributism depended upon individual men who would desire the liberty and self-reliance that private ownership could bring. Unlike socialism, capitalism, and fascism, Distributism could not be imposed on the majority by a narrow coterie of revolutionists or well-financed wirepullers. In the tradition of anarchism, Distributism could not be realized through laws or the sinews of bureaucracy: it had to be desired by common man and would endure only through the will to possess property. Thus the Chesterbelloc had to make people aware of the efficacy of Christian social and economic values as the basis for the intellectual revolution which was the prerequisite for the practical implementation of Distributism. This meant that the nation would have to return to essentially Catholic values; but given Britain's Protestant tradition and the secular and bureaucratic temper of postwar industrial society, such a requirement was probably impossible to fulfill.

In the final analysis, the Chesterbelloc did not fail completely in this Sisyphean endeavor, for their ideas were the inspiration of the Catholic back-to-the-land movements and the mainspring of the neo-Thomistic revival in Catholic intellectual circles. Equally important was their success in breaking down siege Catholicism in England. As Douglas Jerrold put it: ''The Chesterbelloc brought Catholicism out of private and into public life.'' Their aggressive polemical writings destroyed the Catholic intellectual's inferiority complex and offered him some well-thought-out social and political principles with which to challenge the ideological assumptions of the modern world.

The Chesterbelloc alliance was not an imitative movement. There was an obvious parallel with the French Right; indeed, Belloc greatly admired Maurras and Déroulède, and all three propounded similar anti-Semitic themes. But the resemblance was only skin-deep. Distributism developed independently of contemporary continental political thought, though it seemed to have some affinity with nineteenth-century continental romanticism and its cult of the middle ages. Belloc's peculiar conception of Catholicism as culture certainly appears to have been unique for his own generation. His view of monarchy was not the same as that of Maurras, nor did he share the anti-republicanism of the elitist French Right. (pp. 207-08)

The Distributist movement was also unique in the context of English political tradition. Drawing upon a mélange of attitudes and ideas (Chartism, Burkean organicism, French revolutionary thought, socialism, anarachism, populism, and liberalism), the social philosophy of Chesterton and Belloc was a peculiar hybrid of both radical and conservative ideas. Although leaning to the right, many of their intellectual sympathies were with the left. Belloc began his political career as a Radical Liberal, Chesterton always called himself a Liberal in the radical tradition, and both men flirted with anarcho-syndicalism during the prewar years. Most Distributists conspicuously emphasized a loyalty to the social and anarchistic ideals of Ruskin and Morris, as well as to the egalitarian concepts of the early socialists. The Chesterbelloc ultimately rejected the labor movement because of its statism. But on the whole, Distributism seems to have had closer ties to the tradition of English conservatism; it looked to the past for social and political models, recognized man as a fallen creature, and appreciated the practical necessity of hierachy, social deference, religion, and strong family ties. Much like Carlyle, Arnold, and other nineteenth-century romantic conservatives, Chesterton and Belloc were always casting their nets for heroes (Mussolini and Franco were seen to possess heroic qualities), detested the narrow uniformity of industrial society, and placed importance on the necessity of social variety, which, they argued, could only be maintained through the possession of property. Most importantly, the Chesterbelloc was never against the idea of class: as opposed to the left, its attacks were not aimed at the social structure but at those within the occupations who were thought to be perverting the social contract.

The Chesterbelloc alliance championed what it called the politics of reaction, but Distributists refused to have anything to do with British facism (at least before Chesterton's death) or with Conservative reactionaries. Unlike the Tory Right, the Chesterbelloc had strong links with Liberal radicalism and were staunch ''little Englanders'' unalterably opposed to the British imperial tradition. Moreover, some of the *Weekly's* most bitter attacks were directed at the major spokesmen for Tory conservatism—Rothermere, Churchill, and Beaverbrook—mainly because of their designs to perpetuate the status quo. Nor was there much connection between the Chesterbelloc and the writers of the reactionary right. Poets like W. B. Yeats and Ezra Pound talked of the need for a hierachical and ordered society, but this was due to their vision of ordinary men as feeble and despicable beasts. Chesterton and Belloc saw the need for authority because of original sin, and they advocated religion, not totalitarian ideology, as a solution to the problem. The Chesterbelloc wrote for everyman: Eliot, Yeats, and the so-called ''reactionary intellectuals'' aimed their esoteric words at the elite and brooded because they could not find an audience of sufficient intelligence to understand them. . . . For some of these intellectuals, literature—not man or God—became the end. Man was destined to create something more important than man: ''art.'' Thus was the individual subordinated to the cultural ideal. Chesterbelloc and the reactionary intellectuals may have shared an appreciation for the organic society, but the Distributist's sense of priorities stemmed from a completely diffferent legacy—that associated with the radicalism of William Cobbett and the vigorously independent yeoman who owed allegiance to no one but God and country.

The Distributist circle dissipated after Chesterton's death. G. K. himself was partly responsible for this, since, in the end, he found it too painful to criticize Italy, a Catholic power, for the sin of imperialism. The singular Bellocian view of Catholicism as culture blinded the movement to the crimes of Italy. But if the Distributist alliance was seriously weakened after 1936 because of the death of Chesterton, who alone was capable of holding the factions together, it was Belloc and the Latinophiles who delivered the final blow to the unity of the group. The *Weekly Review's* uncritical support of Mussolini's foreign policy, its growing willingness to sanction fascist measures for Britain's domestic ills (despite the fact that Chesterton had persistently condemned the policies of the B.U.F. [British Union of Fascists]), and its proposal for an alliance with the dictators against the Soviet Union, had the cumulative effect of drumming the true Distributists out of the movement.

In the end, the Distributists fell victim to that sin of exaggeration which Chesterton had once called heresy. They stretched a portion of Catholic truth out of its proper and well-balanced perspective. The Latinophiles had been guilty of a special intellectual failing—that heretical oversimplification of one complex of ideas (Bolshevism, Jewish finance, and Catholicism as culture) at the expense of the intricate whole. Distributism lost its balance, and hence its own sanity. (pp. 208-11)

Jay P. Corrin, ''Summing Up,'' in his G. K. Chesterton & Hilaire Belloc: The Battle against Modernity, *Ohio University Press, 1981, pp. 201-11.**

MICHAEL H. MARKEL (essay date 1982)

[Markel is an American educator and essayist who has written studies on the works of William Shakespeare, Andrew Marvell, A. E. Housman, and other prominent English authors. In the following excerpt, he surveys and discusses Belloc's poetry: the work, according to most critics, by which Belloc's name will endure.]

During a writing career of more than forty-five years, Hilaire Belloc turned out almost one hundred and fifty prose works. With only a handful of exceptions, writing these books was an enormous chore for him, what one commentator calls his ''sad campaign for a livelihood.'' Belloc's aggressive and domineering personality prevented him from long remaining anyone's employee, so he turned his antipathy for socialists, atheists, and Darwinians into a lifelong vocation.

But Belloc's real love remained his poetry. What he wished to be remembered for is collected in a slim volume called ***Complete Verse***. Had circumstances been otherwise, he probably would have written ten volumes of poetry and very little else. Whereas the subject of his prose was the struggle of men in the world, their attempt to create a set of reasonable and just institutions that would allow them to lead civilized lives, the subject of his poetry was the perennial theme of man's struggle against his mortality. Belloc put into prose what he wanted the world to hear; he saved for his poetry what he *had* to say.

In addition to his serious poetry, Belloc wrote several books of light verse, most of which is collected today under the title ***Cautionary Verses***. His first book of light verse, ***The Bad Child's Book of Beasts***, appeared the same year as his first collection of serious poems and, much to his delight, sold briskly. (p. 24)

Although Belloc is often linked with [Edward] Lear and [Lewis] Carroll as the third master of nonsense verse, he seems to have been largely indifferent to both of them. (p. 25)

Belloc remained unmoved by Lear and Carroll because he was not principally interested in writing for children. Even though the titles of his light verse collections—such as ***The Bad Child's Book of Beasts*** and ***More Beasts (for Worse Children)***—appear at first glance to be intended for children, the adjectives "bad" and "worse" clearly suggest an adult perspective. Unlike Lear and Carroll, Belloc never tried to assume the viewpoint of the child, and there is very little childlike delight in any of the cautionary tales. Instead, Belloc wrote from the perspective of the stern parent lecturing children on the ghastly consequences of their improper behavior. Belloc achieved his humor by overstating the perils. Most of the bad children in his books die a horrible death: several are eaten by wild animals, one dies in an explosion caused in part by his own carelessness, and another succumbs because he ate too much string. Those lucky children who do not die suffer other unkind fates. Maria, for instance, constantly made funny faces. One day, "Her features took their final mould / In shapes that made your blood run cold . . ." Her sad story is suggested by the title of the poem: **"Maria Who Made Faces and a Deplorable Marriage."** Unlike Lear and Carroll, whose strategy was to bridge the gulf between adults and children, Belloc startled his readers by exaggerating that gulf. Belloc's view of children did not look backward to the Victorian nonsense poets, but forward to the films of W. C. Fields.

The Bad Child's Book of Beasts . . . was the first appearance of Belloc's irascible narrator, who innocently announces his intentions in an introduction:

I call you bad, my little child,
  Upon the title page,
Because a manner rude and wild
  Is common at your age.

The Moral of this priceless work
  (If rightly understood)
Will make you—from a little Turk—
  Unnaturally good. . . .

But the real personality of the narrator soon emerges. (p. 26)

The Tiger on the other hand, is kittenish and mild,
He makes a pretty playfellow for any little child;
And mothers of large families (who claim to common
  sense)
Will find a Tiger well repay the trouble and
  expense. . . .

Enhancing Belloc's humor are the drawings by his friend Basil T. Blackwood that accompany the text. . . . **"The Tiger"** has two sketches: in the first, a hungry-looking tiger is approaching a smiling toddler. In the second, the tiger is walking away, licking its lips. This was one of Belloc's strategies in the book: the words express the seemingly innocent advice; the drawings portray the narrator's—and the reader's—real thoughts.

This kind of macabre humor obviously is not intended for the average child. The parents are the real audience, as several other verses in the collection make clear. **"The Marmozet"** and **"The Big Baboon"** gave Belloc a chance to have a little fun with the evolutionists, with whom he was constantly quarreling, while satirizing the poverty of the modern spirit. (p. 27)

Some of the verses in ***The Bad Child's Book of Beasts*** are funny without being violent or satirical, and many of the drawings are innocently clever, but for the most part Belloc was writing in the tradition of Jonathan Swift and Mark Twain, not Lear and Carroll. Belloc chose animals for his subject not because every child likes to read about them, but because they are strong, self-sufficient, and unaffected. Belloc accepted them as creatures that know what they are, never aspire to be anything else, and never are needlessly cruel. In this way they serve as a perfect contrast to the foolish and vain species called Man. Belloc's book of nonsense verse, reminiscent of Swift's parable of the Yahoos and the Houyhnhnms in Part IV of *Gulliver's Travels*, turns the hierarchy of nature upside down. Published in Oxford, ***The Bad Child's Book of Beasts*** sold out in four days. . . . The critics were very enthusiastic, but, as biographer Speaight remarks, they usually failed to see that the comic verse was not really nonsense.

The critics also applauded ***More Beasts (for Worse Children)*** . . . , which Belloc published quickly to capitalize on the success of the earlier book. Its plan is the same, but on the whole the humor is forced. Several of the verses are clever. **"The Microbe,"** for example, pokes fun at scientists who describe fantastic microscopic organisms they have never seen. "Oh! let us never, never doubt / What nobody is sure about!" intones the narrator solemnly. . . . But the violence and cruelty of many of the verses is gratuitous: the woman who is devoured by a python in this book "died, because she never knew / Those simple little rules and few" about how to care for it. . . . Her fate is neither humorous nor revealing.

Belloc found his mark again the next year with ***The Modern Traveller*** . . . , a satirical parable about imperialism. His criticism of the British role in the struggle with the Boers in South Africa was already taking shape; despite its clever verse and Blackwood's drawings, ***The Modern Traveller*** was obviously intended for adults, not children. (pp. 28-9)

Signs of hasty composition are apparent in ***A Moral Alphabet***, but the book is interesting in that it reveals Belloc's awareness of his audience and his growing self-confidence. Four of the twenty-six rhymes refer directly to this or one of his other books. "A," for instance, "stands for Archibald who told no lies, / And got this lovely volume for a prize." When he comes to the nemesis of all alphabet rhymsters, X, Belloc effortlessly turns the situation to his advantage:

No reasonable little Child expects
A Grown-up Man to make a rhyme on X.
MORAL
These verses teach a clever child to find
Excuse for doing all that he's inclined. . . .

(pp. 31-2)

In 1907 Hilaire Belloc, member of Parliament, must have sensed that the public was ready for another book of light verse. ***Cautionary Tales for Children*** follows in the tradition of his first ***Beast*** book, but it shows a new direction in Belloc's thinking. Almost all of the children in this collection who pay so dearly for their misdeeds belong to the upper class. The title of one verse, **"Godolphin Horne, Who was cursed with the Sin of Pride, and Became a Boot-Black,"** is representative of Belloc's new interest in satirizing the rigid class system of England. His characteristic mask in this book is that of the defender of the class system, but occasionally the real author peeks out and winks at his readers. One example is **"Algernon, Who played with a Loaded Gun, and, on missing his Sister, was reprimanded by his Father."** (p. 32)

Belloc's unorthodox parliamentary career kept him in the public eye. Frequently squabbling with his own party, he became known as something of a national eccentric, with a reputation apart from his literary renown. Just as nobody was surprised when he decided not to stand for reelection in 1910, nobody was surprised when in 1911 he published ***More Peers***, a collection of cautionary verses for adults. One verse describes the unfortunate plight of a physician whose patient, a Lord Roehampton, dies without leaving enough to pay the medical fee. The furious doctor storms away when he learns this tragic news, "And ever since, as I am told, / Gets it beforehand; and in gold." . . . Another lord, Henry Chase, wins a libel suit against *The Daily Howl*, "But, as the damages were small, / He gave them to a Hospital." . . . (p. 33)

Nineteen years were to pass before Belloc got around to ***New Cautionary Tales*** . . . , published near the end of his long career. This collection is tired, partly because Belloc was then sixty years old, but mostly because he feared that the good fight against the forces of privilege had been lost. He could not escape the realization that fifty years of struggle and one hundred and fifty books had not changed the world. . . .

Belloc's last book of comic verse, ***Ladies and Gentlemen***, was published two years later, in 1932. It was quite obviously the work of a weary man who no longer felt that the foibles of society were a thoroughly suitable subject for humorous verse. (p. 34)

The comic verse, except for ***The Modern Traveller***, was collected under the title ***Cautionary Verses*** in 1939. . . . The collection remains Belloc's most popular single volume. An ironic reminder of the extent to which the satirical element in Belloc's comic verse has remained unrecognized is the fact that ***Cautionary Verses*** is generally catalogued among the children's books in the library. Taken together, the comic verse is a remarkable achievement. Belloc wrote too much of it, as he did of everything, but the best represents the extraordinary diversity of his imagination, which could combine pure nonsense of the highest quality and serious political and social satire. . . . The comic verse is of course very funny, but behind the laughter is the sadness of an idealistic man in a real world.

In one of his comic verses Belloc wrote a couplet, "Upon the mansion's ample door, / To which he wades through heaps of Straw . . ." and added a footnote: "This is the first and only time / That I have used this sort of Rhyme." . . . In his comic verse he was scrupulous about following the technical conventions, including such matters as the crispness of the end rhymes. He once wrote that comic verse "has nothing to sustain it save its own excellence of construction, . . . those who have attempted it [find] that no kind of verse needs more the careful and repeated attention of the artificer." This is surely overstatement, for the rate at which he produced his comic verse would have made such refinement and polishing impossible. However, the remark suggests the importance Belloc placed on "the excellence of construction" in all of his verse.

In his relatively few serious poems, in particular, he allowed himself the luxury of slow and careful construction, for in no other kind of writing would he speak so candidly. Almost everything else he wrote was intended to pay the bills. But in his serious poems he expressed his essence, the melancholy and even the despair that tested his Catholic faith. While the rest of Belloc's massive output contains the record of his many opinions, the serious poetry is his purest literary expression.

Belloc's poetic principles were classical. He deplored the contemporary trends in poetry whose origins he saw in the tenets of the Romantics of a century earlier. He insisted that "the greatest verse does not proceed immediately from the strongest feeling. The greatest verse calls up the strongest emotion in the reader, but in the writer it is a distillation, not a cry." (pp. 35-6)

Belloc's respect for the classical conception of poetry is immediately apparent in his first volume of poetry, ***Verses and Sonnets***. . . . Establishing a pattern that he was to follow in all of his books of poetry, Belloc arranged his work according to genre: sonnets, songs, epigrams, and satires. Like the ancients, he believed that poetry is a deliberate and self-conscious utterance and that an idea or emotion has to be expressed in an appropriate genre to achieve its meaning.

Belloc's concern for the plight of the poor, for example, is expressed in two poems, one a satire and one a sonnet. . . . The satire is grimly cheerful, as befitting the confrontation between the rich man and the beggar. The sonnet, on the other hand, is almost a prayer to Christ to alleviate the suffering of the poor. The sonnet, the most popular genre of love poets, is perfectly appropriate for this different kind of love poem.

Social justice was one of Belloc's two major concerns at this time in his life. The other was Elodie, whom he married in 1896, soon after the publication of ***Verses and Sonnets***. **"The Harbour"** dramatizes his frustration in waiting five years for her consent. . . . In **"Love and Honour"** he uses [a] favorite strategy of the Renaissance: the personification of abstract concepts. The impatient male is always Love, the reluctant female is Honour. In the traditional conflict Love tries unsuccessfully to conquer Honour, who retreats and thus conquers him by her virtue. (pp. 38-9)

Time, the enemy of all lovers, is the subject of many of the poems in Belloc's first collection. In **"Her Music"** he expresses the fear that the enchantment of his love will "stir strange hopes" of immortality, "And make me dreamer more than dreams are wise." . . . The theme of mutability is explored in the highlight of the volume, **"Sonnets of the Twelve Months,"** which contain some of Belloc's best descriptive poetry. . . . The brisk March wind is described in a line that combines perfectly the sense and the sound: "Roaring he came above the white waves' tips!" . . . The sonnets of the early summer months provide a gentle interlude before the declining half of the year. In several of the sonnets about the later months Belloc builds the poem around a famous European battle scene. In **"July,"** for instance, he describes the Christian kings returning from the Crusades and states, "I wish to God that I had been with them . . ." . . . . In **"August"** Belloc's historical imagination transports him to Charlemagne's great victory at Roncesvalles. In **"September"** he became a participant in the French Revolution: "But watching from that eastern casement, I / Saw the Republic splendid in the sky, / And round her terrible head the morning stars." . . . The best of the twelve sonnets is **"December,"** which ends with this sestet:

> For now December, full of agéd care,
> Comes in upon the year and weakly grieves;
> Mumbling his lost desires and his despair;
> And with mad trembling hand still interweaves
> The dank sear flower-stalks tangled in his hair,
> While round about him whirl the rotten leaves.

This passage, reminiscent of *King Lear*, is an appropriate conclusion to the sonnet sequence, for it unifies and transcends the individual battle scenes in a final portrait of human suffering. Belloc's love of European history, which was to become apparent in his numerous prose studies, is here given its shape by the poet's sensibility. (pp. 39-40)

With his prose and then his parliamentary career occupying his time, Belloc did not publish his next volume of poetry until 1910. ***Verses*** includes many of the poems from ***Verses and Sonnets***. Distinguishing the new verses from the old is not difficult, however, for the fourteen intervening years had changed Belloc dramatically. Whereas the first volume is marked by a youthful vitality and exuberance, ***Verses*** is permeated by a sense of spiritual fatigue and loss that characterized all of Belloc's work in the second half of his life. The death of his wife and then of his son Louis a few years later was to make this outlook permanent, but in 1910 Belloc was already beginning to characterize his life as a painful battle and to look backward to his youth as a carefree period of harmony with mankind and nature.

Yet the comic spirit is still alive in several poems. **"Lines to a Don,"** for instance, is a comic diatribe against a "Remote and ineffectual Don / That dared attack my Chesterton." . . . (p. 41)

The comic verses, however, represent only a small part of the newer poetry. Belloc's alienation from society is portrayed most characteristically as violent combat. In **"The Rebel,"** for example, he pictures himself as a soldier fighting against the forces of "lies and bribes." . . .

In **"The Prophet Lost in the Hills at Evening"** this violent struggle is transferred to the battlefield of Belloc's soul as he envisions himself as God's warrior. . . . (p. 42)

The more successful poems in the 1910 collection are less self-consciously dramatic. **"The South Country"** pays homage to his native Sussex in simple and natural language. . . . The power of **"The South Country"** is his point that even though his dream [of eventually retiring to a rustic cottage in Sussex, to live out his days surrounded by old friends] is apparently humble, it is as unattainable as any attempt to turn back the clock.

The best poem in the collection, **"Stanzas Written on Battersea Bridge During a South-Westerly Gale,"** dramatizes this thought rather than just stating it. Although Belloc never tired of criticizing Wordsworth, this poem shows that he learned the techniques of the meditative lyric from him. As his title suggests, the strategy of the poem is similar to Wordsworth's in "Lines Composed a Few Miles Above Tintern Abbey." . . . Unlike Wordsworth, whose realization of loss is tempered by a growth of understanding, Belloc sees no redemption in the passage of time. Like A. E. Housman, Belloc characterizes the journey from innocence to experience as a cruel joke. The last stanza is touched by an unreasonable self-pity, the indignation of a man who feels that his country has treated him unfairly—from the time of Oxford's refusal of the fellowship to his more recent struggles in the literary and political arenas. This treatment, Belloc is saying, is particularly unfair, considering the great energy he expended trying to do the right thing. Rather than remain in his "rightful garden"—the sheltered world of poetry—he confronted his enemies tirelessly. (pp. 43-4)

Belloc never did understand the ways in which he made his life more difficult than it might have been. **"Stanzas Written on Battersea Bridge"** is a complete failure as a logical argument, but it is a beautiful and moving evocation of his confusion. (p. 45)

His third book of verse, ***Sonnets and Verse,*** was not published until 1923, thirteen years after his second book, twenty-seven years after his first. By this time he had had a chance to contemplate his disappointments and his grief. Despite his increasing activity as a Catholic apologist, he never was able to integrate his personal experience and his faith. Almost all of the new poems included in the 1923 volume record Belloc's struggle to understand his tragedies; in none of them does he offer a Christian explanation. Like the classic poets whose work he studied and emulated, he remained essentially a pagan. And like the pagans who stoically accepted death, he finally came to an uneasy peace with his fate.

Not all of the poems, of course, concern death. **"Tarantella"** is a song about a subject Belloc knew well—"the fleas that tease in the High Pyrenees"—and **"The Chanty of the 'Nona'"** is a sea song commemorating a sail he took in 1914 along the western and southern coasts of England. For these songs, and for many others he wrote, he composed melodies that he loved to sing aloud. ***Sonnets and Verse*** also contains a number of stinging epigrams, such as **"Epitaph on the Politician Himself."** . . . The mood of the volume, however, is most closely expressed by **"The False Heart":**

> I said to Heart, "How goes it?" Heart replied:
> "Right as a Ribstone Pippin!" But it lied. . . .

The bulk of ***Sonnets and Verse*** is love sonnets to Elodie. Several of them may in fact have been written before her death. The reader cannot tell because Belloc has stripped the poems down to an essential emotion—his love for her—which never changed in the sixty years following their first meeting. (pp. 45-6)

These love poems that Belloc wrought out of his grief were his memorial to Elodie. ***Sonnets and Verse*** thus represented for him a catharesis. By defining himself as Elodie's companion, he was able finally to stop the aching movement of time without his wife, just as in the earlier love poems he was able to create a fixed image of her. (p. 49)

The final volume of poetry, also called ***Sonnets and Verse*** . . . , is distinct from the 1923 volume in that it offers only a few brief lyrics to the memory of Elodie. In all other respects, however, Belloc remained unchanged. The generic classification system that the poet maintained emphasized this continuity. The "Epigrams" section of the 1923 volume, for instance, concludes with **"Partly from the Greek."** The 1938 collection, without skipping a beat, simply continues with the next epigram, **"From the Same."**

"The Fire," a melancholy description of how time has destroyed his hopes, is the best example of Belloc's later poetry. The self-assured pleasures of youth are described in the opening stanza, which gallops along carelessly in tetrameter lines. . . .

The assault by time, however, cannot be resisted: "The golden faces charged with sense / Have broken to accept the years." . . . The speaker, now alone and perplexed, demonstrates Belloc's ability to change the tone radically while maintaining the tetrameter lines:

> Were they not here, the girls and boys?
> I hear them. They are at my call.
> The stairs are full of ghostly noise,
> But there is no one in the hall.

Also characteristic of Belloc are the biting epigrams. One victim is a pacifist: "Pale Ebenezer thought it wrong to fight, / But Roaring Bill (who killed him) thought it right." . . . Another victim, a Puritan, Belloc would classify a religious eccentric: "He served his God so faithfully and well / That now he sees him face to face, in hell." . . . And, as always, Belloc loved to define the political animal, as in **"On Two Ministers of State."** . . . (pp. 49-50)

Belloc's poetic masterpiece, **"Heroic Poem in Praise of Wine,"** is also included in the 1938 ***Sonnets and Verse.*** Both poetically and philosophically, it is his most mature composition. The term "heroic poem" in the title refers to the poetic form: rhymed iambic pentameter couplets, sometimes called heroic couplets or heroic verse. By choosing this demanding poetic form for a work of over two hundred lines, he was distinguishing himself from the world of modern poetry and allying himself with the classical Greek and Roman writers and, in England, with Dryden and Pope. (pp. 50-1)

"Heroic Poem in Praise of Wine" combines a sustained technical virtuosity with Belloc's most sophisticated vision: a subtle mingling of the pagan earth and the Christian sky. He worked on the poem for some twenty years. More important, however, he lived most of his life before he could understand and articulate—just this once—the essential unity of comedy and tragedy on earth. (p. 52)

Michael H. Markel, in Hilaire Belloc, *Twayne Publishers, 1982, 175 p.*

JONATHAN RABAN (essay date 1983)

[*Raban is an English free-lance writer and journalist who has written several book-length works of literary criticism, radio plays, and the popular travel book* Old Glory: An American Voyage *(1981), which recounts the author's journey down the Mississippi River in a small boat. In the following excerpt, he discusses* The Cruise of the "Nona," *noting the mixed qualities of Belloc's outlook and style contained therein.*]

No-one who now reads ***The Cruise of the "Nona"*** for the first time will respond to it without some sense of shock. Most people will come to it (as I did) because of its fugitive reputation as a sea-classic; an enchanting story of a voyage in a small boat down the Irish Sea and up the English Channel, a book full of idyllic solitude, of sunsets, storms, oily calms, wet sleeping-bags, tide races, tangled ropes and the rest of it. Such readers, if they skip judiciously, will manage to find what they want, but they won't be prepared for what ***The Cruise of the "Nona"*** actually is—an extraordinary and disturbing can of worms and glories.

For Belloc's work has mostly been expurgated by the passage of time. . . . The Belloc whom everybody knows is the genial, baa-lamb author of ***Cautionary Tales*** and the ***Bad Child's Book of Beasts.***

The Belloc of ***The Cruise of the "Nona"*** is a very different figure—a genuinely dangerous character. The book begins softly enough, in the language of romantic escapism, but by the time it has run its course it has laid down a seductive programme for the regeneration of England. The programme is explicitly Fascist, and the real hero of this story is Mussolini, who had come to power in Italy in 1922, three years before Belloc's ***Cruise*** was first published. The politics and the romance of the book are intimately, powerfully twined together. It is the weirdest imaginable blend of *Mein Kampf* and *Yachting Monthly.*

In his dedication to Maurice Baring, Belloc suggests with great charm and lucidity that his voyage should be construed as a metaphor. . . . The form of the voyage, with its passages, its long reflective spells at anchor, its visits to port, its anxious navigation, becomes the perfect vehicle for a reckoning with life at large. En route, Belloc comes to terms both with his own personal past and with the history of England, his adopted country. The sea supplies him with distance and perspective; it enables him to stand *aloof*—a nautical term, originally, meaning to "luff-up" into the wind, away from the shore. The *Nona,* his engagingly untidy, leak-prone little sloop, gives him an alternative home. The boat—sailing under no ensign—is really another sovereign state in its own right.

Afloat at sea, Belloc sees Britain as a sinking ship. (pp. vi-vii)

His cruise takes him far out into the most hazardous of political deep waters. By the 1920s his disillusion with parliamentary democracy was absolute. Watching England from a mile or two offshore, he saw a history and geography that he loved with a convert's passion, while at the same moment he saw a contemporary social order that he believed to be utterly degenerate. He characterises parliamentary government as a treacherous delegation of authority to "the slime of the Lobbies". . . . Europe's tragedy, Belloc thought, lay in its return to the "vomit" of parliamentary rule at the end of World War I, "instead of continuing the rule of soldiers as it should have done".

Today it's very hard to swallow such facile advocacy of martial law as a moral imperative. In 1925 it wasn't so. When ***The Cruise of the "Nona"*** first came out, the *London Mercury* called it "the most beautiful" of Belloc's books, while the *Observer* said that Belloc "has never written better". The reviews help to remind one that Belloc was writing in a climate far warmer than ours to the idea of final solutions.

Belloc's solution, inspected with the unearned wisdom of living in the 1980s, is one of terrible banality. Heartsick of contemporary Britain (in which corrupt and lazy politicians and charabancs of day-trippers at Clovelly are treated indifferently with the same blind rage), Belloc dreams of, and prays for, a miraculous return to a "homogeneous" society; a nation of one race and one religion. The sole spark of hope on his horizon is the mirage of Italy under Il Duce.

> What a strong critical sense Italy has shown!
> What intelligence in rejection of sophistry, and
> what virility in execution! May it last!

The word *virility* is a key one in Belloc's vocabulary. It crops up in ***The Cruise of the "Nona"*** over and over again, as if the real choice before the nations of Europe was between impotence and erection. . . . Belloc's hearty, open-air approach to things often led him to make judgements of infantile silliness, and infantile cruelty too. His anti-semitism (violently expressed in ***The Jews,*** a book designed to clear himself of the charge of

Belloc on board the "Nona." Photograph by the late James Hall. Courtesy of Philip Jebb.

being an anti-semite) sprang as much, one feels, from the conviction that Jews were pallid, cerebral people who spent too much time indoors as from any more serious perception.

None of this helps to make ***The Cruise of the "Nona"*** a likeable book, though it does give it real status as a rather odious historical document. The trouble is that the splendour and vitality of ***The Cruise*** is directly linked to its always cranky, often ugly vision of history and politics.

For the *Nona* is held up as a tiny scale model of how an idyllic society might be; it is a ship of state in miniature, and the simple virtues of life at sea are set in counterpoint against the corruption and depravity of modern England as it slides by on the beam. The boat is Belloc's great good place—a temple of virility, comradeship and self-reliance. The sea is the immutable element: while the land gets ravaged beyond recognition by the products of industrial democracy, the sea remains the same as it has always been—a mysterious and lovely wilderness.

When he deals with the sea, Belloc writes at the top of his bent. All the most memorable stretches of ***The Cruise*** are full-length portraits of a particular patch of water—the Sound between Bardsey Island and the Lleyn peninsular in a high gale; the entry to Port Madoc on a still evening; the great tide-races of Portland Bill and St. Alban's Head; sailing through Spithead with its navel history still vividly printed on the surrounding landscape. These set-pieces are beautifully done. There's precious little nonsense about topping-lifts and jib-sheets and the rest of the salty talk that tends to disfigure the writing of most amateur sailors. Belloc's writing is entirely free of heroics: it is a good, plain prose, full of wonder, surprisingly humble. (pp. vii-x)

Belloc is still frighteningly topical. His loathing of "politicians" is probably more widely shared today than it was in 1925. His sense of the degeneracy of society in Britain has turned into a platitude in our own age. His particular strictures on British institutions have an unpleasantly familiar ring sixty years on. . . . If his remarks about Italian Fascism and Jewry make him sound like a political coelacanth, Belloc's basic line on the condition-of-England-question is bang up to date. He would be very much at home in 1984; certainly more at home than he was in his own time.

His cruise, too, strikes a deep latterday chord. When Belloc took to the sea alone, he was one of a small company of gentleman-oddballs. The motives that drove him—to escape from England's overpopulous industrial society, to be self-sufficient and dependent only on the forces of nature, to meditate—were out of the ordinary. They have since become commonplace. Britain's domestic seas are crowded with *Nonas*; and most of their helmsmen would come up with a less articulate version of Belloc's story. Much of what in ***The Cruise of the "Nona"*** is fresh first-hand discovery has now become part of the rolling stock of cliché in the yachting press. To go to sea to come face to face with the eternal verities, and to return to land as a prophet of the Far Right, is now almost as conventional a career as computer programming or chartered accountancy. For some reason, the visions, darknesses and revelations of the sea never apparently turn men into socialists.

So the book survives, still bright; partly for excellent literary reasons, and partly (or so it seems to me) for bad political ones. For every moment of enchantment in it—and there are many—there is a corresponding spell of Mussolini-worship or worse ("Eh, Rosenheim? Eh, Guildenstern?"). The two aspects of ***The Cruise*** are inseparable: each is the inevitable product of the other.

Belloc self-deprecatingly calls the book "a hotchpotch", but it is far more artistically elaborate than that. Land and sea, society and solitude, history and the present, are intricately balanced and woven into a pattern; and the pattern reveals a message as unambiguous as a homily on an embroidered sampler—forsake democracy, or be destroyed by an antlike mass-culture manipulated by tycoons and politicos.

Yet the dominant image of ***The Cruise of the "Nona"*** survives in spite of the crudity of the book's political intentions. Belloc, sitting alone at the tiller of the *Nona,* piloting his boat through the tricky waters of England and Wales, is cantankerously alive. One shares his adventures; quarrels furiously with him along the way; and remembers his own epitaph on himself:

> When I am dead, I hope it may be said:
> "His sins were scarlet, but his books were read."

(pp. x-xii)

Jonathan Raban, in an introduction to The Cruise of the "Nona" *by Hilaire Belloc, Hippocrene Books Inc., 1983, pp. vi-xii.*

A. N. WILSON (essay date 1984)

[*Wilson is an English novelist, biographer, and essayist. Cited by* Spectator *critic Francis King as "one of the most promising of our younger novelists,'' he is best known for his novels* The Sweets of Pimlico *(1977) and* The Healing Art *(1980), works noted for their deftness of characterization, striking irony, black humor, and adroit treatment of difficult subjects. Wilson's biographies include* The Life of John Milton *(1982) and* Hilaire Belloc *(1984). In the following excerpt from his introduction to a recent reprint edition of* The Four Men, *Wilson compares this work, which he considers Belloc's masterpiece, to* The Path to Rome, *praising* The Four Men *as a work that thoughtfully and poignantly portrays a simpler, earthier, and happier era in England's history.*]

The wisdom of Belloc can not endure, for it was too obviously right. It is only by his folly that he will be remembered. Most of his astonishingly varied and prolific output of books has been forgotten today. It is because of their truth that we cannot bear to read them. His works of political analysis—***The Servile State, The Party System of The House of Commons,*** and ***Monarchy***—are crammed with wisdom. But it is an intolerable, pessimistic wisdom; the wisdom of a man who says 'I told you so' after the horse has bolted, and who is not entirely sorry to point out that the stable door, far from being better closed, was warped and torn from its hinges years ago.

His political position was arrived at by circuitous routes. His literary antecedents in this area were Rousseau, Cobbett, and Pope Leo XIII. Of these, Cobbett was perhaps the most important, for he seemed to foresee the whole sorry history of Western 'capitalist' democracies. Belloc, very young, came to realize that he was watching the ancient civilization of Europe in its deaththroes. (p. v)

Belloc's prophecies are therefore melancholy and ultimately desperate. Despair is the note of much of his poetry: 'Ha'nacker's down and England's done.' He was in many ways a cynic. One of his grandchildren once witnessed him, in extreme old age, stagger drunkenly out of the Black Horse at Horsham and scatter what at first appeared to be leaves in the gutter. Then, with his old blackthorn stick, he pushed these 'leaves' along the gutter until they disappeared down the drain-hole. They were not leaves. They were a roll of pound notes. Nor was Belloc ever a rich man. This cynical, drunken gesture is all of a piece with his humour and, which is closely related, his religion. Like other 'Catholic men who live upon wine' (say, Chaucer), he felt on the one hand a *contemptus mundi*; on the other, a jolly sense that this world 'nis but a faire', a passage to a better place and a more abiding city but, because it is such a passage, a place to be infinitely valued, treasured, and enjoyed.

All these preoccupations lurk beneath the surface of ***The Four Men,*** which is subtitled 'A Farrago'—that is a hotchpotch, a jumble, or a mess. It is not a completely solemn book. Like Belloc himself it is a strange mixture of tones, of pathos and irony, of raucous hilarity and heart-broken anger. In 1901 Belloc had walked from Toul, the old garrison town where he had done his national service in the French army. It was a ramble which turned into a pilgrimage. The result of his journey was ***The Path to Rome,*** the book with which his name will always be associated. At first glance it seems a little like Stevenson's *Travels with a Donkey,* an ambling, chaotic, witty Victorian travelogue. But as the journey progresses we see that it is an essay on the delights of being European. It is an extraordinarily, some would say a stridently, self-confident book for a young man of 30 to have written. He is at the centre of the stage all the time talking to himself.

If ***The Path to Rome*** had an underlying theme, though, it could be summed up in the sailor's song from ***The Four Men:***

> Oh, I thank my God for this at the least,
> I was born in the West and not in the East,
> And He made me a human instead of a beast,
> Whose hide is covered with hair.

The Path to Rome was published in 1902, and when he got his copy of the book from the publisher Belloc began to doodle on it the opening sentences of ***The Four Men.*** He conceived the idea of writing a similar travel book. Only this time, instead of making a pilgrimage to the centre of European Christendom, he would journey deep into the county of Sussex where, in his early infancy, his widowed mother had made her home. (pp. vii-viii)

'Myself', the chief character of ***The Path to Rome,*** is joined in this book by three others: a Poet, a Sailor, and a disillusioned old man called Grizzlebeard. They are all, of course, Belloc himself—aspects of his nature. The Four Men ramble through Sussex, as Belloc himself so often liked to do with his friends, in search of the Arun.

It is a hostile criticism of most books to say that they have 'dated'. But to say it of ***The Four Men*** is to encapsulate what is its glory. It is like a series of happy snapshots taken at random before a cataclysm. There will always be those who find Belloc distasteful, just as the squeamish Arthur Benson hated the 'gypsy' atmosphere of King's Land. Certainly, Belloc struts and poses:

> I pray good beef and I pray good beer
> This holy night of all the year,
> But I pray detestable drink to them
> That give no honour to Bethlehem.

But consider the moment towards the end of the book when they go up on the Downs above Chichester:

> The air was pure and cold, as befitted All-Hallows, and the far edges of the Downs toward the Hampshire border had level lines of light above them, deeply coloured, full of departure and of rest. There was a little mist above the meadows of the Rother, and a white line of it in the growing darkness under the edges of the hills. It was not yet quite dark, but the first stars had come into the sky, and the pleasant scent of the wood fires was already strong upon the evening air when we found ourselves outside a large inn standing to the north of the road, behind a sort of green recess or common. Here were several carts standing out in the open, and a man stood with a wagon and a landaulette or two, and dogcarts as well, drawn up in the great courtyard.

This scene of the Sussex/Hampshire border before the popularity of the internal combustion engine, has a terrible poignancy for us. Bellow knew that he was immortalizing a world which was soon to vanish for ever; destroyed not by accident, but by human folly. ***The Four Men*** triumphs by its celebration of detail such as this, juxtaposed with its nonsense, its drunkenness, and the faintly bogus-seeming Merry-Englandism of its Catholic good cheer.

The Path to Rome had been a spiritual journey in which Belloc reaffirmed his place, and that of his readers by implication, in the great European Catholic tradition. That tradition was largely broken by the First World War. ***The Four Men*** makes a less certain journey, rambling like the rolling English drunkard of Chesterton's poem. He described it as a farrago, a hotchpotch, and so it is. But it is also an elegy. However much, in his own person, his own household, and his own writings, he tried to embody the ancient values, he was painfully aware that the battle would be lost. It celebrates a vanishing landscape and an obsolete life-style. Even its humour, much of it, seems pre-Chaucerian. But running through that humour, as through the quest and the conversations of the Four Men themselves, there is the reassuring sense that, though here we have no abiding city, we journey to a place where the broken things will be mended and the lost things found. (pp. xii-xiv)

A. N. Wilson, in an introduction to The Four Men: A Farrago *by Hilaire Belloc, Oxford University Press, Oxford, 1984, pp. v-xiv.*

A. N. WILSON (essay date 1984)

[In the following excerpt from his biography of Belloc, Wilson discusses Belloc's works as being merely faint reflections of their author's "genius."]

[The genius of Belloc] is not to be found in the frequently unsatisfactory 'hack work', nor wholly in the works where his genius flowered—***The Four Men;*** the verse, but particularly the comic verse; almost all his essays, but particularly ***Hills and the Sea*** and the ***Essays of a Catholic;*** the fiction—particularly ***Belinda*** and ***The Mercy of Allah;*** the controversy—***The Servile State, The Jews*** and ***Survivals and New Arrivals;*** the reconstructions of the past in ***The Eye Witness;*** the brilliant mingling of topography and prejudice in ***The Battleground.*** The genius is there in the books. But when we turn away from the books to the letters and the memories of everyone who met him, whether they regarded him with love or hatred, we realise that his literary genius is only a shadow of his full greatness. (p. 378)

[Desmond MacCarthy] rightly praises the 'trenchancy' of Belloc's political and economic thought; the brilliance of his travel books; the wit of his satires, and the skill, as well as the variety, of his verse [see excerpt dated 1950]. There remains an unspoken 'but' in the encomium. And, with the passing of the years since Belloc's eightieth birthday, the 'but' has silenced all appreciation of his work. 'I have visited libraries,' MacCarthy wrote, 'where the works of Hilaire Belloc occupy several long shelves, but I doubt if even his ardent admirers possess them all.' Thirty years later, I have visited the same libraries and found that they have taken Belloc off the shelves and sold him to the second-hand bookshops.

There are two reasons for this. One is that Belloc is an offensive character to the majority of those who know about him. When, as a young publisher at Duckworths, Anthony Powell met him in 1928, he recalled, 'I can't imagine anyone more odiously bad mannered and charmless.' This quality carries into Belloc's 'controversial' prose, his dealings with the heretics, his exposures of the corruptions of the rich. We live in a politer age than Belloc's. We dislike his bluster, his charmless rudeness, and we are nervous of anyone who could express such insensitively strong dislike of the Jews. This last, in my belief, is the chief reason for the obscurity of Belloc's reputation. In our century, for obvious and good reasons, anti-semitism is the unforgivable sin. One can laugh off almost any other psychological aberration in a man of genius. We allow writers to have flirted with Eugenics or Stalinism or the Occult. We forgive Yeats his silly adulation of frauds like Aleister Crowley and we forgive Shaw his unimaginatively blood-thirsty adulation of the Stalinist terror. But we cannot forgive Ezra Pound for snarling about the Jews. And we can forgive Belloc even less, for in his book on the subject, published in 1922, he prophesied what would happen to European Jewry with such eery accuracy, as a direct consequence of liberal 'double-thinking' on the subject.

But the second reason why Belloc's reputation has not survived as well as those of some of his lesser contemporaries is his sheer carelessness as a craftsman. There was good reason for the librarians of the 1950s and 1960s to cart armfuls of Belloc's work into the lumber-room. He 'wrote' carelessly, and in later years he did not even bother to write: he merely strutted about his study dictating at a rapid pace to secretaries. Much of what he dictated in those years is remarkable if we consider it merely as *oratory*. It shows that he was extraordinarily eloquent, and that he thought, not in sentences, but in whole paragraphs. On the other hand, it is all very repetitive stuff. And there is not much in ***Wolsey*** that you cannot also find in ***Cranmer;*** little in ***Cranmer*** that is not to be found, often word for word, in ***Cromwell*** or ***Milton,*** or ***Characters of the Reformation.***

Even in his most excellent work (***The Path to Rome, The Four Men, The Cruise of the Nona,*** some third of the poetry), there is a sense that the literary product does not match the quality of the genius which made it. The work is less than the man. And one realises the force of this if one asks the question, *Would you rather have met Belloc or read one of his books?* He was at the opposite end of the spectrum from Shakespeare, a genius wholly subsumed in his work and who, by all accounts, 'gave' little on actual meeting. He was much more like Dr Johnson, universally believed to be a genius by his intimates, but leaving no one literary work by which this belief could be substantiated.

Unfortunately Belloc left no Boswell, and we only catch half-echoes of his conversational manner in the letters which he dashed off, so voluminously but at such speed, to his friends and relations. His greatness really consisted not even so much in what he said as in what he was. There was no one else in the history of the world remotely like him. He was more strongly, more vigorously, more riotously, more intolerably *himself* than almost any other human being. Turn from almost any other biography to that of Belloc and it is what the palate would feel, having tasted a distinctive thing like coriander, only to be blasted by the hottest curry. The experience may be crude, but it is unforgettable. (pp. 382-83)

A. N. Wilson, in his Hilaire Belloc, *Hamish Hamilton, 1984, 398 p.*

WILFRID SHEED (essay date 1984)

[The son of Frank Sheed and Maisie Ward, founders of the Catholic publishing house of Sheed & Ward, Sheed is an English-born American critic and fiction writer whose works in both fields are marked by his erudition and wit. He has served as a columnist for The New York Times *since 1971. In the following excerpt from a review of A. N. Wilson's* Hilaire Belloc, *Sheed offers an overview of Belloc's accomplishment, describing Belloc as a bellicose bigot and something of a hack writer, whose works seem bound for continued obscurity—all except his light verse. For an opposing view of the value of Belloc's work to the modern reader, see the excerpt by Robert Royal (1985).]*

Hilaire Belloc was a writer who probably can't be revived, but who won't quite fade away either. In his lifetime he saw to it that most of his admirers would be Roman Catholics and precious few of them Jews, but by now I doubt that either group cares much. The old church that he celebrated so stoutly folded its tent for good at Vatican Council II and the Judaism he heckled, that never-never world of Sassoons and Rothschilds and international cabals running everything, seems too farfetched to bother about since World War II.

In fact, most of his admirers now are children. By good chance, Belloc was able to distill the best of his gifts into his children's verse: his delicate touch, exquisite phrasing, metrical wizardry and high spirits. He even managed to smuggle in some of his sardonic world view, purged of its prickles, or some of them, as in the following, which may also serve to introduce him:

> The Llama is a woolly sort of fleecy hairy goat,
> With an indolent expression and an undulating throat
> Like an unsuccessful literary man.

Hilaire Belloc was definitely not that kind of literary man himself—or any other kind one can easily think of. An Edwardian poet whose esthetics owed nothing to the period, a novelist occupying no place at all in the history of the novel, a prose stylist whose very century would be hard to guess: sui generis, his own man, impossible to compare with anyone else, for better or worse.

This was partly the result of Belloc's not seeming to have *read* anybody else, at least anyone born in his lifetime. His own excuse for this was that contemporary stuff (especially newspapers) ruined one's style. But in fact he seems to have been too busy hiking, sailing, singing, cursing, laughing, hating and slamming out his own books to have the time. He was a hyperactive child who remained a hyperactive man, with a bellicose expression and a cannon in his throat, like an unsuccessful military man—which in a sense he was.

What is now best remembered as issuing from that cannon of his is anti-Semitism, but A. N. Wilson is at pains to point that he had other targets. For instance, he was known to refer to his own Pope as a "greasy monsignore" and to his own Saviour as a "milksop." No one was safe when the cannon was loose. . . .

The Jewish mania was a comparatively late bee to land in his bonnet, which was almost full by late adolescence, and his mother, Bessie Parkes, an advanced liberal, deplored it vociferously to the end of her long life. Unluckily for her, Hilaire had done some youthful time in the French artillery where, in those days, one picked up anti-Semitism with one's kit—especially if one was descended from a certain Moses Bloch in Nantes. There was always a note of barracks-room raillery about Belloc's jibes, which points up an element in his makeup that brings all judgments about him up short: to wit, he happened to be very funny.

At least his friends (who were not red-faced bullies, but among England's best and brightest) found him so even at his worst. Wilson describes a scene on a hiking trip in which Hilaire rants endlessly while his friends roar helplessly. This smacks strangely of the nursery to me. As a small boy raised by females, Belloc had apparently delighted his elders by marching up and down the lawn banging a tin drum—and here he was still doing it. "Old Thunder" his mother had called him, and his style was set. (p. 3)

At some point in his prime, he decided to drop everything and devote all his formidable gifts to defending the church—or rather to showing (a) that a first-rate mind could decently belong to it and (b) that anti-Catholicism was provincial and middle-class. On the second count English snobbery came to his assistance and there is no doubt that Rome became a more *chic* place to be in his lifetime. But on the first, all he showed many people, I fear, was the disastrous things the Church could do to a first-rate mind.

For in his perverse zeal, Belloc proceeded to pour out a ream of unsound, underresearched history books blatantly taking the Catholic side of everything. Since he had the qualifications to be a good historian, there is something shabby about this, the last stage of Hack's Progress. "Pay me twice as much and I'll do twice as much research," he once told my father, Frank Sheed, the publisher.

But it wasn't just money: one didn't publish with the likes of Sheed & Ward for money. It was rather a wanton impatience and restlessness that wouldn't burn itself out but kept him pacing the earth instead of his study, until the plug was disconnected by a couple of strokes in his early 70's. To enter the lists for one's faith unarmed with facts is, of course, as arrogant as it is futile, and Belloc's maddened bully-boy charges did not represent the Church as attractively as he might have supposed. Yet some of his intuitions, particularly about the Tudor power struggles, have been quietly absorbed and tamed by mainstream history and his real enemy, Official Protestant History, is by now at least as dead as he is. (p. 17)

Chesterton's mind . . . kept growing to the end, while Belloc's stopped puzzlingly in midflight, at which point he took to repeating himself querulously and endlessly. His political ideas, which had seemed quirkily brilliant in the 1900's, were now just quirky, while as for religious ideas he had never had any, except that the church is a Damn Good Thing. Meanwhile the poet and bellettrist had to stand by helpless as Old Thunder banged his same old drum to an empty house. (p. 18)

Wilfrid Sheed, "Tantrums of a Literary Man," in The New York Times Book Review, *September 2, 1984, pp. 3, 17-18.*

ROBERT ROYAL (essay date 1985)

[Royal works for the Ethics and Public Policy Center in Washington, D. C. In the following excerpt from a review of A. N. Wilson's Hilaire Belloc: A Biography *(1984), he discusses several of Belloc's beliefs and defends Belloc as a writer who deserves, on the strength of his very best books, to be read today. For an opposing view of the value of Belloc's work to the modern reader, see the excerpt by Wilfrid Sheed (1984).]*

The figure in the history of English letters who best bears comparison with Hilaire Belloc is Doctor Johnson. Both were larger than life in natural generosity and wit, religious in eccentric ways, by turns appalling, bullying, and endearing in personal habits and relations. Both were also geniuses who now go largely unread. Johnson survives mainly through Boswell. Belloc . . . seems doomed forever to lack the wider audience he deserves.

For the few Belloc aficionados, the last point needs no explanation. For the many others who, in the current state of our literary culture, have never been introduced to Belloc, I can only offer a suggestion: read ***The Path to Rome, The Cruise of the Nona, The Servile State,*** and the comic verse. . . . In style and substance, these stand out from similar works by better-known writers in the early part of the twentieth century.

Belloc was a prodigiously prolific writer who lived by his pen and produced more than 150 books, many of them poorly researched hack work. But the books I have mentioned, and several others besides, are so obviously brilliant that the reasons for the neglect of them must be sought elsewhere.

To begin with there was Belloc's brusque Catholicism. Belloc was born in France of a French father and an Irish mother, who was a convert. Educated in British schools and at Oxford, he was all his life a violent antagonist of all that was religiously insular in England. The antagonism was sharpened by what he regarded as anti-Catholicism in Oxford's refusing him a fellowship to All Souls. Actually his domineering manner probably contributed more to this result than prejudice, but Oxford dons were to be the objects of unrelieved satire in Belloc's work ever after.

One of his avowed goals was to break through the complacent religious sectarianism and atheistic anti-Catholicism (mostly derived from Gibbon) of his time. As he was to phrase it in the 1920s, he wanted to create a climate in which "a man who does not accept the Faith writes himself down provincial." In these carelessly ecumenical days this may seem needlessly belligerent. When Belloc wrote, however, the Whig View of History was still virulent. Among other things, it disfigured the story of the Reformation and the entire history of Catholicism. That this is no longer completely so owes a great deal to Belloc's willingness to expose himself to ridicule in his striking historical biographies and other studies.

Belloc's often-quoted remark, "Europe is the Faith; the Faith is Europe," Wilson rightly says, has been misunderstood. Belloc was not saying that the Church is a European thing, or that it should be restricted to Europe (he expected Asia and Africa to play a large role in the Church's future). Instead, he meant that European civilization is the product of the Catholic Faith and that without the Faith, Europe was finished. Much of his work is aimed precisely at recovering the *disjecta membra* of true European culture that have managed to survive into the modern world. When he is hiking through a European landscape shaped by centuries of human habitation, or singing the praises of bread and wine (sacred and non), or ruminating on one of the old peasant songs so dear to him, he becomes an almost magically evocative representative of the old, great tradition.

Belloc's views on politics and economics, offshoots of his basic religious vision, are also often misunderstood by the British and Americans because his opinions fly in the face of our simple *idées reçues*. His hatred of Bolshevism was, of course, profound. For him, it willfully sought the end of those unbought graces of life that he most valued in the world. Yet he probably would have found defenses of the spirit of democratic capitalism incomprehensible. In ***The Servile State*** he defined capitalism as the system that made the average man a wage slave and Marxism as the system that enslaved man to the state. The remedy in both cases was the wider distribution of private property. This remedy, which he and Chesterton dubbed Distributism, incorporated ideas derived from medieval guilds to ward off the evils of the two main modern forms of mass organization.

Belloc was a monarchist because he believed that only a king could break the stranglehold of the "money power" on most of the European governments. Paradoxically, he also wrote approvingly of the French Revolution. For him, the Revolution was not the violent utopian impulse described by Burke, but an authentic popular reaction in the best feudal tradition, which sanctioned breaking the bonds of fealty to a lord when the lord was no longer living up to his proper contractual agreements. Louis XVI and his immediate predecessors had simply overstepped the bounds of a king's power; the popular will had set things right again. Because of his religious enthusiasms, however, Belloc regarded the English regicides and the Glorious Revolution as nothing but the fruits of a rich Protestant oligarchy refusing proper submission to their king.

Anti-Semitism is a charge that is often brought against Belloc. Wilson documents that there was often more heat than light in Belloc's remarks about Jews. . . . [While] he discusses Belloc's prejudices frankly he also admits that Belloc identified an irreducible problem in relations between Christians and Jews that the latter have also begun to appreciate. As one Jewish scholar put it recently in *Commentary*, "We cannot hope to smooth away the Jewish-Christian conflict by reducing it to a family quarrel between two groups that are basically akin." Anyone interested in weighing Belloc's views on the subject should take a careful look into his book ***The Jews.*** (pp. 54-5)

Given Belloc's abrasive manner and peculiarities of thought it is not surprising that he has failed to attract a larger audience. But many other authors of the same period—Shaw, for example—are still read in spite of their eccentricities. Belloc has clearly been neglected because of his sharp opposition to almost everything that has become part of the liberal modern world. That world will not care to read Belloc, but those who pick up his best books to savor his historical imagination, the overall keenness of his mind, and the simple force of his prose will need no other reason to return to him again and again. (p. 55)

Robert Royal, "Belloc's Boswell," in National Review, *Vol. XXXVII, No. 1, January 11, 1985, pp. 54-5.*

ADDITIONAL BIBLIOGRAPHY

Adcock, A. St. John. "Hilaire Belloc." In his *Gods of Modern Grub Street: Impressions of Contemporary Authors,* pp. 13-19. New York: Frederick A. Stokes Co., 1923.

A short biographical and critical introduction to Belloc.

Baring, Maurice. *The Puppet Show of Memory*. Boston: Little, Brown, and Co., 1922, 457 p.

Contains scattered references to Baring's and Belloc's long friendship, recounting their initial, unpleasant meeting and their later joint-editorship of *The North Street Gazette,* a newspaper published during 1908 and which ran to one issue.

Braybrooke, Patrick, "Hilaire Belloc As a Novelist." In his *Some Catholic Novelists: Their Art and Outlook,* pp. 37-71. London: Burns, Oats & Washbourne, 1931.

Discusses *The Green Overcoat, Mr. Petre,* and *The Emerald.*

Brome, Vincent. "Hilaire Belloc versus H. G. Wells." In his *Six Studies in Quarrelling,* pp. 170-89. London: Cresset Press, 1958.*

A detailed, quotation-filled gloss of the Wells-Belloc controversy of 1926.

Chesterton, G. K. "Hilaire Belloc." In his *G. K. As M. C.: Being a Collection of Thirty-Seven Introductions,* edited by J. P. Fonseka, pp. 96-102. London: Methuen & Co., 1929.

Personal reminiscences and a brief assessment of Belloc's writing skill.

Eliot, T. S. Review of *The Servile State,* by Hilaire Belloc. *The Monthly Criterion* VI, No. 1 (July 1927): 69-73.*

Reviews a new edition of *The Servile State*, finding it to evidence sloppy composition and little consideration of the weaknesses and practicality of Distributism.

———. Review of *Essays of a Catholic Layman in England*, by Hilaire Belloc. *The English Review* LIII, No. 2 (July 1931): 245-46.
Favorably reviews this essay collection, but notes that Belloc's famed polemical aggressiveness seems heavy-handed, considering the weakness of the opponents he addresses in the volume.

Hynes, Samuel. "The Chesterbelloc." In his *Edwardian Occasions: Essays on English Writing in the Early Twentieth Century*, pp. 80-90. New York: Oxford University Press, 1972.*
Examines the reflection of Belloc's aggressive, occasionally brutal personality in the author's work. Hynes believes that Belloc's more belligerent efforts pale in comparison to his light verse and travel books.

Jago, David. "The Stoicism of Hilaire Belloc." *Renascence* XXVII, No. 2 (Winter 1975): 89-100.
Examines Belloc's melancholia, finding the author "less a writer than a failed man of action."

Jebb, Eleanor, and Jebb, Reginald. *Testimony to Hilaire Belloc*. London: Methuen & Co., 1956, 172 p.
Essays and memoirs on Belloc's life and beliefs, recounted by Belloc's daughter and son-in-law.

Kelly, Hugh. "Centenary of Hilaire Belloc." *Studies* LIX, No. 236 (Winter 1970): 396-403.
A brief survey of Belloc's career.

Kilmer, Joyce. Introduction to *Verse*, by Hilaire Belloc, pp. xi-xxvii. New York: Laurence J. Gomme, 1916.
Praises Belloc as "a poet who happens to be known chiefly for his prose." Kilmer believes that Belloc's Catholicism vivifies the poems most likely to endure.

Las Vergnas, Raymond. "Hilaire Belloc." In his *Chesterton, Belloc, Baring*, pp. 50-87. New York: Sheed & Ward, 1938.
An excellent survey and study of Belloc's life, work, and beliefs.

Lowndes, Marie Belloc. *The Young Hilaire Belloc*. New York: P. J. Kenedy & Sons, 1956, 182 p.
A memoir of Belloc's life up to 1914, recounted by his sister.

Mandell, C. Creighton, and Shanks, Edward. *Hilaire Belloc: The Man and His Work*. London: Methuen & Co., 1916, 143 p.
A study of Belloc's thought and work, examining separately each genre in which the author wrote.

McCarthy, John P. *Hilaire Belloc: Edwardian Radical*. Indianapolis: Liberty Press, 1978, 373 p.
Presents Belloc as a social and political radical-liberal of his day. His life and beliefs are examined against the background of Great Britain's foreign and domestic policies of the late nineteenth and early twentieth century.

———. "The Historical Vision of Chesterbelloc." *Modern Age* 26, No. 2 (Spring 1982): 175-82.*
Delineates the historical vision shared by G. K. Chesterton and Belloc, drawing upon Belloc's *Europe and the Faith, The Crisis of Civilization*, and *Survivals and New Arrivals*, as well as Chesterton's *The End of the Armistice* (1940).

McCarthy, Mary. "Mr. Belloc's Theory of History." *The Nation* CXXXVIII, No. 3574 (3 January 1934): 24-5.
An approbatory review of *Charles the First: King of England*.

Reilly, Joseph J. "The Art of Belloc, Biographer." In his *Dear Prue's Husband and Other People*, pp. 70-98. New York: Macmillan, 1932.
A valuable study of Belloc's skill at biography.

Reynolds, E. E. "The Chesterbelloc." *The Critic*, Chicago 37, No. 17 (March 1979): 2-3, 6.
Surveys Belloc's career, positing that *The Path to Rome* and some of Belloc's poetry will survive to posterity.

Sheed, Wilfrid. "Chesterbelloc." In his *The Morning After: Selected Essays and Reviews*, pp. 259-75. New York: Farrar, Straus & Giroux, 1971.*
A discussion of Belloc and G. K. Chesterton, stressing their roles as promoters of Catholicism and examining their anti-Semitism.

Speaight, Robert. *The Life of Hilaire Belloc*. London: Hollis & Carter, 1957, 552 p.
An important critical biography.

Waugh, Evelyn. "Mr. Belloc in the North." *The Spectator* 161, No. 5762 (2 December 1938): 964, 966.
Review written in praise of *Return to the Baltic*, a work that is unfortunately marred, according to Waugh, by Belloc's refusal to attack the modern enemies of his ideals. Instead, Belloc lashes out at such long-established foes as English dons and the nation's aristocracy.

———. "Belloc Anadyomenos." In his *The Essays, Articles and Reviews of Evelyn Waugh*, by Evelyn Waugh, edited by Donat Gallagher, pp. 472-74. Boston: Little, Brown and Co., 1984.
Reprints a 1955 review of *The Cruise of the "Nona."* Waugh praises the book and outlines many of Belloc's beliefs.

Wilhelmsen, Frederick. *Hilaire Belloc: No Alienated Man: A Study in Christian Integration*. London: Sheed and Ward, 1954, 108 p.
A study of the various aspects of Belloc's outlook which, together, define his Christian humanism.

Williams, Charles. "The Last of the Kings." *Time and Tide* 21, No. 8 (24 February 1940): 198.
Favorable review of *The Last Rally: A Study of Charles II*, which Williams deems "one of the best of [Belloc's] later books; perhaps the best."

Theodore (Herman Albert) Dreiser

1871-1945

American novelist, essayist, autobiographer, journalist, short story writer, dramatist, and poet.

Dreiser was one of the principal American exponents of literary Naturalism. In spite of his numerous artistic failings, critics consider Dreiser one of America's foremost novelists. No other author has withstood so much vehemently negative criticism and retained such a high status—perhaps because no other author displayed such glaring faults of logic and style, while at the same time exhibiting such powerful characterizations and strong ideological convictions.

Dreiser was the twelfth of thirteen children born to a poor Indiana farm family, the members of which were often separated when the parents and older children sought jobs in different cities. Dreiser was a mediocre student at the succession of schools he attended; however, he received encouragement from a high school teacher who offered to pay his tuition to the University of Indiana. The experience was not a beneficial one for Dreiser: he was acutely conscious of the differences between himself and wealthier, better-looking classmates, and after one year he left the university to work as a journalist in Chicago, St. Louis, Pittsburgh, and finally New York, where his brother Paul helped him attain the editorship of *Ev'ry Month* magazine. During this period Dreiser wrote his first novel, *Sister Carrie*. Marital difficulties, together with the poor sales of *Sister Carrie,* left Dreiser deeply depressed. He lost his job and later recorded that for several years he suffered from hallucinations and seriously considered suicide. Paul again helped him find employment, and H. L. Mencken encouraged him to resume work on *Jennie Gerhardt,* his second novel. In the interim, *Sister Carrie* had been received favorably in England, and was reissued to mixed reviews in the United States in 1907.

Sister Carrie was unique in American fiction, departing sharply from the gentility and timidity of Howellsian realism. Many critics were shocked that Dreiser's heroine, a "fallen woman," remains unpunished at the novel's end, and this was the focal point of much early criticism. Dreiser's deterministic philosophy, developed more fully in the Cowperwood trilogy, is evident in what some critics call Carrie's "neo-Darwinian adaptability." She survives and prospers because of her willingness to adjust with equanimity to whatever advantageous situations develop. Conversely, the deterioration and death of her second lover, Hurstwood, is generally agreed to be one of the most powerful and moving portraits of human defeat ever written. Critics of *Sister Carrie* also noted an apparent contradiction, which persisted throughout Dreiser's works, between his determinism—his belief that individuals lacked the ability to shape their own destinies—and his sentimentalism—for though he portrayed their unhappy fates as inevitable, Dreiser evoked considerable pity and sympathy for his defeated characters. Popular legend, reinforced by Dreiser himself, holds that the original publishers of *Sister Carrie* attempted to suppress the book, and failing this, did not advertise it because of virulent early criticism. That Doubleday did not advertise *Sister Carrie* is true; however, the claim that it received an overwhelmingly negative initial critical reaction is not borne out by an examination of the book's earliest reviews. The

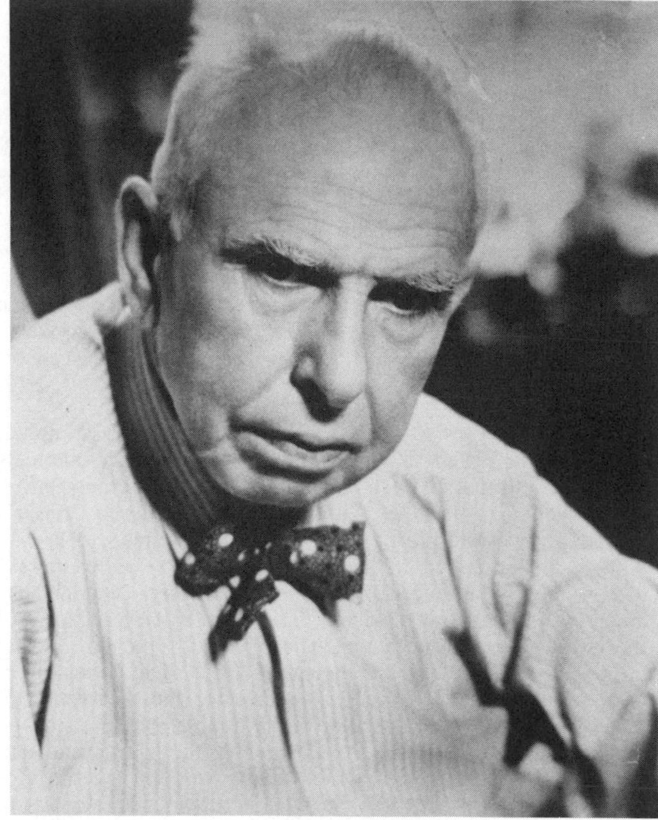

The Granger Collection, New York

circumstances surrounding the first publication of *Sister Carrie* are still under examination.

Dreiser's next novel was *The Financier,* the first work of the Cowperwood trilogy, which details the life and career of successful businessman Frank Algernon Cowperwood. Both *The Financier* and the second volume of the trilogy, *The Titan,* contain somewhat didactic illustrations of Dreiser's determinism and utilize crude Darwinian biological imagery. In these novels Dreiser also outlines his "chemicomechanistic" concept of life as little more than a series of chemical reactions, primarily in the depiction of Cowperwood's relations with women. Cowperwood's rise, fall, and second triumph in the world of high finance are recounted with journalistic attention to detail—indeed, newspaper accounts of the life of streetcar magnate Charles Tyson Yerkes inspired the creation of Dreiser's financier. Dreiser worked on the third volume of the trilogy, *The Stoic,* intermittently for over thirty years. It was completed shortly before his death. Considered by most critics to be vastly inferior to the first two volumes of the trilogy, *The Stoic* concludes with the death of Cowperwood and the dispersal of his fortune. It ends on a note of Eastern mysticism, which was then a concern of Dreiser's second wife.

Dreiser's fifth novel, *The "Genius"*, aroused more genuine controversy than was fallaciously attributed to *Sister Carrie*.

In this thematically scattered but important work, Dreiser portrayed the artist as Nietzschean superman who lives beyond conventional moral codes. Sales of *The "Genius"* were initially good and early reviews approbatory; however, in the year following its publication, *The "Genius"* came to the attention of the New York Society for the Suppression of Vice, which sought to block its distribution. Mencken, though he personally disapproved of the book, circulated a protest against the censorship of *The "Genius"* or of any literary work. The protest was signed by hundreds of American and British authors, including Robert Frost, Sinclair Lewis, Ezra Pound, and H. G. Wells. Although in retrospect critics find *The "Genius"* to be one of Dreiser's weakest novels, Charles Shapiro wrote that it "achieved historical importance as a result of the famed fight over its suppression, a struggle that ranks with the *Ulysses* case as a pivotal victory in the fight for American literary freedom." The legal issues surrounding the book's suppression are unclear. No formal action was taken against the book or its publishers; however, the influence wielded by self-appointed censors such as the Society for the Suppression of Vice was then considerable. The re-relcase of *The "Genius"* in 1923 was a decisive blow against such arbitrary and unqualified censorship.

Published ten years after *The "Genius"*, Dreiser's next novel, *An American Tragedy,* reaffirmed his standing as America's greatest Naturalist and established him as the foremost American novelist of his time. Although critics deplored Dreiser's unwieldy, awkward prose, his stylistic and grammatical flaws—what Mencken called his lack "of what may be called literary tact"—they experienced in *An American Tragedy* an undeniable depth and power of vision. The novel is an indictment of the gulf between American ideals of wealth and power, and the provisions available for their realization. The entire American system is seen to be responsible for the destruction of Clyde Griffiths, a weak-willed individual who aspires to the American dream of success. Curiously, the journalistic tendency of Dreiser's prose, which was frequently the cause of critical complaint in the past, was found by some critics to benefit *An American Tragedy*. Grant C. Knight wrote "In his desire for veracity Mr. Dreiser does lapse into journalism"; nevertheless, while it "is true that Mr. Dreiser is always at pains to spread out every fact that sometimes he even transgresses relevance, . . . in the instance of *An American Tragedy* . . . nothing short of full documentation would have been convincing." However, Dreiser's usual defender, Mencken, felt that the book was a failure and wrote that whole chapters of it should have been deleted—while Knight wrote that "not a chapter, hardly a page . . . could be deleted without injury."

Dreiser's final two novels, *The Stoic* and *The Bulwark,* were published posthumously. Dreiser devoted much of his time during his last twenty years to nonfiction writings and to *The Bulwark,* which remains something of a problem novel. In *The Bulwark* the moral scruples of a Quaker businessman, Solon Barnes, come up against the reality of American business dealings. In a reversal for Dreiser, Barnes, as the upholder of traditional mores and values, is portrayed sympathetically and without the usual implied charge of hypocrisy. Granville Hicks found in *The Bulwark* "a rejection of naturalism as a literary theory."

Dreiser produced four autobiographical works, *A Traveler at Forty, A Hoosier Holiday, A Book about Myself,* and *Dawn*. He also wrote several dramas, which are generally agreed to be unactable; two volumes of poetry, *Moods, Cadenced and Declaimed* and *The Aspirant,* both harshly reviewed and little read; a volume of short stories, *Free,* and one of short stories and novellas, *Chains*. The volumes of essays *Dreiser Looks at Russia* and *Tragic America* reflect Dreiser's growing involvement with socialism. Several of his biographers believe that he joined the Communist Party late in his life. Dreiser's socialist activities included a trip to Russia in 1927 and investigation of labor conditions in Kentucky coal mines in 1931. The extensive press coverage of these activities, Dreiser's political writings, and the fact that he did not produce a novel for twenty-one years, led to the loss of his generally accepted reputation as America's greatest living novelist. Dreiser was critically evaluated as a novelist whose career ended with *An American Tragedy,* until the publication of the two posthumous novels, *The Bulwark* and *The Stoic,* demonstrated the need for reassessment.

Increasingly since his death, Dreiser's importance has been seen as chiefly historical. Critics such as J. Donald Adams and T. K. Whipple believe that Dreiser made his greatest contribution as a "trail blazer" in the field of of modern Naturalist fiction, thus opening the field for other writers. Jack Salzman summarized Dreiser's currrent critical standing when he wrote that Dreiser's "significance in the history of American letters is no longer a matter for dispute. We may continue to debate his merits as an artist, but his importance to American literature has been well established."

(See also *TCLC*, Vol. 10; *Contemporary Authors,* Vol. 106; *Dictionary of Literary Biography,* Vol. 9, *American Novelists, 1910-1945;* Vol. 12, *American Realists and Naturalists;* and *Dictionary of Literary Biography Documentary Series,* Vol. 1.)

PRINCIPAL WORKS

Sister Carrie (novel) 1900
Jennie Gerhardt (novel) 1911
**The Financier* (novel) 1912
A Traveler at Forty (autobiography) 1913
**The Titan* (novel) 1914
The "Genius" (novel) 1915
A Hoosier Holiday (autobiography) 1916
Free, and Other Stories (short stories) 1918
The Hand of the Potter [first publication] (drama) 1918
Twelve Men (sketches) 1919
Hey Rub-A-Dub-Dub: A Book of the Mystery and Wonder and Terror of Life (essays) 1920
A Book about Myself (autobiography) 1922; also published as *Newspaper Days,* 1931
An American Tragedy (novel) 1925
Moods, Cadenced and Declaimed (poetry) 1926
Chains (short stories and novels) 1927
Dreiser Looks at Russia (essays) 1928
The Aspirant (poetry) 1929
A Gallery of Women (sketches) 1929
Dawn (autobiography) 1931
Tragic America (essays) 1931
America is Worth Saving [with Cedric Belfrage] (essays) 1941
The Bulwark (novel) 1946
**The Stoic* (novel) 1947
Letters of Theodore Dreiser (letters) 1959
***An Amateur Laborer* (autobiography) 1983
Theodore Dreiser: The American Diaries, 1902-1926 (diaries) 1984

*These works are collectively referred to as the "Cowperwood trilogy"

**This work was written in 1903.

ROGER ASSELINEAU (essay date 1959)

[*Asselineau, a French poet, critic, and literary historian, has a special interest in American poets and was awarded the Walt Whitman Award from the Poetry Society of America in 1961 for his* The Evolution of Walt Whitman: The Creation of a Personality *(1960). Among his other numerous works are critical studies of Ernest Hemingway and Mark Twain, the poetry collection* Poesies incompletes *(1959), and French translations of works by Whitman and Edgar Allan Poe. In the following excerpt, originally presented as a paper in 1959, Asselineau discusses the influence of transcendentalism on Dreiser's works.*]

Dreiser, like the moon, is composed of two hemispheres, one which meets the eye, his naturalism; the other which generally remains in the dark and which only a few bold critics like Alfred Kazin, F. O. Matthiessen, and Charles Walcutt have ventured to explore, namely his transcendentalism. At first sight, the two notions may seem incompatible. Yet, Dreiser somehow managed to reconcile them. Like a true transcendentalist he was indifferent to contradictions and cared little for logic. He felt that, since life was made up of contraries, he had the right to include them side by side in his mind. (p. 99)

Consequently he saw no inconsistency in describing psychological and social phenomena from a materialistic standpoint with the detachment—and sometimes the jargon—of a scientist, while at the same time expressing the wonder of a child or poet before the mystery of life. He constantly swung between these two extreme positions and the amplitude of the oscillation increased to such an extent in the last few months of his life that he was eventually both a fervent religionist and a member of the Communist Party. But he did not mind being in uncertainties. He confessed it in ***A History of Myself:*** "Chronically nebulous, doubting, uncertain, I stared and stared at everything, only wondering, not solving." So, on his own admission, he never reached any intellectual certainty. His mind restlessly groped for some transcendent reality beyond material appearances, for something which the meshes of scientific laws failed to catch—in short, he was a transcendentalist first and foremost.

Dreiser's transcendentalism is most forcibly expressed in a much-neglected collection of poems in free verse which he very fittingly entitled ***Moods.*** According to his own testimony it was "written between 1914 and 1926" and he kept revising and enlarging it for another ten years, which shows how much he prized it. In his own words, it "represents in the first instance a fair summary of [his] philosophy in mood form, and in the second, an elaborated presentation of it." It is "lyrical philosophy and possibly the first conscious attempt to express an individual philosophy lyrically. . . ." Thus, in ***Wood Note,*** he concludes a brief sketch with lines which suggest a mysterious spiritual presence in the woods and the unreality of matter:

> Of what vast deep is this the echo?
> Of what old dreams the answer? . . .

God, for the poet of ***Moods,*** is present in all things and in the humblest of men:

> God
> To my astonishment
> Is shining my shoes.
> He has taken the form,
> In part,
> Of an Italian shoe black
> Who is eager to earn a dime. . .
> Reading a newspaper
> To learn of Himself
> I presume. . .
> Getting drunk,
> Eating a ham sandwich
> In order to maintain His strength.
> A most varied
> Restless
> Changeful
> Moody
> God. . .

(pp. 100-01)

In his lyrical moods, Dreiser mystically identifies himself with this changeful God. . . .(p. 101)

But, strangely enough, this keen perception of an underlying mystery in all things is again and again spoiled so to speak, by a disquieting sense of the purposelessness and meaninglessness of the world, in ***The Passing Freight,*** for instance, in which the disillusioned poet dejectedly meditates on the passage of a train:

> Out of the mystery
> And meaninglessness of things
> And into it again;
> A train bearing cotton
> With thunder and smoke
> And a flare of fire,
> Yet bearing that
> Which is nothing more than an idea;
> That has come out of the darkness of chemistry
> And will soon return into it. . .
>
> And I, myself,
> Who view it
> And admire—
> Out of the mystery
> And meaninglessness of things
> And into them again. . . .

At such times we seem to be a very long way indeed from Emerson's boundless optimism. Dreiser's position is then almost that of an agnostic. We are reminded of the sceptical utterances with which he had sprinkled ***A Traveler at Forty:***

> For myself, I accept now no creeds. I do not know what truth is, what beauty is, what love is, what hope is. I do not believe any one absolutely and I do not doubt any one absolutely. . . .I indict nature here and now. . .as being aimless, pointless, unfair, unjust. I see in the whole thing no scheme, but an accidental one—no justice save accidental justice. . . .

(pp. 101-03)

But such statements expressed only "moods," to take up his own word. They corresponded to only one facet of his thought. Emerson too did not always yield himself to "the perfect whole," and had to admit that "our torment is Unbelief, the Uncertainty as to what we ought to do; the distrust of the value of what we do, and the distrust that the Necessity (which we all at last believe in) is fair and beneficent." But, like Emerson, Dreiser succeeded in transcending his doubts—even though he never entirely discarded them—and in some of his ***Moods*** he prays "the hidden God," "the substance of suns, and flowers, rats and kings,". . .and worships with the fervor of a true transcendentalist. . . .

Give honor unto him
Who, in the midst of doubt. . .
Still, still can dream
And still build temples—
Not to Christ,
Or Buddha,
But to Beauty—
The human will to loveliness. . . .

(pp. 103-04)

Like the transcendentalists, what Dreiser means by beauty is not plastic beauty, but the mysterious presence behind appearances of something wonderful which escapes his senses. His apprehension of beauty is in fact a mystical intuition, a form of religious worship. . . .

What he keeps seeking and wondering at is the enigmatic force which carries all things forward irresistibly toward an unknown destination. He ultimately equates reality with Life. (p. 104)

He worships life in all its forms–life "as it is," to take the words which he himself used to define his realism (and this incidentally shows that there was after all no fundamental incompatibility between his transcendentalism and his naturalism). He felt a "Creative Force" at work in the world, "the amazing Creative force which has brought 'humanity' along with its entire environment into being." According to him, "man is not really and truly living and thinking, but, on the contrary, is being lived and thought by that which has produced him. Apart from it. . .he has no existence." (p. 105)

"There is in my judgment no death," he declared more explicitly in ***A Traveler at Forty,*** "the universe is composed of life; but nevertheless, I cannot see any continuous life for any individual.". . .

As with transcendentalists, this dynamic vitalism leads up to a wish to live rather than expiate, to self-reliance and the exaltation of individualism. Dreiser did not believe in original sin or the innate corruption of man any more than Emerson. All his characters are men of good will. True, they are eminently fallible, but they are not really responsible for their lapses since they are caught in a tangle of biological and social forces which, to a large extent, determine their behavior. (p. 106)

All these resemblances between transcendentalism and Dreiser's philosophy were not accidental. In his youth, Dreiser read Emerson's works with passion. . . . He was also an admirer of Thoreau. He had compiled a book entitled ***Thoreau's Living Thoughts. . . .*** (pp. 107-08)

So transcendentalism undeniably exerted an influence on his thought. But its importance should not be exaggerated. There was a sort of preestablished harmony between the transcendentalists and himself. Their writings merely encouraged him to preserve and develop, instead of suppressing or repressing, the mystical tendencies of his temperament. Even as a child he was an exceptionally sensitive lover of nature endowed with a keen sense of wonder which he never lost. (p. 108)

This innate sense of the mystery and beauty of the world, which his transcendentalism no doubt reinforced, illuminates not only his poems, but also his so-called naturalistic novels. It glows even in ***An American Tragedy,*** which is probably the most prosaic of his books. Instead of describing "Life as it is," he often looks at it through the wondering eyes of Clyde Griffiths, who stares at the rich and their dwellings and feels "like looking through the gates of Paradise.". . . Reality often gives place to dreams, dreams of beauty and wealth and pleasure. (p. 109)

As to the characters—at least the major ones—they are essentially forces which move forward and come into conflict with other forces, but they have no idiosyncrasies, no minor traits. They are never sharply individualized. They remind the reader of Mayakowsky's "clouds in trousers," for their clothes are carefully described, but though they have bodies full of appetites and desires, they have no faces. Dreiser's point of view is not psychological, but social *and* metaphysical. He is not interested in his characters as individuals, but as social types *and* as manifestations of the central life force which flows through all things, as parts of the "oversoul."

Besides, most of these characters constantly aspire to something beyond the workaday world in which they are caught. They crave a fuller life, beauty, some ideal which they are unable to define, but in whose existence they firmly believe. In ***Sister Carrie*** in particular, Dreiser again and again suggests "that constant drag to something better" which Carrie feels so strongly. . . , but it is not particular to her, it is a universal feeling, according to Dreiser. He makes her face "representative of all desire" and warns us that "her look was something which represented the world's longing.". . . (p. 110)

Thus, Dreiser was a poet and in several respects a belated transcendentalist in his naturalistic novels as well as in his poems. True, his transcendentalism coexisted with lurking doubts that prevented him from giving any dogmatic content to his intuitions and with a tenacious pessimism that made it impossible for him to ignore social and other evils, but, nevertheless, he spontaneously sensed beneath this world of appearances another inward world which he kept wondering at and whose universal presence conferred beauty and mystery on the most banal and insignificant sights. Without this poetical power his works would be nothing but dull naturalistic descriptions of American society, whereas, thanks to it, he has, however massively, sung himself and celebrated—or pitied—himself in the guise of various characters ("Sister Carrie, Cowperwood, Clyde Griffiths, c'est moi," he might have exclaimed), and, at the same time, he sang and celebrated man and the presence in man of the irresistible creative force at work in the world. His transcendentalism is therefore the true source of his greatness. (pp. 112-13)

Roger Asselineau, "Theodore Dreiser's Transcendentalism," in his The Transcendentalist Constant in American Literature, *New York University Press, 1980, pp. 99-114.*

DONALD PIZER (essay date 1976)

[In the following excerpt, Pizer discusses the influences on Dreiser's Frank Cowperwood trilogy.]

Drieser's career as editor, magazine contributor, and novelist up to early 1911 had called upon him to adopt various attitudes toward both the myth of success and its seemingly debunking counterpart of muckraking exposure. As "The Prophet" [the pseudonym with which he signed the monthly "Reflections" column in the magazine *Ev'ry Month*] he had been predictably flexible. In his role as Social Darwinist, he viewed business and political struggle and corruption as inseparable from the American scene. In his role as moralist, he deplored the methods and goals of the politically and financially great. Later, as a well-paid interviewer for Marden, his standard sequence of questions implicitly endorsed the basic values of the myth of success. Such economic buccaneers as Philip Armour, Marshall Field, and Andrew Carnegie, who had clawed their way to the top of their empires, admitted, with the aid of Dreiser's leading questions, that hard work, frugality, and perseverance were the keys to their success and that their principal aim in acquiring great wealth was to aid their fellowmen. It was no doubt Dreiser's sense of the discrepancy between the myth of success and the reality of American business life—the difference between what Armour said about his career and what Dreiser knew about it—which entered into his portrait of Robert Kane in ***Jennie Gerhardt.*** For Robert is a sanctimonious and rigid moralist in his personal affairs and is appropriately self-righteous in his estimation of himself, yet his business values and methods are those of the jungle. And it is Robert, not his more generous-spirited brother, who gains control of the family business and who builds it into a powerful trust.

Dreiser's portrait of Robert is fairly tame, however, for it was no news in 1911 (or indeed in 1901, when the character was first sketched) that there was a difference between the private and public morality of most successful Americans. Dreiser's basic social beliefs were indeed far more radical, as he began to reveal in ***The "Genius."*** For Eugene, with the author's endorsement, does not even profess a personal morality. Impelled during the period following his collapse by a powerful need to fulfill his desires and seemingly unhampered by moral values, he has a great advantage over those who permit themselves to be guided by ethical beliefs while playing the game of life. He fails in the long run because he has not completely purged himself of moral sentiments and because he lacks the strength to pursue his goals with a necessary single-mindedness. But his insight into the amorality of life nevertheless assaults the assumptions of both those who believe that the pursuit of success can occur within moral law and those who cry out at the violation of such law. In effect, Dreiser was saying that there is no law, that anything goes so long as it brings success.

In his many accounts of the origin of ***An American Tragedy,*** Dreiser always claimed that his interest in the situation of a man murdering his pregnant sweetheart in order to pursue a more socially desirable girl long preceded his choice of the Gillette case as a specific instance upon which to base his treatment of this situation. Although Dreiser left no account of the source of his interest in Charles T. Yerkes, this same sequence can be posited for the Cowperwood trilogy. It was not a desire to write a novel about Yerkes which prompted Dreiser to undertake the trilogy but a desire to write a novel about an American financier and the discovery that the career and personality of Yerkes were almost perfectly adaptable to his ends. (pp. 154-55)

Yerkes's full notoriety . . . occurred shortly after his death, when his fame was still great and when it was possible to write about him without fear of libel actions or other forms of retaliation. . . . Yerkes's life was . . . fully recounted. And this life, with its details of Yerkes's Philadelphia prison sentence, his divorce of his first wife, his dramatic rise in Chicago, his freebooting financial methods, his immense expenditures on his private art collection and his New York mansion, and his vast plans for a London traction system, was so inherently dramatic that a newspaper report of it just after his death was titled "The Materials of a Great Novel" and concluded with an appeal for an American Balzac to undertake the project. (p. 155)

Despite this notoriety, the American scene contained financiers both more famous and more wealthy than Yerkes whom Dreiser might have turned to as prototypes. But Yerkes had several major attractions as a model besides the obvious though necessary one that he was dead. His life had indeed been dramatic and could easily be shaped into exciting fiction. But more significantly, Yerkes's methods and expressed beliefs would permit Dreiser to introduce a radical concept of American experience into his narrative. . . . In Yerkes's honest practice of dishonesty Dreiser had an immensely effective tool for an ironic examination of the hypocrisy governing all American social and moral life. And, finally, Yerkes's interest in art and women permitted Dreiser to deal once again with the theme present in so much of his fiction—the desire of the seeking temperament for beauty. (p. 156)

From the very first, even before he began to write ***The Financier,*** Dreiser planned that his study of an American tycoon would have an epic breadth. He would not merely tell the story of a particular "captain of industry" but would attempt to represent as well a whole phase of American social, economic, and moral life.

It was no doubt this epic impulse which Dreiser referred to in a 1912 interview when he commented that "In ***The Financier*** I have not taken a man so much as I have a condition. . . ." He went on in the same interview to note that "It has always struck me that America since the civil war in its financial and constructive tendencies has represented more the natural action of the human mind when it is stripped of convention, theory, prejudice and belief of any kind than almost any period in the world's history." His novel was thus epic not only because it depicted a vital moment in American life, one in which the "condition" of economic piracy flourished, but because it caught in its portrayal of that condition a permanent social and psychological reality. Stated in terms of its origin, the concept of man and society which underlies the Cowperwood trilogy is closely related to Spencer's law of equation or balance. (pp. 156-57)

The "natural action of the human mind" which Cowperwood illustrates within Dreiser's idea of equation is both obvious and complex. Cowperwood is a clear example of the man who realizes that life is a struggle in which the strong battle the weak and that morality is merely a metaphor of this conflict. On a more complex level, Cowperwood's responsiveness to the equation of life is also a responsiveness to the beauty pervading all life, a beauty whose most compelling forms are art and women. And, finally, though Cowperwood (unlike Eugene) succeeds in fulfilling his desires, he nevertheless succumbs on several occasions to the counterpress of the mass in the "equation inevitable."

The idea of equation was thus useful to Dreiser as a metaphor for many of his basic beliefs and feelings. He could use it to express his contempt for conventional morality while affirming through it an order independent of human volition; and he could use its mechanism to attack human pride while affirming the perceptive and feeling mind which could sense the beauty present in a mechanistic world. And always it was a flexible idea, one which could accommodate his otherwise contradictory philosophical "moods." Thus, for most of his career he used it to attack moralistic reform movements, but in the 1930s he could adapt it to sanction reform, including reform through communism, by arguing that the social balance had swung too far in the direction of absolute power by the strong and that reform was the mechanistic response of the social organism to this imbalance.

The idea of equation was not only flexible but amorphous and could absorb Dreiser's various enthusiasms at different moments of his career. The mechanism of Jacques Loeb, for example, which he seems to have encountered about 1914 or 1915 (after completing ***The Titan***), confirmed as a specific biological reality the mechanism which Dreiser's idea of equation posited for all life. And in his essay on "The American Financier" in ***Hey Rub-a-Dub-Dub*** Dreiser offered the thought of Nietzsche and Marx as metaphoric statements of the two poles of individual and mass power within the idea of balance. (pp. 157-58)

[H. L.] Mencken had been a Nietzsche enthusiast for some years, and in 1980 he published *The Philosophy of Friedrich Nietzsche,* a defense and exposition of Nietzsche's thought. He sent a copy to Dreiser, who replied favorably that he considered himself and Nietzsche as "hale follows well met." But in a letter to Mencken ten days later he qualified his earlier endorsement and referred to Nietzsche as "Schopenhauer confused and warmed over." Both remarks suggest that Nietzsche's ideas, as explained by Mencken, served primarily to confirm views already held by Dreiser. He and Nietzsche were "hale fellows well met" because both rejected moral values which arose from supernatural sanctions and because both believed that life was essentially struggle. And Nietzsche appeared to be "warmed over" Schopenhauer because Mencken stated that Nietzsche's will to power was Schopenhauer's will to live and Dreiser himself had already deduced, from Spencerian Social Darwinism, that the struggle to live was principally a struggle for power.

Nietzsche's influence on Dreiser is perhaps clearest in the theme of contempt for the masses with their "slave morality" which runs through the first two Cowperwood novels and which made ***The Titan*** one of Mencken's favorite Dreiser novels. In all, however, Dreiser's encounter with Nietzsche's ideas (through Mencken) resembles his acceptance of many other "philosophies," several of them seemingly contradictory, for the remainder of his career. These beliefs, from socialism to technocracy and from Freudianism to Hindu mysticism, did not alter Dreiser's thought but rather were absorbed into his permanent and emotionally grounded cosmology of the equation inevitable. (pp. 158-59)

Donald Pizer, in his The Novels of Theodore Dreiser: A Critical Study, *University of Minnesota Press, 1976, 382 p.*

JACK E. WALLACE (essay date 1981)

[In the following excerpt, Wallace examines the comic and ironic elements in The Financier *and* The Titan.*]*

In assessing Dreiser's achievement as a novelist, critics often find a difference between the judgment which condemns a particular work and the intuitive response which attests to its power and significance. This is especially true of ***The Financier*** . . . and ***The Titan***. . . . Whether considered as separate novels or as a single epic, the Cowperwood narrative is not highly esteemed, and the general preference for ***The Financier*** suggests that Dreiser failed altogether in achieving his epic design. [In a footnote Wallace states: "The third novel in the Trilogy, ***The Stoic***. . . , was not written until nearly thirty years after ***The Titan***. Aside from being unfinished, ***The Stoic*** is inconsistent in tone and thought with the earlier novels and need not, ought not, be considered in evaluating Dreiser's treatment of the financier in America."] In recent years, however, ***The Titan*** has won the grudging praise of a few distinguished critics. Robert Penn Warren confesses to reading it with "self-indulgent eagerness" and asks if it has not been condemned by criteria inappropriate to its form. Unable to find an answer, Warren concludes that the novel remains "a constant source of puzzlement." This paper proposes first of all, that the cause of this "puzzlement" is not the novel itself but the widely held assumption, shared by Warren, that the story is meant to be experienced as tragedy.

In spite of Dreiser's frequent association of the city, especially Chicago, with the spirit of romance, critics tend to take him seriously only when he describes the city as a tragic place. "Nature is so grim. The city, which represents it so effectively, is also grim. It does not care at all.". . . Not surprisingly, the notion that Dreiser was always secretly hostile to capitalism has enhanced his reputation among liberal critics and helped to locate his novels in the privileged genre of urban tragedy. Dreiser has thus become a key figure in image-of-the-city studies whose prevailing thesis is that serious American fiction is anti-urban and anti-financier. . . In ***Sister Carrie*** and ***An American Tragedy,*** the stories of Clyde Griffiths and George Hurstwood (whose fall is usually considered more interesting than the comic rise of the heroine) conform to this thematic scheme and have become touchstones in assessing Dreiser's significance. It is therefore understandable that Dreiser's supporters should give his epic of the financier the benefit of its best intention and make a case for Cowperwood as tragic hero. For if he is seen as either the victimizer of the urban poor or himself the victim of urban greed, then the novel, whatever its artistic defects, will be ideologically respectable. It is also understandable that these critics should seek evidence of tragic intent in Dreiser's choice of Charles T. Yerkes as the model for Cowperwood. (pp. 56-8)

But the critics who hold to the tragic reading assume that Dreiser was bound both by temperament and moral persuasion, to show the dark consequences of the financier's vaulting ambition. While admitting that Yerkes's story is the stuff of comedy, Philip Gerber argues that Dreiser's only major departure from the source documents was to transform the streetcar tycoon from a cheerfully amoral trickster into a tragic tyrant. Dreiser may have admired Yerkes's genius, Gerber says, but "he despised him as symbolic of capitalistic evil, oppressor of the masses." In short, the tragic reading assumes that the controlling voice in the novel is the echo, at least in an ideological sense, of the collective journalistic voice in the source documents, for the Chicago papers, whatever their differences on other issues, were united in attacking Yerkes as an "oppressor of the masses" and in taking credit for driving him out of Chicago.

While it is true that in other writings Dreiser at times adopted the moralistic style of the newspapers in warning a "liberty-deluded mass" that their chains were being forged by a "financial oligarchy," it was not that voice which spoke in the

Cowperwood narrative. In the epilogues, to be sure, Dreiser loses artistic detachment and attempts to inflate his story with tragic philosophizing, including the generically absurd allusions to *Macbeth*. But the epilogues war against an essentially coherent comic structure and a controlling voice that effectively undermines the themes of urban tragedy. In other words, the alleged tragic voice is heard, nearly always, in an ironic register. (pp. 58-9)

Before the publication of ***The Financier*** in 1912, the typical business novel represented the puritan conflict between good and evil. The city provided an image of ruthless self-interest which threatened to destroy the ideal of a small community based on ethical restraint. This image of the city as jungle was tragic only in the journalistic sense (a terrible but curable condition), and the reader was expected to judge the characters according to traditional moral standards and to believe in the possibility of urban reform. Dreiser differs from the writers of his day, Larzer Ziff observes, in having "the courage to act on his perception that there was no real gap between self-interest and the ethical norm:. . .self-interest was the real force; the ethical norm was a set of terms applied after the fact." But this perception, insofar as it shapes the Cowperwood narrative, does not make Dreiser's city more tragic, as is often supposed. On the contrary, Dreiser's key strategy is to represent the Darwinian city in such a way that the reader is encouraged to take a romantic view of what the anti-urban novelists would consider a really tragic environment. This system of expectation is established in the first chapter of ***The Financier,*** where Dreiser transforms a seemingly tragic premise into a comic line of development. Frank Cowperwood's mother, "a rather prim woman," of "religious temperament," teaches her son the Christian version of the origin and meaning of life, "but he didn't believe it." What he believes is the lesson in the fish tank. Seeing the lobster devour the squid, Frank concludes, "Things lived on each other—that was it.". . . The Victorian mother, upset by the boy's interest in the spectacle, twice orders him to "Run wash your hands"; but Frank intuitively accepts the lesson, internalizes the law of the lobster, and makes himself at home in the Darwinian city. Although the narrator calls the lobster-squid drama a "tragedy," the experience liberates the hero and establishes his ground for comic rebellion. Frank grows up with a good-natured contempt for the sexual and financial squeamishness of his parents and conventional society in general. But this hero is no Hamlet: "so the world was organized, and it was not for him to set it right." His purpose is simply to get rich, and his habitual reaction to the moral order that opposes him is a clue to the reader's experience. "It made him smile.". . . (pp. 62-3)

We find an equally important clue to comic rebellion in the account of Cowperwood's successful courtship of Lillian Semple, a young widow so inhibited by religious training that she is afraid of what people will think if she marries a younger man. Cowperwood therefore sees himself in conflict with "the late Mr. Semple and the force and quality of public opinion.". . . His purpose becomes not simply to possess Lillian but to "rout out all memory of her former life." Commenting on this motive, the narrator says: "Strange ambition. Strange perversion, one might almost say." By setting himself in opposition to a long sequence of father figures, Cowperwood might seem to violate his keen instinct for self-preservation; but the novel's treatment of his "strange ambition" remains comic: the daughters are willing; the fathers are fools or knaves. The quest succeeds.

The comic line is clearly developed when Cowperwood tries to invade the street-railway field that the city fathers of Philadelphia "held sacred to themselves." At the same time he trespasses on a more sacred preserve, the nineteen-year-old daughter of Edward Butler, an Irish Catholic politician who thought of Cowperwood as one "of his own sons.". . . The plot seems to take a tragic turn when Butler discovers the affair and gets Cowperwood sent to prison on a "technical" charge of embezzling city money. But the hero's affair with Aileen (who is perfectly willing) and his extralegal "borrowing" are treated as appropriate signs of heroic ambition. . . . [In the novel] the "bohemian" financier survives, the leader of the conspiracy is broken. Like all the fathers who oppose Cowperwood, Butler is defeated by his own inconsistency, his failure to see that the law of the stronger applies to both economic and sexual opportunities. The irony here is that Aileen, in spite of her convent training, is seduced by home truths. In renouncing her father, she nonetheless follows the code of the financier: "Cowperwood's *laissez-faire* attitude had permeated and colored her mind completely.". . . In the meantime, the hero remains undaunted. Even in prison he is at one with himself and in harmony with the Darwinian universe. Once freed, he quickly makes another fortune and, as the novel ends, plans to divorce the aging Lillian and go west with his young mistress: "I am a millionaire. I am a free man. I am only thirty-six, and my future is all before me.". . . When vast inscrutable forces do all this for a man, that may be a cause for wonder but hardly for pity and fear. Neither does it seem that the Macbeth epilogue has much retroactive effect. There is a parallel lapse at the end of ***The Titan***. Otherwise, Cowperwood's Chicago adventure continues to stimulate and gratify expectations appropriate to comic romance.

The epic intent of ***The Titan*** is announced in the formal invocation where Dreiser identifies himself as the bard of Chicago, he who will deserve the "laurels as laureate of this Florence of the West." Dreiser means to compare the Chicago of the late nineteenth century with the Florence of the Medici and to encourage the reader to see Cowperwood as a modern counterpart to the Machiavellian princes who created great artistic cities. In calling Chicago a "rude, raw Titan," the narrator also foretells that the hero, as agent of the city's titanic growth, will become a titan himself, at once the city's genius and its enemy. Though the descent from liberator to tyrant could assume a tragic form, in fact it eventuates as an urban version of the romance of the west, where profiteering, plunder, violence, "striking it rich," and conspicuous consumption were norms of behavior.

Although technically an easterner, Cowperwood has mythic qualities usual in the western "stranger." He is a loner with a criminal past, a straight-talking, bribe-on-the-table kind of man who soon rises to power with the help of similar "democratic" and Jacksonian types, especially the Irish saloon-keepers who control city hall. Opposing Cowperwood's well-bribed Democratic machine are the Republican silk-stockings, a clique of entrenched millionaires who seek to offset the hero's political advantage by using their newspapers to influence public opinion and keep the aldermen in line. This opposition can readily be transposed into a conflict between two narrative voices, two ways of representing urban life. The controlling voice, the echo of Cowperwood and the Irish Democrats, is comic, amoral, and consistent with the Darwinian order—the "real" order. Throughout the novel, Cowperwood and the cheerfully amoral Democrats are not only the most attractive characters but their policies are clearly best for the city—a

THE TITAN

BY
THEODORE DREISER
AUTHOR OF
"THE FINANCIER," "SISTER CARRIE,"
AND "JENNIE GERHARDT"

NEW YORK: JOHN LANE COMPANY
LONDON: JOHN LANE, THE BODLEY HEAD
TORONTO: BELL & COCKBURN MCMXIV

Title page to the first edition of The Titan.

political reality many Chicagoans still accept. The opposing voice, the echo of church-going Republicans and their newspapers, is morally serious and, in a journalistic sense, tragic. The novel's moral voice, even in such chapter headings as "A Marauder on the Commonwealth," is nearly always heard in an ironic register. What purports to be the "tragic" line, the muckraker's lament for the plundered city, usually serves the stylistic strategies of a controlling comic voice. Probably the most familiar example of this strategy occurs just after the Republicans buy an election and then attempt to establish a "reformed" city government: no payoffs for passing franchises. In response to this communication, Kerrigan says, "none o' that Christian con game goes around where I am," . . . and he leads the aldermen back into alliance with Cowperwood. Kerrigan's retort is often cited as an instance of Dreiser's vivid characterization of ethnic types, but it also supplies a clue to narrative intent. The Irishman's "comic line" speaks out the main narrative line. Throughout the novel every assumption that urban life conforms, or should be made to conform, to a transcendent moral scheme is treated as "Christian con."

The "con" becomes most evident when the Republicans order their newspapers to attack Cowperwood as a tyrant who walks on people as if they were nothing more than "a mass of bent backs, their knees and faces in the mire.". . . Even if Cowperwood were a great deal worse than we know him to be (and we do not see a single poor man suffer on his account), this stale radical rhetoric should weigh in his favor. But a critic disposed to look for tragic tyrants and anti-financier messages is likely to miss the point. F. O. Matthiessen, for example, confused the issue by assuming that the narrator was trying to represent the evils of capitalism but not quite succeeding:

> To be sure, he [Dreiser] gave a generalized description of "the Titans" as those "who without heart or soul, and without any understanding or sympathy with the condition of the rank and file, were setting forth to enchain and enslave them." But the reader never feels that Dreiser is wholly involved in this verdict.

Indeed not, for both the narrator and the reader are involved in a very different experience. In the larger context of this passage, the narrator is reporting, from the perspective of the reform movement, a "feeling" in the "nation at large.". . . This feeling, we soon learn, encourages anti-capitalist legislation which Cowperwood calls "crack-brained". . .and the narrator, in his reliable voice, will later call "fol-de-rol.". . . The reference to men "without hearts and souls" enslaving the "rank and file" is not meant to be a verdict about Cowperwood in particular or financiers in general; it is simply another instance of the naive rhetoric of the reform movement. The novel is focused centrally not on the enslaved "rank and file" but on those sturdy underlings who break their chains and rise in the world.

Probably the most successful strategy of the comic voice is to treat the idea of virtuous poverty as yet another "Christian con." In this respect Dreiser's novel reflects the spirit, perhaps the influence, of Bernard Shaw's comedies. Like Shaw's Undershaft, Cowperwood is a comic offspring of the Nietzschean superman and he consistently draws the reader into sympathy with other amoral survivors. Typical of this group is Berenice's mother, Hattie Starr, who refuses to become a "back-street seamstress," a virtuous occupation on which "the inexperienced so cheerfully comment.". . . Like Shaw's Mrs. Warren, Hattie becomes a prostitute and eventually the prosperous madame of a Louisville brothel, enabling her daughter to attend an exclusive boarding school. The subsequent triumph of Berenice, like that of Carrie, completes the attack on the wages-of-sin moralism of the pulp novel. Another successful adventuress in ***The Titan*** is Claudia Carlstadt, an orphan from the Chicago slums, who uses her beauty and wits to get a job in Washington as a "detective. . .and a sort of smiling prostitute," employed by Cowperwood to spy on Illinois congressmen. . . .(pp. 64-7)

Although the press finally defeats Cowperwood in his attempt to nail down his street-railway monopoly with fifty-year franchises, the narrative treatment remains essentially comic. In attempting to stop Cowperwood at any price, the Republicans order their newspapers to join the general outcry for socialistic reforms, hoping to reconstruct public opinion after Cowperwood is defeated. But before the franchise vote is taken, Eastern banking interests force the Chicago financiers to give up a foolish "scheme of revenge which only stirs up the masses and makes municipal ownership a valid political idea.'. . . Though the silk-stockings finally rally to Cowperwood's side, by then their papers have whipped the public into such a fury that Cowperwood's frightened aldermen vote against him. There is no suggestion, however, that this is a victory for reform principles. The reform movement itself is motivated by self-interest. The universal struggle between the strong and the weak will continue. To be sure, Cowperwood does discover the "law of equation": "in the end a balance is invariably struck wherein the mass subdues the individual or the individual the mass.". . . In a formal sense, this may seem a tragic recognition: but Cowperwood's "great woe" is too squarely inconsistent with our sense of his character and situation. At a deeper level, the "law of equation" proves that he is right after all, not right about the limits of his power but right in his *laissez-faire* principles. For the real consequence of the mob's uprising in Chicago is not to achieve a moral balance between the mass and the individual but to support the argument for Social Darwinism. Such an argument must demonstrate that a free economic system, like the order of nature, protects itself against tyranny that might destroy competitive balance. Just as the "law of equation" maintains stability in the natural world by making sure that no single animal or species can devour all the others, so the city protects itself, blindly and instinctively, from Cowperwood's "octopus-like grip.". . . Though the hero must be stopped, there is nothing tragic about his defeat. Having arrived in Chicago with only a million in his pocket, he departs with over twenty millions. He suffers neither inner division nor guilt, and to the end the narrator praises his "iron policy of courage" and his "stern opposition to fol-de-rol [socialistic] theories.". . . Finally, Cowperwood triumphs over the conservative financiers and makes good his promise at the end of ***The Financier:*** "They caught me once, but they will not catch me again.". . . And, just as the young Aileen was the emblem of his success in the first novel, Berenice Fleming signifies the ultimate realization of his "strange ambition" to supplant the archetypal Victorian father. This movement to Berenice as mistress-daughter is closely related to the main comic line.

The familiar condemnation of Dreiser's handling of Cowperwood's sexual quest rests on two interdependent misconceptions. The first, of course, is that Cowperwood's financial ambition is tragic; the second is that his pursuit of women is idealistic. In attempting to bring the hero's sexual motive into alignment with his *hubristic* drive to wealth, Donald Pizer assumes that Cowperwood is seriously in search of Ideal Beauty. If this is the aim, Pizer argues, then Dreiser violates his generic conception with a happy ending: "To have Cowperwood gain a concrete embodiment of an ideal [Berenice] and to end the novel on this note is to work against the grain of [tragic] experience." But to a reader attuned to the comic voice, Cowperwood no more loves the ideal than he oppresses the masses. Like his "great woe" at losing the franchise war, Cowperwood's sentimental worship of Berenice is a minor false note and does not seriously distort our interest in a hero whose charm for a thousand pages has been his total lack of idealism. "I am selfish and ambitious—a materialist.". . . This is the man to whom we respond throughout two long novels; in the final analysis, it is in those terms that we understand his sexual quest.

While the narrator sometimes suggests that Cowperwood's womanizing is the symptom of his need for Ideal Beauty, this motive is continually discredited by the comic voice. "From one point of view it might have been said of him [Cowperwood] that he was seeking the realization of an ideal, yet to one's amazement our very ideals change at times and leave us floundering in the dark. What is an ideal anyhow?" Whatever it is, the reader can hardly take it seriously when the narrator then gives a long list of Cowperwood's mistresses and concludes: "In the hardy language of Napoleon, one cannot make an omelette without cracking a number of eggs.". . . The principal "eggs," in length of narrative treatment, are Rita Sohlberg and Stephanie Platow, Cowperwood's most "artistic" mistresses and allegedly the forerunners of the "ideal" Berenice. But no one is convinced that this sequence really signifies a growth in the hero's aesthetic and spiritual sensibility. Instead of this familiar progression—Rita, Stephanie, and the "ideal" Berenice—I suggest that Cowperwood's progress is best illustrated by the movement from the young Aileen to Caroline Hand/Cecily Haguenin to the "real" Berenice. I combine Caroline and Cecily because Cowperwood's affairs with them are disclosed at the same time, midpoint in the novel, and both fall into paradigm with the revelation of Cowperwood's affairs with Aileen in ***The Financier.*** When Hosmer Hand, Cowperwood's strongest financial backer, discovers his young wife's adultery, he joins forces with the Republicans and engineers the conspiracies that shape the latter half of the novel. Cowperwood's affair with Cecily Haguenin, the twenty-year-old daughter of his only journalistic supporter, has the same result and provides one of the novel's best comic scenes. Unlike the newspapers who are outraged at Cowperwood's behavior, the narrator finds nothing surprising in Cowperwood's taking the girl, or in her taking him; the surprise is in the way Haguenin takes the news. But then, we are told, he was a "man of insufficient worldliness in spite of his journalistic profession.". . . Though it may be true that Cowperwood's sexual adventures do not always mesh with his business affairs, the underlying comic strategy is clear: those who think that economic life in America can be (or should be) conducted according to traditional moral principles are as naive as those fathers who think that their daughters (or wives) can be made to conform to Victorian standards of sexual conduct.

At the end of ***The Titan*** the reader recognizes in Cowperwood's projected departure from Chicago a repetition of his triumphant departure from Philadelphia some twenty-five years earlier. This event is reproduced in the first chapter of ***The Titan,*** connecting the two novels. In a Philadelphia train station two clerks turn and watch Aileen walk by "with rich, sinuous, healthy strides," and one clerk exclaims, "a man wouldn't want anything better than that." Commenting on the universality of the clerk's tribute to youth and beauty, the narrator says, "On that pivot swings the world.". . . This playful metonomy on the cosmic significance of Aileen's swinging hips defines the materialistic and erotic motive that shapes the narrative. Comedy, after all, is sex worship, a vicarious release from moral rigor and high seriousness, a tribute to the vitality of pagan forces. At the end of the novel the sixty-year-old hero is no less vital as he prepares to leave Chicago with the nineteen-year-old Berenice who is, in looks and temperament, a sophisticated and refined version of the young Aileen. Since Cowperwood has already made Berenice his legal ward, she is now both daughter and mistress, the perfect embodiment of his "strange ambition" to displace the Victorian father figure and re-create the beloved in his own image.

Dreiser no doubt muddles the final pages by inventing a tragic recognition for Cowperwood—"the pathos of the discovery that even giants are but pigmies,'. . .but the comic energy of the novel is not likely to be dissipated in the ill-conceived epilogue. Cowperwood is still a giant and, in the familiar paradox of profiteering, he has made Chicago a great city even as he robbed it. And in the triumphant and illicit union of the criminal financier and the daughter of a prostitute we have a striking variation, at once democratic and Darwinian, of the American success story. (pp. 68-71)

Jack E. Wallace, "The Comic Voice in Dreiser's Cowperwood Narrative," in American Literature, *Vol. 53, No. 1, March, 1981, pp. 56-71.*

RONALD E. MARTIN (essay date 1981)

[*In the following excerpt, Martin discusses the philosophical premises that lie behind Dreiser's works.*]

The two basic facts about Dreiser's intellectual life are that he hungered after experience and explanation, and that he was consistently and deeply in rebellion against both his father's guilt-ridden fundamentalism and the norms and sanctions, the inhibitions and hypocrisies of the whole community of Christian respectability. Omniverousness and rebelliousness are, in fact, about the only elements of consistency in his life and works. (p. 217)

He envisioned himself in the vanguard of thought, in the role of opposing traditional ideas—especially those traditional ideas about religion, morals, or social conventions by which he had been made to feel so oppressed in his youth and early manhood—but his tenuous understanding of tradition and his lack of real critical perspective diminished his philosophizing to the status of self-assertion, self-justification, outcry. His education was intense but random. As he records in the ***Dawn*** volume of his autobiography, he had performed so well in school that his teacher, Miss Mildred Fielding, had sponsored him for a year at the University of Indiana, and urged him, "Read Spencer. Read a life of Socrates. Read Marcus Aurelius and Emerson." He continued the habit of wide-ranging reading and philosophical pondering throughout his lifetime, but his sense of historical culture remained insubstantial, and he got a more compelling education on the streets of Chicago, identifying emotionally with the up-to-the-minute life around him and intellectually with an indiscriminate gaggle of interpreters of that life: scientists, pseudoscientists, popularizers, sensationalizers, philosophers, and spiritualists. (pp. 217-18)

Philosophizing was very real to him throughout his career. His first nonreportorial publications were entitled "Reflections" and signed "The Prophet," and among his early publications are many philosophical discussions and exhortations; during his artistic maturity he wrote and published a set of philosophical reflections, collecting them in 1902 in ***Hey-Rub-a-Dub-Dub!***; in his latter years he diverted a considerable amount of his creative time and energy away from his fiction for researching and writing his gargantuan philosophical fragment, variously titled "The Formula Called Man" and "Notes on Life," never publishable during his lifetime, and only recently abridged, arranged, and edited by Dreiser scholars and published by a scholarly press. Despite criticisms from people whose opinions he otherwise valued (his friend and supporter H. L. Mencken had written him that ***"Hey-Rub-a-Dub-Dub*** largely appeals, I believe, to the defectively educated"); Dreiser persevered in his philosophizing as though he were on the brink of some great discovery: ***"Hey, Rub*** contains the sub-stone of a new and better philosophy, something on which can be reared a sounder approach to life than is now voiced. Some one is going to come along who will get it and make it very clear," he wrote a friend in 1921, and in 1935 he wrote to Simon Flexner, director of the Rockefeller Institute, that "something creatively astounding seems to be waiting for proper biological, chemical and physical attention." He never quite discovered the key, however, and there is no avoiding the conclusion that the expository product of his striving, searching, and dogmatizing is shallow and inconsiderable stuff. Its tenor is set by the commonplace agnosticism he announces as if it were a new revelation, by the Sunday-supplement science with which he demolishes what he conceived of as ordinary men's norms and ideals, by the callow mysticism he hankers after, undercutting both agnosticism and scientific rationalism. (pp. 218-19)

Dreiser's cerebration, as a number of critics have noted, was really closer to feeling than to thinking—he arrived at an attitudinal sense of things rather than a consistent rational paradigm of the universe. As Robert Penn Warren has pointed out, he was a thinker "who automatically absorbed ideas into the bloodstream of his passionate being. He was not concerned with consistency within a logical frame, with rules of the game; he was concerned with how an idea 'felt.'" Thus Dreiser's intellectual consistency was emotional, and, as I shall suggest in analyzing his works, situational, rather than rationally consistent.

His philosophical quest was basically metaphysical. . . . [When] he looked to science or scientific philosophy he was looking for answers to ultimate questions, for a kind of substitute for the religion in which he no longer believed. And although his ideas changed frequently with altering circumstances and new influences, the object of his quest stayed the same. Specifically, his thinking both began and ended in a sense of awe at what he perceived as the harshness and beauty of a universe made up of determining forces indifferent to man and inscrutable; his inveterate philosophizing was an attempt to account for, or at least take an attitude toward that very unsettling perception. It is certainly reasonable to suggest, as several critics have, that Dreiser's habitual philosophical orientation was an advantage to him as a novelist. Vernon Parrington makes the point about him that "the larger view of life gives detachment" and Irving Howe states that "As a philosopher, Dreiser can often be tiresome; yet his very lust for metaphysics, his stubborn insistence upon learning 'what it's all about' helped to deepen the emotional resources from which he drew as a novelist." The philosophy itself might be deplorable, but its effect on the novelist as novelist is certainly another question.

The universe of force was a part of Dreiser's thinking from the very beginning of his career as a writer. As Dreiser traced his own intellectual development in his autobiography, the important and character-forming stages were the rejection of the conceptual scheme of Christianity and the liberating, mind-bending discovery of the awesome new scientific philosophy of the likes of Spencer, Huxley, and Tyndall.

After an early life characterized (by himself) as one of curiosity, questioning, and increasing discomfort with conventional concepts and mores, he came across the new philosophy through Herbert Spencer, and it seems to have struck him with shock and disillusionment, but at the same time to have opened a whole set of new possibilities. His later remembrances of the event differ somewhat in particulars. . . . but they all agree on the import of his discovery of Spencer and the universe of force. (pp. 219-20)

In writing his fiction, Dreiser (as is generally recognized) drew first and most fully on his own personal experience rather than on any intellectual system of abstractions. . . . Realism for him meant truth to his experiential, felt knowledge of things, and out of that primary knowledge grew his affinity for certain fictional motifs, characters, and patterns. Yet the generalizations, although secondary, were essential to him as a writer of realistic fiction, since it also seems to have been an inherent and unquestioned element of his realism that everything—characters, motives, events, social and cosmic meanings—be explained as fully as it was humanly possible to explain them. Of course, one could never hope to attain absolute explanation, as Dreiser would almost grudgingly admit when speaking of the art of fiction—"I know by now that life may not be put down in its entirety even though we had at our command the sum of the arts and the resourcefulness of the master of artifice himself"—but he seems to have felt that it was the business of the writer to try. In explaining or accounting for the phenomena of human experience, Dreiser, again the realist, had little faith in the symbolic and nondiscursive aspects of his art and relied heavily instead on the seemingly literal scientific and pseudoscientific generalizations in which his age had such unbounded faith. It was in this manner that Dreiser relied on the universe-of-force concepts in his work, and the strain that his implicit literary theory put on him as a thinker and on his works (especially his early works) as artistic wholes was considerable.

And since Dreiser was, as we have seen, a thinker who had fixed but sometimes incompatible conceptual responses to different philosophical situations, his works at times could easily veer toward fragmentation of approach, despite their conventionally coherent plot-lines. Richard Poirer perceptively identifies this phenomenon of incoherence in ***Sister Carrie:*** "What is perplexing is that he [Dreiser] creates no plastic coherence among the lurid varieties of self-characterization that emerge from his language. His relationship to the reader and to his material is fragmented." Philosophically, at least, this problem is precipitated in large part by Dreiser's groping and nonce-situational attempts to get everything explained.

By now no one should need further cautioning that Dreiser is not coherent, but another condition exists that needs to be taken into consideration in examining the scientific-philosophical content of his works, and that is the matter of his various collaborators. With the exception of ***Sister Carrie*** all of his novels were worked on by hands other than his own, as he had the habit of sending his manuscripts to others—colleagues, editors, and even girlfriends—who would make revisions as well as offer suggestions about them. The extent to which his various friends affected particular books we do not know; but we do know that he relied on the judgments of several of them quite extensively—the extreme shortening and editing of ***An American Tragedy*** by Louise Campbell and Sally Kusell being a clear example. It is unlikely that any of them added any philosophical material, but they well might have reduced or coordinated it. Thus when Dreiser gets less randomly and sweepingly explanatory, as in ***An American Tragedy,*** it is difficult to know to whom to give the credit.

Dreiser's works manifest universe-of-force orientation and concepts in various ways and degrees. First, his play ***Laughing Gas*** from the collection ***Plays of the Natural and the Supernatural,*** although only a literary curiosity, is the purest, most explicit expression of Dreiser's conception of the relationship between man and the universe of force. In his literary criticism he identifies such an awareness of cosmic relationship as an essential characteristic of profound literary works: "Each [of these works] suggests in its way . . . that unescapable and yet somehow pitiable finiteness in the midst of infinity which, think as we will, contrives to touch and move the understanding." ***Laughing Gas*** explores that relationship both explicitly and symbolically in a form unusual for Dreiser, an expressionistic closet drama. Dreiser attempted a few such ponderous flights of fancy in ***Plays of the Natural and the Supernatural,*** and in ***Laughing Gas*** he had, according to his biographer W. A. Swanberg, the added inspiration of a personal experience with laughing gas, used as an anaesthetic in a minor surgical operation.

The action of thy play is an operation to remove a neck tumor, performed on J. J. Vatabeel, an eminent physician; the substance of the play is his hallucinations while under the anaesthetic, counterpointed with the operating room emergency that occurs when the surgical procedure turns out to be far more serious than had been anticipated and the oxygen supply runs out. After a minimum of preliminaries, Vatabeel is administered the anaesthetic and begins his journey through the force cosmos; first "The Rhythm of the Universe" speaks: "Om! Om! Om! Om!. . ." Then Vatabeel, *"Functioning through the spirit only,"* is *"conscious of tremendous speed, tremendous space, and figures gathered around him in the gloom."*... As the operation proceeds Vatabeel has a flicker of fear of dying, but as *"the arc of his flight bisects the first of a series of astral planes,"* Force speaks:

> Alcephoran (*A power of physics without form or substance, generating and superimposing ideas without let or hindrance. . .*): Deep, deep and involute are the ways and the substance of things. Oh, endless reaches! Oh, endless order! Oh, endless disorder! Death without life! Life without death! A sinking! A rising! An endless sinking! And an endless rising!
>
> The Rhythm of the Universe: Om! Om! Om! Om! Om! Om!

As on the conscious level the crisis develops and more oxygen is urgently sent for, Alcephoran and The Rhythm are joined by Demyaphon, the chemical force of the laughing gas, which speaks climactically the universal truth to man: the depths of the universe are beyond any human knowing—"you are a mere machine run by forces which you cannot understand". . .—and the forces of the universe send man around the same set of experiences again and again—"the same difficulty, the same operation, ages and worlds apart.". . . Vatabeel makes the enormous and arbitrary effort necessary to continue life, and he narrowly comes through, but aware now of the insignificance of man in the vast sea of determining forces, the endlessness and meaninglessness of life in the universe, he comes through the final, the laughing stages of the anaesthetic laughing cynically and sardonically:

> Oh, ho! ho! Oh, ha! ha! ha!I see it all now! Oh, what a joke! Oh, what a trick!Over and over! And I can't help myself!. . .
>
> And the very laughing compulsory! vibratory! a universal scheme of laughing! Oh, ho! ho! ho!. . . I have the answer! I see the trick. The folly of medicine! The folly of life!. . . What fools and tools we are! What pawns! What numbskulls!. . . (His face has a sickly flatness, the while he glares with half-glazed eyes, and shakes his head.)

The Dreiserian irony is that although he survives, he survives disillusioned.

The play reads today like an unconscious self-parody, but its ideas, of course, were the ones Dreiser was most serious about. Perhaps for this reason he wrote to Mencken (incredibly) that ***Laughing Gas*** was "supremely the best—personally I think the best thing I ever did." At any rate, he made the epiphany of this atypical little piece the discovery of the universe-of-force concepts he himself felt so stimulated and threatened by.

In Dreiser's fiction the works most thoroughly and consistently involved with the universe of force are the novels in the Cowperwood trilogy, ***The Financier*** . . . and ***The Titan***. . . especially, and ***The Stoic***. . . to a somewhat lesser extent. Based on the actual career of financier Charles Tyson Yerkes, the trilogy presents the story of the achievement and travail of this new American myth-figure, the tycoon, in the setting of a universe of force and a world of stark Darwinism. Frank Cowperwood's character and actions are perfectly suitable, given a universe where "the large, placid movements of nature outside of man's little organisms would indicate that she is not greatly concerned," a universe whose creator seemingly rewards deception and ruthlessness rather than truthfulness and justice (as Dreiser points out in the zoological parable, "Concerning Mycteroperca Bonaci," at the end of ***The Financier***). (pp. 236-39)

Realizing that conventional morality is only a sham, Dreiser's tycoon forms an ethical philosophy in keeping with the ideas of personal force, Social Darwinism, and cosmic indifference: "'I satisfy myself,' was his motto; and it might well have been emblazoned upon any coat of arms which he could have contrived to set forth his claim to intellectual and social nobility." . . .

One of the principal ways in which he seeks satisfaction is sexually. Throughout the trilogy, Cowperwood's career is twofold—commercial and amorous—and in both realms he is audacious, unscrupulous, and generally successful, despite the considerable complications and dangers involved. Dreiser uses a great deal of universe-of-force terminology to explain the causes and effects of love in Cowperwood's life. Frank Cowperwood's "force" is invariably what first interests a woman in him, and his perception of "force" in her is what assures that a reciprocal relationship is beginning. (p. 240)

Dreiser frequently enough reminds us that with the likes of Cowperwood, Aileen, and Berenice we are dealing with people in whom "the chemistry and physics in life are large." Thus, in simplified terms, the trilogy presents us with an elemental conflict: human will and desire against convention and circumstances. The outcome is determined by the relative strength as forces of the various factors.

In depicting financial competition as a social phenomenon Dreiser's vector analysis is naturally quite prevalent. Some men are social forces (notably Cowperwood and all the men at the top of the economic ladder), and others are not. The forceful men—amoral, thoroughly self-possessed, daring, and blunt—are recognizable by their cool and calculating style, by their unemotional attitude toward business and political affairs, by the clear hard looks in their eyes. And they are thoroughly unself-indulgent; other, lesser people want money for the comforts it will buy them, "whereas the financier wants it for what it will control—for what it will represent in the way of dignity, force, power." . . . Lesser people exist for the financier only to be aligned by his force-field: the little men in business and politics to be manipulated or suborned, like Stener the city treasurer in ***The Financier;*** the women to be used sexually or socially, like the first Mrs. Cowperwood and Aileen Butler; and even the artists to be employed to enhance the great man's dignity and force, like the architect in ***The Financier*** and the painters in ***The Titan***. And of course the masses of people who use the natural gas, ride the street-railways, vote in elections that the financiers are struggling to control are insignificant, unthinking creatures fit only to be led or misled as the men of power choose. The vision is as undemocratic as it is amoral.

Given this system of values in the trilogy, high drama occurs only when there is opposition between men of force. When in ***The Financier*** Cowperwood rises to financial prominence in Philadelphia, opens his own banking house, and begins to gain control in such areas as the street-railway system, the established men of power see him first as a bright, audacious, somewhat helpful man, but later, as his adventures threaten their interests and even their control of the local financial scene, they recognize him as the Darwinian threat that he is and take every action they can to thwart him. Then their personal encounters with him are icily cordial, steely-eyed, fraught with natural antagonism and wariness. Depicting this high-stakes coolness seems to have been one of Dreiser's main interests in writing the trilogy; the basic situation recurs in ***The Titan*** as Cowperwood invades the Chicago financial world to take control of natural gas and assault the street-railway systems, and in ***The Stoic*** as he moves his operations to London to consolidate and control the subway system. In each case, it should be noted, Dreiser the literary realist carefully details the means and machinations of these conflicts, generally from the inside of both sides of the situation. Dreiser's social paradigm in these books is an atomistic, Darwinistic force-vector system, but that system is certainly presented concretely and particularly, rather than abstractly or formulaically.

The social vector system is a highly complex one. The personal financial and political forces interact with erotic forces, social forces, and even the forces of chance to produce the final fate-vector. In each of the three novels Cowperwood is thwarted by some combination of these forces. The specific situation in ***The Financier*** is the most cataclysmic. Cowperwood's early financial alliance with Edward Butler introduces him to Butler's daughter Aileen. The powerful and mutual erotic force between Cowperwood and Aileen sets them at odds with conventional society and, when one anonymous member of that conventional society informs Aileen's father and Cowperwood's wife of the illicit alliance, their forces too are turned against the tycoon. In his financial deals too he experiences a reverse: just as the financial powers of Philadelphia are girding against him, the Great Chicago Fire destoys a number of important businesses and the bottom drops out of the market. This unpredictable force of chance occurs just when Cowperwood, in conspiracy with the city treasurer, had been deeply engaged in illicitly investing the city's money. He is caught short and he finds nothing but hostility from the financial elite, who are spurred on by the revengeful Butler and are anxious for Cowperwood to fail so they can pick up his holdings. The financial forces even turn into political forces working to overcome Cowperwood, as the reform of the city treasurer's office and the freeing of the city from the influence of unscrupulous operators like Cowperwood become a crusade, first among cynical politicians and then in the population at large. Even the reformer (as Dreiser later pointed out in his essay "The Reformer" in ***Hey-Rub-a-Dub-Dub!***) comes on the scene as a kind of reactive force. As a result, Cowperwood fails, not because he broke moral laws or overreached himself, but because the forces—erotic, social, circumstantial, financial, and political—happened to interrelate and combine in opposition to his will, and they were together too strong for him. In ***The Financier*** he recoups his fortune, after his failure and a term in jail, in lightning-fast manipulation during the market crash of 1873, and he heads for Chicago with Aileen. In ***The Titan*** he rises to colossal heights in Chicago finance only to be thwarted again by a combination of social, moralistic, financial, and political forces. In ***The Stoic*** he enters upon a similar course in London only to have it interrupted by his death. (pp. 242-44)

Dreiser in the context of this trilogy seems to regard the course of human affairs principally in terms of dynamic law (every force has a counterforce, every imbalance is ultimately balanced), rather than in terms of a moral law, a divine plan, or even an evolutionary paradigm. Of course, the author being Dreiser, the trilogy has glimpses from other philosophic vantages too, some in keeping with the dominant mechanical perspective and others not. There is a good deal of Darwinism in the narrator's outlook, but it is the "hard" Darwinism of the struggle for dominance and survival rather than the "soft" Darwinism, more characteristic of American thought, of progress toward better, higher things. Appropriately to this framework, Dreiser concludes ***The Financier*** with the postlude parable of the Black Grouper, which demonstrates evolutionary survival through adaptation, deception, and predatoriness. There is no hint of progress or amelioration in this passage; life is as empty of values and purpose in the biological metaphor as it is in the physical. Totally or emotionally consistent with the biological and physical metaphors is the pervading sense of ultimate futility and disillusionment which the novels give. All Cowperwood's yearnings and striving, and all of the turmoil he precipitated finally end in almost nothing. Macbeth's witches pretentiously announce this to him at the end of ***The Financier:*** "Hail to you, Frank Cowperwood, master and no master, prince of a world of dreams whose reality was disillusion." . . . The philosophical pattern is similar to that in ***Laughing Gas,*** where the discovery of the mechanical essence of the universe reveals all human endeavor as ultimately futile, which suggests that possibly all life is illusion. That final point is only intimated in the Cowperwood trilogy in statements like that of the witches, but it is clear that that is one of the constituents of Dreiser's longest perspective on the events of the trilogy.

The last of the three volumes, ***The Stoic,*** has a slightly different emphasis due to the shift in Dreiser's philosophical proclivities in the thirty-odd year period during which he worried it along to near-completion. (He never quite finished it; his widow Helen finally had to put it together and have it published. . . .) Inherently the least interesting novel of the trilogy, it is nevertheless curiously tinged with Dreiser's later religious preoccupations at the same time it reveals him still trying to find meaning in the situation of the embattled, now aging, and still polygamous financier in the universe of force. And finally, after Cowperwood's death and the dispersal of his fortune, his art collection, and his dreams in the litigation that followed, his true love, Berenice, motivated by their past relationship and by what seemed to be the philosophical lesson of Frank Cowperwood, turns to Hindu philosophy and humanitarian works done in his name. The universe of force is never denied in this spiritualized conclusion to the trilogy—in fact a force draws Berenice to India to find a guru ("Something appears to be drawing me like a magnet and I feel I shall not be deflected in any way"). The philosophy at which Berenice arrives views the universe as fundamentally spiritual but, like the universe of force, radically nonanthropocentric, ateleological, nonprogressive. Thus, in Dreiser's last attempt to find meaning in this welter of striving and disillusionment, Berenice's final humanitarianism counteracts the Social Darwinism that had so pervaded the trilogy, but her mystical metaphysic only serves to spiritualize the universe of force. (pp. 244-45)

In some respects, . . . the trilogy is a failure, and they are important respects and not unrelated to the trilogy's originality and strength. Why does the whole Cowperwood saga seem more tedious than compelling? Why do we care so little what happens to Cowperwood? A confluence of factors, imaginative, philosophical, and technical, is involved. To begin with, it is very difficult for a writer to engage an audience by depicting a value-void universe from an essentially amoral point of view. It would be very difficult to locate what would matter to them in such a context, and to hang that in the balance, but if an artist had sufficient imaginative and technical resources it could be brought off, I feel. What Dreiser has done in this trilogy is to give us Cowperwood and his quantitative egotistical aspirations, virtually self-depicted, to care about. He asks us to set aside good-and-bad for a while in vicariously experiencing this life, but he offers us only winning-or-losing in its stead. . . . [But] absent is any sense that we as human beings have some stake in the game. Cowperwood's aspirations give us no more to care about. When, in ***The Titan,*** he is yearning and striving to become the man who exploits the public's need for natural gas and street railway transportation, when he is trying to hire a seducer for his faithful wife Aileen so he can be free to court his teen-aged idol Berenice, and at the same time keep Berenice distant from the other passing sexual affairs he is drawn into by his great magnetic force, it is very difficult to feel some loss, as Dreiser undoubtedly means us to, when some parts of his grand design fail. Our moral categories might well return, and we may feel he deserved his failure and precipitated it himself, which is precisely the sort of reaction Dreiser wanted to prevent in constructing the world of the trilogy around force rather than around what he felt were the outdated categories of good and evil. Finally, we might even feel the trilogy is not the high tragedy Dreiser intended, but a comedy of a selfish man's yearning for infinite gratification, and his ultimate frustration.

Dreiser's depiction of the titan doesn't help matters, either. Cowperwood's force and charm are merely posited, his behavior often seems petulant, and his apologies and explanations are trite and tedious. . . . Cowperwood's magnificence is fudged. Dreiser's imagination and language failed him, and unfortunately produced a kind of superman who was petty at the core, thus reinforcing the reader's ambivalence. The final effect is less one of awe than one of confusion, as Dreiser, despite his great skill in depicting the realms of business and politics, lacked the art and the insight to successfully bring together amoral realism, the business-world hero, and the universe of force.

In ***The "Genius"*** . . . Dreiser attempted some of the same effects, but this time with a hero who was an artist and an intellectual of sorts. The book is richer and more vivid than any of the Cowperwood novels, especially in its depiction of motivation, subjective reflection, and personal relationships (some of the superior aspects of ***An American Tragedy*** first emerge in ***The "Genius"***), but it leads the reader into some of the same sorts of ambivalences as does the trilogy. The hero, Eugene Witla, the genius in quotation marks, is presented by Dreiser as a man of great natural artistic talent, deep emotional stirrings, and considerable though somewhat undirected and undefined capacities. He comes across as more sensitive, more reflective, and more self-aware than Cowperwood, and without the tycoon's single-minded power drive, although in other respects (like their disdain for convention, their fickle and amoral amorousness, their weakness for eighteen-year-olds, their sense of special destiny) they are similar. Both heroes show signs of being self-justifications, self-depictions of Dreiser himself, and in the question of authorial perspective lie some of the problems with the novel's ambiguities. (pp. 246-47)

The universe of force is an important part of the conceptual background of the book. Early in his development the "genius" discerns that social ideals and the people who uphold them "meant nothing in the shifting, subtle forces of nature," and, in a gloomier frame of mind induced by romantic difficulties and a reading of the likes of Darwin and Tyndall he decides that "life was nothing save dark forces moving aimlessly."... As in the Cowperwood trilogy, motivation is seen as force-directed: the narrator explains that "the results of many experiments indicated that the apparently *willful* selection in these cases [of self-destructive behavior] is the inevitable action of definite chemical and physical laws which the individual organism can no more change than it can change the course of gravitation;"... and especially the repetitious erotic motivation is again expressed in terms of force correlations: "She looked into his eyes and felt the impact of that emotional force which governed her when she was near him. There was something in the chemistry of her being which roused to blazing the ordinarily dormant forces of his sympathies."... (p. 248)

But despite this pseudoscientific aspect of ***The "Genuis,"*** various mystical and superstitious ideas are also given credence by the characters and credence-implying function by the narrator. Fortune-tellers twice in the novel provide strikingly accurate foreknowledge for the characters and foreshadowing for the storyteller as well. (Witla's entire career is laid out before him—for a dollar . . . and his wife Angela learns . . . that he was never to marry his eighteen-year-old sweetheart.) Astrology is also invoked, and on one occasion the good luck omen of seeing a cross-eyed boy accurately foretells to the hero (and foreshadows to the novel's audience) that the job interview to which he is hurrying is about to be monumentally successful. . . . A kind of mystical thought transference occurs several times in the novel of which the narrator offers the explanation that

> One could almost accept the Brahmanistic dogma of a psychic body which sees and is seen where we dream all to be darkness. There is no other supposition on which to explain the facts of intuition. So many individuals have it. They know so well without knowing why they know.

What are we to make of the novel's strange mixture of mechanistic materialism and mystical idealism? Simply that Dreiser's own incompatible philosophical enthusiasms, which are always close to expression in this nearly autobiographical work, come through in the novel as an incoherent narrative approach.

The problem of philosophical approach is magnified because the novel is to such a substantial extent the story of the hero's growth in philosophical understanding. Unlike Frank Cowperwood, who as a boy learned for once and for all "how life was organized" in the drama of the lobster and the squid, Eugene Witla gropes, questions, reads, backslides, and, supposedly, *develops* in his view of the nature of things. ***The "Genius"*** is Dreiser's *Martin Eden* in respect to philosophical wisdom, and it is just as inadequate in that respect. But where London's wisdom [in *Martin Eden*] was too narrowly and paradigmatically (and obsoletely) Spencerian, Dreiser's is too diffuse and self-contradictory, though similarly obsolete. Eugene Witla early in his career has his eyes opened by the universe-of-force perspective. As he experiences setbacks in his life, his reading of Spencer, Darwin, and others haunts him with visions of man's helplessness and life's futility. . . . The same ideas, then, which were first tokens of Witla's superior insight become symptoms of a morbid neuroticism, psychologically believable but still philosophically naive. . . . (pp. 248-49)

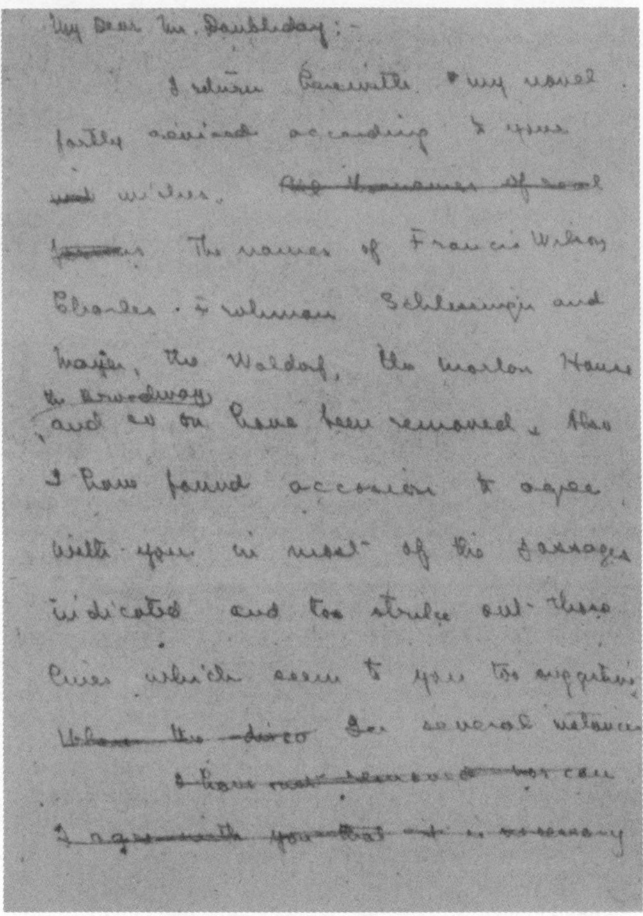

My dear Mr. Doubleday:-

I return [illegible] my novel fairly revised according to your wishes. [illegible] The names of Francis Wilson, Charles Frohman, Schlesinger and Wagner, the Waldorf, the Morton House, the Broadway and so on have been removed. Also I have found occasion to agree with you in most of the passages indicated and to strike out those lines which seem to you too suggestive. [illegible] In several instances [illegible]

Draft of a letter from Dreiser to Frank N. Doubleday criticizing the publisher's censorship of Dreiser's work.

Out of these emotional and philosophical depths, Witla cries for the reassurance of some sort of spiritual or ideal element in nature, and, after his second breakdown, comes up with (not surprisingly, given the intellectual level of the book) Christian Science. Mary Baker Eddy and the idea that God is Love and that evil is man's illusion are preached to Witla extensively (and approvingly) near the end of the novel, and although he never becomes a Christian Scientist, he seems to get some of the reassurance he needs from its principles and from one of its practitioners. At this stage of his recovery he eagerly seizes on ideas of design in nature, of the action of God in cellular growth, and so forth—typical American popularizations of evolutionary philosophy and ones Dreiser himself would later cleave to—as if they were answers to his condition. . . .

Yet there is another, a final stage to Witla's development. . . . Witla moves beyond his religious phase, and he is ultimately pictured as the accomplished artist, his wife deceased and his sweetheart gone out of his world, seated before his fireplace, sadder but wiser, coming to terms with "the unescapable and unstable illimitable" by reading a passage (which Dreiser quotes at some length) from Herbert Spencer's *Facts and Comments*, affirming the unknowability of the ultimate universe. (p. 250)

Although the *content* of the novel's philosophizing is shallow, incoherent, falsely and superficially "modern," disappointing to the educated reader, and demeaning to the stature of the protagonist, the function of that philosophizing makes good novelistic sense. The ultimate lesson of ***The "Genius"*** is a very sincere and valid one, one very close to the warp of Dreiser's own experience: emotions dominate ideas—a man's philosophy is a function of his state of mind. Whether we feel callousness and enmity from the great forces, or ideal and holy purpose, or merely the stimulation of an incomprehensible but awesomely beautiful welter, our comprehension, according to the novel, is a matter of our own personal and emotional adjustment to the universe of force. (p. 251)

Ronald E. Martin, "Theodore Dreiser: At Home in the Universe of Force," in his American Literature and the Universe of Force, *Duke University Press, 1981, pp. 215-55.*

ALFRED KAZIN (essay date 1982)

[A highly respected American literary critic, Kazin is best known for his essay collections The Inmost Leaf *(1955) and* Contemporaries *(1962), and particularly for* On Native Grounds *(1942), a study of American prose writing since the era of William Dean Howells. Having studied the works of "the critics who were the best writers—from Sainte-Beuve and Matthew Arnold to Edmund Wilson and Van Wyck Brooks" as an aid to his own critical understanding, Kazin has found that "criticism focussed many—if by no means all—of my own urges as a writer: to show literature as a deed in human history, and to find in each writer the uniqueness of the gift, of the essential vision, through which I hoped to penetrate into the mystery and sacredness of the individual soul." In the following excerpt, Kazin discusses* Theodore Dreiser: The American Diaries, 1902-1926.*]*

Theodore Dreiser began these diaries [**"American Diaries: 1902-1926"**] in 1902 as a daily medical record, on the advice of a Philadelphia physician who had offered to cure his continuing "neurasthenia" after the failure of **"Sister Carrie."** Dreiser typically ascribed his troubles to "mental exhaustion from past excess both of the sexual passion and mental labor." There is nothing here about what went into his once shocking first novel, nothing of the cuts he and his wife, Jug, made to make the book more publishable in the highly restrictive atmosphere of 1900, nothing of Frank Doubleday's refusal to promote the book when he found he could not get out of his contract with Dreiser. Nor is there anything about his relations with Jug, from whom he was to separate in 1910, about how close he came to suicide in 1903, about his ideas and hopes for the novels he would soon write—**"Jennie Gerhardt," "The Financier," "The Titan," "The 'Genius,'"**

But Dreiser makes a humble and typically ill-written statement in February 1903, after describing his poverty and desperate mental state: "After writing the above I read in my chair in my room until six o'clock, feeling that I might as well use my time to improve my knowledge of current novels since I shall want to be writing another one myself some day."

What he generally put down here is an unrelievedly crass but oddly fascinating account, sometimes hour by hour, of his daily activities. He tells just when he got up, with whom he spent the night, that he bathed and shaved, where he went for breakfast and how much less he paid last week for breakfast at another joint, how many hours he spent on a story or article, how much he withdrew from the bank. Many of the entries are so self-absorbedly factual about eating, drinking, lovemaking and the cost of living that they take on a horrid interest. He notes that toilet paper is up 10 cents from the previous week and deplores that in 1917, at Nickells' on 97th Street, "4 Scotch highballs cost us $1.40!" What he particularly notes is the "round" he had in the early afternoon with "Bo," the round he had a few hours later with "Lill," and his need to keep both from knowing about "Louise."

The boast of these diaries, which often read like a stud book interspersed with a record of daily expenditures, is that he was amazingly outside himself and his feelings. This was not really so, of course; he had recovered from his early breakdown and, though still hard up, was delighted to find that his growing literary reputation attracted women—especially if they shared the conviction (this was Greenwich Village, 1917-1918) that sex was necessary to his, and sometimes their, literary labors.

These diaries by one of the most powerful novelists of the century have no intrinsic literary interest. They are so crude and even illiterate in style (the assiduous editor has bravely retained Dreiser's many misspellings, as well as footnoting the many mistresses and literary folk of the time) that they may well provoke scorn among Dreiser's detractors.

Nevertheless, a novelist's diary is usually not so much a confession as an unwitting display—and practice—of narrative method. Stendhal, Gide, Woolf made superb books of their daily doings; Evelyn Waugh's is as deliberately limited as Dreiser's. But all these diaries, even when they leave out much we would like to know, reproduce the writer's professional habit of mind and gift of observation. Dreiser's is no exception.

Dreiser was crude, inadequately educated, often brutal (particularly as his confidence grew) in his contempt for both the leaders and victims of American society. But one has only to read **"Sister Carrie"** and **"An American Tragedy"** to know that what he put into his greatest characters was a vulnerability he saw as central to their destinies. The "tragedy of desire" (a phrase he uses here in an unusually generous note about a jealous mistress) found in him a perpetually starved and complaining soul. Many poor boys harshly brought up have "made it" by making themselves over; what is amazing about Dreiser is that the artist was always more intelligent, more interesting, more human than the man.

Dreiser the man was a perfect example of what Mark Twain called an American "claimant." He was one of your perpetually starved, rancorous, bigoted victims who usually hide their hatreds in the crowd. He did not have any money until **"An American Tragedy,"** . . . when he was in his middle 50's, and he had no real love in his life until he settled down with his second cousin, Helen Richardson, in 1919. He was not able to marry her until Jug died in 1942 and he was in his 70's. Jarring as his sexual record book is, his whining over every nickel and dime he spends, Dreiser reminds one of Hurstwood at the end of **"Sister Carrie,"** just barely keeping his head above water. (p. 9)

His hunger for women Dreiser might have ascribed to his early feelings of being unattractive and unsuccessful. Here he doesn't ascribe it to anything—he just wants what he wants and even plainly enjoys letting the woman he lives with know that he is "playing" with another. Though the clinical style of the diary virtually precludes general statement, it is obvious from the most interesting section of the book—written in Greenwich Village during the First World War—that Dreiser felt sanctioned by the intellectual unrest of the time and place, with its revolt against "puritanism" and the dizzying way in which the liberated women of the day flocked to him in admiration of his work and sympathy for his many difficulties. He generally managed to combine a love affair with editorial help.

Dreiser felt about his many affairs as he did about his lifelong recoil from American good cheer—he had no choice in the matter. Life just took hold of him and dealt with him as it liked. He had been brought up in the strictest immigrant Catholicism, and like so many writers who came to fruition in the 20's, he had a horror of established religion. "Always life is no good," he writes in 1917, "a horrible nothing." He submitted gratefully to every fresh claim by "science" that determinism was the answer to his intellectual questions.

Dreiser's belief that human beings are essentially passive is a clue to the dreaming inarticulateness of his characters and the extraordinary rhythm of fact he got into his best scenes. On a boat taking him from New York to Savannah, he noted that "nothing is more interesting to me than just the silent passing of moods in the mind, hour after hour, day after day, year after year though nothing is said. . . . I know life to be more or less of a perfect scheme of things (as good as well can be) as bad as I know it to be." The banality of this needs no comment. But Dreiser's conviction that human beings are always at the command of their "moods" actually gives a haunting forcefulness to his preoccupation with such detail. And it is here that the diaries, for all their clinical self-absorption, reveal the novelist who had nothing to say about his own novels or other people's novels. He was relentless. (pp. 9, 27)

Alfred Kazin, "The Records of an American Claimant," in The New York Times Book Review, *August 22, 1982, pp. 9, 27.*

SUSAN WOLSTENHOLME (essay date 1982)

[*In the following excerpt, Wolstenholme discusses the portrayal of women in Dreiser's works.*]

In his acceptance speech for the Nobel Prize that Dreiser thought *he* deserved, Sinclair Lewis paid homage to ***Sister Carrie*** as having descended upon "housebound and airless America" to give fresh air to "our stuffy domesticity." Lewis's use of domestic imagery to describe the world that received Theodore Dreiser's work both recalled the publishing problems that beset the young Dreiser and anticipated the critical battle that would follow for over half a century.

It has become a popular cultural myth to perceive Dreiser as Lewis portrayed him, as a great energetic, virile force that descended upon a female-dominated, enervated literary world. But this myth is as dubious as it is demeaning to women. (p. 243)

Repercussions of the myth that Dreiser came as a great phallic force to liberate male literary strength have shaken not only critical evaluations of Dreiser but the entire literary canon. (p. 244)

Feminist readers of Dreiser must revise traditional notions of Dreiser's place in the canon, but they also have a new vantage point for seeing his work. As a "resisting reader," to use Judith Fetterley's term, a contemporary reader can perceive the profound implications for feminism in Dreiser's fiction. This fiction at its best arises not from hostility toward women or from great phallic strength but from a powerful struggle between male and female psychical values, a struggle perceptible within the fiction rather than in the outside literary world, a struggle that Dreiser at his best confronted honestly and humanely.

In *The Mermaid and the Minotaur*, Dorothy Dinnerstein argues that our prevailing sexual arrangements, rooted in mother-dominated infancy, are destructive to both men and women because, for both male and female children, these arrangements give rise to deep-seated passionate ambivalences toward sexuality. From these arrangements originates, for both male and female children, deep-seated antipathy toward women, along with passionate attachment, arising from one's primary relationship with one's mother. Consequently, adult women in our society are the targets of great primary rage from both men and women; and both men and women, for slightly different reasons, experience a rather precarious sense of identity.

Both Dreiser's life and his work exemplify these deep-seated passionate ambivalences and this precarious sense of identity. Dinnerstein's analysis begins to explain some of the paradoxes in both Dreiser's life and his work: that he was a notorious womanizer while intensely devoted to his mother and sisters; that he could devote his first two novels to sympathetic portraits of women and in his acknowledged masterpiece sympathize with the murderer of a pregnant woman; that he could fill two volumes with stories of women breaking free of societal bonds but still write the three-volume saga of a hero who treats women as objects.

Robert Forrey has explained the biographical roots of the Oedipal structuring principle in Dreiser's work: "His rejection of his father—whom he held responsible for the suffering and humiliation of his impoverished childhood—and his identification with his mother and women were probably the crucial psychological events of his life, for they affected not only his personality and sexuality in a decisive way but his political and religious belief and his art as well." Forrey's "French Freudian" analysis, though it takes account of the entire Oedipal drama, gives the psychic weight of the role of the father. But although, as Forrey reminds us, the French unconscious may be Oedipal "through and through," the American unconscious is at least equally dominated by a "mother complex" that Freud's terms explain only partially. (pp. 244-45)

Robert Penn Warren has remarked that ***Sister Carrie, Jennie Gerhardt,*** and ***An American Tragedy*** were written "under the aegis of the mother," whereas ***The Financier, The Titan,*** and ***The Stoic*** were written "under the aegis of the father." The imagery Warren invokes enlightens the psychological dynamic worked out in these novels. The *aegis* was Zeus's shield, borne by Athene, and later given by her to Perseus to be used in defeating the Gorgons. When Athene later reclaimed the shield as her breastplate, she continued to wear on it the head of Medusa.

In Dreiser's Cowperwood novels, the father's "aegis" protects the protagonist from that same threatening, primitively awesome female power suggested in the myth. For a man, the trilogy fulfills the infantile wish of escape from mother-domination; Frank Cowperwood is the modern equivalent of the successful conquering hero-son. The narrative voice in this novel is very close to the protagonist. The real-life Cowperwood, Charles Tyson Yerkes, was a hero to Dreiser, for such a businessman, as Dreiser saw it, could "do as he pleased"—that is, he might successfully circumvent maternal restriction. Cowperwood's motto is "I satisfy myself."

The famous early scene of the squid and the lobster portends Cowperwood's later dealings in the financial world, as critics have suggested. But its place as a pivotal incident in Frank's childhood suggests that in Frank's psychic development it might also have more primal significance. As the lobster lives on the squid, Cowperwood concludes that men live on men—but Frank isn't really sure. He hesitates before reaching the conclusion. What lived on men?

> Was it other men? Wild animals lived on men. And there were Indians and cannibals. And some men were killed by storms and accidents. He wasn't so sure about men living on men; but men did kill each other.

Finally, when he lights on the idea of slavery as explaining how men live on other men, it is with an air of relieved triumph—and he runs home to tell his mother. Children, locked into symbiotic relationships with their mothers, perceive their mothers as devouring them at the same time that they themselves are torn between the wish to devour their mothers and the wish to preserve them as a source of nourishment. Thus, little Frank Cowperwood's relieved discovery that men live on men serves as a defense against his infantile fear that women might. No wonder Frank is so excited by his discovery!

"The squid couldn't kill the lobster—he had no weapon." What this "weapon" might signify is abundantly clear to any reader of Freud. Whereas the hard, armored lobster and its claws suggest the phallus as "signifier of desire," the squid resembles Dinnerstein's "mermaid" in its symbolic overtones—as representative of "the dark and magic underwater world from which our life comes." But the squid Dreiser describes is not a terrifying creature at all; it is rather "pale and waxy in texture, looking very much like pork fat or jade" (***The Financier*** . . .). In the presence of the lobster's "weapon," the squid is perceived as powerless and as solely a source of nourishment. For the only way to detoxify the infantile fear that women will live on men is to turn the image around.

As Perseus used the reflecting surface of the original "aegis" literally to turn around the Medusa's image, so that what was threatening to him instead destroys her, in the trilogy the infantile threat of female domination is turned around to assure Cowperwood's victory. Perseus then used his phallus-like sword to behead the Medusa; Cowperwood uses the business world.

Appropriately, at the end of the chapter where this incident appears, Frank Cowperwood ponders how he should get along in this world. He has reached the age when he seeks to turn the "shield" of his father's world against his mother-dominated young life. At the end of the chapter, he concludes that "he was sure he would like banking; and Third Street, where his father's office was, seemed to him the cleanest, most fascinating street in the world" (***The Financier*** . . .). The adjective *cleanest* makes sense if the reader acknowledges the psychic significance of the chapter's events. His father's world is "clean" because it enables him to escape from the "dirty" world of the flesh represented to him by home and mother, dirty because, as Dinnerstein suggests, this world reminds one of the constraints of mortality and also because it represents the part of his own nature that a man must suppress if he is to be as successful as Cowperwood will be.

But Clyde Griffiths in ***An American Tragedy*** also seeks an "escape" from what he perceives as female-imposed demands. His escape, without the assurance of the father's "aegis," suggests more fully and clearly the dark implications of both the male adolescent's problem and its threat to women under prevailing sexual arrangements. The psychological significance of the murder of Roberta Alden is made explicit when he first contemplates that means of "escape," in a dream where Dreiser uses a set of images similar in their implications to those of the incident of the lobster and the squid.

Clyde dreams first that he is beset by "a savage black dog that was trying to bite him. Escaping that menace by waking up, he then sleeps again to find himself in "some very strange and gloomy place, a wood or a cave or narrow canyon between deep hills." He leaves the cave by a "promising" path, but that path disappears; and his way back is blocked by "an entangled mass of snakes that at first looked more like a pile of brush." Finally, he turns around again to be confronted by a huge "horned and savage animal . . . its heavy tread crushing the brush." Crying out, Clyde awakens.

This dream seems at first to suggest only that dangers beset Clyde wherever he turns. But the elements of the dream suggest why Clyde sees his situation as so horrible. The lobster and the squid are safely enclosed in a tank, but Clyde's dream does not provide him with a safe vantage point. The black biting dog suggests castration anxiety. In the second dream, the three terms used to describe the place where Clyde finds himself, "a wood or a cave or narrow canyon between deep hills," are apparently not alike except that all suggest female genitalia. Escaping from the frightening but nonetheless fairly safe womblike enclosure, Clyde encounters the Medusa-like cluster of snakes.

Freud tells us that "the terror of Medusa is . . . a terror of castration that is linked to the sight of something." Freud explains that the Medusa's snakes "replace the penis, the absence of which is the cause of the horror. This is a confirmation of the technical rule according to which a multiplication of penis symbols signifies castration."

Freud explains the magical effect of the Medusa's head, its turning the spectator to stone, as a "transformation of affect" that offers consolation to the spectator: "He is still in possession of a penis, and the stiffening reassures him of the fact." In the appearance of the "horned and savage animal," the same transformation of affect is evident. Another parallel: though both the appearance of the horned animal and the petrification of the spectator counteract the threat of the Medusa (Dreiser even tells us that the heavy tread of the animal crushes the same "brush" that the snakes at first resemble), both also threaten the spectator-victim. Clyde's dream, then, suggests both that his own penis, as a defense against the Medusa-snakes, has betrayed him; and at the same time, that the father as alternative to the mother, represented by the Medusa according to Freud, is equally terrifying.

For Dreiser's men, the presence and strength of the father's "aegis" marks the difference between success and the most horrifying defeat. Whereas Frank Cowperwood's father provides him with a "clean" alternative to mother-domination, Clyde Griffiths's father is a failure in Clyde's eyes because he provides no safe clean world as a refuge for Clyde. The character of Lester Kane in ***Jennie Gerhardt*** foreshadows Frank Cowperwood in many ways: like him, Lester Kane is a businessman; and like him, his "perversion" regarding women is that he is attracted to their resistance and to difficulty in working out relationships with them. But he is unlike Cowperwood in that he is more completely mother-dominated. He never escapes from the murky world of the lobster and the squid to the "clean" world of his father's business. One result is that in business he cannot become as successful as Cowperwood or even as his brother Robert; he is not, as Robert notes, "snaky" enough. The other result is that he adopts Jennie as mother to him: "These years of living with Jennie had made him curiously dependent upon her. Who had ever been so close to him before? His mother loved him. . . . His father—well, his father was a man, like himself.". . . (pp. 245-48)

Though Dreiser has been labeled a "naturalist" and his strength has been perceived in his presenting a mechanistic, amoral system, some critics have perceived that his view is sentimental, humanistic, and moralistic. All of his novels written under "the aegis of the mother" suggest a war between these two systems of perceiving reality. In ***Jennie Gerhardt,*** the gap between these two systems must have become clear to Dreiser as resolving this confrontation eluded him. Originally ***Jennie Gerhardt*** had a happy ending; but according to Robert Elias, "Lester's not marrying Jennie and the death of Jennie's child were incidents Dreiser had to contrive in revising his novel, to give the story a 'poignancy' which the original tone demanded but which he had not been able to maintain." The original ending of the novel, though it may have been more sentimental, would have been appropriate to one of the competing sets of values implicit in it. For two-thirds of its length, the novel is a rewriting of the Patient Griselda tale. Dreiser's problem in writing the novel was closely related to his perception of society's ambivalence toward women's role in our own culture.

As Frank Cowperwood is one kind of ideal man to Dreiser, Jennie Gerhardt is his ideal woman, but it is instructive to note the difference between the male and female ideals. Whereas Cowperwood represents complete escape from the dark mermaid world of the mother and the ability to subjugate feminine energy to male will, Jennie represents that mermaid world itself; and that world is both comforting and terrifying. (p. 248)

By the terms of the novel, Jennie becomes for Lester the embodiment of the "all-mother"; and it is her role as mother that makes her, as critics have perceived, the ideal woman Dreiser never found. But the dream that she fulfills for a man has nightmare implications for him: he cannot operate in the socially accepted "male" mode if for him a woman occupies the center of his life. Lester lives with Jennie in a womblike, timeless world, which, nonetheless, is affected by the events of the external time-bound world. In Lester's infantile fixation, he denies that time will ultimately deny him his inheritance; so Jennie must become the admonishing mother to remind him. His marriage allows him to manage a woman as Jennie could not be managed; it puts his relationship with a woman in socially accepted terms partly because it allows him to subordinate a woman to his "clean" business activities, and so it represents his escape from the dark but emotionally satisfying mother-dominated world to the business world of his father and brothers. Therefore, he suddenly gathers great energy in the business world and quickly rises.

For all her self-abnegation, Jennie becomes an Angel of Death, presiding over the deaths of her mother, her father, her daughter, and finally Lester—appropriately, because she embodies life-and-death forces with which Lester's wife has lost connection. But Dreiser establishes in this novel the merits of these forces; he maintains something positive even in Jennie's role as Death Angel. Further, he makes clear why society is unfair to force a woman to assume such a burden, for Jennie herself suffers not as a superpowerful but as a human being. In the original ending of the novel, Jennie and Lester live out a fantasy, the inverse of the Cowperwood fantasy. In that fantasy the threat of maternity is apparently neutralized; consequently, the ending is both 'happy" and sentimental. But in the published ending of the novel, one sees the human, female consequences of a status quo where women are made to bear such an "ideal." After all, the "little individuals" created and limited by "certain processes of the all-mother" who consider this force "very vile" are in power.

In the Cowperwood trilogy, the actual terms of such power are explicitly laid out. As Lester Kane lives the fantasy of a nearly perfect symbiotic relationship with his mother, Frank Cowperwood lives the fantasy of complete escape both from maternal domination, threatening because the mother is perceived as a devouring creature, and from paternal authority, threatening because the father is perceived as castrator. Forrey suggests that Cowperwood's defiance of the father is only posturing because the son cannot escape castration as long as he sees the father as "the other"; Forrey notes, moreover, that Cowperwood's virility is asserted but never authenticated.

Dreiser "authenticates" his hero's virility only in a series of shadow pictures, in Cowperwood's relationships with women. For such a man as Cowperwood, as Dinnerstein suggests, "what makes life under the dominion of other males livable, is in part his ownership of [women]." Cowperwood is successful because, unlike Clyde Griffiths and even unlike Lester Kane, he can so completely separate his needy, childish self from the self that goes forth each day to an exclusively male world. (pp. 249-50)

Cowperwood's relationships with women, so necessary to his business success, are clearly modeled on his relationship with his mother, as Dreiser implies early in ***The Financier***. . . . His three most important relationships, with Lillian, Aileen, and Berenice, suggest in turn the psychological dimensions of the stages of Cowperwood's career. Lillian, older than Frank, is a mother figure; Aileen, though younger than he, is the most nearly his contemporary; Berenice is a daughter figure. But Dreiser also plays the inversions implicit in each of these roles: the mother-figure is, as Dinnerstein suggests she must be, childish. During his courtship of Lillian, Cowperwood picks her up like a child; this action symbolically neutralizes the primitively awesome power she embodies and with which she cannot be comfortable, and also portends the dependent childish role a woman must assume in marriage.

Aileen is the most conflicted of the three because of her anomalous position—the only woman to be both mistress and wife to Cowperwood, she is also mother to the child imprisoned within him and child to his fatherlike mastery of the world—and therefore the most completely robbed and destroyed. In her the need to be both child and mother clash, and she can be nothing but victim. Berenice is safer in her daughter role, though she must still emulate maternal authority. Significantly, only Lillian, the maternal figure, bears children to Cowperwood; Aileen's parents appear in ***The Financier,*** but they disappear in the later books; and Berenice is represented as having a mother—but no father, for Cowperwood assumes that role.

Cowperwood's art collection in the trilogy reflects his relationship with women. During the early days of his affair with Aileen, Cowperwood arranges a little votive shrine to beauty in the house on North Street for her, where he gathers rare objects (***The Financier***. . .); and when they are married, she perceives that her position must be that of a "radiant, vibrating *objet d'art*." Later Cowperwood hangs her trophylike portrait in his Chicago art gallery, where she presides over the riches that conceal the ruin of her life. But Cowperwood has no affectionate loyalty to the items in his collection, including the women; he replaces them as he can afford finer and finer pieces. Finally, in the scene where Cowperwood declares to Aileen his lack of love for her, Aileen pauses before one acquisition—appropriately, a Raphael Holy Family, in which she takes note of the Madonna (***The Titan***. . .) and notes the Virgin's vapid insufficiency for a contemporary woman like herself. Cowperwood's sense of art moves him continually toward more artistic women—Rita Sohlberg, Stephanie Platow, and finally Berenice Fleming, successively finer examples of the Madonna.

Love and art are so closely associated in the trilogy because both, in addition to being social and financial assets, become means for Cowperwood to deny the fundamental fact of mortality. As Dinnerstein suggests, maternal power is particularly threatening because it forces confrontation with this fact. Cowperwood's freedom to replace any woman who cannot give him what he requires fulfills the infantile fantasy of having the power to demand perfect satisfaction from the mother; he believes that he really can satisfy himself. Like his drive for financial power, his control of women and ownership of art confer on him the omnipotence that children imagine themselves to have. Significantly, in the trilogy only the women characters grow old. Love and art are bound to be illusory for Cowperwood so long as he refuses to acknowledge the suggestion of mortality implicit in both. (pp. 250-52)

In ***A Gallery of Women,*** the form of the work itself, a collection of portraits, acts like the fictional "gallery" that Dreiser has Cowperwood create within the fictional world of the trilogy. In effect, Dreiser as author builds for himself the same sort of gallery he attributes to the fictional businessman with whom he so closely identified himself. Though some critics have noted that the ***Gallery*** suggests Dreiser's devotion to "the study of female psychology," it would be more accurate to describe the ***Gallery*** as a study of a man's relationship to women, with the emphasis on the male observer. Warren is much closer to the mark when he describes the ***Gallery*** as "a sort of trophy room in print." His metaphor is again brilliantly suggestive. The "Gallery" is at least as much like a shooting gallery as a picture gallery; and what is striking about the work is not so much the psychology of the women as the psychology of the curious narrator who points to the many portraits to tell their stories, as the Duke of Ferrara in Browning's poem pointed to the portrait of his last Duchess.

In some of the sketches—for example, "Reina"—this narrator seems merely priggish. In others, like "Olive Brand," the narrative voice suggests fear of the protagonist's sexuality, fear that appears not to be under the author's control. The narrator seems unaccountably unaware of some of the most evident suggestions of the stories he tells. For example, the narrator appears not to recognize that Lucia, in volume I, has unresolved Oedipal problems. "Emmanuela," in volume II, presents the classic male fantasy of a frigid woman's suppressing a rape fantasy. But below the smugness, one senses that the narrator's impetus to tell about this life springs not from a desire to justify himself but from a troubled need to make sense of a mutual failure: "I had really wanted," he tells us sadly at the end, "to share her life." Even if the reader perceives that the responsibility for his failure to have done so rests as much with him as with her, the sincerity of the wish is evident.

None of the portraits in the ***Gallery*** is entirely successful; all read more like the sketch of a novel that was never written than a finished work. Some of the least successful are the most essayistic, where Dreiser indulges, as he is wont to do, in pseudophilosophy and rhapsodizes on the vicissitudes of life and its meaninglessness. Nonetheless, these less successful sketches do suggest the force behind the work as a whole. (pp. 252-53)

He speaks of actresses—"female adventurers" he calls them—who must "sell themselves to the highest bidders or fall, and quite uniformly they sold themselves. They had no essential refinement." He perceives that they chase men who are "bounders and dubs and wasters like themselves"(***Gallery***. . .). But he fails to acknowledge that the difference between the male and female "adventurers" is that the males are in power.

Yet this very issue is what troubles the narrator throughout this story. The preoccupations in ***A Gallery of Woman***—the limits of responsibility, the definition of power relationships—are the same themes used, with greater artistic control, in Dreiser's better work. Despite its artistic limitations, the much-neglected ***Gallery*** is a rich source for critical inquiry, a work that may shed some light on the author's better known work. Dreiser suggests, apparently unaware of the implication, why Hollywood must create a "little girl" type for the films such women as Ernestine make. When Ernestine begins to age, the film world, which cannot recognize mortality, discards her. She returns to the scene of her earlier life with her lover and, having failed to gain power over her life, exercises it over her death by committing suicide. "I thought I understood," says the

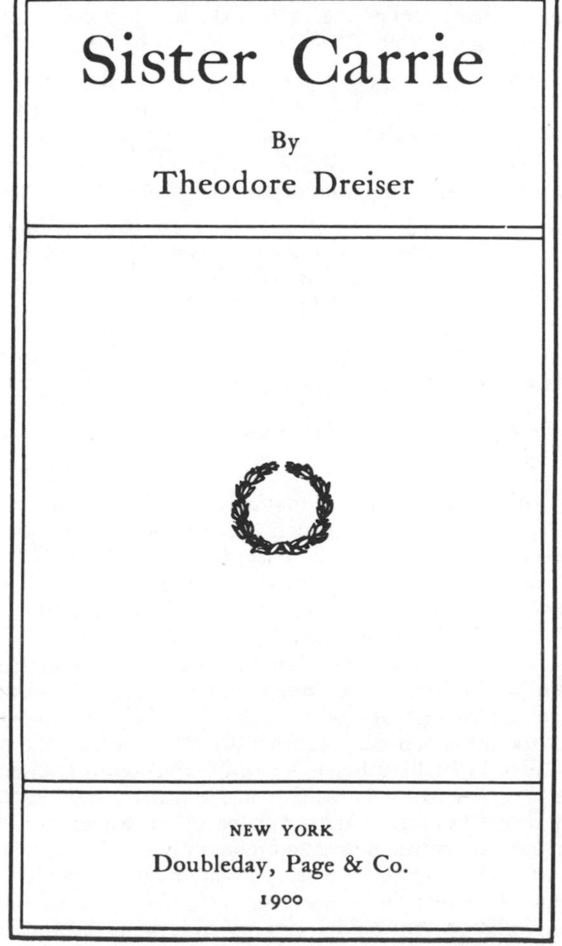
Sister Carrie

By

Theodore Dreiser

NEW YORK

Doubleday, Page & Co.

1900

Title page to the first edition of Sister Carrie.

narrator in the concluding paragraph. "Or did I?"(*Gallery*. . .). Her former lover is "very sad," and the suggestion is that so is the narrator.

That problematic narrative distance in ***A Gallery of Women*** was prefigured in Dreiser's first novel; for in many ways ***Sister Carrie*** is a portrait that has escaped the confines of a "gallery.". . . Like the portraits in ***A Gallery of Women***, Carrie's story has feminist implications: Carrie does better for herself than if she had followed a more conventional path; and the novel suggests that the single life can be worth living whereas the married life often is not. But Dreiser undercuts these implications. Earlier critics perceived Carrie to be unsympathetic and Hurstwood to be the source of the novel's power. Critics accorded tragic stature to Hurstwood, but they perceived Carrie herself to be lacking the human possibilities that make such stature possible. She becomes a comic character, just as within the novel she becomes a comic actress. The narrative voice of Dreiser, counterposing the "tragedy" of Hurstwood as a reproach to Carrie, seems to indicate that Carrie's success suggests her own emptiness.

The character Ames seems to speak for the narrator and to suggest the same thing to Carrie directly. But Ames—like the narrator of the ***Gallery*** portraits, who always takes seriously the women he encounters—does not trivialize Carrie herself but only her role as comedienne. He advises her to take her own power seriously and to use it as a real artist might, to represent "the world's longing." He proposes to Carrie that she employ her talent neither in tragedy nor in comedy, but in "comedy drama." (pp. 253-54)

What is remarkable for the feminist reader of Dreiser is that he so honestly dealt with his own primal rage and rarely reduced either men or women to the simple level of "victim" or "villain." In all his fiction, Dreiser deals with an issue of vital concern to women, the issue of power. (p. 261)

Susan Wolstenholme, "Brother Theodore, Hell on Women," in American Novelists Revisited: Essays in Feminist Criticism, *edited by Fritz Fleischmann, G. K. Hall & Co., 1982, pp. 243-264.*

WALTER BENN MICHAELS (essay date 1982)

[*In the following excerpt, Michaels discusses the thematic unity of* The Financier.]

Many critics have questioned the relevance of ***The Financier***'s love story to its primary subject, the American businessman, complaining, in Donald Pizer's words, about Dreiser's "frequent practice of devoting alternative chapters or parts of chapters exclusively to each of these subjects." Pizer himself thinks that the problem is more than merely formal; "the subjects themselves are incompatible," and Dreiser cannot keep Cowperwood's "two lives, that of the world and that of the spirit," from contaminating each other. Such a reading presumes, of course, the usual hierarchy between spirit and world, and presumes also, in Richard Lehan's words, a vision of Dreiser as unable to "reconcile the selfish and altruistic motives that fought within himself." Whatever the ultimate merits of this critical contrast between love and money, Dreiser's account of the fair-trading wife and the freely giving mistress should help us begin to see that, in his view anyway, Cowperwood's sentimental relations are hardly incompatible with his financial ones. In fact, the sentimental for Dreiser is already financial. Hence I would like to begin this essay by exploring some of the ways in which wife and mistress provide paradigms for the major competing accounts of value in ***The Financier***'s general economy.

Cowperwood's courtship of Lillian Semple, for example, takes place in an atmosphere marked by extraordinary financial turbulence, the panic of 1857. . . . During this decade, Frank Cowperwood had established himself as a successful stockbroker, but the panic and subsequent slide into depression dramatize for him "what an uncertain thing the brokerage business was." He begins to think about getting out of "stock-gambling" and into "bill-brokering, a business which he had observed to be very profitable and which involved no risk as long as one had capital." . . . At the same time, he finds himself attracted by marriage in general—the "home idea" seems to him society's "cornerstone" . . .—and in particular by Lillian, whose "lethargic manner" and "indifference" convey to him a sexually charged sense of "absolute security." . . . (p. 279)

Marriage to Lillian is thus represented as a kind of emotional bill-brokering, where "you were dealing in securities, behind which there was a tangible value not subject to aimless fluctuations and stock-jobbing tricks." This equation of security and securities with "tangible value" enforces a parallel between the "home idea" and the idea of production. Children, obviously, play a role in this parallel (Cowperwood thinks of having babies as if it were a form of capital accumulation—"he liked it, the idea of self-duplication. It was almost acquisitive," . . . but much more important is the stability guaranteed by what Dreiser calls the primacy of "fact." The "fact" of marriage allows "no possibility of mental alteration or change" whereas the problem with the stock market is that it is "all alteration" because "buying and selling must be, and always was, incidental to the actual fact—the mine, the railroad, the wheat crop, the flour mill." . . . Cowperwood imagines himself a producer and imagines in production a refuge from risk; the vision of value that emerges here might almost be called agrarian, an economy shielded from fluctuation by the joint facts of marriage and of commodities themselves.

Yet the appeal of Aileen . . . involves values very different from those represented by Lillian. Dreiser himself insists on the financial implications of this contrast by juxtaposing Cowperwood's growing attraction to Aileen's "vitality and vivacity" . . . with his almost unconscious return to "an atmosphere of erratic and [as it initially seems] unsatisfactory speculation." . . . Entering into an agreement with the Philadelphia city treasurer, George Stener, Cowperwood undertakes to drive a large issue of city loan certificate to par essentially by creating a false demand, buying initially from the city for the city, and thus misleading investors as to the strength of the market. The real attraction of the plan, however, one that makes Cowperwood forget all his reservations, is that as long as the city will "ultimately get par for all its issues," he and Stener can make an extra profit for themselves by speculating in the certificates: "Having the new and reserve issue entirely in his hands, Cowperwood could throw such amounts as he wished into the market at such times as he wished to buy, and consequently depress the market. Then he could buy, and, later, up would go the price." . . . The point here is that the instability Cowperwood fears when thinking of himself as a potential producer of commodities is the phenomenon that makes his success as a speculator possible. "Speculation," as one financial writer defined it in 1909, "is the act of taking advantage of fluctuations in the price of property." Cowperwood, however, not only takes advantage of these fluctuations, he goes one step further; he creates them—they *are* his commodities, the source of his profit. Instead of wheat or steel, the financier produces "fluctuations," "manufactured" by "manipulative tricks." . . . (pp. 279-80)

To speak of Cowperwood as manufacturing fluctuations is, of course, to translate production into an unsettlingly abstract vocabulary, but Dreiser makes it clear that this love of abstraction is central to the financier's career. Cowperwood's first job is in the commission business, brokering flour and grain, but he decides early on that "there was no real money in it," which turns out to mean not simply or even primarily that trading commodities does not provide sufficient opportunity to make big profits. The trouble with commodities, he thinks, is that they are not "mental enough." He has no interest in flour or grain: "Money was the thing—plain money, discounted, loaned, cornered, represented by stocks and bonds—that interested him." The financier's dislike of stability thus emerges even more explicitly as a distaste for commodities, and the opposition between the phlegmatic wife and the passionate mistress, between stability and alteration, finds itself reinscribed in the difference between values that are "tangible" and those that are "mental."

Put in these terms, the conflict between wife and mistress can now be understood as a version of the more general conflict over how, exactly, the value of things will be determined. (pp. 280-81)

[An] alliance between speculation and production helps explain what would otherwise seem some peculiar inconsistencies in ***The Financier.*** We have, for example, already noted Dreiser's identification of marriage with an agrarian commitment to production and "tangible value" while noting at the same time his identification of the mistress with the speculator's "mental" manipulations. But when, in more general terms, he attacks marriage and defends the philanderer, he seems to invert the argument, representing the mistress as a physiocrat and the wife as a manipulator of artificial "conventions": "One life, one love, is the Christian idea, and into this sluice or mold it has been endeavoring to compress the whole world. Pagan thought held no such belief . . . and in the primeval world nature apparently holds no scheme for the unity of two beyond the temporary care of the young." . . . Cowperwood's finances may be as divorced as possible from the physiocratic, but Dreiser still relies on nature to justify his sexual practices. Hence when the "sweet bond" of marital "exchange" becomes "the grasping legality of established matrimony," . . . it is contrasted not only to the love between man and mistress but to the single most powerful paradigm of natural affection, the love of a parent for his or her child, "broad, generous, sad, contemplative giving without thought of return." . . . (pp. 287-88)

[This] juxtaposition of Cowperwood as speculator, profiting from utterly artificial stock fluctuations, with Cowperwood as pagan lover, flaunting nature in the face of Christian law, is not a simple contradiction. For the mistress and the parent are cornucopian lovers; disdaining "exchange," "giving without thought of return," they produce affection with the disruptive and inhuman power of nature making commodities. And if what unites the speculator with nature is precisely the attraction of the cornucopia, what unites the wife and the producer is the fear of unlimited production—of wheat, oil, or love. The hostility of wife to mistress thus turns out to be a version of the producers' mistrust of nature. The mistress, a figure for unproductive manipulation, is also (by nature's illogic of excess) a figure for infinite productivity. (p. 288)

The Financier nicely illustrates the double-edged character of this naturalization of the economy. Nothing about Dreiser is better known than his susceptibility to Spencerian "physico-chemical" explanations of human behavior. And nothing in Dreiser's work provides a better example of this susceptibility than the allegory of the lobster and the squid that opens ***The Financier*** and, from an intellectual standpoint, clears "things up considerably" for the young Frank Cowperwood. The "heavily armed" lobster gradually devours the weaponless squid, and answers in the process a question that had long troubled Frank: "How is life organized?" . . . "Things lived on each other—that was it." The moral of this story, as Cowperwood and Dreiser come to see it, is the irrelevance of anything but strength in a world "organized" so that the strong feed on the weak. Such a moral is, of course, congruent with the Spencerians' Social Darwinist tendency to find in natural law a justification for the robber-baron practices of the most predatory American businessmen. But it is curiously inapplicable to the events of ***The Financier*** itself, which persistently exhibit nature not primarily as an organizing force dedicated to the survival of the fittest, but as the ultimate measure of life's instability, the "mystic chemistry" that embodies the "insecurity and uncertainty of life." . . . (pp. 288-89)

Along these lines, Dreiser presents both the Chicago fire of 1871, which temporarily ruins Cowperwood, and the panic of 1873, which restores his fortunes, as inexplicable and unpredictable *lusūs naturae*. Events like the fire, "unheralded storms out of clear skies—financial, social, anything you choose," make wise men "doubt the existence of a kindly, overruling Providence." . . . Part of his point is that nature can be cruel, bringing "ruin and disaster to so many," but more important is what we might think of as nature's ability (and propensity) to be unnatural. Thus Dreiser's language here anticipates the headlines proclaiming Jay Cooke's failure (Cowperwood's great opportunity) in 1873: "A financial thunderclap in a clear sky," "No one could have been more surprised . . . if snow had fallen amid the sunshine of a summer noon." . . . Nature, in ***The Financier,*** is most herself when she is least like what she usually has been; hence the business crisis, understood by Dreiser as an essentially natural phenomenon, cannot be mastered or even predicted by any system of thought, any account of life's 'organization'—theological, scientific, even economic. "It was useless, as Frank soon found out, to try to figure out exactly why stocks rose and fell." . . . The financier is a gambler "pure and simple."

The financier's inability either to master or confidently predict events in the economic world around him turns out to have more general implications in the drama of judgment that dominates the last few hundred pages of the novel. The emotional and, as it turns out, legal question raised by these pages is one of what Dreiser calls "control," the relation between intentions and consequences. Charged by Aileen's father with having ruined her life, and urged by him to make her do what is right, Cowperwood proclaims his impotence. If "you know anything above love," he tells Mr. Butler, "you know that it doesn't always mean control." . . . His "intentions" toward Aileen were "perfectly good"; "if this panic hadn't come along," he had planned to divorce his wife and marry her. His legal defense against the charge of having stolen sixty thousand dollars from the city is identical; his "intentions were of the best," . . . but the unexpected severity of the panic prevented him from restoring the money to the city treasury before he failed.

Neither Butler nor the State Supreme Court buys this defense, arguing in effect that the consequences of Cowperwood's act constitute the best evidence of the "fact" of his intent. Only the dissenting Judge Rafalsky is convinced, and his agreement is articulated in such a way that its force, like that of the natural economy, is double-edged. The effect of upholding Cowperwood's conviction, Rafalsky writes, is to extend "the crime of constructive larceny to such limits that any businessman who engages in extensive and perfectly legitimate stock transactions may, before he knows it, by a sudden panic in the market or a fire, as in this instance, become a felon." . . . There is, in other words, no necessary relation between intention and consequence, and the court, in convicting Cowperwood, is punishing him for something he never meant to do, making him responsible for events that he did not, in his own words, "create": "I did not create this panic. I did not set Chicago on fire." . . . But to put the argument in this way is, in Dreiser's terms, to expose its weakness. For what does the financier create? What Dreiser calls his "harvest" . . . depends not on hard work, not even finally on his "subtlety," but on his happening to be in the right place when a crisis comes. If the financier has neither "earned" nor "deserved" . . . his success, then the fact that he has not created the conditions of his failure ceases to count as a mitigating circumstance. Rafalsky is right. The court's decision reduces the difference between the businessman and the thief to a matter of "accident": judicially determining guilt and innocence is only "glorifying *chance*." But, of course, Cowperwood's whole career is a glorification of chance, and the constant lesson of ***The Financier*** is that accidents will happen.

In an economy where nature has taken the place of work, financial success can no longer be understood as payment for goods or services. It becomes, instead, a gift, and for Dreiser this economy of the gift functions at every level. We have already seen how it characterizes the love of a parent or mistress and how it also characterizes the winning and losing of speculative fortunes: "Who is it that can do anything it was not given him to do? All good things are gifts." The literal force that Dreiser attaches to this claim cannot, I think, be overestimated. Love and money are gifts, personal identity ("Who by taking thought can add one cubit to his stature? Who can make his brain better.") is a gift, even art, although explicitly dissociated from the making of money, participates in the general economy of the gift.

Of course there are no artists in ***The Financier,*** a fact consistent perhaps with the absence of producers in general. But there is a good deal of art, procured for Cowperwood by an art dealer whose "fiery love of the beautiful" does duty for a less commercial version of the artistic temperament and awakens in the financier a desire "to make a splendid, authentic collection of something." He begins with furniture, buying, "after the Georgian theory," "a combination of Chippendale, Sheraton, and Hepplewhite modified by the Italian Renaissance and the French Louis." The inventory of brand names is appropriate here: Dreiser lists the objects without describing them; what interests him is accumulation. Cowperwood's "passion" for art takes the exclusive form of a desire "to possess" it, and his way of developing an understanding of it is "by actual purchase." Dreiser calls this, astonishingly enough, the love of "art, for art's sake," by which he means that Cowperwood has no desire to make money from the art "business." For him, the simple accumulation of the objects themselves is "distinction" enough. Art for art's sake and accumulation for the sake of accumulation thus come to the same thing.

This identification is, however, by no means a simple one. For in almost the same context that Dreiser equates art with the principle of accumulation, he equates it also with what would seem its opposite, the principle of philanthropy. "Great art," he says, is the only appropriate "background" for the "great beauty" . . . of Cowperwood's mistress, Aileen. But the relation between Aileen and great art is closer than that of foreground to background, for the particular quality of Aileen as mistress, her "sacrificial, yielding, solicitous attitude" toward Cowperwood, is "related to that last word in art, that largeness of spirit which is the first characteristic of the great picture, the great building, the great sculpture, the great decoration—namely, a giving, freely and without stint, of itself, of beauty." . . . Linking acquisition with expenditure, Dreiser defines the love of "art for art's sake" as the love of giving or receiving but never exchanging. Another way of putting this might be to say that art, like mistresses and speculators, has no sympathy for the principles of fair trade, which animate wives, farmers, perhaps even artists. The financier loves a glut. He makes his living on the disruption produced by excess, and he understands philanthropy and accumulation both as a form of excess. Beauty, given "freely," "without stint," "without thought of return," reinscribes excess as the principle of cornucopian generosity. (pp. 289-91)

Dreiser's conception of art as philanthropy is based neither on an attempt to contrast art with business nor on an attempt to bring them together under the rubric of a labor theory of value. If for Cowperwood, "wealth and beauty and material art forms" are "indissolubly linked," what links them is the primacy of the free gift. . . . [Art] in ***The Financier*** offers no refuge from the instability of the market; it embodies that instability and generalizes the principles that identify nature and the market economy. "All good things are gifts." Speculation is nature's way. (p. 293)

Nature in ***The Financier*** is the speculator's ally, not his enemy, but she is for Dreiser . . . implacably uncontrollable. . . . [For] Dreiser not only thinks of capitalist production as natural, he goes on to think of nature in all her manifestations as capitalistic; art and sex are as speculative as the stock exchange. Thus the "new world" . . .—Chicago and the west—toward which Cowperwood lights out at the end of ***The Financier*** seduces by its promise of a "vast manipulative life," sexual, aesthetic, economic. (pp. 293-94)

Walter Benn Michaels, "Dreiser's 'Financier': The Man of Business as a Man of Letters," in American Realism: New Essays, *edited by Eric J. Sundquist, The Johns Hopkins University Press, 1982, pp. 278-95.*

MICHAEL SPINDLER (essay date 1983)

[*In the following excerpt, Spindler discusses Dreiser's portrayal of the nineteenth-century American entrepreneur in the Frank Cowperwood trilogy.*]

During the late nineteenth century a novel social type, the millionaire manufacturer and financier, came to prominence on the American scene and provided writers with compelling literary subject-matter. The spectacle of the entrepreneurs' rise to wealth and power attracted William Dean Howells, whose *The Rise of Silas Lapham* (1885) was the first serious fictional study of this type, as well as Frank Norris and Theodore Dreiser. The ideological perspectives and literary preoccupations they brought to their subject were diverse, and realism of treatment was subjugated to the moralistic or tendentious interpretation of 'the captain of industry' that they each wished to present. (p. 48)

Dreiser's trilogy, [***The Financier, The Titan*** and ***The Stoic***] . . . is the most substantial representation of the nineteenth-century entrepreneur in American fiction in this period and his portrayal of Frank Algernon Cowperwood marks considerable advances over Howells's Silas Lapham and Norris's Curtis Jadwin. In particular, he strips the entrepreneur of any residual Christian morality and redeeming human warmth to present him as nakedly competitive and manipulative. Dreiser rightly saw that the rise of the entrepreneur and *laissez-faire* industrial capitalism had rendered traditional American values irrelevant. He also saw that people were slow to recognise this uncomfortable fact because they continued to structure the social experience of the present according to received models from the past. . . . Dreiser, his journalistic eye keenly observant of the social realities, recognised that the petty-bourgeois ideology of natural rights was demonstrably out of date in the era of the Robber Barons and, responsive to the intellectual climate in the first decade of the century, he adopted the plutocratic rationale of Social Darwinism and propagated it in his trilogy as the only valid explanation of man and society. Partly then, these novels demystify the exploiter and the processes of exploitation and corruption by stripping them of the hollow pieties in which they were usually clothed. But the Social Darwinian perspective also implies an affirmation of business and its methods. By the traditional standards asserted by Howells and other critics the tactics of the captains of industry were indefensible, but in the Social Darwinian view the tycoons were merely obeying the natural law of competition. Dreiser's study of the entrepreneur, therefore, can be read as both an exposé and a celebration of the world of finance capitalism.

Dreiser grounded his trilogy thoroughly in the economic and social life of the late nineteenth century by basing it closely upon the life of Charles T. Yerkes, the traction magnate. Although he was very rich and powerful, Yerkes did not belong to the élite of the Gilded Age financiers composed of the Vanderbilts, Rockefellers and others. Yet Dreiser especially selected him as the model on which to base Cowperwood. He told Masters that he 'had looked into the careers of twenty American capitalists and that Yerkes was the most interesting of them', and he seems to have seen in this particular magnate a figure of almost mythic proportions. . . . Dreiser's high regard for his subject obviously precluded any undercutting irony or debunking over-inflation in his treatment. The result is a sycophantic portrait which has a myth-making function in that it attempts to endow the entrepreneur with epic dimensions—to make him, in fact, a colossus of the age. Dreiser's irony is directed instead at the hypocrisy, as he saw it, of the public and private moral codes. It was Yerke's lack of such hypocrisy, his unabashed practice of dishonesty, which appealed so strongly to Dreiser, providing him with a foil against which to set the hollow sentiments which were supposed to govern American business life. Furthermore, Yerkes had a strong interest in art, as well as a taste for attractive young women, two pursuits which Dreiser adapted and idealised as aspects of Cowperwood's quest for pure beauty.

Dreiser thoroughly researched his material, concentrating on American economic history from the early 1860's, the social and political history of Philadelphia, Chicago and London, and Yerkes's career, including details of his private life. The account of Yerkes's public life in the trilogy is for the most part literally correct, and Cowperwood's financial dealings closely follow those of his original. . . . It is Dreiser's portrait of the financier's personal life that is largely imaginative. Since the documentary content of the business plot is so high, we shall pay scant attention to developments there in order to concentrate upon the ideological and imaginative reshapings which the material underwent at Dreiser's hands.

In the main, the trilogy constitutes one long *Tendenzroman* in which Dreiser sets out to demonstrate the tenets of Social Darwinism and the insufficiency of moral codes. In the opening pages of ***The Financier*** the young Cowperwood, a boy of ten, watches a struggle to the death between a lobster and a squid in a fish-tank. So impatient is Dreiser to establish the dominant perspective that he has Cowperwood, with improbable precocity, draw a Darwinian generalisation from the incident: 'Things lived on each other—that was it . . . men lived on men.' This imposed vision of a fiercely competitive society sustains the financier throughout his career. 'Life was war—particularly financial life', he reassures himself during his trial at Philadelphia, and his general conviction that 'the race is to the swift . . . the battle is to the strong', is reiterated through the three novels. Early in the novel we also learn that he is a 'dynamic, self-sufficient, sterling youth', and that his most powerful motive is the 'desire for wealth, prestige, dominance'. The unchecked individualism which is to be the keynote of his character is expressed early in his motto, 'I satisy myself', and later hardens in ***The Titan*** into the determination that 'he could, should, and would rule alone. . . . By the right of financial intellect and courage he was first, and would so prove it.' Ruthless, egotistic and admitting bonds with no one, Cowperwood represents Emerson's doctrine of self-reliance taken to its inevitable and harsh extreme.

In constructing his myth of financial success Dreiser includes one or two elements from the older Franklinesque myth of self-improvement. Cowperwood, for instance, devotes his life to a strong work ethic and continues to do so even when he has a massive fortune to enjoy. While work and business are hardly sacramental in character to him, they do all the same become ends in themselves. The domination of his life by work becomes an occasion of regret for him in ***The Stoic,*** but because of the 'current American contempt of leisure' it enables him to compare favourably with the emergent American leisure class in the figure of Polk Lynde and with the English aristocracy in the figure of Lord Stane who, although he 'knew how to play', could not match Cowperwood for 'vigour, resourcefulness, naturalness'. The great entrepreneur-hero must obviously not appear deficient in any respect!

Although Cowperwood may be bound to the work ethic, Dreiser is sufficiently alive to the trends of his time to equip his protagonist with a mentality suitable not to an age of early accumulation but to an age of high finance. Contrary to Franklin's admonition, not thrift but credit and risk are necessary in these conditions to amass capital on any scale. 'It was not his idea that he could get rich by saving', we learn in ***The Financier.*** 'From the first he had the notion that liberal spending was better.' He early recognises that the way to wealth in the late nineteenth century lies not so much through manufacture as through the manipulation of stocks and the capital gains accruing therefrom. The stock market was the central institution of the finance capitalism which emerged in the United States after the Civil War, and Dreiser's depiction of its role in the centralisation of capital and his identification of it as, in Engels's words, 'the hearth of extreme corruption' and the medium for 'the annihilation of all orthodox moral concepts' reveal a deep insight into its economic and social effects.

It is a concomitant of Cowperwood's involvement in the competitive milieu of finance, as well as a consequence of his Darwinian view of society, that he should be totally amoral. We learn in ***The Financier*** that he 'was an opportunist' and that 'his financial morality had become special and local in its character', for morality 'varied, in his mind at least, with conditions if not climates'. In stark contrast with Howells's Silas Lapham, there is none of the steadfastness of the morally principled man here. Dreiser expunged any trace of vestigial Protestantism from his characterisation; Cowperwood utterly lacks a conscience and has no 'consciousness of what is currently known as sin'.

It was in order to exemplify the healthy honesty of Cowperwood's rejection of the current conventions governing private and public life that Dreiser invented the Butler family. The adulterous affair between Cowperwood and the daughter, Aileen Butler, is presented by Dreiser as conspicuously lacking in that guilt and remorse which the Puritan moral code asserted was both inevitable and proper. Butler himself, though as corrupt and ruthless in practice as the opportunist financier, still pays lip-service to the ethics which were supposed to rule in business and political life. While his public morality may be hypocritical, however, his family morality is sincerely conservative, and he is genuinely outraged at the affair between his daughter and Cowperwood. As Donald Pizer points out, the discrepancy between Butler's business and family values is cleverly and economically employed by Dreiser as the pivot on which to turn both the public and private plots of ***The Financier.*** Butler's moral outrage against Cowperwood on family grounds is the real motivation for his determination to ruin the financier and bring him to trial for the embezzlement of Philadelphia City Council funds.

Similarly in ***The Titan,*** Dreiser develops two features of Yerkes's experience in Chicago—his failure to gain a place in Society and his many affairs with young women—into major aspects of Cowperwood's personal life in order to highlight the hypocrisy of the Chicago élite. The millionaire businessmen and financiers cloak their economic opposition to Cowperwood by invoking a moral code which looks askance at his history of adultery, divorce and imprisonment, and at his continuing infidelities. In the struggle for control of the Chicago street railways which takes up much of the latter half of the novel both Cowperwood and his opponents, Arneel, Schryhart, Merrill and Hand, wish to satisfy themselves, but this group hides its material motives behind a veil of seeming concern for the public. As Dreiser makes plain during his documentation of the corruption of city politics, these financiers also engage in the bribery and purchase of politicians and the manipulation of the democratic process in order to further their nefarious ends. Yet they use their control of the Press to have Cowperwood branded as the real threat to the city. When the public agitation they have whipped up begins to embrace socialistic demands for the public ownership of *all* street railways (as municipal reformers were pressing for at the turn of the century), then the capitalists, mindful of their own interests, close ranks and withdraw their opposition to Cowperwood's monopoly.

Egotism and the lust for power are hardly sympathetic traits, and to render them acceptable in his financier Dreiser subsumes them as part of a larger, questing temperament. It is frequently impressed upon us that Cowperwood is no ordinary mortal but more a kind of 'superman', and repeatedly we are meant to recognise in him a Renaissance vitality and hunger for the sensuous riches of life. 'To live richly, joyously, fully—his whole nature craved that', we are told in ***The Financier.*** But the two activities in which Dreiser seeks to convey, as opposed to merely insisting upon, the financier's spiritual largeness—his collection of art and pursuit of women—are weak and unconvincing. Both seem rather mechanical extensions of his obsessive acquisitiveness and we never see Cowperwood making anything other than wooden responses to either life or art.

It is also impressed upon us that finance itself is no ordinary, money-grubbing activity. 'Finance is an art', we are informed in ***The Financier,*** and we are meant to view Cowperwood admiringly in the manner of one of his lovers in ***The Titan,*** as 'a very great artist in his realm rather than as a businessman'. When Dreiser attempts to illustrate or define this special artistic quality of Cowperwood's mind, however, the results are only large and vague gestures. His difficulty in successfully realising the attribute he so vehemently insists upon is an index of the imaginative invention required, for the documentary facts militated against this aspect of his conception of the entrepreneur.

Most of the financiers of the Gilded Age were noted for the cultural barrenness of their lives and for their incapacity to sustain interest in, or conversation on, any topic not directly related to the making of money. Yerkes's own maxims—'It's the straphanger who pays the dividends', and 'The secret of success in my business is to buy old junk, fix it up a little and unload it upon other fellows'—may reveal a hard, practical grasp of business but they certainly do not indicate a promising foundation on which Dreiser could erect the philosophic grandeur of a Cowperwood. So concerned is Dreiser to image the financier as the dynamic multifaceted hero of a phase of capitalism which was already passing that he turns a blind eye to the impoverishment a monomaniacal pursuit of money and power could inflict upon the whole personality.

In this trilogy Dreiser dramatised an account of the main drift of American economic development from the Civil War until the early 1900s, and his passion for documentary frequently leads him to lose Cowperwood in his surroundings. So much historical and economic information has to be provided, and so much is done by others to whom attention is shifted for whole chapters at a time, that we never really gain a clear sense of Cowperwood, the arch-manipulator, sitting at the centre of his financial empire and pulling the strings. Norris was able both to keep his entrepreneur in sharp focus and convey some of the excitement of business by concentrating on Jadwin's own activities in the hurly-burly of the Exchange, but in Dreiser's trilogy the events tend to be too vast and abstract (with the possible exception of the bankruptcy) for one ever to feel the drama and sweep of high finance. Dreiser also failed to integrate his adopted ideology of Social Darwinism unobtrusively into his narrative, so that it remains at the level of imposed authorial rhetoric. However, he did see correctly that the financier was a social type of consequence who deserved extended literary treatment, and his trilogy can be read as an education in the methods and corruptions of the Gilded Age, closely documenting the distortion of city politics carried out by the urban plutocracy. (pp. 67-73)

Michael Spindler, "The Rise of the Entrepreneur in the Work of Howells, Norris and Dreiser," in his

THE
BULWARK

BY
THEODORE DREISER

NEW YORK: JOHN LANE COMPANY
LONDON: JOHN LANE, THE BODLEY HEAD
TORONTO: S. B. GUNDY :: MCMXVI

Title page to The Bulwark.

American Literature and Social Change: William Dean Howells to Arthur Miller, *Indiana University Press, 1983, pp. 48-73.**

ELIZABETH LANGLAND (essay date 1984)

[*In the following excerpt, Langland compares and contrasts the Naturalistic elements in the fiction of Dreiser and Emile Zola.*]

Flaubert's *Madame Bovary* . . . has been praised for containing the seeds of the naturalistic novel. . . . Much as Flaubert reveals about the effects of social environment on character, he is primarily interested in his characters and world as an aesthetic object; his principal concern is with the artistic presentation of this object.

Other novelists, however, were then, and had been earlier, interested in the social issues inherent in the object. Their purpose was not simply to shape the novel for aesthetic contemplation but to arouse the social conscience and inculcate a social moral. Thus was born the "social novel" of England's 1840s, as written by Mrs. Gaskell, Benjamin Disraeli, and Charles Kingsley, the later naturalistic novel whose most articulate proponent is Emile Zola, and the American sociological novel of the 1920s dominated by Theodore Dreiser. The public's quarrel with these novelists centered on an aesthetic issue. These writers were accused of using the novel's popular appeal to reach a wider audience for their propaganda, of sacrificing the artistry of the novel, and of reducing characters to mechanisms in order to promulgate a social theory. (p. 125)

Dreiser's naturalism, unlike Zola's [in *Germinal*], expresses little social optimism. Rather than presenting us with images of germination and imminent birth, Dreiser concludes ***An American Tragedy*** with the same scene that began it—except that the boy Clyde has been replaced by his sister's illegitimate son, Russell. The repetition of scene, "Dusk—of a summer night," "up the broad street, now comparatively hushed"; the repetition of experience, "As they sang, this nondescript and indifferent street audience gazed, held by the peculiarity of such an unimportant-looking family publicly raising its collective voice against the vast skepticism and apathy of life"; and the repetition of character, "Of the group the mother alone stood out as having that force and determination which, however blind or erroneous, makes for self-preservation, if not success in life"—all these suggest that Clyde Griffith's tragedy will be repeated in the next generation, that the experience will repeat itself indefinitely because it expresses American life and values.

Zola and Dreiser present an important contrast because they both seek to illuminate the force of society in shaping individual lives, but in this illumination Zola finds cause for hope and Dreiser finds only repetition and defeat. Zola's stress on process and his optimism are achieved by his presenting society as a particular, paradigmatic place. Society, so defined, can become a concrete locus for change. Dreiser prefers to analyze a whole social world.

The scope of Dreiser's fictional society, by comparison, is enormous. Dreiser ranges in locale from West to Midwest to East; from large city to small city, from town to countryside, from impoverished farm to lavish resort. He depicts foreign immigrants, the lower classes, and lower-middle classes from which Clyde comes. He recognizes a distinction between the new rich, like the Finchleys and Cranstons, and the established rich like the Samuel Griffiths. The scope of religious experience ranges from the street preaching of Clyde's youth to the church social functions Clyde attends in Lycurgus. There seems to be no element of society that Dreiser cannot or does not portray. Perhaps his depiction of Lycurgus's frivolous social set includes some falsity of tone, but in this novel that falsity contributes to the sense of unreality and idealism that Clyde himself brings to the upper classes.

Dreiser's society includes not only a broad geography and a sound understanding of class distinctions but also a full depiction of American institutions, businesses, finance, and politics. (pp. 134-35)

Dreiser presents a whole society at a particular period. What unifies these diverse scenes and social classes are common ideals fostered by this society and shared by all its members. These common ideals are expressed in the gaudiness of the Green-Davidson Hotel and reflected, with greater sophistication, in the home of Samuel Griffiths. They can best be summarized as a respect for wealth and all of its manifestations: material success becomes man's highest goal. Clyde's material ambitions not only express the collective aspirations of his society, but they are also sanctioned by all its norms and customs. The religious vocation of Clyde's parents arouses only the contempt and pity of those whom it intends to succor, and it arouses contempt because the Griffiths are obviously financial failures—failures on the one scale of values that confers meaning in this society. Even Clyde's mother, of unquestioned religious integrity and faith, shares her son's hope for some financial assistance from his rich uncle. Later, Roberta Allen, the woman Clyde murders, finds Clyde attractive because he is a "Lycurgus Griffiths." Society, then, in ***An American Tragedy***. . . , depends on the shared materialistic goals and values of a world widely disparate in experience, class, and geography.

Although class relationships in both ***An American Tragedy*** and *Germinal* are determined by economic factors, there are differences. Clyde Griffiths seeks money. He wants to join those at the top and is willing to trample on those below to get there. The protagonists of *Germinal* do not seek simply more money, they seek justice, which for the nontheoretical becomes "A day's pay for a day's work." They do not want to be masters to tyrannize over other men; they want a more equitable system, and they are capable of envisioning such a system. Dreiser's protagonists are not. This is a consequence of Zola's emphasis on social process and Dreiser's concentration on anatomizing society at a particular period.

Implicit in *Germinal,* in contrast to ***An American Tragedy,*** is a distinction between humans and beasts. The protagonists of the former novel face starvation and the attendant degradation of desperate people. Their situation reduces them to bestial behavior, a behavior which, however necessary,. . . is bitterly resented. Their social situation has deprived them of human dignity. The lesson of Zola's Jeanlin is precisely that of man reduced by a social system to his bestial origins.

Dreiser's protagonist never faces starvation. American capitalism allows subsistence for all, but at the same time it has entrenched the gaps between rich and poor. The poor will not starve, but neither will they be allowed to move out of poverty. When Zola makes the social situation of a particular locale a paradigm for society as a whole, he creates the breadth of criticism he wants, yet has a specific locus for conflict and resolution, actual or potential. Dreiser's expanded society provides no locus for challenge, conflict, and change. The protagonist's plight is more desperate in one sense because more amorphous and less remediable.

Poverty has become a source for a kind of humiliation other than that born of the degradation we saw in *Germinal*. Although Dreiser reveals the injustices of the social system and the ways in which those injustices are perpetuated, to the characters themselves, poverty means moral failure. Those who are poor are so because they deserve to be not because of the social system. In that world's perspectives, the genuinely meritorious will succeed, a perspective born of confusing a business ethic with Christianity, a confusion characteristic of American morality. It seems that Dreiser gives Clyde's parents a religious vocation to show the failure of moral absolutes in affecting the community at large. His parents earn contempt for their indigence rather than respect for their devotion.

This confusion of morality and wealth existed in *Germinal*. It usually plays a role in sociological/naturalistic novels. From the wealthy characters' perspectives, their "superior" morality antedated their wealth; indeed, their wealth, as they see it, is a consequence of superior morality. In the narrator's eyes, however, that morality is made possible by social standing, not the other way around. Morality, then, is a luxury; the richer one is the more one can afford it. This issue becomes acute in Dreiser's novel because his protagonist is not starving or suffering physically, yet he murders to improve his social position. (pp. 136-37)

In order to make Clyde Griffiths sympathetic, Dreiser has created and developed his personality and fate in such a way that we become acutely conscious of the social forces that have produced him and that limit him. (p. 138)

Clyde is relegated to one sphere of society; he wants to participate in another. In other novels, those of George Eliot, for example, the protagonist's nature conflicts with dominant values in his society. Dorothea Brooke has qualities that prevent her fate from being decided merely according to custom and "canine affection." Clyde Griffiths's desires, on the contrary, harmonize with society's dominant material values. Appropriately, his parents seem "cheap," a word connoting both tawdriness and insignificant monetary value. He wants to experience the superior life of wealth. He is in conflict with his current position, but he is in harmony with the values of his world.

Dreiser does not pretend that society bears the entire blame for what happens to Clyde. The boy's nature is seriously flawed. His mother early sees that he is "not any too powerful physically or rock-ribbed morally or mentally.". . . The narrator confirms that "he lacked decidedly that mental clarity and inner directing application.". . . The boy possesses a "naturally selfish and ambitious and seeking disposition" and "a temperament that was as fluid and unstable as water.". . . Part of Dreiser's aim, like Zola's, is to use individual weakness to demonstrate the need for social change. Since individuals are already hereditarily determined, the only way to improve humanity is through change in the other determining factor: society.

In light of Clyde's personality, it may surprise us that his life arouses as much sympathy and forestalls as much condemnation as it does. This achievement depends on Dreiser's understanding of character in society, an understanding that parallels Zola's. Clyde's society not only compounds his personal weaknesses, but, more seriously, it perverts his personal strength. Usually, in the novel, a character's strengths will help him fight the spurious in his society. In ***An American Tragedy*** not only do Clyde's weak qualities leave him vulnerable to social determinants, but his strengths—his eager determination, his sensitivity, his keen powers of observation—increase his vulnerability. Other characters remain invulnerable, not because they are represented as superior, but because they neither experienced the pain of Clyde's childhood nor shared his vision. We learn that a minor character, Governor Waltham, who must help decide Clyde's fate, was "a tall, sober and somewhat somber man who, never in all his life had even so much as sensed the fevers or fires that Clyde had known.". . . The Reverend McMillan recognizes that "[Clyde's] hot, restless heart which plainly for the lack of so many things which he, the Reverend McMillan, had never wanted for, had rebelled.'. . . (pp. 138-39)

An American Tragedy works to make Clyde sympathetic precisely because of his greater sensibilities and his desires to attain what is represented in the novel as a better, because it is a more gracious, way of life. . . . Clyde's bellhop friends at the Green-Davidson are safer from the lures than Clyde because they are more limited: "Hegglund, as he could see, was vain and noisy and foolish—a person who could be taken in and conciliated by a little flattery. And Higby and Kinsella, interesting and attractive boys both, were still vain of things he could not be proud of—Higby of knowing a little something about automobiles . . . Kinsella of gambling, rolling dice even.". . . (pp. 139-40)

Not only does Clyde emerge as more sympathetic than these youths, but perhaps more important, no other character in Dreiser's world arouses greater sympathy. Some characters are, of course, superior to others. Clyde's mother certainly wins our admiration for her devotion, dedication, and resourcefulness, but in that milieu much of her effort is futile. She fails to comprehend either her position in that world or the forces crucially affecting and defining her family. Her good qualities lead only to self-preservation, not success in life. . . . Her inadequate response to Clyde's tragedy is to try with young Russell to "be kind to him, more liberal with him, not restrain him too much, as maybe, maybe, she had [Clyde]." . . . (p. 140)

Further to insure sympathy for Clyde as a victim of society, Dreiser early establishes a pattern of description and evaluation that operates throughout. Whenever Clyde is confronted by one of a series of crucial decisions, a particular process is enacted. In the first book, these decisions range from the proposed visit to the house of prostitution, to his mother's request for the money he needs to finance Hortense's fur coat, to the proposed excursion in the stolen car, to the accident culminating in Clyde's flight. First Clyde becomes sympathetic (as opposed to his peers) by experiencing some conflict over the proposed course of action. For example, when the bellhops urge Sparser to take his employer's car for their personal use, we learn that "the only one, apart from Sparser [who fears his employer's imminent return], who suffered any qualms in connection with all this was Clyde himself." What at first seems to be a moral dilemma, that of "taking anything that belonged to any one else," is quickly translated into a dilemma born of potential personal consequences in that society, "They might be found out." The social consequences become even more cogent to Clyde; "he might lose his job through a thing like this." . . . These reflections conclude Clyde's thoughts, and in this way the author keeps us within a frame of judgments more sensitive to social consequences than to any moral imperatives.

Although we appreciate Clyde's vulnerable social position, it is also possible that we might condemn him for his moral inadequacies. Dreiser's decision to leave this episode without stressing any moral inadequacies in Clyde invites our condemnation of the social values that shape his reaction. In fact, it would seem that Dreiser must preclude certain types of moral judgments, or they will interfere with the revelation of an inimical social order. (pp. 140-41)

In ***An American Tragedy,*** there exist no satisfying moral standards provided by the social milieu or by the implied author which may serve as an alternative measure of success.

Indeed, Dreiser precludes such standards in order to intensify the social pressures on Clyde. As in Zola's novel, morality is a function of social class. This phenomenon determines Clyde's shock at the suggestion that he might have had sexual relations with the wealthy Sondra Finchley. . . . Clyde's moral horror here is born of the social differences between Sondra and Roberta, the woman he murders. His morality takes its prerogatives and distinctions from the social system.

Roberta, too, exculpates Clyde by sharing his dream. Just as Clyde hopes to advance himself socially through marriage to Sondra, so Roberta plans to advance herself socially through marriage with Clyde: "For all [Roberta's] fears, even the bare possibility of joining her life with Clyde's was marvelous." . . . To the degree that Roberta shares Clyde's conception of the value of social position and prestige, we modify our condemnation of his actions. Clyde wonders, "Wasn't he of sufficient importance to move in this new world without her holding him back in this way?" . . . As if in response, Roberta worries that "alas, apart from this claim of [her pregnancy], what had she to offer him comparable to all he would be giving up in case he acceded to her request? Nothing." . . . (p. 142)

Sondra and her set, despite the frivolity and snobbishness of certain members, represent not only luxury, but a gracious way of life, in comparison with which the impoverished life of Roberta and the Aldens seems sordid and demeaning. Despite Roberta's worthiness, she actually emerges as inferior to Sondra, and marriage to Roberta becomes a significant failure for Clyde, because everyone in that world makes value judgments within a social framework similar to Clyde's. If they do invoke some moral imperative such as justice or moral turpitude, they seem to do so in the service of their own social well-being, or in consideration of social ends, or in ignorance of social determinants. Clyde's wealthy uncle is willing to consider the family's neglect of Clyde as a partial cause for the murder, but he concludes with Clyde's personal weaknesses. "The wretchedness of such a mind as that—the ungoverned and carnal desires!" . . . However, the implied author does not endorse these judgments. (pp. 142-43)

Clyde's confessor, Reverend McMillan, struggles to determine Clyde's degree of responsibility and guilt, even though he is certain Clyde murdered the woman. . . . While Clyde can finally acknowledge that "his sin was very great. Very, very terrible!" he also has a "feeling in his heart that he was not as guilty as they all seemed to think." . . . Clyde never can completely accept the religious solace his mother and Reverend McMillan offer. (p. 143)

So strong, in fact, are Clyde's doubts that even after he confesses his guilt on the urging of his mother and Reverend McMillan, his religious enthusiasm falters before his doubts. At the end, Clyde shakes the faith and mental peace even of the devout Reverend McMillan: "Had he done right? Had his decision before Governor Waltham been truly sound, fair or merciful? Should he have said to him—that perhaps—perhaps—there had been those other influences playing on him? . . . Was he never to have mental peace again, perhaps?" (p. 144)

While a Clyde Griffiths will never achieve the stature of a tragic hero, he can, through his struggle, evoke sufficient sympathy to render his situation tragic.

Although they stress determinism, these sociological/naturalistic novels move us, not by denying free will, but by making us question the bases for our moral judgments, by representing the arbitrariness of social class and the inescapability of social determinism. (p. 145)

Elizabeth Langland, "The Art of Sociological Naturalism in Zola and Dreiser," in her Society in the Novel, *The University of North Carolina Press, 1984, pp. 124-46.**

ADDITIONAL BIBLIOGRAPHY

Bernheim, Mark. "Florida: The Permanence of America's Idyll." *Modernist Studies: Literature and Culture 1920-1940* 4 (1920-40): 125-45.*

Discussion of the perception during the 1930s of Florida as an image of America's future. Bernheim examines the works of Dreiser, John Dos Passos, and other leading writers of the 1930s, as well as articles in *Vanity Fair* and other popular magazines, to discuss the use of Florida as an image of promise and growth.

Boren, Lynda S. "William James, Theodore Dreiser and the 'Anaesthetic Revelation'." *American Studies* XXIV, No. 1 (Spring 1983): 5-17.*

Documents James's and Dreiser's search for mystical euphoria. Boren discusses both men's interest in the relationship between the human mind, body, and soul; James's experimentation with mind-altering drugs; and Dreiser's dramas and poetry as expressions of a search for scientific proof to support their religious beliefs.

Doctorow, E. L. "The Novelist Who Was Born Old." *The New York Times Book Review* (4 December 1983): 9, 58, 60.

Discussion of Dreiser's *An Amateur Laborer*. Doctorow characterizes the work, which was written in 1903 but not published until 1983, as a frank documentation of Dreiser's poverty, mental breakdown, and recovery following the publication of *Sister Carrie,* and examines the ways in which Dreiser's life mirrors the lives of the characters in *Sister Carrie*.

Hakutani, Yoshinobu. *Young Dreiser: A Critical Study*. Rutherford, N. J.: Fairleigh Dickinson University, 228 p.

Examination of Dreiser's early life. The work focuses on Dreiser's youth, journalistic work, and his career as a magazine editor in an effort to demonstrate the significance of these experiences in the shaping of his earliest short stories and *Sister Carrie*.

Hughson, Lois. 'Dreiser's Cowperwood and the Dynamics of Naturalism." *Studies in the Novel* 16, No. 1 (Spring 1984): 52-71.

Discussion of *The Financier*. Hughson contends that Cowperwood, the protagonist of the novel, has mistakenly been described by other critics as a "superman," when in fact he embodies the natural fullness of humanity through his dreams of unattainable "dominance through the control of material resources."

Huddleston, Eugene L. "Herndon's *Lincoln* and Dreiser's *An American Tragedy*." *The Midwest Quarterly* XXII, No. 3 (Spring 1981): 242-54.*

Compares the formative years of Abraham Lincoln and the fictional Clyde Griffiths. Despite the sharp contrast in the outcome of each subject's life, Huddleston examines the similarities in the family backgrounds, physical traits, ambitions, and sexual problems of the two men.

Hussman, Lawrence E., Jr. *Dreiser and His Fiction: A Twentieth-Century Quest*. Philadelphia: University of Pennsylvania Press, 1983, 215 p.

Examines Dreiser's fiction chronologically to trace spiritual and intellectual growth.

Kazin, Alfred. "*An American Tragedy* and *The Sound and the Fury*." In his *An American Procession*, pp. 334-56. New York: Alfred A. Knopf, 1984.*

Examines the cultural, philosophical, historical, and familial influences on the works of Dreiser and William Faulkner.

Land, Mary G. "Three Max Gottliebs: Lewis's, Dreiser's, and Walker Percy's View of the Mechanist-Vitalist Controversy." *Studies in the Novel* 15, No. 4 (Winter 1983): 314-31.*

Examines the influence of scientist Jacques Loeb's theories of scientific mechanism on works by three novelists.

Riggio, Thomas P. "Dreiser in the Making." *Review* 3 (1981): 175-80.

Critical discussion of Yoshinobu Hakutani's *Young Dreiser: A Critical Study*.

Sinclair, Upton. "Steffens: The Man and the Muckraker." *Institute of Social Studies Bulletin* I, No. 6 (Summer 1952): 62, 71-2.*

Brief discussion of how communists used the names of the sympathetic famous, including Dreiser, as fronts.

Smith, Carl S.; McWilliams, John P., Jr.; and Bloomfield, Maxwell, eds. *Law and American Literature: A Collection of Essays*, pp. 71ff. New York: Alfred A. Knopf, 1983.

Examines the relationship between American law and literature in Dreiser's *An American Tragedy,* James Fenimore Cooper's *The Pioneers,* Herman Melville's *Billy Budd,* and Richard Wright's *Native Son*.

Stronks, James. In a review of *Theodore Dreiser: The American Diaries, 1902-1926*. *Modern Philology* 82, No. 1 (August 1984): 110-12.

Discounts the importance of Dreiser's diaries to a critical or biographical understanding of the author.

Watts, Emily Stipes. *The Businessman in American Literature,* pp. 4ff. Athens: University of Georgia Press, 1982.

Includes references throughout to Dresier's Cowperwood trilogy and *An American Tragedy*.

Wilson, Christopher P. "Notes: *Sister Carrie* Again." *American Literature* 53, No. 2 (May 1981): 287-90.

Examines the unresolved controversy about the publication of *Sister Carrie*.

Thomas Hardy

1840-1928

English novelist, poet, dramatist, short story writer, and essayist.

The following entry presents criticism of Hardy's novel *Tess of the d'Urbervilles.* For a complete discussion of Hardy's career, see *TCLC,* Volumes 4 and 10.

Tess of the d'Urbervilles is a powerful exploration of the conflict between Victorian social convention and the forces of human love and sexuality, as well as a portrait of the destruction of English agrarian culture by modern technology and commercial interests. In particular, the story of Tess Durbeyfield depicts the victimization and condemnation of women by a masculine social order, represented in the novel by Alec d'Urberville, who seduces and impregnates Tess, and by Angel Clare, who marries and rejects her when her ''fallen'' state is revealed to him. The novel's full title, *Tess of the d'Urbervilles: A Pure Woman Faithfully Presented,* suggests both the perspective Hardy maintained throughout the work and the focus of much of the critical discussion surrounding it, for many critics find Tess's behavior too morally ambiguous to fully agree with Hardy's insistence on her purity and innocence. Although initial critical opinion of the novel was polarized on this point, *Tess* has come to be recognized as one of Hardy's most significant novels and a landmark of English fiction.

Published in 1891, *Tess* followed such acclaimed novels as *Far from the Madding Crowd, The Return of the Native,* and *The Mayor of Casterbridge,* all of which were set in the Wessex countryside, a fictional region modeled after Dorsetshire, and all largely demonstrating Hardy's concept that life is determined by forces beyond the individual's command, particularly external pressures of society and the internal compulsions of character. Like the novels which preceded it, *Tess* is set in the Wessex region and reflects Hardy's deterministic vision. Nevertheless, *Tess* markedly differs from Hardy's other novels because of the exceptional degree to which he is emotionally involved with its main character. According to Geoffrey Wagner, *Tess* is ''Hardy's thirteenth novel in order of composition and possibly his first in emotional commitment.'' A descendant of an old Dorset family of landowners which, like the Durbeyfields, had come down in the world, Hardy retained a strong sense of pride in his heritage and concern for the fate of the land once held by his ancestors. Several biographical and critical studies contend that Tess was in part modeled after one of Hardy's distant cousins, but Irving Howe, among other critics, has noted that Hardy's attitude toward Tess is more paternalistically intimate, that he ''hovers and watches over [her] like a stricken father.'' J. Hillis Miller contends that ''Hardy's feelings about Tess were strong, perhaps stronger than for any other of his invented personages. He even obscurely identifies with her. The reader here encounters an example of that strange phenomenon in which a male author invents a female protagonist and then falls in love with her. . . .'' Tess is widely considered an incarnate representation of the beautiful pastoral world Hardy cherished and which was being destroyed by the Industrial Revolution; her character is thus endowed with multiple values of extreme personal and emotional significance to Hardy. More than a lovely, helpless victim descended from a downgraded ancient family, she is, according to Thomas Hinde, ''the daughter of doomed rural England which Hardy loved.''

Tess was scheduled to begin serialization in the *Graphic* in the autumn of 1890, but serialization was delayed for six months when the editors demanded that Hardy make extensive revisions in sections of the novel considered too scandalous for its readership. Hardy was infuriated over the required changes, believing that they destroyed the intent of the work. For example, the crucial seduction or rape scene which concludes the first portion of the novel was changed to a mock marriage in the serialized version. Hardy attempted to restore the altered sections for the first book edition in 1892, but many parts of the text were not reinstated until the 1912 edition. Although *Tess* was harshly attacked by some early reviewers, critical response was predominantly positive and sales were brisk. The most famous—and vehement—critical attack came from Andrew Lang, who charged that the novel was immoral, anti-Christian, and unduly pessimistic, or in his term, ''Tessimistic.'' Hardy addressed Lang's allegations in his preface to the fifth edition, sardonically referring to him as a ''great critic'' who had ''turned Christian for half-an-hour'' to justify his criticisms of the novel. The heated debate between Lang and Hardy affected London literary circles to such an extent that critics often defended the position of one or the other in their own discussions of the novel.

Most critics agree that the characterization of Tess is the novel's controlling element, not only because she is the most complex and well-drawn character, but also because it is through her experience that Hardy explores the dominant thematic issues of hypocrisy in Victorian morality and the destruction of agrarian traditions by modern technology and commerce. While Tess's abundant physical beauty is the catalyst for her tragedy, in that it attracts Alec d'Urberville, it also serves as an apt metaphor for the unspoiled loveliness of the Wessex region which is being ravaged by the designs of the nouveau riche, exemplified by d'Urberville. Hardy uses the consequences of Tess's violation, the birth of her illegitimate child, and her subsequent murder of d'Urberville as vehicles to attack Victorian social opinion, which condemned her as a fallen woman and criminal without considering the wrongs inflicted upon her. Angel Clare is the character most representative of this society which worships material progress but which fails to see the damage caused by harsh and unfeeling moral standards; while Clare superficially appears to be an intellectual and a free-thinker who frequently challenges the established social order, he is ultimately revealed—through his rejection and desertion of Tess after her confession—to embrace the hypocritical moral standards of his day. Richard Carpenter maintains that "Angel believes that there is some mystic purity native to the maid of the lower classes, necessary to her desirability" and that this is a particularly destructive notion because it substitutes false concepts about society for individual human values. William Watson considered the novel Hardy's "strongest protest against the unequal justice meted out to men and women for an identical crime," for while neither d'Urberville nor Clare are socially ostracized for their sexual transgressions, Tess is regarded by herself and society as tainted and unmarriageable, fit only to live as d'Urberville's mistress. Many early reviewers condemned Tess in much the same way as did the society in the novel, fervidly refuting Hardy's subtitle, *A Pure Woman Faithfully Presented.* Nevertheless, the majority of critics agree that Hardy's greatest accomplishment in *Tess* is that he forces the reader to recognize that there is, in Irving Howe's words, "a morality of being as well as of doing, an imperative which weakens the grip of judgment. . . . We do not care to judge Tess at all: we no longer feel ourselves qualified." Thus, novel and character ultimately transcend even the most vigorous attempts to define them in terms of social and moral codes.

Many critics have praised the poetic qualities of *Tess,* noting that in this novel Hardy composed some of his finest descriptive passages. The novel acquires much of its emotional impact from the manner in which Tess's interior state is reflected by the descriptions of the landscape, rather than by disclosure through dialogue or objective analysis. Michael Millgate contends that the novel's power resides in the "externalization of emotional states in terms of the particular colouring given to the accounts of the places Tess inhabits, the work she does, the people she encounters, the treatment she receives. . . . The emotional is evoked and recorded in terms of the sensory." Two scenes are frequently cited as masterpieces of this technique: one takes place at the Flintcomb Ash farm and depicts Tess and other laborers working near the blades of a threshing machine; the other occurs at Stonehenge during the novel's conclusion. In the first scene, the exploitation and peril of Tess and old Wessex are exquisitely represented by their proximity to the dangerous machinery, which Hardy portrays as possessing a nearly supernatural and malevolent power. In the second, Tess sleeps peacefully on the altar slab on which pagan sacrifices were made; upon waking she is taken into custody and hanged, thus fulfilling the novel's most prominent motif of Tess as a passive, sacrificial victim. Another important effect produced by Hardy's skillful blending of poetic and prosaic technique, mythic allusion, and the representation of interior states by exterior landscape, is the pervasive sense that the events in the novel occur in a universe governed by powers indifferent to humanity. The philosophical and theological implications fostered by such a perspective are pessimistic and irreligious: two dimensions of the work which Andrew Lang, and those critics who shared his opinion, found offensive. Nevertheless, it was precisely these qualities which distinguished *Tess* (and indeed all of Hardy's works) from most nineteenth-century English novels. Because of the inevitability of Tess's fate, her nobility of character, her redemptive suffering, and the mythopoeic richness of the novel, many critics agree with D. H. Lawrence's appraisal that it "contains the elements of the greatest tragedy," and a number have drawn extensive comparisons between *Tess* and classic Greek and Shakespearean tragedies. Richard Carpenter concludes that "Hardy wrote in *Tess of the d'Urbervilles* one of the finest novels of the nineteenth century because he lifted the story of a wronged peasant girl into the realm of tragedy through his use of . . . universal qualities; it is not only the tale of Tess Durbeyfield but also the story of wronged and suffering humanity."

Hardy wrote only one novel after *Tess, Jude the Obscure,* which was the subject of especially harsh attacks for its unidealized portrayal of human relationships and the institution of marriage. His reaction to this criticism was to cease writing novels and devote himself to poetry, which he had written intermittently throughout his career. Most critics agree that Hardy's sympathetic and artistic engagement as a novelist reached a pinnacle in the composition of *Tess of the d'Urbervilles* and that this work, in Irving Howe's estimation, "stands at the center of [his] achievement, if not as his greatest then certainly his most characteristic novel."

(See also *Contemporary Authors,* Vol. 104; *Dictionary of Literary Biography,* Vol. 18: *Victorian Novelists After 1885;* and Vol. 19: *British Poets, 1880-1914.*)

ANDREW LANG (essay date 1892)

[Lang was one of England's most powerful men of letters during the closing decades of the nineteenth century, and is remembered today as the editor of the "color fairy books," a twelve-volume series of fairy tales introduced with The Blue Fairy Book *(1889) and ending with* The Lilac Fairy Book *(1910). The stories in these volumes were drawn from various world cultures, the outgrowth of Lang's extensive research into early languages and literature in an attempt to find cultural affinities in the folktales, myths, and legends of otherwise disparate societies. Lang elaborated on these correlations in* Myth, Ritual, and Religion *(1887), a work which inspired a reevaluation and ultimate alteration of the course of anthropology. A romantic vision of the past imbued Lang's writings, coloring his work as a translator, poet, and revisionist historian. Among the chief proponents of Romanticism in a critical battle that pitted late nineteenth-century revivalist Romanticists against the defenders of Naturalism and Realism, Lang espoused his strong preference for romantic adventure novels throughout*

his literary criticism and found little to commend from among the works of Realists or Naturalists. In the following excerpt from his review of Tess, *Lang maintains that it is an important novel but notes aspects of the work that he finds weak or offensive.*]

Tess of the D'Urbervilles . . . demands more space than, in a crowd of hustling books, it is likely to receive. Indeed, the story is an excellent text for a sermon or subtly Spectatorial article on old times and new, on modern misery, on the presence among us of the spirit of Augustus Moddle. That we should be depressed is very natural, all things considered; and, indeed, I suppose we shall be no better till we have got the Revolution over, sunk to the nadir of humanity, and reached the middle barbarism again. . . . The conclusion of ***Tess*** is rather improbable in this age of halfpenny newspapers and appeals to the British public. The black flag would never have been hoisted, as in the final page. But one is afraid of revealing the story to people who have not yet read it. The persistent melancholy they perhaps like, or perhaps can make up their minds to endure. The rustic heroine, in the very opening of the book, explains to her little brothers that our planet is "a blighted star." Her mother possesses "the mind of a happy child," yet coolly sends her into conspicuous danger, remarking, "If he don't marry her afore, he will after." Poor Tess is set between the lusts of one Alec D'Urberville and the love, such as it was, of one Angel Claire. "Now Alec was a Bounder," to quote Mr. Besant; and Angel was a prig, whereas Tess was a human being, of human passions. Here are all the ingredients of the blackest misery, and the misery darkens till "The President of the Immortals has finished his sport with Tess." I cannot say how much this phrase jars on one. If there be a God, who can seriously think of Him as a malicious fiend? And if there be none, the expression is meaningless. . . . It is pity, one knows, that causes this bitterness in Mr. Hardy's mood. But Homer is not less pitiful of mortal fortunes and man "the most forlorn of all creatures that walk on earth," and Homer's faith cannot be called consolation: yet there is no bitterness in him; and probably bitterness is never a mark of the greatest art and the noblest thought.

There are moral passages of great beauty in ***Tess:*** for example, in that scene where the bemused villagers stagger home through the moonlight, which casts halos round the shadows of their heads no less than if they had been happy shepherds on the sides of Latmos. There are exquisite studies of the few remaining idyllic passages in rural life, like that walking of the white-clad women in May, which Mr. Hardy compares to the Cerealia. . . . There are touches highly picturesque and telling, as when the red spot on the ceiling, no bigger than a postage stamp, widens into a broad splash of blood. The style is pellucid, as a rule, but there are exceptions. "Human mutuality" seems, to myself, an ill phrase. "There, behind the blue narcotic haze, sat 'the tragic mischief' of her drama, he who was to be the blood-red ray in the spectrum of her young life." Here is an odd mixture of science and literature. A face is, or rather is not, "furrowed with incarnated memories representing in hieroglyphic the centuries of her family's and England's history." . . . However, tastes differ so much that the blemishes, as they appear to one reader, of Mr. Hardy's works may seem beauty-spots in the eyes of another reader. He does but give us of his best, and if his best be too good for us, or good in the wrong way, if, in short, we are not *en rapport* with him, why, there are plenty of other novelists, alive and dead, and the fault may be on our side, not on his. (pp. 247-49)

Andrew Lang, in a review of "Tess of the D'Urbervilles," in The New Review, *Vol. VI, No. 33, February, 1892, pp. 247-49.*

THOMAS HARDY (letter date 1892)

[*In the following excerpt from a letter to Edward Clodd, Hardy responds to Andrew Lang's criticism of* Tess.]

Lang's article on ***Tess*** in the *New Review* is, of course, Langy. If Andrew, with his knowledge & opportunities, had a heart instead of a hollow place where his heart ought to be, he would by this time have been among the immortals of letters instead of in the sorry position of gnawing his quill over my poor production. Or, if accident forced him to this business, he would have felt the smallness of stooping to pick out the trivial accidents of a first [edition] of a book of 140,000 words, and have put his finger on the real and serious faults of the story, which not one of these gentry has had the wit to find out.

The only clear objection he makes to the novel is that it is tragedy; and every word he says against it in this respect tells with equal force against all the Greek tragic dramatists, Shakespeare, and the Elizabethans. While his Christian (?) objection (I suppose it is meant to be Christian) to the words "President of the Immortals" &c., is evidently factitious—for I distinctly state that the words are paraphrased from Æschylus.

You will be glad to know that there is no check to the sale of the book. Mudie keeps ordering more and more—and others *pari passu*.

Thomas Hardy, in a letter to Edward Clodd on February 4, 1892, in his The Collected Letters of Thomas Hardy: 1840-1892, Vol. 1, *edited by Richard Little Purdy and Michael Millgate, Oxford at the Clarendon Press, Oxford, 1978, p. 257.*

WILLIAM WATSON (essay date 1892)

[*Watson was an English poet and critic who maintained that a writer should be an integral part of the social and intellectual life of an era and contribute to decisions of public policy. One of his primary aims as a poet was to elucidate current affairs; for that reason, he wrote much occasional poetry. He was alien to the aesthetic temper of the 1890s and in fact held more imaginative realms of poetry to be the province of the second-rate. Watson first gained recognition for his poem* "Wordsworth's Grave" *(1890). Selected to compose the official elegy for Tennyson,* "Lacrimae Musarum" *(1892), he appeared to be Tennyson's successor to the position of poet laureate. However, Watson's strong anti-imperialist views, expressed in particular in* The Purple East *(1889) and his numerous denunciations of the Boer War, were probably responsible for his being passed over for that position. Although knighted in 1917, Watson died an impoverished and embittered man. In the following excerpt, originally published in* The Academy *in 1892, Watson appraises* Tess *as a great work, but also points out some minor flaws in the novel which mar its perfection.*]

One may . . . feel the greatness of [***Tess***] profoundly, and yet be conscious of certain alloying qualities; but let it be said at once, such qualities are of the surface only. None the less, with respect to the over-academic phraseology which here and there crops up in this book, I myself have but one feeling—a wish that it were absent. This terminology of the schools is misplaced; I can feel nothing but regret for these nodosities upon the golden thread of an otherwise fine diction. In a certain sense they disturb a reader all the more for the very reason that they are *not*—like Mr Meredith's singularities of speech, for example—ingrained in the very constitution of the style and, obviously, native to the author, nor are they so frequent as to become a habit, a characteristic mannerism which one might get used to; rather they are exceptional and excrescent—foreign to the total character of Mr Hardy's English—and serve no purpose but to impair the homogeneity of his utterance. The perfect style for a novelist is surely one which never calls attention to its own existence, and there was needed only the omission or modification of a score or two of sentences in these volumes to have assimilated the style of ***Tess*** to such an ideal. Nothing but gain could have resulted from the elimination of such phrases as 'his former pulsating flexuous domesticity.' (pp. 71-2)

Fortunately, however, ***Tess*** is a work so great that it could almost afford to have even proportionately great faults; and the faults upon which I have dwelt—perhaps unduly—are casual and small. Powerful and strange in design, splendid and terrible in execution, this story brands itself upon the mind as with the touch of incandescent iron. To speak of its gloom as absolutely unrelieved is scarcely correct. Dairyman Crick provides some genuine mirth, though not in too abundant measure; and 'Sir John,' with his 'skellingtons,' is a figure at once humorous and pathetic. But with these exceptions, the atmosphere from first to last is, indeed, tenebrous; and after the initial stroke of doom, Tess appears to us like Thea, in Keats's poem:

> There was a listening fear in her regard,
> As if calamity had but begun:
> As if the vanward clouds of evil days
> Had spent their malice, and the sullen rear
> Was with its stored thunder labouring up.

The great theme of the book is the incessant penalty paid by the innocent for the wicked, the unsuspicious for the crafty, the child for its fathers; and again and again this spectacle, in its wide diffusion, provokes the novelist to a scarcely suppressed declaration of rebellion against a supramundane ordinance that can decree, or permit, the triumph of such wrong. The book may almost be said to resolve itself into a direct arraignment of the morality of this system of vicarious pain—a morality which, as he bitterly expresses it, 'may be good enough for divinities,' but is 'scorned by average human nature.' . . . Truly a stupendous argument; and in virtue of the almost intolerable power with which this argument is wrought out, ***Tess*** must take its place among the great tragedies, to have read which is to have permanently enlarged the boundaries of one's intellectual and emotional experience.

Perhaps the most subtly drawn, as it is in some ways the most perplexing and difficult character, is that of Angel Clare, with his half-ethereal passion for Tess—'an emotion which could jealously guard the loved one against his very self.' But one of the problems of the book, for the reader, is involved in the question how far Mr Hardy's own moral sympathies go with Clare in the supreme crisis of his and Tess's fate. Her seducer, the spurious D'Urberville, is entirely detestable, but it often happens that one's fiercest indignation demands a nobler object than such a sorry animal as that; and there are probably many readers who, after Tess's marriage with Clare, her spontaneous disclosure to him of her soiled though guiltless past, and his consequent alienation and cruelty, will be conscious of a worse anger against this intellectual, virtuous, and unfortunate man than they could spare for the heartless and worthless libertine who had wrecked these two lives. It is at this very point, however, that the masterliness of the conception, and its imaginative validity, are most conclusively manifest, for it is here that we perceive Clare's nature to be consistently inconsistent throughout. As his delineator himself says of him: 'With all his attempted independence of judgment, this advanced man was yet the slave to custom and conventionality when surprised back into his early teachings.' He had carefully schooled himself into a democratic aversion from everything connected with the pride of aristocratic lineage; but when he is suddenly made aware that Tess is the daughter of five centuries of knightly D'Urbervilles, he unfeignedly exults in her splendid ancestry. He had become a rationalist in morals no less than an agnostic in religion; yet no sooner does this emancipated man learn from his wife's own most loving lips the story of her sinless fall, than his affection appears to wither at the roots. . . . The reader pities Clare profoundly, yet cannot but feel a certain contempt for the shallowness of his casuistry, and a keen resentment of his harsh judgment upon the helpless woman—all the more so since it is her own meek and uncomplaining submission that aids him in his cruel punishment of her. 'Her mood of long-suffering made his way easy for him, and she herself was his best advocate.' Considering the proud ancestry whose blood was in her veins, and the high spirit and even fierce temper she exhibits on occasion, one almost wonders at her absolute passivity under such treatment as he subjects her to; but the explanation obviously lies in her own unquestioning conviction of the justice of his procedure. One of Mr Hardy's especially poetic traits is his manner of sometimes using external Nature not simply as a background or a setting, but as a sort of superior spectator and chorus, that makes strangely unconcerned comments from the vantage-ground of a sublime aloofness upon the ludicrous tragedy of the human lot; and, in the scene of Tess's confession, a singularly imaginative effect is produced by kindred means, where Mr Hardy makes the very furniture and appurtenances of the room undergo a subtle change of aspect and expression as the bride unfolds her past, and brings Present and Future ruining about her head:

> Tess's voice throughout had hardly risen higher than its opening tone; there had been no exculpatory phrase of any kind, and she had not wept. But the complexion even of external things seemed to suffer transmutation as her announcement progressed. The fire in the grate looked impish—demoniacally funny, as if it did not care in the least about her strait. The fender grinned idly, as if it too did not care. The light from the water-bottle was merely engaged in a chromatic problem. All material objects around announced irresponsibility with terrible iteration. And yet nothing had changed since the moments when he had been kissing her; or rather, nothing in the substance of things: but the essence of things had changed.

(pp. 73-9)

After this, D'Urberville's re-intrusion upon her life, and his resumed mastery of it, are matters which, in their curious air of predestination, affect us somewhat in the manner of spectral interferences with human fates; and this impression is incidentally aided by the use made, very sparingly—with that fine, suggestive parsimony which reveals the artist's hand—of the one preternatural detail, the legend of the D'Urberville coach and four. Thenceforward, as the tragedy climbs towards its last summit of desolation and doom, criticism in the ordinary sense must lie low, in the shadow of so great and terrible a conception.

There is one thing which not the dullest reader can fail to recognise—the persistency with which there alternately smoulders and flames through the book Mr Hardy's passionate protest against the unequal justice meted by society to the man and woman associated in an identical breach of the moral law. In his wrath, Mr Hardy seems at times almost to forget that society is scarcely more unjust than nature. He himself proposes no remedy, suggests no escape—his business not being to deal in nostrums of social therapeutics. He is content to make his readers pause, and consider, and pity; and very likely he despairs of any satisfactory solution of the problem which he presents with such disturbing power, and clothes with a vesture of such breathing and throbbing life. (pp. 79-80)

William Watson, "Mr. Hardy's 'Tess of the D'Urbervilles'," in his Excursions in Criticism: Being Some Prose Recreations of a Rhymer, *Macmillan & Co., 1893, pp. 70-80.*

GEORGE MEREDITH (letter date 1892)

[*Meredith was a major English novelist whose career developed in conjunction with an era of great change in English literature during the second half of the nineteenth century. While his early novels largely conformed to Victorian literary conventions, his later novels demonstrated a concern with character psychology, modern social problems, and the development of the novel form that has led to his being considered an important precursor of English Modernist novels. In particular, Meredith is noted as one of the earliest English psychological novelists and as an important experimenter with narrative told from a variety of shifting, unreliable perspectives, reflecting a modern perception of the uncertain nature of both personal motivation and of social or historical events. In the following excerpt from a letter to Frederick Greenwood, Meredith praises the overall quality of* Tess *but also expresses criticism of the latter part of the novel.*]

[***Tess***] is open to criticism, but excellent and very interesting. All of the Dairy Farm held me fast. But from the moment of the meeting again of Tess and Alec, I grew cold, and should say that there is a depression of power, up to the end, save for the short scene on the plain of Stonehenge. If the author's minute method had been sustained, we should have had a finer book. It is marred by the sudden hurry to round the story. And Tess, out of the arms of Alec, into (I suppose) those of the lily necked Clare, and on to the Black Flag waving over her poor body, is a smudge in vapour—she at one time so real to me. (pp. 1068-69)

George Meredith, in a letter to Frederick Greenwood on February 23, 1892, in his The Letters of George Meredith, Vol. II, *edited by C. L. Cline, Oxford at the Clarendon Press, Oxford, 1970, pp. 1068-69.*

[MARGARET OLIPHANT] (essay date 1892)

[*Oliphant was a popular late-Victorian Scottish novelist whose works most often chronicled the lives of independent, resourceful, and unmarried women. Her criticism is noted for its sympathy with the views of the average reader. In the following excerpt Oliphant notes flaws in Hardy's portrayal of Tess and questions his interpretation of fate.*]

Tess of the D'Urbervilles is the history, Mr Hardy tells us, *par excellence*, of a pure woman, which is his flag or trumpet, so to speak, of defiance upon certain matters, to the ordinary world. It is time enough, however, to come to that after we have done justice to the real pictures which an artist cannot help giving, with qualities of life and truth which are independent of all didactic intentions. Tess is a country girl of an extraordinary elevated and noble kind. Everybody knows what Mr Hardy's peasants in Wessex are. They are a quaint people, given to somewhat high-flown language, and confused and complicated reasoning, like, it was at first supposed by hardy guessing, to George Eliot's peasants, yet not really so, except in being more dignified, more grandiose in speech than the usual article, as it comes across the ordinary senses of more common people. They are sometimes a little grotesque, but their sentiments are usually fine. John Durbeyfield, the father of Tess, is an example of this somewhat artificial personage. If he is not good Dorsetshire, he is at least good Hardy, which answers just as well; and the book begins by a very foolish communication made to this rural "higgler" by an old antiquarian parson of the fact that he is the lineal representative of the old race of the D'Urbervilles, whose marble tombs are to be seen in a great church near. The unfortunate weakly and silly straggler by the country roads takes the information to heart, and rears a structure of foolish hopes upon it which lead to nothing but dismay and trouble. . . . [All] but the queenly Tess, who is the flower of it, and who is throughout ashamed of the whole business, is of a very heavy comic kind; but the family, always granted the Hardy element in it, is a vigorous and real picture. The father, too fond of beer; the mother singing at her washing-tub, rocking the cradle with her foot, strong yet slatternly, kind yet mercenary,—quite ready to sell the beautiful daughter for the benefit of the family, and think no harm, yet loving and serving them all in her rude way. . . . It is a pardonable extravagance to make of Tess a kind of princess in this *milieu*, which is a mistake that even the most experienced make from time to time, since there is scarcely a vicaress or rectoress who has not some such favourite in the parish—some girl with all the instincts of a lady, as the kind patroness will tell you. We doubt much, however, whether having passed the Sixth Standard improves the phraseology in the manner believed by Mr Hardy; but this is of little importance. Tess is, we are ready to allow, the exceptional creature whom we have all seen, beautiful in the bloom of first youth, capable of all things, as the imaginative spectator feels, and whom it is dreadful to think of as falling eventually into the cheerful comely slattern, with a troop of children, which her mother is. . . . Tess is plunged at once into the abyss of evil. We need not follow a story which by this time everybody has read, through all its details. It is amusing, however, to find that such a democrat as Mr Hardy, finding nothing worth his while in any class above that of the actual sons of the soil, should be so indignant at the trumpery person who has assumed the name of D'Urberville, having no sort of right to it. What could it matter? We are aware that the name of Norfolk Howard has been assumed in similar circumstances, which has made the world laugh, but had no more serious result. Mr Hardy, however, takes it very gravely, though it is a godsend to him, opening the door for all that follows. The idea of sending Tess to seek her fortune by claiming kindred with the wealthy family which calls itself D'Urberville throws her at once into the hands of the young sensualist and villain of fiction, the rural Lothario with whom we are so well acquainted. Tess is spotless as a lily—that may be granted: but a girl brought up in the extraordinary freedom and free-speaking of rural life would scarcely be entirely ignorant of evil; and indeed, as a matter of fact, she has the instinct to discourage and escape as much as possible from the advances of the seducer and rustic profligate Alec D'Urberville, whose character is well known.

That she should have been taken advantage of, and dragged into degradation by mingled force and kindness, is possible; but not that, pure-minded and spotless, yet already alarmed and set on her guard as she had been, she should have trusted herself at midnight with the unscrupulous young master who was pursuing her, and whose habits she was fully informed of, in order to escape from the drunken and riotous companions who, odious as they were, were still a protection to her. The girl who escapes from her fellow-servants in their jollity by jumping up on horseback (and how about the horse? does that fine animal nowadays lend itself to such means of seduction?) behind a master of such a character, and being carried off by him in the middle of the night, naturally leaves her reputation behind her. . . . [Poor] Tess yields not to any impure suggestion, which is the last thing to be thought of in such a case, but to those mingled motives of vanity and excitement which have so large a share in this kind of moral downfall. The sense of triumph over others left behind, and intoxicating superiority for the moment to all rivals, has far more to do, we believe, with feminine offences of this description than any tendency towards vice. No one could doubt what was to follow: the girl, perhaps, alone might have hoped in some incomprehensible way that she should yet escape. And indeed Mr Hardy, at the last moment, generously gives her an opportunity of running away, of which the real Tess certainly would have availed herself; but then where would the story have been, and all the defiant pleas of the author for that virtue which is proved in his estimation by the breach rather than the observance?

If Mr Hardy had not labelled this poor girl as a specimen of exceptional and absolute purity, nothing could have been more piteous than her story. . . . [Poor] little Tess, at sixteen going back to her house with her young eyes so fatally opened, has nothing but our pity, especially when, after a vague interval, she reappears in the harvest-field, among the other women at their work, with a baby dependent on her. The situation is one which is as old as poetry. Mr Hardy seems to have a notion that he has invented it—but unfortunately it is not so. It has been treated in all the methods, and romance has invariably leant to the charitable side. If it is the woman who pays, at least it is the woman, the inevitable sufferer, who has all the sympathy. And the unfortunate child thus brought into the world is also a most powerful agent in fiction. Generally it has been supposed by the storyteller to be a means of redemption for the fallen woman. One remembers how Mrs Browning treats it in *Aurora Leigh,* elevating and developing the being of the girl Marion, who is a still greater martyr than Tess, by the revelation of maternity and the glory of the new life. But the philosophy of enlightenment and the *fin de siècle* has nothing to do with such imaginations. Naturally a new creed must treat such a situation in a new way, especially when the principles of that creed are indignation . . . and wrath, and have no sympathy with the everlasting reconstruction which another philosophy perceives to be going on for ever in the moral as well as in the material world. Mr Hardy scornfully admits the possibility that the downfall of poor Tess may have been "a retribution,"—it being "a morality good enough for divinities," though "scorned by average human nature," to visit the sins of the fathers upon the children. "Doubtless some of Tess D'Urberville's mailed ancestors, rollicking home from a fray, had dealt the same wrong even more ruthlessly upon peasant girls of their time:" but he does not allow any return in the processes of nature. This silly cant is very unworthy of any man acquainted with the secrets of the heart, and versed were it ever so little in those great problems of humanity which it is the occupation of the poet to fathom; but it is "the height of the fashion," and we know how in the lower walks of life fashion is exaggerated, so that perhaps Mr Hardy, as an exponent of peasant life, feels himself justified in going a little further than the commonest of sense permits. His unfortunate young mother is compelled to look upon her poor baby in a different and original way from all previous sufferers of her kind. She holds it on her lap in the reaping-field, "and looking into the far distance, dandled it with a gloomy indifference that was almost dislike: then all of a sudden she fell to violently kissing it some dozens of times, as if she would never leave off, the child crying at the vehemence of an onset which strangely combined passionateness with contempt."

The moralisings which follow when the unfortunate baby dies are equally remarkable. Tess is in despair, not for the loss of her child but chiefly about its salvation. . . . "She thought of the child consigned to the nethermost corner of hell, as its double doom for lack of baptism and lack of legitimacy; saw the *arch-fiend tossing it with his three-pronged fork* like the one they used for heating the oven on baking days; to which picture she added many other quaint and curious details of torment taught the young in this Christian country." Now, so far as we are aware, except, perhaps, in some quaint piece of medieval divinity still less likely to have fallen under Tess's notice than ours, the arch-fiend with the three-pronged toasting-fork (it is well to be particular), with which she was so familiar as to think that it was like the one used for heating the oven, occurs in certain grim passages of the *Inferno,* but in no more popular reading. We have admitted that we have less faith in the Sixth Standard than Mr Hardy, but it seems probable that we spoke in ignorance. Has it come to that, that Dante is taught and familiarly studied in our village schools? No wonder in that case that to pass the Sixth Standard should be a high test of a liberal education. But we cannot help fearing that Mr Hardy has here incautiously muddled up the views of the poet with those of the Catechism. (pp. 465-69)

The next division of the story begins with something very different from this dreary stuff. It is the picture of the great dairy to which Tess, free of all encumbrances, her baby dead and oblivion closing over all her trouble, goes as "a skilful milkmaid," "between two and three years after her return from Trantridge." She must now have been, therefore, between eighteen and nineteen, and a most accomplished woman; for not only did she know *au fond* the prophecies of Ezekiel and the *Inferno* of Dante, but she had been at sixteen an expert poultry-woman, and now was an exceptional milkmaid, so that her gifts in every way were great. In addition to which she was beautiful—not ruddy and buxom as a country girl, but with the beauty of ancient ancestry and noble blood. The establishment into which she is received is idyllic; and nothing can be more vivid, living, and actual than the great farm, with its innumerable cows, its rustic patriarch at the head, the pretty maids all a-row, the fringe of rougher men. There is, however, a serpent in this Eden,—though it is no vicious person, no deceiver or rustic profligate like poor Tess's previous master, but a gentleman of the last and most painful degree of refinement, studying farming in preparation for emigrating, an Agnostic, a musician, a philosopher, and every other superfine thing that can be conceived. "Mr Angel Clare—he that is learning milking, and that plays the harp"—is how one of the ordinary milkmaids describes him. We do not know whether it is usual for an intending farmer to learn milking, but we are sure that it is not at all usual for a young man of the nineteenth century to carry a harp about with him, which is an inconvenient piece of luggage. . . . However, it is perhaps not less unlikely that a parson's son in Wessex should carry a harp about with him, than that he should be called Angel Clare. He is truly worthy of the name, being the most curious thing in the shape of a man whom we think we have ever met with—at least out of a young lady's novel. . . . It is needless to say that poor Tess finds her doom in the superfine pupil, and that they soon begin to fall in love with each other. (pp. 469-70)

> Being so often—possibly not always by chance—the first two persons to get up at the dairy-house, they seemed to themselves the first persons up of all the world. In these early days of her residence here Tess did not skim going out of doors at once after rising, where he was generally awaiting her. The spectral half-compounded aqueous light which pervaded the open mead impressed them with a sense of isolation, as if they were Adam and Eve. At this dim inceptive stage of the day, Tess seemed to Clare to exhibit a dignified largeness both of disposition and physique, and almost regnant power, possibly because he knew that at that preternatural time hardly any woman, so well endowed in person as she, was likely to be walking in the open air within the boundaries of his horizon—very few in all England. The mixed singular luminous gloom in which they walked along together to the spot where the cows lay, often made him think of the Resurrection hour. He little thought that the Magdalene might be at his side. While all the landscape was in shade, his companion's face, which was the focus of his eyes, rising above the mist stratum, seemed to have a sort of phosphorescence upon it. She looked ghostly, as if she were merely a soul at large. In reality her face, without appearing to do so, had caught the cold gleam of day from the northwest; his own face, though he did not think of it, wore the same aspect to her.
>
> (p. 471)

This wonderful piece of landscape speaks for itself. That the man who can do it should waste his gifts in echoing the mean prose of fashionable philosophy fills one's soul with impatience. However, we have said enough on this subject.

Tess falls in love with Angel Clare; and he, so far as such a vision can, loves her, and asks her to marry him. We may say, however, that all the milkmaids are, as one woman, in love with the gentleman-pupil, and the spectacle of these daughters of the fields, in their fulness of flesh and blood, weeping upon each other's bosoms without jealousy, but with a passion which makes one, alas! take to drinking, and another try to drown herself, when the die is cast, is exceedingly Hardyish, and just a very little grotesque, though also touching. It is idyllic—with a twist—and pretty, yet apt at moments to be laughable. Tess is brought to a sudden pause and horror by her lover's proposal, and declares it to be impossible; but gradually is brought round, though always with the certainty that she must tell him what her antecedents have been. One knows how difficult even in real life it is to make a confession much less serious than this—and in fiction it is inevitable that all the difficulties should be increased. So that the fated days run on, and Tess does not tell. (pp. 471-72)

[The] terrible intelligence is only conveyed to Clare on the evening of the wedding-day, after he himself has made a confession of a similar description to Tess, which of course she forgives at once, and, emboldened, proceeds to tell him. Then, equally of course, the insufferable being whom Mr Hardy has set up as a man and an Agnostic proves what stuff he is made of, and flings his bride from him. He becomes immediately a compound of ice and iron. Pity is not in him, nor understanding, nor common-sense, nor, least of all, love. . . . He deserts the unhappy girl without a struggle—leaving her from that moment to herself. "Tess," he said as gently and as civilly as he could speak, "I cannot stay in the room with you." Now, Mr Hardy is strong on the injustice of the fact that "the woman pays," but he never makes this injustice apparent to his hero. Nor does he apparently disapprove of Clare's action, or of the remorseless abandonment of his heroine, which of course is required by the exigencies of the story.

We need not follow poor Tess in her abandonment. Clare sets off for Brazil, as the farthest point possible, we suppose, and every kind of misfortune happens to lure her on to the fatal conclusion. Her father dies, and the burden of her mother's family falls upon her. She drops out of the prosperous milkmaid condition into the roughest work of the fields, giving room for more and yet more telling descriptions of rural operations. Then Alec D'Urberville comes once more across her path, the destroyer of her youth. He is a revivalist preacher when she sees him next, having been, with grotesque particularity, brought to repentance of his sins by the ministrations of Angel Clare's Low Church father; but Tess changes all that in a moment, partly by the mere sight of her, and partly by her repetition of Mr Angel's arguments against revelation, which are so potent (Mr Hardy wisely does not state them, but only tells us the effect, historically) that D'Urberville flings his religion to the winds, and begins a systematic pursuit of his former victim. He is ready to marry her, but that, of course, is impossible: he shows himself, however, the Providence of her family, and the matter ends as—everything we have been made to understand concerning Tess forbids us to believe that it could do. When Clare finally becomes ashamed of himself and returns home, he hunts down his wife in seaside lodgings and fine clothes with D'Urberville. She has a wild interview with him in her beautiful dressing-gown; then rushes up-stairs to the room in which she has left her lover, stabs him in his bed with the carving-knife, which has been put ready to cut the cold ham for breakfast, laid out in their sitting-room, and, rushing after her husband, joins him—for a brief honeymoon of passion and mad love and enjoyment. Clare, who behaved so brutally to her when he heard of the distant sin of her youth, for which she was so little to blame, receives her out of the arms of the other without a moment's hesitation; and Tess, who, according to any natural interpretation, and of all we know of her, must have died of shame rather than meet the eyes of her husband clothed in the embroideries of the nightgown, which Mr Hardy does not spare us—forgets every tradition of natural purity, and passes from one to another as if, which indeed she says, the murder had made all right.

We have not a word to say against the force and passion of this story. It is far finer in our opinion than anything Mr Hardy has ever done before. The character of Tess up to her last downfall, with the curious exceptions we have pointed out, is consistent enough, and we do not object to the defiant blazon of a Pure Woman, notwithstanding the early stain. But a Pure Woman is not betrayed into fine living and fine clothes as the mistress of her seducer by any stress of poverty or misery; and Tess was a skilled labourer, for whom it is very rare that nothing can be found to do. Here the elaborate and indignant plea for Vice, that it is really Virtue, breaks down altogether. We do not for a moment believe that Tess would have done it. Her creator has forced the *rôle* upon her, as he thinks (or says) that the God whom he does not believe in, does—which ought to make him a little more humble, since he cannot, it appears, do better himself. But whatever Mr Hardy says, we repeat that we do not believe him. . . . She would not have stabbed Mr Alec D'Urberville, her potential husband, with the carving-knife intended for the cold ham (which, besides, awakens all sorts of questions, as—why did Alec D'Urberville, a strong young man, allow himself to be stabbed? and how did it happen that the lodging-house carving-knife, not usually a very sharp instrument, was capable of such a blow?), but have turned him head and shoulders out of the poorest cottage in which he had insulted her with such a proposition. It is no use making men and women for us, and then forcing them to do the last thing possible to their nature. If Tess did this, then Tess, after all her developments, was at twenty a much inferior creature to the unawakened Tess at sixteen who would not live upon the wages of iniquity; and thus two volumes of analysis and experience are lost, and the end is worse than the beginning—which, after watching Tess through these two volumes, and following the progress of her thoughts much more articulately than she could have done herself, we absolutely decline to believe. Whoever that person was who went straight from the endearments of Alec D'Urberville to those of the Clare Angel or the Angel Clare, whatever the image is called, Mr Hardy must excuse us for saying pointedly and firmly that she was not Tess; neither was she a Pure Woman. This is the portion of the book which was served up to keen appetites in the Reviews, and we rejoice to think that it was so. Let the cultivated reader keep the nastiness for which it seems he longs. We are delighted to find ourselves on the side of the honest lover of a story who requires no strong stimulation of criminality thrown in against all the possibilities of natural life.

Mr Hardy's indignant anti-religion becomes occasionally very droll, if not amusing. Against whom is he so angry? Against "the divinities," who are so immoral—who punish the vices of the fathers on the children? Against God?—who does not ask us whether we wish to be created; who gives us but one chance, &c. But then, if there is no God? Why, in that case, should Mr Hardy be angry? We know one man of fine mind whom we have always described as being angry with God for not existing. Is this perhaps Mr Hardy's case? But then he ought not to put the blame of the evils which do exist upon this imaginary Being who does not. (pp. 473-74)

[Margaret Oliphant], in a review of "Tess of the D'Urbervilles," in Blackwood's Edinburgh Magazine, *Vol. CLI, No. DCCCCXVII, March, 1892, pp. 464-74.*

FRANCIS ADAMS (essay date 1892)

[Adams was a Scottish poet, novelist, and short story writer. In the following excerpt from a review of Tess, *he discusses the strengths and weaknesses of the characters of the novel.]*

The central conception of [***Tess of the D'Urbervilles***], the main feature, seems right enough, but it has not been seized strongly, and the story, like all Mr. Hardy's stories, alternately hurries or flags. Parts are good enough as renderings of human and natural life to make one more than astonished at the not unfrequent lapses into the cheapest conventional style of the average popular novelist. What can one make of a piece of writing like this, where the most flagrant puppets for the time being usurp the parts of what he has taught us to feel as something like human characters?

(The Durbeyfield family is discussing a recent visit of Mr. D'Urberville.)

> Her mother hastened to explain, smiles breaking from every inch of her person. . . .
>
> "Mr. D'Urberville says you must be a good girl, if you are at all as you appear; he knows you must be worth your weight in gold. He is very much interested in'ee—truth to tell. . . ."
>
> "It is very good of him to think that," she murmured; "and if I was quite sure how it would be living there, I would go in a moment."
>
> "He is a mighty handsome man!"
>
> "I don't think so," said Tess coldly.
>
> "Well, there's your chance, whether or no; and I'm sure he wears a beautiful diamond ring."
>
> "Yes," said little Abraham brightly, from the window-bench; "and I seed it! And it did twinkle when he put his hand up to his mistarshers. Mother, why did our noble relation keep on putting his hand up to his mistarshers?"
>
> "Hark at that child!" cried Mrs. Durbeyfield, with parenthetic admiration.
>
> "Perhaps to show his diamond ring," murmured Sir John dreamily, from his chair.

And so on, in the same vile and detestable fashion. No one knows better than Mr. Hardy that English agriculturalists do not talk like this, because he continuously shows them talking in quite another way. But his dramatic aberrations lead him into blunders more serious still. To say nothing of the improbability of four milkmaids, all sleeping in one room, and all hopelessly in love with one blameless prig of an amateur gentleman farmer, what a shocking want of the sense of both humour and variety does he show in creating such a situation! It is scarcely to be wondered at that these imaginary dairymaids soon begin to talk as never dairy-maids talked on this earth. One of them has caught another kissing the shade of the prig's mouth against the wall, and as the three were standing that night "in a group, in their night-gowns, bare-footed at the window," amorously regarding the beloved one below, Miss Retty Priddle candidly states the fact.

> A rosy spot came into the middle of Izz Huett's cheek.
>
> "Well, there's no harm in it," she declared, with attempted coolness. "And if I be in love with him, so is Retty too; and so be you, Marian, come to that."
>
> Marian's full face could not blush past its chronic pinkness.
>
> "I?" she said; "what a tale! Ah, there he is again! Dear eyes—dear face—dear Mr. Clare!"
>
> "There—you've owned it!"
>
> "So have you—so have we all," said Marian. . . . "I would just marry him to-morrow."
>
> "So would I—and more," murmured Izz Huett.
>
> "And I too," whispered the more timid Retty.

"At this," observes Mr. Hardy ingenuously, "the listener [Miss Tess Durbeyfield] grew warm," and although she is also in her night-gown, though not at the window, it is no wonder. (pp. 19-20)

Nothing more ridiculous than this has been done by any writer of anything approaching ability in our time, and it is as false in characterization as it is absurd in conception. Even Mr. Hall Caine rarely sinks lower. The same weakness drives Mr. Hardy to mar the evanescent reality of Tess herself. He will make her talk sometimes as the author of ***Far from the Madding Crowd*** is often wont to write. Her lover presses upon her a course of study in history; but she refuses.

> "Because what's the use of learning that I am one of a long row only—finding out that there is set down in some old book somebody just like me, and to know that I shall only act her part; making me sad, that's all. The best is not to remember that your nature and your past doings have been just like thousands and thousands, and that your coming life and doings'll be like thousands and thousands. . . . I shouldn't mind learning why the sun shines on the just and the unjust alike, but that is what books will not tell me."

Tess, it is true, as Mr. Hardy continually remarks, had passed her Sixth Standard; but even agricultural girls of the Sixth Standard are scarcely yet credible with a "criticism of life" of this calibre. It is terrible to see a storyteller so unaware of what constitutes the one possible charm of his chief figure. . . . And it is not that Mr. Hardy is not at times able to render character. D'Urberville, for instance, in the first two parts is recognizably drawn from the life; but that does not prevent a shadowy masquerade of this vicious brute appearing for a short period later on as a ranting preacher. It is not that vicious brutes may not become ranting preachers. They may, and do; but that this particular vicious brute of Mr. Hardy's, thanks to the want of energy in his realization, does nothing of the kind.

One artistic gift Mr. Hardy has which rarely seems to desert him, and that is what Henri Beyle calls so aptly *l'originalité de lieu*. His people are at one with his places, a single harmonious growth of spiritual and natural circumstance, and this, the true artistic charity, covers, or helps to cover, a multitude of sins. The best examples of it reach high, indeed as high as anything of the kind now done among us. What else but this renders credible and even poignantly real the final wanderings of the two lovers world-weary and doomed. [The murder, of course, is absurd.] The love-nest in the empty furnished home of strangers, an incident superficially so improbable, is only less actual than the weird journey to Stonehenge, and Tess's sacrificial sleep on the altar-stone. After all, the book has in it the sob of the earth's suffering, "the sense of tears in mortal things," the vain struggle of the human heart against unjust fatality; and of how many books, not to say of how many novels, that appear in this England in a generation can one say so much?—in this England where the novel has become the helpless prey of the Philistine and Philistiness—where the only variety possible on the banalities of an ignorant and abject conventionality seems to be fantastic revels in the English tongue, and the literary woe and abomination alluded to by more than one of the prophets.

Yet one cannot for a moment hesitate in one's recognition of the fact that Mr. Hardy's novel is not a success—is a failure. It is far too faulty to pass. The gaps that represent bad work are too large and too frequent. One has no desire to come back to it. A second reading leaves a lower estimate of it than the first, and a third is not possible. There is the immense pity of it. The artistic blemishes which were in Mr. Hardy's early books might, and in all probability would, have been eradicated if from the beginning he had had to face anything like genuine criticism, anything like a genuinely critical public. But, as it was, he was praised for his bad work and blamed for his good, until the faculty of distinction in him became hopelessly blurred and bewildered. The grotesque worthlessness of the criticism which he, like all the rest of us, received and receives in the ravenous and whirling columns of the press, he must soon have learned to rate at its true value for a serious writer. But the critical effort (and that comes to mean the effort in what may be called comparative culture) which still alone can prove the salvation of such an one among ourselves, this he does not seem to have made. The result is that his most ambitious work, which should have proved a masterpiece and which contains the elements of a masterpiece, has absolutely missed its aim and falls away. (pp. 21-2)

Francis Adams, in a review of "Tess of the D'Urbervilles," in The Fortnightly Review, *n.s. Vol. LII, No. CCCVII, July, 1892, pp. 19-22.*

A[NDREW] LANG (essay date 1892)

[In the following excerpt from his rejoinder to Hardy's preface to Tess, *which appeared in the American version of the novel's fifth edition, Lang defends and reiterates the criticisms he made in his initial review of the novel (see excerpt dated 1892). For an excerpt from Hardy's preface, see* TCLC, *Vol. 10.]*

Mr. Hardy has just answered the graceless persons—a small minority—who did not admire without qualification his tale, ***Tess of the D'Urbervilles.*** The following extract from his preface is culled out of the *Illustrated London News.* The last sentence, of course, is not Mr. Hardy's:

> In the introductory words to the first edition I suggested the possible advent of the genteel person who would not be able to endure the tone of these pages. That person duly appeared, mostly mixed up with the aforesaid objectors. In another of his forms he felt upset that it was not possible for him to read the book through three times, owing to my not having made that critical effort which 'alone can prove the salvation of such an one.' In another, he objected to such vulgar articles as the Devil's pitchfork, a lodging-house carving-knife, and a shame-bought parasol appearing in a respectable story. In another place he was a gentleman who turned Christian for half-an-hour the better to express his grief that a disrespectful phrase about the Immortals should have been used; though the same innate gentility compelled him to excuse the author in words of pity that one cannot be too thankful for: 'He does but give us of his best.' I can assure this great critic that to exclaim illogically against the gods, singular or plural, is not such an original sin of mine as he seems to imagine. True, it may have some local originality; though, if Shakespeare were an authority on history, which, perhaps, he is

> not, I could show that the sin was introduced into Wessex as early as the Heptarchy itself. Says Glo'ster to Lear, otherwise Ina, king of that country—
>
> As flies to wanton boys are we to the gods;
> They kill us for their sport.
>
> Needless to say that the "great critic" is Mr. Andrew Lang.

Mr. Hardy's argument is logical indeed. 'I said from the first,' he observes, 'that the genteel person'—meaning the Snob—'would not like my book. Some people did not like my book, therefore they are genteel persons.' Nothing can be more convincing. Then Mr. Hardy selects myself (as I signed my notice in the *New Review*), and he makes a reply which, I am sure, is only a petulant expression of annoyance, and does not seriously signify what it seems to signify. Mr. Hardy has no means of knowing what my private shade of theological dogma is. He cannot tell whether I am, as a matter of creed, a Christian or not. Nor can he really suppose that I, being, *ex hypothesi,* an unbeliever, pretended for half-an-hour to belief, in order that I might pick a hole in a phrase of his. The charge of so superfluously playing the part of Tartuffe for a critical and literary purpose is comic or melancholy according to your humour. As Mr. Hardy says, he 'exclaimed illogically against the gods' in the phrase, 'The President of the Immortals (in Æschylean phrase) had ended his sport with Tess.' This was the moral and marrow of his romance, as I supposed, and the phrase must seem equally illogical to an Atheist and a Christian, to a Buddhist and a Bonze. For nobody in his senses now believes in a wicked malignant President of the Immortals, whatever Glo'ster may have said in his haste while Ina was a monarch of the West Saxons. No; one need not be a Christian, nor pretend to be a Christian, before resenting a comment on the 'President of the Immortals' which is confessed to be illogical, and which—if Mr. Hardy does not believe in a malignant 'President'—is insincere and affected. And here I may add the expression of my regret that my quotation, 'he does but give us of his best,' has annoyed Mr. Hardy. For he always does give us of his best—of his best labour and earnest endeavour—and this is a virtue not universal among artists.

As to ***Tess*** and my own comparative distaste for that lady and her melancholy adventures, let me be unchristian for half-an-hour and give my reasons. But, first, let me confess that I am in an insignificant minority. On all sides—not only from the essays of reviewers, but from the spoken opinions of the most various kinds of readers—one learns that ***Tess*** is a masterpiece. One hears the same opinion from a great classical scholar, who seldom deserts the ancients for the moderns, and from a Scot living his life out in a remote savage island, which, by the way, is *not* Samoa. There is no absolute standard of taste in literature, but such a consensus of opinion comes as near being a standard as one generation can supply. So I confess myself in the wrong, as far as an exterior test can make me in the wrong; and yet a reviewer can only give his own impression, and state his reasons, as far as he knows them, for that impression. In the *Illustrated London News* of October 1 there is not only the beginning of a new tale by Mr. Hardy, but an eloquent estimate of Mr. Hardy's genius by Mr. Frederick Greenwood. . . . Mr. Greenwood, greatly admiring, as every one must admire, the talent of Mr. Hardy, says that one of his tales ***(The Hand of Ethelberta)*** is 'forbidding in conception.' Now, to my private taste— and *on n'a que soi,* even when one is a reviewer—***Tess*** is also 'forbidding in conception.' I have not read ***The Hand of Ethelberta,*** but ***Tess*** is not the only one of Mr. Hardy's novels which repels me by what is, to me, the 'forbidding' character of its 'conception.' . . . There is ***Two on a Tower,*** where the heroine, a widow, is not infrequently described as 'warm.' Her child, by a second marriage, through some legal misadventure or mischance, is to be born without a legitimate father. So she marries a clergyman—a bishop if my memory holds good—and imposes the babe on that prelate. It may be my 'gentility,' or it may be my partiality for a married clergy, but somehow I do find the 'conception' of ***Two on a Tower*** to be 'forbidding.' I don't like the practical joke on the clergyman; and the 'warmth' of the widow seems too conspicuously dwelt upon. (pp. 100-03)

I find a similar 'forbidding' quality in ***Tess,*** as I do, and have always done, in *Clarissa Harlowe*. Poor Tess, a most poetical, if not a very credible character, is a rural Clarissa Harlowe. She is very unlike most rural maids, but then she comes of a noble lineage. She is not avenged by the sword of Colonel Morden, but by that lodging-house carving-knife, which seems anything but a trusty stiletto. She does not die, like Clarissa, as the ermine martin dies of the stain on its snowy fur, but she goes back to the atrocious cad who betrayed her, and wears—not caring what she wears—the parasol of pomp and the pretty slippers of iniquity. To say that all this is out of character and out of keeping is only to set my theory of human nature against Mr. Hardy's knowledge of it. I never knew a Tess, as Mr. Thackeray was never personally acquainted with a convict. Her behaviour does not invariably seem to me that of 'a pure woman,' but perhaps I am no judge of purity, at all events in such extraordinarily disadvantageous circumstances. As to purity, people are generally about to talk nastily when they dwell on the word. The kind of 'catastrophe' spoken of by Mr. Hardy has been adequately treated of by St. Augustine, in his *De Civitate Dei*. To my own gentility it is no stumbling-block. Other girls in fiction have been seduced with more blame, and have not lost our sympathy, or ceased to be what Mr. Hardy calls 'protagonists.' . . . It is not the question of 'purity' that offends me, but that of credibility in character and language. The villain Alec and the prig Angel Clare seem to me equally unnatural, incredible, and out of the course of experience. But that may only prove one's experience to be fortunately limited. When all these persons, whose conduct and conversation are so far from plausible, combine in a tale of which the whole management is, to one's own taste, unnatural and 'forbidding,' how can one pretend to believe or to admire without reserve? Of course it may be no fault in a book that it is 'forbidding;' many people even think it a merit. *Le Père Goriot* is 'forbidding;' *Madame Bovary* is 'forbidding,' yet nobody in his senses denies their merit. But then, to myself, those tales are credible and real. ***Tess*** is not real nor credible, judged by the same personal standard. To be sure, ***Tess,*** unlike *Madame Bovary,* is at all events and undeniably a romance. When Angel Clare, walking in his sleep, carries the portly Tess, with all her opulent charms and 'ethereal beauty' to a very considerable distance, he does what Porthos, or Guy Livingstone, could hardly have done when wide awake. It is a romantic incident, but if an otherwise romantic writer had introduced it, the critics, one fears, would have laughed. At all events, when any reader finds that a book is beyond his belief, in character, in language, and in event, the book must, for him, lose much of its interest. Again, if he be struck by such a defect of style as the use of semi-scientific phraseology out of place, he must say so; he must point out the neighbourhood of the reef on which George Eliot was wrecking her English. An example of a fault so manifest, and of such easy remedy (for nobody need write jargon), I selected and reproduce. A rustic wife is sitting in a tavern, taking her ease at her inn. 'A sort of halo, an occidental glow, came over life then. Troubles and other realities took on themselves a metaphysical impalpability, sinking to mere cerebral phenomena for serene contemplation, and no longer stood as pressing concretions which chafed body and soul.' 'Men and hangels igsplain this,' cried Jeames, on less provocation. First, one does not know whether this description of Mrs. Durbeyfield's tavern content is to be understood as her way of 'envisaging' it, or as Mr. Hardy's. It can hardly be Mrs. Durbeyfield's, because the words 'cerebral' and 'metaphysical' were probably not in her West Saxon vocabulary. (pp. 103-04)

Well, for all these reasons—for its forbidding conception, for its apparent unreality, for its defects of style, so provokingly superfluous—***Tess*** failed to captivate me, in spite of the poetry and beauty and economic value of its rural descriptions, in spite of the genius which is obvious and undeniable in many charming scenes. To be more sensitive to certain faults than to great merits, to let the faults spoil for you the whole, is a critical misfortune, if not a critical crime. Here, too, all is subjective and personal; all depends on the critic's taste, and how it reacts against a particular kind of error. (p. 105)

To some tastes faults appear which to others are unapparent. But there are faults and faults, tastes and tastes. We all admit the existence of blemishes in the works which are most dear to us; there are palpable faults in *Rob Roy,* in *Tom Jones,* in *Tartuffe* (they tell me), and, they tell me, in *Vanity Fair.* The question is, how far do these faults offend the reader, and spoil, for him, the merit of the work before him? Here, again,

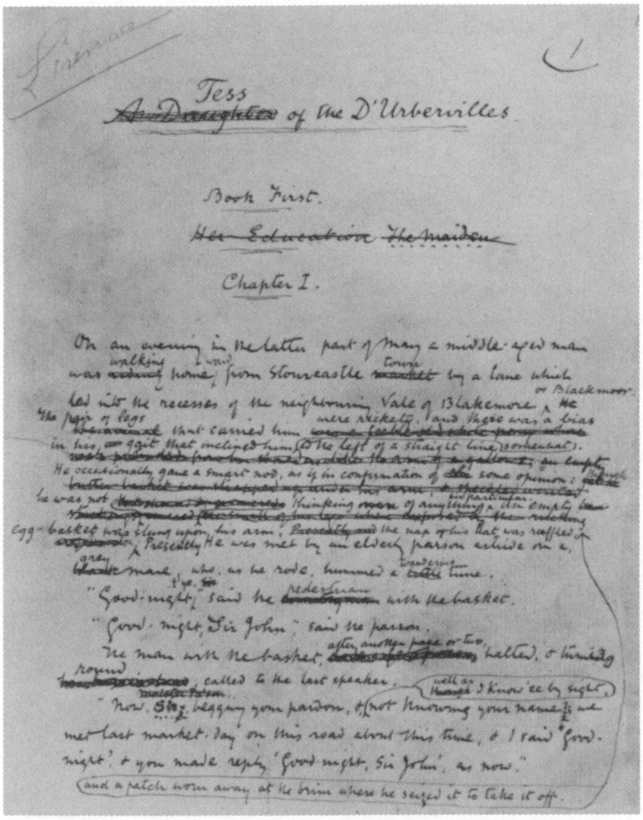

Tess
~~A Daughter~~ of the D'Urbervilles

Book First.

~~Her Education~~ ~~The maiden~~

Chapter I.

On an evening in the latter part of May a middle-aged man was walking home from Stourcastle by a lane which led into the recesses of the neighbouring Vale of Blakemore or Blackmoor. The pair of legs that carried him were rickety, and there was a bias in his gait that inclined him to the left of a straight line. He occasionally gave a smart nod, as if in confirmation of some opinion, though he was not thinking of anything in particular. An empty egg-basket was slung upon his arm, the nap of his hat was ruffled, and a patch worn away at the brim where he seized it to take it off. Presently he was met by an elderly parson astride on a grey mare, who, as he rode, hummed a wandering tune.

"Good-night t'ye," said the pedestrian with the basket.

"Good-night, Sir John," said the parson.

The man with the basket halted, after another pace or two, & turning round called to the last speaker. "Now, Sir, begging your pardon, we met last market-day on this road about this time, & I said "Good-night," & you made reply "Good-night, Sir John," as now."

Holograph copy of the first page of Tess.

we deal with the subjective. A man says that *Pickwick* is 'low' and boisterous; well, my genteelness (or 'gentility') is unoffended by *Pickwick.* . . . On the other hand, I confess that what seem to me faults in ***Tess,*** do not exactly spoil, but leave me less patience than I could wish, to enjoy the book's many and notable merits. Yet what is all this but saying that one prefers ***Far from the Madding Crowd*** to ***Tess*** and some of Mr. Hardy's other works? Arguing about it proves nothing, especially in the face of a consensus of praise from almost everybody who is not 'genteel.' I might say that ***Tess*** is not only a romance, but a *tendenz* story, a story with a moral, that moral, or part of it, being, apparently, the malignant topsy-turviness of things, the malevolent constitution of the world, the misfortunes of virtue, the conspiracy of circumstances against the good and 'pure.' A lurking vein of optimism may make one distrust this conclusion (if this indeed be the conclusion), and one may be comforted by one's very powerlessness to believe; may say, like the unconsciously heterodox old woman, 'After all, perhaps it is not true.' And that is a consolation for oneself, but not good for the novel. So I have ventured to say my say, though I had not intended at any time to speak again about any work of Mr. Hardy's. (pp. 105-06)

A[ndrew] Lang, "At the Sign of the Ship," in Longman's Magazine, *Vol. XXI, No. CXXI, November, 1892, pp. 100-10.*

W. P. TRENT (essay date 1892)

[*An American educator and literary critic, Trent was the founder and editor of the* Sewanee Review, *which was formed to provide the South with a much-needed literary organ. However, although the journal under Trent featured Southern writers, it never sought to evoke a constricted provincialism. As a critic and scholar, Trent was primarily concerned with literature as a contributing force to history; for that reason he stressed the study of the history of literature over analysis of the meaning and import of current literature. Throughout his career, Trent specialized in histories and criticism of American literature, his most notable work being the* Cambridge History of American Literature *(1917-20). In the following excerpt, Trent praises Hardy's achievement in* Tess *and compares its power to that of Greek and Shakespearian tragedy.*]

It would be useless to enter here upon any elaborate account of the plot of a book every one is reading or has read. As we all know Tess, the milkmaid heroine, has fallen from virtue through no fault of her own. Subsequently her great passion for a second and nobler lover sweeps her into a marriage with him after she has failed to tell him of her condition, although she has attempted to do so. Her confession of her secret to her husband is one of the most powerful and painful scenes in all literature. After the weak man has deserted her, she undergoes in patience a life of unspeakable torture, but at last falls again to her former betrayer in order to keep her mother and her family from starvation. Her husband returns to her, and in her remorse she stabs her betrayer to death. After a brief period of ecstatic bliss with the now repentant man, whose desertion has brought her to such a pass, she is seized by the officers of the law and led to the scaffold. Her story ends with the husband and her young sister moving away with averted eyes from the black flag that floats above the gloomy modern jail. In the words of her Creator, "'Justice' was done, and Time, the arch-satirist, had had his joke out with Tess."

"How horrible, how pessimistic," exclaims one reader. "How absurd," says another, "to attempt to prove that such a woman was pure," this last personage being swift to remember Mr.

Hardy's sub-title, "A Pure Woman Faithfully Presented." "What is the good of such stories when they only make one weep?" says a third. "It is the greatest tragedy of modern times," says a fourth. "It is a dangerous book to put into the hands of the young," says a fifth. And so on through a chorus of praise and blame which seems to us to be as a rule beside the point.

In the first place, we see little use in arguing whether or not Tess was really pure. We may see some excuse for her second fall, another may not. But what no one can fail to see is that in Tess Mr. Hardy has drawn a great character, nay, his greatest character, and we venture to say the greatest character in recent fiction. She seizes one at once and never looses her hold. What does it matter to us, from the point of view of art, whether she is pure or not, provided she does not repel us? There is here no allurement to sin, no attempt to make wrong right, no disposition to paint vice in the colors that belong to virtue. We see in her only a beautiful earth-born creature struggling against a fate too strong for her, a fate that brings her to a dishonored grave, and yet not a fate that will cut her off from the peace and joy of another world than this. She is elemental, this peasant's daughter with the blood of a Norman noble in her veins. She has the elemental freshness, the odor of earth, that Mr. Hardy's other peasants have, but she has also an elemental strength and nobility that they have not. This elemental freshness, this elemental strength and nobility, make her a woman fit to set in the gallery of Shakspere's women—which is but to say that she is a creation of genius that time cannot devour. Her story is pure tragedy—the greatest tragedy, it seems to us, that has been written since the days of the Elizabethans—it lacks "the accomplishment of verse," but at least it is told in the strongest and purest prose. If this be true, how vain to call it a horrible book? As well call the "Othello" horrible. Granted that it leaves a sensation of pain that lingers with a reader for hours, still it is the bitter-sweet pain that tragedy always leaves, and the pain is overbalanced by the pleasure we gain from our appreciation of the artist's triumph. Mr. Hardy may take his leave of us with a pessimistic fling, but he has succeeded malgrè pessimism in producing a great work of art. (pp. 19-21)

Viewed in its details, this book impresses one as strongly as it does when viewed as a whole. Its subordinate characters are admirably drawn and all help on the action. The husband, Angel Clare, is scarcely worthy of Tess's love, but Mr. Hardy has the authority of the Greeks for setting the man's selfishness and subservience to conventionalism as a foil to the natural purity and charm of the woman. Euripides makes Admetus serve as a foil to Alkestis. Mrs. Durbeyfield, the silly mother, who is responsible for Tess's fall, is a creature seen time and again among her class. Angel Clare's evangelical father and mother are also touched off in a few strokes which have the inevitableness that a master's hand alone can give. (p. 21)

But this is also a novel of powerful and memorable scenes. That in which Tess christens her child of shame, giving him the name of Sorrow, while her little brothers and sisters act as clerk and congregation, is piercing in its pathos, to borrow an expression of Matthew Arnold's. This scene was omitted from the first American edition of ***Tess,*** and the book was thereby greatly mutilated. No one who has read it can ever forget it or forget the lesson of charity it teaches. Very powerful also are the scenes describing Tess's confession to her husband and the consequences of that confession, although it is impossible to deny that the sleep-walking experiences of the pair are somewhat exaggerated. With the departure of Angel Clare the clouds of doom begin to mass above Tess's head and the tragedy gathers such swift intensity that it is almost vain to speak of scenes. But who will forget Tess's first day at the bleak upland farm, or her frustrated visit to her father-in-law's house, or her second meeting with her betrayer, or her sudden deed of frenzy, or her capture on Salisbury plain under the Shadow of Stonehenge? To forget these scenes would imply the power to forget the sight of Lear upon the wintry heath or of Othello in the death chamber of his "gentle lady."

But ***Tess*** has merits that lie apart from the power of characterization and of dramatic presentation which its author so constantly displays. Never has Mr. Hardy's knowledge of nature stood him in better stead than in the descriptive passages which here and there break the tense thread of the action. They have the effect that all description should have in a novel, of heightening the impression which the author is endeavoring to convey by means of his characters and their actions. We read them only to plunge once more into the narrative of Tess's adventures with a sense of the impotence of nature to avert the doom of her choicest creation. At times it seems as if this modern Englishman were really a Greek endowed with the power of personifying the trees and streams past which his heroine glides, just as he seems to be a Greek in his never-ceasing sense of the presence of an inexorable fate. In fine, the Hardy of this novel is the Hardy who has charmed and impressed us before, but also a Hardy of heightened and matured powers—a master of fiction. (pp. 21-2)

W. P. Trent, "The Novels of Thomas Hardy," in The Sewanee Review, *Vol. I, No. I, November, 1892, pp. 1-25.*

D. F. HANNIGAN (essay date 1892)

[Hannigan was an English critic and translator. In the following excerpt, he attacks Andrew Lang's criticisms of Tess *(see excerpts dated 1892).]*

If the novel is to be a faithful picture of actual life, and not a mere romantic narrative intended mainly to amuse young persons in their hours of leisure, the hackneyed moralisings of such critics as Mr. Andrew Lang must be disregarded as utterly beside the question—What is the proper sphere of fiction?

This well-known critic has thought fit to emphasise his intense dislike of both the conception and the style of Mr. Thomas Hardy's novel, ***Tess of the D'Urbervilles,*** in *The New Review* for February of the present year [see first Lang excerpt dated 1892]. Mr. Lang half-playfully sneered at the pessimism of ***Tess,*** and expressed the belief that its *dénoûment* is quite improbable "in this age of halfpenny newspapers and appeals to the British public." Perhaps the critic had before his mind the case of Mrs. Maybrick, but his observation has, after all, very little force. In Mrs. Maybrick's case there was a conflict of medical testimony, and, rightly or wrongly, the British public had got hold of the idea that the verdict was not warranted by the facts. But it is absurd for Mr. Lang or any other latter-day critic to maintain that a woman convicted of murder would escape death merely because she possessed some personal fascination, or because the circumstances connected with the crime were more or less romantic. . . . [Public] opinion has not yet arrived at such a stage in England as to make it at all certain that, in such a contingency as that indicated in Mr. Hardy's book the culprit would be saved by her sex from the ordeal of capital punishment. (p. 655)

Comfortable critics of this sort cannot sympathise with the temptations, the struggles, the miseries of a noble but half-darkened soul like that of poor Tess Durbeyfield. Mr. Hardy himself has vigorously dealt with the "genteel" reviewer in the preface to the fifth edition of the novel, and most rational persons will be inclined to think that Mr. Lang cuts a very sorry figure under the lash of this novelist's just resentment [see *TCLC*, Vol. 10]. A more modest type of author than Mr. Thomas Hardy does not exist. He shrinks from "blowing his own trumpet." He refers to his book as an "unequal and partial achievement," and seems to be utterly unconscious of the fact that he has written one of the greatest novels of this century. What he tries to avoid is not disparagement but misrepresentation. In the last paragraph of his novel he says: "Justice was done, and the President of the Immortals (in Æschylean phrase) had ended his sport with Tess." This sentence arouses the "virtuous indignation" of Mr. Lang, who cannot give adequate expression to his horror at such a supposed insult to the Deity. Really it is no wonder that the novelist should protest against the assumed wrath of the "gentleman who turned Christian for half an hour the better to express his grief that a disrespectful phrase about the Immortals should have been used."

Some critics would allow a writer of fiction no freedom. He should write conventional stories to please their somewhat valetudinarian tastes. He should draw a veil over all the unpleasant facts of life. (pp. 655-56)

To this school of critics Mr. Andrew Lang belongs. We trace in him the prudishness and exclusiveness of the fashionable preacher who has turned aside from religious paths to wander through the flowery meads of literature. Mr. Lang is perfectly welcome to enjoy what he is pleased to call "Romance," and to praise the blood-curdling Zulu narratives of his friend Mr. Rider Haggard; but why does he attempt to depreciate a novel, which is obviously outside the range not only of his sympathies but of his critical powers?

In the November number of *Longmans' Magazine* Mr. Lang returns to the subject, and says that he considers the book "unreal" [see second Lang excerpt dated 1892]. He admits the theme is capable of treatment in a novel, and refers to *The Heart of Midlothian* and *Madame Bovary*. What an intellectual jumble it is to couple Scott's old-fashioned romance with Flaubert's grimly realistic work! "It is not the question of purity," says Mr. Lang, "that offends me, but that of credibility of language and character."

Mark the egotism of this kind of criticism. "Offends *me*." Is there no criterion for Mr. Lang except the *ego*?

It is idle to say that the criticism of a work of fiction is a mere matter of personal feeling. There is a standard of judgment for a novel as well as for pictures or musical compositions. The critic who can only praise a book which does not "offend" him is the most wretched of critics. (p. 656)

[***Tess of the D'Urbervilles***] is a monumental work. It marks a distinct epoch in English fiction. From beginning to end it bears the hall-mark of Truth on every page of it. It is a more impressive narrative of crushing facts than George Eliot's *Adam Bede*. It is more deep and poignant than anything that either Zola or Guy de Maupassant has written. It is a work worthy of Balzac himself. There is no coarseness in it, no nastiness of detail, and yet nothing essential is avoided. From the time when poor Tess falls a victim to the lascivious pursuit of the base D'Urberville up to her death upon the scaffold, every step in her sad history is recorded. We can follow her career as if we knew her and lived with her. We feel her sufferings; we respect her shortcomings; we lament the chain of circumstances that led to her doom; and finally, we forgive and pity her. The beautiful passages in the book are so numerous that to quote them would be only heaping up extracts and, so to speak, breaking the harmony of an exquisite novel. The descriptions of field-life are clear, forcible, and true. The knowledge of Nature shown by the author is as wonderful as it is rare. The picture of Tess, after the murder, lying down to sleep in her exhaustion beneath one of the pillars at Stonehenge is, perhaps, the most touching and splendid scene in the entire novel. (p. 657)

It is easy to find fault with the style of even the greatest book. Victor Hugo is not free from mannerisms. George Eliot is often pedantic. Thomas Hardy, in this his latest and greatest novel, uses occasionally barbarous words, which are neither English nor Latin. He might have avoided the introduction of such verbal coinages as "juxtapose," "dolorifuge," and "theolatry." What does it matter, however, if an author here and there sins against philology? Small critics grasp at such things; let them! There are spots on the sun. The fact remains that ***Tess of the D'Urbervilles*** is the greatest work of fiction produced in England since George Eliot died. (p. 658)

D. F. Hannigan, "The Latest Development of English Fiction," in The Westminster Review, *Vol. CXXXVIII, No. 6, December, 1892, pp. 655-59.*

ROBERT LOUIS STEVENSON (letter date 1892)

[*Stevenson was a Scottish novelist and poet. His novels* Treasure Island *(1883),* Kidnapped *(1886), and* Dr. Jekyll and Mr. Hyde *(1886) were considered popular literary classics upon publication and firmly established his reputation as an inventive stylist and riveting storyteller. Stevenson is also noted for his understanding of youth, which is evident both in his early "boy's novels," as they were known, and in his much-loved* A Child's Garden of Verses *(1885). In the following excerpt from a letter to Henry James, he levies harsh criticism against* Tess. *For James's response to Stevenson's commentary see the excerpt dated 1893.*]

Hurry up with another book of stories. I am now reduced to two of my contemporaries, you and Barrie—O and Kipling! I did like Haggard's *Nada the Lily*; it isn't great but it's big. As for Hardy— you remember the old gag?—Are you wownded, my lord?—Wownded, Ardy.—Mortually, my lord?—Mortually, Ardy.—Well, I was mortually wownded by Tess of the Durberfields [*sic*]. I do not know that I am exaggerative in criticism; but I will say that ***Tess*** is one of the worst, weakest, least sane, most *voulu* books I have yet read. Bar the style, it seems to be about as bad as [G.W.M.] Reynolds—I maintain it—Reynolds: or to be more plain, to have no earthly connection with human life or human nature; and to be merely the ungracious portrait of a weakish man under a vow to appear clever, as a ricketty schoolchild setting up to be naughty and not knowing how. I should tell you in fairness I could never finish it; there may be the treasures of the Indies further on; but so far as I read, James, it was (in one word) damnable. *Not alive, not true*, was my continual comment as I read; and at last—*not even honest!* was the verdict with which I spewed it from my mouth. I write in anger? I almost think I do; I was betrayed in a friend's house—and I was pained to hear that other friends delighted in that barmicide feast. I cannot read a page of Hardy for many a long day, my confidence [in him] is gone.

Robert Louis Stevenson, in a letter to Henry James on December 5, 1892, in "Tess of the D'Urbervilles'' by Thomas Hardy: An Authoritative Text, Hardy and the Novel, Criticism, *edited by Scott Elledge, second edition, W. W. Norton & Company, Inc., 1979, p. 388.*

HENRY JAMES (letter date 1893)

[*An American novelist, James is valued for his psychological acuity and complex sense of artistic form. Throughout his career, James also wrote literary criticism in which he developed his artistic ideals and applied them to the works of others. Among the numerous conceptualizations he formed to clarify the nature of fiction, he defined the novel as ''a direct impression of life.'' The quality of this impression—the degree of moral and intellectual development—and the author's ability to communicate this impression in an effective and artistic manner were the two principal criteria by which James estimated the worth of a literary work. In the following excerpt from his response to a letter from Robert Louis Stevenson (see excerpt dated 1892), James discusses Stevenson's criticisms of* Tess.]

I grant you Hardy with all my heart and even with a certain quantity of my boot-toe. I am meek and ashamed where the public clatter is deafening—so I bowed my head and let ''Tess of the D's'' pass. But oh yes, dear Louis, she is vile. The pretence of ''sexuality'' is only equalled by the absence of it, and the abomination of the language by the author's reputation for style. There are indeed some pretty smells and sights and sounds. But you have better ones in Polynesia.

Henry James, in a letter to Robert Louis Stevenson on February 17, 1893, in ''Tess of the D'Urbervilles'' by Thomas Hardy: An Authoritative Text, Hardy and the Novel, Criticism, *edited by Scott Elledge, second edition, W. W. Norton & Company, Inc., 1979, p. 388.*

D. H. LAWRENCE (essay date 1915?)

[*Lawrence was an English novelist, poet, and essayist who is noted for his introduction of the themes of modern psychology to English fiction. In his lifetime he was a controversial figure, both for the explicit sexuality he portrayed in his novels and for his unconventional personal life. Much of the criticism of Lawrence's work concerns his highly individualistic moral system, which was based on absolute freedom of expression, particularly sexual expression. Human sexuality was for Lawrence a symbol of the Life Force, and is frequently pitted against modern industrial society, which he believed was dehumanizing. His most famous novel,* Lady Chatterley's Lover *(1928), was the subject of a landmark obscenity trial in Great Britain in 1960, which turned largely on the legitimacy of Lawrence's inclusion of hitherto forbidden sexual terms. In the following excerpt, Lawrence discusses the characters of* Tess *as representations of the male and female elements of human nature.*]

[Every] man comprises male and female in his being, the male always struggling for predominance. A woman likewise consists in male and female, with female predominant.

And a man who is strongly male tends to deny, to refute the female in him. A real ''man'' takes no heed for his body, which is the more female part of him. He considers himself only as an instrument, to be used in the service of some idea.

The true female, on the other hand, will eternally hold herself superior to any idea, will hold full life in the body to be the real happiness. The male exists in doing, the female in being. The male lives in the satisfaction of some purpose achieved, the female in the satisfaction of some purpose contained. (p. 481)

The women approved of are not Female in any real sense. They are passive subjects to the male, the re-echo from the male. As in the Christian religion, the Virgin worship is no real Female worship, but worship of the Female as she is passive and subjected to the male. Hence the sadness of Botticelli's Virgins.

Thus Tess sets out, not as any positive thing, containing all purpose, but as the acquiescent complement to the male. The female in her has become inert. Then Alec d'Urberville comes along, and possesses her. From the man who takes her Tess expects her own consummation, the singling out of herself, the addition of the male complement. She is of an old line, and has the aristocratic quality of respect for the other being. She does not see the other person as an extension of herself, existing in a universe of which she is the centre and pivot. She knows that other people are outside her. Therein she is an aristocrat. And out of this attitude to the other person came her passivity. It is not the same as the passive quality in the other little heroines, such as the girl in ***The Woodlanders,*** who is passive because she is small.

Tess is passive out of self-acceptance, a true aristocratic quality, amounting almost to self-indifference. She knows she is herself incontrovertibly, and she knows that other people are not herself. This is a very rare quality, even in a woman. And in a civilization so unequal, it is almost a weakness.

Tess never tries to alter or to change anybody, neither to alter nor to change nor to divert. What another person decides, that is his decision. She respects utterly the other's right to be. She is herself always.

But the others do not respect her right to be. Alec d'Urberville sees her as the embodied fulfilment of his own desire: something, that is, belonging to him. She cannot, in his conception, exist apart from him nor have any being apart from his being. For she is the embodiment of his desire.

This is very natural and common in men, this attitude to the world. But in Alec d'Urberville it applies only to the woman of his desire. He cares only for her. Such a man adheres to the female like a parasite.

It is a male quality to resolve a purpose to its fulfilment. It is the male quality, to seek the motive power in the female, and to convey this to a fulfilment; to receive some impulse into his senses, and to transmit it into expression.

Alec d'Urberville does not do this. He is male enough, in his way; but only physically male. He is constitutionally an enemy of the principle of self-subordination, which principle is inherent in every man. It is this principle which makes a man, a true male, see his job through, at no matter what cost. A man is strictly only himself when he is fulfilling some purpose he has conceived: so that the principle is not of self-subordination, but of continuity, of development. Only when insisted on, as in Christianity, does it become self-sacrifice. And this resistance to self-sacrifice on Alec d'Urberville's part does not make him an individualist, an egoist, but rather a non-individual, an incomplete, almost a fragmentary thing.

There seems to be in d'Urberville an inherent antagonism to any progression in himself. Yet he seeks with all his power for the source of stimulus in woman. He takes the deep impulse from the female. In this he is exceptional. No ordinary man could really have betrayed Tess. Even if she had had an illegitimate child to another man, to Angel Clare, for example, it would not have shattered her as did her connexion with Alec d'Urberville. For Alec d'Urberville could reach some of the real sources of the female in a woman, and draw from them. Troy could also do this. And as a woman instinctively knows, such men are rare. Therefore they have a power over a woman. They draw from the depth of her being.

And what they draw, they betray. With a natural male, what he draws from the source of the female, the impulse he receives from the source he transmits through his own being into utterance, motion, action, expression. But Troy and Alec d'Urberville, what they received they knew only as gratification in the senses; some perverse will prevented them from submitting to it, from becoming instrumental to it.

Which was why Tess was shattered by Alec d'Urberville, and why she murdered him in the end. The murder is badly done, altogether the book is botched, owing to the way of thinking in the author, owing to the weak yet obstinate theory of being. Nevertheless, the murder is true, the whole book is true, in its conception.

Angel Clare has the very opposite qualities to those of Alec d'Urberville. To the latter, the female in himself is the only part of himself he will acknowledge: the body, the senses, that which he shares with the female, which the female shares with him. To Angel Clare, the female in himself is detestable, the body, the senses, that which he will share with a woman, is held degraded. What he wants really is to receive the female impulse other than through the body. But his thinking has made him criticize Christianity, his deeper instinct has forbidden him to deny his body any further, a deadlock in his own being, which denies him any purpose, so that he must take to hand, labour out of sheer impotence to resolve himself, drives him unwillingly to woman. But he must see her only as the Female Principle, he cannot bear to see her as the Woman in the Body. Her he thinks degraded. To marry her, to have a physical marriage with her, he must overcome all his ascetic revulsion, he must, in his own mind, put off his own divinity, his pure maleness, his singleness, his pure completeness, and descend to the heated welter of the flesh. It is objectionable to him. Yet his body, his life, is too strong for him.

Who is he, that he shall be pure male, and deny the existence of the female? This is the question the Creator asks of him. Is then the male the exclusive whole of life?—is he even the higher or supreme part of life? Angel Clare thinks so: as Christ thought.

Yet it is not so, as even Angel Clare must find out. Life, that is Two-in-One, Male and Female. Nor is either part greater than the other.

It is not Angel Clare's fault that he cannot come to Tess when he finds that she has, in his words, been defiled. It is the result of generations of ultra-Christian training, which had left in him an inherent aversion to the female, and to all in himself which pertained to the female. What he, in his Christian sense, conceived of as Woman, was only the servant and attendant and administering spirit to the male. He had no idea that there was such a thing as positive Woman, as the Female, another great living Principle counterbalancing his own male principle. He conceived of the world as consisting of the One, the Male Principle. (pp. 482-85)

But there is not one principle, there are two, travelling always to meet, each step of each one lessening the distance between the two of them. And Space, which so frightened Herbert Spencer, is as a Bride to us. And the cry of Man does not ring out into the Void. It rings out to Woman, whom we know not.

This Tess knew, unconsciously. An aristocrat she was, developed through generations to the belief in her own self-establishment. She could help, but she could not be helped. She could give, but she could not receive. She could attend to the wants of the other person, but no other person, save another aristocrat—and there is scarcely such a thing as another aristocrat—could attend to her wants, her deepest wants. (p. 485)

And Tess, despising herself in the flesh, despising the deep Female she was, because Alec d'Urberville had betrayed her very source, loved Angel Clare, who also despised and hated the flesh. She did not hate d'Urberville. What a man did, he did, and if he did it to her, it was her look-out. She did not conceive of him as having any human duty towards her.

The same with Angel Clare as with Alec d'Urberville. She was very grateful to him for saving her from her despair of contamination, and from her bewildered isolation. But when he accused her, she could not plead or answer. For she had no right to his goodness. She stood alone.

The female was strong in her. She was herself. But she was out of place, utterly out of her element and her times. Hence her utter bewilderment. This is the reason why she was so overcome. She was outwearied from the start, in her spirit. For it is only by receiving from all our fellows that we are kept fresh and vital. Tess was herself, female, intrinsically a woman.

The female in her was indomitable, unchangeable, she was utterly constant to herself. But she was, by long breeding, intact from mankind. Though Alec d'Urberville was of no kin to her, yet, in the book, he has always a quality of kinship. It was as if only a kinsman, an aristocrat, could approach her. And this to her undoing. Angel Clare would never have reached her. She would have abandoned herself to him, but he would never have reached her. It needed a physical aristocrat. She would have lived with her husband, Clare, in a state of abandon to him, like a coma. Alec d'Urberville forced her to realize him, and to realize herself. He came close to her, as Clare could never have done. So she murdered him. For she was herself.

And just as the aristocratic principle had isolated Tess, it had isolated Alec d'Urberville. For though Hardy consciously made the young betrayer a plebeian and an impostor, unconsciously, with the supreme justice of the artist, he made him the same as de Stancy, a true aristocrat, or as Fitzpiers, or Troy. He did not give him the tiredness, the touch of exhaustion necessary, in Hardy's mind, to an aristocrat. But he gave him the intrinsic qualities.

With the men as with the women of old descent: they have nothing to do with mankind in general, they are exceedingly personal. For many generations they have been accustomed to regard their own desires as their own supreme laws. They have not been bound by the conventional morality: this they have transcended, being a code unto themselves. (pp. 486-87)

It may be, also, that in the aristocrat a certain weariness makes him purposeless, vicious, like a form of death. But that is not necessary. One feels that in Manston, and Troy, and Fitzpiers, and Alec d'Urberville, there is good stuff gone wrong. Just as in Angel Clare, there is good stuff gone wrong in the other direction.

There can never be one extreme of wrong, without the other extreme. (p. 487)

The one extreme produces the other. It is inevitable for Angel Clare and for Alec d'Urberville mutually to destroy the woman they both loved. Each does her the extreme of wrong, so she is destroyed.

The book is handled with very uncertain skill, botched and bungled. But it contains the elements of the greatest tragedy: Alec d'Urberville, who has killed the male in himself, as Clytemnestra symbolically for Orestes killed Agamemnon; Angel Clare, who has killed the female in himself, as Orestes killed Clytemnestra: and Tess, the Woman, the Life, destroyed by a mechanical fate, in the communal law.

There is no reconciliation. Tess, Angel Clare, Alec d'Urberville, they are all as good as dead. For Angel Clare, though still apparently alive, is in reality no more than a mouth, a piece of paper. . . .

There is no reconciliation, only death. And so Hardy really states his case, which is not his consciously stated metaphysic, by any means, but a statement how man has gone wrong and brought death on himself: how man has violated the Law, how he has supererogated himself, gone so far in his male conceit as to supersede the Creator, and win death as a reward. Indeed, the works of supererogation of our male assiduity help us to a better salvation. (p. 488)

D. H. Lawrence, "Study of Thomas Hardy," in his Phoenix: The Posthumous Papers of D. H. Lawrence, *edited by Edward D. McDonald, The Viking Press, 1936, pp. 398-516.*

JOSEPH WARREN BEACH (essay date 1922)

[Beach was an American critic and educator who specialized in American literature and English literature of the Romantic and Victorian eras. Of his work, Beach noted: "I do not aim so much to render final judgments and deliver certificates of greatness, which is something manifestly impossible and a trifle ridiculous, as to analyze and interpret stories and poems as expressions of our humanity and as effective works of art." In the following excerpt Beach discusses Tess's character, the lyricism of Hardy's prose, and the author's compassionate portrayal of his fictional creations.]

Hardy's women are—as with most novelists of his time—his most convincing and attractive characters. And Tess is the crown of all his women. [Eustacia Vye of ***The Return of the Native***] was a wonderful creation, a poetic invention, of strange exotic beauty, fit to be the wicked queen of tragedy. There is nothing of the exotic or nocturnal about our milkmaid, walking out at daybreak with her companions, or working in the harvest fields at noonday with the men and women of Marlott. She has the force of passion of Eustacia without her unscrupulous and somewhat perverse idealism. Among the earlier characters, she has more of [Bathsheba Everdene of ***Far From the Madding Crowd***] than of [Elfride Swancourt of ***A Pair of Blue Eyes***], being a creature of the fields and barns instead of the drawing-room and the study. She is even more deeply tinctured than Bathsheba with the ocherous contact of the earth. She has a dignity of bearing like Bathsheba's; but being no independent farmer but the merest proletarian, she has more than the helplessness of her sex, and is the marked victim of an economic order that spares its Bathshebas.

She is beautiful, and real, too. For her beauty is not too perfect, and not too fully inventoried. Her eyes and mouth are the only features about which her painter is specific—her "large innocent eyes," her "large tender eyes," of indeterminate color, and her "mobile peony mouth." There is one peculiarity of her mouth upon which he dwells more than once—the way her lower lip had "of thrusting the middle of her top one upward, when they closed together after a word." It was this that was so maddening to Angel on the afternoon when he watched her at the milking till drawn to her as by an irresistible charm. Her lips were beautiful but not perfect; "and it was the touch of the imperfect upon the intended perfect that gave the sweetness, because it was that which gave the humanity." It is that which convinces us that the author was here drawing from the life. The same conviction is forced upon us by the charming colloquialism of her speech, bits of ancientry that slipped through the web of her National School training; and above all by the "stopt-diapason note which her voice acquired when her heart was in her speech, and which will never be forgotten by those who knew her." There is something in the phrasing here that makes one sure the author is speaking of an actual woman, whose voice he has heard and cannot forget.

She has every quality to make us admire her: her modesty, her sensitiveness to the disgrace of her father's drunken ways, her motherly concern for her brothers and sisters, the simple earnestness and patience with which she performs the hard tasks imposed upon her, and the scrupulous conscience that brings her so much pain. Above all we find beautiful the wholeness of her devotion to the man she loves, in its combination of qualities traditionally distinguished as proper to woman and to man. "Clare knew that she loved him—every curve of her form showed that—but he did not know at that time the full depth of her devotion, its single-mindedness, its meekness; what long-suffering it guaranteed—what honesty, what endurance, what good faith."

This is a good woman for whom our tears are asked. "A pure woman" he calls her in his title; an adjective he defends in the Preface to one of the later editions. Heretofore Mr. Hardy has been content in his novels to make a "tacit assumption" of the conventional standards of morality. But here, in the interest of truth or of his story, he is impelled to interpose over and over again his own passionate defense of his heroine's character. He represents Tess, in the time of her disgrace, as encompassed with

> a cloud of moral hobgoblins by which she was terrified without reason. It was they that were out of harmony with the actual world, not she. Walking among the sleeping birds in the hedges, watching the skipping rabbits on a moonlit warren, or standing under a pheasant-laden bough, she looked upon herself as a figure of Guilt intruding into the haunts of Innocence. But all the while she was making a distinction where there was no difference. Feeling herself in antagonism, she was quite in accord. She had been made to break an accepted social law, but no law known to the environment in which she fancied herself such an anomaly.

It is a very frank appeal to the law of nature from the law of society. As expressed in the more rustic language of Mrs. Durbeyfield, "Well, we must make the best of it, I suppose. 'Tis nater, after all, and what do please God."

But if the author is so bold in his appeal to nature, he nevertheless takes pains to clear his heroine of too much responsibility for her experience. It may be merely a social law which she had broken; but he wants us to understand that it was only through her extreme ignorance that she "had been made" to break it. It is with great feeling that Tess reproaches her mother for not telling her "there was danger in men-folk." Her fellow-workers in the fields, watching her nurse her baby, reckon that "a little more than persuading had to do wi' the coming o't. . . . There were they that heard a sobbing one night last year in the Chase; and it mid ha' gone hard wi' a certain party if folks had come along." The circumstances of her betrayal were evidently thought out with great care so as to make her seem almost, if not quite, helpless.

It is here if anywhere in the book that we hear the creak of the machinery. Whatever he might think himself of the relative validity of the laws of nature and those of society, the author had still to reckon with his public of Saxon readers; and he must at all cost save his heroine from the slightest imputation of—well—sensuality. The trick, if such it be, was on the whole very neatly turned. It is far from the crude violence of movie and melodrama, in which the heroine is betrayed by mere force or deceit, agreeable to the Saxon persuasion—at least for purposes of romance—that no decent woman ever *can* be seduced by any other means. It is equally removed from the somewhat low-creeping realism of George Moore. . . . The upshot of the whole matter for Mr. Hardy seems to be that the reproach for such an act is in proportion to the degree of responsibility, and that degrees of responsibility are infinite in number.

As for Tess, her responsibility is represented as practically *nil.* She was "an almost typical woman, but for *a slight incautiousness of character* inherited from her race." A slight incautiousness of character, and that inherited, can hardly amount to the *tragic fault* in a protagonist regarded as essential to justify the ruling powers. It would not suit the purposes of Sophocles, of Shakespeare, of Hawthorne, or George Eliot. This is not tragedy in the traditional sense; and the modernity of the author is shown in his bold impiety. "'Justice' was done," he says on recording the execution of Tess, "and the President of the Immortals (in Aeschylean phrase) had ended his sport with Tess." Mr. Hardy, in his Preface, defends his exclamation against the gods with a quotation of Gloster's words in *Lear,*

> As flies to wanton boys are we to the gods;
> They kill us for their sport.

He does not quote the words of Gloster's son,

> The gods are just, and of our pleasant vices
> Make instruments to scourge us.

More in Gloster's vein, again, is Marian's reply to Tess's suggestion that her unhappy life is fair payment for her own wrong-doing. "Wives are unhappy sometimes; from no fault of their husbands—from their own," says Tess. "You've no faults, deary; that I am sure of," is Marian's reply. "So it must be something outside ye both." It is not immorality of which Hardy should be accused. . . . His offense is a more modern one—the great modern crime of impiety.

We are here concerned only with his artistic offense—that against realism—the venial offense, when all is said, of taking for his heroine an exceptionally fine woman, a woman with no other fault than a slight incautiousness of character.

Far deeper crimes than this we can forgive to an artist who knows how to envelop his story in such a dense and shining atmosphere of poetry. We have never had a novelist who made so beautiful a use of that time-vision which is one of the richest resources of the poet. This is not the faculty of reviving in romantic tale the glittering figures and events of a time long past. It is the more elevated and poetic faculty of setting the plainest figures of today in a perspective of ages, in a shadowy synthesis that, while it dwarfs the present scene, yet lends it a grandeur, too, a dignity and a noble pathos borrowed from those of time itself. (pp. 207-12)

A special element of wonder is added to the daylight wonder of Stonehenge by the way it is approached by Tess and Angel, in the darkness of their furtive midnight journey, and ignorant of their whereabouts. Unable to make out anything by sight, they are guided only by the booming sound of the wind playing upon the gigantic edifice, as it plays upon the Egyptian stones of Memnon, and by the sense of touch which informs them of the shapes of pillar and altar stone. It is with a great shiver of awe that they and the reader come at last to the conclusion that "this pavilion of the night" is Stonehenge, the ancient temple, "older than the centuries; older than the D'Urbervilles."

If anything was needed to give a sense of greater depths of time lying behind them, it was the realization that this edifice was probably dedicated to the worship of the sun. For in this reference back to primitive ritual and myth, one measures time not by years and centuries but by the vast cycles of man's religious sense. Many times in the story of Tess we have this appeal to our ultra-historic imagination: the "old-time heliolatries" being suggested to the author by a hazy sunrise in August, when "the sun, on account of the mist, had a curious sentient, personal look, demanding the masculine pronoun for its adequate expression"; the May-day dance of the women of Marlott being traced to the ancient rites of the local Ceres.

As usual, Hardy is very precise in his notation of those geological diversities that antedate Stonehenge and Cybele, and yet give their present expression to the landscape. There is even more occasion than usual for such science in this book, since the changing fortunes of Tess take her into such various parts of the country, and her sympathetic creator is anxious to make us feel the difference, for example, between the rich alluvial character of the Valley of the Great Dairies, where she spent the days of her happiness and the flinty rudeness of the upland where her life was bitter. In her slow journeys on foot or by wagon, the earthy substructure of the scene is always present to her sense, "perceptible to the tread and to the smell." (pp. 213-14)

The sense of encompassment by nature is made even stronger by the author's insistence on the remoteness of his scene from the intrusions of civilization. Especially tender is his treatment of the sleepy Vale of Blackmoor and the limited view of the peasant girl for whom this shut-in nook of country is the world. This was "the vale in which she had been born, and in which her life had unfolded. The Vale of Blackmoor was to her the world, and its inhabitants the races thereof. From the gates and stiles of Marlott she had looked down its length in the wondering days of infancy, and what had been mystery to her then was not less than mystery to her now. . . ."

It is by such means that the figures of the story are all invested with a tender light as of the end of day, with contours softened and every rudeness refined, as in the paintings of Millet or the sculptures of Meunier. It is thus that they sink into the beauty of their setting, at least for us who behold the picture, and half the soreness of life is taken away by the very pathos of their insignificance.

It is in ***Tess of the D'Urbervilles*** that Hardy's pathos culminates—the general envelopment of human nature with his yearning tenderness. It is not merely Tess and her misfortunes that move him. He takes every opportunity of extending his compassionate regard to any creature within his view. He loves to dwell upon the minor solacements which mortals find for anxiety and pain. He dilates more than once upon the comfort of strong drink, which, while it only serves in the long run to deepen trouble, yet for the moment creates an illusion of well-being. (pp. 214-15)

Hardy loves also to dwell on the more healthy solace of nature to sore spirits. He loves to think of Tess, in the time when she hid her shame, watching from under her few square yards of thatch, "winds, and snows, and rains, and gorgeous sunsets, and successive moons at their full." He loves to think of her as taking her solitary walk at the exact moment of evening "when the light and the darkness are so evenly balanced that the constraint of day and the suspense of night neutralize each other, leaving absolute mental liberty," when "the plight of being alive becomes attenuated to its least possible dimensions." And he must have taken a sad joy in her moment of satisfaction when she lay before daybreak upon the stone altar of Stonehenge. . . . "I like very much to be here," she murmured. "It is so solemn and lonely—after my great happiness—with nothing but the sky above my face. It seems as if there were no folk in the world but we two. . . ."

And so it is that the poet throws about his pitiful creatures the purple mantle of his compassion. And we can almost forget the pain of the story in its loveliness. The rage and indignation pass; the tenderness remains. And if we say, how pitiful! it is to say, in the next breath, how beautiful! (pp. 216-17)

Joseph Warren Beach, in his The Technique of Thomas Hardy, *1922. Reprint by Russell & Russell, 1962, 255 p.*

PATRICK BRAYBROOKE (essay date 1928)

[*In the following excerpt Braybrooke discusses the philosophy of determinism presented in* Tess.]

To a certain extent, in ***Tess of the D'Urbervilles*** Hardy appears to be writing something that might be a plea for a very sincere and uncompromising form of Atheism, or, rather, a subtle and almost dangerous Determinism. And perhaps the latter is more serious because it is the more definite. Atheism has no real value in determining human conduct and human responsibility, but Determinism postulates a very definite and, in my opinion, a very detestable type of Deity. For, in ***Tess,*** Hardy seems to be very positive. He is much more positive than in any of his earlier work. His pessimism is no longer merely a possibility; it is stated and insisted on with the utmost show of rational dogma. It is almost gloried in as though the writer took a pleasure in upsetting the illusions of those good people who believe because they have been told, and so often believe greatly because they see with eyes that only see that which falls in with their pious belief. Of course, ***Tess*** is a book that may be interpreted as anti-Christian, but it will have the supreme merit of being anti-Christian because Tess is treated by some power that has no apparent semblance whatever to the God who is said to have walked this earth in the form of a despised Carpenter, a despised Carpenter who has eluded those who have been most zealous in His service.

There are those who see in ***Tess of the D'Urbervilles*** but a very grim and relentless philosophy. They will not be persuaded that there is much to be said for such a philosophy. At least, in the complacency of their own firm beliefs they might realise that Hardy is drawing a woman who all through her life met nothing that could give the faintest inkling of a beneficent power behind the Universe. Of course, it can be argued that Tess is not true to life, or that the woman was her own enemy. But the fact still remains that the outside world can show at every turn men and women who appear to be but the puppets of a world ruled by a callous and heartless Energy.

I say, then, at the outset that I believe very firmly there is a point of view which makes Mr. Hardy's philosophy in ***Tess*** not only reasonable, but inevitable. But there is the other side; and it is probably superficial to be too much prejudiced either for or against his doctrines. We can only try and determine whether Tess in her experiences was apparently a mere automaton driven hither and thither or whether she seems to have fashioned her own tragic destiny.

Tess herself is certainly, like so many of Hardy's heroines, a rather weak kind of woman, uncertain in her affections, to a certain extent illogical, and withal, capable of unbounding affection and possessed of almost limitless emotions.

The physical attractions of Tess appear to have been considerable, and it is again a nice little dilemma that nature which gave these to Tess makes most of her troubles result from them. It is the old curious principle of giving with one hand and taking away with the other.

> A small minority, mainly strangers, would look long at her in casually passing by, and grow momentarily fascinated by her freshness, and wonder if they would ever see her again; but to almost everybody she was a fine and picturesque country girl, and no more.
>
> (pp. 47-8)

In so many of the heroines that Hardy creates there is radiated a "something" that calls for the sympathy of those who encounter these unfortunate women. It is, I think, to be found in the fact that all Hardy's women seem to be possessed of a horrid feeling of coming evil, a feeling of helplessness, a feeling that any happiness cannot last; that though there may be transitory joy, sorrow cometh in the morning. These women strive against the inevitable. It is as though they would prevent the advent of the tide by means of scooping out gallons of water. Is Hardy too gloomy in this inevitable thorny path that poor Tess has to tread? In other words, is her life exaggerated? I must confess I can see no grounds for any affirmative answers to such a question.

The meeting between Tess and "Durbeyfield," the beginning of the horrid tragedy—it is all done with the hand of a master. The artist who does not use too much paint or does not use too little; the thinker who can see the beginnings that can only end in dire misery; the philosopher who looks onwards and onwards and can only see black, black clouds hurrying along, and almost laughing that they are for ever obscuring the sun from some wretched woman.

> Thus the thing began. Had she perceived this meeting's import, she might have asked why she was doomed to be seen and coveted that

> day by the wrong man, and not by some other man, the right and desired one in all respects—as nearly as humanity can supply the right and desired; yet to him who amongst her acquaintance might have approximated to this kind, she was but a transient impression, half forgotten.

We may well wring our hands in despair at such misery. Perhaps a Divine joke, but a very poor one. What purpose can there be in this ill-assorting of people? At least Hardy can see none. It throws him back again and again, almost exhausted, to that pernicious Determinism which leaves us wailing, "No hope, no hope." (pp. 49-50)

So far I have discussed something of the gloom or pessimism of ***Tess of the D'Urbervilles.*** I now propose to enter upon an examination of the next most important part of this book—the love element in it; the love that is the "reason" of the subsequent tragedy. The lack of love that Tess displays for D'Urberville seems to be described by Hardy in quite simple and natural dialogue. The type of dialogue that might well be used by a hundred other novelists, who would never dream of considering their work of the nature of a classic. There is certainly no fault to be found with it. The conversation shows only too well the wrong man making love to Tess. For love never needs to be made; it is there, if it is there at all!

> "Tess, why do you always dislike my kissing you?"
>
> "I suppose—because I don't love you."
>
> "You are quite sure?"
>
> "I am angry with you sometimes!"

Yet there is in this a certain amount of vacillating about Tess, even in this frank admission. She is not quite sure that she doesn't love D'Urberville. Or rather, she isn't absolutely sure that love will not perhaps come. Somewhat later on Hardy, I think, implies this by some subtle dialogue.

> "Tessy, don't you love me ever so little now?"
>
> "I'm grateful," she reluctantly admitted. "But I fear I do not. . . ." The sudden vision of his passion for herself as a factor in this result so distressed her that, beginning with one slow tear, and then following with another, she wept outright.

Tess is in the dangerous position when a woman may let gratitude lay so firm a hold of her that she subsequently mistakes it for love. Hardy seems to make no mistake at all about the curious position between Tess and Alec D'Urberville. All the time there is that sense again of Tess striving against something that is bound to beat her. We never imagine for a single instant that she will ever come out victorious. D'Urberville himself seems to be on the winning side, even in the seemingly impossible task of attempting to make a woman who does not love enter upon that inscrutable and devastating emotion. All through the various pieces of dialogue the vitality of Tess is sapped. Hardy leads on to her tacit surrender with an almost cruel insistence. (pp. 51-3)

The whole affair is so hopeless. Hardy does not allow a single ray of light to make any attempt to penetrate the thick darkness.

There is not the slightest pandering to the reader, who might quite conceivably gasp that he is being slowly but surely drowned in an ocean of tears. The downward process of Tess is painful; the more so that the pain is intimately associated with affection.

We must pass on to the extraordinary episode with Angel Clare. I do feel in some ways that Angel Clare is slightly exaggerated. His priggishness is so detestable that it may be that Hardy dislikes him so much that he has rather overdrawn his unpleasing character. The love that Tess has for Clare is one of those absorbing passions which are absolutely uncompromising and utterly unscrupulous. Tess is absolutely uncompromising in her love for Clare. There is a suggestion of a Shavian position—the utter relentlessness of woman when she is gripped by her most desired passion.

The very slight interest that Clare displays in Tess for quite a long time is well brought out. Yet there *is* interest, and Clare is not wholly indifferent to her. (pp. 54-5)

One of the best quotations to demonstrate the perpetual "fear" that Tess has of life is, I consider, to be found when she has a conversation with Clare, in the stage when there is a certain mutual interest between them. It depicts something of the inability of Tess to "beat" herself; something of an inherent weakness; something, again, of that suggestion that she is in reality but a pathetic puppet. It is not the things in life that terrify her but Life itself.

> "But you have indoor fears—eh?"
>
> "Well—yes, sir."
>
> "What of?"
>
> "I couldn't quite say."
>
> "The milk turning sour?"
>
> "No!"
>
> "Life in general?"
>
> "Yes, sir."

That is it, the worst of all fears—terror of something that cannot be defined. Perhaps really fear of oneself. Men and women do not fear actual concrete things in Life. What they do fear is that inevitable impulse which tells over and over again that they have no real power over themselves; no real and firm Faith; only a sensation of drifting, a hurtling down stream. Tess drifts; she is ever carried onward and onward against her will. Hardy again and again shows her to be afraid, yet never really that rather indefinable thing—a coward.

It is refreshing to be able to show Tess for one short period quite happy. That curious and delicious happiness when two people are gradually falling in love though nothing has been said on either side. (pp. 55-6)

Happiness, that warm glow, that tender emotion that sets every limb on fire; that love which draws another person so near that the contact is delicious pain, that is the happiness, that, loving Clare, Tess experiences. So wonderfully does Hardy write of it. That little bit of Tess's history that is not sadness. It is so pleasing to be able to record it.

> Tess had never in her recent life been so happy as she was now; possibly never would be so happy again. She was, for one thing, physically and mentally suited among these new surroundings.

And she had that happiness that for the moment—what mattered was the present. Again Hardy depicts Tess at her one real stage of unworrying bliss.

> Moreover, she, and Clare also, stood as yet on the debatable land between predilection and love; where no profundities have been reached; no reflections have set in; awkwardly inquiring, "Whither does this new current tend to carry me? What does it mean to my future? How does it stand towards my past?"

So quickly is the unworrying stage over; and we are faced with the unpleasant fact that our new-found indescribable happiness has its vicious perplexities.

The extraordinary magnetism of Clare is, in my opinion, a little inclined to be overstated. But if so, perhaps Hardy could scarcely avoid this, if the love of Tess for Clare was to be reasonable in the terrible lengths to which it was destined to go. I mean, in a word, Clare seems to be a little *made* but Tess is always flesh and blood. Clare is almost the instrument by which is shown the desperate passion of Tess. He is almost, if not quite, an auxiliary. But it is probably unfair to criticise, even a little sternly, Hardy on account of this. (pp. 57-8)

There is also a sad dilemma about the whole thing. Hardy seems to think Tess not worthy of Clare. No doubt a pious standpoint, but a little unimaginative!

> And the thorny crown of this sad conception was that she whom he really did prefer in a cursory way to the rest, she who knew herself to be more impassioned in nature, cleverer, more beautiful than they, was in the eyes of propriety, far less worthy of him than the homelier ones whom he ignored.

Thus Hardy is on the side, I fear, of dull propriety, but the lapse is merely temporary!

The whole attitude of Tess to Angel Clare is one that, as it were, completely turns her round. She is the ardent and insatiable seeker. Her feeling for Clare is one of reverence, amounting to something that can quite easily be interpreted as worship. Her great desire is that he shall call her by her name. It is one of those rather astonishing human touches of Hardy which are in charming contrast to his sombre and rather detached philosophy. For there is, I think, all through ***Tess of the D'Urbervilles*** a relative suggestion that Tess is something of an instrument through which Hardy can express his point of view. The marvellous genius of the whole thing is that Tess is so intensely human. (pp. 58-9)

If Tess is driven irresistibly to Clare—Clare is driven with just as irresistible an urge to Tess. Passion is the hardest thing in the world to avoid. A man may pray all the gods that he may have the strength not to see any more the woman he loves, but his prayer will be a mockery. For it will be a petition to the gods that his prayer may never be accepted literally. This irresistible urge is written with great force by Hardy when he shows Clare more and more under the spell of Tess.

> He was driven towards her by every heave of his pulse.

Driven. Is there any word that interprets Hardy's outlook more forcibly?

Towards the end of the history of Tess we get one or two of the saddest passages, perhaps, any great novelist has written. The one is when Clare finds that his love for Tess has all come back—come back when it is no longer any use. The other when Tess has to leave him for ever, for cruel men must take away to the bitter callousness of the law. I quote the two passages to show their exquisite pathos, the pain of them that hurts like a violent blow.

> "I do love you, Tess, I do—it is all come back," he said, tightening his arms round her with fervid pressure.

Too late—for Tess is a murderess, and so soon her neck will be violently pulled up from her body that her soul may go to see whether after all she was in the hands of a callous monster.

Those lines when Tess leaves Clare. No last dreadful dialogue between two lovers never to meet again has perhaps been more beautifully written than by Hardy.

> "What is it Angel?" she said, starting up. "Have they come for me?"
>
> "Yes, dearest," he said; "they have come."
>
> "It is as it should be," she murmured. "Angel, I am almost glad—yes, glad! This happiness could not have lasted. It was too much. I have had enough; and now I shall not live for you to despise me!"
>
> She stood up, shook herself, and went forward, neither of the men having moved.
>
> "I am ready," she said, quietly.

And so to the last dreadful paragraph in this great book. When Tess has gone and only her poor violently killed body is left that it may lie down with the earth and get a long quiet sleep.

> "Justice" was done, and the President of the Immortals, in Eschylean phrase, had ended his sport with Tess. And the D'Urberville knights and dames slept on in their tombs unknowing. The two speechless gazers bent themselves down to the earth, as if in prayer, and remained thus a long time, absolutely motionless; the flag continued to wave silently. As soon as they had strength they arose, joined hands again, and went on.

Thus we pass on our pilgrimage a little more sad, not only because Tess is dead, but because we are not sure that The President of the Immortals will not "sport" with us in the same way as the "sporting" with Tess. (pp. 60-2)

Patrick Braybrooke, in his Thomas Hardy and His Philosophy, *The C. W. Daniel Company, 1928, 167 p.*

DOROTHY VAN GHENT (essay date 1953)

[Van Ghent was an American educator and literary critic. In the following excerpt, she discusses the ways in which the earth functions as the central dramatic factor in Tess *and examines the fatalistic philosophies of the principal characters.]*

The dilemma of Tess is the dilemma of morally individualizing consciousness in its earthy mixture. The subject is mythological, for it places the human protagonist in dramatic relationship with the nonhuman and orients his destiny among preternatural powers. The most primitive antagonist of consciousness is, on the simplest premise, the earth itself. It acts so in ***Tess,*** clogging action and defying conscious motive; or, in the long dream of Talbothays, conspiring with its ancient sensuality to provoke instinct; or, on the farm at Flintcomb-Ash, demoralizing consciousness by its mere geological flintiness. But the earth is "natural," while, dramatically visualized as antagonist, it transcends the natural. The integrity of the myth thus depends, paradoxically, upon naturalism; and it is because of that intimate dependence between the natural and the mythological, a dependence that is organic to the subject, that Hardy's vision is able to impregnate so deeply and shape so unobtrusively the naturalistic particulars of the story.

In ***Tess,*** of all his novels, the earth is most actual as a dramatic factor—that is, as a factor of causation; and by this we refer simply to the long stretches of earth that have to be trudged in order that a person may get from one place to another, the slowness of the business, the irreducible reality of it (for one has only one's feet), its grimness of soul-wearying fatigue and shelterlessness and doubtful issue at the other end of the journey where nobody may be at home. One thinks, in immediate comparison, of Egdon Heath in ***The Return of the Native.*** Except for one instance—when Mrs. Yeobright has a far walk to Clym's cottage, and Clym, unforewarned, fails to meet her, and she turns away—the heath in ***The Return*** exists peripherally and gratuitously in relation to the action, on the one hand as the place where the action happens to happen (an action has to happen somewhere), and on the other, as a metaphor—a metaphorical reflection of the loneliness of human motive, of the inertia of unconscious life, of the mystery of the enfolding darkness; but it is not a dramatically causative agent and its particular quality is not *dramatically* necessary. . . . In ***Tess*** the earth is *primarily not a metaphor but a real thing* that one has to move on in order to get anywhere or do anything, and it constantly acts in its own motivating, causational substantiality by being there in the way of human purposes to encounter, to harass them, detour them, seduce them, defeat them.

In the accident of Prince's death, the road itself is, in a manner of speaking, responsible, merely by being the same road that the mail cart travels. The seduction of Tess is as closely related, causally, to the distance between Trantridge and Chaseborough as it is to Tess's naïveté and to Alec's egoism; the physical distance itself causes Tess's fatigue and provides Alec's opportunity. The insidiously demoralizing effect of Tess's desolate journeys on foot as she seeks dairy work and field work here and there after the collapse of her marriage, brutal months that are fore-shortened to the plodding trip over the chalk uplands to Flintcomb-Ash, is, again, as directly as anything, an effect of the irreducible *thereness* of the territory she has to cover. There are other fatal elements in her ineffectual trip from the farm to Emminster to see Clare's parents, but fatal above all is the distance she must walk to see people who can have no foreknowledge of her coming and who are not at home when she gets there. Finally, with the uprooting and migration of the Durbeyfield family on Old Lady Day, the simple fatality of the earth as earth, in its measurelessness and anonymousness, with people having to move over it with no place to go, is decisive in the final event of Tess's tragedy—her return to Alec, for Alec provides at least a place to go.

The dramatic motivation provided by natural earth is central to every aspect of the book. It controls the style: page by page ***Tess*** has a wrought density of texture that is fairly unique in Hardy; symbolic depth is communicated by the physical surface of things with unhampered transparency while the homeliest conviction of fact is preserved ("The upper half of each turnip had been eaten off by the live-stock"); and one is aware of style not as a specifically verbal quality but as a quality of observation and intuition that are here—very often—wonderfully identical with each other, a quality of lucidity. Again, it is because of the *actual* motivational impact of the earth that Hardy is able to use setting and atmosphere for a symbolism that, considered in itself, is so astonishingly blunt and rudimentary. The green vale of Blackmoor, fertile, small, enclosed by hills, lying under a blue haze—the vale of birth, the cradle of innocence. The wide misty setting of Talbothays dairy, "oozing fatness and warm ferments," where the "rush of juices could almost be heard below the hiss of fertilization"—the sensual dream, the lost Paradise. The starved uplands of Flintcomb-Ash, with their ironic mimicry of the organs of generation, "myriads of loose white flints in bulbous, cusped, and phallic shapes," and the dun consuming ruin of the swede field—the mockery of impotence, the exile. Finally, that immensely courageous use of setting, Stonehenge and the stone of sacrifice. Obvious as these symbolisms are, their deep stress is maintained by Hardy's naturalistic premise. The earth exists here as Final Cause, and its omnipresence affords constantly to Hardy the textures that excited his eye and care, but affords them wholly charged with dramatic, causational necessity; and the symbolic values of setting are constituted, in large part, by the responses required of the characters themselves in their relationship with the earth.

Generally, the narrative system of the book—that is, the system of episodes—is a series of accidents and coincidences (although it is important to note that the really great crises are psychologically motivated: Alec's seduction of Tess, Clare's rejection of her, and the murder). It is accident that Clare does not meet Tess at the May-walking, when she was "pure" and when he might have begun to court her; coincidence that the mail cart rams Tess's wagon and kills Prince; coincidence that Tess and Clare meet at Talbothays, *after* her "trouble" rather than before; accident that the letter slips under the rug; coincidence that Clare's parents are not at home when she comes to the vicarage; and so on. Superficially it would seem that this type of event, the accidental and coincidental, is the very least credible of fictional devices, particularly when there is an accumulation of them; and we have all read or heard criticism of Hardy for his excessive reliance upon coincidence in the management of his narratives; if his invention of probabilities and inevitabilities of action does not seem simply poverty-stricken, he appears to be too much the puppeteer working wires or strings to make events conform to his "pessimistic" and "fatalistic" ideas. It is not enough to say that there is a certain justification for his large use of the accidental in the fact that "life is like that"—chance, mishap, accident, events that affect our lives while they remain far beyond our control, are a very large part of experience; but art differs from life precisely by making order out of this disorder, by finding causation in it. In the accidentalism of Hardy's universe we can recognize the profound truth of the darkness in which life is cast, darkness both within the soul and without, only insofar as his accidentalism *is not itself accidental* nor yet an ideology-obsessed puppeteer's manipulation of character and event; which is to say, only insofar as the universe he creates has aesthetic integrity, the flesh and bones and organic development of a concrete world. This is not true always of even the best of Hardy's novels; but it is so generally true of the construction of ***Tess***—a novel in which the accidental is perhaps more preponderant than in any other Hardy—that we do not care to finick about incidental lapses. The naturalistic premise of the book—the condition of earth in which life is placed—is the most obvious, fundamental, and inexorable of facts; but because it is the physically "given," into which and beyond which there can be no penetration, it exists as mystery; it is thus, even as the basis of all natural manifestation, itself of the quality of the supernatural. On the earth, so conceived, coincidence and accident constitute order, the prime terrestrial order, for they too are "the given," impenetrable by human *ratio*, accountable only as mystery. By constructing the ***Tess***-universe on the solid ground (one might say even literally on the "ground") of the earth as Final Cause, mysterious cause of causes, Hardy does not allow us to forget that what is most concrete in experience is also what is most inscrutable. . . . The accidentalism and coincidentalism in the narrative pattern of the book stand, thus, in perfectly orderly correlation with the grounding mystery of the physically concrete and the natural.

But Hardy has, with very great cunning, reinforced the *necessity* of this particular kind of narrative pattern by giving to it the background of the folk instinctivism, folk fatalism, and folk magic. If the narrative is conducted largely by coincidence, the broad folk background rationalizes coincidence by constant recognition of the mysteriously "given" as what "was to be"—the folk's humble presumption of order in a rule of mishap. The folk are the earth's pseudopodia, another fauna; and because they are so deeply rooted in the elemental life of the earth—like a sensitive animal extension of the earth itself—they share the authority of the natural. (pp. 201-05)

We have said that the dilemma of Tess is the dilemma of moral consciousness in its intractable earthy mixture; schematically simplified, the signifying form of the ***Tess***-universe is the tragic heroism and tragic ineffectuality of such consciousness in an antagonistic earth where events shape themselves by accident rather than by moral design; and the *mythological* dimension of this form lies precisely in the earth's antagonism—for what is persistently antagonistic appears to have its own intentions, in this case mysterious, supernatural, for it is only thus that the earth can seem to have "intentions." The folk are the bridge between mere earth and moral individuality; of the earth as they are, separable conscious ego does not arise among them to weaken animal instinct and confuse response—it is the sports, the deracinated ones, like Tess and Clare and Alec, who are morally individualized and who are therefore able to suffer isolation, alienation, and abandonment, or to make others so suffer; the folk, while they remain folk, cannot be individually isolated, alienated, or lost, for they are amoral and their existence is colonial rather than personal. . . . Their fatalism is communal and ritual, an instinctive adaptation as accommodating to bad as to good weather, to misfortune as to luck, to birth as to death, a subjective economy by which emotion is subdued to the falling out of event and the destructiveness of resistance is avoided. In their fatalism lies their survival wisdom, as against the death direction of all moral deliberation. There is this wisdom in the cheerful compassion of the field-women for Tess in her time of trouble: the trouble "was to be." . . . It is in the folk code of secrecy—as in Dairyman Crick's story of the widow who married Jack Dollop, or in Joan's letter of advice to her daughter, summoning the witness of ladies the highest in the land who had had their "trouble" too but who had not told. Tess's tragedy turns on a secret revealed, that is, on the substitution in Tess of an individualizing morality for the folk instinct of concealment and anonymity. While their fatalism is a passive adaptation to the earthy doom, the folk magic is an active luxury; the human being, having a mind, however incongruous with his animal condition, has to do something with it—and if the butter will not come and someone is in love in the house, the coexistence of the two facts offers a mental exercise in causation . . . ; yet the magic is no less a survival wisdom than the fatalism, inasmuch as it does offer mental exercise in causation, for man cannot live without a sense of cause. The magic is a knowledgeable mode of dealing with the unknowledgeable, and it is adaptive to the dooms of existence where moral reason is not adaptive, for moral reason seeks congruence between human intention and effect and is therefore always inapropos (in Hardy's universe, tragically inapropos), whereas magic seeks only likenesses, correspondences, analogies, and these are everywhere. (pp. 205-07)

The folk magic is, after all, in its strategy of analogy, only a specialization and formalization of the novelist's use of the symbolism of natural detail, a symbolism of which we are constantly aware from beginning to end. Magical interpretation and prediction of events consist in seeing one event or thing as a "mimicry" of another—a present happening, for instance, as a mimicry of some future happening; that is, magic makes a system out of analogies, the correlative forms of things. Poets and novelists do likewise with their symbols. Burns's lines: "And my fause luver staw my rose, / But ah! he left the thorn wi' me," use this kind of mimicry, common to poetry and

"I would rather take it, sir, in my own hand." Illustration by E. Borough Johnson for the serialization of Tess *in the* Graphic, *July 25, 1891.*

magic. When a thorn of Alec's roses pricks Tess's chin, the occurrence is read as an omen—and omens properly belong to the field of magic; but the difference between this symbol which is an omen, and the very similar symbol in Burns's lines, which acts only reminiscently, is a difference merely of timing—the one "mimics" a seduction which occurs later, the other "mimics" a seduction and its consequences which have already occurred. . . . When a piece of blood-stained butcher paper flies up in the road as Tess enters the gate of the vicarage at Emminster, the occurrence is natural while it is ominous; it is realistically observed, as part of the "given," while it inculcates the magical point of view. Novelistic symbolism *is* magical strategy. In ***Tess,*** which is through and through symbolic, magic is not only an adaptive specialization of the "folk," but it also determines the reader's response to the most naturalistic detail. Thus, though the story is grounded deeply in a naturalistic premise, Hardy's use of one of the commonest tools of novelists—symbolism—enforces a magical view of life.

Logically accommodated by this view of life is the presentation of supernatural characters. Alec D'Urberville does not appear in his full otherworldly character until late in the book, in the episode of the planting fires, where we see him with pitchfork among flames—and even then the local realism of the planting fires is such as almost to absorb the ghostliness of the apparition. The usual form of his appearance is as a stage villain, complete with curled mustache, checked suit, and cane; and actually it seems a bit easier for the reader to accept him as the Evil Spirit itself, even with a pitchfork, than in his secular accouterments of the villain of melodrama. But Hardy's logic faces its conclusions with superb boldness, as it does in giving Angel Clare his name and his harp and making him a minister's son; if Alec is the Evil One, there will be something queer about his ordinary tastes, and the queerness is shown in his stagy clothes. . . . Alec is the smart aleck of the Book of Job, the one who goes to and fro in the earth and walks up and down in it, the perfectly deracinated one, with his flash and new money and faked name and aggressive ego. If he becomes a religious convert even temporarily it is because he is not really so very much different from Angel (the smart aleck of the Book of Job was also an angel), for extreme implies extreme, and both Angel and Alec are foundered in egoism, the one in idealistic egoism, the other in sensual egoism, and Angel himself is diabolic enough in his prudery. When Alec plays his last frivolous trick on Tess, lying down on one of the slabs in the D'Urberville vaults and springing up at her like an animated corpse, his neuroticism finally wears, not the stagy traditional externals of the Evil Spirit, but the deeply convincing character of insanity—of that human evil which is identifiable with madness. Both Angel and Alec are metaphors of extremes of human behavior, when the human has been cut off from community and has been individualized by intellectual education or by material wealth and traditionless independence.

Between the stridencies of Angel's egoism and Alec's egoism is Tess—with her Sixth Standard training and some anachronistic D'Urberville current in her blood that makes for spiritual exacerbation just as it makes her cheeks paler, "the teeth more regular, the red lips thinner than is usual in a country-bred girl": incapacitated for life by her moral idealism, capacious of life through her sensualism. When, after Alec's evilly absurd trick, she bends down to whisper at the opening of the vaults, "Why am I on the wrong side of this door?" her words construct all the hopelessness of her cultural impasse. But her stabbing of Alec is her heroic return through the "door" into the folk fold, the fold of nature and instinct, the anonymous community. If both Alec and Angel are spiritually impotent in their separate ways, Tess is finally creative by the only measure of creativeness that this particular novelistic universe holds, the measure of the instinctive and the natural. Her gesture is the traditional gesture of the revenge of instinct, by which she joins an innumerable company of folk heroines who stabbed and were hanged—the spectacular but still anonymous and common gesture of common circumstances and common responses, which we, as habitual readers of newspaper crime headlines, find, unthinkingly, so shocking to our delicate notions of what is "natural." That she goes, in her wandering at the end, to Stonehenge, is an inevitable symbolic going—as all going and doing are symbolic—for it is here that the earthiness of her state is best recognized, by the monoliths of Stonehenge, and that the human dignity of her last gesture has the most austere recognition, by the ritual sacrifices that have been made on these stones. (pp. 207-09)

Dorothy Van Ghent, "On 'Tess of the D'Urbervilles'," in her The English Novel: Form and Function, *Holt, Rinehart and Winston, 1953, pp. 195-209.*

RICHARD CARPENTER (essay date 1964)

[Carpenter is an American educator and literary critic who has written extensively on Thomas Hardy. In the following excerpt, he discusses the ways in which Tess *functions as a critique of conventional Victorian morality and examines the symbolic and mythic structure of the novel.]*

Although its "message" is comprised in dramatic situations rather than in tractarian statement, ***Tess of the D'Ubervilles*** is a frontal attack on some of the bastions of Victorian *mores,* and was recognized as such. In addition, Hardy emphasized his point by subtitling his novel *A Pure Woman Faithfully Presented,* thus virtually guaranteeing a storm of protest. For Tess is not only once but twice fallen from the point of view of Victorian respectabilities. No matter that she is subjected to intolerable pressure: she has been seduced; she has borne an illegitimate child; she has married, been deserted by her husband, and lived with her seducer. Even Henry James thought that such a novel was "vile" [see excerpt dated 1893]. Hardy drew blood when he tried to write a serious story about a basic moral issue.

Hardy did not intend his novel to be a social tract, but he did want to treat social problems in a mature way. In doing so, he did not confine himself only to the question of moral standards but also considered the effect on ordinary people of economic instability and social climbing. Tess's father initiates the tragic course his daughter pursues by his illusion that he is a somebody because his ancestors were noble Normans.. A chain of circumstance is linked together from this notion, the most important link being Tess's going to her "kinfolk," the d'Urbervilles (who are actually *nouveaux riches*) for help. The constant need for steady income to support the family later takes Tess far away from home, and turns her into an itinerant farm laborer, thus setting the stage for the reappearance of Alec. Part of Hardy's social criticism is thus aimed at the agricultural situation in which poor people lacked even a modicum of security and were subject to any chill economic wind that might blow along. Moreover, the pernicious idea that the members of the "better classes" were really better than the simple country folk is subjected to sharp analysis. Tess is by far the most admirable person in the novel, and the two men in her life—both presumably above her in the social scale—

are shown as the victims of false ideas of human interrelationships coming from their background. Not only Tess's father labors under the illusion that social classes have some intrinsic value in them. . . , but Alec thinks he can play the *seigneur* to the peasant girl and Angel believes that there is some mystic purity native to the maid of lower classes, necessary to her desirability. Both of these are destructive notions because they replace individual human values with false concepts about society. As Hardy had done in such widely differing novels as ***The Hand of Ethelberta*** and ***The Woodlanders***, he demonstrated in ***Tess*** the problems that arise from social prejudices and illusions.

Hardy also includes in his social critique his usual theme of the invasion of the pastoral world by alien forces, here symbolized by the threshing machine, that "buzzing red glutton" with its tender "a creature from Tophet, who had strayed into the pellucid smokelessness of this region of yellow grain and pale soil," a throbbing mechanical monster on which Tess works her heart out. But more pervasive, and evidently more striking because so many readers have been impressed by it, is the metaphysical theme which is, in ***Tess of the D'Urbervilles***, more patent than in any previous novel. Hardy shows Tess the helpless victim not only of society but also of principalities and powers for which no human agency can be held responsible. We saw in ***The Mayor of Casterbridge*** and in ***The Return of the Native*** that these powers might provide situations which character could then exploit, but in ***Tess*** they operate without regard to character. Hardy unwisely puts into Tess's mouth early in the novel the portentous remark that we live in a "blighted world," and throughout his novel he seems determined to prove the point. (pp.126-28)

When all is said and done, however, the *quality* of the novel comes from its characters and setting rather than its more conspicuous themes. Tess is outstanding among Hardy's heroines because she is the only *good* woman who has the role of a protagonist. She has none of the caprice and egotism of a Eustacia or a Sue Bridehead; she is instead the ideal ingenue—Tamsin Yeobright, Marty South—brought centerstage. Unlike these others, however, she is more vitally alive; specifically, she is more female, more sexual, more passionate. In combination with her innocence, her gentleness, and her worshipful loyalty, this sexuality makes her indeed a memorable character. It is as if the voluptuousness of the luxurious Felice had been purified and combined with the virtue of the guileless Tamsin. Tess is also better educated and more intelligent than the ingenues of the earlier novels; and she has greater moral and physical endurance than any of Hardy's other heroines. Most notable of all is what we might somewhat lamely call her genuineness. She has the straightforward sincerity, the natural simplicity of those who live close to nature. No tiresome paragon of virtue, she also has a dash of recklessness in her character (coming, Hardy implies, from her knightly Norman ancestors) that enables her at long last to turn on her tormentor and slay him. Like the peasantry from which she comes, Tess knows nothing of deceit; like Billy Budd, she can only strike out when its evil is fully revealed to her. Beautiful with a full-bodied femininity, staunch in character, passionate in emotion, Tess is Hardy's vision of an ideal woman.

In contrast to her are the two men in her life, who lack not only her genuineness but also her simplicity and passion. Alec d'Urberville is the less interesting of these men, but he has unexpected qualities which come out in the course of the novel. In the beginning he is the typical seducer of melodrama, with his flashy clothes, high-stepping horses, his bold and roving eye, and his "badly moulded" mouth. Only a bit less theatrical than Manston of ***Desperate Remedies*** or William Dare of ***A Laodicean***, Alec acts his stereotyped role so mechanically that we almost feel like hissing him when he strokes his mustache and calls Tess, "My Beauty.". . . Yet there is something in Alec which goes beyond the mere stock seducer, for he does seem torn between his better and his worser selves, and his yielding to the latter indicates the strength of Tess's appeal. (pp.128-30)

Angel Clare is similarly a man who is pulled in different directions by conflicting motives, and he is in some ways the most interesting character in the novel—not the most imaginative creation nor yet the most profound personality, but the most intriguing because of his problems. Angel is as obsessed with the idea of "feminine purity" as any of his namesakes might be, but he is at the same time a rationalistic skeptic lacking in compasssion and tolerance. This ambivalence is compounded by his desirc to break free of his social and religious background, to strike out on his own intellectually and economically. This desire is not, however, strong enough to withstand his early conditioning. When Tess confesses her past to him, he is too blinded by his prejudices to see the reality before him—her fundamental purity and innocence; instead he allows himself to be controlled by his barren notions.

Yet Angel has a genuine love for Tess which lies beneath his conscious self. In one of Hardy's most bizarre scenes Angel walks in his sleep a few nights after the confession and carries Tess across the Froom River to place her in a stone coffin, obviously the act of love and despair. Although contrived (and often censured), this scene is powerfully imaginative in its grotesque distortion of the ordinary, and prepares the reader for Angel's eventual realization of his true feeling for Tess. Like his successor, Jude, Angel is a more "modern" character than other Hardy men; for he has ambiguous and contradictory motives—some overt, others so hidden under layers of ideas that they can come out only at night. His waverings, his rationalizations, his sophistries, his naïve self-deceptions, and his neurotic self-torments ally him to such figures as Stephen Dedalus and Quentin Compson rather than to the typical Victorian hero. Both the sleepwalking and the intensity with which he reacts to Tess's confession may well indicate a hidden sense of sexual guilt, as the emphasis on feminine "purity" usually indicates an obsession with sexuality as something to be feared.

Angel is notably inconsistent, too. He is later tempted to take Liz Huett with him to Brazil as his mistress because he feels cynical about women and would be "revenged on society." The irony of such a double standard, as well as its patent falsity, Angel cannot perceive. He complains about the social ordinances of marriage as restrictive, when his own concept of "purity" in his wife binds him more securely than the law. Not self-destructive like Henchard, Angel is similarly self-alienated; in this respect he is also like Clym and Jude. Except for Jude he is the most complex and contradictory of Hardy's men.

Angel and Tess first meet at Talbothays Dairy, where she has gone to work after the death of Sorrow, her baby. Talbothays is certainly one of Hardy's supreme accomplishments in setting, a superbly realized place and a rich, complex symbol at the same time. It is of the essence pastoral, with its red and white cows, its verdant "water-meads," and its immemorial rhythms of milking, skimming, and churning. Hardy shows it to us through its most fertile seasons of spring and summer, establishing an equation between its serenity and the restoration to Tess of an interest in life after her harrowing experiences. For Talbothays is a means of stressing the integral relationship between man and nature which Hardy so often presents. This setting is, within the properly respectable limits of Victorian fiction, about as much a Dionysia as one could expect. The passions of men and women are not only stimulated by the burgeoning fecundity of nature but are a reflection of it. . . . To mix a figure, it is a pagan paradise where Angel, for instance, experiences an "aesthetic, sensuous, pagan pleasure in natural life and lush womanhood," a land so fecund that it is described in an erotic imagery which should have outraged Hardy's audience if it had been alert to the implications of such comparisons: "The season developed and matured. . . . Rays from the sunrise drew forth the buds and stretched them into long stalks, lifted up sap in noiseless streams, opened petals, and sucked out scents in invisible jets and breathings.". . . If the reader of today did not know that this was Hardy, he might momentarily think it was D. H. Lawrence; for it celebrates the life-giving powers of sex in a similar fashion.

The Talbothays setting, as Hardy indicates, is both mirror and lamp, for it brings about a corresponding sexuality in the characters. Angel, returning to the farm after a journey to his home, finds Tess just awakened from an afternoon nap, "the brimfulness of her nature breath[ing] from her." When she stretches her arm above her head, he can see "its satin delicacy above the sunburn. . . . It was a moment when a woman's soul is more incarnate than at any other time; when the most spiritual beauty bespeaks itself flesh; and sex takes the outside place in the presentation." . . . The sun shines in the window "upon her inclining face, upon the blue veins of her temple, upon her naked arm, and her neck, and into the depths of her hair." Angel clasps her close to him; and, while she will not at first look up, "her eyes soon lifted, and his plumbed the deepness of the ever-varying pupils, with their radiating fibrils of blue, and black, and gray, and violet, while she regarded him as Eve at her second waking might have regarded Adam." . . . (pp. 130-32)

A paradise like Talbothays might reasonably be expected to have within it an Adam and Eve, as Hardy implies in the above episode, and perhaps a Satan lurking in the outer darkness. Indeed it is so, although Hardy gives us less an allegory than a complex of symbolic suggestions. Tess is more clearly a kind of Eve than Angel is an Adam. In her innocence and simplicity, as well as in her worship of him as a "godlike" being; in her naturalness and passion; and in her fall from innocence into the knowledge of good and evil, she is closer to the primordial mother of men than Angel is to the first man. Angel is too much the intellectual and skeptic to fulfill the role of Adam, although Hardy twice refers to him in this way. His name indicates better the ambiguities of his position, for it is partly fitting and partly ironic. He is a rather saintly man who knows little of the real world, but he is also rather inhuman. If angels are not only better than men morally but also superior in their understanding and compassion for erring humanity, Angel is somewhat wide of the mark. It takes much suffering to humanize his "angelic" character and to bring him back to Tess to share in the last unhappy days. Prior to this conversion, his role in paradise, while not overtly destructive like Alec's at Flintcomb-Ash, is damaging enough. A splendid scene in which Angel strums a secondhand harp in the weedy garden at Talbothays most effectively symbolizes the part he is to play in this paradise. As Tess listens to the "thin notes," she is fascinated and draws near to him through the fringe of the garden, which "uncultivated for some years . . . was now damp and rank with juicy grass which sent up mists of pollen at a touch; and with tall blooming weeds emitting offensive smells." Stealthily approaching, Tess gathers "cuckoospittle on her skirts," steps on snails, and gets stains on her arms and hands from "thistle-milk and slug-slime" and from the "sticky blights" of trees. Quite plainly these images imply the corrupting influence on Tess's life of this angel in an unweeded Eden; the physical stains and blights are symbolic of the spiritual stains and blights which will eventuate from her contact with him. It certainly was a bold imaginative stroke on Hardy's part to convey his meaning by having a man named "Angel" play a harp in a garden.

The Devil does not appear in the paradisal Talbothays, but he certainly shows up later on. After the marriage of Tess and Angel, the confession, and the desertion, Tess goes to Flintcomb-Ash, the "starve-acre" farm where she labors like a serf. When Alec appears, she is at the end of her strength and hope, so that his temptation effectively takes advantage of her woman's weakness. Significantly enough, Alec is in the guise of an evangelist, for who can quote Scripture better for his own ends than the Devil? Later, Hardy makes the allusion more specific, having Alec pop up out of an atmosphere of smoke and fire, disguised as a laborer, when Tess is burning grass at Marlott. Alec's joke—"a jester might say that this is just like Paradise. You are Eve and I am the old Other One, come to tempt you in the disguise of an inferior animal"—is perfectly apropos. . . . (pp. 132-34)

Not only is Alec's pursuit of Tess symbolic of the temptation of Eve but it also is more broadly related to the entire complex of scapegoat myths in which an innocent victim becomes the sacrifice for the sins of society. (p. 134)

These overtones are given strength by the movement of the latter part of the novel. When Tess goes from Talbothays to Flintcomb-Ash, with its sterile name and its winter weather, she journeys not only across the landscape but also moves in the direction of her fated sacrifice. The triumph of winter over the fecundity of Talbothays is the prophetic triumph of death over Tess's life; the dominance of the threshing machine is the triumph of mechanism over the vital qualities represented by life close to nature. . . . [She] becomes ever more clearly the victim of the world's inexorable vengeance, the archetypal scapegoat. (p. 135)

When she and Angel finally leave their temporary hiding place at Bramshurst, after she kills Alec, they proceed aimlessly across the countryside in a naïve attempt to escape, and come at night to Stonehenge, which at first they do not recognize. Hardy derives full advantage from this magnificent setting for the climax of his tragedy: the wind playing upon the huge pillars, "like the notes of some gigantic one-stringed harp"; the look and feel of the great stones against the night sky; the associations with the immense past, for as Angel says, it is a heathen temple, "older than the centuries; older than the d'Urbervilles." Tess asks him if the heathens sacrificed to God in this place, and he replies that he thinks they sacrificed to the sun. But that they did sacrifice and that Tess is the modern equivalent of those barbaric ceremonial victims are only too clear. She sleeps on one of the stones; and, when morning comes, so do the police. . . . Tess is allowed to wake naturally; seeing the police she says, "'It is almost as it should be'," because the happiness of the last few days with Angel could not have lasted. "She stood up, shook herself, and went forward, neither of the men having moved. 'I am ready,' she said quietly." . . . (pp. 135-36)

Without a doubt this is one of the most moving scenes Hardy ever wrote, and it shows him at the peak of his talent. The blending of symbol and reality, the mythic meaning combined with the human meaning, the superbly realized description of action and setting match anything in the English novel. Here the folktale of the ruined maid takes on the aspect of universal tragedy. Whatever faults ***Tess of the D'Urbervilles*** may have—and they are no doubt many—they are redeemed in this scene at Stonehenge.

The novel is, however, not entirely done with myth at this point, for the painful scene at the denouement when Angel and Tess's sister Liza-Lu leave the prison just before Tess's execution brings to our attention a theme of rebirth. It would be too grim, even for Hardy, to have his beautiful heroine sacrificed entirely in vain. We are thus allowed to feel that through her husband and her sister, who is significantly described as a "spiritualized image of Tess," there will eventually come about a new order of life. As the two leave Wintoncester, "the drooping of their heads is that of Giotto's 'Two Apostles'"; and, with this plain implication of their task, Hardy tells us that Tess will, in a way, live on.

Myth is, of course, not the rich body of the tale, but rather its soul or spirit. ***Tess of the D'Urbervilles*** is a fine novel from the realistic point of view as well as from the symbolic (although too narrow a construction of that realism has often left critics unable to cope with its symbolism). There is more than a little humor in the illusions of Tess's drunken father with his notions about his social status; in the breathless infatuation of the dairymaids for Angel . . . ; and in the character of Angel's brothers. A subordinate theme of much interest is involved in the question of inheritance in all three of the major characters, especially as it affects Tess through the "decay" of ancient families. Hardy even implies some warped kind of retribution when Alec seduces, or rapes, Tess as her "mailed ancestors rollicking home from a fray" may have "dealt the same measure even more ruthlessly towards peasant girls of their time." . . . He does qualify this idea with some objections to its validity as a principle, but throughout the novel he harps on the idea of heredity and its influence on Tess's life. The novel also emphasizes the effect of abstract concepts on conduct, both with Angel and his family, basically good and tolerant people whose natural feelings are overlaid with the incrustations of a narrow theology. Mr. Clare is a character who demonstrates clearly Hardy's idea that life-denying ideas, no matter how ethical, are destructive.

Social realism of this sort is not, however, what gives the novel its power. The myth does that. When the letter which Tess has written telling Angel about her past slips under the carpet so that he does not see it before the marriage, we know that Chance has made its mystic and malign influence felt once again. We feel, as Frederick Karl puts it, that Hardy is using Chance as his "weapon to strike through surface reality to areas where the poetry of man offers resistance to the drab starkness of a malevolent universe. When the shaft of the mailcart runs poor old Prince through the breast and his life spills out through the hole in his chest, and when the blood-red motif haunts us through the rest of the novel, from the thorns scratching Tess's chin from Alec's roses, to the texts in vermilion letters that tell Tess her "damnation slumbereth not," to the scarlet of the threshing machine, to Alec's blood on the ceiling—when Hardy so boldly uses this symbolism, we know that we are reading a great mythopoeic writer. The ineluctable sense of the earth over which men move and on which they act out their fates is ever before us, from the pearly moonlight of The Chase where Tess becomes a symbol of fallen humanity, to lush Talbothays and stony Flintcomb-Ash, and finally to Stonehenge itself. Hardy wrote in ***Tess of the D'Urbervilles*** one of the finest novels of the nineteenth century because he lifted the story of a wronged peasant girl into the realm of tragedy through his use of these universal qualities; it became not only the tale of Tess Durbeyfield but also the story of wronged and suffering humanity. ***The Mayor of Casterbridge*** is more austere, ***The Return of the Native*** more passionate, but ***Tess*** remains Hardy's most moving dramatization of a pure soul struggling with the inscrutable evils of existence. (pp. 136-38)

Richard Carpenter, in his Thomas Hardy, *Twayne Publishers, Inc., 1964, 223 p.*

IRVING HOWE (essay date 1967)

[A longtime editor of the leftist magazine Dissent *and a regular contributor to* The New Republic, *Howe is one of America's most highly respected literary critics and social historians. He has been a socialist since the 1930s, and his criticism is frequently informed by a liberal social viewpoint. Howe is widely praised for what F. R. Dulles has termed his "knowledgeable understanding, critical acumen and forthright candor." Howe has written: "My work has fallen into two fields: social history and literary criticism. I have tried to strike a balance between the social and the literary; to fructify one with the other; yet not to confuse one with the other. Though I believe in the social approach to literature, it seems to me peculiarly open to misuse; it requires particular delicacy and care." In the following excerpt, Howe discusses Hardy's understanding of women and his portrayal of the character of Tess.]*

As a writer of novels Thomas Hardy was endowed with a precious gift: he liked women. There are not, when one comes to think of it, quite so many other nineteenth century novelists about whom as much can be said. (p. 108)

Throughout his years as a novelist Hardy found steadily interesting the conceits and playfulness of women, the elaborate complex of strategems in which the sexual relationship appears both as struggle and game. He liked the changefulness, sometimes even the caprice, of feminine personality; he marveled at the seemingly innate capacity of young girls to glide into easy adaptations and tactical charms. And he had a strong appreciation of the manipulative and malicious powers that might be gathered beneath a surface of delight. Except perhaps with Sue Bridehead, he was seldom inclined to plunge into the analytic depths which mark the treatment of feminine character in George Eliot's later novels; but if he did not look as deeply as she did into the motivations of feminine character, he was remarkably keen at apprehending feminine behavior. (pp. 108-09)

Throughout Hardy's fiction, even in his lesser novels, there is a curious power of sexual insinuation, almost as if he were not locked into the limits of masculine perception but could shuttle between, or for moments yoke together, the responses of the two sexes. . . . And at the deepest level of his imagination, Hardy held to a vision of the feminine that was thoroughly traditional in celebrating the maternal, the protective, the fecund, the tender, the life-giving. It was Hardy's openness to the feminine principle that drew D. H. Lawrence to his work and led him to see there, with some justice, a kinship with his own. One may speculate that precisely those psychological elements which led Hardy to be so indulgent toward male passivity also enabled him to be so receptive to feminine devices. He understood and could portray aggression; but at least as a writer, he did not allow it to dominate or corrode his feelings about the other sex—and that, incidentally, is one reason he does not care to pass judgment on his characters. The feminine admixture is very strong in his work, a source both of his sly humor and his profound sympathy.

It is in ***Tess of the D'Urbervilles*** that this side of Hardy comes through with the most striking vitality. The book stands at the center of Hardy's achievement, if not at his greatest then certainly his most characteristic, and those readers or critics who cannot accept its emotional ripeness must admit that for them Hardy is not a significant novelist. For in ***Tess*** he stakes everything on his sensuous apprehension of a young woman's life, a girl who is at once a simple milkmaid and an archetype of feminine strength. Nothing finally matters in the novel nearly so much as Tess herself: not the other characters, not the philosophic underlay, not the social setting. In her violation, neglect and endurance, Tess comes to seem Hardy's most radical claim for the redemptive power of suffering; she stands, both in the economy of the book and as a figure rising beyond its pages and into common memory, for the unconditional authority of feeling.

Tess is one of the greatest examples we have in English literature of how a writer can take hold of a cultural stereotype and, through the sheer intensity of his affection, pare and purify it into something that is morally ennobling. Tess derives from Hardy's involvement with and reaction against the Victorian cult of chastity, which from the beginning of his career he had known to be corrupted by meanness and hysteria. She falls. She violates the standards and conventions of her day. And yet, in her incomparable vibrancy and lovingness, she comes to represent a spiritualized transcendence of chastity. She dies three times, to live again:—first with Alec D'Urberville, then with Angel Clare, and lastly with Alec again. Absolute victim of her wretched circumstances, she is ultimately beyond their stain. She embodies a feeling for the inviolability of the person, as it brings the absolute of chastity nearer to the warming Christian virtue of charity. Through a dialectic of negation, Tess reaches purity of spirit even as she fails to satisfy the standards of the world.

Perhaps because she fails to satisfy them? Not quite. What we have here is not the spiritual sensationalism of the Dostoevsky who now and again indulges himself in the notion that a surrender to licentiousness is a necessary condition for spiritual rebirth. Hardy's view is a more innocent one, both purer and less worldly. He does not seek the abyss nor glory in finding it. He is not a phenomenologist of the perverse. But as a man deeply schooled in the sheer difficulty of life, he does recognize that there is a morality of being as well as of doing, an imperative to compassion which weakens the grip of judgment. Once educated to humility, we do not care to judge Tess at all: we no longer feel ourselves qualified. And that, I think, is a triumph of the moral imagination.

In staking out these claims for ***Tess of the D'Urbervilles*** I recognize that Hardy's vision of Tess can hardly satisfy the rigorous morality of Protestantism which was a part of his heritage. Other forces are at work, both pre- and post-Christian: the stoicism of the folk ballad, from whose wronged heroines Tess descends, and the moral experiment of romanticism. Hardy could no more avoid the conditioning influence of romanticism than a serious writer can now avoid that of modernism; it was part of the air he breathed. (pp. 109-11)

There are, to be sure, instances of self-indulgent writing in this novel which can be described as late-romantic, even decadent, but the controlling perception of Tess is restrained and, if one cares to use such terms, "healthy." Tess demands nothing that can be regarded as the consequence of deracination or an overwrought will; she is not gratuitously restless or neurotically bored; she is spontaneously committed to the most fundamental needs of human existence. Indeed, she provides a standard of what is right and essential for human beings to demand from life. And because we respond to her radiant wholeness, Tess stands somewhat apart from, nor can she be seriously damaged by, the romantic excesses into which Hardy's writing can lapse. Tess is finally one of the great images of human possibility, conceived in the chaste, and chastening, spirit of the New Testament. Very few proclaimed believers have written with so complete a Christian sentiment as the agnostic Thomas Hardy.

Simply as a work of fiction, ***Tess of the D'Urbervilles*** is singularly direct in its demands. It contains few of the elements we have come to know and expect in nineteenth century novels. There is little interplay of character as registered through nuances of social manners or the frictions of social class. None of the secondary figures has much interest in his own right, apart from his capacity to illuminate and enlarge the experience of Tess; all of them seem, by Hardy's evident choice, to be dwarfed beside her. The passages of philosophic comment . . . surely do not provide a center of concern for the serious modern reader. And while the social setting—a setting that, in its several parts, forms a history of rural England leveled in space—comes to be quite essential for the development of the action, finally it is not to the world in which Tess moves, nor even the world Tess may symbolize, that we yield our deepest assent.

As for the plot, it seems in isolation a paltry thing, a mere scraping together of bits and pieces from popular melodrama: a pure girl betrayed, a woman's secret to be told or hidden, a piling on of woes that must strain the resources of ordinary credence. Whether Hardy was deliberately employing the threadbare stuff of melodrama in order to transcend it, or whether he shared in the emotional premises of such fiction but through his peculiar genius unconsciously raised it to the level of abiding art (as Dickens repeatedly did), is very hard to say. Perhaps, in the case of a writer like Hardy, it is a distinction without much difference.

There is just enough plot loosely to thread together the several episodes that comprise the book, yet surely it is not here that one looks for Hardy's achievement. ***Tess of the D'Urbervilles*** can, in fact, profitably be regarded as a fiction in the line of *Pilgrim's Progress* rather than in the line of Jane Austen's and George Eliot's novels, for its structure is that of a journey in which each place of rest becomes a test for the soul and the function of plot is largely to serve as an agency for transporting the central figure from one point to another. ***Tess*** is clearly not an allegory and no one in his senses would wish that it were, but its pattern of narrative has something in common with, even if it does not directly draw upon, Bunyan's fiction. There are four sections or panels of representation: Tess at home and with Alec; Tess at Talbothays and with Angel; Tess at Flintcomb-Ash and again with Alec; Tess briefly happy with Angel and then in her concluding apotheosis at Stonehenge. None of these panels is quite self-sufficient, since narrative tension accumulates from part to part; but each has a distinctiveness of place, action and tone which makes it profitable to think of the novel as episodic. One is reminded of a medieval painting divided into panels, each telling part of a story and forming a progress in martyrdom. The martyrdom is that of Tess, upon whom everything rests and all value depends. (pp. 111-13)

What matters in ***Tess of the D'Urbervilles,*** what pulses most strongly and gains our deepest imaginative complicity, is the figure of Tess herself. Tess as she is, a woman made real through the craft of art, and not Tess as she represents an idea. Marvelously high-spirited and resilient, Tess embodies a moral poise beyond the reach of most morality. Tess is that rare creature in literature: goodness made interesting. She is human life stretched and racked, yet forever springing back to renewal. And what must never be forgotten in thinking about her, as in reading the book it never can be: she is a woman. For Hardy she embodies the qualities of affection and trust, the powers of survival and suffering, which a woman can bring to the human enterprise. The novel may have a strong element of the pessimistic and the painful, but Tess herself is energy and joy, a life neither foolishly primitive or feebly sophisticated. Though subjected to endless indignities, assaults and defeats, Tess remains a figure of harmony—between her self and her role, between her nature and her culture. Hardy presents her neither from the outside nor the inside exclusively, neither through event nor analysis alone; she is apprehended in her organic completeness, so that her objectivity and subjectivity become inseparable. A victim of civilization, she is also a gift of civilization. She comes to seem for us the potential of what life could be, just as what happens to her signifies what life too often becomes. She is Hardy's greatest tribute to the possibilities of human existence, for Tess is one of the greatest triumphs of civilization: a natural girl.

Simply as a fictional character, she is endlessly various. She can flirt, she can listen, she can sympathize, she can work with her hands. Except when it is mocked or thwarted, she is superbly at ease with her sexuality. In no way an intellectual, she has a clear sense of how to reject whatever fanatic or pious nonsense comes her way. After pleading with the vicar to give a Christian burial to her illegitimate child, she answers his refusal with the cry: "Then I don't like you! and I'll never come to your church no more!" A mere instance of feminine illogic? Not at all; for what Tess is saying is that a man so seemingly heartless deserves neither human affection nor religious respect. And she is right. Her womanly softness does not keep her from clear judgments, and even toward her beloved Angel she can sometimes be blunt. "It is in you, what you are angry at, Angel, it is not in me," she pointedly tells him when he announces that he cannot accept her. The letter she sends Angel during the Flintcomb-Ash ordeal is a marvelous expression of human need: "The daylight has nothing to show me, since you are not here . . ." At least twice in the book Tess seems to Hardy and the surrounding characters larger than life, but in all such instances it is not to make her a goddess or a metaphor, it is to underscore her embattled womanliness.

The secondary figures in the book have useful parts to play, but finally they are little more than accessories, whose task is not so much to draw attention in their own right as to heighten the reality of Tess. Only one "character" is almost as important as Tess, and that is Hardy himself. Through his musing voice, he makes his presence steadily felt. He hovers and watches over Tess, like a stricken father. He is as tender to Tess as Tess is to the world. Tender; and helpless. That the imagined place of Wessex, like the real places we inhabit, proves to be inadequate to a woman like Tess—this, if message there must be, is the message of the book. The clash between sterile denial and vital existence occurs repeatedly, in a wide range of episodes, yet through none of them can Hardy protect his heroine. And that, I think, is the full force of his darkness of vision: how little can be done for Tess.

If we see Hardy's relation to Tess in this way, we can be a good deal more patient with the passages of intermittent philosophizing that dot the book. These passages are not merely inert bits of intellectual flotsam marring a powerful narrative. They are evidence of Hardy's concern, tokens of his bafflement before the agony of the world. At best, if not always, the characters in ***Tess*** are not illustrations or symbols of a philosophic system; at best, if not always, the philosophic reflections comprise a gesture in response to the experience of the characters. It is Hardy ruminating upon the destruction of youth and hope—and if we thus see Hardy's role in his narrative, we can grasp fully the overwhelming force of the lines from Shakespeare with which he prefaces the book: "*. . . Poor wounded name! My bosom as a bed / Shall lodge thee.*" It is her only rest. (pp. 130-32)

Irving Howe, in his Thomas Hardy, *The Macmillan Company, 1967, 206 p.*

TONY TANNER (essay date 1968)

[Tanner is an English educator and critic specializing in British and American literature. In the following excerpt, he discusses the significance of the imagery in Tess.*]*

Every great writer has his own kind of legibility, his own way of turning life into a language of particular saliences, and in Hardy this legibility is of a singularly stark order. If we can think of a novelist as creating, among other things, a particular linguistic world by a series of selective intensifications of our shared vocabulary, then we can say that Hardy's world is unusually easy to read. The key words in his dialect, to continue the image, stand out like braille. It is as though some impersonal process of erosion had worn away much of the dense circumstantial texture of his tales, revealing the basic resistant contours of a sequence of events which Hardy only has to point to to make us see—like ancient marks on a barren landscape. And Hardy above all does make us see. . . . When he says in his introduction to ***Tess of the D'Urbervilles*** that 'a novel is an impression, not an argument', . . . we should give full stress to the idea of something seen but not tampered with, something scrupulously watched in its otherness, something perceived but not made over. Hardy's famous, or notorious, philosophic broodings and asides are part of his reactions as a watcher, but they never give the impression of violating the people and objects of which his tale is composed. Reflection and perception are kept separate (in Lawrence they often tend to merge), and those who complain about the turgidity of his thoughts may be overlooking the incomparable clarity of his eyes. (p. 219)

For all Henry James's scrupulous indirectness, Hardy's art is more truly impersonal. He goes in for graphic crudities of effect which James would have scorned, yet, as other critics have testified, the result is an anonymity which we more commonly associate with folk-tale, or the ballads. By graphic crudity of effect I am referring, for instance, to such moments as when Tess, shortly after being seduced, encounters a man who is writing in large letters 'THY, DAMNATION, SLUMBERETH, NOT.' There are commas between every word 'as if to give pause while that word was driven well home to the reader's heart.' This is not unlike Hardy's own art which is full of prominent notations, and emphatic pauses which temporarily isolate, and thus vivify, key incidents and objects. . . . [A] 'crudity' is discernible in the characterisation which is extremely schematic, lacking in all the minute mysteries of individual uniqueness which a writer like James pursued. *Angel* Clare is indeed utterly ethereal; his love is 'more spiritual than animal'. He even plays the harp! On the other hand Alec d'Urberville is almost a stage villain with his 'swarthy complexion . . . full lips . . . well-groomed black moustache with curled points', his cigars and his rakish way with his fast spring-cart. If we turn from character to plot sequence we see at once that the overall architecture of the novel is blocked out with massive simplicity in a series of balancing phases—The Maiden, Maiden No More; the Rally, The Consequence; and so on. Let it be conceded at once that Hardy's art is not subtle in the way that James and many subsequent writers are subtle. Nevertheless I think it is clear that Hardy derives his great power from that very 'crudity' which, in its impersonal indifference to plausibility and rational cause and effect, enhances the visibility of the most basic lineaments of the tale.

I want first to concentrate on one series of examples which show how this manifest visibility works. For an artist as visually sensitive as Hardy, colour is of the first importance and significance, and there is one colour which literally catches the eye, and is meant to catch it, throughout the book. This colour is red, the colour of blood, which is associated with Tess from first to last. It dogs her, disturbs her, destroys her. She is full of it, she spills it, she loses it. Watching Tess's life we begin to see that her destiny is nothing more or less than the colour red. The first time we (and Angel) see Tess, in the May dance with the other girls, she stands out. How? They are all in white except that Tess 'wore a red ribbon in her hair, and was the only one of the white company who would boast of such a pronounced adornment'. Tess is marked, even from the happy valley of her birth and childhood. The others are a semianonymous mass; Tess already has that heightened legibility, that eye-taking prominence which suggests that she has in some mysterious way been singled out. And the red stands out because it is on a pure white background. In that simple scene and colour contrast is the embryo of the whole book and all that happens in it.

This patterning of red and white is often visible in the background of the book. For instance 'The ripe hue of the red and dun kine absorbed the evening sunlight, which the white-coated animals returned to the eye in rays almost dazzling, even at the distant elevation on which she stood.' This dark red and dazzling white is something seen, it is something there; it is an effect on the retina, it is a configuration of matter. In looking at this landscape Tess in fact is seeing the elemental mixture which conditions her own existence. In the second chapter Tess is described as 'a mere vessel of emotion untinctured by experience.' The use of the word 'untinctured' may at first seem surprising; we perhaps tend to think of people being shaped by experience rather than coloured by it—yet the use of a word connected with dye and paint is clearly intentional. In her youth Tess is often referred to as a 'white shape'—almost more as a colour value in a landscape than a human being. And on the night of her rape she is seen as a 'white muslin figure' sleeping on a pile of dead leaves; her 'beautiful feminine tissue' is described as 'practically blank as snow'. The historic precedent for what is to happen to this vulnerable white shape is given at the start when we read that 'the Vale was known in former times as the Forest of White Hart, from a curious legend of King Henry III's reign, in which the killing by a certain Thomas de le Lynd of a beautiful white hart which the king had run down and spared, was made the occasion of a heavy fine,' Against all social injunctions, white harts are brought down. And in Tess's case the 'tincturing'—already prefigured in the red ribbon—starts very early.

The next omen—for even that harmless ribbon is an omen in this world—occurs when Tess drives the hives to market when her father is too drunk to do the job. When she sets out the road is still in darkness. Tess drifts, sleeps, dreams. Then there is the sudden collision and she wakes to find that Prince, their horse, has been killed by another cart. 'The pointed shaft of the cart had entered the breast of the unhappy Prince like a sword, and from the wound his life's blood was spouting in a stream and falling with a hiss on the road. In her despair Tess sprang forward and put her hand upon the hole, with the only result that she became splashed from face to skirt with the crimson drops. . . . On one level the death of the horse means that the family is destitute, which means in turn that Tess will have to go begging to the d'Urbervilles. Thus, it is part of a rough cause and effect economic sequence. But far more graphic, more disturbing and memorable, is the image of the sleeping girl on the darkened road, brutally awakened and desperately trying to staunch a fatal puncture, trying to stop the blood which cannot be stopped and only getting drenched in its powerful spurts. It adumbrates the loss of her virginity, for she, too, will be brutally pierced on a darkened road far from home; and once the blood of her innocence has been released, she too, like the stoical Prince, will stay upright as long as she can until, all blood being out, she will sink down suddenly in a heap. Compressed in that one imponderable scene we can see her whole life.

After this Tess is constantly encountering the colour red—if not literal blood, manifold reminders of it. When she approaches the d'Urberville house we read: 'It was of recent erection—indeed almost new—and of the same rich red colour that formed such a contrast with the evergreens of the lodge.' And the corner of the house 'rose like a geranium bloom against the subdued colours around.' Tess, with her red ribbon, also stood out against 'the subdued colours around'. Mysteriously, inevitably, this house will play a part in her destiny. And if this red house contains her future rapist, so it is another red house which contains her final executioner, for the prison where she is hanged is 'a large red-brick building'. Red marks the houses of sex and death. When first she has to approach the leering, smoking Alec d'Urberville, he forces roses and strawberries on her, pushing a strawberry into her mouth, pressing the roses into her bosom. Hardy, deliberately adding to the legibility I am describing, comments that d'Urberville is one 'who stood fair to be the blood-red ray in the spectrum of her young life'. On the evening of the rape, Tess is first aware of d'Urberville's presence at the dance when she sees 'the red coal of a cigar'. This is too clearly phallic to need comment, but it is worth pointing out that, from the first, d'Urberville seems to have the power of reducing Tess to a sort of trance-like state, he envelopes her in a 'blue narcotic haze' of which his cigar smoke is the most visible emblem. . . . It is in a brilliant continuation of this blurred narcotic atmosphere that Hardy has the rape take place in a dense fog, while Tess is in a deep sleep. Consciousness and perception are alike engulfed and obliterated. When Tess first leaves d'Urberville's house she suddenly wakes up to find that she is covered in roses; while removing them a thorn from a remaining rose pricks her chin. 'Like all the cottagers in Blackmoor Vale, Tess was steeped in fancies and prefigurative superstitions; she thought this an ill omen.' The world of the book is indeed a world of omens (*not* symbols) in which things and events echo and connect in patterns deeper than lines of rational cause and effect. Tess takes it as an omen when she starts to bleed from the last rose pressed on her by Alec. She is right; for later on she will again wake up to find that he has drawn blood—in a way which determines her subsequent existence.

After the rape we are still constantly seeing the colour red. The man who writes up the words promising damnation is carrying 'a tin pot of red paint in his hand'. As a result 'these vermilion words shone forth'. . . . We will later see Tess virtually trapped and tortured on a piece of red machinery, and her way will take her past several crosses until she finds her own particular sacrificial place. When Tess is working in the fields her flesh again reveals its vulnerability. 'A bit of her naked arm is visible between the buff leather of the gauntlet and the sleeve of her gown; and as the day wears on its feminine smoothness becomes scarified by the stubble, and bleeds.' Notice the shift to the present tense: Hardy makes us look at the actual surfaces—the leather, the sleeve, the flesh, the blood. One of the great strengths of Hardy is that he knew, and makes us realise, just how very much the surfaces of things mean.

Of course it is part of the whole meaning of the book that there is as much red inside Tess as outside her. Both the men who seek to possess her see it. When Tess defies d'Urberville early on, she speaks up at him, 'revealing the red and ivory of her mouth'; while when Angel watches her unawares, 'she was yawning, and he saw the red interior of her mouth as if it had been a snake's'. When Angel does just kiss her arm, and he kisses the inside vein, we read that she was such a 'sheaf of susceptibilities' that 'her blood (was) driven to her finger ends'. Tess does not so much act as re-act. She would be content to be passive, but something is always disturbing her blood, and all but helplessly she submits to the momentums of nature in which, by her very constitution, she is necessarily involved. (pp. 220-24)

The end of the book is sufficiently well known, but it is worth pointing out how Hardy continues to bring the colour red in front of our eyes. The landlady who peeps through the keyhole during Tess's anguish when Angel has returned reports that, 'her lips were bleeding from the clench of her teeth upon them'. It is the landlady who sees 'the oblong white ceiling, with this scarlet blot in the midst', which is at once the evidence of the murder and the completion of a life which also started with a red patch on a white background, only then it was simply a ribbon on a dress. The blood stain on the ceiling has 'the appearance of a gigantic ace of hearts'. In that shape of the heart, sex and death are merged in utmost legibility. After this we hardly need to see the hanging. It is enough that we see Tess climb into a vast bed with 'crimson damask hangings', not indeed in a home, for she has no home, but in an empty house to be 'Let Furnished'. And in that great crimson closed-in bed she finds what she has wanted for so long—rest and peace. Apart from the last scene at Stonehenge, we can say that at this point the crimson curtains do indeed fall on Tess; for if she was all white at birth, she is to be all red at death. The massed and linking red omens have finally closed in on Tess and her wanderings are over.

Tess is a 'pure woman' as the subtitle, which caused such outrage, specifically says. The purest woman contains tides of blood (Tess is always blushing), and if the rising of blood is sexual passion and the spilling of blood is death, then we can see that the purest woman is sexual and mortal. Remember Tess watching Prince bleed to death—'the hole in his chest looking scarcely large enough to have let out all that animated him'. It is not a large hole that Alec makes in Tess when he rapes her, but from then on the blood is bound to go on flowing until that initial violation will finally 'let out all that animated her'. Hardy is dealing here with the simplest and deepest of matters. Life starts in sex and ends in death, and Hardy constantly shows how closely allied the two forms of blood-letting are in one basic, unalterable rhythm of existence.

I have suggested that the destiny of Tess comes to us as a cumulation of visible omens. It is also a convergence of omens and to explain what I mean I want to add a few comments on the part played in her life by the sun, altars and tombs, and finally walking and travelling. When we first see Tess with the other dancing girls we read that they are all bathed in sunshine. Hardy, ever conscious of effects of light, describes how their hair reflects various colours in the sunlight. More, 'as each and all of them were warmed without by the sun, so each of them had a private little sun for her soul to bask in'. They are creatures of the sun, warmed and nourished by the source of all heat and life. Tess starts sun-blessed. At the dairy, the sun is at its most active as a cause of the fertile surgings which animate all nature. 'Rays from the sunrise drew forth the buds and stretched them into stalks, lifted up sap in noiseless streams, opened petals, and sucked out scents in invisible jets and breathings'. This is the profoundly sensuous atmosphere in which Tess, despite mental hesitations, blooms into full female ripeness. Hardy does something very suggestive here in his treatment of the times of day. Tess and Angel rise very early, before the sun. They seem to themselves 'the first persons up of all the world'. The light is still 'half-compounded, aqueous', as though the business of creating animated forms has not yet begun. They are compared to Adam and Eve. As so often when Tess is getting involved with the superior power of a man, the atmosphere is misty, but this time it is cold mist, the sunless fogs which precede the dawn. In this particular light of a cool watery whiteness, Tess appears to Angel as 'a visionary essence of woman', something ghostly, 'merely a soul at large'. He calls her, among other things, Artemis (who lived, of course, in perpetual celebacy). In this sunless light Tess appears to Angel as unsexed, sexless, the sort of non-physical spiritualised essence he, in his impotent spirituality, wants. (At the end he marries 'a spiritualized image of Tess'). But Tess is inescapably flesh and blood. (pp. 226-27)

Tess drifts into marriage with Angel (her most characteristic way of moving in a landscape is a 'quiescent glide'), because 'every wave of her blood . . . was a voice that joined with nature in revolt against her scrupulousness', but meanwhile 'at half-past six the sun settled down upon the levels, with the aspect of a great forge in the heavens'. This suggests not a drawing-up into growth, but a slow inexorable downward crushing force, through an image linked to that machinery which will later pummel her body. It is as though the universe turns metallic against Tess, just as we read when Angel rejects her that there is in him a hard negating force 'like a vein of metal in a soft loam'. This is the metal which her soft flesh runs up against. Other omens follow on her journey towards her wedding. Her feeling that she has seen the d'Urberville coach before; the postillion who takes them to church and who has 'a permanent running wound on the outside of his right leg'; the ominous 'afternoon crow' and so on. I want to point to another omen, when the sun seems to single out Tess in a sinister way. It is worth reminding ourselves that when Angel finally does propose to Tess she is quite sun-drenched. They are standing on the 'redbrick' floor and the sun slants in 'upon her inclining face, upon the blue veins of her temple, upon her naked arm, and her neck, and into the depths of her hair'. Now, on what should be the first night of her honeymoon we read: 'The sun was so low on that short, last afternoon of the year that it shone in through a small opening and formed a golden staff which stretched across to her skirt, where it made a spot like a paint-mark set upon her'. She has been marked before—first, with the blood of a dying beast, now with a mark from the setting sun. We find other descriptions of how the sun shines on Tess subsequently, but let us return to that crimson bed which, I suggested, effectively marked the end of Tess's journey. 'A shaft of dazzling sunlight glanced into the room, revealing heavy, old-fashioned furniture, crimson damask hangings, and an enormous four-poster bedstead. . . '. The sun and the redness which have marked Tess's life, now converge at the moment of her approaching death. Finally Tess takes her last rest on the altar of Stonehedge. She speaks to Angel—again, it is before dawn, that sunless part of the day when he can communicate with her.

'"Did they sacrifice to God here?" asked she.

"No", said he.

"Who to?"

"I believe to the sun. That lofty stone set away by itself is in the direction of the sun, which will presently rise behind it."' When the sun does rise it also reveals the policemen closing in, for it is society which demands a specific revenge upon Tess. But in the configuration of omens which, I think, is the major part of the book, Tess is indeed a victim, sacrificed to the sun. The heathen temple is fitting, since of course Tess is descended from Pagan d'Urberville, and Hardy makes no scruple about asserting that women 'retain in their souls far more of the Pagan fantasy of their remote forefathers than of the systematized religion taught their race at a later date'. This raises an important point. Is Tess a victim of society, or of nature? Who wants her blood, who is after her, the policemen, or the sun? Or are they in some sadistic conspiracy so that we see nature and society converging on Tess to destroy her? (pp. 227-29)

We see Tess suffering, apparently doomed to suffer; destroyed by two men, by society, by the sun outside her and the blood inside her. And we are tempted to ask, what is Hardy's vision of the *cause* of this tale of suffering. Throughout the book Hardy stresses that Tess is damned, and damns herself, according to man-made laws which are as arbitrary as they are cruel. He goes out of his way to show how Nature seems to disdain, ignore or make mockery of the laws which social beings impose on themselves. The fetish of chastity is a ludicrous aberration in a world which teems and spills with such promiscuous and far-flung fertility every year (not to say a brutal caricature of human justice in that what was damned in the woman was condoned in the man). So, if the book was an attempt to show an innocent girl who is destroyed by society though justified by Nature, Hardy could certainly have left the opposition as direct and as simple as that. Social laws hang Tess; and Nature admits no such laws. But it is an important part of the book that we feel Nature itself turning against Tess, so that we register something approaching a sadism of *both* the man-made *and* the natural directed against her. If she is tortured by the man-made threshing machine, she is also crushed by the forge of the sun; the cold negating metal in Angel is also to be found in the 'steely stars'; the pangs of guilt which lacerate her are matched by the 'glass splinters' of rain which penetrate her at Flintcomb-Ash. Perhaps to understand this feeling of almost universal opposition which grows throughout the book, we should turn to some of Hardy's own words, when he talks of 'the universal harshness . . . the harshness of the position towards the temperament, of the means towards the aims, of today towards yesterday, of hereafter towards today'. When he meditates on the imminent disappearance of the d'Urberville family he says, 'so does Time ruthlessly destroy his own romances'. This suggests a universe of radical opposition, working to destroy what it works to create, crushing to death what it coaxes into life. From this point of view society only appears as a functioning part of a larger process whereby the vertical returns to the horizontal, motion lapses into stillness and structures cedes to the unstructured. The policemen appear as the sun rises: Tess is a sacrifice to both, to all of them. Hardy's vision is tragic and penetrates far deeper than specific social anomalies. One is more inclined to think of Sophocles than, say, Zola, when reading Hardy. The vision is tragic because he shows an ordering of existence in which nature turns against itself, in which the sun blasts what it blesses, in which all the hopeful explorations of life turn out to have been a circuitous peregrination towards death. (pp. 236-37)

Tess is the living demonstration of these tragic ironies. That is why she who is raped lives to be hanged; why she who is so physically beautiful feels guilt at 'inhabiting the fleshly tabernacle with which Nature had endowed her'; why she who is a fertile source of life comes to feel that 'birth itself was an ordeal of degrading personal compulsion, whose gratuitousness nothing in the result seemed to justify'. It is why she attracts the incompatible forces represented by Alec and Angel. It is why she who is a lover is also a killer. Tess is gradually crucified on the oppugnant ironies of circumstance and existence itself, ironies which centre, I have suggested, on the fact of blood, that basic stuff which starts the human spot moving across the white vacuity. Blood, and the spilling of blood; which in one set of circumstances can mean sexual passion and the creation of life, and in another can mean murderous passion and death—two forms of 'red' energy intimately related—this is the substance of Tess's story. And why should it all happen to her? You can say, as some people in the book say fatalistically, "It was to be". Or you could go through the book and try to work out how Hardy apportions the blame—a bit on Tess, a bit on society, a bit on religion, a bit on heredity, a bit on the Industrial Revolution, a bit on the men who abuse her, a bit on the sun and the stars, and so on. But Hardy does not work in this way. More than make us judge, Hardy makes us see; and in looking for some explanation of why all this should happen to Tess, our eyes finally settle on that red ribbon marking out the little girl in the white dress, which already foreshadows the red blood stain on the white ceiling. In her beginning is her end. It is the oldest of truths, but it takes a great writer to make us experience it again in all its awesome mystery. (p. 237)

Tony Tanner, "Colour and Movement in Hardy's 'Tess of the d'Urbervilles'," in Critical Quarterly, *Vol. 10, No. 3, Autumn, 1968, pp. 219-39.*

MICHAEL MILLGATE (essay date 1971)

[Millgate is an English-born educator and critic specializing in English and American literature and the author of the most complete biography of Hardy to date. In the following excerpt, he examines the interrelationships of character, heredity, and environment with destiny in Tess.*]*

Tess, it has often been pointed out, is not a psychological novel in the sense understood and practised by George Eliot and Henry James. It does offer, however, a continuous and remarkably precise record of Tess's mental condition, and a sharp if less developed sense of the thoughts and feelings of other characters, at least at the moment when their lives impinge most nearly upon Tess's own career. This perception of internal states is only partly achieved by direct analysis, or even by the dramatised revelations of dialogue. More important and more powerful than either of these is the externalisation of emotional states in terms of the particular colouring given to the accounts of the places Tess inhabits, the work she does, the people she encounters, the treatment she receives, the natural and climatic conditions she experiences. The emotional is evoked and recorded in terms of the sensory. The constant disturbance of the narrative surface reflects the intensity of Tess's own internal life.

Ian Gregor, in a fine essay on ***Tess,*** speaks of the way in which "at every stage of the tale interior states are visualized in terms of landscape" [see *TCLC,* Vol. 4]. Irving Howe has more recently compared the novel to *Pilgrim's Progress* in that its structure is "that of a journey in which each place of rest becomes a test for the soul and the function of plot is largely to serve as an agency for transporting the central figure from one point to another" [see excerpt dated 1967]. Both insights are relevant: the chief locations of the novel serve both as testing places for Tess and as expressions of her states of mind. Even the names of places—Marlott, the Valley of the Great Dairies, Flintcomb Ash—seem freighted with significances both experiential and moral. Alec d'Urberville's home, "The Slopes", is aggressively modern and bright: "Everything looked like money—like the last coin issued from the Mint." . . . It is clear from the maps he drew that Hardy was extremely conscious of the journeying aspects of Tess's career, and not only do possible allusions to *Pilgrim's Progress* occur in the course of the novel—Dairyman Crick's wife is called Christiana, for example, the Trantridge villagers on their visit to the fair and market at Chaseborough are referred to as "pilgrims" . . . but a pattern of pilgrimage seems to govern the book as a whole. As in *Pilgrim's Progress* the physical experience of walking through the countryside is very faithfully evoked, and like Christian (or Christiana) Tess encounters and reencounters many other pedestrians who both relate immediately to her and yet possess a more generalised significance: the text-painter, the man who knows of her Trantridge past, the changeable shape of Alec d'Urberville himself.

Tess's tragedy is that her pilgrimage has no possible goal. It is true that some of the profuse paradisal imagery creates a sense of Tess herself as an earthly paradise capable of surviving the discovery of the tree of knowledge, and such a feeling certainly pervades the Talbothays chapters and the heavily charged and almost magical atmosphere of the days spent with Angel in the empty house. Yet despite that eventual satisfaction of the "appetite for joy" . . . and the sacrificial apotheosis at Stonehenge, Tess's terrestrial journey ends on the scaffold, and in the final pages images from *Pilgrim's Progress* blend with others from *Paradise Lost* as Angel and Liza-Lu emerge "through a narrow barred wicket" . . . and set off, with bowed heads and joined hands, as if on a fresh attempt to arrive at the Celestial City. ***Tess*** is not allegory. Its allusions, like its philosophical formulations, are unlikely to carry relevance for more than their immediate context. At the same time, the allegorical landscape of Bunyan's work and its population of moral types seem not impossibly remote from symbolic landscapes such as those of Talbothays, Flintcomb Ash, and Stonehenge, or from characters called Mercy Chant, Sorrow, and Angel Clare—"who but Hardy," asks Dorothy Van Ghent [see excerpt dated 1953], "would have dared to give him the name Angel, and a harp too?"

As in *Pilgrim's Progress* so in ***Tess,*** the significance embodied in places and in people emerges all the more powerfully and believably from their location within a concretely realised fictional world. Indeed, the richness and sheer solidity of Hardy's creation both of this rural setting and of Tess's situation—her controlling environment of work and social victimisation, of agricultural economics and the English class system—enables him to venture upon further expressionistic techniques. Despite the heavy rurality of her surname (Durbeyfield) and the deliberately "pastoral" Christian names (John and Joan) of her parents, Tess's immediate family situation is fairly consistently presented in realistic terms, with a conscientious concern for the actual conditions of rural life and for the precise quality of the human relationships involved: the character and attitudes of Joan Durbeyfield, for example, are developed with some amplitude and given an important role in the novel as a whole. But Hardy does not hesitate to exaggerate the characterisation of the members of Angel Clare's family circle, while Alec d'Urberville and his mother are often treated with a degree of caricature which verges on the grotesque. To some extent such distortion may image Tess's own view of people and manners previously outside her experience, and there is also the obvious element of contrast between those examples of emotional rigidity . . . and the atmosphere of uncritical acceptance which pervades Tess's own background. But the Durbeyfield household—in its casual irresponsibility and general fecklessness a doubtful representative of "the agricultural community"—is itself portrayed in highly critical terms, and one aspect of the novel is clearly its concern with the failure of human relationships within all the family groups and with the repeated efforts of Tess herself to create and sustain a basic family unit of a more viable kind. In view of Tess's remarks shortly before her capture, the closing description of Angel hand in hand with Liza-Lu can be seen as representing her final gesture, and perhaps achievement, in this direction.

When Tess is living with Alec, at Trantridge and Sandbourne, the emphasis is on luxurious artificiality: the villa at Sandbourne . . . bears a striking resemblance to the white Mediterranean villa with which Rochester tries to tempt Jane Eyre to a similar surrender. Tess's marriage with Angel, on the other hand, is associated with sterility and unnaturalness. The honeymoon becomes funereal, the mistletoe bough withers unused, the symbols of domesticity lose all their positive force. . . . If Tess is trapped by the fatalities of her heredity and environment, she is equally caught between the contrasted personalities of the two men—both superior to her in class, wealth, and education—who dominate her life. If Alec now and then suggests the unchastened Rochester, Angel sometimes echoes the principled inhumanity of St John Rivers—though it is Alec, ironically enough, during the period of his conversion, who begs Tess to become his partner in a missionary enterprise, while Angel permits himself to make a brutally frank proposal to Izz Huett. Hardy probably did not have *Jane Eyre* specifically in mind, but the double inversion of role for Alec and Angel is deliberate enough, constituting one element in a pattern of opposition which runs throughout the novel.

The basic norms from which Alec and Angel thus momentarily depart can perhaps be crudely identified in terms of the polar

The threshing scene. Illustration by Hubert Herkomer for the serialization of Tess *in the* Graphic, *December 5, 1891.*

opposites of ''Paganism'' and ''Paulinism'' which Hardy invokes in his description of Alec's conversion. . . . Alec adopts Paulinism for a while, but his basic creed is closer to ''animalism.'' Angel affects to have revolted against the Paulinism of his temperament and upbringing, but at the crisis of his relationship with Tess he proves to be still its slave. Soon after Tess's revelation to Angel she is presented as a personification of ''Apostolic Charity'' who ''sought not her own; was not provoked; thought no evil of his treatment of her.'' . . . The ironic allusion is to St Paul's own words in the thirteenth chapter of the first epistle to the Corinthians, and Hardy may well have intended to prompt recollection of the famous opening verse of that chapter: ''Though I speak with the tongues of men and angels, and have not charity, I am become as sounding brass, or a tinkling cymbal.'' It is Angel himself—quoting the first epistle to Timothy . . .—who first invokes the word ''charity'' just before the exchange of confessions with Tess . . . , yet in practice he proves to be, even in a conventional sense, much less charitable than Alec himself, who does at least take pains to improve the material circumstances of Tess and her family.

Angel's rigidity and lack of charity constitute the terrible flaw in a man who seems—if only because Tess loves him with such unquestioning fervency—to possess unusual potentialities for goodness and right action. Little enough can be expected of Alec after his first introduction as the typical villian of melodrama, and in some ways he turns out better than anticipated. Angel, for all his obvious superiority to Alec, does even greater damage to Tess, and it is made clear—from the emphasis on his resolute and unnatural resistance to Tess's beauty—that he could have done with a little of Alec's unreflecting animality. . . . If Alec sacrifices Tess to his lust, Angel sacrifices her to his theory of womanly purity. The one obeys a natural law, the other a social law, and Hardy has no hesitation in assigning to the latter the greater blame. Angel is saved from utter condemnation by the quasi-redemptive effect of his own sufferings in Brazil and by the transforming power of Tess's love during their brief period of ecstasy, made magical by Tess's serenity and by their strange suspension within a kind of social and moral vacuum, itself directly symbolised by the empty house. Even at this point in the novel, however, when the moral Angel has abandoned himself to the power of Tess's love and will—despite the knowledge that she is now adultress and murderer as well as maiden seduced—he still cannot free himself from dogma: when Tess urges him to marry Liza-Lu, he can only object that she is his sister-in-law; when Tess, like Hester Prynne in *The Scarlet Letter,* begs to be allowed to hope for the reunion of lovers after death, he, like Dimmesdale, remains silent. Angel's humanity fails him in these passages, and it receives a proper rebuke in those final words of Tess herself which reveal a love so profound as to comprehend a clear-sighted recognition of the beloved's inadequacies and of what must inevitably have followed a descent from magical suspension into social actuality:

> 'What is it, Angel?' she said, starting up. 'Have they come for me?'
>
> 'Yes, dearest,' he said. 'They have come.'
>
> 'It is as it should be,' she murmured. 'Angel, I am almost glad—yes, glad! This happiness

> could not have lasted. It was too much. I have had enough; and now I shall not live for you to despise me!'
>
> (pp. 272-77)

Alec and Angel between them leave Tess so devastated in mind and spirit that Angel, returning "too late" to find her installed in the lodging house as Alec's mistress, realises "that his original Tess had spiritually ceased to recognize the body before him as hers—allowing it to drift, like a corpse upon the current, in a direction dissociated from its living will." . . . The moment has been prepared for by Tess's earlier talk of separating soul from body. Coming at this point in the novel it serves as a moving image of Tess's whole tragedy—the recalcitrance of circumstance to the most refined aspirations of the human spirit, the most passionate imperatives of the human emotions. Against the coarse animalism of Alec and the sterile intellectualism of Angel—alike inhumane, life-denying, destructive of the individual—Tess can muster only the forces of that generous and spontaneous "naturalism" so richly evoked in the harvest episode and elsewhere. She can offer, in fact, only the passive defence which comes from sheer instinctual resilience, a quality akin to that "endurance" which Faulkner attributed to his rural poor.

There are many aspects of ***Tess*** which seem to look forward to Faulkner, and particularly to what Cleanth Brooks has described as the nature poetry of *The Hamlet:* the idyllic aspects of Ike's love for the cow, for example, might well have been suggested by the lush summer evocation of Angel's courtship of Tess in the meadows near Talbothays dairy. Faulkner also resembles Hardy in his readiness to exploit literary and legendary allusions for local rather than structural purposes, and in his capacity to retain, even during the most ecstatic merging of natural description with emotional fervour, a firm grasp on actuality, on the irreducible conditions of rural existence. In Lawrence—whose debt to Hardy and especially to ***Tess*** he himself was only the first to remark—there is a tendency for the world of tangible objects to become progressively swept away by the rising emotional tide: in the scene in *The Rainbow* in which Will and Anna stook the sheaves of wheat the rhythm of their work becomes, is absorbed wholly into, the rhythm of their sexual passion. In Hardy, as in Faulkner, the merging never becomes quite so complete. His novels constitute a kind of peaceable kingdom of the imagination, capable of accommodating as discrete yet interconnected elements both the emotion and the natural or climatic phenomenon which prompts or reflects it, the emblem and the concrete presentation, the narrative quirk and the thread of the thematic pattern. His method is not to blend together the disparate constituents of the fiction but to leave them—individual, identifiable—in permanent suspension. If there is incongruity, Hardy himself is not disturbed by it. He takes, indeed, a curious satisfaction in touches of the macabre, in inversions of situation or role, in life's little ironies. In ***Tess,*** because the unity of the work radiates so strongly from the profoundly apprehended and powerfully created central figure, and from a richly evoked sense of the Wessex world in which she moves, the fictional structure can accommodate an extraordinary diversity of narrative and descriptive modes, from the theatrical to the poetic, without danger of fragmentation.

This technique of multiple juxtaposition produces unusual richness of texture. It also permits Hardy to establish a pattern of constant reverberation to and fro within the world of the novel. This is not merely a question of "prefigurations" such as the death of Prince and Tess's pricked chin, or of early thematic statements—such as Parson Tringham's "our impulses are too strong for our judgment sometimes" . . . whose full force is only appreciated at a later stage. It is rather a method of constantly recalling crucial moments of the action in such a way as to keep those moments alive in the reader's mind. The sight of Tess on the altar at Stonehenge looks back to Alec on the d'Urberville tomb and beyond that to Angel laying Tess in the abbot's tomb. Angel finding Tess in her dressing-gown at Sandbourne recalls the time, equally rich in sexual overtones, when he returned to Talbothays to meet her descending fresh from sleep. The recollection twists the knife of regret, of what might have been. Moments of prefiguration become, at a later stage in the narrative, points for retrospective reference, heightening the emotional intensity of each successive crisis, keeping the past continuously alive for the reader as it is always so cruelly alive for Tess herself. (pp. 277-79)

Tess may be essentially the victim, and we may from an early stage feel that she is doomed, if only because of what myths and ballads and melodramas have taught us to anticipate as the life pattern of seduced country maidens. But Hardy makes clear that Tess herself has choices to make, even though they can only lead her into worse difficulties. She is not entirely helpless in the grip of a mechanistic universe, and a less passive, more self-confident character might have found avenues of escape not discovered by Tess herself. In handling the question of Tess's ultimate responsibility for her most decisive acts—the sexual surrender to Alec, the failure to confess to Angel, the second surrender to Alec, the murder—Hardy achieves an entirely valid ambiguity. He nowhere suggests that Tess is *right* to do these things, and he metes out to her, in terms of mental suffering and the final legalised execution, punishment enough to satisfy the sternest moralist. Yet his compassionate presentation of Tess makes it impossible to make attribution of responsibility co-extensive with assignment of blame, especially since the avoidance of analysis in favour of dramatic and expressionistic techniques forces the reader to an extraordinary degree of participation in Tess's career.

With a restraint that is eloquent of artistic maturity, Hardy does not present the actual moments of surrender or crisis: the seduction on the Chase, the subsequent period of co-habitation, the telling of her story to Angel, the murder at "The Herons". Faulkner once said of *The Sound and the Fury* that it seemed more "passionate" not to present his heroine directly; in ***Tess*** the important elements in Tess's crises are precisely the pressures she experiences, and once we see these as irresistible we need see no more. It is, in this respect, a marvellous touch of Hardy's to present the murder as if through the uninvolved, commonplace eyes of Mrs Brooks, the Sandbourne landlady, and in terms which suggest a lurid newspaper report, or evidence given at Tess's trial. Tess's career, so Hardy seems to insist, can be made to fit many stereotypes, from ballad maiden-no-more and melodrama victim-heroine to "the woman" in a sordid domestic "tragedy"; yet she evades all such restrictive social classifications to emerge at the end of the novel as a figure at once representative and individual whose evident sexuality in no way compromises that triumphant purity which Hardy's sub-title so properly, if polemically, asserts. (pp. 279-80)

Michael Millgate, in his Thomas Hardy: His Career As a Novelist, *Random House, 1971, 428 p.*

GEOFFREY WAGNER (essay date 1972)

[In the following excerpt, Wagner examines Tess *from a feminist perspective and discusses the ways in which Tess's sexuality and*

individuality are in conflict with the Victorian social order and so contribute to her destruction.]

Hardy asks—What is love? In ***Tess of the D'Urbervilles,*** his thirteenth novel in order of composition and possibly his first in emotional commitment, we have the heroine as victim, 'a visionary essence of woman—a whole sex condensed into one typical form.' She is perhaps the most firmly fleshed-out person in these pages, as also the most fully sexed. What is more, Hardy takes pains to present her as both a living, breathing, individual woman and one trying hard to defer to the models in her culture. In short, she exemplifies what one feminist has defined as modern woman's true tragedy—'the sad thing for women is that they have participated in the destruction of their own eroticism'.

It is important to be clear about Hardy's intentions here from the start. For his own reticences, compounded with those of his time, sometimes obscure—certainly for the contemporary student steeped in libertine literature—what shimmers through the imagery, in a manner in which of course it does in life. Tess liked sex. (pp. 183-84)

[Between] Phase The First ('The Maiden') and Phase The Second ('Maiden No More,' explicitly enough) there is an interval or lacuna during which Tess must be conceived as having been carried away by her sexual side, to which she obviously yielded with a degree of pleasure. Alec's initiation into sex—bully though he is—was not, in short, wholly unpleasant. She was, in Hardy's words, 'stirred to confused surrender awhile . . . ', and, in her own to Alec, 'My eyes were dazed by you for a little, and that was all.' (pp. 184-85)

We must establish all this securely at the start since it influences so much later on. The structural response comes in the pivotal confession scene with Angel, whom Tess realizes she could at this point win over by the wiles of sex yet refrains from so doing, sensing that (in a shame-culture for women) seduction can be no solution—'she might have used it promisingly', we read here, 'it' being 'her exceptional physical nature'. Hence Tess hates herself for her initial weakness, really a little rape when we compare its similarity with that of the dying pheasants later on when she again sleeps outside. So at the very beginning of her destiny she turns with flashing eyes on Alec to cry, 'My God! I could knock you out of the gig! Did it never strike your mind that what every woman says some women may feel?' (p. 185)

As with *Jane Eyre,* an initial (anti-familial) breach with convention starts out others. In Tess's case, of course, for she is surely one of the most charming heroines in literature, this breach of convention is based on obeisance to another. For if it had not been for her father's egregious infatuation with aristocracy, Tess would never have been urged forward by her mother in the first place (pimped by her maternal parent would be the less polite, if more accurate, term). Flatteringly described as 'foolish', her mother blames her oldest daughter for not having got Alec to marry her, later chides her again for telling Angel the truth about the resulting bastard ('christened' Sorrow, in book form), and can still round on her at the end for not having practised general sexual deception as a life principle—'O, Tess, what's the use of your playing at marrying gentlemen, if it leaves us like this!'

Finally, the 'maternal' Joan Durbeyfield is responsible for pressuring Tess to marry Angel, and so sets in train the eventual tragedy. In fact, Hardy's ironies can become a shade heavy-handed in these contexts, at least for modern taste, as when he has Alec d'Urberville, who has watched Tess tortured by treadmill-like labour on the steam thresher all day long, tell her—the woman he himself had seduced—'You have been the cause of my backsliding.'

But a novel, as Hardy wrote in a Preface to this one, is 'an impression, not an argument'. (pp. 186-87)

[Hardy] was not writing the conventional nineteenth-century novel, what Ford called the 'nurvole', as his contemporary critics appear to have been anticipating. He was writing for and on behalf of women and made, for his society, the ultimate trespass of what he himself called 'a full look at the worst'—not only in Tess, but also in Eustacia Vye of ***The Return of the Native,*** and (though somewhat differently) in Bathsheba Everdene of ***Far From The Madding Crowd.*** These heroines he saw as archetypes, essences. It was only parenthetically that he ventured into the sociology of his stories, though distinctions like this are hardly separable.

The picture of dairy farming, cleaning a field of garlic plants, of the first steam threshing (long before the coming of the combine harvester), are powerful adjuncts to the novel, as to Tess's inner life. Passages on the cheapness of female field labour (particularly in the section 'The Woman Pays') could be set beside the statistical findings reported at the start of de Beauvoir's *The Second Sex* (e.g. her Chapter V, 'Early Tillers of the Soil'), and parenthetically remind us that, for the Tesses of those days, the now much-despised housework would have been nothing less than a glorious treat.

But though Hardy was writing not long after Zola's *Earth* (mainly composed in 1887), he was not rewriting it. Some contemporary reviewers seemed to think he was: there is, after all, the same sexual determinism, the same tragic sense that all women can do until they revolt is endure. Hence Hardy was considerably judged by those standards of verisimilitude belonging to a kind of narrative in which he was uninterested. Improbabilities were early pounced on, in a way they would not be now. (p. 194)

The debate about the coincidences in the book seems to have been rather pointlessly continued, therefore. Pointlessly because Hardy did not need to have the Dickensian recurrence of characters like dark Car, once Alec's paramour, nor make Groby, 'floored' by Angel, crop up as the exploiting farmer later (though here the theme of male revenge contributes to the story, it is true). Hardy's coincidences have been variously explained, e.g. as 'the persistence of the unforeseen' (Samuel Chew) [see TCLC, Vol. 4] and thus an aspect of Immanent Will which hung over Hardy's whole view of life, or again as almost the reverse, no chance at all but rather a sort of miraculous element characteristic of folk feeling and literature (Donald Davidson). The reader must be left to himself/herself to sift through such suggestions and decide whether they are or are not so many rationalizations for a kind of writing Hardy merely inherited.

The reviews of the time, in fact, laid so much stress on Hardy's supposed lack of realism that Arnold Kettle's Marxist interpretation of ***Tess*** as 'the destruction of the English peasantry' seems somewhat falsely syllogistic. Almost any great novel about the English countryside of this date is likely to be about this. Moreover, Kettle carefully points out the realistic imperfections throughout. If, then, the novel is guilty of departing so from verisimilitude, how may we, in the same breath, trust it as a vehicle of social insight?

No, Hardy was moving into a far more symbolic sort of fiction. (p. 195)

Tess Durbeyfield grows up to a strong country girl, able to face a walk of twenty-five miles with equanimity and to write a long impassioned letter to her husband after stoically enduring a dawn-to-dusk thumping on the platform of a steam-thresher at Flintcomb-Ash (a Hardy name, if ever there was one). It is important to stress her physique since it is made much of, and is clearly meant to fit her character as a Gea-Tellus, Earth Mother. At the end she kills a strong man with evident ease with a table knife ('Fulfilment' is the title of this section, or Phase).

Now it is far from frivolous to suggest that a great deal of the present ranting about feminine inferiority in a pretentiously egalitarian world is a sort of tight-shoes syndrome . . . women are told, and therefore feel, they have inferior physiques. A firm way of classifying men, that is, appears to be by the fact that they are physically stronger. Our laws embed this distinction within them at points.

But is this a biological parentage or a social construct? It seems hard to discern. (p. 196)

[Sexual equality] doesn't mean sameness, and I for one think Hardy was trying to show this. (p. 202)

When Angel Clare, by this time married to Tess, makes his proposal to Izz Huett to come to be his mistress in Brazil, he footnotes the offer as follows: 'But I ought to remind you that it will be wrongdoing in the eyes of civilization—western civilization, that is to say.' The accent is on western, and it is the man he meets in South America who shrugs his shoulders at Angel's erotic problem.

Under Roman law, at the end of the Antonine jurisconsults at any rate, women were legally equal with men in most matters, a position of which the matrons seem not to have profited. As we know, the troubadour period later perfected a form of matrism which, while it undoubtedly turned men's minds to the Virgin Mary in another world, concomitantly civilized their behaviour to the Lauras and Beatrices of this. 'It may be questioned', Burckhardt wrote of the Holy Virgin, 'whether, in the north, a greater devotion was possible.' Under such matrism women certainly began to emerge more as fellow-beings than they had for some while before, thus making the Portias and Rosalinds of a later century possible. 'The period soon became one of enhanced status for women. They were given an education similar to that of men, and were regarded as their equals, even if it was held to be proper for them to work by influencing men rather than to engage directly in politics.

Such is stressed here since Hardy has been called, by Lord David Cecil, one of the last of the heroists. Two strains meet in Tess, the Gea-Tellus or all-powerful fecundator (*queen* in the original sense, one shared with *quim*) and, of course, the all-too-human equal and companion of man. For it is likely that Bachofen's famous study overstressed the feminine quotient in the alleged early matriarchies of the Mediterranean basin. De Beauvoir shows herself uncomfortable with the Bachofen view:

> These facts have led to the supposition that in primitive times a veritable reign of women existed: the matriarchy. It was this hypothesis, proposed by Bachofen, that Engels adopted, regarding the passage from the matriarchate to the patriarchate as 'the great historical defeat of the feminine sex'. But in truth the Golden Age of Woman is only a myth. To say that woman was the *Other* is to say that there did not exist between the sexes a reciprocal relation: Earth, Mother, Goddess—she was no fellow creature in man's eyes; it was *beyond* the human realm that her power was affirmed, and she was therefore *outside of* that realm.

With Molly Bloom, Tess very much wanted to be within that realm; she earnestly longed to be a fellow creature in man's eyes here and now. By this route we can come logically back to Lawrence and his twin insights concerning her plight. For she is very strong physically and quite unafraid of Groby at the end: 'To have as a master this man of stone, who would have cuffed her if he had dared, was almost a relief after her former experiences.'

Tess's physicality has been thoroughly insisted on since she is the flower of her sex and race: so much so that it sometimes suggests her as older than she is. She is thoroughly natural, a 'pure' woman, and 'her exceptional physical nature' causes her to ask Angel to marry her sister after she has been hanged, as if she were some generous tree, giving off another branch of life. By this request, too, to which Angel evidently accedes, she urges him to join her on the other side of convention: of her own crime Hardy had at once commented, 'She had been made to break an accepted social law, but no law known to the environment in which she fancied herself such an anomaly.'

It must be clearly established, too, that Angel Clare was far more anti-conventional than a modern reader (certainly a modern American reader) might assume. Dairyman Crick tells us that he is 'one of the most rebellest rozums you ever knowed', he is described as 'un-Sabbatarian' and 'preferred sermons in stones to sermons in churches'. At one point the adverb 'communistically' is used of him, the word only having acquired English currency around 1850. But Angel fails at the brink and can only go the whole way 'Too late, too late!' (in Tess's terms before the murder).

The story is archetypally simple. A young country girl is seduced, has an illegitimate child which dies in infancy, marries another and tells her husband the truth before consummation of the wedding. The latter cannot tolerate the idea and abandons her to go to Brazil. Now at this turn in the narrative we may, in fact, tend to judge Angel too harshly. But his identity and whole relationship with the world depended on things being what they were. (pp. 203-05)

Pestered by her first lover, Tess gives in to live with him since he will then support her family—the words 'He bought me' in the 1892 text were expunged by Hardy from the later Wessex edition. On her husband's return and subsequent discovery of her new ménage, Tess kills her paramour, has a few days' elegaic happiness with her new-found husband and is apprehended for her crime lying, like a sacrificial victim, on an altar at Stonehenge, an episode of overcrude symbolism for many critics. She is hanged.

We see that Hardy carefully arranged for chance to interfere with Tess's first confession of her supposed fault and then for Angel, before the marriage consummation, to see fit to make his own admission of sexual 'backsliding'. Overjoyed, Tess then makes hers 'because 'tis just the same'.

But of course it isn't, given the society. Convention intervenes and though 'nothing had changed since the moments when he had been kissing her', ignorant of her lapse, 'the essence of things had changed'—the essence, not the existence. Tess slides to her knees and begs for forgiveness, saying 'I will obey you like your wretched slave', and asking, from the depths of her instincts, how he can suddenly stop loving her on the mere receipt of information—'It is in your own mind what you are angry at, Angel.' In truth, it is. Angel's position is put in the following exchange:

> 'In the name of our love, forgive me!' she whispered with a dry mouth. 'I have forgiven you for the same!'
>
> And as he did not answer, she said again—
>
> 'Forgive me as you are forgiven! I forgive you, Angel.'
>
> 'You—yes, you do.'
>
> 'But you do not forgive me?'
>
> 'O Tess, forgiveness does not apply to the case! You were one person; now you are another.'

If we have been correct in tracing two themes working through Tess so far, fecundating Earth Mother and social and political equal, we can see that there is far more at stake here than a simple attack on the double standard of male convention. (pp. 205-06)

For Tess is longing to be *whole* and neither man in her life will let her be so. (p. 206)

Angel was the classic case of the Puritan. But [D. H.] Lawrence proceeds astutely to observe that you can't have the one without the other, the Puritan without the Cavalier; and his interpretation of the other social pole repressing sex by exploiting it, and also refusing full consciousness to woman, is extremely interesting [see excerpt dated 1915?].

For him Alec d'Urberville is the opposite of Angel Clare, he has 'killed the male in himself, as Clytemnestra symbolically for Orestes killed Agamemnon'. So his is really another way of hating the flesh (indeed Hardy writes, 'd'Urberville gave her the kiss of mastery'). 'It is a male quality to resolve a purpose to its fulfilment', Lawrence here claims, 'to receive some impulse into his semen, and to transmit it into expression'. Woman, that is, needs the mediation of the male, the reverse view, of course, of a feminist sexologist like [Ruth] Herschberger ('The male functions to produce sperm to give to the female'). Thus Alec 'seeks with all his power for the stimulus in woman. He takes the deep impulse from the female'. (p. 207)

What Lawrence is saying is structured to show the destruction of a woman's psyche: this happens in two ways—*(a)* Angel denies woman, *(b)* Alec identifies woman and destroys her by betrayal. The result is death since in neither case is the woman left whole. In short, 'The female is the victim of the species.'

Thomas Hardy was one of the last great heroic writers—'Elizabethan' for Cecil—lodged in a time that was running down. His God, or anti-God, was Immanent Will, President of the Immortals, The Spinner of the Years, a purblind Doomster (the diffidence of specification, in Hardy's semantic here, is itself an 'ironic' acknowledgement of taboo). (pp. 207-08)

With one side of himself (the rational) Hardy tried to adumbrate a universe of sheer fatality, chance, 'hap'. As the fields are cut in ***Tess*** rabbits and rats, friend and foe alike, cluster together in panic and misery, then run for their lives. Like humans, it is a matter of luck which of them is killed, and which escapes. We are all, that is, in the words of one of Hardy's best poems ('**Neutral Tones**'), 'Alive enough to have strength to die.'

There is a whole philosophy in that line, which seems to be Hardy's inheritance from those urns of Zeus of which the weary Achilles talks to Priam at the end of the *Iliad*. Angel once confesses to his father 'that it might have resulted far better for mankind if Greece had been the source of the religion of modern civilization'. And again, after the chance but most important meeting with the stranger in Brazil, a cosmopolite who thought Tess's slip 'of no importance beside what she would be', Angel reflects that he had himself 'persistently elevated Hellenic Paganism at the expense of Christianity, yet in that civilization an illegal surrender was not certain disesteem'.

This is all very well, but Hardy proceeds to people his fiction with omens, and his poetry with ghosts. Intuitions, hauntings, spectral voices usually have a habit, with Hardy, of coming true. (pp. 208-09)

Tess may be part of nature, but she *has to be* part of society. 'Thus Tess walks on, a figure which is part of the landscape. . . .' This is the existentialist Hardy who could write, with some fervour in his prose:

> Tess was no insignificant creature to toy with and dismiss; but a woman living her precious life—a life which, to herself who endured or enjoyed it, possessed as great a dimension as the life of the mightiest to himself. Upon her sensations the whole world depended to Tess; through her existence all her fellow-creatures existed, to her. The universe itself only came into being for Tess on the particular day in the particular year in which she was born.

This could be straight Camus, and in fact it really is for, as Cecil suggests, Hardy's mnemonic side had to concede what the Greeks called a human nature. We can, after all, talk about persistence beyond death; rabbits and rats cannot. 'Despairing literature', as Camus once put it, 'is a contradiction in terms'.

So society executes Tess, as did Camus's Meursault, and for not entirely dissimilar reasons. In neither case is the murder the guilt; the revolt against convention is the real guilt. Meursault is decapitated 'in the name of the French people'. Tess is hanged in the name of male society. And yet her touching, tentative revolt against inhuman laws affirms something irreducibly human, and makes us all her murderers, as well as her fellow-condemned.

Of course, the great difference, aesthetically, between Hardy's brand of existentialism and Camus's is that the latter writer could already locate his in a social situation where the values of solitude, alienation, revolt (during German occupation) were normatively heroic. As a matter of fact, there may even have been an artistic penalty for this; however sympathetic Camus's fiction was, he was again giving testimony, acknowledging public truths, rather than (or just as much as) writing out of private discovery, apart. We feel he is as honest as Hardy all the way, but does he maintain the same creative energy over long stretches (his best work is short)? As Irving Howe once put it, 'Camus has not yet given himself irrevocably to the powers of art, he has not yet taken the final step that would bring him from the realm of reflection to the realm of imagination.' Yet Camus's tragic optimism replies to, rounds out, Hardy's ironic pessimism. (pp. 209-10)

So Tess, this 'mere child of the soil', is also a child of our time, a truly delicate organization of appetencies. No wonder Tolstoy approved her (at least in serial shape). She is 'Alive enough to have strength to die', all right, and cannot imagine no further life for the true lovers of this world. She speaks closely to women since she lives 'under an arbitrary law of society which had no foundation in Nature'. For although we may all be pawns in the hands of the purblind Doomster, there is a sense of joy in the very copiousness of nature: as we read in ***Tess:***

> The 'appetite for joy' which pervades all creation, that tremendous force which sways humanity to its purpose, as the tide sways the helpless weed, was not to be controlled by vague lucubrations over the social rubric.

Nature itself is guiltless, and Tess a sample of its innocence. For, if not the first, Hardy is certainly one of the best of our writers to use landscape as psychic state, and sometimes one of the most daring (in ***Tess*** there is a lengthy description of the Vale of the Var as a vaginal cleft). So Hardy makes his 'pure' woman cry out for all the women when, exhausted by field labour, she lashes at Alec with her glove, then sinks on the straw, on which his blood is dropping, to cry out in agony, 'Now, punish me. . . . Whip me, crush me; you need not mind those people under the rick! I shall not cry out. Once victim, always victim—that's the law!' (pp. 210-11)

Geoffrey Wagner, " 'Tess of the D'Urbervilles': The 'Pure' Woman," in his Five for Freedom: A Study of Feminism in Fiction, *1972. Reprint by Fairleigh Dickinson University Press, 1973, pp. 183-211.*

THOMAS HINDE (essay date 1976)

[*An English novelist and critic, Hinde was one of the Angry Young Men, a group of British writers of the 1950s whose writings expressed bitterness and disillusionment with society. Common to the work of the Angry Young Men is an anti-hero who rebels against a corrupt social order in a quest for personal integrity. Hinde is particularly concerned with the effect of social change and progress on the individual. His well-plotted novels are most successful when examining the tangled motives and delusions of his characters and their ineffectuality before some implacable truth. In the following excerpt, Hinde examines the ways that Tess's fate mirrors the destruction of the agricultural class in England at the end of the nineteenth century.*]

The plot of ***Tess of the D'Urbervilles*** turns on a succession of accidents and coincidences. Again and again Tess's tragic fate depends on some disastrous mischance. One or two of these may seem possible—life after all is full of mischance—but heaped on top of each other they produce a final effect of gross improbability. Does this matter? Are we to see them as blemishes on an otherwise fine novel; or are they such a pervasive part of it that they must either condemn it or form part of its success?

At its face value the novel suggests not only that these accidents and misfortunes are included by intention but that it is the author's view that life does give human beings just such a succession of kicks downhill to disaster. The refrain 'where was Tess's guardian angel?' is more than an attack on the conventional Christian idea of a benevolent and protecting Almighty; it implies the exact opposite. Our problem, if we don't share this view, is that we see Tess as not so much the victim of Fate, nor as the victim of her own character and circumstances, but as Hardy's personal victim.

It is he who appears to make her suffer her improbable sequence of accidents. In criticizing this effect I do not imply that probability is a criterion by which we should universally or invariably judge. A novel sets its own standards, and no one, to take an obvious example, expects the same 'realism' from Kafka as from Tolstoy. The problem with Hardy's novels is that in most other ways they set up expectations of a quite conventional realism. It is against this self-established standard that the plot of ***Tess,*** as much as that of any of his novels which came before it and which it otherwise excels, at first sight appears equally to offend.

I say at first sight because my purpose is to suggest a way of looking at ***Tess*** which sees its many accidents and coincidences neither as blemishes, nor as valid samples of Hardy's neither credible nor particularly interesting view of the part played in life by a persecuting fate; if encouragement were needed to search for such a view it would be provided by ***Tess***'s many admirers who seem undismayed by its improbabilities, though these begin on the very first page and feature regularly throughout the book.

Setting the scene, and necessary if there is to be any novel at all, is the coincidence of names: the rich north country manufacturer Stoke who buys his way into the southern landed gentry has arbitrarily chosen from a British Museum list of defunct families the name d'Urberville to add to his own, and this is the original name of the family from which Tess Durbeyfield is distantly descended. The story opens with Parson Tringham telling Tess's father about his aristocratic ancestors, which till now he has not known about. John Durbeyfield puts two and two together and makes five, concluding not only that he is related to the Stoke-d'Urbervilles but that he probably belongs to the senior branch.

Up to this point all could be said to be reasonable enough. If it is an accident it is one which sooner or later seems possible if not probable. In any case, even a realistic novelist may, without offending against his own criterion of probability, precipitate his story with such a single event, then stand back to demonstrate with no further interference the inevitable consequences. (pp. 74-5)

There seems no such inevitability about the next kick downhill which Fate gives Tess. Driving her father's cart to market at night because he is too drunk to go, she is run down by the mail coach, and Prince, the horse on which his livelihood as a haggler depends, is pierced to the heart by the mail coach's shaft. Tess's guilt at what she has done persuades her to agree to her mother's plan that she should visit the *nouveaux riches* Stoke d'Urbervilles in the hope of making a prosperous marriage.

Here she meets the young and buckish Alec d'Urberville; once again a flavour of managed accident surrounds her seduction by him. Her quarrel, late at night in open country, with the drunken Trantridge village women provides her with just the motive which makes plausible her acceptance of Alec's offer of a pillion ride when he spurs up at a convenient moment. Criticism is only disarmed by the splendid dramatic quality of this scene, set as it is with sinister omen and diabolic detail.

At Talbothays, where Tess goes a few years later and after the death of her child to become a milkmaid, who should she meet but Angel Clare, the young man who, in a more insidious but surer way, is to lead her to her tragic end. (p. 75)

From this moment the plot turns on Angel's plan to marry Tess, and on whether or not Tess can bring herself to confess her sinful past with Alec d'Urberville before their wedding day. Though she can't tell Angel to his face she at last makes herself write to him and late at night pushes the letter under his door. Only on her wedding eve does she discover that Fate has struck again: she has accidently pushed it under the carpet as well as the door and Angel has never received it.

Her confession after her marriage leads to their separation, Angel to go to Brazil, Tess to return to Marlott. He has left her an allowance but a succession of minor misfortunes—in particular the neediness and imprudence of her parents—leaves Tess destitute by the time winter comes. Angel has told her that she should go to his parents if she is ever in need, but Fate, which has already put him personally beyond her reach, closes this escape too. She walks to Emminster and finds Angel's father, the vicar, out. Before she can try his door again Angel's brothers discover her walking boots which she has hidden on the outskirts of the village and Miss Mercy Chant bears them off for charity. Tess's courage fails her and she turns for home. 'It was somewhat unfortunate,' Hardy writes, 'that she had encountered the sons and not the father, who, despite his narrowness, was far less starched and ironed than they, and had to the full the gift of Christian charity.' Though we may read this as a confession of clumsy plotting, that is far from Hardy's intention. His tone is ironic. The world may consider that Tess here suffered an improbable and untypical stroke of ill luck, but Hardy, better informed about the working of Fate, knows that such accidents are in fact typical and probable.

Meanwhile Tess has taken on the humblest and most oppressive sort of agricultural labour: work on arable land. The description of her grubbing up swedes for cattle food, creeping across the icy uplands of Flintcomb Ash in drenching rain, is one of the most memorable in the book. And who should turn out to be her employer but a farmer who knows her past and whom Angel once struck on the jaw when he insultingly hinted at it during the last days before their marriage. Inevitably he takes his revenge on Tess. (pp. 75-6)

Alec d'Urberville's conversion to evangelical Christianity—coincidentally performed by Angel Clare's father—now gives Alec the chance to harass Tess again and, more important, weakens her power to resist him. The scene is set for her final disastrous return to Alec. The various letters Angel ultimately receives from her and from others reach him at moments which time his return exactly too late to save her from the murder of Alec and ultimately the gallows.

Though this is only a brief selection of the blows which Fate strikes Tess, I hope it is sufficient to show that the plot of the novel turns on a succession of disastrous accidents which far exceeds realistic probability. But as in all such abstracts, vital elements which seem unrelated to the book's plot have been left out, in particular one to which Hardy persistently returns even though his attention is overtly directed towards Tess and her personal tragedy. This is the equally sure and tragic destruction of the traditional society of the English village.

Twice he shows us mechanized agriculture at work; on the first occasion he describes how the reaping machine, with its red arms in the shape of a Maltese cross, gradually reduces the standing corn.

> Rabbits, hares, snakes, rats, mice, retreated into a fastness, unaware of the ephemeral nature of their refuge, and of the doom that awaited them later in the day when, their covert shrinking to a more and more horrible narrowness, they were huddled together, friends and foes, till the last few yards of upright wheat fell also under the teeth of the unerring reaper, and they were every one put to death by the sticks and stones of the harvesters.

It needs little intuition to see that Hardy is here describing by parallel the fate of the human inhabitants of such a village as Marlott.

Humans themselves are the victims on the second occasion: Tess and her fellow workers who feed the monstrous itinerant threshing machine at Flintcombe Ash, with its diabolical master.

> By the engine stood a dark motionless being, a sooty and grimy embodiment of tallness, in a sort of trance, with a heap of coals by his side: it was the engineman. The isolation of his manner and colour lent him the appearance of a creature from Tophet, who had strayed into the pellucid smokelessness of this region of yellow grain and pale soil, with which he had nothing in common, to amaze and to discompose its aborigines.
>
> What he looked he felt. He was in the agricultural world, but not of it. He served fire and smoke; these denizens of the fields served vegetation, weather, frost, and sun. He travelled with his engine from farm to farm, county to county . . . He spoke in a strange northern accent; his thoughts being turned inwards upon himself, his eye on his iron charge, hardly perceiving the scenes around him, and caring for them not at all.
>
> (pp. 76-7)

Apart from the implications of such incidents, Hardy as author continually comments on the changing and deteriorating condition of rural Wessex. The May Day dance, for example, where we first meet Tess, is 'a gay survival from Old Style days when cheerfulness and May were synonyms'. The refreshments which the rural labourers of Trantridge drink on Saturday nights are 'curious compounds sold to them as beer by the monopolizers of the once independent inns'. Still more important, it is the tenant farmers, deprived of their independence, who are 'the natural enemies of bush and brake', and to whom Tess falls victim at the lowest point of her decline at Flintcombe Ash.

And it is because Tess's family are victims of another aspect of this destruction of rural independence that she is finally exposed once more to Alec d'Urberville. As soon as her father dies her mother loses her right to their cottage, and the family must join all those other labourers' families which take to the road on Lady Day, their worldly goods loaded on to hired waggons, to hunt for new jobs and homes. Oppressed by responsibility for her family, she no longer feels she has the moral right to resist his advances when they could bring with them the financial help she so badly needs.

Indeed, a good many of Tess's misfortunes turn out, on closer inspection, to have economic causes which seem almost as important as the random vengefulness of Fate to which Hardy attributes them. It is only a short step from realizing this to wondering whether Hardy is not—consciously or unconsciously—concerned throughout the book not so much with Tess's personal fortune as with her fate as a personification of rural Wessex.

Just why Tess should be an appropriate figure to play this part is clearly explained in Chapter LI, in a passage which holds the clue to the book's social message.

> The village had formerly contained, side by side with the agricultural labourers, an interesting and better-informed class, ranking distinctly above the former—the class to which Tess's father and mother had belonged—and including the carpenter, the smith, the shoemaker, the huckster, together with nondescript workers other than farm labourers: a set of people who owed a certain stability of aim and conduct to the fact of their being lifeholders like Tess's father, or copyholders, or, occasionally, small freeholders. But as the long holdings fell in they were seldom again let to similar tenants, and were mostly pulled down, if not absolutely required by the farmer for his hands. Cottagers who were not directly employed on the land were looked upon with disfavour, and the banishment of some starved the trade of others, who were thus obliged to follow. These families, who had formed the backbone of the village life in the past, who were the depositaries of the village traditions, had to seek refuge in the large centres; the process humourously designated by statisticians as 'the tendency of the rural population towards the large towns', being really the tendency of water to flow uphill when forced by machinery.

At once much that appeared arbitrary becomes logical. The destruction of the haggler's daughter no longer seems a cruel mischance, but inevitable. And many more of the accidents she suffers, which on a personal level seem so excessive and gratuitous, become those which her class *must* suffer.

The mail coach which runs down the haggler's cart and kills his horse is the vehicle which will destroy the livelihood of all hagglers, whether they are drunkards like John Durbeyfield, or sober and hard-working. Deprived of their former independence, the children of this village middle class will be driven downwards into just the sort of menial labouring jobs that Tess is forced to take. Her downward progress from milkmaid to arable worker of the lowest sort is the path ahead for all of them. (pp. 77-9)

Tess is of course many other things as well. She is, for example, the embodiment of 'nature' and in particular of natural womanhood. 'Women whose chief companions are the forms and forces of outdoor Nature retain in their souls far more of the Pagan fantasy of their remote forefathers than of the systematized religion taught their race at later date.' And however much she may stand for a principle or a passing society, she remains a lost and frightened human being in a world which misleads then persecutes her. Scenes such as the splendid but appalling one in which she baptizes her dying child in her bedroom wash basin may indeed seem to establish her tragedy too clearly as a personal one for the interpretation I am suggesting.

But such a view of Tess becomes less and less satisfactory as Hardy inflicts on her a less and less probable sequence of accidental and coincidental misfortune. It is only when she is seen to some extent also to be a daughter of the doomed rural England which Hardy loved, and in particular of that class in the rural community from which Hardy himself came and which was once 'the backbone of the village life' that her fate no longer seems arbitrary and author-imposed but inescapable. (p. 79)

Thomas Hinde, ''Accident and Coincidence in 'Tess of the D'Urbervilles','' in The Genius of Thomas Hardy, *edited by Margaret Drabble, Alfred A. Knopf, 1976, pp. 74-9.*

H. M. DALESKI (essay date 1980)

[Daleski is a South African-born educator and critic who has written extensively on English literature. In the following excerpt, originally written in 1980 and slightly revised in 1984, he examines the ways in which the principal character traits of the protagonists of Tess *influence their tragic fates]*

The form of ***Tess of the d'Urbervilles*** is at first sight deceptively simple: the life of the protagonist is divided into ''phases,'' and her adventures in love seem to be shaped by no more than a traditional triangle. But the antagonists in the triangle, Alec d'Urberville and Angel Clare, are not merely oposed as alternate lovers of Tess Durbeyfield; like Heathcliff and Edgar, and Stephen and Philip, they clearly figure oppugnant principles of being. The nature of this opposition and of the triangle in which it is contained has been suggestively described by D. H. Lawrence:

> Angel Clare has the very opposite qualities to those of Alec d'Urberville. To the latter, the female in himself is the only part of himself he will acknowledge: the body, the senses, that which he shares with the female, which the female shares with him. To Angel Clare, the female in himself is detestable, the body, the senses, that which he will share with a woman, is held degraded. . . .
>
> The one extreme produces the other. It is inevitable for Angel Clare and for Alec d'Urberville mutually to destroy the woman they both loved. Each does her the extreme of wrong, so she is destroyed.
>
> The book is handled with very uncertain skill, botched and bungled. But it contains the elements of the greatest tragedy: Alec d'Urberville, who has killed the male in himself . . . ; Angel Clare, who has killed the female in himself . . . : and Tess, the Woman, the Life, destroyed by a mechanical fate, in the communal law [see excerpt dated 1915].

One need not subscribe to Lawrence's view of the constituents of the male and female principles to grant that he has seized on an opposition that is fundamental to Hardy's vision of life. It is an opposition that runs through Hardy's work, from ***The Return of the Native*** . . . , with its insistence on 'the mutually destructive interdependence of spirit and flesh'—the terms in which Hardy chooses to formulate the conflict—to ***Jude the Obscure*** . . . , with its searing corroboration of Jude Fawley's intuition that his life is one of "constant internal warfare between flesh and spirit." The conflict, moreover, is so much a question of general principles of being that Hardy duplicates the kind of opposition that is established between the two male rivals in ***Tess*** in his presentation of the two women whom Jude loves. (pp. 69-70)

The opposition, however, is neither as simple nor as fixed as Lawrence makes it. In the Hardy universe "flux and reflux—the rhythm of change—alternate and persist in everything under the sky" . . . , and both Alec and Angel are caught up in that rhythm. If Alec has killed the male in himself, has denied the spirit, that is, he would also appear to hanker after it, for he undergoes a "conversion" and becomes a "ranter," even though his career as an itinerant preacher may be shortlived. And if Angel is pure male and lives by the spirit, he repudiates the Church, which he is expected to enter as a minister, and aspires to a life of the senses, for he seeks a down-to-earth existence as a farmer. Hardy would thus appear to be concerned with a conflict between flesh and spirit that is not only externalised in the opposition between Alec and Angel but also internalised in each of the men. As it is, of course, in Tess herself, for perhaps Hardy's boldest manipulation of his traditional form is the rhythmic duplication of its triangular dynamics: with the swing of a pendulum, Tess moves from Alec to Angel, and then back to Alec before returning to Angel, thus imaging the degree to which she is pulled between one man and the other. What is also suggested is her inability to reconcile within herself the conflicting principles they preeminently embody, as she first negates the spirit in relation to Alec and then the flesh in relation to Angel. And since she moves freely between the two men, choosing her own way though subjected to intolerable pressures, her tragedy would seem to lie not so much in her mutual destruction by Alec and Angel, as has been the critical consensus since Lawrence, as in her own failure to integrate flesh and spirit. It is true that Tess sees herself as a victim—"Once victim, always victim—that's the law!" she bitterly cries out towards the end of her story . . . ; and that is how the novelist, as he sets the scene for Tess's arrest at the sacrificial slab at Stonehenge, would seem to wish us finally to see her. But she is as much a victim of herself as others, and should be regarded as ultimately responsible for what happens to her. (pp. 70-71)

The sort of relationship Alec wishes to impose on Tess is figured when she rides with him in his smart gig on the way to Trantridge. Alec is a "handsome, horsey young buck" . . . , and when they reach a long, steep descent and he begins to drive recklessly down it, it seems at first as if this is merely an expression of his natural flamboyance and high spirits. . . . But it soon becomes apparent there is more to his driving than that. For one thing, the horse is a mare; and as the dashing young male urges it into a full gallop, the description of the pell-mell drive downhill, with "the figure of the horse rising and falling in undulations before them" . . . takes on insistent sexual overtones. These are still further emphasized when, before the end of the drive, Tess is reduced to desperation and "her large eyes [stare] at him like those of a wild animal." . . . (p. 72)

Once Alec has loosened the rein and given the mare its head, what he demonstrates in the ride is the degree to which he can impel it to a wild abandon while he himself coolly—if high-spiritedly—retains control of it. . . . The motif of abandon, so sharply concretized in the mare's plunge downhill, is of central importance in Tess's story, and indeed may be said to frame it at its very beginning, if only by way of light adumbration. . . . [Though] Tess's fatal involvement with Alec might appear to be quite literally determined by a force beyond her control since she is asleep when Prince is killed, I think she must be seen as abandoning herself to the sleep which overtakes her, despite the fact that she knows she should stay awake. There is, after all, a point at which one *allows* oneself to fall asleep.

As the gig speeds along, alternative possibilities in the development of Tess's relationship with Alec are nicely juxtaposed. At first Tess clings to him, and it is only when they safely reach the bottom of the hill that she disengages herself and realizes how completely she has given way to impulse: "She had not considered what she had been doing; whether he were man or woman, stick or stone, in her involuntary hold on him." . . . Alec then "[loosens] rein" again, they go shooting down a second hill, and the only way Tess can persuade him to stop is by agreeing to let him kiss her. She implores him not to claim his due, but he is "inexorable," and gives her "the kiss of mastery" . . . —a phrase which draws together related significances of the drive. When they come to "yet another descent" and Alec tries to extort another kiss, however, Tess defeats him by allowing her hat to blow off and refusing to get back into the gig after she has retrieved it. Demonstrating that she can take a stand, Tess walks the rest of the way to Tantridge. . . . (p. 73)

But she is not always prepared to walk, and the way in which she "abandons herself to her impulse" on another occasion is premonitory of what is to come. She has been drawn into a fierce quarrel with the Queen of Diamonds when suddenly Alec appears on horseback. He urges her to jump up behind him in order to get away from "the screaming cats." . . . This episode immediately precedes Tess's seduction; and being a culminating instance of her capacity for abandon in relation to Alec, would strongly seem to suggest that it is a seduction, and not a rape, that follows. This is the general critical view, but Tony Tanner, in one of the very best studies of the novel, repeatedly refers to what happens as a rape [see excerpt dated 1968]. This gives one pause and makes one realise that what happens in the Chase is not, in the formulation of Ian Gregor, "both a seduction *and* a rape," [see *TCLC,* Vol. 4] but so ambiguously presented as to invite the mutually contradictory readings.

Though Hardy is constrained by the conventions of his time to leave us to find our way by indirection, his sudden change of direction is startling. Prior to the scene in the Chase, Alec has certainly not been presented as a rapist. For "near three mortal months" he has pursued Tess, and though riled by her "trifling" with him, has accepted her rebuffs. . . . On the night in question he tells her that he loves her, and asks whether he may not treat her "as a lover." . . . He also reveals that on that day he has presented her father with "a new cob" to replace Prince, and given toys to the children of the family. . . . Most revealingly of all, when he leaves Tess to try to find out where they are, he is compassionate to her: "'Nights grow chilly in September. Let me see.' He pulled off a light overcoat that he had worn, and put it round her tenderly. 'That's it—now you'll feel warmer,' he continued. 'Now, my pretty, rest there; I shall soon be back again'." . . .

Neither his concern nor his tenderness suggests the rapist, yet when he returns to "the white muslin figure" which seems to have been swallowed up in the darkness—"everything else was blackness alike"—suggestions of violation become insistent. . . . And for good measure the description of Alec's return to Tess ended, in the first edition of the novel, with the following passage (subsequently omitted from later editions):

> Already at that hour some sons of the forest were stirring, and striking lights in not very distant cottages; good and sincere hearts among them, patterns of honesty and devotion and chivalry. And powerful horses were stamping in their stalls, ready to be let out into the morning air. But no dart or thread of intelligence inspired these men to harness or mount, or gave them by any means the least inkling that their sister was in the hands of the spoiler; and they did not come that way.

This pronouncement is echoed in the edition we now have in the comments of a villager on Tess's baby: "A little more than persuading had to do wi' the coming o't, I reckon. There were they that heard a sobbing one night last year in The Chase; and it mid ha' gone hard wi' a certain party if folks had come along." . . . (pp. 73-5)

If it is difficult to reconcile this view of the matter with what precedes it, with the way in which both Tess and Alec have been presented, it is equally hard to relate it to what follows, to the way in which Tess responds to the experience. It is possible to imagine—or, at any rate, to conceive how a novelist such as Hardy could lead us to imagine—that a woman might fall in love with her rapist; but Tess, both before and after the night in the Chase, repeatedly states that she does not love Alec and has never loved him—and yet, though this episode takes place on "a Saturday in September" . . . , it is not until "a Sunday morning in late October" . . . that she leaves him, having freely lived as his mistress, that is to say, for about a month after it. Hardy, apparently, both wishes it to be clear it is not only a rape that is in question (if it is a rape at all) and wants to minimize the extent of Tess's transgression. He is led into inconsistency, it seems to me, not so much because he is intent on presenting Tess as "a pure woman," as has been asserted, as because he wants her to be seen as a victim. Tess is asleep when Alec returns to where he has left her in the Chase, just as she was asleep when the accident with Prince takes place, but it is as a responsible tragic agent—not helpless victim—that we should view her.

Tess emerges as such an agent, and any dispute as to whether she has been raped or seduced becomes supererogatory, in what she reveals about her attitude to Alec during the period she is his mistress. What is most striking about her feeling when she leaves Trantridge is her self-loathing, her self-disgust. When Alec catches up with her, she says to him: ". . . if I had ever sincerely loved you, if I loved you still, I should not so loathe and hate myself for my weakness as I do now! . . . My eyes were dazed by you for a little, and that was all." . . . And when her mother tells her she should have got Alec to marry her, she reflects bitterly how little her mother knows the feeling towards him which has made her "detest herself":

> She had never wholly cared for him, she did not at all care for him now. She had dreaded him, winced before him, succumbed to adroit advantages he took of her helplessness; then, temporarily blinded by his ardent manners, had been stirred to confused surrender awhile: had suddenly despised and disliked him, and had run away. That was all. Hate him she did not quite; but he was dust and ashes to her, and even for name's sake she scarcely wished to marry him....

Tess loathes and hates herself so strongly, it now appears, because she despises and dislikes Alec. Her feeling for him fills her with revulsion from her own body as well as his, and it is not only he who is "dust and ashes" to her. She herself is reduced to dust and ashes because she now realizes that what she gave Alec was a body uninformed by spirit, devoid of the love which could animate it—and which could alone redeem it in her eyes. (pp. 75-6)

When Tess, at the beginning of Phase the Third: The Rally, sets out for Talbothays, where Angel is staying, it is not only in a literal sense that her journey is "now in a direction almost opposite to that of her first adventuring." . . . (p. 77)

Tess's passionate nature . . . is not much in evidence at Talbothays—despite the novelist's lavish celebration of the lushness of her surroundings. . . . Tess's own assurance of a fullness of being while she is together with Angel at Talbothays would seem to posit her achievement of a new wholeness, but in fact from the moment she comes to the farm she seems to wish to dispossess herself of her own body.

This tendency first becomes apparent during a conversation with Dairyman Crick at breakfast:

> 'I don't know about ghosts,' [Tess] was saying; 'but I do know that our souls can be made to go outside our bodies when we are alive.'
>
> The dairyman turned to her with his mouth full, his eyes charged with serious inquiry, and his great knife and fork (breakfasts were breakfasts here) planted erect on the table, like the beginning of a gallows.
>
> 'What—really now? And is it so, maidy?' he said.
>
> 'A very easy way to feel 'em go,' continued Tess, 'is to lie on the grass at night and look straight up at some big bright star; and, by fixing your mind upon it, you will soon find that you are hundreds and hundreds o' miles away from your body, which you don't seem to want at all.' . . .

Tess, we remember, may be said to have made her soul go outside her body in her relationship with Alec, but that was by way of leaving her body unimpeded; now what she seems to aspire to is the liberated soul that may burgeon from a discarded body. But that such a severance, in this case as in the other, will no less surely issue in dust and ashes is strikingly suggested by the gallows simile—a comparison which only Hardy could have made. At the very outset of this "phase," what is proleptically implied is that, with her predilection to set aside the body, Tess takes her first step to the gallows, for this will lead her in due course to return to Alec, giving him her body then to do with as he likes, and so to the murder when Angel comes to claim her. (pp. 79-80)

When Tess knows that Angel loves her and wants to marry her, she cannot decide whether or not to tell him of her relationship with Alec. Her mother, when appealed to, tells her not to be a fool, and Tess concludes that silence would seem to be "best for her adored one's happiness." . . . Tess does not hold to the decision to keep her relationship with Alec secret, but when her attempt to inform Angel of it by letter miscarries, she fails—though "in her conscience" she knows there is "still time" before the marriage . . .—to tell him. For all the mitigating circumstances, Tess must be seen as responsible for this failure, which is at the very heart of her story. It is the kingpin of the plot, for it results in Angel's abandonment of her; it is the essential cause of her tragedy, for it is an irreparable error and leads, in the end, to her murder of Alec and her execution; and it is the crux of her attitude to Angel, for it signifies her shrinking from the facts of flesh in relation to him. (pp. 81-2)

When Tess finally confesses to Angel, she is appalled to find that he will not "forgive" her, as she begs him to. "O Tess," he says, "forgiveness does not apply to the case. You were one person; now you are another. My God—how can forgiveness meet such a grotesque—prestidigitation as that!"—and he insists that the woman he has been loving is "another woman in [her] shape." . . . Angel's response suggests that his is a case of love in the head, as Lawrence might have called it; and his recourse to the word "prestidigitation" in such circumstances reveals how he takes refuge in words from the woman in front of him. Angel, that is to say, when shocked back into an old mode of being, is as much given to intellectual altitudes as Tess to spiritual; and in his relationship with her the flesh is as surely and mutually denied as is the spirit in her relationship with Alec.

The mode that Angel slips back to, annulling his hard-won freedom from trammeling creeds, is described when he announces to Tess it is "advisable" they should part:

> Tess stole a glance at her husband. He was pale, even tremulous; but as before, she was appalled by the determination revealed in the depths of this gentle being she had married—the will to subdue the grosser to the subtler emotion, the substance to the conception, the flesh to the spirit. Propensities, tendencies, habits, were as dead leaves upon the tyrannous wind of his imaginative ascendency. . . .

Angel's harshness to Tess is in part occasioned by his sense of having been deceived by her, is in part "the cruelty of fooled honesty . . . after enlightenment" . . . ; but, more fundamentally than that, it springs from an involuntary revulsion from what he takes to be her defilement, a recoil from tainted flesh that is not unlike her own. He realizes this long afterwards in Brazil and then is "struck" by remorse, perceiving that what he has "inherited with the creed of mysticism" is an "abhorrence of the un-intact state." . . . It is a tyrannous will that now forces him to smother his natural feeling for Tess, all such "propensities" being scattered like so many "dead leaves." The will to subdue the flesh to the spirit meets a capacity to withdraw spirit from flesh in a common sterility, in dead leaves, for on the night of Tess's seduction it was in "a deep mass of dead leaves" that Alec made "a sort of couch or nest" for her . . . , and it was to "the white muslin figure he had left upon the dead leaves" that he returned. . . . Alec's struggle to master Tess, moreover, is juxtaposed to Angel's to master himself. As he steels himself against her, his air is "calm and cold, his small compressed mouth indexing his powers of self-control; his face wearing still that terribly sterile expression which had spread thereon since her disclosure." . . . Coldness, it appears, is the condition of his kind of mastery as of Alec's, but Angel's coldness is more inhuman, for it is the coldness of metal: though he is generally "gentle and affectionate," deep within him there lies hidden "a hard logical deposit, like a vein of metal in a soft loam, which [turns] the edge of everything that [attempts] to traverse it," and blocks his acceptance of Tess, no less than of the Church. . . . (pp. 82-3)

After Angel deserts her, Tess is brought back to earth with a vengeance; and, reduced to hard physical labour in the swede-fields of Flintcomb-Ash, she now lives in a place which is "bosomed with semi-globular tumuli—as if Cybele the Many-breasted were supinely extended there," and where are to be seen "myriads of loose white flints in bulbous, cusped, and phallic shapes." . . . If Tess succeeds in resisting the temptation of going to Alec when he pursues her at Flintcomb-Ash, she is unable to withstand him after her father dies and she and her family are forced to leave their village home and seek refuge in a nearby town. When even the rooms they hope to rent in Kingsbere are not available to them, and the family is literally in the street, she finally succumbs to Alec's offer to provide for them. This is a new lease of life for her mother and the children, but, though she herself moves with Alec to "a stylish lodging-house" at Sandbourne . . . and has all the material comfort she can want, we are to understand that the spirit goes out of her at this point. "These clothes are what he's put upon me: I didn't care what he did wi' me!" she tells Angel when he returns to England and seeks her out at Sandbourne; and Angel receives an impression then that Tess has "spiritually ceased to recognize the body before him as hers—allowing it to drift, like a corpse upon the current, in a direction dissociated from its living will." . . . Tess, of course, is labouring here under the shock of Angel's unexpected return and of the realization that "it is too late" . . . , but it is into her whole renewed relationship with Alec that she has, in effect, drifted as mere flesh, like a corpse. In agony, she goes back to Alec, who is still in bed, and with "her lips . . . bleeding from the clench of her teeth upon them," says to him: "O, you have torn my life all to pieces . . . made me be what I prayed you in pity not to make me be again! . . . My own true husband will never, never—O God—I can't bear this!—I cannot!" . . . Tess's situation is tragic; but, wanting Angel and having given herself to Alec (like Catherine caught between Heathcliff and her husband in *Wuthering Heights*), it is she who has torn her life to pieces—and breakdown is her only recourse. It is in a "moment of mad grief," Angel later supposes, that "her mind [loses] its balance" and she kills Alec in final desperate abandon. . . . (pp. 85-6)

Tess then runs out after Angel in order to tell him what she has done:

> By degrees he was inclined to believe that she had faintly attempted at least, what she said she had done; and his horror at her impulse was mixed with amazement at the strength of her affection for himself, and at the strangeness of its quality, which had apparently extinguished her moral sense altogether. Unable to realize the gravity of her conduct she seemed at last content . . .
>
> It was very terrible if true; if a temporary hallucination, sad. But, anyhow, here was this deserted wife of his, this passionately-fond woman, clinging to him without a suspicion that he would be anything to her but a protector. He saw that for him to be otherwise was not, in her mind, within the region of the possible. Tenderness was absolutely dominant in Clare

at last. He kissed her endlessly with his white lips, and held her hand, and said—

'I will not desert you! I will protect you by every means in my power, dearest love, whatever you may have done or not have done!' . . .

It is a moving scene, as Tess, after all her suffering, finds acceptance at last. But for her there is now nothing left except the week's happiness she snatches with Angel before her arrest at Stonehenge. For Angel, as he comes to believe that she has, at the least, attempted murder, the wheel comes full circle in the rhythm of change, and he is now called on to respond to a Tess whose "taint" is far worse than when he first rejected her, a being whose "moral sense" seems to be altogether "extinguished." What is remarkable is that he is equal to the occasion, his self-mastery being attained now not through a cold self-control but a readiness to let go. His instinctive reaction of horror at her deed is at once mediated by a deeper understanding of what has led her to it. Faced by a supreme test, Angel does not this time subdue substance to conception: taking "the gravity of her conduct" into account, he nevertheless fully sets beside it the woman who is clinging to him, accepting the "passionately-fond woman" as his "deserted wife"; and it is now that woman in all the anguish of her frailty and strength who is his first concern. This reconciliation of hitherto contending forces in Angel is epitomized in the "tenderness" that is "absolutely dominant" in him at last, in his tender kisses and protectiveness, for it is in such tenderness that spirit bespeaks itself flesh and flesh is made one with spirit.

Only now, when it is tragically too late, are Tess and Angel ready for full relationship. Within the house in which they take refuge there may be "affection, union, error forgiven," but outside is "the inexorable." . . . The closing pages of the novel imply that for Angel there may still be left the possibility of a new union with Tess's younger sister. But when he joins hands with 'Liza-Lu after Tess's execution and "[goes] on," he leaves ruin behind him. Angel may be said to have found himself in the end, but the lives that have been lost are now irredeemable. (pp. 86-7)

H. M. Daleski, "'Tess of the d'Urbervilles': Mastery and Abandon," in his The Divided Heroine: A Recurrent Pattern in Six English Novels, *Holmes & Meier Publishers, Inc., 1984, pp. 69-87.*

J. HILLIS MILLER (essay date 1982)

[*An American critic, Miller is associated with the "Yale critics," a group which includes Harold Bloom, Paul de Man, and Geoffrey Hartman. Although the Yale critics are generally considered the most influential critical group in America today, they have little in common beyond the fact that they all teach at Yale. Throughout his career Miller has successfully applied several critical methods to literature, including New Criticism (which examines a literary work as an object complete in itself through a close analysis of symbol, image, and metaphor, and which holds that literature should not be interpreted as a manifestation of ethics, history, or an author's psychology), the existential phenomenology of Georges Poulet (which views each author's work as the product of a unique individual consciousness with specific understandings of nature, society, time, and space, and thus cannot be understood in terms of generalizations about an era or period), and deconstructionism. Based on the thought of French critic and philosopher Jacques Derrida, deconstructionism asserts that language can never express a speaker's intended meaning, and that in itself language can convey no objective meaning. This concept opposes the traditional critical view that the study of literature is the search for meaning, ideas, and truths in a text. Deconstructionists concentrate solely on the linguistic elements of a text, denying the representational function of words and delineating instead the way a work is constructed of verbal forms. Deconstructionism, then, posits a basic similarity, if not sameness, in all works of literature. Miller and his colleague de Man are the most prominent American practitioners of deconstructive method. In the following excerpt, Miller discusses how several repetitive thematic patterns provide the possibility of various interpretations of the theme and meaning of* Tess.]

The narrative fabric of ***Tess of the d'Urbervilles*** is woven of manifold repetitions—verbal, thematic, and narrative. At the same time, it is a story about repetition. * * * * (p. 116)

I shall concentrate on the interpretation of a single important passage in the novel, the one describing Alec's violation of Tess. This passage is one in which many forms of repetition are both operative and overtly named. I have called what happens to Tess her "violation." To call it either a rape or a seduction would beg the fundamental questions which the book raises, the questions of the meaning of Tess's experience and of its causes. Here is the passage:

D'Urberville stooped; and heard a gentle regular breathing. He knelt and bent lower, till her breath warmed his face, and in a moment his cheek was in contact with hers. She was sleeping soundly, and upon her eyelashes there lingered tears.

Darkness and silence ruled everywhere around. Above them rose the primeval yews and oaks of The Chase, in which were poised gentle roosting birds in their last nap; and about them stole the hopping rabbits and hares. But, might some say, where was Tess's guardian angel? where was the providence of her simple faith? Perhaps, like that other god of whom the ironical Tishbite spoke, he was talking, or he was pursuing, or he was in journey, or he was sleeping and not to be awaked.

Why it was that upon this beautiful feminine tissue, sensitive as gossamer, and practically blank as snow as yet, there should have been traced such a coarse pattern as it was doomed to receive; why so often the coarse appropriates the finer thus, the wrong man the woman, the wrong woman the man, many thousand years of analytical philosophy have failed to explain to our sense of order. One may, indeed, admit the possibility of a retribution lurking in the present catastrophe. Doubtless some of Tess d'Urberville's mailed ancestors rollicking home from a fray had dealt the same measure even more ruthlessly toward peasant girls of their time. But though to visit the sins of the fathers upon their children may be a morality good enough for divinities, it is scorned by average human nature; and it therefore does not mend the matter.

As Tess's own people down in those retreats are never tired of saying among each other in their fatalistic way: "It was to be." There lay the pity of it. An immeasurable social chasm was to divide our heroine's personality there-

> after from that previous self of hers who stepped from her mother's door to try her fortune at Trantridge poultry-farm.

I have said that this passage describes Tess's violation. Yet, as almost all commentators on the scene have noted, the event is in fact not described at all, or at any rate it is not described directly. It exists in the text only as a blank space, like Tess's "beautiful feminine tissue . . . practically blank as snow as yet." It exists in the gap between paragraphs in which the event has not yet occurred and those which see it as already part of the irrevocable past. It exists in the novel as a metaphor. Doubtless Hardy was not free to describe such a scene literally. The reader will remember in this connection the notorious fact that in the first periodical version of ***Tess*** in *The Graphic*, Hardy had to have Angel Clare wheel Tess and the other girls across a puddle in a wheelbarrow rather than carry them across in his arms. The episode of Tess's violation by Alec does not occur in *The Graphic* version at all. Even so, the effacement of the actual moment of Tess's loss of virginity, its vanishing from the text of the finished novel, is significant and functional. It is matched by the similar failure to describe directly all the crucial acts of violence which echo Tess's violation before and after its occurrence: the killing of the horse, Prince, when Tess falls asleep at the reins, the murder of Alec, the execution of Tess. Death and sexuality are two fundamental human realities, events which it seems ought to be present or actual when they happen, if any events are present and actual. In ***Tess*** they happen only offstage, beyond the margin of the narration, as they do in Greek tragedy. They exist in the novel in displaced expressions, like that gigantic ace of hearts on the ceiling which is the sign that Alec has been murdered, or like the distant raising of the black flag which is the sign that Tess has been hanged.

The sign in the novel of Tess's violation, the metaphor which is its indirect presence in Hardy's language, has a deeper significance than those of the more straightforward ace of hearts or black flag. Tess's rape or seduction exists in the novel in a metaphor of drawing. 'It is the marking out of a pattern on Tess's flesh. "Analytical philosophy," says the narrator, cannot explain "why it was that upon this beautiful feminine tissue there should have been traced such a coarse pattern as it was doomed to receive." This metaphor belongs to a chain of figures of speech in the novel, a chain that includes the tracing of a pattern, the making of a mark, the carving of a line or sign, and the act of writing. * * * * (pp. 116-18)

Hardy's feelings about Tess were strong, perhaps stronger than for any other of his invented personages. He even obscurely identified himself with her. The reader here encounters an example of that strange phenomenon in which a male author invents a female protagonist and then falls in love with her, so to speak, pities her, suffers with her, takes her to his bosom, as Hardy's epigraph from *Two Gentlemen of Verona* affirms he did in the case of Tess: "Poor wounded name, my bosom as a bed/Shall lodge thee." * * * * (p. 119)

The emotional experience of following through the novel no doubt forms that background of agreement about the novel which is shared by almost all readers and forms the basis for

The Crown Inn, Marnhull, Dorset, the original for The Pure Drop, Marlott, in Tess.

discussions of it and even for disagreements about what the novel means * * * * (p. 119)

It is because all good readers of ***Tess*** would agree that Tess suffers and even tend to agree that she does not wholly deserve her suffering, and it is because all good readers of ***Tess*** share in the narrator's sympathy and pity for that suffering, that we care about the question of why Tess suffers so. At the same time, apparently casual, peripheral or "abstract" elements, such as the use of the figure of writing to describe Tess's deflowering, are not foreign to her suffering or to the reader's re-experience of it. The figures are a major vehicle for the communication of the emotional rhythms the novel and its adjacent poem create in the reader. What could be more moving than to know that Tess's self-hatred or self-disparagement is so great that, thinking of her life as having made an ugly inscription on the world, like a shocking graffito on a wall, she wants every "trace" of herself obliterated. Because the reader is moved, he may want to understand just what is implied by Hardy's repeated use of this metaphor.

The metaphor of the tracing of a pattern has a multiple significance. It assimilates the real event to the act of writing about it. It defines both the novel and the events it presents as repetitions, as the outlining again of a pattern which already somewhere exists. Tess's violation exists, both when it "first" happens and in the narrator's telling, as the re-enactment of an event which has already occurred. The physical act itself is the making of a mark, the outlining of a sign. This deprives the event of any purely present existence and makes it a design referring backward and forward to a long chain of similar events throughout history. (pp. 119-20)

Sex, physical violence, and writing all involve a paradoxical act of cutting, piercing, or in some way altering some physical object. The paradox lies in the fact that the fissure at the same time establishes a continuity. It makes the thing marked a repetition and gives it in one way or another the power of reproducing itself in the future. The word "paradox," in fact, is not, strictly speaking, appropriate here, since it presupposes a prior logical coherence which the paradox violates, going against what is normally taught or said * * * * (pp. 120-21)

The acts of sexual conjunction, of physical violence, and of writing create gaps or breaks, as, for example, "an immeasurable social chasm was to divide our heroine's personality thereafter from that previous self of hers."

All three of these acts in ***Tess*** converge in the multiple implications of the metaphor of grafting used to describe the relation of Tess and Alec. The metaphor is overt when the narrator says that though the spurious Stoke-d'Urbervilles were not "of the true tree," nevertheless, "this family formed a very good stock whereon to regraft a name which sadly wanted such renovation" . . . , or when Tess's father says of Alec, "sure enough he mid have serious thoughts about improving his blood by linking on to the old line" . . . , or when her mother says, "as one of the genuine stock, she ought to make her way with 'en, if she plays her trump card aright.". . . The metaphor of grafting may be present covertly, according to a characteristically complex conjunction of motifs, when the rapid ride Tess takes with Alec in the dog cart, the ride that leads to Alec giving her "the kiss of mastery" . . . , is described in the metaphor of a splitting stick: "The aspect of the straight road enlarged with their advance, the two banks dividing like a splitting stick; one rushing past at each shoulder." * * * * (p. 121)

The "kiss of mastery" which anticipates Alec's sexual possession of Tess is "imprint[ed] . . . , as though it were a design stamped with a die, and Tess tries to undo the kiss by "wip[ing] the spot on her cheek that had been touched by his lips". . . , as though the kiss had left a mark on her cheek. The word "graft" comes from a word meaning carving, cutting, or inscribing. "Graph" has the same etymology. With "graft" may be associated another word meaning a traced or carved-out sign, "hieroglyph." * * * * (p. 122)

The novel itself is defined in the prefaces as a mark imprinted on Hardy's mind, as a die strikes a coin, and repeated or re-inscribed in the words of the text. The novel is, Hardy tells his readers in his preface to the fifth edition, "an impression, not an argument.". . . (p. 124)

The novel proper is repeated by its title, but its subtitle, by the epigraph, and by its sequence of four prefaces or explanatory notes. These prefaces discuss the way the novel and its subtitle are repetitions. ***Tess of the d'Urbervilles,*** says Hardy in the note to the first edition, is "an attempt to give artistic form to a true sequence of things." The sequence existed first. The novel repeats it in a different form. "To exclaim illogically against the gods, singular or plural," he says in the preface to the fifth edition, "is not such an original sin of mine as he [Andrew Lang, who had attacked the novel] seems to imagine" [See *TCLC,* Vol. 10]. The novel is the repetition of an older sin, Shakespeare's sin in *King Lear,* or the historical Gloucester's sin before that. In the preface of 1912 Hardy says that the subtitle, "A Pure Woman/Faithfully Presented," "was appended at the last moment, after reading the final proof." It is a summary of the whole, another form of duplication.

Besides calling attention to the way the book is a repetition, the prefaces are also themselves reaffirmations of the novel. They are attempts to efface it or to apologize for it which in that apology reiterate it or admit that once it is written it cannot be erased, as, within the fiction, Tess's life, once it has happened, can never not have been. The novelist in his own way repeats the fate of his heroine. Neither can escape from the reiteration of an act performed in the past. (p. 125)

The episodes of ***Tess of the d'Urbervilles*** take place in a line, each following the last. Ultimately they form a row traced out in time, just as Tess's course is traced across the roads of southern England. Each episode in Tess's life, as it occurs, adds itself to previous ones, and, as they accumulate, behold!, they make a pattern. They make a design traced through time and on the landscape of England, like the prehistoric horses carved out on the chalk downs. Suddenly, to the retrospective eye of the narrator, of the reader, and ultimately even of the protagonist herself, the pattern is there. Each event, as it happens, is alienated from itself and swept up into the design. It ceases to be enclosed in itself and through its resonances with other events becomes a sign referring to previous and to later episodes which are signs in their turn. When an event becomes a sign it ceases to be present. It becomes other than itself, a reference to something else. For this reason Tess's violation and the murder must not be described directly. They do not happen as present events because they occur as repetitions of a pattern of violence which exists only in its recurrences and has always already occurred, however far back one goes.

In one way or another most analyses of prose fiction, including most interpretations of ***Tess of the d'Urbervilles,*** are based on the presupposition that a novel is a centered structure which may be interpreted if that center can be identified. This center will be outside the play of elements in the work and will explain and organize them into a fixed pattern of meaning deriving from this center. Hardy's insistent asking of the question "Why does Tess suffer so?" has led critics to assume that their main task is to find the explanatory cause. The reader tends to assume that Hardy's world is in one way or another deterministic. Readers have, moreover, tended to assume that this cause will be single. It will be some one force, original and originating. The various causes proposed have been social, psychological, genetic, material, mythical, metaphysical, or coincidental. Each such interpretation describes the text as a process of totalization from the point of departure of some central principle that makes things happen as they happen. Tess has been described as the victim of social changes in nineteenth-century England, or of her own personality, or of her inherited nature, or of physical or biological forces, or of Alec and Angel as different embodiments of man's inhumanity to woman. She has been explained in terms of mythical prototypes, as a Victorian fertility goddess, or as the helpless embodiment of the Immanent Will, or as a victim of unhappy coincidence, sheer hazard, or happenstance, or as the puppet of Hardy's deliberate or unconscious manipulations.

The novel provides evidence to support any or all of these interpretations. ***Tess of the d'Urbervilles,*** like Hardy's work in general, is overdetermined. The reader is faced with an embarrassment of riches. The problem is not that there are no explanations proposed in the text, but that there are too many. A large group of incompatible causes or explanations are present in the novel. It would seem that they cannot all be correct. My following through of some threads in the intricate web of Hardy's text has converged toward the conclusion that it is wrong in principle to assume that there must be some single accounting cause. For Hardy, the design has no source. It happens. It does not come into existence in any one version of the design which serves as a model for the others. There is no "original version," only an endless sequence of them, rows and rows written down as it were "in some old book," always recorded from some previously existing exemplar.

An emblem in the novel for this generation of meaning from a repetitive sequence is that red sign Tess sees painted by the itinerant preacher: THY, DAMNATION, SLUMBERETH, NOT. Each episode of the novel, or each element in its chains of recurrent motifs, is like one of these words. Each is a configuration which draws its meaning from its spacing in relation to the others. In the strange notation of the sign-painter, this gap is designated by the comma. The comma is a mark of punctuation which signifies nothing in itself but punctuation, a pause. The comma indicates the spacing in the rhythm of articulation that makes meaning possible. Each episode of the novel is, like one of the words in the sign, separated from the others, but when all are there in a row the meaning emerges. This meaning is not outside the words but within them. Such is the coercive power of pre-established syntactic sequences, that a reader is able to complete an incomplete pattern of words. Tess completes in terror and shame the second sign the painter writes: THOU, SHALT, NOT, COMMIT——, and the reader knows that the relation of 'Liza-Lu and Angel will repeat in some new way the universal pattern of suffering, betrayal, and unfulfilled desire which has been established through its previous versions in the book.

Tess wanders through her life like a sleepwalker, unaware of the meaning of what she is doing. She seeks a present satisfaction which always eludes her until her final happiness in the shadow of death. Her damnation, however, slumbereth not. This "damnation" lies in the fact that whatever she does becomes a sign, takes on a meaning alienated from her intention. Hardy affirms his sense of the meaning of Tess's story not by explaining its causes but by objectively tracing out her itinerary so that its pattern ultimately emerges for the reader to see.

Hardy's notion of fatality is the reflex of his notion of chance. Out of the "flux and reflux—the rhythm of change" which "alternate[s] and persist[s] in everything under the sky" . . . emerges as if by miracle the pattern of repetitions in difference forming the design of Tess's life. Such repetitions produce similarity out of difference and are controlled by no center, origin, or end outside the chain of recurrent elements. For ***Tess of the d'Urbervilles*** this alternative to the traditional metaphysical concept of repetition emerges as the way the text produces and affirms its meaning * * * * (pp. 139-42)

Tess of the d'Urbervilles, like Hardy's other novels, brilliantly explores the implications for an understanding of human life of a form of repetition which is immanent. Such a sequence is without a source outside the series. (p. 142)

On the basis of this definition of immanent repetition, it is possible to identify what Hardy means by the first half of his definition of ***Tess of the d'Urbervilles*** as "an attempt to give artistic form to a true sequence of things." The artistic form is the novelist's interpretation of the events. This interpretation does not falsify the events, but it imposes meaning on them by reading them in a certain way, as a sentence may have entirely different meanings depending on how it is articulated. The meaning is there and not there. It is a matter of position, of emphasis, of spacing, of punctuation. (p. 142)

Attention is insistently called to the act of reading, in the broad sense of deciphering, throughout ***Tess.*** One way is the many examples of false interpretation which are exposed by the narrator. These include the comic example of the bull who thought it was Christmas Eve because he heard the Nativity Hymn, or the more serious dramatization of Angel's infatuation with Tess and his interpretation of her as like Artemis or like Demeter. . . , or the description of Tess's "idolatry" of Angel . . . , or Tess's false reading of nature as reproaching her for her impurity. All interpretation is the imposition of a pattern by a certain way of making cross-connections between one sign and those which come before or after. Any interpretation is an artistic form given to the true sequence of things. Meaning in such a process emerges from a reciprocal act in which both the interpreter and what is interpreted contribute to the making or the finding of a pattern * * * * (pp. 143-44)

To add a new interpretation to the interpretation already proposed by the author is to attach another link to the chain of interpretations. The reader takes an impression in his turn. He represents to himself what already exists purely as a representation. To one purity the reader adds a subsequent purity of his own. This is Hardy's version of the notion of multiple valid but incompatible interpretations * * * * (p. 144)

In ***Tess of the d'Urbervilles,*** in any case, the narrator always presents not only the event with its "objective" elements, but also his interpretation of the event. At the same time he shows his awareness that the interpretation is "purely" imposed not inherent, except as it is one possibility among a limited repertoire of others. An example would be the "objective" description of the sun casting its beams on Tess. This is first interpreted as like the act of a god, but that interpretation is then ironically undercut: "His present aspect . . . explained the old time heliolatries in a moment.". . . The narrator's act in not only describing the true sequence of things but also giving it artistic form is shown as what it is by its doubling within the text in the interpretative acts of the characters. The narrator always sees clearly what is "subjective" in Tess's reading of her life, but this insight casts back to undermine his own readings. These multiple acts of interpretation are not misinterpretations in relation to some "true" interpretation. Each telling, even the most clear-sighted one, is another reading in its turn. The bare "reality" Angel sees when he falls out of love with Tess is as much an interpretation as the transfiguration of the world he experiences when he sees her as a goddess and the world as irradiated by her presence.

The power of readings to go on multiplying means that Tess's wish to be "forgotten quite" cannot be fulfilled. The chain of interpretations will continue to add new links. Tess can die, but the traces of her life will remain, for example in the book which records the impression she has made on the narrator's imagination. Her life has a power of duplicating itself which cancels the ending her failure to have progeny might have brought. The life of her sister will be, beyond the end of the book, another repetition with a difference of the pattern of Tess's life. Beyond that, the reader comes to see, there will be another, and then another, ad infinitum. If the novel is the impression made on Hardy's candid mind by Tess's story, the candid reader is invited to receive the impression again in his turn, according to that power of a work of art to repeat itself indefinitely to which the novel calls attention in a curious passage concerning Tess's sensitivity to music. Here is a final bit of evidence that Hardy saw the principle of repetition, in life as in art, as impersonal, immanent, and self-proliferating rather than as controlled by any external power, at least once a given repeatable sequence gets recorded in some form of notation or "trace." The "simplest music" has "a power over" Tess which can "well-nigh drag her heart out of her bosom at times." . . . She reflects on the strange coercive effect church music has on her feelings: "She thought, without exactly wording the thought, how strange and godlike was a composer's power, who from the grave could lead through sequences of emotion, which he alone had felt at first, a girl like her who had never heard of his name, and never would have a clue to his personality." . . . In the same way, ***Tess of the d'Urbervilles,*** as long as a single copy exists, will have its strange and godlike power to lead its readers through some version of the sequences of emotion for which it provides the notation. (pp. 144-46)

J. Hillis Miller, " 'Tess of the D'Urbervilles': Repetition as Immanent Design," in his Fiction and Repetition: Seven English Novels, *Cambridge, Mass.: Harvard University Press, 1982, pp. 116-46.*

ADDITIONAL BIBLIOGRAPHY

Abercrombie, Lascelles. "Epic Form." In his *Thomas Hardy: A Critical Study,* pp. 129-52. New York: Russell & Russell, 1964.

Compares Hardy's use of epic form in *Tess* and *Jude the Obscure*.

Bonica, Charlotte. "Nature and Paganism in Hardy's *Tess of the d'Urbervilles.*" *E.L.H.: A Journal of English Literary History* XLIX, No. 4 (Winter 1982): 849-62.

Discusses Hardy's anthropomorphic depiction of nature.

Brick, Alan. "Paradise and Consciousness in Hardy's *Tess.*" *Nineteenth-Century Fiction* XVII, No. 2 (September 1962): 115-34.

Examines Hardy's use of Biblical imagery with particular emphasis on allusions to an Edenic paradise and to humanity's fall from grace.

Brooks, Jean R. *"Tess of the d'Urbervilles:* A Novel of Assertion." In her *Thomas Hardy: The Poetic Structure,* pp. 233-53. Ithaca, N.Y.: Cornell University Press, 1971.

Examines Tess's struggle to assert her individuality against laws of nature, heredity, society, and economics operating in the novel.

Brown, Susan Hunter. " 'Tess' and *Tess:* An Experiment in Genre." *Modern Fiction Studies* XXVIII, No.1 (Spring 1982): 25-44.

Examines *Tess* by using criteria generally applied to discussions of the short story.

Davis, W. Eugene. *"Tess of the d'Urbervilles:* Some Ambiguities about a Pure Woman." *Nineteenth-Century Fiction* XXII, No. 4 (March 1968): 397-401.

Questions Hardy's conception of Tess's purity.

Draper, R. P., ed. *Hardy: The Tragic Novels.* New York: Macmillan Press, 1975, 256 p.

Includes discussion of character in *Tess* by Douglas Brown and essays on the novel's imagery by Tony Tanner and David Lodge.

Eakins, Rosemary L. *"Tess*: The Pagan and Christian Traditions." In *The Novels of Thomas Hardy,* edited by Anne Smith, pp. 107-25. New York: Barnes and Noble, 1979.

Discusses allusions to Christian and pagan beliefs in the novel.

Enstice, Andrew. "Wessex Vignettes: *Tess of the d'Urbervilles.*" In his *Thomas Hardy: Landscapes of the Mind,* pp. 111-54. London: Macmillan Press, 1979.

Detailed discussion of similarities between the real Dorset county and Hardy's fictional Wessex.

Friedman, Alan. "Thomas Hardy: 'Weddings Be Funerals'." In his *The Turn of the Novel,* pp. 38-74. New York: Oxford Univerity Press, 1966.

Discusses Tess's innocence, destruction, and symbolic replacement by her younger sister.

Gose, Elliott B., Jr. "Psychic Evolution: Darwinism and Initiation in *Tess of the d'Urbervilles.*" *Nineteenth-Century Fiction* XVIII, No. 3 (December 1963): 261-72.

Discusses Hardy's application of Darwin's theory of evolution in *Tess*.

Griffith, Philip Mahone. "The Image of the Trapped Animal in Hardy's *Tess of the d'Urbervilles.*" *Tulane Studies in English* XIII (1963): 85-94.

Discusses the symbolic identification of Tess with trapped or hunted animals.

Hamilton, Horace E. "A Reading of *Tess of the d'Urbervilles.*" In *Essays in Literary History Presented to J. Milton French,* edited by Rudolf Kirk and C. F. Main, pp. 197-216. New York: Russell & Russell, 1965.

Examines the interconnected allegorical patterns of Christian theology and pagan belief in *Tess*.

Hazen, James. *Tess of the d'Urbervilles* and *Antigone.*" *English Literature in Transition* XIV, No. 4 (1971): 207-15.

Explores the significant relationships and resemblances between *Tess* and Sophocles' tragedy.

Hornback, Bert G. *"Tess of the d'Urbervilles."* In his *The Metaphor of Chance: Vision and Technique in the Works of Thomas Hardy,* pp. 109-25. Athens: Ohio University Press, 1971.

Discusses weaknesses in the novel generated by Hardy's attempt to write a tragic work as well as an attack on Victorian morality.

Horne, Lewis B. "The Darkening Sun of Tess Durbeyfield." *Texas Studies in Literature and Language* XIII, No. 2 (Summer 1971): 299-311.
Discusses the significance of sun and earth imagery in *Tess*.

Kelly, Mary Ann. "Hardy's Reading in Schopenhauer: *Tess of the d'Urbervilles*" *Colby Library Quarterly* XVIII, No. 3 (September 1982): 183-98.
Draws a connection between Hardy's familiarity with Schopenhauer's "godless and fatalistic philosophy" and his indication in *Tess* that the individual's "continual loss of happiness is directly related to the fact that he has no real conscious choices in life."

Kettle, Arnold. "Thomas Hardy: *Tess of the d'Urbervilles.*" In his *An Introduction to the English Novel,* Vol. II, pp. 45-60. London: Hutchinson University Library, 1953.
Discusses *Tess* as a "social document" that portrays the inevitable destruction of the English peasant class by modern commercial interests.

Laird, J. T. *The Shaping of "Tess of the d'Urbervilles."* London: Oxford at the Clarendon Press, 1975, 193 p.
Provides detailed textual analysis of the composition of the novel and "traces [its] gradual evolution from the Ur-version to its final printed form."

Marshall, George O., Jr. "Hardy's *Tess* and Ellen Glasgow's *Barren Ground." Texas Studies in Literature and Language* I, No. 4 (Winter 1960): 517-21.*
Compares the similarities in theme, tone, and detail in both novels.

McDowall, Arthur. "The Tragic Novels." In his *Thomas Hardy: A Critical Study,* pp. 79-84. London: Faber and Faber, 1931.
Discusses the emotional impact of Hardy's prose in *Tess* and describes the novel as being "plainly written from the heart."

Meisel, Perry. *"Tess of the d'Urbervilles."* In his *Thomas Hardy: The Return of the Repressed,* pp. 118-35. New Haven and London: Yale University Press, 1972.
Examines how Tess's psychological battle between her "natural and social components" brings about her tragedy.

Morrell, Roy. "A Note on the Machine in *Tess.*" In his *Thomas Hardy: The Will and the Way,* pp. 29-34. Kuala Lumpur: University of Malaya Press, 1965.
Examines the symbolic significance of the threshing machines in *Tess.*

Paris, Bernard J. "A Confusion of Many Standards: Conflicting Value Systems in *Tess of the d'Urbervilles." Nineteenth-Century Fiction* XXIV, No. 1 (June 1969): 57-79.
Discusses the novel's lack of thematic unity.

Roberts, Marguerite, ed. Introduction to *"Tess" in the Theatre,* pp. xv-cviii. Toronto: University of Toronto Press, 1950.
Provides information regarding the adaptation of *Tess* for the stage. The text also includes three versions of the play: Hardy's original script, a dramatization by Lorimar Stoppard, and Hardy's 1925 revision of his original play.

Silverman, Kaja. "History and Female Subjectivity in *Tess of the d'Urbervilles." Novel* XVIII, No. 1 (Fall 1984): 5-28.
In-depth semiotic discussion of the novel.

Simmons, James. "Ambiguities of Tess as a 'Pure' Woman." *American Notes and Queries* X, No. 6 (February 1972): 86-8.
Discusses symbolism concerning the nature of Tess's sexuality.

Sommers, Jeffrey. "Hardy's Other *Bildungsroman: Tess of the d'Urbervilles." English Literature in Transition* XXV, No. 3 (1982): 159-68.
Argues that Tess embodies "many of the features denominated as typical of the *Bildungsroman.*"

Stewart, J. I. M. *"Tess of the d'Urbervilles."* In his *Thomas Hardy: A Critical Biography,* pp. 162-83. New York: Dodd, Mead & Co., 1971.
Discusses Hardy's composition of *Tess* and autobiographical aspects of the novel.

Van Dyke, Henry. *"Tess of the d'Urbervilles."* In his *The Man Behind the Book: Essays in Understanding,* pp. 283-305. New York: Charles Scribner's Sons, 1929.
Claims, based on an interview with Hardy, that he "loved" Tess over all of his characters and that the novel marks him "at the height of his tragic powers."

Vigar, Penelope. *"Tess of the d'Urbervilles."* In her *The Novels of Thomas Hardy: Illusion and Reality,* pp. 169-88. London: Athlone Press, 1974.
Contends that, more than any of Hardy's novels, the distinctiveness of *Tess* is dependent upon "Hardy's consistent use of suggestion and implication" in narrative technique.

Williams, Randall. "Novels of Character and Environment." In his *The Wessex Novels of Thomas Hardy,* pp. 20-7. New York: E. P. Dutton & Co., 1924.
Considers Tess's struggles with her circumstances "axiomatic [of] Hardy's interpretation of Life."

T(homas) E(dward) Lawrence

1888-1935

(Also wrote under pseudonymns of T. E. Shaw, John Hume Ross, and Colin Dale) English autobiographer, translator, diarist, essayist, poet, and critic.

Lawrence, popularly known as Lawrence of Arabia, is an enigmatic figure whose literary works have often been overshadowed by his dramatic personal life. Yet today most critics agree upon the importance of his autobiographical work *Seven Pillars of Wisdom,* an epic literary documentation of the Arab Revolt during World War I. The continuing appeal of this work is evident in the remarkably diverse critical treatment that it has received, including examinations of *Seven Pillars* as military history, poetic autobiography, self-created myth, spiritual confession, and journal of psychosexual pathology. Its evident resistance to precise classification, as well as its stylistic versatility and vivid, often macabre war scenes, continues to elicit considerable critical analysis. But perhaps the primary reason that Lawrence's masterpiece is still read and studied today is for its revelation of Lawrence himself—one of the most singularly complex and engaging personalities of modern times.

Psychologists and biographers frequently point to Lawrence's illegitimate birth and punishments by his religiously strict and guilt-ridden mother as key factors underlying his partially megalomaniacal, masochistic, and insecure nature, which he progressively disclosed in his autobiographical writings. Lawrence's father was an Irish baronet named Chapman; his mother was an Englishwoman named Madden who became housekeeper to Chapman and his wife. A strong romantic attachment formed between Chapman and Madden, prompting him to relinquish his title and estate and set up residence with Madden elsewhere in Ireland. During the course of a series of relocations the two adopted the name Lawrence. By the time they finally settled in Oxford, England, in 1896, their second child, Thomas Edward, was eight years old and recognized by them as markedly intelligent and talented, if rambunctious and independent. Although in letters written years later Lawrence admitted to a troubled relationship with his domineering mother, he shared with his father an intense interest in geology, archaeology, and medieval architecture, and often occupied himself by taking stone and brass rubbings of various artifacts in the area or by excavating in and around the city. In 1907, Lawrence entered Jesus College, Oxford, with a history scholarship. There he met noted archaeologist David Hogarth, whom the young Lawrence impressed with his sizable knowledge and interest in archaeology and related studies. Conducting extensive research outside his regular coursework, Lawrence immersed himself in his chosen specialty, the Middle Ages, by readings in history, military history, Provençal poetry, and French chansons de geste.

In 1909, with the encouragement of Hogarth, Lawrence traveled to Syria and Palestine to study the ancient castles and fortresses of the Middle East, hoping to prove his hypothesis that Western builders had heavily influenced construction in the East at the time of the twelfth-century Crusades; Lawrence's findings were later published as *Crusader Castles*. After graduating with first-class honors in 1910, Lawrence was offered a postgraduate traveling scholarship from Magdalen College

The Granger Collection, New York

so that he might participate in an extended dig near the ancient Hittite city of Carchemish. He willingly accepted the offer and returned to the Middle East, working there sporadically for the next three years under Hogarth and Orientalist Leonard Woolley, and readily assimilating Arab language, customs, and culture. In 1914 Lawrence joined Woolley in a British military intelligence expedition to the Sinai, followed by work as an aide to the war office's map department. After Britain's declaration of war on Turkey, Lawrence was officially stationed in Cairo as a military intelligence officer. Accompanying Sir Ronald Storrs in 1916 to the Hejaz region of what is now Saudi Arabia, Lawrence met with the sons of Husain ibn Ali (Sherif of Mecca), who had proclaimed a revolt against the Turkish empire. Lawrence soon established a close relationship with Husain's son Emir Feisal, and was assigned to work within Feisal's camp as a British liaison officer. Well educated from earlier extensive study of the classic military theoreticians, Lawrence proceeded during the next two years to play an instrumental role in marshalling and inspiring the Arab tribes to carry out highly effective guerilla raids against Turkish forces. In 1918, after the revolutionaries defeated the Turkish-German forces, Lawrence returned to England a national hero.

Wishing to ensure sovereignty for the Arabs to whom he had become both emotionally and ideologically attached, Lawrence participated in the Paris Peace Conference as technical advisor to the British and interpreter and spokesman for Feisal, who had emerged as coleader of the Arab forces along with his brother Abdullah. His efforts to secure complete Arab rule of Syria and Iraq, however, were not realized by the close of the conference. In later negotiations, acting as Middle East advisor to then-colonial secretary Winston Churchill, Lawrence did obtain Iraq and Transjordan for the Arabs in 1921. By then, however, Lawrence had grown weary of politics and the unwelcome publicity sparked by journalist Lowell Thomas's sensational travelog series covering Lawrence's part in the Arab Campaigns. To compound matters, Lawrence, encouraged by friends to document his wartime experiences, had exhausted himself with the completion of two massive drafts of *Seven Pillars of Wisdom,* the first of which was mysteriously lost; the second was later destroyed by Lawrence after he had revised it into the "Oxford" version, so called because he had eight copies made by the *Oxford Times* for safekeeping. Lawrence's letters dating from this period reveal the enormous emotional strain under which he was writing as he effectively relived many painful events of the war, causing speculation that the original draft was purposely mislaid due to Lawrence's trepidations concerning both the quality and content of his bulky manuscript.

In a seemingly abrupt decision, Lawrence renounced his fame and several promising career opportunities and enlisted in the Royal Air Force under the name John Hume Ross, informing only his closest friends as to his whereabouts. Regarding his motives to commit what one biographer has described as "social suicide," Lawrence explained in a letter to Robert Graves: "It was a necessary step, forced on me by an inclination towards ground-level: by a despairing hope that I'd find myself on common ground with men:. . . . by an itch to make myself ordinary in a mob of likes. . . ." Later, describing his contentment with the cloistered, ordered existence offered by the R.A.F., Lawrence wrote to Lionel Curtis: "There has not been presented to me, since I have been here, a single choice: everything is ordained—except that harrowing choice of going away from here the moment my will to stay breaks down. With this exception it would be determinism complete—and perhaps in determinism complete there lies the perfect peace I have so longed for." However, Lawrence's contentment was destroyed in early 1923 when the press discovered and revealed his identity. Unwilling to accept the "respectable" life that his friends urged him to assume, Lawrence enlisted in the Royal Tank Corps as T. E. Shaw.

Lawrence reentered the R.A.F. in 1925 and, until his retirement ten years later, employed his mechanical and organizational talents in several developmental projects. Although many of his friends considered this decade of Lawrence's life an extremely unfortunate and needless waste of genius, Lawrence himself found it the happiest of his life; as far as literary endeavors, it was certainly his most productive. Aided editorially by George Bernard Shaw, Lawrence readied *Seven Pillars* for private, limited circulation in 1926, commissioning illustrations by young artists and personally supervising the typographic design. To cover the extra production costs incurred, an abridged edition entitled *Revolt in the Desert* was issued for mass circulation the following year. Although publication of his other major work, *The Mint,* was delayed until 1955 to protect the privacy of numerous individuals, Lawrence did assemble the contents—diary notes of his experiences in the R.A.F.—into manuscript form. In addition, Lawrence published translations of Adrien le Corbeau's *Le gigantesque* and Homer's *Odyssey,* several pseudonymous book reviews, introductions to works by other English writers, and wrote numerous letters in which he offered sound critical advice to such writer-acquaintances as Siegfried Sassoon, E. M. Forster, Henry Williamson, and C. Day Lewis. During these years Lawrence also developed a keen interest in motorcycling. Shortly after his retirement from the R.A.F. in 1935, Lawrence was involved in a motorcycle accident and died as a result of his injuries.

Critics discussing *Seven Pillars* commonly acknowledge Lawrence's indebtedness to the panoramic grandeur of Charles Doughty's classic *Arabia Deserta* (1888). An ardent admirer of Doughty, both as a writer and man of action, Lawrence strove to create a highly mannered Victorian prose that would lend his story a lyrical, ageless quality. Viewing Lawrence as an artist-warrior who continually reveals his inner self to the reader, critics find that *Seven Pillars* transcends conventional historical narrative through its emphasis on the narrator's psyche as well as outward events and the actions of other figures of the Arab Revolt, modulating from self-obsession to self-detachment to create in effect a spectrum of narrative modes. Despite Lawrence's claim that *Seven Pillars* represents a largely accurate documentation of the revolt, Richard Aldington has charged that Lawrence was simply a self-propagandist interested in enhancing his own historical stature. Most critics, however, have emphasized the value of *Seven Pillars* not as history but as modern epic. Uncovering a direct correspondence with Homerian and Vergilian epic, scholars point to paeans following battles as well as heightened battle descriptions peopled with such memorable characters as Auda Abu Tayi, Lawrence's modern equivalent of Homer's brave Achaean warriors. Also prevalent are numerous medieval and chivalric motifs that reflect Lawrence's strong identification with that age and evidence his predilection for the romances of William Morris and for Thomas Malory's *Morte d'Arthur,* which he carried with him in the desert throughout the revolt.

Despite its classical, medieval, and romantic influences, *Seven Pillars* is unmistakably modern in outlook. Irving Howe has asserted that "it is as necessary for comprehending the twentieth century as Brecht's poems or Kafka's novels or Pirandello's plays," while the introspective tone and a profusion of narrative modes in the work have led to comparisons with the works of Marcel Proust and James Joyce. The unifying element of the work is the character of Lawrence—a self-conscious leader straddling two cultures who alternates between extreme confidence and profound pessimism regarding his personal identity and earthly purpose. Readings of *Seven Pillars* as spiritual autobiography or confessional testament focus especially on this last aspect, perceiving Lawrence as a sexually confused ascetic preoccupied with purity and salvation and yet simultaneously attracted to the animalistic and the grotesque. Considered the pivotal focus of the work from a psychological standpoint is the chapter covering the Deraa episode, in which Lawrence, while on a spy mission, is captured by Turkish soldiers and tortured and sodomized. His detached description of this traumatic experience is written in consonance with the conventions of flagellation literature and exposes Lawrence's fascination with the subject of sadomasochism. Consequently, his puritanical attitudes toward sexual matters (he claims to have remained celibate throughout his life) create heightened tension when counterpoised with his reaction to the torture directed by the Turkish leader: "I remembered smiling idly at him, for a delicious warmth, probably sexual, was swelling through me. . . ." This masochistic urge has been linked thematically to the progressive denial of self in *Seven Pillars,* in which pain, dissolution, and death appear increasingly attractive to Lawrence as he questions his role as a leader of the Arabs. Contrary then to such classics of autobiography as the confessions of St. Augustine and Jean-Jacques Rousseau, *Seven Pillars* moves toward a largely pessimistic and spiritually distraught, rather than optimistic and spiritually renewed outlook.

Although lacking the epic traits of *Seven Pillars, The Mint* is equally essential, critics contend, to an understanding of Lawrence. It remains particularly interesting from a linguistic standpoint as Lawrence abandoned the artificial prose of *Seven Pillars,* for which he had been criticized, and wrote in his own unique, vivid style of life in the R.A.F. Structurally, *The Mint* has been termed cinematic in form for its measured movement from scene to scene and has earned Edward Garnett's declaration that it possessed "the just precision of Maupassant at his best." Indeed Garnett, editor of the manuscript, considered *The Mint* superior to *Seven Pillars* as he believed it revealed more of Lawrence the man and displayed a more natural prose. *The Mint* links with and distinguishes itself from its precursor through a continuation of the identity theme; whereas *Seven Pillars* demonstrates a definite decrescendo in the narrator-hero's self-esteem and raison d'être, *The Mint* displays Lawrence reaffirming himself within the brotherhood of the R.A.F. Although Lawrence's major, nonautobiographical writings—the prose translation of the *Odyssey* and the *Letters*—are much less discussed than these works, they have nonetheless been admired, particularly the *Letters* for their insight into the keen critical and philosophical mind of Lawrence.

A recent revival of interest in Lawrence's works has served to reaffirm his immense significance for our age and to insure that *Seven Pillars* is recognized as a twentieth-century classic. As Stanley and Rodelle Weintraub have concluded: "What will survive, as license of language turns *The Mint* into a period piece and new translations of the *Odyssey* become annual nonevents, are those works which illuminate the unforgettable Lawrence personality: his letters and the *Seven Pillars*. Few epics are lived and fewer written. As authentic epic, despite its stridency and posturing, the *Seven Pillars of Wisdom* passes almost beyond literary criticism, for in it life and art are fused."

(See also *Contemporary Authors,* Vol. 115.)

PRINCIPAL WORKS

Carchemish: Report on the Excavations at Djerabis on Behalf of the British Museum, Part I [with C. Leonard Woolley] (archaeological study) 1914
The Wilderness of Zin [with C. Leonard Woolley] (archaeological study) 1915
Carchemish: Report on the Excavations at Djerabis on Behalf of the British Musuem, Part II [with C. Leonard Woolley] (archaeological study) 1921
Seven Pillars of Wisdom: A Triumph (autobiography) 1922; also published as *Seven Pillars of Wisdom: A Triumph* [revised edition], 1926; also published as *Revolt in the Desert* [abridged edition], 1927
**Crusader Castles.* 2 vols. (archaeological study) 1936
The Diary of T. E. Lawrence MCMXI (diary) 1937
The Letters of T. E. Lawrence (letters) 1938
T. E. Lawrence to his Biographers Robert Graves and Liddell Hart (letters) 1938
Oriental Assembly (essays) 1939
Men in Print (criticism) 1940
The Essential T. E. Lawrence (letters, diary, criticism, poetry, autobiography) 1951
***The Mint* (autobiography) 1955
Evolution of a Revolt: Early Postwar Writings of T. E. Lawrence (essays) 1968
Minorities [editor] (poetry) 1971

*This work was written in 1910.

**This work was written from 1922 to 1928.

E. M. FORSTER (letter date 1924)

[Forster was a prominent English novelist, critic, and essayist, whose works reflect his liberal humanism. His most celebrated novel, A Passage to India *(1924), is a complex examination of personal relationships amid the conflicts of the modern world. Although some of Forster's critical essays are considered naive in their literary assessments, his discussion of fictional techniques in his* Aspects of the Novel *(1927) is regarded as a minor classic in literary criticism. Forster enjoyed a close friendship with Lawrence beginning near the time of the latter's enlistment in the R.A.F.; the two shared through numerous letters a lively exchange of views regarding each other's literary works and theories. In the following excerpt, Forster offers some critical thoughts on* Seven Pillars of Wisdom.*]*

Have still about 20 chapters of [***The Seven Pillars of Wisdom***] to read, but should like to start putting down a few notes on it. I think it's a great affair, and am much obliged to you for allowing me to read it. I told Sassoon, also Mrs. Hardy, how much I liked it, and won't go on to you, because you probably prefer criticisms, tips. I will try and send some, on the faint chance of their helping you. My own qualifications: have written some novels, also done journalism and historical essays; no experience of active life, no power of managing men, no Oriental languages, but some knowledge of Orientals. Have been a bit in Egypt and India. Now you can discount.

Dividing literature into fluid and granular, you come into the latter class. It's not merely your subject matter that makes me say this. You do present (though you don't see) life as a succession of items which are organically connected but yet have some sort of intervals between them. i.e. you give a series of pictures. I see people on camels, motionless, I look again and they are in a new position which I can connect with its predecessor, but is similarly immobile. There never can have been a Movement with so little motion in it! It all goes on, it's never unreal, practically every sentence and word is alive, but life unprintable—in the spaces between the words—is absent. Trying to think of a big book to clear my ideas (no good thinking of small ones) I hit on *War and Peace*. It's years since I read it, but there's an incident where Natasha & Nicolai (I think) ride through open country to pay a call on an uncle which gives me a clue. There's the fluid. Not the succession of positions, but the actual slide into the uncle's house, round it, and out again into the air.

Your scenery is perfect. Scenery always waits—comparatively speaking. Rum stumped you rather, perhaps, but nothing else, not Azrak. I noted ch. XLI par. 13, as an example of your power to hold the eye and excite the mind, but any thing else would have done. I suppose you know Geology. How we who don't can expect to convey any thing except slush I don't know. At any minute you can tell us what we are standing on and looking at. This gives a tremendous sense of security in your work.

Animals wait less. The fidgetiness of men—it seems, even of Arabs—is remarkable. How far can the granular method present them? With the big exception of pathos, (which I'll try to touch presently)—I find some thing not quite satisfactory in your presentation of the human race. I'll tell you what to do about it too!! Put in more conversations. Inverted commas are a great help for this sort of writing. I have Auda in view particularly here. He seemed to me your most elaborate character, you had taken great trouble over him, but he was always going—not dead but quiet. All your characters tend to go *quiet* when the eye is removed, including your own character [presentations are what I am discussing throughout of course]. Well to counteract this static tendency, while at the same time keeping your method, you should introduce more conversation. Auda—and you—gained enormously when you ragged his epic style. I was suddenly rolling about among you. And in this connection, you'd do well to have more funny passages. ['There was no more fun.'—I daresay, but that's not my job]. Turn King Hussein oftener on to the telephone. Shoot your own camel oftener in her neck. Talks and bits o' fun—not sardonic reflections, they congeal—are awfully useful, they are hostages given by the human mind to the human surface. You've got some and you want a few more. I think of what I can test your presentations by: I have seen Murray for 2 minutes, Feisal for 10, Storrs for an hour, and all years ago. 'Yes, he does them all right' is my valuable verdict, 'but they give out something he hasn't given them'.

Well well, this leads me to your style. Discount an undergraduate petulance here. I do not think it is a Cambridge style. And I disagree hotly with the gauntlet thrown down in I. 2. I'm damned if I ever lift a phrase of yours knowingly though my loyalty to your book is real and will be lasting: have never read a book with such sympathy: am not sympathetic to Tolstoy——Well. Book being lengthy, you have very rightly several styles, one for R.E.8s, and that sort of thing, another for normal narrative, another for reflections, another for crises of emotion or beauty. The criticism I'd offer is that your reflective style is not properly under control. Almost at once, when you describe your thoughts, you become obscure, and the slightly strained sense which you then (not habitually) lend words, does not bring your sentence the richness you intended, imparts not colour but gumminess. (pp. 58-60)

I saw what you could do over some dead Turks early on, and soon after you did something more difficult in describing the disillusion on reaching Akaba. Best of all— a philosophic glory was added—was the dumb way-farer by the water-bath at Rum. Now there comes that breathing sliding reality that I do so love and that is always sliding away from me over a precipice.

I must end these notes some how. There is the tedious question as to whether the book's a whole. Of course it is. It would have been even if some one else had written it, because the subject matter imposes unity, and you reinforce that unity although your personal purpose may have been double. An awfully sad book. (pp. 61-2)

By the way your book helped me to finish a book of my own. Seemed to pull me together. You have only to go on showing it to people to get praised, but it is itself an exposure of that very process and of all that is second rate in public life. You will never show it to any one who will like it more than I do: its subject and incidentals suit me: also my critical sense never stops telling me it's fine. (p. 62)

E. M. Forster, in a letter to T. E. Lawrence in February, 1924, in Letters to T. E. Lawrence, *edited by A. W. Lawrence, Jonathan Cape, 1962, pp. 58-62.*

G. BERNARD SHAW (essay date 1927)

[*Shaw is generally considered the greatest and best-known dramatist to write in the English language since Shakespeare. Following the example of Henrik Ibsen, he succeeded in revolutionizing the English stage, disposing of the romantic conventions and devices of the "well-made play," and instituting the theater of ideas, grounded in realism. During the late nineteenth century, Shaw was also a prominent literary, art, and music critic. In 1895 he became the drama critic for* The Saturday Review, *and his reviews therein became known for their biting wit and brilliance. During his three years at* The Saturday Review, *Shaw determined that the theater was meant to be a "moral institution" and "elucidator of social conduct." As Samuel Hynes has noted, Shaw was driven by a rage to better the world. A Fabian socialist, he wrote criticism which is often concerned with the humanitarian and political intent of the work under discussion. Shaw's friendship with Lawrence, which began in the early 1920s and lasted until Lawrence's death, has been the subject of much discussion and study. Acting as both a paternal and editorial influence, Shaw encouraged Lawrence in his work and completed a page-by-page revision of the original or "Oxford version" of* Seven Pillars of Wisdom. *In the following excerpt from a review of* Revolt in the Desert—*an abridged version of that revision designed for a popular audience—Shaw praises the work as one of the great achievements in modern literature.*]

This abridgment [***Revolt in the Desert***] of the famous ***Seven Pillars*** (itself an abridgment) contains as much of the immense original as anyone but an Imam has time to read. It is very handsomely and readably printed, and has not a dull or empty sentence from end to end. . . . The book does not, like the original, leave you with a sense of having spent many toilsome and fateful years in the desert struggling with Nature in her most unearthly moods, tormented by insomnia of the conscience: indeed it is positively breezy; but that will not be a drawback to people who, having no turn for "salutary self-torture," prefer a book that can be read in a week to one that makes a considerable inroad on a lifetime.

Among the uncommon objects of the worldside, the most uncommon include persons who have reached the human limit of literary genius, and young men who have packed into the forepart of their lives an adventure of epic bulk and intensity. The odds against the occurrence of either must be much more than a million to one. But what figure can estimate the rarity of the person who combines the two? Yet the combination occurs in this amazing age of ours in which we sit holding our breaths as we await wholesale destruction at one another's hands. In Mr. Apsley Cherry-Garrard's *Worst Journey in the World* we have a classic on Antarctic exploration written by a young man who endured it at its blackest. And within ten years of that we have "Colonel Lawrence" (the inverted commas are his own) appearing first in the war news from Arabia as a personage rather more incredible than Prester John, and presently emerging into clear definition as the author of one of the great histories of the world, recording his own conquests at an age at which young company officers are hardly allowed to speak at the mess table.

The fate of the man who has shot his bolt before he is thirty, and has no more worlds to conquer, may be compared curiously with that of the genius who dies unwept, unhonored and unsung, and is dug up and immortalized a century later. Nobody will ever be able to decide which is more enviable. But it is mitigated if the hero has literary faculty as a second string to his bow; and Colonel Lawrence has this with a vengeance. He can re-create any scene, any person, any action by simple description, with a vividness that leaves us in more complete possession of it than could "the sensible and true avouch of our own eyes." He packs his narrative with detail that would escape nine hundred and ninety-nine out of a thousand observers; so that when he has made you see the start of Feisal's motley legions as plainly as he saw it himself, he has also left you with an exact knowledge of how an Arab mounts a camel and arranges his outlandish clothes for riding, and how he manages to carry a slave with him (when he has one) as a western might carry a portmanteau. As to the landscape painting, no padding novelist gravelled for lack of matter ever approached Col. Lawrence's feats in this art. And the descriptions are not interpolated: they are so woven into the texture of the narrative, that the sense of the track underfoot, the mountains ahead and around, the vicissitudes of the weather, the night, the dawn, the sunset and the meridian, never leaves you for a moment.

You feel, too, the characters of the men about you: you hear the inflections of their voices, the changes in their expression, all without an instant of reader's drudgery. There is a magical brilliance about it; so that you see it at once with the conviction of reality and with the enchantment of an opera. Auda after his roaring camel charge, with his horse killed, his field glass shattered, and six bullet holes through his clothes, unhurt and ascribing his escape (under Allah) to an eighteen-penny Glasgow Koran which he had bought as a talisman for a hundred and twenty pounds, is at once a squalidly realistic Arab chieftain and a splendid leading baritone. The description has the quality of orchestration. Lawrence's own famous camel charge, which was checked by his having the camel shot under him, and ended, after a whole Arab tribe had thundered over him, in the irresistible anti-climax of the discovery that he had shot the camel himself, makes a page that reduces Tennyson's *Charge of the Light Brigade* to minor poetry.

These blazing climaxes of adventure stand out from an inferno of tormented bodies and uneasy souls in which one is glad to meet a rascal for the sake of laughing at him. The subjective side which gives Miltonic gloom and grandeur to certain chapters of ***The Seven Pillars,*** and of the seventy and seven pillars out of which they were hewn, plays no great part in this abridgment: Lawrence's troublesome conscience and agonizing soul gives place here to his impish humor and his scandalous audacities; but it will interest the latest French school of drama to know that their effect remains, and imparts an otherwise unattainable quality to the work, even though they are not expressed.

G. Bernard Shaw, "The Latest from Colonel Lawrence," in The Spectator, *Vol. 138, No. 5150, March 12, 1927, p. 429.*

LEONARD WOOLF (essay date 1927)

[*Woolf is best known as one of the leaders of the "Bloomsbury Group" of artists and thinkers, and as the husband of novelist Virginia Woolf, with whom he founded the famous Hogarth Press. The Bloomsbury Group, which was named after the section of London where the members lived and met, also included Clive and Vanessa Bell, John Maynard Keynes, Lytton Strachey, Virginia Woolf, Desmond MacCarthy, and several others. The group's weekly meetings were occasions for lively discussions of philosophy, literature, art, economics, politics, and life in general. Although the group observed no formal manifesto, Woolf and the others generally held to the tenets of philosopher G. E. Moore's* Principia Ethica, *the essence of which is, in Moore's words, that "one's prime objects in life were love, the creation and enjoyment of aesthetic experience, and the pursuit of knowledge." In the following excerpt, Woolf favorably reviews* Revolt in the Desert.]

I began Colonel Lawrence's **"Revolt in the Desert"** . . . with interest, but with, I daresay unreasonable, prejudice. One had heard so much about the previous, private, unexpurgated edition and how the author had given a copy to X and had refused a copy to Z, though Z prayed on bended knee for it, and how copies were already selling for £200 each in the agony column of the TIMES, that one began to have suspicions of a mixture of mystery and advertisement. And then why should a man whose name appears to be T. E. Lawrence print it in inverted commas on the title page of his book? The answer is, I suppose, "Why shouldn't he?" At any rate, as soon as I had read fifty pages of the book, my prejudices began to evaporate, and by the end they had vanished.

At first, indeed, prejudice became confirmed. This was due to Colonel Lawrence's style. It is so imitative of Doughty's in "Arabia Deserta" as to be near parody. It imitates Doughty even to the sweeping itself absolutely bare of conjunctions, so that every sentence begins again with a full breath and ends with a really full stop. It often acquires the same gnarled texture with the same habit of an order twisted with queer adjectives and adverbs. . . . But the moment of irritation at this sham Doughty soon passed. After all, why should not a man imitate Doughty? The more you read "Arabia Deserta," the more you feel that it is Arabia itself that has made the style, that nothing could give so immediately the feel of its sands and its nomads than those gnarled and twisted sentences, so swept and bare of even a conjunction. Perhaps it is the desert itself which makes a man write like that if he once gets the feel of the desert. At any rate it did not take fifty pages before I had lost my irritation with Colonel Lawrence's style.

The book very soon begins to hold one, and once held you are not released until the last page. It has that rare thing, an epic quality about it. It is not a great book in the sense that "Arabia Deserta" is a great book, a great piece of literature. Colonel Lawrence has not, I suppose, Doughty's stature or quality of imagination. But he has a great story to tell, a story of precisely that stuff which Homer, Virgil, and their kind were moved to turn into epics. That the story is of things that happened the day before yesterday makes no difference, or that aeroplanes and motor-cars take the place of spears and chariots. The story of great racial adventure, with its heroes, its fights, its sufferings, its journeyings, its visions, and its sacrifices, has a poetry of its own which many people would have said had died out of the modern world. This book proves that is not so. Colonel Lawrence has really seen and felt those things in his story which are of the stuff which make the poetry of the epic. That he has done so and coloured the fabric of his book with their colour is the reason why his little tricks and affectations and imitations fade into the background, and you gladly surrender to the sweeping fascination of the tale.

The book is a minor and a modern epic. Part of its fascination consists in its extreme modernity. You see this epic adventure through the eyes of a very queer and very modern man. . . . Colonel Lawrence tells [his story] extremely well. He makes it very vivid and exciting: the wild Arab fighting and looting, the raids on the railways, the intolerable marches through the furnace or bitter cold of that terrible country, the horrors of the Turkish retreat, and the intoxication of the entry into Damascus. If he had only done that, he would have written a superior travel book. But Colonel Lawrence has the sensitiveness, the psychological fidgetiness, the uneasy egomania, which seems to be characteristic of our age. What makes his epic adventure so much better than a superior travel book is the vision of it through this shifting, sensitive, peevish modern mind. In all ages men have found themselves, voluntarily or by chance, involved in romantic odysseys or high adventures, conquests, or wars of liberation, or voyages and discoveries, and many have written down their own account of them. . . . Compare the mind of Caesar in his Commentaries, of Marco Polo in the story of his travels, and of "T. E. Lawrence" in **"Revolt in the Desert,"** and you will see that the first two belong to the same species of animal, but one which is entirely different from that of "T. E. Lawrence." Yet thirteen hundred years separated Marco Polo from Caesar, and only six hundred separate "T. E. Lawrence" from Marco Polo. The differences is in the whole mental attitude, in the reaction of the mind to things, scenes, events, and the universe. The species to which Caesar and Marco Polo belonged, and which began to die out, I suppose, in the eighteenth century, took everything, life and death, mystery, romance, adventure, themselves and other people, quite simply and at their face value. They never looked round the corner or beneath the surface; they had a peculiar calm and dignity. Colonel Lawrence will never leave anything alone. He is in a perpetual fidget and psychological St. Vitus's dance, prying into his own psychology and picking over the minds of Feisal and Lord Allenby and all the Nasirs, Abdullas, and Audas who throng his pages. There is no calm, no simplicity, no dignity here. Or, if there is, they are always questioned, mocked by the jazz-tune which is the appropriate accompaniment of all the modern man's thoughts and feelings. This accounts for the queer atmosphere of almost peevish disillusionment which hangs over Colonel Lawrence's book. It is the epic of the modern man.

Leonard Woolf, "The Epic of the Modern Man," in The Nation and The Athenaeum, *Vol. XL, No. 24, March 19, 1927, p. 857.*

JOHN BUCHAN (essay date 1927)

[*Buchan was a Scottish politician, historian, and crime novelist whose* The Thirty-nine Steps *(1915) was made famous when adapted to the screen by Alfred Hitchcock. In the following excerpt Buchan, who was a friend of Lawrence, offers a laudatory review of* Revolt in the Desert.]

[**"Revolt in the Desert"**] is a masterpiece of production, for Lawrence has always made a hobby of such matters. It is superbly printed, and illustrated with many striking drawings by Augustus John and others.

First for the story. It is written with the uttermost candor, and with a notable command of English prose. It has none of Doughty's Elizabethan and Biblical archaisms, but the style has the grace of sound scholarship, and at times its vividness and realism are almost cruel. It is both a record of great deeds and the presentation of the soul of a land and a people and the soul of a man. . . .

[It is] an Odyssey and an Iliad combined completed before the age of thirty. But the book is not an epic, for there is none of the gusto and swing of epic. The scholar has become a superb man of action, but he remains a scholar—reflective, sensitive, tormenting himself with doubts and subtleties, analyzing each emotion with a terrible precision. He stands outside himself and comments like an impartial spectator. It is his psychological profoundity which makes his book so great a piece of literature. Lawrence owed his success mainly to the fact that his dream rode him like a passion.

It is easy to see why Lawrence desired his work to have a limited number of readers. The book is full of a noble beauty, but it is full also of terrible things, which are not for every eye. Such is the account of his capture as a spy in Deraa and what happened to him before he escaped. (pp. 659-60)

Once in 1918 I talked to a great Frenchman. He was of opinion that in the years to come few of the protagonists of the Great War would be remembered, since it had been a war of peoples rather than a war of leaders. The names of generals and statesmen would, he thought, pass into oblivion; but two figures would survive in the world's memory because they were the material of legend. One was d'Annunzio, and the other was Lawrence. This book gives the writer a second title to fame, for it is hard to believe that it will not live. It is a great work and a most paradoxical one, for here is romance acted and written of by one who despises it; supreme adventure narrated by one who cares nothing for it; war to the death waged by a scholar and a thinker; the wildest ambition of youth realized by a man whose dream burned to a white heat and in the moment of triumph died. (p. 660)

John Buchan, "Of Such Is History," in The Saturday Review of Literature, *Vol. III, No. 34, March 19, 1927, pp. 659-60.*

HERBERT READ (essay date 1927)

[*Read was a prolific English poet, critic, and novelist. Several convictions are central to his discussions of literature, the foremost being his belief that art is a seminal force in society and human development, and that a perfect society would be one in which work and art are one. He also believed that art and material progress are the result of conflicting forms of thought. In literature, the most dynamic conflict is between classicism and romanticism: "categories usually known as classicism and romanticism are related to their psychological origins in the individual, and shown to be, not alternatives equivalent to right and wrong, but tendencies which must be accepted as equally inevitable and reconciled in some more universal concept, which with due caution might be described as Humanism." Read's discussions of poetry are informed by his definition of two basic poetic forms, the organic and abstract. Organic form is that in which imagination dictates the form of a poem and fuses structure and content, as in free verse; abstract forms are those in which structure follows a fixed pattern, such as the sonnet. Read's preference for the former is central to his criticism. Read's work as a poet and novelist gave him special insight into the creative process; his tolerance of various literary theories enabled him to appreciate the works of many diverse artists and made him one of the more interesting English critics of the twentieth century. In the following excerpt from an article which first appeared in 1927 and was reprinted in* The Bibliophile's Almanac for 1928, *Read unfavorably appraises* Seven Pillars of Wisdom. *For Lawrence's response to Read's views, see the excerpt dated 1927.*]

By the time this note appears, the topical interest in Colonel Lawrence's book will have subsided. The heartless neglect which descends on all modern books, whatever their scale or quality, after their brief day, will descend on this book; and the meditative reader will wonder if, after all, it *was* a great book: whether all that the reviewers said about it was really true; whether Bernard Shaw is to be trusted as a *critic* of literature; and what good, finally, is the newspaper reputation of any book. In the end the reader finds himself alone: he has to decide for himself, to make up his own mind. (p. 35)

The Seven Pillars is a difficult book. Not difficult to read, in the ordinary sense, but difficult to bring into any definite focus. So much of it is vivid, but the author's mind behind it all is dark, and obscured by divided aims. It is this core of darkness which more than anything else puts one in doubt as to the essential greatness of the book. Great books are written in moods of spiritual light and intellectual certainty, and out of any other mood there only emerges an imperfect work of art. It might be less uncompromising to say that out of any other mood there only emerges a *romantic* work of art, but about the best romantic moods, moods held openly and consistently, there is a positiveness which relieves them from the charge of darkness and doubt. I do not, however, see this openness in ***The Seven Pillars of Wisdom.***

Why an affectation of mystery? Why give this title to your book, to which it has no relevant or perceptible application? Why produce it with an expensive parade of eccentricity and bad taste? I am no professed bibliophile, but in *The Bibliophile's Almanack* I would venture to say that this book is a monstrous exhibition of all that a book should not be. It is an amateur's nightmare. It is heavy and ungainly; it is printed in a small type and illustrated by an incongruous array of artists. It is rather like a grangerized album of the 'sixties. For the decorations and drawings of Edward Wadsworth and William Roberts I have a great admiration, but they consort oddly with the splendid pavement portraits of Eric Kennington and the politer drawings of Professor Rothenstein and others. In many walks it is a good thing to discard tradition and invent new forms and fresh proportions; but there are no dogmas more rightly and immutably established than those which govern the margins of the printed page and its accompanying illustrations. Eric Kennington's portraits, however, slip off into the infinite space around them; their titles get printed on any patch of colour that comes in the way.

All these matters would perhaps be trifles were there not evidence that they are perversions which have been the intense care of the author. He has even gone to the length of ruthlessly cutting his text to suit his page. His dogma is: that an initial letter must be placed in the left-hand top corner of the page, and nowhere else; and that it must none the less start a paragraph. Pages and paragraphs are arranged accordingly. It is pleasant at any time to see an example of devotion to an abstract cause, and journalists are commonly made to suffer this form of torture. But journalism is one thing, and ***The Seven Pillars of Wisdom*** another—at least, so the reviewers would have us believe. Perhaps Colonel Lawrence himself has no such pretensions, and considers himself as no more than an honest hard-working scribbler, with superb 'copy', it is true, but what is the finest 'copy' in the world worth in the balance against an abstraction, a cause, an initial letter in the left-hand top corner of the page? I am not speaking ironically, for I think it is conceivable that Colonel Lawrence does really think in this way. He is sufficiently an analyst of minds to be under no illusions about his own.

The story of ***The Seven Pillars of Wisdom*** is splendid 'copy', but is it anything more? If it is, it is so by virtue either of its matter or its manner. By virtue of its matter, because if a story is of epic quality it will transcend its manner, passing from one story-teller to another until it perhaps receives that most immortal manner—the anonymous tradition. But in the present case we begin with a doubt—who is the hero of the story: Colonel Lawrence or the Arabian army? If Colonel Lawrence, then the story fails to reach epic quality because Colonel Lawrence, however brave and courageous he may have been, is not heroic. About the epic hero there is an essential undoubting directness: his aim is single and unswerving; he questions neither himself, his aims, nor his destiny. He may share his glory with his chosen band, his *comitatus,* but essentially he is self-possessed, self-reliant, arrogant and unintelligent. Colonel Lawrence was none of these things; in all these things he was at the contrary pole—full of doubts and dissemblings, uncertain of his aim, his pride eaten into by humility and remorse, his conduct actuated by intellectual and idealistic motives. It is no disparagement to say that out of such stuff no hero is made. Out of such stuff we only get a case of conscience, a problem of personality. Such problems, though of profound interest to the contemporaries and co-sufferers of a man, tend to dissolve with the circumstances which produced them. They are only saved from such a fate by their universal elements, as when the personality of Hamlet stands for the general mood of the Renaissance, or, in a lesser degree, as when Rousseau seems to embody the spirit of an epoch. But even Rousseau is a pathological case rather than a hero, inciting our curiosity rather than arousing our admiration.

To this limited extent Colonel Lawrence is representative: a lame duck in an age of lame ducks; a soldier spoilt by introspection and self-analysis; a man with a load on his mind.

But if Colonel Lawrence is not the 'hero' of this epic, can we discern one in the Arab nation? Surely not. We learn from this book, as from *Arabia Deserta,* that the Arabs have qualities which we can admire, such as a capacity for hardship and endurance: the possibilities, at least, of fine perceptions; and a real religious force. But these qualities cannot for long blind us to the overwhelming venality, pettiness, fanaticism and ignorance of the mass of them. This realization is present in Colonel Lawrence's own mind, and acts as a blight on whatever there is of epic quality in that fine effort of strategy and cunning which culminated in the fall of Damascus. But let us realize this fact too: the Palestine Campaign was merely the romantic fringe of the war. In France and Belgium men of infinitely finer quality than these Arabs were enduring day after day, without the inspiration of the open horizon and all that that conveys of adventure and surprise, the dull and dispiriting agony of trench warfare. No one will be fool enough to make out of that horror an epic story, or to see in our armies a race of self-reliant heroes; but this Arabian adventure was no more than a dance of flies in the air beside the magnitude of that terrific earthy conflict. To see one of these adventurers, then, so to speak, 'get away with' the heroic buncombe in a literary press mostly in the hands of non-combatants, inspires me with a certain bitterness of which I ought to be ashamed, but which at any rate I am not ashamed to confess.

Perhaps this is all beside the point. I read ***The Seven Pillars of Wisdom*** with keen interest, and what more can man want? Nothing, if you will leave it at that. But if I am expected to pay the book the lip service I willingly pay to *Arabia Deserta,* then I revolt. ***The Seven Pillars of Wisdom*** is not in the same category. Doughty fills me with wonder, with reverence, and gives me unfailing enjoyment. 'Who touches this book touches a man'—and at every page: a man who was a great mind, a great patriarch among men, a great enduring character, pensive but self-possessed, inquiring but full of certainty. In ***The Seven Pillars of Wisdom*** I am only conscious of a bold adventurer; of an Oxford graduate with a civilian and supercilious lack of the sense of discipline; of a mind, not great with thought, but tortured by some restless spirit that drives it out into the desert to physical folly and self-immolation, a spirit that never triumphs over the body and never attains peace. (pp. 35-41)

Herbert Read, "'The Seven Pillars of Wisdom'," in The Bibliophile's Almanack for 1928, *edited by Oliver Simon and Harold Child, The Fleuron Limited, 1928, pp. 33-41.*

T. E. LAWRENCE (letter date 1927)

[*In the following excerpt from a letter to Edward Garnett, Lawrence responds to Herbert Read's criticism of* Seven Pillars of Wisdom *(see excerpt dated 1927).*]

This is going to be mainly about Read's very excellent note]see excerpt by Herbert Read dated 1927]. . . . (p. 547)

He starts off on a defeatist note, about the brief life of modern books. He may be talking in periods of geology, and be deploring the present neglect of Aurignacian letters; if he is thinking post-Homeric, then I call his sentiments rot. There has never been such interest in books as there is today, nor so much writing, nor so much book-publishing nor so much book-buying, nor so much reading of books, or about books. This century holds the record in every particular. A book's life only begins when the newness has passed off its covers, and when the reviewers have stopped talking. He is confusing the news-value of a book with its being read. Go to . . . *'Great books are written in moods of spiritual light and intellectual certainty'*.

I would maintain against him that these moods never produced an imaginative work the size of a mouse from any of the people sterile enough to feel certain. My notion of the world's big books are *War and Peace, The Brothers Karamazoff, Moby Dick,* Rabelais, *Don Quixote*. Of course we treat of prose. There's a fine set of cores of darkness! But of course his idea of a great book may be different. Probably he uses 'romantic' in some special sense, as a word of abuse. I do not know how the coteries transcribe it now-a-days. We used to mean by it books like the *Odyssey*, as compared with the 'classical' works, which were the *Iliad* or *Marmion* sort of thing.

Drawing of Lawrence by Augustus John. The Granger Collection, New York.

The title of my book [***Seven Pillars of Wisdom***] was a reminiscence, for my ear, of a destroyed book of mine. But it fits the new ***S. P.*** better than it fitted the old. Perhaps Read is not fond of Jewish symbolism? I hate bibliophiles, and did my best to throw them off the track with ***The S. P.;*** so I did not number my copies, or declare how large the edition was (the published guesses are wide of the truth) or have a standard binding, or signatures, or index, or anything posh. It is heavy, so as to be little carried about. Its type is too large for my taste, but the Lanston people hadn't a decent 11 point in 1923. It is grangerised of course. I said why, in my preface to the Illustrations. Why shouldn't I grangerise my own book? I bowdlerised it too.

The Rothenstein drawing was not asked to consort with the Kennington. It is not possible to put a coloured illustration on a page of type. So all my plates were segregated at the back of the book, in an appendix like a picture gallery. They had no connection, except that of needle and thread, with the text. When he says that the Kennington drawings slip off into the infinite space around them, he puts it better than I ever managed to explain my aim to myself. One doesn't bother, usually, to verbalise one's aspirations. Titles were printed where they went best, because they were just titles superposed on colour reproductions of drawings. He would have had me try to turn them into pictures, perhaps. I wanted them to remain outside the book, and be what they were.

Ruthlessly cutting the text to suit his page . . . any evidence of ruthless cutting, or of cutting, either? I am not aware of it. Of course 15% was cut in making this text from the Oxford version; but my aim and standard of cutting was always the betterment of the prose, and those people who have compared the versions generally give me best with the new one. There are plenty of initial letters not in the top left-hand corner of the page, by the way . . . unless he has the heresy of thinking each page is separate, and not, like trousers, inseparable as pairs. In which case we will not argue where the stress comes on a sheet of type-script.

Of course ***The S. P.*** is not a work of art. Who ever pretended it was? I write better than the majority of retired army officers, I hope; but it is a long way from that statement to literature. Yet ***The S. P.,*** if not art, is equally not 'scribble'. It is the best I could do—very careful, exact, ambitious; and a hopeless failure partly because my aim was so high. I think it better to have burst oneself overthinking and overtrying, than to do Max Beerbohmish little perfections. So I have pretensions—and haven't. . . . (pp. 547-49)

Isn't he slightly ridiculous in seeking to measure my day-to-day chronicle by the epic standard? I never called it an epic, or thought of it as an epic, nor did anyone else, to my knowledge. The thing follows an exact diary sequence, and is literally true, throughout. Whence was I to import his lay-figure hero? Leaders of movements have to be intelligent, as was Feisal, to instance my chief character. Read talks as though I had been making a book, and not a flesh-and-blood revolt. (p. 550)

Agreed a thousand times about Doughty. If only the people who run about after my farthing dip would go and read Doughty. But D. is partly to blame for that. These fellows here, with whom I have lived the last five years, are not so sure in their English as to enjoy *Arabia Deserta*. D. uses hard words for which they would need a dictionary, and his Scandinavian syntax puzzles them. He closed his goodness off from the world by not being as honest and simple in manner as he was in mind . . . and so people like Rosita Forbes and Mrs. Hull and me can still write about the desert.

His last six lines are, I'm sure, very near the truth; except that there too he must pursue his quarrel against the word adventure. He seems beset with whims and bogies. Has he in some way a grudge against something in life? In his writing I see a lack of happiness and of carelessness. In me there is so much of the cold-blooded calculator that I can understand him, I think, more or less by myself. The emotionalism of my ***S. P.*** is what sticks in his gizzard, and what he means when he girds at its romance and adventure . . . as if these forms of activity had some lien with emotion. You told me he was too intellectual:—perhaps, but not in this bit of work. Here he puts on paper his feelings towards the book, in the purest manner of the impressionists, for whom Middleton Murry has lived in vain. So he is much to my taste, for I feel through the appearance of those who would make criticism a science. (pp. 550-51)

T. E. Lawrence, in a letter to Edward Garnett on December 1, 1927, in his The Letters of T. E. Lawrence, *edited by David Garnett, Jonathan Cape, 1938, pp. 547-51.*

ROBERT GRAVES (essay date 1927)

[*Graves is a prolific English man of letters who is considered one of the most accomplished minor poets of the twentieth century. Strongly influenced by both World Wars and by his literary and emotional attachment to American writer Laura Riding, Graves displayed in his work a mixture of disquietude and cheerful romanticism. Although his subject matter is often characterized as traditional, he is credited with ingenious structural and linguistic experimentation. In addition to his achievements in verse and other creative genres, notably with the historical novel* I, Claudius *(1934), Graves is equally esteemed for his theoretical and critical works. The study* The White Goddess: A Historical Grammar of Poetic Myth *(1948) examines the appearance and importance of the mythical female deity in poetry—a reflection of a provocative and recurrent theme in his own work. In the following excerpt from one of the two biographies of Lawrence authorized by Lawrence himself (see also the Liddell Hart entry in the Additional Bibliography), Graves explains why he prefers the original "Oxford" text of* Seven Pillars of Wisdom *to* Revolt in the Desert.]

Seven Pillars of Wisdom is, beyond dispute, a great book; though there is such a thing as a book being too well written, too much a part of literature. Lawrence himself realizes this and was once, indeed, on the point of throwing it into the Thames at Hammersmith. It should somehow, one feels, have been a little more casual, for the nervous strain of its ideal of faultlessness is oppressive. Lawrence charges himself with 'literary priggishness,' but that is unfair. His aim was, all the time, simplicity of style and statement and this he achieved in the most expert way. He has, somewhere, confessed to a general mistrust of experts and it may be that he should have carried it further, and dispensed with expert advice in literary matters too. (Possibly, though, in actual practice he did; he was always a difficult pupil.) On the whole I prefer the earliest surviving version, the so-called Oxford text, to the final printed book which was the version that I first read consecutively. This is a physical rather than a critical reaction. The earlier version is 330,000 words long instead of 280,000 and the greater looseness of the writing makes it easier to read. From a critical point of view no doubt the revised version is better. It is impossible that a man like Lawrence would spend four years on polishing the text without improving it, but the nervous rigor that the revised book gave me has seemingly dulled my critical judgment. I may add that Lawrence had foreseen the effect that the book would have on me and refrained for many years from letting me see it. (pp. 407-08)

The Seven Pillars of Wisdom will not be reprinted in Lawrence's lifetime. It is not a book, people agree on Lawrence's behalf, that should be published for a popular audience. (A simple member of the public, an electrician, was shown the most painful chapter while proofs were being passed. Then he could do no work for a week, but walked up and down the pavement outside his house, unable to rid his mind of the horror of it. The chapter about the Turkish hospital is almost as painful.) Also popular publication might, they say, involve Lawrence in a series of libel actions: he seems to spare nobody in his desire to tell the whole story faithfully (least of all himself). Again, the censor might, it is suggested, ban as obscene some of the more painfully accurate accounts of Turkish methods of warfare. But in any case Lawrence never intended publishing the book, except privately, so these remarks are really irrelevant. The book was first written as a full-length and unrestrained picture of himself, his tastes, ideas and actions. He could not have deliberately confessed to so much had there been any chance of the book coming out. Yet to tell the whole story was the only justification for writing anything at all. And once written a strictly limited publication of the book promised to remove the need of even thinking about that part of his life again.

The historical accuracy of Lawrence's account has been jealously questioned by some overseas reviewers of ***Revolt in the Desert:*** he has been accused of self-interested exaggeration. However, as there were forty or fifty British officers, besides Arabs, as witnesses of his activities and as no one of them has challenged the accuracy of his statements, this criticism hardly calls for answer. Moreover, all the documents of the Arab Revolt are in the archives of the Foreign Office and will soon be available to students, who will be able to cross-check Lawrence's account and are likely to find that his chief fault has been telling rather less than the truth. (pp. 410-11)

Robert Graves, in his Lawrence and the Arabs, *Jonathan Cape, 1927, 454 p.*

EDWARD GARNETT (letter date 1928)

[*Garnett was a prominent editor for several London publishing houses, and discovered or greatly influenced the work of many important English writers, including Joseph Conrad, John Galsworthy, and D. H. Lawrence. He also published several volumes of criticism, all of which are characterized by thorough research and sound critical judgments. Through a common admiration for writer Charles Doughty, Lawrence met Garnett and the two quickly became close friends. Because Lawrence greatly valued Garnett's editorial instinct and insight, he entrusted him with the task of producing an abridgment of* Seven Pillars of Wisdom *and with the safekeeping of the* Mint *manuscript. In the following excerpt from a letter, Garnett applauds Lawrence for a masterful refinement of his art between the writing of* Seven Pillars *and* The Mint.]

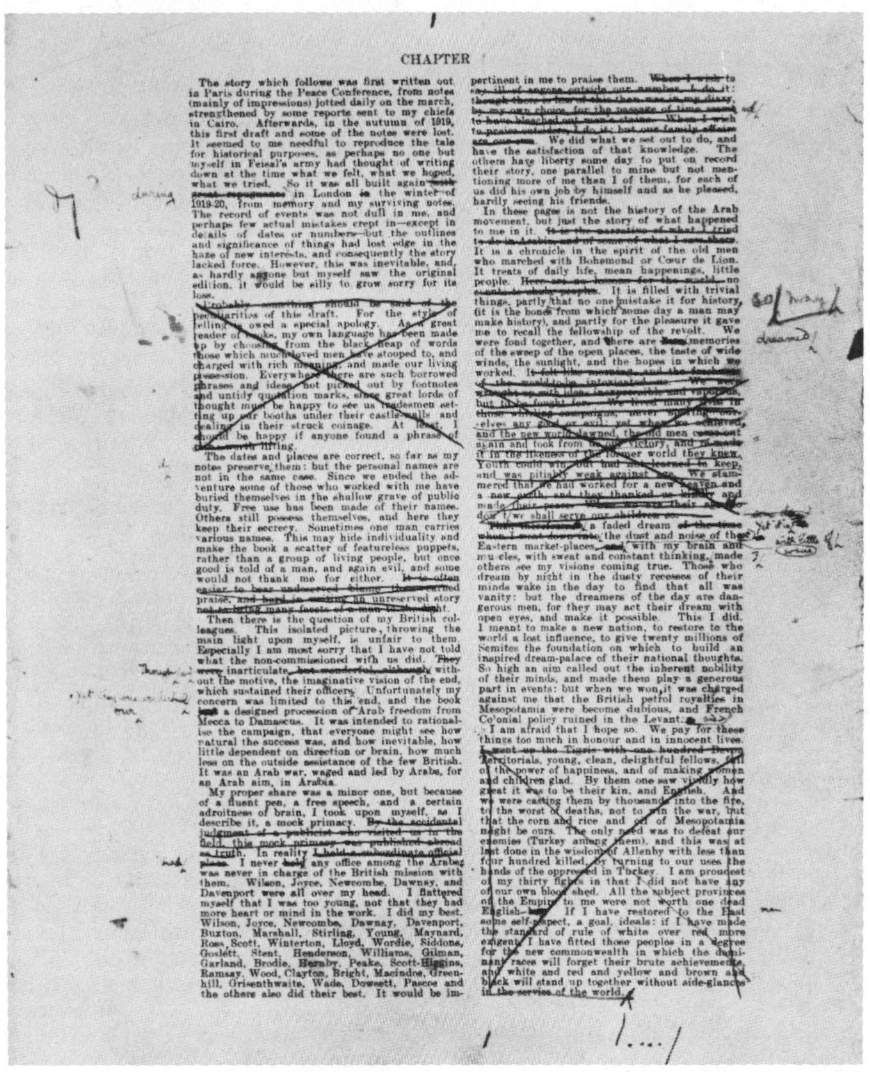

CHAPTER

The story which follows was first written out in Paris during the Peace Conference, from notes (mainly of impressions) jotted daily on the march, strengthened by some reports sent to my chiefs in Cairo. Afterwards, in the autumn of 1919, this first draft and some of the notes were lost. It seemed to me needful to reproduce the tale for historical purposes, as perhaps no one but myself in Feisal's army had thought of writing down at the time what we felt, what we hoped, what we tried. So it was all built again ~~with great repugnance~~ in London ~~in~~ the winter of 1919-20, from memory and my surviving notes. The record of events was not dull in me, and perhaps few actual mistakes crept in—except in details of dates or numbers—but the outlines and significance of things had lost edge in the haze of new interests, and consequently the story lacked force. However, this was inevitable, and, as hardly anyone but myself saw the original edition, it would be silly to grow sorry for its loss.

~~Probably something should be said of the peculiarities of this draft. For the style of telling is owed a special apology. As a great reader of books, my own language has been made up by choosing from the black heap of words those which much-loved men have stooped to, and charged with rich meaning, and made our living possession. Everywhere there are such borrowed phrases and ideas, not picked out by footnotes and untidy quotation marks, since great lords of thought must be happy to see us tradesmen setting up our booths under their castle walls and dealing in their struck coinage. At least, I should be happy if anyone found a phrase of mine worth lifting.~~

The dates and places are correct, so far as my notes preserve them: but the personal names are not in the same case. Since we ended the adventure some of those who worked with me have buried themselves in the shallow grave of public duty. Free use has been made of their names. Others still possess themselves, and here they keep their secrecy. Sometimes one man carries various names. This may hide individuality and make the book a scatter of featureless puppets, rather than a group of living people, but once good is told of a man, and again evil, and some would not thank me for either. ~~It is often easier to bear undeserved blame than unearned praise, and hard in writing an unreserved story not to bring many facets of a man to the light.~~

Then there is the question of my British colleagues. This isolated picture, throwing the main light upon myself, is unfair to them. Especially I am most sorry that I have not told what the non-commissioned with us did. ~~They were~~ inarticulate, ~~but wonderful, although~~ without the motive, the imaginative vision of the end, which sustained their officers. Unfortunately my concern was limited to this end, and the book ~~is~~ a designed procession of Arab freedom from Mecca to Damascus. It was intended to rationalise the campaign, that everyone might see how natural the success was, and how inevitable, how little dependent on direction or brain, how much less on the outside assistance of the few British. It was an Arab war, waged and led by Arabs, for an Arab aim, in Arabia.

My proper share was a minor one, but because of a fluent pen, a free speech, and a certain adroitness of brain, I took upon myself, as I describe it, a mock primacy. ~~By the accidental judgment of a publicist who visited us in the field, this mock primacy was published abroad as truth.~~ In reality ~~I held a subordinate official place.~~ I never ~~held~~ any office among the Arabs; was never in charge of the British mission with them. Wilson, Joyce, Newcombe, Dawnay, and Davenport were all over my head. I flattered myself that I was too young, not that they had more heart or mind in the work. I did my best. Wilson, Joyce, Newcombe, Dawnay, Davenport, Buxton, Marshall, Stirling, Young, Maynard, Ross, Scott, Winterton, Lloyd, Wordie, Siddons, Goslett, Stent, Henderson, Williams, Gilman, Garland, Brodie, Hornby, Peake, Scott-Higgins, Ramsay, Wood, Clayton, Bright, Macindoe, Greenhill, Grisenthwaite, Wade, Dowsett, Pascoe and the others also did their best. It would be impertinent in me to praise them. ~~When I wish to say ill of anyone outside our number, I do it: though there is less of this than was in my diary, by my own choice, for the passage of time seems to have bleached out men's stains. When I wish to praise outsiders, I do it; but our family affairs are our own.~~ We did what we set out to do, and have the satisfaction of that knowledge. The others have liberty some day to put on record their story, one parallel to mine but not mentioning more of me than I of them, for each of us did his own job by himself and as he pleased, hardly seeing his friends.

In these pages is not the history of the Arab movement, but just the story of what happened to me in it. ~~It is the narrative of what I tried to do in Arabia, and of some of what I saw there.~~ It is a chronicle in the spirit of the old men who marched with Bohemond or Cœur de Lion. It treats of daily life, mean happenings, little people. ~~Here are no lessons for the world, no disclosures to shock peoples.~~ It is filled with trivial things, partly that no one mistake it for history, (it is the bones from which some day a man may make history), and partly for the pleasure it gave me to recall the fellowship of the revolt. We were fond together, and there are ~~keen~~ memories of the sweep of the open places, the taste of wide winds, the sunlight, and the hopes in which ~~we~~ worked. ~~It felt like morning, and the freshness of the world-to-be intoxicated us. We were wrought up with ideas inexpressible and vaporous, but to be fought for. We lived many lives in those whirling campaigns, never sparing ourselves any good or evil: yet when we achieved, and the new world dawned, the old men came out again and took from us our victory, and re-made it in the likeness of the former world they knew. Youth could win, but had not learned to keep, and was pitiably weak against age. We stammered that we had worked for a new heaven and a new earth, and they thanked us kindly and made their peace. When we are their age no doubt we shall serve our children so.~~

~~[illegible]~~ a faded dream ~~of the time when I went down into~~ the dust and noise of the Eastern market-places, ~~and~~ with my brain and muscles, with sweat and constant thinking, made others see my visions coming true. Those who dream by night in the dusty recesses of their minds wake in the day to find that all was vanity: but the dreamers of the day are dangerous men, for they may act their dream with open eyes, and make it possible. This I did. I meant to make a new nation, to restore to the world a lost influence, to give twenty millions of Semites the foundation on which to build an inspired dream-palace of their national thoughts. So high an aim called out the inherent nobility of their minds, and made them play a generous part in events: but when we won, it was charged against me that the British petrol royalties in Mesopotamia were become dubious, and French Colonial policy ruined in the Levant.

I am afraid that I hope so. We pay for these things too much in honour and in innocent lives. ~~I went up the Tigris with one hundred Devon Territorials, young, clean, delightful fellows, full of the power of happiness, and of making women and children glad. By them one saw vividly how great it was to be their kin, and English. And we were casting them by thousands into the fire, to the worst of deaths, not to win the war, but that the corn and rice and oil of Mesopotamia might be ours. The only need was to defeat our enemies (Turkey among them), and this was at last done in the wisdom of Allenby with less than four hundred killed, by turning to our uses the hands of the oppressed in Turkey. I am proudest of my thirty fights in that I did not have any of our own blood shed. All the subject provinces of the Empire to me were not worth one dead English~~ [illegible]~~. If I have restored to the East some self-respect, a goal, ideals: if I have made the standard of rule of white over red more exigent, I have fitted those peoples in a degree for the new commonwealth in which the dominant races will forget their brute achievements, and white and red and yellow and brown and black will stand up together without side-glances in the service of the world.~~

First page of Edward Garnett's copy of the 1922 "Oxford" edition of Seven Pillars of Wisdom. *Editorial markings are Garnett's. By permission of the Houghton Library, Harvard University.*

Well, you've gone & done it this time! & knocked all your feeble pretences of not being a writer, etc etc. into final smithereens. I received the precious MS. [of ***The Mint***] on the 18th & read it, very carefully, in the next two days & the deeper I got the more delighted I was. It is a most *perfect* piece of writing. I call it a *classic* for there's not a word too much. It's elastic, sinewy, terse: & spirit & matter are the inside-out of its technique, perfectly harmonious throughout—inseparable as in all first rate stuff. Its very original in its effect, for having given us the essential in its living body, it smites one much harder than if you had made 'a book' of it, or told us more. That terse, sinewy, yet elastic form, all lean & athletic, is just what is right: the descriptions of the men, China, Sailor, Corp. Abner, Taffy, Stiffy, the Commandant, etc. are wonderfully drawn, mere thumbnail sketches, with the lines bitten in with a marked precision. Then, the atmosphere that grows more hard & bitter & north-easterly as the men get branded, or 'minted' in the struggle. There's nothing like it in the least in English: there may be in French? The style has the just precision of Maupassant at his best; but has of course, quite a different quality. And the narrative goes on justifying itself in its actuality—in its tensity of fact, just as 'The House of the Dead' does, so that one forgets it is a book. These chapters, XV Church, XIX Shitcart, XX Air commanding officer, XXVI China: Trouble, XXX Discipline, XXXV Intemperate, XLV Offensive, XLIX In the Guard Room, LVIII The Hangar, LX Funeral, LXIII Police Duty, LXI The Dance, LXVII The Pond; LXVIII A Thursday Night LXIX, Interlude. These chapters I single out, not because there are not others equal to them, but because their art is faultless in feeling & in expression. I abused you for not recording your own sensations & emotions in ***The Seven Pillars***—& here you have marvellously fused the whole objective picture with *your* breath, *your* sensations & *your* self. What strikes me specially is the *justesse* of it all. No tricks, & no self-consciousness here. Just your own sensations & your judgement, impartial, as any one finite man's can be. The *book has a perfect spiritual balance*. For a *book* it is. One has no feeling of 'notes' at all. The 'lubricant' you have added, does right away with any scrappiness. It all flows, one out of another perfectly. If you had 'written up' the stuff, as Kipling would do, you would have ruined it. The phrasing is perfect: often *most* original. That chapter—'The Funeral' is magnificent *as* writing. You have found *the* word. It knocks one endways. I don't speak of the early chapters I-XV—because I want to reread them—but you wind into your subject with an uncanny art. Chaps 4-10—go on deepening & deepening, as the recruits sink deeper into R.A.F. mud. The feeling of the Hut & Fatigue life, sweeping out of existence all former states of consciousness rivets one horribly—& the sensations of the breathless struggle with time, to get things done *in time*, is nightmarish. The Cadet College comes as a relief to the blackness—& it's also admirably written; but you grow a little sententious in your Airman propaganda. Yes, that's overdone a trifle. I don't mind *that* because luckily it dries up: & you wind up with three fine, last chapters, fine in their ease & naturalness. Well, you've done it, now! I don't advise you ever to write 'a book'. A man who can write 'Funeral'—can write anything—whenever he pleases:—whether he takes 'notes' or doesn't. He's only got to write tersely of what he *sees* & *feels* & there it is. (pp. 96-8)

Yes by God, its extreme naturalness & concise simplicity & frankness make it a masterpiecc. (p. 98)

Edward Garnett, in a letter to T. E. Lawrence on April 22, 1928, in Letters to T. E. Lawrence, *edited by A. W. Lawrence, Jonathan Cape, 1962, pp. 96-8.*

DAVID GARNETT (letter date 1928)

[*Garnett, an English publisher, bookseller, novelist, and son of editor Edward Garnett, is most often remembered for his biological fantasy* Lady Into Fox *(1922). In this debut novel Garnett demonstrated a clear and expressive style which he consistently upheld in later works and for which he has earned repeated critical acclaim. In the following excerpt from a letter written before Lawerence and Garnett had met, Garnett praises* The Mint.]

For a fortnight or so I've been living with ***The Mint,*** which at this moment is lying in the drawer of my writing-table beside its great black stable companion ***The Seven Pillars.*** I want to thank you again & again for letting me read it. It has been a great experience. My father has told you that ***The Mint*** is a masterpiece. No praise I can give the book will satisfy him:—how then shall I satisfy you? Or appear but as a feeble and almost reluctant echo of him?

There is a real difficulty in being Garnett II or III or IV. (I don't know where you start the dynasty!) Perhaps I should write more easily if I changed my name—& should choose Moore. That might help me to pitch my praises differently from my father's. But of course I agree that it's a masterpiece.

My first impression is that you are a queerer man than I took you to be from ***The Seven Pillars:*** (you have probably become queerer) queerer & less intellectual. You don't strike me from ***The Mint*** as intellectual at all: I see you as much more a man with the gift of words, a poet, an orator, a preacher, than a man of ideas or thinker. Like ***The Seven Pillars*** the book is half record of fact, half spiritual experience: my father did well to compare it with Dostoevsky's *House of the Dead*. Your experience was far worse than his: convicts do not enlist for prison; they do not pretend willingly to give up being men in order to become a chain-gang.

There is an odd streak in ***The Mint*** which crops up now & then—perhaps due partly to its date: what I should call a survival of the war-spirit in you. I mean there is a tendency for you to regard all sort of incidents as illuminating & valuable which are neither . . . just because you are so keen. There is a flavour of 1915 (a flavour of Rupert's sonnets!) To me this gives a touch of insanity such as I always feel in reading of—battles—wars—religious revivals & similar aberrations of humanity. I see all such proceedings with the eyes of Candide. I dislike your keenness & the keenness about flying. Even if you were a scientist doing physics it would seem exaggerated. (pp. 82-3)

The Mint is valuable not because you were in the R.A.F. but because it is finely written, & because of its subject:—Not the R.A.F. but an account of the prolonged torture of the individual & his heroic but incomplete resistance to the torture. He even preserves detachment while it is going on. There are some subjects which are too narrow & too painful to lend themselves to an artist. The tortures of the damned, & the temptations of the saints. But ***The Mint*** succeeds where all such fail. (pp. 83-4)

The agony is finely graduated of course—with immense, wonderful, wholly admirable art. The form of the book: the way you have drawn out your string of sausages, is wonderful. Beyond all praise from me.

Perhaps I am exceptional in feeling the horror of institutional life so strongly.

I am the most pleased by life, and all its processes—eating—drinking—sleeping—talking—making love—of anyone in the world. They come naturally to me, easily, I am never constipated. In ordinary life this emotion is never aroused this instinct or emotion of a weasel in a steel trap. When I feel it my intelligence falls away, even my cunning is gone, I am tooth & claw as I was at school or in the doctor's forceps at the moment of my birth. So the shock of the book on me has been very great: reminding me on every page of this emotion & making me live through it vicariously which I have felt strongly in the past but which I had forgotten: the emotion of the weasel in the steel trap, biting the keeper's boots. To go back to ***The Mint.*** I don't think it could be improved on, except here & there (for example I don't care about the reflections at church before Stiffy's wonderful lecture: I don't care for the reflections about the Air Force etc in the 3rd part). But being born of notes has somehow made the book, has given it the quality of a distilled essence . . . It is in every way a work of art, and could only have been written by a great writer (a careless one—sometimes).

All through it there are very beautiful passages; I should have known at once you were a great writer from the 1st chapter. Words are your medium, words, not deeds, and not thoughts. *Words.* ***The Mint*** is full of beauty, though you have purposely pruned it too hard for many flowers to show—& only rarely, till the 3rd part is there the splendour & the colour of ***The Seven Pillars.*** That book was a triumph—this an agony. Instinctively I pick out to remember in ***The Mint*** its least valuable, least characteristic parts:—(because they don't hurt) the first afternoon watching the footballers, the sleepless man rambling under the autumn moon at night & the sentry's coppers:—Alexandra in Marlborough House—shopping in Lincoln (What steep streets! What a disappointing cathedral!) I do so in self-defence—but no self-defence will keep out the maddened tortured—torturing—crippled figure of the Commandant. Marvellous! (pp. 84-5)

David Garnett, in an extract from a letter to T. E. Lawrence on May 20, 1928, in Letters to T. E. Lawrence, *edited by A. W. Lawrence, Jonathan Cape, 1962, pp. 82-5.*

E. M. F[ORSTER] (letter date 1928)

[*In the following excerpt, Forster critiques the manuscript of* The Mint; *for Lawrence's response to Forster's comments, see the excerpt dated 1928.*]

Book finished and *is* good. Read it all today in the garden and wood. Kept stopping to think about myself, and that the writer, if he chose, could be sitting in similar comfort.

If I just say 'book's good—masterpiece' you'll be neither helped nor amused. If I begin talking about your character you'll be amused but not helped. Yet technically—which is what a writer does want—I haven't much to say. I refuse however to be sidetracked by the subtitles of Notes. Notes may be literature, as in Alexandria: a history and a guide: or are literature, as here. So I shall refer to the book as a book. The first two parts are superbly written—the third part is a little odd: will come to it later. The style (I & II) is constricted and yet fresh—exactly what is needed to express the guts of men, and they have never been expressed before: spirited or scientific detachment or licentious sympathy have all 3 had their try, and all failed. You have got the new view point and the words in which it can be put. I am awfully glad. (pp. 66-7)

Now you give good reasons both for the style [epistolary] and for the matter of Part III, so what I am about to say is empty, but what I wish is that you could have taken up your narrative from the moment you left the depot, described your dismissal, touched on the Tanks, described your readmission, and then gone ahead.—Plenty of reasons, dynastic and personal, against this, no doubt: I am only saying what I wish. As it is, the transition is into another medium, into a sort of comforting bath water, where I sat contented and surprised, but not convinced that I was being cleansed. Your habit, that's to say, communicated your happiness to me. Which is difficult to do, we know. But I think more could have been done if you hadn't made that big leap in time and could *also* have put away from your head and heart the notion that you ought to be fair, and emphasise the pleasanter side of the R.A.F. before laying down your pen. 'For the fairness' sake' (Part III An Explanation) were the words that caused me to prick up my literary ears, and I am trying to keep to literature for the reason that I am unlikely to be useful as any other sort of animal.

Summing up as such, I inform you that ***The Mint*** is not as great a work as ***The Seven Pillars*** either in colour or form; but it is more new more startling and more heartening than either ***The S.P.*** or anything else I've read.

> The two most brilliant items are —after all— in Part III: Queen Alexandria, and the chapter that follows her—'Dance-Night'—which is so charming, so pretty: these are actually the words I must use. All through the book there's charm: lovely the descriptions of the Park, the Hangar, the final wait in the grass, and much of the smut.

There seems to me now no reason why you shouldn't write all sorts of books. I hadn't, before, known whether you could use many kinds of experience, or whether—as far as creation was concerned—you would stop at Arabia. I rather wish you would make yourself examine and describe women: many of them are about, and reluctance can lead us to profitable discoveries. (pp. 67-8)

[Your book is] heartening because it justifies the flesh through describing it; the reader comes away awfully wise. (N.B.—I don't involve you here!! what you give us, not what you are or may be, is my affair.) It's heartening because it shows that cruelty is accidental and abnormal, not basic: I have known this sitting in drawing rooms & gardens, but you have gone to places where I should smash and scream in 30 seconds, and bring back the same news. A world of infinite suffering, but of limited cruelty; that's what one has to face. (p. 68)

E. M. F[orster], in a letter to T. E. Lawrence on July 5, 1928, in Letters to T. E. Lawrence, *edited by A. W. Lawrence, Jonathan Cape, 1962, pp. 66-8.*

T. E. LAWRENCE (lettter date 1928)

[In the following excerpt, Lawrence responds to E. M. Forster's comments (see excerpt dated 1928) on The Mint *and describes the composition of the work.]*

Dear E.M.F., Your wonderful letter about ***The Mint*** has given me about eight readings of unalloyed pleasure, so far. It is a gift that, of mine, of being able to read so loosely that I can go on reading a thing for time after time, and enjoy it always. (p. 618)

The (Hitherto) youngest Garnett wrote me a most queer letter [see excerpt dated 1928] about ***The Mint*** (forgive my egoism in talking about it all the time. To write an unpublished book is to hear nothing, except from you & the Garnetts and the Shaws, what sort of a book it is . . . and one does wonder, you know). He said that it was a study in pain, and that it had hurt him; I did not think it very horrible anywhere. Now there were things I did write about the Tank Corps which were horrible . . . but ***The Mint*** is not abysmally cruel or crude. Surely not. You get on the side I'd like to stand, when you deduce from it that cruelty is not universal nor basic in humankind. I am sure it is not.

You put the first & second parts before the third, as writing. I am interested by that word. Every night in Uxbridge I used to sit in bed, with my knees drawn up under the blankets, and write on a pad the things of the day. I tried to put it all down, thinking that memory & time would sort them out, and enable me to select significant from insignificant. Time passed, five years and more (long enough, surely, for memory to settle down?) and at Karachi I took up the notes to make a book of them . . . and instead of selecting, I fitted into the book, somewhere & somehow, every single sentence I had written at Uxbridge.

Now tell me. Did my mind select at the time . . . or is there no truth that art is selection . . . or does my book lack selection. Is the whole affair there, and the trees cluttered up by redundant twigs & blossoms?

I wrote it tightly, because our clothes are so tight, and our lives so tight in the service. There is no freedom of conduct at all. Wasn't I right? G.B.S. calls it too dry, I believe. I put in little sentences of landscape (the Park, the Grass, the Moon) to relieve the shadow of servitude, sometimes. For service fellows there are no men on earth, except other service fellows . . . but we do see trees and star-light and animals, sometimes. I wanted to bring out the apartness of us.

You wanted me to put down the way I left the R.A.F., and something about the Tanks. Only I still feel miserable at the time I missed because I was thrown out that first time. I had meant to go on to a Squadron, & write the real Air Force, and make it a book—a BOOK, I mean. It is the biggest subject I have ever seen, and I thought I could get it, as I felt it so keenly. But they broke all that in me, and I have been damaged ever since. I could never again recover the rhythm that I had learned at Uxbridge, resisting Stiffy . . . and so it would not be true to reality if I tried to vamp up some yarn of it all now.

The notes go to the last day of Uxbridge, and there stop abruptly.

The Cranwell part is, of course, not a part, but scraps. I had no notes for it . . . any more than I am ever likely to have notes of any more of my R.A.F. life. I'm it, now, and the note season is over. The Cadet College part was vamped up, really, as you say, to take off the bitterness, if bitterness it is, of the Depot pages. The Air Force is not a man-crushing humiliating slavery, all its days. There is sun & decent treatment, and a very real measure of happiness, to those who do not look forward or back. I wanted to say this, not as propaganda, out of fairness, the phrase which pricked up your literary ears, but out of truthfulness. I set out to give a picture of the R.A.F., and my picture might be impressive and clever if I showed only the shadow of it . . . but I was not making a work of art, but a portrait. If it does surprisingly happen to be literature (I do not believe you there: you are partially kind) that will be because of its sincerity, and the Cadet College parts are as sincere as the rest, and an integral part of the R.A.F.

Of course I know and deplore the scrappiness of the last chapters: that is the draw-back of memory; of a memory which knew it was queerly happy then, but shrank from digging too deep into the happiness, for fear of puncturing it. Our contentments are so brittle, in the ranks. If I had thought too hard about Cranwell, perhaps I'd have found misery there too. Yet I assure you that it seems all sunny, in the back view.

Of Cadet College I had notes. Out of letters on Queen Alexandra's Funeral (Garnett praises that. Shaw says it's the meanness of a guttersnipe laughing at old age. I was so sorry and sad at the poor old queen), for the hours on guard, for the parade in the early morning. The Dance, the Hangar, Work and the rest were written at Karachi. They are reproductions of scenes which I saw, or things which I felt & did . . . but two years old, all of them. In other words, they are technically on a par with the manner of ***The Seven Pillars:*** whereas the Notes were photographs, taken day by day, and reproduced complete, though not at all unchanged. There was not a line of the Uxbridge notes left out; but also not a line unchanged.

The only photographic chapter of ***The Seven Pillars*** was the account of the tribal feasts, in Wadi Sirhan, when we stuffed meat and rice till we were sick. For that I had photographic notes, which only required rearranging. I wrote ***The Mint*** at the rate of about four chapters a week, copying each chapter four or five times, to get it into final shape. Had I gone on copying, I should only have been restoring already crossed out variants. My mind seems to congest, after reworking the stuff several times.

To insist that they are notes is not side-tracking. The Depot section was meant to be a quite short introduction to the longer section dealing with the R.A.F. in being, in flying work. Events killed the longer book: so you have the introduction, set out at greater length.

'You hadn't, that is to say, communicated your happiness to me'—nor convinced my rational side of it. The happiness is real: but sensory, only, I think.

'The Mint is not so great a work as ***The Seven Pillars':***—but possibly better, as Garnett thinks. It is so tiny a theme and work; perhaps I have a cherry-stone talent. ***The Seven Pillars*** is a sort of introspection epic, you know: and it would have taken a big writer to bring it off.

'There seems no reason why you shouldn't write all sorts of books'. Why, I feel as dry as a squeezed orange. I do not think it is at all likely that I will ever be moved to write anything again. ***The Mint*** dates from 1922, when I hadn't looked back in cold blood at ***The Seven Pillars,*** & seen how they fell short of my fancied achievement. Too ambitious, the little soul was: and so he's come a fearful cropper. (pp. 619-21)

T. E. Lawrence, in a letter to E. M. Forster on August 6, 1928, in his The Letters of T. E. Lawrence, *edited by David Garnett, Jonathan Cape, 1938, pp. 618-21.*

CLIFTON FADIMAN (essay date 1935)

[*Fadiman became one of the most prominent American literary critics during the 1930s with his insightful and often caustic book reviews for* The Nation *and* The New Yorker *magazines. He also reached a sizable audience through his radio program from 1938 to 1948. In the following excerpt from an obituary essay, Fadiman discusses various aspects of Lawrence's psychological makeup which he believes give rise to the strong "brooding character" of* Seven Pillars of Wisdom.]

To write scrupulously of T. E. Lawrence it is necessary first to clear the atmosphere. Wittingly or unwittingly, willingly or unwillingly, he exhaled during his lifetime a vapor of silly mystification. This fog settled in the pen barrels of most of those who wrote about him. The result is a literature that is part hysterical hero-worship, part violent detraction, and part—too large a part—circus-poster ballyhoo. A cool reading of his books, a cool review of his Arabian achievement, compel the conclusion that he was a man of great force and originality, quite possibly a strategist of genius, and a wielder of a vigorous, personal English prose. It is when one tries to pin down his personality more closely that the Lawrence myth rises to confound one's efforts. No doubt there is a real Lawrence, but he is shrouded in all the queer, pseudo-Lawrences the real Lawrence created—or which were created for him by amateur publicity agents. My guess is that the key will some day be provided, as with Poe and Rimbaud, not by the historian or the biographer but by the psychoanalyst. (p. 65)

[Lawrence] was a field in which operated dozens of mutually antagonistic lines of force. But one basic opposition can be traced, because he himself gives us the clue. "There was a craving to be famous," says Lawrence, "and a horror of being known to like being known." On the one hand, he was filled with Napoleonic ambition, all the more intense because he really was a superior personality who found leadership natural. On the other hand, he was undoubtedly a masochist or, as he would put it, an ascetic, and part of his self-punishment consisted in nursing a sense of frustration and immediately after achievement, in denying himself the honors to which he was entitled, in a symbolic killing of his personality. Thus T. E. Lawrence becomes Private Shaw, the most publicized pseudonymity of all time. Thus his book is lost, burnt, printed in a crazily limited edition—and again all the world knows about it. Lawrence was not, in the simple sense, a publicity-seeker. One part of him strove to punish, to vilify himself, and another part insisted, often with extreme subtlety, on letting everyone in on the punishment and the vilification.

Hence, when he says "My achievement as a writer falls short of every conception of the readable," don't pay too much attention to him. This is neither humility nor inverted bombast. It is part of his split personality, whose roots reach back into his probably abnormal sexual temperament and can be traced only by an expert in psychoanalysis. Similarly, we must not be confused when he, whose powers of strategy have been praised by no less an authority than Liddell Hart [see Additional Bibliography], speaks of himself at one point as "militarily incompetent" and at another refers, with quiet arrogance, to the Arabian revolt as "a hobby of mine." Throughout he denigrates himself and his capacity for leadership, yet in the strange verses "to S. A." which precede his book, he writes, "I drew these tides of men into my hands and wrote my will across the sky in stars." Masochism and megalomania are linked deviations.

At the end of his story, Lawrence lists four motives that led him to direct the Arab revolt. The least of them was "historical ambition." More important was "curiosity," the longing to feel himself "the node of a national movement." More important still was "a pugnacious wish to win the war." But the strongest motive, he writes, "had been a personal one, not mentioned here, but present to me, I think, every hour of these two years." What this personal motive may have been is anybody's guess. Lawrence will not tell us, but the thing to ponder is that he tells us that he will not tell us. Again the conflict, the desire to conceal his soul versus the desire to reveal the concealment.

All this may seem far from "**Seven Pillars of Wisdom**" itself. But I do not believe one can be just to the book until one has engaged in a little preliminary purgative reflection about the Lawrence myth and the Lawrence mystery, by no means one and the same thing.

Logically there is no reason for **"Seven Pillars"** selling eighty thousand copies in England in three weeks—at thirty shillings, too. About half of it is straight military narrative, the dullest, as it seems to me, of all varieties of narrative. Anyone else would have produced unreadable copy. Lawrence, whose light cannot be hid even under a bushel of tactical operations, manages to make it barely readable. But I seriously doubt whether eighty thousand Englishmen are really interested in a detailed account of a series of raids, however brilliant, conducted in a remote wilderness of unpronounceable place names.

For Americans, I think, the historical interest is limited. It is as a work of art, uneven but unforgettable, that **"Seven Pillars"** will be remembered. Certain sections are simply superb—the opening chapters analyzing the social, racial, and geographic bases of Arab character; the descriptions of Bedouin life and desert landscape; the scattered generalizations on strategy; the terrible scene in which Lawrence, refusing to surrender his chastity to a Turkish officer, is tortured until his spirit, no less than his body, is broken; the scattered reflections, acrid and ironic, on the shortcomings of the military mind; and the Hamlet soliloquies on the hopeless complexity of his own. For these things Lawrence will live as a writer.

He makes even clearer than he did in **"Revolt in the Desert"** that his whole Arabian adventure was a tragic personal failure. Drawn to the Arabs by his early archeological experiences in the Near East, by his unquestionably abnormal admiration for their Spartan, super-masculine, primitive, "heroic" character, and by his interest (subconsciously Fascist) in the romantic idea of nationalism, he organized their revolt, worked the strings attached to Feisal, their chieftain, and led them to victory against the Turks. But he was deceived by the British imperialism that unwittingly he served. As the book draws to a close he realizes with a clarity he should have exercised at the beginning that he will never be able to keep his promises to the Arabs, that England is using him and them for her own chilly, Machiavellian purposes. It is this increasing frustration, which he sees not under the aspect of history but in terms of his own personality, that gives the book its brooding character and turns it at times into something that more nearly resembles a tragedy by Sophocles than a military chronicle by Xenophon.

He still awaits explanation—this Proteus who carried the "Morte d'Arthur" in his saddle bags and could transform himself on the instant into a genius of action; who bruited to the world his renunciation of fame and publicly became Private Shaw; who had "a contempt, not for other men, but for all they do;" who preferred objects to persons, and ideas to either; who was horrified at procreation and hated women; who was always preventing himself from being read, and sold a single story half a dozen times; who was always resigning from active service and always being sent back with increased powers; who to William Bolitho was "Desperate Desmond in green whiskers" and to most Englishmen a demigod—and who was neither; who spoke of himself as a coward and was clearly one of the bravest of men; who was born to lead but was always, almost pathologically, on the alert for a master to whom he could enslave himself; who spoke of his senses as "sluggish beyond the senses of most men" and yet drank only water because he claimed the differences among wines were too coarse and obvious; and who died because he used speed as a method of escaping from a self that he could never compel to stillness. (pp. 65-8)

Clifton Fadiman, "T. E. Lawrence," in The New Yorker, *Vol. XI, No. 33, September 28, 1935, pp. 65-8.*

HENRY SEIDEL CANBY (essay date 1935)

[Canby was a professor of English at Yale and one of the founders of The Saturday Review of Literature, *which he served as editor in chief from 1924 to 1936. He was the author of many books, including* The Short Story in English *(1909), a history of that genre which was long considered the standard text for college students. Canby always considered himself primarily a teacher, and his declared aim was "to pass on sound values to the reading public." In the following excerpt, Canby describes* Seven Pillars of Wisdom *as an English puritan tragedy, akin in purpose and feeling to the* Confessions *of St. Augustine.]*

I wish to study **"The Seven Pillars of Wisdom"** as a book not as a war history, one of the few unique books written in English in our time. And I trust I will not be accused of bad perspective or lack of interest if in this review, necessarily short for so much matter, I pass over the brilliant episodes of guerilla combat, the incisive Arab portraits, the sweep of a difficult war, in order to search for the quality that makes **"The Seven Pillars"** more than a record of adventure, more than first-hand historical evidence, much more than first-rate description and narrative that when it runs clear is also first-rate. "More," not "better" in any absolute sense. Caesar's Gallic Wars is a much shrewder presentation of a campaign than Lawrence's memoir; but it stops there. There is very little Caesar in the Gallic Wars. Lawrence, like Gibbon and Burton and Bunyan, has put himself into his book.

If **"The Seven Pillars"** seems to me a description and sometimes a manifestation of a genius, it nevertheless is far from being a masterpiece of composition. It is definitely a disorderly book, in which it is like many of those vital books of the seventeenth century which most resemble it. The reader would

Lawrence photographed during World War I. The Granger Collection, New York.

be well advised to go over Lawrence's own outline before he begins, and then to skip judiciously, although he will return later to his omissions. It is a book badly compounded from notes of activity—bombings, charges, strategies, perils in scouting, intrigues, and sometimes most humorous politics—and passages of self-criticism, racial philosophy, and analysis of motives carried far beyond Arabia. As a story of a campaign and its characters, the abridgment hitherto published and called **"Revolt in the Desert,"** is much more coherent than this narrative—just as a map of a scene is much more understandable than a picture. Nor is the style satisfactory. Sometimes it is negligent, often tortured, seldom does it run smooth for more than a page. Lawrence was quite right in deprecating his skill as a writer; quite right also in knowing that at his best he was superb, as his toil and sacrifice in thrice writing this book, and seeing it into print at ruinous cost proves, at least to me.

He was an amateur in writing and an amateur in war, and a genius in both. "It was a hard task for me to straddle feeling and action," he says in a key passage.

"I had one craving all my life—for the power of self-expression in some imaginative form—but had been too diffuse ever to acquire a technique. At last accident, with perverted humor, in casting me as a man of action, had given me place in the Arab Revolt, a theme ready and epic to a direct eye and hand, thus offering me an outlet in literature—the technique-less art. Whereupon I became excited only over mechanism. The epic mode was alien to me, as to my generation."

In other words, having been given by accident materials which needed only expression, he could not use them as an epic story because to his skeptic eye neither himself nor the Arab nor the revolt was really heroic. The fallacy in this statement designates the amateur in Lawrence. Literature is the opposite of technique-less. When his opportunity came he had a fiery prose at his hand and a stocked imagination to express in it, but lacked precisely that art of composition which would have made of **"The Seven Pillars"** a classic book to satisfy all the formalists of literature. But it was just because his life-long need for self-expression found its opportunity in the record of heroic things that to him were not heroic, not epic, but sham and illusion and moral distress, that **"The Seven Pillars,"** in spite of its many faults, is clearly one of the outstanding English books that invite no comparison even with each other because they are unique. This will need some explaining.

The truth of the matter is that Colonel Lawrence was a Puritan, perhaps the last great English Puritan. (Mr. Santayana has just written a novel about the last American Puritan—a very different life, but in some respects a resemblant character.) It is this that marks him, that makes his genius so intensely English in its violent nonconformity; it is this which gives blood, as it is Arabia that gives flesh and bones, to his book.

I find a curious but natural resemblance between the self-torturings of the triumphant Cromwell as John Buchan reports him and Lawrence's confessions of conscience. Both men were supremely successful in the organizing of energy; both were tormented by self-doubt when success was in their grasp; both were ill content with the judgment of their fellows. (pp. 3-4)

Skeptic as he was, Lawrence never lost faith in the supremacy of the moral determinant. He believed it to be behind courage, behind character, behind destiny. If **"The Seven Pillars"** is, among other things, an extraordinary gallery of portraits of men, this is because its author in addition to his gift for vivid description, saw every Arab, Turk, Englishman in his book, from the tumultuous Auda to the shepherd boy caught by the raiders and knowing only his duty to his sheep, as a mind and body driven by the moral tensity which lies somewhere in all of us. In particular, he so viewed himself, "this furnace in my brain," which, since he could not approve of his own desire for action he lent to the ideas of other men.

All this, to readers of seventeenth century English, must seem a familiar picture. Abstract the theology, extend the horizon, of those great Puritans who wrestled with God, and you have fellow minds to Lawrence who wrestled with his conscience. The religion is different, the moral philosophy extraordinarily like, the bursts of intense energy wreaking itself upon words or upon practical achievement, or upon both, almost identical. Lawrence is far closer to Jonathan Edwards, to George Fox, to Roger Williams, to Milton, to Cromwell, than to Beaverbrook, Lloyd-George, Robert Cecil, or to Wilson who was the Puritan perfectionist freed from the inhibitions and the safeguards of self-criticism.

It is possible now to see why Lawrence's career and Lawrence's book are both extraordinary. This guarded flame of will, this tool seeking a master, is released by the Arab Revolt, a surge toward personal freedom by men whose wills were as ruthless as Lawrence's own. And at the same time it was such a revolution as Cromwell led in England, designed to turn the scales of empire, end a war, bring a world peace, and thus be an enterprise of such scope and difficulty as alone could satisfy the frustrated perfectionist who dashed his head in vain against the wall of his own personality.

By chance Lawrence was the man for the opportunity. Already deeply experienced in the East, a master of language and custom, he was a passionate student of military history, and as confident of his own genius as he was uncertain of his right to use it.

And so he enters upon a great make-believe, a deception of others, and a self-deception encouraged by fatigue, danger, incessant planning—the man of action leading the man of morbid self-scrutiny against his better judgment. He knows that he is bound to betray the Arabs by the very energy he puts into their cause. He knows that they are being used for alien purposes of victory for nations of the West and will be let down in the end. And even in this victory, which he desires, he has no faith as an absolute good. He knows that his triumph will satisfy neither his Arabs nor his own conscience, which holds as its central tenet that only a moral success is viable for humanity. And the clash and conflict of skepticism, need for self-expression, and the momentum of great opportunity, reverberate in the tireless energy, the exploit after exploit of the book, and most of all in the uncanny insight of this man whose mind is set above the battles into the military, the political, the executive needs of a wholly practical campaign.

Viewed this way, the title of the book is appropriate and significant. Here are the seven pillars hewn out by wisdom for her house, hewn with pain and self-scrutiny; for what is wisdom, and of what shall her house be builded? It should (as he said) have been an epic or direct action, and for that the materials were abundant, and indeed the best of them are all in this book—the exalted action, the exciting adventure, the characters of an epic, noble, imperfect, tragic, or pitiable, all lifted upon the plane of a great endeavor. But the mood of the writer is not epic, and the book is not epic. It is a Puritan tragedy, a drama of energy scanned and scrutinized by wisdom and constantly condemned by the hero himself— really a confession like Augustine's, who also lived mightily and found it was nought in the sight of God. Lawrence is too much of a Puritan and a modern to think it was nought. He is proud of his energy, proud of his courage, exulting even in the frightful degradations of his tortures in the Turkish camp, aware that when for moral reasons he shot the Moroccan in cold blood he was revenging upon his own fastidious mind the lust for action which had led him into a leadership morally indefensible. And so with penetrating irony he subtitles his thrice-written book "A Triumph." A triumph in the great war, a triumph for Colonel Lawrence, which Lawrence the Puritan acknowledges by divesting himself of his orders and his rank, refusing all reward, and coming close to starvation within a few years of the climax of his success. But a triumph also for wisdom, who here makes her distracted comment on a tale which, without the self-scrutiny, might have been written like Southey's "Life of Nelson," or Wellington's unreflecting comments on how he saved Europe from the menace of France. "Pray God," says Lawrence, "that men reading this story will not, for love of the glamour of strangeness, go out to prostitute themselves and their talents in serving another race."

Postscriptum: Since writing the above review, I have had the privilege of consulting Colonel Isham's unique copy of **"The Seven Pillars of Wisdom,"** which contains the original first chapter, included elsewhere only in the five original copies printed from the uncondensed manuscript. This chapter, which was deleted from **"The Seven Pillars"** by the advice of George Bernard Shaw, not only confirms the theory of moral responsibility outlined in the review above, but explicitly states that **"The Seven Pillars"** was essentially a book about himself. It is to be devoutly hoped that this chapter will later resume its proper place in the book. It contains not only one of the finest paragraphs of English prose which Lawrence ever wrote, but the best and most specific account of his reasons for encouraging the Arab revolt, and his hopes for saving his Arabs from what he knew would be their probable fate when the war was won. (pp. 4, 14)

Henry Seidel Canby, "The Last Great Puritan," in The Saturday Review of Literature, *Vol. XII, No. 22, September 28, 1935, pp. 3-4, 14.*

R. P. BLACKMUR (essay date 1940)

[Blackmur was a leading American literary critic of the twentieth century. His early essays on the poetry of such contemporaries at T. S. Eliot, W. B. Yeats, Wallace Stevens, and Ezra Pound were immediately recognized for their acute and exacting attention to diction, metaphor, and symbol. Consequently, he was linked to the New Critics, who believed that literature was not a manifestation of sociology, psychology, or morality, and could not be evaluated in the terms of any nonliterary discipline. Rather, a literary work constituted an independent object to be closely analyzed for its strictly formal devices and internal meanings. Blackmur distinguished himself from this group of critics, however, by broadening his analyses through discussions which explored a given work's relevance to society. Inspired by the moral thought of the American autobiographer Henry Adams, Blackmur conceived the critic's role as that of a crucial intermediary between artist and reader, for the dual purpose of offering literary insight as well as social commentary on the age. His belief that criticism also represented an art form in its own right led him to an increasingly poetic, impressionistic style best demonstrated in his posthumously published lecture series Anni Mirabiles 1921-25: Reason in the Madness of Letters *(1967). In the following excerpt, Blackmur discusses the "obsessed sensibility" of Lawrence as demonstrated in* Seven Pillars of Wisdom *and* The Mint.*]*

In thinking of T. E. Lawrence we are bound up in the web of action and event—of the war, the air force, the motor cycle—which made the man a legend while he yet lived, a myth, and almost a Cause, lost but lurking: as who should call a king great because his country perished during his reign. The fate of Arabia, of Europe, the no less irrelevant fate of Lawrence himself: these as they work together to the merest look of recognition make the image that goes before us—Will o' the Wisp if you will—in our present adventure, shared or imminent. Lawrence wrote it down himself in the introduction to the Oxford text of the ***Seven Pillars of Wisdom***: "We were wrought up with ideas inexpressible and vaporous, but to be fought for. We lived many lives in those whirling campaigns, never sparing ourselves any good or evil: yet when we achieved and the new world dawned, the old men came out again and took from us our victory, and remade it in the likeness of the former world they knew. Youth could win, but had not learned to keep, and was pitiably weak against age. We stammered that we had worked for a new heaven and a new earth, and they thanked us kindly and made their peace. When we are their age no doubt we shall serve our children so." Lawrence wrote it down as a statement of fact, but on the advice of Bernard Shaw omitted it from later editions; for Lawrence was docile, in the very measure of his scrupulousness, and in imagination as well as act, to those whom he admired. He walked always with pebbles in his boots.

But he put it down and we put it back. It is there: all the power—of persuasion, of enactment—that comes from the ability to put things down: the power without which Lawrence could not have become a legend or a myth, for without that power he could not have revealed his cause, its strength, its weakness, its necessity. At least he could not have done so in our western world, however it may be in the east; for in the west the old men habitually obliterate every power short of the rational imagination: imagination rising from a Cause through the written word. Lawrence would have been made nothing or wholly falsified, as at the Peace Conference or in the newspapers, if he had not written a book. (pp. 1-2)

It may be as well to begin with an emphasis upon Lawrence's own view of himself as a craftsman: his love of the minute mechanics of writing and his aspiration towards major form—towards what he called, along with many, the architecture of his book. The emphasis cries for plain citation. Here are a few sentences and phrases isolated from the letters, of which the first set deal with words.

"That frenzied aching delight in a pattern of words that happen to run true. . . . My deepest satisfaction [is] in the collocation of words so ordinary and plain that they cannot mean anything to a book-jaded mind: and out of some such I can draw deep stuff. . . . Prose depends on a music in one's head which involuntarily chooses & balances the possible words to *keep tune* with the thought. The best passages in English prose all deal with death or the vanity of things, since that is a tune we all know, and the mind is set quite free to think while writing about it. . . . Only occasionally in things constantly dwelt upon, do you get an unconscious balance, & then you get a *spontaneous* and perfect arrangement of words to fit the idea, *as the tune*. Polishing is an attempt, by stages, to get to what should be a single combined stride. . . . The worst of being a habitual translator is that one gets in the way of trying to squeeze every sponge dry—and so few authors ever really *intend* all the content of their sponges. Words get richer every time they are deliberately used . . . but only when deliberately used: and it is hard to be conscious of each single word, and yet not at the same time self-conscious. . . . What you say about the emphasis I get on simple words like Moon or chocolate bisquits, mayn't it be partly because I do try & feel every article and emotion that comes into the book? I tie myself into knots trying to re-act everything, as I write it out. It's like writing in front of a looking-glass, and never looking at the paper, but always at the imaginary scene. That, and a trick of arranging words, so that the one I care for most is either repeated, or syllable-echoed, or put in a startling position."

So much for the craft of words. The citations are emphatic, it seems to me, of the high degree in which Lawrence was a deliberate craftsman. It is not easy to make the emphasis as plain with regard to the more formal aspects of craft, because the citations seldom appear in compact phrases or sentences. Any reader of the Letters may find for himself instance after instance of Lawrence's effort to shape his books for sequence and balance and drama.

The chief labour that went into ***The Mint,*** for example, seems to have been the labour of re-arranging its items so as to reach a satisfactory pattern. As it happens, there is one passage about ***The Mint*** compact and self-complete enough to quote. "You are right about the absence of flowers in ***The Mint.*** There is a severe beauty in some buildings, which would only be reduced if creepers were grown over them. I tried—deliberately—for that. You see, as I suppose every writer who reads it will see—how deliberate the construction and arrangement of ***The Mint*** is. I called its proportions the worst side of ***The Seven Pillars:*** and was determined that (what Siegfried Sassoon calls the architectonics of) whatever else I wrote should be, at any rate, calculated." We shall see later the irredeemable fault which made the proportions of ***The Seven Pillars*** what Lawrence called their worst side. Meanwhile we can note that Lawrence was quite aware of the worth of a few flowers on even the severest of buildings; for he continued the letter just quoted with this paragraph. "Your liking for the first-afternoon-football-match pleases me. That page was meant like a seat for anyone tired with the idea of effort. So was the whole third book put in like a benediction after a commination service: and the very occasional landscapes and lyric paragraphs, between stresses."

Finally, just as a general statement selected from among many for the ambiguity at its centre—for just that ambivalence and sense of defeated judgment which has afflicted so many writers—there is this paragraph, taken from the letter containing the quoted passage about words as sponges. "I mustn't slip again into the technique of writing. Writing has been my inmost self all my life, and I can never put my full strength into anything else. Yet the same force, I know, put into action upon material things would move them, make me famous and effective. The everlasting effort to write is like trying to fight a featherbed. In letters there is no room for strength."

This is the declaration of vocation at the strongest value Lawrence ever reached: the co-operative sentiment of doubt was here no stronger than the sentiment of vocation. Conviction, which alone makes mastery possible, he never reached; for reasons of sensibility which it will be the main effort of these notes to show. His general sentiment was more nearly at the level of the following statement, which he made in a letter to Robert Graves shortly before he died. "Almost I could be an artist, but there is a core that puts on the brake. If I knew what it was I would tell you, or become one of you. Only I can't."

The everlasting effort nevertheless went far before the brake was felt. It was forced writing, seldom discovered writing, never the writing of momentum. Lawrence *forced* his eyes into the looking-glass with all the impetuosity which is characteristic of the complex dread of letting go, of missing, and of going forward. His writing acquired ease, I think, only in the sense that impetuosity became a habit. Usually his best effects are conspicuously either struck off or seized at, snatched from a near physical collision of his sensibility with the object. How strong his predilection was for violence of imagery is perhaps suggested by his choice of a first paragraph for ***Revolt in the Desert.*** It is taken from the second paragraph of chapter VIII of ***Seven Pillars,*** where the first, in a more composed writer, would have served more masterfully. "When at last we anchored in Jeddah's outer harbour, off the white town hung between the blazing sky and its reflection in the mirage which swept and rolled over the wide lagoon, then the heat of Arabia came out like a drawn sword and struck us speechless."

It is an excellent passage in its kind, but it is quoted here because of the initial position Lawrence assigned to it in the ***Revolt:*** which leads us immediately to understand in ***Seven Pillars*** that it is the violence of the first two pages there that gives them their principal relevance to the book, for, without the yoking consideration of violence, they deal with matters not otherwise explored. I refer particularly to the description of casual homosexuality among the Arab troops. A "cold convenience" he called it, and proceeded: "Later, some began to justify this sterile process, and swore that friends quivering together in the yielding sand with intimate hot limbs in supreme embrace, found there hidden in the darkness a sensual coefficient of the mental passion which was welding our souls and spirits in one flaming effort. Several, thirsting to punish appetites they could not wholly prevent, took a savage pride in degrading the body, and offered themselves fiercely in any habit which promised physical pain or filth."

The reader will remember that these sentences occur in a general consideration of the Arab Revolt and Lawrence's relation, as an alien Englishman, to it. They come down like a fist struck on a table during an otherwise steady argument, without significance to it but the contrary, yet forcing attention upon it beyond the confines of logic. Memory is invested; whether the shock or the argument is better remembered is no question, the association is permanent: kept, say, as the sense of smart. This mode of persuasion is well recognised, whether in conduct or in art; is often the deliberate substitute for mastery (the more inviting because in the instance it amounts to mastery); and Lawrence furnishes an extreme, perhaps a heroic, example of a writer for whom it constituted a chief resource. It overcame in the act one of his major obstructive obsessions—which we shall come to in another form; it overcame his sense of "many humiliating material limits" by declaring that there were "no moral impossibilities," and overcame too, by enacting it, that "physical shame of success" which was the reaction to victory. It gave him the means to say, or partly say, what he at once knew and did not know, otherwise unsayable. (pp. 3-8)

There are at least three easily separable sub-species of writing in which Lawrence reached through the rules of his mode into handy use. One is the expression of atmosphere, landscape, setting, through imagery which, by coupling close observation, that might be dead, with far-fetched simile, that might often be *distrait,* gave a created effect of actuality. The strain of sensibility becomes thus equivalent to the tension of the object. Citation of this species is easy because brief examples offer. One is the figure of the heat and the drawn sword quoted above. Another, especially apt here, is when Lawrence remarks of tactics that nine tenths are teachable, "but the irrational tenth was like the kingfisher flashing across the pool, and in it lay the test of generals." He proceeds immediately, and here is the characteristic interesting point: "It could be ensued only by instinct (sharpened by thought practicing the stroke) until at the crisis it came naturally, a reflex." The reader will note how vivid, and useful, and how created out of whole cloth is General Kingfisher. Again, when Lawrence told the Arabs of Allenby's successes: "My hearers' minds drew after me like flames. Tallal took fire, boasting." Here the apposition seems at first sight so logical that no amount of analysis—which the reader may make for himself—will reduce its aptness to the level of yoked superficies where logically it belongs. What was created by the first stroke cannot afterwards be cut down, except by an uncalled for act of will. ***Seven Pillars*** is full of such strokes, some simple and some complex, e.g., balls of dead thistle "careered like run-away haycocks across the fallow"; an airplane "climbed like a cat up the sky"; and "black-white buildings moving up and down like pistons in the mirage"—which last gains its virtue perhaps precisely because it will not bear analysis at all. (pp. 8-9)

It is not easy to cite either of the other two principal sub-species in Lawrence's practice in his natural forced mode. The difficulty is partly in length and partly in clear identification. The best citations will therefore be fragmentary and themselves forced. One sub-species is to be found in the series of Arab portraits that extend through ***Seven Pillars***—the full-dress characterisations of such men as Hussein, Feisal, Abdulla, and Auda, given sometimes all at once, but more often a page or so at a time as the history called for comment. My point is that these portraits are marvellous forced creations, quite removed from but parallel to their unrealiseable originals: pictures Lawrence kept with him, let us say, to remind himself of the complete men with whom he had to deal—preach to, persuade, and command.

The connection between the picture and the man is analogous to that between the minds that drew after Lawrence like flames and Tallal taking fire, not logical but putative. For Lawrence, they were limited acts of forced attention, for us they are created possibilities of human character, violent and incomplete, not open anywhere to analysis. They are characters not achieved or discovered but asserted. Lawrence lacked the power, or the rare abiding charity, to make, or even to see, character complete; but he had inexhaustibly the power to make a willed substitute for it. To put it unkindly, his Arabs, and his Englishmen, and himself, too, all play character parts; they all work on formulas, however unpredictable and unusual; but, to make it praise, the formulas are intensely felt and the working out all fits into the game recorded. Two things need hardly be added, one that these remarks have no bearing on Lawrence's private intuition of character, which may have been perfect, but apply only to what he put down; the second, that what he did put down has only a lesser value, in the experience of character, than the productions of those who have put down, not so much more, but what was more complete. What is said here only makes another clue to help us discriminate the class of writer to which Lawrence belongs. Let us say merely that he was a man of feelings, which are fundamental, and of emotions, which are sometimes perfect products of feelings; but that, as a writer, he was governed by a driven and imperfect intellect, an intellect not ever his in the sense that his feelings were his, and not ever completing his feelings as his emotions might have completed them, and, as he knew, they were meant to. It is a matter of dominance, of hierarchy, of productive order, and not a matter of whether or not he owned the various talents which he did, uneasily.

The remaining, or third principal sub-species in which Lawrence shows himself characteristic of his mode, has been saved till now because its great complexity is everywhere based on the relative simplicity of the first and second sub-species, and because it makes up, if we can cite it, evidently the very bloodstream of his imagination: the medium—the food and the habitat—of what he had to say. It will be understood that we speak really of the whole ***Seven Pillars*** and of ***The Mint,*** too, at least by extension, and that it is merely to focus attention that we bring up on a single passage: namely, chapters thirty-one to thirty-three of ***Seven Pillars.***

These chapters contain Lawrence's account of his journey from Wejh to Wadi Ais to find out why Abdulla had done nothing with his army for two months. During the journey he is sick with dysentery, boils on his back and heavy fever, commits judicial murder, and discovers the major strategy by which the Arab revolt can be successfully conducted. The sickness—the physical suffering and the biological dismay—together with a concomitant sense of landscape and quotidian actuality may be said here to furnish what I. A. Richards calls the coadunating power of imagination and so give meaning and location to the murder, and the strategy, and compose, on top, a new meaning possible to these pages alone. Certainly not the sickness only, and impossibly the landscape only, made these images their fertile apposition. Lawrence's wilderness had need to be spiritual as well as physical before it could breed vision out of observation, and the pang of conceptual feeling needed a direct base in bodily pain before it could be forced, by imagination, into emotion or, as it happened, the plot of action.

We can say if we like, looking for the technical aspect of these chapters, that we have just an example of old-fashioned straightforward first-person narrative, limited by the historical facts and enriched by the forced data of a special sensibility. Lawrence went, was sick, did murder, and conceived strategy; these things were so; this is how they were seen; no more. But this is to remove both the sense of the deliberate artist and of the driven intellect, which furnish the true setting of the narrative and produce the true meaning. So far as Lawrence was aware of his writing—and in terms of precision of feeling he was supremely aware—what he wrote was not narrative at all, but a re-seizure, highly selective and deeply canalised, of the focal material of experience: to which the mere narrative line can never be more than apposite. That is why the sickness and the landscape count for so much, while the narrative counts relatively for so little in defining the murder and enforcing the strategy come upon. Any other narrative would have done as well or as poorly; for Lawrence did not compose by narrative means, the story does not come first. In fact the composition comes the other way round: the story, the events, serve to enrich and to prune a little the native superabundance of the sensibility engaged. The events, say, served as a mechanical closing focus—the iris of a camera—upon the actual material of experience, just as his intentions, the residual pattern or habituated eyesight of his sensibility served as the evaluing focus. They reduced, and thereby concentrated, the scope of his attention sufficiently to permit the valuing act to occur.

This is, I think, the only way Lawrence knew how to write; it explains the predominance of the fragmentary and the violent over the evidently integrating and reserved factors in two books which had the express aim of presenting whole pictures. Wholeness, for Lawrence, lay in the sensibility; so far as its elements could be expressed, they would make a unity that might be taken as complete if taken at all: the unity of obsession.

The problem of Lawrence, if there needs to be a problem, is the problem of the obsessed sensibility, which beyond or beneath its obsessions is disparate, without conviction, altogether homeless, nearly lost. (pp. 10-14)

Lawrence wrote always about himself, the individual who, ultimately, could not cope,—with nothing, no plan or frame or conception, to fit himself into to make his tale objective in immediate import. His plain ambition is, as it were, untested; he could not steer for it, whether instinctively or deliberately; which is the difference in value between his books, and his life, and the books of the "Titans" [Fëdor Dostoevsky, Friedrich Nietzsche, and Herman Melville] he desired so to emulate. The ungrounded idealism which was fatal to him as a man comes out in his writing as compositional weakness, and is indeed the rough counterpart to what we feel as the lack of an abiding conviction. What is meant here by composition is the sum of those inner modes and outward manners by which the materials of experience are set together so that they make a whole so secure that the mere intention of the writer becomes immaterial to the book. In Lawrence, the intention everywhere counts, which is to say is questionable: uncomposed. It was his only operative weakness; other weaknesses hardly count, hardly exist, so tenaciously, with such strength of sensibility, did he fasten upon just those major aspects of experience which he could not compose. Few with that strength *and* that weakness—for it is a weakness that inhabits especially the whole class of great but eccentric sensibilities—few in the measure of Lawrence have done more. Not Melville, certainly not Nietzsche; only Dostoevsky on Lawrence's list, and he by that inexhaustible charity of imagination which produced, quite superior to the insult, the injury, and the humiliation which attracted Lawrence to him, a vast host of what we call "characters." Characters are an end-product, an objective form, of imaginative composition, and their creation depends on the deepest-seated of human convictions, so humanly full of error, by the occasion of genius so superhumanly right. When we say that Lawrence never produced a character, not even his own, if we add that he produced nevertheless almost everything that makes for character, we have said very nearly what is necessary. It was his everlasting effort. (pp. 36-7)

R. P. Blackmur, "The Everlasting Effort: A Citation of T. E. Lawrence," in his The Expense of Greatness, *1940. Reprint by Peter Smith, 1958, pp. 1-37.*

V. S. PRITCHETT (essay date 1951)

[*Pritchett is a highly esteemed English novelist, short story writer, and critic. Considered one of the modern masters of the short story, he is also one of the world's most respected and well-read literary critics. Pritchett writes in the conversational tone of the familiar essay, a method by which he approaches literature from the viewpoint of a lettered but not overly scholarly reader. A twentieth-century successor to such early nineteenth-century essayist-critics as William Hazlitt and Charles Lamb, Pritchett employs much the same critical method: his own experience, judgment, and sense of literary art are emphasized, rather than a codified critical doctrine derived from a school of psychological or philosophical speculation. His criticism is often described as fair, reliable, and insightful. In the following excerpt from an essay originally published in 1951, Pritchett examines Lawrence the man as revealed through* Seven Pillars of Wisdom.]

Forgetting all one has read and heard of T. E. Lawrence, what portrait can one build up from his writings? He has the total, sanguine, efficiency of genius, of course. After that, the Anglo-Irish and Highland Scottish parentage makes a bold and distinctive general outline. Courage, militancy, imagination, clear separation of close-packed thought from withdrawn feeling, the ability to get "inside the skin of the participants" in an action—which Sir Ernest Dowson noted—without losing oneself in the process, a dizzy sexless energy, irony—but that is the militant tradition—an instinct for mischief and intrigue, vanity and a core of diffidence, weakness, insecurity. History suggests that their insecurity as the lonely conquerors of a savage and treacherous country is a profound element in the general character of the Anglo-Irish and (as Lawrence's brother thought) the weakness provoked in T. E. Lawrence that transcendent will which is incessant in men and women of genius. Other Anglo-Irish traits are suggested by a comparison with Bernard Shaw. There are the continuous histrionic touch and the remorse that follows—an unavailing remorse because it, also, is theatrical. There is the merciless mental energy which pours out endlessly in words or action, and turns upon the character with humiliating self-criticism. There is the special kind of idealism: ascetic, bodiless, rational, unromantic, and it keeps a place for the inevitable cynicism of tactics. Unlike English idealism it is unsentimental and without hypocrisy. Lawrence's guilt about betraying the Arabs could not be dis-

Lawrence at Miranshah. National Portrait Gallery, London.

solved by useful moral arguments; it was hard. An objective thinker cannot get rid of the objects he sees or deceive himself by turning them into something else. Lawrence's dislike of Imperialism was traditional; on the other hand, he was drawn irresistibly to the military fascination of Imperial power. Thus, to hold Alexandretta for ever is vital; to lose British soldiers for Mesopotamian oil is squalid and wicked. In this kind of judgment Lawrence may have been a strategist and not a political economist, but he was chiefly a kind of aesthete, plumping for abstract power which was, in some way, connected with honour. It had nothing to do with the squalid, practical interests of the oil trade. (His reading at this time is suggestive: Homer, the *Morte d'Arthur* and Blake; the epical, chivalrous and mystical.)

At any rate the attitude of Lawrence is not that of a 19th-century Romantic. Nor is there any Rupert Brooke in him. Of all those who wrote about the first World War, he is the only one to go into it with his eyes open. He had been studying castles, military science, the actual terrain of his war and its people in his youth scientifically. The disillusion of the other war writers of that generation arose because war was not what they thought it would be; the strong ruling and military bent of the Anglo-Irish seems to have preserved Lawrence from illusion. What he experienced after the war was the disgust of success, the disgust following intoxication; perhaps the affront that he was no longer a king-maker; and, of course, the frustration of the guerrilla soldier's ideal of freedom for a race of soldiers.

I do not say this is to whittle down the sincerity of his desire for Arab Freedom, but to underline the importance of the idea of honour in his character. It goes back to the Elizabethans in Ireland, not to the English public schools; and his feeling for the Arabs—though there was always some part of him that was the observer—seems to have been a natural response to people who lived by honour, the corruption of honour by eternal quarrels, and its ironies. It is an exquisite moment in ***Seven Pillars of Wisdom*** when Feisal discreetly shows that he has guessed Lawrence is doctoring the telegrams from Mecca; there is an Elizabethan taste for the conceit, for the subtle arabesque of innuendo. When Feisal says to Lawrence "You always prefer my honour to your own," the words have the ambiguity of a verse cut by the diamond of a betrayed Tudor. For, as Lawrence said many times in the *Arab Bulletin* and ***Seven Pillars,*** he *used* the honour of the Arabs; he was stronger because he had a motive unknown to them. He had the demon inside him, the will of the Allies; and he was strong also because he had to make an enormous moral effort to live with his own guilt. . . . (pp. 38-40)

The precocious Lawrence who, as a boy of five, could read a newspaper upside down, who became a technician, an archaeologist and an historian while he made himself into a deep and original military thinker, was a "thought-riddled" man. He was the kind of man of action who did not value what men of action valued. He was made to bear the Hamlet-like burden of the double role; he became a legend, perhaps because he was a new and prophetic prototype. The guerrillas of the 1939 war, the equipped individualists, the educated men or the sensitive who had to stick out the promiscuous living of the Nissen huts, were foreshadowed by him. He stands, rather flamboyantly guilty, at the beginning of a new age to which the conflicts of ***Seven Pillars*** were to become soberly familiar. In everything, from the hold-ups, the executions, the intrigue and the tortures to the final nihilism, he was the first guinea-pig of the underground. What a guilt-eaten book ***Seven Pillars*** is and how subtle. True to the feeling of his period (for the book is very much of the Twenties in its artifice, its mastery and egoism) and true to his own nature, it is theatrical; but it has to be so to make its corrosive mark as a new, progenitive kind of mind in war. ***The Mint*** was a good title for its successor, because it was Lawrence's place to stamp the hurt contemporary face on the new coin.

The theme of ***Seven Pillars*** seems to be ecstasy, guilt and suffering. In action, that means the satisfaction of the well-laid mine, the provision of timely loot, excitement and slaughter for the tribesmen; it means blood-guilt; and it means the martyrdom of leadership—having to shoot a man oneself in order to prevent a blood feud—and a curious moment like the one when, after a massacre, Lawrence went round and arranged the dead in more seemly positions. The self-questionings have the rhetorical touch—later Lawrence criticised the "foppishness" of his mind—but the manner he adopted, one feels, was simply his device for screwing the last ounce out of sensibility, or a kind of flagellation. . . . (pp. 40-1)

The pages on self-surrender, obedience and abasement are, in their way, religious and, indeed, were observed among believers in a warlike religion. The final desire is for physical solitude. Lawrence could not bear to be touched, unless, one supposes, he was hurt.

And so one could go on about this strange actor whose aim—realised only among the Arabs—was to be notable for being unnoticeable, an actor both morally and physically. His self-analysis is not really the best part of ***Seven Pillars;*** what holds one is more than the story; it is the brain. Travellers have told before how they have stopped a quarrel by a well-turned tale, especially (one seems to remember) in the East, the home of convenient formulae; but Lawrence giving an impromptu parody of an Arab story-teller, at a bad moment, to an audience who (he tells us) had never heard parody before, is superb in assurance. Or again, Lawrence dominating his illness by thinking out his campaign, shows us the will at work hour by hour. Throughout a swift, masterly narrative, packed with action, character and personal emotion, we have the extraordinary spectacle of a brain working the whole time. It is as if we could see the campaign thought by thought. The close texture of genius in action has rarely been so livingly done by an active man; it has been left, as a rule, to the self-watching invalids. And this density of thought was present from the beginning. If there had been no war in Arabia, and no epic to live, Lawrence would still have been a vivid, trenchant and sardonic historian. Hardly classical in manner (for that was "out" in the Twenties and writers were looking for manners which would bring home their nervous singularity) ***Seven Pillars*** is the solitary classic of the self-conscious warrior, as Doughty is of the great self-conscious traveller. (p. 42)

V. S. Pritchett, "A Portrait of T. E. Lawrence," in his Books in General, *Chatto & Windus, 1953, pp. 37-42.*

L. P. HARTLEY (essay date 1955)

[*Author of the acclaimed novel trilogy* Eustace and Hilda *(1944-47), Hartley was an English novelist and short story writer whose fiction is unified by the theme of the search for individuality and meaning in the post-Christian era. In his examination of moral dilemmas he is often compared to Nathaniel Hawthorne, while his effective use of symbolism and close attention to craft and plot unity evoke frequent comparisons to the works of Henry James. As a literary critic, Hartley contributed reviews for many years to* The Saturday Review, Time and Tide, The Spectator, *and other periodicals. In the following excerpt, Hartley questions whether* The Mint *merits recognition as a prose masterpiece.*]

The name of Colonel Lawrence has always meant different things to different people, and now, after the appearance of Mr. Richard Aldington's 'biographical inquiry' [see excerpt dated 1955], it is more than ever controversial. One begins to wonder whether a man whose life and character are capable of such diverse and contradictory interpretations can ever have existed in the flesh. But he did—I can testify to that—for I once met him.

It was at All Souls College, where in the autumn of 1919 he had been elected a Research Fellow. It was about this time that he leaped into fame, but I had hardly heard of him when I met him, so I talked to him as to an ordinary man, not as a celebrity. I remember he was wearing a blue suit, while everyone else was wearing a dinner jacket, and that he was small and slight and fair and girlish-looking. His manner was extraordinarily quiet and gentle. We talked—at least he talked, for I had nothing to contribute to the conversation—about coding and decoding, a subject which had no special interest for me, and yet he made it fascinating, and I was aware of a compelling magnetism in him, which grew on me as we talked. It was slightly but not disturbingly hypnotic, and its seat was in his eyes, which were dark blue and very large. No other person I have met has had the same effect on me.

After this small contribution to the Lawrence legend, I must proceed to discussing ***The Mint.*** The author's name is given as 352087 A/C Ross, which was Lawrence's alias when in 1922 he joined the ranks of the Air Force. He kept a day-to-day record of his experiences in the depot at Uxbridge where the recruits were being licked into shape, and this book is the fruit of them. . . .

On the jacket of ***The Mint*** it says that the book is not self-pitying. To me the Uxbridge sections seem one long wail of self-pity—a self-pity that if not always stated is continually implied. One feels sorry for him, of course: he was thirty-four, and a sensitive plant; the other men were for the most part many years younger and much less sensitive to material hardships. When it came to P.T. and such-like exercises, he was inevitably at a great disadvantage. But he had himself been in the Army, as an officer, for many years: he knew what conditions in the Services were like, and yet for reasons of his own he deliberately chose to live among them. He was not a conscript: no one asked him to join up: indeed, many people must have done their utmost to dissuade him. He brought it on himself, but when it came to the point, he could not take it—at least, not without making a great fuss. If he entered the R.A.F. to spy on its proceedings and afterwards make them public, then one's sympathies with him would be less than ever: but there is every evidence that he did not.

Nuns fret not at the convent's narrow room: the discipline which enables a soldier to endure the terrors of war is no doubt partly the outcome of being shouted at and bullied by N.C.O.s. Lawrence may have been right that such rigours need not form part of an airman's training; indeed, that is one of his main grievances; but in general his criticism of service conditions is really a criticism of war itself. (p. 658)

Is ***The Mint*** a masterpiece, as the ambiguous dedication suggests that Lawrence thought it might be? He was one of the most conscientious and self-conscious craftsmen; nothing less than a masterpiece would satisfy him. Of ***The Mint*** he says, 'I wrote it tightly because our clothes are so tight and our lives are so tight in the service'. To my mind it is too tightly written, too condensed; polishing is a great feature of military life, and it has been overpolished. Consequently, neither the pressure nor the tempo varies; the same pitch of intensity is maintained throughout; the trivial and the important receive equal emphasis; the prose is too well drilled. One longs for a casual, limping sentence that would relax the tension. On the other hand, there is something to admire in almost every paragraph, some feat of compressed expression or some striking thought. One cannot say that the book is very enjoyable or that it is very readable, except in small doses, but it is continuously impressive. Even the spaces left blank for the obscenities with which servicemen eke out their meagre vocabularies form part of the pattern; they are as studied as the rest.

Egocentric as it is, ***The Mint*** is not lacking in humanity or even in humour. The sketches of Lawrence's companions in the depot are brilliantly drawn, and often drawn with affection. Lawrence was capable of both objectivity and feeling, though not of losing himself in what he saw and felt. That was impossible to him, for he was always in search of himself. It is both his strength and his limitation as a writer, but he was well aware of it. He could never have said with the Indian sage, 'It is Thee I seek from fountain to fountain', for it was always himself he sought. I think one would call the book a failed masterpiece, but the failure is grander than many successes.

And Lawrence himself? What light does ***The Mint*** throw on him? How does he come out of it? How does one feel towards him? Inevitably, I think, as one feels towards the man with a grievance, the man with a chip on his shoulder. A writer can get only a small part of himself across in a book: the Lawrence I remember, who talked so compellingly to an unknown undergraduate, is absent from it. The magnetism does not work. The mystery, which his personality undoubtedly held in such rich measure, the flower that was in him, he crushes in the iron hold of his too well turned out prose. It is an ironical commentary on someone who chafed so bitterly at spit and polish that those should be the very qualities that prevent his prose from being as good as he wanted it to be.

His trouble was that he was far too complex a human being to be single-minded about anything. Even in the matter of cruelty his attitude is self-contradictory. He inveighs against the bullying N.C.O.s, but he observes of the barrack-room scraps his companions had among themselves (and in which he joined): 'There's hardly a night without its mirthful accident of bloodletting'. He complains bitterly of the punishments meted out to the recruits, but he also says, 'Men will never work for long, unpunished'. One feels he was perversely determined to play the Spartan Boy. (p. 659)

L. P. Hartley, "A Failed Masterpiece," in The Listener, *Vol. LIII, No. 1363, April 14, 1955, pp. 658-59.*

JEAN BERAUD VILLARS (essay date 1955)

[*In the following excerpt, Lawrence's French biographer Villars offers a high assessment of* Seven Pillars of Wisdom, *but finds* The Mint *to be weakened by the author's masochism.*]

It is difficult to give an opinion of a work which, with all its faults, long-windedness, omissions, obvious inaccuracies, and passionate bias, remains without any doubt one of the finest books of our generation. Through its complexity it escapes analysis; to appreciate its originality, its faults and its power alike, one must hold it in one's hand. (p. 294)

[At] Carchemish Lawrence had written on Seven Cities of the Orient, a work which he destroyed in 1914. He had entitled it ***The Seven Pillars of Wisdom,*** drawing his inspiration from a verse in Proverbs: "Wisdom hath builded her house, she hath hewn out her seven pillars" Proverbs ix. 1. This fine title, which had remained unused, never ceased to haunt his memory, and he made use of it for his new work.

This title, with all its poetic content, places the ***The Seven Pillars*** on the level on which it was conceived, not on that of wisdom—never was a book less wise—but on that of lyricism; further, Lawrence was thus able to connect the story of his war experiences with his former life, heavily charged for him with the memories of a carefree and happy youth in a Syrian Arcadia.

Above all else, the book is in fact a work of art, a literary monument. To underline his aesthetic intentions, Lawrence had placed a poem of Shakespearean inspiration at the beginning of his work with an introduction which transports us to the highest summits of sensitivity and fervour. These are the first movements of the *Pathétique*. The reader is warned, he is on the threshold of an epic and not of a staff report.

This tone is maintained throughout the ***The Seven Pillars.*** The story is told with control, the excitement is gradually built up from the opening of the situation right up to the feverish pages of the final battle and the triumphant entry into Damascus. In truth the work has the sweep of an epic poem or of a tragedy. Spell-bound by this seething work, the reader comes across successively philosophical considerations, stories of battles and diplomatic negotiations, descriptions of landscapes, and portraits and confessions of brutal accuracy. The size of the work, the multiplicity and diversity of the subjects of which it treats could have made of it an incoherent jumble, but throughout its thousand pages the interest never sags for a moment, so skilful are the transitions and so powerful the architecture.

The style, sometimes too laboured and taut, has a flawless solidity. Lawrence has the mastery of language, of the evocative word full of suggestions and echoes. He handles the familiar, the scholarly, the trivial, the classical, and the crude without ever losing his distinction. It is difficult to find prose that is more colorful, more vibrant, and more full of imagery. The vast and dense vocabulary, steeped in the ancient sources of the language, brings it close to the Elizabethans, and for a Frenchman recalls the vigorous authors of the end of the Renaissance: Montluc and d'Aubigné or yet Retz.

The profundity of the introspection and the nakedness of the confessions make one think of Rousseau or rather of Proust or Gide. Though a book on war it contributes to our researches into the obscurities of the human heart. In the course of a painful quest into a rent and complex self, and behind a screen of dignity and gravity can be perceived some very dangerous problems; few authors have described the troubled twistings of the serpent with so much penetration and sincerity.

The book when it appeared struck a new note: its balance between romanticism and naturalism was the essence of a new form of literature. Traditional in form, the ***The Seven Pillars*** is in many ways revolutionary. The public of the time, especially the English public, was not accustomed to so much precision in the depicting of the horrors of war nor to such confessions of the inner life. In the pages of the ***The Seven Pillars*** one sees in detail men killing other men with their hands; the veil of modesty which the majority of authors of war books have drawn across the technical details of the immense collective murder is withheld. Certain passages in the *Débâcle* by Zola, certain episodes in *Feu* by Barbusse had alone attained to this degree of horror; but still one felt of these two authors that their literary gift was greater than their personal experience, that they had held neither the knife nor the machine-gun which Lawrence, the intellectual and artist, had handled in twenty engagements; no great writer had ever told how he had executed one of his men at point-blank range, finished off a wounded comrade, been successively tortured and sodomised by a squad of soldiers; no veteran of the trenches had revealed what happened after an attack or analysed the state of his soul.

Thirty years ago, these accounts plucked at fibres that were not accustomed to vibrating. Into the ***The Seven Pillars*** he dragged in the musty smells of homosexuality, of cruelty, and of death. A certain sadism mingled with the stories, a sadism which had been carefully expurgated from the accounts of the other war writers, who by tacit consent presented themselves as martyrs and paladins that were not supposed to have known such troubled sensations.

Lawrence proved to be the forerunner. Before Malraux, the Koestler of *Darkness at Noon,* Kafka and Jean-Paul Sartre, before the writers of the Resistance and those who described the Nazi and Soviet atrocities (without speaking of recent commercial novels, hybrid offsprings of brutality and pornography), he invented a style which was to be largely exploited by a whole generation of writers.

So much art was not expended gratuitously. Immersed in his work, living in the hallucinating world of the writer in the process of creating his work, Lawrence allowed himself to be carried away by purely aesthetic considerations, but he never lost sight of his aim, his plea for the Arab cause, and his service to the nation whose champion he had made himself; he never hesitated before an exaggeration, an omission or if necessary a lie.

When very young he had once said to one of his brothers who was in the process of studying history, "Political poems are the only thing not dry in History." In writing the ***The Seven Pillars*** he wittingly composed a political poem, a work of propaganda as tendentious as *Renard, The Song of Roland,* Shakespeare's *Henry V* or Napoleon's *Mémorial.*

Now it is not possible for a writer to be at once the painter of a large lyrical fresco, an inflamed partisan, a faithful memorialist and also the recorder of the confessions of a soul in torment. One must of necessity ask what is the historical value of a testimony in which truth is quartered on so Procrustean a bed.

If we are to go by what Lawrence himself said, this value would be definitely questionable. In the first introduction which he wrote for the ***The Seven Pillars*** he allowed himself to say some disturbing things. "It seemed to me historically needful to reproduce the tale, as perhaps no one but myself in Feisal's army had thought of writing down at the time what we felt, what we hoped, what we tried." And further on: "In these pages the history is not of the Arab Movement, but of me in it."

And he finished with: "I began in my reports to conceal the true stories of things and to persuade the few Arabs who knew to an equal reticence. In this book also, for the last time I mean to be my own judge of what to say."

The reader must choose between three such contradictory professions of faith.

Bernard Shaw realising that these preliminary statements would remove all credence from the work, persuaded Lawrence to suppress them, but T.E.'s brother, with some naïvety, published them posthumously to the great concern of future historians.

It does not seem, however, that we ought to take literally lines that were written from differing motives, and despite the author's imprudent statement we can consider that the ***The Seven Pillars,*** cross-checked and verified with other writers, and brought into focus by a critical mind, remains a relatively accurate story, and the only one which can give us any idea of this complex, multifarious and confused movement called the Arab Revolt.

It will always be possible to raise doubts on the authenticity of a number of incidents related in the book and to which there was no other witness than the author himself. We appear, however, to have proof of the veracity of the story as a whole, which for being indirect is none the less a strong one. It is the attitude of the officers and the soldiers who, having been Lawrence's companions during the war, came to know the ***The Seven Pillars of Wisdom*** in 1926.

We know that Lawrence sent a copy of his work to most of the Englishmen who had been with him in Arabia; now none of them ever raised a protest against the author's allegations. This silence is all the more significant since Lawrence dealt with some of them rather unkindly. Such colleagues as he had treated badly had a fine opportunity for getting their own back. Now, if some have had reservations to make on points of detail or have criticised the character, the methods, the strategy, or the political views of the author, nobody has said that he did not play a major rôle in the campaign, nor above all that he boasted of personal exploits which he did not accomplish. The tacit acquiescence of Allenby, of Clayton, of Storrs, Newcombe, Joyce, Young, Wavell and Dawnay, to speak only of them, guarantees the authenticity of the work. They might possibly have let a few inaccuracies go out of a spirit of comradeship or for political reasons, but their tolerance, if it existed, must have had its limits, and one cannot for a moment imagine soldiers and officials of that quality keeping a conspiracy of silence in order to cover up for a braggart or an imposter. (pp. 294-99)

As an impartial witness Lawrence would have given us an accurate account of confused battles in a secondary theatre of operations. Subjective, partisan and violently egotistical, he leaves us a work of art, a monstrous but unique book which is a combination of *War and Peace, The Confessions* of Jean Jacques Rousseau, and the *Châtiments* of the old Victor Hugo and which has a much greater chance of survival than the sincere accounts of so many of the actors of the war, more faithful but lacking in genius. (p. 302)

Sincerely or not, [Lawrence] declared that the ***The Seven Pillars*** had been a fiasco. He wished in fact to produce a great work.

At the depôt at Uxbridge, whilst he was experiencing the most painful side of the soldier's profession, he had taken some notes of a melancholic mood, pouring out his spleen in vitriolic comments on the harsh training to which he had submitted. At Karachi, he put the finishing touches to what he considered to be the book of his life and sent the manuscript to Edward Garnett with this dedication: "You dreamed I came one night with this book crying, "Here is a masterpiece. Burn it. Well as you please." Needless to say, Garnett did not burn it.

The book was entitled ***The Mint,*** a word which conveys the idea of violently stamping an indelible mark on coarse material. The Army, which moulded the soldier's body and soul into a uniform pattern, was the Mint.

It is legitimate for a conscientious objector to rebel against military discipline, but it is the less so for a man who has freely chosen the career of a soldier, and the violence of the diatribe written by Lawrence is astonishing. There were, however, some legitimate reasons for his project: he was in revolt against the clumsy methods with which it was intended to train the recruits for a technical army whose task was either flying or delicate mechanical work, and against the application of the very harsh, almost Prussian methods of the old English mercenary army.

His starting point is therefore just and many of Lawrence's criticisms went far, but the artist and the fanatic betray the logician, and the violence of the satire weakens the scope of the work. The adventure was too petty for the misfortunes of the hero to be moving, the persecution mania is obvious and it is difficult to feel sorry for the *declassés* (whom the author besides describes in pretty unattractive colours) subjected to the abuse of the sergeant-major and the classical punishments of the barracks. The righteous wrath of the author falls flat. The inspiration of *Le train de 8 h. 47* or *Les Gaiétés de l'Escadron* are not worthy of the whip of a Juvenal.

Certainly there are some pages in this book in which one recognises the fist of a great writer, his vigorous prose, the choice of words, the imagery, and the magical power of evocation: ***The Mint*** is composed of short chapters of two or three pages, of which some are excellent, such as those which describe the Church Parade, the sermon on the sin of the absurd padré, barrack-room life, drill, and such passages as depict the mentality of the English people, and their finicky and complicated formalities. But apart from these pages of quality, there are unfortunately others of either an odious cruelty or in very bad taste, and others which leave the impression of childishness and, even worse, are deadly boring. The almost physical hatred which the author nourished for the officers is insupportably dragged out, and he describes with a sadistic pleasure the camp commander, a war-cripple, falling into the mud and unable to get up, being dragged along the ground by his dogs. What he says of the N.C.O.s makes one think that they are worse than the worst re-enlisted men charged with drilling the habitual inmates of Biribi, which is not very likely. Here again the excess of realism detracts from its credibility and one is regrettably aware of a certain baseness in this literary vengeance on his old officers.

Lawrence wanted to write the whole book in the language of the English soldier which (like that of all soldiers) is candidly and constantly obscene and filthy. The effect is disagreeable, because if for the soldiers who use them the foul words have lost some of their evocative power, it is different for the reader who has forgotten his barrack life, and the marching songs he used to sing. It is painful to see in black and white the song, once so funny, which the soldier sang. Some of the expressions ought never to be printed. One detects the influence of *Feu,* which Lawrence had read, but Barbusse, despite his brutality, used the argot of the soldiers with much greater discretion and the subject of his book—the trench war—allows of licences which the infinitely less tragic theme of the tribulations of recruits in a barracks, does not.

Meanwhile, despite the poverty of the story and the incongruity of the vocabulary, ***The Mint*** attains in places a tragic intensity which is astonishing for such a subject, but one realises that it is moving because it reveals the anguish of an unbalanced mind.

It exposes Lawrence's persecution mania, his morbid need to suffer, and above all his unhealthy desire to humiliate himself morally and physically. The author rolls himself deliciously in his own filth, and the enjoyment with which he describes himself eating the remains in the kitchens or splashing through pig dung is distinctly pathological. If ***The Mint*** is not the artistic peak which Lawrence hoped it would be, it remains a curious human document which is indispensable to the understanding of the latter part of his strange life. (pp. 334-36)

Jean Beraud Villars, in his T. E. Lawrence; or, The Search for the Absolute, *translated by Peter Dawnay, Sidgwick and Jackson Limited, 1958, 358 p.*

RICHARD ALDINGTON (essay date 1955)

[*Aldington is perhaps best remembered as the editor of the Imagist periodical* The Egoist *and as an influential member of that movement, which included Hilda Doolittle—who became his first wife in 1913—Ezra Pound, and Amy Lowell, among others. The Imagists viewed themselves as the saviors of a dead language; their major goal was to free poetry from excessive verbiage and vague generalities and to utilize precise imagery. Aldington's work with this group was cut short by his service in World War I, which had a damaging effect on his mental health and his career. It took him years to recover from his experiences, and once he did he virtually gave up writing poetry for prose. However, as a novelist he achieved some success with his angry yet honest attacks on war and on his native England. As a literary critic and biographer, Aldington combined his skills as a poet, his perceptiveness as an extremely sensitive reader, and his personal reminiscences to produce criticism which is creative as well as informative. In the following excerpt from a biography commonly regarded as malicious in intent, Aldington attempts to dismantle the Lawrence myth.*]

The business of a biographer is to tell a life-story and thereby also to portray a character by gathering, arranging and interpreting the discoverable facts about his subject. Where the facts are uncertain or contaminated or embellished, as in this case, the biographer finds himself in the position of counsel who puts his client in the box only to discover a faulty witness; or, if that seems too lofty a comparison for so humble a labour, he may be likened to a bricklayer who finds some of the bricks given him true and straight, others faulty and misshapen, and yet others crumbling to dust when handled. Whatever Lawrence's part in the 1914 war it can probably never be estimated exactly because so much of the evidence rests on his own testimony. Lawrence has recorded that Lord Allenby could not determine how much in him was "genuine performer" and how much "charlatan," and Lord Wavell comments that Allenby never solved the problem; but "always suspected a strong streak of the charlatan in Lawrence." Lloyd George more vaguely hints a similar opinion.

From this arose the necessity for careful checking of all the claims and picturesque anecdotes which were circulated directly by Lawrence or indirectly by him through his more or less credulous friends. But in so doing the biographer must keep in mind that no man is rigidly consistent and accurate, especially a man like Lawrence whose unstable temperament is illustrated by the constant variations in his scrawled handwriting; that everyone changes with the passage of time, so much so that a man of forty looks back with some astonishment and dismay at his half-forgotten self of twenty, unless indeed roseate idealisation of the past sets in early; that the universal miseries of life induce fibbings and subterfuges in us all, and that in our letters we all tend to vary our expression according to the person addressed. He must keep in mind the old fable of the shepherd who cried "Wolf" too often, and remember that Lawrence may sometimes be speaking the truth. Above all, he must recollect that many of the embellished tales are not without some basis of fact, and avoid denying all Lawrence's accomplishments because they were outrageously exaggerated. He was, for instance, a very good revolver shot, though he did tell an absurd tale of intentionally shooting a man in the little finger, and the different and highly-coloured versions of the episode he circulated do not mean that no such encounter occurred. His bicycle was not designed by Lord Nuffield and himself, as he claimed, but he did have a light racing bicycle, and did cover long distances, though demonstrably in some instances (and probably in most) not as long as he asserted. (pp. 110-11)

A careful study of Lawrence's psychology, taken with what has been recorded of his medical history, by some really competent specialist, would be of great interest and doubtless enable us to understand and to condone much which now seems merely impudent. Meanwhile from the standpoint of common sense and common knowledge we may point out that a certain amount of boasting, more or less, is usually inseparable from that stage of adolescence which Lawrence so queerly seemed in some respects never to outlive. . . . We can go further, and say that such boasting is a universal human failing or trait, from young Red Indian braves to elderly retired mariners and field officers. What is different in Lawrence's case is that the stories were told deliberately, and found their way into print while he persuaded two biographers [Robert Graves (see excerpt dated 1927) and B.H. Liddell Hart (see Additional Bibliography)] to publish statements misleading their readers into thinking he had no responsibility for them. If it be asked why these stories were believed by his biographers and by the numerous friends who have left their personal memories, the answer is perfectly simple. Not one of these stories was published until after Lowell Thomas's propaganda had worked up public hysteria to an almost unprecedented extent, and had made Lawrence the popular war hero, creating an atmosphere in which such stories were readily acceptable, on the strength of achievements which Lowell Thomas himself had not witnessed—his lecture and his book are based on what he was told by Lawrence and Lawrence's friends [see Additional Bibliography]. (pp. 111-12)

Some of the Lawrence stories . . . are absurd and trivial, but they happen to be among those where Lawrence can be shown definitely to be romancing. . . . As an example of the self-glorifying story which cannot be definitely disproved but which sounds highly improbable, let us look into the much-publicised interview between Lawrence and Kitchener which is alleged to have occurred before the war. As it links up with a claim (supported also by no evidence beyond Lawrence's own assertions) that early in 1915 he was the real author of the strategic plan for a landing at or near Alexandretta, the enquiry is not without interest.

The first mention of this interview occurs in Lowell Thomas's book. According to this, Lawrence "with his intimate knowledge of history" thought that the proposal to run a branch line to Alexandretta from the main Berlin-Baghdad railway was "a bold Prussian threat against British power in Asia" and therefore instantly hurried to Cairo, "demanded an audience with Lord Kitchener" and asked him why "Germany had been permitted to get control of Alexandretta." Unfortunately for posterity no film or photograph exists to show the expressions moving across Lord Kitchener's swivel-eyed features as he was thus bluntly challenged by an unknown non-military Oxonian of twenty-five. According to Thomas's version of Lawrence's tale there was no explosion but the mild reply: "I have warned London repeatedly, but the Foreign Office pays no attention. Within two years, there will be a World War. Unfortunately, young man, you and I can't stop it, so run along and sell your papers." Why "sell your papers?" What papers? Can this refer to the well-known practice of Oxonians who help to pay their way through college by hawking copies of the *Saturday Evening Post* on Carfax? However that may be, the story itself was told to Mr. Thomas by "Major Young, of the Near Eastern Secret Corps," whatever that was. Probably Major Sir Hubert Young of the Indian Army is meant, but his book, *The Independent Arab,* is discreetly silent on this tale. It is, however, repeated by Graves (and hence with Lawrence's knowledge) in agreement with the assertion that Lawrence was "a student of world politics," of which there is not the slightest evidence in his pre-1914 letters and writings, and with the change of Kitchener's last words to: "So run along, young man, and dig before it rains." Thus, through Graves, Lawrence gave his acquiescence to a story which Lowell Thomas had already picked up from someone in a slightly differently form, thereby glorifying himself as one on familiar terms before the war with the ruler of Egypt, as a student of world politics and one intimately acquainted with history.

But did this interview ever take place? It is true Lawrence was in Egypt with Petrie in 1912, when Kitchener was Consul-General, but when Liddell Hart asked Lawrence at what date he met Kitchener, Lawrence replied that he "first met Kitchener in 1913 and again in 1914." It is only negative, but there is no evidence that Lawrence was in Cairo at any time during 1913-14 until December, 1914, and Sir Ernest Dowson has certainly mis-dated Lawrence's first reporting for duty at the Surveyor General's office. Of course, it is possible that Lawrence did make a brief trip to Cairo between January, 1913 and June, 1914 (when Kitchener left for good), and that the journey went wholly unrecorded at the time. He may have had an interview, even, though it seems quite incredible that he could have refrained from boasting of having met so eminent a person to some of his friends; yet not one of the pre-war letters or reminiscences mentions it. Lowell Thomas only heard the story in 1918, by which date Kitchener was dead. Not the least incredible part of the tale is that a man in Kitchener's responsible position would have been so utterly indiscreet as to prophesy a World War to a casual civilian caller aged 25.

And how unaware Lawrence was of the approaching catastrophe is proved by his 1913 letter . . . in which he hopes for several more years at Carchemish and then another and another "nice place." If a man so important as Kitchener had really warned him that a war was coming, how could Lawrence have indulged in such false hopes?

In the 17th-18th century vogue of "the ruling passion" psychology Lawrence's would certainly have been set down as amour-propre, vanity. But, as La Rochefoucauld, one of its chief exponents, pointed out, vanity is a universal passion; and it is not necessarily to be condemned, since it may be and often is a strong motive to effort and action. What is curious in Lawrence's case is that he was so lacking in pride that he was quite content to let himself be celebrated in anecdotes which he knew to be untrue or exaggerated since he himself had originated them and connived at their circulation. Yet this preposterous vanity co-existed with a desire to be thought modest and retiring in the English Public School boy tradition; and indeed in some moods it became partly genuine when he discovered what nuisance newspapers and public made of the notoriety he himself had so eagerly courted. But the familiar propaganda which represents him as the shrinking victim of a notoriety thrust upon him against his will is just one more myth—of his own creation. (pp. 112-14)

Our problem here is not to attempt an assessment of ***The Seven Pillars*** as a "titanic" work of literary art, but to ask how far it is history, how implicitly it can be relied on for the facts. This is a problem which can never be really solved, because the principal witness is Lawrence himself. In the first part of this book, examples have been brought forward of Lawrence's methods of building up his legend. While trying to preserve a reputation for shrinking modesty, he circulated through his friends exaggerated or wholly invented stories always to his advantage, stories which eventually got into print and now form the principal basis of his reputation, and in almost every case they were stories which could only have originated with himself.

The difficulty is to find any adequate means of verifying Lawrence's statements, and one danger is that his unsupported testimony may be doubted when it is in fact as reasonably true as human tendency to error permits. It is the inevitable penalty for the many fanciful stories he unquestionably did tell about himself. How far, for example, are we justified in believing or questioning Lawrence's version of his relations with staff and general officers in Cairo, Ismailia and Basra? His standard of judgement was that those who shared Lawrence's views about "the Arabs" were heroes or at any rate "good men," while those who disagreed with him were ignorant, foolish and incompetent. Everybody accepts Lawrence's version without question, omitting to observe that, even if the officers in question had wished to reply to the insults rather than criticisms of an amateur, they were debarred by professional etiquette from doing so while they held their commissions. (pp. 160-61)

The story of the production of ***Seven Pillars of Wisdom*** is long and complicated, and highly characteristic of Lawrence's pretentious egotism. To write a clear, straightforward account of the Arab war and of his own share in it did not suit him at all. While affecting a shrinking modesty and protesting how much was owing to others, he was all along casting himself for the leading part. Then the book had to be a literary masterpiece, a "titanic book," self-consciously and pretentiously planned as such, according to Lawrence's Oxonian ideas of what constituted a masterpiece, looking to literature, not to life. People influential in the literary world were enmeshed as advisers and approvers during the revision; and, according to Lawrence, Bernard Shaw improved every paragraph. So we are left uncertain as to how much of the book was in fact rewritten by Shaw over Lawrence's rhetoric. The completed work then had to be illustrated by colour reproductions of specially commissioned portraits and pictures, and produced in accordance with Lawrence's notions of typography. By a series of brilliant manoeuvres, he contrived to enjoy the reputation of having sacrificed his fortune to produce a book beautiful for the happy few, while arranging for a popular cut-down edition which sold in tens of thousands and repaid all his losses. After which, he gave all his royalties to charity; but, when the book was withdrawn in England, these royalties can only have continued from abroad.

Lawrence had considerable gifts as a rhetorical and propagandist writer, though he lacked spontaneity and naturalness and the "tact of omission." He was a persuasive and plausible advocate with a decided taste and ability for descriptive writing. He was not naturally an observer, but could force himself to note and to remember when he felt that it was called for, and must have kept elaborate notes during 1917-18. (His private 1911 diary of his walk is one of the most jejune travel productions ever printed.) It is Lawrence's perpetual conscious effort to write up to this artificial level which puts a strain on the admiration of his readers. (pp. 313-14)

In addition to this straining for a "titanic" style, the book imposes on its readers the additional strain of watching the author's painful mental and spiritual contortions as he suffered the onslaught of a severe nervous breakdown. What Herbert Read called the "splendid 'copy'" and Lawrence himself the "Boy Scout" appeal of the book is spoiled by pretentiousness and an irrelevant self-torture, for the author's acute psychological sufferings arise from a cause totally unconnected with the Arab rebellion, though possibly brought to consciousness by its hardships, responsibilities and dangers.

At the same time that the reader has inflicted on him this extraneous neurosis, he is often irritated by Lawrence's cynical contempt and frivolity. Obviously Lawrence had a perfect right to give his book a meaningless Biblical title passed on from a destroyed work of his youth, and there was nothing to stop him from pulling about, cutting and adding to his laboriously composed and Shaw-aided text merely to gratify his amateurish typographical fads. But he cannot at the same time claim the merit of a serious recorder of an intensely-felt experience which he longed passionately to convey to others, for them to share and to take warning, not for self-glorification and the plugging of some political "cause." Something like six thousand words of fine writing are devoted to a two-days' camel-ride from the coast to Feisal's camp, which shows a singular contempt for his readers' patience. I cannot agree with those who think that Lawrence's style resembles Doughty's, though it is true that both write a self-consciously assumed and mannered prose—Doughty, a 19th-century pastiche of 16th-century English, and Lawrence, a 20th-century version of 19th-century aesthetic prose. Little unimportant details may stem from Doughty, such as "bouncing camels" and sheiks as "worshipful men of the desert," but the style of ***Seven Pillars*** is not pseudo-Elizabethan. On the other hand, Doughty's influence may be to blame for the confused structure, the long-winded digressions, the ruthless translation into the chosen idiom of every detail jotted down as notes. Yet Lawrence was aware of the drawbacks to Doughty's style. He rightly regrets Doughty's use of foreign constructions, his archaic vocabulary and his use of hundreds of Arabic words which have perfectly good English equivalents. Lawrence's dictum: "Camel is a better word than thelul," should be noted and obeyed by all writers tempted into verbal local colour. On the other hand, Lawrence, like Doughty, sometimes forgets—or rather does not care—that his reader may not share his interest in endless descriptions of obscure desert features and persons. There is always a moment, too often several, in these books on the Arabian Desert when we are called on to thrill, Robinson Crusoe-like, to such a transcendent revelation as the spectacle of dried camel dung fretted by the drifting sand. And Lawrence's narrative is apt to be loaded with unknown or forgotten names, almost like those "begat" chapters in the Old Testament. (pp. 328-29)

On the other hand, there is certainly literary talent here, especially that talent for persuasion and plausible propaganda so noticeable in his *Arab Bulletins* and in his political reports and letters to the Press. Only a man widely conversant with literature, and in possession of a genuine gift for fitting words to thought and experience, could have worked out a style so high-flown and exacting and have maintained it through so long a book. This virtuosity in words, this meticulously mannered type of style had been much admired in the tardily aesthetic Oxford of Lawrence's youth. And is it too fanciful to see in him something of that Irish or Celtic love of playing with words, which has produced how many verbal preciosities down to the enormous word-bog of *Finnegans Wake*? But, however that may be, Lawrence as a writer was also skilful in the art of using words so as to suggest or to imply something more or something less than is actually stated. This was often a useful defence, making it as hard to lay hold of his real meaning as to grasp a naked man smeared with grease. But that kind of verbal dodging is the virtue of a politician and intriguer, not of a writer. Almost the hardest and least often achieved triumph of the heart-breaking craft of words is to use them so that they

"The Mound of Carchemish," *from the sketch by Lawrence. From* The Letters of T. E. Lawrence, *edited by David Garnett. Cape, 1938. Reprinted by permission of Jonathan Cape Ltd, on behalf of the Letters of T. E. Lawrence Trust.*

will mean to the reader exactly what they meant to the writer. Suggestion is too easy. One example among many—Lawrence used the appeal to puritan prejudice of the word "clean" in the most unscrupulous way. Thus he warmly recommends his Farraj and Daud (who, on his own showing, were a couple of unwashed desert homosexuals) as "so clean." He praises "the sword"—i.e., the archaic symbol for War, with all its filth and degradation—as "clean." He tries to place Allenby above question or discussion by calling him "clean-judging." And elsewhere we hear that Lawrence admired a private soldier because he was "the rugged *clean*" type of Englishman, which leaves one musing over those dirty, slick English types one sees furtively bolting about all over the world.

May it be questioned whether a style so mannered, so literary and so inexact was really the most suitable for an honest war narrative? True, every personal war narrative is autobiography; but War is action, whatever it may involve of plans and preparations, and however much the neurotic intellectual who is writing may have been plagued by mental conflict and divided aims. Action does not ask a too sophisticated style, but rather a speech which is vigorous, direct, and unaffected, where the very existence of the sayer is forgotten in the vividness and meaning of the thing said. Is there a page of ***Seven Pillars*** in which we are allowed to forget Lawrence of Arabia? He might have written much better if he had not striven so painfully to write too well. (pp. 329-30)

It has been said that Lawrence had "no real self," that he was merely an actor who played many parts. But there was "a real self," which is fairly plainly shown both in ***Seven Pillars*** and in the letters to Lionel Curtis and Charlotte Shaw—an unhappy, wistful, tortured, hag-ridden self, floundering between heights and depths, aspiring to the rôle of a knight of the Round Table and tumbling with Hibernian awkwardness into grotesque and even terrible accidents and misfortunes—who can think of that flogging at Deraa without a shudder of pity for the victim? Yet he had the courage, the skill—the cunning, if you like—and the force of will and character to impose on the world his over-valued persona as reality, and to receive world-wide acclaim—for what? for the clever patter and pictures of a glib showman untroubled by the majesty of truth. (p. 350)

Richard Aldington, in his Lawrence of Arabia: A Biographical Enquiry, *Collins, 1955, 448 p.*

COLIN WILSON (essay date 1956)

[*Wilson is an English novelist, critic, and philosopher. His first book,* The Outsider *(1956), began a series of works, both fiction and nonfiction, whose central purpose has been to investigate mental and spiritual faculties of an exceptional kind latent in certain individuals. These faculties, which Wilson characterizes as those of the visionary, have as their basis the capacity and need to experience a sense of meaning and purpose in human life. The frustration of this need, according to Wilson, is observable in the predominantly negative tone of such modern authors as Samuel Beckett and such modern philosophers as Jean-Paul Sartre. Whereas Sartre's philosophy of existentialism demands a recognition of the basic absurdity and futility of human existence, Wilson's "new existentialism" proposes that "man should possess an infinite appetite for life. It should be self-evident to him, all the time, that life is superb, glorious, endlessly rich, infinitely desirable." In the following excerpt from* The Outsider, *Wilson views Lawrence as representative of the "outsider" personality; that is, a personality whose discontent with the world of commonplace existence leads to a state of unresolved psychological conflicts and unfulfilled spiritual goals.*]

The Seven Pillars of Wisdom is one of the most important case-books of the Outsider that we possess. From the beginning, Lawrence's interest in ascetic religious discipline is apparent. In an early chapter dealing with the religion of the Semitic peoples, he writes:

> The Arabs said there had been forty thousand prophets. . . . Their birth set them in crowded places. An unintelligible, passionate yearning drove them out into the desert. They lived there a greater or lesser time in meditation and physical abandonment; and thence they returned, with their imagined message articulate, to preach it to their old, and now doubting associates. The founders of the three great creeds fulfilled this cycle; their possible coincidence was proved a law by the parallel life histories of the myriad others, the unfortunate who failed, whom we might judge of no less true profession, but for whom time and disillusion had not heaped up dry souls to be set on fire.

(pp. 73-4)

Throughout ***The Seven Pillars,*** Lawrence's sympathy with these prophets reveals itself. The desert becomes a symbol of purity; of escape from the human:

> The Bedouin of the desert, born and grown up in it, had embraced with all his soul this nakedness too harsh for volunteers, for the reason, felt but inarticulate, that there he found himself indubitably free. . . . This faith of the desert was impossible in the towns. It was at once too strange, too simple and too impalpable for common use.

The chapter on religion ends with an important affirmation of the basis of Lawrence's 'religion':

> They were a people of starts, for whom the abstract was the strongest motive, the process of infinite courage and variety, and the end, nothing. They were as unstable as water, and like water, would perhaps finally prevail. Since the dawn of life, in successive waves, they had been dashing themselves against the coasts of the flesh. Each wave was broken but, like the sea, wore away ever so little of the granite on which it failed, and some day, ages yet, *might roll unchecked over the place where the material world had been,* and God would move on the face of those waters. One such wave (and not the least) I raised, and rolled before the breath of an idea, till it reached its crest, and toppled over and fell at Damascus. [Italics mine.]

There are times, in later scenes of violence and bloodshed, when Lawrence seems to be driving home Hemingway's conclusion, Most men die like animals, not men. There are even passages when the unemotional detachment seems to be callousness, or a disguised sadistic pleasure, and this would be difficult to reconcile with the picture of Lawrence drawn by his friends. It is then that passages like the one above provide the key to Lawrence's attitude. His detachment is like Hemingway's, a desire to 'stand for truth'. But there is an element present that Hemingway lacks completely, that element of *religious creed* that conditions his way of seeing. The violence and cruelty of the desert, and its contempt for the flesh, weigh equally in opposite balance-pans. The creed that reconciles them is the belief that the aim of life is the conquest of matter by spirit. (pp. 74-5)

What becomes undeniably apparent in reading ***The Seven Pillars*** is that Lawrence *did not regard himself as a soldier*. It was as the prophet of an idea that he 'raised the wave'; his power is the power of a man who can be *possessed by an idea,* and communicate his feeling to others. Again and again he repeats that the Arab war was a war of preaching, not of fighting. His frequent periods of misery and discouragement are due to a simple fact: he cannot believe in the idea that he is preaching:

> If I had been an honest advisor of the Arabs, I would have advised them to go home and not risk their lives fighting for such stuff. . . .

In spite of this disbelief, the role of preacher and leader afforded Lawrence the self-expression he needed. Elsewhere he confesses:

> I had one craving all my life—for the power of self-expression in some imaginative form. . . .

This war affords him an insight into himself. . . . It gives him a clear glimpse of that which is not trivial and unheroic.

His power of self-analysis is profound. He cannot see himself and his mind as a whole, but he can construct the picture in fragments, and in ***The Seven Pillars,*** none of the fragments is missing. His most characteristic trait is his inability to *stop thinking*. Thought imprisons him; it is an unending misery, because he knows the meaning of freedom, from such experience as this:

> We started on one of those clear dawns that wake up the senses with the sun, while the intellect, tired after the thinking of the night, was yet abed. For an hour or two, on such a morning, the sounds, scents and colours of the world struck man individually and directly, *not filtered through or made typical by thought:* they seemed to exist sufficiently by themselves, and the lack of design and of carefulness in creation no longer irritated.

When asked to become Feisal's advisor:

> I said I hated responsibility . . . and that all my life, *objects had been gladder to me than persons, and ideas than objects.*

The statements of those who knew him corroborate this. E. M. Forster wrote of him:

> Though I was frank with him, he was never frank in return, nor did I resent his refusal to be so. This explains in part why he was a great leader of men; he was able to reject intimacy without impairing affection.

Essentially, Lawrence was not interested in human beings. . . . (pp. 74-7)

For such a person, the world is an unbelievably colourless place, without vivid perception of sights and tastes to remove the attention from human beings and their inanities. The result is a state of unending mental strain:

> It was only weakness which delayed me from mind-suicide—some slow task to choke at length this furnace in my brain: I had developed ideas of other men . . . but had never created a thing of my own, *since I could not approve creation.* [Italics mine.]

This disapproval of creation is of the same nature as Oliver Gauntlett's 'The ignorant, the deceived, the superficial, were the happy among us', and consequently, the creative among them. It is dislike of human beings, 'the mob', 'chattering, snivelling, scolding'.

We can see that Lawrence combines the central characteristics of Roquentin [in Jean Paul Sartre's *Nausea*] and the Barbusse Outsider [in Henri Barbusse's *Hell*]. Roquentin had said: 'I was like the others—I said with them, the ocean *is* green, that white speck up there *is* a seagull, but I didn't feel that it existed.' Lawrence's inability to escape his 'thought riddled nature' has the same effect upon him; *everything is unreal*. And like Barbusse's hero, he cannot be happy in society, because he 'sees too deep and too much'. The desert war provided Lawrence with the same kind of peep-show into human suffering that Barbusse's hero found in his hotel room. These experiences were necessary to him, as they were necessary to the Barbusse Outsider, because their violence left no room in his mind for the irrelevancies of a civilization based on compromise. (pp. 77-8)

Lawrence's [capacity] to bear physical pain is of central importance in understanding him. His clear-sighted intellect could not conceive of moral freedom without physical freedom too; pain was an invaluable instrument in experiments to determine the extent of his moral freedom. His nihilism was fortified when he found himself unable to bear extremes, when, for instance, beaten by Turkish soldiers, the pain mastered his will not to cry out. Yet his conclusions point towards ultimate moral freedom:

> During [our revolt] we often saw men push themselves or be driven to a cruel extreme of endurance, yet never was there an intimation of physical break. Collapse arose always from a moral weakness eating into the body, which of itself, without traitors from within, had no power over the Will.
>
> While we rode we were disbodied, unconscious of flesh or feeling, and when, at an interval, this excitement faded and we did see our bodies, it was with some hostility, a contemptuous sense that they reached their highest purpose, not as vehicles of the spirit, but, when dissolved, their elements served to manure a field.

The will is supreme, but, as for Schopenhauer, it can exercise its ultimate freedom only by willing negation. Yet the belief in its fundamental importance gives us the key to Lawrence's life; he had never ceased to experiment to test the power of his will.

> Such liberties [abstaining from food and sleep] came from years of control (contempt of use might well be the lesson of our manhood) and they fitted me peculiarly for our work; but in me they came, half by training, half by trying . . . not effortlessly, as with the Arabs. Yet in compensation stood my energy of motive. Their less taut wills flagged before mine flagged, and by comparison made me seem tough and active.

There is, admittedly, a sort of contradiction involved in the two paragraphs quoted above. The Emersonian parenthesis, 'Contempt of use might well be the lesson of our manhood', follows logically from his earlier statement that 'his senses . . . needed the immediacy of contact to achieve perception'. His asceticism is an attempt to 'cleanse the doors of perception' (in Blake's phrase). Yet this does not fit in with the earlier paragraph and its complete denial of the body. One line of thought leads to the conception that the body reaches its highest purpose with perfect 'immediacy of perfection achieved', which is the conclusion of the mysticism of Boehme and Blake. The other leads to complete contempt, a cleansing of the senses that ultimately leads to throwing the senses away too.

Obviously, Lawrence's metaphysics does not form a self-complete system, and where it shows contradictions, it does so because he never worked systematically at self-analysis. This particular contradiction is inherent in mysticism—the saint who sees all existence as holy, and the saint who is completely withdrawn from existence—and if Lawrence had ever empirically resolved it, the last fifteen years of his life might have been much easier to understand. The 'mind suicide' of joining the R.A.F., and thereby involving himself with 'the ignorant, the deceived, the superficial', might have been rejected in favour of some less frustrating form of asceticism. Lawrence deliberately complicated the difficulty of self-realization by refusing to believe that he had any self to realize. He stated: 'Indeed, the truth was I did not like the "myself" I could see and hear', but had no notion of how to proceed to unearth the self he *didn't* dislike, the self he was aware of on that 'clear dawn that woke up the senses with the sun, while the intellect . . . was yet abed'. Lawrence has all of the powers of a man who is capable of making tremendous efforts of will; he fails beause he has no purpose towards which to direct the will. His failure is due to his inability to analyse the vague urges that stir in him, and bring them into the light of consciousness. (pp. 79-81)

The popular ideas of a 'Lawrence enigma' have culminated in Mr. Aldington's attempt to explain Lawrence in terms of Freud's inadequate psychology. But the 'Lawrence enigma' was cleared up by Lawrence himself in ***The Seven Pillars.*** Man is not a unity; he is many. But for anything to be worth doing, he must become a unity. The divided kingdom must be unified. The deluded vision of personality that our Western civilization fosters and glorifies, increases the inward division; Lawrence recognized it as the enemy. The war against it is therefore inevitably a revolt against Western civilization.

Lawrence's achievement takes us even further. The war is not to be fought by mere reason. Reason leaves the personality comfortable on its own ground. The will's power is immense when backed by moral purpose. Reason's only role is to establish moral purpose by self-analysis. Once the enemy is defined, the will can operate, and the limit of its power over the body is only the limit of moral purpose to back it.

If our reasoning is correct, the Outsider's problem is not new; Lawrence points out that the history of prophets of all time follow a pattern: born in a civilization, they reject its standards of material well-being and retreat into the desert. When they return, it is to preach world rejection: intensity of spirit versus physical security. The Outsider's miseries are the prophet's teething pains. He retreats into his room, like a spider in a dark corner; he lives alone, wishes to avoid people. 'To the thinkers of the desert, the impulse into Nitria had proved ever irresistible.' He thinks, he analyses, he 'descends into himself': 'Not that probably they found God dwelling there, but that in solitude they heard more certainly the living word they brought with them.' Gradually the message emerges. It need not be a positive message; why should it, when the impulse that drives to it is negative—disgust?

The prophet is a man of greater spiritual integrity than his neighbours; their laxness revolts him, and he feels impelled to tell them so. In his embryonic form, as the Outsider, he does not know himself well enough to understand the driving force behind his feelings. That is why his chief concern is with thinking, not with doing. (pp. 83-4)

Colin Wilson, "The Attempt to Gain Control," in his The Outsider, *Houghton Mifflin Company, 1956, pp. 70-106.**

JAMES A. NOTOPOULOS (essay date 1965)

[In the following excerpt, Notopoulos "aims at understanding Lawrence through two metaphors of literature, the epic and the tragic, which he felt in literature and experienced in his brief life."]

There have been brave men after as well as before Agamemnon. A glance at the United States Printing Office book on our winners of the Congressional Medal of Honor shows acts not unworthy of Achilles or Ajax. "Only they lack a poet," as Horace says. They also lack an ethos of society where "the delirium of the brave," as Yeats calls it, is the highest value in life. The *Iliad* has this quality, while the *Aeneid* and *Paradise Lost* lack it, compensating for it by their larger symbolic themes. The capacity for gallant living and dying is more appealing when it is rooted in that core of darkness called the tragic sense of life. Though the epic-tragic is a quality largely enveloped in the greatness of the Homeric epic wherever it appears in subsequent literature, it never ceases to captivate the human heart.

I believe that modern life has found a unique manifestation of this quality in T. E. Lawrence who, even when stripped of the myth that has shed glamor upon him, possesses the last glow of the Homeric splendor. His attraction is now the battleground between psychiatric and literary analysis. He exhibits the dilemma of a modern figure who experienced the Homeric delirium of the brave and wrote of it with the requisite magic of literature, yet was condemned to tragic frustration by the anachronism of the heroic act in our times. Lawrence is now an enigma to his stream of biographers who veer more and more to psychoanalysis. His enigma is stripped of the glamorous myth with which Lowell Thomas invested him in the 'twenties. His life, writings, and conduct involve symptoms of abnormality which excessively fascinate an age addicted to psychoanalysis. He may be a "sick soul," but we need to be reminded that great literature also deals with sick souls like Achilles in Homer, Ajax and Philoctetes in Sophocles, Othello and Hamlet in Shakespeare. Though Lawrence received many wounds and beatings in the war, and inwardly many more in his postwar career, his enigma becomes clearer if set against the metaphors of great literature. (pp. 331-32)

It is one of the oddities of English literature that in the desert of Arabia were born two of its prose masterpieces—Doughty's *Arabia Deserta* and Lawrence's ***The Seven Pillars of Wisdom.*** Doughty was one of Lawrence's literary heroes and his own experience of desert life increased his admiration for him and indebtedness to him for style, structure, and understanding of Arab psychology and ways of life. Yet Lawrence's book is not a travel masterpiece but an epic which any student of Homer will call Homeric despite its many differences from Homer. It has the touchstone of the delirium of the brave, that basic impulse in the Arab warriors which Lawrence moulded into a "Triumph," the subtitle of his book. Yet at the very moment of victory it became a defeat for Lawrence ever after. Historians of English literature have pointed out that after Milton the epic was taken over by the novel. This is only superficially true. There are two modes of epic in English, Milton versus *Beowulf* and Malory. The former is a symbolic epic, the latter are genuine epics. The direct descendant of Beowulf and Malory is to be found in Lawrence's ***The Seven Pillars of Wisdom,*** which outside of verse depicts the heroic ideal and way of life in a society where fighting is a necessary and noble activity. Yet Lawrence could not write the simple direct kind of epic. It had to be an epic fashioned out of complex factors. (p. 332)

The book has multiple levels and one can get lost in them. It contains blocks of sense and thought in its cursive progress. Lawrence was aware of this motley architectural pattern and tries to account for "its wild mop of side-scenes and side issues: the prodigality and profuseness: and the indigestibility of the dish" by saying "for this the whole experience and emanations and surroundings (background and foreground) of a man are necessary." He conceived of his book not as a work of art but "a summary of what I have thought and done and made of myself in these first thirty years." These are valuable hints for the reader to have. The twisted strands that make the whole of the ***Seven Pillars*** are open for inspection. It is in part biographic but not in the usual sense of war memoirs. It is historical in part, but the Revolt of the Arabs is not written as history but as art, for which he devised a unique style which pleases the ear and eye and mind together.

Its archaic style has been misunderstood by some critics. Lawrence could write as contemporary English as any, and this is shown in ***The Mint.*** He deliberately chose a style nearer to Doughty's to enhance the outmoded epic gesture of his theme. He stops the flow of narrative with pages or even chapters of Thucydidean analysis of motives, portraiture of the *dramatis personae*. It even includes a Platonic analysis of strategy as *epistêmê* (knowledge) versus *doxa* (appearance or opinion). Some of these take the form of prose choral odes of a tragedy which comment on the previous episode or action. It is Herodotean in its digressions, again another favorite author of Lawrence. It exhibits the archaic joy in the fulness of reality, yet he strives to subordinate this to key ideas. He writes in a letter, "in all my life objects had been gladder to me than persons, and ideas than objects." He sees the remarkable in the obvious because he used all of his eyes to see it. This is the clue to his art. Yet what Lawrence saw he sees in such a way that there is a radar refraction from the object seen into Lawrence's own mind. In the Arab we can see much of Lawrence's submerged self. "These lads," he says, "took pleasure in subordination; in degrading the body: so as to throw into greater relief their freedom in equality of mind: almost they preferred servitude as richer in experience than authority, and less binding in daily care." *De te fabula* ["The story relates to you"]. Lawrence had become so much an Arab that this sentence is the explanation of his later self-flagellating life in the RAF, so vividly described in ***The Mint.*** Lawrence took pains to reveal himself by indirection. He writes to Garnett, "By avoiding direct feeling I would keep the emotional expression on the plane of the rest of the construction. That's the reason of all that resolution of the personal, the indirectness of which offends you: and my temptation is to go more abstract, more complex, rather than more open." (pp. 333-34)

The ***Seven Pillars,*** subtitled *A Triumph,* became, as Lawrence said, "in essence a tragedy—a victory in which no man could take delight."

The nature of this tragedy awaits clarification. The tragedy was twofold, political and personal. For Lawrence, who put his heart into the Revolt and tuned the Arabs to such a pitch of faith in him that they believed he personally embodied England's policy, the Revolt began on false pretences. Aware of the Sykes-Picot treaty between England and France, which involved the annexation after the war of some promised areas and the respective spheres of influence over all the rest, Lawrence was constantly and bitterly ashamed. He was privy to a deceit and he put on the "mantle of fraud," which made the "bravest, simplest and merriest of men" dupes. The Peace Conference brought all this out, and though Churchill later made some amends, Lawrence continued to look upon his war triumph as a tragedy, a mockery of the cause he inspired in the Arabs.

The tragedy was also a personal one. It was a tragedy in the classical sense of the word. The central conflict in Lawrence is best explained in terms of a problem Sophocles saw long ago. Lawrence's tragedy is but a newer version of Sophocles' *Philoctetes*. No one who reads the ***Seven Pillars*** needs convincing about Lawrence's epic role for which he was to the manner born. The heroic act began with the romantic impulses in his childhood, was matured by his favorite authors: Homer, Malory's Arthurian epics, Doughty's *Arabia Deserta,* Caesar's *Commentaries on the Gallic Wars*. Later Melville's *Moby Dick* was to join the list. As we shall see later, the heroic world was the focus of his inner and outer life. Yet no one more than Lawrence was conscious of the absurdity and anachronism of the heroic act in the world of the twentieth century. He could not let himself go and enjoy the heroic act with the simplicity, the directness, the passionate dedication of the Homeric or Arab hero to his *timê*, the value of the heroic act. The corrosion of doubt, his consciousness of the betrayal of Arabs, the visitation of the introspective moods of the futility of life which reach a crescendo in the letters to Lionel Curtis, restrained him from a whole-hearted acceptance of the heroic act. . . . His self-denial of the heroic amounted almost to a stoic suicide. It took the form of an impossible return to the Ithaca of normalcy. The nightmare is vividly described in ***The Mint,*** which is his Golgotha. Yet even this self-immolation of normalcy had its momentary cracks, such as his incognito visits to Lowell Thomas' film and talk on Lawrence of Arabia; his circulation of the eight copies of ***Seven Pillars,*** printed in sheets by the *Oxford Times* staff, to his friends; his allowing Garnett to abbreviate the original text into the ***Revolt of the Desert*** so as to raise money for Eric Kennington's beautiful illustrations of the limited edition of 1926 of about 107 copies. All this attests to his fascination with the heroic gesture. The very title of ***The Mint*** reveals further Lawrence's fascination with the heroic. It was minted from Housman's line,

> They carry back to the coiner the mintage of man,
> The lads that will die in their glory and never be old.

Lawrence suffered not from Miniver Cheevism but from what Edmund Wilson calls "the wound and the bow," a phrase he coined in his famous essay on Sophocles' *Philoctetes* to symbolize the hero, the artist, who pays the price of the wound for his *aretê*. Sophocles in this play dramatizes the hero out of joint with the pragmatic world; the dilemma of the unbending Homeric hero whose myth is so manipulated by Sophocles that he is made to face a new world, the realities that Sophocles saw at work in the fifth century. A new kind of hero is required in such a complex world, the Odysseus who is aware of the obsolescence of the Homeric *aretê* in a modern world. Thus in the play Homeric ram-rodness is made to confront diplomacy, compromise, use of people as means to an end. This confrontation is irreconcilable even for Sophocles himself, who in this play alone makes use of a *deus ex machina* to resolve the conflict. So too with Lawrence who carried in his soul a dialogue between the Homeric hero and a nonheroic world. Yet he could not find any *deus ex machina* except retreat into anonymity and the self-effacement of a recruit's life. (pp. 335-37)

If the core of darkness in Lawrence cannot be understood without the metaphor of Philoctetes, his splendor as a human being and a writer cannot be understood without the metaphors of the *Odyssey* and the *Iliad*. Both of these poems enter into his experiences, his writing, and into shaping his outlook. Homer was a lifelong study with Lawrence and he emerges as one of his finest translators. . . . In translating the *Odyssey* over a period of four years he was consciously reliving his own Homeric life which prior to the Revolt fits into the *Odyssey* pattern. While an undergraduate at Oxford he traveled to Syria and Palestine following the trail of medieval castles in order to write his special Oxford thesis. This was written completely through a personal odyssey involving hardship, stinking steamers, dysentery, risk of life, beatings by native Kurds.

His archeological career at Carchemish by the Euphrates for three years is a veritable odyssey as we read of it in his letters. So is his mission into Mt. Sinai desert to map, in the guise of an archeologist, the district for Lord Kitchener. It may truly be said of him that he lived the opening lines of the *Odyssey:* "the various minded man . . . made to stray grievously about the coasts of men, the sport of their customs good or bad." He lived the *Odyssey* not as a simile but as a metaphor. . . . Lawrence did not produce a translation that is antiquarian. He calls it a "novel," which justified his choice of prose over verse and gave to him the license to excise, transpose, be free with moods and tenses. His preface is somewhat eccentric to the classical scholar. As one who had lived with Arab oral bards, to such an extent that he even made an amusing parody of the formulaic style in a story to parody Auda's incorrigible epic addiction, Lawrence failed to perceive the oral style of the *Odyssey*. Yet one will go far to match such touches as his characterization of Nausicaa who "enters dramatically and shapes, for a few lines, like a woman—then she fades, unused"; or such fine touches as his description of the hanging of the faithless maidservants of Odysseus: "A little while they twittered with their feet—only a little. It was not long." His translation of the *Odyssey* reveals a side of Lawrence essential to the understanding of him as a Homeric man. No scholar has ever brought such non-armchair knowledge as Lawrence to the translation of the *Odyssey*.

The most significant event in Lawrence's life, the Revolt of the Arabs which he organized and led to success, can only be understood by the metaphor of the *Iliad*. In the midst of the Revolt there flashed to him the meaning of his role—the role of destiny which, in an unheroic age, thrust him into a heroic way of life. He speaks of "the incongruity in my answering the infectious call of action. . . . I had had one craving all my life—for the power of self-expression in some imaginative form—but had been too diffuse ever to acquire a technique. At last accident, with perverted humour, in casting me as a man of action had given me place in the Arab Revolt, a theme ready and epic to a direct eye and hand, thus offering me an outlet in literature, the technique-less art. Whereupon I became excited only over mechanism. The epic mode was alien to me, as to my generation. Memory gave me no clue to the heroic, so that I could not feel such a man as Auda in myself. He seemed fantastic as the hills of Rumm, old as Malory."

Despite all the complex levels, ***The Seven Pillars*** is, as Lawrence himself notes, "a theme ready and epic." It is this theme that is the focal point in the book. . . . Lawrence had witnessed at first hand an epic society which, outside of clothing, differed little from the Homeric way of life. But without Homer and Malory, Lawrence could not have made ***The Seven Pillars*** the masterpiece that it is. They awakened in him on the occasion of this epic experience an inner and outer idiom to feel and to express the experience. Read in his review saw this very quality and insisted that the book be measured by the epic standard [see excerpt dated 1927].

In the epic we have heroic actions arising out of events and out of character. ***The Seven Pillars*** contains both. There is epic action in the hit-and-run tactics of dynamiting the trains, in the interplay of design and accident that ever characterizes wars. But one cannot have an epic out of such, only military history, war memoirs. For epic or tragedy we must look for character spinning the plot. There are two such in ***The Seven Pillars***—Lawrence himself, and Auda. Lawrence is everywhere the source of the strategy and action and his unique position as one detached from the British Army, acting independently as *agent provocateur* and leader of the Arab Revolt, is such that he emerges as a lone-wolf, and not a general. This enables him to find direction to the heroic through indirection. His upbringing as an Englishman prevents him from seeking the heroic directly; it enables him to envelop the epic with introspection. His epic quality is cerebral even though he does not spare us his descriptions of straining his body and spirit to out-Arab the Arabs in their endurance. He is aware that he is an actor playing the role of an Arab but never can be a complete Arab. His heroic impulses are muffled by his awareness of the ludicrousness of the heroic role in modern society. It can be used as a means in modern society, not as an end in itself. Yet Lawrence's book achieves its epic quality by reason of his fascination with the heroic act as an end in itself. This finds fulfilment in Auda, who embodied for Lawrence the primitive epic hero and whom he models closely to his Homeric prototype. In the portrait of Auda we find the envy of Lawrence himself.

A study of Auda in ***The Seven Pillars*** shows epic action emanating out of epic character. Lawrence realized the importance of Auda to the success of the Revolt. Only by means of Auda and "his immense chivalrous name" could Lawrence swing the tribes from Maan to Akaba to take Akaba. His unique role is seen in Lawrence's conscious use of Homeric adjectives and phrases to describe him: "the old lion," "the implacable warrior," "child of battle who had never known a master," "lordly in his delight of war," "drunk with a life-time wine of self-will." (pp. 338-41)

Lawrence's chief fascination with Auda . . . was the warrior's delight in war and the delirium of the brave. The crescendo of the epic action in the book coincides with Auda's exhibition of the delirium of the brave. The terror of Auda emerges in several scenes. Always in charge of his Arab warriors, like Achilles over the Myrmidons, he ever strikes terror in the enemy: "The Howeitat spread out along the cliff to return the peasants' fire. This manner of going displeased Auda, the old lion, who raged. . . . So he jerked his halter, cantered his mare down the path and rode out plain to view beneath the easternmost houses of the village. There he reined in, and shook a hand at them, booming with his wonderful voice: 'Dogs, do you not know Auda?' When they realized it was that implacable son of war their hearts failed them." Lawrence's description of Auda's furious charge at Aba el Lissan, after he taunted Auda on the Howeitat's "shooting a lot but hitting a little," is sheer Homeric. Slaking his thirst with countless slaughters Auda comes to Lawrence: "Auda came swinging up on foot, his eyes glazed over with the rapture of battle, and the words bubbling with incoherent speed from his mouth. 'Work, work, where are words, work, bullets, Aub Tayi . . . and he held up his shattered field-glasses, his pierced pistol-holster, and his leather sword-scabbard cut to ribbons. He had been the target of a volley which had killed his mare under him, but the six bullets through his clothes had left him scathless."

Finally we have a scene reaching a crescendo before the triumphal entry into Damascus, where ***The Seven Pillars*** finds tangency to Achilles' reaction to the slaying of Partroclus. The Turkish slaughter of Tallal's kinsfolk, with pregnant women bayonetted, rouses Tallal, Auda's bosom friend. . . . The slaughter that ensued, as the price of Tallal, "the splendid leader, the fine horseman, the courteous and strong companion of the road," is Achillean. Here and nowhere else in modern literature do we catch the last delirium of the brave. Here we glimpse in ***The Seven Pillars*** the last vestige of the epic. (pp. 343-45)

In his preface to the *Odyssey* Lawrence said of Homer, "He . . . was driven by his age to legend, where he found men living untrammeled under the God-possessed skies." Lawrence so lived and died that he has become a legend gracing an unheroic age. It is an age to which the epic mode is alien and whose memory gives no clue to the heroic. Hence its misunderstanding of Lawrence's dilemma, its futile attempts to solve him through the world of Freud, its lack of comprehension of the personal price he paid, the price of Greek heroes who are "bound hand and foot to fatal destiny." The metaphors of great literature are requisite for the understanding of such. (p. 345)

James A. Notopoulos, "The Tragic and the Epic in T. E. Lawrence," in The Yale Review, *Vol. LIV, No. 3, March, 1965, pp. 331-45.*

ROBERT PAYNE (essay date 1972)

[An English poet, novelist, and historian, Payne has also written a book-length study of Lawrence's life (see Additional Bibliography). In the following excerpt, Payne discusses Lawrence's prose style in Seven Pillars of Wisdom.]

There are very few great prose writers, and all the truly great passages of English prose could probably be contained in an anthology of about a hundred pages. Half of these pages would come from Shakespeare and the King James version of the Bible, and most of the remaining pages would come from Sir Thomas Browne, Thomas Traherne, John Donne, John Keats and Herman Melville, and there would be a dozen pages reserved for fragments culled from a half a hundred authors. (p. 91)

The truth is that great prose is much rarer than great poetry, for the genius of the English language seems to reside in poetry. . . . (p. 92)

Almost the last of the great prose writers was Thomas Edward Lawrence, whose ***Seven Pillars of Wisdom*** was an attempt to match a great adventure with a prose worthy of its subject. He wanted to give the reader a sense of the physical splendor of Arabia, and its wide spaces, and the people he encountered, and their fierce struggles, so that they would rise from the page and enter the imagination cleanly, luminously, without any barrier between reader and writer. He had a story to tell as wildly adventurous as the *Iliad,* and even more bloody. The book would inevitably assume the aspects of an epic, and it would be necessary to invent a style possessing an epical quality capable of reflecting the swift march of events and the slow unfolding of intrigues. There must be a place for his own sombre self-questionings, and sometimes, like Homer, he would allow himself to interrupt a battle scene with a digression for no other purpose than to prolong the suspense. He would try, wherever possible, to eliminate himself or place himself in the background till he was no more than a speck on the horizon, and he must have known that this would be the most difficult task of all. Throughout the book his presence can be felt as a pervading spirit, for he is not only the narrator but also the principal actor, and the more he enlarges on the acts of others, the more he is present. Yet, strangely, when we have finished the book, it is not so much Lawrence we remember as the rush of armies, the faces of the Arabs and the blazing sun.

This, of course, was his intention, and that he succeeded so well was due largely to the epic form in which he conceived the book. He was not writing an historical account of the Arabian campaign so much as an imaginative re-creation of events, pouring life into the characters and painting the air in which they moved. To do this, he needed a style which was not only epical in its larger dimensions but also intensely vivid in its details, relying on rhythm and cadence to mould the shapes of things, making a virtue of his own sensuousness, and orchestrating each passage as though he had a musical score beside him. The effect is often magical, for the thing read becomes the thing seen, and the reader, caught up in the sensuous music, has no defenses. Lawrence knew he was attempting the impossible. On rare occasions he falters, and we are aware that he is no longer in command of the orchestra, but more often than not we hear the full orchestra with every note shining clear.

Read, for example, his description of the Turkish dead lying on the battlefield of Abu el Lissal. The Arabs are feasting noisily over their booty, while Lawrence, horrified, wanders over the bloody plain where the Turks lie stripped of their clothes in the moonlight:

> The dead men looked wonderfully beautiful. The night was shining gently down, softening them into new ivory. Turks were white-skinned on their clothed parts, much whiter than the Arabs; and these soldiers had been very young. Close round them lapped the dark wormwood, heavy with dew, in which the ends of the moonbeams sparkled like sea-spray. The corpses seemed flung so pitifully on the ground, huddled anyhow in low heaps. Surely if straightened they would be comfortable at last. So I put them all in order, one by one, very wearied myself, and longing to be of those quiet ones, not of the restless, noisy, aching mob up the valley, quarrelling over the plunder, boasting of their speed and strength to endure God knew how many toils and pains of this sort; with death, whether we won or lost, waiting to end the history.

Such passages may be criticized as too romantic in their coloring or too deliberate in construction: the faultless control of rhythm seems almost inhuman. Essentially the miracle has come about through the marriage of words and music, the musical phrase giving the words a resonance they would not otherwise have possessed. From the dark wormwood and the white bodies in the moonlight he has composed a threnody and a prayer. There is no feeling of despair; only an aching tenderness, which he has transformed into music so clearly defined that it would be quite possible to score the entire passage.

Yet this music, which appears to be so spontaneous and to move so effortlessly, was not achieved easily. The true marriage of words and music and color comes about only as the result of almost inhuman pressures, of endless hours of remorseless concentration and heartbreaking revisions. (pp. 93-5)

Lawrence was fascinated by the way words and sentences can be shaped to evoke a scene. The shaping and the evocation partakes of magic, for there exist no laws, no body of experience, to help a writer put down on paper the things he sees in his imagination. (p. 96)

Nothing in Lawrence's early prose writings prepares us for the concentrated energy and brilliant coloring of ***Seven Pillars of Wisdom.*** His early study of mediaeval architecture, which he called ***Crusader Castles,*** and the passages written by him in ***The Wilderness of Zin,*** and the voluminous articles he wrote for the *Arab Bulletin* in Cairo, could have been written by any reasonably talented writer of his generation. The stuff of genius is not in them, and we read them today only because he wrote them. With the ***Seven Pillars*** a totally unexpected music emerges. Describing generalship he wrote: "Nine-tenths of tactics was certain enough to be teachable in schools; but the irrational tenth was like the kingfisher flashing across the pool, and in it lay the test of generals." So with his prose. Nine-tenths of it could be acquired by study, but there remained the irrational tenth, the new music, the new words, the kingfisher flashing across the pool.

Above all he was concerned to give his prose a strenuous, resilient and shining quality, hammering out words and sentences until they gleamed like bronze. Grammatical constructions would be bent to serve his own purposes. The noun erect and resolute, the adjective in motion, the adverb pointing the direction, the verb flashing and leaping, each paragraph a cavalcade. Not that he hoped to accomplish so rich a tapestry on every page, but this was the ideal to be reached as often as possible, for an epic demands a highly wrought and intricate prose close to poetry. No one since Malory had accomplished such a tapestry, and Malory was writing about imaginary battles, while Lawrence was writing about real battles which had left twenty wounds in his flesh. (pp. 97-8)

The haunting quality of his prose derives from the intensity of his vision, his power to re-create scenes in the full glare of the imagination. He has described in his letters how he would write for twenty-four hours at a stretch, without food or rest, until he reached a kind of trance state in which he would find himself transported from his study in Oxford to the sands of Arabia. Almost he would lose himself in the imagination, and sometimes he was in danger of not returning. He sees with the clarity of madmen or visionaries, or so it seems, until we remember that Arabia is full of visionary landscapes. When he writes about the valley of Rumm, we have the feeling that he is describing a valley seen only in dreams—so vast and magnificent it is, with the two towering walls of reddish mountains looking down on an avenue so wide that it might once have served as a processional way for the gods—but in fact he depicted it exactly as it is. (pp. 100-01)

Like all great works ***Seven Pillars*** is derivative. The rhythms of Malory's prose and Doughty's verse flow through it in many-colored streams. He had read deeply in the five great masters—Browne, Traherne, Donne, Keats and Melville—and he had a special affection for *Moby Dick,* which perhaps of all writings was the one closest in spirit to ***Seven Pillars.*** (p. 104)

Not long ago Cyril Connolly invented the term "Mandarin English" to describe a kind of writing which uses all the arts of rhetoric and invention. As the prime example he gave Walter Savage Landor's description of a lioness:

> On perceiving the countryman she drew up her feet gently, and squared her mouth, and rounded

"Laying Out the Dead Turks," *from a sketch by Lawrence* (Seven Pillars of Wisdom). *From* The Letters of T. E. Lawrence, *edited by David Garnett. Cape, 1938. Reprinted by permission of Jonathan Cape Ltd, on behalf of the Letters of T. E. Lawrence Trust.*

> her eyes, slumberous with content, and they looked, he said, like sea-grottoes, obscurely green, interminably deep, at once awakening fear and stilling and suppressing it.

This splendid passage moves us with its slow and sinuous music like the uncoiling of a serpent. *Slumberous, obscurely* and *interminably* are all weak words, but they set the languorous mood that Landor desired, while *sea-grottoes* comes as a necessary illuminating shock which has the effect of bringing the languor into focus. What Lawrence wanted, and strove for, was a more strenuous Mandarin English, more direct and uncompromising, yet using to the utmost all the riches of the language in color and imagery. He demands of prose that it should have muscle and claws and that it should move swiftly and accurately, and that there should be a glory about it.

Here is Lawrence describing a feast in the tent of Ali abu Fitna, one of the Howeitat chieftains:

> The bowl was now brim-full, ringed round its edge by white rice in an embankment a foot wide and six inches deep, filled with legs and ribs of mutton till they toppled over. It needed two or three victims to make in the centre a dressed pyramid of meat such as honour prescribed. The centre-pieces were the boiled, upturned heads, propped on their several stumps of neck, so that the ears, brown like old leaves, flapped out on the rice surface.

And again:

> Feisal looked very tall and pillar-like, very slender, in his long white silk robes and his brown head-cloth bound with a brilliant scarlet and gold cord. His eyelids were dropped; and his black beard and colourless face were like a mask against the strange still watchfulness of his body.

So Shakespeare would have written if he had lived in the modern age. (pp. 107-08)

Robert Payne, "On the Prose of T. E. Lawrence," in Prose, *No. 4, 1972, pp. 91-108.*

KEITH N. HULL (essay date 1975)

[*In the following excerpt, Hull discusses Lawrence's sense of personal and corporate identity in* The Mint.]

In these days of wholesale identity crises T. E. Lawrence deserves the respect due a pioneer in the field. Few have ever undertaken such extremes of behavior directed at establishing a firm sense of self. ***Seven Pillars of Wisdom*** is an extraordinary chronicle of combat, torture, and intrigue whose central theme is less revolt in the desert than it is the question of who the devil Lawrence really is. Torn at least three ways by British versus Arab interests versus personal motivation, the Lawrence of ***Seven Pillars*** sees himself as lacking any identity: "In my case, the effort for these years to live in the dress of Arabs, and to imitate their mental foundation, quitted me of my English self, and let me look at the West and its conventions with new eyes: they destroyed it all for me. At the same time I could not sincerely take on the Arab skin: it was an affectation only. . . . [Such a detached man] plodded on mechanically, while his reasonable mind left him, and from without looked down critically on him, wondering what that futile lumber did and why."

When the book ends, the reader is left with a non-Lawrence, one whose roles have so undermined each other that the confidence man no longer knows which is the real self: "Accident, achievement, and rumour . . . had built me such a caddis-shell as almost prompted me to forget the true shape of the worm inside." ***The Mint,*** on the other hand, chronicles Lawrence's efforts to establish a firm identity. . . . In several ways ***The Mint*** is the reverse of the earlier book; the action and exoticism of ***Seven Pillars*** are absent, and the focus on identity is sharper; ***Seven Pillars*** shows the progressive breakdown of Lawrence's grip on who he is, while the later book dramatizes the deliberate effort to regain it. In ***Seven Pillars*** Lawrence's personal difficulties are interwoven with the military, political, and social problems of Arabia; in ***The Mint*** the characters are few and English, and the issues are simple, though the problems they involve are not necessarily easily overcome. ***Seven Pillars of Wisdom*** can perhaps be reduced to the image of Lawrence's despairing, nihilistic, self-mocking laughter amid the rotting corpses of the Turkish military hospital; ***The Mint,*** however, is a haltingly hopeful book that reaches its culmination with Aircraftman Lawrence lying momentarily contented in the fickle English sunshine. (pp. 340-41)

In the RAF, as ***The Mint*** makes plain, Lawrence was seeking not oblivion but a corporate identity in which he could share. There were of course other institutions he could have attached himself to—Oxford or the Civil Service were real possibilities for him—but the RAF offered particular advantages to a man in Lawrence's state of mind; in the Air Force he could be among those he considered his own kind—failures, even frauds—who were seeking a new life. (p. 341)

Slowly, incompletely, and with much backsliding, Lawrence in ***The Mint*** becomes a part of this group. Their corporate life, under the rigors of basic training, begins to flourish and to an indeterminant extent Lawrence partakes of it. (p. 342)

When the section on basic training ends, Lawrence's comments on what has happened describes precisely the nature of the collective self: "Our hut used to arrive at an opinion by discussion, by contradicting the early word that the first fool rushed out. Later this turned into instinct. We have come, unknowing, to a corporate life. Today we think, decide, act on parade without a word said. . . . We have attained a flight-entity which is outside our individualities. The self-reliance each has singly lost is not lost to us all. . . . The person has died that to the company might be born a soul." . . . (pp. 342-43)

The degree of Lawrence's involvement in the corporate life is not all mystery, however. In ***The Mint*** two clear barriers exist to Lawrence's ever completely becoming "just like any other" in all ways: sex and extreme self-consciousness. Because of the passages in ***Seven Pillars*** about Arab homosexuality and the Turks' homosexual rape of Lawrence, the subject of sex has preoccupied many of his readers; ***The Mint,*** however, goes far toward clarifying Lawrence's attitude toward sex, since he had to face up to the preoccupation which enlisted men have with the subject. In ***The Mint*** Lawrence's unwillingness or inability to share in this preoccupation prevents his ready entry into the recruits' fellowship; yet among them it is a strong bond, a recurrent theme in their thoughts and conversation, and an often tapped though limited store of figurative language: "Enlistment brought the shock of rediscovery of the basis of life:—in the troops' phrase, that every jack-man had his bicycle pump and tool-bag. In our boldest thrustings across the furtherest airs, we carry that equipment with us: and uniformed men mean too much to each other to leave room for paracletes. Each of us is a little part of all the rest—as all the rest of us." . . .

Lawrence's reaction to this situation is not unsympathetic—as ***Seven Pillars*** is not unsympathetic to Arab homosexuality—but his role is that of a bystander who is sometimes repulsed by the grossness of others' sexuality, sometimes sympathetic, sometimes amused, sometimes detached. In fact, some of the liveliest moments of ***The Mint*** depend on Lawrence's situation as observer rather than participant. On one occasion a drunken airman returns from enjoying his first sexual experience and insists on telling Lawrence, who earlier loaned him money, about his good time. In a remarkable monolog he bends over Lawrence in bed and explains, "Made me jump, this did, like two hundred volts. . . . I can't ever do it the first time again: but Christ, it was bloody wonderful." And he concludes, "I say, what've I got to do now? Wash it, I s'pose. Got any dope?" . . . (p. 343)

In the end Lawrence cannot be involved in sexuality for reasons as mysterious as ever, and he acknowledges with erudite humor that this fact keeps him an outsider: "So I shall never be quite happy, with the happiness of these fellows who find their nectar of life, and its elixir, in the deep stirring of some seminal gland." . . . Yet Lawrence in ***The Mint*** leads a life of sensuality bordering on the erotic; music, for example, moves him as it has moved few people since Il Pensoroso. In a paragraph preceded and followed by passages full of sexual references he describes "exquisite moments when myself goes suddenly empty." Then, foreshadowing the nearly deadly 200-volt intercourse of his drunken hut-mate, Lawrence goes on, "Each time lasts an instant only: more, and I should die, for it holds still my breath and blood and vital fluid." . . . (pp. 343-44)

The concluding chapters of ***The Mint*** are dominated by a motorcycle—Boanerges or "Boa" for short—that provides a similar near-sexual experience. After leaving basic training Lawrence acquired a series of motorcycles, on the last of which he suffered his fatal accident; on these motorcycles he took advantage of his limited leave time to travel long distances to visit friends. ***The Mint,*** however, would have us believe that the relationship between Boa and his owner was far more important than the destinations of any journeys together: "A skittish motor-bike with a touch of blood in it is better than all riding animals on earth, because it is the logical extension of our faculties, and the hint, the provocation, to excess conferred by its honeyed untiring smoothness. Because Boa loves me, he gives me five more miles of speed than a stranger would get from him." . . . Interestingly, for our purposes here, Boanerges brings Lawrence and his fellow airmen together. On his speed binges around the countryside Lawrence stops at various merchants to pick up groceries which he takes back to his base to sell at prices below the canteen's. The airmen welcome the inexpensive variety in their diets and affectionately refer to Lawrence's travels as "split-arse work." . . . (p. 344)

Looking back, Lawrence by his own admission and by his literary treatment of sexuality is unable to enter the community of airmen to the degree that he does not share their sexuality. Yet it is also true that he did have sensual pleasures that may have given him a measure of sympathy for those of his fellows and allow him some degree of acceptance among them. However, one other barrier existed between him and Air Force corporate life.

One of the most tortured facets of the Lawrence of ***Seven Pillars of Wisdom*** can be seen in one distinction he makes between himself and the Arabs. They, he says, "knew only truth and untruth"; contrasting to such simplicity is Lawrence's own difficulty, "our modern crown of thorns"—doubt—joined to "metaphysical difficulties" and, most importantly for ***The Mint,*** "introspective questionings." . . . In ***The Mint*** the other airmen have the same function as the Arabs in ***Seven Pillars.*** Echoing the earlier book, Lawrence says in ***The Mint*** that "our ranks were too healthy to catch this diseased Greek antithesis of flesh and spirit. Unquestioned life is a harmony . . .". . . . (pp. 344-45)

For a change the collective pronoun clearly does not include Lawrence. Repeatedly he distinguishes among parts of himself—intellect, spirit, flesh, "I"—admitting strenuously that the parts of the thing called Lawrence are not in harmony and that the thing suffers for its awareness of the fact. Of the rigors of physical training he says, "If [my insignificant body] fails me now I shall break it" . . . ; or again, critically, "my soul [is] always looking for fear to salt its existence" . . . ; and still again, "reason may be stung into new activity when it hears there's yet a part of me which escapes its rule." . . . As one looks at the sum total of these passages it seems that the "I" cannot be exclusively body, soul, or reason, and that it is capable of standing back and looking at the very instruments of its own awareness—its various faculties. This, I think, is what Lawrence means in ***Seven Pillars*** by "metaphysical difficulties" and "introspective questionings"; the self is composed of at least three parts and has the capability of recognizing and distinguishing among these parts. Despite the vagueness of all these ideas, Lawrence clearly names rationality as the villain. Sounding very much like Blake—"I am a disciple of Blake," he once wrote—he proclaims in ***The Mint:*** "Man, who was born as one, breaks into little prisms when he thinks. . . ." . . . (p. 345)

Apparently Lawrence thought that this potential for dividedness exists in all humans but that they do not exercise it; the Arabs and Airmen do not, while Lawrence does: "here [in the RAF] are men so healthy that they don't chop up their meat into mince for easy digestion by the mind: and who are therefore intact as we are thereby diseased." . . . A lack of metaphysical, introspective difficulties is, like sex, a common ground among the airmen. Their "health" binds them together; furthermore the harmony of the parts resonates with the harmony of the group in a closed system. During physical training, for instance, they enjoy games together, their individual abandonment begetting a "mass-effort" that contributes in turn to their individual well-being: "Airmen are so healthy and free of the joints, that they exult to fling their meat about. Activity does not remind them, yet, how man hangs in his body, crucified. So we drill hard, desperately hard, exercising our bodies. It is a kind of fun, just to pant them out. The raggedness of the mass-effort testifies that, after his own time, each man is caring to the utmost for his good health and muscularity." . . . (pp. 345-46)

Lawrence, whose trouble may have been due at the time as much to the physical difficulties of age as to metaphysical problems, insists repeatedly that he cannot join the airmen in the community of physical activity. At times his reaction is to feel tortured by physical pain; at other times he mocks his own awkwardness, but at all times he cannot overcome his own physical limitations as he wishes to and plunges into a renewed sense of the intellect/spirit/body division. Still there is hope in his situation. As he was able to enjoy enough of the sensual life to enable him to sympathize with his fellows, he recognizes that to the extent that the metaphysical difficulties can be overcome, he can join the corporate identity. Continuing the Blakean thought to its conclusion Lawrence goes on to say in one of his most revealing meditations: "Man, who was born as one, breaks into little prisms when he thinks: but if he passes through thought into despair, or comprehension, he again achieves some momentary onenesses with himself. And not only that. He can achieve a oneness of himself with his fellow: and of them with the stocks and stones of his universe . . .". . . .

Thus ***The Mint*** contrasts with ***Seven Pillars,*** the chronicle of despair, by its exercise in comprehension, the recognition and analysis of the problem and solution to loss of identity; the very act of comprehending and seeking to solve the problem leads not to oneness but at least to "onenesses." Or, to make the whole issue even more paradoxical, we might say that self-awareness destroys the oneness of identity, but that despair at or comprehension of this awareness restores partially the oneness which it destroys. Lawrence's analysis of the reasons for his exclusion from the airmen's corporate self and his description of the limited ways available to him for overcoming exclusion become in themselves the chief means to what he seeks. (p. 346)

[In] the end all problems of identity in ***The Mint*** find their solution in the corporate identity of the airmen. The planes are theirs, not the pilots', the aristocracy of the RAF is composed of craftsmen, not officers, and service pride is in craftsmanship, not tradition.

When Lawrence enters the Air Force at the beginning of the book it is this identity that he seeks and which he partially achieves. Then, through this newly defined RAF, Lawrence in the last chapter makes the final leap to one of the onenesses with "the stocks and stones of the universe." In a moment of contentment, having sent a well-cared-for "kite" on its way and with nothing to do but await its return, Lawrence and his fellow airmen lie on the grass in the sun. At first the reader might be suspicious that the "we" does not include Lawrence, but the "everywhere" of the last sentence of the book does include him:

> From the turf beneath our moist backs there came up a sister-heat which joined us to it. Our bones dissolved to become a part of this underlying indulgent earth, whose mysterious pulse throbbed in every tremor of our bodies. The scents of the thousand-acre drome mixed with the familiar oil-breath of our hangar, nature with art. . . .
>
> Such moments of absorption resolve the mail and plate of our personality back into the carbohydrate elements of our being. They come to

> service men very often, because of our light surrender to the good or evil of the moment. . . . In winter we struggle undefined along the roadway, and the rain and wind chivy us, till soon we are wind and rain. We race over in the first dawn to the [Air Cadet] College's translucent swimming pool, and dive into the elastic water which fits our bodies closely as a skin:—and we belong to that too. Everywhere a relationship: no loneliness any more. . . .

(p. 348)

Keith N. Hull, "Lawrence of 'The Mint', Ross of the RAF," in South Atlantic Quarterly, *Vol. 74, No. 3, Summer, 1975, pp. 340-48.*

STANLEY WEINTRAUB AND RODELLE WEINTRAUB (essay date 1975)

[Stanley Weintraub is an American scholar known for his studies of several major authors and artists of the late nineteenth century, including Oscar Wilde, Aubrey Beardsley, and James MacNeill Whistler. He is also highly regarded for his editorship of various collections of George Bernard Shaw's writings. His wife Rodelle, an authority on technical writing, has worked closely with him on several publications and shares with him an intense interest in Shaw's work. In the following excerpt from their critical study of Lawrence, the Weintraubs discuss the transformation of autobiography into legend in Seven Pillars of Wisdom.*]*

The basic question which must be asked about ***Seven Pillars of Wisdom*** as a work of literature is whether it would still be read if the author were not the near-mythic "Lawrence of Arabia." Yet the question is unanswerable, for the man cannot be separated from his work, and the best of the uneven parts of ***Seven Pillars*** rise from superior journalism to high art. "Certain sections," Clifton Fadiman wrote soon after the book's posthumous publication [see excerpt dated 1935], "are superb—the opening chapters analyzing the social, racial, and geographic bases of Arab character; the descriptions of Bedouin life and desert landscape, the scattered generalizations of strategy; the terrible scene in which Lawrence, refusing to surrender his chastity to a Turkish officer, is tortured until his spirit, no less than his body, is broken; the scattered reflections, acrid and ironic, on the shortcomings of the military mind; and the Hamlet soliloquies on the hopeless complexity of his own. For these things Lawrence will live as a writer." Fadiman might have equally noted other scenes and other portraits, including the defeat-in-victory in Damascus.

Most of the criticism of ***Seven Pillars*** has concerned itself with its synthesis of man-of-action and man-of-letters, creating a critical psychology which will usually preclude a narrowly literary approach to the work. It is difficult, also, to separate the artless from the artful in Lawrence's use of the confessional mode. That he lived much, if not most, of his introspective epic makes it seem almost coincidental, for example, that he was reading Conrad's *Lord Jim* at about the time he was writing ***Seven Pillars,*** for the life of the Byronic, guilt-ridden, white-rajah hero bears an uncanny resemblance to that which Lawrence had already lived and largely recorded. The facts of the work's conception and development challenge a purely literary judgment. R. A. Scott-James [in *Fifty Years of English Literature*] would go further. The ***Seven Pillars*** to him is not merely the rare product of a man of action who was also by chance a man of letters: "The distinctive qualities which fitted him for literature were qualities without which he could not have succeeded in Arabia; and his literary ability needed, or appeared to need, important events shaped by himself for subject matter. He had an epic theme to handle; there would not have been this epic theme if he had not forced events to take that shape; and he produced the epic. His book is as full of heroes as the *Iliad,* and its Achilles is the author himself. What amazing egotism, one may be tempted to say, what colossal arrogance." Yet after some discussion of Lawrence's Doughty-inspired prose, Scott-James writes of the work's "muscular" language and "drama and splendor in the portraits of the chiefs," concluding that "The story has the distances of heroic legend, yet the closeness of autobiography."

Whether or not a search for "distance" caused Lawrence to falsify or romanticize his Arabian experience, it is unquestionable that many events differ in details from the "facts" he reported in the *Arab Bulletin,* in his letters home or to friends, and in the accounts written by contemporaries on the scene. . . . It is likely that studies of the discrepancies will continue to appear in reassessments of the ***Seven Pillars***. . . . Certainly Lawrence exaggerated and even invented some of the details in his narrative, but an analysis of these, rather than denigrating his achievement, only establishes his flair as a writer. One such episode picked apart by [Suleiman Mousa, see Additional Bibliography]—and it is typical—is Lawrence's description of a raid on a Turkish train which took three pages in the *Arab Bulletin* for October 21, 1917, but thirty-two pages (and fourteen thousand words) in the Subscription Edition of ***Seven Pillars.*** In the later account T. E. wrote of having looked after "an ancient and very tremulous Arab dame" and assured her that she would not be harmed. Months later, he wrote, he received from Damascus "a letter and a pleasant little Baluchi carpet from lady Ayesha, daughter of Jellal el Lel, in memory of an odd meeting."

"I believe this to be a fabrication," Mousa declares, "and that the carpet was part of the booty plundered from the train. Lawrence may have fabricated the episode to forestall the charge that he shared with the bedouin this primitive custom of plundering the enemy." To prove his point—and there seems no question that it is proven—Mousa quotes a letter from Lawrence to a friend dated September 24, 1917, two days after his return from the raid. "The Turks . . . nearly cut us off as we looted the train," T.E. wrote, "and I lost some baggage, and nearly myself. My loot was a superfine red Baluchi prayer-rug." Did Lawrence alter his story to protect himself from charges of looting? More likely the alteration of details was for literary reasons and as such was a successful touch. More of the same can be found on almost every page of ***Seven Pillars:*** it is Lawrence transmuting autobiographical chronicle into legend. It is the marrying of the "distance of historic legend" with the "closeness of autobiography" that makes ***Seven Pillars*** (despite the technical flaws which close analysis of its text and texture may uncover) unique in literature.

Whether facts were falsified or magnified, invented or suppressed, belongs to history rather than to literature. (pp. 53-6)

[Yet, one] of the problems raised by consideration of ***Seven Pillars*** as a major twentieth-century work of literature is that despite its confessed inexactitude and subjectivity it *is* a work of history—a work which has the poetry of history. G.B.S. seems to have hoped as he saw it in progress that it would become history on the Thucydidean model, where the events were brought to vivid life, however great the cost was in the loss of exactitude; but Lawrence's book of the Arabian revolt is only history as is the *Iliad* history. As *literature* it does not approach so great a work as the *Iliad* but rather has the inaccuracies, extravagances, diffuseness, artificiality—and sustained genius for language—of an epic in the Miltonic manner but misplaced in time: misplaced because in its frank subjectivity and its naturalism we see its peculiarly twentieth-century aspects.

Henri Montherlant in his *Threnody for the Dead of Verdun* talked of the war "nostalgia" of veteran soldiers and claimed that one could say that it had been, ironically, the most "tender" human experience of contemporary life. His countryman, the Jesuit Teilhard de Chardin, wrote that the most compelling fascination of the battlefield was that in action one discovered a lucidity not otherwise vouchsafed: "This heightening is not got without pain. All the same it is indeed a heightening. And that is why in spite of everything, one loves the front and regrets it." The power of ***Seven Pillars of Wisdom*** lies not only in its mannered prose and its epical evocations but in its dramatizing such paradoxes. (p. 62)

[Of Lawrence's writings, what] will survive, as license of language turns ***The Mint*** into a period piece and new translations of the *Odyssey* become annual nonevents, are those works which illuminate the unforgettable Lawrence personality: his letters and the ***Seven Pillars.*** Few epics are lived and fewer written. As authentic epic, despite its stridency and its posturing, the ***Seven Pillars of Wisdom*** passes almost beyond literary criticism, for in it life and art are fused.

Lawrence is the only major character astride his own pages, subject as well as objecct of the literary impulse that persisted when every other ambition he had for himself proved transitory or distasteful. Whatever the literary merits of his small output, it will be discussed—and sometimes even read—as long as men's imaginations are stirred by "Lawrence of Arabia." (pp. 137-38)

Stanley Weintraub and Rodelle Weintraub, in their Lawrence of Arabia: The Literary Impulse, *Louisiana State University Press, 1975, 175 p.*

THOMAS J. O'DONNELL (essay date 1976)

[O'Donnell is an American critic whose writings on Lawrence have been praised by Stephen Ely Tabachnick as a "pioneering attempt to see Lawrence's work—including The Mint*—as art and to assign it to a tradition." In the following excerpt, O'Donnell discusses* Seven Pillars of Wisdom *and* The Mint *as works belonging to a tradition of confessional literature which includes the autobiographical works of St. Augustine, Oscar Wilde, and Jean-Jacques Rousseau.]*

Critics consider Lawrence an anomaly in literary history—intriguing, a master of prose, but a writer who resists classification. They most frequently note his affinities to travel literature. But he had greater aspirations: "If mine had been simple stuff it wouldn't have mattered. It could have gone into the Hakluyt category as a good yarn; but it is elaborate and self-conscious: ambitious if you like: and that makes failure a discredit. It doesn't matter missing if you don't aim. . . ." Among Lawrence's contemporaries, ***Seven Pillars*** was art, not history and Lawrence generally wrote of it as art, even "an artificial straining after art."

Seven Pillars and ***The Mint*** can best be understood in the context of the confessional tradition in which they originate. Lawrence knew well literary precedents; he had read and admired, for example, the rare prewar edition of Henry Adams' confession. Like other works in the genre, Lawrence's confessions are book-length, nonfictional narratives in prose exploring an aspect of the writer's life which determines his moral standing in a system of belief. The belief is public and shared in the religious confession, private in the secular. Highly selective, the writer reads his life under one sign or organizing principle. The prominence of the principle is deceptive, for it provides occasion for the writer's review of his entire life focusing on those aspects he deems most significant and revealing. "Did my mind select at the time. . . ," Lawrence asks anxiously of ***The Mint,*** "or is there no truth that art is selection . . . or does my book lack selection?" [see excerpt dated 1928]. . . (pp. 7-8)

The confessional writer establishes a pattern or myth by means of which he defines himself. (p. 8)

The organizing principle may be religious, as in Augustine and Bunyan, or secular, as in Wilde and Lawrence. The confessions of Wilde and Lawrence are imitative of clearly established Romantic literary patterns. Just as the narrative of an exemplary conversion unifies Augustine's confession, so the process of growth and contraction of self endured by a late Romantic hero unifies Lawrence's. In ***The Mint*** Lawrence delineates the Romantic myth his confessions embody: "Man, who was born as one, breaks into little prisms when he thinks: but if he passes through thought into despair, or comprehension, he again achieves some momentary onenesses with himself.". . . "Onenesses" indicates Lawrence's constant ambivalence about the validity of the pattern he imposes. (p. 9)

Though the form of the genre remains influential, the twentieth-century confession departs radically from its religious origins, for there can be no moral norm common to author and reader. Henry Adams, following the lead of John Stuart Mill in his *Autobiography,* broadens the theme of the hero's conversion to that of his education. In a comment on his own confession, *The Education,* Adams admirably summarizes the difference: "his great ambition was to complete St. Augustine's 'Confessions,' but . . . St. Augustine, like a great artist, had worked from multiplicity to unity, while he, like a small one, had to reverse the method and work back from unity to multiplicity. The scheme became unmanageable as he approached his end."

The public, Christian myth is useless as an organizing principle for twentieth-century writers. As in other literature of this century, the myths used to present a concept of self become increasingly esoteric and idiosyncratic; even the ability to create a private myth has atrophied. [Michel Leiris, author of *Manhood* (1946)] argues that the modern writer can and should avoid establishing any unifying pattern. . . . (p. 11)

"Even as I write," Leiris complains, "the plan I had devised escapes me, and one might say that the more I look into myself the more confused everything I see becomes, the themes I originally hoped to distinguish proving inconsequential and arbitrary. . . ." Such statements, common in the modern confession, serve as persistent evidence of the natural and moral chaos the writer perceives and intends to express; frequently, as in Lawrence's confessions, conflicting presentations of self are left unresolved in the face of such confusion. The modern confessional writer, like his counterparts writing poetry and fiction, becomes obsessed with himself and the act of composition. . . . ***The Mint,*** for example, constantly portrays Lawrence recording events in the midst of its narrative. The heroes of *The Education of Henry Adams, Manhood,* Fitzgerald's *The Crack-Up,* and Mailer's *The Armies of the Night* are similarly engaged. The act of writing the confession becomes a way to cope with the moral chaos the writer perceives, a vital instrument to which he clings and which enables him to survive.

Didactic, public motives for writing decrease as private intentions to use confessions to make sense out of one's life or to change its course increase. The modern confession's purpose is, as Leiris says, "to elucidate . . . certain still obscure things." Leiris' intention is "to engage myself completely. Within as without: expecting it to change me, to enlarge my consciousness, and to introduce, too, a new element into my relations with other people, beginning with my relations with those close to me, who could no longer be quite the same once I had exposed what may have been already suspected, but only in a vague and uncertain way. This was no desire for a brutal cynicism, but actually a longing to confess everything in order to be able to start afresh, maintaining with those whose affection or respect I valued relations henceforth without dissimulation." Analogously, Lawrence's writing of ***Seven Pillars*** slays the will of its author: "it was a real beast, and this book its mangy skin, dried, stuffed and set up squarely for men to stare at.". . . Lawrence argues that the creation of ***Seven Pillars,*** not the war, destroyed his will and forced his postwar enlistment as an airman; the book took "all my nights and days till I was nearly blind and mad. The failure of it was mainly what broke my nerve, and sent me into the RAF. . . ." (pp. 11-13)

In the modern confession the relationship between reader and author is more ambivalent than it was for Augustine and Bunyan. Whatever his overt stance, the writer needs his audience and has a certain responsibility to it. The justification for the existence of the confession is dual; as Leiris emphasizes, one must *"illuminate certain matters for oneself at the same time as one makes them communicable to others."* The modern confession is primarily written for a coterie or addressed to a single individual and is often published privately, as *The Education of Henry Adams* and ***Seven Pillars,*** or posthumously, as Wilde's *De Profundis*. Frequently the confessional writer defines himself in opposition to a public code of morality. He apparently assumes that his intimate audience identifies with him rather than with the imaginary general reader, for he sets out to outrage and antagonize this wider audience. Arthur Adamov's "The Endless Humiliation" is characteristic: "For what follows I do not expect sympathy or even understanding. I know that most of you will soon abandon me, paralyzed by an insuperable disgust. You will be the same ones who, confronted with the deepest conflicts of sexuality and neurosis, either maintain a stubborn silence or burst into odious sniggers to protect your meanness of spirit and your fear of facing a horrible and unspeakable problem." The humiliation of Adamov is a consequence not only of the acts he narrates but also of the putative audience to which he exposes himself. Lawrence's attitude toward his readers vacillates between abasement and exalted egotism, and in this he closely resembles Rousseau and Adamov.

The general reader is assumed to have moral values antithetical to the author; he establishes his own values as an ethical norm and escapes the pessimism and bondage in which the author finds himself. Augustine and Bunyan wrote in triumph, indeed because of triumph, but secular confessions after Rousseau dramatize failure and humiliation. The self-integration characteristic of the religious confession now yields to portrayal of disintegration. "Pray God," Lawrence begins, "that men reading the story will not, for the love of the glamour of strangeness, go out to prostitute themselves and their talents in serving another race.". . . (pp. 13-14)

Despite their declarations, the secular writers still seek absolution from the reader by means of their confessions. The confession, as Leiris writes, is an attempt "to seduce my public into being indulgent, to limit . . . the scandal by giving it an aesthetic form, . . . to find in my neighbor less a judge than an accomplice." (p. 14)

As seen clearly in Augustine's *Confessions,* the genre's archetype, both religious and secular writers reveal an inordinate and growing contempt for flesh and an increasing overvaluation of spirit and mind. This tendency reflects the religious origins of the genre, but may also be an inevitable consequence of intense self-observation, attempting to distinguish the core of one's identity from the acts and flesh which veil it. "Indeed," Lawrence concludes, "the truth was I did not like the 'myself' I could see and hear.". . . Confessions are Puritan in temper, yet their writers assume an erotic viewpoint, for sexuality is the most obvious and central denial of the primacy of spirit. Confessional writers, particularly the modern ones, are deeply wounded in their sex. One must triumph over the sexual, sublimate it, or prostrate oneself to it. Sexuality is central to the confessions of Augustine, Abélard, Rousseau, Lawrence, Leiris, Adamov, Genet, and Mailer, central not only to their lives but to the shape they give their lives. (pp. 14-15)

As the confession becomes secularized, soul becomes a vague concept of "self," a shrinking core or citadel to which identity withdraws. Bunyan's *Grace Abounding* provides several revealing comparisons to Lawrence's work; both ***Seven Pillars*** and ***The Mint*** are in the English Puritan confessional tradition—the former in spirit, the latter in spirit and form. In the works of both writers act and self, what you do and what you are, are irremediably separated. Grace and redemption are given, not earned; damnation and salvation are foreordained. But there are significant differences. As Bunyan is to God, Lawrence is to an aspect of himself which judges, which is implacable, and which remains independent—untouched and uncorrupted by good or evil acts. For Lawrence no appeal beyond the self and its phantasms is conceivable. . . . In twentieth-century confessions there is constant struggle among the absurd demons inside each writer rather than with the great God outside.

In both religious and secular confessions, extremes within the self are frequently defined and opposed. For example, both Bunyan and Lawrence vacillate perpetually between extremes. Lawrence asks, "What was this hoarding of extremes, this laying up of the highest and lowest. . .?" . . . Perhaps this is caused by the hypersensitivity of the writers. With his exquisite sensibility Bunyan identifies the feeling that generates the vacillation; his "former frights and anguish were very sore and deep, therefore it did oft befall me still as it befalleth those that have been scared with fire: I thought every voice was Fire, fire—every little touch would hurt my tender conscience." To Bunyan security "is the very kingdom and habitation of the wicked one." The vacillatory narrative rhythm of both confessions is expressed in Bunyan's statement that "sometimes I should lie under great guilt for sin, even crushed to the ground therewith, and then the Lord would show me the death of Christ . . . that in that conscience where but just now did reign and rage the law, even there would rest and abide the peace and love of God through Christ." (pp. 16-17)

Pascal argues that one must seek the *via media:* "Man must not think that he is on a level either with the brutes or with the angels, nor must he be ignorant of both sides of his nature. . . ." But Lawrence and his contemporaries can live only at one extreme or the other: "Once I fancied I was very near the angels. . . . Angels, I think, we imagine. Beasts, I think, we are.''. . . Lawrence argues that his own confessions are divided in this way: ''The S.P. [***Seven Pillars***] was man on his tip-toes, trying very hard to fly. These notes [***The Mint***] are men on their very flat feet, stumbling over a sticky and noisome earth.'' Lawrence, however, records no passage between the extremes, establishes no cause-effect relationship; he simply judges the same acts differently. In the sixteenth century, Montaigne identified a similar process: ''I have ever observed that supercelestial ideas and subterrestrial conduct are singularly suited to each other. . . . People try to get outside of themselves, and escape from the man. That is foolishness: instead of transforming themselves into angels, they transform themselves into beasts. Instead of raising they degrade themselves.''

The author of ***Seven Pillars*** and ***The Mint*** first presents his hero as angel, then beast, as war narrator, then introspective self. Which is the true angel, which the proper beast is a problem he cannot resolve. These presentations of self are never linked; no transition between them is psychologically possible for either self. Lawrence vacillates between the two and is unable to extinguish one or the other pole or to desire a middle position. . . . The introspection of ***Seven Pillars*** and ***The Mint*** portrays contraction of self, dissolution of the self under pressure of analysis. The main formal problem of Lawrence's confession is this division. Lawrence's attempts to bridge the division by means of structure are relatively ineffective, and the various manuscript versions of ***Seven Pillars*** attest to the vargaries of this attempt. Lawrence, while never abandoning the war narrator and his pride in his power to act, increasingly comes to emphasize the introspective hero and his paralysis. The opposing concepts of self are allied to the classic psychological notions of sadism and masochism, though these simplify the complexities of Lawrence's vision to some degree. In traditional literary terms, the war narrator begins in the optimistic, expansive stage of the young Romantic protagonist. After a time his will is thwarted and he must withdraw, contract the boundaries of self to the point of annihilation; this second stage is most clearly presented in the introspection of ***Seven Pillars of Wisdom*** and in the first two sections of ***The Mint.*** In his final stage the hero rejects personality and says he feels absorbed by society and by matter, ideally achieving ''a oneness of himself with his fellows: and of them with the stocks and stones of his universe.''. . . This stage is asserted in an unconvincing, contradictory manner in Part Three of ***The Mint*** and is never adequately dramatized. (pp. 17-19)

Both ***Seven Pillars*** and ***The Mint*** display a precious style, reveal Lawrence's inability to characterize, emphasize the effects of discipline on the common soldiers, and dramatize the hero's alienation from his comrades. These similarities might be expected, for Parts One and Two were composed at the same time extensive revisions of ***Seven Pillars*** were going forward. ***The Mint,*** like ***Seven Pillars,*** focuses intensely on the self, and the reader's interest is in the impact of this brutal life on a man of sensitivity. Never was there a documentary with less detachment or objectivity. The form also has parallels to that of ***Seven Pillars.*** Though the whole of ***The Mint*** portrays the private self, direct introspection increases as the strain of Lawrence's enlistment is relieved. The final third of the book is decidedly less concrete and less concerned with any specific event than the first third. Like the last books of ***Seven Pillars,*** by Part Three ''the note season is over.'' . . . But formal differences from ***Seven Pillars*** are also significant, for the complex dramatic design and balance of the earlier work is absent. What Forster said of ***Seven Pillars*** is more appropriate for ***The Mint;*** Lawrence presents ''life as a succession of items which are organically connected but yet have some sort of intervals between them, i.e., you give a series of pictures'' [see excerpt dated 1924].

Lawrence's will is not destroyed after Deraa nor is its strength lessened. Rather the object of the will has changed from domination of the outside world to domination of the inner. He asserts that the lesson of Arabia is that the body does affect the will, that there is flesh, perhaps only flesh. The boundaries of the self contract. Now the ''circle centres bit by bit on myself: and therefore turns faster and is dangerous. People who lived in Nitrea, in the old days, to fight down the world, did grow their eyes inward: only inside me is too vacant a place to take much exploring.'' . . . Contraction of self is at once punishment for his expansive role as redeemer and a means to restrain his will. (pp. 165-66)

The Mint is a confession, and has a single, unifying pattern: the process of stamping out personality, of annihilating the self by giving it over to the R.A.F. machine, for he had ''struck a false image'' of himself on the coin current. But it is more clearly a private confession than ***Seven Pillars*** and depends heavily on the reader's close familiarity with the earlier book and Lawrence's biography. For instance, he assumes his reader will know that the marks on his back queried by an officer in the book's opening chapter are from the beating at Deraa; otherwise his dry remark that the beating was not intended as punishment, but was ''more like persuasion'' would be meaningless. His audience is to be Forster, David and Edward Garnett, the Shaws—literary figures. Besides, he writes Forster, ''it isn't a book. It's a note for your private eye: a swollen letter.'' . . . (p. 169)

The Mint begins with Lawrence's defecating as a nervous response to his enlistment in the ranks of the Royal Air Force; the ''melting of the bowels before a crisis'' supposedly illustrates the moral that he is not a man of action. . . . Then he is stripped naked and his body scrutinized, as if it were an object. The body and its functions are to be the subject of ***The Mint,*** its image of the absolute; everything in it is ''designed to emphasize the flesh of men, leading a life which is only of the body, and therefore growing . . . very natural souls.'' R. P. Blackmur finds in ***The Mint*** ''the continuous cultivation of the intolerable'' [see excerpt dated 1940]. Lawrence says this more precisely: he displays the ''attraction of unlikeness.'' . . . (pp. 169-70)

The assertion of absorption with which ***The Mint*** ends seems to be belied by the form and style of the work, as well as by Lawrence's own admission in his correspondence that this absorption has not in fact occurred. The conviction of separation from other soldiers, openly stated in Parts One and Two, is implicit in Three. E. M. Forster [see excerpt dated 1928] finds the affirmation less successful than the expiation; he prefers ''the 3rd part, as a whole, less than its predecessors.'' The transition to Part Three, Forster believes, ''is into another medium, into a sort of comforting bath water, where I sat contented and surprised, but not convicted that I was being cleansed. You hadn't . . . communicated your happiness to me.'' The form of ***The Mint*** militates against the self's achieving absorption, for at the beginning of Part Three the narrator steps forward, out of character, to declare that this section is not based on his Depot notes, like the previous two, but only on a few ''extracts, mainly from letters to my friends. . . . There is no continuity in these last pages. . . . How can any man describe his happiness?'' . . . The inability to complete the intended form of the work, the destruction of the continuity of the process, demonstrates that Lawrence has not joined the men, that his conviction of being absorbed is questionable at best. The relation of the third part to the first two is that of "benediction after a commination service." . . . (pp. 171-72)

The title of the minor work is as ironic as that of the major one. In his letters, Lawrence repeatedly asserts that he feels separate from the men. He has lived five years in the barracks and "can honestly confess that I've never been really one with my fellows. I have sometimes, for a moment, imagined myself into a unity with them: and before I could seize it and settle down into it, like a rabbit into a burrow, I'd be whisked off to another existence, incontinent." . . . Frequently in ***The Mint*** he shows himself at the center of events busily recording them. . . . He has "learned solidarity with them here. Not that we are very like, or will be. I joined in high hope of sharing their tastes and manners and life: but my nature persists in seeing all things in the mirror of itself, and not with a direct eye." . . . Lawrence finds himself odder in the ranks than before . . . ; only the pattern of physical movement "could momently absorb my mind." . . . (p. 172)

The use of "we" in ***The Mint*** seems contrived and, as in ***Seven Pillars,*** jars the reader throughout the work. The style of ***The Mint*** constantly pulls away from the content. Yet Lawrence believes that its "style well fitted its subject: our dull clothed selves; our humdrum, slightly oppressed, lives; our tight uniforms: the constriction, the limits, the artificial conduct, of our bodies and minds and spirits, in the great machine which the R.A.F. is becoming. I had to hold myself down, on each page, with both hands." . . . In fact, mannered throughout, ***The Mint*** generally has only a painted style. Of course this quality is heightened in landscapes . . . , but there is no real division in style because no significant public action is narrated. The book is primarily introspective, or at least reflective, in purpose, and direct emotional expression is not checked, as it is in the war narrative of ***Seven Pillars. The Mint*** heals the split in ***Seven Pillars*** by eliminating its active side, for this narrator is always his literary, introspective self, always filtering out those passages which do not confirm this self. (pp. 172-73)

As in ***Seven Pillars,*** Lawrence exhibits little feeling for nature. The sentimentality, the pathetic fallacy, the gloomy Romantic figure contrast strongly and consciously with the crude barracks and the animals inside.

The distance between Lawrence's elaborate prose and the soldiers' speech, fucking this and fucking that, is immense, even comic. Yet Lawrence's ear for speech rhythms in ***The Mint*** is remarkable; he seldom uses this faculty in ***Seven Pillars.*** The authenticity of the cadences of the obscenities is indisputable. Nonetheless Lawrence records only exclamations and isolated sentences, not conversations. Perhaps he is not interested in dialogue, for it would distract from the focus on himself.

Virtually no significant public events are narrated in ***The Mint.*** As heroic events become anti-heroic in ***Seven Pillars,*** here anti-heroic becomes heroic—or, more accurately, mock-heroic—by virtue of the style. There is no clear, direct, vigorous style, no war narrator certain of his identity who dominates a scene. The narrator expresses his feelings openly and directly about each event; he is angry, frightened, meditative by turns, and he analyzes each emotion. . . . (pp. 173-74)

In seeking to become like the airmen, Lawrence emphasizes his essential difference and consistently defines himself against them. Theoretically the self would be representative if this were truly a minting process. Lawrence seeks the convergence of private and public self, but part of him remains willful, undegraded, unbroken, as style and form demonstrate. Indeed, if the form of the work is fragmentary . . . , as Lawrence declares, using this form to express harmony of body and spirit is incongruous.

Absorption is never achieved by ***The Mint***'s hero, and the search for the absolute again ends in failure. In a single letter Lawrence says ambiguously that Part Three is "vamped up," but "sincere." He "shrank from digging too deep into the happiness, for fear of puncturing it." . . . In fact in his confessions Lawrence never moves beyond the stage of withdrawal and contraction of the self. The confessions of Augustine, Bunyan, and Rousseau portray the inner life absorbing and eventually transforming the outer. In Lawrence the outer life simply withers away. (p. 175)

Lawrence is the offspring of the literary and philosophical ideas of the nineteenth century, and by exaggerating them to destructive extremes he acts out the unconscious impulses of his age in a radical and direct way. Lawrence makes the creation and presentation of self his life's work after the war. His spiritual crisis—an inheritance from the nineteenth century—is never resolved. Indeed, his problem is the paralysis of will associated with the sadomasochistic character and cannot be resolved. Lawrence analyzes himself as a case-study of the abnormal. Yet as Emerson says of a writer's confessional impulse, "the deeper he dives into his privatest, secretest presentiment, to his wonder he finds this is the most acceptable, most public, and universally true." It is Lawrence's unsystematic translation of the optimistic Romantic myth of self into the pessimistic psychological myth of our century that gives his confessions power, universality, and complexity. (pp. 180-81)

Thomas J. O'Donnell, in his The Confessions of T. E. Lawrence: The Romantic Hero's Presentation of Self, *Ohio University Press, 1979, 196 p.*

JOHN E. MACK (essay date 1976)

[Mack is a distinguished American psychologist who is particularly interested in the use of psychology in biography. In explanation of his approach to research in this area, Mack states: "The value of psychology in biography is that it deepens our appreciation of the inner life of public figures, and illuminates some of the motivating determinants of action. But psychology is only useful in a greater context that includes the political, social, and economic factors that form the weave of history." In the following excerpt from his Pulitzer-prize winning biography of Lawrence, Mack uncovers the motivating factors behind Lawrence the war hero through an examination of the more introspective elements of Seven Pillars of Wisdom.*]*

A decade after the desert campaigns were over, Lawrence wrote Robert Graves: "During the Revolt I had a motive, within me, for activity, and therefore became capable of imposing my will on others. The very accident that normally I am empty of motive, helped make the rare motive, when it finally came, overpowering." With this statement Lawrence draws our attention from the activity itself to the motive behind it.

A discussion of someone's motivation in relation to events in which he has taken some vital part implies the possibility of choice: that he was not simply performing actions required by a situation he had no part in creating, or to which he was drawn by circumstances beyond his control. The more effectively a person like Lawrence can impose his will upon events, shape their course or influence their outcome, the stronger our fascination with the psychology of his motivation becomes—even stronger if these events have a sufficiently sharp impact and continue to affect our own lives. For we recognize then among the determinants affecting the course of history—and ourselves with it—the internal drives and purposes of an unusual person. We wish to understand him, to learn why he chose the directions he did. (p. 187)

Lawrence's importance as a historical figure derives from his ability to impose his will not only through actions and decisions of his own, but through his unusual capacity to influence his superiors—men like Allenby and later Churchill—to act in directions of his choice. "Allenby, Winston, Trenchard. I have a fine taste in chiefs," Lawrence wrote to another British officer many years later.

But beyond his work through such men as these Lawrence gains importance as a historical figure by virtue of his introspective nature and gifts of psychological perceptiveness regarding the motivation of himself and others. He teaches us what "a person like Lawrence" is like, insofar as it is possible to generalize from his psychological characteristics to those of others who live out their inner fantasies and conflicts in the public domain. (p. 188)

Lawrence was particularly aware of the multiple levels of his motivation, and taught us to expect to find a number of motivational levels in any leader, rather than to conclude that he or anyone else is likely to be motivated by one purpose alone. I believe the efforts of Lawrence's biographers to find *the* definitive motive for important periods of his life, such as the years of his participation in the Arab Revolt, to be in error.

Lawrence retained, as is well known, the child's pleasure in teasing and making riddles—for example, the merry chase he has led his biographers regarding the identity of "S.A.," the object of his dedicatory poem in ***Seven Pillars of Wisdom.*** Like Rumpelstiltskin he provoked interest in his own identity and piqued his audience with clues, but at the same time he seemed to dread their really "finding" him. (pp. 188-89)

In the early chapters of ***Seven Pillars of Wisdom*** Lawrence reveals a fantasy of himself as a kind of contemporary armed prophet, the most recent in the history of prophets, inspired in the desert, who had been spiritual and military leaders of the Semitic peoples since the beginning of recorded history. The Arabs of the desert, he writes, were "incorrigibly children of the idea" and "could be swung on an idea as on a cord; for the unpledged allegiance of their minds" (and by implication their susceptibility to the development of an allegiance with one, such as Lawrence, who would choose and be able to lead them and to "arrange their minds") made them "obedient servants." The awesome scope and form of this prophet fantasy does not seem to have become fully apparent to Lawrence until after the campaigns were over and he turned to writing his narrative. However, the shape of his continuing ambition, the quickening "root of authority," and his power to convert fantasy into reality clearly evoked fear in Lawrence and played a part in his personal retreat after the war. (pp. 192-93)

Lawrence wrote in ***Seven Pillars of Wisdom*** that as he approached his thirtieth birthday (August 15, 1918) he looked back upon medieval-Napoleonic fantasies of glory and achievement that he had previously entertained: "It came to me queerly how, four years ago, I had meant to be a general and knighted, when thirty." But his intensely self-critical nature rejected what he called "crude ambition" and his "detached self" eyed "the performance in the wings in criticism." The favorable opinion he was receiving of his successes made Lawrence anxious and he sought to dissect and examine his motives, to be truthful with himself. "Here were the Arabs believing me, Allenby and Clayton trusting me, my bodyguard dying for me," Lawrence observed, and felt that the good reputation was due to his acting, to a "craving for good repute among men," and to fraud. He asked himself whether "all good reputations were founded, like mine, on fraud." He observed how his "self-distrusting shyness held a mask, often a mask of indifference or flippancy, before my face, and puzzled me."

But Lawrence recognized behind this a powerful, egoistic, aggressive drive for fame and ambition (he called it his "egoistic curiosity"), whose proportions frightened him and which he ultimately rejected. He knew that his studied indifference "was only a mask; because despite my trying never to dwell on what was interesting, there were moments too strong for control when my appetite burst out and frightened me." A few paragraphs later he wrote: "Self-seeking ambitions visited me, but not to stay, since my critical self would make me fastidiously reject their fruits. Always I grew to dominate those things into which I had drifted, but in none of them did I voluntarily engage. Indeed, I saw myself a danger to ordinary men, with such capacity yawing rudderless at their disposal."

For Lawrence there seemed to be some conflict over all strong passions, as if he distrusted powerful feelings of any kind. His insight into this quality in himself was unusual. "I was very conscious of the bundled powers and entities within me," he wrote; "it was their character which hid. There was my craving to be liked—so strong and nervous that never could I open myself friendly to another. The terror of failure in an effort so important made me shrink from trying; besides, there was the standard; for intimacy seemed shameful unless the other could make the perfect reply, in the same language, after the same method, for the same reasons.

"There was a craving to be famous; and a horror of being known to like being known. Contempt for my passion for distinction made me refuse every offered honour."

Anis Sayigh, a Lebanese of Palestinian origins and a well-known Arab nationalist writer, has written a perceptive analysis in Arabic of Lawrence's prophet fantasy and role among the Arab peoples. Sayigh sees Lawrence as being in the tradition of Englishmen who had for three centuries exercised in the Middle East "a prophethood directed toward humanitarian aims." But Lawrence's prophethood, according to Sayigh, was not a religious one, for he was not religious and his age was more complex. The call to prophethood of previous ages would not have been appropriate in the early part of the twentieth century. Lawrence's mission, as Sayigh understands it, was one of reconciling the aims of Arab nationalism, which he supported, with the mission of Britain in the Middle East, as he tried to influence it, and each had responsibilities to the other. Lawrence "wished to save the Arab world from Turkish occupation and the greed of the French, Germans and Russians and to give the Arabs a place in the family of liberated nations." Lawrence, in Sayigh's view, saw Britain as having a special mission or responsibility in the underdeveloped world, and he in turn had the responsibility for defining Britain's mission, fixing its boundaries, and supervising it.

Sayigh stresses also Lawrence's belief that in return the Arabs would, in the psychological sense, liberate the Western mind. (pp. 193-94)

Sayigh, in my opinion, answers effectively the question of whether Lawrence's "real" motive was to serve the British or the Arabs during the campaigns. Clearly, in this Arab view he was trying to reconcile the complex and often conflicting aims of both. His intolerant conscience occasioned him much suffering over the limitations of the success of his efforts. Writings about Lawrence abound with discussions of whether he "really cared" about the Arabs. It is clear that the Arab peoples played a part in the fulfillment of vast dreams and historical fantasies on Lawrence's part and in this sense he "used" them. On the other hand there is no inherent contradiction between this larger purpose of personal ambition and caring at a personal level. It is the kind of discourse which often fails to be effectively joined because it is carried on at different levels. (p. 195)

A biographer needs to exercise special caution as he approaches the question of deeper personal motives, those inner drives which the subject tries to mold to the opportunities and requirements of external reality. This is not less true of Lawrence. For even though his introspective nature, his need to wash his mental linen in writings that would inevitably become public, gives us more opportunity than is usually available when studying historical figures to gain insight into the psychological roots of significant actions, direct evidence for interpretations, even in his case, is nevertheless limited. Only inferences that are no more than likelihoods can be drawn.

The pivotal concept linking Lawrence's passionate pursuit of his "mission" in the Arab cause with his background and personal development lies, in my opinion, in the idea of redemption. Arnold Lawrence understood well his mother's hope that her sons would redeem her guilt. With the deaths during the war of Frank and Will, the burden fell upon T. E., . . . [who] urgently . . . felt the need to become more active in the campaigns after they died. His reference in ***Seven Pillars of Wisdom*** to the Germans in Syria as "the enemy who had killed my brothers" suggests this personal element.

The language of renunciation and redemption pervades ***Seven Pillars of Wisdom.*** Lawrence saw the Arabs of the desert as exemplifying the ideal of renouncing the desires of the world, and his identification with this element he saw (or wished to see) in them played an important part in the structure of the private fantasy by which he was propelled during the campaigns. "The common base of all the Semitic creeds, winners or losers, was the ever present ideal of world-worthlessness," Lawrence wrote in ***Seven Pillars.*** "Their profound reaction from matter led them to preach bareness, renunciation, poverty; and the atmosphere of this invention stifled the minds of the desert pitilessly." Or: "The desert Arab found no joy like the joy of voluntarily holding back. He found luxury in abnegation, renunciation, self-restraint. . . . His desert was made a spiritual ice-house, in which was preserved intact but unimproved for all ages a vision of the unity of God."

The Arabs were idealized as his own ancestors were devalued. He wrote of the "fine-drawn Arabs whom generations of inbreeding had sharpened to a radiance ages older than the primitive, blotched, honest Englishmen." But the Arabs were a subject people, held in bondage by the Turks, fallen from the former prosperous state of their civilization. In fitting his image of the Arab condition to the outlines of his personal dream, Lawrence condensed time and smoothed out the irregularities of historical fact and detail. "With the coming of the Turks," he wrote "[Arab] happiness became a dream. By stages the Semites of Asia passed under their yoke, and found it a slow death. Their goods were stripped from them; and their spirits shrivelled in the numbing breath of a military Government."

The struggle to create and redeem runs throughout ***Seven Pillars of Wisdom,*** and Lawrence's personal identification with the Arabs is striking. His redemption and theirs are so intertwined as to be indistinguishable, and he became fully aware that he had attempted to achieve the former through the latter. He would sacrifice himself on behalf of the Arabs and redeem thereby the lowly state (as he perceived it) of both. But the profound egoist root of this self-sacrifice could not escape his ruthless self-examination. It confirmed his belief in his deceitfulness, his illegitimacy, and deepened the sense of sin and guilt, lowering his self-regard still further. "To endure for another in simplicity gave a sense of greatness," Lawrence wrote. "There was nothing loftier than a cross, from which to contemplate the world. The pride and exhilaration of it were beyond conceit. Yet each cross, occupied, robbed the latecomers of all but the poor part of copying: and the meanest of things were those done by example. The virtue of sacrifice lay within the victim's soul." (pp. 195-97)

Much has been written of Lawrence's need to dramatize himself, to seek publicity while simultaneously eschewing it, to "back into the limelight." But he was critical of that aspect of himself which, in spite of himself, gave in, often unconsciously, to self-dramatizing. He was aware of his inclination to mislead in his writings: he wrote, for example, to Mrs. Shaw, in 1927: "The reviewers [of ***Revolt in the Desert,*** his abridgment of ***Seven Pillars of Wisdom***] have none of them given me credit for being a bag of tricks—too rich and full a bag for them to control."

But I believe that this insight was to some extent the rationalization of the tendency to dramatize, which seemed to be outside Lawrence's control and which was spawned by psychological needs of which he was unaware. This tendency reached its fullest expression in ***Seven Pillars of Wisdom.*** One of Lawrence's purposes in writing the book was to invite his public to create with him a new and different self, a mythological Lawrence, larger than life, a self that would be immune to or beyond personal pain and conflict, and one that would replace the self he felt he had debased. The new self would be ideal in its honesty and integrity, a participant in epic events described in the epic mode, committing great deeds in war and yet responsible for war and rejecting it as no commander before had been or done, a Lawrence that was to be merciless if not all-seeing in his self-scrutiny.

The irony is that, objectively, the real Lawrence corresponded in so many ways to the ideal one he sought to create through his dramatizing and embroidering. But from his inner psychological perspective the real self was debased by the war and his experiences in it, and fell far short of the ideal self he had to invent, with the help of others, through legend-making.

The dramatic richness of ***Seven Pillars of Wisdom*** is widely acknowledged. Its value as a contemporary epic derives in part from its power to lift everyday events and personal struggles to a higher plane. Some of these events contained an intrinsic drama. In other instances Lawrence brought, through his passionate literary descriptions, drama and beauty to events of the Revolt—even the arrangement of corpses—that would otherwise have been merely horrible, painful or ordinary. (p. 222)

In passage after passage of ***Seven Pillars of Wisdom*** Lawrence provides accounts which throw the spotlight on himself and credit him with a central place in actions whose grandeur is raised to epic proportions. Yet this self-elevation (unnecessary from a purely objective standpoint in view of his actual accomplishments) is invariably matched with countervailing passages of self-disparagement, and proclamations of the baseness of his position and of his deceit, which become a kind of litany. Similarly, events in which Lawrence focuses credit upon himself, such as the capture of Aqaba ("Akaba had been taken on my plan by my effort. The cost of it had fallen on my brains and nerves"), seem always to be matched by accounts, such as his description of his role at Tafas, that exaggerate negative, even almost criminal, activity. Grand success and spectacular failure seem to alternate throughout the book. In the passages of horror—and there are many—even brutality, cruelty and gore are made somehow glorious; and tortures are stretched in intensity beyond belief. It is as if there is operating in Lawrence in writing this book—and I am treating it here as a psychological document rather than as a literary work—a balance scale controlling the economy of his self-esteem. The glorification of himself, and of the great events of the Arab Revolt in which he took part, seems to serve to overcome his low self-regard. But some internal monitor, or busy conscience under the control of a low self-estimate, seems always to swing the pendulum of judgment back in the direction of self-disparagement.

Seven Pillars of Wisdom has been criticized as a work of history because of alleged distortions of fact. The historian L. B. Namier, who considered Lawrence "a man of genius, a great artist," wrote gently of him that "he seemed to dislike the precision of dates" [see A. W. Lawrence, ed., *T. E. Lawrence by His Friends* in Additional Bibliography]. There are distortions in the book, but they come not, in my opinion, from a simple alteration of facts—it is remarkable how much valuable historical information the book does contain when its psychological and literary purposes are considered. Rather, the distortions and inaccuracy result from Lawrence's need, deriving from the conflicts and his self-regard, to elevate the tale to epic proportions and to make of himself a contemporary legendary figure.

The legend-making did not of course end with ***Seven Pillars of Wisdom.*** The Lawrence of myth continued to grow and be enriched by the tales he told his friends (from which, once they are retold, it is impossible to distinguish the embellishment and embroidering that is Lawrence's from that of his friends and biographers) and especially from the accounts he supplied his biographers. Sometimes Lawrence seemed unable to resist writing as if the whole Middle Eastern campaign, even the capture of Damascus, were related to his personal wishes, motives and accomplishments. For example, afer teasing Liddell Hart with a cryptic note about the relationship between his dedicatory poem ("To S.A."), and his sadness at the end of the campaigns over the death of Dahoum (he never just comes out and says he felt grieved about the loss of Dahoum), Lawrence wrote: "The unhappy 'event' happened long before we got to Damascus. *I only took D.* (so far as that motive was concerned) for historical reasons" [italics added]. (pp. 223-24)

Lawrence's personality was replete with paradoxes and contradictions. These relate to the complexities and ambiguities of his origins, family relationships, and childhood development, but are not explained by them. They have made him fascinating to biographers and may account in part for the attraction of his example. He retained on the one hand a childlike immaturity—like a gifted schoolboy—and a responsiveness to the child's world, while at the same time he assumed throughout his life extraordinary adult responsibilities. He possessed an unusual capacity for relationships with many different sorts of human beings, while retaining an essential isolation and aloofness. He was highly open to sensuous experience yet remained always an ascetic who rejected many of the pleasures of the flesh, especially sexual ones. Self-absorbed and egocentric, he was nevertheless unselfish in giving of himself. He suffered troubling forms of psychopathology and was "neurotic" in many ways. Yet out of his sufferings he found new solutions and values, and was often able to convert his personal pathology to creative public endeavors. His own moral conflicts became irreconcilable and he never fully recovered a full sense of his own worth. Yet he continuously helped others feel more worthwhile in themselves.

Lawrence was a great creator of myths in the sense that his exploits and his own rich account of them—so vivid at times as to give the impression of fiction—served as the basis for the creation by others of the distorted legend that grew around him. Yet he represented such fundamental truthfulness in his being that David Garnett once told me Lawrence was the only man he had known in whose presence he could never lie. He was to a degree a hero fashioned along the lines of the Victorian revival of medieval romanticism. Yet he may contribute ultimately to the destruction of this form of heroism and help to replace it with a model of a hero more self-aware, responsible and realistic. He was the representative of British colonialism in the Middle East, but became a spokesman for the end of traditional imperialism. A war hero and modern military leader—perhaps, next to Churchill, Britain's best known—Lawrence could become a figure who represents the renunciation of war. (pp. 457-58)

Lawrence has been hurt by both his idolators and his denigrators. The latter, especially Richard Aldington and Malcolm Muggeridge [see excerpt dated 1955 and Additional Bibliography], have found Lawrence to be a charlatan and a liar. My own examination of the evidence has led me to different conclusions. Lawrence had a compelling need to tell stories, which grew in part out of his deep doubts about his self-worth. Profoundly uncertain about his value, he laid the foundation for the creation alongside of the actual Lawrence of a legendary personality built on the dramatizations and elaborations of his tales. So extraordinary are some of these stories that they have seemed at times to have been made up. Yet my research led me repeatedly to the conclusion that Lawrence's accounts of his accomplishments were largely accurate and, if anything, he would customarily leave out information that was to his credit, or allow to stand distorted depictions of events that have invited the attacks of his detractors. I have not found Lawrence to be a liar.

Lawrence's struggles form one of the most moving personal sagas I have ever encountered. He could not ultimately resolve his inner personal disorder. Had he been able to, he might have lived to make a contribution in Britain's hour of need in World War II. But though he could not quiet his own inner demons, he was, in Irving Howe's words, a "prince of our disorder" and one of its civilizing forces. (p. 459)

John E. Mack, in his A Prince of Our Disorder: The Life of T. E. Lawrence, *Little, Brown and Company, 1976, 561 p.*

ELIE KEDOURIE (essay date 1977)

[Kedourie is an Iraqi critic living in England who has written several sociopolitical studies of the Middle East. In the following

excerpt from an essay that is largely a critical attack on several biographies of Lawrence, Kedourie denounces Seven Pillars of Wisdom *as a romantic aggrandizement of an ordinary military event. This essay originally appeared in the July 1977 issue of* Commentary *under a different title.*]

During his lifetime, and even more so after his death, Colonel T. E. Lawrence, 'Lawrence of Arabia', was the subject of a great deal of curiosity and speculation. The literature about him is voluminous and varied, ranging from accounts of his military career during World War I and his political activities afterward to investigations of his private life and explanations—sometimes involved and far-fetched and sometimes downright sensational—of his personality and behavior. (p. 261)

For many years, Lawrence's friends and admirers pitched the merits of his writings very high indeed. To take one example, the *Times Literary Supplement* has recently revealed that it was Lawrence's patron and friend, D. G. Hogarth, who anonymously reviewed in its pages ***Revolt in the Desert*** when it appeared in 1927. Hogarth, we find, ends his review by affirming that 'the book leaves from first to last an impression of absolute truth'. Hogarth, who was as deeply involved in the Arab revolt as Lawrence himself, should have known better. It was this kind of glorification, repeated over the years *ad nauseam,* which no doubt led Aldington to speak somewhat unkindly of what he called the Lawrence Bureau.

Lawrence's most recent admirers have been more circumspect, less sweeping and categorical, in their praises. In [*Lawrence of Arabia: The Literary Impulse,* see excerpt dated 1975], the Weintraubs explain that though Lawrence 'exaggerated and even invented some of the details in his narrative,' this only serves to establish 'his flair as a writer'. Lawrence, they tell us, was simply engaged in 'transmuting autobiographical chronicle into legend'; and, 'despite its confessed inexactitude and subjectivity, it *is,*' they insist, 'a work of history—a work which has the poetry of history'. [In *Prince of Our Disorder,* John E. Mack], for his part, advances a number of explanations for what he describes as 'distortions and partial truths' in ***Seven Pillars*** [see excerpt dated 1976]. He tells us in one place that their purpose is either embellishment 'for dramatic purposes', or the protection of other people. In another place he claims that 'the distortions and inaccuracies result from Lawrence's need to elevate the tale to epic proportions and to make himself a contemporary legendary figure'. Again, he explains that Lawrence's 'tendency to fictionalize his experiences, to turn his life into a legend', was most prominent when Lawrence was feeling particularly troubled in his self-regard. 'At these times,' Mack's diagnosis runs, 'he would give way to an unconscious need to create a fictional self, drawn on lines of childish heroism, to replace the troubled self he was experiencing'. In yet another passage, Mack invites us to consider Lawrence's literary labours as so many attempts to overcome the 'continuing effects of traumatic experiences'. Since these writings were meant to reach the public, Mack also invites us to look upon Lawrence as a benefactor—albeit an unwitting one—of the cause of mental health: 'He would be glad, I am sure.' Mack solemnly opines, 'if his public self-exposure could contribute to human understanding and to the relief of suffering. He would, I am quite certain, want others to benefit from any knowledge or insights gained from studying and analyzing the struggles he could not resolve altogether for himself.'

On the face of it, ***Seven Pillars*** is simply the account of a wartime episode. It requires some ingenuity to turn it into a myth, or a neurotic's confession requiring the analyst's transformative logic to unlock its esoteric meaning and unveil its hidden significance. But whatever the analyst's skill, it is difficult to see ***Seven Pillars*** as a myth, like Gilgamesh or Prometheus or Oedipus. And if the book is a piece of self-exposure, the maunderings of a neurotic on his psychoanalyst's couch, it is not clear why it should benefit humanity at large: at the most the benefit will accrue to the patient himself and to his doctor. All this laborious huffing and puffing, in short, sounds uncommonly like apologetics—which are necessary, since the fact cannot be gotten over that at certain points, some of them crucial, ***Seven Pillars*** is knowingly and deliberately untruthful. Lawrence, for instance, knew that Faysal, third son of the Sharif of Mecca, whose champion he became, was a timid, perhaps even a cowardly, man in battle, and lacking in judgment, and yet he portrayed him in ***Seven Pillars*** as a heroic figure, 'the leader who would bring the Arab revolt to full glory'. He chose to disguise the truth because—as he later told Liddell Hart—it was 'the only way to get the British to support the Arabs—physical courage is an essential demand of the typical British officer'. This may have been a necessary—albeit questionable—proceeding when Lawrence was acting as Faysal's champion. To perpetuate the deception in a work later composed at leisure is to take advantage of the reader's good faith. But perhaps the most flagrant example of this abuse is Lawrence's account of the fall of Damascus. The reader of ***Seven Pillars*** is led to believe that the city was captured by Faysal's forces, when the truth was—as Lawrence well knew—that on Allenby's orders all Allied forces were forbidden to enter Damascus, only Faysal's being allowed to do so, and thus—falsely—to claim its capture.

Lawrence's book, we may then fairly say, is a corrupt work, which deliberately sets out to induce in its readers—by means of falsehoods—feelings of admiration, pity, indignation and guilt, in respect of events which in reality do not possess that tragic quality for which such emotions are appropriate. The political and military events in which Lawrence was mixed up, and which in his fashion he later recounted, involved conflicting interests and ambitions, no single one of which was, however, particularly righteous or signally elevated. ***Seven Pillars*** pretends to the contrary, and by transforming the mediocre and the shady into noble and exalted beings, the book is not only corrupt but also corrupting—corrupting in a manner particularly familiar to the modern age, when political causes have come to be endowed with transcendental significance, to warrant the greatest sacrifices and justify the most heinous crimes. This kind of corruption may properly be called romantic, since it rests on yearning for a harmonious or paradisaical existence to be established or regained by means of political action.

Evidence of such romanticism is abundant in Lawrence's writings. Consider, for instance, the dedicatory poem which stands at the beginning of ***Seven Pillars.*** It is not known for sure to whom the poem is dedicated, but such evidence as exists points to Dahoum, a donkey boy who was employed on the diggings at Jerablus, and with whom Lawrence established a close relationship. But whatever the identity of the person to whom the poem (and the book) is dedicated, the poem itself is clearly erotic. It begins: 'I loved you', and its third stanza constitutes a typically romantic amalgam in which love and death are simultaneously and nostalgically evoked:

> Love, the way-weary, groped to your body, our
> brief wage ours for the moment
> Before earth's soft hand explored your shape,
> and blind worms grew fat upon
> Your substance.

Not only is this love poem—memorial of a private relationship—made to stand at the head of a book dealing with public events, but it is also itself made to affirm that the writer's actions in war and politics were motivated by a desire to give pleasure to the loved one. The first stanza reads:

I loved you, so I drew these tides of men into
my hands
and wrote my will across the sky in stars
To earn you Freedom, the seven-pillared worthy
house,
that your eyes might be shining for me
When we came.

We may add that the poem, as it figures in ***Seven Pillars,*** was amended and toned down by Robert Graves, and that Lawrence's original version—as Knightley and Simpson show in their book [see Additional Bibliography]—was palpably more explicit. It is all very peculiar.

Equally peculiar is the fact that while Lawrence's biographers have speculated a great deal on the identity of the person to whom it is dedicated, they have seldom paused to consider the significance of what the bare text of the poem so revealingly discloses about Lawrence's attitude to politics and public affairs. The poem, and other statements by Lawrence, indicate that he was perhaps homosexually inclined. Mack quotes a passage from some unpublished notes made for a projected autobiography in which Lawrence declares 'I take no pleasure in women. I have never thought twice or even once of the shape of a woman: but men's bodies, in repose or in movement—especially the former, appeal to me directly and very generally.' Side by side with this disgust for the female sex went hatred for generation and childbirth which, he told Mrs. Bernard Shaw, was 'so sorry and squalid an accident . . . if fathers and mothers took thought before bringing children into this misery of a world, only the monsters among them would dare to go through with it'. Such an outlook, so much at variance with the common experience of mankind, has for its corollary a view of politics in which are entirely absent those aims usually held to justify political activity—namely, the preservation and perpetuation of a human group. Hence perhaps Lawrence's occasionally wild and nihilistic outbursts, such as this one which occurs toward the end of ***Seven Pillars:*** 'To the clear-sighted, failure was the only goal. We must believe, through and through, that there was no victory except to go down in death fighting and crying for failure itself.'

In the dedicatory poem which inaugurates ***Seven Pillars,*** Lawrence boasts that 'I drew these tides of men into my hands and wrote my will across the sky in stars'. Here the self, by a sheer exercise of will, claims to master the world. In ***The Mint,*** which consists of sketches describing his life as an enlisted man in the Royal Air Force, Lawrence's attitude is the very opposite. The self is now wholly mastered by the world, governed by abject fear which, however, is perhaps as pleasurable as absolute domination: *les extrèmes se touchent*. He writes: 'The root-trouble is fear: fear of failing, fear of breaking down.' And: 'My soul, always looking for some fear to salt its existence, was wondering what seven whole years of servitude would do against the hasty stubbornness which had hitherto buttressed my values.' Having, in his search for a superhuman harmony, attempted (and failed) to soar to the heights, he would now seek the ineffable by immersing himself in a bovine existence where 'unquestioned life is a harmony': 'here are men so healthy that they don't chop up their meat into mince for easy digestion by the mind: and who are thereby intact as we are thereby diseased.' Therefore, deliberately, now preferring his world 'backwards in the mirror', Lawrence abandoned himself to the 'urge downwards, in pursuit of the safety which can't fall further'. It did not work: *qui veut faire l'ange,* as Pascal said, *fait la bête;* but not vice versa.

Lawrence's record, then, shows bravery in war, a great capacity for physical endurance, ingenuity as a guerrilla leader, and later some literary talent. But it also shows that he was self-centered, mercurial and violently unstable. In his concluding chapter Mack notes that Lawrence 'sought *new possibilities* for the self'. But this cannot redound to his praise, as Mack evidently means it to do. For these possibilities and the quest for them can be mischievous and even catastrophic. So in Lawrence's case they have proved to be—not only in his own restless and unhappy life, but also in the example which he set, and which his legend (which he took such care to put together and to promote) made immensely popular. Mack's further verdict, that Lawrence was a civilizing force, cannot therefore stand. The cause of Arab nationalism which he embraced (and which he falsely claimed to have been double-crossed and betrayed by his country) was not more virtuous or worthy than any similar cause. Why a foreigner should so fervently embrace it, and what it has contributed to civilization, are both quite obscure. Lawrence, on the other hand, promoted a pernicious confusion between public and private, he looked to politics for a spiritual satisfaction which it cannot possbily provide, and he invested it with an impossibly transcendental significance. In doing so, he pandered to some of the most dangerous elements to be found in the modern Western mentality. His influence and his cult, here at their most extensive and enduring, we may judge to be not civilizing, but destructive. (pp. 271-75)

Elie Kedourie, "Colonel Lawrence and His Biographers," in his Islam in the Modern World and Other Studies, *New Republic Books/Holt, Rinehart and Winston, 1981, pp. 261-75.*

JEFFREY MEYERS (essay date 1977)

[*Meyers is an American critic who has written extensively on T. E. Lawrence, George Orwell, and Katherine Mansfield, as well as on the interrelationships of various social issues with modern literature. In the following excerpt, Meyers discusses the psychosexual aspects of Lawrence's complex personality as revealed in* Seven Pillars of Wisdom *and his letters.*]

Seven Pillars of Wisdom . . . is the story of Lawrence's growth in personal and political awareness. The meaning of the book is determined by the juxtaposition of his psychological needs and the pattern of historical events, by the conflict between the man who acts and the conditions of his action. Lawrence's role in the Arab Revolt combined self-discipline with freedom and power, and his devotion to the higher cause of a 'holy war' enabled him to define his identity. But for Lawrence this self-discovery was destructive rather than enlightening. He gradually realized that he had been transformed from a man who had once valued each human life and had given himself in the service of freedom, to one who had been caught up in a repellent and fascinating slaughter and had lost his idealism. When he was tortured and raped at Deraa, this insight deepened into the horrible realization that he had achieved sexual pleasure from physical pain.

The Deraa experience completely destroyed his elaborately constructed network of defences and exposed his all-too-human vulnerability, broke his spirit and extinguished the possibilities of creative freedom. This crucial moment—what Erik Erikson calls 'The Event', or culmination and turning point of a man's experience—dramatizes the central opposition of body and will, and forms the core of ***Seven Pillars*** as well as of Lawrence's life.

Lawrence's post-war career—his political activities, the composition of ***Seven Pillars,*** the enlistment in the ranks, the flagellations and even the suicidal motorcycle rides—followed inevitably from the events described in the book. For just as the idealism and repression of his early life seemed to prepare for and lead up to his crisis in Arabia, so everything that happened after it seemed to be a direct result of those two years, 1916-18, that synthesized the experience of a lifetime.

Nietzche's concept of the will to power provided a philosophical foundation for Lawrence's idealistic ambitions, and the expression of the will through action was his means to self-knowledge. (pp. 114-15)

Nietzsche's theory that the will to power could dominate corporal needs and be employed as a creative force, not only gave Lawrence ideological support for his leadership of the Arab Revolt but also reinforced his hatred of the body. In a late chapter of ***Seven Pillars*** on the Turkish hospital, he writes of the 'slow physical corruption, a piecemeal rotting of the envelope of flesh about the hopeless spirit longing to escape'. . . . Much of Lawrence's life was an unsuccessful attempt to subjugate his body, and he tried to escape the humiliation of the physical ('Everything bodily is now hateful to me') through starvation, asceticism, masochism and even flagellation. To test and prove his will he would sometimes resort to trials of physical endurance, a degradation of the body that threw the mind into greater relief. . . .

Lawrence's revulsion in the Tank Corps from the raw, lecherous carnality and the 'animal reek here which keeps me awake at night with the horror that mankind should be like it', is very similar to Gulliver's horror and astonishment when he observes in the abominable Yahoo a disturbing likeness to himself. (p. 115)

The bitter and enigmatic personality of Jonathan Swift provides a suggestive analogy to the divided Lawrence. Swift, a posthumous child and Lawrence, an illegitimate one, had radically disturbed and covertly hostile relationships with their parents. Each had a proud and anguished character, a horror of the physical side of life, a compulsive cleanliness, a perverse sexual attitude; and they also had a considerable achievement in both literature and politics, a number of brilliant and powerful friends, a soaring ambition briefly gratified and then permanently disappointed. The last part of their lives was spent in obscurity, amidst humble and adoring mediocrities.

Lawrence's mother was the dominant influence in his life. She too was an illegitimate child, brought up under the rigorous regimen of Presbyterian puritanism, which she powerfully impressed on her son. She was sent to Ireland as a young woman to be a maid in the house of Sir Thomas Chapman, Lawrence's father, who had long been married to an unstable, unattractive and unsympathetic woman. Though passion momentarily overcame repression when she ran off with Sir Thomas (who could never obtain a divorce), she soon reverted to an even more fanatical religion as the 'sinful' birth of her five sons repeated her mother's 'crime' and intensified her own fears of damnation. (p. 116)

The origins of Lawrence's sexual pathology can be clarified by Shakespeare's *Hamlet,* for both Hamlet and Lawrence react to the guilt-ridden, irregular marriage of their mothers, to whom they are unusually close, with a violent sexual revulsion. Hamlet's nauseated condemnation of living

> In the rank sweat of an enseamed bed,
> Stewed in corruption, honeying and making love.
> Over the nasty sty . . .

is an accurate portrayal of Lawrence's sexual morbidity and of the impossibility of escaping the 'corruption of lust'. As D. H. Lawrence writes of the tortured Prince: 'A sense of corruption in the flesh makes Hamlet frenzied, for he will never admit that it is his own flesh.''

Undoubtedly disturbed by his parents' sexual relationship. Lawrence adopted David Hogarth as a 'purer' surrogate father and Charlotte Shaw as his substitute mother. Lawrence felt he could confide in the older married woman (he believed women are unfortunate when they have sexual relations with men) and Mrs Shaw was 65 when she first met Lawrence in 1922, the year his mother left for China. Charlotte Shaw, who shared Lawrence's idea of 'sexlessness' and inviolate virginity, never slept with her husband, Bernard Shaw. Lawrence established a surprising intimacy with her, adopted her name in 1925, and made some extraordinary revelations about his family and himself in his letters to her. (pp. 116-17)

Lawrence grew up in an atmosphere of overwhelming sin and guilt, and discovered the source of this guilt just as he was entering the vulnerable period of adolescence. His statement that he 'didn't care a straw' is a rather unconvincing whistling in the dark. It is difficult to assess (but easy to underestimate) the influence of Lawrence's illegitimacy on his personality, but it must have intensified, if not determined, his odd combination of shy reserve and provocative aggressiveness, his intense alienation and isolation, and his sense of shame and degradation. (p. 118)

Because of their strong similarity, Lawrence developed a keen insight into his mother's puritanical shame and guilt. This perception did not liberate him from his mother's feelings, but led to a revulsion and disgust that prevented him from ever having sexual relations with women. (pp. 118-19)

One of the ways that Lawrence came to terms with his body was through a kind of Greek idealization (inspired by Achilles and Patroclus) of male love. This homosexual union in an exclusively masculine society, represented in ***Seven Pillars*** by the love of Farraj and Daud, Lawrence considered more honest, innocent and spiritual than heterosexual love. . . . In an essay on *Arabia Deserta,* the homosexual novelist, Norman Douglas, coyly writes: 'We could have been given glimpses into certain secret things, certain customs of profound significance in Oriental life and of interest to the European students. Doughty, with a kind of maidenly modesty, barely hints at their existence.' Lawrence amply provides what Doughty omits, and portrays the permissive atmosphere of Arabic male love, first made notorious in Gide's *The Immoralist,* where young Arab boys reveal their golden nudity beneath soft, flowing robes.

Male passion had to be satisfied in the desert, sometimes through bestiality with the flocks of sheep or with the raddled meat of prostitutes. In the very first chapter Lawrence challenges conventional morality and writes that 'friends quivering together in the yielding sand with intimate hot limbs in supreme embrace, found there hidden in the darkness a sensual co-efficient of the mental passion which was welding our souls and spirits into one flaming effort.'. . . For Lawrence, the clean, indifferent male bodies are not only a comparatively pure alternative to venereal disease, but also have the advantage of providing political as well as sexual unity. Lawrence's desire for 'these partnerships of man and man, to supply human nature with more than the contact of flesh with flesh' . . . was realized not only in his writing but also in his life, where there is continual evidence of homosexuality, especially in his relations with Sheik Ahmed, to whom he dedicated ***Seven Pillars***.

Sheik Ahmed or Dahoum (he was known by both names), of mixed Arab and Hittite blood, was 14 when the 23-year-old Lawrence met him with the other workers at the Carchemish archeological site in 1911. Leonard Woolley, Lawrence's colleague and co-author, reproduces some photographs of the lovely but 'not particularly intelligent' boy in *Dead Towns and Living Men*. . . . (pp. 119-20)

Lawrence also attracted a number of sensitive, intelligent and creative men (as well as elderly maternal women), and had extremely close friendships with Vyvyan Richards and Ernest Altounyan (both of whom have suggested they were in love with Lawrence); with the homosexual writers James Hanley, Frederic Manning and E. M. Forster; and with young airmen like the beautiful, blond and blue-eyed R. A. Guy (whom he called 'Rabbit' or 'Poppet') and to whom he writes: 'My pleasure in the R.A.F. was partly, largely, due to the pleasure I got from your blue and yellow self: I owe you a deep debt for many happy times.'

A . . . letter to Charlotte Shaw, written a year later revives the earlier themes of his mother's dominance, his frightening similarity to her, his ambivalent attraction-repulsion, her probing search into his privacy, her vicarious existence in her children's lives, and her insatiable demand for love, especially after the death of two sons in the war.

> She is monumental really: and so unlike you. Probably she is exactly like me: otherwise we wouldn't so hanker after one another, whenever we are wise enough to keep apart. Her letters are things I dread, and she always asks for more of mine (I try to write monthly: but we haven't a subject we dare to be intimate upon: so they are spavined things) and hates them when they come, as they do, ever so rarely. I think I'm afraid of letting her get, ever so little, inside the circle of my integrity: and she is always hammering and sapping to come in. A very dominant person: only old now, and, so my brother says, very much less than she had been. She has lived so in her children, & in my father, that she cannot relieve herself, upon herself, and from herself, at all. And it isn't right to cry out to your children for love. They are prevented by the walls of time and function, from loving their parents.

Lawrence's language in [this letter] . . . is strikingly close to his description of his torture and rape at Deraa. His mother's 'sapping' is a metaphor of siege and assault, and also has the suggestion of sexual debilitation. Lawrence's terror that 'if she knew [his feelings] they would be damaged: violated: no longer mine' and his fear 'of letting her get . . . inside the circle of my *integrity*' is emotionally and psychologically connected to the last sentence of the Deraa chapter: 'the passing days confirmed how in Deraa that night the citadel of my integrity had been irrevocably lost'. The greatest childhood fear of his mother was realized in the most horrible and degrading moment of Lawrence's life.

Though Lawrence was often the only witness to the events he records, and his veracity has been questioned, most notably by Richard Aldington [see excerpt dated 1955], the memoirs of his comrades and enemies confirm the essential accuracy of his account of the Arab Revolt. Similarly, the longer Oxford edition of ***Seven Pillars*** and Lawrence's extremely frank letters to Charlotte Shaw give the complete revelation of what is portrayed only indirectly in the published version of his book.

Like Proust, Lawrence subjects this experience to a minute and introspective analysis, as if he wanted his mind to be an objective observer of his flesh's suffering in order to understand it and make it bearable. But this event was extremely difficult for him to record; and even Lawrence, with his capacity for Proustian self-revelation, was unable to write the distinct truth and was forced to portray it obliquely. (pp. 121-22)

Chapter 80 on Deraa, in which Lawrence discusses his greatest personal failure, appears within the context of Book 6, which narrates his greatest military failure: his inability to destroy the railway bridges in the Yarmuk Valley. And Chapter 80, the antithesis of his triumphs at Aqaba, Jerusalem and Damascus, is closely related to the avenging massacre of the Deraa police battalion in the battle of Tafas, where Lawrence ordered that no prisoners be taken.

In this chapter, Lawrence describes his torture with a nearly intolerable precision that has become a model for the torture scenes in books like *Days of Wrath* and *1984*. Disguised as a Circassian, Lawrence is captured on a reconnaissance behind enemy lines, and after violently rejecting the depraved assault of a Turkish Bey, he is tortured into submission. (pp. 122-23)

The sadistic ingenuity of the depraved torturers is a fearful as humiliation, suffering or death; and this extreme moment represents the ultimate punishment for the accumulated fear and guilt—personal, political and military—of a lifetime. (p. 123)

In ***Seven Pillars*** Lawrence is taken to the Turkish Bey who 'rejected me in haste, as a thing too torn and bloody for his bed' . . . who instead of Lawrence takes a Turkish soldier for his pleasure. But in an agonizing letter to Charlotte Shaw, Lawrence admits the truth: that he lost his nerve and sexually surrendered when he could no longer bear the pain.

> You instance my night in Deraa. Well, I'm always afraid of being hurt: and to me, while I live, the force of that night will lie in the agony which broke me, and made me surrender . . . For fear of being hurt, or rather to earn five minutes respite from a pain which drove me mad, I gave away the only possession we are born into the world with—our bodily integrity. It's an unforgivable matter, an irrevocable position: and it's that which has made me forswear decent living, and the exercise of my not-contemptible wits and talents.
>
> You may call this morbid: but think of the offence, and the intensity of my brooding over it for these years. It will hang about me while I live, and afterwards if our personality survives. Consider wandering among the decent ghosts, hereafter, crying 'unclean, unclean!'

The phrase, 'will hang about me', is an allusion to the albatross in 'The Ancient Mariner', and the final words refer to the pariah-leper in Leviticus 13:45 who rends his clothes, bares his head, covers his lips, and cries 'unclean, unclean' through the deserted streets. Like the leper, Lawrence feels he is to blame for his uncleanness. (p. 124)

Lawrence's sexual surrender at Deraa and his homosexuality that was so inextricably a part of it led to a desire for self-punishment and humiliation. After the war he became an 'extinct volcano' and, like Conrad's Razumov and Lord Jim experienced a moral self-betrayal and dishonourable fall from self-esteem that intensified his guilt. Lawrence told Lionel Curtis that his masochism remains and will remain, and emphasizes that self-degradation is his aim. 'I long for people to look down on me and despise me', he writes to Charlotte Shaw, 'and I'm too shy to take the filthy steps which would publicly shame me, and put me in their contempt'.

This intense desire for self-degradation manifested itself in two significant ways. First, Lawrence abandoned the unlimited possibilities of a career in public life and voluntarily returned to his mother's class (the class that 'gave themselves away') in the 'lay monasticism' of the masculine military ranks: 'I'm afraid (physically afraid) of other men: their animal spirits seem to me the most terrible companions to haunt a man . . . What is it that makes me so damnably sensitive and so ready to cry out, and yet so ready to incur more pain? Secondly, while serving in the Tank Corps in 1923, Lawrence persuaded a young Scotsman, John Bruce, to flog him at regular intervals, which sometimes occurred on the anniversary of the Deraa torture and extended over a period of eleven years. (p. 127)

Though the precise reasons for Lawrence's scourging are complex and obscure, it is likely that the series of beatings exemplify the 'repetition-compulsion' which Freud discusses in *Beyond the Pleasure Principle* (1920) and relates to the death-instinct. The whippings are a re-enactment of Lawrence's terrible traumatic guilt, and allow him to redeem his eternal and existential debt by enduring what had once crushed his body and spirit, and to displace the death-instinct with self-punishment instead of self-destruction.

The desire for death is a powerful theme in ***Seven Pillars*** ('instinct said die'): in the opening lines to S. A. ('Death seemed my servant on the road . . .'), in his weary longing to be among the quiet and strangely beautiful corpses that he carefully arranges, and in his desire, after the destruction of his will, to have the winds blow his empty soul away. The death wish could be displaced but never eliminated, and was embodied in the frenetic speed passages in 'The Road' section of the masochistic ***Mint*** and finally realized in the pointless and fatal motorcycle accident.

Lawrence's death wish is significantly related to his passion for personal cleanliness and to his love of baths (his one sensual indulgence) as well as to the important theme of cleanness in ***Seven Pillars***. Lawrence often describes the desert as clean ('the desert landscape cleansed me'), and it is a strong contrast to the 'filth' (blood, vomit and sperm) that is wiped off Lawrence as he lies 'retching and sobbing for mercy' after his flogging. In the last chapter of ***Seven Pillars*** Lawrence, on the verge of a nervous breakdown after the ultimate horrors of the Turkish hospital, laughs hysterically at an Australian major who then smacks him in the face. This symbolic slap recalls the slap of the Bey's bedroom slipper across his face before the torture at Deraa, and from this moment Lawrence becomes 'so stained in estimation that afterward nothing in the world would make him feel clean.'. . . Only death 'would be a clean escape'. The epigraph stamped on the cover of the book—'the sword also means clean-ness and death'—reinforces Lawrence's connection of cleanness with death, rather than with life. He specifically associates birth with uncleanness and filth, and invites the astonished Arabs to imagine the birth of children, who 'crawl worm-like out of the mother [a] bloody, blinded thing.'. . . The core of Lawrence's, and Swift's, sexual pathology is their inability to accept the natural life-processes of birth and sex which are inevitably linked with women, and the terrible paradox that man is born between urine and feces, that 'Love has pitched his mansion in/The place of excrement'.

Lawrence's inability to accept this physiological fact is a cause of his hatred of the body, masochism, fear of his mother, revulsion from heterosexual love and homosexuality. (pp. 127-29)

In ***Seven Pillars of Wisdom*** inversion is dichotomized either as 'carnal marriage complemented by spiritual union' among the Arabs or sickening sodomy among the Turks. But in Lawrence's case, homosexuality is the manifestation of the body's weakness in relation to the will. Lawrence hated his body's vulnerability and feared his barely repressed desires; and by disciplining and subjecting his corporal self he was able to channel his libido into war, achieve the outstanding feats of physical endurance and earn the respect of the Bedouin, which was vital to his leadership. But the assault by the despised Turkish enemy on his point of greatest weakness, his sexual core, subverted his will and powers of endurance, betrayed the high ideals of the dedicatory poem to S. A. ('the inviolate house as a memory to you'), ravished his bodily integrity and precious virginity, and set him on the path of renunciation and destruction. (pp. 129-30)

Jeffrey Meyers, "T. E. Lawrence: 'Seven Pillars of Wisdom' (1926)," in his Homosexuality and Literature: 1890-1930, *McGill-Queen's University Press, 1977, pp. 114-30.*

DESMOND STEWART (essay date 1977)

[*Stewart was an English novelist and authority on Middle Eastern culture and history. In the following excerpt, he analyzes* Seven Pillars of Wisdom, *centering on the "Deraa incident" in which Lawrence is raped.*]

No twentieth-century writer has set out with higher ambitions [than T. E. Lawrence]. As well read as James Joyce, a good deal better read than his namesake D. H. Lawrence, he sought to produce, at whatever cost in hunger, thirst, exhaustion and self-exposure, a masterpiece in the western tradition. He was no *faux naif* or subliterate genius. His literary perspective went back to Homer and Virgil, of whom there are significant echoes in his pages. Along with the *Iliad*'s acceptance of killing as a human activity, Homer's use of repeated epithets suited the authoritarian streak in Lawrence, with his tendency to fix men in uncomplex stereotypes. Although he later earned a considerable sum from translating the *Odyssey*, its echoes are in reverse: for the sea the desert, for an Ithaca with Penelope and waiting hound, a Damascus empty of Sharif Ali and Dahoum. Lawrence, as post-Christian, is closer to the immediately pre-Christian spirit of the 'maidenly' and Celtic Virgil. The *Aeneid*'s structure—the wanderings of a remnant from Troy who eventually establish a new state in Italy—has affinities with Lawrence's ten-book recital of how Arabs, awaking from centuries

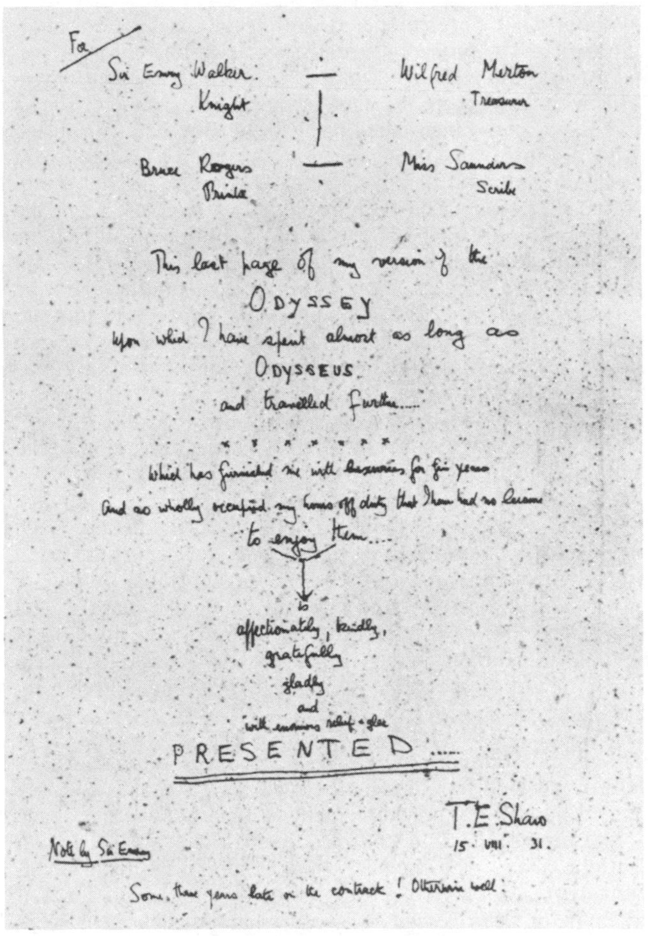
For
Sir Emery Walker: — Wilfred Merton
Knight | Treasurer
Bruce Rogers — Miss Saunders
Printer Scribe

This last page of my version of the
ODYSSEY
upon which I have spent almost as long as
ODYSSEUS
and travelled further....

* * * * * * *

which has furnished me with luxuries for five years
and so wholly occupied my hours off duty that I have had no leisure
to enjoy them....

to
affectionately, kindly,
gratefully
gladly
and
with enormous relief & glee
PRESENTED....

T.E.Shaw
15. VIII. 31.

Note by Sir Emery
Some, three years late on the contract! Otherwise well.

Holograph manuscript of the last page of Lawrence's translation of the Odyssey.

of neglect, embark on a journey whose end is summed up in the title of Book X: *The House is Perfected.* Lawrence's portrayal of Feisal is as reverent (and lifeless) as the pious Aeneas of Virgil and the mood in which Lawrence subtitled his epic 'A Triumph' is close to Virgil's distinctive blend of imperial confidence and Celtic pessimism. Ostensibly hymning the birth of Rome and, by implication, the genius of Augustus, Virgil gives his last line to the defeated Turnus, whose soul flees *indignata sub umbras.* Lawrence concludes with the author-hero's bitter departure from Damascus. (pp. 235-36)

[The abridged version of ***Seven Pillars***], ***Revolt in the Desert,*** as a result of its bowdlerization, is neither a work of literary significance nor historical interest. Lawrence was correct in seeing it as a pot-boiler, right in suspending its sales once they had paid the debts he had incurred in producing and illustrating an expensive, limited edition of the 'real' book. No one interested in the Arab campaign would bother to consult the pot-boiler; those interested in Lawrence will never discard ***Seven Pillars of Wisdom;*** if only for its effect on his contemporaries it will remain on the library shelves.

After a legible version of his 'real' book existed, in August 1922, Lawrence was to tell [editor Edward] Garnett that he had 'collected a shelf of titanic works, those distinguished by greatness of spirit, *Karamazov, Zarathustra* and *Moby Dick.* Well, my ambition was to make a fourth.' Since two of the three are novels, and in the third, Nietzsche attributes his own, nineteenth-century ideas to the historical Zarathustra, the level of truth is plainly that of imaginative literature, not official history.

But if ***Seven Pillars of Wisdom*** shares elements with two great novels, it does not manifest the usual attributes of successful fiction: character is not delineated in incident and dialogue; the story, as even his greatest admirers have conceded, lacks narrative movement. 'His book was not a great narrative,' André Malraux has written. 'What sort of existence did these people lead?' he asks, qualifying Lawrence's portrayal of the Arabs as scarcely going 'beyond the picturesque, that of the English beyond a crude sketch. What reader, the book closed, "knows" Joyce, Young, Clayton? The most characterized person, Feisal, is he not a sort of official portrait?'

In ***Seven Pillars of Wisdom*** Lawrence's self-baffling personality plays the role which the philosophy of the Superman plays in Nietzsche's *Zarathustra* or the struggle between man and the absolute in *Moby Dick.* 'Every priest,' once more to quote Malraux, 'knows that confession in the abstract costs little.' Hence the concrete questions from behind the grille: with whom? how many times? in what manner? Yet 'Lawrence's nature was opposed to confession both by the violence of his pride and by that of modesty.'

To surmount the problem, Lawrence adopts the technique which Perseus used when facing the Medusa. The Greek hero confronted the petrifying monster by looking at her, indirectly, in the mirror of his shield. Lawrence invents myths in whose polished steel he, too, can face the unfaceable. The myths become oblique confessions. And like confessions they look first to the past and then to the future. In the myth of Daud and Farraj he looks back to his own idyllic days in Carchemish and Lebanon with Dahoum; he also looks forward, through the prism of Deraa, to his post-war self. The name Daud was not chosen without care. While having the same initial and vowels as Dahoum, it is also the Arabic for David, a name which gains significance when we read the passage in which Lawrence describes his final parting from Sharif Ali. The parting comes at the end of the period in which Lawrence sets the myth of Deraa. The exchange of clothing is also significant. It repeats, on a different social level, his pre-war game of dressing up as Dahoum. (pp. 239-40)

The Deraa incident . . . is structurally and emotionally the pivotal incident in the book. (pp. 240-41)

Beyond its function in his epic, the Deraa incident is also the most important of Lawrence's myths; in its shield-light he faced the crucial truths about himself. His movements (known at the time to Wingate and Hogarth and recorded in his own skeleton diary and letters) rule out this pointless sortie from Azrak. The myth further conflicts (as has been established by the Arab historian Suleiman Mousa and the authors of *The Secret Lives of Lawrence of Arabia*) with what is known of the Bey of Deraa, as much a historical personage on the Ottoman side as Clayton on the Allied.

The story's internal lack of coherence is a yet more decisive factor for rejecting it as true in the sense of historically accurate.

What is supposed to have happened?

According to the version he had printed at the *Oxford Times,* instead of resting himself and his camels at Azrak for ten days, Lawrence goes off on a reconnaissance mission to the key railway junction between the Hejaz Railway and the spur into Palestine. While he is surveying the aerodrome, a Turkish N.C.O. seizes Lawrence but ignores his Arab companion: he is marched into a compound before a 'fleshy Turkish officer, one leg tucked under him': Lawrence gives his name as Ahmed Ibn Bagr [besides echoing an English synonym for sodomite, the name in Arabic can have connections with the verb to eviscerate] and claims to be a Circassian from Kuneitra [the capital of modern Syria's Jolan province] and thus exempt from military service: [Lawrence had startled Sharif Abdullah by his knowledge of Turkish regiments; he must have known that military service had been obligatory for all Ottoman subjects, whatever their race or religion, since the Young Turk Revolution.] He is led to a guard-room, consoled by Turkish soldiers, fed their food, and told he may be released next day if he fulfils the Bey's pleasures [in this first version Lawrence simply names the governor as Hajjim, or 'my Hajji', a term of respect]; is, after nightfall, conducted across the railway to a somewhat remote, detached and guarded house: is conducted upstairs to the Bey's bedroom: the Bey, who is in bed, fondles Lawrence, 'saying how white and clean I was' [Lawrence had ridden for weeks without a proper bath; was covered with boils and saddle sores]; promises military favours [apparently without checking his papers or military status]; flies into a rage when Lawrence resists him: has him stripped: gapes at the bullet-wounds [which had vanished when Meinertzhagen saw him undressed less than eighteen months later]; tries again: gets Lawrence's knee in his groin: shouts for the corporal: has Lawrence pinioned while he slippers his face, bites his neck, kisses, has bayonet-fun; states he knows who Lawrence is; seems not to mean what this implies: [or if he does, sacrifices the chance of a huge reward]; hands the still obdurate Lawrence over to the soldiers: they take him outside, stretch him on the guard-bench [apparently kept outside the Bey's bedroom]; hold him down till the corporal returns with a Circassian riding whip [which Lawrence somehow observes in every detail from his disadvantageous position]; 'a thong of supple black hide, rounded, and tapering from the thickness of a thumb at the grip (which was wrapped in silver) down to a hard point finer than a pencil.'

Four paragraphs are now devoted to the subsequent whipping. Again, despite being held so that his eyes are on the ground (two soldiers grasp his ankles, another two hold his wrists over his head) he can apparently see the area of flagellation, his back, where 'at the instant of each stroke a hard white mark like a railway, darkening slowly into crimson, leaped over my skin, and a bead of blood swelled up wherever the ridges crossed.' His use of language is revealing: 'they [the blows] hurt more horribly than I had *dreamed of* . . . [this the author's emphasis.]

In the second paragraph he forgets to count the blows after the first twenty.

The third paragraph suggests that the 'men'—squabbling over whose turn would be next, resting, twisting Lawrence's head round to observe their handiwork, easing themselves, playing with him a little—are enjoying the performance. In a supreme display of his command of the language, Lawrence shrieks only in (apparently perfect) Arabic [a high percentage of the Ottoman soldiers in Syria were Arabic speakers].

The fourth paragraph has him lying on the floor 'panting for breath but vaguely comfortable.'

The paragraph that follows is important. The corporal kicks him with his nailed boot, turning 'yellow and lacerated' his whole left side. 'I remembered smiling idly at him, for a delicious warmth, probably sexual, was swelling through me; and then he flung up his arm and hacked with the full length of his whip into my groin.' One soldier giggles; another shows pity. Lawrence is then taken back to the Bey who, disgusted by the results of what one is meant to assume is a normal Deraa evening, rejects him. 'So the crestfallen corporal, as the youngest and best looking on the guard [and as we have seen, the toughest and most sadistic] had to stay behind while the others carried me down the narrow stairs and out into the street.' He is put in a lean-to shed on a pile of quilts; his knife [can it be the gold Sharifian dagger?] is apparently returned to him: an Armenian dresser tends his wounds: a soldier whispers 'in a Druse accent' [whatever that may be, it reveals him as an Arab] 'that the door into the next room was not locked.' Lawrence [with most of his readers] wonders if 'it was not all a dream': he remembers the 'hospital at Khalfati where something of the same kind had happened to me.' In the next room hangs a convenient 'suit of shoddy clothes.' Next morning Lawrence puts them on and in escaping stumbles on a 'hidden approach to Deraa for our future raiding party.' [Deraa was no unmapped mystery town such as Philby looked for in Arabia proper. A railway junction, it appeared in detail on British maps. Local Arabs, who knew every inch of the district, were to support the final assault on Deraa eleven months later. No British officer in the Anglo-Arab forces has mentioned this secret approach.]

For this extraordinary story ***Seven Pillars of Wisdom*** (in its Oxford and then its edited, published text) remains the only source: along with the supplementary details Lawrence gave to Meinertzhagen, who confided them to his diary, and to Charlotte Shaw, who bequeathed his letters to the British Museum. Had Lawrence so chosen, no one would have known of the myth or been forced to guess what lay behind it. (pp. 241-43)

Deraa represented the discovery that for him, as for Swinburne before him, pain was the vital ingredient, if not for pleasure, then release. Deraa is not historical in the sense that Allenby's capture of Jerusalem was historical. It embodied an approach to truth which Lawrence shared with such writers as George Borrow, Ford Madox Ford and George Moore. 'Such writers,' David Wright has written, 'take truth as the warp into which a weft of imagination may be woven. The web or embroidery that results is myth, but often an emblematic myth that recreates, makes explicit or at least illuminates some inherent truth or quality that strict fact may sometimes obscure.'

The truth that Lawrence discovered in the War was more than he could totally reveal: only his long concealed post-war actions, his attendance at beating-parties in Chelsea organized by an underworld figure known as Bluebeard, his requests, sporadic but in one case regular, to be birched by soldiers, would uncover a truth as absurd as it was painful. In his predicament, as well as in his fame, Lawrence had a predecessor: the Byron who had dominated the imagination of the Napoleonic generation and whose marriage collapsed in mysterious ruin. Byron's *Don Juan*, like Lawrence's epic, conceals as well as reveals. The scandal in the poet's marriage seems to have been the applicaton to his wife of sexual techniques he had learnt with young men. The legend of incest with his half-sister, as well as *Don Juan*'s portrayal of an obsessive womanizer, help disguise a less acceptable truth. Lawrence disguises the discovery of his physical masochism behind what seems its opposite. Lawrence offsets Deraa—probably the transubstantiation of a genuine experience at Azrak with Sharif Ali—with a plethora of sadistic incidents and overtones. (pp. 243-44)

To forge his myths Lawrence devised a prose style which has probably alienated as many readers as the mysterious dedication to ***Seven Pillars of Wisdom*** has intrigued. That it was not natural to him is shown by the letters and articles which he published about the Middle East in the British press.

When the book existed only in the cumbrous print of the *Oxford Times,* Bernard Shaw discussed the literary influences on it with his fellow-Fabian, Sidney Webb. The William Morris who had been the aesthetic idol of Lawrence's youth was too much of the north to have given a model for this epic of the east. With his dislike for latinate words Morris would have condemned such Lawrentian passages as '. . . to Wadi Agida, wherein the Egyptians were taking counsel pavidly with one another.' While Webb discerned Borrow's influence, Shaw was so certain that the influence was Doughty that he took the trouble of reading *Arabia Deserta* the better to appreciate what Lawrence had written. But Shaw was in part misled by Lawrence's admiration for Doughty as a writer and his practical efforts on the old man's behalf. (Lawrence went to commendable lengths to get *Arabia Deserta* reissued and its author awarded a government pension.) There are of course affinities in the background to both works and to a lesser extent in their chief characters: Doughty disguised as the Christian-Arab physician, 'Khalil', and Lawrence as himself. Also, Doughty shared Lawrence's interest in pain, if not his attitude to it. 'Khalil' first puts himself at risk, the third night of the pilgrimage caravan, 'when curiosity led him to the aga's tent to see execution going forward on the person of an Arab thief. Compassion drew from him a hakim's [physician's] protest against further flogging.' Like Lawrence, Doughty subtly changed, in retrospect, his point of view. His contemporary journals reflect none of the prejudice against the pilgrims and their faith evident in the bitter narrative he subsequently published. But Doughty's influence did not lie in his style, whose distinctive tedium, the transliteration of Arabic terms for which English equivalents existed, Lawrence avoided. It lay in Lawrence's acceptance that a carefully wrought style was a necessity. When he had asked Doughty what had prompted him to visit Arabia, the old man gave reply which has become famous: 'to redeem the English language from the slough into which it had fallen since the time of Spenser.' Lawrence had taken a complete Spenser with him to Carchemish; Malory's *Morte d'Arthur* had accompanied him into the desert.

The influence he missed, not the influences he accepted, constituted Lawrence's misfortune. At a time when he could have been affected by Ezra Pound—whom his brother Will had invited to address an Oxford literary society—Lawrence was still too conformist to see the value of the American's innovatory demands. When Pound did visit Lawrence in his rooms at All Souls, it was too late. ***Seven Pillars of Wisdom*** had already been written in a style echoing the Butcher and Lang translations of Homer and heavily influenced by the Georgian poets whom Pound demolished.

Georgian poetry, in its now forgotten day linked with Sir John Squire and his friend Eddie Marsh, represented the anaemic old age of Victorian vigour. How disastrously Lawrence was committed to its values is shown in the handwritten anthology of poems, [***Minorities***], 'in a minor key', or 'my box of moral éclairs', which he presented to Charlotte Shaw in 1927. The first half of what finally numbered 112 poems were written down during the four years when he was composing and revising ***Seven Pillars of Wisdom.*** Apart from poems by such friends as Sassoon and Hardy, Lawrence selected the flowery, the weakly sad. He copied three complete poems by Swinburne, the poet in one respect so close to him. They derive from *Songs Before Sunrise,* composed after the poet had withdrawn to Putney, not from the period of Swinburne's revolutionary and self-revelatory strength.

The brutality of Lawrence's material helped to offset the 'faintly Ninetyish-plus-Edwardian flavour' which Cecil Day Lewis, otherwise an admirer, found in his poetic taste. 'The poet's secret', Graves complains, 'Lawrence envisaged as a technical mastery of words rather than as a particular mode of living and thinking.' Yet Lawrence's way of living and thinking gives ***Seven Pillars of Wisdom*** much of its interest, whether we account him 'one of the greatest beings alive in our time' [see Winston Churchill's essay in *T. E. Lawrence by His Friends,* edited by A. W. Lawrence, in Additional Bibliography], 'a disgusting little thing', or simply a fascinating human puzzle. If Pound's correcting pencil had deflected him for archaizing diction and the over-use of adjectives, it would surely have been as helpful to him as it was to Eliot and Hemingway. The narrative would have moved faster; the reader would have lost the sensation of swimming, for much of the time, through fudge. Too late, Lawrence discovered the merits of post-Spenserian prose. On receipt of Hogarth's life of Doughty he was to write: 'He [Doughty] loved Spenser and Chaucer—with so little love of literature and poetry that he loved them for what they did not have in common with the trunk of greatness in English letters.' But Lawrence wrote this when his career as a creative writer was over. (pp. 246-48)

If [his other full-length prose work, ***The Mint,***] had been published in the 1920s—perhaps, like *Ulysses* and *Lady Chatterley's Lover,* in France—it could have won Lawrence new fame as a literary innovator. For if ***Seven Pillars of Wisdom*** looked back, ***The Mint*** anticipated what the social realists of the 1930s were to attempt with infrequent success. Lawrence had made a writer's most generous sacrifice: it was also the price for continuing a service career which satisfied him and seemed to his prominent male relations a safe way of keeping a deviant hero under control. (p. 268)

Desmond Stewart, in his T. E. Lawrence, *Harper & Row, Publishers, 1977, 352 p.*

STEPHEN ELY TABACHNICK (essay date 1978)

[*In the following excerpt from his biographical and critical study of Lawrence, Tabachnick discusses the literary style of* Seven Pillars of Wisdom *and* The Mint.]

Although we no longer see [Lawrence] as portrayed in the posed photographs of Lowell Thomas, another figure in the Rudolph Valentino "Sheikh of Araby" texture of the 1920s, his life remains interesting as a true paradigm of the conflicts of romantic men who live into our century. In his role as a character in his own poetic autobiography, he proves one of the first examples in our century of the phenomenon of culture shock, and ***Seven Pillars*** becomes a glaring and unsettling mirror of his plight.

Our question, however, is not whether Lawrence led an interesting life (he did), but whether or not he produced good literature from it. The literary critic must use Lawrence's life to illuminate his books, and not vice versa. Biographers may share with historians the hard task of sifting documentary evidence; but the literary critic has ***Seven Pillars*** and ***The Mint*** before him. A cool, impartial, and scrupulous literary analysis of both books inevitably leads to the conclusion that Lawrence the artist speaks to us in a voice different and greater than that of Lawrence of Arabia, and certainly much more permanent. (pp. 26-7)

If style—the right word in the right place, according to Coleridge—is important in fiction, it is particularly and even more so in poetic autobiography, where the author's *primary* concern is not the presentation of an exciting plot or the depth psychology of a group of characters, but the forceful exposition of his own personality, which he does not fully understand. The poetic autobiographer reveals himself to the reader most clearly not by recording inner and outer events, the significance of which he does not always fully grasp himself, but through his manner of expressing himself. This manner clues us in as it were on what he really thinks about the events he describes, and hence on who he is. And in fact poetic autobiographers, like Thoreau, Whitman, Yeats, and James (to name only a few), are all masters of style.

As R. P. Blackmur correctly noticed, the true unity of Lawrence's ***Seven Pillars*** lies not in the military framework, which only superficially holds the book together, but in Lawrence's own sensibility, those elements of his personality which make Lawrence who he is and not someone else. . . . (p. 124)

His method of styling his work was first to write down his sentences quickly and spontaneously, as we see in his claim that Book 6 "was written entire between sunrise and sunset" . . . and that ninety-five percent of Text II was written in thirty days. Then he would return over the sentences again and again, making sure that each captured his individuality. So Lawrence's style has both a romantic spontaneity, a very deep expression of his feelings at the moment of writing, *and* a very deliberate and conscious polish. (pp. 125-26)

[The] result of Lawrence's polishing is highly complex, sophisticated, artificial (in the sense of being unlike normal speech) prose rather than a Mozart-like purity and simplicity and clarity. Although Lawrence felt that "Simplicity is as often the mark of a first-class work as complexity is of second-class work," . . . he also felt that . . . his own complex style grew naturally out of his own personality and experience and thus suited the post-World War I age even as it appeared to be a throwback to the nineteenth century. (p. 126)

Even if Lawrence is always complex, even when appearing simple, the alert reader notices that ***Seven Pillars*** is written in more than one style. . . . [Hence, some] critics stress the adventure story, and thus see the book as highly structured; others, following without understanding the story of the two veils, see only fluctuating confusion. Some critics stress the "limpid" style of the narrative sections, while others decry Lawrence's style as involved or muddy because they emphasize the "gummy" reflective style. The end to this confusion lies in the realization that ***Seven Pillars*** is a whole poetic autobiography which follows the principles of its genre.

The thing that all Lawrence's styles in ***Seven Pillars*** have in common is a high-powered complexity, the response Lawrence found most suitable for his own personality and the age, and which reminds us of his love for powerful motorcycle, motorboat, and airplane engines. The whole of the "Strangeness and Pain" chapter is written in a prose influenced by the throb of airplane engines, as Lawrence tells us himself. (pp. 127-28)

By arranging his styles across a spectrum of the amount of personality they contain, we see the full range of Lawrence's psyche and ability as a writer. (p. 129)

When we speak of the "amount of personality" in each of Lawrence's styles, what we mean is the *degree of involvement* of Lawrence in his subject matter that the reader detects by observing stylistic features. If the prose is highly complex, involuted and "gummy" (to use Forster's term [see excerpt dated 1924]), Lawrence is too deeply involved in his subject matter to view it objectively—and this is the case with his chapters on his own personality, 99, 100, and 103. If the prose is full of closely observed details but is basically clear and cool, we have the strange mixture of involvement and detachment that we get in scenes of horrors, like the beating at Deraa and the Turkish military barracks, and the earlier execution of Hamed.

If, on the other hand, the prose is cool, lacking in highly colored adjectives, and composed of simple elements rather than many interlocking parallel elements, then we have the analytical distance of the Lawrence who considers military alternatives or views the Arab Revolt only as a tool for British victory or describes the desert: but even in these instances of relative uninvolvement we should notice that some amount of involvement, of personality, is always present, that Lawrence never wrote one sentence that did not indicate some kind of involvement, at least in ***Seven Pillars.*** We can call those styles in which a relatively high degree of involvement is indicated Lawrence's "Arab veil" styles; and those which reveal distance and detachment, his "British veil" styles. Arranged in a spectrum, the styles look like this:

Maximum
involvement
and introspection

Lawrence's Arab Veil

1. Reflective: Chapters 99, 100, 103—Lawrence's personality.
2. Romantic: "Strangeness and Pain," Death of Ferraj, "S. A." poem, Charge of Tallal, Portraits of Feisal and Auda
3. Horrorific: Torture at Deraa, Massacre at Tafas, Turkish barracks at Damascus, Execution of Hamed
4. Action Narrative: Blowing up railway, Rush on Akaba, Battle of Tafileh

Lawrence's British Veil

5. Patriotic: British desire to better world (Introductory chapter); Allenby; Capture of Jerusalem
6. Descriptive: desert, seasons
7. Strategic: Chapter 33, "House of War"
8. Historical-Analytical: Syria in Chapters 4 and 58; Criticism of Feisal, Arab Revolt, and British commanders before Allenby

Minimum
involvement
and introspection

(pp. 129-30)

Lawrence's stylistic spectrum reveals much of the man as he saw himself during the period of the Arab Revolt. But as much as he manages to project through the formal elements of ***Seven Pillars,*** a good part of his personality remains veiled, hidden, and impervious to scholarly unraveling—just as he intended it to be. Each reader must create his own Lawrence, perhaps after his own image, and this effect may be Lawrence's greatest achievement as an artist. Whichever Lawrence the reader takes away from ***Seven Pillars of Wisdom*** will be one of the greatest characters in all literature. (p. 136)

In ***The Mint,*** we have only the British veil—in plot line at any rate—and a more constricted one than in ***Seven Pillars.*** Instead of grand strategy, interesting description of exotic scenery and equally exotic historical events and the pressures of war, ***The Mint*** contains only the daily hardship of basic training and Lawrence's feeling of the importance of air travel. Neither the men nor the events—internal and external—match the keyed-up excitement of the earlier book, and the deliberately anti-romantic style of clipped sentences and abrupt chapters reveals the new straitjacketed constriction of the life of the narrator-protagonist. By joining the R.A.F., Lawrence deliberately forced himself into a "mint" which would amputate his will and hold his fragmented self together with external pressure. Unfortunately, as a literary character he is much more interesting when the pressure of strangeness, pain, and war causes his personality to come apart at the seams, and when his struggle to hold himself together is embodied in a wide variety of styles and situations. ***The Mint*** follows "a hard act to follow," ***Seven Pillars,*** and by contrast is simply too attenuated and narrow a view of life—despite the adventure of speed and air—to excite strong partisanship.

At the same time that we make this comparative artistic judgment, we should bear in mind that ***The Mint*** contains the important story of Lawrence's reintegration as a person and his reintegration into society—somewhat analogous to Henry Fleming's journey into himself in Crane's *Red Badge of Courage* and Ishmael's reconciliation with man and nature in *Moby Dick*—of his reconciliation with his own body and psyche and that of other human beings through a newfound opening of the sense of touch, hitherto experienced only with Dahoum if at all. ***The Mint*** thus completes the process of alienation and detachment with a joyous fulfillment unglimpsed in ***Seven Pillars.***

Like ***Seven Pillars, The Mint*** is clearly a poetic autobiography, in which we glimpse aspects of the narrator-protagonist's personality even more clearly than in the earlier book; ultimately however he remains a mystery. The central question of *why* he joined the R.A.F. as a private is imperfectly answered, and the book thus contains an element almost as shadowy as the S. A. and Deraa stories of ***Seven Pillars.*** Again like ***Seven Pillars, The Mint*** contains first and foremost the story of Lawrence's personality rather than that of recruit training or the development of the air force. All events in the book are seen through his eyes, filtered through his personality, and the spotlight shines fully only on him. This is not the tale of any man undergoing training, but that of T. E. Lawrence, or Ross, or Shaw, the fallen colonel, submitting himself to a new but inherently less interesting and exciting trial of self-control and willful self-debasement.

As in ***Seven Pillars,*** the core of ***The Mint*** is a personal chapter . . . , "Odd Man Out," in which Lawrence analyzes the elements of his character in clearer language than he does in the "Myself" chapter of ***Seven Pillars.*** We notice the same elements; a love of physical testing and the power to withstand pain; the intellectual shyness and selfconsciousness that makes life in public a torture *and* the forcing of the self into public life, again as a test; fear of failing to measure up to impossible, absolute physical and mental standards that only Lawrence could set for himself; a fear of sexuality and touch which is largely resolved by the end of Part 3; and a fascination with pain and degradation, shown especially in the portrait of "Our Commanding Officer" . . . ; and finally an aestheticism which informs his whole view of his surroundings.

The difference in personal content between the two books is that ***The Mint*** presents an experiment, Lawrence's conscious attempt to "end his civil war and live the open life, patent for everyone to read." . . . He wants to overcome his fears and fragmentation and amazingly succeeds by the end of the book. (pp. 137-39)

Seven Pillars has made Lawrence's distress so intimate and interesting to us that we are reluctant to accept the fact that he actually reconciled his fragments, solved his civil war, and became on the whole happy; but his letters make plain that such was the case, that he was very reluctant to leave the R.A.F. and that at some intellectual expense became to a large degree the gifted but normal R.A.F. mechanic who wrote **"A Handbook to the 37½ Foot Motor Boats of the 200 Class"** (1933). In 1934, he writes John Buchan that he is resigning from the R.A.F. because of his age, "But if I could have remained perpetually young, nothing would have pleased me better" than to remain enlisted. And in a fragment from a projected sequel to ***The Mint*** he states this even more clearly: "The wrench this is; I shall feel like a lost dog when I leave—or when it leaves me, rather, for the R.A.F. goes on. The strange attraction in the feel of the clothes, the work, the companionship. A direct touch with men, obtained in no other way in life." . . . (pp. 141-42)

Lawrence's sincerity in making these statements and in writing the conclusion to ***The Mint*** may be called into question by critics who have not themselves been in the army, and who are therefore skeptical about the positive aspect of army experience about which Lawrence writes so simply and truly. Military service can in fact offer the kind of comradeship and satisfaction that would be available in no other way to an intellectual like Lawrence. The fact that two excellent critics [E. M. Forster and V. S. Pritchett] have found the most sincere and direct writing in the book in its third section further substantiates the feeling of Lawrence's honesty that the reader experiences in this section. Fortunately or unfortunately, intelligent readers frequently prefer their heroes to remain unhappy rather than totally fulfilled at the end of a book. Ironically, the personal happiness revealed in ***The Mint*** makes far less interesting reading than the intense and exotic suffering that forms the basis of ***Seven Pillars.*** Perhaps it is true that suffering is essential to the highest art.

In addition to the difference in content, ***The Mint*** displays two formal differences from ***Seven Pillars:*** the use of the present tense and the tight, clipped style including the brief, abrupt chapters. ***Seven Pillars*** was composed under the pressure of immediate recollection, but apart from dialogue, it is written in the past tense. Since ***The Mint*** is transcribed directly from notes written on the spot (in its first two sections) and from notes and letters at a somewhat greater distance in time (in its third section), Lawrence chooses present-tense narration throughout. . . . Thus ***The Mint*** is autobiography that tends in the direction of the diary, and it gains a certain immediacy as a result. Its strikingly etched, memorable scenes are not mirror images of reality, but rather photographs taken through the distorting lens of his personality, and they have the immediate impact of photographs. (pp. 142-43)

The effect of the stringing together of this series of distorted photos and the summing up of their meaning . . . is like that of a documentary film narrated from a certain point of view, with a certain message to impress, very immediate but restricted in content—like an unusually artistic military training film in fact. This filmlike immediacy is also the result of the book's style of writing. Clipped, abrupt, generally lacking in but not without rich diction, Lawrence's style in ***The Mint*** keeps us rivetted to the surface of immediate events rather than propelled to airy heights of thought or writhing in involuted uneasiness. Lawrence chose this style deliberately to express the new constriction of his self, and his changed circumstances. . . . (p. 143)

The fact that this new situation is not nearly as interesting as the old, and that Lawrence's personality is less pressured and consequently less divided and mysterious for us, should not blind us to an interesting experiment in autobiographical form. For ***The Mint*** is poetic autobiography, but in the form of a documentary film, complete with distorting lenses, a series of sharp frames (or chapters) moving past us, rather than a rich deep mysterious self-portrait in oils. As Lawrence pointed out in a letter to Mrs. Shaw in the British Library collection, neither ***The Mint*** nor ***Seven Pillars*** owes anything to Joyce. But in its fast-moving immediacy, as in its paean to the air force, ***The Mint*** remains a tribute to twentieth-century technology. It is the first autobiography to meet the film on its own ground. (p. 144)

Stephen Ely Tabachnick, in his T. E. Lawrence, *Twayne Publishers, 1978, 174 p.*

M. D. ALLEN (essay date 1984)

[*In the following excerpt, Allen examines the medieval sensibility of Lawrence as it relates to his works.*]

As a schoolboy and young man, Lawrence threw himself into antiquarian pursuits with formidable thoroughness. Perhaps the first awakening of interest in the past occurred when he watched his father at his various hobbies, which included the study of the architecture of castles and cathedrals; and any smoldering enthusiasm for the Middle Ages would have been fanned into flame by the reminders of the past to be found in many of Oxford's streets. Turn-of-the-century Oxford may have lost a little of its former glory, but only forty-three years before the Lawrences moved there, "Oxford was still in its outward aspect a medieval city, 'a vision of grey-roofed houses and a long winding street and the sound of many bells,' as William Morris later described it." Morris's disciple Lawrence found himself in a more modern environment; even so, had he been offered the opportunity, he could hardly have chosen a place that would have better stimulated interest in the past. (p. 53)

Lawrence studied Oxford's Gothic buildings, especially those of the Perpendicular, "late" Gothic period, such as Merton College and the Cloisters of New College. He frequented the Ashmolean and University museums and the Bodleian and Radcliffe libraries; he studied medieval pottery and made a collection of brass rubbings. One expert reports Mrs. Lawrence as informing him that "a few of her son's best efforts [at brass rubbing] were presented to the Ashmolean Museum, Oxford, as they were found to be of superior quality to some of the examples housed in the collection there." The museum's manuscript catalog, prepared by the Oxford Architectural and Historical Society, was "largely amended and corrected by Lawrence himself, and the characteristic handwriting appears on many of its pages." Obviously, this argues for a great deal of erudition on Lawrence's part.

A thorough knowledge of monumental brasses demands a knowledge of armor and heraldry, for it is impossible to understand a brass properly if one cannot date it roughly by any armor borne by the engraved figure, and "the heraldry of a brass can, to the discerning, be almost as informative about those commemorated as the inscriptions." Lawrence made a friend of Charles J. ffoulkes, who lectured on armor at Oxford University in 1909-10. On ffoulkes's behalf he later looked in Syria for a man who still practiced the "mystery craft" of chain-mail making. With a schoolboy friend he compiled heraldic rolls of arms, "painted in their proper tinctures. . . . A herald's jargon eventually enriched the vocabulary of the ***Seven Pillars***." By the time he was fifteen, Lawrence had traversed the southern and eastern counties on brass-rubbing expeditions; two years later he had exhausted most accessible British examples of Gothic architecture and in the summer of 1906 began a series of vacation trips to France.

To read the letters to his family dating from these tours is to receive an impression of intellectual and physical vigor, of a rather precarious pride, and of a consciousness of latent capacities. Disbarred from smooth social or even unquestioned acceptance in many "suitable" careers by his illegitimacy and personal eccentricity, Lawrence found comfort and involvement in exploration of another age, and, to a great extent, identification with its values. Lawrence's interests enabled him to distance himself, emotionally and physically, from the combination of town and time that made demands he could not or would not fulfill.

Lawrence's interests were also in tune with some of the artistic and literary preoccupations of the day. The Pre-Raphaelites praised medieval Italian painting. Ruskin claimed that the ugly was not a suitable subject for treatment in art: this seemed to exclude much of the contemporary world of an increasingly industrial England. (Lawrence closely read "The Nature of Gothic," the chapter of *Stones of Venice* in which the social implications of Ruskin's medievalism are made clear, and its influence in theme and phrase on ***Seven Pillars*** and ***The Mint*** is plain to see. Lawrence saw in Ruskin's distinction between "servile ornament" and "the mediaeval, or especially Christian, system of ornament" a parallel to—it was probably an inspiration for—his own differentiation between the natures and roles of regular armed forces and Arab guerrillas). Morris, whom Lawrence resembled so much and whose rebellion against late Victorian England and its values took a practical turn, as Lawrence's own was later to, made plans as a young man for an "Order" or "Brotherhood," and wrote to a friend that "We must enlist you in this crusade and holy warfare against the age."

In the summer of 1906 Lawrence cycled vigorously and pursued his medieval interests with satisfying completeness. Technical terms pepper the loving and detailed letters sent back to Oxford, and Lawrence's capacity for imaginatively reconstructing his period in practical specifics is in evidence. . . . (pp. 54-5)

However, the writing by which we should judge Lawrence's intellectual development as an adolescent and young man is the thesis that he presented in addition to his Finals papers in 1910, then entitled "The Influence of the Crusades on European Military Architecture to the End of the Twelfth Century" and now known as ***Crusader Castles***. . . . It is impossible for a layman to comment on the validity of the work, which, in direct opposition to the generally accepted view of the time, claimed that "the Crusading architects were for many years copyists of the Western builders." In other words, according to Lawrence, the Crusaders did not take back to Europe from Byzantine examples their knowledge of engineering and fortification but brought it with them to the East from their home countries. The dispute has still not been finally settled, but it seems that Lawrence, with characteristic originality and self-consciousness, overstated his case. Modern experts believe that there was more mutual influence than earlier scholars had accepted or—in the other direction—than Lawrence admitted. Lawrence's work assisted in the modification of views, but he went too far.

As a definitive statement on the evolution of twelfth-century military architecture, ***Crusader Castles*** may not therefore be acceptable. As evidence of remarkable reading and traveling, consequent remarkable knowledge, and the ability to master ideas and handle them to suit a purpose, it is eminently so. Lawrence is sufficiently sure of his grasp of the topic to interpret, in a prose that is consistently fluid and self-confident, a mass of complex and technical detail in a way that supports his thesis (he had made up his mind before leaving Europe, of course). (pp. 56-7)

The B.A. thesis is something of a triumph. Not only is it a precocious work of learning still treated with respect (although with caution too) by experts today, but it also represents the successful imposition of a view that its holder finds comfortable and heartening onto a large amount of technical detail of absorbing interest—and hence by extension onto chaotic life itself, which—challenges, threats, promises, and all—was just opening before Lawrence. This imposition does no violence to the understanding of author or reader. (p. 58)

When, six years after writing his thesis, Lawrence began fighting with the Arabs, he found a number of similarities between the societies depicted in his favorite reading and that society he was trying to influence to fight the Turks. At one point in ***Seven Pillars*** Lawrence refers to the "chivalrous semi-feudalism" of the Druses, but the phrase will do well to describe a Beduin society too. The nomadic Beduin obviously did not (or do not) have a system that revolves around service in exchange for land tenure. But they are represented as having a flexible hierarchical society with hereditary privileges, the Sherif of Mecca and his sons, descendants of the Prophet, being at the summit. The revolt involves curiously anachronistic fighting.

Pen-and-ink sketch by Lawrence of Sahyun, from Crusader Castles I: The Thesis. *By permission of the Houghton Library, Harvard University.*

In real contrast to the battles taking place in Flanders, the outcome of Arab engagements can be visibly affected by the courage and prowess of an individual warrior; men fight under their territorial (i.e., tribal) leaders; a man can make a speech to his sword, by name, before beginning to fight. . . . Arab society tends toward intertribal warfare, which is the means of obtaining honor and profit (Auda Abu Tayi, the possessor of an "immense chivalrous name," . . . is careful to have quarrels with all his neighbors), but rules are observed and the Arabs are horrified when they are broken. . . . The Turks are not chivalrous enemies, and ***Seven Pillars*** contains more than one account of bloody massacre, Turk and reciprocal Arab. But the elements of medieval conflict at its best are present; and an eccentricity such as the "confirmed smoker" Feisal's sending pack animals loaded with cheap cigarettes to a tobaccoless enemy garrison is an incident from a war that is personal, individual, archaic, as is Abdullah's writing an exultant letter to a Turkish commander (Fakri Pasha), telling him of an important capture of Turkish booty and leaving it where it would be found and passed on.

The war is, moreover, fought upon historic ground, sometimes under "the old Crusader fort of Monreale . . . very noble against the night sky." . . . (pp. 58-60)

A medievalist's account of such a war, fought in such a region, will produce some interesting results. So far we have seen an idealistic and somewhat dreamy attitude toward the place and circumstances in which Lawrence, by extraordinary good luck (or, more portentously, fate), found himself. But he was not fighting in the heyday or even the decadence of chivalry, but in the twentieth century, and this fact must make itself evident.

Lawrence tries to link his war to the Crusades by his use of heraldic language in ***Seven Pillars***. His study of heraldry had made its jargon part of his idiolect. . . . Lawrence, furthermore, was growing up at a time when the study of heraldry was becoming intellectually respectable again. He read not only genuinely medieval works but also the poetry of Tennyson and the Pre-Raphaelites, who inherited something of the romantic attitude toward heraldry. (pp. 60-1)

The letter of 9 August 1906 (which should be read in this context) describing Léhon Abbey in northern France shows Lawrence to be a competent, if not omniscient, amateur herald. He is familiar with the stylized depiction of an eagle when a charge on a coat of arms; he knows the heraldic use of *badge*, and what is meant by *billets or*. Heraldic terminology invaded his letters in nonheraldic contexts, precursors of his usages in ***Seven Pillars:*** "All the country is of one colour," he wrote home of Syria, "a murrey brown, but very subtly beautiful." The OED reports "murrey" as historical or archaic, and gives no example of it in literary use after 1847. "[Indian] wall hangings are usually stamped with yellow figures of tigers ramping" he told a brother—"ramping" almost certainly being inspired by "rampant." When he read *Le Petit Jehan de Saintré* in 1910, he would have learned about the duties of heralds and improved his knowledge of explicitly French heraldic language, for chapter fifty-eight consists largely of a list of the men who, la Sale claims, accompanied Saintré on crusade and their coats of arms, described in properly technical language. (p. 61)

How then does Lawrence apply this learning? The Arabs did bear before them the plain crimson flag ("crimson" is Lawrence's word, and nonheraldic) of the Hashemites, the family claiming descent from Mohammed. The flags are referred to as banners and the men who carry them called standard bearers, somewhat inconsistently. With that exception, heraldic terminology must be used in ***Seven Pillars*** in a transferred sense, not describing concisely and unambiguously lines and shapes on a shield but lines and shapes in the writer's surroundings. (But it may be noted here that a standard—a swallow-tailed flag bearing badges and motto, with the arms themselves perhaps in the hoist—was last used in war in the Palestine campaign of 1917, by Commander and Lt.-Col. H. Pirie-Gordon of Buthlaw. Pirie-Gordon does not appear in ***Seven Pillars,*** but he was a friend of Lawrence's.) It is characteristic of Lawrence's borrowings that not even the most unbending purist could object to them as abusing heraldic language. They create resonances for any reader of ***Seven Pillars*** who has even a tyro's knowledge of heraldry. (pp. 61-2)

During the Arab Revolt, Lawrence was sustained by chivalric dreams, and took refuge in them when reality was discouraging ("In my saddle-bags was a *Morte d' Arthur*. It relieved my disgust." . . .) But even ***Seven Pillars,*** in which a high-minded antique campaign is high-mindedly recalled, is invested by some suspicions about the contingency of the chivalric ethos. In ***The Mint*** . . . Lawrence is wary of phlegmatic northerners:

> Perhaps, in days of Chivalry, even the north took the parade of arms lovingly, and throbbed at the feel of swords, the sight of banners. Perhaps: though I've chased through mediaeval literature after the days of chivalry, and found their revivals, and legends or reminiscences or ridicule of them, but never the real thing. Today these modes are right out of tune with the social system, whose firm-seatedness makes one doubt if an Englishman's blood can ever have flowed hotly enough for him to swallow a tomfoolery divorced from alcohol.

The writing of ***Seven Pillars*** was an attempt to add a book to the shelf of "titanic" works Lawrence admired. One of these "big books" is *Don Quixote,* which, by recounting the absurd adventures of the deluded would-be knight-errant (who is not quite as anachronistic as the "Arabian knight"), satirizes romances inspired by the chivalry Lawrence here fears never really existed, at least in the North. (pp. 63-4)

Lawrence knew that he lived in an age of the relative outlook. He contrasted himself with C. M. Doughty, who "had a fixed point in his universe, and from one fixed point a moralist will . . . build up the whole scheme of creation." He contrasted himself with Herbert Read, who, in reviewing ***Seven Pillars*** [see excerpt dated 1927], said that "Great books are written in moods of spiritual light and intellectual certainty." He knew that he was not the only twentieth-century medievalist to be aware of the conflict between relative and absolute. James Branch Cabell, the American author of a number of stories set in a fictional Poictesme of the Middle Ages, had a cynical explanation for chivalry's popularity. It appeals to man's pride "through an assumption of man's responsibility in his tiniest action." The chivalrous man considers himself God's representative on earth; he is supported by a "flattering notion of divine vicarship. . . . There is no cause for wonder that the appeal was irresistible, when to each man it thus admitted that he himself was the one thing seriously to be considered."

Lawrence had read Cabell's *Jurgen* (1919), an ironic retelling of the solar myth of regained youth, and admired it. The eponym of the "comedy of justice," possessor of a young body and an experienced heart, spends some time at the court of Glathion, where the chivalric ethos is highly regarded but imperfectly practiced. Jurgen spends his time not unpleasantly, seducing the Guenevere who will later marry Arthur (and finding her much like other women when the barriers are down, and before), but he is made uncomfortable by the inability to believe in the wisdom of an omnipotent creator and the doubts that flow from that inability. "And all the while he fretted because he could just dimly perceive that ideal which was served in Glathion, and the beauty of this ideal, but could not possibly believe in it. . . . Jurgen abode among these persons to whom life was a high-hearted journeying homeward. God the Father awaited you there, ready to punish at need, but eager to forgive, after the manner of all fathers: that one became a little soiled in traveling . . . was a matter which fathers understood." Serving the king is an idea not to be taken seriously, for the king "was a person whom Jurgen simply could not imagine any intelligent Deity selecting as steward." The chivalic conception of courtly love cannot be taken seriously: "when it came to serving women, what sort of service did women most cordially appreciate? Jurgen had his answer pat enough, but it was an answer not suitable for utterance in mixed company." Everywhere is self-deceit. In the week of tourneys and feasting preceding Guenevere's being taken to London for marriage, "dukes and earls and barons and many famous knights" contend for honor "and a trumpery chaplet of pearls."

Cabell, Jurgen, and Lawrence believe they have asked for bread and have been given a stone. It is impossible not to fail one's vision and high-colored ambitions after adolescence, despite one's longing for a world in which they could be honored. Jurgen, second time round, kills the man who in reality married Dorothy la Désirée, the local lord's daughter, whom, for one idyllic youthful summer, he had loved and been loved by. Jurgen's words to his victim are "it is highly necessary you die tonight, in order that my soul may not perish too many years before my body."

They are words that Lawrence remembered. Sherif Nasir is one version of the perfect warrior. The same romantic aura surrounds him that surrounds Auda Abu Tayi, whose first appearance is followed by a page and a half of almost infatuated description ("knight-errant . . . saga . . . heroic . . . poems of old raids and epic tales of fights" . . .), that surrounds the armed prophet Feisal, "black against the sun, whose light threw a queer haze about his slender figure, and suffused his head with gold, through the floss-silk of his head-cloth." . . . But Nasir, with his sophisticated Medina background, is the Arab most like Lawrence. He stands out in the glorious court and military life of Arab warriors and aristocrats. He lives in an alien world. "[H]e was body-weary after months of vanguard service, and mind-weary too, with the passing of youth's careless years. He feared his maturity as it grew upon him, with its ripe thought, its skill, its finished art; yet which lacked the poetry of boyhood to make living a full end of life. Physically he was young yet: but his changeful and mortal soul was ageing quicker than his body—going to die before it, like most of ours." . . . "[I]n most men," Lawrence later writes, "the soul grew aged long before the body." . . . (pp. 65-7)

Lawrence always maintained a belief in the possibility of chivalric action, in the twentieth century and before. But after the horrors of the war, particularly the traumatic Deraa episode, he forsook honor for himself. Although Lawrence was able to lose himself in idealistic effort and ambition when writing ***Seven Pillars*** (and thus recalling earlier efforts), true heroism otherwise seemed often nebulous and far away. This pessimistic view is reflected in a letter written after a trip to Glastonbury in 1924 to see a musical version of Thomas Hardy's *The Famous Tragedy of the Queen of Cornwall*. Glastonbury is identified by Giraldus Cambrensis with Avalon; it is where the tomb of Arthur and Guenevere was found in the reign of Henry II. "[I]ts tremendous past makes one walk expectant in the streets, so that the smallest sign is a wonder: only why (except to try us) is all the wonder of the Abbey sunk to a perfectly-preserved kitchen?" The principal actors did not impress. Perhaps Tristram gave most offense. "[He] was fat faced, & shiny-faced, with a long turned-up nose, & glittering lecherous eyes. His mouth slobbered, & when he hugged, or was hugged by the pair of Iseults the satisfaction on his face was too horrible for words. Of course it may have been true, & Tristram far from being heroic may have been just a stout greasy snarer of women." That last sentence gives us some indication of Lawrence's final submission. (pp. 67-8)

M. D. Allen, "Lawrence's Medievalism," in The T. E. Lawrence Puzzle, *edited by Stephen E. Tabachnick, The University of Georgia Press, 1984, pp. 53-70.*

ADDITIONAL BIBLIOGRAPHY

Anderegg, Michael A. "Lawrence of Arabia: The Man, the Myth, the Movie." *Michigan Quarterly Review* XXI, No. 2 (Spring 1982): 281-300.*

Focuses primarily on cinematic technique and theme in David Lean's 1962 film "Lawrence of Arabia" and offers insight into the Lawrence persona.

Armitage, Flora. *The Desert and the Stars*. New York: Henry Holt and Co., 1955, 318 p.

Detailed account of Lawrence's life.

Bonsal, Stephen. "The Arabs Plead for Freedom: Emir Faisal, Colonel Lawrence, and Gertrude Bell—The Desert Queen." In his *Suitor and Suppliants: The Little Nations at Versailles*, pp. 32-51. New York: Prentice-Hall, 1946.*

Diary account discussing the actions of the Arab delegation to the Peace Conference in 1919.

Brent, Peter. *T. E. Lawrence*. New York: G. P. Putnam's Sons, 1975, 232 p.

Biographical treatment which emphasizes the connection between Lawrence's illegitimacy and his self-deprecatory behavior.

Clements, Frank. *T. E. Lawrence: A Reader's Guide*. Hamden, Connecticut: Shoe String Press, 1973, 208 p.

Annotated bibliography of works by, about, and relevant to Lawrence.

De Rougemont, Denis. "Prototype T.E.L." In his *Dramatic Personages*, translated by Richard Howard, pp. 135-51. New York: Holt, Rinehart and Winston, 1964.

Searches for the essence of Lawrence's political morality.

Eden, Matthew. *The Murder of Lawrence of Arabia*. New York: Thomas Y. Crowell Publishers, 1979, 271 p.

Fictional reconstruction of the events leading up to Lawrence's death.

Graves, Richard Perceval. *Lawrence of Arabia and His World*. New York: Charles Scribner's Sons, 1976, 127 p.

Heavily illustrated general study of Lawrence.

Howe, Irving. "T. E. Lawrence: The Problem of Heroism. *The Hudson Review* XV, No. 3 (Autumn 1962): 333-64.

Finds that the progressive revelation of Lawrence's personality in *Seven Pillars of Wisdom* is the central factor underlying the book's profound impact on the reader.

Hull, Denis Boak. "Malraux and T. E. Lawrence." *Modern Language Review* LXI, No. 2 (April 1966): 218-24.*

Examines the philosophical and aesthetic ties between Lawrence and the author considered his French counterpart, André Malraux.

Hull, Keith N. "T. E. Lawrence's Perilous Parodies." *The Texas Quarterly* XV, No. 2 (Summer 1972): 56-61.

Investigation of Lawrence's concept of parody as related to his employment of conventional military tactics during the Arab Revolt and to his accompanying battle accounts in *Seven Pillars of Wisdom*.

Hyde, H. Montgomery. *Solitary in the Ranks: Lawrence of Arabia as Airman and Private Soldier*. New York: Atheneum, 1978, 288 p.

Study of the latter period of Lawrence's life from his initial entry into the R.A.F. until his death. Hyde supports his study with numerous excerpts from letters written by Lawrence as well as his close acquaintances.

Knight, G. Wilson. "T. E. Lawrence." In his *Neglected Powers: Essays on Nineteenth and Twentieth Century Literature*, pp. 309-51. New York: Barnes & Noble, 1971.

Overall assessment of Lawrence in which Knight compares him to Lord Byron.

Knightley, Phillip, and Simpson, Colin. *The Secret Lives of Lawrence of Arabia*. New York: McGraw-Hill Book Co., 1969, 333 p.

Revealing account of Lawrence's personal life, informed by John Bruce's exposure in 1968 of the masochistic side to Lawrence's personality and by other materials and information previously unavailable to the public.

Lawrence, A. W., ed. *T. E. Lawrence by His Friends*. Garden City, New York: Doubleday, Doran, & Co., 1937, 538 p.

Collection of appraisals and reminiscences of Lawrence by numerous personal and professional acquaintances, including Leonard Woolley, Lord Allenby, Winston Churchill, Chaim Weizmann, and Jonathan Cape.

Lewis, Wyndham. "Perspectives on Lawrence." *The Hudson Review* VIII, No. 4 (Winter 1956): 596-608.

Addresses several issues raised by Richard Aldington's biography, questioning in particular Aldington's claim that Lawrence's knowledge of his parents' true background had a profound psychological effect on him. Lewis concludes by recommending Flora Armitage's biography for its beautiful and, on the whole, accurate narrative of Lawrence's life.

Liddell Hart, Basil Henry. *T. E. Lawrence: In Arabia and After*. London: Jonathan Cape, 1934, 491 p.

Authorized biography focusing primarily on Lawrence's war years. Liddell Hart provides a high appraisal of Lawrence as a military strategist.

———. "T. E. Lawrence, Aldington, and the Truth." *The London Magazine* 2, No. 4 (April 1955): 67-75.*

Rebuts Richard Aldington's scathing biography of Lawrence.

Lönnroth, Erik. *Lawrence of Arabia: An Historical Appreciation*, translated by Ruth Lewis. London: Vallentine, Mitchell, & Co., 1956, 102 p.

Biographical and psychological assessment of Lawrence's life and work.

Malraux, André. "Lawrence and the Demon of the Absolute." *The Hudson Review* VIII, No. 4 (Winter 1956): 519-32.

Attempts to explain Lawrence's multifaceted personality and its relationship to *Seven Pillars of Wisdom*.

Meyers, Jeffrey. "E. M. Forster and T. E. Lawrence: A Friendship." *The South Atlantic Quarterly* LXIX, No. 2 (Apring 1970): 205-16.*

Examination of the views exchanged by Forster and Lawrence through letters concerning each writer's literary projects and sensibilities.

———. *The Wounded Spirit: A Study of "Seven Pillars of Wisdom."* London: Martin Brian & O'Keefe, 1973, 200 p.*

Proposes that three writers—Charles Doughty, Leo Tolstoy, and Friedrich Nietzsche—largely influenced the shape of *Seven Pillars*, either stylistically, philosophically, structurally, or thematically.

———. *T. E. Lawrence: A Bibliography*. New York: Garland Publishing, 1974, 48 p.

Unannotated list of works by and about Lawrence.

Mills, Gordon. "T. E. Lawrence as a Writer." *Texas Quarterly* V, No. 3 (Autumn 1962): 35-45.

Studies *Seven Pillars of Wisdom* in light of Lawrence's literary theory that the writer must maintain an aesthetic distance in his work.

Mousa, Suleiman. *T. E. Lawrence: An Arab View*, translated by Albert Butros. New York: Oxford University Press, 1966, 301 p.

Biography of Lawrence with special treatment of the actual nature of his contribution to the Arab Revolt. Mousa calls into question several previously held assumptions concerning these years. Appended to the biography is a commentary by A. W. Lawrence, who challenges the validity of several of Mousa's conclusions.

Muggeridge, Malcolm. "Poor Lawrence." *New Statesman* LXII, No. 1598 (27 October 1961): 604, 606.

Believes that Lawrence was "congenitally untruthful" and finds the prose in *Seven Pillars of Wisdom* lifeless: "each adjective tastefully chosen, like a virginal lady's clothes, delicately matched, fragrantly draping inviolate flesh."

O'Donnell, Thomas J. "The Confessions of T. E. Lawrence: The Sadomasochistic Hero." *American Imago* 34, No. 2 (Summer 1977): 115-32.

Analyzes *Seven Pillars* and *The Mint* as psychosexual confession.

Payne, Robert. *Lawrence of Arabia: A Triumph*. London: Almat Publishing, 1962, 256 p.

Narrative of Lawrence's life.

Philby, H. St. John. "T. E. Lawrence and His Critics." In his *Forty Years in the Wilderness*, pp. 82-109. London: Robert Hale, 1957.

High appraisal of Lawrence's literary abilities and contribution to the Arab Revolt conjoined to a denunciation of Richard Aldington's iconoclastic biography.

Phillips, Jill M. *T. E. Lawrence: Portrait of the Artist as Hero*. New York: Gordon Press, 1977, 441 p.

Biographical study. "What this book is meant to be," Phillips says, "is a critical, if at times, self-indulgent version of the life of a man whose greatness defies the word itself, whose talents were unorthodox, and whose very life wavered in the wistful balance between tragedy and comedy for a gross period of the time." This study devotes its last hundred pages to a critical examination of the major works written about Lawrence.

Rattigan, Terrence. *Ross: A Dramatic Portrait*. New York: Random House, 1962, 180 p.

Dramatic representation of Lawrence as an anonymous corpsman in the R.A.F. recalling his two-year participation in the Arab Revolt.

Richards, Vyvyan. *Portrait of T. E. Lawrence: The Lawrence of the "Seven Pillars of Wisdom."* London: Jonathan Cape, 1936, 255 p.

Biographical account by a close friend of Lawrence. Richards regards Lawrence as "a mystery to himself, and the *Seven Pillars* is his great effort, not perhaps to solve, but to face up to that mystery."

Robinson, Edward. *Lawrence: The Story of His Life*. London: Oxford University Press, 1935, 250 p.

Biography for the young reader.

Rutherford, Andrew. "The Intellectual as Hero: Lawrence of Arabia." In his *The Literature of War: Five Studies in Heroic Virtue*, pp. 38-63. New York: Harper & Row, 1978.

Study of Lawrence as a disillusioned hero of war.

Sperber, Manès. "False Situations: T. E. Lawrence and his Two Legends." In his *The Achilles Heel*, translated by Constantine FitzGibbon, pp. 175-204. Garden City, New York: Doubleday & Co., 1960.

Study of Lawrence's legendary dual nature. Sperber describes these two components as 1) "the glory of Napoleon" and 2) the "proud repentance" of Victor Hugo.

Steffens, Lincoln. "Armenians Are Impossible: An Interview with Lawrence of Arabia." *Outlook and Independent* 159, No. 7 (14 October 1931): 203-05, 222-24.

Interview on the subject of "backward" nations and imperialist policy (conducted in Paris during the Peace Conference in 1919).

Storrs, Ronald. *Orientations*. London: Nicholson & Watson, 1945, 532 p.*

Memoirs by a British official who served in the Middle East with Lawrence at the time of the Arab Revolt.

Tabachnick, Stephen E., ed. *The T. E. Lawrence Puzzle*. Athens: University of Georgia Press, 1984, 342 p.

Essays covering the major aspects of Lawrence's literary works and public life.

Thomas, Lowell. *With Lawrence in Arabia*. Garden City, New York: Doubleday and Co., 1967, 320 p.

Biographical study of Lawrence and the Arab Revolt which is inspired by Thomas's postwar travelog of the same name.

Weintraub, Stanley. *Private Shaw and Public Shaw: A Dual Portrait of Lawrence of Arabia and G.B.S.* New York: George Braziller, 1963, 302 p.*

A biography which explores the evolution of the Shaw-Lawrence friendship.

———. "Bernard Shaw's Other Saint Joan." *South Atlantic Quarterly* LXIV (1965): 194-205.*

Discusses the degree to which George Bernard Shaw's character Saint Joan may have been modeled on Lawrence.

Williamson, Henry. *Genius of Friendship: 'T. E. Lawrence.'* London: Faber and Faber, 1941, 78 p.

Account of the close friendship that developed between Lawrence and Williamson.

Ada Leverson

1865-1936

(Also wrote under pseudonym of Elaine) English novelist, short story writer, dramatist, poet, essayist, and journalist.

Described by Oscar Wilde as "the wittiest woman in the world," Leverson was an English novelist of the early twentieth century who belonged to London's world of wealth and fashion, and who is primarily remembered for her friendships with prominent authors and artists. In particular, she is known for her unconditional support of Wilde during and after his trial and imprisonment for committing homosexual acts. Of a retiring nature and repelled by the thought of personal publicity, much less notoriety, Leverson has, ironically, been more widely known for her involvement in Wilde's scandal than for her literary career. Her six novels, published between 1907 and 1916, are noted for their predominantly lighthearted treatment of love and marriage, their urbanity, and their clever dialogue, all of which have led some critics to underestimate the serious sentiments frequently underlying her work.

Born in London to affluent parents, Leverson was educated privately in the classics, French, German, and the broadest spectrum of English literature. Her mother, one of the best amateur pianists of her day, at times displayed more interest in entertaining contemporary musicians than in overseeing the education of her several children, evincing a passion for the arts that Leverson herself would later emulate. Well-dowered and anxious to escape parental control, Leverson was married at age nineteen to a man twelve years her senior, the son of a prosperous diamond merchant. They had two children, a son who died in early childhood and a daughter. Her husband soon demonstrated an obsessive love for gambling that superseded domestic concerns, and Leverson discovered that the remainder of her marital life was to be a compromise between the security of a marriage—however unhappy—and her need for social, sexual, and cultural fulfillment; on a holiday in Monte Carlo, for example, Ernest Leverson abandoned his wife for days at a time, leaving her to struggle with and then renounce romantic attachments she developed for the Earl of Desart and novelist George Moore. Although Leverson no longer loved her husband, her fear of scandal and solicitous concern for her family's welfare would not permit her to pursue extramarital relationships or divorce; she later chronicled the dilemma of the loveless marriage in her novels revolving around Edith Ottley, a character who, in sentiment and principle, was largely modeled after Leverson herself.

In 1892 Leverson met Oscar Wilde for the first time at one of the gala gatherings of prominent social and literary figures which was a feature of fashionable London life at the time. To Leverson, Wilde, even when answering the demands of late Victorian propriety with inflammatory candor, appeared to be a man who genuinely cared for others and was capable of eliciting their best qualities. A brilliant conversationalist during a period when such ability was admired and cultivated, Wilde established an atmosphere conducive to the flowering of Leverson's own repartee, later demonstrated in her novels' masterful dialogue. Wilde found in Leverson a woman who had a wit to match his own. Once when Wilde boasted of an admiring apache (a Parisian ruffian) who accompanied him everywhere with a knife in one hand, Leverson was heard to reply, "I'm sure he had a fork in the other!" In London literary and social life, Leverson found respite from the disappointments of her marriage. For a number of years she was the nucleus of a successful artistic salon, surrounded by an assortment of writers, wits, musicians, and people whom she considered attractive or interesting. So influential was she in furthering the careers of some struggling participants of these coteries that Grant Richards, who had been introduced to Leverson years before he became her publisher, affirmed that an "introduction to Mrs. Ernest Leverson was one of the most important things that could happen to a young man at that time."

Upon discovering that Leverson was the author of parodies and sketches which had appeared anonymously in the popular periodical *Punch,* Wilde urged her to continue her efforts. On July 21, 1894, when a parody by Leverson of his poem "The Sphinx" came to Wilde's attention, he immediately dubbed her "Sphinx," an epithet she retained throughout their friendship. Leverson wrote several stories for *Black and White* and *St. Stephen's Review* until 1895, when the editors of the distinguished periodical *The Yellow Book* invited her to become one of its contributors. However, the pleasure that Leverson should have experienced in the publication of her first story by *The Yellow Book* in 1895 was diminished by the onset of

Wilde's litigation and eventual imprisonment for homosexual practices. Because of the nature of the scandal involved, none of Wilde's friends but Leverson, who braved adverse publicity to support an individual who had always been generous to her, would agree to shelter him in the months between his trials. Wilde's rapid degeneration upon his release from prison troubled Leverson deeply, and she felt a profound sense of loss when he died.

Shortly after Wilde's death Leverson's marriage ended. Thereafter, while forced to restrain many of her generous monetary gifts, Leverson lived comfortably on her dowry and the income from writing a women's column in the *Referee*. In 1905, Leverson abandoned the *Referee* to devote her energies to a novel, *The Twelfth Hour,* published two years later. This novel and its five successors were well-received by contemporary reviewers, and Leverson enjoyed a resurgence of popularity in literary and social spheres which she had not known since her association with Wilde. She continued to be a patroness of the arts, persuading Richards to publish the writings of Edith, Sacheverell, and Osbert Sitwell, the last of whom included his impressions of her in his autobiography. Although in the last decade of her life deafness impeded Leverson's greatest pleasure—conversation—the affliction did not cause her to withdraw from the company of others. During these years Leverson spent much time abroad, particularly in Italy, where she contracted pneumonia, from which she died in London in 1936.

Ennui is the real or imagined malady most feared by the individuals who people Leverson's novels, the most important of which are *Love's Shadow, Tenterhooks,* and *Love at Second Sight,* which were originally published separately and later collected under the title *The Little Ottleys*. Leverson's fictional world faithfully reflects the appearances of her own social milieu in its definitive class distinctions between uniformed or liveried domestics and those moneyed masters and mistresses, relieved of all responsibilities short of occupying opera box seats and engaging in idle gossip. Beneath this polished veneer, which has compelled some critics to find Leverson's works insubstantial, conflicts of individual will are waged against a backdrop of conjugal loyalty independent of law or faith. In *Love's Shadow,* the activities of Edith Ottley and her husband Bruce, an insufferably conceited Foreign Office clerk, remain largely diversionary; secondary characters in the novel, they are presented as merely a mildly amusing, mismatched couple moving up in the social ranks. It is not until *Tenterhooks* that the Ottleys become principal characters, with Bruce, the comic bore, now a visible burden to his wife, who patiently endures his vanity out of a sense of duty, doggedly persevering despite the remonstrations of Aylmer, an attractive widower who is her equal in intelligence and sensitivity. Edith's sense of responsibility is unwavering when Bruce abandons her to run off to Australia with another woman, rightly anticipating that Bruce, in turn, will be jilted and will return to her. Only in *Love at Second Sight* can Edith relinquish her unhappy marriage with a clear conscience, knowing she has done all she could. World War I has begun and a wounded Aylmer returns to England from the front. The lovers' dilemma remains unchanged until Bruce again deserts Edith. While some have found Leverson's characters merely vehicles for her wit, others believe she conveys accomplished characterization deftly and swiftly in the epigrammatic dialogue which both mirrors the lively conversational style of her contemporaries and serves, much like the playbill in a drama, to decisively identify characters throughout her works. Her manner, too, of cutting briskly from one scene to another is reminiscent of drama. Leverson's open-minded acceptance of all but the mean and self-important is consistently reflected in her novels, where her tone may range from that of playful affection to one of gentle irony, but rarely dissolves into open contempt.

Despite the necessarily lighthearted aspects of her work, employed to capture the essence of Edwardian society, most commentators have noted that Leverson's astute observations on human nature are slyly insinuated and often couched in the casual witticisms of her characters. For some, who remember her solely for her kindness to Oscar Wilde or who dismiss her as the superficial recorder of a frivolous age, Colin MacInnes has observed that, though Leverson may seem "apparently uninvolved, in tone urbane, she really holds humane and moral views that determine a whole vision."

PRINCIPAL WORKS

"Claude's Aunt" (short story) 1892; published in journal *Black and White*
The Twelfth Hour (novel) 1907
**Love's Shadow* (novel) 1908
The Limit (novel) 1911
**Tenterhooks* (novel) 1912
Bird of Paradise (novel) 1914
**Love at Second Sight* (novel) 1916
Letters to the Sphinx from Oscar Wilde, with Reminiscences of the Author [editor] (letters and memoirs) 1930

*These works were published as *The Little Ottleys* in 1962.

THE BOOKMAN, LONDON (essay date 1907)

[*In the following essay, the critic disparagingly reviews* The Twelfth Hour.]

We have carefully read **"The Twelfth Hour,"** but have only hazy ideas as to what it is all about. It is present-day, the scene is London, the characters are wealthy, flippancies abound, there is nothing in the way of a plot, and the style is intended to be epigrammatical. A central figure is Lady Chetwode, a woman of great beauty and low-grade brainpower, who flirts with Society young men in the absence of her husband at race-meetings and on quests of old furniture. Lady Chetwode has a sixteen-year-old brother, a precocious young man, who is no doubt meant to be a character of the kind so successfully represented on the stage by Mr. Alfred Matthews. The author, however, has not Mr. Matthews' gift of characterisation, and the brother is only tiresome. The brother's name is Savile, and describing him, the writer, in a burst of brilliance, says:

> Savile would never eat *Reading* biscuits, because he feared that some form of condensed study was being insidiously introduced into his system.

The italics are Miss Leverson's, who has thoughtfully employed them in case the duller of her readers might miss the Great Jest. The book is freely peppered with italics . . . This is typical of its pleasantries:

> "Oh, I don't like so many flowers in the drawing-room, papa. But, if you like, I might send them

> to one of the hospitals. Perhaps the 'Home of Rest for Chows and Poodles' might—"
>
> "Ridiculous, child. They would not be appreciated there. What do our canine friends care for carnations?" He smiled with satisfaction at the phrase.

One has the impression that Miss Leverson has frequently, in the making of this book, "smiled with satisfaction" at the phrases—and with just as much justification as the parent who spoke of canines and carnations.

A review of "The Twelfth Hour," in The Bookman, *London, Vol. XXXII, No. 191, August, 1907, p. 180.*

THE ACADEMY (essay date 1908)

[*In the following essay, the critic favorably reviews* Love's Shadow.]

What a delightful group of people it is which Mrs. Ernest Leverson has selected for our delight in her latest novel [**"Love's Shadow"**] and described with a lightness of touch and a sureness of observation, a sparkling wit and penetrating humour rare indeed among novel-writers. Her book is at once a joy to readers and a model to those who feel a call to write a story of modern frivolous society, of life as lived—or played, if you will—by people whose chief object is to kill time in the pleasantest way. As a rule novelists who treat of these people have a bad habit of making them out to be hopelessly idiotic or unlikelily vicious. Mrs. Leverson has no need to conceal a want of talent or invention by such subterfuges. She does not find it necessary to be foolish in order to tickle, or nauseous in order to whet, jaded appetites. She takes her characters, just such as any one may meet every day in any drawing-room, and with her observant humour—in spite, one might almost say, of her mordant wit—she makes exquisite miniatures of them, so perfect that one might be in danger of not noticing the skill, the reticence, the restraint which unite to get the effect. The story is slight, yet full of interest—just the tale of a girl, Hyacinth, who falls in love with a young man, Cecil Reeve, who imagines himself to be in love with a fascinating widow, but who finds in the end that Hyacinth was really what he wanted. In their little love story are involved a group of people who each have an interest, an individuality of their own, and who assist the central theme in a most natural and unconscious way. All the men are more or less in love with Hyacinth, but quite nicely. *We* know it, as we see the effect their devotion has on them; but it delights us, and it makes no one in the book miserable. Even the women are attracted by her, especially her old companion Anne Yeo, the most sensible of women in everything which doesn't concern herself. The chief subsidiary couple are "the little Ottleys," so called rather from the size of their flat and their interests rather than for physical reasons. They make a perfect picture of a *ménage* only kept satisfactory by the tact of the wife, who knows exactly how to treat her husband—a good-looking, stupid, and conceited young Foreign Office clerk. They have a child who is one of the triumphs of the book; not more life-like than its elders, but how rare is it to find a child in a novel who is the child of real life, which pleases, amuses, bores us, and scores off us by its inconsequent yet direct chatter. The cleverest man, the most tactful woman, is easily "stumped" by a child, and Archie routs his elders with the most perfect ease and the most innocent intentions. It is not too much to say that all the characters are entirely satisfactory; in a few lines the author brings them before our eyes, and they remain perfectly consistent till we take leave of them. Most of them, it must be admitted, are very amusing people; but the clever things they say are neither forced nor unreal; their verbal fencing is deadly, but not strained. And the one or two bores in the book never bore the reader. They are indeed, as enjoyable as the clever people; their stupidity, their dulness are never allowed to make the reader feel dull or stupid. Even Raggett, whom Ottley introduces to his wife and then proceeds to be jealous of, is a joy with his clumsy love-making; and Lady Cannon, who in real life would be unbearable, is a figure of gorgeous fun. But it is not only in her character-drawing that Mrs. Leverson shows her delicious humour and powers of observation. The incidents by which the tale progresses are described with a truth which makes them echoes of every one's personal experience. The chapter entitled "Hyacinth Waits" is an excellent example of this. Lightly and delicately written, it yet has real power; it is a little tragedy which is being enacted as Hyacinth watches the clock, a tragedy we have all experienced, and it is described with a choice and economy of words worthy of Maupassant. It is just this careful brevity, in which nothing essential seems left out, which so remarkably distinguishes the author's work from the general. Her dialogue is so good, so apparently natural and yet so incisive, that much of it could be transferred as it stands to the stage. One knows that the lines would "tell," just as one feels certain that the characters would "get over the footlights." Surely there is here material for a charming light comedy. We are grateful for so brilliant an example of what can be done by delicate wit and humour playing upon characters which a less talented writer would either make heavy in the process of putting them on paper or extenuate to nothingness. Mrs. Leverson has proved herself an artist of rare quality. (pp. 909-10)

A review of "Love's Shadow," in The Academy, *Vol. LXXIV, No. 1885, June 20, 1908, pp. 909-10.*

OSBERT SITWELL (essay date 1933)

[*The brother of the poets Dame Edith and Sir Sacheverell Sitwell, Sir Osbert Sitwell was an English novelist and poet whose works are marked by satirical humor and whose extensive autobiography colorfully records the history of his literary family and cultured life of their wide circle of associates. In the following excerpt from Leverson's obituary notice, he eulogizes Leverson's personality and literary skill.*]

The death of Ada Leverson removes a clever novelist and a remarkable woman, who was greatly loved by her friends. Her books, for the most part published between 1910 and 1914, are delightful reflections of her witty, sympathetic personality and a lively record of the Edwardian period, in which they were written. In them she betrays the greatest dexterity, lightness of hand, and some of fantasy; the same characteristics, indeed, which showed themselves in her conversation and made of her so entrancing a companion.

Osbert Sitwell, "Mrs. Leverson: Edwardian Novels," in The Times, *London, September 1, 1933, p. 17.*

INEZ HOLDEN (essay date 1950)

[*In the following excerpt from a general essay on Leverson's novels, Holden compares and contrasts Leverson's craft with that of various other authors of her era and discusses her technical skills.*]

Ada Leverson did not write, as both the literary giants and the prolific dwarfs were then doing, of current political trends. It would be possible to read all her novels without becoming aware that the Fabians were already on the footpath, that Woman's Suffrage was a subject of violent controversy or that the 'New Woman' was forever putting on her bloomers for the next spin on her bicycle. Ada Leverson was not preoccupied with intellectual agnosticism, and her novels are equally free from the morbid gloom that permeate the books of her friend Miss Violet Hunt. Even Miss Braddon, best selling authoress of *Lady Audley's Secret, Cut By The County* and seventy other popular novels, was bringing a little 'social consciousness' into her novels; and in *One Thing Needful* I recently found a young Lord who goes so far as to say that he is no longer certain that 'the well born' are necessarily 'the best people.'

The people she wrote about she did not think 'the best people' or for that matter 'the worst people'; they were, for her, the people she knew best and the people she knew the worst about—talking as she had heard them talk and acting as she had seen them act, as they played out their dramas of happy and unhappy love, despair, frustration and exaltation against an easy background of bourgeois security. Lady Kellynch, Hyacinth Verney, Miss Yeo, Harry de Freyne and the rest could only be creatures of their own epoch; whereas Ada Leverson was in some ways ahead of her period. At the end of ***The Limit*** we find Romer dreaming of the back of Harry de Freyne's neck, as he had seen it while Harry was sitting at a desk writing a letter. Romer dreams, too, of the Japanese dagger he had noticed hanging on the wall; and he becomes aware in his dream of a desire to take down the dagger and plunge it deep into Harry's neck. At this time Freud had discovered the Theory of the Unconscious; but it is doubtful if Edwardian society had yet discovered Doctor Freud's discovery.

In Ada Leverson's day, of course, people read a great many novels; and they wrote a great many novels, too, many of them with weighty plots, counter-plots, sub-plots and stupendous surprises. All the characters turned up in the last chapter in their true colours: the good girl got her man and the bad girl got her just deserts. Although Mrs. Leverson's novels tended to end happily, they were always written with a delightful, well-balanced lightness, and she had such an extraordinary sense of situation that each novel appears to be a series of well-turned situations rather than an elaborately contrived plot. She was able to do this, I think, through her masterly use of dialogue. There were very few writers with her ear for dialogue then, and very few who can equal her dialogue now. (pp. 430-31)

Ada Leverson's novels did not have very large sales, though they usually went into a second edition soon after publication. But the reviewers appear to have been not quite sure what to make of her as a novelist. In the few contemporary reviews I have been able to find they constantly refer to her as 'the English Gyp.' Yet Colette was a writer with whom she had far more in common.

Ada Leverson's first novel, ***The Twelfth Hour,*** was published in 1907. The *Daily Mail* thought it deserved 'abundant popularity,' the *Referee* considered it 'decidly amusing,' and the *Dundee Courier* found it 'well stocked with smart sayings.' When ***Love's Shadow*** was published, the next year, a reviewer observed that 'to say that the author has the gift of writing smart dialogue would be to say far too little.' Perhaps Ada Leverson's two greatest qualities—readability and lightness of touch—somehow had the effect of hoodwinking reviewers into under-rating her as a novelist. Wilde, Wells, E. M. Forster, Hardy, Bennett, G. K. Chesterton, Bernard Shaw and Conrad were all writing at this time, and minor writers of the period may well have been overlooked. But Ada Leverson's ***The Limit*** strikes me as more witty than Anthony Hope's *Dolly Dialogues;* and I find her novels funnier than Saki's short stories which have been reprinted seventeen times since 1930.

The Limit is probably Mrs. Leverson's best novel. The story is lightly, wittily and, apparently, almost carelessly told, and yet within the framework of the Fancy Dress Ball there is a sort of secondary sadness. The adults prepare for their party and, like children at play, the details of their game absorbs their interest, so that the tragedies, conflicts and complicated inter-relationships, which rule their lives, are for the moment as if removed from them. Yet these conflicts are all the more menacing, still in the shadows, and still, as it were, within shouting distance. (pp. 432-33)

Mrs. Leverson is writing about a world where 'a servant opened the door' and people said, quite naturally, 'Shall I ring for tea?' The girls go out for a spin in a motor-car wearing their motoring veils to enjoy a gossip about 'the dear boys,' and then come home to tea on the lawn. In ***The Limit*** much is going on, but all within an atmosphere of leisure and ease; and in the other novels it is the same thing. (pp. 434-35)

Henry James's 'Gentle Reader' was always the 'Gentle Writer,' and had none of Saki's cruel hatred of young children and interest in old aunts. She did not possess either Ronald Firbank's gift for using words like delicate music, or the slow melancholy tempo of Maurice Baring; but one notices that these writers are linked by sudden inconsequences, a kind of occasional near-silliness in style, which seems to distinguish the writer of a leisured class, and comes perhaps from social confidence. (p. 435)

It is surprising that Ada Leverson did not write for the Theatre. She had a remarkable gift of characterisation; and, without referring to ***The Limit,*** I find that I can summon up each of the *dramatis personae*. Besides those at the Fancy Dress Ball, there is Mrs. Foster, the 'baby Guardsman's' mother, with her sweet country cottage and her penchant for writing erotic poetry, and Gladys Brill, daughter of Tom Brill, the landlord of the Bald Faced Stag. Gladys has been bespoken since birth to the son of a neighbouring publican; and poor Gillie Hereford-Vaughan, the successful playwright with the modest and unassuming nature, is in love with her. There is also Miss Luscombe, the actress, a *grande dame* on the stage and an actress in society.

'She had got into the habit of talking always as if she were surrounded by crowds, and she said so much about the celebrities who ought to have turned up that one felt almost as depressed as if they had really been there.' Miss Luscombe's friend, John Ryland Rathbone, has, it is revealed, a frustrated passion to go on the stage, and her mother Mrs. Luscombe 'has no nonsense about her.' Lady Walmer is also startlingly downright; and discusses frankly the unfortunate situation of Alec, her heiress daughter, who is so desperately in love with Harry de Freyne that she can only talk to him in excruciating slang.

But, at second hand, it is impossible to give a fair account of Ada Leverson's talent. Trying to reproduce someone else's wit is rather as if one should say: 'I saw a woman to-day who had exceptionally beautiful eyes—I have had one copied for you. Here it is—in glass.' Like Tommy Handley and the Marx

Brothers, Ada Leverson was both 'High-brow' and 'Low-brow,' but, of course, never 'Middle-brow'; and to read her is to belong to some strange esoteric sect, all of whose members have gone through the exhausting ritual of raking the second-hand bookshops of the Faringdon and Charing Cross Roads in search of old copies of her six once-celebrated novels. (pp. 437-38)

Inez Holden, "The Art of Ada Leverson," in The Cornhill Magazine, *No. 983, Summer, 1950, pp. 429-38.*

C. P. SNOW (essay date 1951)

[*Snow was an English scientist and novelist whose writings address the moral dilemmas spawned by the atomic age. In the following excerpt, Snow favorably reviews* Love's Shadow *and* The Limit, *contrasting Leverson's technique with that of Ronald Firbank, one of the author's contemporaries.*]

Ada Leverson and Ronald Firbank were both writing during the 1914-18 war. They both belonged to the upper-class Edwardian world at a time when only the imaginative could foresee that this particular kind of privilege and cultivation was already doomed. Neither of them was happy in that world, so far as one can judge from Sir Osbert Sitwell's moving descriptions: but it was where they belonged, it was the England they knew. The rest of England did not know much about this small sector of society; if you talk of Edwardian England, you must not forget the England of Bennett, or Wells, or Firbank's exact contemporary, D. H. Lawrence, to whom the Firbank environment seemed as remote as it does to us, and more forbidding. In 1951, that tiny, glittering Edwardian society has taken on a shimmer of its own; and part of the interest of such writers as these, particularly of Mrs. Leverson, is one of period.

Nevertheless they have considerable interest in their own right, though it is asking for trouble to put their claims too high. Ada Leverson was an agreeable and entertaining novelist with a great deal of wisdom about the emotions of love. She lacked altogether the force, the appetite, which make the characters in a novel stand out as though they are embossed: unlike Anthony Hope, whom she in certain respects resembles, one does not feel that she had great powers, and through diffidence or perversity or both, half-deliberately threw them away. There is nothing in her novels which approaches the best pieces of *The King's Mirror* (a sad book because of its overwhelming impression of a fine novelist wasted). Yet she is readable: she is witty, often conscientiously and elaborately so; she is very honest about love, and treats her characters with the disillusioned tenderness of one who has suffered much. Both ***Love's Shadow*** . . . and ***The Limit*** . . . , her second and third books, . . . reveal her in what I imagine (I have not read her other four) to be characteristic form. They are much more worth reading than any but a handful published in 1950.

For most people, they are also much more worth reading than any of Firbank's—though he was an original writer in a sense which Ada Leverson was not, though he is one of the pioneers of the moment-by-moment novel. The moment-by-moment fashion has now outlived its usefulness, but it dominated a certain kind of sensibility for thirty years; and so it is worth while to go a little further into Firbank's brand of originality. In *Inclinations* (1916) and ***Love's Shadow*** there happens to be a closely similar situation. A young woman is going to bed, thinking of a man. This is how Ada Leverson deals with it.

> Hyacinth felt somewhat soothed, and resolved to think no more of Cecil Reeve. She then turned up the light again, took her writing materials, and wrote him three long letters, each of which she tore up. She then wrote once more, saying—
>
> "Dear Mr. Reeve,
>
> I shall be at home today at four. Do come round and see me."
>
> She put it under her pillow, resolving to send it by a messenger the first thing in the morning, and went to sleep.
>
> But this letter, like the others, was never sent. By the morning light she marvelled at having written it, and threw it into the fire.

Here is Firbank's treatment.

> "I shall never sleep. I don't see how I can. The die is cast! There's no telling, child, how it will end! . . ."
>
> ". . . Via Tiber . . . Countess P-a-s-t-o-r-e-l-l-i. Via Tiber . . . O Tiber, Father Tiber, *to whom the Romans pray*. Impossible! . . . If they did, it was a perfect scandal."
>
> "And suppose he made me too? Oh, good gracious!"
>
> By the bedside, mellowing among a number of vellum volumes, were the *Nine Prayers* of the Countess of Cochrane and Cray.
>
> Who would do the burning?
>
> That eighth one! What a clamour for a crown!
>
> On the subject of jewels there wasn't much she didn't teach.
>
> *Two loose diamonds made a charming tic-toc sound.*
>
> At a dinner-party, now, who would work in first? She or Lady Cray? One would push past her probably, in any case—"the *Italian* woman!" . . . *"The Pasto* Countess thing!"
>
> She played her eyes and flung out a hand towards a sugar-crystal-rose.
>
> No; one couldn't exactly tell how it would end.
>
> "My dear, I shouldn't care to say! . . ."
>
> There were those Beer-Hall voices . . . Fal de rol di do do, *di do do*! Fal de rol—"
>
> Miss Collins turned her pillow.
>
> "I suppose I've to lie and listen! . . . Oh, Good gracious!" . . .

If you analyse the two passages textually, you will find many interesting contrasts. Firbank's is far more variegated: it is throbbing with sensation: but it contains nothing but sensation. Emotionally, it is ice-cold. The words of Ada Leverson are flatter, less individual: you may find them dull at a first reading, but at a second they will make you aware of a sharp, sarcastic mind and a warm heart. In terms of sensation, they convey nothing, nor, indeed, does any of Ada Leverson's writing. Between these two writers, neither of them first-rate in their own school, you can see two different approaches to human beings with caricature-like exaggeration—Firbank apprehending them with brilliant senses, but with weak or inhibited emotion and little mind: Ada Leverson, not photographing them with a tenth of his vividness, but responding to them with strong feeling and an acute intelligence. If I have to choose, I do not hesitate a moment about which approach gives the truer picture.

C. P. Snow, in a review of "Love's Shadow" and "The Limit," in The Spectator, *Vol. 186, No. 6395, January 19, 1951, p. 82.*

ANTHONY WEST (essay date 1951)

[The son of Rebecca West and H. G. Wells, West is an English author who has written several novels concerned with the moral, social, psychological, and political disruptions of the twentieth century. As a critic he has written a study of D. H. Lawrence in addition to his many reviews published in various magazines. In the following excerpt, West disparages The Limit.*]*

Ada Leverson was a woman of talent and courage. She followed Bernard Shaw and preceded Max Beerbohm as dramatic critic of the English *Saturday Review,* and when her friend Oscar Wilde had exposed himself to criminal proceedings by his ill-advised libel suit against the Marquis of Queensberry and was waiting for the final blow to fall, she took him into her house and sheltered him. So far so good, but she would write novels. Some of these are now being revived in England, and one, **"The Limit,"** has been brought out, for the first time in this country, by Norton. My British colleagues are apparently being bowled over by them. "Their wit seems as fresh as ever and they date only in the sense that in them wealth, domestic servants, and leisure are abundant and taken completely for granted," somebody remarks in the *Observer.* (Messrs. Norton have been kind enough to suppress the names of the critics concerned.) Someone else, in the *Daily Mail,* remarks that "It is astonishing how they have stood the test. . . . Period pieces, if you like . . . but period pieces from which some of our sententious, repetitious, and long-winded modern novelists need not be ashamed to take a hint." And the *Times* Literary Supplement goes on record as believing that "her wit, and—at its best—her understanding of life, are second to none among her contemporaries. Her style has an economy and directness that belong to a later school." If "understanding of life" means what I take it to mean, and "contemporaries" means what I take it to mean, we have here a discovery—an equal of, say, Hardy and Conrad.

However, we have **"The Limit"** itself to look at as well as the critical opinions that festoon its jacket. It opens with Romer Wyburn and his wife, Valentia, discussing their friends and their affairs in a long stage conversation that is an exact copy of the exchange between maid and valet that introduced the cast in the conventional machine-made play of the eighties:

> "Oh, Romer dear, really! . . . You see, Harry is giving this dinner *on purpose* so that Daphne shall meet Van Buren by accident. You know all about Van Buren, *the* Van Buren—the millionaire, who turns out to be a dear creature and quite charming! . . ."

When I read this passage, I found myself instinctively rising from my seat and preparing to leave a theatre, and it was with some amazement that I remembered I was at home reading a novel. This stagy opening scene also contains a low-class booby trap, or swindle, in which the author breaks in on the characters to present the reader with some deliberately misleading information about Romer Wyburn:

> In a superficial way Romer was very effective, fair, and good-looking, well-made and distinguished; but the entire absence of all expression from his empty, regular face, and of all animation from his dry, colorless voice and manner, soon counteracted the effectiveness. . . . His personality was so extraordinarily *nil* that it was quite oppressive.

This is to prepare the reader for the dénouement, in which Romer, by sheer force of character, moral strength, and integrity (I am for the moment taking Mrs. Leverson's opinions of her man at their face value), wins his wife back from the villain of the piece. In short, Romer is the equivalent in the realm of literary manners of an exploding cigar. (p. 82)

One can only presume that Mrs. Leverson's publishers were inspired by the biographical sketch of her included in Osbert Sitwell's "Noble Essences" and by the current vogue for revivals to rescue this dismal stuff from the slag heap. If Mr. Michael Sadleir can succeed in persuading the critics and the public that the long-winded, pedestrian novels of Trollope are worth reading; if Firbank's rhinestones can pass muster; and if the five-eighths of Scott Fitzgerald's work that was drink-blurred and offhand can be smuggled through on the strength of "The Great Gatsby;" then it must seem that anything goes. But this book won't even get by as fashionable entertainment, to be read on the beach by young ladies in the shade of de Chaldée. This type of reader has gained a great deal of literary muscle since Mrs. Leverson's day. She has now a healthy appetite for such things as the bracing pessimisms of Graham Greene, and for the real wit and more authentic snob stuff to be found in Evelyn Waugh and Nancy Mitford. As for the lesser members of the smart, glossy-paper school of writing, their work (whatever else it may or may not have) at least has the vitality of the current mode. The fashionable writer of today is, moreover, a technician infinitely superior to his predecessor of forty years ago. He has read Gide, Colette, Henry James, Virginia Woolf, Cocteau, Chekhov, Aldous Huxley, and Proust, and has learned from them not only a good deal about writing but as much psychology as he has from his analyst. He is no more capable of perpetrating a husband who can claim, after five years of the marriage bed and shared life, never to have said a word or done a thing his wife didn't like than he is capable of stooping to Mrs. Leverson's seedy stage mechanics for getting people "on" and "off." If **"The Limit"** is worth reading at all, it is as a demonstration of the vast improvement in taste, technique, and plain common sense in the fashionable novel that has resulted from the triumph of feminism and the disappearance of the overdressed, overfed, underexercised, undereducated, and intolerably idle nineteenth-century middle-class woman. It is only in the proletarianized literature of the pulp magazines and in advertising copy that one now encounters beings of the order of Valentia Wyburn, a compound of ignoble wish-fulfillment dreams of a love that involves no gift of self but only an unending taking of gifts and services. (pp. 83-84)

Anthony West, "Out of the Dead Past," in The New Yorker, *Vol. XXVII, No. 27, August 18, 1951, pp. 82-4.*

JOHN MASON BROWN (essay date 1951)

[*Brown, an influential and popular American drama critic from the 1930s through the 1950s, wrote extensively on contemporary British and American drama. He had a thorough knowledge of dramatic history and his criticism often displays a scholarly erudition in addition to the qualities of popular reviewing. In the following excerpt from a review, Brown offers high praise for* The Limit.]

A few days before Ada Leverson died in London in August 1936, a man, an old friend, dropped by to ask how she was. Her condition was serious but not too serious for her to insist upon making up her face before he was allowed to see her. When her daughter showed him in she was guilty of one of those sickroom lies all of us tell out of kindness. "Isn't Mother wonderful!" she exclaimed. "She'll soon be the same as everyone else." With effort Ada Leverson managed to sit bolt upright in bed. "That, thank God," she said, enunciating very clearly, "is one thing I shall never be!" Nor was she.

It is Sir Osbert Sitwell who tells this engaging story about her, along with many another, in *Noble Essences*. But it is Ada Leverson herself who demonstrates her singularity on almost every page of ***The Limit,*** that novel of hers, one of the six she wrote between 1907 and 1916, which has just been published in America for the first time some forty years after it appeared in England. (p. 11)

Her novel is a joy—light, slight, and mannered, but with wisdom shining through its absurdities and delectable because of the polish and distinction of its artifice. If it speaks engagingly for Mrs. Leverson, giving us shimmering indications of what her prowess must have been in conversation, it speaks no less wittily for Wilde. English critics, I notice, have endeavored to capture the merits and texture of ***The Limit*** by likening it to the work of a more amiable Saki, a less fantastic Ronald Firbank, or a more substantial Hope of *The Dolly Dialogues*. Yet in their search for a fit comparison it seems to me they have, in the best tradition of *The Vision of Sir Launfal,* traveled far and overlooked a figure who was right at their doorsteps and in her heyday at Ada Leverson's. I mean Oscar himself.

For ***The Limit*** reads the way a Wilde comedy ought to be played. Not a revival of one of his earlier dramas such as *Lady Windermere's Fan, A Woman of No Importance,* or *An Ideal Husband,* tarnished as their brilliance was by plots borrowed from French problem plays. No. A revival of a comedy by the Wilde who had escaped from Dumas-fils, Augier, and Sardou, and who in *The Importance of Being Earnest* had come wholly and jubilantly into his nonsensical own. Moreover, ***The Limit*** is a revival uncursed by any indifferent actors who cannot master the artificiality of the style, the ping-pong of the epigrams, or the deliciousness of the fooling. It would be ridiculous to say that it has Wilde's final polish, his ultimate arrogance of mind, grace of paradox, elegance of mockery, or brilliance. Even so, the spirit is often the same. And so is the tone. (pp. 14-15)

The world into which ***The Limit*** leads us is a vanished universe. This is a part of the novel's fun and charm. It is a world within a world, confident of itself, minuscule in its interests, and trivial in its hopes. Love and profitable courtship are the chief worries of its characters. To these, as to marriage, they bring submerged, if any, emotions. When its men and women do not live by their wits, they live for them. No one, including themselves, could take them seriously. They do not have to tell jokes; they are jokes. They are sophisticates, protected, pampered, and spoiled, whose sole fear—a groundless one in their case—is the dread of being commonplace.

Readers who thrive on anguish, who like their reading purposeful, and who want all novels to be centered in the silo, the soil, or the soul, will find little to please and much to annoy them in ***The Limit.*** Most decidedly it is not their dish of tea. Instead, it is meant for those who find laughter no hardship, high comedy a delight, nonsense relaxing, and who are not made uncomfortable by worldlings both comfortable and conscienceless.

If, in spite of the good time I have had reading ***The Limit,*** I feel no particular urge to rush out and devour Ada Leverson's other five novels at one sitting, it is because a little of this kind of writing can go a long way. Nonetheless I am delighted to have made Ada Leverson's acquaintance and not to have missed ***The Limit.***

Her novel is the kind of comedy at which the English excel. At least it is the kind of comedy at which they have excelled. It is the production of a top-drawer people at their top-drawer moment of international domination and personal security. It springs from the worldly prosperity, snobbishness, and class-consciousness in which high comedy flowers. Three hundred years of a Britannia that ruled the waves lie behind its assumptions, hence its values and laughter. Britons such as Evelyn Waugh and Nancy Mitford may write in a changed and threatened world wittily and brilliantly about the passage of an old and once entrenched society. One wonders, however, what will happen to the artifices of high comedy when that society has disappeared and the wealth is gone which enabled it to be not only idle but frivolous. (pp. 16-17)

John Mason Brown, "Edwardian Sphinx," in his As They Appear, *McGraw-Hill Book Company, Inc., 1952, pp. 11-17.*

COLIN MACINNES (essay date 1961)

[*MacInnes was an English essayist and novelist known for works reflecting the troubled lives of people who belong to London's various subcultures. In the following excerpt, he seeks to undermine the legends surrounding Leverson which, he believes, have impeded a more judicious appraisal of her work, and then surveys her career as a novelist.*]

It is an unjust fate for a great artist to become so much entangled in a legend that a personality is better known than an achievement. This has been the lot of Ada Leverson, whose name is so honourably remembered, and whose writing remains disproportionately unread. The legend is a particularly obstinate barrier to her art, because it is threefold: one part of it misleadingly surrounding her own self, the other two parts willed on her by fellow artists whom she loved and served.

To dispose first, if one can, of the most tenacious of these legendary reputations: the one arising from her friendship for Oscar Wilde. (p. 46)

[Anyone] who thinks, as I most surely do, that Ada Leverson is in her own right and by her own achievement a very great artist indeed, may feel that from the point of view of her own literary reputation (which is, of course, a factor that her generous soul would not even have considered), the most fatal step she ever took was to behave, to Wilde, so well and so unselfishly. For Wilde, most unquestionably, is in the matter of his "legend" a terrible vampire: like some strange, greedy planet, his name and repute have absorbed and flung into orbit round his memory so many human moons—and even, in the case of Ada Leverson, one rare star. It is surely high time that as an artist she be rescued from this association most honourable to herself; and that it be realised, as I hope to demonstrate, that save for *The Importance of Being Earnest,* Ada Leverson was certainly Wilde's equal and, I believe, ultimately a finer writer.

The next legend that must be unravelled, or set in its fit proportion, is that woven round Ada Leverson's name by Sir Osbert Sitwell in the fifth volume of his autobiographical *Left Hand, Right Hand!;* and called, it will be remembered, *Noble Essences, or Courteous Recollections*. . . .

[When] we come to read the *Noble Essences*—which are, of course, in a sense a book apart—the impression is often, to be frank, unpleasant. It is but damning with faint praise to say that one is grateful for the information the author gives about these splendid men and women; and in the case of Ada Leverson herself, I must own it was not until I read this book that I knew she was a writer. But the great defect is this: it is precisely *not* as a writer that, in the book, Ada Leverson is portrayed. It is as a sort of adjunct, or satellite, or mascot even of the author: loved and admired, certainly, and greatly esteemed, but condescended to; and not seemingly cherished for what ought to be the most important thing about her—that she was an artist also; and in her case, a great one. (p. 47)

The third "legend" shrouding Ada Leverson which one must also try to peel aside, is the one created unintentionally by herself. It is a regrettable reality of the "literary world"—yet one of which any writer concerned with his ultimate "reputation" must take some account—that writers, to a great extent, are valued in their day, and even by posterity, very much at the value which they seem to place upon themselves; or which they permit, by genuine indifference or neglect, their contemporaries to place upon them. Of course no reputation, be it nursed however ardently, can be sustained without the presence of a talent; and it is true that later reassessments of neglected or self-neglected artists, sometimes do take place. Yet because it is hard to learn and easy to forget, "the world," if not reminded, will prefer to leave a talent in oblivion.

As an artist, no one could have been more careless of her "literary reputation" than was Ada Leverson (which is one of the many attractive things about her). Although in quantitative fact and, as I hope to show, by quality, she was in the most entire sense a professional writer, she never was, nor cared to be, a *femme de lettres:* the notion would have seemed to her preposterous, a bore. Throughout the 1890s, she printed innumerable occasional pieces in topical magazines—many of which are only now being disinterred; and between 1907 and 1916 she published six novels of outstanding merit. But all this was made to seem "effortless" in two ways. The style itself, and the whole tone of these six volumes, convey—unless one is attentive—the impression that the thing is all too easy: as if it were set down, in random moments, by a beautiful and brilliant lover of life and art between outings on idle afternoons. So far as her own attitude to her work went, she was the kind of person—as wonderful as rare—whose sense of *chic* and inborn dislike of all pomposities (not least among "creative" people) would forbid her to make claims for herself that others would not spontaneously make for her. Her chief delight was in the victorious achievement of her friends; for friendship was as dear to her as love, and she was in both an artist. Thus, one can imagine her joy if on the publication of a novel, a friend told her he admired it (the more so if he could tell her, very exactly, why). But to imagine her pressing a volume into a friend's hand, let alone undertaking that kind of artistic lobbying which helps to establish and preserve a literary "name," is quite impossible. Of Edith Ottley, heroine in three of her novels, and whom one may with little doubt assume to be something of a self-portrait, Ada Leverson has this to say:

> Such vanity as she had was not in an uneasy condition; she cared very little for general admiration, and had no feeling for competition. She was without ambition to be superior to others.

It is thus that the notion has arisen—and has been sustained in many a preposterous study of "the nineties" or of "the Edwardian era"—that as well as being a literary acolyte (albeit one greatly cherished) Ada Leverson was a gifted, casual non-professional. To this absurd impertinence, her writings now may make reply.

The Twelfth Hour, her first novel, was published when she was already reaching her middle years. The competence of plot and structure, the swift, sharp establishment of character, and the easy, laconic urbanity of style, suggest—which was indeed the case—that although a "first novel," this is the work of an experienced writer. Subsequently to be developed in depth and range, the essential Ada Leverson themes and tone are already apparent. Her two chief themes are: first, the relations of men and women bound by marriage or—put less conventionally—the reconciliation of the eagerness for individual life and personal fulfilment, in each of the two partners, with the moral imperative of their promise to each other: for marriage, or love-in-marriage (rather than love before it, or outside it) is seen in terms of a bond of loyalty—the free promise—much more than of ties imposed by faith or law. And since she clearly approves of and delights in the life-loving individuality of the wife and husband, and yet as equally believes a promise *is* a promise and that full personal self-realisation can best be achieved through keeping this primal vow, the central conflict of her books is always the way in which their chief protagonists, the married man and woman, will confront and resolve this situation. Her secondary theme—though almost of equal weight—is friendship, to which it is clear she attached great human value. It is often believed that friendship is a masculine specialty. In the Ada Leverson world, at all events, it isn't: for though there are competent descriptions of friendships between men, the most sensitive and complex are those she creates between women and men (and these *are* real friendships, not failed or potential love affairs) and just as effectively—if surprisingly—friendships between women themselves. As for the Ada Leverson tone or mood, it is one of amused, affectionate, and occasionally ironic or contemptuous acceptance of her characters' behaviour: often presented in scenes of such deadpan absurdity that the reader must be alert indeed to catch, in so many throw-away lines, each double meaning. This is not to say that her attitude to her characters (and hence to life) is uncritical: indeed it is, and the "detached" urbanity of tone never entirely masks (unless the reader wishes to see no further) her underlying seriousness about life, and what matters most in it. But she never "judges:" never bullies her characters, or erects them to knock them down; and never forces her own views (while making them quite apparent) upon the reader, to whom she clearly feels her duty is to entertain and, if "instruct," only to do so by providing all the clues by which the reader can do this for himself if he so wishes.

Ada Leverson belongs, in fact, to a category of writer rather unusual in England—and of which Congreve may be the great exemplar—the classic author of the comedy of manners. This sort of art reveals itself, in form, by a harmonious construction, parts deftly related to the whole, subsidiary themes neatly tucked away in echoing counterpoint; next, in language, by a studied but easy and relaxed precision, with flights of dialogue tossed to and fro like aery but well-directed shuttlecocks; and then in theme, by the perpetually underlying presence, amid all this apparent accident of episode, of an essential drama: sometimes hinted at with such obliqueness that the sudden glimpses of its dangerous deep turbulence can be, to the reader (if he does not miss them), quite alarming; and at last, after phrases and chapters have skimmed like butterflies or birds over a clear still pool, there is the abrupt, positive confrontation—often on the very brink of irredeemable disaster—with the conflict in its total, perilous reality. Once it is thus realised what the writer is about, the gay, flitting, entertaining and, apparently, ''inconsequential'' chapters soon assume their other as yet unstated, but already fully present, dramatic dimension. The ''frivolity'' becomes meaningful, the nonsense potentially sad. This is not farce, not ''witty writing,'' but true comedy: and of it, Ada Leverson is a master.

Though one mode of writing may not be more or less ''difficult'' than another (to whoever may be good at either), it would seem the classic writer must be technically more assured. To appear not to be saying what in fact you are, to achieve, save in rare ''moments of truth,'' effects of feeling (those both of characters and writer) by implication, demands a tight-rope dexterity, since to hit the wrong note is to tumble at once into sentiment or farce; and to develop all the themes, major and minor, hold them in a firm yet delicate grip, and conduct them at the correct pace in each episode—and as if by the wish of nature—with a swift final sweep to their ''inevitable'' resolution, requires enormous talent and self-discipline. It will escape no attentive reader of Ada Leverson's books that she has surely been much influenced—or helped—in achieving some of these effects by her love for and knowledge of the theatre: indeed, many of her scenes in which the dialogue develops entirely without ''author's interjections,'' seem almost borrowed from an unpublished play. More peculiar still (although admittedly, the bioscope was well enough known by the turn of the century—but not yet the innovations of D. W. Griffith) is her frequent use of film scenario devices: ''cutting'' briskly from scene to scene, or situation to situation, without any ''explanation'' (of which indeed, so neatly is it done, there is no need); and even more strangely, ''editing in'' scenes and themes apparently unrelated to the one that, in realistic terms, she is just then evoking.

A final but persistent error about her art (one held, I suppose, by those who have not read her or with one eye open only) must be assailed before her novels are examined in more detail: and this is that Ada Leverson is an ''Edwardian,'' or ''period'' writer. Our custom, in thinking of the past (especially the recent English past), would seem to be to get into our heads some notion about an epoch (the ''nineties,'' the ''twenties,'' or whenever it may be), and then imperatively demand that any actual ''figure'' of that period should conform to the stereotype of our imaginings; and also, fail wilfully to remember (in our blindfold thirst for ''period atmosphere'') that the past always was, at one time, its own present. The word ''Edwardian,'' for example, conjures up a host of clichés about which the chief point, so far as Ada Leverson is concerned, is that even were these all exact she could never have herself conformed to them, as a woman or a writer, because she was, in every page of everything she wrote, an acutely devastating critic of her own age. It is hopeless to look in her books for ''Edwardian raw material'' which we of to-day may then digest and comment on: for she herself, anticipating us by a half-century, has already performed this task. The key to ''situating'' her in this respect is to grasp (as on reading her, one so swiftly can) that she was not an ''Edwardian natural'' at all, but a most sharp (albeit most indulgent) observer of all things Edwardian. As a writer, in consequence, she is in no sense ''period:'' no one, in fact, could be of her own day more ''modern:'' which is precisely what gives to her books—except for their inevitable account of the accessory paraphernalia of Edwardian life—their timeless actuality.

As a corollary to this, she has also dourly been reproached with a culpable unawareness of social and material factors of her period. This seems to me an amazingly blind charge, since how things work, and what things cost, and how it feels to be rich or poor (she had, in her own life, experience of both)—often, indeed, precisely demonstrated with figures spelled out in pounds shillings and pence—are constantly recurring preoccupations. As for the social structure of her day, the variety of social groups her characters are drawn from, and the fullness of her knowledge of them all, are equally apparent. (As one would expect, when the 1914 war comes, it also comes organically into her picture of the new Georgian society.) In short, although a classicist in form, she is most certainly a realist in content. Edwardian ''society'' evidently interested (and diverted) her, and she knew very much about it; but it is the social relations of human persons, and not ''society'' itself, that is her chief and most cherished raw material.

In ***The Twelfth Hour,*** then, the central situation is that the young marriage between Felicity and her husband Chetwode is imperilled not because of dangers from without, but because he (who loves horses and antique furniture second only to herself) is taking her fidelity outrageously for granted, and she is too proud—or respects herself too much—to tell him so. The sub-plots are the love of Felicity's younger sister, Sylvia, for Woodville, who is ''eligible'' in every way except for the essential financial; and of the divided love of Felicity's younger brother Savile (who is sixteen) for Dolly (fourteen) and, at the same fatal time, for the celebrated *diva* Mme. Adelina Patti. Subsidiary characters are the brother and sisters' devotedly bullying Aunt William (so called because her late husband, Uncle Mary, seemed to them less a man than she); Sir James Crofton, their father, a pompous, self-contradictory, good-hearted parliamentarian; Mr. Ridokanaki, the Greek financier, initially (and vainly) in love with Sylvia, and ultimately to be the *deus ex machina;* the ''artistic'' (''in a continual state of vague enthusiasm'') Vera Ogilvie; and such fleeting figures as Agatha, Mrs. Wilkinson, so named by the family because, although a commoner, her mien is decidedly aristocratic. (pp. 47-50)

The Limit has essentially the same theme as ***The Twelfth Hour*** but with developments in depth and even harshness: since in this case the husband and wife, Romer and Valentia, are not such amiable persons as were Chetwode and Felicity; and the potential lover, Harry de Freyne, in addition to being an unworthy ''charmer,'' is clearly a more real danger to the marriage than was, in ***The Twelfth Hour,*** the vacuously agreeable Bertie Wilton. Thus, of Romer the husband his creator says, ''Apparently cool and matter of fact, he was in reality a reticent fanatic.'' And as for Valentia his wife, she is the nearest thing in Ada Leverson's books to an ''immoral''—at any rate an unprincipled—woman: playing with two fires at once, and knowing it. This situation between the trio reaches danger points that are dramatic—almost melodramatic; and only at "the limit" (beyond, even, the "twelfth hour") is the marriage saved from wreckage by three factors: that Romer, the husband, behaves though with violence, with nobility; that Harry the lover is revealed at last to Valentia as a creature lacking all profundity; and that Valentia herself, once her all too silent husband's devotion is splendidly disclosed, has still sufficient love in her, and honour, to react passionately in his favour.

Decidedly, this book is more imperfect than some others: the "plot" creaks at times, with "coincidences" rather nonchalantly contrived; there is even, most unusually for Ada Leverson, some padding; and the final resolution, though effective and credible psychologically, seems hurried and "theatrical" (the last words of the book, one feels, should be not THE END but CURTAIN). Nor are the secondary characters so assured: there are a "funny" American and a "funny" Belgian who are not so very; though Mrs. Wyburn, Romer's mother, is a splendidly-drawn monster ("Eagerness, impatience, love of teasing and sharp wit were visible in her face to one who could read between the lines"). What is happening in this book, one feels, is that the writer is stepping boldly outside her usual range (almost like her heroine, Valentia) to see just what will happen: thus attaining, as an artist, to her own "limit" of naturally manageable theme. So that though one may "fault" ***The Limit,*** there is little doubt that writing it enabled Ada Leverson, in the next books, to profit by the wider experience it gave her and develop, within her natural artistic boundaries, situations and characters of greater complexity and depth. (p. 51)

In ***Love's Shadow*** the tone is light. The Bruce-Edith dialogues (delicious in print, but oh how dreadful they would be in fact!) are purest fun. Edith, a young wife as yet, is still at the stage of putting up with much too much and letting Bruce pontificate and get (apparently) his "way." These two key personages are also introduced most subtly to this first book in which the reader meets them, as subsidiary characters—the main "intrigue" being elsewhere: they are still so far—as everyone in the novel calls them—"the little Ottleys:" at present acting as a comic foil to the major, but much more conventional "drama," of the apparent heroine Hyacinth Verney, of her adoringly jealous friend Anne Yeo, of her vapid lover Cecil Reeve, and of the (not unamiable) *femme fatale* of Cecil's vacillating predilection, Mrs. Eugenia Raymond (whose presence is, in Cecil's fresh love for Hyacinth, "love's shadow"—though we may come to feel it is over Edith that the darker shadow really looms). And since the courtship of Hyacinth by Cecil takes up much more of the book than does the brief description of their ensuing marriage, there is contrasted to the mere drama of marrying, the much more important drama (always, to Ada Leverson), in Edith and Bruce's case, of being married. (p. 52)

[In ***Tenterhooks***] Edith is both more resigned, and yet more brusque, with Bruce; she still respects marriage, but no longer her husband simply because he is her partner in it; and . . . the Ottleys are this time presented, from the outset, with the authority of chief characters.

Vincy (in full, Vincy Wenham Vincy) is next introduced as Edith's confidant and friend: and the clear definition that he is no more than this (and that neither he nor she wish it to be otherwise) prepares us for the introduction of the third (apart from the children) essential character in Edith's life—Aylmer Ross, who soon loves her and awakes her love. Aylmer enters the book—and Edith's existence—so decisively and powerfully that the reader is at once certain this is no Bertie, Harry, or Cecil, as before, but the essential man who will combine the qualities that Edith (and her creator) seek in their ideal figure of the husband-lover; and since Edith's devotion to her marriage is known to be so absolute, the question at once assails the reader's mind (as it was no doubt intended to) as to whether and how the writer will contrive, within her own now well-defined concept of what marriage is, and what its obligations, to unite Edith with Aylmer, or whether the conflict of love and honour (rather than "duty") will perhaps destroy her.

In this book, at last, the central theme (because the protagonists are now worthy of it) is confronted boldly. And although, for quite logical reasons of the characters' psychology, no "affair" outside marriage does actually take place, the sexual dilemma of the heroine is now brought frankly into the open. It is not that the writer loses any of the reticence about this that is natural to her and which was, in earlier books, appropriate to their lighter or more superficial tone and characters: the fact of sex is not, I mean, unnecessarily projected—used merely to heighten "drama." But it is present now, and stated: both by what the characters are made to say, and by the injection of an element of physical violence that is directly related to the revealed realities of the chief characters' desires. Thus, for the first time in the novels, we have scenes of physical assault (though not reaching their "culmination") when Aylmer embraces Edith, and even Bruce "uses force." Edith herself is also driven by her feelings into coquetry, at moments "provoking" Aylmer almost as if she were an inferior person like Valentia of ***The Limit;*** and in her rejoinders to her husband, speaking with undisguised tartness that barely veils (from the reader, if not from obtuse Bruce) a threat of infidelity. All three of them are now "on the brink:" wife, lover, and even husband: for Bruce, who of course supposes that any intrigue by a "devoted married man" (such as himself) is not one, and who, like so many "good sorts," is an inveterate flirt, involves himself first with his children's governess (which Edith, as much by style as by a consciousness of her own faithlessness of heart if not yet of fact, forgives), and then decisively deserts her in favour of one Mavis Argles. To Aylmer Ross the lover, this desertion seems (as it might well, initially, to the reader) the perfectly honourable (and socially acceptable) pretext for Edith to leave her husband, sue for divorce and marry him: for realising that Edith's love can only be fully given within a totally embracing vow, and being himself a man of such quality as despises, in the case of anyone he values and respects, a mere "affair," Aylmer longs now to marry her. But it was Bruce's all unconscious master-stroke to elope with somebody like Mavis Argles, and do so to, of all places, Australia. For Edith knows better than he does that the adventure will be a failure (Mavis in fact "gets off" with someone else while still on the high seas), that he will return, and that if she abandons him he will not just be the failure that he is, but shrink into a ruin. So she rejects her freedom—and her love. (pp. 53-4)

With the final book, ***Love at Second Sight,*** it is clear that the writer has committed herself to re-shaping Edith's life in terms satisfactory to Edith herself, to the writer's clearly enunciated code, and to the reader's heightened expectations. How, short of some sudden death or dire fatality—neither of which, the reader may rightly feel, would be appropriate—is she to accomplish this? The answer will be that with entire credibility and consummate art, she will transform Aylmer, the lover, into the "husband" whom, to win Edith, he must first become: not, I mean, "husband" merely in fact, but in psychological reality.

To achieve this, we see, first of all, how the two earlier Edith Ottley books (and more tangentially, the three others) will serve their purpose. Edith is now thirty-five, Aylmer forty-two, so it is "now or never." They have been entirely separated, since Edith's earlier rejection of him, by three years of time, during which their feeling has not waned but deepened. Bruce has learned nothing, is more dreadfully himself than ever—so much so that, to anyone who had not read of his earlier behaviour to her, it would seem from his attitude to Edith that she has nothing to forgive him. The children are older, and are beginning to see through their father. The 1914 War (as I hinted earlier) is also pressed organically into service: for while Bruce has not joined the New Army (he suffers from a "neurotic heart"), Aylmer, disguising his age, has gone to the Front and—doubly subtle touch—his son by a first marriage, Teddy, also disguising his (he is under-age to fight), is in khaki too. . . .

The means to the final union of Edith and Aylmer (though not the essential reason), and the catalyst of the whole situation, is one of Ada Leverson's most original, appalling, and hilarious creations, Mme. Eglantine Frabelle. Mme. Frabelle (English, but the relict of a French wine merchant) is a woman who gets everything wrong, never stops saying so, but who is so affably and so predictably mistaken, and so unfeignedly interested in whoever, at that moment, is her interlocutor, that everybody (except, significantly, Aylmer and Edith's boy Archie) likes her.

> People were not charmed with Eglantine because she herself was charming, but because she was charmed.

She has descended on the Ottleys with a letter of introduction from a friend who, it later transpires, knows nothing whatever about her—and indeed, once Mme. Frabelle has settled like a benevolent cuckoo in the Ottley's house, this friend asks *them* to tell her who this woman she introduced into their midst, may be. Bruce, flattered by her attention (despite her being older than he, and far from beautiful—or perhaps even because of this), is quite enchanted with her indefatigable solicitude. And so, in a different way, is Edith: for when in doubt—as she is often, now—a conversation with her guest will serve to resolve perplexities because of Edith's faith in Eglantine's sure instinct for giving to any question an answer unfailingly and reliably incorrect. (p. 54)

So Mme. Frabelle provides, initially, the atmosphere of almost crazy unreality in which reality can best declare itself. Meanwhile, Edith's visits to Aylmer, who is wounded and on leave in London, become increasingly tense and desperate. The word love, and the fact of it, are now openly declared between them. And so are even—though in conversations not with Aylmer, but with one of Edith's confidants, Sir Tito Landi, the composer—the possible facts of infidelity, of divorce, of second marriage. . . . The visit to Eastcliff is of course (and of course with Bruce's indifferent agreement) to see Aylmer, who is convalescing there; and during it, Edith at last commits herself. Aylmer is soon to return to the war in France; and Edith tells him she will leave Bruce—who, they both accurately assess, will not want to keep the children (too much bother)—and henceforth they are, in their own eyes and hearts, "engaged." In this almost final scene, the writer establishes two essential things: that Edith, sure of his love and hers, and sure as she can be of the children's future, is prepared to "desert" her husband and accept "social disgrace;" and that in spite of the urgencies of their feeling for each other, and of the overhanging war, neither he nor she wish for physical union until they can be pledged entirely to each other.

And now Mme. Frabelle plays from afar (in fact, from Liverpool) the unexpected and unhoped for final card that will give Edith not only the whole game, but game with honours. For Mme. Frabelle is waiting to cross the Atlantic, and Bruce is going to cross it with her: this time, we know, in a grasp far more irrevocable than Mavis Argles'. On his earlier flight with Mavis, Bruce had announced it to his wife by letter; but now her lingering doubt will not be satisfied with less than an avowal from her husband. This—as necessary psychologically to both Bruce and Edith, as artistically to the writer—Bruce provides her with: and tells her face to face why it is "I can't endure married life any longer." The last link breaks finally when Edith, accepting this (not on this occasion as we know, without relief) asks Bruce if he would wish to see their child Dilly before he goes. He doesn't want to; and she no longer wants him in any way at all.

In this book, the chief themes of all her art are finally united and resolved: friendship, love and honour become one. Technically, it is her most perfect: even the decorative chapter headings of the earlier five books have vanished in the assured pace with which she sets down her final testament. Two decades of Ada Leverson's life remained to her, but she never wrote another novel; and one may conjecture this was most because the meaning that life held for her had now been given, in her art, entire expression.

On the evidence of these books, we now see clearly defined what Ada Leverson most admired in men and women, and most disliked; and can so deduce, from the consistency with which she reveals these attitudes through her characters' sayings and behaviour, what is the nature of the essentially moral instinct on which her whole outlook as an artist was ultimately based. One may say first of all, on the positive side, that she loved those who loved life, who were spirited yet considerate and kind, and that she liked good manners (while caring nothing whatever for conventional "status"). She adored the young (including the special category of children), and she admired poised old age. She liked women as well as men (whom she liked even more), and to both she could give friendship, of which she well knew the boundaries, as well as she could give love (of which she knew all the rareness and the peril and the need for nourishing it with absolute devotion). She liked people who did things, but didn't mind when they did nothing if they did it with style. She respected most of all men and women who, involving themselves in a human situation, take their due share of responsibility, and try to preserve it and enrich it.

She disliked the mean, the self-important, the tale-bearers, and those lacking candour when to withhold it can do damage: though she disliked equally the indiscreet, and the superfluously "outspoken." She despised duplicity, but did not mind artifice. Most of all, I think—and this is perhaps the only cardinal sin in Ada Leverson's indulgent and forgiving code—she detested cruelty, especially when wanton and aware. Yet almost all these blemishes she was ready enough to pardon, or to make allowances for, if the culprit—as culprits often are—was really unconscious of his fault.

In its simplest essence, one may say of her vision that it is—though this is an odd word to use—a healthy one: where life glowed, there her heart was, and her active sympathy. Although, as a writer, she is "worldly" (in the sense of knowing precisely what the rules are), she emerges from her pages as an artist who, however knowledgeable and difficult to deceive, is innocent and pure. To her readers—even to her characters . . . and even to the most dreadful among these—she is like a fairy godmother: eager to bestow gifts; courteous and considerate to her public, and too good-natured, often, even to hurt her own creations when they most deserve it. Really to know life, and to accept it—while always wishing it were better and striving, in one's own human relations, to make it so—and once knowing it, to grow to love it more and more in spite of its conditions, is the indication in any human person of maturity and wisdom. Such a person Ada Leverson was, and of this kind of being all her writing is a celebration. (pp. 55-6)

Colin MacInnes, "The Heart of a Legend: The Writings of Ada Leverson," in Encounter, *Vol. XVI, No. 5, May, 1961, pp. 46-56.*

JULIAN MITCHELL (essay date 1962)

[Mitchell is an English novelist and short story writer. In the following excerpt from a review of The Little Ottleys, *he commends Leverson's technical skill and artistic viewpoint.]*

There must, I suppose, be others besides myself for whom the reissue of Ada Leverson's novels in 1950-51 might just as well not have taken place for all the notice we took. If we had heard of her at all, it was as a shadowy figure of the nineties, vaguely to do with Wilde and Egypt (something about a sphinx)—one of those people who could be placed once and for all in a couple of paragraphs in 'The Handy Guide to the Rise of Modernism in English Literature 1890-1930', if only someone would *write* the thing. (p. 80)

[But] The Handy Guide is going to have to find room for a good deal more than a couple of paragraphs on Ada Leverson. She is an admirably serious and genuinely witty writer who blew on the fag-end of Edwardian social comedy and lit from it a highly original brand of her own. She exposes the myth of the 'golden' years before 1914 like Saki, but with none of his intense bitterness: the surface gaiety of the period is shown betrayed by a curious exhaustion, moral, social and personal, that surely contributed significantly to the strange death of Liberal England. After reading her we can understand how for a lot of upper-middle class people, living in Knightsbridge and St John's Wood, the outbreak of war seemed at first a merciful release from the tedium of social life. She has the compassion essential to any serious novelist, and she has the intelligence, as well as a high degree of technical skill in counterpoint and contrast.

These virtues are exhibited in all the novels which have Bruce and Edith Ottley as characters, though to least advantage in the first, ***Love's Shadow*** . . . , in which the Ottleys have subsidiary rôles. (It seems doubtful that Ada Leverson had a series in mind when she wrote ***Love's Shadow.***) Like the others, the novel has marriage as its subject, but its hero and heroine are rather colourless, their squabbles are of little interest, and the comedy of Wilde can be watched staggering to an inglorious end as the characters swap epigrams with the grimness of schoolboys playing conkers ('Wam! My paradox is more meaningless than yours!' 'Bam! No it's not!'). Yet the novel is full of original observations. Here is, for instance, a most sympathetic and delicate study of the heroine's Lesbian companion, resigned to doing without what she most wants, clear- and dry-eyed amidst a good deal of romantic mush.

Resignation, acceptance of one's rôle in other people's lives, is a main theme of the novels, and notably of ***Tenterhooks*** . . . , the second and most impressive of them. Bruce Ottley, the civil servant and comic bore, is a burden to his more intelligent and sensitive wife Edith. But she bears his vanity and hypochondria with forbearance and a sense of duty more subtle than most: she has 'taken him on', and for all his inanity it is as much for his sake as for the children's that Edith insists on keeping the marriage going. When she falls in love with a widower as intelligent and attractive as herself she has to choose between duty and happiness: she picks duty. When Bruce runs away to Australia with a girl it seems that she has the excuse and opportunity to pick happiness instead, but much to her lover Aylmer's chagrin she refuses the divorce Bruce asks for. She guesses that the girl will abandon Bruce (which indeed she does) and that his need for Edith will be greater than ever: she must, therefore, stick by him, and she does. Bruce returns, Aylmer goes abroad, Edith is resigned. All this is beautifully handled, and full of perception.

Love at Second Sight . . . has an almost identical plot. The war has begun and Aylmer returns wounded from the front. The lovers' dilemma remains the same, but this time Bruce runs away to America with a woman as crass as himself: she is, however, a great deal tougher, and won't let him go. Edith feels that she is now free, someone else has taken him on: the ending is happy. There is more sentimentality than in ***Tenterhooks,*** but the two novels are admirably balanced. In both, the moral situation is illuminated by the social background. The detail is marvellous. Dotty hostesses, intimate friends, disappointed lovers, dinner companions—all are observed with great acuteness. Ada Leverson's world is a small one, but it is brought vividly to life.

She wrote no more novels after ***Love at Second Sight,*** and one can see why. The war was too big a subject for comedy, even comedy of her seriousness: besides, it was to kill many of her characters and to destroy for ever the background of social triviality against which she moved them. Its appearance is most uneasily handled. Yet Ada Leverson's novels are not diminished by the dramatic change which came over her world. They are extremely readable, they deal with serious subjects with enormous adroitness, they have great charm. (pp. 80-1)

Julian Mitchell, in a review of "The Little Ottleys," in London Magazine, *n.s. Vol. 2, No. 9, December, 1962, pp. 80-1.*

V. S. PRITCHETT (essay date 1964)

[Pritchett is a highly esteemed English novelist, short story writer, and critic. Considered one of the modern masters of the short story, he is also one of the world's most respected and well-read literary critics. Pritchett writes in the conversational tone of the familiar essay, a method by which he approaches literature from the viewpoint of a lettered but not overly scholarly reader. A twentieth-century successor to such early nineteenth-century essayist-critics as William Hazlitt and Charles Lamb, Pritchett employs much the same critical method: his own experience, judgment, and sense of literary art are emphasized, rather than a codified critical doctrine derived from a school of psychological or philosophical speculation. His criticism is often described as fair, reliable, and insightful. In the following essay, Pritchett applauds Leverson's style and economy of expression in The Little Ottleys.*]*

Why do the novels of Ada Leverson survive? How is it that these water ices of the Edwardian drawing room have kept their

Ada Leverson, from a portrait by Walter Sickert that originally appeared in The Yellow Book.

crispness and have not melted away? One can put it down to the Wilde revival; one can regard it as a side-effect of the present turdish taste for chichi; or as a passing nostalgia for the tritenesses of small, safe, set, satiny world of teacups and little dinners, where the gravest dangers are things like being seen riding in a hansom with a wan Bohemian girl from the wrong side of the Park. Ada Leverson's urban males are vulnerable to pity for ill-provided females through whose designs any well-appointed woman can see. We are offered a life lived according to "the rules," which smoothly prevent the emotions from becoming more than inconvenient. To cover the inevitable boredom there are always the bitchings and counter-bitchings of the Knightsbridge kennels. Thus, a rather too jolly Mr. Mitchell will be "almost any age between sixty and sixty-five"; a Sir Charles is "distinguished to the very verge of absurdity." All this is pleasant enough, but—I agree with Colin MacInnes who writes an ardent preface to Ada Leverson's best-known trilogy ***The Little Ottleys***—it has little to do with her merits. The only unconvincing touches that occur in her last novel are those that are closest to the modern world: they record one or two glimpses of the outbreak of the 1914 war. It is natural that they should be unconvincing, for that war killed the comedy of manners. She survives because she is an original and considerable artist.

A writer can be a considerable artist without being more than a minor novelist. If they are to last, the minor novelists depend on sparkle, a freshness of view and a perfection of means; if they are comedians, on the gift of living in a perennial present. Economy and distinction of style and—in Miss Leverson's case—skill in construction are indispensable. They must delight in their limits if we are to delight in them: they must always refuse—and how few middling novelists do make this refusal!—to borrow the courage of other people's convictions. Miss Leverson understood this. It is possible that the pleasure she gives owes a lot to a clever adaptation of the methods of the theatre: the two-dimensional tale passes as quickly as an expert charade. A scene never lasts too long; it is as sharp as repartee. She is careful, even when moralizing, to keep to the surface of life and it is often when she appears to be most trivial that she is life-enhancing and most serious.

To the somewhat extravagant praise given by Mr. MacInnes, I would add the warning that she has not the range of, say, an Edith Wharton; and although it is true that, in a general way, she writes in the tradition of Congreve, she dilutes with the very different comedy of *The Diary of a Nobody,* the Ottleys being the Pooters, but younger and smarter and moved from Finchley to Knightsbridge. They are little Somebodies. This is the comedy of "life's little ironies" which came in during her lifetime. When the clownish Bruce Ottley and his wife chase from one Hamilton Place to another in London looking for where they are supposed to be dining and find they have got the week wrong; above all, in Bruce Ottley's querulous time as an amateur actor, we have pure Grossmith:

> "I told Mitchell what I thought of him in very plain terms. I went so far as to threaten to throw up my part, and he said, 'Well, all right, if you don't like it you can give it up any time.' I said 'Who else could you get at the last minute to play a footman's part?' and he said 'Our footman.'"

The other strain in her comedy is her concern for integrity. She rejoices in the banality of her characters; but in her heroine, Edith Ottley, she has created a young wife who clings to the conservative conventions of her world yet is disturbed to find that she may in her marriage be sacrificing herself to them when she supposes she is doing something sensitive and fine. In other words, Miss Leverson introduces the question of personal truth into her comedy. There is a point at which Edith, despite her coquettishness, is in danger of becoming as tiresome as Thackeray's Amelia; it is no great credit to Edith's probity that she is rescued from having to solve her dilemma by her husband's inane flight with the chief comic character of the book and, ultimately, by the breakdown of the standards of Knightsbridge in the war. I find Edith a shade calculating. Her asinine husband is at his shamefaced worst when the marriage collapses and, in a wonderful scene, comes out with the one honest remark of his life, a ridiculous, fierce *cri de coeur* that punctures the basic assumption of her ethic and her comedy:

> "No, Edith. I can't endure married life any longer. It doesn't suit me."

This cry from a prime domestic fusspot who is always carrying on about being master in his own house is marvelously funny, but it has a wildness about it suggesting that the Ottleys, like the rest of this Edwardian world, had somehow begotten two children without having done more than meet socially.

It is sometimes said that artificial comedy in English suffers from a lack of brain. It really celebrates the English genius for hardening off, refusing to face issues and creating an ennui which will be the great guarantor of social, moral and emotional eventlessness. The most boring and self-centered of men, Bruce Ottley, thrives on boredom and develops, in consequence, a character so eccentric that it never ceases to fascinate his friends.

Our comedy, like our way of life, depends on the evasion of ideas or knowledge and on the creation of character. Edith is about to marry a fine fellow at the end of the novel, but as far as comedy is concerned he is a dead loss: he bores us with his £5,000 a year and his undoubted enlightenment. And it is an odd conjunction of life and art that, after she wrote this novel in 1916, Miss Leverson wrote no more.

But she had by then created a comic character far more original than the lunatic Bruce—Madame Frabelle. This portrait is satisfying because it is not caricature. It is the truth about Madame Frabelle that is so funny; and the fact that she is a likable monster makes her funnier. She is the Life Force gone dowdy, shady and kind, but never dormant. Indeed, advancing years make her phoniness redoubtable. It is she who runs off with Bruce in the end—one can imagine her picking him up like a puppy in her teeth and wobbling off with him—and anyone who is interested in skill in writing must admire the cleverness with which Miss Leverson insinuates the stages that lead to this dénouement. The splendid thing about Madame Frabelle is that she is absurd, false, but sympathetic—this comes from Miss Leverson's truthfulness:

> Madame Frabelle (of course) was dressed in black, *décolletée* and with a good deal of jet. A black aigrette, like a lightning conductor, stood up defiantly in her hair. Though it did not harmonize well with the somewhat square and *bourgeoise* shape of her head and face, and appeared to have dropped on her by accident, yet as a symbol of smartness it gave her a kind of distinction. It appeared to have fallen from the skies; it was put on in the wrong place, and it did not nestle, as it should do, and appear to grow out of her hair, since that glory of womanhood, in her case of a dull brown going slightly grey, was smooth, scarce and plainly parted. Madame Frabelle really would have looked her best in a cap of the fashion of the Sixties. But she could carry off anything; and some people said that she did.

Madame Frabelle's great gift is that of being wrong about everything. She is a monument to the failures of feminine intuition. She is an exciting store of inaccurate facts and false conjectures. She is the queen of nonsensical law-giving, masterfully inhabiting a very heaven of self-deception, as dotty as a horoscope. But people are charmed—again Miss Leverson's truthfulness—because Madame Frabelle is helplessly charmed by them. When she carries off Bruce, no one really minds. Two absurdities will have fulfilled themselves. Edith's excellences bored Bruce: he needed the dramatic companionship of a fellow self-deceiver.

Miss Leverson's admired males are too psychologically decorative: they are "connoisseurs of human nature," "urbane observers," "collectors of experience." They call Edith "*impayable*" when, frankly, she is really a moral coquette. But Miss Leverson's wit and perceptions are original. There are Lady Cannon's florid and massive clothes which, like her furniture, "express a violent, almost ominous conventionality, without the slightest touch of austerity to tone it down." Edith Ottley's appearance has "the rather insidious charm of somehow recalling the past while suggesting something undiscovered in the future." The random dialogue of parties turns, with hardly a pause, from the disturbing perception—"something in his suave manner of taking everything for granted seemed to make them know each other almost too quickly, and gave her an odd sort of self-consciousness"—to the hilariously vapid:

> Captain Willis lowered his voice to a confidential tone and said:
>
> "D'you know what I always say is—live and let live and let it go at that: what?"
>
> "That's a dark saying."
>
> "Have a burnt almond," said Captain Willis inconsequently as though it would help her to understand.

Writers of comedy have to bear as best they can the charge of triviality, in spite of the fact that their eye for detail and their instinct of selection give them an exceptional power to render the surface of life. How rarely do realists catch that surface. The other charge that they are evasive or, of all things, not "serious" is even more stupid, for they above all convey by their laughter the sense of danger that is inseparable from delight in the moment. In artificial comedy and the comedy of manners this sense of danger is intense. Miss Leverson lives by this. But the quality that has helped most to keep so much of her work in the perennial present is, quite simply, her feminine appetite for news:

> All women love news of whatever kind; even bad news gives them merely a feeling of pleasurable excitement . . .

Heavier novelists die off in a decade or two from a surfeit of information. (pp. 263-69)

V. S. Pritchett, "Knightsbridge Kennels," in his The Living Novel & Later Appreciations, *revised edition, Random House, 1964, pp. 263-69.*

CHARLES BURKHART (essay date 1970)

[Burkhart is an American educator, essayist, and editor who has written the only book-length critical study of Leverson's works to date. In the following excerpt, he compares and contrasts Leverson's early magazine work with the works of Oscar Wilde.]

Even though the friendship formed in 1892 [between Mrs. Leverson and Oscar Wilde] lasted uninterruptedly until Wilde's death in 1900, Mrs. Leverson's early admiration often took the form of parody. She began to contribute stories and sketches to *Black and White* and to *Punch,* inspired by Wilde's triumphs and by his urging. Parody often has its origin in malice but the four sketches she wrote for *Punch* in 1893 to 1895 are cool and harmless and funny skits, based on, in order, *The Picture of Dorian Gray, The Sphinx, An Ideal Husband,* and *The Importance of Being Earnest.*

"An Afternoon Party," the first and best of the sketches, is a lively dialogue among a highly assorted group of contemporary "celebrities," including Charley's Aunt, Madame Santuzza (the heroine of *Cavalleria Rusticana*), Mrs. Tanqueray, Nora (of *Doll's House*), Lady Windermere, Princess Salome, Captain Coddington, Lord Henry Wotten, and Lord Illingworth. The conversation is a disconnected succession of jokes, puns, and Wilde-like mock-epigrams, such as Lord Illingworth's "Valour is the better part of indiscretion." Princess Salome is amusing parody whether or not one is acquainted with Wilde in his pretentiously lyric vein:

> "Is that mayonnaise?" asked the Princess Salome of Captain Coddington, who had taken her to the buffet. "I think it is mayonnaise. I am sure it is mayonnaise. It is mayonnaise of salmon, pink as a branch of coral which fishermen find in the twilight of the sea, and which they keep for the King. It is pinker than the pink roses that bloom in the Queen's garden. The pink roses that bloom in the garden of the Queen of Arabia are not so pink."

In the following year, 1894, she published **"The Minx—A Poem in Prose,"** which is in the form of an interview of the Sphinx by "a Poet." Earlier in this year Wilde's poem *The Sphinx,* a long Baudelairean erotic fantasy, had appeared in elaborate format with decorations by Charles Ricketts. In Ada's version, the Sphinx is a prima donna who rattles through the events of Egyptian history in a casual, *haut-monde* sort of way. Her glib slang is in sharp contrast to Wilde's hothouse cadences, as is also the illustration to **"The Minx"** by Edward Tennyson Reed, a caricature of Ricketts' design for the cover of Wilde's poem. From then on, to Wilde, and to many others, Ada Leverson was herself known as "the Sphinx."

The other two Wildean parodies are even shorter than **"The Minx."** The first is called **"Overheard Fragment of a Dialogue"** and consists of a conversation between Lord Goring and Lord Illingworth which mocks both the epigrammatic Wilde ("If one tells the truth, one is sure sooner or later to be found out") and the lyric Wilde ("The sky is like a hard hollow sapphire"). The second is called **"The Advisability of Not Being Brought up in a Handbag: A Trivial Tragedy for Wonderful People."** The title is almost as long as the dialogue itself, which includes remarks like, from a character named Algy, "It is such a blessing, Aunt Augusta, that a woman always grows exactly like her aunt. It is such a curse that a man never grows exactly like his uncle. It is the greatest tragedy of modern life." (pp. 194-95)

[Much] that Wilde's and Mrs. Leverson's writings have in common they have in common with the age.

One of the paradoxes of the Nineties is that side by side with aestheticism and decadence, wit and comedy flourished. A rococo spirit pervaded the age, in everything from house decoration and food to women's clothing, yet at the same time the era saw the beginning of Max and the heyday of *Punch.* The two tendencies could be combined in the same person: Oscar Wilde wrote both *Salome* and *The Importance of Being Earnest.* There is considerable effeteness in the latter, but no comedy, or none that is intentional, in the former. The excessive modishness of the age, when the chic and the elegant were far more central to the general tenor of the times than they had been in the earlier Victorian period, offered itself easily as a target for wit. The fin-de-siècle overripeness produced its obverse, the chastening astringency of comedy. In Wilde there are both sides of the coin; in Mrs. Leverson, only the latter.

Civilized, even overcivilized, London preferred its humor light. The London of the Nineties responded to the short comic sketch, the caricature, the quip and the cartoon; the parodies by Mrs. Leverson, as any issue of a popular Nineties periodical like *Punch* will show, are typical. It would even seem that wit had not been so highly prized since the Restoration, a period which has other points in common with the end of the nineteenth century. Conversation, especially witty conversation, was one of the chief arts of the Nineties. The greatest talker of all was Wilde, and Ada Leverson was famous as a wit before she ever wrote a word. Wilde is best known for his plays, and Mrs. Leverson's novels are like plays in that they are almost pure dialogue.

There are numerous other resemblances between the two writers. Their milieu, Mayfair, and their interest in the fads and foibles of their immediate society are the same. Paradox, epigram, and simple joke or *plaisanterie* abound in both writers. And both are satirists. But Mrs. Leverson's satire is more human than Wilde's and governed by a more traditionally humane philosophic outlook. Her wit does not have the sting of his, and her epigrams are more self-amused and indulgent, less bristling and brilliant than his. More frequent than epigrams in her novels are aphorisms flavored with paradox. For example, from ***The Limit:*** "It is an infallible sign of the second-rate in nature and intellect to make use of everything and everyone." And from ***Love at Second Sight,*** in a description of the composer Sir Tito Landi: "There was something in his mental attitude that was not unfeminine, direct and assertive as he was. He had what is generally known as feminine intuition, a quality perhaps even rarer in women than in men." She was much more interested in what human nature was like than Wilde was, and she seldom sacrificed her interest for merely verbal comedy. Wilde's pose or persona is highly polished, while one of the chief appeals of Mrs. Leverson's writing is its directness and spontaneity.

Characterization is not Wilde's strong point; the types who populate his plays are facile sketches who have in common the ability to express themselves often with wit and always with elegance. To compare the two-dimensional Lady Bracknell in *The Importance of Being Earnest* with Mme. Frabelle, a character in Mrs. Leverson's last novel, ***Love at Second Sight,*** is to see with what range and richness Mrs. Leverson could capture personality. Mme. Frabelle is absurd, in her great air of wisdom which is always mistaken, in her professional sympathy where none is needed, in her careful sensitivities to what is banal and obvious; and she is appalling, in the rocklike structure of her ego. She entirely deserves the man she elopes with, Edith Ottley's husband Bruce, for Bruce is another monster of vanity, and with qualities all his own of petulance and acidulous spite. Comedy springs out of character in Mme. Frabelle and Bruce Ottley; they have not an epigram between them.

A final difference between Wilde and Ada Leverson has already been suggested. It is simply that Mrs. Leverson's novels are *about* something; underneath their lively surface they are a serious exploration of human relations—in friendship, in courtship, and, especially, in marriage. One doesn't find fault with *The Importance of Being Earnest* because it lacks a true subject; its glitter is certainly sufficient. But Mrs. Leverson is quite traditionally concerned with values, with human error and frailty and virtue and strength.

Even if Mrs. Leverson's novels have more humane depths and make more fundamental enquiries than Wilde's plays, it is clear that, in life, Wilde's wit and affection and elegance were enough for her. Long after she had stopped writing novels, the memory of her great friend was fresh, and in memoirs and diaries and letters of the Twenties, when we catch a glimpse of her, she is always linked with Wilde: she is recalling some Wildean anecdote or jest of thirty years before. Because Wilde had been dead so long, her association with him gave her, in her last years, the aura of a legend. Just as she had written for the famous *Yellow Book* in the Nineties, she wrote for Eliot's famous *Criterion* in the Twenties, and the subject of her essay in it, **"The Last First Night,"** was reminiscences of Wilde. It is quite fitting that her last published work, ***Letters to the Sphinx from Oscar Wilde,*** concerned the friend who had helped to inspire the beginning of her career forty years earlier. Such loyalty is a kind of love, a tribute both to Wilde and to his "Sphinx of gilded memory." (pp. 197-98)

Charles Burkhart, "Ada Leverson and Oscar Wilde," in English Literature in Transition, *Vol. XIII, No. 3, 1970, pp. 193-200.**

CHARLES BURKHART (essay date 1973)

[In the following excerpt, Burkhart explores plot, characterization, theme, and style in a number of Leverson's minor works.]

Ada Leverson's London comes to life just as topically and immediately [in her short pieces] as it does in the novels. An incisive and energetic social commentator, she shows in her very first published work the born skill of the anatomist. Another interest of her minor pieces is the light they cast on the novels. Like most writers, she repeated herself; she was not one to drop a successful *mot*. What amused her once was likely to amuse her again, so that we find jokes, phrases, situations, and even characters making a return engagement in the novels after a trial run in *Black and White* or *Punch*. (pp. 59-60)

Whether or not her very first publications were those in *Black and White,* they offer an interesting portent of the way in which her career was to develop. In this weekly, Mrs. Leverson published three short stories—**"Claude's Aunt," "Mimosa,"** and **"In the Change of Years"**—and a series of twenty-four **"Letters of Silvia and Aurelia."** The first of the three short stories is a comedy; the second, a tragedy; the third, primarily comedy but with serious overtones.

"Claude's Aunt," if it were a Restoration comedy (and it only lacks earthiness to be one), could have the subtitle: "The Marriage Maneuver." When Claude Ferguson visits the country house of his aunt Gladys, he falls in love—as in innumerable rites of initiation in novels and plays and movies, largely French—with an older woman, Mrs. Vervaine, a professional flirt who is estranged from her husband. Claude's aunt, wishing to acquire Claude for her stepdaughter Lucy, who is Claude's own young age, arranges for the unexpected arrival of Colonel Gray, Mrs. Vervaine's lover, and for Claude, "by accident," to witness the loving reunion between Colonel Gray and Mrs. Vervaine. When the strategem succeeds, Claude transfers his affections to Lucy. Another situation, earlier in the story, which is also lifted from familiar stage devices, is the discovery by Lucy of a love letter written by Claude to Mrs. Vervaine.

Other characters include a young married couple, Arthur and Sylvia, whose newlywed bliss adds to the atmosphere of matchmaking and marriage; Mr. Thorne, a bachelor; and Mr. Vincent, an 1890's dandy. Vincent, in his bossy elegance, is an amusing figure; with him, Mrs. Leverson's preoccupation with boutonnieres begins to be evident: Vincent has "prize carnations . . . sent down from town in a cardboard box, twice daily. . . ." The characters have only one, two, or three traits, never more: Claude is emotional, impetuous, and romantic, in a word, young; Lucy, the same; Mrs. Vervaine, sly and flirtatious; Gladys, Claude's aunt, shrewd; Colonel Gray, no traits at all. Mrs. Vervaine has tired "Japanese" looks that foreshadow the Japanese-looking lady Mrs. Raymond in ***Love's Shadow,*** whom Cecil Reeve loves and whom Lord Selsey, Cecil's uncle, marries. Certainly the characters in **"Claude's Aunt"**—the title is probably an echo of *Charley's Aunt*—are as flat as Oscar Wilde's. When one of the flattest, Colonel Gray, appears on the scene, we read: "Gladys rose to greet a man of fifty, who had exactly the appearance that an actor would 'make up' for a conventional middle-aged cavalry officer."

"Claude's Aunt" shows that Mrs. Leverson was a humorist from the beginning, and the quick pace and the brevity of the paragraphs reveal that, whatever she had earlier written or published, she was already accustomed to a short, snappy type of journalistic paragraph; and, more important, her instinctive turn was for dialogue. The dialogue is theatrical in nature, and the story is arranged in a series of conversational exchanges, like a play with many short scenes; it is divided into parts—they could be called acts—like a play. The story reads like a scenario, and there is a climactic ball scene, as there is in everything from *The Cherry Orchard to My Fair Lady*. Was it Wilde's influence or her own natural bent that led her to a quasi-dramatic form?

The dialogue of **"Claude's Aunt"** is lively, if not brilliant, and an occasional remark already has the authentic Leverson ring: "Mr. and Mrs. Ferguson [Claude's parents] were very pleased with the letters they received from Claude, though they were shorter than his telegrams and less numerous." **"Claude's Aunt"** is a workmanlike trifle, which could have been made into a trifling and probably charming play; but Mrs. Leverson . . . attempted only one play for production—**"The Triflers"**—which was never finished.

"Mimosa," Mrs. Leverson's second story, is a tragedy more in intention than in effect. It is most uncharacteristic, in that only a certain dry restraint keeps it from mawkishness. In this simple story about a young country girl with the appropriate country name of Annie Croft, and with the pet name of Mimosa, given to her by the young artist Cecil Thorpe, who comes to stay at her father's farm, Mrs. Leverson aims at sentiment and at romance. Cecil paints Mimosa's portrait and declares his love for her, which the naïve girl ardently returns. When Cecil leaves, Mimosa is as innocent as he had found her, and he promises to return. When he does return, he is too late; he arrives just on the eve of her marriage to the neighboring young farmer—who is, of course, named "John." During Cecil's absence he had achieved success and fame with his portrait of Mimosa, but Mimosa herself gradually came to despair of his return. On her wedding day, after the ceremony—Cecil has left her, this time irrevocably, on learning of her marriage—she is close to taking poison. But "then the influence of the simple religion, in which she had been brought up, asserted itself . . . ," she joins her new husband, and the story ends. Religion, which hardly ever appears in Mrs. Leverson's writings, has an operative if unconvincing role in this story.

If this simple tale were more Wordsworthian or more allegorized, it might achieve the pathos at which it aims. The theme may concern the selfishness of art; for, when Cecil returns to Mimosa, he has realized that her portrait is the best thing he has ever done, and he tells her, "my *art* is really dependent on *you.*" Moreover, though he loves her, he loves his painting, or himself, more. In contrast to Mimosa's deep, unselfish love, Cecil's is shared with another mistress, his painting; and his love for Mimosa and his art is shallow, since he can barely be troubled to write a letter to her and since, as he well knows, he is not a very good painter.

The impression the story makes is that of a step taken in the wrong direction. There is a clear narrative line, but the anecdote is hackneyed. The closest to humor the story comes is in a description of Cecil's success: "he was made much of by a section of Society, the feminine members of which are free from all solicitudes except that of looking prettier than their neighbors." Pale, only remotely poignant, **"Mimosa"** shows Mrs. Leverson as divesting herself of her sense of comedy and thereby as depriving herself of her most attractive talent.

The title of Mrs. Leverson's last *Black and White* story, **"In the Change of Years,"** apparently refers to certain changes wrought by time, particularly the transfer of the heroine's—Alice Herbert's—love of her fiancé, Frederick Langton, to a less pompous suitor, Lance Challoner. The change does not seem much for the better: though Fred is pompous and money-minded, Lance is vain, handsome, and silly. When Alice considers the change in Fred, who has returned after making a fortune in South Africa, her mixture of shallowness, true feeling, and girlishness (she is eighteen) is an interesting one: "He was earnest, poor and had a moustache. It's not the same man I was engaged to, or, perhaps, I am not the same woman? If he shaved his beard, and lost all his money would he be possible again?" When Alice breaks her engagement to Fred, he promptly proposes to another girl, the horsy "modern" Ida Hurst. Alice thinks she has been abandoned by Lance, who has returned to London from the northern seaside village where most of the action takes place; but an inflammation of the lungs has been the cause of his silence. After a sickbed reconciliation, the story ends happily—except for Dormer Ellis.

Dormer is Lance's close friend, with whom he has shared a flat; and Dormer is as sober and conservative a barrister as Lance is frivolous and romantic. When the story ends a month after the marriage of Alice to Lance, the last lines portray Dormer's sadness: "Dormer, upstairs, surrounded by cigars and drinks, was supposed to be struggling with a brief. He looked sad. He knew that he now took the second place in the heart of Lance, who was very dear to him. From the room below came the sound of their young laughter. . . ." Even if the language is trite, its effect is to show that the "change"of the title is also a change in Dormer Ellis' life.

The surprisingly melancholy conclusion of the story just quoted may be consonant with the theme, but it is not with the prevailing tone of the story, which is light. Alice Herbert's mother is the first of those studies of comic dowagers, like Lady Kellynch and Lady Cannon, which enliven the novels. Authors often overdo a first inspiration, which additional practice refines; and Mrs. Herbert, with her neurasthenia, her self-indulgence, and her innocent preoccupation with social trivialities, is coarsely executed in comparison with her descendants in the novels. Lance is a harmless fop with his guitar and warbling of sentimental songs, but we wonder why Alice is in the least interested in him. Alice is like a girlish study of Edith Ottley, heroine of three of the novels, in her sensitivity, interest in the arts, and quiet beauty.

There are two complexly conceived scenes in the story. The first is on a fishing boat expedition where, amid the landing of small fish and the jealous intervention of Ida Hurst, Lance declares his love to Alice. The other is the scene of Alice alone by the sea in the little northern town of Sandby. She has rejected Fred, and Lance has apparently abandoned her:

> The little place was full of memories, and she would sit alone, watching the serene irony of unconscious nature, wondering at the harshness, the cruel, unmeaning futility of life.
>
> Supreme summer was over. The first chill of autumn was in the air. The falling leaves had the poetic grace of fading things. Soon the whole earth would be dying of old age and weariness. Already the frequent showers fell like tears, like bitter tears of resignation to the inevitable approach of winter.
>
> But there is always a feeling of life and hope in the restless movement of the sea.
>
> Alice was watching it one day, as she sat on the beach, while a crude, belated band played a valse. It was a commonplace valse, and one that she associated in her mind with rose-coloured tulle, the scent of stephanotis, small social remarks, and polite struggles for ices and plovers' eggs.

As a whole, the passage fails. It might be suitable for Tolstoy's Anna Karenina, but not for Alice Herbert, whom we barely know. Yet the single-sentence third paragraph is a higher order of cliché than what precedes it, and it tempts us to speculate on what might have been Mrs. Leverson's future as a writer if she had pursued the purely romantic vein. However, the last sentence of all in the quoted passage, with its quick, witty, and close social observation, is an example, and a fine one, of the course she did follow.

"In the Change of Years" is not so satisfactory a story as **"Claude's Aunt"** because of divided intention; it was only later, in the Edith Ottley novels especially, that Mrs. Leverson could blend comedy and romantic love convincingly. (pp. 60-5)

Letters to the Sphinx, the tribute to Wilde which ended Mrs. Leverson's literary career is, happily, one of her finest pieces of writing. (pp. 86-7)

In style, the three parts of the essay of reminiscences are of a piece; and the style is at once the most graceful and the most weighty that Mrs. Leverson ever achieved. She turns each anecdote into a little story of its own, with elements artfully spaced and arranged. Her sentences tend to be longer, more complex, more obviously rhythmic, but her habitual one-sentence epigrammatic paragraph, as in the novels, also appears. The tone of unembittered gaiety deepens often into sensitive, graver notes. Even with the intimacy of her portrait, she never says, "It is I who sheltered Wilde"; nor, on the other hand, does she disguise her good deeds and his gratitude for them and his affection. Throughout her writing, her candor is coupled with a fine restraint. Wilde himself so much admired manner and manners (in that order, I think) that he surely would have approved the Sphinx's style in her reminiscences, just as he had lavished praise on her sketches and parodies of the early 1890's. (p. 87)

What Mrs. Leverson does in **"The Importance of Being Oscar"** is to set the scene for the rest of the essay by delineating the character of the early 1890's and by showing how Wilde dominated the period. She describes how London in 1894 and 1895 "bloomed out into a sudden flamboyance of taste and of expression. Art, poetry, beauty, dress and decoration became the fashion." She well remembers the enthusiasms of those days—the Overture to *Tannhäuser, Mrs. Tanqueray,* The Gaiety Theatre, the revival of mid-Victorian decoration, Whistler, the de Rezskes. Of Wilde himself, she says, in pungent summary,

"The most soft-hearted, carelessly-generous, and genial of men, his great fault was weakness, and, with all his brilliance, a fatal want of judgment." She ends with a splendid series of Wilde's conversational epigrams (some of which he printed in *Intentions*), such as his famous opinion of Meredith:

> "Will you kindly tell me, Mr. Wilde, in your own words, your viewpoint of George Meredith?"
>
> "George Meredith is a prose Browning, and so is Browning."
>
> "Thank you. His style?"
>
> "Chaos, illuminated by flashes of lightning."

In this first third of the essay, Mrs. Leverson's method is one often used in novels, and especially in movies: she has given a panoramic view, then she has focused on this or that detail, and then she has centered upon where the view and the details have been carefully selected to lead her—upon the central human figure, Wilde himself.

The arrangement of the central section, **"The Last First Night,"** follows another familiar literary form, which could be called the sandwich pattern, or the bracket effect. Mrs. Leverson begins with a description of one tonality and ends with one the same, or nearly the same; but between the two, the bulk of **"The Last First Night"** is a sharp contrast to the prologue and epilogue. The first sentences are: "On Valentine's Day, the 14th February 1895, there was a snow-storm more severe than had been remembered in London for years. A black, bitter, threatening wind blew the drifting snow. On that dark sinister winter's night . . ." and the last sentences are nearly identical.

Between this beginning and this end is a brilliant, light-filled evocation of the first night of *The Importance of Being Earnest* at the St. James's Theatre. Oscar had commanded that the flower of the evening be the lily-of-the-valley, and the stalls were filled with women whose large puffed sleeves were adorned with sprays of lilies and with young elegants whose boutonnieres were also that flower. "What a rippling, glittering, chattering crowd was that! . . . Whoever still lives who was present on that night will remember the continual ripple of laughter from the very first moment, the excitement, the strange almost hysterical joy with which was received this "Trivial Comedy for Serious People.' . . ." (pp. 88-90)

The first two sections of the essay are static, but the third, **"Afterwards,"** has considerable narrative interest. It covers the Sphinx's relationship with Wilde from the time of his first trial in early 1895 until his death in 1900. The central section concerns, of course, the Leversons' granting asylum to Wilde during the period between his trials. Most biographies of Wilde during his latter years have made use of this part of Mrs. Leverson's memoir, and the events are too well known to warrant more than a summary: the loyalty of the Leversons' servants to them and to Wilde, his residence on the nursery floor, the arrangements made for his escape from England and his rejection of them, his two years' incarceration in prison, his reunion with the Sphinx and other friends on the morning of his release, his final years in Paris and the Sphinx's last visit with him there.

Into the narrative line she works many a small, vivid glimpse of Wilde, examples of his wit, his generosity, his capacity for sympathy and for sorrow. For biographical interest, this last part of the memoir is remarkable. Her artistry has a great moment at the end when she is witty, in no callous way, even if her subject is his death; and the wit is, generously, not her own, but Wilde's, and from his last play:

> One of the hits in *The Importance of Being Earnest* is when the clergyman says that Mr. Bunbury expressed a desire to be buried in Paris. "I fear," says the clergyman, "that this doesn't seem a very desirable state of mind at the last."
>
> Oscar is buried in Paris under Epstein's magnificent monument given, ten years after his death, by a lady whose friendship remained steadfast to the end.

(pp. 90-1)

Charles Burkhart, in his Ada Leverson, *Twayne Publishers, Inc., 1973, 171 p.*

PENELOPE FITZGERALD (essay date 1983)

[*Fitzgerald is an English biographer and novelist who has written lives of Edward Burne-Jones and of her relatives, the Knox brothers. She has written: "I believe that people should write biographies only about people they love, or understand, or both. Novels, on the other hand, are often better if they're about people the writer doesn't like very much." In the following excerpt, Fitzgerald favorably reviews a recent reprint edition of* The Little Ottleys.]

[Ada Leverson] was enchanted by the times she lived in. The three novels which make up ***The Little Ottleys*** change subtly with the passing years, not only in reference, but in atmosphere. In ***Love's Shadow*** there are aging poets surviving from the Nineties, *nouveau art*, amateur theatricals. In ***Tenterhooks*** you can choose whether to take a hansom or a taxicab, Debussy and Wagner are 'out', and at dinner-parties 'one ran an equal risk of being taken to dinner by Charlie Chaplin or Winston Churchill.' The Turkey Trot is discussed along with Nijinsky and Post-Impressionism: 'please don't take an intelligent interest in the subjects of the day,' the hero begs. In ***Love at Second Sight*** he is in khaki, and wounded. At the same time the viewpoint grows, not less intelligent, but more sympathetic to the absurdity of human beings in a trap of their own making.

Unashamedly her friends are pictured in her novels, and her own unhappiness, and, for that matter, the courage with which she faced it. Perhaps because of this, they show a great advance on her *Yellow Book* stories, **'Suggestion'** and **'The Quest for Sorrow'. *Love's Shadow*** is a set of variations on the theme of jealousy: Ada herself felt that jealousy was allowable, but envy, never. Hyacinth Verney's guardian is in love with her, Hyacinth is in pursuit of the fashionable Cyril, Cyril has a hopeless *tendresse* for Mrs. Raymond, who is neither young nor beautiful, but seems merely 'very unaffected, and rather ill'. For counterpoint, there is Edith Ottley, who is beginning to be tired of her own patience with her husband, but who is not yet the victim of human emotion. Critics, and even the Sphinx's own family, found the book frivolous, but I don't know that any book which proclaims so clearly the painful value of honesty can be frivolous. Its real heroine is the uncompromisingly plain Anne Yeo, hideously dressed in a mackintosh and golf-cap, and 'well aware that there were not many people in London at three o'clock on a sunny afternoon who would care to be found dead with her.' Sharp-tongued Anne is in love with Hyacinth, the only genuine passion in the novel. When she has done all she can to help Hyacinth to capture Cyril in marriage, she is seen for the last time on her way to Cook's. She has decided to emigrate.

Whether Ada Leverson originally intended it or not, the Ottleys become central to the next two novels. Grandly careless in small details, she changes Edith's age and the colour of her hair, and makes her far more witty and admired. Bruce is, if possible, more monstrously selfish and witless. (When Ernest Leverson came back on one of his infrequent visits from Canada, it was said that 'he talked just like Bruce.') Possibly the Sphinx is too hard, at times, on her creation. Faultless is Edith's clarity, ruthless are the sharp-eyed inhabitants of the nursery. But, after all, Bruce is well able to protect himself. 'With the curious blindness common to all married people, and indeed to any people who live together', Edith has not noticed that Bruce is making sly advances to the governess. Meanwhile, she herself has fallen in love with the impulsive Aylmer Ross, but 'how can life be like a play?' she asks sadly, and to Bruce's relief (for he can now feel injured) she simply gets rid of the governess. In contrast to her self-restraint, there is the interlocking story of her devoted friend, Vincy. A dandyish observer of life, Vincy has a mistress, Mavis, an impoverished young art student whose red hair is 'generally untidy at the back'. Her poverty, which brings her close to starvation, is disquieting, but Vincy discards her without pity: '"Shall you marry her?"—"I'm afraid not," he said. "I don't think I quite can."' For all their humour and good humour, these novels can sometimes seem unrelenting. At length, the easily-persuaded Bruce runs off with Mavis. Edith, however, for the sake of her children, rescues him once again.

But Ada Leverson is writing in terms of comedy, and Edith Ottley must be left happier than she was herself. To bring this about, she introduces, in ***Love at Second Sight,*** a grotesque creation, powerful enough to dominate the situation. Eglantine Frabelle, perfectly well-off and perfectly self-satisfied, is a guest in the Ottleys' small London house and shows no signs of ever going away. She is, wrote Siegfried Sassoon, like 'a really great impressionist picture by Whistler or Manet', who, 'to tell you the truth, rather dumps the others, dear Sphinx'. Sassoon was right. Edith and Aylmer are less interesting than this stately, tedious widow of a French wine-merchant, whose name has undertones of *frappant* and *poubelle*. Always knowledgeable, and invariably wrong, she is detestable, and admired by everybody: even Edith is devoted to her. When Bruce (it is 1916) finds that listening to the war news is affecting his health, and he must leave for America, he elopes—and we know he will never escape again—with Madame Frabelle. Once she has left the book, even though Aylmer and the delightful Edith are free to marry, the interest fades. We seem to be waiting for her to come back.

How can Bruce manage to think that he must 'throw in his lot' with her? Through wilful misunderstanding. Their day out on the river is tedious. The only boat left for hire is *The Belle of the River,* as battered as an old tea-chest, and they find that they have very little to say to one another. But both of them have the impression that it has been a great success. With such non-events or anti-events, Ada Leverson is marvellously skilful. Oscar Wilde had wanted *The Importance of Being Earnest* to be not paradoxical, but nonsensical—pure nonsense, he said. The first act ends not with an epigram, but a wail: 'But I haven't quite finished my tea!' This is the art of inconsequence, possible only in a society where consequences can still be grave. The Sphinx, also, had a most distinctive ear for nonsense. 'With a tall, thin figure and no expression,' she writes, 'Anne might have been any age, but she was not.'

Penelope Fitzgerald, "Dear Sphinx," in London Review of Books, *December 1 to December 21, 1983, p. 19.**

ADDITIONAL BIBLIOGRAPHY

Bergonzi, Bernard. "Woman of Some Importance." *The Spectator* CCIX, No. 7001 (31 August 1962): 311.

Favorably critiques Leverson's use of dialogue and sense of comedy.

Sitwell, Osbert. "Ada Leverson." In his *Noble Essences,* pp. 127-62. London: Macmillan & Co., 1950.

Biographical sketch of Leverson based on Sitwell's reminiscences of her.

Wyndham, Violet. *The Sphinx and Her Circle*. London: Andre Deutsch, 1963, 128 p.

Biographical portrait of Leverson, with emphasis upon those who influenced her.

Detlev von Liliencron

1844-1909

(Born Friedrich Adolf Axel von Liliencron) German poet, novella and short story writer, novelist, and dramatist.

Ranked among the foremost lyric poets of Germany during his lifetime, Liliencron is today considered important to modern German poetry primarily for his stylistic innovations. A Prussian soldier rather than a man of letters, Liliencron utilized themes of war, love, and death and a style unmindful of literary convention to create works praised for their originality and freshness. Although Liliencron disavowed allegiance to any literary school or movement, the realism and forcefulness of his poetry led to his being acclaimed the leader of "Youngest Germany," a group of writers who sought to purge German literature of triviality and sentimentality. Today Liliencron's works are valued for their profound effect on late nineteenth-century German poetry.

Liliencron was born into an impoverished family of the baronial class in the German province of Schleswig-Holstein. After an undistinguished school career he entered the Prussian army in 1863 and served with distinction in the 1866 war against Austria and the Franco-Prussian war of 1870-71, rising to the rank of captain. He loved the life of a soldier, about which he later wrote, "Oh, those glorious years as a young officer! The good friends and comrades; the fine acceptance of duty and service; the subduing of self!" However, debts, as well as injuries incurred in battle, forced him to resign his commission in 1875. He emigrated to the United States, where he had connections through his maternal grandfather, who had been a member of George Washington's military staff. After two years of struggling to earn a living as a house painter, piano player, language teacher, and stable master, Liliencron returned to Germany, where he was granted a series of minor civil service posts. According to Liliencron, he wrote his first poem in 1879, at the age of thirty-five; however, dated notebooks attest to steady literary activity from the time of his return to Germany in 1877, and evidence exists that he actually began writing as early as 1863. His first volume of poetry, *Adjutantenritte,* was published in 1883 to critical but not popular acclaim: according to critic Jethro Bithell, the book sold only twenty-three copies in two years. Although his numerous volumes of poetry and fiction eventually gained him an enthusiastic following, Liliencron lived close to poverty through most of his life; during the cholera epidemic of 1892 he wrote of his financial difficulties: "What's a little mass death in comparison?" In 1909, as the result of a visit to the battlefields around Metz where he had fought in 1870, Liliencron contracted pneumonia and died.

Liliencron's early poetry, of which the poems in *Adjutantenritte* are the best known, established him as an independent force in the post-Romantic era of German poetry. Critic Detlev W. Schumann attributes the acclaim Liliencron received from his contemporaries to historical circumstance, noting that German literature of the 1880s was dominated by inferior imitators of Johann Wolfgang von Goethe and Heinrich Heine, which resulted in a literary atmosphere of stale conventionalism. By comparison, Liliencron's spirited, unconventional verses appeared as an invigorating force, and Liliencron was proclaimed leader of the movement of young, iconoclastic writers seeking to revitalize German letters. Liliencron's direct and vivid style, dominated by elements of Naturalism and Impressionism, constituted a significant departure from traditional poetic forms. His most famous poem, "Die Musik kommt," demonstrates his successful use of impressionistic techniques and unconventional use of language in depicting the passing of a military band. Critics note Liliencron's contribution to German poetic vocabulary in the introduction of countless neologisms, unconventional compounds and metaphors, and colloquial expressions previously considered unsuitable for poetry. Liliencron is also praised for his ability to capture the rhythm of his subject, as typified by "Zwei Meilen Trab," the poetic rendering of a two-mile trot on horseback, and "Auf einem Bahnhof," which depicts the noise and bustle of a train station. The dominant subjects in Liliencron's work are derived from the life of the soldier and the outdoorsman, and his poems are often placed in natural settings, particularly on the North Sea or in the heath and marshland of his native Schleswig-Holstein. His treatment of war, military life, hunting, death, and love is direct and nonintellectual, favoring the assembly of a series of straightforward descriptions and images to analysis or moralizing. Critics find Liliencron's poetry outstanding for its spontaneity and vigor, and note that when Liliencron did attempt to examine metaphysical themes, the natural force of his writing degenerated into banality. Liliencron's later poetry, including the popular epic *Poggfred*, lacks the compactness of his earlier work, and is generally considered inferior due to its diffuseness and lack of narrative structure.

In addition to his poetry, Liliencron wrote numerous dramas and prose works, all of which are regarded by critics as much less successful than his poetry. Although his shorter prose works—particularly the stories in *Kriegsnovellen*, which are based on his war experiences—are praised for the immediacy of their descriptive passages, they suffer from the same careless structure and discontinuity as Liliencron's later poetry. Most critics concur that Liliencron's strength lay in the creation of brief, impressionistic pieces rather than complex, sustained works. His novels feature disconnected plots interspersed with unrelated commentary, reminiscences, and critical evaluations, and are almost universally regarded as unsuccessful. *Breide Hummelsbüttel* is considered the most cohesive of the four novels, and *Leben und Lüge* of some interest for its autobiographical aspects. The dramas, written early in Liliencron's career, are similarly dismissed as weak in characterization and overburdened with unnecessary conflict and narration.

The enthusiasm with which Liliencron's works were greeted during his lifetime has long since subsided. In comparison with the work of his successors Rainer Maria Rilke, Hugo von Hofmannsthal, and Stefan George, Liliencron's unsubtle, nonintellectual poetry now appears crude and even vulgar. While modern critics therefore no longer regard Liliencron among Germany's foremost poets, they continue to acknowledge his substantial contribution to the evolution of German poetry.

PRINCIPAL WORKS

Adjutantenritte (poetry) 1883
Knut der Herr (drama) [first publication] 1885
Die Rantzow und die Pogwisch (drama) [first publication] 1886
Der Trifels und Palermo (drama) [first publication] 1886
Arbeit adelt (drama) [first publication] 1887
Breide Hummelsbüttel (novel) 1887
Die Merowinger (drama) [first publication] 1888
Unter flatternden Fahnen (short stories) 1888
Gedichte (poetry) 1889
Der Mäcen (novel) 1889
Mit dem linken Ellbogen (novel) 1889
Der Haidegänger (poetry) 1890
Krieg und Frieden (short stories) 1891
Neue Gedichte (poetry) 1893; also published as *Nebel und Sonne* [enlarged edition], 1900
Kriegsnovellen (short stories) 1895
Eine Sommerschlacht (short stories) 1895
Poggfred (poetry) 1896; also published as *Poggfred* [enlarged edition], 1908
Aus Marsch und Geest (short stories) 1900
Bunte Beute (poetry) 1903
Pokahontas (drama) [first publication] 1904
Balladchronik (poetry) 1906
Leben und Lüge (novel) 1908
Gute Nacht (poetry) 1909
Letzte Ernte (short stories) 1909
Gesammelte Werke. 10 vols. (poetry, dramas, novels, novellas, and letters) 1910-12

Translated selections of Liliencron's poetry have appeared in the following publications: *Contemporary German Poetry* (translated by Jethro Bithell); *Contemporary German Poetry* (translated by D. Yarmolinsky); *German Lyrics and Ballads from Klopstock to Modern Times;* and *The World's Best Literature*.

A. VON ENDE (essay date 1900)

[In the following excerpt, Von Ende praises the versatility and emotive power of Liliencron's poems.]

It is almost impossible to open a volume of poems by one of the young Germans without finding a dedication to Detlev Baron von Liliencron, who, though about fifty-six years of age, is always considered as belonging to the young school, and by its members called their master and fellow. His art is more likely to appeal to a wider circle of readers than that of most of his admirers and brothers in song, for finding beauty even in some features of life that are not included in the programme of the future, his genius has established a link between the Old and the New. The scion of an old noble family, Liliencron has seen active service in several campaigns, and has served his country in official capacity. A true German "Junker," he loves the simple pleasures of the country as much as he appreciates the whirl and artificial glamour of the metropolis. A man of the world and a child of the Holstein heath, a soldier and a singer, a true poet and a true man, his charming naïveté and spontaneous humor make him a most amiable personality. An artist by instinct, the versatility of Liliencron is amazing. He makes one realize the fascination of uniforms and epaulettes, the clink of spurs and sabres, the sound of fife and drum, and all the dash of military life; but he also paints the carnage and horror of the battlefield with the power of Verestchagin's brush. With exquisite playfulness he can describe little scenes of society life, and with stirring pathos he can record the tragedies of lowly life. His religious feeling is intense; one of the most beautiful of his longer poems is **"Pieta,"** where he tells how Mary bends over the form of the Crucified. . . . Liliencron's verse has a harmony, a strength, and a spontaneousness which are truly unique. All the elements of the *Zeitgeist* are there, but no longer in a fermenting chaos, for the poet has known life and learned that man has to bide his time. (pp. 239-40)

A. Von Ende, "The Poets of Young Germany (Conclusion)," in The Critic, *New York, Vol. XXXVI, No. 3, March, 1900, pp. 238-42.**

R. C. K. ENSOR (essay date 1909)

[Ensor was an English journalist, educator, poet, and author of works on history and politics. In the following excerpt, he examines the themes and techniques of Liliencron's poetry.]

Liliencron . . . stands rather outside the current [of German poetry]. He is extremely individual. He had a strong, keen personality; he cared passionately for certain ideas; he was withal an astonishing *virtuoso* in verse. Like Swinburne he felt the need of revealing new music in, and imposing new fetters on, a language long used for poetry. He tabooed the easy half rhymes—*Liebe* and *trübe*, or *Freude* and *Leide*—which Goethe and Heine had accepted from folk-song; and he wrote a witty little skit on their use. Like his friend Hugo Wolf in music, he took the popular medium, song, and liked to banish its conventions, to alter its outlines, to mould subtler forms, expressing more perfectly the inmost meaning of the artist. He was saved from overdoing this tendency by his soldierly robustness and his sincere concern with what he had to say. Some of his metrical exploits are not less remarkable than Swinburne's; but he never (as Swinburne seems to have done) composed stanza after stanza simply to employ certain rhymes or achieve a certain metrical effect. The man always matters in him more than the artist, consummate artist though he be. (pp. 448-49)

He was not a great play-wright, nor a great novelist, but his lyrical power enabled him to write passages of much distinction in nearly all his books. In the lyrics this power takes its natural course. Among them should really be included his "epic" poem, **"Poggfred"**—a brilliant lyrical medley of the most contrasted materials, tragedy and comedy, battle-pieces and idylls, genre-painting and landscape. It is written in the metre of "Don Juan," and shows perhaps more family likeness to that masterpiece than to any other long poem of modern Europe. But there are great differences between them; where Byron declaims, Liliencron sings, and his high spirits exhibit little of the Byronic cynicism. Such cynicism as there is in him is rather that of the reckless, full-blooded "superman" than that of the soured voluptuary.

The advent of his **"Adjutantenritte"** in 1883 was a veritable trumpet-blast. It synchronised with the first trumpet-blasts of Nietzsche, and called men to the same resurrection. Germany before 1870 had reached an intellectual *impasse*. . . . [About] 1880 came the definite revolt, in which Nietzsche and Liliencron were both leaders. This is not the place to discuss all its aspects, and winnow its wheat from its obvious chaff. Fundamentally and instinctively it embodies two valuable ideas—the reclaiming of the individual's freedom from the pressure of modern environment, and the reassertion of the joy of life as against its burden. No doubt Liliencron's glad, strong military heroes, when you analyse them, embody with this a good deal of the Bismarckian cult of sheer force; no doubt the brutality, which he sometimes affects, goes much beyond a mere counterblast to the namby-pambyism of the romantic school. Considering who the man was by birth and up-bringing, and what part he had personally played in the great movement which Bismarck and Moltke directed, who can wonder? What is perhaps more surprising is the comparative frequency with which the conservative and Bismarckian poet is driven by his artistic conscience and his real human sympathy to appeal to our emotions of pity and tenderness, and our protest against injustice between man and man. Moreover, he is never guilty of that amateurishness and those mistakes of pure ignorance which are so distressing in Nietzsche. The would-be philosopher fought his battle in a sphere for which he was very imperfectly equipped. Liliencron's equipment for the sphere in which he chose to fight—lyric poetry—was beyond cavil.

A German who wanted to appraise him shortly would probably describe him as the perfector of the "realistic lyric.". . . [A poet who] challenges superficial comparison is Mr. Kipling. In his soldier subjects, his ballad forms, and his outspoken cult of force and virility he is an obvious parallel; and it would be interesting to know if he had read him. There is between them, however, not only the disparity in technique and compass, but also a wide difference of temperament. Mr. Kipling has the materialism of the English middle-class, and his worship goes rather to the engineering type of man; the Freiherr von Liliencron is an aristocrat, and his idols are the fighter and the singer.

Liliencron's realism is very steady. He can describe details by fire-flashes just as brilliantly as Mr. Kipling, but he always attends to the effect of his whole poem. In general he abhors the moralising, dear to Mr. Kipling's Anglo-Saxon nature, and fights shy of large abstract phrases. His method is to pick out and collocate the eloquent facts, and let them speak for themselves. . . . [His] striking ballad, called **"Midsummer in the Forest,"** . . . describes how a poor distracted artisan goes to the edge of the forest and hangs himself. Without a word of moralising, three ideas are hammered into us—the pity of it; the total failure of the victim's fellow-men to throw him any sort of a life-line; and the gay indifference of the forest, which goes its own splendid way, unheeding that humanity should lose its path and beat its life out. All this is given not in so many words, but simply in a rapid succession of unexaggerated facts, driven in so cunningly that the pain is well-nigh intolerable. (pp. 449-51)

But realism is only one of the two factors in the realistic lyric. The other is song, and here Liliencron's intimacy with great music and great musicians becomes important. He has an almost unique power of seizing the rhythm of modern things. Has anyone ever rendered so well that of a railway train? (pp. 451-52)

Or consider the music of **"Festnacht und Frühgang"**—a magnificent dance, all whirl and life and colour, and then the lovers' walk of two dancers that have left it, spell-bound in the tender dawn. Great skill he has too in writing poetry that musicians can compose. (p. 452)

Liliencron's stories are often based on his military experiences, but his purely military lyrics are not prominent. On the other hand his experiences as forest-warden and dyke-surveyor off the Schleswig coast were of the utmost artistic value to him. . . . This stern lonely region—half land, half sea—with its vast expanses and vistas, its mists and clouds, its cold air and pale colouring, its dreary heaths, its pines and winter snow, is constantly present to the poet's imagination. His set descriptions of it, as in the **"Haidebilder,"** or the little **"Einsames Haus am Aussendeich,"** have an extraordinary magic; and often it enters as something more than a background—a sort of Greek chorus—to the tale of human passion. (pp. 452-53)

This bare, gaunt, grandiose sternness and beauty of the North Sea is heard as a sort of pedal-bass in most of Liliencron's poetry. The themes written above it are rapid and swift. At one time it is the fierce exultation of the elemental warrior. "Forth! forth!" he exclaims in a celebrated passage, "To battle and war, for man must fight man!" And again more deliberately, "I was born for war, for war is in the nature of things, is it not as old as the world? Know that war and hatred, envy and spite, will only end when the world ends." At another time it is love—the merry downright love of the boisterous Northern conqueror, which now leaps and sparkles like a reckless mountain cascade, and now slips into pools of loveliest dreaming, but is seldom or never self-analysing or self-torturing. (p. 454)

On the loveliness of passages like these comment is needless. Their richness is all the richer by contrast with the Scandinavian saga-like tone which prevails in their author's work. But even within that sterner key he could write with a surpassing tenderness, an unexpected revelation of sentiment, recalling rather those extraordinary letters, compounded of romance and passion and Beethoven, which Bismarck wrote to his wife from his quarters outside bombarded Paris. (p. 455)

In poems like these the realist Liliencron goes back to the romantic school, and opens a door to sentiment which is characteristically and familiarly German; but in doing so he takes with him a strong breeze of reality to keep the romantic air fresh.

Liliencron had certainly his measure of the Nietzschean scorn. There is a fine poem in which he apostrophises a vision of Frederic the Great, and applauds his misanthropy. . . . (p. 456)

But aristocrat though he was, he was no spoiled child of fortune. The income of a Prussian captain on half-pay was not much above starvation point; and his appointment on the Schleswig coast was not one that a man of his genius and lively disposition could have coveted, had anything better been available. These adversities were blessings in so far as they saved Liliencron from being narrowed to a mere sympathiser with the successful and the strong. He has a lordly contempt for "the mob," for the low tastes and ephemeral aims of the people who flock to vulgar theatres, but he feels, much as a Tory of Scott's type could, the wealth of essential human interest in poor people's lives. So too he exposes with a sort of zest the sham which human honours and titles become in the presence of Nature and at the touch of Time. In this vein is his well-known poem, **"The New Railway,"** in which some rough navvies dig a line across the grave of a forgotten grandee. Their coarse ears do not hear his disinterred skull protesting piteously his titles, his great embassy, his place in history; like Hamlet's grave-diggers they play at loggats with it, and bestow his insignia and ornaments on the nearest barmaid.

The fame of poets is perhaps less fleeting than that of ambassadors; yet it, too, has its day. How will Liliencron's stand a century hence? On the whole it seems likely to stand high. . . . Of the lyrists since 1870 Liliencron towers easily above the rest; and his work has just those qualities—brevity, lucidity, intensity, and impeccable form—which, though they do not exhaust the possibilities of merit in literature, are its surest passports to immortality. (pp. 456-57)

R. C. K. Ensor, "Detlev von Liliencron," in Contemporary Review, *Vol. XCVI, October, 1909, pp. 448-57.*

PERCIVAL POLLARD (essay date 1911)

[*Pollard was a German-American playwright, novelist, and highly regarded critic who was known for his attacks on sentimentality and puritanical morality in American literature. In the following excerpt from* Masks and Minstrels of New Germany, *a work that introduced many little-known German writers to American readers, Pollard discusses Liliencron's works as those of a man who subordinated literature to life, resulting in poetry distinguished by its immediacy and freshness.*]

Not until Detlev von Liliencron came was there a revival of an actual note of truly German nationalism. No such naïvely singing soul had been heard since Goethe. Only Verlaine, in France, equalled him in lyric spontaneity. He was utterly a German; he lived as a German; he put that life directly into his songs and his stories. He lived first, wrote afterwards; the note of life, of actual experience illumines his every line. You forget, reading him, any question of craft, just as he himself forgot it, to all appearance. Only nature—the German nature, the German scene, the life of himself, a German—had anything to teach him; he followed in no footsteps, obeyed no formulas.

He was soldier, huntsman, cavalier, country magistrate first; he lived his life vigorously and variously; literature was a last resort. You never smelt literature in what he wrote; what you smelt was life; the blood and powder of battles, the soil of his northern lands, the glitter of uniforms; always life, life. Few men, anywhere, led a life more full of color; few put more of that color into their writing. He spanned the gulfs from the swagger officer to the vagabond; from the magistrate to the infidel; from the rank feudalist to the soldier in liberty's cause; from the balladist of wedlock to the egoistic Don Juan; from a birthright of Danish allegiance to a supporter of the Prussian standards. He lived at top pressure; it is for that reason, when he came, late in life, to express his experience in words, those words went straight, full pressure also, to the mark. (pp. 55-6)

The natural note in the poems of Liliencron startled an audience that had long been accustomed to weak dilutions of what, in Goethe and Heine, had been genuine sentiment. The lyrics of the day were written in lavender water. With the publication of his **"Adjutantenritte" ("Rides of an Adjutant")** and the following volumes of verse, the discriminating few found that a new man had come to be reckoned with. Here was war in all its color and dirt and tragedy; here was nature at first, not third or fourth, hand; here was love as it had come to life and song in the arms of a flesh-and-blood girl, not a lay figure patterned upon the formulas of other poets. (p. 64)

To readers who do not read German it is impossible to convey a notion of the graphic swiftness of movement in the early military verses of Liliencron. The musical and dramatic values of short words, and even of syllables, are used most effectively. Sharp, staccato strokes seem to cut out for us slices of breathing, glowing life. (p. 65)

Since Mr. Kipling sang rather of the barracks and departments of peace, than of war, I do not know where to look in English for equivalents to the qualities Liliencron showed in his prose and verse versions of war. In the war stories of Ambrose Bierce you will, I think, come nearest to the color and the irony in this German. He gives us the glitter of the sun shining on the cavalry charge, and he also gives us the eternal irony of things, just as did Bierce in his picture of the splendid horseman riding splendidly and futilely across a bullet-pelted space; just as did Tennyson when he sang of the mad charge at Balaclava, and just as did Bernard Shaw when he declared in "Arms and the Man" that what made a certain cavalryman's ride into apparently sure death possible was not heroism but the fact that his horse was running away with him. The irony of things was constant in Liliencron, but it was an irony tinged with melancholy, with pity. (pp. 66-7)

The only poet who in English achieved similar effects of direct sensation, who seemed to cut slices straight out of the actual and serve them to you lyrically was William Ernest Henley. . . . Of Liliencron's military songs the most popular was always his **"Die Musik Kommt,"** which is as if you said "Here comes the band." No wonder that in the days of the Überbrettl' it was hummed and sung all over Germany. (p. 69)

He sang as much of love and of nature as of things martial, and, whatever he touched in his singing, you forgot manner, and heard the matter of it going directly into your heart. The ability to express the individual impression was peculiarly his. You felt, always, that it was a battle he had seen, a girl he had kissed, of which he sang to you, not of some lithographed melodramatic moment or some model Daphnis or Chloe. In his **"Nach dem Ball"** you can almost smell the violets, see the tired eyes of the little countess sleeping on his shoulder.

The actual tone of life, that was what he always gave us, and it was because he was always more the lover of life than anything else. He was the first artist in almost two generations who was not a mere literary man, but man. The literary man never showed through his work; here was nothing of the abstract academician to whom all things human are vile; here was a plain, hearty German personality: an officer, baron, country gentleman, with all the peculiar qualities and defects of his class. (p. 71)

Beyond the poetry Liliencron's work expressed itself in several volumes of drama, and short stories. Those of the latter which deal with his army experiences are to be counted with the best in that sort anywhere, with the pictures of war that De Maupassant in France, Verestchagin in Russia, and Bierce in America, have produced. (p. 72)

Liliencron expressed, as no other since Goethe, the oneness of nature and the individual. He brought freshness and genuineness into a land that had forgotten both. (pp. 76-7)

Percival Pollard, "Detlev von Liliencron," in his Masks and Minstrels of New Germany, *John W. Luce and Company, 1911, pp. 55-83.*

OTTO EDUARD LESSING (essay date 1912)

[In the following excerpt, Lessing offers a survey of Liliencron's works, beginning with those written during the poet's stay in America, and discusses the characteristic subjects of his poetry: "war, chase, hatred of philistinism, consciousness of life's duality, erotic passion, tender sympathies, love of nature, a romantic longing for the unattainable."]

The literary reflex of Liliencron's American episode are a few fine lyrics: **"Departure", "Return"**, and **"Thou my country"**; a tragic love story the scene of which is New York, and two dramatic efforts: ***The Nobility of Labor*** and ***Pokahontas.*** These as well as the plays ***The Merovingians, Trifels and Palermo, The Rantzows and Pogwisch's, Knut the Lord*** were all written before the poet had attained to that perfect mastery of form which characterizes his lyrics. They are painfully amateurish. With the exception of the first one mentioned each contains enough dramatic elements to make half a dozen effective plays: unbounded ambition, base envy, demonic jealousy, cold-blooded assassinations crowd the scenes. But what there is of dramatic possibilities is suffocated by an overgrowth of lyricisms and epic narrations. The plays are successions of past events, sometimes fascinatingly told in dialogic form, rather than present unfoldings of inner conflicts, of causes and effects. "Tell me now", begins ***The Merovingians.*** This is typical.

While his dramas share all the conventional faults of a rhetorical age, Liliencron's war poetry is distinguished by the strict conciseness, concrete plasticity, and directness of imagery that mark the modern epoch of German Literature. It is the lyrics and short stories of an ***Adjutant's Rides*** that made Liliencron one of the admired leaders of Youngest Germany. (pp. 38-9)

"A Backward Glance" ("Rückblick") expresses the sentiments before, during, and after a battle. When the attack is about to be made, the poet's thoughts wander back to the fairyland of childhood, to the wild life of the man of the world.

Holograph manuscript of a poem by Liliencron.

Then comes the quick plunge into bloody combat—peril, wounds, victory. After all is over, in the night, by the gleaming campfire, the musings of the morning are continued, to be dissolved into the elating consciousness that the fierce encounter has led the restless youth to firm manhood. The battle itself fills only six brief strophes. There is nothing said directly of the thousands taking part. The figure of the individual alone appears in sharp outlines; and yet our imagination easily rounds the segment out to a circle. Landscape, men, objects are designated by their most characteristic names and set in motion by means of a few verbs, scarcely any explanatory adjectives being required. (pp. 40-1)

Such limitation of horizon, such condensation of material is the secret of Liliencron's art. It is the suggestive force of personal life that creates the impression of world-wide reality.

In his war stories he never attempts to describe a battle in its entirety, as did e.g. Grabbe, Bleibtreu, and Frenssen. What he does is this: he narrates most graphically a connected series of important actions, shows their effect upon their immediate vicinity, and concludes with a grand finale. Consequently we, his readers, go through all the thrilling experiences in one part of the battlefield, constantly realizing that, at the same time, similar scenes take place everywhere around us, until at last the isolated details merge into their combined result, into the all-embracing catastrophe. So, as our attention was never distracted, as our eyes were not compelled to stray over an endless procession of images, a few images are clearly and permanently inscribed upon our souls with the ultimate effect of one overwhelmingly great phenomenon.

Horrible as many or most of these war-stories are—Liliencron can, indeed, be appreciated only by men and women of strong minds—the mild light of humor is not altogether missing, nor is the spirit of love. Quite in contrast to Zola, Daudet, and Maupassant with their fanatic exaggerations and falsifications, Liliencron never utters a word of hatred against the enemies of his people. True to his aristocratic name, he is always chivalric and admires the tenacious energy, the daring élan of the opposing army as much as the bravery of his own. "The enemy's wonderful army", he once exclaims in purely esthetic delight. (pp. 41-2)

In his poems and stories of war—always, in fact—Liliencron places man in close contact with nature. The dismal moods of rainy weather, the manifold hues of sunsets, the splendor of starry nights, the chaste briskness of the hour before sunrise, the heat of summer afternoons, the majestic flight of a heron through clouds of mist far above advancing cavalry, the playful flutter of butterflies among the bleeding wounds of the fallen—such motives contribute essentially toward visualizing the action proper, either by contrasts of color and light or by plastic symbolization.

Liliencron has often been praised for his extraordinary keeness of observation. Indeed, the soldier, the horseman, the hunter had his senses trained to extreme acuteness. Like an Indian on the warpath he seems to hear and see everything. But it is not only, as overwise and underread critics would have it, the detached detail, the surface of things which he grasps. The external, individual phenomenon has always a deeply typical meaning for him. (pp. 42-3)

When as an adjutant he has to carry an important message from one part of the battlefield to another, he is stopped by a wounded soldier. His heart goes out to the poor wretch whom a drop of water might save. But there stands Dame Duty, solemnly commanding: "Forward!" to save the thousands instead of the one. A vision, a dream, and yet the very essence of present reality. "Forward, look not behind you!", this cruelly saving call that sounded to him so often amidst the ghastly slaughter of battle, became the motto of his whole life. It guarded him against Weltschmerz, that despair over the world's irreparable misery to which sensitive natures so easily succumb.

Liliencron was a passionate hunter, not because he enjoyed killing, but because chase kept awake in him the chivalric virtues of war, gave constant exercise to body and mind, and brought about the most intimate communion with nature. On horseback or on foot, accompanied by his faithful dogs, rambling through the solitude of heath, marshes, and woods means ever new revelations of beauty to him. And as war, so chase assumes symbolical significance. Wolfhunting and heronhawking, brilliantly depicted in two pendants, **"Feudal"**, change through almost imperceptible irony into symbols of social evolution. The modern poet revives the memory of ancestral times, when a serf's life meant no more than the life of a wild beast. (p. 44)

Similarly a prose-sketch **"Hetzjagd"** is an allegory of human life. A motley cavalcade of hunters marches past our eyes: first Fortuna. "She looked behind her, laughing, laughing, laughing so that the little gold crown upon her head glistened and sparkled." She is followed by an endless procession of woes and passions. "All that is inflicted upon man by himself and others, disease and distress, misery and want, all and everything, move by, the horses always in rapid gait." The most horrible of all vexations is Poverty, and in the same line with her comes Care; then follow Hatred, Revenge, Calumny, Scorn, Grudge, Jealousy, and, singled out as one of the very meanest, "she with the face of an old spinster, in a lilac-colored dress with a grassy green bow in her hair": Thoughtless Gossip. Close upon her comes Gambrinus, the curse of the nation, the god of the Schützen-and-Sängerfest-Germans, the god of those Philistines who despise whatever is original, whose stupid apathy causes the ruin of poets and artists. Last is Satan with his two mistresses Falsehood and Infamy. The scene is shifted for a moment. The procession seems to be transformed into an advancing regiment of cavalry. Military signals and orders are heard which are suddenly relieved by hunting-cries. Again appear the Vices and Cares. They are chasing a man. In the forest stands Adam, the man who is you and I, naked, lonely. Frantic terror seizes him, when he hears the wild chase approach. He knows that he is the game. He runs, hard pressed by the bloodthirsty pack. An abyss bars his way. He glides down the slope, clings despairingly to the edge. But Fortuna, still leading, leaps from her horse, and tramples upon his fingers. He sinks, falls, is lost. Now Fortuna, waving her hand, gives the signal for a general shout of triumph.—Slowly, from the distance, Satan upon his elephant draws near. He takes his time; for he is sure of success.

This somewhat lengthy extract is given, since the content comprises an essential part of Liliencron's philosophy, and since the method of composition applied here is used over and over again. With a rigidly realistic technique he expresses romantic sentiments. No poetry in recent times contains a greater number nor a greater variety of visions than his who is labeled as a naturalistic writer. This bold vision of the wild chase grows out of a most accurately observed, trivial reality. The time is a weary, hot September afternoon. The scene changes between woods and bush, where the author is engaged in grouse-hunting, and a village-tavern. The model of Fortuna is a buxom waitress who does not dislike flirting. Yet the moods of sunny day and spectral apparitions do not, except once, neutralize each other. Both intermingle, supplement each other as insensibly as in Grillparzer's dream play.

The vision comes very near the sublime without being wholly sublime. Liliencron rarely mastered the gesture of solemnity. Here, in what is only a sketch—Übungsblatt—he did not want to. Humor and irony relieve the tragic tension. Jolly flirtation introduces, unconscious drollery of the girl closes the vision. There is one real break, however. An unveiled personal confession separates this sketch from pure art to which its subject points. The horror of the Gambrinus-worshipping German philistine misleads our poet here as elsewhere to direct polemics. An enthusiastic patriot, he hated, as relentlessly as did Friedrich Schlegel or Brentano, the worst enemy of his people, the philistine who, over beer and skat, forgets the ideals of liberty and energetic activity; who strangles with his envy whatever is great, original, natural, in order that he may not be disturbed in his dull indolence; the philistine who is the absolute negation of creative spirit. (pp. 45-7)

War, chase, and love are the "three green spots" Liliencron has discovered in the arid sands of life. In his erotic poetry there is no trace of that withered morbidity which has been ascribed to his epoch with more or less justification; nothing hysterically incensed—and no carnal pruriency covered up by pretentious spiritualism. Liliencron is equally far remote from D'Annunzio as from D. G. Rossetti. He is natural; strongly sensual, and at the same time capable of most delicately graded feelings. As for all great creators, the sexual passion is for him the center and source of his emotional life. In it he finds the hope for the permanency of the race, while he is painfully conscious of the transience of individual existence, of individual happiness in love. In accordance with his own sensuality he believes that man's nature is polygamic, woman's on the contrary monogamic: their mutual interests consequently never fully agree; happiness is limited to brief periods. His love-poetry has, then, of necessity a tragic undertone which, however, so rarely makes itself heard directly that professional criticism for a long time failed to notice it at all. (pp. 49-50)

Charming idyls, often enlivened by delightful humor, take turns with melancholy motives. Love, with Liliencron, as a rule flames up suddenly, kindled by the magic touch of the elves' queen. Man and woman are drawn into each other's arms by an irresistible magnetism. The moment is grasped, bliss enjoyed; for it escapes those that tarry. It vanishes soon enough, at best. Happiness is always short. Either the lovers are separated by the same uncontrollable fate which united them, or the man is unable to bind himself permanently, or envy and jealousy of others are the cause of disunion. Repeatedly the poet sounds the warning to guard the secret. For thief Envy will not rest, until he has robbed you of your treasure. But if you hesitate at the call of happiness, if you do not make use of an opportunity, you will be punished by everlasting grief over the irretrievable. The sorrow for bliss once enjoyed and then lost is mild compared to the bitter repentance for opportunities unused. Nothing is more terrible than a "too late". (p. 51)

Liliencron would not be a noble man, if he had satisfied his craving for happiness by excess or by violating the rights of others. Upon his banner he has inscribed the great word "Self-control". Sensuous he was, but not a libertine. He did not go astray with Robert Burns whose lyrics are rivalled in naturalness by his. With all his polygamic instinct he recognized monogamy as the pillar of social organization. His own married life he praised as the source of his highest bliss. The poet of those impassioned **"Stammelverse"** at the same time sung the naive charms of child-life. A soothing, fine lullaby, sweet, free from weakly sentimentality, closes the circle of his love-poetry.

Out of his family sense grows social sympathy. No one took the misery of the common people more to heart than this son of a feudal race. The tragic ballad of a tramp whom starvation drives to suicide, is a severe condemnation of the wrongs of our economic system. However, here too, in this ever present war for mere existence, the harsh command must be heeded: "Forward, look not behind you!" The desirability of universal love he acknowledged, its possibility he denied as a Utopia. His heart was governed by the same logic as Nietzsche's which demands moderation even in charity. Like Nietzsche he despises "society", admires the leading geniuses. Hannibal, Julius Caesar, Frederic the Great, are his favorites. (pp. 53-4)

It would take a book to give an approximately adequate idea of the variety of Liliencron's lyrics. His balladry can only be mentioned. He occupies a place of honor with Germany's greatest writers of ballads. Historical subjects, tragic or humorous, he treats with as great perfection as the uncanny supernatural, which merges into hazy dusk, or the glaring light of everyday reality. Murder and revenge, punishment for long forgotten crimes, violent abductions, barbarous feuds, battles, surprises from ambush, destruction of cities, death-defying defense of personal freedom, love-adventures, heroic self-sacrifice—in brief we find all the traditional motives of balladry. But to all he has given the impress of his own graphic style. Even in his old age he succeeded in immortalizing events from Germany's African war.

Whatever he possessed of dramatic talent came to life in his ballads. In a few lines he gives the presuppositions together with the first steps of the action which then moves in breathless haste to its climax. There are no epic intermissions, nor rhetorical devices for superficial decorations. Here as everywhere the expression is rigidly concise; the final effect that of some elemental force. (pp. 54-5)

About one half of Liliencron's stories treat of erotic subjects. They are partly clothed in historical garb, reading like ballads in prose, partly they are taken from the life of modern society. As with the poems there is a tragic undertone common to all: a last greeting from the deathbed of a deserted girl and late repentance of the seducer; adultery, abduction and cruel retaliation, bitter resignation, mortal jealousy between father and son, brutal revenge of a disappointed rival, the touchingly modest love-token of a poor maid, and so forth. (p. 55)

Hardly ever the poet attains or strives for the uniformity of structure usually expected of the Novelle. Hunting or leisurely rambling through fields and woods, in some indifferent country-inn, conversing with friends, he seems to pick up his stories. Often the frame attracts as much attention as the picture itself. As in **"Hetzjagd"**, dream and reality, present and past, intermingle. The poet's imagination builds bridges from the Holstein forests to the streets of New York, from his tavern to the age of Charles V. If the whole is sometimes rather dismembered, if there are uninteresting interludes, there are always charmingly vivid details. Liliencron is at his best, whenever he sins against the rule of objective narration, whenever he appears in persona, telling us of his own emotions. He is not like his fellow-countryman, Theodor Storm, a lyric poet and a novelist at once. He is always a lyricist who, owing to his marvellous power of visualizing, occasionally, as if by chance, may produce great epical effects. His war-stories, then, came to be his best epic performances, not so much because of a truly narrative talent, as because his personal feelings were identical with the outer events. (p. 56)

The Maecenas (Der Mäcen) and ***Life and Lie (Leben und Lüge)*** are, though written at different periods, two closely connected parts of an autobiographical romance. (p. 58)

While in ***The Maecenas*** no attempt was made toward connected narration, ***Life and Lie*** is intended to be a "biographical novel". Nevertheless it is very deficient as regards its structure. It was not given to Liliencron to carry out long compositions. (p. 59)

Like most of Liliencron's prose this novel, too, is interspersed with things which, having little or nothing to do with the plot, serve only to illustrate the hero's literary taste or the trend of his thought: War reminiscences, aphorisms, poems by himself or others, historical data, letters, even a complete novelette. Still, the whole book is filled with one sweet, melancholy mood. It is the retrospect of a wise man over a long life with moments of heavenly bliss and decades of unfulfilled yearning. (p. 60)

In a chapter "Something about poetry" Liliencron characterizes himself as an artist. The majority of his writings, he thinks, will perish with his person; only one will survive: ***Poggfred.*** "In this will be perceived the irony of life; and a later period will find in it many experiences of our time: the philistine pettiness of every day life; the social, moral, and religious hypocrisy; the cowardly negation of all strong instincts; the none the less unchecked flight of individual imagination; the indelible pleasure in mere existing, in the adventures of love, of war, and travel; first of all, however, the unrestrained humor of a perfectly independent man of the world who defies every meanness of human fate with the formula: 'Je m'en fiche!' ['I laugh at it!']. Therefore, he believes, ***Poggfred*** will sometime be recognized as a landmark of brave irony."

Liliencron was no doubt too modest. The indications are that not only ***Poggfred*** will continue to live but also a stately number of his ballads and love-poems. As a composition ***Poggfred,*** which the author calls an epos, is no less imperfect than the novels. The work, nominally consisting of twenty-nine cantos, is in fact a collection of separate ballads, visions, realistic idyls, grotesques, meditations. The connection established consists only in the identity of the author and in the metrical system: groups of ottave-rime alternate with groups of terza-rime. Indeed, there is the refreshingly courageous irony; for the poet was an affinity of Byron's whose Don Juan he cherished. This is a personal union, as it were, not an esthetic unity. However, many individual parts are of inimitable beauty.

The intelligent reader will not cease to admire the profusion of visions, the brilliancy of colors, the melodiousness of rhythm, the plasticity of characters, the smoothness and vitality of language. These verses reach up and down the entire scale from sublime tragedy to the exuberant frolic of carnival. And the poet builds up his imaginary castle Poggfred, where, secure from the world, he reigns over the world by force of his phantasy, so concretely that fiction is changed to truth. This wealthy grand seigneur and tiller of his own soil, this hotblooded Epicurean and humble devotee of nature, this earnest godseeker and frivolous cynic, this lonely misanthrope and brave fighter in life's struggles, this romantic dreamer and realistic artist, this melancholy humorist, this freest of all free men: the poet and hero of ***Poggfred*** is Detlev von Liliencron. (pp. 60-2)

Otto Eduard Lessing, "Detlev von Liliencron," in his Masters in Modern German Literature, *1912. Reprint by Books for Libraries Press, 1967; distributed by Arno Press, Inc., pp. 35-62.*

LUDWIG LEWISOHN (essay date 1917)

[A German-born American novelist and critic, Lewisohn was considered an authority on German literature, and his translations of Gerhart Hauptmann, Rainer Maria Rilke, and Jakob Wassermann are widely respected. In the following excerpt, he contends that Liliencron, a man of action rather than a man of letters, singlehandedly returned "vigor and life and expressiveness" to German literature with his poetry collection Adjutantenritte.*]*

In every ancient and highly developed literature it happens recurrently that the language of poetry once fresh and significant sinks into mere conventional verbiage and that both words and thoughts lose touch with their basis in reality. That happened in England at the end of the eighteenth century when Wordsworth announced his new theory of poetic diction and bade the poet write "with his eye on the object." To a much smaller degree but very definitely the same thing happened in German literature between the death of Heine and the advent of the moderns. The late, post-romantic versifiers repeated the same forms and rhythms and barren tales indefinitely; the few lyrical masters of the period—Hebbel, Meyer, Keller—did not come into their own until years later. The poet who with one memorable and already classical volume brought back to German verse vigor and life and expressiveness was Detlev von Liliencron.

He belonged by birth to the minor nobility of Schleswig-Holstein. During a lonely boyhood he spent much time in the out of doors, untroubled by any literary ambitions. He wanted to be a soldier as befitted his birth and traditions, served as a lieutenant in some seventeen garrisons, took part in the campaigns of 1866 and 1870, rose to a captaincy in the Prussian army but was forced to resign on account of his wounds and his debts. He went to America and suffered many hardships, returned and tried the life of a subaltern government official. At this time—he was now forty—the literary instinct suddenly overwhelmed him and he published his famous **'Adjudantenritte.'** He was always in difficulties, despite the devotion of his friends Richard Dehmel, the poet, and Emanuel Reicher, the eminent actor, and despite a pension granted him by the emperor. But he was always of a virile serenity and spiritual wholesomeness—a strong, humorous, soldierly man.

These biographical facts are of very great importance. It is not often that something very like a revolution in any modern literature has been accomplished by a man of Liliencron's type, a man removed as far as possible from scholarship or letters in the narrower sense, essentially a man not of reflection but of action. What enabled him to do his work was his sheer temperament, his character, the peculiar endowment of his very senses. Untroubled by literary memories, not tormented for years by a desire for expression, he saw the world with consummate vividness and closeness and naïveté for forty years before he began to embody his impressions in verse. His observation had not been the calculating exercise of the modern realistic novelist or playwright: he had seen things with the eyes of a soldier, a hunter, a wanderer. The result might, of course, have been crude enough. But Liliencron was born with an entirely noble and incorruptible sense for style and form. He is utterly careless, utterly unmindful of any conventions in regard to choice of subject or mood or words: he is quite unconscious of the old distinctions of noble and ignoble, fit or unfit for art. His form is always of a final firmness and distinction.

The result is a body of lyrical work which, in its own way, stands alone in modern literature. One might compare Liliencron to Burns and, of course, Burns has a more piercing note and a more immortal note of pure song. But Burns did not have Liliencron's magnanimous manhood. Or one might compare him to Henley, if Henley had had his serenity, his ultimate wholesomeness and virile strength. It is only to the works of such poets, however, that one can compare his wonderful straightforwardness and reality, his complete and immediate translation of experience and vision into art.

Unlike most moderns he is not, then, a poet of reflection or analysis at all. Love and war and the chase and (in his ballads) the historical legends and events of his native province—these are his themes. The wind of the North Sea is in his verses, the sun on his Saxon heaths, or the sounds and sights of the battles which he shared for the fatherland. Yet from the totality of his work, naïve and spontaneous as it is, there arises a final impression that is characteristic, above all others, of the life of modern Germany. Liliencron is an asserter, an affirmer of life—of its goodness and power and worth—of life as a whole—accounting energy above conformity, joy above sickly scruples, self-discipline above an outer yoke, the yea above the nay.

The influence of his work upon his countrymen was immediate and has proven permanent. No German poet of the thirty years that have just passed but has written more directly, concretely, and, in the highest sense, manfully, not only for the verse but for the character of Detlev von Liliencron. (pp. 9058a-58b)

Ludwig Lewisohn, "Detlev von Liliencron, 1844-1909," in The World's Best Literature, Vol. 15, *edited by John W. Cunliffe and Ashley H. Thorndike, Warner Library Company, 1917, pp. 9058a-9058b.*

WILLIAM A. DRAKE (essay date 1928)

[Drake was an American editor, journalist, translator, and author of several studies of European and American literature. He also adapted European plays for the American stage. In the following excerpt, Drake refers to the decline of Liliencron's reputation as a poet, maintaining that his fiction rather than his poetry will ensure him an enduring place in German literature. His view contrasts with that of the majority of critics writing in English on Liliencron's work.]

The appearance of [Liliencron's] first volume of verse, ***Adjutantenritte und Andere Gedichte,*** in 1883, is an event in German literature comparable with the publication of Kipling's *Departmental Ditties* three years afterwards. . . . All that ***Adjutantenritte*** promised was more than fulfilled in the succeeding volumes, ***Der Heidegänger*** and ***Bunte Beute,*** published respectively ten and twenty years later. Here was a man, standing erect and singing the songs of men—songs of war and of the chase, of human passions and human emotions—in a frank, clear utterance that cared for naught save honesty, but achieved much else besides. And all that he did not fully express in his poetry, he elaborated in the short stories in his volumes ***Eine Sommerschlacht, Unter Flatternden Fahnen, Der Mäcen*** and ***Krieg und Frieden,*** which Pollard [see excerpt dated 1911] has so aptly compared with the war stories of Ambrose Bierce. It is a safe conjecture that, although only a handful of Liliencron's verses may live, a dozen of these stories will enter into the classic literature of Germany. (pp. 326-27)

[Liliencron's] present reputation suffers somewhat from the iconoclasm of the young, from the singular astigmatism of history which makes the epoch which we have just passed seem more remote to us than another passed a century ago, and above all, from the circumstance that Liliencron wrote too much and without artistic tact—that, lacking an accurately functioning faculty of self-criticism, he allowed his writings to be published in an imperfect state, and preferred of his works such a confection as his humorous epic ***Poggfred*** to his splendid ballads, or an allegorical tidbit like ***Hetzjagd*** to his powerful realistic prose. (p. 327)

But the whole genius of Liliencron's writings lies in their spontaneity; in the perfect naturalness of their thought and diction, whatever the faults of these qualities may be. Living and exulting in action, he translated rugged action into his poems and stories. If he had attempted revision, he would doubtless have taken away, not their imperfections, but that very impact of living experience which we find to be their most moving quality. He lived as naturally as he wrote, cherishing his independence, accepting the inconveniences of poverty, seeking the graces of love and friendship, and all the while, stoutly maintaining his pride as a man, an aristocrat, an officer, and a German. (p. 328)

William A. Drake, "Detlev von Liliencron and Richard Dehmel," in his Contemporary European Writers, *The John Day Company, 1928, pp. 324-33.**

Poggfred.

Kunterbuntes Epos in 12 Cantussen

von

Detlev von Liliencron.

Berlin.
Verlag von Schuster & Loeffler.
1896.

Title page of the first edition of Poggfred.

JETHRO BITHELL (essay date 1939)

[In the following excerpt, Bithell praises the freshness and originality of Liliencron's poetry, but dismisses his prose as "negligible" and his dramas as "unreadable."]

[Liliencron's] pride of race and training allied with genuine *bonhomie* and readiness to rub shoulders with the roughest people and his openly expressed disgust with literature as a profession give him a place apart among the class-proud poets he frequented. He was a Bohemian, but still an aristocrat. There is naturalism enough in his work, but it is rather the outrightness of a blunt soldier or the free-and-easy raciness of a hunting gentleman, not a programmatic choice. ***Adjutantenritte*** revealed him as one of the new characters which *Moderne Dichtercharaktere* were calling for to create the new verse; and the new leader was found far from all *cénacles,* absolutely unconscious of iconoclast theory, creating the new style out of the freshness of his originality. The date of ***Adjutantenritte*** is actually a year before that of *Moderne Dichtercharaktere;* and the strange thing is that these poems by virtue of their double sense or symbolism—Liliencron is fond of a quizzical glance at death or of a light-hearted but penetrating reference to man's mutability in the permanence of nature—point forward beyond the short fashion of naturalism to the succeeding school of impressionism. There are also in his work generally the elements of *Heimatkunst* [''regional art'']. *Holsatia non cantat* was an old saying; but Detlev von Liliencron is yet another in the list (Hebbel, Klaus Groth, Theodor Storm) of poets of the first rank born and reared in Schleswig-Holstein; and he closely follows Theodor Storm (as Timm Kröger and Gustav Frenssen follow him) as a delineator of his native province; the virile martial note which the title of his first volume announces is doubled and relieved by the most vivid descriptions of *Marsch* [''marsh''] and *Geest* [''heath''] of the leagues of rolling heather by oozy mud-flats (*Watten*) bared by the ebb of the tide on the coast of Holstein. His love of soldiering comes out in poem after poem; typical are **'Kleine Ballade'** or **'Die Musik kommt,'** which quaintly pictures the passage through a village street of a regiment of soldiers with the band going on before and all the girls gazing at the haughty captain and the rosy-faced lieutenants. There is a deeper note in certain lyrics which show the sadder side of soldiering (**'Tod in Ähren'** and above all **'Wer weiss wo?'**). Improvisator and academically unschooled as he is, he is a master of rhymecraft and of certain stanza forms, certainly of the *Siziliane*. . . . In the volumes of verse that followed there is no development except that the form grows both more supple and mannered.

In the historical panorama of German verse Liliencron stands out as one of the most significant poets. Intellectually his range is low; that is, he was no thinker. But he makes history by his style. This marks an advance or a new direction in two main aspects. Firstly, he flouts poetic diction. He accomplishes the reform—an abandonment of traditional artificiality in favour of a language new-coined to pass current in a new, less idealistic life—for which Conradi and his merry men had been clamouring; but whereas they had despite their theories carried on with the old style of language Liliencron renews the language of verse without premeditation by the mere trick of abolishing such devices as the *Dichter-e* [''poetic 'e' ''] (*spielet* for *spielt*), and above all by admitting as poetically effective words from everyday life (such as *Bureau, Zigaretten, Einglas*) previously regarded as too tawdry for the purpose. The second main element of his style is what is now interpreted as impressionism: Liliencron gives, not (like the naturalists) a drab section of a continuous state, but momentary, very vivid impressions of something unusual, or a series of such impressions with everything unnecessary eliminated. The difference is that between a photograph and a film; the naturalists freeze life, Liliencron shows it in flashes of movement. This verbal magic is enhanced by other qualities, above all by his delightful rough humour, which may come out in a juggling with words (*Tigert er auf dich heraus, / Tatz' ihn! wie die Katz die Maus*) or in a startling pretence of coarseness (*Das war der König Ragnar, / Der lebte fromm und frei. / Ertrug gepichte Hosen, / Wie seine Leichtmatrosen, / Die rochen nicht nach Rosen, / Das war ihm einerlei*); he is a master, too, of sound-painting (*die Quelle klungklingklangt*) and of metaphor (*Ein Wasser schwatzt sich selig durchs Gelände; Es schleicht die Sommer-nacht auf Katzenpfoten*). His ballads, mostly in the old pattern of rough quatrains, are best where they deal with historical episodes of his native province; savage frays and stark revenge is their theme. They may not pull at the heart-strings, as the best ballads do, but they have that fierce delight in fighting for its own sake which is the oldest element of German poetry. Liliencron's waywardness unshapes but lends a charm to his higgledy-piggledy epic (*'kunterbuntes Epos'*) ***Poggfred*** . . . , in the style and stanza of Byron's *Don Juan* slowed down in the more serious parts by *terza rima*. The title is Low German for 'frog's peace', a pious fiction for the poet's country mansion (more likely his abode at the time of composition was in plain lodgings at Altona); the poem is a panorama of the memories and fancies of the poet's life shaped as humorous episodes or allegorical visions. Very much indeed of Liliencron's best poetry is (like Theodor Storm's Novellen) *'Rückblickspoesie'* ['poetry of reminiscence']; often, for instance, in bald blank verse he calls to mind some simple episode of his past, and suddenly the lines fill with a rush of intense feeling. . . . (pp. 118-20)

Of Liliencron's prose there is little to say, but more than of his dramas, which are unreadable. His novels are written anyhow, and apart from his ***Kriegsnovellen*** . . . , which often have the literal truth of experience, even his short stories are negligible; the mass of them (***Aus Marsch und Geest, Könige und Bauern, Roggen und Weizen*** . . .) have too much of the swagger of his famous poem **'Bruder Liederlich'**: the bold bad baron comes and conquers some delightful female or other (peasant wench or princess is all the same)—and departs; or the episode leads up to such a sensational picture as that in **'Auf der Marschinsel'**—the narrator as dike captain is fetched by his underling to the outer dike to see two naked corpses washed up: a white female of delicate build and a Herculean negro crucified together on a plank, with the negro's left fingers touching the right ones of the woman. One of his novels, ***Leben und Lüge***. . . , might be read for its autobiographical interest, but the picture is somewhat fanciful; his true self stands out best from his ***Briefe*** [''letters''] collected by Dehmel. (p. 121)

Jethro Bithell, ''From Bahr to Dehmel,'' in his Modern German Literature: 1880-1938, *Methuen & Co. Ltd., 1939, pp. 97-142.**

DETLEV W. SCHUMANN (essay date 1945)

[*In the following excerpt, Schumann examines Liliencron's stylistic techniques and evaluates his career.*]

In contrast to the majority of . . . evaluations it is my own conviction that the living Liliencron of 1944 is primarily the early Liliencron, the author of the ***Adjutantenritte*** and other poems contemporaneous with those contained in that volume. (p. 66)

What is it . . . that distinguishes the best of these early poems? It is their spontaneity and compactness; it is the concreteness and vividness which the author imparts to the most fleeting impressions. . . . [With] a few sparse suggestions, with a minimum of words . . . Liliencron succeeds in evoking an intense atmosphere, in creating an entire picture—or rather, in forcing us to create it. . . . Altogether radiant sunshine is most typical of Liliencron's sceneries. . . . But other nature moods, too, are rendered with equally suggestive terseness. . . . [The **''Haidebilder''**] give sharply differentiated, utterly characterisic pictures of the solitary heath in the four seasons. In comparing the cycle to Storm's treatment of the same locale—and quite definitely Liliencron is here under his influence—[Berthold] Litzmann points out how much more subjective, more introverted the older poet is; with the younger one, soldier and passionate hunter, all sensory elements, especially the visual ones, are sharply defined, individualized. . . . What German spring poem between Storm's ''April'' and Hofmannsthal's ''Vorfrühling'' or Rilke's ''Aus einem April'' is so fraught with mood as Liliencron's **''Märztag''** . . .? Here we have the very essence of vernal wistfulness against the background of a wide North-German horizon. . . . (pp. 66-8)

Liliencron's death mask.

And then there are the impressionistic pictures from the battlefield: **"Tod in Ähren"**, . . . **"Wer weiß wo,"** . . . **"Fühler und Vorhang."** . . .

In a lighter vein the military theme is treated in **"Die Musik kommt,"** . . . with its somewhat boisterous onomatopoeia. This poem, owing to phonographic recording, first made the broad public aware of Liliencron, and it has doubtless remained his most popular one to the present day.

"Siegesfest" . . . transcends the bounds of an individual situation and gives us—again with a brevity that discards syntactic completeness—fleeting glimpses of many co-existent human destinies, blissful and tragic. Such kaleidoscopic impressionism reaches an artistic climax in the **"Schwalbensiziliane,"** . . . where the odd lines express the transitoriness of human existence, while the identical even ones indicate the eternal sameness of nature. . . . (p. 68)

Prominent among the many polarities in Liliencron is that between the picaresque and the feudal element. The latter is represented especially by his ballads and balladesque poems. . . . (p. 69)

In the narrative ballads, whose themes are taken largely from the history of Schleswig-Holstein and Denmark, a deeper psychological penetration and emotional differentiation are on the whole conspicuous by their absence; nor is there that touch of cosmic mystery which characterizes Agnes Miegel or Börries von Münchhausen. "Ruck, Zug, Bumsfallera," that is what delights Liliencron in Strachwitz, while Platen and C. F. Meyer, both of whom he otherwise greatly admires, according to him lack the essentials of the ballad: fire, blood, swollen veins, and clanking of arms. . . . The true ballad, he insists, should send a shudder down our spines . . . , but in his own case this shudder tends to be brought about rather exclusively by a gory violence which often fails to rise above the level of colorful fury and slaughter. . . . A strong regional and historical flavor is produced by the extensive use of proper names, as when in **"Das Haupt des heiligen Johannes auf der Schüssel"** . . . the canonesses from the old feudal families of Schleswig-Holstein are enumerated. . . . (p. 70)

One must agree with Wolfgang Kayser that Liliencron can hardly be acclaimed as a creative renewer of the German ballad; but he did keep it alive in an age of middle-class and therefore essentially unballadesque mentality. He stands between Strachwitz and Börries von Münchhausen, smaller, to be sure, than either; and it is significant that all three are of feudal origin.

Two poems among these early ones stand out in a negative sense. **"Unheimlicher Teich"** . . . is written in free verse that altogether lacks a sustaining rhythmical force, and it must be regarded as typical of its author in that respect. Even more fundamental is the weakness of the long diffuse poem **"Die Nixe."** . . . It is weak *because* it is long, and in this sense likewise typical. Impressionistic, non-intellectual, and subject to abrupt momentary impulses as he is, Liliencron, with rare exceptions, excels only when he imposes upon himself the discipline of brevity.

And it is this brevity which often is lacking in his later poems. Too few have those qualities which we found to be characteristic of the author of ***Adjutantenritte*** (and other contemporary poems) at his best: compactness, concreteness, vivid suggestiveness. There is an astonishing number of sprawling, unintense, and banal poems that leave no deeper impression whatsoever. He no longer makes sufficiently strict demands upon himself in composing, and he is not selective enough in publishing. (p. 71)

If we seek the reasons for this deterioration, the following factors seem to be involved: Firstly, to put it baldly, the progressive spiritual bankruptcy of the author. . . . Both [Heinrich] Spiero (reluctantly) and [Johannes] Elema (emphatically) have . . . a low opinion of the poetical harvest of the Munich year, ***Der Haidegänger und andere Gedichte.*** But: "Ich war so glücklich" ["I was so happy"]—does not Liliencron thus sum up the experiences of this period? Precisely, answers Elema. . . . This famishing of the poet by the hedonist—which is, of course, not limited to the sojourn in Munich but goes on year after year—manifests itself in a lack of discrimination both as to content and form. And later, when Liliencron settles down as a *pater familias* ["father of a family"], he is, despite all spurts of a tumultuous affirmation of life, fundamentally a tired, embittered old man.

Secondly: it was in Munich that Liliencron really came into personal contact with the naturalists, and their doctrine of direct imitation of empirical reality would seem to have had a harmful effect upon him, as it was the reason for their own lyrical sterility. (pp. 71-2)

A third point stands in contrast, but not in contradiction, to the second. There is in Liliencron, as in some members of the naturalistic age-group, the desire for vindication on a supra-empirical level, the desire to penetrate to the sphere of fundamentals and to emerge as a symbolist. But since he depends on the direct stimulus of sensory reality, since he is by nature unspeculative and utterly unmetaphysical, his visions are apt to appear forced and uncompelling, his symbols to congeal into brittle allegories.

There are, of course, some excellent individual poems among the later ones. To mention but a few:—**"Einen Sommer lang"** . . . succeeds for once in fusing an aesthetically sublimated erotic experience with a very delicate feeling for nature. **"Tragisches Liebesmahl,'** . . . though formally uneven, is compelling through the intensity with which it expresses the ethos and pathos of companionship in arms. **"Die Zwillingsgeschwister,"** . . . which has the destruction of Jerusalem by Titus as a background, combines perfection of rhythm and imagery with great tragic depth, recalling C. F. Meyer, as Wolfgang Kayser points out. And **"Das Schlachtschiff Téméraire,"** . . . a free adaptation of Henry Newbolt's "Fighting Téméraire," is a masterpiece of the lyrical ballad with its merely suggestive pictures of the good ship before, during, and after the battle.

Considerations of space forbid our entering into a detailed critical discussion of Liliencron's later phases, in which, when all is said and done, we see predominantly a decline. Let us rather, disregarding chronology, concentrate on a few general aspects of his poetry.

In the first place his style is . . . characterized by exact observation, especially of visual elements. . . . In a cavalry attack he sees the points of the saddle-cloths sweep over the grass like the wind. . . . Crows do not walk, but stumble through the garden, and from the fields is heard not a voice in general, but that of a boy scolding his cows. . . . The sensations are primarily those of a hunter, a landowner, or a soldier. Descriptions of urban and industrial scenes are the exception and seem, where they do occur, attributable to the influence of naturalism.

On the other hand Liliencron has a definite fondness for exotic motifs. Moors and Syrians with gold plate in their noses and ears carry litters through the streets of the ill-fated city of Rungholt. . . . How superior is the succinct suggestiveness of the short poems that breathe the breath of the native soil, poems that activate the reader's imagination into creativity instead of weighing it down and stifling it with elaborate description.

Imagery often reaches a high degree of visual intensity. . . . In [a] threnody, **"Und ich war fern,"** . . . Liliencron beautifully symbolizes the despair caused by three successive dreams of a beloved person's death by the thrice repeated image of black flowers encompassing his bed.—"Rote Perlenküste" ["a red pearl coast"] . . . for a girl's mouth is a striking (if somewhat baroque) metaphor, "groschengroße Tropfen" ["groschen-sized drops"] . . . a robustly effective simile.

But by no means always is he so fortunate in his imagery. A dissonance is introduced into mood and style when in **"Rückblick"** . . . the fleeing enemy is coarsely referred to as "tollgehetzte Hammel" ["madly pursued mutton"]. The comparison of the *two* lieutenants guarding the colors in **"Die Musik kommt"** . . . to a fence is visually impossible. . . . Forced and trivial is the conception of foliage washed by "die große Gießkanne des Wolkengärtners" ["the great watering can of the gardener in the clouds"] . . . , or the likening of the moon to a comma . . . , of a beautiful rose to melting butter. . . . (pp. 72-5)

One of Liliencron's favorite tropical forms is anthropomorphic personification—a very dangerous one. Sometimes, to be sure, he succeeds in striking that naive note which here alone creates illusion. . . . But too often the anthropomorphic element is so obtrusive that it weakens rather than intensifies the mood. . . . The sun lending his jewelry to the snow . . . , fir-trees touching each other's finger-tips . . . , morning squeezing his finger-tips through the cracks in the shutters . . . , the storm pressing his rude forehead against the panes . . . , the wind clipping off pearls from (?) the dew . . .—all these personifications show a certain element of strain. The concepts of solitude vying with stillness for precedence . . . or of summer stretching out his hot arm for ever earlier hours (i.e., the days are lengthening . . .) are distressing in their tortuousness. (p. 75)

Altogether Liliencron's desultory temperament, unchecked by intellectual discipline, leads him to badly inconsistent and mixed metaphors. . . .

As for Liliencron's vocabulary, a distinctive trait is his use of substandard and dialect words, often chosen with a view to their onomatopoetic qualities. . .

Even more characteristic are the frequent neologisms. (p. 76)

Liliencron speaks of himself as a "deutscher Sprach-Fanatiker" ["German language-fanatic"], indeed as an ardent disciple of Wustmann, the schoolmasterly, irascible purist and author of *Sprachdummheiten*. Moreover, it is an established fact that he spent much time and care on the revision of his poems. All the more astounding are such cases of negligent, indeed illogical diction. . . .

Masterful is often the expressiveness of Liliencron's rhythm. **"Zwei Meilen Trab"** . . . trots and the first part of **"Festnacht und Frühgang"** . . . waltzes; a gentle breeze blows in the first half of **"Mit der Pinasse,"** . . . a squally storm in the second. . . .

There remain to be said a few words about ***Poggfred,*** the dramas, and the prose. (p. 78)

The form [of ***Poggfred***] is predominantly the *ottava rima* of Byron's *Don Juan;* extensive parts are in the Dantesque *terza rima*. With *Don Juan* it shares the ironical note produced by startling rhymes and by the insouciance with which the author, disdainful of illusion, lets the reader watch the composition in process, chatting with him and taking him into his confidence with regard to motifs, diction, and rhyme; but Liliencron's touch is not quite so light as Byron's. There is no continuous plot, rather a medley of scenes, anecdotes, and fantasies, held together by the individuality of the author himself. . . . [Spiero] greatly admires the poem, at least its earlier parts. . . . [But] does ***Poggfred*** really exert a compelling force? . . . It did have such an effect on many of the poet's contemporaries; on the other hand . . . later critics (Ermatinger, Elema, Nadler) altogether fail to respond with enthusiasm. Whence this discrepancy? Because we have since, in George, Rilke, Hofmannsthal, Carossa, witnessed a depth of spiritual experience, a sustained perfection of form, and a flawless integration of both that are simply beyond Liliencron individually and his age collectively. Naturalistically bound, both lack an upbearing metaphysical consciousness; moreover he is personally desultory in temperament, he lacks direction and concentration in his manner of experiencing life—at least after the triple breakdown of his career, his faith, and his first marriage. To a given situation he reacts instantaneously and violently, rather than continuously and profoundly. His emotional waves are stormy, but also choppy and short; there is no deep, enduring groundswell. (p. 79)

Sharp of perception and quick of reaction, he is a master of the short poem; the more extensive the project, the less intensive is its emotional density, and the less cogent its spell. And so it is with ***Poggfred.*** There are strong passages in it, vivid and forceful pictures. But it does not gather momentum as it goes along. One stimulus gives way to another; we are thrown from motif to motif, from scene to scene, from mood to incongruous mood. And when the poet ventures beyond his proper sphere of sensory reality altogether into that of the spiritual, the universal, the cosmic, his visions become fantastically and allegorically abstruse more often than magically and symbolically plastic.

In the years 1882-87 Liliencron wrote a series of historical plays: ***Knut der Herr, Pokahontas, Die Rantzow und die Pogwisch, Der Trifels und Palermo, Die Merowinger.*** Their general tenor reminds of Wildenbruch; individual passages show the influence of Shakespeare, and especially of Kleist's blank verse with its peculiar staccato cadence. Truly dramatic qualities are lacking. The characters, as far as they are individualized at all, are deficient in plastic roundness and fullness; most of them can be reduced to a single dominant trait. Attempts to draw a complex figure, as in the case of the Emperor Henry VI (***Der Trifels und Palermo,***) are not convincing. The knot of dramatic action is not tightly drawn: entrances and exits are inadequately motivated. The historical illusion is marred by anachronisms. There is a certain colorful balladesque quality in these dramas, but we have seen that a deeper and subtler human element is absent in Liliencron's ballads themselves. (pp. 80-1)

While Liliencron's dramatic works belong to one definite period of his life, he turned to the novel at various times. In Kellinghusen he wrote ***Breide Hummelsbüttel*** and ***Der Mažen; Mit dem linken Ellenbogen*** grew out of his sojourn in Munich, and ***Leben und Lüge*** was completed in 1908.

Breide Hummelsbuttel has many traits in common with his creator. The scion of an old landed family whose history resembles that of the Liliencrons, he loses his estate through irresponsibility and bankruptcy. The relations between him and his wife, in whom we clearly recognize Helene von Bodenhausen, are strained, but in calamity she stands by him. As a small railway official he manfully sets to work to build up anew his shattered existence; he dies rescuing a proletarian child from an on-rushing train. Quite obviously he thus embodies a moral wish-image of the author, who has his *alter ego* master misfortune, retain (or rather, regain) the love of a proud but loyal woman, and ultimately sublimate a wayward life by a crowning self-sacrifice. A second wish-image, on a different level, is represented by Count Heesten, a fabulously rich grandee and literary connoisseur; we have previously seen in Liliencron's correspondence the would-be grandseigneur reveling in such fantasies.

In ***Der Mažen*** this same type appears in Wulff Gadendorp, who lives as a patron of the arts and in his last will makes stupendous provisions for needy German authors. The word novel is here really a misnomer, for instead of a plot we have a medley of scenes from country life, polemics against the aesthetic apathy and moral squeamishness of the German public, assorted critical remarks and evaluations (a list of "great authors" and "great books" takes up almost two pages), together with copious selections of favorite poetry dating from Uhland and Platen to the naturalistic era; interspersed are descriptions of gallant adventures and of lusty pleasures of the palate. Gadendorp's *buen retiro* Poggfred foreshadows the later epic thus entitled.

Mit dem linken Ellenbogen, in contrast, is brimful of lurid happenings. The heroine, a South-German village girl, goes through many ups and downs—poverty alternating with affluence, rape, true love, infanticide, etc.—before she is finally poisoned by the wife of her rich lover. The plot is in places pure melodrama, the style a mixture of *Papierdeutsch* with naturalistic and symbolistic elements; the development of the central figure from a dialect-speaking country lass to a self-assured woman on the outskirts of high society is unconvincing.

Leben und Lüge, the biographical novel of Kai Vorbrüggen, has a considerable fullness and warmth in the first part, where Liliencron draws upon memories from his own childhood; later it becomes sketchy, disjointed, and pale. Kai, who has come into an enormous fortune, again plays the rôles of a limitlessly open-handed grandseigneur and of a spokesman through whom Liliencron utters various and sundry opinions on life and literature.

Of these four novels ***Breide Hummelsbüttel*** has the most closely knit plot and the best drawn characters. ***Mit dem linken Ellenbogen*** hardly rises above the level of pulp literature. ***Der Mažen*** is no real novel at all, and ***Leben und Lüge*** is one properly only in its early chapters. In all of them except the second, where the South-German milieu is alien to the author, we do find from time to time a strong local coloring and excellent descriptive passages. . . . On the other hand there are, as in the poetry, slovenly and illogical sentence structures; and the dialogue style is not free from the banalities of the trash novel. . . . (pp. 81-2)

On the whole, even Liliencron's staunchest admirers have failed to applaud his novels whole-heartedly.

The inverse ratio between his formative power and the quantitative scope of his themes applies to his prose as well as his poetry. He is not made for tasks which refuse to yield to the first impressionistic *élan,* he cannot integrate a complex subject matter through a firm structure and a sustained mood. Thus his shorter prose pieces are, on the whole, greatly superior to his novels. The best are found among the very briefest.

The more closely he approaches the genuine *novelle* (*i.e.,* the more the emphasis lies on the narrative element), the more disappointing is in general the result. The clear epic line is apt to be obscured by extraneous material; often he reaches his plot in a long, roundabout way and then rushes helter-skelter to the conclusion. Or, where a greater structural unity and clarity are achieved, the characters are not convincingly drawn. Melodramatic solutions may tax our credulity, and the dialogue occasionally be wooden. But perfect is **"Schmetterlingsgedanken"** . . . , in which two parallel actions of the deepest pathos, beautifully interwoven with a melancholy nature symbolism, are compressed into four pages. Similarly concentrated, similarly worked out to a perfect intensity of mood are the three pages of **"Verloren,"** the first of the ***Kriegsnovellen***. . . . Most of the latter, to be sure, are not *novellen* at all, but semi-fictionalized sketches from the wars of 1866 and 1870/71. Wonderful—and wonderful because based on experience—are the vivid descriptions, stark but not crude. Only **"Portepeefähnrich Schadius"** ventures deeper into the realm of the genuine *novelle;* and although the proper plot again gets under way somewhat slowly, it is led to a powerful conclusion; the characters are sharply drawn, and the motif of the mysterious French mountain fastness introduces a romantic trait which yet fuses harmoniously with the dominant realistic tenor.—Also of the historical *novellen* some are no stories at all, but sketches from the past of the Cimbrian peninsula, more or less touched up with fictional or balladesque elements. The rhythmical prose ballad **"Josua Qualen"** (inserted in **"Auf meinem Gute"** . . .) has a demonic depth and an intensity of atmosphere that are rarely equaled.

Whether Liliencron's shorter prose pieces are *novellen* or not, their strength lies preeminently in the descriptive passages; and it is on account of the latter that the critics have invariably ranked them next to, or even with, his poetry. . . . The descriptions range from straight naturalistic impressionism to a highly symbolical variation that, since it rests on the firm foundation of observation, is infinitely more forceful than pictures of Aldebaran or other cosmic visions not prompted by terrestrial sensory stimuli. . . . (pp. 83-4)

Very strong is Liliencron's chromatic sense; it is characteristic that his colors are stark, undifferentiated. . . . In the historical sketch **"Die Dithmarschen"** he shows us the glow of the watch fires as they eerily light up the black, gleaming faces of the Danish king's Ethiopian body-guard . . . ; and after the battle the black water of the marsh ditches is mixed with blood. . . . (p. 85)

Altogether this love of chromatic intensity often appears, as in the poems, in close connection with exotic motifs. We have already mentioned the Ethiopians in the retinue of the king of Denmark. Africans also wait on Gorm the Old, the Viking chief who rides a milk-white steed covered with a purple saddle-cloth and has stirrups of Arabian workmanship. . . .

Also acoustic elements are strongly in evidence. . . . Especially bird sounds are constantly reproduced. . . . Melodiously the oriole sings "gigliaglio, güliaio gülio gigliaglio" . . . , and mournful is the yellow-hammer's "never never never never more" (*sic!* . . .).

Despite all the strong points in Liliencron's prose sketches the quality of his style is as uneven here as elsewhere; he is just not cut out to be a perfectionist. Ugly and entirely unnecessary participial constructions and infinitives used as nouns mar his diction. (pp. 85-6)

As we look back upon Liliencron and try to see the man and the author as a whole, we may find the intense enthusiasm with which he was once acclaimed hard to understand. It can be explained only from the historical circumstances. There is abundant evidence that by about 1880 the great recent, and even the great living poets had well nigh fallen into oblivion: Mörike, Storm, Keller, etc. The foreground of the literary scene was occupied by the epigons. . . . (p. 86)

Against this vacuous triviality the young naturalists directed their onslaught, giving no quarter. Together with them Liliencron fought the battles of the eighteen-eighties; and they saw in him, in the field of the lyric, the fulfillment of their own aspirations as we have observed. . . . Indeed, owing to his spontaneity, his closeness to nature, they regarded him as one who saved naturalism from itself, from its wordy theorizing, its anaemic dialectics; and as time went on and the young generation began to grope beyond strict naturalism, he appeared as the inaugurator of a new imaginative poetry.

Such evaluation was enhanced by Liliencron's human personality and way of life in an age which, under the impact of Nietzsche, reveled in moral iconoclasm, blissfully unaware of its fall into an inverted smugness and priggishness. (pp. 86-7)

The verdict of these over-enthusiastic contemporaries we can no longer accept. Liliencron the poet does not appear to us as the one on whom the mantle of Goethe descended, Liliencron the man not as the "Tänzer und Sieger" ["dancer and conqueror"]. In art and life he lacked discipline, and thus formative power. There is in him a similar amorphousness as in Whitman. Such a comparison may come as a surprise to the reader, but if we make allowances for the enormous differences in tradition and environment (here the Prussian officer and monarchist, there the product and prophet of equalitarian American democracy), enough basic likeness remains to justify it. Both poets are non-intellectual and can be naive to the point of absurdity; both lack self-limitation and self-criticism; both are therefore artistically uneven: masters in expressing the concrete individual perception, but incapable of sustaining a uniformly high level, of forming a comprehensive structural whole.

Lacking the power of integration, Liliencron lacked greatness. But he did create a number of unforgettable poems. (p. 87)

Detlev W. Schumann, "Detlev von Liliencron (1844-1909): An Attempt at an Interpretation and Evaluation, Part II," in Monatshefte, *Vol. XXXVII, No. 2, February, 1945, pp. 65-87.*

ADDITIONAL BIBLIOGRAPHY

Burkhard, Arthur. "The Language of Detlev von Liliencron's Lyrics and Ballads." *Journal of English and Germanic Philology* XXX, No. 2 (April 1931): 236-54.

Examines Liliencron's unconventional poetic style in relation to poetic tradition, citing his creation of new words and unusual metaphors as the distinctive feature of his poetry.

———. "Progress in Poetry: A Comparison of the Poems of Conrad Ferdinand Meyer and Detlev von Liliencron." *Journal of English and Germanic Philology* XXXI, No. 2 (April 1932): 173-99.*

Compares the poetry of Liliencron, an innovator in the modern movement of German verse, with that of his contemporary Meyer, a representative of the conservative poetic tradition, in order to investigate the nature of progress in poetry.

Field, G. Wallis. "Lyric Poetry from Poetic Realism to Impressionism and Symbolism." In his *A Literary History of Germany: The Nineteenth Century, 1830-1890,* pp. 131-54. London: Ernest Benn, 1975.*

Provides a brief discussion of the themes and techniques of Liliencron's poetry.

Krappe, Alexander Haggerty. "The Source of Detlev von Liliencron's 'Abschied'." *Journal of English and Germanic Philology* XXV (1926): 79-83.

Demonstrates that Liliencron's poem was derived from an Aesopian fable.

Rose, Ernst. "The Fighting Téméraire." *Germanic Review* XV, No. 4 (December 1940): 273-80.*

Examines the history of the English battleship and Liliencron's adaptation of Henry Newbolt's "The Fighting Téméraire," concluding that Liliencron "transposed by a few deft strokes Henry Newbolt's sentimental poem into a powerfully German tragic ballad."

Schumann, Detlev W. "Detlev von Liliencron (1844-1909): An Attempt at an Interpretation and Evaluation: Part I." *Monatshefte* XXXVI, No. 8 (December 1944): 385-408.

Biographical essay, prefaced by a summary of critical reaction to Liliencron's works. For comments from Part II, see excerpt dated 1945.

Masaoka Shiki

1867-1902

(Born Masaoka Tsunenori) Japanese poet, short story writer, essayist, diarist, and critic.

Shiki is considered responsible for the early twentieth-century revitalization of haiku and tanka, two traditional Japanese poetic forms composed, respectively, of seventeen and thirty-one syllables. In his verse and numerous critical essays, Shiki established guidelines for preserving the essential aspects of the Japanese poetic heritage, while at the same time incorporating new techniques which would make traditional verse forms useful for poets in the swiftly-changing Meiji Period. The Meiji Period corresponded with the rule of Emperor Mutsuhito (1868-1912) and marked the beginning of Japan's modern era, during which the country underwent profound change in attempts to shed its isolationist past and embrace elements of Western culture. While the Japanese were receptive to Western technological advancements, they found a fundamental conflict between their culture's reverence for Eastern tradition and spirituality and the new Western ways. An additional source of conflict was the concentrated interest Japanese writers took in contemporary European literature. By the late nineteenth century, translations of European authors acquainted the reading public with fresh and unfamiliar writing and encouraged many Japanese writers to abandon traditional forms they believed had grown dated and stale. Shiki's campaign to reestablish haiku and tanka as relevant modes of poetic expression occurred at a time when both forms were lapsing into obsolescence. The cumulative force of his critical theory, his recruitment of other poets to the movement, and the application of his theories in his own verse establish Shiki as one who, according to Donald Keene, "almost singlehandedly restored the haiku to an important place in Japanese poetry. . . ."

Shiki was born in the Iyo Province, now the Ehime Prefecture, to a modest samurai family. After the early death of his father, Shiki became the ward of his maternal grandfather, a respected Confucian scholar and strict samurai, who instilled in him a deep regard for scholarship, Japanese tradition, and the samurai values of stoicism and contempt for material wealth. Shiki revealed in his memoirs that as a young boy he dreamed of surpassing his grandfather's scholarly excellence, but that he despised school and frequently neglected his studies to write poetry, the only activity of which he never tired. His talent in language and literature emerged early: by age eleven he was fluent in Chinese and had composed his first poem in that language, and by age thirteen he had formed his first literary group with several schoolmates—the Poetry Lover's Society—which met in his cluttered bedroom. In 1883, Shiki left his provincial middle school and moved to Tokyo, where he passed an entrance examination for the University Preparatory School. Although his academic interest shifted from politics and law to philosophy, Shiki's study of literature remained consistent and his commitment to it grew stronger, so that once again he began ignoring conventional study to write poetry. In 1889, while still a student, Shiki contracted tuberculosis, which would eventually kill him; when he coughed blood for the second time, he took the pen name Shiki, the Chinese word for a legendary cuckoo bird that coughed blood when it sang. The year 1892 marked a turning point in Shiki's life. After failing his examinations, he withdrew from the university and devoted himself to intensive reading through the entire history of haiku and working on a novella. This concentrated literary activity contributed to the development of his poetic theory, which was first presented in serial form in the newspaper *Nippon*. Shiki was the poetry editor of *Nippon* from 1892 until his death and used his column as a lively literary forum for both his opinionated criticism and his poetry. In 1893, the two-hundredth anniversary of the death of the revered haiku poet Bashō, Shiki published a controversial series of articles entitled *Bashō Zatsudan,* in which he attacked the quality of Bashō's work and challenged the validity of his adulation by Japanese readers. In spite of his frail physical condition, Shiki went to China in 1894 as a correspondent for *Nippon* during the Sino-Japanese War. On the return voyage he suffered a lung hemorrhage and nearly died. Although he was largely confined to bed for the rest of his life, Shiki remained exceedingly active in Tokyo literary life, producing voluminous amounts of criticism and poetry and holding frequent meetings with disciples at his bedside. In this weakened condition and in constant pain, Shiki wrote his important essay on the eighteenth-century haiku poet and painter Yosa Buson, which maintained that his poetry was equal, and in many ways superior, to that of Bashō, and which established him as a model for modern haiku poets. During his final years, Shiki wrote three sickbed diaries which included much of his finest verse and in which he recorded his poignant, yet unself-pitying, reflections of his battle with death.

Shiki's most significant contributions to modern Japanese poetry can be found in his critical essays. Rather than calling for the abandonment of traditional Japanese poetic standards, Shiki's essays on haiku and tanka reform present suggestions for the renovation of these traditional forms so that they retain their essential nature, but also accommodate the needs of an increasingly changing culture. In *Dassai Shooku Haiwa,* his initial call for haiku reform, Shiki stressed the potential of haiku as a viable art form while simultaneously criticizing past haiku poets, maintaining that their largely stale and unimaginative work was responsible for the degraded state of the art. Shiki followed this harsh evaluation of the haiku crisis with the publication of a series of articles on Bashō, the finest haiku poet of the Tokugawa period (which preceded the Meiji era) and one of the most honored figures in Japanese literature. In *Bashō Zatsudan,* Shiki levied harsh criticism at the "Saint of Haiku," questioning his cult status and asserting that "the majority of Bashō's haiku are bad or even doggerel, and not more than a tenth can be called first rate." With this essay, Shiki attacked the sancrosanct values of the literary community and attracted an audience for his suggestions for haiku reform. In 1894, a fortuitous combination of Shiki's discovery of the haiku poet Buson and his meeting the Western-style painter Nakamura Fusetsu resulted in the formulation of the core of his poetic theory, which was published several years later in his seminal essay *Haijin Buson.* In this work Shiki praises the objective and pictorial quality of Buson's verse, a principle called *shasei* ("copying life") by realist painters such as Fusetsu. Shiki considered haiku the literary form closest to painting, because of its emphasis on the spatial relationships of objects in the poem, and believed it could be revitalized if poets strove to attain the same sense of immediacy and realism sought by the innovative Japanese painters of the day. Unlike the lofty and intellectualized quality, traditionally termed "negative beauty," found in work of Bashō and other haiku masters, Shiki thought the shasei principle endowed poetry with realistic vitality and strength, or "positive beauty." While Japanese art was characteristically created on the principles of negative beauty, Western art was traditionally positive. By Shiki's introduction of this Western aesthetic principle to the traditional haiku and tanka, modern Japanese poetry was able to preserve its heritage even as it began to reflect the occidental influence in the Meiji culture.

Shiki's own haiku and tanka, composed between 1885 and his death, reveal the development of his poetic theory. While many critics agree that his early verse exhibits mundane subject matter and banal realism, his later work masterfully illustrates the objectivity and descriptive precision he promoted in his criticism. Although Shiki's poetry, like that of his predecessors, focused on the traditional Japanese theme of nature, his work was distinctive for its inclusion of Westernized vocabulary and frequent contrasts of nature with modern inventions—ranging from railroad tracks to toothpaste. The finest of Shiki's haiku and tanka employ the shasei technique and attempt to sketch nature accurately and dispassionately. Unlike old-fashioned haiku, which lacked a sense of the poet's mediating presence—an absence which Shiki contended contributed to its bland quality—his subject was the poet's relation to nature. In Shiki's haiku and tanka, the poet's presence is implicit, and his skillful use of shasei and absolute understatement of emotion result in verse which demonstrates his distinct intelligence while presenting the surrounding world with crystalline accuracy. In order to fully capture the realism he sought, Shiki advocated "sequential composition," the practice of writing haiku or tanka in sequence so that the individual poems acquire additional significance when considered collectively. Sequentially composed haiku or tanka were to be unified by a single motif, with each poem presenting a different aspect of that motif. Shiki maintained that through varied treatment of one subject the poet could more successfully capture a range of realistic nuances. Because he was confined to bed for the last five years of his life, many of Shiki's poetic sequences describe his sickroom, the flowers at his bedside, or the garden as viewed from his bedroom window. While suffering through the final stages of tuberculosis, Shiki's work focused almost exclusively upon his physical condition and approaching death. The poems he wrote about the diseased state of his body are marked by graphic description and clinical objectivity, the best example of these being his famous deathbed sequence, written in his diary *Byōshō Rokushaku* (*A Six-Foot Sickbed*), which describes the agony of his last hours with accuracy and samurai stoicism.

Shiki is remembered today as a pioneer of haiku and tanka reform whose diligent efforts not only preserved these traditional forms, but also made them vital for modern Japanese poets. For his perceptive critical assessments of classical Japanese literature, as well as his skillful application of his innovative poetic theory in his own work, Shiki is considered—along with Bashō and Buson—one of the great masters of haiku.

PRINCIPAL WORKS

Dassai Shooku Haiwa (criticism) 1892; published in journal *Nippon*
"Tsuki no Miyako" (short story) 1892
Bashō Zatsudan (criticism) 1893; published in journal *Nippon*
Bunkai Yatsu Atari (criticism) 1893; published in journal *Nippon*
Haikai Taiyō (criticism) 1895; published in journal *Nippon*
Meiji Nijūkunen no Haiku Kai (criticism) 1896-97; published in journal *Nippon*
Haijin Buson (criticism) 1897; published in journal *Nippon*
Hyakuchū Jisshu (poetry) 1898; published in journal *Nippon*
Utayomi ni Atauru Sho (criticism) 1898; published in journal *Nippon*
Bokujū Itteki (poetry and diary) 1901 [*A Drop of Ink,* 1975]
Gyōga Maroku (poetry and diary) 1901-02
Byōshō Rokushaku (poetry and diary) 1902
Shiki Zenshū. 15 vols. (poetry, essays, and diaries) 1924-26
A Verse Record of My Peonies (diary) 1969; published in *Japanese Poetic Diaries*
Peonies Kana (poetry) 1972

Translated selections of Shiki's poetry and prose have appeared in the following publications: *Anthology of Haiku Ancient and Modern, The Bamboo Broom, A Chime of Windbells, From the Country of Eight Islands, Haiku, Haiku Harvest, A History of Haiku, An Introduction to Haiku, Japanese Haiku, Japanese Literature in the Meiji Era, Landscapes and Portraits, Modern Japanese Haiku: An Anthology, A Net of Fireflies,* and *The Penguin Book of Japanese Verse.*

HAROLD G. HENDERSON (essay date 1958)

[*Henderson was an American educator and authority on Japanese language and literature. In the following excerpt, he discusses the difficulty Western readers have understanding the predominantly Japanese subject matter of Shiki's verse.*]

Shiki loved his country—its scenery, its people, its customs, its history, its traditions—and he wrote about them constantly and much more consciously than previous haiku masters. His poems about Japan are likely to be among his finest, because in these his emotion is not only genuine, but also strong. They do, however, present special difficulties to foreigners. Sometimes these difficulties can be cleared up by explanation. Take for example:

Of those who pass
with spears erect, there are none.
Plumes of pampas grass.

Here the reference is to the daimyō processions that in the days of the Tokugawa Shogunate used to go regularly between Edo (Tokyo) and the provinces. Shiki himself had never seen them, but many older Japanese had, and must have often described them to him. They can be visualized from illustrations, such as those by Hiroshige, who had died less than twenty years before Shiki's birth. These show a long cortege of retainers, not all spearmen, and among them a number carrying long poles with colored tufts at the end, which acted as identifying standards. It was probably such standards, rather than the spears themselves, which the pampas plumes suggested to Shiki's mind.

Or take as another example:

Atsumori's tomb—
and here there is not even
a cherry tree to bloom!

Every literate Japanese would know of Atsumori, a gallant young samurai of the twelfth century who was killed in battle at the age of fifteen, and would instantly recognize the traditional connection between such young samurai and falling cherry-blossoms—a connection so strong that Shiki did not even have to mention the blossoms. And most of all, he would feel, with Shiki, the wickedness of letting the past go wholly into oblivion. (pp. 156-58)

[What] can one do with this, which is deservedly one of Shiki's most famous poems?

Persimmons; as I chew,
a temple bell begins to boom
from Hōryū.

It is possible to explain that Hōryū Temple (Hōryū-ji) dates from the seventh century; that it is the oldest wooden building in the world; that it contains wonderful old wall paintings and sculptures; that it has been venerated for ages. It is possible to explain that Shiki liked persimmons; that Shiki's persimmons did not have the same taste or consistency as Western ones; that their slight astringency is indicated by the "k" sounds in the first line *kaki kueba;* etc., etc. But no foreigner can have quite the same feeling about Hōryū-ji that a Japanese has; and how can anyone get the subtle connection—and there is one—between a taste he has never tasted and a sound he has never heard?

Of course, Shiki did not always write poems that are purely nationalistic. Such a poem as:

Treading the clouds,
inhaling the mist:
a soaring skylark.

might have been written by any real poet, no matter what his nationality. (pp. 158-59)

Shiki was very fond of using the purely objective type of haiku, the effect of which he likened to that of a painting.

One full moon;
stars numberless; the sky
dark green.

If anyone should ask what this "means," Shiki has already answered that only a tyro asks what a poem "means"; the only thing that matters is what effect it has. And certainly in such a poem as this, where Shiki is writing about universals, both foreigners and Japanese can get the same picture and the same effect. (pp. 159-60)

The real trouble comes when Shiki gives the description of a purely Japanese scene—which he usually does. No foreigner, unless he has lived most of his life in Japan, can visualize it clearly; and unless one can get the picture, it is impossible to get the underlying emotion.

Through the center of the town
flows a little river; here
willow trees hang down.

For this even the translation has to have redundant words like "hang down" to show that the trees are weeping willows. The town is certainly very different from any town in Europe or America. As I visualize it, in Shiki's time "modern improvements" are creeping in. There is probably a factory; almost surely electric-light or telegraph poles; and only the river and the willows to keep the original closeness to nature. But I may be wrong.

It is a great pity that we non-Japanese cannot appreciate more of these poems, because the technique of purely objective word painting is a very good one, and Shiki used it to perfection. By means of it he could run the gamut of emotion, from the most delicate suggestiveness to powerful, stark realism. (pp. 160-61)

Shiki died before his powers reached their full maturity, but before he died he and his colleagues had won the battle against artificiality and had brought to haiku a new sense of youth and freshness. It is possible that the victory went too far. Shiki had a habit of using haiku to record any genuine emotion, no matter how ephemeral or unimportant it might be, and to me it seems that this habit resulted in his publishing a great deal of very second-rate verse. But this, of course, is the judgment of a foreigner. (p. 162)

Harold G. Henderson, "Shiki," in his An Introduction to Haiku: An Anthology of Poems and Poets from Bashō to Shiki, *Doubleday Anchor Books, 1958, pp. 149-74.*

ROBERT H. BROWER (essay date 1971)

[*In the following excerpt, Brower discusses Shiki's poetic theories.*]

Shiki's notions of what was good and bad in the waka remained fairly conventional until 1894. At this point he experienced a rather sudden change of heart—an emotional revulsion against the classical *Kokinshū* and a correspondingly fervent conversion to the *Manyōshū,* the first great anthology of Japanese poetry, compiled in the eighth century, and revered by the National Scholars of the Tokugawa period as the supreme expression of the pure Japanese spirit. The suddenness of the conversion suggests that it was prompted more by men and events than by any deep study of the tanka tradition. (p. 388)

The first and most extended major statement of his views was the ten installments of his **"Open Letter to the Waka Poets"** (***Utayomi ni Atauru Sho***), published in *Nihon* in February and March, 1898. Coming in the midst of Tekkan's already well-advanced campaign of reform, Shiki's manifesto was something of an anticlimax. Nevertheless, its forceful language impressed Shiki's following and the readers of *Nihon,* and the **"Open Letter"** has since become a kind of classic of modern Japanese literary polemics. (p. 389)

[In the **"Open Letter"** Shiki excoriates] contemporary waka poets for knowing nothing about haiku or Chinese poetry; for being smugly convinced that no form of literature can be as fine as their tanka; for refusing to recognize the beauty of any but a smoothly mellifluous poetic cadence, and the like. Despite the obvious unfairness of his sweeping charges, however, his specific criticisms of poets and poems are often lively and pointed, and his arguments also have the considerable merit of treating poetry for the most part in the proper literary terms. At the same time, notwithstanding the expansiveness of his avowed principles—his call for complete freedom of diction, or to "study and learn from all literature, old and new, high and low, East and West"—the conclusion of the **"Open Letter"** shows that Shiki's basic esthetic ideal was actually rather more conservative than revolutionary. Fundamentally, it was the haiku standard of *fūryū,* or "poetic elegance"—an ideal significantly different from the waka concept of elegant beauty, but in its way just as traditional. The ultimate test of what should and should not be treated in poetry therefore came down to the question of whether the material was "beautiful," or could be rendered beautiful by the basic techniques of composition, contrast, and arrangement (*haigō*) of the haiku:

> When I say to treat new and unusual materials in your poems, some people will bring forth such "machinery of civilization" as trains and railroads, but such notions are very mistaken. The machinery of civilization consists for the most part of inelegant, unpoetic things, which are difficult to put into poems. However, if one wishes to make the attempt, there is nothing for it but to arrange and harmonize these things with other materials that are tasteful. To treat them without such harmonizing material—to say, for example, "The wind blows along the railroad tracks"—this is utterly flat and tasteless. It will give at least a somewhat better appearance if one combines these things with other materials, saying, for example, that violets are blooming beside the railroad tracks, or that the poppies scatter or the pampas grass waves in the wake of the passing train, and the like. Another good way of treating such unpoetic materials is from a distant point of view. One means of effacing their prosaic, tasteless qualities is to say, for example, that the train can be seen across the field of rape flowers, or that the train is passing in the distance beyond the broad fields of summer grass.

The basic conservatism of Shiki's view of the poetic suggests that by "realistic description" he really meant something rather different from describing whatever happens to be at hand "just as it is." . . . Shiki's realistic description in the tanka is basically a poetic mode, a way of treating certain poetic materials. The effect of the treatment when it is successful is to give the illusion of reality—to present a scene or a situation that seems somehow "objective" and "true"—but the techniques may be as conventional and "artificial" as the careful arranging of the haiku masters, or the conceits of Tsurayuki.

For the first public demonstration of his principles, Shiki asked eleven friends, mostly haiku disciples and newspaper people connected with *Nihon,* to select ten poems each from among his tanka. The results were published . . . [in 1898] under the title **"Ten Poems from a Hundred"** (***Hyakuchū Jisshu***). Many of the poems are surprisingly conventional in view of Shiki's announced program of reform; some have no more strikingly novel effect than is conveyed by an unusual word or image. Such touches, however, seemed considerably more bold and daring to Shiki's Japanese readers in 1898 than they do to a Japanese or a Westerner today. The traditional aspect of Shiki's approach to tanka composition is perhaps best shown by the simple fact that nearly all of the poems in the series are "compositions on topics" (*daiei*). In both the conventional waka and haiku the great majority of poems were *daiei,* and the imagery, tone, and even details of treatment of such poems were determined in greater or less degree by their imagistic or situational topics, which were conventional and often fictional. The poet's task was to compose a poem on the topic that expressed its "essential nature" (*hon'i*) in terms of his own imaginative experience. (pp. 392-94)

Shiki composed tanka almost constantly from 1898 on. His poems are often in groups of eight or ten, treating the same topic, or all ending with the same word. The following poem is from a sequence of eight, all ending in *ware wa* (I . . .). . . .

> Yoshiwara no
> Taiko kikoete
> Fukuru yo ni
> Hitori haiku no
> Bunrui su ware wa.

> From the Yoshiwara, the sound of a drum is heard, while all alone in the deepening night I sort haiku.

The contrast between the gay world of the pleasure quarters implied by the sound of the drum and the solitary Shiki absorbed in his work suggests a tone of loneliness—a lyrical element that is lacking in so much of Shiki's poetry. Indeed, the biographical reference—it is said that it refers to a time two years before, when Shiki was working intensively on haiku—makes the poem one of Shiki's most admired today. It is also valued for its "pictorial quality." The order of the Japanese syntax cannot be reproduced in English, but the effect of the final *ware wa* is as if Shiki were explaining a photograph—saying, "Here I am, sorting haiku late at night. . . ."

Another poem is from a set actually composed on a series of pictures, and all ending with the substantive *tokoro* (place, time).

Ko no moto ni
Fuseru Hotoke o
Uchiogami
Zō hebidomo no
Nakiiru tokoro.

The elephants and serpents weeping and worshipping the reclining Buddha under the tree.

The picture on which the poem was based depicted the death of the Buddha. Shiki was trying, of course, to capture the essential details of the picture, and to render them "realistically." The effort to achieve this realistic description absorbed and excited him and the followers who gathered about him, but the poetic result in this instance is flat and prosaic, like a caption.

The "realistic" technique of such poems is based on the premise that what is objectively true can be discovered and expressed "objectively." It also implies the assumption that the truth so expressed has an importance both to the poet (or the speaker of his poem) and the audience. It is perhaps not surprising that the quasi-scientific ideal should impel Shiki characteristically to eschew some of the basic subjective means—metaphor, symbol, and other techniques—by which poets commonly convey their imaginative apprehension of what is true and significant and their feelings and attitudes towards experience. But Shiki's obsession with Realism also often led him to neglect the expression of feeling which is the life blood of such a brief poetic form as the tanka, and in turn has led some later critics to characterize him as "anti-lyrical."

The effort to express the real in as exact terms as possible sometimes leads in Shiki's poetry to the treatment of greatly reduced materials almost microscopically observed—to "painting the stripes on the tulip," as in this poem. . . .

Kurenai no
Nishaku nobitaru
Bara no me no
Hari yawaraka ni
Harusame no furu.

The spring rain falls softening the thorns of the rosebush, whose canes have grown to two feet of crimson.

Shiki's esthetic ideal of beauty in nature—the *fūryū* of haiku—is conveyed by the traditional tonal associations of the spring rain and the lovely contrast it makes with the crimson canes of the rose bush. But the significance of the realistic technique lies rather in the minute detail of the thorns and the exact qualification in the second line: the rose canes have grown not "quickly" or "suddenly," but to "two feet." Our response must depend on the extent to which we can appreciate the importance of Shiki's choice.

The "accuracy" of "two feet of crimson" is basically more subjective and impressionistic than scientific, and in poetry such details inevitably involve the feelings as well as the intellect. While denying himself so many of the traditional resources of Japanese poetry, Shiki argued that his kind of "objectivity" (i.e., description) should evoke an emotional response just as surely as more avowedly subjective kinds of poetic treatment. (pp. 399-400)

Another feature of Shiki's poem should be pointed out. This is the function of the adverbial phrase *yawaraka ni* (softly) in the fourth line. In the Japanese syntax, the phrase is a kind of pivot word, serving not only as an adverbial phrase to qualify the falling spring rain in the last line, but also as a predicate for the noun *hari* (thorns). The effect is not the conventional word play of the *kakekotoba* or pivot word, but a kind of "yoking," or zeugma, it may be called. The quality of softness is attributed to the thorns, and a relationship established between the thorns and the rain that touches them. The softness of rose thorns is a subjective impression of the speaker of the poem; it is not describing things objectively, "just as they are."

Shiki's critics have not failed to notice his use of the technique in this poem, but the discovery of such rhetorical "tricks" has made them uneasy, and many have either denied the technique or, failing that, denied that Shiki was conscious of what he was doing. Conscious or not, the technique, as well as many other elements of Shiki's ideal and practice of *shasei*, may be found in the poetry and ideals of a period and group of the very Court poets whose tradition Shiki so flatly rejected. In the late thirteenth century and early fourteenth, the innovating Kyōgoku-Reizei Court poets attempted to bring a new freshness and intensity to their tradition and to express their poetic impressions of the natural world through a descriptive poetry in many ways strikingly similar to Shiki's. The motives behind the poetic results were also similar in some respects. The realism of the Kyōgoku-Reizei poets was intellectually motivated by their interest in such things as Zen Buddhism and Chinese poetry and painting of the Sung period—not by the techniques of illusionist realism in Western painting or the desire to return to the "artless realism" of the *Manyōshū*. But in their effort to express as "realistically" as possible the quasi-Platonic essences of their conventional topics, they explored as completely as they could the possibilities of the descriptive mode in their nature poetry. In their new styles they avoided the more obvious kinds of subjective wit of the traditional "*Kokinshū* style," using colloquial diction and images and such techniques as repetition to convey the exact nature of a moment of experience. (pp. 401-02)

It is doubtful that Shiki more than glanced at the poetry of the Kyōgoku-Reizei poets, and his use of a similar technique is probably not due to conscious borrowing. Nevertheless, the coincidence is but one similarity between Shiki's descriptive techniques and those of the Kyōgoku-Reizei poets, as more extensive comparison would show. It also helps to clarify the underlying subjectivity of Shiki's poetry of "realistic description."

The treatment of greatly reduced materials "exactly as they are" often results in a greatly decreased esthetic distance between the poet and his materials and an increased distance between the poet and us, his audience. We may concede that the thing itself and the experience of perceiving it are of overriding significance to the poet, but it often becomes extraordinarily difficult to follow him into the experience. The difficulty is particularly great with such a brief form as the tanka if the experience is not presented in terms of conventional tonal symbols or even of normal values and experience that we can understand. The problem is crucial to Shiki's poetry, and deserves to be examined in some detail.

The following poem has been extravagantly admired by the poets and critics of the *Araragi* School, the heirs of Shiki's reforms.

Kame ni sasu
Fuji no hanabusa
Mijikakereba
Tatami no ue ni
Todokazarikeri.

The spray of wisteria put in the vase is so short
that it does not reach the floor.

Taken by itself, the poem seems very flat and prosaic. The subjectivity of the conception is of course implicit in the selection of imagistic detail, and explicit in the statement that because one thing is so, another is not—a rhetorical element that again reminds us of the practice of the late classical poets. But what does the poem mean? we ask. What is the tone of the poem?

Within the tanka tradition in which Shiki was perforce working, the obvious thing is to look first to the natural images of the poem for clues to meaning, for centuries of poetic development had endowed such images with complex tonal associations of beauty or transcience or sadness. The single natural image in this poem is the wisteria, a spring image traditionally treated in terms of appreciation for the graceful shape and color of the flowers, whether purple or white, often compared by the Court poets to the waves of the sea (*fujinami*) and the like. Unlike cherry blossoms or autumn leaves, which suggest evanescence as well as beauty, the wisteria is more neutral; it is simply beautiful. Is the poet, then, complaining that the wisteria in this instance is not graceful because it fails to sweep to the floor like the conventional wisteria of older poetry? Probably not, for such treatment would violate the convention that the wisteria must be presented as beautiful—the convention that governs this similar poem by Shiki's older contemporary, Ochiai Naobumi.

Kogame o ba
Tsukue no ue ni
Nosetaredo
Mada mada nagashi
Shirafuji no hana.

Though I have placed the vase upon the table,
the spray of white wisteria is still too long, yes,
too long.

The images of the wisteria and the vase are very similar in the two poems, and like Shiki's (which might almost be taken as an allusive variation on it) this poem treats the length of the wisteria spray. The conventional beauty of the flower is conveyed by the image and the speaker's appreciation of it by exclaiming over its length. We may not respond to Naobumi's poem with appreciation, but at least we feel we can understand it.

It might be concluded that Shiki's poem plays itself off, as it were, against convention; that is, that it might have such an implication as, "The wisteria of tradition is beautiful because of its graceful length, but this real spray before me is so short that it does not reach the floor. This is the beauty of truth as opposed to the elegant fictions of literary convention." Such an interpretation of the "meaning" of Shiki's poem may be far-fetched, but it is not entirely unjustified unless one is to disregard the tanka tradition completely. (pp. 402-04)

Much of the discussion that has centered about the poem has been concerned with the significance that should be attached to the crucial adjective form *mijikakereba* ("because it is short," "is so short that . . .") in the third line. The expression gives the poem the cause-and-effect construction that in many forms and guises typifies the "wit" or "reasoning" (*rikutsu*) of the "*Kokinshū* style," and is often found in such a milder, less witty form as this in the poetry of the Kyōgoku-Reizei poets. The consensus seems to be that Shiki did not really mean "because"—that he intended instead a simple statement of fact: "The spray of wisteria is short *and* does not reach the floor." As one commentator has put it,

> The gist of the arguments is that *mijikakereba* does not express a reason (*rikutsu*). Rather, the poem expresses straightforwardly the appearance of the spray of wisteria just as the poet saw it just as he lay there on his back. In other words, this is a work in which the poet directly demonstrates the method of realistic description that he has advocated. If we repeat the poem over a number of times to ourselves, bearing in mind the feelings expressed in the headnote, we will soon cease to feel that there is any reasoning involved, and will be able to sense the breathing of the invalid poet Shiki. By *mijikakereba,* he has expressed pretty much the meaning of *mijikakute* ("is short, and . . ."), and in the deliberate choice of *mijikakereba* with its extra syllable, we must also consider that Shiki was giving attention to the poetic cadence.

It is so easy to read things into a tanka, and so easy to scoff at those who do. If biography seems to play an unwontedly large role in creating the reputation of some of Shiki's more prosaic compositions, it is still possible to appreciate such a poem as this within the context of the mixed prose and poetry of Shiki's journal and the tone of sad melancholy that pervades the whole.

Shiki's poetry necessarily became more circumscribed as he turned increasingly to his immediate surroundings for subjects and materials. He had earlier tried his hand at the new-style poetry, particularly in the years before embarking on his tanka reform in 1898. He also wrote patriotic chōka on the Emperor's Birthday or **"Celebrating the Marriage of the Crown Prince"** in 1900, and called upon the readers of his column in *Nihon* to send in poems on such topics as "On Reading the *Heike Monogatari*." But when one considers the wide range of subjects and themes treated in older poetry or the almost graphic references to love making in the sensationally autobiographical poems of Yosano Akiko, Shiki's poetry seems almost unduly restricted. He wrote no love poetry, for example, apart from a few early treatments of fictional topics. Within the framework of the total cumulative development of the tanka tradition, even some of his best nature poetry seems pale and bloodless by comparison with the more exciting poems of the Kyōgoku-Reizei poets, who made a comparable attempt to present the real.

In avoiding the higher flights and even the fictional treatment of such subjects as love, Shiki was no doubt following the natural inclinations of his "anti-lyrical" temperament as well as directing his intense energy into the effort to present the real. If he was often prosaic, he seems to have felt in the poetry of the "idealists"—that is, such exponents of the more strongly lyrical as the poets of the *Myōjō* school—something of the uncomfortable self-dramatization that often mars their work. Like his friend Sōseki, Shiki seems to have had a kind of exaggerated dread of appearing ridiculous. Such concerns led him away from certain poetic subjects and treatments, and to the end of his life underlay his preoccupation with *shasei*. In June, 1902, only a few months before his death, he wrote in his journal ***Byōshō Rokushaku:***

> In both painting and poetry there are many who advocate what is called idealism, but such people do not even understand the flavor of realistic description. . . . I do not mean to say that idealism is necessarily bad, but it is a fact that the majority of works in which the conception is expressed as idealism are bad. . . . A work of realistic description may appear at first sight to be shallow, but the more deeply it is savored, the greater its variety and the deeper its poetic taste. . . . It often happens that that fellow idealism tries to reach the top of the roof in one jump but only succeeds instead in falling into the pond. Although realistic description may be plain and flat, it does not fail in this way. And when one has succeeded in embodying the height of poetic taste within the plain and simple, its marvelous effect is indescribable.

Despite Shiki's "anti-lyricism," his poetry became increasingly autobiographical as he turned more to his immediate surroundings for poetic inspiration. That is, the speaker of his later poems is almost always avowedly himself, so that we are increasingly aware of the particular circumstances of Shiki the poet and the man in the background or context of the poem. This confusion or blurring of the distinction between the poetic speaker and the poet can be found in poetry throughout the tanka tradition. Even in periods most given to "compositions on topics," there was a strong undercurrent of autobiographical poetry as well as a latent feeling that somehow such poetry was more "sincere." As the autobiographical strain becomes more pronounced in Shiki's poetry, the poetry becomes more traditional in this sense, and perhaps feeling himself more in the mainstream of Japanese poetry, Shiki began to turn more to tradition—specifically, the *Manyōshū*—and to incorporate recognizable elements of traditional rhetoric and diction into his poems. (pp. 408-11)

Shiki's use of the *Manyōshū* is not for metaphor as the evocation of the ancient anthology in the allusive variations of the classical poets contrasts the past with the present to convey the sense of the sad passage of time. Shiki's *Manyō* poetry is, in short, imitation. . . . The argument for it seems to be very like the usual arguments for imitation. The *Manyōshū* is simple, forthright, direct, and full of realism and vigor. These are all qualities of good poetry. Consequently, if we imitate the *Manyōshū,* our own poetry will have these qualities; it, too, will be simple, forthright, direct, and full of realism and vigor. (p. 417)

Shiki's poetic reputation today rests primarily on his haiku and on a body of plain descriptive poetry that has the haiku-like vividness of precise detail. His principle of "realistic description" was a quasi-scientific principle directly influenced by conceptions of illusionist realism in Western-style painting. His advocacy of the *Manyōshū* was an echo of the antiquarianism of Kamo no Mabuchi and the scholars of National Learning. Underlying these two very differently inspired aspects of Shiki's reform movement, however, can be seen the ideal of "sincerity"—that peculiarly Japanese virtue so often brought forward to justify the products of the struggle to create a modern literature in the Meiji period. The basic "sincerity" combined with the very simplicity of Shiki's two main enthusiasms made it possible for his followers to elaborate upon them. (p. 418)

Robert H. Brower, "Masaoka Shiki and Tanka Reform," in Tradition and Modernization in Japanese Culture, *edited by Donald H. Shively, Princeton University Press, 1971, pp. 379-418.*

JANINE BEICHMAN (essay date 1982)

[Beichman is an American educator and critic specializing in Japanese literature. In the following excerpt from the only book-length study of Shiki in English, she discusses the important themes in Shiki's poetry and diaries.]

The expression or depiction of individual character had not been the objective of Tokugawa period writers. With the Meiji period, suddenly and almost without being consciously articulated, there appeared the unspoken assumption that the individual was important, more important than her or his context or situation. The history of Japanese literature since the Meiji period can be seen from one point of view as an attempt by the individual to break out of the molds cast for her or him. Haiku, of course, lent itself especially badly to the expression of individuality and the articulation of complex emotion. One reason was its brevity; another was the importance in it of the seasons.

In the traditional haiku, each poem must have a season word, of which there is a detailed and lengthy catalogue. Furthermore, only certain events and images are considered appropriate to each season word. For example, the way to write a good poem based on the season word "spring rain" (*harusame*) is to find an image or event that goes well with "spring rain" and evokes the natural phenomenon itself—as does this poem by Shiki himself:

> spring rain:
> browsing under an umbrella
> at the picture-book store

The quiet feeling of spring rain is splendidly evoked, but the identity of the browser is deliberately left vague in order to better evoke the quality of the rain. This vagueness (which can sometimes result in the fertile ambiguity we have seen in the snow and cockscomb poems) is an intrinsic part of the traditional haiku.

One of Shiki's most important accomplishments in the haiku was to make his own individual situation and emotions an essential part of the poem. In his haiku (and his tanka as well), he is as important as the season. Many of his poems still evoke a season or time, but the natural context is usually there because of Shiki, not vice versa. For example. . .:

> the nettle nuts are falling . . .
> the little girls next door
> don't visit me these days . . .

When the nuts of the nettle tree began to fall in autumn, the young daughters of Kuga Katsunan (Shiki's neighbor and the editor of *Nippon*), stopped coming to his house to play. In summer, the heat had sometimes driven them indoors to his home; but now, with the fine fall weather, they spent all their time outdoors, forgetting about him. The poem has a bittersweet quality that evokes at once the season and Shiki's emotion, half-rueful because of the absence of his young visitors and the passing of the season, half-glad, because of the lovely weather. (pp. 68-9)

Other, earlier poets seem to be talking to us directly, as when Kakinomoto Hitomaro . . . in his *chōka* on parting from his wife . . . tells us that he thought he was a brave man but now his sleeves are wet with tears. Still others, like Bashō, speak of their inner thoughts, but in a tone far more exalted than Shiki's. Bashō's deathbed haiku was:

ill on a journey,
my dreams wander
over withered moors

Bashō's tone is a public one. The poem is a good example of what Shiki called Bashō's "tone of grandeur." To mention his illness and in the same breath to draw an image of overcoming it in dream—there is a grandeur and nobility to the poem, the grandeur and nobility of the artist proclaiming or still believing that in the end imagination is stronger than mortality. This tone is totally lacking in Shiki, who would never have made any such assertion.

Shiki's beauty was, in his own words again, "the beauty of precision." Shiki worked with the small, the finite, the close to home. His tone is completely private. Where Bashō speaks as the artist, and the vastness of his image makes one imagine the entire universe, Shiki speaks as a sick man; his tone of voice seems soft, almost a whisper, and he could only be speaking to himself or, at the most, a few friends. One must, as I have said, imagine oneself physically very close to him to appreciate many of his poems. In

how much longer
is my life?
a brief night . . .

there is hardly a concrete image. . . . One has to construct an image in one's mind of Shiki, lying in bed at dawn, commenting on the brevity of a summer night—the heat, his own discomfort, his despair over his pain, his ambivalence about living and dying. (pp. 71-2)

The night was short because of the season, but what Shiki must really have felt as short was his own life. Hence, there is an oblique comparison between the night and Shiki's life. At the same time, his pain sometimes made him (we know this from his diaries ***Stray Notes While Lying On My Back*** and ***A Drop of Ink***) desire a quick death as relief from suffering. The poem expresses, using the barest understatement, the tormented wish to die quickly, regret at the ebbing of life, and the wish for his life to continue, all at once. At the same time, beneath the specific question concerning his own life, there is a universal question—how long is life itself?

If there is a continuum from the private to the public along which one may progress by gradually adding more and more "clothing" to one's naked emotions, then Shiki sought to catch himself much earlier along on that continuum than had earlier poets. That is why he tried to dispense with metaphor, simile, and other literary tropes. He wished to depict himself emotionally naked, yet he did so with a restraint and an objectivity that saves his work from vulgarity. Still, for some, the lack of esthetic distance between poet and audience in Shiki's work may make it distasteful, or too demanding. Others can accept both the close-up view of Shiki's poems and the majestic vision of Bashō's. In any case, it is certain that through his unique combination of intimacy and objectivity, artlessness and intensity, Shiki imbued the haiku with a new psychological complexity, and made it a poetic form that would survive into the modern period. (p. 73)

Shiki did not initiate his tanka reform until 1898 and his knowledge of the tanka remained quite limited as late as 1895. His earliest tanka dates from 1883, but for at least another decade he followed the conservative *Kokinshū* style against which he later rebelled. Nevertheless, the assumption that a reform of the tanka was necessary underlay all his poetic criticism from the first, and he had a clear idea of the direction that reform should take as early as 1893.

In the essay ***Bunkai Yatsu Atari*** (***Indiscriminate Attacks on the Literary World . . .***), he presented in embryo form two of the central ideas of his tanka reform, ideas reminiscent of those presented in his haiku criticism: first, that the tanka must end its artistic isolation and seek to fulfill the more universal standards of literature; and second, that it must broaden its range of subject and vocabulary if it were to survive. (p. 74)

Shiki's early tanka were conventional and dull. (p. 80)

By 1898, however, when he began his tanka reform, Shiki had arrived at some original ideas and begun to put them into practice. The number of his tanka suddenly increased, as though his criticism and discussions stimulated his creativity. This momentum continued through 1899 and 1900, reflecting the development of the Negishi Tanka Society. The poems of these years can best be understood within the context of the ideas expressed in ***Letters to a Tanka Poet.***

Letters to a Tanka Poet was a fiercely polemical work, full of Shiki's characteristic mordant wit. The opening sentences illustrated both aspects: "As you say, the tanka these days is ailing. To speak bluntly, it has been ailing since the *Manyōshū* and Sanetomo.". . . The second letter began: "Tsurayuki was a bad poet and the *Kokinshū* a worthless anthology.". . . By comparison with the *Kokinshū,* he went on, the *Shinkokinshū* seemed rather good: "It has more good poems than the *Kokinshū;* but one can count them on one's fingers.". . . (pp. 80-1)

From the thirteenth century on, the *Manyōshū,* with its great variety of themes and styles, came to stand for a freedom and directness of expression opposed to the mainstream of the tanka, the courtly style of the imperial anthologies. Unorthodox poets used the *Manyōshū* as justification for rebellion against the conventions of the courtly style, appealing to the "Manyō spirit" as their ideal. . . . With the opening statements of ***Letters to A Tanka Poet,*** Shiki was deliberately placing himself in the rebel, "Manyō" line and outside the classical tradition of the tanka. Much has been made of this rejection, and it was indeed important. Laying too much stress on this aspect of the essay, however, obscures Shiki's basic ideas, which were positive.

Shiki's primary concern was not to tear down the old poetry, but to create a new poetry vital enough to survive the Meiji period. We know from ***Talks on Haiku from the Otter's Den*** that he feared the tanka and the haiku might literally become extinct. He believed that the tanka could not even survive unless it enlarged its limited vocabulary, tone, and range of subjects, and unless tanka poets began to judge themselves by the standards of literature as a whole. In ***Letters to a Tanka Poet,*** he wrote that since the vocabulary of the classical tanka was restricted to words that had been used in the 10th century *Kokinshū,* and no words of Chinese or other foreign origin were permitted, the subjects were naturally severely restricted as well. Furthermore, the tone of the tanka was supposed always to be gentle and flowing; a forceful or even slightly humorous tone was looked at askance.

Shiki's remarks in ***Letters to a Tanka Poet*** and the style of ***Ten Poems in a Hundred*** stemmed from two basic critical concerns, which never changed from 1898 until his death four years later: the wish to bring the tanka within the perimeters of literature, as those were newly conceived in the Meiji period, and the need to enrich the tanka (in tone, subject and vocabulary) with elements from other genres and other cultures, in order to prevent its extinction.

In ***Letters to a Tanka Poet #3,*** Shiki discussed the use of strong tone as one way to enrich the tanka. Tanka poets proudly boasted that the tanka, unlike the haiku, had tone, or melody (*shirabe*), he said; but this was because they misunderstood the nature of tone, supposing that the gentle, flowing one of the traditional tanka was the only one possible. In fact, there were many possible tones, and poets should use those appropriate to their subjects and themes. (pp. 81-2)

The best of Shiki's later poems, whether haiku or tanka, are descriptions of nature in the sketch from life style. Usually no attempt is made to distinguish between the different kinds of poems within this one category. There is in fact, however, a crucial distinction to be made, between those poems which simply describe nature and those which, while describing nature, have as their subject the relation between the poet himself and nature. It is in the latter that Shiki worked out his relation to the world as he prepared to leave it, moved from resistance to his fate to a kind of resignation that suggests a final spiritual transcendence and reconciliation.

Two examples of the first type of poem—pure natural description, in which the poet himself does not figure—are these haiku from 1900 and 1902:

wisteria plumes
sweep the earth, and soon
the rains will fall . . .

purple unto
blackness:
grapes!. . .

The first poem vividly conveys the pregnant dampness of early summer heat in Japan through the full, heavy plumes of the wisteria. The second . . . is an emphatic declaration of the purpleness, a celebration of a natural beauty that particularly impressed Shiki. The center of the first poem is the wisteria and the summer; of the second, the color of the grapes. In neither do we feel the personal presence of the poet himself. (pp. 97-8)

There was also a different sort of poem, however, in which the poet's presence was implied or overtly stated. The effectiveness of the first type of poem, the objective description of nature, comes solely from the beauty of the description itself, but that of the poems in which the poet himself figures comes from the relationship between the poet and the natural beauty he is observing. In the poems which express this relationship least ambiguously, the poet and nature are depicted in simple juxtaposition, and nature is something which consoles him by its mere existence. For example, in 1900 Shiki wrote this tanka as part of a sequence on some peonies he had received:

to where I lie,
sick upon my bed,
they brought for me
these potted peonies . . .
their petals' trembling never ends . . .

Peonies were Shiki's favorite flower, and here one feels that he takes their delicate trembling as a way of speaking to him. (p. 98)

Nature's influence on the poet is not always as benevolent and life-enhancing as in this poem. For example, this tanka from the ten-poem sequence in ***A Drop of Ink*** entitled "I can't help taking up my brush":

as if to cheer me
on my bed of pain,
the peony spreads
its petals wide and
seeing this I grieve . . .

Similarly, in this tanka of 1902, part of a series of six on a bonsai he received, the flower's beauty only increases the poet's sense of loneliness:

when to my pillow
no friend comes
I lie alone,
turned to face
the potted plum . . .

The closer Shiki came to death, the stronger became his sense of separation from nature and of alienation from the human world. In the diaries, his sense of alienation was most often expressed in subjective tones of petulance and self-pity, sometimes relieved by irony. Shiki's last writings, however, were not in prose, but in poetry, specifically haiku. In the three haiku he wrote just hours before his death, he abandoned the attachment to this world felt in earlier poems and moved to resignation and a final transcendence.

The first of these poems was:

the gourd flowers bloom,
but look—here lies
a phlegm-stuffed Buddha! . . .

Here, the poet is no longer characterized as a sick man but as a dead man, and the separation between himself and the world he observes has become complete and final. In the poems discussed above, Shiki either identified with nature (as in the poems on the plum bonsai) or else, while feeling separate from it, lamented the separation. There was always a sense that he was trying to overcome the distance between himself and the beauty he observed, trying to hang onto life, or, at least, regretting the leaving of it.

The juice of the gourd, gathered from the plant before it bloomed, was used to relieve coughing such as Shiki's. However, as his condition became past remedy, the juice had become useless and the flowers allowed to come into bloom. The blooming of the flowers, lovely in itself, has a sinister meaning, for it signifies the hopelessness of Shiki's condition, implies his death. Living flowers mean a dying Shiki—again two opposites, held at once in the mind.

In the next two of the three final haiku, the poet says that even if there were gourd water it would not help. In other words, he is already dead and there can be no turning back to life:

a quart of phlegm—
even gourd water
couldn't mop it up . . .

they didn't gather
gourd water
day before yesterday either . . .

With the negatives ("can't," "didn't") of these poems, Shiki was declaring the end of his relation to this world. He had left behind the "infinite ambition" of his youth for the "zero wish" of Enlightenment. (pp.102-03)

Shiki dealt with his own death by creating literary works which had him for their protagonist and of which the theme was his own confrontation with mortality. In ***A Drop of Ink*** and ***A Sixfoot Sickbed,*** Shiki created a literary character, a persona, which was a refined and distilled version of the everyday Shiki we know from the private diary ***Stray Notes While Lying On My Back*** and some of the letters.

It might be argued that the private self of ***Stray Notes*** and the letters should be relegated to biography and the public self of ***A Drop of Ink*** and ***A Sixfoot Sickbed*** to literature, but in fact the two selves existed on a continuum, with the public self being a subtler, more refined version of the private, and, to some degree, created in the very act of writing. In this sense, the diaries are the stage on which Shiki finally achieved the equation of life and literature that followed from his sketch from life realism and which he asserted on a personal level as well. Just as Shiki's conscious aim as an artist practicing sketch from life realism was to create the illusion of an identity between art and reality, so his unconscious aim as a human being was to achieve an identity between his life and his literature. (p. 123)

From 1895, Shiki knew he would die young. For the seven remaining years of his life, much of the energy that was not devoted to his work as haiku editor for *Nippon* and as leader of his own literary movements, was taken up with meditation upon his own death. This was not due to a morbid fascination with the subject; it was forced upon him by the constant pain in which he lived.

In the end, writing was almost all he could do. As it came to be one of the last remaining physical activities he could perform voluntarily, more and more it became for him a metaphor for life itself. To write was to live, and when he could not lift the brush himself, he dictated to a friend. The title of ***A Drop of Ink*** shows how closely he identified his words with life, for the ink of the title was a metaphor for his life's blood.

From 1895 on, though he was uncertain when death would come, Shiki lived each day with its presence unbearably close. Time as he experienced it had qualities it does not have for most healthy people. First, it moved unbearably slowly and seemed extremely long, so that boredom was one of his chief torments. Second, and paradoxically, it seemed very short, moving swiftly and inexorably toward his own death. A sense of urgency . . . coexisted with a sense of enormous tedium. Thirdly, time had no firmly imaginable future, for he felt he could not plan for more than a few hours ahead. There was only a past and a present. Death, though he knew it would come, was a darkness, unimaginable; he did not believe in an afterlife. These are the qualities time has when experienced in the midst of great anxiety over a portending and dreaded, but in some ways desired, event.

Shiki's anxiety over death was intimately bound up with his pain. An increase in physical pain, which signified the further deterioration of his body, always brought in its train depression, anxiety, and ultimately great mental agitation. These emotions then increased the pain itself.

To his anxiety and his pain, the twin prisons in which he lived, Shiki considered a limited number of solutions—to dream or go mad, to destroy himself, or to beguile the time by activity. Although he expressed the wish to go mad, he was too incurably rational to do so. He seems, however, to have often had dreams in which he walked and even flew in painless freedom, or else found a blissful death. In the entry of April 24 from ***A Drop of Ink,*** he wrote,

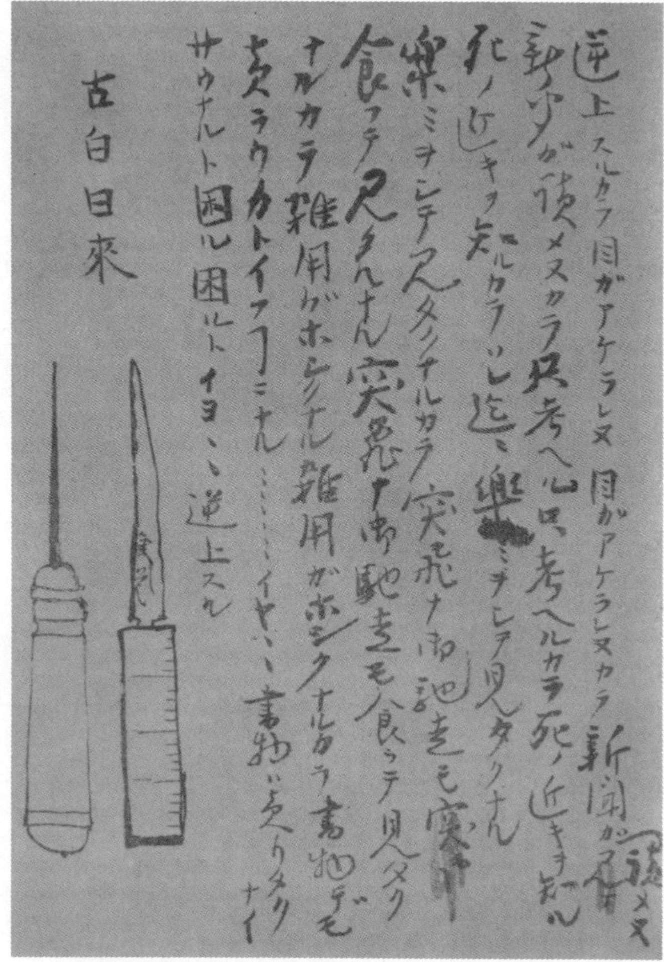

Holograph copy of a page from Shiki's manuscript of Gyōga Maroku. *Reprinted with permission from Kodansha International.*

> Last night I had a dream. I had come to a place where many animals were playing. One of them was rolling about in such agony that I was certain it was about to die. A gentle rabbit went up to the tormented beast and offered its paw. The animal at once took the rabbit's paw in both of its own and pressed it to its lips. Just as it joyfully started to kiss the paw, its suffering ended and it died as though falling into a blissful sleep. The rabbit then did the same for another animal who was raving in the throes of death; and that animal also yielded to death as if to a pleasant sleep. I have woken from my dream but I shall never forget that rabbit. . . .

(pp. 123-25)

The three diaries of 1901 and 1902 represent part of Shiki's efforts to distract himself by activity. The impulse to write and publish ***A Drop of Ink,*** in particular, was rooted in Shiki's need to reaffirm his existence daily as he watched the daily, visible wasting away of his body. In the January 24 entry of this journal, he wrote that he meant it only as a diversion for himself from the tedium of illness and did not expect anyone else to take it seriously. Yet, there is no doubt that he himself took it very seriously, if not as literature then as in expression of his life, for he begged shamelessly to have it published serially in *Nippon,* even though the editors were far from enthusiastic. (p. 127)

Shiki's ever present sense of death made him need a daily reminder that he was alive. If words were life to him . . . then his published diary must have been tangible proof to him of his own survival. In that sense, the "short pieces" of ***A Drop of Ink*** were Shiki's own life transfigured into words, expressions of an effort to recreate himself in words as his body literally decayed before his eyes. They were his way, as well, of clinging tenaciously to this world.

An attachment to life provided the basic impulse for all three diaries. This attachment is expressed most concretely in the private diary ***Stray Notes,*** which stresses the physical aspect of his life almost to the point of tedium. The typical entry begins with a comment on how he slept, a listing of all food eaten that day, with exact quantities, the number of bowel movements he had, the weather, the events in his garden (what birds came, what flowers were in bloom), and the general state of his illness. Some entries add nothing more. Others, if he felt well enough, note the day's social events, such as the names of visitors and the presents, if any, they brought. Rather frequently the physical concerns are expressed in or provide the background for poems. There are a few very long entries—one in which he vents his rage against his sister Ritsu and another in which he vents it against Nakae Chōmin, the author of *Ichinen Yūhan* (*A Year and A Half*); and a third, in which he describes a brush with suicide. . . . Aside from these three expressions of pent-up emotion, most of the entries are short.

In ***Stray Notes,*** which Shiki did not intend anyone else to see, he made little effort to achieve literary interest. . . . [The] work as a whole gives the impression of the barest sort of diary. Yet it has tremendous fascination. It is liberally sprinkled with poems and drawings, as though these were so natural to Shiki that they poured from his pen even when he was at his most literal. The contrast between the completely physical and raw concerns of most of the prose and the more refined emotions expressed in the bulk of the poetry is very striking, creating a strange mixture of a grossly material perception of experience with a refined distillation of it in the form of art. I doubt that there has been anything like it in Japanese literature before or since.

The tenacious grasp on life that Shiki expressed through writing the diaries was accompanied by a paradoxical desire to be rid of it; living itself had become an agony. The extreme of this desire was reached in the suicidal thoughts already quoted from ***Stray Notes.*** But other reactions indicate that his inner resources were deeper than the account from ***Stray Notes*** suggests and also help one understand how he was able to carry on his literary activities for so long. In ***A Sixfoot Sickbed*** for June 2, 1902, he wrote,

> Until now I had mistaken the "Enlightenment" of Zen: I was wrong to think it meant being able to die serenely under any conditions. It means being able to live serenely under any conditions. . . .

(pp. 128-29)

Pain was as great a factor in Shiki's despair as boredom and was at least partly responsible for his ambivalence toward life. Sometimes he wished to die as an escape from his suffering; but always, or almost always, his attachment to life conflicted with this. This ambivalence, treated so directly in ***Stray Notes,*** was conveyed more subtly and humorously in ***A Drop of Ink*** and ***A Sixfoot Sickbed,*** probably because both of the latter were intended for publication. (In the May 11 entry of ***A Drop of Ink*** Shiki wrote, "Put some poison beside my bed. Would I take it or not?"; this was not published in *Nippon.*) In ***A Drop of Ink*** especially, Shiki treated his conflict with humor and irony, transmuting the theme of ambivalence into a kind of game in which he sought out death only to engage it in shadowboxing, playing with it, teasing it, asking it to come take him, then suddenly getting cold feet. For example, in the entry of April 9 he addressed a letter to the Four Elements:

> 1902
>
> Earth, Water, Fire, Wind & Co.:
>
> Re: One Human Being.
>
> I return same. However, please accord it special dispensation to return to this world from time to time as a spirit.
>
> Yours truly,
>
> Masaoka Shiki . . .

(p. 130)

One basic, single-minded wish underlay Shiki's ambivalence: to be released from suffering. It was a hopeless wish; no human being could do more than distract him from it for a time. His most intense physical experience, that of pain, was one that no other human being could share, though to him it was so overwhelmingly real that it sometimes blotted out consciousness of all else. In ***A Sixfoot Sickbed*** for May 28, 1902, he wrote that his pain was "indescribable" and only someone who had died once or was on the verge of death could understand what he experienced. (p. 132)

In ***A Sixfoot Sickbed,*** Shiki became able, perhaps thanks to morphine, to forget his pain at intervals and achieve a kind of quiet joy. Whether his painting had actually improved I cannot say, but his response to beauty seems to have become more intense as he became closer to death. Paradoxically, the closer he came to the final dissolution, the more he came to feel he understood the secret of creation. . . .

In ***A Drop of Ink,*** Shiki has written, "I feel the pain and see the beauty." This ability to hold two opposites in suspension, preserving both yet yielding to neither, has already been described in the poetry, and it characterized Shiki himself as well, for he tended both to perceive and to describe in dualities.

A Drop of Ink, for example, abounds in discussions of dualities: city life versus country life, the old calendar versus the new, Japan versus the West, good poetry versus bad, subjectivity versus objectivity, as well as the already mentioned oppositions of pain and beauty, sickness and health, the desire to live and the desire to die. (p. 140)

Taken as a whole, the diaries give a full picture of Shiki's physical and mental state during the last two years of his life. The contents are amazingly varied, ranging from haiku, tanka and Chinese poetry, to personal reminiscences, literary and art criticism, still-life watercolor sketches, lists of presents received, ethnological notes, tormented outpourings of his pain and frustration, minor essays on his daily life, and humorous reflections on the world outside his sickroom as mediated by the newspapers and magazines of the day. Yet the premise and central theme of each was his physical deterioration. Running like a stream through the diaries, sometimes disappearing while poetic or intellectual interests take the lead, then abruptly surfacing for a time only to go underground again, were the anger, frustration, despair, and self-pity of a man who had to wait helplessly for death. Even the reader who has never suffered as Shiki did can identify with the feelings Shiki expressed: his experience was but an extreme form of the universal confrontation with suffering and death. Anyone who has ever had the barest intimation of this confrontation will be caught by the truth of the diaries and find it hard to turn away from Shiki's voice as it speaks so clearly across the barriers of language, culture, and time. (pp. 142-43)

Janine Beichman, in her Masaoka Shiki, *Twayne Publishers, 1982, 174 p.*

MAKOTO UEDA (essay date 1983)

[*Ueda is an educator and scholar specializing in Japanese literature. In the following excerpt, he examines Shiki's poetic theory.*]

Generalizations about Shiki's theory of poetry are difficult to make because it not only changed considerably in the course of his career, but also contained contradictions. Yet, on the relationship between art and nature, three ideas stand out. These are *shasei* (''sketches from life''), selective realism, and *makoto* (''truthfulness'').

Of the three, shasei is the most famous, and has had the greatest effect on the practice of other poets. The idea was inspired in part by the realistic qualities Shiki saw in Western art, especially its attention to accurately observed perceptual detail and its claim to present the entire spectrum of experience. (pp. 9-10)

Shiki made shasei the basic principle of composition in his many essays intended to guide beginning poets. In **''Haiku Wastebasket,''** for example, he likened an amateur versifier to a mother trying to help dress up her teenage daughter. More often than not the mother would put on too much face powder and select too gaudy a kimono, so that the daughter would end up looking either ridiculous or sickening. Decorative words chosen to emphasize the poet's emotional reaction or to heighten the effect of a scene were like the gaudy kimono and excess powder, but a composition that copied an actual scene with no verbal ornamentation would never be the worst kind of poem, even if it had other weaknesses. (pp. 10-11)

Such heavy emphasis on shasei had special pertinence in Shiki's time, when poetic composition was too often merely an intellectual exercise. Most haiku and tanka poets were in the habit of writing about imaginary scenes, stirred by a title such as ''Plum Blossoms'' or ''Harvest Moon'' and producing trite, emotionless poems. . . . Shasei was a revolt against [this practice]; moreover, by invoking the Western idea of realism shasei placed haiku and tanka in the context of world literature, thereby proving that these forms were not parochial or outmoded.

Yet intrinsically the principle of writing from direct observation was too simplistic, a tool for beginning students only. For more advanced writers, Shiki refined his theory by introducing the principle of selection. Students with some experience in shasei were to exercise choice in sketching nature. As he explained:

> Shasei or realism means copying the subject as it is, but it necessarily involves a degree of selection and exclusion. . . . A writer sketching a landscape or an event should focus on its most beautiful or moving aspect. If he does this, the subject described will automatically begin to live its own life. It should be noted, however, that the most beautiful or moving aspect does not necessarily correspond to the most substantial or conspicuous or indispensable part of the subject. The aspect I speak of often lies in the shade, showing itself only partially in one's range of sight. A red camellia blooming in an ominously dark forest would strike one as exceedingly beautiful and attractive. In a case like that, a writer should sketch the scene focusing on the camellia. The flower does not have to be described in detail. It will deeply move the reader if the writer first describes the ominous darkness of the wood in some detail, then presents the camellia in the briefest words.
>
> (pp. 11-12)

Shiki seems to have thought that a student who had mastered the art of selective realism could increase the amount of subjectivity in his poetry if he saw fit. ''At times,'' wrote Shiki, ''the poet may even change the relative positions of things in an actual scene or subjectively replace a part of the scene by something that is not there. An actual scene is like a beautiful woman without makeup. She will not be free from imperfections, so that the artist must correct her eyebrows, but on rouge and powder, and dress her up in beautiful clothes.'' Shiki, who discouraged amateur versifiers from putting ''makeup'' on nature, here encouraged more advanced poets to do just that. He seems to have believed that an artist—a master artist—does not merely imitate nature but corrects her imperfections. Here an element of idealism modifies Shiki's basic commitment to realism: once he has established a basic truthfulness to things, as artist should also be truthful to his own wishes and ideals.

In order to correct nature's imperfections, the artist must have his own vision of how nature should be. Shiki was not blind to the pitfalls into which realistic poets sometimes fall. ''Too realistic a poem,'' he once said, ''is prone to be commonplace and lacking in surprise. . . . A poet too bent on realism tends to imprison his mind within the confines of the tiny world his eyes can see, forgetting about rare and fresh motifs that lie distant in time or space.'' It was from this angle that Shiki praised Buson's poetry. While recognizing objective beauty in Buson's works, Shiki was also fascinated by the poet-painter's fertile imagination. In his opinion, Buson was the only premodern haiku poet whose mind roamed freely between heaven and earth: he could ''soar to the sky without wings and sink into the ocean without fins.'' (pp. 13-14)

Shiki's view of the relationship between poetry and external reality was, then, a flexible one. Although it may look self-contradictory, from a pedagogic viewpoint it is coherent. He stressed the value of realistic representation for beginners, but for more advanced students recommended selective realism and allowed expert poets considerable freedom to choose between extremes of direct observation and imaginative creation. (pp. 14-15)

Shiki's own practice reflected the broad range of his theory, for although he wrote more and more poems based on shasei as he grew older, the doctrine of realism was never strong enough to stifle his occasional fanciful impulse. For example, in the last year of his life, when he was a staunch advocate of shasei, he wrote these poems:

> Across the summer moor
> walks a traveler—on his back
> a *tengu* mask.

> At Akabane
> Village, an embankment
> covered with shoots of horsetail,
> so many my sister and I
> will never pick them all.

That these poems describe imaginary scenes is evident, since Shiki was confined to bed at the time he wrote them. A *tengu* is an imaginary monster with a fiery face and a long nose: the image of the grotesque mask adds an almost Gothic element to the otherwise normal haiku on a natural scene. The tanka is more realistic, because horsetail shoots were Shiki's favorite food, and his younger sister often went out to the fields to pick them. It presents an imaginary picture based on wishful thinking. Akabane Village was located near Tokyo, and one of his leading disciples, Kawahigashi Hekigodō . . . , had gone there to collect horsetails shortly before Shiki wrote the poem.

However, in the Shiki canon non-shasei poems like these are in general inferior to realistic ones. Shiki gained his rank among the major poets of modern Japan through works based more directly on his actual life, especially on his last few years, spent in a losing battle with tuberculosis. At that time, his poetic sketches from life gained great vigor from the intensity of his sensations, heightened by the knowledge of approaching death. (pp. 15-16)

These poems differ from those [by Bashō, Taigi, and Sane Sada that] Shiki praised as embodiments of shasei and selective realism. . . . [These] works concentrate on internal, psychological reality. They can be called ''sketches from life'' only if ''life'' is interpreted to mean internal life-force, an invisible energy that keeps man living on, and they can be related to selective realism only if it means copying internal, rather than external, reality. Shiki had a different word to denote this principle: makoto.

Shiki borrowed the term ''makoto'' from the writings of a past tanka poet he much admired, Tachibana Akemi. In an essay entitled **''Akemi's Poetry,''** he praised Akemi as a rare latter-day poet who tried to capture the spirit of the ancient poetry anthologized in *The Collection of Ten Thousand Leaves*. That spirit was makoto. ''Makoto is the essence of Akemi's poetry,'' explained Shiki, ''and that of *The Collection of Ten Thousand Leaves*. It should be the essence of all tanka. The principle I have been advocating—'copy reality as it is'—is nothing other than makoto.''. . . Makoto, then, is shasei directed toward internal reality. It is based on the same principle of direct observation, except that the object to be observed is the poet's own self. The poet is to experience his inner life as simply and sincerely as he is to observe nature, and he is to describe the experience in words as simple and direct as the ancient poets—so simple and direct that they seem ordinary.

Shiki further clarified his concept of makoto in an essay called **''My Haiku,''** which traces the vicissitudes of his haiku poetic. In the initial phase he tried, he said, to present both subjective impressions and objective reality whenever he wrote haiku. Apparently he thought of subjective impressions and objective reality as two separate things, and felt composing haiku required a skillful blending of the two. Too frequently, however, he found decorative words, ornamental language, and self-conscious imaginings intruding, and soon he became tired of such haiku. Thereupon he strove to purge subjectivity from the poem, sketching objects unadorned and leaving readers to form their own impressions. . . . With his characteristic terseness he described this shifting emphasis: ''At first, I copied nature objectively. Later I became fond of copying humanity objectively.'' By ''humanity'' he must mean human nature and its manifestation in the form of emotions and feelings. Makoto is the truthfulness that enables the poet to copy such manifestations (and what lies underneath) ''objectively,'' with no artifice interfering. It is a higher principle of selection—by being true to his own inner life, the poet is drawn to scenes, and within those scenes to objects, that express his inner life (and beyond it humanity) most directly. (pp. 16-18)

Shiki died, however, before he had a chance to expound the principle of makoto very extensively. It is likely that he arrived at the principle from an intensive reading of ancient tanka, which he did fairly late in his career. Yet examples are sometimes more eloquent than theory, and lack of theoretical exposition is not to be equated with lack of importance. Unless in Shiki's poetic makoto carries as much weight as shasei and selective realism, there is no way to account for some of his best poetry. (pp. 18-19)

In his writings, Shiki was concerned less with the nature of the aesthetic effect than with its range. His concept of poetic beauty was considerably more inclusive than the traditional one: before his time, the average poet thought of beauty as characterized by elegance, grace, or exquisiteness, sometimes tinged with a sense of life's sadness, at other times blended with calm resignation. Shiki expanded the concept to include all kinds of effects, and comprehensiveness characterized his aesthetic. For instance, in attacking contemporary tanka poets he charged that they should prize not only ''elegance'' but also ''the sublime,'' ''the antique,'' ''the novel,'' ''the stately,'' and ''the light.'' He mentioned still more possible effects in his discussion of haiku. Once, in classifying haiku, he referred to those that are: ''vigorous,'' ''genteel,'' ''magnificent,'' ''delicate,'' ''shady,'' ''exquisite,'' ''mysterious,'' ''lucid,'' ''stately,'' ''light,'' ''novel,'' ''plain,'' ''complex,'' ''simple,'' ''serious,'' and ''humorous.'' At another time he distinguished 24 styles of haiku and cited examples of each. (p. 28)

Shiki's classification of poetry beauty was far from exhaustive or methodical; it was not intended to be. His chief aim was to show that poets can explore many types of aesthetic effects. More than anything else he disliked a stereotyped poem written with the sole aim of achieving one or another of the effects valued within the narrow confines of traditional Japanese aesthetics. In his view, a poet who would write such a poem had a mind like water in an abandoned well. He urged that the poet bail out all the stagnant water until the bottom was bare so that new, clear water could begin to seep in little by little. Possible sources of aesthetic pleasure were countless. ''O poets,'' Shiki addressed his colleagues, ''the universe is wide, and the material for poetry boundless. Why do you think there is no fitting material outside of the moon, dewdrops, singing insects, tear-soaked sleeves, friends, the fields, and leaves of grass?''

In his eagerness to extend the realm of poetic beauty, Shiki went so far as to discover—or rediscover—the beauty in excrement. In an essay called **''Haiku on Excrement,''** he demonstrated that the old masters produced beauty out of this unlikely material, citing 41 poems (most of them haiku) on feces,

18 on urine, 4 on farts, 24 on toilets, and 21 on loincloths. (p. 29)

At the conclusion of **"Haiku on Excrement,"** Shiki made clear that he was not especially fond of using this sort of material for poetry; he only wanted to show how widely a poet might explore. In discussing the 24 styles of haiku, he did not specify which he preferred, yet despite his general evenhandedness, he seems to have harbored a predilection for the sublime and the plain. He especially admired the former in his younger days, and was more attracted to the latter in later years. (p. 30)

Shiki liked the sublime because it was fresh. Traditionally the Japanese had valued the opposite effect, elegance, and the result was an overabundance of elegant poems, with an inevitable decline in quality. . . . Shiki emulated, and urged other poets to emulate, the ancient poets represented in *The Collection of Ten Thousand Leaves,* who wrote from their own experience. Those poets were able to write sublime verse because they were motivated by deeply felt emotions; they did not try to adorn their language for the sake of an elegant appearance. Later poets merely tried to imitate classical court poetry and ended up producing pseudoelegant poems that were trite and stereotyped, with no emotional appeal.

The effect of some of Shiki's more successful poems can be explained in terms of the sublime. Here are four examples:

Hot spring in the mountains:
high above the naked bathers
the River of Heaven.

Quietly it lies asleep:
a hamlet, after all its
lamplights are gone . . .
Only the River of Heaven
white above the bamboo grove.

The wintry gust:
they have left a temple bell
by the roadside.

New leaves on a tiny
weed in my yard, and I think
of heaven and earth
limitlessly spacious,
filled with spring green.

The first two poems share a common image, the Milky Way flowing in heaven. The image creates a sense of magnitude and eternity, which is further enhanced in the haiku by the addition of another grand image, the towering mountains. Amid the great expanse of the natural setting, human beings strip off their petty manners and customs. In the tanka, the villagers are all asleep. With not a single lamp burning, the stars in the sky sparkle even more brightly, looking ready to come down in a shower of light. In contrast, the bamboos below are dark and grow straight up, their stalks pointing toward the sky. Here is a communion of heaven and earth on a grand scale, approaching the sublime.

In the third poem the juxtaposition is more striking than harmonious. A huge black bell has been left by the roadside when the team of parish volunteers carrying it to their temple go to their night's lodging at the end of day. The bronze bell sits all alone, and the winter wind blows on it. The gust hits the bell so hard that it seems ready to begin ringing at any monent; yet it does not: silent and immobile, it looms in the growing dark.

The fourth poem starts on a smaller scale. The poet is ill and has been confined to bed; his yard is all of the outside world that he can see. Intently observing it as he does every day, he notices several new leaves on a familiar weed. Thereupon his imagination quickly expands: he visualizes the whole universe filled with verdant vegetation. The universe is all the more spacious, and the green all the fresher, because physically the poet is imprisoned.

If the last poem seems not quite as sublime as the other three, it shows the difficulty a bedridden poet has in writing a large-scale poem. To write such a poem he has to depend on his imagination, not on shasei. Whether for this reason or not, Shiki wrote fewer and fewer poems in the sublime vein as years went by. He became increasingly attracted to another type of beauty, plainness.

To designate this effect, Shiki employed such words as *heitan* ("flatness"), *heii* ("plainness"), *tanpaku* ("lightness"), and *jinjō* ("ordinariness"). Its connotations are more difficult to delineate than are those of the sublime. The concept of plain beauty seems to have originated, and is still used, in areas other than poetics. In painting it denotes a light layer of paint as opposed to a thick one; in cooking, the taste of light foods, such as salad, as opposed to that of heavy, greasy ones; in stylistics, plain, lucid language as opposed to elaborate, ornate diction; and in craftsmanship, simplicity and naturalness as opposed to complexity and artifice. When referring to a landscape, it implies a flat, smooth terrain as opposed to a rugged one. (pp. 31-3)

Shiki's finest poems are plain in this sense:

Ill on a winter day
I have moisture wiped off
the glass door by my bed—
revealed on the other side,
socks hanging from the clothesline.

My nurse
awaking from a nap
swats a fly.

Outside the glass door
how bright the moonlight!
A bank of white clouds
extends far across the sky
above a forest of trees.

Blossoms have fallen
and the water is flowing
southwards.

The first two poems depict a trivial occurrence in the ailing poet's life. Shiki, utterly bored, has someone wipe the fog off the glass door near his bed. Through the cleared pane he sees no breathtaking sight—merely a few socks hanging from a clothesline. But even that is fresh to his eyes. There is an added poignancy in that he has no use for socks; he is too weak to stand on his feet. The next poem also describes a seemingly trivial occurrence. This time the season is summer. The day is hot and humid, as summer days usually are in Japan. Shiki's nurse, probably a young woman, is tired from her chores and dozes off while sitting by his bedside. The sick man, however, cannot sleep. When she awakes, their eyes meet. She is embarrassed, realizing that she has dozed in front of a young male patient. Without thinking, she grabs a flyswatter and swats a fly.

The next two poems are so plain and ordinary that they may seem trite. They are poems of pure shasei, describing common, familiar things—the moon, a forest, white clouds, blossoms, water. Yet in these ordinary scenes something mysterious and eternal is suggested. The bank of clouds trails far into the distance, the water flows toward the far south, and no one knows their destinations. In the process of observing nature, the poet senses an unknown force, manifest in phenomena such as these. Yet things simply follow their destiny without trying to solve the mystery. There is a tone of calm acceptance in both the tanka and the haiku; the haiku, in particular, is almost a Zen poem. (pp. 35-6)

Shiki's ideas of shasei, makoto, and selective realism do not explain his lifelong devotion to two traditional verse forms, haiku and tanka, nor does his predilection for the sublime or the plain. Indeed, longer literary forms might seem more suited to the complexities of realistic representation, and an extended treatment more capable of producing a sense of magnitude and power. Shouldn't Shiki have been attracted to write in prose or in shi, a newer and freer verse form that imposed no restrictions on length or lineation?

Shiki did have an interest in prose composition. He is considered the founder of a new prose genre called *shaseibun* (literally "shasei prose"), short prose pieces objectively describing a scene or incident that especially interests the writer. The piece has to be true to fact, but the writer is free to select in order to focus his presentation. Stylistically, the piece must be plain, lucid, and devoid of adornment. The new genre had a considerable effect of the Japanese literary scene in the first decade of the twentieth century, and many of Shiki's friends and disciples in poetry tried their hands at it. Later, it developed into a type of autobiographical prose fiction and in its own way helped to promote realism in the modern Japanese novel. Shiki himself, however, wrote only about a dozen shaseibun and penned no autobiographical novel. Although he did produce nine short stories, all but one show little realism, and all are without much literary merit. There is no doubt that Skiki's oeuvre as poet far outweighs his work as a writer of prose.

Shiki was interested in shi, too. When Tōson's *A Collection of Young Herbs* appeared in 1897, in a review in [the newspaper] *Nippon* Shiki said he saw great potential in the new form. Even before Tōson's debut, when the success of the new poetic experiment was still very much in doubt, Shiki had defended the experimentalists by comparing them to military heroes who lost their lives for better times to come. Indeed, he once asserted that of all writers in contemporary Japanese literary genres, those writing shi had shown the most remarkable progress in modernization. He placed haiku poets next and tanka writers last.

Shiki's pessimism about haiku and tanka resulted in a shocking forecast. Since these verse forms have limited syllable counts, he speculated that one could calculate the maximum number of haiku or tanka that could possibly be composed. In his rough calculation, the last good haiku had already been written, and even if that were not true, haiku would surely exhaust its poetic potential by the end of the current Emperor's reign. Tanka, which has more syllables, theoretically would have a longer life expectancy, yet since it was more restricted in vocabulary, Shiki felt it had run out of energy in premodern times. When someone who noticed a recent trend of writing haiku in eighteen or nineteen syllables suggested that haiku might in time lengthen itself into a Western-style poem, Shiki agreed, saying he was not saddened by haiku's predicament because his loyalty was to literature in general, not to haiku alone.

That comment notwithstanding, as a poet Shiki was loyal to haiku and tanka throughout his career. He did write shi, 38 all told. These poems are interesting as experiments, especially because some attempt to use rhyme, a device previously unknown in Japanese poetry. Yet by and large they are devoid of poetic merit. Most are stereotyped in theme (as can be surmised from such titles as **"My Father's Grave"** and **"Mourning the Death of the Empress Dowager"**), monotonous in rhythm (based largely on a 7-5 pattern), and lacking in emotional appeal. Thirty-eight poems is not a large number in view of the fact that Shiki wrote some 2,300 tanka and 18,000 haiku in his lifetime.

Shiki's attachment to haiku and tanka may have been rooted in a traditional upbringing. Born into a former samurai family in the nineteenth century, in early childhood he acquired a premodern education, which emphasized reading and writing traditional forms of poetry. As a young student he developed such a passion for haiku and tanka that he indulged in writing them when he should have been doing his schoolwork. "Charmed by the demon of haiku," he recollected later, "I was helpless. I failed the annual examinations in 1892." His illness, which lasted much of his adult life, may also have contributed to his preference for short verse forms. One needs sheer physical endurance to write a novel or a long shi, and Shiki did not have it.

In addition, Shiki felt that the Japanese people excelled in short verse forms and therefore should try to cultivate them. He postulated two reasons why short verse forms developed in Japan. First, Japanese poetry had been reared within a self-contained culture, where it had become a kind of sophisticated party game; in such a situation, short poems function best. Second, Japanese poetry concentrated on depicting natural landscapes rather than communal events or personal feelings. Long literary forms better served to depict events or sentiments, which tend to be complex, but short forms sufficed to present landscapes. Nature, according to Shiki, was simple to depict because it followed a regular course. Cherries always bloom in spring; chrysanthemums in autumn. People's lives are more irregular, he felt. To account for why Japanese poetry traditionally focused on nature, Shiki observed that his country, because of her geographical isolation, had enjoyed relative peace from ancient times and that his forefathers had no strong cause to protest political, social, or religious injustice. Furthermore, Japanese poets always had beautiful settings to inspire them. To recount his reasoning: Japanese poets were traditionally fond of writing poems on nature; nature poems were relatively simple; and therefore short poetic forms developed in Japan.

Personal preference aside, however, Shiki was receptive to all verse forms. The most important consideration for him was that the content fit the form. "In brief," he said, "various kinds of verse forms should be allowed, each in the situation appropriate to it. There is no reason for a poet to be restricted to 5-7 or 7-5 lines, nor need he try to create an unusual rhythm with extralong or extrashort lines. A fine poem will emerge when form matches feeling." Unknowingly, Shiki was advocating free verse, for it is in free verse that form aspires to mirror feelings exactly. (pp. 38-41)

Shiki himself never conceived of haiku or tanka as unrestricted by syllable count, but he was quite generous in allowing extra syllables. He wrote, and encouraged others to write, haiku in 18 or more syllables and tanka in 32 or more syllables if a particular occasion warranted. When more conservative poets attacked this practice, he vehemently defended his stand on the ground that form should be determined by content. He also argued that the 17- and 31-syllable forms had been in existence for so many centuries that some variation would create refreshing effects. Moreover, the traditional 5-7 rhythm seemed to him so smooth, melodious, and elegant that he sometimes wanted to break away from it to produce something irregular. Being more anxious to write a fine poem than to write a haiku or tanka, he did not care if old-fashioned masters objected to his calling his extralong poems by those names. . . .

Many of Shiki's haiku and tanka have extra syllables. Of the 920 haiku in one of the standard selections from his works, 155, or one out of every six, have 18 or more syllables. The proportion is ever greater for tanka: for 544 poems included in *Bamboo Village Tanka,* 164 have more than 31 syllables. That is about 30 percent, a high ratio indeed. Most of the poems with an extra syllable or two are very successful. (p. 41)

Another notable feature of Shiki's concept of form is a principle of internal harmony. He wanted a poem to place two or more images side by side in a way that creates an aesthetically pleasing impression. Because each person has his own sensibility, Shiki's principle of harmony is ultimately subjective, but he probable felt that Japanese poets, with their centuries-old cultural tradition, shared the same taste to a great degree. A poet's task, therefore, was to seek a new combination of images that most people would consider harmonious. (p. 42)

Although Shiki was the first to advocate internal harmony as a poetic principle, the method of juxtaposing images had been practiced in haiku long before his time. In fact, there is evidence that Bashō was already aware of the technique, and Shiki himself referred to it in **"Elements of Haiku."** It is definitely to Shiki's credit, however, that he advocated applying it to tanka. No poet before him had thought of using the haiku technique in tanka, since the two verse forms had evolved different poetics over the centuries, and a poet would specialize in one form or the other but not in both. Shiki wrote poetry in both forms, and saw nothing wrong with applying the technique of the one to the other. (p. 43)

Finally, Shiki's concept of form is distinguished by what he called *rensaku,* or "sequential composition." This term refers to the practice of writing haiku or tanka in sequence, usually in such a way that the poems, although autonomous, take on additional significance when seen as a group. The practice was not unknown before Shiki's time, but seldom was it carried out with a conscious artistic aim. Shiki was the first to see a new poetic possibility in the technique; indeed, he seems to have invented the term *rensaku.* Although it does not figure prominently in his statements on theory, he practiced rensaku a number of times, with such successful results that he started a trend, especially among the tanka poets who looked to him for leadership.

Shiki's interest in rensaku seems to have had its beginnings in a pedagogic, rather than a poetic, motive. He taught that a student of haiku should compose as many poems as possible on a given subject and then choose the finest as his final product. Shiki did this himself, and at times he found it difficult to narrow down his choice to a single poem, especially when some of the draft poems expressed different aspects of the same subject. At such times, he would retain two or more poems and present them under a common title or headnote. A good example of this practice is recorded in his journal, ***A Drop of Ink.*** In the spring of 1901, one of Shiki's disciples presented him with three live carp in a tub. The gift was to help the bedridden teacher visualize spring visiting the spacious waters in the world outside. Overjoyed, Shiki began to write a haiku, with the tub by his bedside. The task was not easy, however. "I rethought and rewrote time and again," he said of the experience, "until the number of poems I drafted reached ten. These were, and were not, ten separate poems. They were nothing more than ten attempts to express the same theme." In the end he retained the ten haiku, all describing carp in a tub on a spring day, but each with a slightly different nuance. (pp. 45-6)

For Shiki, the usefulness of literature derives from the pleasure that it gives. Initially he saw this pleasure merely as recreative, but in his later years it began to take on greater importance, as an absorption in poetry came to provide him with the strength to remain calm and human in the face of suffering and eventual death. (pp. 48-9)

Shiki's diaries provide a concrete example of the usefulness of positive pleasure by revealing the irreplaceable moral support poetry provided during the years he was an invalid dying of tuberculosis. When he became unbearably bored, he could always turn to poetry. When he had a sleepless night (and he had many), he could draft haiku in his head. When an unseasonably hot spell tormented him, he could console himself by writing poems about it. When an overgrown pine tree in his garden bothered him, he could vent the frustration in tanka. He was quite honest when he said:

> People praise me for my studiousness, but actually I read and write because I have this prolonged illness and do not know how to overcome boredom otherwise. Even those who will have nothing to do with books in normal life are said to become fond of reading novels and biographies, or even of composing amateurish tanka and haiku, when they suffer from a long illness. I have been living this way for so long that if for any reason someone should want me to abandon it he might as well sentence me to instant death.

We have already seen that Shiki wrote three haiku—and good ones, too—within 24 hours of his death. As two of the three poems imply, at the time his throat was stopped up with mucus, and he could hardly breathe. But it is clear why he made the desperate attempt to write them, his chest heaving hard, his hand shaking uncontrollably, and his energy all but exhausted. It was an assertion of humanity in the face of immutable fate. Although not a religious man, Shiki had an ultimate faith in art as the only way to confront death with courage and dignity. His last three haiku are unmistakable proof of the usefulness of poetry. (pp. 51-2)

Makoto Ueda, "Masaoka Shiki," in his Modern Japanese Poets and the Nature of Literature, *Stanford University Press, 1983, pp. 9-52 [the excerpts of Shiki's poetry used here were originally published in* Modern Japanese Haiku: An Anthology, *edited and translated by Makoto Ueda, University of Toronto Press, 1976].*

DONALD KEENE (essay date 1984)

[Keene is one of the foremost translators and critics of Japanese literature. In the following excerpt, he surveys Shiki's poetic theories and discusses characteristic examples of his work.]

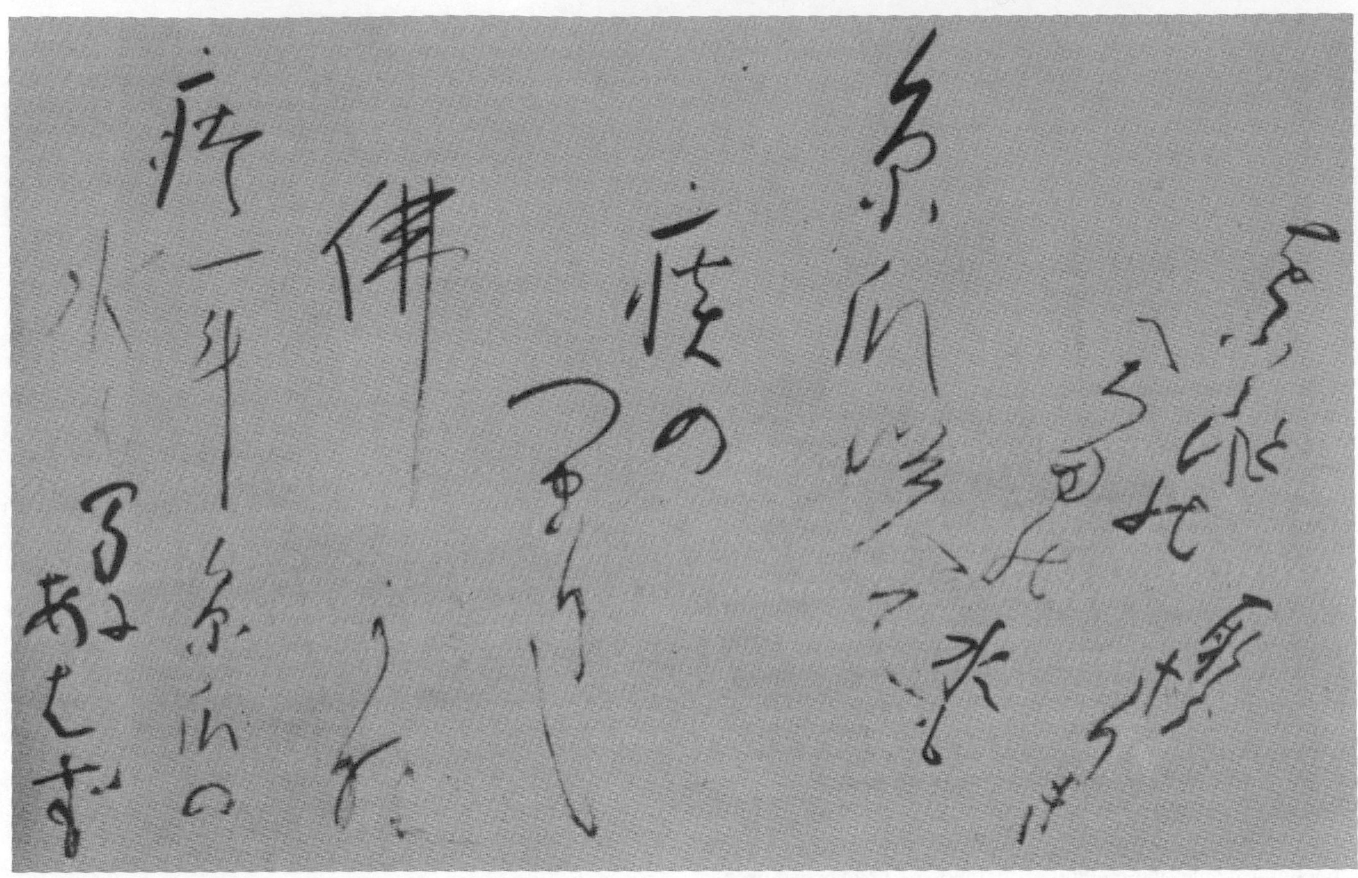

Holograph copy of three haiku written by Shiki on the day of his death, 19 September 1902.

Masaoka Shiki . . . almost singlehandedly restored the haiku to an important place in Japanese poetry after first subjecting it to devastating attacks. Katō Shūson . . . declared that there had been two great "waves" in the history of haiku, represented by Bashō and Shiki, and that no modern practitioners could ignore either man.

Shiki's first important statement of his view on haiku was presented in a series of articles published in 1892 under the title ***Dassai Shooku Haiwa (Talks of Haiku from the Otter's Study).*** He opened with a brief recapitulation of the history of hiakai poetry. This section contains few surprises, but his account picks up interest when he reaches his predictions of the future of haiku. He began, characteristically in a man of the modern age, with a reference to a new science, mathematics: "Present-day scholars who have studied mathematics say that the number of possible waka, haiku and similar forms of Japanese poetry is unquestionably limited, as one can easily calculate from the number of permutations possible with a mere twenty or thirty syllables. In other words, the waka (generally called the tanka) and the haiku must sooner or later reach their limits. We have already reached the point where it is quite impossible to compose a wholly original poem." Shiki deplored the ignorance of those who supposed (out of ignorance of science) that it would always be possible to compose new tanka and haiku. "In fact, both the tanka and the haiku are already fast approaching their death throes." The innumerable thousands upon thousands of tanka and haiku composed since ancient times all seem different on first glance, but under careful examination it becomes apparent how many are alike. Pupils plagiarize their teachers, and men of later generations plagiarize their predecessors. A man who can convert the stone of old poems into the jade of new ones is acclaimed as a master poet, even though he never presents an original idea. (pp. 92-3)

Shiki's simplistic calculation of the potential number of tanka and haiku in terms of permutations of the seventeen or thirty-one syllables was not really essential to his judgment that the tanka was already exhausted and the haiku would certainly be dead before long. This statement was far more sweeping than any previous attack on traditional Japanese poetry. Shiki did not merely point out the inadequacies of traditional poetry to express the life of the new age, but insisted that it could no longer fulfill any literary function. He recognized that "contemporary affairs and things are totally unlike those of the past." Not only had swords given way to guns, but the peculiar features of Japanese society were fast vanishing. Formerly people rode or walked according to their station in life, but now commoners rode in the same vehicles as noblemen. The waka, Shiki asserted, was totally unable to respond to this changed situation because of its rigorous insistence on purity of diction, and the haiku, though it did not absolutely reject new words, certainly did not welcome them.

Shiki followed this challenging section of ***Talks on Haiku*** with a rather bland discussion of Bashō's disciples and of the birds and plants most commonly mentioned in Japanese poetry. Only when he turned his attention to a book on haikai poetry by a contemporary poet did he let loose with his familiar sarcasm in an attack on the author's opinions on the grammar of the haiku. "The author urges poets to adopt the ancient grammar in writing haiku today, but I would like to ask him one question: When he speaks of ancient grammar, to which age does he refer? Remote antiquity? The Nara period? The Heian period? Or perhaps the Muromachi period? Whatever age he may have in mind, why must we cling to the grammar of the past? Is grammar incapable of changing with the times?'' Shiki was especially distressed by the examples of modern haiku given by the author: ''My first reaction to this book was one of weariness and boredom, but the extreme ineptness and superficiality of the haiku given as examples finally made me want to vomit.'' Such intemperance must have startled readers, but there can be no doubting the genuineness of Shiki's disgust.

On the whole Shiki was pessimistic about the future of the haiku, but his very expressions of despair suggested that he did not in fact consider the haiku beyond redemption. At first he confined his attacks to the tsukinami poets of recent times, but in a series of articles published in 1893 in the newspaper *Nippon* . . . he chose a new subject, the hitherto sacred poetry of Bashō himself. By Japanese reckoning 1893 marked the two-hundredth anniversary of the death of Bashō. Irritation over the excessive adulation offered the Master at innumerable celebrations may have inspired Shiki to produce in ***Bashō Zatsudan (Chats on Bashō)*** what was probably the harshest criticism ever directed at the Saint of Haiku. Shiki explained the worship of Bashō in terms of the popular appeal of his poetry, which had endeared him to the public at large, but questioned whether such adulation was a true indication of its literary worth. From these doubts he passed to an examination of what he labeled Bashō's ''bad poems,'' declaring his intention of analyzing Bashō as a literary figure rather than as the object of cult worship. Even though he attacked specific haiku, he paid Bashō the indirect tribute of referring to his works as literature (*bungaku*), using a term that was normally reserved for compositions in Chinese and similarly elevated forms of writing.

Shiki opened his discussion of the ''bad poems'' with a bombshell: ''I would like to state at the outset my judgment that the majority of Bashō's haiku are bad or even doggerel, and not more than a tenth can be called first-rate. Even barely passable verses are as rare as morning stars.'' He listed eleven haiku by Bashō that were generally acclaimed as masterpieces and analyzed each. Only the first, the celebrated haiku on the frog jumping into the pond, elicited his praise; he called it ''the most necessary verse in the history of haiku,'' a poem that exists on a plane of its own, without reference to the conventional considerations of good or bad. Apart from its historical significance as the work that heralded Bashō's characteristic style, it was highly exceptional in its unadorned expression, which defied the common preference for ingenuity and decoration.

Shiki's praise of the frog poem bore no resemblance to the normal inarticulate cries of wonder on the part of Bashō's devotees who, if asked the meaning of the poem, would answer that it was a mystery, incommunicable in speech. His opinions had the precision associated with Western-oriented scholars: Bashō, he explained, was able, thanks to the use of suggestion, to convey the silence of the ancient pond, remote from the city and the clamor of men's voices, without once mentioning it. Shiki believed that the poem, like the Zen adept's calling a willow green and a flower red, described as exactly as possible an actual experience. The poem, he was sure, had flashed into Bashō's head in the form of the second and third lines: ''A frog jumps in/ The sound of the water.'' There was no statement of subjective impressions, no prolongation of the experience either spatially or temporally. Bashō later added the first line, ''The ancient pond,'' merely in order the establish the setting.

Shiki's treatment of the other ten haiku by Bashō was much harsher. . . . [Several] famous poems by Bashō were denounced as plagiarism or close adaptations of earlier haiku, and Shiki was especially irritated by any display in ingenuity. His final judgment was that Bashō's poetry, all in all, was no more than a junk heap of bad and good works indiscriminately thrown together.

Shiki, however, denied that he thought Bashō's poetry was worthless; on the contrary, his good haiku possessed the qualities most lacking in Japanese literature: masculinity and grandeur. Poetry embodying these qualities is found in the *Manyōshū* and even earlier works, but with the exception of Minamoto Sanetomo, no poet of later times possessed them. The haiku of the Teitoku and Danrin schools had reeked so much of stale vulgarities as to be unworthy of the name of literature; Bashō's poetry was the first in centuries to display virility and amplitude. . . .

Conversely, [Shiki's] dislike of the feminine qualities in Japanese literature reflected his samurai background and his basically unromantic nature. On occasion, it is true, he admired poetry in a romantic vein, but his greatest enthusiasm was reserved for the *Manyōshū* and for poets working in the *Manyōshū* traditions.

By this time Shiki was thoroughly contemptuous of the ''three masters of the Tempō era'' and poets of their line, whom he characterized as frogs in a well, unable to discern the great sea. As yet he had not discovered Buson, and his praise for Bashō, though grudging, represented the limit of his admiration for haiku. (p. 96)

[His] essay on Bashō exudes the brashness of youth, and no one could assent to all of Shiki's judgments, but even his mistakes effectively awakened people from complacent admiration for the Master. Bashō could no longer be taken for granted as the incarnation of the spirit of the haiku; his defenders would have to prove his excellence.

Shiki's writings between 1894 and 1896 revealed a steadily deepening admiration for Buson. . . . [After] praising Buson in 1894 as the greatest haiku poet after Bashō, he never afterward wavered in this opinion. . . . The climax of his writings on Buson came in the long essay **''Haijin Buson'' (''Buson the Haiku Poet,''** 1896). It opened with a reiteration of Shiki's doubts concerning the divinity of Bashō, the Saint of Haiku. He complained that Buson was neglected: ''The haiku of Buson are the equal of Bashō's and in some respects superior. He has failed to win the fame due him mainly because his poetry is not for the masses, and because the haiku poets after Buson were ignorant and lacking in discrimination.''

In the section on the ''positive beauty'' he found in Buson's haiku, Shiki declared, ''In general, oriental art and literature tend toward negative beauty, occidental art and literature toward positive beauty.'' However, in both Orient and Occident negative beauty was typical of the past and only later gave way to positive beauty. Bashō's art, he insisted, was essentially negative, though he wrote some haiku of grandeur and sublimity. Most of Bashō's successors considered negative beauty to be the only kind, and rejected sensual charm, vivacity or originality as aberrations of expression, much as devotees of oriental art decried Western art as vulgar. Buson, by contrast, was a poet of positive beauty, and summer, the most "positive" of the four seasons, was the time of year he loved best. Bashō rarely wrote about peonies, a voluptuous summer flower, but Buson composed no fewer than twenty haiku on the subject, including several masterpieces. "Young leaves," another "positive" summer subject, appeared in Bashō's haiku merely as seasonal appurtenances, but Buson wrote ten haiku about them, capturing their particular brilliance.

Shiki next discussed Buson's pictorial qualities. Shiki's interest in this subject was aroused by his meeting in 1894 with the Western-style painter Nakamura Fusetsu . . . , from whom he learned about the principle of shasei (copying life). At first Shiki showed not the least appreciation of Western paintings, but under Fusetsu's guidance he learned to distinguish the qualities of Japanese and Western art. After six months of conversations with Fusetsu he came to believe that haiku poetry and painting were in essence identical arts. The aspect of Fusetsu's theory of art that most powerfully impressed Shiki was the central importance he gave to shasei in reproducing sights and experiences. Shiki first attempted to incorporate shasei in his haiku when he went on an excursion in August 1894 with Fusetsu and the haiku poet Naitō Meisetsu. . . . He composed various poems, including

The stone flight of steps
Looms high in early autumn
Amidst the cedars.

Fusetsu commented that such a poem would be easy to convert into a painting. (pp. 97-8)

Shiki believed that haiku poetry was closest of all literary forms to paintings. In other forms of poetry the emphasis is on time, rather than on space, but the haiku is too brief to go beyond the present moment, and must therefore evoke space instead.

Shiki's interpretation of the meaning of shasei changed over the years, especially after he had come to appreciate the Chinese ideal of *heitan* (plainness and blandness), but he continued to relate poetry to painting. In 1892 Shiki had advocated the "positive beauty" of Western art, but he admitted in ***Wa ga Haiku (My Haiku,*** 1896) that he had changed his mind: "A man who formerly loved the extremely unusual and the grandiose has come to love plainness and blandness instead. This surely must indicate that he has reached a state at which his emotions have developed sufficiently for him to make more subtle distinctions.". . . A haiku written in this style might seem bland and unprovocative, but the apparent blandness was merely the surface under which lay hidden deep flavors that could be appreciated only after careful savoring. By 1902 he stated, "Shasei is heitan." In his last years Shiki, confined to his sickbed, had little direct contact with nature, and perhaps that was why he came to think of shasei not as a means of depicting nature in the raw but as the heitan surface beneath which the poet's deepest emotions could be glimpsed. (pp. 99-100)

Shiki's activities as a critic earned for him the reputation of having been the founder of modern haiku. He occupied a similar position with respect to the modern tanka too, though this form was not so close to him as the haiku; his first and last poetic impulses were expressed in the haiku. He was by nature an unusually practical and intellectual poet, despite his repeated insistence on simplicity and his rejection of "intellectualization." His training in the Confucian classics as a young man probably accounted for this strong element of rationalism, which went better with the haiku than the more lyric tanka. He was at times able to approach the "positive beauty" he admired in Buson, but rarely the loftier realm of Bashō's poetry.

Shiki's first haiku of distinction was composed in 1890, the year after he coughed blood and took the name "Shiki." During the course of his short life he composed over eighteen thousand haiku, as well as many tanka and other varieties of poetry. The early haiku are occasionally of interest, whether because of a perception of nature or a glimpse of his personal life, but only after his meeting with Nakamura Fusetsu in 1894 and his adoption of shasei as his guiding principle did his haiku acquire maturity. In the summer of 1894, in between jobs, he spent his days wandering in the suburbs, notebook in hand, composing haiku in the shasei manner. According to his own account, it was then that he first came to make the shasei techniques a natural part of his expression, as in:

See how low it flies,
That locust on the paddy walk—
The sunshine weakens.

It is autumn. The rice has been harvested, and the locust, deprived of a place of concealment in the paddy field, rests on the raised path. At Shiki's approach it flies up, but so weakly it does not rise very high. The sunshine has also lost its summer intensity. Shiki's close observation of the locust is saved from triviality (always a danger in shasei haiku) by his perception that not only the locust but the sun itself has weakened.

In 1895 Shiki volunteered as a war correspondent. He should have realized that his delicate health would be unequal to the strain, but he persuaded himself that life would not be worth living unless he could see service at the front in China. His stay there (mainly at Chin-chou) lasted little more than a month, but the poetry he composed was important to the development of his shasei style; he described unfamiliar scenes with accuracy and evocativeness:

The long days—
The shadow of a lash
Chases a donkey.

Shiki captured the spaciousness of the Chinese landscape with the long shadows of a spring day stretching into the distance. Other haiku composed in China were more closely associated with the warfare; one described the sickening sight of corpses strewn around a gun emplacement, another the fewness of the swallows after a battle had ended. Shiki also wrote some tanka and poems in Chinese on the same experiences, evidence of how deeply they had affected him. None of these poems ranks among Shiki's major poems, but travel abroad extended the range of his shasei expression. (pp. 100-01)

More and more frequently Shiki's haiku alluded to his illness, as in this verse written late in 1896:

Snow When I Was Sick
Again and again
I asked the others how much
Snow had fallen.

Behind the apparently straightforward statement lies the unspoken anguish of the man who cannot leave his sickbed even to step into the garden and measure the snowfall for himself. Yamamoto Kenkichi wrote of this haiku: "In such sickbed compositions Shiki was already exploring a unique poetic domain which was not that of either Bashō or Buson. . . . His style, intentionally borrowed from Buson's ever since discovering Buson's haiku in 1893, came in this year to possess at last individuality of expression.''

When Shiki became immobile toward the end of 1896 his tiny garden became virtually his only source of poetic inspiration. The love he expressed for the flowers he could glimpse from his bed was quite extraordinary; his life seemed to have become one with the plants. ''The objects he saw were so restricted in numbers that his eyes truly began to see. Shiki's shasei reached its heights at this point.'' Other men in Shiki's predicament might have yielded to self-pity, but his samurai training made him shun overt expressions of weakness in his poetry.

Even Shiki's impromptu poems were often tinged with deep pathos because of the implicit circumstances of his illness. Some of them, written in the impersonal shasei style, were for long overlooked because their implications were not detected. The following haiku, ignored by most professional haiku critics for years, is now often acclaimed as his masterpiece:

> Cockscomb—
> I'm sure there are at least
> Fourteen or fifteen stalks.

This verse unfortunately loses everything in translation, but even the original excited derisive remarks from various poets who, questioning the absoluteness of its terms, made such substitutions as ''seven or eight stalks'' or ''withered chrysanthemums'' for ''cockscomb.'' One critic defied anyone to define the differences between seven or eight stalks and fourteen or fifteen stalks; but, as Yamamoto Kenkichi pointed out, the sound of the words is important, and anyone who argues exclusively on the basis of meaning does not understand the nature of poetry. The slight differences in shading (rather than of meaning) given the haiku by the grammatical particles and verb endings also communicate overtones to a sensitive Japanese reader that cannot be analyzed in translation. Yamamoto wrote:

> Every masterpiece is a flower on a precipice, to be picked only with spiritual danger. The risk is life itself. It is too much to hope every poetry-lover will unfailingly grasp all subtleties of the creative act, but no artistic masterpiece exists without the danger of its being misunderstood. It is a tremendous assertion for the poet to have said, ''There must be fourteen or fifteen stalks of cockscomb.'' After we read this poem we cannot imagine the possibility there could have been more or fewer cockscomb than fourteen or fifteen.

The first discoverer of this poem was Nagatsuka Takashi, a disciple of Shiki's in tanka rather than haiku, who was struck by the profound impression it conveyed of Shiki's emotions as he gazed from his bed at the cockscomb in his garden. Shiki, watching the proudly erect plants, wishes he could be like them, though he knows that his bedridden life is fast ebbing away. Probably Shiki composed the haiku easily, even artlessly, as he looked at the garden, unaware that he had created a masterpiece of haiku; but the depth of his feelings and his skill at shasei composition revealed themselves in a work that was uniquely his own. (pp. 103-04)

Shiki is today remembered above all as a critic, a pioneer in the revival of both haiku and tanka who wrote at a time when it seemed most unlikely traditional poetry could survive in the complex new world of Meiji Japan. His harsh criticism of linked verse all but killed this art, and if he had continued to attack haiku and tanka he might well have obtained the same results. It is true that his sharp criticism of Bashō did little to diminish the Master's reputation, but that may have been because Shiki's criticism of Bashō was always tempered with expressions of admiration. He borrowed much from Buson, but remained a totally different poet, never taking on Buson's romanticism or his absorption with the Heian past. His best haiku are given their particular coloration by his samurai stoicism and his suffering. Few are truly memorable, but he stands nevertheless at the head of the twentieth-century revival of the haiku. (p. 105)

Donald Keene, ''The Modern Haiku,'' in his Dawn to the West, Japanese Literature of the Modern Era: Poetry, Drama, Criticism, *Holt, Rinehart and Winston, 1984, pp. 88-190.**

ADDITIONAL BIBLIOGRAPHY

Blyth, R. H. ''Shiki: The Critic,'' ''Shiki: On Furu-ike ya,'' and ''Shiki: The Haiku Poet.'' In his *A History of Haiku,* Vol. II, pp. 21-45, 46-76, and 77-100. Tokyo: Hokuseido Press, 1964.
Examines Shiki's importance as a critic and poet.

Isaacson, Harold J. Preface to *Peonies Kana,* by Masaoka Shiki, pp. xi-xxii. New York: Theatre Arts Books, 1972.
Discusses Shiki's stature in Japanese literature and his contribution to the development of modern haiku.

Keene, Donald. ''Masaoka Shiki.'' In his *Some Japanese Portraits,* pp. 195-204. Tokyo: Kodansha International, 1978.
Discusses Shiki's contributions to tanka and haiku reform and his development as a critic.

Kimata, Osamu. "Shiki Masaoka: His Haiku and Tanka." In *The Modernization of Japan: A Special Edition in the Philosophical Studies of Japan,* Vol. VIII, compiled by the Japanese National Council for Unesco, pp. 41-66. Tokyo: Japan Society for the Promotion of Science, 1967.
Examines the dominant characteristics of Shiki's haiku and tanka.

Miner, Earl. ''The Verse Record of My Peonies.'' In his *Japanese Poetic Diaries,* pp. 47-50. Berkeley: University of California Press, 1969.
Provides biographical background to Shiki's diary.

Okasaki Yoshie. *Japanese Literature in the Meiji Era.* Translated by V. H. Viglielmo. Tokyo: Obunsha, 1955, 673 p.*
Contains scattered references to Shiki's contributions to the development of Meiji literature.

Yasuda, Kenneth. *The Japanese Haiku: Its Essential Nature, History, and Possibilities in English.* Rutland, Vt.: Charles E. Tuttle Co., 1957, 232 p.
Contains references to Shiki's role in modernizing haiku.

Vladimir (Vladimirovich) Mayakovsky

1893-1930

(Also transliterated as Maiakovskiĭ, Mayakovski, Mayakovskiy, and Majakovskij) Russian poet, dramatist, essayist, and autobiographer.

Mayakovsky is considered the central figure of the Russian Futurist movement and the premier artistic voice of the Bolshevik Revolution of 1917. The Russian Futurists, who denied any association with the Futurist movements developing in Italy and France in the early decades of the twentieth century, saw their work as the quintessential mode of aesthetic expression for their historical epoch, which was distinguished by violent social upheaval and the subsequent downfall of Russia's established government. The Futurist poets aimed to destroy traditional poetic precepts through the disregard for metonymic and grammatical convention, the use of bizarre imagery and invented vocabulary, and techniques borrowed from avant-garde painting, including irregular typefaces, offbeat illustrations, and the author's handwriting. Mayakovsky is generally considered the leader of the Futurist movement and one of the most innovative poets in twentieth-century literature.

The only son of a Georgian forester, Mayakovsky was an intellectually precocious child who developed an early appreciation for literature, but demonstrated little interest in schoolwork. After the death of his father in 1906, Mayakovsky's mother moved the family to Moscow, where he attended public secondary school and joined the Social Democratic Worker's party, a subversive, anticzarist organization. Between the ages of fifteen and sixteen, Mayakovsky was arrested three times by undercover police who had amassed evidence linking him with such criminal activities as running an illegal printing press, bank robbery, and organizing a jailbreak of political prisoners. He was imprisoned for six months after his third arrest in connection with the jailbreak charge, and proved such an agitating presence among other inmates that he was frequently moved and eventually placed in solitary confinement. Upon his release from prison, Mayakovsky entered the Moscow Institute of Art, hoping to become a painter. There he met the Russian Cubist painter David Burlyuk, who introduced him to avant-garde trends in the visual arts and poetry and who soon became the organizer and promoter of Futurist road shows that toured Russia before 1917. Dressed in outrageous garb, such as the yellow tunic which became his trademark, the tall and ruggedly handsome Mayakovsky soon became the dominant and most popular poet-performer of the group, frequently captivating audiences with his loud, dramatic recitations. Mayakovsky's early poetry mirrored this egotistic and theatrical quality through its use of a first-person poet-protagonist. In 1913, he wrote and performed in his first drama, the "tragedy" *Vladimir Mayakovsky,* which played to full houses of curious and sometimes heckling spectators. Two years later Mayakovsky met Osip and Lilya Brik, beginning a relationship that greatly affected his personal and professional life: Osip Brik, a wealthy lawyer with strong literary interests, became Mayakovsky's publisher, and Lilya—Osip's wife—became his mistress and the inspiration for most of his impassioned love poetry, including *Fleita pozvonochnik* (*The Backbone Flute*) and *Pro eto* (*About That*).

The Granger Collection, New York

The outbreak of the Bolshevik Revolution in 1917 provided Mayakovsky with an opportunity to combine his political commitment and artistic talents, and he plunged headlong into the cause of promoting the new regime. Victor Shklovsky, a leading Russian critic, wrote in his memoirs, "Mayakovsky entered the Revolution as he would enter his own home." Soon considered the official poet of the Revolution, Mayakovsky applied his poetic skill toward writing songs, slogans, and jingles expounding Bolshevik ideology, and also used his abilities as a painter and illustrator to produce a voluminous number of propaganda posters and cartoons. He was proud of his ability to create utilitarian literature without compromising himself as a poet, and critics also marvel at his achievement, often citing his 3,000 line poem *Vladimir Ilyich Lenin*—written on the leader's death in 1924—as one of his finest works, a communist equivalent of a religious epic. In the mid-to-late 1920s, Mayakovsky traveled in Europe, Mexico, and the United States as an official representative of the Soviet government. On these trips abroad he kept a grueling schedule of public appearances and recorded his impressions of the capitalist societies he visited. Mayakovsky expressed his admiration for American technology and architecture in his *Amerikanskiye stikhi* (*America*) cycle, which includes one of his most famous poems, "Brooklyn Bridge," a eulogy to American engineering and the universal plight of the common laborer.

During the last few years of his life, Mayakovsky experienced a succession of personal disappointments and critical attacks from Soviet officials, all of which eroded his confidence and stamina. A serious love affair he had begun in Paris failed when the woman, a Russian émigré, refused to return with him to Moscow, and he was denied a visa to remain in France. Mayakovsky's relationship with the Communist party was also strained, for he had been growing increasingly disillusioned by the expanding party bureaucracy and the infiltration of bourgeois values into the new order. At the same time, the conservative Bolshevik leaders charged that Mayakovsky's writing was too individualistic and that its prerevolutionary Futurist tenets were incompatible with the ideology of Joseph Stalin's Five Year Plan, which advocated collectivization of agriculture and art alike. Under extreme political pressure, Mayakovsky was forced to abandon his editorship of *Novyi LEF* (*New LEF*), a revival of the Futurist magazine *LEF*, and joined the Russian Association of Proletarian Writers (RAPP), a conservative, state-controlled literary organization. Mayakovsky satirized the philistine Soviet bureaucrats in his plays *Klop* (*The Bedbug*) and *Banya* (*The Bathhouse*), which were written and performed in the last two years of his life. Considered outrageous offenses to the state, the plays received scathing reviews and were banned in the Soviet Union until 1955. Although in the last months of his life Mayakovsky maintained his usual hectic public schedule, biographers indicate that he was emotionally devastated, having regarded the critical rejection of his work as a personal attack. Torn between the flamboyant originality of his art and a desire to "stamp on the throat" of his talent in service to the party, Mayakovsky played Russian roulette, a pastime he favored when despondent, and died by his own hand on April 14, 1930.

In the appraisal of Russian critic D. S. Mirsky, "Mayakovsky's poetry is very loud, very unrefined, and stands absolutely outside the distinction between 'good' and 'bad' taste." It is marked by powerful rhythm, often evocative of an invigorating march cadence, which along with the declamatory nature of the verse, makes it best appreciated when read aloud. Mayakovsky virtually abandoned metric structure in his poetry; on the page his verse is arranged in irregular lines—often in a step formation such as that found in the work of the modern American poet William Carlos Williams—and is generally held together by strong, but unpredictable, internal rhyme schemes. Much of Mayakovsky's originality as a poet is attributed to his use of hyperbolic imagery, often blasphemous or violent, in a verse which simultaneously speaks sorrowfully of unrequited love. Critics concur that the long poem *Oblako v shtanakh* (*A Cloud in Trousers*), written in 1914, is one of his finest and most characteristic works, for it exhibits not only the boisterous form and language that distinguishes his verse, but it also contains many of the themes that are repeatedly addressed in his writing.

One of the most important features of *A Cloud in Trousers* is its introduction of the first-person poet-persona, Mayakovsky's megalomaniacal "I" which dominates most of his writing. It is from the perspective of the "beloved self" that all action in Mayakovsky's work is presented, making this persona inestimably significant as it assumes multiple roles and introduces key themes. One role the poet-persona frequently assumes is that of a social critic and prophet of the Revolution who severely chastises the bourgeoisie for their complacency and foretells the impending destruction of their world. This speaker democratically equates himself with the "street thousands—students, prostitutes, contractors" in a manner reminiscent of Walt Whitman, whose poetry Mayakovsky had read in translation. Like Whitman, Mayakovsky was also essentially an urban poet whose work more often describes and celebrates city life and the press of humanity than the serenity and beauty of nature. Mayakovsky's speaker sustains the thematic element of time throughout his verse by consistently rejecting all belonging to the past, while placing hope in the future and its promise of change. In *A Cloud in Trousers* the self-proclaimed forerunner of the Revolution declares, "I inscribe 'Nihil' ['Nothing'] over everything done before me."

While the speaker in Mayakovsky's poetry is a vital and heroic presence, he is also distinguished as a tragic figure who is rejected, and ultimately destroyed, by both the cause and the individuals he loves. In the politically oriented verse, the persona is frequently depicted as a self-sacrificing savior who lays down his life for the Revolution. Mayakovsky often used distorted religious imagery and litany in these works, of which *Chelovek* (*Man*), a parody of the life of Christ, is the best example. By skillful and recurrent use of this theme, Mayakovsky defined the poet-persona as a mythic hero who could, according to Jurij Striedter, "be transposed from the sphere of religion and metaphysics to that of worldly, social, political revolution; and as he is made into an abstract myth, embodying the sacrifice for the sake of world redemption, he can take on the vital function of worldwide redeemer in the 'new myth' of revolution." Mayakovsky also portrays his speaker as a persecuted sufferer in his love poetry, which is consistently woven into the social verse. In these passages, the speaker is tormented by the rejection of a single woman, rather than by an entire nation. Mayakovsky's frustrating relationship with Lilya Brik was the inspiration for much of his love poetry, which contains some of his most grotesque and violent imagery. Unlike the persona of the political verse—who stoically endures the torment of "crucifixion," or persecution by uncomprehending philistines—the victim of unrequited love is often portrayed as being mutilated or dying by his own hand. *The Backbone Flute* and *About That,* written and dedicated to Brik, are considered by Victor Terras "quite as gory as the most cruel scenes in *Voina i mir* (*War and the World*), which depicts the horrors of war."

The growing despair and ambivalence Mayakovsky felt toward his own life and the future of his nation is clearly reflected in his late works, the satirical dramas *The Bedbug* and *The Bathhouse,* but perhaps most eloquently in "Vo ves golos" ("At the Top of My Voice"), an unfinished long poem, which many critics consider a masterpiece. In this work, written in 1930, the poet unleashes a lyrical deluge of personal emotion, which had been consistently underplayed in the revolutionary verse: confessions of pain and anger at the rejection dealt him by women and the Soviet regime, agony caused by trying to play the dual roles of public apostle and private poet, and an uncharacteristic sense of exhaustion and surrender. Mayakovsky quoted several lines from the poem in his suicide note.

In Joseph Stalin's assessment, "Mayakovsky was, and remains, the greatest Soviet poet." In the Soviet Union today, his poetry follows only Alexander Pushkin's in terms of popular readership. Not only the preeminent artist of the Revolution, Mayakovsky is also one of the most distinctive poets of this century, whose work has had tremendous influence on younger Russian poets, such as Yevgeny Yevtushenko, as well as on contemporary poets throughout the world.

(See also *TCLC*, Vol. 4 and *Contemporary Authors,* Vol. 104.)

PRINCIPAL WORKS

Poshchochina obshestvennomu vkusa [with David Burlyuk,

Velimir Khlebnikov, and Aleksey Kruchonykh] (manifesto and poetry) 1912
Vladimir Mayakovsky (drama) 1913
[*Vladimir Mayakovsky: A Tragedy* published in *The Complete Plays of Vladimir Mayakovsky,* 1968]
Ya (poetry) 1913
Oblako v shtanakh (poetry) 1915
[*A Cloud in Trousers* published in *Mayakovsky,* 1965]
Chelovek (poetry) 1916
Fleita pozvonochnik (poetry) 1916
Rossii (poetry) 1916
Sebe, lyubimomu, avtor posvashchaet eti stroki (poetry) 1916
Voina i mir (poetry) 1916
Misteria-Buff (drama) 1918
[*Mystery-Bouffe* published in *The Complete Plays of Vladimir Mayakovsky,* 1968]
Vse sochinennoe Vladimirom Mayakovskim (poetry and drama) 1919
150.000.000 (poetry) 1920
Liren (poetry) 1921
Lyublyu (poetry) 1922
Nash byt (poetry) 1922
Ya sam (autobiography) 1922
[*I Myself* published in *Mayakovsky and His Poetry,* 1942]
Pro eto (poetry) 1923
Vladimir Ilyich Lenin (poetry) 1924
[*Vladimir Ilyich Lenin,* 1970]
Amerikanskiye stikhi (poetry) 1926
Kak delat' stikhi? (essay) 1926
[*How are Verses Made?,* 1970]
Khorosho! (poetry) 1927
Klop (drama) 1929
[*The Bedbug, and Selected Poetry,* 1961]
Banya (drama) 1930
[*The Bathhouse* published in *The Complete Plays of Vladimir Mayakovsky,* 1968]
Mayakovsky and His Poetry (autobiography and poetry) 1942
Polnoe sobranie sochinenii Mayakovskogo. 13 vols. (poetry) 1955-1961
The Complete Plays of Vladimir Mayakovsky (dramas) 1968

D. S. MIRSKY (essay date 1926)

[*Mirsky was a Russian prince who fled his country after the Bolshevik Revolution and settled in London. While in England, he wrote two important and comprehensive histories of Russian literature,* Contemporary Russian Literature *(1926) and* A History of Russian Literature *(1927). In 1932, having reconciled himself to the Soviet regime, Mirsky returned to the U.S.S.R. He continued to write literary criticism, but his work eventually ran afoul of Soviet censors and he was exiled to Siberia. He disappeared in 1937. In the following excerpt, Mirsky discusses the distinctive features of Mayakovsky's poetic style and cites the ways in which it radically differs from the Symbolist poetry that preceded it.*]

In 1911 [Mayakovsky] came in contact with the beginning Futurists and began writing verse. He was hardly distinguished at first from the other Futurists, but gradually he began to emerge as something essentially different from the rest. His poetry was not intended for the studio, but for the street; it was free from "trans-sense"; it was full of human interest; and it was frankly rhetorical—only rhetorical in a very new and unexpected way. (p. 270)

Mayakovsky's poetry is extraordinarily unlike that of the Symbolists: he recognizes as the only poet who at all influenced him (except the Futurists) the satirist Sasha Cherny. . . . In prosody Mayakovsky is a continuer of the Symbolists; but the destruction of the classical syllabism of Russian verse which with them was only one of many tendencies becomes a fully developed system with Mayakovsky. His versification is based on the number of stress-accents (which in Russian is equivalent to the number of words) in a line, and completely disregards all unstressed syllables. His rhyming system is also a development of Symbolist tendencies, but here again Mayakovsky has made a coherent system of what was only a tendency with the Symbolists: the principal stress is laid on the consonants preceding and following the rhyming vowel; the quality and even the number of vowels that come after the stress is indifferent. He revels in long rhymes composed of more than one word and in punning rhymes—his whole method of rhyming would vividly remind the English reader of Browning: *ranunculus* and *Tommy-make-room-for-your-uncle-us* would be a good equivalent of the more conservative type of Mayakovskian rhyme. Mayakovsky's new versification has had a very wide influence on Russian poetry, but it has not succeeded in superseding the old syllabic system, which is, after all, much more various and full of resource than his.

Mayakovsky's poetry is very loud, very unrefined, and stands absolutely outside the distinction between "good" and "bad" taste. He uses the diction of every day in its cruder forms, deforming it to suit his needs in a direction opposite to that of the older poetical tradition. His language is free from "trans-sense" elements; but, considered as a literary language, it is a new dialect, a dialect which is entirely his own creation. For the way he puts to use the elements of spoken language makes them sound quite different from the usual. The harmony of his verse with its heavy emphatic beat and its rude "unmusical" choice of sound is like the music of a drum or of a saxophone. There is a certain affinity between Mayakovsky and Mr. Vachel Lindsay. But, apart from the difference of spirit animating the two poets, Mr. Lindsay's poetry is essentially musical, intended to be sung in chorus—Mayakovsky's cannot be sung at all; it is declamatory, rhetorical—the verse of an open-air orator. Judged but by "Victorian" standards, his verse is simply not poetry at all; and judged by Symbolist standards, it is no better. But it is largely owing to our Symbolist education, which has widened to such an extent our poetical sensibility, that we are capable of appreciating this rowdy and noisy rhetoric. Mayakovsky is genuinely popular and read by a very wide circle of readers. His appeal is direct and simple, his subjects can interest the most uncultured, while the high originality of his craftmanship makes him a paramount figure in the eyes of the professional poet.

Mayakovsky's favourite method of expression comprises (besides purely verbal effects based on the utilization of "unpoetical" diction) metaphor and hyperbole. Both his metaphors and his hyperboles are developed in a realistic way, which recalls to a certain extent the *concetti* of the seventeenth century. He indulges in what his commentators call the "realization of metaphor," which is a powerful way of giving life to worn-out clichés: if he introduces the hackneyed metaphor of his heart burning with love, he heightens it by developing a whole realistic picture of a fire with firemen in casques and

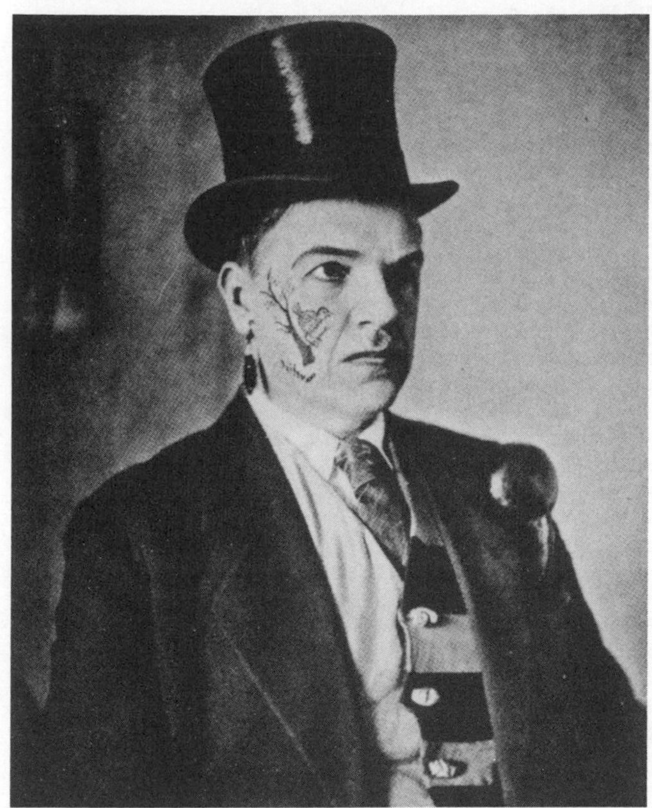

Mayakovsky's friend and benefactor David Burlyuk, dressed and made up in a Futurist manner. Leonard Hutton Galleries, New York.

top-boots infesting the burning heart. If he symbolizes the Russian people in the colossal figure of the *moujik* Ivan, the champion of Communism, he describes in detail how he wades the Atlantic to fight in single combat the champion of capitalism, Woodrow Wilson. The inspiration of Mayakovsky's poetry is materialistic and realistic—this is his principal ground in common with atheistic Communism. His credo is expressed best of all in four lines of the prologue to the ***Mystery-Bouffe:***

> We are fed up with heavenly candies,
> Give us real rye-bread to feed on!
> We are fed up with cardboard passions,
> Give us a live wife to live with!

But of the genuine spirit of Communism, there is very little in Mayakovsky, and the responsible Communists easily discern in him a dangerous individualism. Though "Mayakovsky," who is the hero of most of Mayakovsky's early poems, may be interpreted as a synthetic impersonation, he is more naturally taken as the actual man, and in his political poems the pathos is revolutionary, to be sure, and atheistic, but it is only superficially dyed in Socialist colours. Mayakovsky is not a humorist; in his satires he inveighs instead of ridiculing. He is an orator, and even his crudities and coarseness serve the ends of serious poetry. This is one of his most original features.

Mayakovsky's principal works are his longer poems. Those written before 1917 are mainly egotistic in inspiration. There is a distinct decadent and neurasthenic element at the bottom of their loud clamour. The most remarkable of these poems are ***Man,*** an atheistic apotheosis of self, and ***The Cloud in Trousers,*** a "sentimental" poem with definite revolutionary "premonitions." . . . The lyrical poem ***I Love*** . . . is perhaps the most immediately attractive of his poems for the general poetry-reader: it is free from excessive crudities, but constructed throughout on a system of elaborate *concetti*. His latest big poem is also on the subject of love. It is far less attractive, and, on the whole, is tedious. It appeared with the portrait of the woman to whom it is addressed, whose name is universally known and who is the wife of one of his literary an personal friends. It marks a certain decline of his powers, and the same is noticeable in all his recent work . . . , much of which is again satire or propaganda written to order. (pp. 271-73)

D. S. Mirsky, "Poetry after 1910," in his Contemporary Russian Literature: 1881-1925, *Alfred A. Knopf, 1926, pp. 253-80.**

ALEXANDER KAUN (essay date 1941)

[*Kaun was an American educator and translator specializing in Russian literature. In the following excerpt from an essay originally published in 1941 in the* Slavonic Year Book, *he defines Mayakovsky's stature as a poet of the Revolution and examines the language of some of his well-known works.*]

Mayakovsky must be treated . . . as *the* poet of the revolution, which stimulated his growth and absorbed fully his strength, talent, and time. After 1917 he personified whatever was vital and creative in futurism, and his desperate efforts at harnessing his Pegasus to the chariot of a proletarian revolution proved pathetic. From 1923 to 1930, the year of his death, Mayakovsky made at least four public shifts of his position in the direction of proletarian orthodoxy. These shifts showed the catastrophic maladjustment of Mayakovsky, whose suicide brought an end to the chapter of futurism in its various ramifications. (p. 40)

Whatever came from his pen had the sparkle of his talent, the unmistakable Mayakovsky touch that distinguished every utterance of his, regardless of the subject matter. Form was to him all-important: the form in which the revolution could be expressed was to be as fresh and new as the very contents of the new life. Thus futurism was not an external whim with Mayakovsky, but an inseparable essence of his creative self—and of the revolution. (p. 43)

A Cloud in Pants . . . is the most characteristic long poem of Mayakovsky. Here primitive exuberance alternates with sophisticated satire and venomous hatred of the modern environment. The pattern is intricate; extremely individualistic notes are interwoven with social motives. This complexity is foreshadowed in the Prologue, wherein he "teases" the smug reader with the alternative of being now "ferocious," now "changing tones like the sky, irreproachably tender, not a male but a cloud in pants." The poet's "I" dominates the poem from the beginning to the end, varying in mood and key, the sardonically arrogant note prevailing. Thus: "I, insolent and caustic, shall satiate myself with mockery. There is not one white hair in my soul, nor any senile tenderness. Bethundering the world with the might of my voice, I march—handsome, twenty-two-years-old." Or, farther down: "Glorify me! I am no match for the great. I inscribe 'Nihil' over everything done before me." . . . Here and there megalomania gives place to humility and the groan of an aching heart. Mayakovsky, loather of sentimentalism and hackneyed words, holds his own even when he faces so ancient a theme as unrequited love. Old words and much-used similes he employs with ironic exaggeration that lends to his personal grief a Gargantuan aspect, the tragic mingling with the comic and tempered by it. When "Maria" rejects him, he telephones to his mother: "Hello! . . . Mama? Mama! Your son is superbly sick! Mama! He has a conflagration of the heart. . . . He has no place to go. Every word of his, even the jest which he belches through his singed mouth, is hurled out like a naked prostitute from a bawdy house on fire." Then he proceeds to picture the conflagration in his heart, with firemen in brass helmets and heavy boots scaling his ribs, and himself making a desperate and vain effort to "leap out of his heart." This method notwithstanding, Mayakovsky fails to hide the genuineness of his yearning pain.

Indeed, he is most genuine and convincing when he opens his heart and becomes "human—all-too-human." Pretensions are then discarded, obsessions of grandeur are replaced by the humble cry of a big, an "enormous" body which "at night craves to hide its resonance within something soft, womanly." His entreaties to Maria, despite all hyperboles, betray his helplessness before a primitive emotion. (pp. 44-6)

Parallel with this personal lyricism, the poem contains a motive of rebellion. Mayakovsky addresses the "street thousands—students, prostitutes, contractors," not as a superior, but as one of the lowly, "vomited by a consumptive night into the palm of Moscow." He is a twentieth-century François Villon, a singer of the rabble, of criminals and harlots, of the miserable and the destitute. The poet, "a lip-shouting Zarathustra of today," he of "the most golden mouth, whose every word newbears the soul, angeldays the body," he calls upon the crowds to show self-respect: "You are not beggars, you dare not beg for alms!" He advises them that, though convicts and lepers, they are "purer than Venetian azure." They may be pockmarked and besmudged, yet "the sun would grow dim on beholding the gold quartz of their souls!" The poet himself, "derided by today's tribe like a long, scabrous anecdote," assures the masses that he is capable of perceiving ahead, where "men's docktailed eyes stop short." Indeed, he prophesies, proving wrong only by one year, "the advent of the year Sixteen, in the thorny crown of revolutions." Mayakovsky proclaims himself the "forerunner" of the pending event: "I am where there is pain—everywhere. On every drop of a flowing tear I have crucified myself." The "event" he describes graphically enough, allowing for the savage war censorship of 1915: "Suddenly both stormclouds and the other cloud folk raised an unheard-of racket in the sky, as though bloused workmen scurried, upon declaring a furious strike against heaven. Raging, thunder crept out from behind a cloud, saucily blew its gigantic nostrils, and for a second the skyey face twitched in the stern grimace of an iron Bismarck."

Unlike the majority of the Russian intelligentsia who had dreams of a gentle, fairy-tale transformation, Mayakovsky envisages the revolution as a bloody affair. He foresees another "General Galliffet come to shoot the rebels! Take the hands out your pockets, you strollers, pick up a stone, a knife, or a bomb, and he who has no hands let him come and butt with his forehead!" . . . Clearly, Mayakovsky's vision of the revolution did not go at the moment beyond riot, anarchy, and slaughter.

I have dwelt at some length on ***A Cloud in Pants,*** because this poem epitomizes Mayakovsky's art both before and after 1917. For although with the revolution he matured politically, and as a tribune of the people he began to write more simply, Mayakovsky remained essentially the same as a man and as a poet. This brings us back to the question of his style, which ought to be discussed, if only briefly.

By his upbringing and make-up Mayakovsky was an enemy of the social order as it existed up to 1917. He detested everything connected with it; above all, its aesthetics, in which he saw the reflection of its tyranny and smugness. From his very first attempt at writing he steadfastly eschewed the use of words that comprise the stock in trade of conventional poetry. In all his voluminous output you will not find a single worn epithet for the description of nature or man or emotions. When he does employ canned phrases, he obviously holds his tongue in his cheek, as some of the quoted excerpts may show. Yet Mayakovsky's rich and colorful (at times even gaudy) vocabulary has little if any of the *zaúm,* irrational, element introduced by the futurists. He does not coin entirely new words, but rather multiplies and variegates existing roots by means of the endless choice of prefixes and suffixes that make the Russian speech so elastic, precise, and suggestive. By taking liberties with grammar and syntax, by the unexpected juxtaposition of sounds and words, he lends freshness and newness to otherwise familiar language. He does not hesitate to abbreviate or augment words, or to combine two into one for the sake of nuance and euphony, nor to change adverbs into adjectives, verbs into nouns, and *vice versa,* nor to omit prepositions when the meaning is clear without them, especially when their presence threatens cacophony. His language thus escapes being smooth and neat, calm and correct "like the pulse of a corpse," to use one of his characteristic similes. It is not the language of the salon or the study, but one of street harangue, and is therefore bold, irregular, trenchant, and laconic.

Similarly, in prosody Mayakovsky revolts against canonized aesthetics. The melodiousness of the Russian tonic-syllabic verse nauseated him by its trim regularity. His verse, not unlike Russian folk poetry, is based on the number of stressed syllables in a line, with no regard for the nonstressed syllables; this results in flexible tonality and greater freedom of rhythm. Coupled with metric irregularity is the typographic feature of broken lines. Mayakovsky writes not for silent reading, but for loud declamation. Not trusting punctuation marks, which he uses very sparingly, he directs the reader's intonation by making each line an accented unit. . . . (pp. 46-9)

Mayakovsky's verse, when not free or blank, is rhymed in the most whimsical way. He has discovered a wealth of consonant possibilities, for the most part unprecedented in Russian poetry. He alternates subtle inner rhymes with clusters of words combined to echo the ending of a previous line. Some of his rhyming tricks verge on puns, and make one question the poet's earnestness.

A more important feature of Mayakovsky's style is his metaphors. Here he manifestly differs from both realist and symbolist poets, for his images are neither of the everyday variety, like the former's, nor do they represent abstractions, like the latter's. In the language of the Schoolmen, he strives after *realiora.* He is never abstract, and even supernatural images he drags down to earth and renders concrete and sensory. At the same time, he clothes his metaphors in a hyperbolic form, deliberately, and often not without humor, exaggerating dimensions and concepts. The description of his heart on fire, quoted above, may illustrate the point. After 1917, especially in his ***Mystery Bouffe*** . . . and in ***150,000,000*** . . . Mayakovsky made abundant use of this hyperbolic style. The revolutionary upheaval, complicated by wars, invasions, the blockade, and their concomitant misery and suffering, heightened the tone of life, quickened its tempo—in a word, lent life a heroic style. Mayakovsky felt in his element, employing and even enhancing his hyperbolic method, now that his country and his people have made the improbable real by defeating seemingly insurmountable obstacles. There is elemental grandeur in the scene of his Unclean Ones storming the universe (***Mystery Bouffe***), or in his titanic Woodrow Wilson, personifying the capitalist order, and equally gargantuan Ivan, the collective embodiment of the victorious proletariat (***150,000,000***). The revolutionary period, its formative years, its groping efforts at destroying and building, its Homeric aspect, found a suitable poet in Mayakovsky.

It would be futile to search for Mayakovsky's indebtedness to other poets. He was not a man of books; traditions and clichés revolted him. There was no Russian poet, before him or during his lifetime, whom he even remotely resembled. It might be easier, indeed, to discover a kinship between Mayakovsky and certain poets of the Western world, specifically the *poètes maudits*. The term need not here be applied only to the French group of the Baudelaire-Rimbaud variety, but to all poets with whom Mayakovsky shared an extreme accentuation of the personal ego, a bent for the sublimation of base subjects and common "street" words, a fondness for new, striking forms and rhythms, and similar unorthodox leanings. This kinship is of a general nature, however. One may point out, in the same way, Mayakovsky's affinity for Verhaeren's note of urbanism, not forgetting how differently the two men treated city themes and voices. Mayakovsky's preoccupation with his self sounds often like an echo of Walt Whitman. (pp. 50-1)

As already noted, Mayakovsky wrote about nine-tenths of his work after 1917. During the last thirteen years of his life he grew to his full stature. The revolution and its multiple tasks filled his void, and gave meaning and contents to his resentments, grievances, and vague aspirations. His style, too, matured, became free from obscurity, from trickery, from an excessive burden of smiles, and from dispensable coarseness. A style of the street, it now represented not the street of strutting philistines, criminals, pimps, and prostitutes, but the streets and squares of a country jolted from age-old apathy to a desperate struggle for its existence and a finer life. Mayakovsky was proud to consider himself a worker, a sharer in the national travail, never too squeamish about using his pen or brush or voice for "propaganda." "I feel as if I were a Soviet workshop, manufacturing happiness. I do not care to be plucked after a day of toil, like a flower off the meadow. . . . I want the Gosplan [State Planning Commission] to sweat while discussing the assignment of my year's tasks. I want the pen to be put on the same footing with the bayonet. I want Stalin in the name of the Politbureau to present reports on the production of verse along with reports on pig iron and steel."

During these arduous years, in the rare moments of leisure he could find, what with his daily "attacks" waged against the enemies of the new order and his frequent travels at home and abroad, Mayakovsky managed to compose a few long poems and plays, in addition to his shorter writings. One of the plays, ***Mystery Bouffe,*** was in verse, a heroic rhapsody of the revolution. The two prose plays, ***The Bedbug*** . . . and ***The Bathhouse*** . . . , castigated philistine smugness that began to raise its head in the "normal" years following the civil wars. Among his travel poems, the cycle on the United States . . . is noteworthy: he caught the rhythm of the country, mingling his admiration for its technological advancement with his revulsion from the wastage and cruelty of its economic order. Of the long poems of that period, mention has been made of ***150,000,000,*** with its theme of the clash between Wilson, personifying Western capitalism, and the peasant Ivan, who symbolizes the Russian masses. ***Of This*** . . . sounded like a relapse into preoccupation with his self and a futile quest of completeness in love. Unlike this poem, his ***'Tis Good!*** was exuberant and social in motive, voicing a militant optimism about the land of Soviets. His most ambitious long poem is *Vladimir Ilich Lenin* . . . written shortly after the death of the man. Here the poet's ever-present note of personal lyricism merges with the broad notes of a national epic. Kalinin's announcement of Lenin's death to the Congress of Soviets, and the scene of the funeral, are among Mayakovsky's highest achievements. There is not one loud word or obvious emotionalism, and the author's unwonted reserve intensifies the tragic sense of the moment.

The life and work of Mayakovsky have been an open book, largely owing to the extrovert nature of his verse. He has turned himself inside out, flaunted intimate details of his past and present, painted a self-portrait of full length and depth. Everything about him, as suggested previously, was elemental and elementary, therefore simple and lucid. Everything, except for one thing: his end. (pp. 53-4)

The death of Mayakovsky . . . came as a surprise, for he had given no obvious signs of maladjustment.

Quite to the contrary. Five years previously, Yesenin, a popular imagist poet, cut his wrists and hanged himself, a victim of drunken debauches, ill-digested fame, and notoriety, and of an ideally mismatched marriage (to Isadora Duncan). Dipping the pen into the blood of his slashed wrists (there was a shortage of ink at the time), Yesenin scribbled a note that ended with the lines:

> In this life 'tis nothing new to die,
> Nor is it, of course, more novel to live.

Mayakovsky felt a need of counteracting Yesenin's gesture. In a later essay, **"How to Make Verses,"** reminiscent of Poe's would-be confession of how he wrote his "Raven," Mayakovsky explained his methods and moods in composing the poem **"To Sergey Yesenin,"** . . . as well as his main motive. Yesenin's final lines, he was convinced, precisely because they were *verse* (italics his), "would draw many vacillating citizens into the noose and in front of the revolver muzzle." Although Mayakovsky's poem was written in his usual bantering tone, one feels keenly its warmth of emotion and the personal concern of a poet chiding his brother for a fainthearted act. He admits that "this time is rather hard for the pen," but then, he asks, "where, when, what great man has chosen a worn and easy path?" Life must be remade—such is the task of the moment. He ends with a paraphrase of Yesenin's lines:

> In this life
> 'tis not hard to die.
> To mold life
> is far more difficult.

This sentiment deceived the public with respect to Mayakovsky's state of mind. He probably deceived himself into believing that he was perfectly at home and at ease under the Soviet regime. There is no question about the sincerity and loyalty of his attitude toward the new order. His service to the "attacking class" was both wholehearted and effective, the latter merit being acknowledged even by Lenin, who personally failed to appreciate Mayakovsky's poetry. But neither can there be any question about the inner split that he experienced most of the time, even—or especially—when protesting his buoyant faith the loudest. For him the difficulty of "molding life" consisted in harmonizing the moods and whims of the bohemian individualist he had been up to 1917, with the convictions of the disciplined Bolshevik he valiantly strove to be thereafter. His last poems, especially ***Of This*** and ***In Full Voice*** . . . , show the cumulative intensity of his inner contradictions, which proved catastrophic. He tells us that again and again he endeavored to stifle the individualist in him, that he "put his foot on the throat of his song." The half-smothered note persisted, however, as an overtone, and insinuated itself now and then as a moan. I refer to such recurrent motives as loneliness, suicide, unrequited love, being misunderstood and underrated by his contemporaries. Here belongs his masterly ***Jubilean,*** wherein he takes the bronze Pushkin for a stroll, after removing him from his pedestal in the famous Moscow square. In a half-jesting tone, behind which one is aware of his profound pain, he pours his heart out to his great predecessor, another rebel who smashed his head against the wall of environment. Mayakovsky confides to Pushkin that soon he too will be dead, and then their names will stand not so far apart in the alphabet of the great. (pp. 55-7)

It is clear—"clear to the point of hallucination," as Mayakovsky would say—that the poet was not a monochrome (Soviet writers prefer the word "monolith"). His inner conflicts and contradictions made his life a tragedy; but they were hardly detrimental to his poetry. The two—or more-selves of this monumental child of nature were voiced forcefully and with unique skill. Regardless of his emotional "deviations," Mayakovsky's work will live chiefly as an expression of the Will to Revolution and, therefore, as most representative of contemporary Russia. (p. 58)

Alexander Kaun, "Postsymbolists," in his Soviet Poets and Poetry, *University of California Press, 1943, pp. 35-97.**

HERBERT MARSHALL (essay date 1945)

[*Marshall is an English editor and translator who has compiled many anthologies of contemporary Russian literature, including the first selection of Mayakovsky's work to appear in English. In the following excerpt, he discusses some of the prominent motifs and technical innovations of Mayakovsky's poetry.*]

Mayakovsky is the poet of the city and the worker. Throughout his works there are practically no images of the countryside, there is very little of "nature" or "nightingales," nothing of the usual clichés of poetry. But you will find boulevards, squares, the bustle of the street, the polish of the asphalt, the noise of machines, the glass eyes of houses, the backbones of roofs, the work of man, the rhythm of revolution, the struggle of society.

He said in one of his speeches . . . "Why must I write about the love of Jack and Jill and not consider myself part of the social organism which is building life? A poet is not he who goes about with long hair and bleats on lyrical love themes. A poet is he, who in an era of sharpened class struggle, gives his pen into the arsenal of the armed proletariat, and fears no job, however prosaic, and fears no theme, whether of revolution, or the reconstruction of our national economy." (p. 3)

Translating Mayakovsky is a tough job, but my feeling is that he fits more easily into the English language than into any other except his own. It is interesting to note that his style was foreshadowed by our own Coleridge, in his poem "Christabel," in which Coleridge made an attempt to break away from the rigid metrical forms of classic poetry. In his preface to his poem Coleridge wrote: "I have only to add that the metre of 'Christabel' is not, properly speaking, irregular, though it may seem so from its being founded on a new principle: namely, that of counting in each line the accents, not the syllables. Though the latter may vary from seven to twelve, yet in each line the accents will be found to be only four. Nevertheless, this occasional variation in number of syllables is not introduced wantonly, or for the mere ends of convenience, but in correspondence with some transition in the nature of the imagery or passion." (p. 8)

But Coleridge's innovation, which broke the rigidity of traditional metric forms, did not find its right and proper usage until over a hundred years later in another language, in the works of a poet who never knew how exactly his revolutionary style was foreshadowed by his English predecessor.

For Mayakovsky developed it still further; his real unit is the expressive gesture of the orator, the accent of *meaning;*

Not:

> My verse with labour thrusts through weighted years
> emerging ponderous, rock-rough, age-grim,
> as when to-day an aqueduct appears
> firm-grounded once by the branded slaves of Rome.

But:

> My verse
>   with lábour
>   thrústs through weighted yéars
> emérging
>   pónderous
>   rock-róugh,
>   age-grim,
> as whén to-dáy
>   an áqueduct appéars,
> firm-gróunded once
>   by the bránded sláves of Róme.

Almost at a glance the difference is felt, and even more so when read out aloud. Let the reader try it, and he will see that Mayakovsky's staccato lines are not just whims.

These lines may vary from a single syllable

> I

to an unbroken line like

> and not like the light of long-dead stars arrives,

where the length and alliteration are appropriate to the image. And of course such a method immediately dispenses with capital letters, except where they should be, at the beginning of a new sentence, or for proper names.

Mayakovsky also made his own punctuation and his own words, but not formalistically. He said: "Our usual punctuation with full stops, commas, etc., is far too poor and limited in expression in comparison with those shades of emotions which the complex man to-day compresses into his poetic productions." That is also a reason why he punctuates, as it were, spatially.

Mayakovsky did not despise rhymes, on the contrary he valued them very much, worked very hard on them. But they are rarely used at short intervals, they echo rather, and that with dissonant resemblance. And his rhyme is for the most part regular through every other main line. Here, of course, is where translation pales the original. Mayakovsky's rhymes are superb, they are apt in meaning, unique in their originality and endless in their variety. (pp. 8-9)

Herbert Marshall, in a foreword to Mayakovsky and His Poetry *by Vladimir Mayakovsky, edited by Herbert Marshall, revised edition, 1945. Reprint by Transatlantic Arts Inc., 1946, pp. 1-10.*

M. L. ROSENTHAL (essay date 1961)

[*Rosenthal is an American poet, critic, and editor. Among his most influential studies are* The Modern Poets *(1960) and* The New Poets *(1967), which analyze the verse of some of the most important poets of the twentieth century. Rosenthal's critical method is marked by its independence from any particular school of criticism and by its emphasis on individual poems, which the critic attempts to place within the general context of modern literature. According to Robert Langbaum: "His strength as a critic comes from the consistency of his criteria, from the theoretical power behind the flexible judgments of individual poems and poets." In the following excerpt, Rosenthal examines the emotional intensity of Mayakovsky's poetry and discusses the ways in which it revealed his ambivalence toward the new social order in postrevolutionary Russia.*]

Almost everything, good or bad, I have ever read by Vladimir Mayakovsky—or heard about him—has suggested that vibrant order of human presence without which ideas and faiths are but abstractions and art is but ritual or affectation. I associate his poetry, somewhat arbitrarily, with the memory of certain Yiddish poets and actors I heard declaiming in my childhood; it has the same gloriously rhetorical manner unknown to most English-speaking poets today. At its best, this manner is not bombast but the acting out of a role to its hilt, like the rhetoric of *King Lear*. In someone like Mayakovsky it is the realization, through passion, of feeling so intense it seems to break the shell of art within which it came to birth and to go on to a life of its own:

> I feel
> my "I"
> is too small for me.
> Stubbornly a body pushes out of me.
> Hello!
> Who's speaking?
> Mamma?
> Mamma!
> Your son is gloriously ill!
> Mamma!
> His heart is on fire.
> Tell his sisters, Lyuda and Olya,
> he has no nook to hide in. . . .

A poet who writes like this has gone beyond his formal technique, like a scientist who, having solved his problem, is no longer concerned with the laboratory equipment. He has got to where he was going. That may be why some poets burn up the resources of their art at such an early age, abandoning it as Rimbaud did or, at the saddest extreme, committing suicide as Hart Crane and Mayakovsky both did in their thirties, and as Dylan Thomas did less deliberately. Whatever poetry at so intense a pitch of projection may say to the reader, to the poet it is an irrevocable commitment, an end in itself, an achieved state that leaves him naked in the wind.

It is the same anguish that dominates his last note: "This is not a way out (I do not recommend it to others), but I have none other. . . . Seriously—there was nothing else I could do. Greetings."

Greetings! It is as from Jesus on the cross, if we imagine a Jesus completely absorbed in the compulsion to sacrifice himself and in the sensation of crucifixion rather than in spiritual indoctrination. (But there is also an elusive but inescapable "spiritual" side to Mayakovsky, particularly in his pursuit of the meaning of love in so many poems. In this respect, he is not far from the paradoxical Christianity of William Blake.) And indeed, in **"The Cloud in Trousers"** Mayakovsky had written:

> I am where pain is—everywhere;
> on each drop of the ear-flow
> I have nailed myself on the cross. . . .

An earlier poem, **"I,"** written before he was twenty, brings out the anguish of realization in a hard ironic imagery of cruelty. The poet in a personal way, the Russian people in their revolutionary break from the past, are seen awaking to the death of their previous, childlike innocence and to the horrors behind the awakening:

> I love to watch children dying.
> Do you note, behind protruding
> nostalgia,
> the shadowy billow of laughter's
> surf?
> But I—
> in the reading room of the streets—
> have leafed so often through the
> volume of the coffin.

Hart Crane is the only American poet who could have written these terrifying lines. They strike with an unforgettable authority that is the key to Mayakovsky. "Behind his manner," writes Pasternak, "Something like decision took one by surprise, decision when it is already put into action and its consequences can no longer be averted. His genius was such a decision, and a meeting with it had once so amazed him that it became his theme's prescription for all times, for the incarnation of which he gave himself without pity or vacillation."

It was Mayakovsky's fate to be dramatically "present," in a way that Pasternak, with his tangential subtleties and fastidiousness of personality, could not have been. Given his background as a Communist in early youth, expelled from school, imprisoned; and given his need to dominate the occasion, he had to become *the* spokesman of that electric Russian moment in which his exuberant and tragic youth realized itself. It was he who made his poetry a bridge between the devout past and the Bolshevist future of Russia. . . . (pp. 211-212)

Then, just as war converts individual men with opinions into uninformed soldiers, the Soviet State partially converted the *poète maudit* and prophet into a civil servant, a slogan-coiner and jingle-maker and official bard. Since he was one of those people who must be noticed, must be heard, whether "right" or "wrong" and under whatever system they live, he allowed himself to be used this way and even pitched himself into it with great enthusiasm. Yet he realized clearly that he was sacrificing himself in this work, and tried in the poem **"An Extraordinary Adventure Which Befell Vladimir Mayakovsky in a Summer Cottage"** to construct an image of heroic expenditure of energies for the common good that would justify the stupendous waste of talent:

> Suddenly—I
> shone in all my might,
> and morning rang its round.

Always to shine,
to shine everywhere,
to the very deeps of the last days,
to shine—
and to hell with everything else!
That is my motto—
and the sun's!

This vision of sacrificial service seemed appropriate enough for the poet who had once expressed the wish to glorify "men as crumpled as hospital beds" and "women as battered as proverbs." Mayakovsky was sure he could reconcile it with his own extravagant, original personality, and it took a dozen hectic years to wear his morale down to the point at which he could no longer find reassurance in the meaning of the world he had helped create. Probably, too, as with Hart Crane at the end, his poetry was no longer a source of strength to him; the battery had gone dead. What wore him down, [in the opinion of Patricia Blake] was not so much hostile criticism as a growing sense of the coming terror of the Stalin period. But until these two kinds of breakdown, personal and political, combined to destroy him, Mayakovsky handled himself confidently.

Moreover, despite propagandistic poems like ***150,000,000*** (categorized by Pasternak as "uncreative"), he continued to write in the old intransigent brooding way. The 1922 sequence **"I Love"** is not political but psychological, self-analytical. It traces his pursuit of an ultimate, essential experience of a love made spiritual to the bitter deprivations of childhood when his "little heart" had had to content itself with nothing human but only the sun, the river, and a "hundred mile stretch of rock." In Paris the poet became entangled with the most un-proletarian of creatures, the elegant White Russian émigrée who is the subject of **"Letter from Paris to Comrade Kostrov on the Nature of Love."** The poem is brilliant in its evocation of the sensuousness and turmoil of this love, and explicit in its defiance. . . . (p. 212)

In the year of his death Mayakovsky summoned up all his indignation and disdain in the merciless, unfinished **"At the Top of My Voice."** He contrasts himself with the sycophantic operators, phonies and effeté half-poets of the new order (attacking them by name). He chooses a deliberately unglamorous but extremely sardonic figure (when we consider that the Revolution had originally meant *freedom* to its finest proponents) for the meaning of his own career:

My verse
by labor
will break the mountain chain of years,
and will present itself
ponderous,
crude,
tangible,
as an aqueduct,
by slaves of Rome
constructed. . . .

Then came the crackup. Until that moment he was one of those people of such stature, with voices so ringingly and hypnotically sure, that they survive and make themselves felt long after weaker mortals have lost both courage and perspective. Look at his ***The Bedbug. . . .*** It is a kind of miracle, but it really was produced. In the first act its protagonist, Prisypkin, is a comic villain, a formerly militant worker who abandons his class-consciousness and his true love to make himself a comfortable marriage and gain all the vulgar, bourgeois satisfactions. Amid the clowning and the marvelous incidental satire he shows up as a pretty contemptible fellow. A drunken quarrel at the wedding leads to a fire in which everyone except Prisypkin is killed. He is preserved in the ice formed from water the firemen's hoses have poured into the zero-cold cellar and is found fifty years later. The second part of the play concerns the unfreezing of Prisypkin in the Utopian world of the future, a world completely if benevolently regimented—scientific, hygienic, banal, and free of art, romance, or, indeed, any kind of purely personal meaning. Now Prisypkin, that same drunken, self-centered, unclean, unpredictable lout, becomes a tragic hero. Before he can infect too many others with his "diseases," he is isolated in the zoo, while the bedbug preserved with him from an earlier era is hunted down and put away as a rare and valuable specimen. At the end we see him pleading with his fellow citizens of the advanced Socialist society to become "unfrozen" and rejoin him in his suffering ordinary humanity.

First produced in 1928, the play was no great success. In 1955, however, it was revived and became, according to Miss Blake, a "smash hit." Actually, the play was first produced before the most reactionary era had set in, so that as Miss Blake suggests few people gave it very serious attention. But the very fact that it had been produced probably created a certain "tolerance" for it (though Meyerhold, its first producer, is said to have died in a concentration camp after 1939). In any case, it seems hard to doubt that the play means what it seems to mean, and that it reveals the two sides of Mayakovsky—his devotion to the Soviet cause and his hatred and fear of the mediocrity and the taming of the soul that cause nourished in its bosom. If this is true, then his Prisypkin is the poor, crucified Everyman of *Ulysses* and of *Waiting for Godot,* as well as of the beveled-and-leveled future envisioned by the publicists and planners of East and West alike. (pp. 212-13)

M. L. Rosenthal, "No Nook to Hide In," in The Nation, *Vol. 193, No. 10, September 30, 1961, pp. 211-13.*

VICTOR ERLICH (essay date 1962)

[Erlich is a Russian-born literary critic specializing in Slavic languages and literature. In the following excerpt, he examines Mayakovsky's poetry for evidence of the tension generated by the poet's attempt to maintain the voices of both a spokesperson for the Revolution and that of a highly individualistic artist.]

In a recent memoir Iurii Olesha, one of the most sophisticated Soviet prose writers, recalls a conversation he once had with V.E. Meyerhold regarding a film version of Turgenev's *Fathers and Sons* which the famous *avant-garde* director was then contemplating. "I asked him whom he had in mind for the part of Bazarov. He answered, 'Mayakovsky'."

The resemblance between one of modern Russia's foremost poets and Turgenev's harshly antipoetic hero may not be immediately obvious. Yet a close look at Mayakovsky's poetry, especially at his earlier, Futurist lyrics, reveals the presence of what might be called the Bazarov syndrome. The tenor of these Surrealist urban still-lives (**"Night," "Morning," "The Street,"** etc.), these impassioned lyrical manifestoes (**"I," "Man," "A Cloud in Trousers"**), is *total negation of the status quo*. (p. 433)

It is the savage intensity of this scorn, powerfully projected and strikingly phrased, that propelled Mayakovsky into the first ranks of prewar Russia's angry young men, the Futurists. It is the desperate urgency of his protest, magnified by a booming voice and a blatantly bold imagery, that made the twenty-year-old art student a recognized standard-bearer of the poetic *avant-garde* shortly after he had been "discovered" and hailed as a genius by that erratic yet shrewd impresario of the movement, David Burlyuk.

Though the point has already been tellingly made by Roman Jakobson in his brilliant essay "On the Generation Which Has Squandered Its Poets," it may be worth restating here: the mainsprings of Mayakovsky's revolt, as reflected in his pre-1917 lyrics and his most revealing Soviet poems, were not primarily political. His radicalism was that of a Bohemian rather than of a doctrinaire Marxist. This is not to deny such relevant facts as Mayakovsky's early involvement with the revolutionary movement, which cost him eleven months in prison when he was still a high school boy, or to question the sincerity of the retrospective statement in the poet's brief autobiography: "No work of art has ever fascinated me more than Marx's 'Introduction' [to *Critique of Political Economy*—V.E.]." Yet the image of the lone rebel which emerges from the violent, apocalyptic phraseology of his early works is more akin to François Villon or Verlaine than it is to either Marx or Lenin. It is as a *poète maudit,* a spokesman for, and a natural ally of, the metropolitan riffraff, "a twisted-lipped Zarathustra/ of convicts of the city/ leprosorium" that the "I" confronts here the hostile crowd of solid citizens. . . . (pp. 433-34)

Several years later the main target of the poet's anger was to be identified in political or topical terms, be it the Entente (**"Left March"**) or world capitalism (**"150,000,000"**). But in his 1916 credo **"Man,"** whose commanding images were to reverberate through much of Mayakovsky's Soviet period, the poet's chief "rival and foe" is that archenemy of the modern artist—and, we may add, of the Russian intelligent—Philistinism. What is challenged here is not a definite social order but the very principle of order or stasis, everything that smacks of tradition, of habit, of routine, everything that sets limits to the Creator's disheveled, colossal sensibility. In a word, a cluster, which an angry young Englishman is likely to call the Establishment, but which in Russian literary usage is covered by the virtually untranslatable word *byt* (the closest approximations, depending on the context, are "circumstance," "mores," "everyday life," "daily grind"). The quixotic one-man warfare against *byt* clearly could not be won; hence the pessimism of the seldom quoted passage from **"Man,"** where the poet's inveterate foe, the epitome of smug respectability, is addressed thus: "Revolutions shake carcasses of kingdoms/ Changes its drivers the human herd./ But you, the uncrowned ruler of souls/ no rebellion can unseat."

The sense of battling against overwhelming odds is closely bound up here with the motif of an imminent defeat, of an impending doom. In **"A Cloud in Trousers," "The Spine Flute,"** and **"Man,"** and in a short tragedy bearing the characteristic title **"Vladimir Mayakovsky,"** the lyrical protagonist appears time and again as one born too early, a precursor and a martyr of a revolutionary utopia, a St. John the Baptist of "the days to come," doomed to destruction at the hands of the invincible Philistines, or conversely the "last Mohican" of poetic sensibility: "I am bringing my soul on a plate/ to the banquet of the ages to come." . . . "Trickling down the unshaven cheek of a square/ like a superfluous tear/ I am/ perhaps/ the last poet." . . . The pervasive theme of a martyrdom occasions here a wealth of religious imagery, striking in a poet so militantly secular and so blatantly materialistic. Mayakovsky is keenly aware of this contradiction: "I who sing of machines and England/ am perhaps no more than the thirteenth apostle/ in the most ordinary gospel."

The existential anguish that pervades these lines raises emotional frustration to the dignity of cosmic despair. In the savagely tender **"A Cloud in Trousers,"** unrequited love becomes a paradigm of ultimate rejection and homelessness. ("I have no place to go.")

Was Mayakovsky's political commitment an attempt to escape the sense of moral alienation which he expressed so poignantly in his lyrical masterpiece? Or was he, on the eve of a major social upheaval, yielding to the temptations of political action and political power, yielding the more eagerly since Lenin's brutally decisive break with the old seemed to offer the closest equivalent to the Bohemian gospel of total negation and a shortcut to utopia? Be that as it may, in November, 1917, Mayakovsky was ready to give his all to the revolution, or, in his own words, "to offer all my sonorous powers of a poet to you, the attacking class."

Mayakovsky's verse, written in the first years of the revolution, breathe an almost physical exhilaration. In the city in turmoil, in the square, gripped by revolutionary excitement, he found an ideal resonator for his thundering voice, for his boisterous oratory. He felt at home amid the chaos and flux, when routine was displaced and "business as usual" discarded. Joyously Mayakovsky summoned into the street the "Futurists," the "drummers," and the "poets." He celebrated the "second tidal flood" in the powerful staccato of **"Our March,"** a rare instance of fundamentally nonobjective revolutionary poetry, where bursts of released consonantal energy provide an auditory correlative for a revolutionary euphoria. He sang the imminent world revolution is a satirical morality play ***Mystery-Bouffe,*** and in a Communist epic **"150,000,000."** . . . (pp. 434-35)

Interestingly enough, the party leaders were none too impressed. Lenin is known to have walked out on a vigorous rendition of Mayakovsky's **"Our March."** But then Lenin was avowedly a literary conservative, who had little use for modern poetry. ("I prefer Pushkin," he said to a vociferous admirer of Mayakovsky.) The testimony of Lev Trotsky, whose literary sophistication was definitely superior to Lenin's, is of greater moment. In a perceptive, if somewhat priggish essay on Futurism in *Literature and Revolution,* the Bolshevik statesman-turned-critic opined that "Mayakovsky's revolutionary individualism poured itself enthusiastically into the proletarian Revolution, but did not blend with it." [See *TCLC,* Vol. 4] Trotsky shrewdly noted in the very savagery of Mayakovsky's ultramaterialistic attack on "the world-Romantic" accents of negative romanticism and expressed annoyance with the poet's "individualistic and Bohemian arrogance," which, ironically enough, was most apparent in the poem intended as an epic of mass heroism, **"150,000,000."** The idea of portraying the final showdown between the revolutionary masses and world capitalism in the form of a hand-to-hand combat between Woodrow Wilson "swimming in fat" and a Russian superman, Ivan, bearing a distinct resemblance to V. Mayakovsky, struck Trotsky as extravagant and frivolous. Actually, one does not need to share Trotsky's impatience with that creative playfulness which to this reader is the most attractive, indeed the redeeming feature of **"150,000,000"** to concur in his basic diagnosis: Mayakovsky's strenuous attempt to submerge in the collective will his elephantine ego ("no one is the author of this poem of mine'') resulted in another act of self-dramatization. ''Our poet,'' says Trotsky aptly, ''is a Mayako-morphist. . . . When he wants to elevate man, he makes him be Mayakovsky.'' (p. 436)

[While] Trotsky was chiding Mayakovsky for his Bohemian arrogance, A. V. Lunacharsky, the first Soviet commissar of education and Mayakovsky's most influential protector, was gently taking the poet to task for his excessively ''humble'' or humdrum notion of poetry. Lunacharsky was mildly shocked by Mayakovsky's insistence that ''today the poet's chief task is to complain in brisk verse about the bad pavements on Miasnitskaia street'' (a street in Moscow). The traditional roles are reversed here, with the cultural bureaucrat upholding the dignity and glamour of the poet's calling, while the poet strenuously urges a narrowly topical and utilitarian view of his job.

This curious polemic epitomizes an important facet of Mayakovsky's political commitment: no propagandistic chore was too menial for him. He wrote marches, versified slogans and Soviet commercials; he produced thousands of posters and captions deriding the opponents of the regime and eulogizing the Soviet institutions, including the dead Cheka. In his moving farewell poem, **''At the Top of My Voice''**, written on the eve of his suicide, he spoke of himself as a ''latrine cleaner and water carrier/ by the revolution/ mobilized and called to colors/ who went off to the front/ from the aristocratic garden/ of poetry/ the capricious wench.'' He debunked any poetry which was not immediately useful: ''In our days only he is a poet who will write a march and a slogan.'' . . . This eagerness to ''serve'' would occasion such passages as the embarrassing plea for party control over poetry found in a 1925 poem: ''I want/ the Gosplan [State Economic Planning Commission—V.E.] to sweat/ in debate/ assigning me/ goals a year ahead./ I want the factory committee/ to lock/ my lips/ when the work is done/ I want/ the pen to be on a par with the bayonet/ and Stalin/ to deliver his Politburo/ reports about verse in the making/ as he would about pig iron and the smelting of steel.''

It is not easy to disentangle all the implications of the above. Was Mayakovsky affirming the importance of poetry in the only language that Russia's iron age could understand—in that of technology and political expediency? Was this another expression of the Futurist innovator's urge to depoeticize poetry, to eschew the hieratic solemnity of the Symbolist pundit and the sweet mellifluousness of traditional lyrics for the sake of a harsher and more vigorous poetic fare? Perhaps. And yet the spectacle of the impudent rebel begging the party for directives is a profoundly disturbing one. The total loyalty to a political blueprint of the future verges here on aesthetic masochism.

It would not be historically accurate to blame this frenzied ''conformism'' on external pressures alone. That during the last years of his life Mayakovsky was often harassed by envious hacks and zealots is a matter of record. But his act, to use his own words, ''of stepping on the throat of my song'' for the greater glory of the cause was largely a voluntary, spontaneous gesture. (pp. 436-38)

Did Mayakovsky's eagerness to subordinate his work to extrapoetic demands and criteria lead to a debasement of his art and a corrosion of his creative powers? Boris Pasternak seems to imply as much when in *I Remember* he speaks of Mayakovsky's political verse as ''clumsily-rhymed sermons, cultivated insipidity, those commonplaces and platitudes set forth so artificially, so confusedly, and so devoid of humor" [See *TCLC,* Vol. 4].

Many will find this too harsh and too broad an indictment. The qualities which characterized the early Mayakovsky—verbal inventiveness, coarse but vigorous wit, delight in and an uncanny adeptness at striking, unorthodox rhymes—are present in varying degrees in his Soviet productions and make many a jingle of Mayakovsky a more vital work of poetry than the most ambitious poems of dutifully proletarian versifiers. In fact, when viewed against the background of the Kazins, the Zharovs, and the Bezymenskys, Mayakovsky looms up like a giant among pigmies; or should one rather say, a crippled giant?

For when all is said and done, there is hardly anything in Mayakovsky's bulky post-1917 output to rival the striking power and the imaginative freshness of **''A Cloud in Trousers.''** Eloquent passages in Mayakovsky's two programmatic poems, **''V.I. Lenin''** and **''Well Done!,''** the deftly ingenious rhymes of some of his occasional verse, the vitality and gusto of several ''American poems,'' for example, **''The Brooklyn Bridge,''** celebrating the encounter of a Futurist imagination with American technology . . . none of this can quite compensate for the reams of journalistic bombast, of strenuous red-flag waving, not devoid of rhetorical effectiveness but unworthy of Mayakovsky.

It is probably no accident that this poetic champion of Bolshevism is most genuinely and effectively himself in his nonconformist or nonpolitical works. Mayakovsky's plays, ***The Bedbug*** . . . and ***The Bathhouse*** . . . , eloquently attest to his gift for savage satire, sharpened by his growing dismay at the rise of Soviet neo-Philistinism. In **''About This,''** . . . or **''A Letter from Paris to Comrade Kostrov on the Nature of Love,''**. . . the pent-up lyrical urge, bursting the fetters of self-imposed restraint and of civic taboos, ''sweeps everything else aside'' (**''About This''**) to proclaim the uncontrollable, elemental power of personal emotions.

Clearly, Mayakovsky's bondage to the future was taking a heavy toll from the poet and the man alike. By the middle of the twenties the ebullience of **''Our March''** had given way to somber stoicism tinged with weariness. In 1925 the future suicide was chiding his fellow poet, the wayward peasant lyricist, Sergei Esenin, who had just hanged himself in a Leningrad hotel, for having taken an easy way out: ''In this life it isn't difficult to die; to build life is much more difficult.'' The main advantage of life seems now to lie in its being the ''harder'' course of action. Two years later, in one of the most spirited poems of that period, **''A Conversation with a Tax Collector about Poetry,''** Mayakovsky was confessing: ''There is less and less love/ there is less and less daring/ and time/ is a battering ram/ against my head/ then comes the deadliest of all amortizations/ the amortization of the heart and soul.'' In 1928 Mayakovsky was engaged in writing the poem **''Badly Done!,''** clearly a polemic with his own earlier epic of the October Revolutionary, **''Well Done!''** He was telling his friends that only a good, great love could save him from what was apparently a growing depression and disillusionment. (pp. 438-39)

[The keylines in his much quoted suicide note] are chilling in their uncanny casualness, in their thoroughly unmayakovskian restraint: ''As they say, the incident is closed./ Love boat has smashed against circumstance.'' In the original the last word is characteristically *byt,* Mayakovsky's chief term of opprobrium. The stolid, ordinary ''reality'' has caught up with Mayakovsky and defeated him, as back in 1916 he said it would. But this time the dull force that crushed the poet's ''great love'' was to a large extent a matter of artificial barriers erected by the very regime that Mayakovsky had embraced as a major ally in his losing battle against the deadly pull of routine.

Was it ideological disenchantment or emotional frustration that triggered the catastrophe? The matter is too complex to permit of a single explanation. Clearly, the ultimate causes of Mayakovsky's self-destructive act lie deeper than that. Both the *émigré* publicists who saw in Mayakovsky simply another victim of Communist dictatorship and the dutiful Soviet hacks mumbling sheepishly about a sudden and totally unexpected loss of nerve were properly reminded by Roman Jakobson that the theme of the Poet's suicide, of gambling one's life away, had haunted Mayakovsky's poetry ever since 1915. The death wish, the tragic crack *(nadryv),* the Kirilov- or Bazarov-like loneliness had been there from the beginning. The *engagement* had not eliminated these attitudes. It had merely driven them underground. In the last years of the poet's life the despair that howled in his Futurist lyrics seems to have reasserted itself with a redoubled force.

The millennium so eagerly anticipated,, so ardently sought, eluded the poet's grasp. Bolshevism let Mayakovsky down; but so, in all fairness, would have any political system, any stabilized mode of societal existence. More important, voluntary sacrifices made en route to the ever-receding utopia proved costly and self-defeating. The grim singlemindedness of the Bolshevik creed, espoused with an *outré* Bohemian frenzy, encouraged lyrical suicide and thus threatened the very qualities affirmed in the initial act of total defiance—untrammeled self-expression, emotional spontaneity.

Herein lies the tragic irony of Mayakovsky's predicament: it is primarily as an embattled artist that he refused the entrance ticket to the world he never made. Yet in his headlong rush toward a future worthy of a poet, he had propelled himself into a situation that rendered all genuine poetry impossible. One is reminded of that archetypal *poète maudit,* Arthur Rimbaud, who, in recoiling from the stifling Philistinism of the French provincial bourgeoisie, ran all the way, only to land at the trading posts of Africa, where the poet's voice was wholly lost. (pp. 439-40)

Victor Erlich, "The Dead Hand of the Future: The Predicament of Vladimir Mayakovsky," in Slavic Review, *Vol. XXI, No. 3, September, 1962, pp. 433-40.*

LAWRENCE LEO STAHLBERGER (essay date 1964)

[*Stahlberger is an American educator and literary critic who has written an important study of Mayakovsky's symbolism. In the following excerpt, he discusses the religious and mythical dimensions of Mayakovsky's poetry.*]

Everything about Majakovskij had the quality of the extraordinary, a hyperbolism of life and letters. Since he had modeled his life on such a grand scale, his death was strangely appropriate to his life. His suicide, although it does not add to the esthetic value of his work, stamps it with an authenticity that could be achieved by no other manner of death. Majakovskij was determined to be the master of his own creation, both in literature and life, to the end.

Kierkegaard has said, "Between poesy and religiosity, worldly wisdom presents its vaudeville performance. Every individual who does not live either poetically or religiously is stupid." Majakovskij's entire poetic creation is a testimony of his inability or refusal to live "between", by the standards of "worldly wisdom", but to live poetically. He was not religious in any doctrinaire, accepted meaning of the term, and his suicide would be incompatible with a religiously motivated life, but it was equally incompatible with what was assumed to be his socially motivated life as a Soviet citizen-poet. (pp. 9-10)

Later when the event had already become history, the problem was often solved by simply ignoring the fact of suicide; the makers of chronologues simply wrote, "1930—Death of Majakovskij". For the Soviets, Majakovskij's death was a betrayal, an act of unforgivable weakness in one who was later hailed as "the best, the most talented poet of our Soviet era".

Of course, it is obvious that Majakovskij himself contributed to the dilemma of the official historians. He apparently tried to and to a certain extent succeeded in concealing his true self by adopting various poses, among them those of the "dandy" and the professional newspaperman, and by deliberately disguising his true feelings. Majakovskij's outward "hooliganism" was seen through rather early by Pasternak, who wrote in his autobiography.

> And besides this the mainspring of his [Majakovskij's] lack of shyness was a wild shyness, and beneath his pretended freedom hid an apprehensive lack of freedom, inclined toward purposeless moroseness. The mechanism of his yellow coat was just as delusive. With its aid he was not fighting against the middle class jackets at all, but against the black velvet of the talent in himself, whose luscious dark-browed forms began to trouble him earlier than happens with less gifted people.

It is not uncommon, of course, for the poet to adopt a pose, but what is unusual in Majakovskij's case is that the pose he adopted was that of the anti-poet. In this he continued the Romantic tradition, which was based on a "conception of life as the life of the poet, and which had been adopted by the Symbolists, but at the same time he inverted it". But it is not only poets who adopt a pose—modern psychology has introduced us to the idea of the "persona", the conscious or unconscious acquiring of what are considered to be the characteristics of the role the person is to play in society. Majakovskij chose the "persona" of the anti-poet principally to flout the conventional conception of the "poet" which was held by the society of his day. This "persona" was mistakenly accepted by many of his contemporaries as the real Majakovskij, and to a certain extent by Majakovskij himself. The last role that Majakovskij assumed, and one that he tried to fulfill diligently from the Revolution of 1917 until 1930, was that of the Soviet citizen. At times the mask slipped and revealed the essential features of Majakovskij's problems and beliefs, with which he struggled in his poetry. It must be asserted that Majakovskij cannot be understood outside the framework of his poetry. R. Jakobson has said, "All Majakovskij's poetry is 'autobiographical' in that it points to his suicide. This is not the same as the vulgar conception of constructing the poet's biography from his poetry."

Soviet critics often ignore or minimize the poetry of Majakovskij which was written before the Revolution of 1917, that is, before the poet consciously assumed his role of Soviet citizen. Majakovskij, after the Revolution, made a sincere effort to make his poetry serve the ends of the new Soviet State. When he succeeded, he carried the mask of the Soviet citizen into his work and disguised the essential nature of his problems.

Propaganda posters drawn by Mayakovsky during the Russian Civil War. From Mayakovsky and His Circle, *by Viktor Shklovsky. Edited and translated by Lily Feiler. Reprinted by permission of Dodd, Mead & Company, Inc.*

Thus the Revolution served as a temporary means for Majakovskij to repress the inherent and most vital questions that he had to ask of life. There is a certain amount of truth in the assertion that the Revolution offered to Majakovskij a way out of his personal dilemma, that the Revolution "saved him", but in accepting this way out he only drove his problems beneath the surface from where they were to burst out in all their unassuaged fury thirteen years later.

If a true understanding is to be gained of Majakovskij's relation to his world, one must do so primarily through an analysis of his system of images and symbols. In this way both the man and the poetry can be illuminated, for Majakovskij stood upon the stage of his poetry as few poets have. This is not a mere figure of speech—in his first long work, the poetic drama ***Vladimir Majakovskij, a Tragedy,*** Majakovskij was both author and hero. . . . This emphasis on the "self" was to be an important characteristic of much of Majakovskij's creation. His "I" is not only the "hero" of his first long work, the *Tragedy,* but also of the following four most ambitious and significant works written before 1917, ***A Cloud in Trousers, The Backbone Flute, War and the Universe,*** and ***Man.*** Majakovskij made of his "I" a symbol, serving not only as a pronoun designation of the author, but also reaching out to include such conceptions as the Promethean rebel and martyr, Christ, and "man" (or mankind).

In the poetry of Majakovskij, the poet is modern man, suffering as both those two archetypes of the martyr had suffered. The "I" of the poet aspires to the position of a "culture-hero" of modern times, to establish a meaning for life for himself and others. He must fill in the Nietzschian void that modern man faces. He must either find or create a significant myth. If man finds a significant myth, he can come to some sort of terms with the human paradox, while if he does not, he must remain in a state of anxiety and despair. The more sensitive the individual involved, the greater and more dynamic is the search he conducts.

For long periods of history, the Christianity of the Gospels formed the basis of the significant myth of the West. Whatever the divergences due to differences in doctrine, the essential basic core of the Gospel myth as exemplified in the life of Christ answers for man the problem of life and death. Hence as Karl Jaspers has indicated, a Christian tragedy would be a paradox: "The tension of tragic knowledge has been released from the outset with the experience of man's perfection and salvation through grace." However, for ever increasing numbers of people, the Christian myth has ceased to be significant, and man has attempted to fill the vacuum with various secular myths of the nation or state or even that pseudo-entity, the race. These then take over the functions of the religious myth, apparently for great numbers of people, who testify to their significance by their willingness to die for them. (pp. 10-12)

The basic test of any myth . . . is the answer it gives to the problem of death and the corollary problem of life. The myth may be religious, social or scientific and the corresponding "culture-hero" will be the one who can convince himself and others of the significance of his myth. True tragedy results when the one who aspires to the role of the "hero" cannot find or create a significant myth.

This brings us to the second element of Majakovsky's creation, the element of the tragic. Majakovskij's attitude toward the Christian myth was not one of simple acceptance or rejection. He could not accept the God of either the Old or New Testament, and at the same time he could not reject the figure of Christ. Therefore, he tried to adopt elements of the Christian myth to his own particular purposes—to create a new myth. His poetry may be conveniently studied under the double aspect of his adaptation of the Christian myth and his attempt to create another. A study of this type may be conducted in two principal ways: it may attempt to classify objects of the given myth (in this case, images and symbols), and through a process of analysis and comparison with similar material clarify their meaning and/or it may study the myth as evidence of a certain perspective or way of looking at reality on the part of the artist. Both methods give fruitful results when applied to a study of Majakovskij's poetry.

In stressing the importance of the "self" in Majakovskij's poetry and the omnipresent "I" an indication of the first approach (that of classifying the objects-images and symbols) has already been given. The meaning of the symbol, in turn, can only be determined from the whole context in which the symbol appears and in terms of its relation to other images and symbols. Majakovskij's symbolic "I" is what has been called a "symbol of congruence", that is, its appeal or meaning is not intrinsic but is validated by its use within a given context. If the "I" of the poet is, as has been stated above, a symbol of the Promethean rebel and martyr, Christ and man, this can only be justified by reference to its environment in a given poem or poems. The method applied to the poem ***Man*** will serve as an example.

In the poem ***Man*** a dominant motif is that of "bondage" expressed by a group of related images in conjunction with the "I" of the poet. The poet ("I") is "driven into the terrestial pen", pulls the "daily yoke", has "a chain, religion" on his heart, is "imprisoned", is "fettered" by the earth, has the globe of the earth "chained" to his feet and is "enclosed" in a meaningless tale. . . . This and similar symbolic complexes in Majakovskij's poetry which express motives of bondage, torture, and aloneness, may be summed up under the term "martyrdom" and build up the "I" as the symbol of the martyr. The linkage to both Prometheus and Christ (culture-heroes) is apparent: Prometheus is fettered and staked to the rock, Christ is imprisoned and nailed to the cross, the poet is locked up in a meaningless tale, and man is bound to the earth (confined within space and time). The "I" of the poet also appears as martyr (or scapegoat) in ***Vladimir Majakovskij, A Tragedy, A Cloud in Trousers, The Backbone Flute, War and the Universe,*** and other poems.

The comparison of Majakovskij's "I" with the martyr-heroes of the Christian and Greek myths is also validated by the constant use of religious imagery (for the most part Christian) in his earlier poems. This characteristic of the poet's creation has been largely ignored by Soviet and Western critics, and where it has been remarked it has usually been misinterpreted. For example, V. Šklovskij, a Russian critic and friend of Majakovskij, says:

> The symbolists wrote about Dionysus, about the eternal feminine, about Demeter, and Majakovskij, seeking the most simple and most available mythology, seeking a new imagery, in Moscow, which was entirely decorated with crosses, accepted the religious image, destroying it. The quantity of these religious fragments in the first volume [of Majakovskij's works] is striking . . . it would be ridiculous to demonstrate, and it is perfectly clear to everyone, that the wearied individual was not religious. But these simple images are understandable to all. . . . These are not religious but blasphemous lines, the lines of an assault on an existing enemy, cutting-off the emotion associated with him.
>
> (pp. 13-15)

In view of Majakovskij's use of the religious image, which is both positive and negative, it hardly seems valid to assert that he "destroyed it". These images are often used in conjunction with the "I" of the poet and in a way which is neither ironical nor derisive. . . . Majakovskij's "I" as a symbol for the poet as martyr, has the characteristics both of Christ and Prometheus. For the Western mind they are archetypal martyrs. In spite of the similarities, there are essential differences between the two. They both suffer a form of crucifixion, but it is Zeus (the god) who martyrs Prometheus, while it is man who martyrs Christ. Prometheus reacts with rebellious pride and views his punishment as unjust: Christ acquiesces in his crucifixion. Prometheus acts in opposition to the will of Zeus in conferring the boon of fire and knowledge on man, while Christ acts in accordance with the will of God in bestowing grace and the hope of salvation on man. Both may be viewed as partaking of the qualities of God and man.

Since Majakovskij's symbolic "I" represents the martyr who rebels (or blasphemes, according to Šklovskij), the question arises, rebellion against what or whom? The simplest answer would seem to be God, that is, the Christian God, for Majakovskij's society is a Christian one. Although there are good reasons for identifying the "Commander of All", as he is called in the poem ***Man,*** with the Jehovah of the *Old Testament,* attentive reading of the poetry seems to complicate the problem. With the progression from the poetic drama, ***Vladimir Majakovskij, A Tragedy*** to the poem ***Man*** . . . , there seems to be an increasing philosophical depth to the poet's conception of his opponent. What in earlier poetry appears as simple blasphemy, later . . . , becomes a much more complicated attack against an enemy who becomes more and more empirically elusive. In the poem ***Man,*** which may be viewed as a central or crisis point in his creation, the "I" of the poet is opposed to the "Commander of All", my opponent, my implacable foe", who is hailed by the people, reads Locke, and commands the Greek sculptor, Phidias, god, and Galileos. He is the "uncrowned possessor of hearts", who is never touched by rebellion. . . . [This] "implacable foe" cannot be simply defined as God, but represents the antithesis of the poet's symbolic "I". The "foe" is the one who martyrs, and a closer understanding of his character depends upon an analysis of his actions and the surrounding imagery of the poetry. At best Jehovah or Zeus or any other divinity appears to be only one of his aspects or manifestations—his essence can only be determined as a coalescence of many conceptions, and it may be that the poet himself is unsure of the character of the enemy. At any rate, the "foe" of the poet is a more complicated and difficult symbol to decipher than the "I" of the poet.

A martyr of the type of Prometheus or Christ, and the mythical culture-hero in general, usually occupies a position midway between man and the divine; he is a superman or semi-divine. In this respect Majakovskij's symbolic "I" is also true to form. The poet martyred by man and for man, like Christ, is man. This question cannot be explained in detail now, but the comparison is obvious from the structure of the poem ***Man,*** as well as ***War and the Universe*** and other works of Majakovskij.

The creation of Majakovskij can then be viewed as incorporating the trinity of man, culture-hero, and the force or power which the culture-hero must overcome. The culture-hero, represented by the "I" of the poet, is engaged in a "spiritual combat" with his "implacable foe". In his "spiritual combat" the "I" of the poet must solve or at least give hope of solving the problems relating to birth, life, and death, which in themselves may be regarded as subsidiary to the general problem of time. For the individual, birth and death represent the two end-points which must remain in some sort of equilibrium in finite time (and space) from a purely rational point of view. Thus any attempt to overcome either birth or death must leap beyond the boundaries of rational thought, and this is just what mythic-religious thought does. The overcoming of death and the fear of death is the great boon which the culture-hero or religious leader must gain for man, and in this respect the poetic thought of Majakovskij is mythic-religious.

To call the poetic thought of Majakovskij mythic-religious is, of course, to syncretize rather arbitrarily a vast amount of phenomena ranging from the myths of primitive peoples to the more highly developed myths of the world's great religions and cultures. In justification, however, it can be proposed that Majakovskij's poetry exhibits just such a process of syncretization, resulting from the multiplicity of his images and their various sources. His creative work is mythopoetic and his perspective, his way of presenting the surrounding reality, is basically mythic. This does not imply that the poet is not influenced by ideas of a more disciplined or philosophical nature, but these only appear in his work as mythically disguised.

Majakovskij's world is principally an animate world and his relation to it is dynamic and emotional. It has been said that the basic distinction between the scientific and the mythic view of the world is that for the former the world is an "it", while for the latter it is a "thou", and Majakovskij certainly prefers to see his world as a "thou", for like the world of myth, Majakovskij's world would refuse to recognize an impersonal, mechanical, functioning of causality. On the contrary, he looks for a "who" rather than a "how".

Because myth is from its very beginning "potential religion", it would be a contradiction in terms to speak of Majakovskij as non-religious. In opposition to V. Šklovskij, therefore, it would be perhaps more rewarding to view Majakovskij's work as the creation of what has been called "a religiously-disoriented religious mind". (pp. 15-19)

Lawrence Leo Stahlberger, in his The Symbolic System of Majakovskij, *Mouton & Co, 1964, 151 p.*

ROBERT PAYNE (essay date 1968)

[*Payne is an American educator and literary critic. In the following excerpt, he summarizes the plots and discusses the major themes of Mayakovsky's four plays.*]

In 1913, when he was twenty, [Mayakovsky] wrote, produced, and acted in his first dramatic work. Characteristically he called it ***Vladimir Mayakovsky, A Tragedy.***

He made no attempt to disguise the theme of the play, which was the celebration of his own poetic genius and apotheosis as the divine poet crowned with laurel leaves, ascending to heaven while intoning his own name. The naked exuberance, the ferocity of the self-adulation, and the brilliance of the imagery seemed to indicate that he had reached the stage of egotistic romanticism beyond which it was impossible to go. In time he was to show that this was the merest beginning. He later extended the range of his exuberance and self-admiration until they encompassed vast unexplored regions of his ego, and he continued to display an extraordinary power to invent images which sent the mind reeling.

Vladimir Mayakovsky, a Tragedy was a tragedy only in the sense that the *Divina Commedia* was a comedy: there was simply no available poetic description for it. Most of the characters, even those who offer tribute to Mayakovsky, were Mayakovsky. The Man Without a Head, the Man with One Ear, the Man with One Eye and One Leg, the Man with Two Kisses, the Man with a Long Drawn-out Face, the Conventional Young Man, and the Old Man with Scrawny Black Cats were all Mayakovsky in his various manifestations, and there is some question whether The Enormous Woman, fifteen to twenty feet tall, was not a projection of the Mayakovsky who in his final appearance wishes he had breasts large enough to feed everyone. Even the Woman with a Tiny Tear, the Woman with a Tear, and the Woman with a Great Big Tear may be regarded as projections of Mayakovsky's devouring self-pity. "Things must be destroyed," says the Old Man with Scrawny Black Cats, and since "things" includes "people," who are no more than bells on the duncecap of God, the poet seems inclined to view the prospect of universal destruction with jaunty indifference. His true habitation is not the world but abstract Time, which buries all things in its capacious belly. As for love, this is just one more of the encumbrances which must be destroyed. "If you had loved as I have loved, you would murder love," says the Man with a Long Drawn-out Face, offering as an alternative the promise of celestial debauchery with "the shaggy, sweat-dripping sky and the milky-innocent stars." It is an unlikely promise, and Mayakovsky does not pursue it farther, although at intervals he will introduce the vast abstractions of Sky, Space, Time, Universes. Time is his special bugbear, for he knows that Time alone can destroy him; and in a strange and wonderful image the Man with One Eye and One Leg describes the ultimate terror:

> . . . the snouts of the years that came crawling out;
> on the foreheads of cities
> anger swelled up into rivers
> of thousand-mile-long-veins.
> Slowly,
> in terror,
> arrows of hair
> rose up on the bald pate of Time.

Not all of the play, of course, reaches that height of terror. Sometimes the game is played as a farce, with Mayakovsky clowning his various roles and turning metaphysical cartwheels. He was an intellectual anarchist, and he soon tired of those huge and ponderous images set in the warring heavens. There is, for example, the question of supplying sufficient electricity to run the tramways. The Old Man with Scrawny Black Cats suggests that it could be done by stroking the backs of his cats and catching the electricity:

> . . . streetcars will start off in a rush;
> the flame of wicks
> will glow in the night like triumphant banners.
> The world, in gay greasepaint, will stir into action;
> the flowers in the windows will strut, peacock bright;
> people will travel on rails—
> always trailed
> by cats, more cats, lots of black cats!
> We'll pin the sun on the gowns of our sweethearts;
> we'll adorn them with glittering brooches of stars.
> Leave your apartments!
> Go stroke cats—
> stroke cats that are black and scrawny!

The cats, you observe, have nothing whatsoever to do with the tragedy of Mayakovsky, who is merely improvising in the intervals of superintending his flock of worshipers; and it is precisely these improvisations which give pleasure to the reader who, without them, would find the going hard and the rewards uncertain. Happily, nine-tenths of the time Mayakovsky forgets to posture in front of distorting mirrors, and displays a gift for comic improvisation. Nevertheless, the mirrors are always waiting for him. So, too, are those vast cosmological arguments which continually tempt him to measure himself against the heavens. The comic interlude with the cats is inevitably interrupted with some pious nonsense about pinning the sun on the gowns of our sweethearts and adorning them with glittering brooches of stars. At such times he was no longer fooling; he was merely imitating himself.

When Mayakovsky first acted out the part of Mayakovsky on the stage of the Luna Park Theater in St. Petersburg, he was still little known. He had been writing poetry for a little more than a year under the guidance of his friend, the painter David Burlyuk, who on the evidence of a single poem assured him that he was a genius. ***Vladimir Mayakovsky, A Tragedy*** was an act of such prodigious effrontery that it brought him to public attention. He was sometimes booed, but never shouted off the stage, for he had a louder voice than all the combined voices of his audience. He took the play on tour, and learned to shout down hecklers in all the dialects of provincial Russia. On that small stage in Luna Park, against a backcloth depicting a spider's web of streets which he had painted himself, he had his beginnings as an actor; and he was to continue to act out the role of the tragedian Mayakovsky as long as he lived. (pp. 3-6)

Above all Mayakovsky wanted to be known as a dramatic poet. In August, 1917, he had already sketched out ***Mystery-Bouffe,*** his twentieth-century version of a medieval morality play, in which the workers receive the rewards of the blessed and the monarchs and capitalist politicians are consigned to eternal damnation. He called it "a heroic, epic, and satiric representation of our era," but in fact it was a brilliant farce in six acts designed to reflect his anarchist vision of the world. There was nothing particularly Bolshevik about the play: the Russian Anarchists, Social Revolutionaries, and Mensheviks all agreed that the workers would inherit the earth. He worked on the play at intervals during the first year of the Revolution. It was finished in October, 1918, and immediately produced by Meyerhold, with the author designing the sets. He wrote in his diary: "Finished ***Mystery-Bouffe.*** Read it, much talk about it. Acted three times, then hammered. Replaced by Macbeths." A second, somewhat longer version was produced in 1921 as an entertainment for the benefit of visiting delegates to the Congress of the Comintern.

The plot of ***Mystery-Bouffe*** is charmingly simple. A flood has overwhelmed the world, leaving only the North Pole above the surface of the waters. The survivors consist of seven pairs of Clean and seven pairs of Unclean. The Clean are typical representatives of the capitalist world which has been swept away in the flood. They include the Negus of Abyssinia, Clemenceau, Lloyd George (indistinguishable from an Arctic walrus), a Russian speculator, and an American with a large bank account. The Unclean are the workers of the world, now at last united in adversity. They include a miner, a lamplighter, a carpenter, a laundress. The Unclean build an Ark, but the capitalists with their usual perversity take command of it. Then The Unclean revolt and toss The Clean overboard, having observed that the Negus of Abyssinia eats all the food and the politicians issue all the commands. So The Unclean set out on their voyage to Ararat, the Promised Land, without benefit of monarchs or any commandments but their own.

Ararat is in sight, or they think it is in sight, when they are presented with an extraordinary apparition—a man walking across the waters toward them. On the stage the role of the apparition was played by Mayakovsky. "My Paradise is for everyone *except* the poor in spirit," says the mysterious stranger, as he steps on the deck. In his deafening voice he offers them the promise of the earthly kingdom:

> Come unto me
> all you who have calmly stabbed the enemy,
> and then walked away from his corpse
> with a song on your lips!

This is not blasphemy: this is merely the age-old portrait of the Christ who has no sympathy for the rich and the powerful of this world. "Heaven is within your reach," he says, "and the poor shall be under my protection and given the wealth of the earth." Then mysteriously he vanishes, and the chorus intones:

> Who is he?
> Who is that free spirit?
> Who is he—
> that nameless one?
> Who is he,
> with no country of his own?
> Why did he come?
> What prophecies did he utter?

It is a moment of extraordinary poignancy: the echoes of one mystery, written in church Slavonic, irrupting into the mystery of the proletarian victory. Mayakovsky knew what he was doing when he played the role of the stranger coming over the sea, for he liked to keep the best verses for himself.

In the following scene we learn that The Unclean by their inexpert seamanship have blundered into Hell, a true medieval Hell inhabited by savagely laughing devils with tails, horns, and pitchforks. A few Clean have somehow survived in the hold, and the devils make short work of them. The Unclean have no difficulty breaking down the portals of Hell, advancing rapidly through Purgatory, and reaching Heaven, where Methuselah, in the company of Tolstoy, Rousseau, and St. John Chrysostom, serves as official greeter. When the saints ask what the horny-handed sons of toil are doing in Heaven, The Unclean reply: "We ourselves are Christ and Savior."

The journey through Heaven, like the journey through Hell, is the purest slapstick, and Mayakovsky has some difficulty in restraining his natural impulse for clowning. The workers steal the lightning of Jehovah, complain about the absence of heavenly chairs, wine, and the ordinary comforts of life. Why wings, when it would be more sensible to install elevators? But when they escape at last from heaven, they are in no better plight, for they find themselves in Chaos, a country inhabited by Marxist doctrinaires. A celestial steam engine now appears and takes them to the Promised Land:

> The gate flies open, and the city is revealed. What a city! The lattice-like forms of transparent factories and apartment buildings tower up toward the sky. Trains, streetcars, and automobiles stand wrapped in rainbows. In the center is a garden of stars and moons, surmounted by the radiant crown of the sun.

One might have known that the Splendid City of Mayakovsky's imagination would resemble New York's Park Avenue at Forty-eighth Street during Christmas week. Happily the vision soon fades and we are presented with a procession of Machines, Things, and Edibles. They offer bread and salt to the workers as a sign of peace, then swear eternal friendship and ask pardon for the crimes they have been forced to commit under capitalism. "All food is free," say the Edibles. "Take and eat." It is only the last of the many borrowings from the New Testament. Just as Mayakovsky imitates the verse patterns of the hymns sung in Russian churches, so he finds himself inescapably bound by Christian images and Christian concepts. He does not turn Christianity upside down; he merely tilts it, so that it can be observed freshly. In the last scene a massed chorus sings Mayakovsky's revised version of the "Internationale." It sounds, and perhaps was intended to sound, like an angelic choir.

It was a lame ending, and Mayakovsky was aware that he had not resolved his difficulties. ***Mystery-Bouffe*** was a failure, and rarely performed. Yet simply because it attempted the impossible feat of rewriting and rescoring a medieval mystery in terms of the proletariat's rise to power, mixing farce and folly with lyrical exaltation and wild invention, it deserves to be remembered with gratitude. He never wrote with more gusto. One does not easily forget the man walking across the waters, the clowning at the North Pole, the rape of Jehovah's lightning. Mayakovsky wore his prophetical robes when he wrote this play, for he speaks of storming the planets by airships of the commune fifty years hence. He saw electricity spreading a mantle of light across the earth, and his faith in the ultimate victory of The Unclean was unshakable. For a brief while he played the role of Aristophanes reborn in the Soviet age—and never was Aristophanes more needed.

When Mayakovsky turned to writing dramatic poetry again, Lenin was dead, and the light had gone out of the sky. In the cruel years of Stalin he wrote with bitterness and despair. The iron bureaucracy, which Lenin brought into being and later dreaded, held all the arts in its hands. At a time when the great purges had already begun, Mayakovsky wrote his two last plays, ***The Bedbug*** and ***The Bathhouse,*** satirizing the bureaucracy and the all-powerful dictator. (pp. 7-11)

The Bedbug, written in the fall of 1928, was a ferocious satire on communist bureaucracy. The proletarian hero Ivan Prisypkin possesses all the conventional virtues of a Soviet bureaucrat, being an ignorant vulgarian who loudly protests his loyalty to the common cause, toadies before higher officials, and insists on the proper deference being paid to his exalted station in life. He has changed his name to Pierre Skripkin, as being more euphonious and more in keeping with his new-found elegance as the wooer of Elzevira Renaissance, a manicurist and cashier in a beauty parlor. He has abandoned Zoya Berezkiina, the working-class girl whom he loved until he met Elzevira, and he is entirely unmoved when she shoots herself. His future mother-in-law is delighted to have a Soviet official with impeccable credentials in the family. He has calloused hands, a Party card, a trade-union card, a vulgar manner. He is continually scratching himself, drinks prodigious quantities of vodka, and strums pleasantly on a guitar. What could be better? But the wedding feast ends abruptly when the bride's veil catches fire and all the wedding guests perish in the conflagration.

Fifty years later, when communism has been established throughout the globe, some workmen excavating on the site of the wedding feast are astonished to discover Prisypkin frozen in a block of ice in the cellar, and the Institute of Human Resurrection offers to restore him to life on condition that it receive world approval for an experiment fraught with danger to contemporary society, for who knows what diseases the corpse may have suffered? The newspaper representatives of *The Chicago Soviet News, The Madrid Milkmaid, the Shanghai Pauper, the Roman Red Gazette,* and all the other newspapers give their unqualified approval. Prisypkin's corpse is revived. So is the bedbug which accompanied him loyally in death. The Institute of Human Resurrection, having brought him to life, has no further use for him, and he is presented to the local zoo, where he inhabits a cage labeled *Philistinius vulgaris*.

From the moment he is resurrected, Prisypkin proves to be a rebel against the new communist state. He wants to play the guitar, sing romantic songs, drink, curse, and make love, but the frailties of a former age are no longer encouraged by the communist rulers. He insists on being human. For a brief moment he is permitted to step out of the cage under armed guard, and the last words are a despairing cry from the heart:

> Citizens! My people! My own people! Dear ones! How did you get here? So many of you! When did they unfreeze you? Why am I alone in the cage? Dear ones, my people! Come in with me! Why am I suffering? Citizens!

The zoo director orders the resurrected Prisypkin to be thrown back into the cage. It was all a mistake; he should never have been let out. "The noise and bright lights brought on hallucinations," he explains, and orders the band to strike up and drown the words spoken by the doomed man.

Though the play was written as a comedy, Prisypkin remains a tragic hero who derives in direct line of descent from ***Vladimir Mayakovsky, a Tragedy.*** Mayakovsky was perfectly aware that he was Prisypkin, or at least that there was a good deal of Prisypkin in him. He took care that the actor Ilyinsky, who played the role at the premiere in the Meyerhold State Theater in February, 1929, should look and behave as much as possible like his creator, even to adopting the same mannerisms and the same raucous voice. Mayakovsky was burlesquing Mayakovsky, and at the same time he was burlesquing the Soviet state, which had produced so many Prisypkins. Under Stalin it was necessary to pretend that the play was nothing but comic buffoonery. With Stalin dead, Soviet audiences were able to see the play performed tragically, as Mayakovsky had originally intended.

The Bedbug was a success and played for three months; the Soviet critics found little to attack in it, preferring to believe that it was a comic fantasy without relevance to anything happening at the time. They were more severe with his next play, ***The Bathhouse.*** This time Mayakovsky made no attempt to conceal his motives. His attacks on Soviet bureaucracy, and the aimless wanderings of the bureaucratic mind, were almost too successful, for long stretches of the play are devoted to parodies of bureaucrats at their labors, and it must be admitted that their speeches are excruciatingly boring, stupid, and distasteful. In particular the speeches of Pobedonosikov (Nose for Victory) are filled with the cliché of bureaucratic power. Pobedonosikov stands at the pinnacle of the Soviet state, for he is the chief coordinator of everything. A notice outside his office reads: "IF YOU HAVEN'T BEEN ANNOUNCED, DON'T COME IN!" Few people are announced, and the dictator spends the greater part of his time making pompous speeches in defense of his own bureaucratic methods. (pp. 12-14)

The Soviet bureaucrats who tolerated ***The Bedbug*** because it was largely incomprehensible found little to tolerate in ***The Bathhouse.*** The cutting edge was too sharp; the parodies of bureaucratic double-talk were too accurate; and the portrait of Pobedonosikov was too evidently based on the reigning dictator. Although the play was performed—for Mayakovsky had too much authority and renown to be rejected from the theater—the literary bloodhounds were in full pursuit. Mayakovsky was sternly admonished. It was hinted that he was a reactionary, a Trotskyist, or worse.Stalin, who had been keeping a watchful eye on Mayakovsky, encouraged the attacks. Vladimir Ermilov, a literary bureaucrat and hack writer who wrote innocuous studies of Dostoyevsky and Chekhov, delivered the most bitter

Mayakovsky and Boris Pasternak in 1924. Reproduced by permission of Agence Strassova.

attacks. In reply Mayakovsky hung a huge banner inside the theater with the words:

> It is hard to get rid of
> The swarms of bureaucrats:
> Not enough bathhouses,
> Not enough soap.
> Bureaucrats like Ermilov
> Are comforted by the critics.

(pp. 15-16)

Yet Mayakovsky knew there could be no fighting against Ermilov. He died because he could no longer breathe the polluted air of Russian bureaucracy, and because the Soviet system could no longer tolerate his genius. (p. 17)

Robert Payne, in an introduction to The Complete Plays of Vladimir Mayakovsky *by Vladimir Mayakovsky, translated by Guy Daniels, Washington Square Press, Inc., 1968, pp. 1-18.*

R. D. B. THOMSON (essay date 1970)

[In the following excerpt Thomson, a Canadian educator and literary critic specializing in Slavic literature and languages, examines the tension existing between the past and future in Mayakovsky's poetry.]

The concept of time is written into nearly everything that Mayakovsky did and wrote. He was one of the leaders of the literary movement called futurism, and as such he was dedicated to the task of creating a new art of the twentieth century. It may be objected that literary titles don't mean a great deal, and that anyway the word futurism isn't quite so meaningful to a Russian as it is to a western reader. Mayakovsky, however, frequently pointed to this connection, as in the following lines:

> We had the reputation of chatterboxes
> on the subject of futurism,
> but isn't it with us that the future
> shines like a rainbow of chasubles?

And this is not a mere liiterary pose . . . Pasternak declared that Mayakovsky really was a man of the future tragically out of place in the present. (pp. 181-82)

Mayakovsky seldom talks about time in the abstract; he almost always distinguishes sharply between time past and time future. One might even say that he makes a moral distinction between the two: time past is invariably bad, while time future is almost always good. The basic conflict of Mayakovsky's works is a sort of cosmic struggle between past and future with the soul of the present as the main issue at stake. He could interpret even the class struggle in these terms:

> To be a bourgeois . . .
> is the heel of the dead on the throat of the young . . .
> to be a proletarian . . .
> is . . .
> to love the future
> that has blown up the filth of our cellars.

But before going on to this struggle we must look more closely at the protagonists, time future and time past.

The future is usually synonymous with Utopia, whether communist or not, and Mayakovsky often uses the word 'time' by itself to mean the future; the meaning is plain from the context, or from the emotional colouring, as, for example, in the following quotation, where, consistently enough, he declares that only the future is qualified to judge him:

> Time!—you are my only judge.

From treating future time as a judge it is only a short step to regarding her as a Muse, as at the beginning of ***Vladimir Ilích Lenin:***

> Time—I begin my tale of Lenin.

(the word *vremya* ["time"] appears twice more in the next few lines). It is, of course, not because the people of the future will need to be told about Lenin, but because Mayakovsky himself is appealing for inspiration. (p. 182)

The poet's mission is also to proclaim the future, and so hasten its coming. . . . Sometimes he compares himself to Noah and Christ, the leaders of a small band of followers out of a wicked past into a better future; sometimes he tries to drag the present bodily after him into the future. . . . (p. 183)

The future then is associated with movement and change. The past, on the other hand, is static, partly because it is over and done with and, as yet, unalterable; it seems dead, but it is still powerful in the form of outmoded forms of society, religion and aesthetics. This leads to the image of sleep; at the end of ***Oblako v shtanakh:***

> the universe sleeps.

Its very indifference to Mayakovsky's blasphemies indicates its impregnability. Conversely, Mayakovsky hailed the revolution with the words:

the sleep of ages is shattered.

Sleep, in turn, leads on to the image of the feather-bed (*perina*), a traditional symbol of bourgeois values in Russian literature; echoes of this feather-bed can be heard in ***Klop*** in the image:

the musty mattresses of time.

(Here it is plain from the context that Mayakovsky is speaking of time past). In the same way the old world is frequently compared to *'star ýe'* (old clothes), and the associations of this image are again of dust, of musty smells, and a stifling atmosphere, the old world which the poet rejects in its entirety. . . . (p. 184)

The road from the present to the future is obstructed in Mayakovsky's poetry by mountains. . . . And at the end of his life he wrote:

My verse will reach over the ranges of mountains.

Why this recurrent image of mountains? Chiefly, of course, because they obstruct the clear view of the future, so that many people have lost faith in it. Secondly, in order to explain why it is that only Mayakovsky perceives this vision—he can see over the top of the mountains: hence he is often compared to the sun, or flies up into the sky, and even when he remains with both feet firmly on the ground, achieves fantastic dimensions. . . . (pp. 184-85)

The image of mountains is also suggestive of difficulties and hardships that have to be overcome, before the Future can be attained. . . . The overcoming of . . . obstacles is not just a test of men's worthiness; it ennobles them and enhances the value of the future.

Now that time past and time future have been characterised, we may attempt to trace the development of this imagery in Mayakovsky's works. Surprisingly, the word 'time' is not found in his earliest poetry, but none the less it is an essential element in the composition. These poems are set in the city, which is depicted as a dead world, a Hell, reminiscent of Blok's St Petersburg poems. Yet if we compare Mayakovsky's descriptions with those that Blok was composing at about the same time, the differences are clearly marked. Take for example the famous poem: *Noch,́ ulitsa, fonar,́ apteka*. . . . Here the return of the opening nouns at the end of the poem serves to reinforce the impression of meaningless repetition:

And everything will repeat itself as of old.

The poem has no title; it is utterly impersonal, even the second person singular has no one in mind, while the absence of any colour or poetic imagery only confirms the impression of frozen immobility and emptiness.

In all these respects Mayakovsky's early poems provide a sharp contrast. They are full of unexpected imagery, vivid colours and fantastic distortions. It would be tempting to explain this by Mayakovsky's training as an art-student, and his early fascination with cubism; but these differences of technique reflect also the essential differences in the responses of the two poets. Blok was horrified by the prospect of eternal repetition, and his poem, even in its structure, reflects his sense of powerlessness. Mayakovsky, however, experiences not just Blok's impotent horror, but also rage and profound pity for the victims of the city. Accordingly, he uses vigorous imagery in his poems to pass on his sense of indignation to his readers and force them to participate. Even his titles are often challenges. . . . In other words, Mayakovsky feels bound to do something about the city, to change its contours, exaggerate its colours. This imaginative transformation serves as a kind of sympathetic magic; perhaps in this way the city really will be transformed physically.

This peculiar need to invervene, to participate, to change the contours of something apparently eternally fixed, leads Mayakovsky on to his theme of the poet as saviour and redeemer, superbly expressed in the poem ***A vse-taki*** . . . Here he provides a horrifying picture of the sufferings and disease that the city has brought; but he is not content merely to say that something ought to be done about it; he actually tries to *do* something about it. He identifies himself with the prostitutes and syphilitics of the city; and innocently takes upon himself their guilt and suffering. They hold him up in their arms, so that finally even God is touched by Mayakovsky's sacrifice, and is stirred out of his apathy. But what is particularly interesting is the way in which the sequence of tenses in the poem illustrates this process. There are five stanzas in all: the first two are devoted to the dead hand of the past on the city of today. Although the scene is set in the present, the verbs are past and perfective, implying that the actions described have taken place once and for all. . . . Finally, the last two stanzas move into the future tense, for the theme of change and redemption.

They will bear me up in their arms like something
sacred and show me to God . . .
and God will weep . . . and run around Heaven,
and will . . . read [me].

The past and the future are set against one another in the very structure of the poem, and struggle for the soul of the present set between them. (pp. 185-87)

Within a mere five years (1912-17) Mayakovsky's themes had led him into an impasse. He had begun to doubt the possibility of a future in any meaningful sense; the past seemed invincible and eternal. It is difficult to see how or where Mayakovsky could have developed further if it had not been for the events of 1917, which seemed to him to have miraculously shattered the power of the past. (It was, incidentally, the revolution of February 1917, rather than the bolshevik coup of October that effected this transformation in Mayakovsky's thinking.) As he wrote in his poem ***Revolyutsiya*** . . . of April 1917:

Citizens! Today the thousand-year old "before" is
collapsing.
Today the foundation of the world is to be re-examined.
Today down to the last button in our clothes
We shall make life anew.

For the first time in Mayakovsky's work, the present is cut away from the past and linked with future. (pp. 188-89)

In his immediate post-revolutionary poems Mayakovsky constantly returns to this idea of the revolutionary change in time; he treats it above all from an aesthetic point of view, for the historic role of the futurists had at last paid off. (pp. 191-92)

The first break in Mayakovsky's confidence in the future came with the introduction of the new economic policy in 1921. Hitherto he had been able to identify his own time-mythology with Marxism (he had been a member of the bolshevik party in his teens). For the Marxist the course of history is controlled by scientific laws, which can be mastered and harnessed by human beings for their own ends; once one has grasped the dialectic of history, one can and indeed should intervene to accelerate its development. Ideologically, therefore, Mayakovsky had no difficulty in equating his own beliefs with communist theory.

But the NEP, justified by Lenin as a tactical step backwards, he found very much harder to accept. With his strong sense of the past, its tenacious grip on the present and consequently its threat to the realisation of the future, he felt that the past and the future could not be played off against one another in this way. The re-introduction of elements of capitalism, the growth of new class distinctions and the restoration of bourgeois values, were all so many hostages to the past, a betrayal of the dynamic of the Revolution. Although in his propaganda poems of these years he continued to parrot the official line, in his more personal works he expresses his doubts openly. This can be seen clearly in the imagery; the deluge of revolution has now become a stagnant marsh:

> the storms of the revolutionary seas have subsided,
> the chaos of Soviet Russia has been covered with scum.
> (p. 192)

It is . . . in the longer poems of 1922-23 that Mayakovsky's concern over the restoration of the past reaches its most agonised and poignant expression. The poem, ***IV Internatsional,*** contrasts the enthusiastic beginnings of the revolution with the contemporary reality of the NEP period. . . . Every advertisement seems to shout ['October is finished!'] The spirit of the past has completely infected the whole system, and Mayakovsky ends with an appeal to prepare for a new revolution. . . . (p. 193)

The greatest achievement of these years is, of course, ***Pro eto.*** It is perhaps the most complex of Mayakovsky's works. The train of thought leaps backwards and forwards across the normal categories of time and place, but these leaps, whether to contemporary Paris, or to the death of Lermontov, are all related by one common feature—they are confined to the bourgeois past, which is threatening to take control of Soviet reality once again. Like ***Oblako v shtanakh, Pro eto*** is concerned with love, art, and society, only to reject them all in their contemporary static forms. The poem was originally centred round New Year's Eve, but significantly, Mayakovsky later changed this to Christmas Eve, a reminder of the religion he hated, and whose appeal he feared.

The idea that nothing has effectively changed since 1917, in spite of two revolutions, is effectively indicated by the constant references to ***Chelovek,*** the most despairing of the early long poems. Once again Mayakovsky's readiness for self-sacrifice proves quite meaningless. He is humiliated and destroyed by the age-old bourgeois system around him. He survives only in the red flag, the symbol of revolution, which now hangs in tatters, waiting for the revolution that must one day occur. (p. 194)

The final section of the poem begins with the ark of Noah approaching the quay—but at the crucial moment the poet wakes up and realises that the prospect of arrival was merely a dream. In the sections 'Life', 'Grief', 'Hatred', and 'Sadness', he gives way to an orgy of bitterness and recriminations. He realises that he will never live to see the future now. One last refuge remains; he appeals to the conscience of posterity to resurrect him. For the privilege of living in the future, he is ready to undertake the most menial of tasks, and the poem ends pathetically with a glimpse of what ideal happiness could mean, where loneliness, unrequited love and suicide will be inconceivable. But Mayakovsky does not really believe in this resurrection; the prospect of the thirtieth century when these miracles will come about is now not a matter of belief, but a psychological, almost a religious necessity. The final sections are headed 'Faith', 'Hope' and 'Charity', hardly futurist sentiments any of them. The future has been given a definite date—a thousand years hence—and to that extent is placed in time, unlike some of Mayakovsky's earlier visions of Utopia, but this figure is suggestive only of remoteness—the thirtieth century is not one for which even Mayakovsky could draw up blueprints.

The unclouded optimism of the earlier revolutionary poems has evaporated, for Mayakovsky now suspected that the revolution had not after all escaped from this world or from the power of the past. The vision of a triumphal march through Heaven and Hell into the promised land disappears. Instead Mayakovsky leaps into a distant future, when communism will at last have been successfully established; but for the time being its links with the present have been broken; between then and now there is a great gulf fixed. (pp. 194-95)

But if the future is no longer to be perceived in the present, but only in some such fantastic leap, then a new problem presents itself: that the poet himself will not live to see it. Hence the growing importance of the theme of the resurrection of the dead, which comes to the fore, significantly enough, in the works written during the months after Lenin's death, and above all, in the long poem, ***Vladimir Il'ich Lenin,*** which actually ends with the resurrection of Lenin in the form of a rejuvenated communist party.

Although Mayakovsky may seem to have moved out of the centre of the stage to make way for Lenin, in fact he has only been able to compose this poem by identifying his own fate with that of Lenin. He too is resurrected at the end of the poem as he merges his personality into that of the masses. Above all, he is concerned with answering his own doubts about the contemporary scene. (pp. 195-96)

Of course, in the majority of his poems, Mayakovsky is content simply to repeat loyal clichés about the revolution, such as that time is on our side, that the revolution even today is a rejuvenating force, that Russia is the land of youth, and so on. There is no need to examine every one of these poems, for they seem to have been composed out of poetic inertia, not out of a fresh experience. It is the deviations from this pattern that are more interesting, and there are two lines in an otherwise totally undistinguished poem that suggest a real confusion in Mayakovsky's mind about the nature of the times that he lived in. The poem was written for the ninth anniversary of the revolution, and consists mainly of a mechanical re-arrangement of traditional images. But then we come to the following lines:

> The mole of time rises up,
> the waves of the days are powerless to resist it.

Time here is, of course the future, and it is equated with the building of communism. It is seen as an impregnable fortress; the daily passing of time is a wave. The sentiment seems to be unexceptionable—Utopia is invincible; but in fact Mayakovsky's usual imagery has been turned inside out. Earlier it was the hateful past, not Utopia, that was compared to a static fortress, and the revolution, not the forces of reaction, to a flood-tide. Some awareness of this reversal can be detected in Mayakovsky's terminology. The wave beats against the mole, but is unable to resist. . . . (pp. 196-97)

Slowly but surely a note of nostalgia, that least futurist of sentiments, creeps into Mayakovsky's works. He begins to look back to the years 1917-1921 as a touchstone. In the poem ***Perekopsky entuziazm*** he welcomes the purges of 1928-29, because they seemed to be returning to the ruthless dedicated spirit of 1918. But the most revealing indication is to be found in the structure of his poems. In these heroic marches, hymns to the five-year plan, appeals to the Komsomol, time after time Mayakovsky rounds off his poem with a repeat of the opening quatrain. This of course is done for emphasis, and it is usually the most effective stanza which is exploited in this way. All the same, the result is curiously static, and conflicts with the content of the poem. The poem seems trapped: he is bravely singing of the future, and the need to get there as quickly as possible, but the actual poems are simply running on the spot, and get nowhere at all. (p. 197)

To return in 1930 to the subject-matter and solutions of his pre-revolutionary poetry was an even more terrible admission of defeat than the return of ***Pro eto*** to the world of ***Chelovek.*** Mayakovsky never completed this work, on which he had set so much store, and a few months later he committed suicide. Stahlberger argues that his suicide resulted from a 'refusal to bow to *byt* and time, and—paradoxically enough—a refusal to accept natural death.' This seems a curious reason for committing suicide; we have many witnesses (Roman Jakobson and Lilya Brik among them) to the close connections between Mayakovsky's everyday life and the themes of his poetry. This relationship is of course essential to the whole purpose of Mayakovsky. Rather Mayakovsky's suicide was not in any sense a way of defying time in general theoretical terms, but an acknowledgment on his own flesh and bone of the total capitulation of the future to the might of the past. In the words of an earlier quotation:

> The mole of time rises up,
> the waves of the days are powerless to resist it.

Time had turned into a fortress again, and the waves of revolution were powerless against it. (p. 200)

R. D. B. Thomson, "Mayakovsky and His Time Imagery," in The Slavonic and East European Review, *Vol. XLVIII, No. 111, April, 1970, pp. 181-200.*

EDWARD J. BROWN (essay date 1973)

[Brown is an American educator and essayist who has written extensively on post-Revolution Soviet literature. Notable among these studies is what some critics consider the standard work on the period, Russian Literature since the Revolution *(1963). In the following excerpt from a later work on Mayakovsky, he discusses the themes of the poetry Mayakovsky wrote during his trip to America and analyzes the poem* "Brooklyn Bridge."*]*

[Mayakovsky's] visit to America in the summer of 1925 was the realization of a plan entertained at least since 1923. . . . The journey provided a rich yield of both poetry and journalistic prose, and, as is usually the case with Mayakovsky, it is more interesting and immeasurably more illuminating to give attention first to the poetry. In fact, Mayakovsky always treated the **"Poems About America"** as a special cycle of his work, and he published them separately as such. They provide a far more reliable diary of his visit than do the sketches he subsequently published under the title ***My Discovery of America.***

The cycle is framed, so to speak, by the two poems about ocean voyages with which it begins and ends, **"The Atlantic Ocean"** and **"Homeward!,"** . . . not a surprising circumstance in view of the fact that the journey itself began and ended with transatlantic crossings. Yet the two poems, and a third that we shall examine, do remind us of the frequent occurence of water in Mayakovsky's poetry and the symbolic meanings that may be attached to it.

The poems inspired by the visit are more interesting than the prose chiefly because Mayakovsky's ambivalence appears in many of them, though never in the prose. For instance, **"I Bear Witness"** . . . complains of simplistic propaganda of the kind that he himself must occasionally be charged with, and **"Camp Nitgedaige"** is an abortive effort at escape into purely lyrical motifs. As in the poems of the Parisian cycle, Mayakovsky's range is incredibly wide, from the ill-natured and humorless triviality of **"Six Nuns"** . . . to the ecstatic wonder of **"Brooklyn Bridge."**

"The Atlantic Ocean" . . . [is] a meditation on deep matters composed on shipboard. Also in a meditative mood he produced a short piece called **"Shallow Philosophy in Deep Places"** . . . , which seems out of character for Mayakovsky since it treats time not as a creator but as a destroyer: the poet, as he experiences the deliberate movement of the ship over boundless ocean and observes the accumulating evidence of its passage through space, reflects on the equally imperceptible movement of the years and the disappearance with them of—everything. The idea of constant flow, change, and passage is deeply embedded in the poem and is set forth in a number of images. . . . (pp. 272-73)

As we continue to consider the poems in the American cycle in the approximate order in which Mayakovsky arranged them for publication, it will be necessary to perform an evaluation: some of them are poor poems and interesting only because Mayakovsky wrote them, others are interesting also because of the political message they contain, and a few belong with the best of Mayakovsky's work. In the first group, **"Black and White"** reveals the American phenomenon of a bitter class struggle complicated by racial hatreds, and is apparently based on some observations made during a brief stay in Havana. The highly political audiences that gathered to hear him read it in New York and other places may well have "raised the roof," as the *Chicago Daily Worker* reported, at Mayakovsky's advice to black Willy, the oppressed worker:

> How was he to know
> that his question
> should be directed
> to the Comintern
> in Moscow?

"Syphilis" is a lame effort to blame the exploiters for the spread of disease among the colonial peoples. **"Christopher Columbus"** employs once again the irreverent approach to greatness of **"The Sun," "Jubilee Year,"** and **"Notre-Dame,"** but the effect is lost when the poem (also a ringing success with his highly selected American audiences) lowers itself to simple propaganda:

> You're stupid, Columbus— / I tell you straight.
> As for me / why I / personally—
> would have closed America / cleaned it up a little
> and then / I would have opened it again / a second time. . . .

(pp. 275-76)

But then the propaganda note disappears without a trace in the poem **"The Tropics,"** conceived on the railway journey from Vera Cruz to Mexico City, which is a purely lyrical impression of the onset of a tropical night, full of botanical wonders, strange colors and fragrances, and "packed" with stars so numerous that even the best accountant could not total them up. **"Mexico"** is probably the most successful piece of pure agitation in the American cycle, and the reason for its success is that it engages both the poet himself and the reader in the cause of liberating the colonial people: the poet's own memories of the Indian games he played during his childhood when, like so many Russian children, he drank deeply from the works of Fenimore Cooper and Mayne Reid, serve as introduction to the actual Indians of Vera Cruz who lift his suitcases, and no longer have any of the pride and beauty of Montihomo Hawk's-Claw: "The pile of suitcases / takes the place / of arrows / that couldn't miss—" The poem contains also a beautiful evocation of past glory and ancient wars, and moments of historical meditation (rare in Mayakovsky): "That / was / so long ago / it almost never was.". . . The poem is so rich with actual images of Indians, with memories of the past in ironic contrast with the present: "Heroism / is not for now. / Montezuma is only a brand name of beer . . .". . . . and with unfeigned sorrow (the word is not too strong) at the humiliation and poverty of the aborigines, that Mayakovsky's closing agitational shout seems natural, and artistically acceptable in the context of the poem: "Soon / crimson flag, / fly over the Mexican melon!" (p. 276)

The poem **"Mexico"** succeeds as propaganda because its message grows naturally out of a personal disenchantment. Others of the same cycle seem to be based on anecdotes or newspaper stories that Mayakovsky could have known only at second hand. . . . (pp. 276-77)

"The Young Lady and Woolworth's" . . . is amusing as a genre picture of American urban promotion methods of the twenties, as an image of the complete failure of communication between extremes of language and attitude, and as pure verbal play. Mayakovsky deftly sketches a familiar street situation of the time: a pretty girl sits in a Woolworth window demonstrating the use of a new "stropper" for Gillette razor blades:

A Commercial Artist Discovers America

Although / it's out of the question
that she should have a moustache
She runs the blade / along her upper lip
pretending to take it off—
As though to say— / very simple,
just sharpen then shave. . . .

(pp. 278-79)

She then performs a manual gesture (no doubt well rehearsed) indicating that the potential customers should by all means come into the store and buy the gadget. The poet, repelled by this crude example of capitalist huckstering (and wholly forgetful of his own contributions to store-window promotion) speaks to her through the window in Russian, being careful to move his lips as though he were speaking English. His remarks concerning her and her job are most uncomplimentary, but she translates everything into romantic compliments:

". . .You're the worst fool." (*dura iz dur*)
But the girl only hears:
"Open
open di dor"
. . . .
Look
they've set you here
like a blockhead (*kak duru elóvuyu*)
But the girl's imagination
swells out at full sail
And she only hears / *"Ai lóv yu."*. . .

(p. 279)

The message from Moscow is lost on a young lady who is only capable of imagining that the handsome youngish man is a rich Wall Street operator who would like to marry her.

The word play is interesting as a preview of the language used in the play ***The Bathhouse*** by the Englishman Pont Kich, whose foreign gibberish consists entirely of actual Russian words in combinations that mean nothing but sound like English. Also, it is characteristic of Mayakovsky's verse procedures, and perhaps lends evidence to the contention that his verse should be thought of as "rhyming" rather than "tonic," that the message, misunderstood though it is, is conveyed entirely by alternating end rhymes. Here we have an example, clear to the point of caricature, of the extent to which rhyme bears the emphasis, rhythm, and movement in a poem of Mayakovsky.

Most other poems of the cycle have less content or verbal interest than this one, though all carry (**"Brooklyn Bridge"** is an interesting exception) the clear stamp of the revolutionary poet speaking about bourgeois America to other revolutionaries who readily take this meaning. Perhaps the poem **"A Skyscraper in Cross-Section"** . . . may be studied as typical of the genre, since it offers an example of a familiar situation: the tourist who is conditioned to see only what he already knew before he came. The poet (is it Mayakovsky or just one of his episodic masks?) is at first astonished by the power and beauty of a thing like New York, but he has learned about the decay of capitalism, and so in his poetry, he "sees through" the industrial miracle of the age—a skyscraper—to the rotting human corpses it encases. We shall see that the circumstances of his visit—his lectures, interviews, and meetings were, with few exceptions, sponsored and arranged for him by Russian or Jewish Communist groups, and he had almost no free contact with American life—helped him, indeed required him, to maintain at all times a dogmatic Marxist stance. One must remember also that in the twenties a large segment of American intellectual society, whether Marxist or not, held a negative view of the American money-culture, its Babbitts, Daddy Brownings, and Pinkertons, its "American tragedies," its hypocrisy built into law, as well as of the mute nonentity who presided over the official show. A surprisingly large number of Americans were ready to accept as sober history the "myth" of the world revolution that Mayakovsky propagated, and to turn hopefully, as he bade them do, to the Comintern. Many of the poems that now carry little conviction even to American radicals were probably not uncongenial to the taste of radical intellectuals in the twenties, and indeed some of them were translated and published in *The Nation*. The hindsight we now have on the Russian revolution, the Comintern, and the Russian Party dictatorship should not blind us to the fact that Mayakovsky's propaganda, dated and forced though it seems to us now, was not out of tune with the intellectual attitudes of his time. But that does not mean at all that it is poetry or should be studied as such.

We now turn to a truly magnificent thing before which criticism either stands mute or lapses into superlatives and even the most eloquent efforts at interpretation seem tongue-tied.

"Brooklyn Bridge" was written in New York City in the late fall of 1925, recited to audiences there, and published in Moscow in the magazine *Projector* in December of that year. The poem as originally conceived is the purest lyricism, a hymn of praise by a modern artist of futurist antecedents and constructivist convictions to those unnamed artists who "made" their own great poem, the bridge. The poem is an abstraction from immediate reality. The poet confronts the bridge in a kind of solitude: the noises of New York are barely audible to him, the lights are distant and ghostly, the ships in the river below are foreshortened to an infinite smallness, and time is displaced to make way for a "geologist" of the far-distant future who examines the fragmental remains of New York and the bridge.

The poem is itself interesting as a structure. It consists of an elated "exordium" addressed to President Coolidge, a set of similes that establish the poet's variegated emotions as he views the bridge, a description of the setting and background from the high vantage point of the bridge, a personal statement of Mayakovsky's affinity with the builders ("I'm proud . . ."), a difficult reconstruction of the bridge and of the history of the times by that "geologist," and a conclusion that expresses the very personal and deep admiration of a maker of poems, Mayakovsky, for another kind of artistic structure.

There are a few lines that seem out of tune with the work as a whole, and the story of how those lines found their way into the poem, duly reported by our Soviet authorities, is instructive as to the nature of the pressures that were constantly at work on Mayakovsky throughout the twenties, making difficult if not impossible the cultivation of his lyric gift. The lines in question read:

> Here / life / for some / was carefree
> for others / it was a long / and hungry howl.
> From this place / men without work
> threw themselves down / into the Hudson. . . .
> (pp. 279-81)

Those lines appear in the handwritten copy of the poem as a later addition, and would seem to be an afterthought forced upon the poet by the hostile reaction of one of his American audiences, as reported in the New York Communist paper *Russian Voice:* "When Mayakovsky had recited his new poem **'Brooklyn Bridge'** before a large working-class audience in New York, a poem in which he expressed his rapture at technology and the greatness of human genius, someone in the balcony shouted: 'Don't forget, Comrade Mayakovsky, that unemployed men often jump off of that bridge into the water. . . .'" . . .

The pure flight of the poet's imagination, unencumbered by a social theme, was not what his audience wanted, and he readily adjusted himself to their spontaneous "censorship." We shall see another instance of his adjustment to quite unofficial censorship in the case of the poem **"Homeward!"** and these examples help us to understand the extremely complex nature of the psychological as well as social pressures under which he labored.

But let us return to the poem itself. What I have called the exordium bids Coolidge (that block of Vermont granite) "give a shout of joy" over Brooklyn Bridge. And "I too will not spare words when it comes to a really good thing," adds the poet. The country may not have been converted to communism by his anti-capitalist propaganda lectures, but "At my praise / you'll blush all red / like our flag, / however / United-States-of-America / you may be." (pp. 281-82)

There follows a set of three parallel similes that establish the poet's humility, his elation and pride, and the open-mouthed awe that one artist experiences before the work of another.

> As a crazed believer / enters / a church,
> . . . .
> so I / in evening's / gray haze
> humbly / set foot on Brooklyn Bridge.
> As a conqueror / marches / into a smashed city
> . . . .
> so, drunk with glory / ready for life,
> I climb / full of pride / onto Brooklyn Bridge.
> As a stupefied painter / fixes his eye
> lovesick and shrewd / on a museum madonna,
> so I / from the star-scattered height
> look / at New York / through Brooklyn Bridge. . . .
> (p. 282)

Mayakovsky, alone with this monster work of art, identifies himself with it completely, associates the work of the builders with his own futurist artistic creed, and insists that he too is above all a careful craftsman:

> I am proud / of just this / mile of steel.
> My own visions have come to life / and stand erect.
> My struggle / for structures / instead of style,
> the stern / calculus / of bolts and steel. . . .
> (p. 283)

These lines are the best, quite possibly the only, poetic realization of the theories about art and literature developed in the *Lef* milieu. . . . The bridge seemed to Mayakovsky a supreme example of what he would call "production-art," an art involved with everyday life and the needs of people, an art both developing out of and molding industrial processes; such an art must be explicitly rational, its effects fully explicable in mathematical terms (the "stern calculus"). Yet the poem is miraculously free of the sectarian dogmatism that usually characterized *Lef* theorizing. We sense no rejection of the "stupefied" (*glupyi*) artist adoring an ancient madonna in a museum, nor indeed any rejection of the past or of museums. Mayakovsky seems rather to associate his experience of reverence for creative power with the experience of all artists at all times.

The poet then invites us to imagine the end of the world and the planet smashed to pieces, with the only thing remaining this bridge "rearing above the dust of destruction.". . . (pp. 283-84)

At this point the lines quoted above on the unemployed workers who threw themselves from the bridge intrude upon the movement of the poem. We may recognize the fact that much human misery went hand in hand with the development of capitalism in America, and that the bridge was indeed the scene of frequent suicides, but still insist that those lines are in disaccord with the rest of the poem, and do not at all fit the remarks of the "geologist," whose sole effort has been to reconstruct the *technology* of a former era from the evidence of the bridge; that evidence would tell him nothing about the class structure of the society that built it. After this interruption the "geologist" completes his remarks:

> And the rest / of my picture / is now very clear.
> Along cable-strings / it reaches to the stars.
> And I see / that here / Mayakovsky
> stood / and composed / verses, syllable by syllable. . . .
> (p. 284)

The last lines have also seemed to some critics an intrusion on the movement of the poem, but we are accustomed to the fact that, whatever the theme or setting of his lyric poetry, the center of apperception and feeling must always be the poet himself. The "chemist" of the distant future is called upon to "resurrect" Mayakovsky; why shouldn't the "geologist" also find a trace of Mayakovsky in the ruins of the bridge?

At this point the poet himself speaks again in his own person, to give a final statement of his total fascination:

> I stare / as an Eskimo stares at a train,
> I fasten on it / as a tick fastens on an ear.
> Brooklyn Bridge—
> Yes—
> It is really a creation! (*veshch*) . . .
>
> (pp. 284-85)

The final word, *veshch*, suggest a self-quotation. The word *veshch* has two meanings here: 1) a thing, an object; and 2) a long poem, a major artistic undertaking; and it is the word he used as a subtitle of the poem *Man*. The pun upon the two meanings in the reference to the bridge—it is both an object, a structure, and a great work of art—reminds us once more of the futurist orientation in the mid-twentites toward art as the production of objects both useful and beautiful. The word serves as an accolade that accepts the bridge and its American builders into the company of modern artists to which Mayakovsky belonged. (p. 285)

Edward J. Brown, in his Mayakovsky: A Poet in the Revolution, *Princeton University Press, 1973, 386 p.*

MARC SLONIM (essay date 1977)

[*Slonim was a Russian-born American educator, literary critic, and editor who wrote extensively on Russian literature. In the following excerpt, he discusses the futuristic aspects of Mayakovsky's poetry that contributed to his emergence as the premier poet of the Bolshevik Revolution.*]

While [Sergey] Essenin, the peasant poet, reflected the tragedy of the victims [during the Bolshevik Revolutions], Vladimir Mayakovsky expressed the aggressiveness and hopes of the masters. Essenin personified the spirit of loss and defeat; Mayakovsky sang of strength and victory. Yet their fate was similar: both ended as suicides. (p. 19)

At nineteen Mayakovsky emerged as the most turbulent of the militant cubo-futurists. He attacked "the academy and decrepit old literature," demanded a revolution in the arts in the name of modernity, speed, dynamism, and direct colloquial means of expression, and was ready to support avant-garde theories with his fists. A tall athletic-looking youth endowed with a violent temperament and the voice of a heckler, he loved to "shock the bourgeois," went around in a bright yellow blazer, and treated the stage where he read his poems as a boxing arena. He enjoyed **"A Slap in the Public's Face"** as the futurist manifesto was entitled in 1912, showered abuse on opponents in his public appearances, which often ended in free-for-alls, and invented all sorts of stunts and hoaxes. It would be useless to deny a great deal of exhibitionism and pose in the challenges and extravagances of the futurists (who often went around with carrots instead of flowers in their buttonholes), but their purpose was serious, and they reflected the inner crisis in literature and art. And the poems which Mayakovsky started publishing in 1915, despite the provocative titles of his two booklets—***A Cloud in Trousers, The Spine Flute***—were unusual in their form but sad and almost tragic in their essence. Excerpts from his **"War and Peace"** and **"Man"** appeared in Gorky's monthly *The Annals* which followed a mild line in poetry and fiction. In all these works of exceptional vigor Mayakovsky used futuristic diction and eccentric, broken meters, *outré* near-rhymes, assonances, topiary arrangements, and whimsical punctuation, while his vocabulary was ostentatiously colloquial and crude. What made his poems highly original was the combination of rebellion and lyricism, of force approaching brutality of expression and hidden emotional sensitivity. He interwove in them the story of a tragic love with the negation of art, of state, and of religion; intimate confession followed his thrusts against social conditions. He complained that his sufferings and inner void came from "the loss of feelings on the city pavements." His heart, he claimed, was like a bordello on fire, and his words were the prostitutes leaping out of its blazing windows. He spoke incessantly of his torments: "I burned my soul where tenderness was bred; it is more difficult than the storming of a thousand Bastilles." His stanzas, filled with extravagant similes, aimed at a complete break with the tradition of the genteel, the sublime, or the esoteric: Mayakovsky wanted to be loud, coarse, impetuous, anti-aesthetic. He loathed the watery sentimentalism of patrician poets, and the verbal vagueness of the symbolists. The debasement of language and metaphor, as well as the ironical or grotesque twist in his verse and its conversational tone, were intentionally directed against the "spirituality" and "purity" of traditional poetry. A considerable part of Mayakovsky's work was inspired by poetical polemics. But the passion and anger of ***A Cloud in Trousers*** and ***The Spine Flute*** make them outstanding poems; they certainly belong to the best works of Mayakovsky though Communist critics are reluctant to admit this. In general, they prefer to underestimate Mayakovsky's futurism and pass over in silence the fact that all his poetic characteristics were evident before 1917. (pp. 19-21)

Mayakovsky considered his poetry a weapon. He served the Revolution with his word just as others served it with the sword. There is no doubt that he did it deliberately and wholeheartedly: he was the poet of the Kremlin by conviction and not by appointment. It is well known that Lenin, who had a very conservative taste in literature, did not like and did not understand his works. But Mayakovsky sang of the same Lenin and taxes and government bonds not because he expected a reward but because his civic and poetic credo demanded it; he was convinced that modern poets had to "turn themselves inside out" and "rush into the morrow, strain forward so that their pants would split." It is easy to mock such tropes and object that splitting one's trousers is not exactly the best way to write good verse, but the point remains that despite all his excessive energy Mayakovsky was a true poet. Some critics have compared him with Nekrassov, the popular bard of the 1860's, who also wanted to merge poetry with life and who wrote topical poems, but despite this similarity, the two poets are far apart. Nekrassov's muse is one of grief, tears, and repentance; Mayakovsky's is active, dynamic, and displays a vibrant acceptance of life. His motto was "To shine like the sun," as he affirmed in one of his best poems **"A Most Extraordinary Adventure"** . . . , which depicts a visit paid by the sun to the poet's country house.

While psychological and ideological motives predominate in Nekrassov, Mayakovsky's poems are for the most part satirical descriptions, ardent appeals, or oratorical formulations of Communist aims. It would be futile to look for complex ideas in

Mayakovsky. He is forceful rather than deep. His philosophy is quite primitive; it can be summed up as revolutionary materialism, based on the superiority of reason and social service over idealistic romanticism or inertia.

His poems, with their obvious and simple meaning, were aimed at the mass reader. He addressed the multitudes in the naïve and and crude language of broad hyperbole, lush sarcasm, and coarse humor; he resorted to sensuous metaphors, and stressed the visual, the palpable, the earthy. This anti-metaphysical poet captured the imagination of his audiences by evoking the notions of mass and quantity: Woodrow Wilson's silk topper is as high as the Eiffel Tower, Chicago has 12,000 streets, the army of the proletariat numbers 150,000,000 Ivans. He shouts at the top of his voice, his sentences roll like drums, and he plays masterfully the complex keyboard of assonances, changing rhythms, unusual rhymes, and rollicking jests. His virtuosity in sounds, meters, and the intergration of colloquialisms into the brittle pace of his lines give his poems a unique verbal expressiveness. As loud (and effective) as circus posters, they are yet full-blooded and sonorous: they demand to be read from a rostrum; they have a thunderous declamatory quality that only the eighteenth-century poet Derzhavin—Mayakovsky's formal predecessor—had achieved previously. But Derzhavin glorified the splendors of the Empire under Catherine the Great in well ordered syllabic-tonic odes, while Mayakovsky sang revolutionary passions in words that marched in military step. Mayakovsky's manner is oratorical and rhetorical, and consists of short, broken lines, printed in staircase fashion; single words and sentences are heavily accented, the stress is on intonation and meaning, the emphasis on syllabic variations of rhymes and the auditory effect of intentionally "difficult" words. He aimed at the "de-poetization" of the language and also "corrected" the current prosody by adopting a meter in which primarily accents (or stresses) in each line were counted. He thus initiated a whole school in Russian poetry, which will be linked with his name regardless of the fate of his individual poems or of the ideas he tried to put across. Toward the end of the 1920's Mayakovsky was convinced that his style truly represented the spirit of the Revolution. With his usual boastfulness (like many people basically unsure of themselves, he despised humility and designated modesty as stupidity or hypocrisy), he claimed that he and his friends were "carrying the literary load." He had a strong sense of responsiblity and often chose a topic because he felt it to be a social and political obligation and not any spontaneous choice prompted by preference or attraction. In an unfinished poem written just before his tragic death he remarked:

> I am also fed up
> with the agit-prop;
> I too could compose
> ballads about you—
> it is pleasanter and pays more—
> but I forced myself
> by planting my foot on the throat of my own song.

In **"A Cloud in Trousers"** he spoke of "the blood-stained rag of my heart," of the "scream which is my crucified soul," and challenged the skies, reproaching them for the torments of his love. He led an intense and turbulent life of emotions—and love lyrics have as important a part in his works as the songs of Revolution. He was the poet of the first decade of Russian Communism with all its exaggerations, wild hopes, and tempestuousness, but he was also a tender, ironical, and sensitive sufferer of the "high disease" compounded of sentiment and imagination—and the two opposing drives within him and in his poetry were not always reconciled.

The New Man he portrayed did not give a rap for "lyrical nonsense," in fact Mayakovsky bragged about strength, rationality, and a revolutionary approach to personal matters. Yet so many of his poems, such as **"A Letter from Paris Concerning Love,"** . . . and his beautiful **"At the Top of My Voice,"** are confessions of wistfulness and amorous longing. And others contain poignant notes of solitude and inner dissension. He was unable to get rid of that romantic "melancrockery" he condemned so dashingly in his didactic verse. As a revolutionist he banned "individualistic emotions" and rejected the lyricist in his literature. But, in an uncanny act of revenge, the lyricist killed Mayakovsky in real life. The drives, dreams, and doubts the poet had tried to chain and imprison escaped and tore their jailer to shreds. Mayakovsky, who jeered at sentimental lovers and announced the replacement of the soul by steam and electricity, fell victim to erotic and emotional failure: he committed suicide mainly because of unrequited love.

By 1930 this trumpeting poet of loud optimism felt lonely and frustrated. He no longer had any illusions about the drawbacks of the regime he was serving, and his satirical plays, ***The Bedbug*** . . . and ***The Bathhouse*** . . . , were bold denunciations of the red tape and triviality that were undermining the heroic dreams of the Revolution. ***The Bedbug*** depicts the pseudo-Communist Prisypkin, a stupid and vulgar parasite who survives by anabiosis; future generations keep him and put him in a zoo as a curious specimen of some savage tribe—together with the bedbug they find on his collar. In ***The Bathhouse*** a fierce attack against the smugness of petty leaders is combined with an exposé of Communist bureaucracy. Meyerhold produced both plays in his theater with brilliant inventiveness, but they were dubbed subversive by the Party press, and disappeared from the Soviet stage. It took almost three decades before they made a comeback in the late 'fifties after the death of Stalin.

Criticism of the plays was not the only conflict between Mayakovsky and the rigid Party line. It should not be forgotten that Lenin disliked Mayakovsky and rejected futurism and all forms of revolutionary art. In his *Reminiscences* Gorky writes: "Lenin distrusted Mayakovsky and was irritated by his works. In his opinion the poet was shouting, invented crooked words, and made difficult reading. Lenin never changed this negative attitude. In 1921 he called Mayakovsky's ***150 Millions*** "stupid, pretentious junk." (pp. 25-9)

At the age of thirty-seven, after a long career of struggle and sacrifice Mayakovsky felt himself isolated and doomed; all the pangs of unhappy love, unsatisfied sex, and of practical and emotional instability added to his ennui. Thus the irrational, non-utilitarian aspirations he had wanted to eliminate gripped him irresistibly—and he must have felt humiliated and baffled by this discrepancy between his real emotions and the principles he had proclaimed in poems.

As a young man he had written:

> The heart longs for a bullet:
> the throat craves for a razor;
> the soul trembles between walls of ice—
> and it will never escape the ice.

Suicide seemed the only way out of this glacial prison. . . . (pp. 29-30)

The impact of his poetry and personality on Soviet literature was tremendous. Not only did he enjoy the love of vast audiences who acclaimed him as the poet of the Revolution and of the working class, but a whole generation of poets recognized him as their leader and imitated him. Even those who did not want to jettison all the themes and traditions of the past felt Mayakovsky's influence and evinced an intention to transform literature into an active means for changing reality. This latter tendency became prevalent in Soviet poetry, and it was accepted as indisputable truth by all Communist poets and many fellow-travelers; thus Mayakovsky promoted a literary trend which is fundamental to the aesthetic credo of the USSR: to approach a work of art as a social phenomenon and to evaluate it in terms of the conribution it makes to the common cause. (p. 30)

Although Mayakovsky was recognized as the greatest poet of the Revolution and his fame thoughout the Soviet Union grew steadily, his official canonization did not really begin until the end of the 1930's (following his suicide there was a definite reluctance in higher circles to glorify his work). But from the moment Stalin called him "the best and most gifted poet of our Soviet epoch," his work was treated as a classic and the study of Mayakovsky became an obligatory part of every school program and textbook. The latter mostly distorted his image and deliberately ignored some of his controversial pieces (***The Bedbug*** and ***The Bathhouse,*** for instance). Pasternak said in his *An Essay in Autobiography* that Mayakovsky "began to be introduced forcibly, like potatoes under Catherine the Great. This was his second death, but he had nothing to do with it." (p. 31)

Statistics show that after Pushkin, Lermontov, and Nekrassov, Mayakovsky is the most widely read poet in the Soviet Union. Between 1917 and 1954 more than 23 million copies of his works were sold in Russian and in 51 languages of the Republic. Villages, streets, and squares were named after him, and so were *sovkhozes, kolhozes,* schools, libraries, theaters, steamships, and a station of the Moscow subway. M. Maslin, one of his biographers, offers a typical explanation of this popularity: "The Soviet people love and appreciate Mayakovsky for the ideological strength and popular spirit of his verse, for the novelty and monumental scope of his images, for his humanity and for the moving intensity of his emotions." When the series "Literary Heritage" published in 1958 new materials on Mayakovsky, bringing out his contradictory nature and his personal tragedy as well as unknown details of his love life, the Central Committee of the Communist Party deemed it necessary to approve a special resolution against this publication as being "dangerous and offering arguments for *émigré* critics." It shows the extent to which Mayakovsky is today considered the official bard of the Communist Revolution. (pp. 31-2)

Marc Slonim, "Vladimir Mayakovsky: The Poet of the Revolution," in his Soviet Russian Literature: Writers and Problems 1917-1977, *revised edition, Oxford University Press, 1977, 19-32.*

JURIJ STRIEDTER (essay date 1979)

[In the following excerpt Striedter, a German educator and critic specializing in Russian Formalist and structuralist criticism, examines Mayakovsky's incorporation of myth into his prerevolutionary poetry.]

In wild destruction
Sweeping away the old
We will thunder out into the world
A new myth. . . .

In these lines from Vladimir Mayakovsky's revolutionary poem ***150,000,000*** . . . revolutionary action is linked to the demand for a "new myth"; out of them arises the question of the extent to which revolution can be mythicized, the relation of the old myth to the new, and the function of poetry in the creation of new myths. (p. 357)

Mayakovsky's cry for a "new myth" harks back indirectly to the Romantics' discussion of myths, and directly to Nietzsche's demand for "new myths." The introduction of this term brought the myth discussion to life, and also complicated it. It did, however, show that where "late horizons" of myth are under discussion, a difference has to be made between: (a) the adoption and reshaping of particular motifs, techniques, and structures of traditional myths in fulfillment of nonmythical intentions, dispensing with a "'mythical view of life,'' and (b) the intention of reviving this "mythical view of life" and creating "new myths," either through recourse to the tradition of myth, or with the aid of new themes and new techniques of mythicizing. (pp. 357-58)

Nietzsche, regardless of his classical education and his embodiment of the Apollonian and Dionysian, as creator of "new myths" usurped the name Zarathustra, founder of a religion, and defied Christ, founder of a religion, thus playing to the full his role of provocator and usurper. And Mayakovsky, who in his very first poem calls himself "the scream-lipped Zarathustra of the present day," . . . constantly usurps the figure of Christ, both for his new revolutionary myth and for himself, as the poetic harbinger of the revolution.

This allusion to the link between the German "new Zarathustra" of the nineteenth century and the Russian of the twentieth is worth making insofar as the striking preference for Christian motifs and ideas, together with the almost total lack of classical mythology in Mayakovsky's pre-revolutionary works, suggests certain specifically Russian premises. Through Russia's link with East Roman-Byzantine—as opposed to West Roman—tradition and through the correspondingly oriented, centuries-old dominance of the orthodox church in almost all spheres of culture, the heritage of classical antiquity played a far smaller part in Russia than it did in Roman Catholic regions, including those that were later to become Protestant. The Christian tradition was thus all the livelier, both as a religious and as a cultural factor. In veiw of this, reference to Christian ideas was bound to be infinitely more effective than evocations of classical mythology. This, of course, applies also to Mayakovsky. (p. 359)

As regards the question why and in what way Christian ideas influenced Mayakovsky's revolutionary myth and poems, a good deal can be learned simply from the selections he made out of the general fund of Christian tradition and, more especially, from his different evaluations of individual elements. He shows an obviously polemic attitude towards the God of the Old Testament, God the Father, who, as creator and ruler of the world, is made responsible for the imperfection and injustice of it: either he is made the object of pathetic protest, or he is ridiculed as a foolish old man. There is a similar attitude towards the church and clergy, who, as administrators of this type of religious order and as followers of the ruler, are also ridiculed or attacked with bitter passion. The church sits with its front steps at the throat of the rebelling street, threatening to choke it, and when the street shakes it off, one awaits the approach of the *deprived* Father God to inflict punishment.

While God the Creator and his church are held responsible for the defects of this world, the "other world" of Christianity is seen primarily as a polemic counter to demands for a better world on this earth. Some works show this in the form of a simple negation. The poet wants liberation from personal and social suffering, not later, in the other world, but in this, his own world; as perfect love he does not want that of heaven but that of earth; he wants the happiness of himself and everyone else to come, here and now. But this other world can also be directly represented in the poem: the poet Mayakovsky, suffering on earth, is personally raised up into heaven; but there he finds a familiar, hated bourgeois idyll, with Verdi's music, small-talk, etc. As a man with a *heart* and with lusts of the flesh he has nothing in common with fleshless, sexless angels and saints ("Where do the bodiless have their heart?"), and he hastens longingly down again to the earth, even though he may not have his longing fulfilled there either. And what the proletarian poet experiences is experienced by the proletarians themselves—the *impure ones,* who do manage to reach the the heavenly paradise, but are bored stiff and leave it again at once, handing it back to its inhabitants Chrysostom, Methuselah, Leo Tolstoy, and Jean-Jacques Rousseau. Thus the Christian "other world" is used as a poetic foil, the renunciation of the other-worldly ideal intensifying the grievance over the imperfections of this world, while the satirical image and style of the other world provide an effective conrast to the pathetic sufferings of this and so give fuel to the revolt against both types of world.

The attitude towards Christ is quite different. No other figure in the early poems and plays is referred to directly or indirectly with such frequency as Christ. These references are without any satirical overtones, and indeed he is often set parallel to or on a level with the poet himself. This striking integration is based on a view of Christ as a human god in the broadest sense. Unlike the distant Father God, inhuman in his severity towards personally guiltless beings, Christ is the god that became a man in order to suffer like a man and through his personally guiltless sufferings to redeem suffering mankind. As god of the poor, the afflicted, the humiliated, he is closely akin to the poet of the hungry and rejected, of the rogues and whores, as the young Mayakovsky sees himself. And so it is with this image of the guiltlessly martyred and crucified Christ that the poet identifies himself. What is vital in this conception of Christ and its poetic application to the revolution, is that he is no longer seen as the human, redeeming embodiment of that same god whose creative and law-giving aspects are personified in God the Father, but as the human *antitype* to this god. As a guiltless expiatory sacrifice he stands implicitly as a bitter accusation against the one who, as creator and ruler of a bad world-order, first arranged this sacrifice, as he arranged all sacrifices and sufferings of the innocent. Inherent in this new interpretation and application of the Christ figure is a strong element of protest, even though Christ himself, as the loving and innocently suffering one, is not portrayed as a protester. Apart from his purely charitable features, the figure is given clearly defined social-revolutionary traits, implying a general revolt against this whole world-order. And this is what makes it possible for the Christ figure to be integrated into the revolutionary myth.

Anyone who knows the history of Russian thought and literature in the nineteenth and twentieth centuries will see at once how deeply rooted Mayakovsky is in Russian traditon. One need only think of Dostoyevsky, who was led by experience of the limitless suffering of innocent children to return to God his "entrance ticket" to this world, and yet on the other hand saw in the meekly suffering Christ or his imitators the ideal, indeed the only, way to overcome the social injustice and other defects of this afflicted world. It is not possible to deal here with the whole history of this idea and its translation into literary form, but a word of warning should be given against offering too narrow a definition of it as "specifically Russian." Certainly this trend was particularly marked and particularly styled in Russia from the middle of the nineteenth century onwards. But there were sources and adherents all over Europe, not the least of them being Pierre Joseph Proudhon, whose influence on Russians such as Dostoyevsky and Mayakovsky is as clear as that on the most important West European theorist of the "new myth" at the turn of the century: Georges Sorel. The idea of justice as the driving force and criterion of historical progress, experience of the injustice of the prevailing world-order, and the resultant endeavor to "recognize the reality and intensity of evil, to seek out its causes, and to discover the cure"—these were the determining factors behind Proudhon's *Idée générale de la révolution*. This gave rise to the possibility of playing off one's own social-revolutionary ideas of justice against the church, and its close ties with the prevailing injustice . . . ; it also gave one the chance to equate love of one's neighbor and expiatory sacrifice, as personified in Christ, with one's own social-revolutionary actions and the socialist revolution. And this was the view taken by many West European as well as Russian revolutionaries. This, then, is the tradition in which stands the equation of Christ with social revolution in Mayakovsky's pre-revolutionary writings. (pp. 361-64)

As the humanized God Christ is reduced to a loving, suffering man, he can be transposed from the sphere of religion and metaphysics to that of worldly, social, political revolution; and as he is made into an abstract myth, embodying the sacrifice for the sake of world redemption, he can take on the vital function of worldwide redeemer and renovator in the "new myth" of the revolution.

The linking of a traditional myth with a new one presupposes the abstraction of both according to a common schema, a mythical "archetype." The mythical archetype, or archetypal myth, that forms the basis of all the revolution myths in Mayakovsky's pre-revolutionary poetry, can be outlined as follows: the world of personal and general experience is a world of imperfection, injustice, and undeserved suffering, and hence a sick world. A cure is possible only through a radical upheaval and a new beginning. Everything existing, rigid, binding, must be released, must be returned through fire and flood back into its original state of chaos, so that the new year of a new chronology for new people in a new world can begin; and this new era will be a golden age or the paradise regained of a new Adam. An indispensable part of this mythical process is the sacrifice which, as a personal and general purification, is a pre-condition, a turning-point, and a ritual sign of the process of redemption.

It is only against this background of the archetypal myth that one can understand the full significance of the Christ figure in Mayakovsky's revolution myth, and that one can follow the different variations in the relation between Christ, revolution, and revolutionary poet Mayakovsky. When Christ is seen as

Mayakovsky and Lilya Brik in 1915. Reproduced by permission of Agence Strassova.

the Redeemer, the *whole* of the revolution (as redemption) can be compared or equated with him. When he is seen as the "new man," he is comparable to the *aim* of the revolution. When he is seen as the indispensable sacrifice, the scapegoat for the redemption, he can be compared to pre-conditions and elements of the revolutionary process, and those that suffer for and before the revolution can be compared to him. In the first instance—the equation of Christ and revolution as a single whole—the revolutionary poet, as herald of the revolution, becomes a "prophet" or "apostle"; in the last instance, when he sees himself as a martyr and a sacrifice for the revolution, he can be identified with Christ, he is a "new Christ." (pp. 364-65)

Thus the poem **"Man,"** for instance, draws a consistent parallel between Christ and Mayakovsky. In direct line with the birth, passion, and ascension of Christ and with the liturgy that refers to these, the poem is divided into the following sections: *Birth of Mayakovsky, Life of Mayakovsky, Passion of Mayakovsky, Ascension of Mayakovsky, Mayakovsky in Heaven, Return of Mayakovsky, Mayakovsky to the Centuries,* and *The Last*. As far as theme and style are concerned, the poem revolves round the contrast between the sacredness of the model and the satirical banality of the blasphemy. The technique used in the poem **"Cloud in Trousers"** is more complex and more refined, as it is continually moving from one type of coordination to another. This poem orginally bore a title that relates very closely to our theme but was censured as being offensive to religion: "The Thirteenth Apostle." The poet's designation of himself as the "thirteenth apostle" is also to be found in the text. (pp. 365-66)

For the person who regards Christianity as a binding religion of tradition, the equation of Christ with the revolution (and with the revolutionary poet) will act as a provocative usurpation of Christian revelation; for the non-Christian reader, the poetic and the religious elements interact as different realizations of the same mythical archetype, with the poetic "new myth" bringing to life what for him is the real point of reference—namely, the "old myth." (p. 368)

Jurij Striedter, "The 'New Myth' of Revolution—A Study of Mayakovsky's Early Poetry," in New Perspectives in German Literary Criticism: A Collection of Essays, *edited by Richard E. Amacher and Victor Lange, translated by David Henry Wilson & others, Princeton University Press, 1979, pp. 357-85.*

PETER FRANCE (essay date 1982)

[In the following excerpt, France discusses the imagery and emotional language of several of Mayakovsky's longer poems.]

It is fascinating—and pointless—to speculate how Mayakovsky's poetry might have developed if there had been no October Revolution. As it was, he immediately identified his cause with that of the Revolution. What is more, he claimed that only the Futurists had an idea of art which was equal to what was happening in politics; in 1918 he wrote in an 'open letter to the workers':

> The revolution of content—socialism-anarchism—is unthinkable without the revolution of form—futurism [. . .] No one can know what immense suns will light the life of the future. Perhaps artists will transform the grey dust of cities into hundred-coloured rainbows [. . .] One thing is clear to us—the first page in the new history of the arts was turned by us.

This belief was not shared by the new rulers of Russia. Although Soviet scholars have looked hard and found certain pieces of evidence to the contrary, it seems clear that Lenin never really thought much of Mayakovsky and preferred more traditional writing. Lunacharsky, the Minister of Culture and Education, was more sympathetic, and gave a certain amount of support, but he also reacted sharply against the destructive 'hooligan' side to Mayakovsky's activity and to what he saw as his extreme subjectivism. So too Trotsky in *Literature and Revolution:*

> Mayakovsky is closer to the dynamic quality of the Revolution and to its stern courage than to the mass character of its heroism, deeds and experiences . . . The individualistic and Bohemian arrogance—in contrast, not to humility, which no one wants, but to a necessary sense of the measure of things—runs through everything written by Mayakovsky. [See *TCLC*, Vol. 4]

Trotsky was relatively friendly; many others were far more hostile. (pp. 172-73)

Many of Mayakovsky's views on poetry and the other arts were expressed in the journal *Lef* (an acronym for Left Front of the Arts), which between 1923 and 1925 grouped many of the former Futurists and some of the 'Formalist' students of literature. In the teeth of hostility from other more conservative literary groups, including the proponets of Proletarian Culture, *Lef* printed both excellent new poetry and programmatic articles defining the nature and function of literature in a revolutionary society. Much of the poetry (such as Pasternak's 'Lofty Malady' and indeed much of Mayakovsky's own work) seems far removed from the theory, but the theory is consistent enough. It is conveniently summed up in these words of Mayakovsky, written in 1928:

> One of the slogans, one of the great achievements of *Lef* is the deaestheticization of the industrial arts, constructivism. The poetic application is the propaganda poem (*agitka*), together with economic propaganda, advertising. In spite of all the hullaballoo of poets I consider [one of his advertising jingles] as poetry of the highest order. . . .

So art should be applied to life; the poet takes his place alongside the craftsman or the engineer. And just as the visual artist was to devote his skill to design, so the poet was a master of words whose services were needed in public life. Notions such as creativity (or worse still inspiration) were ousted by that of skill (*masterstvo*). For Mayakovsky there was nothing degrading in devoting as he did a lot of his energy to such things as the design of tea-packets. As he told an artist who worked with him, 'these wrappings are worth more, not less than the pictures you paint for exhibitions'. This position is reminiscent of the Bauhaus—or indeed of William Morris; for Mayakovsky the point was that it was in precisely such spheres as industrial design or journalism that the battle had to be fought against the old aesthetic, social and moral habits. (pp. 176-77)

In all this it is striking how much Mayakovsky's notion of poetry is centred on conflict. The conflict may be between 'you' and 'I', the poet and the bourgeois audience, as in the early Futurist poems. Later, the poet is more often a combatant in the service of the Revolution, and his poems are weapons for fighting the enemies of the cause, military adversaries, capitalist survivals, bourgeois habits, old ideas of poetry. One such poem is **'To Sergey Esenin'** . . . , written in 1926, and particularly interesting not only because of its subject but because Mayakovsky used it as an example to demonstrate, in the manner of Edgar Allen Poe's 'Philosophy of Composition', 'how to make verse'. The newspaper article with this title . . . is designed to help other writers, but it is also a provocative manifesto of the *Lef* conception of poetry. Stressing the need for the poet to work in accordance with a 'social demand', Mayakovsky praises 'tendentiousness' and pours scorn on the poetry of self-expression. His poem is cited as a successful application of this doctrine.

Esenin, on committing suicide, had written a farewell note in his own blood which ended with the lines:

> In this life to die is nothing new,
> But of course to live is nothing newer.

Mayakovsky saw his poetic task as being to neutralize the harmful influence of Esenin's poem, which could not only be effectively countered by another poem, not by pontificating articles. He describes his own poem in strictly rhetorical terms, showing how all the various elements (tone, length, diction) are designed to produce the right effect. It was a difficult task; he had to avoid sentimentality, sententiousness and flippancy, never forgetting the probable reactions of an audience who were very much under Esenin's spell. (pp. 177-78)

'To Sergey Esenin' is therefore presented as a persuasive poem. It is also a beautiful and moving poem, which gives every appearance of springing from strong emotion. Nor should it be thought that there is any contradiction between didactic intention and the apparent expression of powerful feeling. Since ancient times oratory and passion have been allies rather than enemies. It is true that in describing his poetic practice, Mayakovsky lays provocative stress on conscious choice and craft to the detriment of inspiration. His remarks are a simplification of the real process, as he himself says, but the result of this simplification is a suggestive account of the generation of a poetic text. In some ways he is doing for his own poem what his friends the Formalists did for the literature of the past: explaining how it is made, what makes it work. Inevitably though, his account differs from theirs in emphasizing less the finished work than its production. And what should be noticed here is that, unlike certain old rhetoricians (or indeed modern structuralists), Mayakovsky sees the maker of poems not as one who conforms to certain pre-existing rules and formulae of the art, but as one who has acquired the habits that make him capable of generating new poetic forms. At the opposite pole from, say, Mandelstam, for whom poetry gave us the 'joy of recognition' of ancient things, Mayakovsky the Futurist believed that 'novelty is essential in a poetic production'. To be capable of making new things, the poet needs to be constantly working on the language, 'filling the reservoirs, the barns of the skull with necessary, expressive, rare, invented, renewed, manufactured and other words'. He must also possess 'habits and ways of working with words, infinitely individual habits which only come with years of daily work: rhymes, metres, alliterations, images, ways of lowering or heightening the tone, endings, titles, etc., etc.' He gives examples of some of these in his article—the rhymes of the first quatrain or the manipulation of stylistic registers—not so that others can imitate them, but so that they can see any poem as the new solution to new problems.

In all this discussion of the craft of verse, one element stands out as somewhat different from the rest; rhythm, which Mayakovsky calls 'the fundamental force and energy of verse', is seen as something inexplicable, like magnetism or electricity. The poet must cultivate his sense of rhythm, but rhythm itself appears as something which is given. Mayakovsky does not know whether it comes from within him or from outside (more likely the former he thinks); whatever its origins he uses for it the same word that Blok had used for the roar in his ears as he wrote *The Twelve*—*gul*. He may not believe in the poetic process as 'the inspired throwing back of the head in expectation of the heavenly spirit of poetry which will descend on his bald patch in the form of a dove, a peacock or an ostrich', but his picture of himself listening to this *gul* recalls many descriptions of the inspired poet, visited by a divine frenzy: 'I walk about, waving my arms and roaring almost without words, now speeding my pace so as not to hinder the roaring, now roaring more quickly to keep pace with my feet.' This corresponds exactly with numerous reminiscences left by those who knew Mayakovsky. It is true that the process is not simply a passive one, but it certainly gives an impression of the poet as an unusual being, cut off from his fellows by an irresistible power.

Mayakovsky was sincere in his attempt to demystify the craft of poetry, and his example is worth meditating by those who make a religion of it. Even so it is often a traditional, Romantic picture of isolation and combined vulnerability and strength that predominates in descriptions of his activities and in certain of his major poems of the 1920s. To be sure, most of his work of this period was propagandist, didactic, heroic or satirical, and two of the longer poems, ***Vladimir Ilich Lenin*** and ***Good*** . . . are impressive large-scale examples of 'tendentious' poetry. Nevertheless, one is always being reminded of the voice, the powerful presence and the personal concerns of the poet, all of which find open expression in his great poem of 1923, ***About That***. . . . (pp. 179-81)

In his brief autobiography, Mayakovsky wrote that ***About That*** was 'personal, on social themes.' It explicitly refers back (in an epigraph and in the body of the poem) over a gap of seven years to one of his major pre-revolutionary poems, ***Man;*** in its tone and general movement it also resembles ***A Cloud in Trousers.*** The original impulse of the poem was a difficult period in Mayakovsky's long love affair with Lili Brik. . . . He was passionately and jealously attached to her, and ***About That*** begins, like ***A Cloud in Trousers,*** with vehement cries of possessive and thwarted love. The opening sequence dramatizes the poet's isolation in the form of a telephone call, and extravagant images evoke his desperate attempts to communicate. The whole world, conjured up in a grandiose enumeration, is seen waiting breathlessly for the outcome of the call, like spectators at a duel, and the person at the other end of the line becomes the duellist D'Anthès, the man who killed Pushkin.

Driven wild by jealousy, Mayakovsky then imagines himself transformed into a bear in a world of swirling water and ice-floes. The rest of the poem alternates between fantastic dream images and more realistic, satirical scenes set in Moscow houses at the Christmas holidays. This juxtaposition points up the contrast between the poet's inner world and Moscow society of the NEP period. For this is the society of *byt,* the cosy new world in which Karl Marx's portrait has become a chic decoration. . . . The bear-like poet tries to pull Lili away from this corrupting life, but above all he must save himself from compromising, accepting, or perhaps simply growing old. One of the most powerful moments comes when from the ice of the River Neva he sees on a Petrograd bridge his younger self, the suicidal hero of ***Man***. . . . Once again water is set against the everyday world, but here the water of deliverance is also the water of death. In ***At the Top of my Voice*** the stone aqueduct carries the water to posterity. Here the bridge stands in the middle of the water and the poet is tied fast to it by his poetry (the poetry of constructive life, the verse for ROSTA perhaps); if he throws himself over he will be broken on the stone of the pillars. . . . (pp. 181-83)

The tone is emphatic, as it is throughout this poem, and indeed in most of Mayakovsky's work, with all sorts of oratorical repetitions, both of words and ideas, and with the characteristics direct address. . . . The poem shifts rapidly and without warning from one to the other, momentarily confusing the reader as one voice follows another and fantasy and realism intertwine. ***About That*** is not an easy poem to understand at first reading. Nor indeed is much of Mayakovsky's best poetry; without ever creating the *zaum'* ('trans-sense' language) which some of the Futurists experimented with, he retained in his post-revolutionary period the urge to 'make things strange', to provoke his reader or listener to imaginative activity by unexpected shifts of perspective, elliptical constructions, new words and so forth. His verse may be oratorical and at times inflated; only rarely does it sink to the easy flow of most public speaking and much public poetry. It was this difficulty, this inaccessibility, that was held against him by his critic of the 1920s. (pp. 183-84)

Although the October Revolution obviously gave a new direction to Mayakovsky's writing, the continuity of themes in his work is striking. From beginning to end, though in varying proportions, we find non-acceptance of the existing world, provocative attacks on the smug and philistine, the aspiration to create a new art and a new life, pain and frustration at the resistance offered by reality, the desire for love, and a utopian vision of the future coupled with an image of himself as sacrificial victim. He writes for others, but always by way of himself; he is in his own constant hero, not loath to see himself as another Christ. Certain images recur, mainly strong elemental ones; this chapter has shown the importance of water, whether in sea or river, aqueduct or water pipe. But water is ambivalent, it can mean both death and life, the friend and the enemy, and one finds a similar ambiguity in other of these elemental images.

Another recurrent group, less ambiguous than water, has not appeared in this chapter, though it meant a great deal to Mayakovsky: these are the animals, whom he loved. He liked to draw himself as a giraffe or a dog, and one of his best early poems, 'Good Attitude to Horses' . . . , is about the sufferings of an exhausted horse on the city streets. Animals appealed to Mayakovsky for their vulnerability, and I think it is fair to say that this is the quality which many readers now find appealing in the poet himself. Vladimir Markov writes: 'He was also a lonely, self-centred, sentimental boy who was obsessed with suicide and sang about unrequited love all his life.'

This anguished figure finds a natural response in many readers of poetry, but it should not allow us to forget the other side to his achievement, the constructive and innovative drive which he celebrates in ***At the Top of my Voice.*** This was already there in his work before the Revolution, but the challenge of a new order gave it greater force and direction. In the work for ROSTA and in his poems of the 1930s, he launches a real attack on orthodox ideas of poetry. Of course he had grown up in a milieu where traditional notions prevailed, he himself knew many of the classics off by heart, and like many earlier poets he was obsessed with himself and his personal problems. But if he set himself up as a rival to Pushkin (in his 'Jubilee' poem of 1924) it was as someone who was writing a new kind of poetry for a new time. This, I think, is what he did—and it demands to be taken seriously by people of all political persuasions.

Nor indeed should one overstress the 'hysterical' element in his writing. Both from his poetry and from a life that was lived and ended in a dramatic way, the dominant impression that remains is one of vital energy. Not only in body, Vladimir Mayakovsky was a big man, a presence that could not be ignored. (pp. 186-87)

Peter France, "Vladimir Mayakovsky," in his Poets of Modern Russia, *Cambridge University Press, 1982, pp. 159-87.*

VICTOR TERRAS (essay date 1983)

[Terras is an Estonian-born educator and literary critic specializing in Russian language and literature. In the following excerpt, he examines the distinctive stylistic features of Mayakovsky's verse and summarizes the critical consensus of the poet's achievement.]

Mayakovsky's originality was very pronounced in the form of his verse, and most of all in his versification, which confused critics and scholars for decades. A controversy over the metric structure of Mayakovsky's verse raged for a long time and was ultimately resolved only by exhaustive statistical analysis conducted by scholars with mathematical expertise, such as A. N. Kolmogorov, A. M. Kondratov, and Mikhail Gasparov.

Mayakovsky himself claimed total ignorance of metric theory and said he could not tell an iamb from a trochee. He could, of course, and he also had an unerring rhythmic sense which allowed him not only to duplicate, but also to parody any meter or rhythm known to Russian poetry. Mayakovsky's verse is declamatory, and hence he early formed the habit of printing his verse "stairway fashion," that is, breaking down his lines by moving one space down after each pause:

Comrade tax collector!
                        Pardon the intrusion.
Thank you . . .
                don't bother . . .
                                I'll stand. . . .

Very often this technique conceals a conventional syllabotonic meter. (p. 117)

The formalist scholar Boris Eichenbaum spoke of "melodic" and "rhetorical" types of poets: the former is concerned more with euphonic and rhythmic effects, the latter with expression. Mayakovsky belongs to the latter type. Whenever his verses have a soft lilt or an irresistible driving rhythm, that regularity is invariably symbolic of their content. Mayakovsky uses rhythm and meter as an expressive device, rather than as a rigid form for his poems. This has caused some scholars to speak of Mayakovskian "free verse." Actually, Mayakovsky's poetry exhibits every form, including the extremes of conventional syllabotonic verse and free verse (that is, lines with a random number of syllables and stresses) and a variety of forms between them. Mayakovsky's verses are, however, always rhymed. Very rarely are they stanzaically structured.

Rhymed lines of varying length (*raeshnik*) are known in Russian folk poetry. . . . Mayakovsky employed it frequently, especially in his earlier propaganda poetry, and in much of ***150,000,000.*** In this type of line Mayakovsky comes closest to prose. But even here a distinct shift away from the rhythm of prose and toward that of verse is possible. Mayakovsky accomplishes this by introducing a significantly higher rate of alliteration, assonance, and inner rhyme than would normally occur in prose discourse, as well as by emphatic stresses and pauses that would not appear in ordinary speech. . . . Printing a line "stairway fashion" is Mayakovsky's way of indicating such pauses.

Statue of Mayakovsky in Moscow. From Mayakovsky and His Circle, *by Viktor Shklovsky. Edited and translated by Lily Feiler. Reprinted by permission of Dodd, Mead & Company, Inc.*

More often than not, Mayakovsky's apparent "free verse" is really stress verse, meaning that the number of stresses in a line is a constant (usually two, three, or four), while the number of unstressed syllables varies. In Russian versification, stress verse in which the number of unstressed syllables between stresses alternates between one and two in a random way is called *dol'nik,* and stress verse in which the number of unstressed syllables is unspecified is called *aktsentnyi stikh* ("accentual verse"). Much of Mayakovsky's poetry consists of lines belonging to one of these two types. "Accentual verse" is his proper domain, however: it was called "Mayakovskian verse" at one time, although Mayakovsky was not the first Russian poet to use it. (pp. 117-18)

Mayakovsky is a great master of the ditty (*chastushka*), usually a quatrain of rhymed trochaic tetrameters with a "punch line." He uses the form most effectively in his didactic and propaganda verse.

Finally, Mayakovsky was a virtuoso of parody who could imitate any meter or rhythm: that of a romance; of "Pushkinian" iambs (in **"Anniversary Poem"** or in the parody of *Eugene Onegin* in the fourth episode of ***Good!***); of Lermontovian trochaic pentameter; or of Aleksey Tolstoy's ballad of the 1840s (in amphibrachs) "Vasily Shibanov" (in **"Ballad about the Bureaucrat and the Worker-Correspondent,"** 1928). Naturally, the section of ***About That*** entitled "The Ballad of Reading Gaol" starts out with Oscar Wilde's meter—but only as a tease, since Mayakovsky quickly moves on to other rhythms.

Mayakovsky's longer poems are remarkable for the variety and elasticity of their rhythmic composition. Not only does he constantly shift from stress meters (or free verse) to syllabotonic meters and back, he also uses different syllabotonic and accentual meters (or *dol'niki*) in lines of different length. (pp. 119-20)

Mayakovsky considered rhyme an indispensable part of his verse. "Why?" he asked. "Because without rhyme the verse will fall to pieces. Rhyme returns you to the preceding line, forces you to remember it, holds together all the lines that form a single thought." . . .

This view is shared by students of Mayakovsky's verse. One of them, Mikhail Shtokmar, thought it more important than stress, so that Mayakovsky's verse should be called "rhymed verse." This is a misconception, for rhyme is to a large extent an integral part of the rhythmic structure of Mayakovsky's verse. Line boundaries are marked by rhyme, while inner rhyme, exceedingly common in Mayakovsky, creates a pause ("caesura") within a line. Rhyme has other functions as well: often rhyming words, or groups of words, form a meaningful juxtaposition, either serious or funny. Then too, Mayakovsky frequently plays with the suspense which the anticipation of a rhyme may produce. (p. 120)

Mayakovsky's rhymes differ significantly from those of nineteenth-century poets. The latter created rhyme by repetition of the last stressed vowel of a line and the vowels and consonants following it, for example, *kupéts: otéts; móre: góre*. In Mayakovsky's poetry the rhyme shifts to the left: the correspondence to the right of the last stress is only approximate (sometimes nonexistent), while a correspondence to the left of it is actively pursued, for example, *zvenó: zvonók*; sir*é*nnye *rókoty*: vr*é*mya-d*óktor* (***About That***). The latter pair is a closer rhyme than the transcription suggests, since *rókoty* may be slurred into *rókty*. The extension of the rhyme to the left is not obligatory. Thus, in the example just given, the rhyme *zvenó: zvonók* is supported even further to the left, while the rhyme with which it alternates has no such support. (p. 121)

Of course Mayakovsky also uses a large number of rhymes that are correct even by nineteenth-century standards. The share of genuine trick rhymes is not very large, but Mayakovsky occasionally treats his audience to rhyming fireworks. (pp. 121-22)

Mayakovsky, who consistently broke through the conventional constraints of poetic form, assiduously cultivated the free forms of sound patterning, such as alliteration, assonance, and inner rhyme. In this area he stayed with his futurist predilections to the end.

Mayakovsky is a virtuoso at using sound patterns symbolically. In ***About That,*** for instance, sound symbolism appears in massive doses. Thus, the lapping of the imaginary water which fills the poet's flat is described in several lines in which the word *voda* (pronounced *vadá*) seems to be everywhere:

Chórt*ova vá*nna!
          Vodá za *divá*nom.
P*od* stolóm,
          za shká*fo*m *vodá*.
S *divá*na,
          sdvínut *vodý* za*devá*n'em,
*v o*knó proplýl chem*odá*n.

Damned water!
          Water behind the sofa.
Under the table,
          behind the wardrobe.
Pushed from the sofa
          by the water,
my suitcase swims out the window. . . .
(pp. 123-24)

Mayakovsky's imagery displays the same breadth as his versification and sound patterning. One area in which he took little interest is nature imagery—he left the birch groves and corn flowers to Esenin. The great range of Mayakovsky's imagery is attributable not only to his extraordinary receptiveness, mobility, and curiosity, but also to the fact that he worked in an exceptionally wide spectrum of poetic genres.

None among Mayakovsky's contemporaries—if we limit ourselves to poets of his caliber—was a consistent writer of panegyric, solemn, celebratory, and occasional odes, as he was. Hence one finds in Mayakovsky's poetic arsenal certain archaic vocabulary and imagery which link him directly to eighteenth-century classicism. These archaic images are mixed with modern prosaisms, but this was also true—*mutatis mutandis*—of Gavriil Derzhavin, Russia's greatest poet of the eighteenth century. An example from Mayakovsky's **"Comintern"** . . . will illustrate this:

Gazing
          into the approaching storm,
                    into approaching thunder clouds,
     thundering ahead through waves of time,
                    through waves of space,
     the rudder
          of stormy days
                    in mighty grip,
along the Moscow river
          sails
               the dreadnought of
                    the Comintern. . . .

Every word in these lines could have been taken from a solemn patriotic ode of the eighteenth century except for the phrase "the dreadnought of the Comintern." The image of the ship of state, guided through stormy seas by a trusted helmsman's mighty hand, is as old as Western poetry: we find it in Alcaeus, who flourished in the seventh century B.C. Incidentally, the lines quoted here are also saturated with alliteration and are exceedingly well suited for declamation. Poetically, this piece—and many others like it celebrating the October Revolution, Red Army Day, Lenin and other communist heroes, the physical fitness of Soviet athletes, the anniversary of the Paris Commune, the Komsomol, the Soviet police, and other such things—all these pieces are as a rule woefully pedestrian. But they also contain a tremendous amount of imagery testifying to the breadth of Mayakovsky's imagination. (pp. 126-27)

It is quite in accord with Mayakovsky's aesthetics that his muse should address herself to minor topics of mundane interest: he would versify on absolutely any topic. He will address an ode to **"Comrade Typist"** extolling the virtues of that much maligned toiler; he will bemoan the poet's futile search throughout Moscow for a decent pair of socks to fit his feet (**"In Search of Socks,"** . . .)—in short, Mayakovsky wrote versified feuilletons dealing with the prose of everyday life, and did as conscientious a job of it as of all his other work. The journalistic genre, then, in conjunction with his didactic, edifying, and commercial verses, accounts for a large portion of Mayakovsky's imagery and vocabulary. And all of that, once conquered by verse, spills over into those of Mayakovsky's poems which few will deny the status of "art." Thus Mayakovsky vastly expanded the range of poetic expression, rather as Pushkin had in his day. (p. 128)

Like his classicist predecessors, Mayakovsky wrote a great deal of versified literary criticism and polemics. Besides great poems, such as **"To Sergey Esenin"** or **"Conversation with a Tax-Collector aboout Poetry,"** he wrote many minor pieces, such as **"Marxism is a Weapon, a Method of Firearm Quality—so Use this Method Knowledgeably!"** . . . , **"Fourfold Hackwork"** (. . . "fourfold" means Gosizdat, criticism, reader, and writer), and **"To Workers in the Field of Verse and Prose, Who will Spend this Summer on a Collective Farm."** . . . Mayakovsky even composed at least one versified theater review: **"Let's have Some Rotten Eggs! Review No. 1"**. . . . In this case Mayakovsky had made a public show of disapproval (whistling as loudly as he could, which was very loudly) during a performance of Vsevolod Pushmin's play *A Room to Pass Through*. He disapproved of the play's eroticism, which he found vulgar, and gave a detailed account of it in a 110-line poem.

Mayakovsky, a poet of great histrionic talent and a master of parody, could produce lines in any style or manner he wished. This also broadened the range of his imagery, which came to include images and phrases from the popular ditty, from the sentimental romance (for example, **"Marusya Poisoned Herself,"** 1927, a ballad in iambics and entirely in the manner of "urban folklore"), from cabaret verse, and even from proletarian verse *à la* Vasily Kazin: "And in the palaces / a different life: // When you've had your fill / of fun by the water, // go, worker, / and lie down // in a Grand-Ducal / bed. // The mountains blaze / like furnaces, // the sea is blue / like a worker's coveralls, // as a speedy repair job / of people proceeds // in that huge / Crimean smithy." . . . (pp. 128-29)

Despite his professed hostility to all "literature," and especially that of the past, Mayakovsky frequently incorporated allusions to the works and images of Russian and foreign authors in his poetry. Pushkin, Lermontov, Gogol, Nekrasov, Tolstoy, Dostoevsky, Blok, Esenin, Goethe, Hugo, Maupassant, Wilde, Whitman, Longfellow, and many other major as well as minor authors enrich Mayakovsky's verse by their presence. (p. 129)

Mayakovsky is among the most inventive masters in all of Russian poetry of the artful conceit (which smacks of the baroque and of the seventeenth century!). Soviet critics, by and large, have tended to reject the notion that Mayakovsky indulged in verbal play the way Gogol did in his prose. But it is fairly obvious that in many instances Mayakovsky's poetic phrase is generated by the power of verbal or visual association, rather than by the logic of a preconceived idea. In a way, Mayakovsky's poems are propelled by two forces: one of emotional energy or rational purpose, and one of an inexhaustible, often metaphysical, imagination. Mayakovsky put it very well in ***The Backbone Flute:*** "I strung out my soul across an abyss, like a cable, // juggling words, I am swaying over it.". . . (pp. 130-31)

Mayakovsky's imagery often veered toward the hyperbolic, the grotesque, and the violent, even before the war and the Revolution gave him ample reason to see the world as grotesque and violent. Some of Mayakovsky's most violent imagery, involving various horrible forms of execution, occurs in ***The Backbone Flute,*** a love poem. Some of the imagery in another love poem, ***About That,*** where the poet's persona is literally shot to pieces in the end, is quite as gory as the most cruel scenes in ***War and the World,*** which depicts the horrors of war.

By and large, Mayakovsky's violent images are not really terrible. His grotesque visions of death and destruction are most often those of a satirical cartoonist. Their violence is that of realized metaphor, not of immediate experience. The bayonets which triumphant communist soldiers ram into the fat bellies of cigar-chomping capitalists in his cartoons are metaphoric, not real, and the same is true of most of his poetic images. (pp. 131-32)

Considering the extraordinary richness of Mayakovsky's imagery, metaphoric as well as nonmetaphoric, it is difficult to delineate any categories or groups of images as characteristic of his poetic style. Lawrence L. Stahlberger has established a pattern of archetypal images—such as "bondage," "eternal recurrence," and "cosmic alienation"—in Mayakovsky's poetry. Certainly these motifs appear prominently in some of Mayakovsky's poems (***The Cloud in Trousers, The Backbone Flute, Man, About That***), but not consistently enough to be considered an integral part of Mayakovsky's *Gestalt* as a poet. Stahlberger sees as a characteristic trait of Mayakovsky's poetry a tendency to present the poet's persona as a martyr, a dandy, or a clown and often all of these together. There is much to be said for this: certainly this trait is intimately linked with Mayakovsky's declamatory style, and he assumed all three roles in life as well. But then, these roles, though perhaps not this particular combination of them, are found in many other poets. Esenin, a very different poet in almost every way, assumed quite similar roles. (p. 133)

Mayakovsky's verbal range is just as wide as the range of his imagery. He obliterates the boundary between poetic language and the language of prose, which exists even in Russian symbolism. The whole lexicon of the Russian language, from pompous archaisms and biblical language to technical jargon and the vilest slang, enters the crucible of Mayakovsky's poetry. Sometimes Mayakovsky utilizes the social connotation of a word for purposes of irony, pathos, mockery, solemnity, etc.; sometimes he will ignore it. . . . Mayakovsky can use his lexicon quite discriminatingly when he wishes to convey a certain impression. He laces his American poems with ample Anglicisms or outright English words. (pp. 133-34)

All in all, Mayakovsky's verbal usage is rich and varied, rather than "different," as Khlebnikov's is. Mayakovsky's numerous neologisms (the subject of a book-length monograph) are often ingenious and sometimes colorful, but they remain within the confines of the rules of Russian derivation. Aristophanean compounds such as *verblyudokorabledrakonii* ("camelshipdraconian," from **"The Fifth Internationale"**); emotionally charged adjectives such as *molotkastyi, serpastyi* ("sporting a hammer and sickle," from **"Verses on My Soviet Passport"**); abstract nouns derived from concrete nouns, for example, *slonovost'* ("elephantine thickskinnedness," from *slon,* "elephant"); all these and many other formations are qualitatively well within the limits of normal creative speech. It is the sheer quantity of Mayakovsky's output which is so impressive.

In assessing Mayakovsky's poetic personality as a whole, one is initially struck by a basic and pervasive contradiction. The most egocentric and self-assertive of Russian poets, Mayakovsky was also the bard of a collectivist society and of the Soviet ideal of man, which is profoundly anti-individualist. But this contradiction may be only apparent. Mayakovsky, though egocentric, reveals little of what must have been his inner life. He functions rather as a persona, or "image," or even as an allegory, instead of an individual. His self, assertive though it is, does not resemble the conscience of a religious person, the intense self-consciouness of the existentialist hero, or the persona of psychological fiction. It is an "outer-directed" self of the sort well described in Trotsky's *bon mot:* "In order to uplift man, he raises him to the level of Mayakovsky." Trotsky's irony was justified. Mayakovsky was a genuine lover of Mayakovskian man, but most intolerant of un-Mayakovskian men.

Mayakovsky's titanism, a striking trait of his prerevolutionary poetry, fuses with the revolutionary titanism of the Soviet period. As early as **"The Fifth Internationale"** . . . , Mayakovsky perceives himself as a hero / Svyatogor of epics of the future.". . . (Svyatogor [**"Holy Mountain"**] is a mythic giant of the Russian folk epic.) (pp. 134-35)

[In] a variety of ways, Mayakovsky's art has two sides: one spontaneous and aesthetically motivated, the other disciplined and in the service of the Soviet regime. This is true even of his revolutionary poetry. The relationship between the Revolution and left art was a complex one. At one point it seemed that their paths might merge. But then left art entered its death throes while Mayakovsky was still alive. The Revolution was continuing, though, as Stalin hammered out a wholly new society which turned its back on the avant-garde, even though Mayakovsky was declared by Stalin himself to have been "the best and most talented poet of our Soviet epoch." The constructivist art of *New Lef,* to whose program Mayakovsky heartily subscribed, would have served Stalin's objectives loyally and well. Yet it was abandoned in every art form, including even architecture, abandoned largely for so-called "socialist realism," which was actually a version of nineteenth-century naturalism with a tendency prescribed by the various exigencies of the Soviet government.

Although Soviet critics would like to deny it, there is a rift between Mayakovsky's more personal moods and the attitude of the poet's persona in his civic poetry. The latter is basically optimistic, despite the criticism of the Soviet system found in the civic poetry. But whenever Mayakovsky speaks for himself, his prevailing mood is one of pessimism; moreover, a pessimism born of frustration, boredom, and resignation. . . . The suicide theme is ever present in Mayakovsky's personal poetry. The Revolution must have given some meaning to his life, but disillusionment soon cast its shadow even over his political poems. The message of **"To Sergey Esenin"** is really that there is little to cheer about in life. Mayakovsky's exhortations to young communists who are cruelly disappointed by the good life of the NEP-men and the bleak life of devoted communists have a ring of resignation (**"What Did We Fight For?"** . . .). What is even worse, at moments Mayakovsky doubted even the value of his own poetry:

In our country of Soviets,
one can live
well enough,
and work together well.
Except for the fact
that there are no poets
here, I'm sorry to say—
However, maybe
none are needed, either. . . .

This statement contrasts markedly with Mayakovsky's stubborn defense of the poet's position in the forefront of progress. (This quite aside from the fact that Mayakovsky claims there "are no poets" in Russia at a time when Pasternak, Akhmatova, Mandelshtam, and Esenin, to name but a few, were at the height of their powers.). . . In **"At the Top of My Voice,"** written five years later, Mayakovsky conceives of his immortality differently: it will not be the immortality of his name and oeuvre, but the anonymous immortality of the honest worker for a better life. In a sense, then, Mayakovsky finds even here a way to make Mayakovsky the mouthpiece of the Soviet regime a logical continuation of Mayakovsky the futurist genius. (pp. 137-38)

An assessment of Mayakovsky the poet cannot be based on a separation between his "genuine poetry" and his "propaganda poetry." Like most artists, Mayakovsky matured and became more skillful at his craft as he grew older. A good deal of his "Soviet" poetry is technically superior to the best of his prerevolutionary verse. It makes even less sense to glean from Mayakovsky's oeuvre those lines which can be readily accepted as "poetry" according to nineteenth-century norms, for these are not always his best lines. . . . We must accept or reject Mayakovsky as a whole, though our evaluation is made difficult by several factors. It is not easy to dismiss from one's mind Mayakovsky's flamboyant and generally attractive personality, his "poetic life," as Pasternak put it. Nor can Mayakovsky's histrionic talents, his brilliant delivery of his poetry, and his spirited defense of his own work be dismissed as irrelevant to the question of his poetic worth: these things certainly contributed to his great stature among his contemporaries. Furthermore, Mayakovsky was the acknowledged leader of a school. He did not invent any of the truly innovative tenets of Russian futurism, but since Khlebnikov, Kruchonykh, and Kamensky, bolder innovators than Mayakovsky, never acquired anything approaching his fame, he recieved most of the credit for the achievements of that school.

Soviet critics and scholars have suggested that Mayakovsky created a new aesthetic by transferring the viewpoint of lyric poetry from a personal to a social stance, by "poeticizing man the creator of his social existence," or by creating a "new poetic 'I' where the 'I' is grandiose, but not with romantic grandioseness, by which an exalted 'I' is juxtaposed to a lowly world of reality, but a different grandioseness which encompasses the whole world and feels responsible for it." But surely in this repect Mayakovsky is anything but unique. His stance—whether one calls it "social," "collective," "civic," or something else—often recalls, *mutatis mutandis,* that of the poets of classicism as well as of Nekrasov and other civic poets of the nineteenth century. Osip Mandelshtam, a keen judge of talent, recognized the basically didactic quality of Mayakovsky's poetry:

> Mayakovsky's merit lies in his using the powerful resources of visual education to educate the masses. Like a schoolteacher, Mayakovsky carries a globe representing the Earth, and other emblems of the visual method, with him at all times. He has replaced the repulsive newspaper of recent times, where nobody could understand a thing, with simple, healthy school work. A great reformer of the newspaper, he has left a deep mark on poetic language, having greatly simplified syntax and assigned to the noun a place of honor and primacy in the sentence.

Mandelshtam is thinking of ***Mystery-Bouffe*** here, but the context suggests that he speaks of Mayakovsky in general.

To be sure, Mayakovsky's message was modern. Pasternak recalled that Mayakovsky once said to him: "Well, sure enough. You and I are different, indeed. You like lightning in the sky, and I like it in an electric iron." While didactic poetry was nothing new, didactic poetry dealing with the construction of hydroelectric power plants was.

Perhaps the most innovative aspect of Mayakovsky's poetry was that a poet of his remarkable talent could devote almost all his energies to the production of utilitarian pieces, many of them utterly banal. Mayakovsky did not see in this any "death of poetry," but rather a recapturing of its proper social role. In this regard, the position of Mayakovsky the Soviet poet was diametrically opposed to that of Mayakovsky the futurist, who had advocated a poetry of pure form.

Mayakovsky has influenced more Soviet poets, Russian and non-Russian, than any other twentieth-century poet, partly because Soviet youth has been exposed to his poetry vastly more than to the work of his contemporaries Pasternak, Mandelshtam, Akhamatova, Tsvetaeva, and Zabolotsky, all of whom may have been greater poets than he. (pp. 149-51)

Mayakovsky has held a strong attraction for poets of the leftist avant-garde everywhere. Bertolt Brecht and Johannes R. Becher in Germany, Paul Eluard and Louis Aragon in France, Wladyslaw Broniewski and Witold Wandurski in Poland, S. K. Neumann in Czechoslovakia, Pablo Neruda among several Latin American poets, and many others have expressed their appreciation of Mayakovsky's art and acknowledged his influence on their own work.

While Mayakovsky's style has stood up well under the wear and tear of time, and while his utilitarian aesthetic is very much alive, his poetry has been "dated" for a long time. While the verses of Pasternak or Mandelshtam are as fresh and fascinating today as they were sixty years ago, one reads Mayakovsky's for their historical and technical interest rather than for aesthetic enjoyment. Mayakovsky's prediction that his verses would reach the future much the way a Roman aqueduct has reached us has come true. (p. 152)

Victor Terras, in his Vladimir Mayakovsky, *Twayne Publishers, 1983, 170 p.*

ADDITIONAL BIBLIOGRAPHY

Alvarez, A. "Giant? Monster? Showman? Charlatan? Genius? Yes!" *The New York Times Book Review* (7 March 1971): 1, 48-9

Favorable review of *The Bedbug and Selected Poetry,* with considerable biographical information.

Barooshian, Vahan D. *Brik and Mayakovsky.* New York: Mouton Publishers, 1978, 157 p.

Explores the relationship between Mayakovsky and Osip Brik as well as their roles in the Russian avant-garde movement between 1915 and 1930.

Beveridge, Nancy. "Mayakovsky and Cubism." *Rackham Literary Studies* (1972): 89-96.

Examines the tenets of Cubism as evidenced in Mayakovsky's poetic images.

Charters, Ann, and Charters, Samuel. *I Love: The Story of Vladimir Mayakovsky and Lili Brik.* New York: Farrar Straus & Giroux, 1979. 398 p.

Discussion of the Mayakovsky Brik love affair which includes examinations of Mayakovsky's poetry related to the relationship and many photographs.

Chénetier, Marc. "Knights in Disguise: Lindsay and Maiakovski as Poets of the People." *MidAmerica II* (1975): 47-62.*

Discusses the "belief in an ideal of communal brotherly life" as similarly evidenced in the poetry of Mayakovsky and Vachel Lindsay.

Clark, Fred M. "Oswald and Mayakovsky: *O homem e o cavalo* and *Mystery-Bouffe.*" *Revista de Estudios Hispanicos* XVI, No. 2 (May 1982): 241-56.

Discusses the influence of Mayakovsky's drama on the work of Brazilian playwright Oswald de Andrade.

Déak, František. 'The AgitProp and Circus Plays of Vladimir Mayakovsky.'' *Drama Review* XVII, No. 1 (March 1973): 47-52.

Discusses the little-known dramatic works Mayakovsky wrote for political occasions.

Ehrenburg, Ilya. "People, Years, and Life." In *Dissonant Voices in Soviet Literature,* edited by Patricia Black and Max Hayward, pp. 236-58. London: George Allen and Unwin, 1964.*

Reminiscences of the revolutionary years in Russia with some discussion of Mayakovsky's involvement in politics.

Gifford, Henry. "Pound, Mayakovsky and the Defence of Human Nature." *PN Review* V, No. 2 (1977): 15-18

Discusses the political involvement of both poets and how they "confused too often the roles of poet and publicist."

Henderson, Elizabeth. "Majakovskij and Eisenstein Celebrate the Tenth Anniversary." *Slavic and East European Journal,* XXII, No. 2 (Summer 1978): 153-62

Compares two works created in celebration of the tenth anniversary of the October Revolution: Mayakovsky's poem "It's Good" and Sergej Eisenstein's film *October.*

Hyde, G. M. "Russian Futurism." In *Modernism: 1890-1930,* edited by Malcolm Bradbury and James McFarlane, pp. 259-73. New York: Penguin Books, 1976.*

Discusses the importance of Mayakovsky's role in the Russian Futurist movement.

Jakobson, Roman. "The Contours of *The Safe Conduct.*" In *Semiotics of Art: Prague School Contributions,* edited by Ladislav Matejka and Irwin R. Titunik, pp. 188-96. Cambridge, Mass.: MIT Press, 1976.*

Discussion of Pasternak's poem with numerous comparisons of his poetic style to that of Mayakovsky.

Jangfeldt, Bengt. "Russian Futurism 1917-1919: I. An Outline. II. Majakovskij and October." In *Art, Society, Revolution: Russian, 1917-1921,* edited by Nils Åke Nilsson, pp. 106-37. Uppsala, Sweden: Almqvist & Wiksell, 1979.*

Discusses "Majakovskij's immediate reactions to the events of October."

Keefer, Lubov. "The Musical Imagery of Vladimir Mayakovski." *The American Slavic and East European Review* V, Parts 14-15 (November 1946): 109-20.

Musically oriented discussion of the profound influence of the work of various composers on Mayakovsky's poetry.

Kreymborg, Alfred. "Revolutions in Poetry." *The Saturday Review of Literature* XXIX, No. 30 (27 July 1946): 45.

Favorable review of *Mayakovsky and His Poetry,* a compilation in English of poems, dramatic sketches, and cartoons.

Laufer, Leo. "Vladimir Mayakovsky and the 'New Look' in Soviet Literature." *Problems in Communism* III, No. 4 (July-August 1954): 15-20.

Discusses conditions in the Soviet Union during Mayakovsky's life which may have contributed to his suicide.

Mirsky, D. S. "Vladimir Mayakovsky." *The Slavonic Review* IX, No. 25 (June 1930): 220-22.

Obituary which claims that Mayakovsky "had a genuinely communal appeal, and did more than anyone to bring poetry . . . out of the closet into the street, and to make of an art for connoisseurs . . . an art for the masses."

Moser, Charles A. "Mayakovsky and America." *The Russian Review* XXV, No. 3 (July 1966): 242-56.

Biographically oriented discussion of the impressions Mayakovsky formed of the United States during his visit in 1925.

Nes Kirby, Victoria. "Moscow Is Burning: Introduction." *The Drama Review* XVII, No. 1 (March 1973): 64-7.

Discusses the production of Mayakovsky's last play.

Nilsson, Nils Åke. "Two Chekhovs: Mayakovskiy on Chekhov's 'Futurism'." In *Chekhov's Great Plays: A Critical Anthology,* edited by Jean-Pierre Barricelli, pp. 251-61. New York: New York University Press, 1981.*

Examines Mayakovsky's attitudes toward and criticisms of Chekhov in terms of his adaptation of Futuristic principles in his work.

Oille, Jennifer. "Vladimir Mayakovsky: Parody and Propaganda." *Theatre* X, No. 2 (Spring 1979): 63-7.

Discusses the plays, posters, and other artistic propaganda Mayakovsky produced for the Bolshevik Party.

Peterson, Dale E. "Maiakovskii's *Lenin:* The Fabrication of a Bolshevik *Bylina.*" *Slavic Review* XLI, No. 2 (Summer 1982): 284-96

Detailed discussion of Mayakovsky's epic poem "Vladimir Ilich Lenin."

Shklovsky, Viktor. *Mayakovsky and His Circle.* Translated by Lily Feiler. New York: Dodd, Mead & Company, 1972, 259 p.

Loosely ordered commentary on the distinctive features of Mayakovsky's poetry and those individuals involved with him in the Russian Futurist movement.

Soviet Literature VI, No. 423 (1983).

Issue devoted to Mayakovsky. Notable among the essays in this issue is the article "My Son's Childhood and Youth," by the poet's mother.

Stapanian, Juliette R. "Vladimir Maiakovskii's 'From Street into Street' as Cubo-Futurist Canvas: A View through the Art of Kazimir Malevich." *Slavic Review* ILI, No. 4 (Winter 1982): 639-52

Compares the similar techniques in Mayakovsky's poem and in several paintings by Russian artist Malevich.

———. "V. Majakovskij's 'To Signs' ('Vyveskam')—A Cubist 'Signboard' in Verse." *Slavic and East European Journal* XXVI, No. 2 (Summer 1982): 174-86.

Discusses the similar motifs and vision in European avant-garde painting and Mayakovsky's early poem.

Thompson, R. D. B. "Andrey Voznesensky: Between Pasternak and Mayakovsky." *The Slavonic and East European Review* LIV, No. 1 (January 1976): 41-59.*

Discusses the influence of Mayakovsky and Pasternak on the contemporary Russian poet Andrey Voznesensky.

Woroszylski, Wiktor. *The Life of Mayakovsky*. Translated by Boleslaw Taborski. New York: Orion Press, 1970, 559 p.

Biography with many reminiscences of Mayakovsky by prominent Russian literary figures.

Jean Moréas

1856-1910

(Pseudonym of Johannes Papadiamantopoulos) Greek-born French poet, essayist, dramatist, novella and short story writer.

An eminent literary figure in late nineteenth-century France, Moréas advanced the cause of an emerging generation of Symbolist writers through the example of his poetry and through his manifestoes in defense of the then-controversial movement. However, while he began his career as the leader of the young Symbolist poets whose masters were Paul Verlaine, Arthur Rimbaud, and Stéphane Mallarmé, Moréas rejected Symbolism and eventually arrived at a poetic theory and practice founded upon classical ideals. His greatest work, *Les stances,* consummately conveys the austere, yet evocative style he achieved in his mature verse. Characterized by both a strong mood of ennui and by a stoic acceptance of life's hardships, this work is esteemed for its philosophic as well as poetic power.

Both in Athens, Greece, to a family of aristocratic background, Moréas was exposed to French culture at an early age, learning the language from his French governess. When he was ten years old he vowed to become a French poet. While he initially prepared for a law career planned by his father, a high-ranking magistrate on the Greek Court of Appeals, Moréas quickly abandoned this field of study. Sent to Paris in 1879 to continue his legal education, he pursued a literary life instead. Through his regular appearance at the literary cafés and his *Tourterelles et vipères,* a volume of verse primarily in Greek which contained a few poems in French displaying a mastery of his adopted language, he became accepted as a serious new writer. Two years later his first major collection of French poetry, *Les syrtes,* appeared. The musical, suggestive quality of these poems aligned Moréas at once with a growing movement of poets inspired by Charles Baudelaire's *Les fleurs du mal* (1857; *The Flowers of Evil,* 1909) and by Edgar Allan Poe's conceptions of art for art's sake and of the beautiful as an amorphous ideal reality which exists beyond the visible world. The movement, struggling to gain validity, received considerable adverse criticism at this time. Paul Bourde, a writer for the *Temps,* attacked the "decadent" style of Moréas and his contemporaries in an article of 1885, addressing in particular the obscurity and esoteric nature of the verse in *Les syrtes.* Moréas responded in the journal *Le XIXème siècle* with an essay defending the search for a new language, one removed from previous conventions of French versification, which could intuitively convey a poetic reality that went beyond the mere description of things. "Thus, in this art," Moréas wrote, "the pictures provided by nature, the actions of men, all concrete phenomena, cannot manifest themselves as themselves: they are perceptible appearances intended to represent their esoteric affinities with primordial ideas." In his essay Moréas coined the term "Symbolist," believing it a more accurate and less derogatory term than decadence to describe himself and his contemporaries. In a continuation of the debate over the validity of this movement, Moréas printed "Manifest littéraire de l'École Symboliste" a year later in one of the leading French dailies, *Le Figaro,* in effect proclaiming Symbolism as the dominant school of French poetics.

The same year Moréas published another volume of verse, *Les cantilènes,* and joined with Gustave Kahn and Paul Adam to found *Le symboliste,* a short-lived periodical which was formed to further the cause of Symbolist literature. During the next few years Moréas's status among his fellow writers rose rapidly, and he gained the high regard of Verlaine and others. With the appearance of *Le pèlerin passionné* in 1891 Moréas's reputation as a talented, outspoken poet and theoretician was firmly established. The volume includes Moréas's first experiments in free verse and displays an elevated, evocative language. In honor of this work, which was enthusiastically hailed in friendly literary circles as the new cornerstone of the Symbolist movement, a banquet was sponsored by the Symbolist journal *La plume.* The work was, however, somewhat antithetical to Symbolist poetic practice in its rationality and verbal simplicity, thus foreshadowing Moréas's philosophical about-face two years later when he issued a revised edition of *Le pèlerin* that excised overly ambiguous poems and included new pieces which adhered to a clearer, more orthodox use of language. In his explanatory preface to this collection, Moréas declared that his earlier poetry had been aesthetically misguided and that Symbolism was dead. He now proposed to master instead the simplicity and economy of medieval French and Latin verse. Consequently, Moréas founded a movement devoted to this cause, the L'École Romane, with Charles Maurras, Maurice du Plessys, Raymond de la Tailhede, and Ernest Raynaud.

In his next few volumes of verse Moréas moved progressively toward a further refinement of language, which resulted in his most distinguished work, *Les stances*. Published in seven volumes, *Les stances* exhibits a highly personal and carefully evolved poetic and philosophic outlook which combines a Symbolist concern with the ideal of beauty and a classical emphasis on clarity. In consonance with this restraint, Moréas produced the Euripidean verse drama *Iphigénie*, first performed in 1903. After this time Moréas's literary production gradually declined due to prolonged suffering from a degenerative disease, from which he died in 1910.

Although relatively little is known of Moréas's private life, critics have extrapolated through examinations of his poetry that, in contrast to his ebullient, charismatic public persona, Moréas was deeply introspective and often melancholic—in large part due to severed artistic friendships resulting from his abandonment of Symbolism. In his early verse Moréas was concerned with themes of love, sadness, separation, and despair, yet failed to attain the maturity and restraint that critics find evident in his later work. With the small volume *Sylves nouvelles* he crystallized a stoic philosophy emphasizing a balance of intellect and emotion in the literary expression of basic human problems and stressing both the forms and philosophy of classical literature. In poems dedicated to his friends and aesthetic compatriots du Plessys, Verlaine, and Raynaud, he urges them in their own work to heed the examples of Pindar, Virgil, and Sophocles and adopt in their work the same serene acceptance of life and death. Recognized as the mature, extended development of this position, *Les stances* conveys a sense of emotional trauma, through recurrent use of powerful symbols such as bleeding wounds and fire, as well as the negation of trauma, through simple language and a carefully modulated tone. Assessing the collection, John Davis Butler has concluded that Moréas "achieved not only a consummate artistic skill, but concurrently, his own soul's answer to the insistent challenges of fate, of living and dying."

Moréas has been criticized, as have most Symbolists, for deliberate obscurity and syntactical complexity. However, scholars confirm his successful avoidance of these in *Les stances*, a work commended for its masterful fusion of the best elements of Symbolism and classicism. Despite the dearth of studies on Moréas in English, he is considered a poet and theoretician of central importance to the development of French poetry in the late nineteenth century.

PRINCIPAL WORKS

Tourterelles et vipères (poetry) 1878
Les syrtes (poetry) 1884
Les cantilènes (poetry) 1886
"Manifeste littéraire de l'école symboliste" (essay) 1886; published in newspaper *Le Figaro*
Les premières armes du Symbolisme [with Paul Bourde and Anatole France] (essays and manifestos) 1889
Le pèlerin passionné (poetry) [first edition] 1891; also published as *Le pèlerin passionné* [revised edition], 1893
Enone au clair visage (poetry) 1894
Eriphyle (poetry) 1894
**Sylves* (poetry) 1894
**Sylves nouvelles* (poetry) 1895
Les stances. 7 vols. (poetry) 1899-1920
Iphigénie (drama) 1903
Esquisses et souvenirs (essays) 1908
Oeuvres de Jean Moréas. 2 vols. (poetry and drama) 1923-26

*These works were published as *Poèmes et sylves* in 1907.

Translated selections of Moréas's poetry have appeared in the following publications: *Chantecleer: A Study of the French Muse, A Century of French Verse, Contemporary French Poetry, Fleurs-de-Lys, French Lyrics in English, A Mirror for French Poetry 1840-1940, The Poets of Modern France, The Lost Wine*, and *French Symbolist Poetry*.

ANATOLE FRANCE (essay date 1890)

[*France is one of the most conspicuous examples of an author who epitomized every facet of literary greatness to his own time but who lost much of his eminence to the shifting values of posterity. He embodied what are traditionally regarded as the intellectual and artistic virtues of French writing: clarity, control, perceptive judgment of worldly matters, and the Enlightenment virtues of tolerance and justice. His novels gained an intensely devoted following for their lucid appreciation of the pleasures and pains of human existence and for the tenderly ironic vantage from which life was viewed. A persistent tone of irony, varying in degrees of subtlety, is often considered the dominant trait of France's writing. In his critical works this device of ironic expression becomes an effective tool of literary analysis. In the following excerpt France, writing just after the appearance of* Le pèlerin passioné, *examines the Symbolist traits of Moréas's verse.*]

The author of ***Les Syrtes*** and ***Les Cantilènes*** has published this very day, through the "bibliopole," Léon Vanier, a new collection of verse [***Le Pèlerin passioné***], whose appearance will be loudly celebrated in the Latin country in which M. Jean Moréas goes his way, followed, it is said, by fifty younger poets, like a young Homer leading his youthful Homerides. (p. 138)

He is descended, if we may believe his biographers, from the navarch Tombazis, whom the sailors of the Archipelago still mention in their songs, and from Papadiamontopoulous, who died like a hero in Missolonghi. But by his intellectual training, and by his feeling for art, he is wholly French.

He fed his mind upon our old romances of chivalry, and it seemed as though he did not wish to meet the gods of ancient Greece save under the refined forms which they assumed on the banks of the Seine and the Loire, in the days when the *Pléiade* was shining. His childhood was spent in Marseilles, and he is no doubt reviving and transforming the first memories of his childhood when he paints for us, in the first poem of ***Le Pèlerin passionné,*** a Levantine harbour, quite in the style of Vernet's marine landscapes, in which we see "tall old men at work on the feluccas, along the piers and the quays." But Marseilles, a Greek colony and a port of the Levant, was not for M. Moréas his adoptive country, his chosen home. The true home of his spirit is further north; it begins where we see blue slates beneath a soft grey sky, where rise those jewels of stone on which the Renaissance has set symbolic figures and subtle devices. M. Jean Moréas is one of the seven stars of the new *Pléiade*. I regard him as the Ronsard of symbolism.

He would fain have been its du Bellay also, and in 1885 he issued a manifesto [**"Manifest li Héraire de l'École Symbol-**

iste"] which somewhat recalls the *Deffense et illustration de la langue françoise* of 1549. He displays in this a curiosity concerning his art, and a love of form rather than a critical or philosophical spirit. The æsthete of the school is rather that M. Charles Morice in whom I divine a certain depth although I do not always hear it, for he is cloudy. But one must always put up with a certain amount of obscurity in the symbolists; if one cannot, one should never open their books. As for M. Jean Moréas, difficult as he is in certain passages, he is certainly a poet; a poet in his own manner and a fine artist in his own fashion. His new book, ***Le Pèlerin passionné,*** is especially deserving of mention: firstly, because here and there it contains pleasant and even exquisite things; and, secondly, because it affords the critic an opportunity of explaining himself in respect of certain questions which are connected with the art of poetry. M. Jean Moréas and his school have rejected the rules of the old prosody. They have rid themselves of the false cæsura, which is still retained by the romantics, in their broken lines, and by the Parnassians. They reject the systematic alternation of masculine and feminine rhymes. This is not all: they employ rich rhymes when they please, and when they please content themselves with mere assonance. They permit themselves the hiatus: they often elide the *e* mute before a consonant, and finally, they write verses in all sorts of measures; verses which, as M. Félix-Fénéon has drily remarked, are "still suspect"; lines whose six and a half feet distress the ear, and lines even longer than these, in which syntax is observed with the greatest facility. The reader must excuse me for entering thus into the technique of the art; we are considering poetry, and it is well to inquire whether these novelties are successful, or permissible. (pp. 138-40)

The beginnings of our poetry are so barbarous and uncouth that no poet would dare to look at them if he had the misfortune to be acquainted with them. Rhyme was originally a clumsy artifice of mnemotechnics, and verse an aid to memory for people who could not read. And if you find it hard to believe that a mnemotechnical expedient has been transformed, in the course of time, into a beautiful artistic resource, it is enough to reflect that in Greek architecture a beam laid upon wooden pillars became the architrave and that either end of the framing of the roof became a marble triglyph.

When we examine the details of versification we perceive that all the prescriptions which the poets obey are recent and arbitrary. They do not last long. They would last an even shorter time were not the sense of imitation very powerful in men, and, above all, in artists. Indeed, a form of verse does not last much longer than through one generation of poets. If we examine the changes lately introduced into French verse we shall, I think, find sufficient reasons for resigning ourselves and saying: "It was inevitable." The suppression of the cæsura is only one step further upon a path which has long been followed. The broken line of our old romantics is to-day regarded as an example and is accepted by all men of letters. The prosodic reforms of 1830 are accepted by every schoolmaster capable of putting together, at random, selected passages for his classes; by the most mechanical of anthologists, the most conventional of collectors; by a Merlet, in short. Now the broken line must needs lead to the line with the shifting and multiple cæsura; that was necessarily the case. And Malherbe teaches us that we should not seek remedies for irremediable ills.

I have not much to say concerning the alternation of rhymes. This is a fairly novel obligation, which did not yet exist in its full rigour in the days of Ronsard. I confess that I am shocked when a poet fails to observe this rule by mistake; the painful impression proceeds less, perhaps, from a delicate ear than from the feeling that an irregularity has been committed which disturbs my sense of the customary. At all events, I am quite aware that I no longer feel this distress when the non-alternation is deliberate and intentional. Undeniably the effect may be agreeable. This is the opinion of M. Théodore de Banville, the most skilful of poets in the management of rhyme.

M. Moréas and his friends take certain further liberties in the matter of rhymes which may also be defended. I used of old to recite, devoutly, like a good Parnassian, the litanies of Sainte-Beuve to Our Lady of Rhyme: rhyme, the dip of the oar, the golden bridle, the brooch of Venus, the diamond ring, the keystone of the arch. I do not deny my faith. But without apostasy I can recognize that the prosody now going out of fashion was bookish and pedantic when it demanded that the rhyme should satisfy the eye as completely as it satisfies the ear. The poet, in this case, surrenders too far to the scribe. It becomes too plain that he burns the midnight oil, that he works on paper, that he is a grammarian rather than a singer. It is the misfortune of our poetry that it is too literary, too much a written thing; this quality should not be exaggerated. And if the symbolists to some extent diminish the graphic symmetry of the rhyme I shall not blame them over-much. And here is another question: should we blame them for permitting the hiatus when the ear permits it? No: they are only doing what the worthy Ronsard used to do. It is pitiable, when one comes to think of it, that for two hundred years the French poets should have been forbidden to say *tu as* or *tu es* in verse! This alone is a remarkable proof of the strict behaviour of the French people, of their obedience to the laws.

Must we call it a barbarous offence if M. Moréas writes:

> Dieu ait pitié de mon âme!
> ["God have pity on my soul!"]

On the contrary, who is there that does not feel that certain hiatuses please the ear? Those crystalline encounters between the vowels in such names as *Néère* or Leuconoë, which are really no more than pleasing hiatuses within the word—by what magic do they become unmusical when they occur between two adjacent words of a line of verse? But it is enough to have read Ronsard to realize how the hiatus may enter into the melody of a poem. Taking them all in all, the novelties of the symbolists are rather examples of a return to ancient usages. Thus they reckon a line of five feet, *nommée Mab,* to be equivalent to four syllables, as it was of old. We shall presently consider an example. Yet they permit themselves at times, if only rarely, as in popular songs, to elide the *e* mute before a consonant, according to their taste. They say: *nommé Mab.* The licence is great, but without this licence, or that preceding it, it is impossible to insert *prie-Dieu* in a line of verse. I have, I think, enumerated all the audacities of ***Le Pèlerin passionné,*** and, taking them all in all, there is not one which would not have been called for and desired and blessed beforehand by Banville, our father, who has said: "The hiatus, the diphthong making a syllable in the line, and all the rest of those things which have been forbidden, and above all the optional employment of masculine and feminine rhymes, furnish the poet of genius with a thousand opportunities for delicate effects, continually varied, unexpected, inexhaustible." And has not Banville, loosing the reins of his Pegasus, further declared: "I could wish that the poet, liberated from all empirical conventions, had had no other master than his delicate ear, subtilized by the tenderest caresses of music. In a word, I wish knowledge, inspiration and life, continually renewed and varied, could have replaced a fixed and mechanical law."

The symbolists have sought to realize the most tuneful dreams and desires of our poets. They have done enough and more than enough to please him. It is said that the master is now alarmed and astonished by innovations which he formerly invoked. This is very natural. He would not be an artist who did not love above all things and with a jealous love the forms in which he himself has inshrined the beautiful. The poet divines new forms; he urges their employment; but as soon as they appear they seem intrusive and he cries: "I have lived long enough!" Alas! the critic must not surrender to the charm of regret; he must follow out in all its evolutions, fearing to regard as incorrect and barbarous that which is a new discovery, a new refinement.

For my part, I find that M. Moréas' prosody somewhat disconcerts my taste without wounding it too severely. It satisfies my reason well enough:

> Et mon cœur en secret me dit qu'il y consent.
> ["And my heart secretly tells me that it consents."]

As for his language: that, to tell the truth, one has to learn. It is unusual and at times impudent. It abounds in archaisms. But upon this point, which is the chief point, I do not wish to be unreasonably conservative and to quarrel with the future. Experience shows that the language changes just as prosody changes. It even wears out more quickly, since it is employed more abundantly. In times of intellectual activity it gains largely and loses largely from year to year, I might almost say from day to day.

I do not know whether we think correctly nowadays; I rather doubt it; but we certainly think a great deal, or rather, we think about a great many things, and we are making a horrible mess of the language. M. Moréas, who is a philologist and interested in linguistic problems, does not invent very many words, but he restores a great many, so that his verses, full of terms taken from old writers, are like the Gallo-Roman villa at Garnier, in which we see the shafts of ancient columns and the remnants of architraves. The result is an amusing and fantastic combination. Paul Verlaine called Moréas:

> Routier de l'époque insigne,
> Violant des vilanelles.
>
> ["Old Stager of the good old times, / playing
> country airs upon the viol."]

It is true that he belongs to the good old times, and that he always seems to be wearing a black velvet doublet. And I have a bone to pick with him. He is obscure. And we feel certain that he is not naturally obscure. On the contrary, he will suddenly put his hand on the exact word, the definite image, the precise form. And yet he is obscure. He is so because he wishes to be so; and if he wishes to be so it is because his æsthetic demands it. For that matter, all things are relative: for a symbolist he is limpidity itself.

But make no mistake: with all the faults and all the oddities of his school, he is an artist and a poet; he has a manner, a style, a savour of his own, an individual way of seeing and feeling things. Now and again he is exquisite. . . . (pp. 141-46)

At all events he is not commonplace, this delicate Athenian, in love with archaisms and innovations, who strangely combines in his poetry the graceful scholarship of the Renaissance and the vague perturbation of decadent verse. It is said that he goes through the Latin quarter followed by fifty poets, his disciples. I should not be surprised if he did. He has, to attach them to his school, the erudition of an old-world humanist, a subtle mind, and a love of fair long arguments and encounters of the intellect. (pp. 147-48)

Anatole France, "Jean Moréas," in his On Life & Letters, fourth series, *edited by J. Lewis May and Bernard Miall, translated by Bernard Miall, Dodd, Mead and Company, Inc., 1924, pp. 138-48.*

STÉPHANE MALLARMÉ (letter date 1891)

[*Mallarmé is considered the leading poet and theorist of the Symbolist movement. His verse, notably* "Après-midi d'un faun" *(1876;* "Afternoon of a Faun"*), evokes a transcendant ideal of beauty through an elaborate use of symbol and metaphor and through innovative experiments with rhythm and syntax. In the following excerpt, Mallarmé commends Moréas's verse.*]

Your written melodies seem exquisitely to faint away in voice and coloring, and thus the page you write them on is virginal in the spaces that surround the words. The words themselves—even the most recent of them—imply that you are the only one who has ever spoken them. And surely the chief magic in all this is the particular touch a foreigner gives these Poems in French, while still remaining a son of his own true native land. You do so excellently, and so we come to feel that the language you propose is here forever; that it has, in fact, been the timeless and limitless property and heritage of all poets through the ages.

Stéphane Mallarmé, in a letter to Jean Moréas on January 5, 1891, in his Mallarmé: Selected Prose Poems, Essays, & Letters, *edited and translated by Bradford Cook, The Johns Hopkins University Press, 1956, p. 102.*

T. S. PERRY (essay date 1892)

[*In the following excerpt from an article devoted to the then-contemporary movement of Symbolism, Perry describes the characteristics of this literary school and Moréas's relationship to it.*]

It is not in political matters alone that France is a perpetual torment to the conservative half of the world. Its literature is always a subject of hot discussion, and not of discussion alone, for endless experiments are continually made by young men who are glad to break with every tradition. The fact that they all have logical minds only lends fresh fuel to the fire, for there is nothing denied a logical mind; it can prove anything it accepts. (p. 359)

There are, for example, the Symbolists, who yearn to convince an incredulous world that they, and they alone, possess the secret of literary excellence. If they do possess it they keep it very well concealed, for anyone who says that he understands them and knows what it is that they mean to say, should be listened to with great caution. And this not because they are reticent, for they write abundantly and expound, or go through the form of expounding, their theories in many manifestos, and all the other schools or kindergartens are equally eloquent. (p. 360)

It may be unkind to say that some of the verse of the Symbolists is obscure, but the only alternative is silence. There are poems, and a great many of them, that would sound most admirable if read aloud in the next room, so that only their sonority would reach us, and we should be spared the delusive intellectual effort to seize their sense. The word *or* (gold) is used with almost barbaric profusion, as if Poe's alleged reason for choosing "Nevermore" as the refrain of his "Raven" because the long o was the most sonorous vowel, and the word was "in the fullest possible keeping with that melancholy which [he] had predetermined as the tone of the poem," had been taken seriously. However this may be, Poe is the only foreigner whose verse has had any influence on the work of these modern men from Baudelaire to Mallarmé, both of whom have translated him. (p. 362)

From [Paul Verlaine, the Symbolists] have learned a delicate and subtile art, though they have sometimes employed this when they have had nothing to say. Jean Moréas, a Greek, struggles hard to interest a cold world, and even advertises a new school, the École Romane, in which he breaks away from Verlaine and Mallarmé, and promises to go back to the principles of the sixteenth century. He is often very successful in giving his verse about that amount of remoteness.

But this statement is far from being a complete definition of Moréas or of the general movement of which he is one representative. His ***Pèlerin Passioné*** contains pieces that are wonderfully melodious, though often he is very obscure, and, evidently, wilfully obscure, in the deliberate attempt, not so much to copy, as to make a tracing of forgotten methods. If the poets of the Latin decadence had not written as they did, Moréas would not write as he now does. (p. 363)

T. S. Perry, "The Latest Literary Fashion in France," in Cosmopolitan, *Vol. XIII, No. 3, July, 1892, pp. 359-65.**

RÉMY DE GOURMONT (essay date 1896)

[*Gourmont was a prominent man of letters in late nineteenth- and early twentieth-century French literature. One of the founders of* Le Mercure de France, *which for a time served as a forum for the Symbolist writers of the period, Gourmont was a prolific novelist, short story writer, dramatist, and poet. His creative works, however, were never as highly regarded or influential as his literary criticism. These works, particularly* Les livre des masques *(1896;* The Book of Masks, *1921), are important for Gourmont's sensitive examinations of the Symbolists and for his adherence to a critical style that made him a significant influence on modern English and American poetry and led T. S. Eliot to call him "the perfect critic." As critic Glen B. Burne explains: "Symbolism meant for [Gourmont] the absolute freedom of the artist to follow and express the impulses of his individual sensibility." Gourmont's criticism also follows this criterion of subjectivity, reflecting in his case a sensibility that combined a keen artistic intuition with a background of scientific learning. Both were employed throughout the body of his literary and philosophical writings. His most esteemed intellectual achievement was in articulating the concept of the "dissociation of sensibility," a method of thought whereby familiar ideas—such as the idea of liberty or justice—could be abstracted from their conventional meanings and associations, chiefly in order to separate sentiment from truth. This type of intellectual discipline, along with a mystical temperament which he shared with the Symbolists of his generation, make clear Richard Aldington's description of Gourmont as "a mixture of a Romantic artist—poet and novelist—and an eighteenth-century philosophe." In the following excerpt from* The Book of Masks, *Gourmont provides a general assessment of Moréas's poetry.*]

[Moréas's] verses are romances, that is, of a poet to whom the romantic period is but a witch's night where unreal sonorous gnomes stir, of a poet (this one has talent) who concentrates his efforts to imitate the Greeks of the Anthology through Ronsard, and to steal from Ronsard the secret of his laborious phrase, his botanical epithets, and his sickly rhythm. As for what is exquisite in Ronsard, since that little has passed into tradition and memory, the Romantic school had to neglect it on pain of quickly losing what alone constitutes its originality. There is I know not what of provincialism, of steps against life's current, of the loiterer, in this care for imitation and restoration. (pp. 213-14)

Arrived in Paris like any other Wallachian or Eastern student, and already full of love for the French language, Moréas betook himself to the school of the old poets and frequented the society of Jacot de Forest and Benoit de Sainte-Maure. He wished to take the road to which every clever youth should vow himself who is ambitious to become a good harper; he swore to accomplish the complete pilgrimage: At this hour, having set out from the *Chanson de Saint-Léger,* he has, it is said, reached the seventeenth century, and this in less than ten years. It is not as discouraging as one supposes. And now that texts are more familiar, the road shortens: from now on less halts. Moréas will camp under the old Hugo oak, and, if he perseveres, we shall see him achieve the aim of his voyage, which doubtless is to catch up with himself. Then, casting aside the staff, often changed and cut from such diverse copses, he will lean on his own genius and we will be able to judge him, if that be our whim, with a certain security.

All that today can be said is that Moréas passionately loves the French language and poetry, and that the two proud-hearted sisters have smiled upon him more than once, satisfied to see near their steps a pilgrim so patient, a cavalier armed with such good-will. (pp. 214-16)

Thus Moréas goes, quite attentive, quite in love, and in the light robe of a pilgrim. When he called one of his poems ***le Pèlerin passionné,*** he gave an excellent idea and a very sane symbolism of himself, his role and his playings among us.

There are fine things in that ***Pèlerin,*** and also in ***les Syrtes;*** there are admirable and delicious touches and which (for my part) I shall always joyfully reread, in ***les Cantilènes,*** but inasmuch as Moréas, having changed his manner, repudiates these primitive works, I shall not insist. There remains ***Ériphyle,*** a delicate collection formed of a poem of four "sylvae", all in the taste of the Renaissance and destined to be the book of examples where the young "Romans", spurred on by the somewhat intemperate invectives of Charles Maurras, must study the classic art of composing facile verses laboriously. (pp. 216-17)

Moréas, like his Phoebe, has tried to put on many diverse countenances and even to cover his face with masks. We always recognize him from his brothers: he is a poet. (p. 217)

Rémy de Gourmont, "Moréas," in his The Book of Masks, *translated by Jack Lewis, 1921. Reprint by Books for Libraries Press, 1967; distributed by Arno Press, Inc., 1967, pp. 213-20.*

LALLA VANDERVELDE (essay date 1910)

[*In the following excerpt from an obituary tribute, Vandervelde provides an overview of Moréas's work.*]

"*Je suis un Baudelaire avec plus de couleur*" ["I am a Baudelaire with more color"], said Moréas, with his curiously

"Be a Symbolist": Paul Gaugin's caricature of Moréas, c. 1891.

metallic, rather impertinent voice. Though not a Frenchman, it cannot be said that his accent was foreign; it was peculiar and very personal. He was not a Baudelaire; he was Jean Moréas, who, some thirty-five years ago, came from Athens to Paris to become a French poet. . . .

Moréas was a poet who was imbued with a passionate desire for perfection in expression, and his relentless self-criticism, combined with an instinctive feeling for form, very often enabled him to realise his aspirations. It was this thirst for perfect beauty of form and expression which caused the continual changes in his poetic career. A poem was hardly published before he disowned it, and each new book of poems marked an advance on the previous one. ***Les Syrtes*** . . . , though influenced by Gautier and Baudelaire, and ***Les Cantilènes*** . . . classed Moréas amongst the Symbolists, whose great champions were Verlaine and Mallarmé. He was noisily acclaimed as the new Symbolist—he himself wrote articles setting forth his poetic creeds, which were eagerly read by his adherents and regarded as the exegesis of the new poetry. (p. 378)

Les Cantilènes are more varied [than ***Les Syrtes***]. They contain popular French legends, poems inspired by Edgar Allan Poe and others, of an extraordinary sweetness, in which Moréas begins to show his own personality. . . . (p. 379)

When Moréas published ***Le Pèlerin passionné,*** in 1890, his admirers gave him a banquet which has remained famous in the annals of French literature, and Anatole France, in an article which appeared in the *Temps* [see excerpt dated 1890], wrote a flattering appreciation of the ***Pèlerin.***

In publishing this new work, Moréas had disowned ***Les Syrtes*** and ***Les Cantilènes.*** What was the horror and disgust of his admirers and followers when, two years after the publication of the ***Pèlerin,*** a new edition of it appeared eliminating certain portions (they were edited separately as a little volume entitled ***Autant en emporte le vent***), adding fresh material (***Gnome au clair visage, &c.***) which, provisionally, he considered was much superior. The new portions were written in flamboyant style, full of archaisms of mythology, and to understand them a glossary would sometimes be useful. . . . (p. 380)

Shortly after, Moréas, with Charles Maurras, Hugues Rebell, &c., founded the *École romane* and abjured Symbolism. At this period of his life, Moréas was mistrusted and treated as a renegade by his former admirers and imitators, and was regarded with suspicion also by the classical school of poets. For, although he had partly reverted to tradition and sought inspiration in classical subjects and models, he was at the same time influenced by Ronsard, Villon, Joachim du Bellay, &c. As Anatole France had attempted in his novels, such as *Jérome Coignard* and *La Rôtisserie de la Reine Pédanque,* so Moréas wished to enrich the French language and to resuscitate the forms of poetry used by the *Pléiade.*

His next volume, ***Les Stances*** . . . is considered his masterpiece. In a series of short poems, composed of one, two, or three quatrains, which are linked together and in reality form only one poem, we find the perfection of Ronsard's or of Bellay's sonnets without any imitation whatever, for Moréas's language is his own and his varied experiments all went to making it strong, simple, and clear. *''Les poèmes,''* says Rémy de Gourmont, *''presque tous parfaits, ont eu leur influence sur la poésie française, et une influence heureuse. Nous avions besoin d'une riche simplicité. C'est l'art suprême. Elle nous y a conduits peu à peu. Mais on n'y est arrivé, comme Moréas lui-même, qu'après mille détours''* [''the poems, almost all perfect, have had their influence on French poetry, and a fortunate influence. We were in need of a rich simplicity. That is the supreme art. It has guided us there little by little. But one only arrives, like Moréas himself, after a thousand detours'']. In ***Les Stances*** Moréas expresses the resignation of the philosopher who has learnt to judge persons and events dispassionately. . . . (p. 381)

Iphigénie is a neo-classic tragedy in five acts, which was first performed in the open-air theatre of Orange in August 1903, at the Théâtre de l'Odéon (Paris) in December of the same year, and at Athens in 1904. . . . Silvain, the tragedian, who has played the part of Agamemnon in both Racine's and Moréas's *Iphigénie,* has expressed the following opinion on the two plays to Jules Claretie, director of the Comédie française:

'''L'Iphigénie' de Racine est une jeune princesse qui, dans les plus beaux vers du monde, soupire les sentiments les plus exquis et fait entendre de son immortelle voix les plaintes les plus touchantes. 'L'Iphigénie' de Moreas est—comment dirai-je?—une sorte de Jeanne d'Arc hellène qui donne des leçons à Achille lui-même avant de mourir pour son pays'' [''The 'Iphigénie' of Racine is a young princess who, in the most beautiful verse in the world, sighs the most exquisite sentiments and makes heard with her immortal voice the most touching complaints. The 'Iphigénie' of Moréas is—how should I say—a sort of Hellenic Joan of Arc who gives lessons to Achilles himself before dying for her country''].

Original in his tragedy as he had been in his poems, Moréas has not followed the example of Corneille or of Racine. Their regular alexandrines engender a certain monotony. Moréas has brought back to us the variety of the Greek drama and has made an epic of a tragedy. At the same time, as Sophocles, Homer, and Virgil have influenced him much more than the French dramatists, the continual changes of rhythms and of metre, and the contrast between the lyric and the dramatic element all go to make his ***Iphigénie*** ''divine'' in the Platonic sense. (p. 382)

Lalla Vandervelde, ''Jean Moréas,'' in The English Review, *Vol. V, May, 1910, pp. 377-84.*

RICHARD BUXTON (essay date 1911)

[In the following excerpt, Buxton discusses Moréas's major works and poetic theories.]

It is a singular fact that, while in England poetry is usually divorced from poetical theory, yet in France, since Bellay's ''Defence and Illustration of the French Language,'' innovating poets have attempted to describe in as exact terms as possible their objects and their methods of attaining them. In the nineteenth century manifesto rapidly followed manifesto, but one theorist stands out from the rest by his energy in controversy, by his two changes of opinion, and by his mastery in all three forms of poetry.

This man was Jean Moréas, by birth Diamantopoulos, a native of Athens, educated and domiciled in France. If there were no other cause for his glory, he might justly be remembered as the man who invented the word ''Symbolist'' as an alternative to the word ''Decadent,'' then used to describe Verlaine and his followers. Moréas published his first book, ***Les Syrtes,*** in 1884, and immediately plunged into the literary war with manifestoes, prefaces, and literary documents of all kinds. In 1886 he published ***Les Cantilènes.***

These two volumes cover the period during which Moréas considered himself an official Symbolist, though many of the poems in them do not come under that head, and many of his poems published afterwards bear the mark of the symbol. One is even a little startled in opening ***Les Syrtes*** to find poems which appear hardly to have felt the existence of Verlaine. The series with which the volume opens, **''Remembrances,''** musical and glowing with colour as it is, has no mystery, none of the power of suggestion upon which the Symbolists prided themselves. (p. 518)

But for all this the symbol is present in these two volumes, not by any means in the extraordinarily difficult form in which it is sometimes presented to us by Kahn and Régnier, but at its simplest, only one step removed from the metaphor. Take this poem, one of the sections of **''Accalmie,''** in which it is employed in a plain straightforward manner.

My heart, my heart was the swinging light
That lit the brothel up by night;
My heart, my heart was the rose that spread
Over the dunghill its flowering head.

My heart, my heart is the taper alight
By a maiden's coffin, pure and white;
My heart, my heart on a pond afar
Floats, a chaste white nenuphar.

Here we have before us, easily comprehensible, the method upon which the Symbolists worked; the attempt to paint mental states by a series of images which should gradually build up one composite image in the mind of the reader. Nowhere in Moréas' first two volumes do these series of images become unintelligible; always they are of the simplest description, and penetrating in their simplicity:

Dans nos cœurs aussi, pauvre amante,
Il va neiger, il va neiger.
[''In our hearts too, poor beloved, It will snow, it will snow.'']

This, reminiscent of Verlaine's ''Il pleure dans mon cœur'' [''It rains in my heart''], and yet distinct from it, is wonderful in its suggestion of love that dies.

While asserting the simplicity of Moréas' symbols in these volumes, I would not be taken as asserting his complete simplicity of idea and language. The series entitled **''Le Pur Concept''** is extremely obscure and wilfully so. It would seem that at this time the poet was desirous of finding some philosophical thread to run through his works as ''L'Inconscient'' is the groundwork of Laforgue's poetry; but his attempt was a failure, and **''Le Pur Concept''** is a riddle hardly worth the trouble of guessing. Much more valuable are the ballads in ***Les Cantilènes,*** which appear in startling contrast to the poems amid which they are placed. Agha Véli is feasting in his palace when a rose-coloured bird enters and says:—

"Your blue-eyed girl, your blonde,
Your blonde with lips so red,
To-morrow she is to wed
The king's son of Trebizond."

He rises and rushes off on horseback.

They leave the hills behind,
Behind, the brown, parched plain,
Moonlit, in the hurricane,
Like devils they pass on the wind.

At the last they meet a funeral procession and Agha Véli demands the name of the corpse.

"'Tis the blue-eyed girl, the blonde,
The blonde with lips so red;
To-morrow she should have wed
The king's son of Trebizond."

This and the accompanying ballads far more resemble the work of Bürger, Byron, and Scott than that of any other French poet. It is plain that the literature of his adopted country was not the only one that influenced the young Greek. Indeed, **"Remembrances"** bears a certain faint resemblance to the lyrics of Heine.

Moréas was always of opinion that the new idea in poetry required not only a new style, but a new vocabulary; and from the first he advocated the revival of the words used before Malherbe. The use of such words as "antan" and "malitorne" gives already an archaic flavour to his early poems. In 1891, however, he published a volume, ***Le Pèlerin passionné,*** which was to be the starting point of a new school, based largely on this revival of the antique vocabulary. A long new manifesto was issued announcing the foundation of the "Ecole Romane," which had for its object "the renewal of tradition." The restoration of the speech of the Pléiade and of writers earlier still was a difficult task, but to write modern poetry in such a form was more difficult still; and it is hardly surprising that even Moréas himself was guilty of numerous failures. He rallied round him a school of enthusiastic disciples, chief among whom were Charles Maurras, Raymond de la Tailhède, Ernest Raynaud, and Maurice du Plessys. . . . But three dangers beset the new method, and from all three Moréas suffered—extravagance, obscurity, the pastiche. If **"Le Dit d'un Chevalier"** is extravagant, and **"Epître"** obscure, then no less is the **"Eglogue à Francine"** a pastiche, brilliant as it is. But occasionally a fine height of vigorous expression is reached, in which his vocabulary and complicated method are handled lightly by the poet and not as an exercise. Take, for example, the poem **"Against Juliette"**—

To keep you in your evil power
With flags and gonfalons of Love,
I gave you love locks black as waves
When the north-west wind blows above.

For shields with tender words on them,
For crowns of deepest loyalty
I gave you my proud hands against
Your natural vulgarity.

A cup of melody and balm,
That you might drink and charmèd be,
I gave to you my living mouth,
Red as the roses on the tree.

For tiring-maids and waiting-maids
Attentive to your fidgeting,
I gave you my hands, more noble far
Than any gold that crowns a king.

And all the treasures of my thought,
The hoarded treasures that were mine,
I gave you, I, the prodigal,
I cast them down like pearls to swine.

It was Moréas' habit when he published a new book to disown all his previous volumes, and ***Le Pèlerin passionné*** followed ***Les Syrtes*** and ***Les Cantilènes*** into limbo on the publication of ***Enone au Clair Visage.*** Here we have the Ecole Romane at its most extravagant and most arid period. These poems of Moréas are of no more value than those of his disciples. Elisions, archaic words and forms, compounded words, new loans from Latin, and obscure construction are the distinguishing characteristics. Only very occasionally does the verse free itself from the chains of these mannerisms. Maurice du Plessys, the most ardent follower of Moréas, exhibits the same faults. In their anxiety for style and vocabulary, the poets of the Ecole Romane forgot the importance of subject, and nearly all their poems which are not on classical themes, so treated as to bear no relation to the human life of to-day, are glorifications of one another. In du Plessys' book, "Le Premier Livre des Pastorales," out of twenty-seven poems no fewer than nine are devoted to the Ecole Romane or to its individual members!

After the publication of ***Eriphyle et Sylves Nouvelles,*** Moréas executed another volte-face and produced his last and greatest work. No volume of poems is at once so simple at first sight or so difficult justly to appraise. At the first reading it appears as though Moréas had slipped into the easy and unproductive way of traditionalism because age had narrowed his outlook and fossilised his mind. But at the second reading you may catch a glimpse of something above and beyond this, and at the third the book becomes a permanent delight.

In criticising it, one falls naturally into the fine old phrases of the classical era. The images are just and the language elegant and exact. Here is none of the fine, unequal fervour of youth; all is restraint, self-criticism, conscious artistry. The work is not cold, because it is restrained and calm; a strong life is perceptible beneath the measured movements of the surface. The prevailing note is a noble Stoic melancholy. The style is not bizarre, but it is most certainly not commonplace. If, as one critic has observed, it is not the French of any one period, it is, in some sense, the French of all periods. It is by its perfect style that the book will live. The thoughts expressed are not anywhere startlingly original, but they are always startlingly true. Here, indeed, is a criticism of life.

Two specimens, one translated and the other not, will serve to show the quality of ***Les Stances,*** as far as any extract can show it, for this is not a collection of poems, but one poem.

Say not that life's a joyous festival;
He that thus speaks is madman or buffoon.
Above all say not; sadness is it all;
That from a coward soul that tires too soon.

Laugh as in springtime waves the leafy bough,
Weep as the wind weeps, or the ruffled stream,
Taste every pleasure, suffer every woe;
And say; it is much, and the shadow of a dream.

Adieu, le vapeur siffle, on active le feu;
Dans la nuit le train passe ou c'est l'ancre qu'on lève;
Qu'importe! on vient, on part; le flot soupire; adieu!
Qu'il arrive du large ou qu'il quitte la grève.

Les roses vont éclore, et nous les cueillerons;
Les feuilles du jardin vont tomber une à une.
Adieu! quand nous naissons, adieu! quand nous mourons,
Et comme le bonheur s'envole l'infortune.

Maurice Barrès once dubbed Moréas "le poète grammairien," and the title was justified. He was ceaselessly seeking the method by which to express himself to the world, and first and foremost he experimented with words. Three distinct styles are visible in the small body of his poems, and it is difficult to believe that the same man could have written **"Accalmie,"** ***Sylves,*** and ***Les Stances.*** But his untiring experiments brought him at last to the perfect medium, and ***Les Stances*** is immortal because of the harmony between thought and style. If there is any book which can provoke a classical revival in France it is the work of this Athenian. (pp. 518-19)

Richard Buxton, "Jean Moréas," in The New Age, *n.s. Vol. IX, No. 22, September 28, 1911, pp. 518-19.*

G. TURQUET-MILNES (essay date 1921)

[*In the following excerpt from* Some Modern French Writers: A Study in Bergsonism, *Turquet-Milnes discusses philosophical aspects of Moréas's poetry, which he aligns with the ideas of Henri Bergson.*]

All the activities of intellectual life which form, as it were, the common atmosphere of an epoch, may start from different points, but they run on parallel lines and encourage one another, like groups of school-boys running through a playing field, each group bent on its own particular game, but catching zest and enthusiasm from the others. The man of letters, when he reaches a certain stage in philosophical research, cannot help discovering the eternal types of action and passion, and is moreover forced to ask himself what is their *raison d'être:* are the categories by which the intellect perceives phenomena, manifestations of a superior reality; and after all is not the artist's invention, which he himself believes to be conscious, rather the surrender of his being to the suggestions of some superior principle, be it called intuition, or abstract reason?

It may seem a far cry from the works of M. Bergson or of M. Ravaisson to the poems of Jean Moréas, and yet when we understand Ravaisson's or Bergson's philosophy as well as Moréas' stanzas we realize that at bottom we are dealing with the same hellenic, generous philosophy, the same striving to be independent of mere intellect, the same aspiring towards all the conditions of a musical art.

By Hellenism I do not mean that hellenism which is only a canon, a system of rules which the Greeks are supposed to have imposed upon their artists and all those thereby inspired, a somewhat passionless range of effects which looks like a cold sensualism without any inner ideals. On the contrary, the great Greek philosophers and artists were the first to see that a work of art is a living organism, and genius an essence apart, anticipating, and even creating, facts. The Bergsonian conception of reality brings us nearer this hellenism so well understood by Renaissance and Nineteenth-Century humanists. Human thought, thus spiritualized and refined by ages of aspiration and suffering, seeks now only this unity, this solidarity of beings, which the great philosophers of antiquity also sought. The artist who seeks to limit himself to the concrete—truly Greek therein—submits to what Bergson calls the Immediate. For the desire to reproduce the expression and individual character of every being and every thing, to write as it were the private history of every soul, is to be essentially both ancient and modern in character.

Fromentin called the Nineteenth-Century school of painting the "sensation school." The name could be applied to the more famous works of Nineteenth-Century literature; Bergson or Moréas are the last comers among the impersonations of their age: all that was intense and original in it is crystallized in them. The pedant will probably deny them the title of pure hellenists, but they are both Renaissance men, actuated by the same desire as the great men of the Sixteenth Century to translate the movement of life which is carried on in shaping itself, of the eternal becoming which is ever new.

The symbolism of the French poets aims at expressing these efforts of the writer who tries, by means of a perfect identification of form and matter, to arrive not only at a reproduction of reality, but to suggest something behind it, more distant, more divine if possible. . . . In order to give real expression to what was in their hearts, and yet to remain always hostile to all declamation and false sentiment, the great Renaissance artists, and those of our day, have recourse to a kind of incomplete effect, something not quite finished which we see in their sculptures and poems, something of that reluctance to arrive at conclusions which Flaubert considered was an attribute of God. It is this infinite suggestiveness that holds us in the statues of Michelangelo and of Rodin, in the poems of Joachim du Bellay or of Moréas.

But the art which, far more than sculpture, painting or literature, is a matter of pure perception is the art of music. "De la musique avant toute chose" ["music before everything else"], cried Verlaine, echoing the dearest wish of his age. We know what help music has lent to Bergson's theories; on the other hand, after studying [***Les Syrtes, Les Cantilènes, Le Pèlerin Passionné, Eriphyle,*** and ***Stances***] . . . , we realize that in spite of his avatars, which we will presently consider, Moréas was always an *intuitif* whose expression, though very clear (for he has a holy horror of the theatrical), was laden with the multiple meaning of the most general feelings of the human mind. His art might be defined by saying that his aim was to sum up the most original or quintessential sensations of life in phrases often archaic in form, but which were always original, but, and before all, musical. (pp. 195-97)

After a certain amount of Ronsardizing and Symbolizing, Moréas in his later years was purely and simply a classic poet. The reader remembers perhaps his words to Maurice Barrès on his deathbed: "There is no such thing as Classic and Romantic, that's all nonsense . . . if only I felt better I could explain what I mean." We shall never know what arguments Moréas would have used: but we do know that after writing what seemed to many Frenchmen a somewhat tortured poetry, he finally produced the noblest and most classic. And in this he is symbolic of the evolution of the young school of 1890-1914. He is a represenative man. (pp. 200-01)

Moréas began to write, or rather to publish, in 1884, when he was twenty-three. Vanier, the publisher of Verlaine and Mallarmé, published his ***Les Syrtes*** about this time: then, in 1886, ***Les Cantilènes*** appeared. The influence of Baudelaire—the symbolistic Baudelaire—is very marked therein, and also the influence of Verlaine. What is most striking in these compositions of a young writer is not only the effort to note the mysterious, the fleeting and sad, the reaction against the Parnassian poetry and vulgar realism, but also the way in which the old classic instinct is seeking for expression.

Towards 1890 those young American or English artists who are always fond of lionizing French poets were able to enjoy the spectacle of poor, sad old Verlaine limping along in his bedraggled trousers side by side with young Moréas, a perfect dandy with his eyeglass in his eye, looking rather like the *Ruffian* of his splendid poem.

Moréas's life was going to be a journey, not only through the *cafés* of Paris and Europe, but through French literature, starting from that of the Middle Ages: and when he died in 1910 his poetry had returned to the source of all true poetry, enriched by all that it had reflected, but calmed down into an ordered stoical nobility. (pp. 203-04)

But, in order to realize the roads he had trod, one should read his ***Pèlerin Passionné,*** which scandalized the world of letters on its appearance in 1890.

Anyone who wants to know what the Parisian younger generation thought of the ***Pèlerin Passionné*** must consult the newspapers and pamphlets of the day. In one of them, called *Fin de Siècle et Décadence* [by Maurice Monteil], I find the following judgment:—"Le titre emprunté à Shakespeare n'a aucun rapport avec les poésies contenues dans le volume: il n'y a ni pélerinage ni passion. Les vers sont libres; ils ont la rime, mais la mesure est absente . . . ; certains ont jusqu'à vingt et un pieds. . . ." ["The title, which is borrowed from Shakespeare, has nothing to do with the poems in the volume: there is neither pilgrimage nor passion. The verses are free; they rime, but metre is absent . . . ; some have up to twenty (metrical) feet. . . ."]. And the hostile critic quoted among other lines the following, which are certainly rather bewildering to a scholar fresh from his Virgil:—

On a marché sur les fleurs au bord de la route,
Et le vent d'automne les secoue si fort en outre.
La malle-poste a renversé la vieille croix au bord de la route,
Elle était vraiment si pourrie en outre.
L'idiot (tu sais) est mort au bord de la route,
Et personne ne le pleurera en outre.

["Someone has walked over the flowers on the side of the road, / And the autumn wind shakes them so hard, besides. / The mail-coach has knocked down the old cross on the side of the road. / It was actually quite rotted, anyway. / The idiot (you know the one) died on the side of the road, / And no one will cry for him, besides."]

It has been said that Moréas was lacking in emotion: such things are easy to say. It is not always those who are continually whimpering who have the most feeling. Ready tears are things of little count, like those rivulets which never run dry because they flow through chalky and infertile soil.

Moréas had discovered that our lives, like our speech, were encumbered with a great deal of unnecessary repetition, and he used the literary trick of piling Pelion upon Ossa in images, with no apparent logical connection. These three lines are the pattern of the style he most readily cultivated in his youth:—

Pire que bonne vous fûtes, et je fus sage.
Vous aviez un bouquet de cassie au corsage,
Et votre cou cerclé d'un collier de ducats.

["You were worse than good, and I was wise.
You wore a corsage from the acacia tree, / and a string of gold coins around your neck."]

That was his manner. He exaggerated a trick of which Verlaine, Rimbaud and Tristan Corbière had set the fashion, and which can be discovered by the careful seeker in most great poetry. But it was the originality of the latter Nineteenth Century to emphasize the process. There were painters with the same way of working, arranging splashes of color one beside the other, without any preconceived agreement of design, and leaving the public to compose the harmony of the picture with a mosaic of colors and shades. The hearer of Debussy's works is in the same manner confronted with a whirlwind of dancing musical atoms,—painter and composer toy, the one with every bar, the other with every tint, progressing slowly, seeking rare sonorities or minute subtleties of color; and often they succeed in obtaining penetrating effects which rival those of Nature. Such work is the image of our own souls, which are like those great rooms in old châteaux whose echoes are so memory-laden that they repeat the cries of joy and pain of all humanity. To produce that effect there have striven, each in his own way, poets so different as Francis Viélé-Griffin, Henri de Régnier, Paul Fort, Camille Mauclair, and Charles Guérin.

Next, still in pursuit of his Renaissance ideal, Moréas took to studying old French, adapted *Aucassin et Nicolette,* translated the *History of Jean de Paris, King of France*. It was at this period, when he was under the influence of the old French poets, and of Ronsard and du Bellay, that he wrote his ***Eriphyle,*** which for every Romanist is a pure masterpiece. (pp. 204-06)

The appearance of the ***Pèlerin Passionné*** in 1891 had given rise to a manifestation which was soon followed by the foundation of the *Ecole Romane*. The members of this new Pléiade were Raymond de la Tailhède, Maurice du Plessys, Charles Maurras, Ernest Raynaud, and Hugues Rebell. Moréas was the acknowledged leader. But it was a constitutional monarchy, and the prime minister was a young man of subtle and penetrating mind whose hour of fame had just struck; for had not the great Taine climbed up the six flights of stairs leading to the young man's flat and all because of an article which this same young man had written? This prime minister was Charles Maurras. Since those days he has attained a certain amount of fame. M. Faguet, in his *Histoire de la Littérature Française,* boldly declares: "The masters of French literature at the present day are Messieurs Bergson, Barrès, and Maurras." Maurras at twenty was the same firm, complete character he is at fifty, and there is little doubt that it was he who pointed out to Moréas whither his excessive decadence and so-called symbolism were leading him. Moréas realized himself, thanks in great part to Maurras, and in this way, after his somewhat disturbed linguistic revolution, his verbal punctiliousness, and his turgid lucubrations, he returned little by little to classic order.

As he grew older he came to appreciate Malherbe, since in a sense Malherbe is the continuation of Ronsard and his art essentially an intellectual reasoning art. Moréas renounced his *vers libre* and the other novelties which had amused him in his youth. He saw, as Malherbe had seen, that the great beauty of the French language is that it is analytic; he realized that it is unwise to strain one's talent; further, he became convinced that the only true art is hellenic art and its pupil French art.

The soul of Moréas is revealed to us in ***Les Stances,*** a kind of breviary for stoic unbelievers. Moréas, like his friend Charles Maurras, believed only in Reason, and Reason in the Greek sense, or as the French classicists of the Sixteenth and Seventeenth Centuries understood it. The perfection of art is the approach of the divine.

Me voici seul enfin, tel que je devais l'être:
    Les jours sont révolus.
Ces dévouements couverts que tu faisais paraître
    Ne me surprendront plus.
Le mal que tu m'as fait et ton affreux délire
    Et ses pièges maudits,
Depuis longtemps déjà les cordes de la lyre
    Me les avaient prédits.
Au vent de ton malheur tu n'es en quelque sorte
    Qu'un fétu ballotté.
Mais j'accuse surtout celui qui se comporte
    Contre sa volonté.

["Here I am alone at last, as I ought to be: / The days are over with. / These displays of devotion that you cast above / No longer catch me beneath them. / The pain you have caused me and your hideous delirium / And its accursed snares, / For sometime the strings of the lyre / foretold them to me. / In the wind of your misfortune you are in some way / only a blown straw. / But I especially accuse the one who acts / Against her own will."]

Of a different order from that of Alfred de Musset is this poetry, with its conciseness, its bitterness against the woman who betrays, its loftiness of tone and its perfection. Here a thoroughly disillusioned heart took refuge in poetry, seeking a cure for the malady of life. (pp. 206-08)

Moréas came at an equivocal moment, as he himself said. None of the themes dear to the heart of the symbolists corresponded with his real temperament. He was too Græco-French to be a pantheist in the German manner, too Greek to have any real Christian faith. There is nothing of a Villon or a Hugo in him, nor of a Byron or a Swinburne. So that the only way open to him was to sing the poems of his destiny and to take refuge in the theatre. The ***Iphigénie*** of Moréas calls for comparison with that of Racine. Racine's is much more French, Moréas' much closer to the Greek text; yet both may fitly be cited as examples of that classic art whose aim is to paint the universal and attain the eternal beauty of which Greece has given imperishable models.

That is the great lesson Moréas teaches us. He is a Platonist in the same sense as Charles Maurras. In the eyes of these two writers the human being, be he poet or statesman, so long as he has not grasped the eternal reason which lies behind the ephemeral aspect of things, can only have fevered visions of reality. It is impossible to understand Moréas without having read Maurras's masterpiece, *Anthinea*. For many a young Frenchman ***les Stances*** and *Anthinea* are the *vade mecum* which enables them to see themselves and their destiny according to the eternal laws which the Greeks discovered. (pp. 208-09)

G. Turquet-Milnes, "Jean Moréas," in his Some Modern French Writers: A Study in Bergsonism, *Robert M. McBride & Company, 1921, pp. 195-211.*

PIERRE DE BACOURT AND J. W. CUNLIFFE (essay date 1923)

[In the following excerpt, de Bacourt and Cunliffe trace the poetic development of Moréas.]

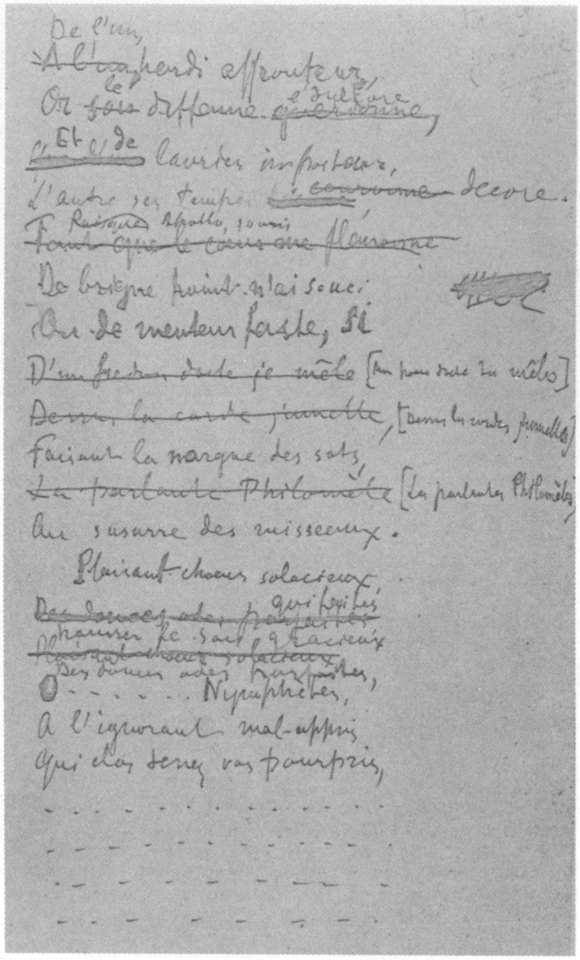

Holograph manuscript of a poem by Moréas.

All French poetry from Charles d'Orléans to Rimbaud was familiar to [Moréas]; he tried to bring back into honour the old and forgotten poetic forms of the masters of the Renaissance and of the fifteenth century. In 1894 he published **'Ériphyle'** and four **'Sylves'** which his friends heralded as the most perfect poems written since 'Sagesse'; the style is of a fluidity and charm which made of these little poems all but masterpieces and permitted Maurras to foretell the admirable perfection of the **'Stances.'** Maurras had an enormous influence on the poet's development; to their friendship may be safely traced the latter's reversion to pure classical forms, and the **'Stances'** is a classic in inspiration as well as in technique. Moréas does not strive for originality. His themes are of everyday topics; his ideas, the very same which have been sung by Homer, Virgil, La Fontaine, but also the ideas of a man of the twentieth century. Like the classics, he does not seek the exceptional, but what men hold in common. These simple themes are expressed with such force, such loftiness, such subtle balance that we find in his work all the charm, the everlasting youth of the true classics. This masterpiece of a Greek had fulfilled the aim of the 'École Romane' which was to prove that the themes and technique of the classics were still worthy of admiration. In 1904 Moréas produced **'Iphigénie'** at the Odéon, a classic drama worthy of the **'Stances.'**

Four different periods may be discerned in his life work. First of all, he was a Symbolist. His theories were expressed in various manifestoes and newspaper articles, collected under the title of **'Les Premières Armes du Symbolisme.'** . . . For him concrete facts have "poétiquement " ["poetically"] no existence; they are mere appearances behind which are shown the ideas. These ideas must never be expressed in plain words under their abstract form, but only in symbols derived from concrete phenomena which our senses can perceive. The mode of expression of the classicists or even of the romanticists is inadequate for such symbolistic expression; hence the necessity of a new language independent of all former rules. The verse must be rejuvenated and metric forms must be as diverse as our ideas. But it never occurred to Moréas that he could get rid entirely of the old rules. He never went as far as "vers libre" ["free verse"]; what he wanted was "vers libéré" ["freed verse"]. In **'Les Syrtes'** the symbols are easy to understand and few in number. In **'Les Cantilènes'** he went much further in that direction, but in neither are found the peculiar forms which he recommends in his manifestoes. His greatest originality as to prosody is the constant use of odd numbers—nine or eleven syllables. After all, he uses the old technique, but freer, lighter, more subtle in its effects. In his first manifesto he urged a reversion to the language, vocabulary and forms of the ancient poets, but it was merely with the idea that the French ought to make use of all the wealth of their literature. This leads us to his second period, that of the first part of the **'Pèlerin Passionné,'** in the preface of which he insists more earnestly on the necessity of coming back to these forms: "I think that since the end of the sixteenth century our language has been impoverished, dessiccated, and fettered." He wants to revert to Malherbe, to adapt the prosody and vocabulary of the poets of the Malherbe period to the needs and taste of his contemporaries, to recreate "the communion of the French middle ages and of the French Renaissance fused and transfigured in the principles of the modern soul." The **'Pèlerin Passioné,'** which represents what has been called his conversion to the middle ages, is the work of a consummate artist in prosody; he uses with the most astounding cleverness all metric forms from assonance and blank verse to the regular alexandrine. At the same time, it becomes more and more apparent that Moréas has never really assimilated symbolistic philosophy, but that he remains content with an adroit reform of language and poetics. It is worthy of note that he alone among the Symbolists attempted that reform and succeeded, at least, in attracting serious attention to this phase of the movement.

Classicism had for him an unconquerable lure, which, however, he himself did not yet fully realise. The Symbolist movement was tending more and more toward mystery, dream, abstruse expression, and this hurt deeply his instinctive love for logic, clearness, light; the affected pessimism borrowed from the nebulous northern literatures grated on the optimism of this son of Greece; the time came (that of his third period) when he was ready to disown his first work, even the first half of the **'Pèlerin.'** "In my opinion my real work in this book begins at the page where the romance influence is felt." From now on his aim was to reject all German vagueness and pessimism and to imitate "the men of the middle ages and the Renaissance, the true sons and grandsons of the Latins and of the Greeks." It is then that he founded the "L'École Romane," with Charles Maurras, Raymond de la Tailhède, Ernest Raymond, and Maurice du Plessis; but this did not satisfy the attraction he felt for true classicism and, after years of thought and inner struggle, he came out as a genuine classicist in **'Les Stances,'** one of the most perfect poems of modern times, and characteristic of his fourth period. "I have abandoned free verse, realising that its effects are purely material and its liberties illusory. Traditional prosody has more nobility, more stability, although permitting infinite variety in the rhythm of the thoughts and of the feelings; but one must be a trained craftsman." Thus Jean Moréas, said a French critic, "succeeded in one of the most extraordinary manifestations of a poetic soul that France has seen in years and years." (pp. 269-72)

Pierre de Bacourt and J. W. Cunliffe, "The Symbolist Movement," in their French Literature During the Last Half-Century, *The Macmillan Company, 1923, pp. 251-84.**

JOHN DAVIS BUTLER **(essay date 1967)**

[Butler has written the most extensive study in English of Moréas's life and work. In the following excerpt from that study, Butler traces the development of Moréas's verse from Les syrtes *to* Les stances.*]*.

Before the publication of the ***Syrtes*** in 1884 Moréas had published several poems in various numbers of the *Chat-Noir* which he helped to direct. While many of these showed some talent, it was not until the appearance of his first volume that the evolution of his career as a poet began in earnest. (p. 65)

The first poem in the volume, **"Remembrances",** which is one of the more successful, is written in octosyllabic quatrains characterized by rich rhymes. The form is Parnassian and classical. However, Moréas expresses a Villonesque or more specifically, a Verlainian nostalgia and melancholy. . . . The selection entitled **"Conte d'Amour"** is one of the fairly long poems, rather well done and obviously of Baudelairean and decadent inspiration. . . . Many of the poems are decadent by virtue of the poet's use of rare words, of neologisms, his richness of imagery, expression of anxiety and ennui, and his slightly satanic melancholy. In like manner it is not difficult to detect the influence of Verlaine for many of the lines sing the sweet, sad music of regret and of the frustration of love and life *à la* Verlaine. . . . There is also the Verlainian melancholy, imprecision and musical suggestion. However this volume is far from being entirely or clearly Symbolist in spite of the elliptic, suggestive, and musical style that obtains in many of these offerings. In many of the poems not only does the poet use the traditional Parnassian form but he engages in direct expression as well. Thus **"Accalmie"** is clearly classic in sound and construction.

Even though Moréas travels far in the development of his art from the ***Syrtes*** to the ***Stances,*** nevertheless it is next to impossible not to recognize in this early work the indications, at least, of the buds from which the ***Stances*** will grow. There is the lyricism overflowing the simplicity of the classical form; there is the tendency toward control of this lyricism in some of the pieces, the tendency toward a classical sobriety. There is also some personal emphasis, a concern with the *moi,* but not the excessively personal frenzy of Romanticism. In addition, there is the Symbolist effort to establish a correspondence between the poet's inner feeling or sensation and exterior phenomena, as well as the ability, though nascent here, to condense and capture an entire experience in a few lines, an art which will reach its acme in the ***Stances.***

Thus while this volume has obvious defects, most of which stem from the poet's desire to write poetry exemplary of externally conceived standards, while it hosts no profound ideas or originality of material, nevertheless in it the poet does achieve (somewhat unconsciously, I submit) a fusion of the elements of Classicism, and Decadentism-Symbolism, a fusion of modernity of sentiment with Classicism of form. This combination results in a volume which contains many pieces that are not only readable but thoroughly enjoyable and rewarding. Moréas' second volume of poetry, ***Les Cantilènes,*** was published in 1886 . . . when the poet was thirty years of age. The word *cantilènes* is given the dictionary definition of "a lyric and epic song; a sentimental melody with a moderated movement". It is derived from the Italian, *cantilena,* which in turn comes from the Latin, *cantare,* to sing. Edouard Maynial, author of an anthology which includes a representative selection of Moréas' poetry, defines *cantilène* as a "chant profane, par opposition au chant sacré, puis toute mélodie ayant un refrain monotone" ["profane hymn, as opposed to a sacred hymn, having an entirely monotonous melody"]. Moréas himself has defined his ***Cantilènes*** as "Airs et récits sur de vieilles légendes" ["songs and recitals about the old legends"]. As the title implies Moréas manifests here a predilection for the legendary ditties and lyric snatches from the epics of the Middle Ages. . . . There is little trace of the depth of feeling, the bitterness, the moving sincerity, bound by determined stoical control, that we have in the ***Stances.*** It is true that Moréas skilfully recaptures a sense of spontaneity and the folk-feeling in some of the adaptations from the Middle Ages, and some of the ***Cantilènes*** are delightful. These appear intermittently throughout the sections titled **"Assonances"**, **"Cantilènes"**, and **"Histoires Merveilleuses"**. Most of them are interesting and well done. This popular poetry in the mode of Béranger is inspired by courtly love and chivalric gallantry as revealed in the *fabliaux, chansons* and *lais* of Medieval France. Such are **"Tidogolain"**, **"Le Ruffian"**, **"Air de danse"**, **"L'Epouse fidèle"**, and **"La Comtesse Esmerée"**. Although the poet tries to adhere to decadent manners, and in some respects succeeds, nevertheless his images are frequently fresh and clear and compellingly vivid. This is particularly true in these popular pieces which are enjoyable for their charm, and their facility in the evocation and recapture of the freshness of genuine folk art.

However, there is little genuine and personal spontaneity. There is too often recourse to learned neologisms, archaisms, decadent vocabulary and preciosity. The syntax, characterized by inversions and ellipses, is frequently Mallarméan. In some of the poems this results in an obscurity that is practically hermetic in quality. This is true of some of the stanzas of the section called **"Le pur concept"**. It is particularly true of one of the poems from the last section. In this poem, called **"Melusine"**, the allegorical meaning is so vaguely suggested and the choice of words is so frequently bizarre as to deny the reader any direct access or sense of communication whatsoever. (pp. 66-9)

Nevertheless [the volume] is of interest to the Moréas student and to the student of Symbolism since it shows facets of the poet's artistic evolution, indicates his thorough grounding in French literature and poetry from their very beginnings, and depicts the workings of a Symbolist who is still reluctant to shed completely the marks of tradition. (p. 71)

[Although Moréas' next work, the ***Pèlerin passionné,***] was far from being typically Symbolist, it was accepted by the critics and poets of the day as the long awaited demonstration piece of the movement. It was the first work that deliberately and sufficiently embodied the theories of the new movement and its youthful writers. Thus it earned for Moréas recognition as the incontestable leader of the movement. (p. 72)

[The] extent of his acclamation by the public and his peers reached heights which were not to be surpassed even when he was later to publish his masterpiece, ***Les Stances.*** It seems that for a while, Moréas overshadowed even Mallarmé and Verlaine. (p. 73)

In spite of this wide acclaim, there were of course some who did not appreciate what Moréas was attempting in ***Le Pèlerin passionné*** and this lack of unanimity caused some controversy. Laurent Tailhade expressed a preference for his earlier volumes, the ***Cantilènes*** and ***Syrtes.*** Huysmans, speaking of Moréas' aim as expressed in the preface to the ***Pèlerin passionné*** said: "Ce rêve! Faire du moderne avec la langue romane! Quelle folie! . . . Enfin, . . . n'en parlons plus" ["This dream! To make something modern with the Roman language! what madness! . . . Finally, . . . let us speak no more of it"]. . . . This volume, so controversial at the time of its appearance and nevertheless of interest only to the specialist at the present time, contains poems written from 1886 to 1890. . . . It is a definitive break, not with Symbolism (at least not in the first edition), but with a certain period or phase of the movement. At the same time it marks the initiation of a new phase demonstrative of a personal dream of the poet. However, the perceptive reader of the poems soon becomes aware that the poet's dream has 'Roman' overtones, for this volume is really a nucleus from which the Ecole Romane will grow in the latter part of 1891. (p. 75)

This return to the ancients which he advocates in the preface and demonstrates in the poems of ***Le Pèlerin passionné*** is in one sense a reaction against Symbolism. Nevertheless, in the expression of his solitary, courageous disdain for that which was taking on the quality of tradition for the movement, he is at once Symbolist in a broader significance of the term—that is, within the confines of its allowance for, indeed insistence upon, the right of the poet to individuality of expression and to emancipation from all tradition whatever. (p. 77)

The ***Pèlerin passionné*** is also more specifically Symbolist by the use of free verse (the first volume in which he uses it), by the numerous hiatuses, and by the use of assonance. The work is characterized by a liberty or prosodic license which is, however, under control; there is indeed a recognizable "désordre savamment ordonné" ["skillfully arranged disorder"]. . . . In spite of the obeisance paid to Mallarmé in some of the poems of the ***Syrtes*** and his great respect for the master, Moréas was not *"septentrionale"* ["northern"] in his poetic orientation and always had an inclination for clarity and order. He did defend obscurity in his bout with Bourdes and in his first tiff with Anatole France, but this was at the time of his arrival in Paris when he was temporarily ravished by the excitement of the Decadent dandies. It was also before he had so thoroughly initiated himself to the genuine and basic character of French poetry. Many of the poems, in the ***Cantilènes*** for example, are difficult to read, too learned and researched or too Decadent (that is, replete with neologisms, inversions, oddities of syntax) as are a few in the ***Pèlerin.*** However, in most of the poems of this latter volume any obscurity of meaning and consequent dilution of the reader's pleasure and appreciation do not stem from an impossible esoterism. . . . Any obscurity present is that created by a linguistic and literary savant, a philologist and professional student of the poetry and the language from its beginnings. It stems from a conscious, deliberate, and reasoned use of archaisms in vocabulary and syntax. (pp. 77-8)

The poetry of the ***Pèlerin passionné*** . . . harks back to DuBellay and Ronsard, to the *chansonniers* of the Middle Ages such as

Thibaut de Champagne to whom Moréas frequently refers, and to the vocabulary and syntax of early French when it was still heavy with Latinisms. It is a disparate collection, a mosaic rather than a genuine fusion, a mixture rather than a compound. In it there occurs a juxtaposition of words from different centuries, a mingling of learned and popular jargon put together with a variety of rhythms. In occasional offerings the poet achieves a gem of rare beauty where the theme and form complement each other in a felicitous manner, thus anticipating the ***Stances,*** but only occasionally. There is virtuosity enough, but this to the extent of constituting a fault. As a whole, the volume smacks of pedantry or thesis poetry. (p. 80)

With the second edition of the ***Pèlerin passionné*** Moréas officially inaugurates his celebrated *Ecole romane*. The seeds were planted in the ***Syrtes*** and ***Cantilènes*** and had already begun to sprout in the first edition. As we have seen, this first edition although not typical of the Symbolist doctrine was accepted as its poetic embodiment. Its obvious departure in some respects from the options of the Symbolists was dismissed as simple ramifications or modifications, merely manifestations of the fundamental *droits* [''rights,'' ''license''] of the young poets—individuality of expression. Now, however, with the foundation of the *Ecole romane* there is no doubt that Moréas has quit Symbolism. (p. 92)

Thus, Symbolism, of which Moréas was the godfather, is summarily relegated to a *position démodée* [''outmoded position'']. Now it is only a movement that had a good intention and aim but has served its purpose and therefore, like Romanticism, must be shed and left behind in quest of 'more stately mansions'. There is in the works comprising the *Ecole romane* some shift in the idea or theme of the poetry. This shift in content, however, is not as consciously conceived or as much emphasized as is Moréas' concern with language, the prime matter of poetry. Moréas is plainly abashed and dismayed at the negative influence upon the French language of foreign literatures and their trends toward excessive mystery, wilfull obscurity, and vagueness of expression. Now Symbolism, successor to Decadentism, was the chief and most recent offender in this verbal license that many considered so deleterious to the language. The more Moréas became oriented toward the classicism of the literary heritage of his native land, the more it became necessary for him to repudiate the abuses of the movement of which he could say, ''que j'ai un peu inventé'' [''that I invented very little of'']. Thus in the manifesto of the new movement he declares forthrightly and sincerely: ''. . . je me sépare du symbolisme que j'ai un peu inventé. Le symbolisme, qui n'a eu que l'intérêt d'un phénomène de tradition, est mort'' [''I separate myself from the symbolism that I invented very little of. Symbolism, which has had interest only as a phenomenon of tradition, is dead'']. The *Frechheit* [''brashness''] of the man is almost refreshing. So confident is he in his role of oracle for the muse that he states as simply as though it were a *fait accompli* that Symbolism is dead because he has pronounced it so. However, what Moréas does in this case as in all of his theorizing in the genre, one must be convinced, is not done with the goal of consciously aspiring to tyranny. He sincerely believed that, on the basis of the knowledge derived from his devoted, life-long study of the genre and its expression in the language, he knew what was best for the development of poetry in French. . . . Just as the Pléiade advised constant and assiduous study and imitation of the ancients, so Moréas advised diligent study and adaptation of the best works of the Renaissance and of 17th century and ancient classicism. DuBellay sought to make his language more rich, nuanced and expressive for the writing of a better poetry; similarly, Moréas, a nineteenth-century DuBellay, sought to extract from the French idiom and French thought the proper aesthetic assigned to them by history. (pp. 93-6)

In his insistence upon rejuvenation of the language and the renewing of the gallic tradition, Moréas was seeking more than a return to clarity of expression which itself would make for greater intelligibility. He was concerned with these, but less as distinct, individual goals than with their contribution to a certain dignity of tone characteristic of all great poetry, a certain linguistic savor which, though elusive of definition, must be a component part of poetic language. He was interested not so much in virtuosity of versification *à la* Marot and the Rhetoriqueurs as he was in a purity of verbal expression. Moréas was seeking to form a language peculiarly proper to the domain of poetry (in the French language), a pure language, distilled from all of French poetry, from its earliest avatars to his own day. (pp. 96-7)

The additions to the ***Pèlerin*** are not vastly different in mood or theme of poetic expression. They are, however, different. The most noticeable difference is in the modification of the versification. Many of the poems are written in regular verse, characterized by a more stable caesura, fewer incidences of *enjambement,* and only sporadic incidence of *vers libres,* ***Enone au clair visage*** containing none at all. Moreover, there is a greater frequency of Alexandrine couplets with an over-all simplification of scansion. With the appearance of each work there is a noticeable moulting of the *écorce* of Symbolism which the poet had donned on his initiation to Parisian poetic palavers and a perceptible progress toward classicism. . . .

Enone au clair visage, the first work admittedly and consciously done in the style of the *Ecole romane* after the announced break with Symbolism was the poem which André Thérive has called an ''élégie amoureuse''. When one recalls that Voltaire has used this same term to qualify all of French tragedy, one is given an insight into the essence of Moréas' poem. (p. 99)

In the poem ***Enone*** are reflected some of the themes that will make up the essence or the quintessence of the ***Stances.*** There is the expression of some of the same themes voiced not only by the Existentialists, but by practically all the poets since Villon, for example, the deceptions and frustrations of life, the sense of failure and of the inexorable flight of time. There are, too, the pains of unrequited passions, a finely nuanced appeal to nature, and the lineaments of the sublime philosophical resignation to the blows of fate that appear so beautifully and insistently in the ***Stances.*** Even though the name ***Enone*** appears in classical mythology, and though critics have made much of her idealization in Moréas' poem, nevertheless, it does depict a real-life personal experience. It is difficult to ignore such lines so pregnant with a Racinien intensity of passion, as:

> Eros, fils de Venus, me possède à jamais.
>
> [''Eros, son of Venus, possess me always.'']

or,

> Je ne me flatte plus, je brûle pour Enone.
>
> [''I flatter myself no longer, I burn for Enone.'']

It is quite possible that the poem may be the disguised expression of a personal experience of its writer, furnishing the point of departure for the similar treatment, though even more idealistically, of yet another woman of Greek legend in his poem ***Eriphyle.*** It does mark a more definite turn toward classicism of structure and content, Symbolism appearing rather rarely and then in a diluted or generalized form.

The ***Sylves*** which, with ***Enone*** appeared in 1893, consist of twenty-two brief poems on a diversity of subjects, and contain material written between 1866 and 1896. The title is derived from the Latin *silva* meaning forest and was used in Latin literature to designate metaphorically a volume of poems. Some of Moréas *sylves* form a polemic against those poets whose influence he considers inimical to the proper development of French poetry. These he variously designates as those ''qui se pensent savants'' [''who think themselves knowing''] (**''Contre quelques-uns''**), as ''le rustre, l'immonde ignorant'' [''filthy, ignorant boors''] (**''A Raymond de La Tailhède''**) or again as ''le rustre au barbare parler'' [''ill-spoken boors''] (**''Les Armes des Dieux''**). Accordingly, and in consonance with the aims of the *Ecole Romane,* he exhorts the espousal of a poetry conscious of its national heritage or a ''poésie de race'', rallying his colleagues with poems or lines addressed to them (e.g., **''A Raymond de La Tailhède''** and **''A Charles Maurras''**). The ''lys français'' [''French lily''] should now take its place in line behind the ''laurier latin'' [''Latin laurel''] and the ''olivier de la Grèce'' [''Greek olive-tree''] (**''Emblème''**). (pp. 102-03)

There are still imitations of the manner of the Pléiade and the classical allusion *à la* Chénier, and there is at least one poem in which Moréas explicitly sings the praise of the poets of Provence (**''A Charles Maurras''**). Nor is the language freed of archaisms and too frequent repetition of such words as *sagette, pertuiser, gaber*. However, in spite of these evidences of continued excessive interest in language there are portions of poems and a few entire pieces where the poet expresses his evolving philosophy so beautifully and poignantly that these exterior trappings are almost overlooked. In the first place the poet is consistent in his decision, following the ''Enone'' experience, to find a melancholy joy or reflection of his soul state in Autumn. In the very first ***Sylve,*** **''L'Equitable Balance''** which immediately follows the ***Enone,*** Moréas vows:

> Mais, pareil au Troyen, à présent je moissonne
> Les prophétiques dons du feuillage écarté,
> Et mon esprit prendra la charmante beauté
> D'un éclatant soleil amorti par l'automne.
>
> [''But, like the Trojan, I now gather / the prophetic gifts of the scattered leaves, / And my spirit will seize the charming beauty / of a brilliant sun deadened by autumn.'']

Then mid-way the ***Sylves*** in the poem **''Aemilius, L'Arbre laisse'',** the poet expresses his recently attained philosophical acceptance of time and age, of the frustrating frailties inherent in the human condition:

> Hélas! déjà l'Eté décline sur ma tête,
> Et cette Automne qui s'apprête
> Viendra bientôt sur moi, comme sur la forêt.
> Ainsi, de mes jeunes ans, ami, je n'ai regret;
>
> [''Alas! already the summer is declining above me, / And this Autumn that readies itself / Will be upon me, as upon the forest. / So, of my young years, friend, I have no regret;'']

Again toward the end of the ***Sylves*** appears the same theme, insistent, with the tone of victory gained, of that classical control of the emotions that is expressed with so many subtle variations in the ***Stances.*** (pp. 103-04)

The only remnant from the Symbolist period is the musicality and fluidity of the verse, but written in the traditional Alexandrine. There is the simplicity of utterance, the personal feeling and the absence of prosodic pyrotechnics that all point toward the ***Stances,*** a succession of sweet lyrics composed . . . on commonplace themes. (p. 105)

The work called ***Sylves nouvelles*** contains but six brief poems; however, these six alone are worth as much or more than the whole of ***Les Cantilènes*** or ***Le Pèlerin passionné*** in its first edition. The poet has not yet attained the classical nudity and emotional concentration of his masterpiece, but these ***Sylves nouvelles*** most assuredly inform us that he is not far from the perfection of the ***Stances.*** They are not much different from the best of the earlier ***Sylves,*** such as **''Aemilius, L'Arbre laisse''**; **''Ore que dessus ma tête''**; and **''Alcinoüs et Rhodope''**. However, they show a progressive emotional and philosophical development that is more in the tone of ***Eriphyle*** than of ***Enone.*** There is more distinctly a tone of acceptance and resignation. One senses in these poems, that the crises precipitating his decision and crystallizing his philosophy of Stoicism have been met in their most intense forms. They will arise again and again, indeed will not die out completely except with the death of the poet, but while they ever threaten, they are defeated, and will be defeated continually. Now there is not the thought that the poet, subsequent to the disillusions of life and the deceptive instability of the material, *will* seek an affinity with the Autumn season and the more melancholic aspects of nature. Rather the tone is one of fact, the identification being expressed as if the decision has been implemented. (pp. 112-13)

Some critics, profoundly impressed by the mastery of the ***Stances,*** tend to consider the ''before the ***Stances***'' production unreadable. This is either because they have not taken the time to read thoroughly the ***Syrtes, Cantilènes,*** *et cetera,* or because, dazzled by the brilliance of the ***Stances,*** they put down the ***Pèlerin, Sylves, Enone,*** or ***Eriphyle*** too soon. (pp. 121-22)

[However, in] spite of the attention brought to Moréas with and following the ''banquet ***Pèlerin passionné***'', and notwithstanding acceptance of the ***Pèlerin*** as a model of the Symbolist doctrine and a work of artistry and merit, notwithstanding the beauty of some of the productions of the Ecole Romane and the salutary effect of its lessons, none of these, or all of them together, did not, do not, suffice to categorize their composer as other than a virtuoso showing sparks of genius that signify the potential of a good or near great poet. Though they bear reading and are rewarding to a good student of the literature, they are for the most part forgotten and scarcely read even by students of the literature, except those specializing in the period of their appearance. It remained for the ***Stances*** and ***Iphigénie*** to forge for Jean Moréas a clean-cut cleft in the rock of poetic masterpieces if not in the granite of immortality. Perceptively enough, these are the only two works that Moréas valued once he reached moral and artistic maturity. Of these two it seems that he was more intensely interested in the ***Stances*** and gave to their composition more sustained and painstaking care. (p. 131)

As one reads Moréas' ***Stances*** the mood that most persistently manifests itself is one of an ennui that is almost metaphysical in nature. In some of the poems it is manifested in an evident disillusion and bitterness, in others by an expression of nostalgic regret and in still others by a melancholic sadness, vaguely defined, yet immanent and pervasive. This ennui or sustained mood of melancholy that possessed Jean Moréas seems to have been a potential facet of his personality since his youth and early maturity. As he grew older and experienced more of the ills of living, it became increasingly intense and refined until at the time of the writing of the ***Stances*** it had developed into a credo and formed an integral part of the poet's philosophy. (p. 134)

Of course Moréas is not the first person to write poetry or prose that is moving and lyrical by virtue of its expression of soul solitude and ennui. There were the Romantics: one thinks of Chateaubriand, Lamartine, Musset, and especially of de Vigny. And of course there was the precursor of the Symbolists and of modern French poetic expression, Baudelaire. . . . However, Moréas' expression of ennui is different from that of the Romantics as well as from that of the author of *Les Fleurs*. Though the sentiment as it appears in all three—Romantics, Baudelaire and Moréas—is of the essence of Romanticism, to wit: a melancholic *état d'âme* [''state of soul''], an unusually developed sense of individualism in society, fed from the *moi* [''self''], and an inclination for confession of the soul *malaise*, nevertheless, Moréas' sentiment is different, and refreshingly so, in that it lacks the maudlin character, the plebeian, unbraked confession and expression of despair of the Romantics, and the morbidity and splenetic vitriol of Baudelaire. In other words, Moréas' ***Stances*** do contain Romantic elements, as well as Symbolist ones, but these are fused into a work that is thoroughly classical.

In vain one searches the prose works of Moréas to find some mention of specific events or experiences in his life which might be considered the *causa praecipitans* of the ennui of his middle age and older life. It is almost equally vain to search the poetry, but at least here we are afforded glimpses, intimations, and even statements—generally expressed—of the categories of irritations and losses, or disappointments that furnished the fuel for the fire of his innate sensitivity of spirit. . . . Although we can point out resemblances to, if not imitations of the style of these three masters of Symbolism, Baudelaire, Mallarmé, and Verlaine, nevertheless by far the greater number of expressions of ennui are individual and in a sense personal, while still remaining impersonal. Thus Moréas refers not infrequently to a ''fire'' which burns within his psyche. . . . This feeling of ennui and spiritual enervation is frequently expressed by other symbols from nature, particularly in the melancholic aspect of Autumn and the falling of dead leaves. . . . (pp. 135-37)

In some of the poems Moréas chooses to employ . . . the symbol of the bleeding wound to express his chagrin. . . . These two symbols—of fire and of a bleeding wound—are aptly chosen to represent the consumptive and enervating force of Moréas' chagrin. . . . [A close examination of] the ***Stances*** has revealed to this writer certain shocks or blows of fate that were sustained by Moréas during his later life and which, when combined with his natural *sensibilité*, were responsible for the terse poetic gems that constitute the ***Stances***. These experiences are the commonplace ones with which we all become acquainted actively or vicariously, sooner or later. (pp. 137-39)

Moréas' chagrin at the loss of friends [precipitated by his defection from Symbolism] is expressed in the very first poem of Book One, recurs at least once in Books Three through Six and is implicit in at least one poem (number fourteen) of Book Two and one (number six) of Book Seven. . . . Closely allied to this keen sense of pain from the loss of friendship is a pang even more guardedly expressed but which undoubtedly plays an integral and important role in the crystallization of the poet's disillusioning experiences into a credo. I refer to the theme matter *par excellence* of lyric poetry, namely, disappointment in love. The whole volume is infused—but very subtly—with the ''eternal distress'', the emotion that prompted Adam to incur the divine wrath rather than risk separation from Eve. (pp.139-41)

The third poem of the third book is notable for its calmness of tone, for its faculty of saying so much by intimation, its piquing of imagination by means of a poetic ambiguity that results from the poet's classical restraint. The language is simple, the theme commonplace, and yet the poet has created a drama in little that is at once personal and universal. The ultimate tone, that is the one most obviously communicated by the words is one of resignation and acceptance, of victory gained over the painful pangs of passion. Nevertheless, there is implicit in the poem the fury of former passions and the drama of the struggle to overcome, to platonize them. . . . (pp. 143-44)

[Another] element of chagrin . . . [is Moréas'] keen sense of the brevity of life and of the transience and vanity of all things earthly. It is upon this theme that some of the most beautiful stanzas are woven as the poet philosophically acquiesces to the intrinsic flux of all creation, both natural and human. [Stance seventeen] from the first book is particularly arresting for the onomatopoetic semblance of the hurried coming and going, the vehicular arrivals and departures of humanity. There is something staccato about the style, the interspersion of the quickly uttered ''adieu!'', the brevity of the sentences contained in the first and third lines, resulting in a jerkily moving rhythm, all of which contribute as effectively as the words to the communication of a sense of flux and change, birth and death. . . . [In stance four of the fourth book] there is a contrast of style; here the tone is one of the serene contemplation of an architectural symbol of ruin and of the mutilation of the poet's personal psyche. It reminds one of Shelley's ''Ozymandias'', and yet is more lyrical, more musical, and more truly poetic because it is less prosaic and less didactic than Shelley's piece. . . . This poem, a particularly successful one, owes much of its beauty to the felicitous compounding of the symbol with the mood or soul-state symbolized. The poet, as he gazes wistfully upon the remains of a once glorious monument sees therein a fitting symbol of all his past glory, that like the mortar of the temple, has crumbled bit by bit, leaving an abandoned genius who is all too conscious of the tragic sublimity of his plight. But the poet realizes that such a collapse or, rather erosion, is the inevitable end of all that is so prized by the soul, the mind, and the ego. By generalization the ruined temple represents the destiny of man himself, created or evolved from dust and doomed to return to dust. (pp. 146-48)

One of the most interesting facets of Moréas' personality, as revealed in his poetry is his ''classical smile''. This classical smile is a bit difficult to elucidate, for it is compounded of several elements, among which are heroic and steadfast courage, patience, suffering, grief, love of life, respect for (but not fear of) death, independence, pride, and again courage! Carlo Levi, author of the novel *Christ Stopped at Eboli* has come close to, but has not comprehensively attained the denotation and the connotations of the term classical smile as we use it here. He has written for a nationally known daily newspaper:

> True courage smiles. It cannot express itself otherwise. Courage is the virtue, the necessary element of existence, the birth of everything.

> Because it is in itself happy—the only happiness—and a smile is the only form it can take on the human face.
>
> The archaic smile of the ancient gods and heroes identified them. In less mythological times, such as ours, the same smile returns on the humble features of unknown men and women, when they find in themselves the basic form of courage: the courage of living.

The smile of Moréas' ***Stances*** is not exactly the Paliachian smile of Laforgue, about whom these words have been written: ". . . c'est par une singulière pudeur qu'il joue au rire pour ne pas laisser voir qu'il a trop envie d'éclater en sanglots" ["it is due to a curious modesty that he plays at laughing, so that it will not be seen that he too much desires to burst into sobs"]. Neither is it the smile so pregnant with wit of Voltaire, nor the *sourire jaune* ["sickly smile"] of Corbière, but is more subdued, and melancholic. It is, however, similar to the mysterious, undying smile revealed in the poetry of Henri de Régnier, whose evolution bears some similarity to that of Moréas. . . . The poet, in the ***Pèlerin passionné,*** had already promised that by his artistic "rite" from new flowers the bees of Greece "butineront un miel français" ["will gather a French honey"]. With his ***Stances*** Moréas succeeded in creating a honey whose flavor is not only French, but Greek as well. It is a flavor recognized by those of all cultures who are given to pondering "the practice of existence". . . . Moréas always succeeded in finding even in the bitterest dregs of experience, a trace of sweetness, the flavor of honey. It is this that contributes largely to the poignant impression of his poetry, that saves it from sinking into a bog of utter pessimism *à la* Musset and other Romantics. (pp. 157-59)

Even though in the ***Stances*** Moréas manifests somewhat of a predilection for death and the tomb, the "ennui" is indeed different from the "spleen" of Baudelaire. The difference is not so much in quality, for in truth Baudelaire's "spleen" was compounded of too keen and obsessive a recognition of the frailty of the human condition, but the difference is in intensity and degree. . . . Moréas' philosophy does not look to death alone for relief or surcease of the sentiment of the absurdity of life, but makes room for hope and takes comfort . . . from the recall of the past and of brighter days. . . . However, Moréas' philosophy does capture something of the spirit of one of Baudelaire's less splenetic compositions, "Elévation" in which the spirit of the author fain would take a "libre essor, plane sur la vie, et comprend sans effort / Le langage des fleurs et des choses muettes!" ["free flight, soars above life and effortlessly comprehends / The language of flowers and of mute things!"] The author of the ***Stances*** turns to the trees—solitary, silent denizens of the plain—and learns the lesson of classical reason, that is, a sad but sane acceptance of the *données* of the cosmos. . . . Thus Moréas' philosophy, as manifested particularly in his volume ***les Stances,*** is one of stoic acceptance of the *anima mundi,* implemented or enhanced by a Hellenic subordination of the personal drives and passions. (pp. 163-66)

Upon reading the ***Stances*** one can appreciate that it is tragic in a sense that a purely Romantic work could never be, for not only does the writer exercise and maintain strict control over the form but over the *fond* ["heart," "essence"] as well. In his volume Moréas does manifest ennui and suffering, a suffering caused as much by the sacrifice of a part of himself (his baser, weaker, more fleshly self) as by the blows of fate or necessity. Moréas' work, his later life and his calm confrontation with death show "the beauty of the human character fighting against fate and circumstance". Again, in the ***Stances*** as in his life, if he did not hide the communication of his pain and humiliation, he certainly hid from his friends and from his readers, their ugliness. (pp. 171-72)

Above all, the ***Stances*** are characterized by what we shall call *measure* which includes the connotations of restraint of the passions, restricted scope, conservatism, dominance of reason, and "good sense." . . . With this restraint Moréas has combined a "classical" Symbolism, that is the suggestive quality of expression which piques the imagination and sometimes makes for an artistic ambivalence of interpretation but which does not seek or end in obscurity. (pp. 177-78)

It is interesting to note that during Moréas' singular evolution from the ***Syrtes*** to the ***Stances*** the underlying themes of the poetry did not change radically. Excluding the popular ditties, recreations of the *chansons* of the Middle Ages interspersed through the ***Cantilènes,*** and the sometimes polemical *art poétique* pieces occurring in the ***Pèlerin passionné,*** all Moréas' poetry consists in variations upon basic themes such as a mystical love, a longing nostalgia for beauty and self-integration, lassitude of life, and a vague ennui. The motivating themes have not changed much but the poet's use and treatment of the themes have and herein lies the explanation of the difference between the mediocrity of the ***Syrtes, Cantilènes*** or ***Pèlerin passionné*** and the consummate artistry, the classic perfection of the ***Stances.*** Though there are occasional *trouvailles* in these earlier works they are largely characterized by artificial inspiration from the Middle Ages, or Nordic mythology, by deliberate erudition and research of rare words, preciosity of expression, affected archaism, capricious syntax, and general liberty of versification. (p. 183)

[One] factor that certainly must be considered in any attempt to account for the superiority of the ***Stances*** over Moréas' earlier work and for its poetic power is that having learned the rules of technique and having learned and absorbed the lessons of study and imitation of the classic masters, ancient and modern, he left off conscious imitation and drew with classical restraint from the lyric potential of his own soul's tragedy. (pp. 202-03)

Thus in their attempt to account for the perfection and power of Moréas' volume, Gillouin, Embiricos, Lalou, and many others have placed emphasis upon the congruity between the life and the lyrics of the poet, the urgency and appeal deriving from the feeling that the poet has lived what is expressed in his poetry. Certainly this does result in a lyrical "meatiness" if we may coin so unpoetic a term, and a sense of sincerity that validates and ennobles the thought. We submit, however, that Moréas could not have achieved so felicitous a rendition of this fusion without the years of technical training and preparation embodied in his evolution with all its launching of manifestoes, its planting the banners of new schools of poetry, and the assumption and abandonment of new aesthetic positions. Without the discipline that such activity constituted; without his careful knowledge and frequent criticism of Romanticism, and his personal experience in Decadentism-Symbolism; without the lessons of the Ecole Romane and its emphasis upon language enrichment; and finally, had he not experienced the disappointments incurred because of his evolution, Moréas' griefs and ennui would not have reached the jewel-like form of "pleurs crystallisés" ["crystallized tears"]. . . . (pp. 203-04)

John Davis Butler, in his Jean Moréas: A Critique of His Poetry and Philosophy, *Mouton, 1967, 236 p.*

ADDITIONAL BIBLIOGRAPHY

Balakian, Anna. "Mallarmé and the Symbolist *Cénacle*." In her *The Symbolist Movement: A Critical Appraisal*, pp. 72-100. New York: Random House, 1967.*

States that Moréas "sought renovations in a return to medieval verse forms and in the use of irregular verse length. . . . Strangely enough, he hardly practiced what he preached, so that there is nothing particularly baroque in his classically inspired neoparnassian poems."

Cornell, Kenneth. *The Symbolist Movement*. New Haven: Yale University Press, 217 p.*

Detailed history of the Symbolist movement, with numerous references to Moréas throughout.

Kronik, John W. "The Introduction of Symbolism into Spain: A Call to Arms." In *Waiting for Pegasus: Studies of the Presence of Symbolism and Decadence in Hispanic Letters*, edited by Roland Grass and William R. Risley, pp. 31-8. Macomb: Western Illinois University, 1979.

Discusses Leopoldo García-Ramón's critical essay written in reaction to Moréas's "Manifeste littéraire de l'École Symboliste."

Lehmann, A. G. *The Symbolist Aesthetic in France: 1885-1895*, pp. 11ff. Oxford: Basil Blackwell, 1950.

Study of Symbolist theory and philosophy which contains several references to Moréas.

LeSage, Laurent. "Jean Moréas: 1856-1910." In his *The Rhumb Line of Symbolism*, pp. 161-64. University Park: Pennsylvania State University Press, 1978.

Biographical and critical sketch of Moréas. LeSage concludes: "As a poet, Jean Moréas has scarcely survived today. His place in literary history is assured chiefly as a theorist and as a personality that conjures up a colorful prewar Paris. Yet the homage paid his verse during his lifetime was not entirely undeserved. . . ."

Lewisohn, Ludwig. Introduction to his *The Poets of Modern France*, edited and translated by Ludwig Lewisohn, pp. 1-72. New York: B. W. Huebsch, 1918.

General summary of Moréas's career. Lewisohn believes that: "It was the Hellenic soul in him, one must suppose, that made his last work [*Les stances*] so memorable an example of the classical spirit in modern poetry."

Philip, Stephan. *Paul Verlaine and the Decadence: 1882-90*. pp. 7ff. Manchester: Manchester University Press, 1974.

Study of one of Moréas's major influences which contains several references to Moréas and his work.

Robertson, William John. "Jean Moréas." In his *A Century of French Verse: Brief Biographical and Critical Notices of Thirty-Three French Poets of the Nineteenth Century with Experimental Translations from Their Poems*, pp. 335-37. London: A. D. Innes & Co., 1895.

Description of Moréas's poetic style. Evaluating Moréas as a poet, Robertson states: "Jean Moréas is a scrupulous and accomplished artist. He differs from Jules Laforgue inasmuch as he always has something to say and does not depend for his effects on the violence of incongruous symbols and startling neologisms. Much of his verse is novel, romantic and picturesque. Many of his forms are singularly felicitious."

George Jean Nathan
1882-1958

(Also wrote under pseudonyms of Owen Hatteras and William Drayham) American critic, essayist, journalist, autobiographer, dramatist, and novelist.

Pictorial Parade, Inc.

Considered a pioneer in the iconoclastic movement in early twentieth-century American dramatic criticism, Nathan is widely acknowledged to have been the most influential critical voice in the transformation of the American stage during the early twentieth century. Entering the sphere of dramatic criticism during the years just before World War I, a period when it had largely degenerated into obsequious or, at best, innocuous theatrical reviews of still more innocuous dramas, Nathan sought to elevate public taste and critical criteria. Through his sprightly erudition and sophisticated, often cynical, derision of contemporary producers and playwrights, his introduction of modern European works into the mainstream of American theater, and his promotion of important dramatists unknown to the general public, Nathan irrevocably altered both the quality of the American stage and the body of critical standards that served it.

Nathan was born in Fort Wayne, Indiana, to an American mother and a wealthy French-born father who owned vineyards in France and a coffee plantation in Brazil, and whose widely traveled cosmopolitanism was later emulated by his son. When Nathan was six, he and his family moved to Cleveland, where he attended school and began to develop an omnivorous interest in reading, particularly dramas and dramatic criticism. During his youth, Nathan spent alternate summers in Europe, studying languages and dramatic literature in Paris, Rome, and Heidelberg, and acquiring an international perspective on life and art. Entering Cornell University, Nathan took part in numerous campus literary and dramatic organizations, becoming editor of the Cornell daily newspaper as well as a champion fencer. After receiving a degree in literature, drama, history, language, and psychology in 1904, Nathan secured a position as cub reporter for the *New York Herald*. Although never caught or reprimanded for the liberties he took, he frequently covered special assignments with more fancy than fact. Nathan was later promoted to backup drama critic, covering some of the less important productions until, suffocated by what he considered both an intellectually servile atmosphere and cowardly and dishonest editorial policies, he left the paper. For the next several years Nathan, writing principally on drama, contributed articles to various magazines, including *Munsey's* and *Harper's Weekly*.

In 1908 Nathan's work was brought to the attention of Norman Boyer, managing editor of the *Smart Set,* who hired Nathan as a drama critic. It was in the New York office of this magazine that Nathan met H. L. Mencken, a literary critic whose ambitions had also been constrained by a career in newspaper work, and who shared Nathan's deep disgust at the state of contemporary American life and art. Both writers believed that reckless iconoclasm was necessary to bring about cultural change, and their immediate friendship and shared vision led to a renowned partnership that lasted for nearly twenty years. At the *Smart Set,* each developed his characteristically vivid, biting critical style and found a podium from which to assail the low standards of American literature and theater. Acquiring the magazine's joint editorship in 1914, Nathan and Mencken attracted new, sophisticated contributors to its pages and transformed the *Smart Set* from a moderately literary magazine of spicy romance into a respectable forum of realistic fiction and drama. The *Smart Set* introduced America to the works of Eugene O'Neill and F. Scott Fitzgerald, and featured writings of such comparatively unknown authors as James Joyce, James Branch Cabell, Aldous Huxley, Ben Hecht, and Thomas Beer. Nathan was responsible for gaining O'Neill wide exposure, persuading producer John D. Williams to stage his first long play, *Beyond the Horizon* (1920), and printing several short plays in the periodical. In his monthly column in the *Smart Set,* Nathan routinely attacked with robust humor many of the reigning American dramatists and producers—notably David Belasco, as well as other purveyors of sentimentality, predictability, and shallow moral uplift—and demanded higher critical standards. As Isaac Goldberg has noted, the *Smart Set* "projected new attitudes, it revealed new gifts, it campaigned for a free, virile, open-air joy in the arts. It had an honest aphrodisiac filip that often verged upon vulgarity, but it was usually the coarseness of a finer nature—Rabelais rather than the barber-shop. . . . It freed the muses from their chaperones." When Mencken and Nathan were themselves denounced in print for their irreverence and unsolicited opinions, these undaunted *enfants terribles* countered with such stunts as publicly announcing their candidacy for president and vice-president of the United States, and publishing within the pages of the magazine their platform of one hundred and twenty-two planks, including the celebrated promise that if elected they would shave off the whiskers of New York Governor Charles Evans Hughes. Two enormous spittoons adorned the offices of the *Smart Set,* symbolizing the deliberate heresies of the two critics; Nathan and Mencken earnestly assured the rest of the staff that these would be duly draped with chintz when poets entered the premises.

During the years before American military involvement in World War I, a period of growing anti-German sentiment in the United States, Mencken—a man fiercely proud of his ethnic heritage and a writer whose essays were sprinkled with German expressions—was vilified in the national press as a "Hun" sympathizer. Because of this, the *Smart Set* suffered through declining sales and contributions, and Nathan and Mencken were forced to write much of the magazine's copy under any of several dozen pseudonyms. Although the *Smart Set* eventually regained its popularity, by the early 1920s Nathan and Mencken had tired of the constraints set by the magazine's somewhat tawdry physical appearance and history, and each desired a freer hand at all stages of the editorial and production process. With the financial backing of publisher Alfred A. Knopf, Nathan and Mencken left the *Smart Set* and founded the *American Mercury* in 1924. Embraced by the nation's college students and sophisticated "flaming youth," the new magazine immediately became one of the most widely read and influential periodicals of the era. Its stance was mockingly skeptical of established American values, and it included some of the best writing of the 1920s, not the least of which was Nathan's monthly column on "The Theatre," Mencken's column "The Library," and the coeditors' jointly written feature "Clinical Notes." But the partnership of the two coeditors ended soon after the *Mercury* was launched, as Mencken sought to create in the *Mercury* a journal of social and political opinion, while Nathan wanted the periodical to be primarily a review of the arts. Unable to resolve their differences, Nathan resigned his position and Mencken became sole editor of the magazine, although Nathan continued as a contributing editor until 1930. The two remained relatively amicable after the separation and until Mencken's death in 1956.

In 1932 Nathan joined Theodore Dreiser, Ernest Boyd, O'Neill, and Cabell in forming the *American Spectator,* a magazine which, like the *Smart Set* and the *Mercury,* was devoted to social commentary, literature, and the arts, and was characterized by a satirical view of American life and culture, (the *American Spectator*'s impressive editorial board, headed by Nathan, was augmented in 1933 by the addition of Sherwood Anderson.) But personal and professional differences between the editors led to their dissatisfaction with the magazine; in a letter to Nathan, Dreiser, echoing Mencken's complaint of the early days of the *American Mercury,* accused Nathan of being an editor less interested in American life and letters than in "the frothy intellectual and social interests of the stage, the Four Hundred, the Bohemian and mentally dilettante worlds." Despite tensions on the editorial staff and the difficulties of publishing a newly formed periodical during the Great Depression, the *American Spectator* sold well and was highly respected, but folded during the mid-1930s after the editors announced that they had "tired of the job." For the rest of his career, Nathan reviewed drama for various magazines, including *Newsweek* and the *Saturday Review of Literature*. As he had before endorsed such writers as O'Neill, he now championed Irish dramatist Sean O'Casey and the American author William Saroyan. O'Casey became a personal friend of Nathan, and one of few individuals permitted to glimpse Nathan's less scathing side, which was generally well camouflaged by his caustic wit. Throughout the rest of his life, Nathan lived—as he had lived throughout most of his career—in Manhattan's Royalton Hotel, in a two-room suite cluttered with a staggering collection of books. During the last year of his life Nathan, a lifelong skeptic, converted to Roman Catholicism, thereby adding an ironic coda to an assessment written by the militantly atheistic Mencken during the friendliest of the former coeditors' "heathen days": "With his last gasp he will make a phrase to flabbergast a dolt."

In 1926 Nathan told Goldberg: "To me, a nation is its metropolis. To that extent, as an American I am a New Yorker of New Yorkers. I do not like the country; I am a cockney. The country, as I see it, is for yokels and cows. In the city, life reaches its fullest flower." A self-proclaimed boulevardier and hedonist, Nathan was frequently held to be a poseur, whose unconventionality and innovativeness were as carefully donned as his dandy's garb. Considering himself to be no reformer or shepherd to the American public, Nathan prided himself thoroughly on his selfishness, both professionally and privately. Commentators of ensuing decades have maintained that contemporaries who considered Nathan a poseur failed to realize that he was completely a man of the theater, for whom the entire panorama of life represented so many fascinating stage settings. All art, Nathan insisted in such critical collections as *Passing Judgments* and *Testament of a Critic,* is hedonistic, and good drama as flexible as the imagination of its audience. For this reason while drama may satisfy certain broad requirements, it need not strictly adhere to conventional dramatic theory and technique. He did not denounce the unimaginative productions he witnessed by pedantically listing their deficiencies; rather, one of his favorite stratagems in scoffing at devotees of the dramatic rulebook was to cite, for each generally accepted axiom, a play that had successfully ignored it. Occasionally, Nathan answered what he considered low melodrama by critically sketching out one of his own, so ludicrously wrought that any dignity remaining in the targeted play disintegrated. Treatment, not the choice of subject matter, was crucial to Nathan, who not only minimized the importance of presenting an artistic message but decried sincerity in art altogether. The true artist, Nathan averred, is seldom, if ever, sincere; if the artist should confine himself to what he believes, his works are mere confessions of his limitations. Even more lamentable to Nathan was the adoption of sincerity as a critical criterion: "Whenever a critic says something is 'heartwarming,' he means he is bewildered by what he saw or read or is ashamed for having liked something that his better sense tells him he should not have liked. In other words, he is confessing mediocrity." The suppression of intellectual freedom and perpetuation of mediocrity were abhorrent to Nathan, who collaborated with Mencken in writing *Heliogabalus,* a bedroom farce which served as a thinly disguised attack on the literary censorship exercised by the narrow-minded rabble. Expecting denunciation by morally offended critics, the authors prepared in advance a rebuttal bristling with indignation, but because of limited exposure no opposition to *Heliogabalus* arose, though one admirer, Dreiser, considered the play "a scream." Like many of the dramatic critics of his day, Nathan had entered the field of criticism during a time when the reviewer's first consideration was that of insuring his managing editor's continued receipt of advertising revenue from Broadway producers, and this was accomplished by routinely submitting favorable appraisals of plays. Mediocrity, to Nathan, had infected the very core of dramatic criticism, which he saw as having inviolably enthroned the most nonsensical precepts, and as having barred its own disciples from commenting as colleagues upon one another's efforts. More than the exchange of brickbats or bouquets, however, criticism was an art to Nathan, and its province was truth, not the box office. Nathan gained notoriety for abruptly stalking out of performances he disliked, and he contended that any critic unable to evaluate a production after viewing the first twenty minutes was a rank incompetent.

Few appraisals of Nathan's work have been ambivalent. More often than not Nathan's criticism elicits either high praise or bitter contempt. Most agree that in his ongoing war against meretriciousness and banality both onstage and in the critical arena, Nathan's ready artillery was his erudition. But his puns, epigrams, inversions, and other verbal stratagems were not welcomed by all readers; some commentators have observed that Nathan's purportedly scintillating style became as artificial as the triviality it condemned, while others have simply protested that Nathan's books were written, not in English, but in dialect. Burton Rascoe related in a letter to Cabell that, in discussing Cabell's work with him, Nathan had mentioned what he considered Cabell's difficult, involved style. Rascoe went on to wryly indicate that this came "from a man who often writes a sentence covering almost an entire page, with verb so far away from subject that you have to read the sentence through twice or three times to get his meaning. . . . Nathan aims at a very complex and involved style . . . and yet his admiration (expressed) is all for lucidity and simplicity."

Despite the obstacles presented by his idiosyncratic style, which has prevented some people from noting the vast knowledge and extraordinary perception in his critical essays, Nathan is generally acknowledged to have been the most learned and influential drama critic in the United States to date. He, more than any other individual, helped the American public to distinguish between popular theatrical merchandise and the more considered works of such dramatists as O'Casey and O'Neill. In the 1920s and much of the 1930s, the weight of one of Nathan's reviews could close a production immediately after its opening night or insure its extended run. Nathan's influence was such that in 1932 he was threatened with congressional investigation on the grounds that iconoclastic criticism such as his own had destroyed the American theater. Irwin Edman spoke for many critics when he observed: "It is a pity that Mr. Nathan through a long exuberant life as a writer . . . has felt it necessary to wear cap and bells and constantly to jingle the bells. For the jingling has often obscured the common sense, the nice perception, the high standards of esthetic integrity that Mr. Nathan has maintained with respect to theatre and other arts. . . . [However,] below the tomfooleries there is a serious critic here and a well stocked and uncorrupted mind."

(See also *Contemporary Authors,* Vol. 114.)

PRINCIPAL WORKS

Europe after 8:15 [with H. L. Mencken and Willard Huntington Wright] (travel sketches) 1914
Another Book on the Theatre (criticism) 1915
Bottoms Up (criticism) 1917
Mr. George Jean Nathan Presents (criticism) 1917
Pistols for Two [as Owen Hatteras; with H. L. Mencken] (sketches) 1917
The Popular Theatre (criticism) 1918
Comedians All (criticism) 1919
The American Credo [with H. L. Mencken[(aphorisms) 1920
Heliogabalus [with H. L. Mencken] (drama) 1920
The Theatre, the Drama, the Girls (criticism) 1921
The Critic and the Drama (criticism) 1922
The World in Falseface (criticism) 1923
Materia Critica (criticism) 1924
The Autobiography of an Attitude (aphorisms) 1925
The New American Credo (aphorisms) 1927
Art of the Night (criticism) 1928
Monks are Monks (novel) 1929
Testament of a Critic (criticism) 1931
The Intimate Notebooks of George Jean Nathan (memoirs) 1932
Since Ibsen (criticism) 1933
Passing Judgments (criticism) 1935
The Theatre of the Moment (criticism) 1936
The Morning after the First Night (criticism) 1938
Encyclopaedia of the Theatre (criticism) 1940
The Entertainment of a Nation (criticism) 1942
The Theatre Book of the Year. 10 vols. (criticism) 1942-51
The Theatre in the Fifties (criticism) 1953
The Magic Mirror (criticism) 1960

[GORDON CRAIG] (essay date 1918)

[An English actor, set designer, and writer on the theater, Craig is known primarily for his innovations in scenery, lighting, and stage management in London and throughout Europe. In 1903 he founded the influential School for the Art of the Theatre in Florence, Italy, where he also edited the respected review of Western drama The Mask *(1908-29). In the following excerpt, Craig applauds Nathan's colorful style and sound critical judgment in* Another Book on the Theatre.*]*

I think [**"Another Book on the Theatre"**] is the best book on the theatre that America has produced.

First reason is that it is American . . . . very American; it is good-tempered, rollicking, sufficiently paradoxical, well written and alive. It 'gets there' more times than not; it is what we in England call 'all right'; and for my part is a book I can turn to again and again, not one of the least reasons for this being that it has style, and its Americanisms are perfectly delightful.

For instance, writing of some incidents in one of Stanley Houghton's plays, he suddenly exclaims. "what sweetish, highly laquered pish; what old-fashioned facetious immateriality; what elegant popgunnery!. . . is this not pure rouge-stick walla-walla?"

Maeterlinck he calls "arch-arbiter of the after-life rumble-bumble". And of a certain prince who was an exceptional waltzer, he writes; "dancing with a lovely actress in Paris during his gay days, the good prince, so goes the story, marathon'd all the other couples off the wax".

In his essay on **"The Unimportance of being Earnest",** he says; "Anyone who knows the first thing about Shakespeare, for instance, knows that of all men, he was a glutton for mendacity, and rarely meant a philosophy he wrote save, of course, when he wrote of rum and women. Did not the fellow himself, forsooth, once admit as much? "Why", he was asked by Robert Peele, "are you ever so persistently insincere in your labours?" To which he offered the now celebrated rejoinder: "Bob, you give me a pain in the ear. No sincere man who is or hopes to be regarded as an artist descends to so low and so facile a means as sincerity to trick fame and repute and moneys. That is reserved for the mahogany heads, the vacant gourds, who have nothing to sell *but* sincerity. Do you get me, old tosspot?" . . . . I do not remember the exact wording.

Whenever I wish to feel cheerful I remember that phrase, "Bob, you give me a pain in the ear". And as dozens of such phrases are to be found in Mr Nathan's book, and as there are hundreds of people going about the world who want cheering up, here is something that will do it.

The secondary value that the book has, that of being admirable sense, is thrown in as an extra: and very many people will want to know much more about the theatre, having enjoyed themselves in the society of a critic who can be profound without being dull.

[*Gordon Craig*], *in a review of "Another Book on the Theatre," in* The Mask, *Vol. 8, No. 1, 1918, p. 4.*

ALEXANDER WOOLLCOTT (essay date 1919)

[*Woollcott is best known as one of America's most eccentric wits and raconteurs, as well as an influential pioneer of modern drama criticism. During his years as a critic for* The New York Times *and several other New York newspapers, he brought such performers as Paul Robeson, the Marx Brothers, and Fred Astaire to the public's attention. With his gossipy approach to reviewing—a style that focused on personalities, trivia, and general impressions of the plays—Woollcott attained and wielded the power of success or failure over Broadway's offerings. His reviews are characterized by the gushing admiration expressed for performers and performances Woollcott liked and by the cruel blasts he reserved for those he did not. Retiring from drama criticism in 1928, Woollcott turned to reviewing books as a much sought-after magazine columnist and radio personality. His popularity as a book reviewer, both on the air and in the pages of* The New Yorker, *soon rivalled that which he had earlier enjoyed as a theater critic. Woollcott and Nathan were completely different in their styles and professional preferences, and were frequently at sword's-point on their respective likes and dislikes in the American theater. In a famous* Smart Set *article, Nathan pilloried Woollcott as "The Seidlitz Powder in Times Square" for evidencing a style that "is either a gravy bomb, a bursting gladiolus, a pappitating missa cantata, an attack of psychic hydrophobia, or a Roman denunciation, unequivocal, oracular, flat, and final." In the following excerpt from an essay written two years before Nathan's article, Woollcott offers a bitingly sarcastic, though partially favorable, review of* Comedians All, *noting with disapproval Nathan's dislike of one of Woollcott's lifelong idols, actress Minnie Maddern Fiske.*]

If, as it sometimes seems, the vocation of writing pieces about the plays and players of the New York stage is scarcely an adequate occupation for an adult mind, what shall be said of one whose mission in life is evidently to write pieces about those who write pieces about the plays and players of the New York Stage? This is the stern mission of the faithful and tireless George Jean Nathan, whose new and pretty continuously entertaining book called **"Comedians All"** shows that he has lost nothing of that well-selected tone of contemptuous disparagement which has been his stock in trade these many years. . . .

[Nathan] whacks and trounces and jibes the local Hazlittry with great gusto in his own private and personal "Smart Set." Their ignorance, bred by decades of low entertainment, is quite general and familiar. But, as targets, none of them is beneath Nathan. Not even the docile and nervous little fellows who write sweet nothings about plays and players with one eye on the clock and the other on the advertising manager. Not even the late William Winter, whose colossal unfamiliarity with the modern drama, what it had done, and what it was trying to do, ever afforded a fine opening for the witty and inexhaustible Nathan. Winter comes in for a parting shot in **"Comedians All."**

With Winter gone, Nathan finds a tempting mark in the venerable J. Ranken Towse of The New York Evening Post, whose wistful feeling that nothing has ever seemed quite so good as the otherwise forgotten efforts of one Samuel Phelps at Sadler's Wells in Mr. Towse's salad days, lays him wide open to the nimbler and more widely cultured chronicler of "The Smart Set." Then he also engages in several lively brushes with the sages of Morningside Heights—Brander Matthews and Clayton Hamilton. Sage brushes, Mr. Nathan would doubtless call them, for he will have his little joke, even if it's a bad one, which it by no means always is. Dr. Matthews did, in his chatter about stage conventions, inattentively expose a peculiarly tempting and accessible reach of pedagogical trouser to the Nathan slapstick, to borrow a familiar and somewhat overworked Nathanism. These are only the more palpable hits. No one 'scapes whipping.

Many popular misconceptions and dislikes begotten by the Nathan mannerisms (for he is as manneristic as Louis Mann or Madge Kennedy) should not betray his not inconsiderable public from profiting by the soundness of much that he writes. For instance, there is no reason why the puzzling, nay, the unaccountable, note of self-importance which, appearing in his chapter "The Foremost American Producer," stands out even in a book not notable for a lack of complacency, should be allowed to vitiate the worth of a really sensitive and discerning essay on the priceless Arthur Hopkins.

Nor should it be thought that the array of and sometimes facetiously imaginary information on the theatre in other lands with which Nathan is wont to obliterate his neighbors, is just that "Smart Set" jackanapes showing off again, as his irritated victims are likely to believe. It is true that he labors to make his fellow-babblers believe that no one who has not seen all the productions up some side street in Odessa or Osaka is a poor creature, unfit to analyze the art of Eva Tanguay. It is true that no local farce is too paltry to inspire him to some windy dissertations on certain Swedish and Bulgarian prototypes. But this is not prompted by an itch for self-display, as is popularly believed. It is simply the output of a naturally punditical mind, whose true professorial quality is never quite concealed by his sedulous jocosity.

Then it is all wrong to laugh at Nathan's judgements in the matter of actors. His periodic approvals and disapprovals are forever being misread by his followers as facetious and greeted with what must be disconcerting hilarity. This is as cruel an injustice as it would have been to have laughed at the untrained Trilby's first croaking of "Ben Bolt" in the studio in the Rue Notre Dame des Champs. In matters of acting Nathan is incurably tone-deaf. He probably knows more about modern dramatic literature than any one now writing regularly on that subject in England or America, but he knows nothing at all about the player's art. He really thinks Mrs. Fiske is a muddle-headed, ineloquent, third-rate actress and that Margaret Illington is the greatest comedienne of her time. He honestly does, and it isn't fair to laugh.

Alexander Woollcott, "Mr. Nathan's Criticisms of Dramatic Criticism," in The New York Times Book Review, *October 26, 1919, p. 598.*

H. L. MENCKEN (essay date 1919)

[From the era of World War I until the early years of the Great Depression, Mencken was one of the most influential figures in American letters. His strongly individualistic, irreverent outlook on life and his vigorous, invective-charged writing style helped establish the iconoclastic spirit of the Jazz Age and significantly shaped the direction of American literature. As a social and literary critic—the roles for which he is best known—Mencken was the scourge of evangelical Christianity, public service organizations, literary censorship, boosterism, provincialism, democracy, all advocates of personal or social improvement, and every other facet of American life that he perceived as humbug. In his literary criticism, Mencken encouraged American writers to shun the anglophilic, moralistic bent of the nineteenth century and to practice realism, an artistic call-to-arms that is most fully developed in his essay "Puritanism as a Literary Force," *one of the seminal essays in modern literary criticism. A man who was widely renowned or feared during his lifetime as a would-be destroyer of established American values, Mencken once wrote: "All of my work, barring a few obvious burlesques, is based upon three fundamental ideas. 1. That knowledge is better than ignorance; 2. That it is better to tell the truth than to lie; and 3. That it is better to be free than to be a slave." In the following excerpt, Mencken examines Nathan's outlook and technique.]*

One thinks of Gordon Craig, not as a jester, but as a very serious and even solemn fellow. . . . Nevertheless, there must be some flavor of low, barroom wit in him, some echo of Sir Toby Belch and the Captain of Köpenick, for a year or so ago he shook up his admirers with a joke most foul. Need I say that I refer to the notorious Nathan affair? Imagine the scene: the campus Archers and Walkleys in ponderous conclave, perhaps preparing their monthly cablegram of devotion to Maeterlinck. Arrives now a messenger with dreadful news. Gordon Craig, from his far-off Italian retreat, has issued a bull praising Nathan! Which Nathan? George Jean, of course. What! The *Smart Set* scaramouche, the ribald fellow, the raffish mocker, with his praise of Florenz Ziegfeld, his naughty enthusiasm for pretty legs, his contumacious scoffing at Brieux, Belasco, Augustus Thomas, Mrs. Fiske? Aye; even so. And what has Craig to say of him? . . . In brief, that he is the *only* American dramatic critic worth reading, that he knows far more about the theater than all the honorary pallbearers of criticism rolled together, that he is immeasurably the superior, in learning, in sense, in shrewdness, in candor, in plausibility, in skill at writing, of—

But names do not matter. Craig, in fact, did not bother to rehearse them. He simply made a clean sweep of the board, and then deftly placed the somewhat disconcerted Nathan in the center of the vacant space. It was a sad day for the honest donkeys who, for half a decade, had been laboriously establishing Craig's authority in America, but it was a glad day for Knopf, the publisher. (pp. 208-09)

What deceived the Drama Leaguers and other such imposing popinjays for so long, causing them to mistake [Nathan] for a mere sublimated Alan Dale, was his refusal to take imbecilities seriously, his easy casualness and avoidance of pedagogics, his frank delight in the theater as a show-shop—above all, his bellicose iconoclasm and devastating wit. What Craig, an intelligent man, discerned underneath was his extraordinary capacity for differentiating between sham and reality, his catholic freedom from formulae and prejudice, his astonishing acquaintance with the literature of the practical theater, his firm grounding in rational aesthetic theory—above all, his capacity for making the thing he writes of interesting, his uncommon craftsmanship. This craftsmanship had already got him a large audience; he had been for half a dozen years, indeed, one of the most widely read of American dramatic critics. But the traditional delusion that sagacity and dullness are somehow identical had obscured the hard and accurate thinking that made the show. What was so amusing seemed necessarily superficial. It remained for Craig to show that this appearance of superficiality was only an appearance, that the Nathan criticism was well planned and soundly articulated, that at the heart of it there was a sound theory of the theater, and of the literature of the theater no less.

And what was that theory? You will find it nowhere put into a ready formula, but the outlines of it must surely be familiar to any one who has read **"Another Book on the Theater," "The Popular Theater"** and **"Mr. George Jean Nathan Presents."** In brief, it is the doctrine preached with so much ardor by Benedetto Croce and his disciple, Dr. J. E. Spingarn, and by them borrowed from Goethe and Carlyle—the doctrine, to wit, that every work of art is, at bottom, unique, and that it is the business of the critic, not to label it and pigeon-hole it, but to seek for its inner intent and content, and to value it according as that intent is carried out and that content is valid and worth while. This is the precise opposite of the academic critical attitude. The professor is nothing if not a maker of card-indexes; he must classify or be damned. His masterpiece is the dictum that "it is excellent, but it is not a play." Nathan has a far more intelligent and hospitable eye. His criterion, elastic and undefined, is inimical only to the hollow, the meretricious, the fraudulent. It bars out the play of flabby and artificial sentiment. It bars out the cheap melodrama, however gaudily set forth. It bars out the moony mush of the bad imitators of Ibsen and Maeterlinck. It bars out all mere clap-trap and sensation-monging. But it lets in every play, however conceived or designed, that contains an intelligible idea well worked out. It lets in every play by a dramatist who is ingenious, and original, and genuinely amusing. And it lets in every other sort of theatrical spectacle that has an honest aim, and achieves that aim passably, and is presented frankly for what it is.

Bear this theory in mind, and you have a clear explanation of Nathan's actual performances—first, his merciless lampooning of the trade-goods of Broadway and the pifflings of the Drama League geniuses, and secondly, his ardent championing of such widely diverse men as Avery Hopwood, Florenz Ziegfeld, Ludwig Thoma, Lord Dunsany, Sasha Guitry, Lothar Schmidt, Ferenz Molnar, Roberto Bracco and Gerhart Hauptmann, all of whom have one thing in common: they are intelligent and full of ideas and know their trade. In Europe, of course, there are many more such men than in America, and some of the least of them are almost as good as our best. That is why Nathan is forever announcing them and advocating the presentation of their works—not because he favors foreignness for its own sake, but because it is so often accompanied by sound achievement and by stimulating example to our own artists. And that is why, when he tackles the maudlin flubdub of the Broadway dons, he does it with the weapons of comedy, and even of farce. Does an Augustus Thomas rise up with his corn-doctor magic and Sunday-school platitudes, proving heavily that love is mightier than the sword, that a pure heart will baffle the electric chair, that the eye is quicker than the hand? Then Nathan proceeds against him with a slapstick, and makes excellent practice upon his pantaloons. . . . And does some fat rhinoceros of an actress, unearthing a smutty play by a corn-fed Racine, loose its banal obscenities upon the vulgar in the name of Sex Hygiene, presuming thus to teach a Great Lesson, and break the Conspiracy of Silence, and carry on the Noble Work of Brieux and company, and so save impatient flappers from the Moloch's Sacrifice of the Altar—does such a bumptious and preposterous baggage fill the newspapers with her pishposh and the largest theater in Manhattan with eager dunderheads? Then the ribald Jean has at her with a flour-sack filled with the pollen of the *Ambrosia artemisiaefolia,* driving her from the scene to the tune of her own unearthly sneezing.

Necessarily, he has to lay on with frequency. For one honest play, honestly produced and honestly played, Broadway sees two dozen that are simply so much green-goods. To devote serious exposition to the badness of such stuff would be to descend to the donkeyish futility of William Winter. Sometimes, indeed, even ridicule is not enough; there must be a briefer and more dramatic display of the essential banality. Well, then, why not recreate it in the manner of Croce—but touching up a line here, a color there? The result is burlesque, but burlesque that is the most searching and illuminating sort of criticism. Who will forget Nathan's demonstration that a platitudinous play by Thomas would be better if played backward? A superb bravura piece, enormously beyond the talents of any other American writer on the theater, it smashed the Thomas legend with one stroke. In the little volume called **"Bottoms Up"** you will find many other such annihilating waggeries. Nathan does not denounce melodrama with a black cap upon his head, painfully demonstrating its inferiority to the drama of Ibsen, Scribe and Euripides; he simply sits down and writes a little melodrama so extravagantly ludicrous that the whole genus collapses. And he does not prove in four columns of a Sunday paper that French plays done into American are spoiled; he simply shows the spoiling in six lines.

This method, of course, makes for broken heads; it outrages the feelings of tender theatrical mountebanks; it provokes reprisals more or less furtive and behind the door. . . . No writer for the theater has been harder beset, and none has been less incommoded by the onslaught. What is more, he has never made the slightest effort to capitalize this drum-fire—the invariable device of lesser men. So far as I am aware, and I have been in close association with him for ten years, it has had not the slightest effect upon him whatsoever. A thoroughgoing skeptic, with no trace in him of the messianic delusion, he has avoided timorousness on the one hand and indignation on the other. No man could be less a public martyr of the Metcalfe type; it would probably amuse him vastly to hear it argued that his unbreakable independence (and often somewhat high and mighty sniffishness) has been of any public usefulness. I sometimes wonder what keeps such a man in the theater, breathing bad air nightly, gaping at prancing imbeciles, sitting cheek by jowl with cads. Perhaps there is, at bottom, a secret romanticism—a lingering residuum of a boyish delight in pasteboard and spangles, gaudy colors and soothing sounds, preposterous heroes and appetizing wenches. But more likely it is a sense of humor—the zest of a man to whom life is a spectacle that never grows dull—a show infinitely surprising, amusing, buffoonish, vulgar, obscene. The theater, when all is said and done, is not life in miniature, but life enormously magnified, life hideously exaggerated. Its emotions are ten times as powerful as those of reality, its ideas are twenty times as idiotic as those of real men, its lights and colors and sounds are forty times as blinding and deafening as those of nature, its people are grotesque burlesques of every one we know. Here is diversion for a cynic. And here, it may be, is the explanation of Nathan's fidelity.

Whatever the cause of his enchantment, it seems to be lasting. To a man so fertile in ideas and so facile in putting them into words there is a constant temptation to make experiments, to plunge into strange waters, to seek self-expression in ever-widening circles. And yet, at the brink of forty years, Nathan remains faithful to the theater; of his half dozen books, only one does not deal with it, and that one is a very small one. In four or five years he has scarcely written of aught else. I doubt that anything properly describable as enthusiasm is at the bottom of this assiduity; perhaps the right word is curiosity. He is interested mainly, not in the staple fare of the playhouse, but in what might be called its fancy goods—in its endless stream of new men, its restless innovations, the radical overhauling that it has been undergoing in our time. I do not recall, in any of his books or articles, a single paragraph appraising the classics of the stage, or more than a brief note or two on their interpretation. His attention is always turned in a quite opposite direction. He is intensely interested in novelty of whatever sort, if it be only free from sham. Such experimentalists as Max Reinhardt, George Bernard Shaw, Sasha Guitry and the daring nobodies of the Grand Guignol, such divergent originals as Dunsany, Ziegfeld, George M. Cohan and Schnitzler, have enlisted his eager partisanship. He saw something new to our theater in the farces of Hopwood before any one else saw it; he was quick to welcome the novel points of view of Eleanor Gates and Clare Kummer; he at once rescued what was sound in the Little Theatre movement from what was mere attitudinizing and pseudo-intellectuality. In the view of Broadway, an exigent and even malignant fellow, wielding a pen dipped in *aqua fortis,* he is actually amiable to the last degree, and constantly announces pearls in the fodder of the swine. Is the new play in Forty-second Street a serious work of art, as the press-agents and the newspaper reviewers say? Then so are your grandmother's false teeth! Is Maeterlinck a Great Thinker? Then so is Dr. Frank Crane! Is Belasco a profound artist? Then so is the man who designs the ceilings of hotel dining rooms! But let us not weep too soon. In the play around the corner there is a clever scene. Next door, amid sickening dullness, there are two buffoons who could be worse: one clouts the other with a *Blutwurst* filled with mayonnaise. And a block away there is a girl in the second row with a very charming twist of the *vastus medialis*. Let us sniff the roses and forget the thorns!

What this attitude chiefly wars with, even above cheapness, meretriciousness and banality, is the fatuous effort to turn the theater, a place of amusement, into a sort of outhouse to the academic grove—the Maeterlinck-Brieux-Barker complex. No critic in America, and none in England save perhaps Walkley, has combated this movement more vigorously than Nathan. He is under no illusion as to the functions and limitations of the stage. He knows, with Victor Hugo, that the best it can do, in the domain of ideas, is to "turn thoughts into food for the crowd," and he knows that only the simplest and shakiest ideas may undergo that transformation. Coming upon the scene at the height of the Ibsen mania of half a generation ago, he ranged himself against its windy pretenses from the start. He saw at once the high merit of Ibsen as a dramatic craftsman and welcomed him as a reformer of dramatic technique, but he also saw how platitudinous was the ideational content of his plays and announced the fact in terms highly offensive to the Ibsenites. . . . But the Ibsenites have vanished and Nathan remains. He has survived, too, the Brieux hubbub. He has lived to preach the funeral sermon of the Belasco legend. He has himself sworded Maeterlinck and Granville Barker. He has done frightful execution upon many a poor mime. And meanwhile, breasting the murky tide of professorial buncombe, of solemn pontificating, of Richard-Burtonism, Clayton-Hamiltonism and other such decaying forms of William-Winterism, he has rescued dramatic criticism among us from its exile with theology, embalming and obstetrics, and given it a place among what Nietzsche called the gay sciences, along with war, fiddle-playing and laparotomy. He has made it amusing, stimulating, challenging, even, at times, a bit startling. And to the business, artfully concealed, he has brought a sound and thorough acquaintance with the heavy work of the pioneers, Lessing, Schlegel, Hazlitt, Lewes *et al*—and an even wider acquaintance, lavishly displayed, with every nook and corner of the current theatrical scene across the water. And to discharge this extraordinarily copious mass of information he has hauled and battered the English language into new and often astounding forms, and when English has failed he has helped it out with French, German, Italian, American, Swedish, Russian, Turkish, Latin, Sanskrit and Old Church Slavic, and with algebraic symbols, chemical formulae, musical notation and the signs of the Zodiac. . . .

This manner, of course, is not without its perils. A man so inordinately articulate is bound to succumb, now and then, to the seductions of mere virtuosity. The average writer, and particularly the average critic of the drama, does well if he gets a single new and racy phrase into an essay; Nathan does well if he dilutes his inventions with enough commonplaces to enable the average reader to understand his discourse at all. He carries the avoidance of the *cliché* to the length of an *idée fixe*. It would be difficult, in all his books, to find a dozen of the usual rubber stamps of criticism; I daresay it would kill him, or, at all events, bring him down with cholera morbus, to discover that he had called a play "convincing" or found "authority" in the snorting of an English actor-manager. At best, this incessant flight from the obvious makes for a piquant and arresting style, a procession of fantastic and often highly pungent neologisms—in brief, for Nathanism. At worst, it becomes artificiality, pedantry, obscurity. (pp. 210-21)

At all events, I seem to notice a gradual disentanglement of the parts of speech. The old florid invention is still there; one encounters startling coinages in even the most casual of reviews; the thing still flashes and glitters; the tune is yet upon the E string. But underneath I hear a more sober rhythm than of old. The fellow, in fact, takes on a sedater habit, both in style and in point of view. Without abandoning anything essential, without making the slightest concession to the orthodox opinion that he so magnificently disdains, he yet begins to yield to the middle years. The mere shocking of the stupid is no longer as charming as it used to be. What he now offers is rather more *gemütlich* [good-natured]; sometimes it even verges upon the instructive. . . . But I doubt that Nathan will ever become a professor, even if he enjoys the hideously prolonged senility of a William Winter. He will be full of surprises to the end. With his last gasp he will make a phrase to flabbergast a dolt. (pp. 222-23)

H. L. Mencken, "George Jean Nathan," in his Prejudices, first series, *Alfred A. Knopf, 1919, pp. 208-23.*

Nathan and Mencken in 1923 at the summer home of Alfred A. Knopf, in a photograph taken during planning sessions for the founding of the Mercury. *Reprinted by permission of Alfred A. Knopf, Inc.*

EUGENE O'NEILL (letter date 1920)

[O'Neill is generally considered America's foremost dramatist. His plays consistently examine the implacability of an indifferent universe, the materialistic greed of humanity, and the problems of discovering one's true identity. Because O'Neill's plays are bleak portraits of a world without ultimate meaning, critics have come to regard him as the most pessimistic of American dramatists. He is credited with creating the traditions of twentieth-century American drama and is considered as integral to modern world literature as the playwrights Bertolt Brecht and August Strindberg. O'Neill's rise to critical recognition was greatly aided by Nathan's influential championing of his plays. In the following excerpt from a letter, O'Neill responds to one of Nathan's Smart Set *articles on his drama, thanking Nathan for his comments and defending several of his plays against the latter's adverse criticisms of them.]*

Dear Mr. Nathan:

I mailed a letter to you on a trip to the village yesterday—after which I bought the July *Smart Set* and read your article on American playwrights. . . . Your criticism of me and mine in the magazine is sure invigorating—grateful as keen salt breeze after much hot air puffing from all sides. If my sublime head were bumping the stars askew, your acid test would sure put a blister of truth on my heinie that would disturb any squatting at ease on the softest complacency. However, I honestly don't need blistering—on that account. My head retains its proper proximity to sea level, I think. But your weighing in the balance is a tremendous lift to me in other ways. For one thing, it gives me the added urge of attempting to make you out a false prophet—in ten years or so. For I refuse to accept your serious doubt, but rather snatch at your "But it may be . . . that I am wrong," and will try to prove it to you, given the time. (p. 149)

"In the Zone"—your "vaudeville grand guignolism" is my own verdict—but I am out of that zone now, never to return. As for "The Rope," I do believe that is sound enough, although it's a year or more since I looked at it and perhaps I'd agree with you now. But where did you get the idea that I really valued "Where the Cross Is Made"? It was great fun to write, theatrically very thrilling, an amusing experiment in treating the audience as insane—that is all it means or ever meant to me. You will see by my last letter how I came to write it, that it was a distorted version of a long play idea and never intended for a one-act play in my mind. And, by the way, it was not "Where the Cross is Made" that you advised me to tear up for reputation's sake. You must have confused it with another I submitted to you—"Honor Among the Bradleys"—a very false and feeble piece of work which you "bawled me out" for writing—now in limbo.

To make sure of my accuracy in this matter of "Where the Cross Is Made." I have been looking up your old letters and I find this in one written in October, 1918: "I have read 'Where the Cross Is Made' and like it very much indeed. It would please me to print it in the *Smart Set*. But I fear that the performance of the play by the Provincetown Players around the first of December would interfere with such publication. It would be impossible for us to use the play before our January issue," etc. So you see you have confused "The Cross" with that other play. I am at pains to state all this merely to show you that it was not "The Cross" you advised me to destroy. (pp. 150-51)

In the light of what you say in your article that you hope I may top my writings from year to year, your later opinion that "Gold" is a better piece of work than "Beyond the Horizon," is more than ever welcome to me. . . .

And again let me thank you for your estimate in the *Smart Set*. Those are the things that count. A prod in the rear and a pointing to a distant goal, not without hope—that is what it means to me. (p. 152)

Eugene O'Neill, in a letter to George Jean Nathan on June 20, 1920 in The Theatre of George Jean Nathan: Chapters and Documents toward a History of the New American Drama *by Isaac Goldberg, Simon and Schuster, 1926, pp. 149-52.*

H. L. MENCKEN (letter date 1920?)

[*In the following excerpt from a letter to critic Burton Rascoe, Mencken compares and contrasts his own writings and outlook with those of Nathan. For further discussion of the personal and professional relationship between Mencken and Nathan, see the essay in the Additional Bibliography by Alfred A. Knopf, who describes relations between the two as fraught with a great deal more tension and animosity than the public was allowed to see.*]

[Nathan and I] are constantly accused of imitating each other. This is absurd. No two men could possibly be more unlike, in style and thought. Nathan detests philosophical questions, and particularly political questions; he sees life purely as idiotic spectacle. I delight in such questions, though I reject all solutions. Nathan aims at a very complex style; I aim at the greatest possible lucidity. Our point of contact is our common revulsion from American sentimentality. We are both essentially foreigners. But he is more French than anything else, and I am more German than anything else. We work together amicably because we are both lonely, and need some support. He dislikes the *American Language* book because it is full of facts, and has never read it. I dislike his interest in the theatre, which seems to me to be an intellectual hogpen. But we come together on several essentials, e.g. our common disinclination to know authors or to belong to literary coteries, our lack of national feeling, and (perhaps most important) our similar attitudes toward money, religion, women, etc. We seldom disagree on literary judgments; it is very rare for either to exercise his veto in buying stuff for *The Smart Set*. both of us think the same, for example, about Cabell, Dreiser, Cather, Dunsany, Conrad, Anatole France, etc. Both have the same (almost pathological) aversion to worldy failure; we dislike having anything to do with men who are so bad at their jobs that they can't live decently by them. Neither regards writing books as a job: it is the *reward* of a job. Both of us detest martyrs of all sorts. (p. 185)

H. L. Mencken, in a letter to Burton Rascoe in the Summer of 1920? in his Letters of H. L. Mencken, *edited by Guy J. Forgue, Alfred A. Knopf, 1961, pp. 184-90.*

BERTON BRALEY (poem date 1920)

[*Braley wrote newspaper verse during the early decades of the twentieth century. In the following often-quoted poem first printed in* The New York Sun *in December, 1920, he caricatures Mencken's and Nathan's esotericism, basing his poem on Eugene Field's nursery rhyme* "Wynken, Blynken, and Nod."]

There were Three that sailed away one night
  Far from the madding throng
And two of the three were always Right
  While every one else was wrong;
But they took the other along, it's true,
  To bear them companee,
For He was the only one ever knew
  Why the other two should Be,
    And so they sailed away, these three,
      Mencken
        Nathan
          And God.

And the two they talked of the Aims of Art
  Which they alone understood,
And they quite agreed from the very start
  That nothing was any good,
Except some novels that Dreiser wrote
  And some plays from Germanee.
When God protested they rocked the boat
  And dropped Him into the sea,
"For you have no critical facultee,"
      Said Mencken
        And Nathan
          To God.

Mencken and Nathan came sailing home
  Over the surging tide,
And trod once more on their native loam
  Wholly self-satisfied,

And the little group that calls them great
Welcomed them fawninglee,
Though why the rest of us tolerate
This precious pair, must be
Something nobody else can see
But Mencken
Nathan
And God.

(pp. 11-12)

Berton Braley, "Three Minus One," in his Hurdy-Gurdy on Olympus, *D. Appleton and Company, 1927, p. 11-12.*

WILLIAM LYON PHELPS (essay date 1921)

[*Phelps was for over forty years a lecturer on English at Yale. His early study* The Beginnings of the English Romantic Movement *(1893) is still considered an important work and his* Essays on Russian Novelists *(1911) was one of the first influential studies of the Russian realists. From 1922 until his death in 1943, he wrote a regular column for* Scribner's Magazine *and a nationally syndicated newspaper column. During this period, his criticism became less scholarly and more journalistic, and is notable for its generally enthusiastic tone. In the following excerpt, Phelps favorably reviews* The Theatre, the Drama, the Girls, *though he expresses disapproval both of Nathan's world-weariness and the slang he employs.*]

Although Mr. Nathan has been on earth less time than I by seventeen years, I shall never be so old as he. Indeed, I think he was older as an undergraduate than I shall be at 80. If Scott Fitzgerald is "a baby with rouged lips," how came it that Mr. Nathan was born a world-weary, disillusioned child? It is unfortunate for his own happiness that even his earliest writings show the "knowing wink"; both unfortunate and dangerous; for sometimes the "knowing wink" becomes the St. Vitus's dance.

Out of his knowledge, critical judgment and experience he ought to write better books about the theatre than he has thus far produced; he is surely well equipped for first-class dramatic criticism. But his books, instead of being written in English—a language he knows well—are written in dialect; and the solid good sense at the basis of his work is marred by faults which make the judicious grieve. One is reminded of a statement by Brunetière; to write about certain things in a certain way is said to require courage; "really it does not require courage; all that is required is bad taste."

One is all the more distressed when one remembers that these excrescences are not the offspring of conversational heat, not mere thinking out loud, not impromptu. I once had the misfortune when dining out to find a hairpin in the potato; but I do not think that implement was deliberately inserted. Anyhow, when the waiter's attention was called to it, he seemed to regard it not as an asset, but as a liability. Now, in the preparation of this book Mr. Nathan originally wrote its pages for the magazine of which he is an editor, then read them in proof, then put them in the periodical; they were then revised and prepared for publication in book form, again read in proof and finally published. How they could all pass the scrutiny of the writer four or five times, with final approval, is hard to understand.

Chronic cocksureness becomes irritating. To use a frequently quoted comparison, the Pope is not so sure of anything as Mr. Nathan is of everything. And his remarks on art and life are expressed not in English, but in the jargon of musical comedy. . . .

It may be that his long experience as a critic has robbed him of something valuable. In replying to the charge made against him by "The Manchester Guardian," he says his attacks on the American theatre are justified; or, as he expresses it, "For one memorable night in the theatre, I have gladly and willingly suffered the empyreuma of 300 crabapples; for one splendid, beautiful and haunting evening, the gases of 300 boob-machines."

We ought, perhaps, to have more sympathy for the professional critic. I go to the theatre only when I want to, and only to the plays I think I shall enjoy. Thus I never see musical comedy, cheap and sentimental melodrama and other rubbish heaps. But Mr. Nathan is compelled by the duties of his profession to go to everything; it is no wonder that at times he becomes violent.

In spite of its defects [**"The Theatre, The Drama, The Girls"**] is emphatically worth reading—both for its passages of serious criticism and for its humor. With reference to the latter, all I can say is that while reading it on the subway I burst out laughing, and could not control myself for a long time.

Some of the most valuable pages are the Confession of Faith, the Literary Drama, the American Librettist, W. Somerset Maugham, Zoe Akins; on the criticism of drama and acting, Eugene O'Neill, Brieux, the propagandist, writing versus playwriting. I hope it won't make him question his own judgment if I say that I heartily share his enthusiasm for George Ade and Tarkington's "Clarence."

Just by way of variety, I wish Mr. Nathan would write one book which he is fully able to produce. This would be written entirely in English—its humor and force gaining rather than losing in such a medium—and it would say more about the genius of Rostand and Hauptmann and less about millinery.

William Lyon Phelps, "New York Drama and Dramatic Criticism," in The New York Times Book Review, *February 6, 1921, p. 9.*

GEORGE JEAN NATHAN (essay date 1923)

[*In the following excerpt, Nathan reveals the personal reasons underlying his abiding interest in the theater.*]

No less than once a week I am asked by some otherwise amiable person why I, after all these years, persist still in consecrating my time and what measure of talent I may possess to a critical consideration of the theatre. "You have said your say," they tell me. "The theatre is too trivial for your later years. Why continue? Why not devote your effort to books on other and more important subjects?" I have been told this so often of late that it has begun to disturb me a bit. It is time, I conclude, to seek counsel with myself. Why, then, let me ask of myself, *do* I persist?

Performing, in the first volume of his "Prejudices," a critical phlebotomy upon me, H. L. Mencken made the following observation: "At the brink of forty years, he remains faithful to the theatre; of his books, only one does not deal with it, and that one is a very small one. In four or five years he has scarcely written of aught else. I doubt that anything properly describable as enthusiasm is at the bottom of this assiduity; perhaps the right word is curiosity. . . . I sometimes wonder what keeps such a man in the theatre, breathing bad air nightly, gaping at prancing imbeciles, sitting cheek by jowl with cads.

Perhaps there is, at bottom, a secret romanticism—a lingering residuum of a boyish delight in pasteboard and spangles, gaudy colours and soothing sounds, preposterous heroes and appetizing wenches" [see excerpt dated 1919]. . . .

It is true that enthusiasm does not figure in my effort. I am, constitutionally, given to enthusiasm about nothing. But it is not true that curiosity is at the bottom of my effort. While curiosity is an habitual impulse with me, it has no part—or at best a very small part—in my devotion to the theatre. To the final indictment, however, I offer a plea of guilty, though with reservations. The theatre is, to me, a great toy; and upon the toys of the world what Mr. Mencken alludes to as my lingering residuum of boyish delight concentrates itself. What interests me in life—and my years have since he wrote marched across the frontier of forty—is the surface of life: life's music and colour, its charm and ease, its humour and its loveliness. The great problems of the world—social, political, economic and theological—do not concern me in the slightest. I care not who writes the laws of a country so long as I may listen to its songs. I can live every bit as happily under a King, or even a Kaiser, as under a President. One church is as good as another to me; I never enter one anyway, save only to delight in some particularly beautiful stained-glass window, or in some fine specimen of architecture, or in the whiskers of the Twelve Apostles. If all the Armenians were to be killed tomorrow and if half of Russia were to starve to death the day after, it would not matter to me in the least. What concerns me alone is myself, and the interests of a few close friends. For all I care the rest of the world may go to hell at today's sunset. I was born in America, and America is to me, at the time of writing, the most comfortable country to live in—and also, at the time of writing, the very pleasantest—in the world. This is why, at the time of writing, I am here, and not in France, or in England, or elsewhere. But if England became more comfortable and more pleasant than America tomorrow, I'd live in England. . . . My sole interest lies in writing, and I can write as well in one place as in another, whether it be Barcelona, Spain, or Coon Rapids, Iowa. Give me a quiet room, a pad of paper, eight or nine sharp lead pencils, a handful of thin, mild cigars, and enough to eat and drink—all of which, by the grace of God, are happily within my means—and I do not care a tinker's dam whether Germany invades Belgium or Belgium Germany, whether Ireland is free or not free, whether the Stock Exchange is bombed or not bombed, or whether the nations of the earth arm, disarm, or conclude to fight their wars by limiting their armies to biting each other. . . . (pp. ix-xii)

Such, I appreciate, are not the confessions that men usually make, for they are evil and unpopular confessions. My only apology for them is that they are true. That is the kind of dog I happen to be, and, I take it, a curse upon me for it!. . . I am not glibly posing myself here as an "artist," an aloof, exotic and elegant fellow with a maroon bud in his lapel and his nose in the air. I am merely a man gifted, as I see it, with an admirable practicability: one who believes that the highest happiness in life comes from doing one's job in the world as thoroughly well as one knows how, from viewing the world as a charming, seriocomic, childish circus, from having a few good, moderately witty friends, from avoiding indignation, irritation and homely women, and from letting the rest—the uplift, the downlift, the whole kit and caboodle—go hang. Selfish? To be sure. What of it?

But what has all this directly to do with the theatre? The theatre, as I have said, is to me one of the world's pleasures. On such occasions as it devotes itself to fine art is one of the world's genuine pleasures. On such occasions as it devotes itself instead to the spectacle of Dutch comedians alternately kicking each other in the scrobiculus cordis and falling violently upon their amplitudina emphatica, it is a pleasure no less, albeit of a meaner species. It is, of course, not to be denied that for one evening of real pleasure in the theatre one often has to undergo a number of profound tortures, but the same thing holds true of the aesthetic satisfaction to be derived in an art gallery, where bogus art is often no less relatively in evidence than in the theatre. One reads a dozen new books before one encounters one that imparts a glow. One sits through a dozen new plays before one encounters a "White-Headed Boy," or a "March Hares," or a pas seul by George Bickel—and through nine or ten dozen before one encounters a "Caesar and Cleopatra." To hold against the theatre on that score is to hold as well against most of the other sources of human gratification.

With all its faults, the theatre has amused and improved the spirit of man for centuries on end. Like the doll, it is the one toy that has outlived, and will continue to outlive, the horde of attacking years. It has now and then risen to greatness; it has now and then fallen to triviality—so have literature, and music, and sculpture, and painting. William Shakespeare and Owen Davis, Michelangelo and Paul Manship, Peter Paul Rubens and Penrhyn Stanlaws, Johann Sebastian Bach and Raymond Hubbell. There is no argument in contrasts; there are always contrasts. But aside from the question of the theatre's place in art, it remains that the theatre is good fun—and it is of good fun of one kind and another that I am, at the moment, speaking. My days are spent professionally in the channels of literature—my mornings with reading, my afternoons with writing. When evening comes, I am occasionally very glad to have done with literature. . . . There is left, as Goethe agreed, the theatre. There is left, between the demi-tasse and the bedtime cigarette, this night "Romeo and Juliet," that night Sam Bernard, this night "Electra," that night Ann Pennington, this night a smash of beauty and that, a smash of slapsticks. A farce by the younger Guitry, an operetta from the Kärntner-Ring, a burlesque show down in Fourteenth Street, the monkeyshines of Robert B. Mantell, a Eugene O'Neill play, a touch of double meaning from Budapest, an unintentionally jocose English "society play," a tune by Oscar Straus, or Emmerich Kalmann or Victor Herbert, a Ziegfeld show, something by Dunsany or Synge or Rostand or Thoma, a revival of some excellent comedy or merely, perhaps, a trim ankle, a sudden, surprising, lightning flash of real poetry, a comedian with an allegorical nose—one pays one's money and takes one's choice. It is the grab-bag nature of the theatre that makes it what it is. It is not curiosity that takes me there, but hope.

But all this has to do with the theatre merely as a diversion, and not as the peg for a writing man on which to hang, as I have more or less hung, a career. Pleasure is one thing, serious work quite another thing. Well, let us see. The theatre, as I look at it, is one of the best subjects in the world from which to fashion a variegated assortment of predicates. It is almost impossible for the writer on politics to use politics as a hook whereon to hang his opinions, say, of music or cow diseases. The same thing holds true of writers on music itself, or painting, or architecture, or sports, or science, or archaeology, or economics, or religion, or almost anything else save books. The theatre, to the contrary, by the very nature of its diverse constituent elements and its peculiar ramifications offers to the man who writes about it a hundred convenient opportunities to air his views con sordini on nearly everything under the sun, and what a writer craves are such opportunities. What is more, these digressions from the main theme are not, in dramatic and theatrical criticism, so patently or objectionably out of key as they would be in other forms of critical exposition. Furthermore, if Mr. H. G. Wells is justified in using the history of the whole world to work off his implied opinion of Lloyd George, I see no reason why objection should be made to me for using a single line in a play by Mr. Samuel Shipman to work off my opinion of unipolar induction, sex hygiene, the political situation in central Siam, or anything else.

For such meditations, the theatre provides an admirably provocative field. One of the best ideas I ever got for a digressive essay on humour came to me while I was watching the characters in a Strindberg play go crazy. The best essay on Shakespeare that I ever composed was inspired by a play written by the Hattons. My most valuable sardonic ideas on the labour problem came to me while a two hundred pound blonde in strip tights was being chased around the stage of a fifty-cent burlesque theatre by an Irish comedian, as the soundest theory I ever achieved on the flaw in Regulus' African campaign in the first Punic war was inspired by a shapely leg in a Gaiety show. This is why my critical writings deal at times with trivial and obscure plays and playwrights. The trivial is often the inspiration of something that is not trivial. Shakespeare so engrosses the mind that it cannot wander, cannot stray into other meadows. It is in the tensest moment of a Broadway crook play that one philosophizes upon the initiative and referendum, the life and habits of the bee, the condition of the babies in the southern provinces of Russia, the art of Henri Emmanuel Félix Philippoteaux, and the battle of Bull Run.

I am, of course, not so vainglorious as to imply that what I personally am able to derive from the trivial is always unfortunately also not trivial; I address myself simply to the theory, which is, at least in the instance of others more talented than I, sound enough. The common notion that only great art can inspire and produce great criticism does not entirely convince me. Great criticism often from little acorns grows. Dryden's "Defense of an Essay of Dramatic Poesy" grew out of a third-rate preface to his brother-in-law's book of fourth-rate plays, as his "Of Heroic Plays" and "Defence of the Epilogue" grew out of Buckingham's inconsiderable "The Rehearsal." Some of the greatest criticism in Lessing's "Hamburg Dramaturgy" grew out of completely negligible theatrical performances. . . . A thousand trivialities are placed in the test tubes of aesthetics that a single piece of sound criticism may endure. Ten thousand unknown men die in battle that history shall record—and the human race take inspiration from—the name of a hill.

This, then, is one way in which I, hopeful of worthy critical accomplishment on some future day, look on the theatre. I do not deny, plainly enough, that I might perhaps more profitably devote my efforts to writing on a subject or subjects of conceivably graver importance to the world we live in; some such subject, say, as a theory for the improvement of the condition of the working classes, or birth control, or civil service reform, or international peace, or Peggy Hopkins; but I know nothing about such things, and, as I have already said, care less. What interests me are not the troubles or problems of the world, but its joys. Art, the thrill of beauty and the aesthetic happiness of the minority are among these joys. And in so far as the theatre can provide them, the theatre engages me.

Life, as I see it, is for the fortunate few—life with all its Chinese lanterns, and sudden lovely tunes, and gay sadness. In so far as I have any philosophy at all, it is founded upon that theory. For the Nietzchean "Be hard!" I have no use, however. It savours too much of cannon, thong and overly intense purpose. For myself I substitute "Be indifferent." I was born indifferent; and at forty I find myself unchanged in attitude. (pp. xii-xxii)

It is in this spirit that I seek the theatre as an outlet for my ideas. An idea, on whatever subject, seems to me to be more in key with my attitude toward life if it is predicated upon an art. I like the notion of that kind of ideational genealogy. Art is, in the view of nine-tenths of the human race, bootless, "unpractical." Thus, whether good or bad, art provides an admirable postulate for my philosophical snobberies. Life, to me, is artificial; all my criticism of drama is based upon the theory that drama is artificial life. There isn't so very much difference, in my way of looking at things, between life as it actually is and life as it is shown in the theatre. I have often been accused of this attitude by critics of my criticism, and often been lambasted for it; I plead guilty to the charge. The theory that drama while admittedly mimicking life yet in some esoteric way departs violently and absurdly from life is maintained chiefly by persons whose life departs violently and absurdly from drama. "That isn't true to life," said the Harlem shoe-dealer, as he watched "Lord and Lady Algy." "That isn't true to life," echoed the flapper, as she watched "Rosmersholm.". . .

Artificiality is often a premise from which one may draw sound and ponderable conclusions. There is no more logical reason why a sound philosophy may not be extracted from such variably factitious a thing as a play by Björnson than there is why a sound philosophy may not be extracted from some such equally variable and factitious a thing as the naturalist transcendentalism of Lorenz Oken or the Kirkcaldyan gospel of unscrupulous Mammonism. If there is in all this an air of what Mr. Burton Rascoe alludes to as the intellectual practical joke that I frequently play whereby I may have my little laugh on the reader, I hasten to make assurance that it is the fault of my defective writing alone, and not of my convictions. That I am not always able, alas, to make the most of the opportunities that the theatre and its drama offer in this direction, that the ideas I am able to develop from the artificiality of the theatre are not often notable or even remotely interesting, is nothing against the doctrine and everything against the meagreness of my talents.

Drama, to come more intimately to cases, is—to me—one of the most interesting of the seven arts. With music and literature, it appeals to me more than all the others in combination. Unlike sculpture and painting, it is alive. It is quick, electric; genius in flame. It *is* literature: they are Siamese twins. It *is,* in Shakespeare and even in such as Rostand, music: music on the violins of metaphor, on the 'cellos of phrase, on the drums of rumbling adjectives and verbs. There is for me a greater aesthetic thrill in the second scene of Act II of "Midsummer Night's Dream" alone than in all the paintings in the two Pinakotheks. There is for me a greater aesthetic pleasure in Synge's little "Riders to the Sea" than in all the sculpture in the whole of Italy.

But, the argument goes, the theatre does not always, or even often, vouchsafe such agreeable and tonic reactions. Well, neither does the printed book page in literature nor the concert hall in music. . . . Art, whatever her platform, is sparing, even miserly, with her genuine gifts.

But, unlike in the instance of the other arts where it is a case of art or nothing, a case either of aesthetic satisfaction or aesthetic irritation and disgust, the theatre is often immensely agreeable in an obscene way when it is not concerning itself with art of any size, shape or colour. When it is concerning itself with art, the theatre is at once great, noble and hugely delightful. When it is not concerning itself with art, the theatre is neither great nor noble, but it is often hugely delightful just the same. . . . There is, in the theatre, a surprise ever around the corner. It may be a great performance of "Hamlet," or it may be a good new blackface comedian—or it may be a memorable night of superb awfulness such as that provided by the play called "Survival of the Fittest" down in the Greenwich Village Theatre. Each, in its different way, is excellent diversion.

If one goes to a concert hall and hears a bad performance or to an art exhibition and sees only bad paintings, one's disappointment is complete. In the theatre, contrariwise, the worst play and performance of the year may provide the greatest hilarity. I have been going to the theatre professionally now for more than eighteen years, and the four most thoroughly amusing evenings I have engaged during that period were provided by as many exhibitions so excessively bad that they baffle description, to wit, the play named above, the showing of "The London Follies" at Weber's Theatre about a dozen years ago, the play called "The Sacrifice" written, produced and financed by a Brooklyn banker with his fat daughter in the star rôle, and the late Charles Frohman's production of Bataille's "The Foolish Virgin." Nor do I set down merely a personal experience. There is not a man who saw any of these who will not whole-heartedly agree with me. For the theatre is never more entertaining than when its effort to entertain skids, and when the species of amusement that it provides is not strictly of the species that it has intended to provide. (pp. xxii-xxviii)

That, in essence, is the theatre as I see it; that, the theatre to which I devote my pen, and with a pestiferous catholicity of taste that embraces "Medea" and "The Follies," Eleanora Duse and Florence Mills. I do not take it very seriously, for I am of the sort that takes nothing very seriously; nor on the other hand do I take it too lightly, for one who takes nothing very seriously takes nothing too lightly. I take it simply as, night in and night out, it comes before my eyes: a painted toy with something of true gold inside it. And so it is that I write of it. I criticize it as a man criticizes his own cocktails and his own God. (pp. xxviii-xxix)

George Jean Nathan, in a foreword to his The World in Falseface, *Alfred A. Knopf, 1923, pp. ix-xxix.*

A. A. MILNE (essay date 1923)

[*Although today known almost exclusively for his Christopher Robin books for children, Milne was also a poet, essayist, and dramatist. Many of his plays achieved considerable success on the London and New York stages during the 1920s. In the following excerpt from a review of* The World in Falseface, *Milne characterizes Nathan as a critic inflated with his own self-importance.*]

Mr. George Jean Nathan comes from the "Mother, look at George!" school of criticism, and is now enjoying a post-graduate course of "Oh, Mr. Nathan, you *do* say things!" As a professional dramatic critic he has been saying things for years, and [***The World in Falseface***] is a collection of his best bits. Evidently he is a person of some consequence in America just now. "Much is made of the fact that I often leave the theatre in the middle of the second act of a play," he tells us. Under this stimulus he writes (and who would not?) with a buoyant swagger which is delightful, but which may lose some of its buoyancy when the fact that he has left the theatre in the middle of the second act is made much of no longer. Meanwhile, he is sufficiently exciting. When he says: "The lesser British playwrights . . . such playwrights as A. A. Milne, for example. . . . The net impression that one takes away from their exhibits is of having been present at a dinner-party whereat all the exceptionally dull guests have endeavoured to be assiduously amusing"—when he says this, he may give more pleasure to my friends than to me; but I do not leave the theatre. I stay to the end, and am rewarded a hundred pages later by the most charming piece of ingenuousness imaginable. He is telling us that, during the last year, he has met personally eleven men whose work he had criticized: four sound artists whom he had praised, seven incompetents whom he had damned. "When I met the seven incompetents I found them agreeable and amiable men, interesting to talk with and extremely companionable." But as for the four sound artists, "I could scarcely bear them. They were devoid of social grace; they were stupid; they were as heavy as lead; they were bores." It is a fascinating picture. Mr. Nathan and the seven amiable second-raters getting on charmingly together. . . . Mr. Nathan, the smile from his last good thing still on his lips, moving confidently across to the four first-raters. . . . I must not spoil it by a word of comment. Let us leave it here, with all its delightful implications. (pp. 61-2)

A. A. Milne, "Dramatic Art and Craft," in his By Way of Introduction, *E. P. Dutton & Co., Inc., 1929, pp. 61-8.**

ERNEST BOYD (essay date 1924)

[*An Irish-American writer and translator, Boyd was a prominent literary critic known for his erudite, honest, and often satirical critiques. In the candidly wrought essays which form his important studies of Irish literature,* Ireland's Literary Renaissance *(1916) and* The Contemporary Dramas of Ireland *(1917), Boyd evaluated Irish literary works apart from English literature. He was also a respected translator, especially of French and German works, and his* Studies in Ten Literatures *(1925) demonstrates his knowledge of modern foreign literature. In the following excerpt, Boyd praises Nathan as the perfect dramatic critic, whose indifference to everything outside the theater is justifiable and commendable.*]

Improving upon the playwright, as is the dramatic critic's privilege, George Jean Nathan has modified Shakespeare's dictum, "all the world's a stage," restricting it to that portion of the world which is his own universe. George Nathan's world is a drawing-room comedy, which might be called "The Importance of Not Being Earnest," in which he plays the part of John Worthing; his life is a stage from which he surveys the real world as though it were a darkened auditorium filled with people whose actual preoccupations are utterly remote from those of the play in which he is perpetually engaged. He is completely absorbed in his art, his part in that comedy within whose three walls all his reality is confined. That reality is the reality of sophisticated comedy, in which an adept and skillful bachelor passes through a crisis induced by blonde tresses and sparkling wines, or is the benevolent spectator of some family tangle whose solution is effected by his friendly acquaintance with the eternal weaknesses of human nature. (p. 197)

When Charles Lamb argued that the Restoration dramatists must not be damned as immoral because the society they described was fictitious, a convention not to be measured by normal standards, he adopted an attitude which must be adapted by those who would appreciate George Jean Nathan. His confessions would indicate him as a monstrosity, as an inhuman and intolerable person. But the truth is he is a highly entertaining and pleasant fellow, whose very hypochondria is not distressing, even when it take the strange form of perpetually plugging his nostrils with pink cotton over which some medicinal incantation has been pronounced, or of unceasingly inhaling a tube of menthol—these being apparently his chief winter sports. The clew to the enigma is the fact, which cannot be to frequently emphasized, that all his world is a comedy, a stage, upon which the eruption of naïve spectators would be as unseemly as the hooting of the villain in a melodrama by untutored rustics righteously indignant on behalf of an outraged and harried heroine. When John Worthing appears in mourning for the imaginary Ernest of Wilde's play, one does not protest against this misuse of the habiliments of grief. The scene is one of the most amusing in the three diverting acts of "The Importance of Being Earnest." It would certainly be disingenuous to the point of complete ingenuousness to forget where Nathan was and to make him step out of his part.

In George Nathan, then, we have the perfect dramatic critic, the archetype, the *Kritiker an sich,* as Kant might say. He is the complete man of the theater, his mind is as uncontaminated with irrelevancies as that of a politician with ideas or that of a professional moralist with a sense of decency or fair play. Everything human is alien to him unless it concerns the theater, of which his lore is profound and extensive and of which he never tires. Of the thirteen volumes which stand to his credit, two are plays, six are specifically devoted to the drama, and the character of the remaining five is well summed up in the title of one of them **"The World in Falseface."** That, after all, *is* his world, whether he be in New York, London or Vienna; whether his topic be Sam Bernard or Eleonora Duse, Ann Pennington and Bert Savoy or Ibsen and Synge. When he writes his impressions of travel he is really drawing attention to the sets for his comedy. (pp. 202-03)

In his critical capacity he has fewer limitations than any other dramatic critic to-day and can enjoy "Krausmeyer's Alley" as much as "Anna Christie"; Rostand's conventional romanticism holds him but does not detract from his enjoyment of "Rosmersholm" or "Man and Superman." He welcomed the Irish Players in "The Whiteheaded Boy" when most of his American colleagues were supercilious, but he joined them in praise of "The Miracle" and the Moscow Art Theatre. When one remembers the catholicity of his tastes it would seem as if he must have devoted his years of criticism to an amiable acquiescence in whatever happened to be fashionable, but his record is one of the harshest censure, involving him in conflicts with personages accustomed to deference or at least discreet silence. He is singing captive in his profession, for he cheerfully attends the opening performances of plays which, on the face of it, could not interest him and are probably worthless, as he gayly demolishes the plays of friends, ignoring the polite conventions for the sake of freedom of opinion. He is as enthusiastic and full of gusto when he holds up Zoë Akins to ridicule as when he first greeted her as the author of "Papa."

His destructive efforts are more frequently remembered, although he has championed many a lost play, and might be satisfied alone by his immediate recognition of Eugene O'Neill. As might be expected, he denies the existence of constructive criticism, in the sense that it is clearly useless to point out how a play should have been written, except as a satisfaction to oneself. The author does not and cannot, as a rule, profit by the suggestions. On the famous occasion when he re-wrote a play by Augustus Thomas, simply reversing the order of the scenes, and showing that it might just as well begin at the end and work back to the beginning—the criticism was constructive, but he had no reason to believe he was doing more than amusing himself. He has a pleasant habit of divulging the obscure linguistic origins of plays which have been accepted as translations from the more familiar French, German or Spanish. This helpful pedantry has by no means established his reputation for learning, because his style is not so genteel as that of the late William Winter. Hazlitt's name never occurs in his essays unless written without a capital and used as a generic term for theatrical journalists. It would be rash to conclude from this that Nathan has never read him.

George Jean Nathan is the American counterpart of the Englishman A. B. Walkley. Two dissimilar men in every respect save their common profession of complete worldliness and their insatiable joy in the theater. Walkley takes the same pleasure in parading his French and his classical education as Nathan in concealing his omnivorous consumption of dramatic literature, and in exhibiting his apparently boundless knowledge of acted plays. (pp. 205-06)

When he becomes unintelligible he does it as a gentleman gets drunk, without becoming objectionable. He never forgets his part in that quintessential comedy which is his existence. Thus he can say of his one passion, the theater: "I do not take it very seriously . . . nor . . . do I take it too lightly, for one who takes nothing very seriously takes nothing too lightly. I take it simply as, night in and night out, it comes before my eyes: a painted toy with something of true gold inside it." (p. 207)

Ernest Boyd, "George Jean Nathan," in his Portraits: Real and Imaginary, *George H. Doran Company, 1924, pp. 197-207.*

A. B. WALKLEY (essay date 1926)

[An English dramatic critic, Walkley was a cultured and dedicated writer whose unfailing urbanity and mellow sense of irony made him an opponent of dramatic sentimentality and extravagance. In an essay on the reviewer's craft, he once wrote: "Your critic is a sedentary person with a literary bias. His instinct is to bring to the play the calm lotus-eating mind with which he day-dreams over a book in his library. To this frame of mind the boisterous flesh-and-blood element of the actor comes as a rude distraction." Following this dictum with some degree of success, Walkley is considered a critic whose reviews are more literary than dramatic. In the following excerpt, Walkley finds Nathan's style altogether refreshing and replete with lively Americanisms, but faults Nathan for what he considers an overly casual critical approach.]

In writing about [Mr. George Jean Nathan,] I feel painfully aware of the delicacy of my task. For one thing he is a fellow critic, and hawks do not pick out hawks' een. For another, he has singled me out for friendly eulogy which warms the cockles of my heart towards him and at the same time will tend to mark my praise of him with the damning footnote, "For Value Received". But the simple fact remains, that he is the one critic, whether American or English, whose writings I read with unfailing delight. His very faults—bombast, super-omniscience, intoxication (as in the famous case of Mr. Gladstone) with the exuberance of his own verbosity—only add to my pleasure. . . . The most astounding (yet always amusing) lingo, culled from every vocabularly . . . baffles, startles and now and then crushingly defeats the ordinary unsophisticated reader, bred on "back numbers" like Gibbon and Hazlitt and Newman.

In my callow days I worried through the *Poetics* and the *Essay of Dramatic Poesy* and the *Hamburg Dramaturgy* and *A View of the English Stage* and Janin and Weiss and Jules Lemaître and Heaven knows how many more classics of dramatic criticism in the fond hope of one day becoming a dramatic critic myself. I thought at any rate I had laboriously acquired a knowledge of what dramatic criticism was, its methods and its limits. Then came Mr. Nathan—*enfin Malherb vint*—and knocked my theories and my poor little accumulations of knowledge endways. I had never guessed that criticism could be like *that*.

Yet prudence bids me pause to remember that there is no effect without a cause and no organism without a creative and moulding environment. I must not let myself be misled by the accident of my geographical position—so remote from America, American literature and American newspapers. Mr. Nathan cannot be the isolated phenomenon, the unique thing, I take him to be. His style must have a literary pedigree and affinities. Well, I can only again plead ignorance, and throw myself on the mercy of the American reader, who must be quite used by this time to the abysmal nescience of the common English ignoramus. But I wonder if he (or Mr. Nathan, either) will forgive me if I say that what chiefly pleases me in the American critic is not so much his criticism as (again) his Americanism?

His criticism, I venture to think, is not his cardinal virtue. It is honest, it is penetrating, it is seldom profound. I suspect he distrusts profundity as probably humbug (or "blatherskite" or "hornswoggling" or whatever) or temperamentally turns from it as dull reading. To the dull it *is* dull. But criticism is something else than easy reading for the lazy or the illiterate. Plays of serious thought demand serious thinking about them. No adequate criticism is possible of, say, *The Cherry Orchard* or *The Master Builder* without equivalent brain-work. You can treat them superficially. You may say you prefer a Manhattan cocktail to either. You may declare them too occultly Muscovite or too frumpishly Scandinavian for your taste. But that is not criticism, it is only "lively" reading. Antics in the presence of great drama are no substitute for the difficult business of explanation. The conscientious critic feels he must rise to the occasion; it is a point of honour; he must needs think out the blessed thing and explain it, or die in the attempt. Now you cannot always, in these crises, count upon Mr. Nathan's alacrity in rising. And so I like him best when his soul is not adventuring among masterpieces but accompanying his body among cocktails and the bosh and tosh which make up the average drama of any country whatsoever. He is particularly good, incisive and sarcastic, on downright bad plays. I have never seen *Abie's Irish Rose* but I have always wanted to, since reading Mr. Nathan's coruscations of contempt over it.

Then, I respectfully submit, his criticism is a little too *dégoûtée* for the average sensual man. He has seen too many plays in every living language to accept the one in hand; his nimble mind skips round all the analogous plays from the Moscow Art Theatre to the old Bowery, from Dan to Beersheba and finds all barren, especially the one under review. For this habit of damning the new with the old, the present with the distant, his criticism has been called "destructive"—not unfairly, I think, for it destroys actual, instant vitality by the weariness of past globe-trotting experience. What *is* the play? What virtue has it for me at this moment? These, I think, are the questions the intelligent play-goer asks himself, rather than what other play do I happen to have seen, or heard of like it?

As for Mr. Nathan's Americanism, it is, I suppose, at the same time a species of anti-Americanism. I mean, it seems to represent the revolt and the protest of the American artistic minority against the American inartistic majority. This particular struggle is, of course, world wide, but probably much more bitter in America than elsewhere, for the simple historical reason that Puritanism, with its attendant Philistinism, is more tenacious, more aggressive, there than elsewhere. And so I seem to detect in much of Mr. Nathan's prose the shrill note, the emphatic hand brought down with a whack on the reading desk, of a man who is speaking in presence of a formidable opposition. With what impish delight he pours out the vials of his wrath upon Rotarians, Elks, Knights of Pythias, Klu-Kluxers, Comstockery and other fearful wild fowl! The American genius for organization is here conspicuous. In England, the same kind of people are quite tame fowl; they will eat out of your hand like Mr. Sothern's *Antony* or the squirrels in Central Park. But the effect of the opposition on Mr. Nathan's style is also conspicuous; its persistent bravado—and *bravura*—its ringing tones of defiance, its calculated "cockiness", its audaciously far-fetched similes, and—most American and most delightful of all—its overwhelming, headlong, Rabelaisian catalogues, cheerfully sacrificing what pedants call "form" and measure to the indigenous fancy for impressive volume and breathless rapidity. Indeed, Mr. Nathan is now and then almost disconcertingly Rabelaisian. It is all the fault of Comstockery—whatever (as Mr. Micawber said of the "Gowans") whatever

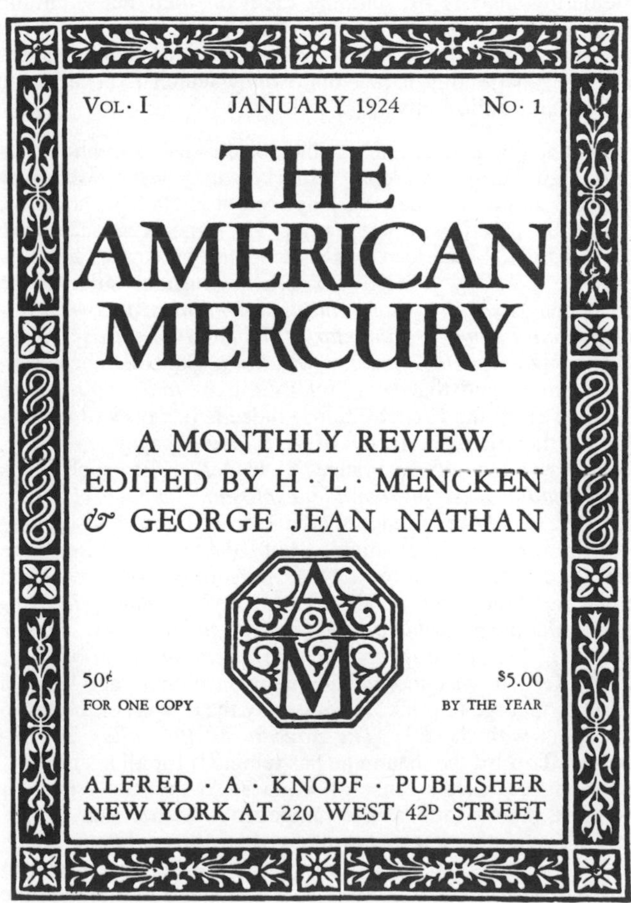

The cover of the first issue of the American Mercury. *Reprinted by permission of Alfred A. Knopf, Inc.*

Comstockery may be. . . . And so I say, with Labiche, *"Oh quel dentiste! il n'y a que lui!"* More soberly, and indeed, in all seriousness, I hold him to be what Matthew Arnold called Heine, "a brilliant soldier in the Liberation War of humanity." (pp. 69, 120)

A. B. Walkley, "The American Stage," in Vanity Fair, *Vol. 26, No. 3, May, 1926, pp. 69, 120.**

ISAAC GOLDBERG (essay date 1926)

[*As a critic, Goldberg's principal interests were the theater and Latin-American literature. His* Studies in Spanish-American Literature *(1920) and* Brazilian Literature *(1922) are credited with introducing two neglected national groups of writers to English-language readers. In the following excerpt, Goldberg examines the characteristics of Nathan's critical outlook and style, comparing and contrasting Nathan's work with that of English drama critic A. B. Walkley.*]

There are numerous times when Nathan's matter is the victim of his manner. This should not blind us to the important fact that no study of him, however cursory, may safely omit a consideration of his style, which, in essence is the verbal mirror of the man. His gusto for words is organically related to his facility and dexterity in the employment of them. His fondness for burlesque effects is a stylistic commentary upon life itself, rooted in his very attitude towards all creation. His instinct for elucidating matters by standing them on their head, turning them inside out and placing them before a distorting mirror is an active philosophy of life unconcerned with much beside the material functioning of that philosophy which is at the same time an anti-philosophy.

Upon that noble instrument which is English speech he has committed *lèse-vocabulaire*. Mencken may write with witty erudition about an American language; it is Nathan, however, who really practises it. Or, rather, his lingo is at once more and less than "American"; it is rampant Nathanese. In a few years his books will need glossaries. Consider such choice specimens as *yokelry, one-building universities, jerkwater Solons, boob-bumper, boobletariat, soup-coloraturas, yokel-yanker, jake-machine, hazlittry, Rialtors*. Consider such verbs as *moronize*, and that beautiful infinitive, *to sardou*. In the infinitive from the French drama, indeed, lies packed the history of a theatrical era. If, out of the *Iliad* we may get *to hector*, why not *to sardou* from France? Consider, again, such nouns as *sardoudlesocks, marmalade explosion, commercial mismanager, joy-boys*, (denoting the eternal enthusiasts among the reviewers, as, for example,—but "the task of filling in the names I'd rather leave to you."); *mezzotints* (for the colored gentry, and recalling, to me, Thackeray's "mahogany children"); *the unspeakable drama* (correct: the movies), *abattoir* (theatre!), Jack-the-Rippers (actors!), *pfui opus, dooflickus, hickpricker*. It was more than happy accident that led this unsaintly George to prick, if not to slay the dragon of the cheap sex drama with the title, *The Adventures of Phallus in Wonderland*. Toward the theatre he has retained, for all his raillery, something of Alice's sense of wonder. At the same time, he has more than a mite of the rampageous humor that led the preacher-mathematician Carroll to write those books which some children think are fit only for children. The man who versified about the slithy toves that gyred and gumbled in the wabe would have recognized a certain, if remote, kinship to this unpreacher-like and unmathematical roisterer of the Royalton.

Mencken, in an early essay upon his associate, has commented, with his wonted gusto, upon the Nathanian vocabulary. "He has hauled and battered the English language into new and often astounding forms," he writes in *Prejudices: First Series* [see excerpt dated 1919], "and when English has failed he has helped it out with French, German, Italian, American, Swedish, Russian, Turkish, Latin, Sanskrit and Old Church Slavic, and with algebraic symbols, chemical formulae, musical notations and the signs of the Zodiac. . . ."

More even than Americanisms the "deliciously intriguing" phrases and cadences that so beguile Mr. Walkley are Nathanisms. They are the prose of criticism on a drunken spree, and "even when he becomes unintelligible," as Mr. Boyd has written, "he does it as a gentleman gets drunk, without becoming objectionable" [see excerpt dated 1924]. To argue from this, as Walkley seems to do, that "his criticism is not his cardinal virtue" [see excerpt dated 1926] is to state the corollary of the dubious proposition that profundity is always clothed in sober garb. Nathan, to be sure, has no talents for the deeps where criticism and mysticism effect a hazy, yet a genuine assimilation. He is too skeptical of those very emotions without which art cannot be; he can, on occasion, smother sense in wit just as surely as a pedant can smother emotion in learning. It is a mistake, however, to dissociate too decisively his language from his lore.

The admiration that Walkley and Nathan have expressed for one another, tempered as critically it should be, is rooted, one may imagine, in resemblances that balance the differences. If there is an imp in Nathan, there is an elf in Walkley; the insinuated erudition of the Englishman makes him as charming to read as the intellectual slumming of Nathan makes him pungent. The Gown and the Town. There are still, in England, mistaken souls who regret that Sir Arthur Sullivan devoted himself too consistently to the form of the light opera; such as they, in our own country, if they think of it at all, may regret that Nathan never sat him down to do something in the grand style. It is to wish that he were another; it is, subtly, to annihilate him,—and to betray oneself.

Nathan's "Americanisms" (read *Nathanisms*) are the very voice of his outlook. And so, to stretch a hand across the sea, are Walkley's paragraphs most delightfully laden, not with Anglicisms but with "Walkleyisms." Nathan without his coruscations of sallies, exaggerations, puns and paradoxes would be as disconsolate as Walkley bereft of Croce, Samuel Johnson, the French language and the Stagirite. The New Yorker has chosen to make of his criticism not grand opera, not oratorio, but burlesque and opera comique. (pp. 132-35)

It is in his inversions, I believe, that we find the central Nathan. Here his strange commingling of the burlesque and the balanced, his transformation of convexities into concavities, his general playing fast and loose with the laws of intellectual gravity, reveal the essence of his critical self. Here is the hallmark of the man complete. Here are his pitfalls and his heights. It is a familiar—and a deadly—device of Nathan's to criticize an inferior play simply by restating it in literal terms. No comment, except, of course, the overtones and undertones of his style. In much the same way, when it comes to criticizing the American *booboisie*—its beliefs, its superstitions, its entire intellectual impedimenta,—he simply catalogues the articles and lets them tell their own sad tale in ***The American Credo.*** The pun, epigram, the inversion, the topsy-turvy,—all the elements of the virtuosity behind these sonatas played by bladders upon buttocks,—are an organic aspect of Nathan's mentation.

He thinks, if I may put it in terms of erethism, orgastically. And as he thinks, he writes. Nathan, appreciably, is one of our few genuine *décadents*. He is, to use the word coined by the American translator of Oswald Spengler, a megalopolitan. He belongs, not to the civilized, but to the hypercivilized, minority.

Nathan has wondered what could impel a man like Mencken to waste his time and substance upon such idiotic spectacles as political conventions. In the same fashion, Mencken, in the chapter in *Prejudices: First Series* devoted to his alter ego, has asked himself "What keeps such a man in the theatre, breathing bad air nightly, gaping at prancing imbeciles, sitting cheek by jowl with cads." His answer does as well for himself as for Nathan: it is the world seen as rollicking, ribald show. "Perhaps there is a secret romanticism—a lingering residuum of a boyish delight in pasteboard and spangles, gaudy colors and soothing sounds, preposterous heroes and appetizing wenches. But more likely"—and here I think Mencken hits upon the crux of the explanation, for both Nathan and himself—"it is a sense of humor—the zest of a man to whom life is a spectacle that never grows dull—a show infinitely amusing, buffoonish, vulgar, obscene. The theatre, when all is said and done, is not life in miniature, but life enormously magnified, life hideously exaggerated." A step above the sublime, said Napoleon, is the ridiculous. A step above the sense of sublimity, however, is the sense of humor. When God had made the earth, on the seventh day He did not rest; He laughed. And ever since, His elect have echoed that laughter.

Nathan's laughter is not exclusively Homeric. Its cruelty is as often surgical as sardonic; it is, at times, finely malicious, but rarely cruel for its own sake. It is rather, Mephistophelian, which is not so strange, since the Devil is only God surveying Himself in a trick mirror. And behind the mirror lies an indifferent void, just as, behind Nathan's indifference, lies a sense of that void which conditions, even determines, his indifference. "Yes," says Don Juan, in Scene IV of the First Part of Rostand's *The Last Night of Don Juan*. "Yes, since All is Nothing"—whereupon the Devil breaks in, "Then let us make of a nothing an All." George "Juan" Nathan is both the Devil and Don Juan. Life and its replica, the drama, are the All that is his Nothing; they are the Nothing that he has made his All. And was it not Don Juan's punishment—the proud Don Juan's—to be transformed into a puppet? Theatrical symbol of that symbolistic theatre which is Life! (pp. 136-39)

Isaac Goldberg, in his The Theatre of George Jean Nathan: Chapters and Documents toward a History of the New American Drama, *Simon and Schuster, 1926, 269 p.*

WALTER LIPPMANN (essay date 1928)

[*Throughout much of the twentieth century, Lippmann was considered the "dean" of American political journalists. He began his career as an investigative reporter for Lincoln Steffens's* Everybody's Magazine *and later helped found the liberal* New Republic *in 1914, serving for several years as associate editor and literary critic. During the 1920s, the focus of his interests swung from literature to politics, and he worked as editor and political writer for various major American periodicals for the rest of his life. In the following excerpt, Lippmann acknowledges Nathan's critical prowess, but attacks his indifference to politics.*]

> *Politics:* I have no interest in politics. I have too humorous a disesteem for the democratic form of government to be guilty of any such low concern. . . .

This passage is taken from the testament of Mr. George Jean Nathan which he recently set down in the *American Mercury* for the guidance of his biographer. I should like to say a few words about it. . . .

Were Mr. Nathan a mathematician, I should be overawed if he declared that in comparison with the austere elegance of mathematical thinking, politics was a sleazy affair. I should be impressed if he were a philosophical poet, or a Buddhist saint, or an Arctic explorer, or the mother of five slim and handsome boys, or a grower of American beauty roses, or a good and not too rapacious dentist. But Mr. Nathan is a theatrical critic. He is a man who devotes most of his life to considering the New York theatre, and that, it seems to me, removes him from the circle of those whose taste is too exquisite for ordinary mortal companionship. A man who can endure all that Broadway has to offer, who can make a life work talking about the Broadway theatre, is neither so humorous nor so delicately attuned, but that he could endure the grossness and the stupidity of politics under the democratic form of government. For after all popular government is not wholly contemptible if you compare it with popular entertainment.

I do not agree with Mr. Nathan's opinion that his humorous disesteem for politics is due to his superior taste. I think it is due to an inferior education, to a somewhat lazy incomprehension of what politics deal with, and to an imagination which is defective in dealing with realities that are complex, invisible and elusive. Attending a show is much easier than observing the political scene. The whole story is presented at once, and in less than three hours, whereas in politics the show goes on forever, and all that anyone can watch is an episode here and there. That, of course, makes it difficult to discern the plot and to realize the significance of any one episode in the whole story. In the theatre, moreover, the idea has become a story, whereas in politics it remains entangled in the rough confusion of reality. To the mass of men politics are therefore almost never interesting until they can be presented as theatre. For the ordinary human mind insists upon the dramatization of events. This is the only form which it finds easily interesting, and where, as in the theatre, there is not only dramatization but visualization, imagination is aroused with the least possible effort. (p. 39)

In plays you have reality selected, ordered and explained for you, often by a superior mind. You have reality composed inside a frame with a definite beginning, middle and an end. You have the meaning brought into relief, extricated from its qualifications and its contradictions, and simplified to a conflict in which you can vicariously participate. All this is much easier and pleasanter and more satisfactory than reading the papers and the documents, listening to speeches and studying statistics. All the sweat it takes to reduce reality to order and significance has been done before Mr. Nathan enters the theatre. It has been done, I have no doubt, by men dealing with material as refractory as the material of politics, by men who, if they were as easily stopped by their capacity for humorous disesteem as Mr. Nathan confesses he is, would never write and produce a play. For the spectator and the reviewer the theatre is relatively effortless because the creative effort has been done in advance. But when Mr. Nathan picks up a newspaper, he is driven, if he is to make head or tail of it, to know much that is not apparent, to disentangle the sense from the nonsense, in short, to do his own creative sweating.

There is nothing morally reprehensible in being too busy or lazy to go to that much trouble about politics in a democracy. Mr. Nathan is free, white and twenty-one, and if he chooses to live in an ivory tower or at a Broadway hotel, as blandly unconcerned as my dog with the historical process of which he is a part, I salute him and pass on. But when he has the brass to make a virtue out of his unconsciousness, noting it down carefully as one more item in the already rather long list of his superiorities, I suggest to him that this is nothing but Philistinism masquerading as high disdain. The Philistine is a man who comforts himself with the notion that there can't be much in anything which he can't get much out of. He can't read poetry so he laughs at poets. He can't enjoy ideas so he snorts at highbrows. If he can't play golf he calls golf chasing a little white pill around a meadow. Whatever he can't do he does his best to show is not worth doing. (pp. 39, 120)

The art of governing is often practiced by absurd amateurs. Like all the arts, especially the theatre, it attracts a host of second raters and fakers. I do not think Mr. Nathan could surprise me with any new stupidity in politics. But when I am told that this art is a low concern, I set down the man who tells me that as just a trifle dumb.

Dumb in spots. Mr. Nathan is far from being wholly dumb. To my taste he knows the theatre as well as anyone between Thirty-fourth and Fifty-ninth Streets. He knows the theatre better than I shall ever know politics. I sincerely admire him. I think that in addition to being a very shrewd critic he has created a character called George Jean Nathan which is as interesting as any I have seen for a long time on any stage. I think too that he is by way of being a connoisseur of human folly, not a connoisseur of the first order, for he lacks education and sympathy, but nevertheless a man of unusual taste. A sort of gourmet with dyspepsia. Not a man of the world, but at least a man of his own world. But when he talks about matters he doesn't understand he talks through his hat. (p. 120)

Walter Lippmann, "The Enormously Civilized Minority: A Consideration of Mr. George Jean Nathan's Celebrated Distaste for Things Political," in Vanity Fair, *Vol. 30, No. 1, March, 1928, pp. 39, 120.*

CONSTANT READER [pseudonym of DOROTHY PARKER] (essay date 1928)

[*An American critic, short story writer, poet and dramatist, Parker is noted for the liveliness and caustic humor of her literary works and of her often-quoted epigrams. A woman whose writings reveal an alternately tender and sardonic personality (described by her friend Alexander Woollcott as "so odd a blend of Little Nell and Lady Macbeth"), Parker achieved her greatest fame as the author of the frequently anthologized short story* "Big Blonde" *(1929) and as the literary and drama critic for* Vanity Fair, Esquire, *and* The New Yorker. *Central to her criticism is a withering contempt for pretentiousness, for predictability, and for unoriginality, as well as high praise for innovation and sophistication. In the following excerpt, Parker favorably reviews* Art of the Night.]

[George Jean Nathan's ***Art of the Night***] acted upon me like so much black coffee, and this in spite of the fact that any book with "Art" in its title usually renders me unconscious as soon as I've cracked it.

In several reviews of his book that I have seen, his critics have taken Mr. Nathan to task—and taking Mr. Nathan to task ranks as a productive pastime with beating the head against a granite wall—for repeating himself. I cannot see that this is so grave a charge. Mr. Nathan has written many books on the theatre, his convictions are always his convictions, and they are invariably present in his writings. This would not seem to be unintentional, so far as I can fathom. Perhaps he emphasizes the same points that he has long been emphasizing, but he has always something more to say on them, and he always has new points to make.

Art of the Night, it seems to me, is the most valuable of his works on the theatre, as well as the most entertaining. The piece called **"Advice to a Young Critic,"** though it be frequently phrased in flippancy, is deeply sound and thoughtful, and the papers on **"Writers of Plays"** highly important. Mr. Nathan has his enthusiasms, but they do not attack his control, as do the penchants of many of our other dramatic critics besiege theirs, causing them to produce not so much compilations of critical papers as bundles of fragrant love-letters. George Jean Nathan does his selected subject the courtesy of knowing about it. He writes of it brilliantly, bravely, and authoritatively. He can, in short, write. And so he makes almost all of the other dramatic commentators (I can think, in fact, of but three exceptions, and I'm not sure of two of those) look as if they spelled out their reviews with alphabet blocks. (pp. 93-4)

Constant Reader [pseudonym of Dorothy Parker], "Ethereal Mildness," in The New Yorker, *Vol. IV, No. 5, March 24, 1928, pp. 93-4.**

WILLIAM SAROYAN (essay date 1929)

[*Saroyan was a popular American novelist, dramatist, and short story writer whose works are noted for their optimistic spirit and celebration of the common individual. He is best known for the story collection* The Daring Young Man on the Flying Trapeze *(1934) and the drama* The Time of Your Life *(1939). In the following excerpt, Saroyan hotly attacks Nathan, H. L. Mencken, and Emanuel Haldeman-Julius for what he considers their destructiveness, shrillness, and prejudice. Nathan's shining endorsement of* The Time of Your Life, *despite the venom of Saroyan's criticism in 1929, was later instrumental in launching Saroyan's dramatic career.*]

There are evidently people in America who imagine they are becoming beautifully civilized merely because they laugh at things Babbitt is supposed to be worshipping, but really isn't. . . . And it must be a most singularly uncivilized audience, composed mostly of the type of people who find it highly gratifying to assume they belong to the sophisticated minority and who suppose themselves not to be Babbitts. They are the ones who want to be among the few with sense enough to laugh at things. Things like God and Coolidge and Virtue. It never occurs to them, apparently, that such laughter is neither wholesome nor pleasant. In fact, that it is not laughter at all, but is sneering and snickering, and a thing of no good to the soul.

The point is: It would be perfectly fine for these people to laugh at the Deity and the President were it not for the fact that in jeering one Deity they are worshipping another, which is very bad business. . . .

It is a thing only intellectual Babbitts do. A person who doesn't believe in a God certainly has no business worshipping a mere man. It is twice as intelligent for a person to worship himself than to worship another man. That is why Mencken, Nathan, and Haldeman-Julius are only twice as intelligent as their humble worshippers.

In view of the fact than no one else cares for the job, I, myself, shall try to give these three gentlemen a regular, old-fashioned horse-laugh. . . .

In the first place all three of these critics are unreasonably intolerant in almost everything they write, and more or less prejudiced as well. . . . Mr. G. J. Nathan is famous as the only theatrical critic in the history of the world who makes it a point to criticize everything that he happens to view. That . . . is nothing, and Mr. Nathan's method is neither a secret nor a puzzle. It remains only for another to try to be as unreasonably critical as Mr. Nathan without losing his sense of humor. (p. 77)

[Let us consider] Mr. George Jean Nathan, who if he is not always rational, but most always is, is always positively amusing, in much the same manner and degree as Mr. Mencken, but a thing of startling impossibility with the great Haldeman-Julius.

Mr. Nathan's sense of humor is of the keen variety and he can make more people laugh than any one else writing today other than Ring Lardner, Robert Benchley, and Stephen Leacock. And even if his profession seems to be that of criticizing the American Theatre (which he does nothing else but) his Clinical Notes in the *Mercury* have always been criticism of the first order as well as sophisticated humor. Even though Mr. Nathan is also somewhat too intolerant to do most of his subjects justice, when he likes he can show a bit of tenderness and understanding and pity. And he never becomes so delirious over apparent things as to write lengthily of them and in a serious mood. He tells what he supposes to be the truth in all matters and he does not bother with what anyone else might think of what he has written. He says, he is entitled to change his opinion of anything as often as he likes, because he is liable to error, and that is a thing most critics do not admit.

Mr. Nathan, like the other two gentlemen already mentioned, also takes *only* himself seriously. For has he not written in the preface to his ***New American Credo*** that "the philosophical treatise (that's what he calls the ***Credo***!) was received with *appropriate* seriousness, despite its surface air of jest." The Credo, as anyone who has laid hands on it knows, is a mere collection of an intelligent man's jokes. And Mr. Nathan is the first and only joke collector to call his jokes philosophy. It is a collection of the things most Americans are supposed to believe, for no reason at all, according to Mr. Nathan.

Let us take a look at the first thing an American is supposed to believe, according to Nathan. "1. That the elephant tusks, swamp moss and specimens of old arrow-heads periodically brought back by explorers from the African jungle are of great value in adding to the store of human knowledge."

If that is the manner in which an American philosophical treatise commences, then we had better read Emanuel Swedenborg on the explanation of the Apocalypse.

In order to finish reading the book it is necessary to wade through only 1231 thats, all of which are equally irrelevant as the first.

Witness another: "374. That a guinea pig performs the act of adultery on an average of five hundred times a day."

And another. "736. That when one asks a bell-boy in a hotel in Buda Pest to get one's suit pressed, he reappears in a few minutes with a large blonde."

And yet the author and the publisher of this book seem so pleased with it that on the last page appears: "A NOTE ON THE TYPE IN WHICH THIS BOOK IS SET. This book is composed on the Linotype in Bodoni, so-called after its designer, Giombattista Bodoni (1740-1813)" etc., etc.

And so here again is a fine critic who makes the mistake of taking his work and himself seriously which is also a sin punishable by eternal censure. (pp. 78, 92)

[These] three gentlemen pursue the uncivilized method of exposing shams and idiocies by pointing them out directly instead of carefully and quietly reporting them in the manner of Anatole France. The latter has undoubtedly done more with his pleasant writings to murder superstition, ignorance, cruelty and intolerance than these three gentlemen combined. But that is saying nothing that might injure these gentlemen, for it will be considerable time before the world will see another Anatole France. Of course, this unrefined method of pointing out superstitions and idiocies is probably entertaining if written by a Mencken or a Nathan. It is however too harsh for the person who is ignorant and superstitious, to see it as the author does, and for that reason, the ignorant remains ignorant and the uncivilized remain uncivilized.

As before stated, there is certainly a lack of intelligent tolerance in these critics, which is regrettable, for what good is a critic who cannot see two sides to every question?

These men are much too prejudiced. So much so that they cannot give such persons and things as the following a half-way decent hearing, but continually dismiss them with gestures of disgust: Eddie Guest, Los Angeles, James Oliver Curwood, moving pictures, idiots, Billy Sunday, song and dance men, English literature, Democracy, Gertrude Atherton, politicians, psychoanalysts, prohibition, Rotary, censors, love, William Randolph Hearst, and God.

But on the other hand they worship and endlessly praise anything they prefer. Thus Mr. Mencken bows his head humbly to medicine, Mr. Nathan to pretty legs and fair faces, and Mr. Haldeman-Julius to himself.

Today it is popularly believed that of these three critics Mr. Mencken is the greatest, with Mr. Nathan a close second. And in the vague and dim distance Mr. Haldeman-Julius is also noticed, but in no wise connected with the other two gentlemen, who are, if not actually, brothers, at least so by adoption and preference.

But they are an intolerant group of men and intolerance is a terrible sin, punishable, at least, with horse laughing and nose thumbing.

Is it any wonder then, when the supposedly sophisticated publications of the land are given to so much unnecessary breast beating on the one hand over trivialities and to an unending haw-haw of a horse laugh at ignorance on the other hand, that more and more people are burying themselves in the pages of such things as *The Saturday Evening Post, The Ladies' Home Journal,* and The Holy Bible? (pp. 92-3)

William Saroyan, "The American Clowns of Criticism—Mencken, Nathan and Haldeman-Julius," in Overland Monthly and Out West Magazine, *Vol. 87, No. 3, March, 1929, pp. 77-8, 92-3.**

EDMUND WILSON (letter date 1929)

[*Wilson, considered America's foremost man of letters in the twentieth century, wrote widely on cultural, historical, and literary matters, authoring several seminal critical studies. He is often credited with bringing an international perspective to American letters through his widely read discussions of European literature. Perhaps Wilson's greatest contributions to American literature were his tireless promotion of writers of the 1920s, 1930s, and 1940s, and his essays introducing the best of modern literature to the general reader. In the following excerpt from a letter written while serving as literary editor of* The New Republic, *Wilson reassures Burton Rascoe about the critical accuracy of a highly unfavorable review of Nathan's* Monks Are Monks *that Rascoe had recently contributed to* The New Republic. *For a fuller understanding of the review discussed by Wilson, see the excerpt by Rascoe (1929).*]

Dear Burton: I don't know why you were visited by all those misgivings about your article. I don't think it sounds in the least unamiable, and it is the only real overhauling which [George] Nathan has had. I think that his insolence has intimidated people, so that they have been afraid to point out how badly he writes and thinks a good deal of the time. Either that, or we are all so used to reading him that as soon as we take up something he has written, we pass into a state of mind where we are unconscious of defects which we should never forgive another writer.

Edmund Wilson, in a letter to Burton Rascoe on September 23, 1929, in his Letters on Literature and Politics: 1912-1972, *edited by Elena Wilson, Farrar, Straus and Giroux, 1957, p. 169.*

BURTON RASCOE (essay date 1929)

[*Rascoe was an American literary critic who served on the staff of several influential periodicals during the early and mid-twentieth century. Noted for his perceptiveness in recognizing new or obscure talent, Rascoe was, at one time or another during his career, the chief literary critic of such publications as the* Chicago Tribune, New York Herald Tribune Books, The Bookman, Esquire, Newsweek, *and* The American Mercury. *In the following excerpt from a review of* Monks Are Monks, *Rascoe elucidates what he considers the major faults in Nathan's style and critical thought. After writing this critical attack, but before its publication, Rascoe suffered misgivings about the harshness of the article, believing that his severity was unwarranted, and confided this suspicion to* The New Republic's *literary editor, Edmund Wilson. For his reply to Rascoe, see the excerpt by Wilson (1929).*]

The first two sentences in [**"Monks Are Monks"**] reveal all of Mr. Nathan's faults of style and thought, at their worst. These faults are not always displayed in his writings, but they occur frequently enough to be deplored by those who, like myself, believe that Mr. Nathan is a gifted writer who has not always respected his gifts. At his best Mr. Nathan is extraordinarily percipient, clear-headed, analytical; he has exposed a greater variety of fallacies than has Mr. Mencken; he is a sound critic, erudite, interesting, and intelligent; and the breath of life is in his prose. At his worst, he is as we find him in these first two sentences.

The faults of style I speak of are bad syntax, redundancy, use of false similes and analogies, misapprehension of the meaning (and sometimes even the spelling) of words and, as he might put it, polysyllabophilia or esotericonomenclature. He has a colored man's and Percy Hammond's delight in long and unusual words.

The faults of his thought are expressed in an irrelevant and specious snobbery, failure to relate his parts of speech to common or even plausible experience, attempts at extravagant paradox which fail to come off, and a tendency to play the buffoon in circumstances which do not justify buffoonery.

Let us examine these first two sentences one by one. First: "Gilbert Hemingham, like most fattish, socially impotent gentlemen slightly past forty and as children deprived of the advantages of a governess, was in the habit of discoursing frequently and not without obvious satisfaction on the length of his fibula."

(1) I don't know whether Mr. Nathan meant the *as* in that sentence to be an adverb of time or a relative pronoun, or whether he made the common mistake of assuming that both *like* and *as* are prepositions. I submitted the sentence to several persons. They disagreed over the interpretation of it. Some held that Mr. Nathan had inserted an unnecessary *and* into the sentence and that, properly written, the sentence would read: "Gilbert Hemingham, like most fattish, socially impotent gentlemen slightly past forty (*who were*) deprived of the advantages of a governess as (or, *when they were*) children was in the habit, etc." Others held that Mr. Nathan had introduced two similes into the sentence, thus: "Gilbert Hemingham, like most fattish, socially impotent gentlemen slightly past forty and like (or *as are*) children deprived of a governess, was, etc."

(2) Let us take the first interpretation of the sentence to be the correct one. The simile assumes that it is a recognized fact that certain men past forty are in the habit of talking often and boastingly of their fibulas—which certainly is not true. There are no men generally known to talk about the length of their shanks (and it would be more natural for them to talk about the length of their shanks than about their fibulas) or even about the length of their tibias. The tibia is the more important of the shank bones and the length of the fibula corresponds in every leg with the length of the tibia. What end did Mr. Nathan seek to gain by the use of that false simile and the use of the word *fibula?*

(3) I think I have read somewhere that the late Ward McAllister was "socially powerful," so I suppose Mr. Nathan is privileged to coin the expression "socially impotent." But he is justified in doing so only if he gives us some indication of what he means by it. He does not and we are left to the conclusion that it is merely a harsh-sounding and ugly synonym for "socially negligible" or "socially unimportant." So many millions of us are socially negligible without our being cut up about the fact that the expression has little force as a descriptive.

(4) When he writes "children deprived of the advantages of a governess," I feel that, in the interest of clarity, he might better have worded it, "children deprived of the discipline (or instruction) of a governess," because the children enjoy the advantages, not the nurse; but, syntax apart, the expression is an exmple of that specious snobbery which often mars Mr. Nathan's writings. I say "specious" snobbery, because there are forms of snobbery natural to the humblest people as well as to the most cultivated; they are unconscious displays of snobbery that are self-protective and inevitable; but Mr. Nathan's implication is that a child that has a governess acquires better manners than a child that is trained by its mother. That is the snobbery of cash money. It is cheap and blatant.

The second sentence reads: "The topic never seemed to tire him, in fact, the length of his fibula appeared in his mind to be at one with his belief in his own superiority to the common run of his fellows and in true mark of him as a sovereign animal."

Because of the faulty syntax of that sentence, involving the use of the word *appeared,* it is not easy to guess what Mr. Nathan intended to say. He may mean, ". . . the length of his fibula was to him evidence in support of his belief in his superiority to the common run of men," or ". . . .the length of his fibula appeared to be associated in his mind with his belief in his superiority, etc." or "his belief that a long fibula denotes the true mark of a sovereign animal was at one with his belief in his superiority to the common run of men." But whatever he intended to say, he has not said it in the sentence I have quoted.

Mr. Nathan's aversion to repeating a word leads him into extravagant synonymns. In this same first paragraph from which I have been quoting, the fibula becomes *osseous tissue;* and pride in ancestry becomes, first, *genealogical peacockery* and later *linear* (sic) *eminence*. Now, tissue cannot be osseous and *linear* is not a synonym for *lineal*. In the next paragraph, Hemingham's talk about his fibula becomes "Hemingham's tibiofibular brio." (pp. 211-12)

By exercising greater care in composition, Mr. Nathan could easily eliminate from his work such flaws as those I have mentioned. But I, as one who for many years has owed much to Mr. Nathan for the pleasure and stimulation I have derived from his writings, am beginning to wonder whether or not Mr. Nathan will ever be able to do anything about that split personality of his which has been responsible for his failure to develop, in any appreciable degree, during the past ten years. In Mr. Nathan we have on the one hand a serious student of life and esthetics, a brilliant mind quick to see the absurdity of certain ideas solemnly accepted by his critical colleagues, a man of profound intellectual integrity, and a courageous critic with a sound sense of values; and on the other hand we have the Broadway epicure prattling of rare wines and cordials, the comic writer relying for laughs upon references to the "sit-spot," and the competent old-style wit reeling off yards and yards of epigrams in the vein of the Yellow Nineties. And the one is constantly being obscured and defeated by the other.

"Monks Are Monks" was a source of real annoyance to me. I resented it in the same way that I have resented a poor performance by a favorite actor, a performance wherein the actor was shirking his work. Hitherto Mr. Nathan has collected the best of his pieces which have appeared in magazines, edited them and made a book out of them. In **"Monks Are Monks"** he has collected these magazine pieces as usual, but has used them as dialogue in a makeshift framework of narrative. The narrative recounts the vain efforts of a young woman, with leanings toward literary men, to lose her virginity to one of them. Mr. Nathan presents us in turn with several grotesque caricatures of writers who spout George Jean Nathanisms to her by the hour but fail to oblige her. One of them is the mouthpiece for a sentence which runs to over 1,500 words in length.

Mr. Nathan calls this makeshift means of utilizing his old magazine paragraphs a work of *criticobiografiction,* a word he has evolved, he says, to describe a literary work which is neither criticism, nor biography, nor fiction, but a combination of the three. Furthermore, we learn that "through the eyes of the central character we are presented with pictures of various conspicuous and representative characters in the American arts and of their philosophies and personal peculiarities."

We are presented with nothing of the kind. If, in permitting his book to be thus described on the jacket, Mr. Nathan is indulging in a hoax, he should be rebuked. If he believes that his book is as it is described, Nathan the critic has lost much of his sense of values. His caricatures of himself and Mencken in the figures, Morton and Norton, are faintly reminiscent of Rube Goldberg's "Mike and Ike, They Look Alike." It is curious, though, that even here he should permit Mr. Mencken to speak in the written style of George Jean Nathan. The experience of his heroine, says Mr. Nathan, taught her what was wrong with American literature. . . . Perhaps, perhaps. (pp. 212-13)

Burton Rascoe, "Criticobiografiction," in The New Republic, *Vol. LX, No. 775, October 9, 1929, pp. 211-13.*

VLADIMAR KOZLENKO (essay date 1930)

[In the following excerpt, Kozlenko extols Nathan's scrupulous honesty and perseverance against adverse criticism, praising Nathan as an individual who is steadfast in his own convictions, and who is a "finer artist" than H. L. Mencken.]

[In Nathan's] writings one is aware of an aristocratic temperament. He never caresses the mob into a respect for him, nor is he in any way mindful of their censure or praise. As he often says, he doesn't give a good damn for them. The mob means but one thing to him. It is present, ergo and alas, it exists. He is not like Mencken who complains of colic whenever he must speak to the Babbitts, yet continues enthusiastically to talk to them. Nathan does not concern himself with them at all. If he must bump against them—well, it can't very much be helped; if not, it is better still. He merely accepts them, like the ancient philosophers, serenely and indifferently.

This gesture of disdain should not be mistaken for misanthropy. He is too healthy to stoop to such a pathological form of aversion. His is a mild but potent form of scorn. There is a certain amount of pity, sentimental pity, but yet an understanding pity in his aloofness. He is too broad and tolerant to hate. He does in a way feel sorry for dolts shackled to the chains of ignorance, superstition and Sklavenmoral, but it isn't long before this mood is punctured by hilarity. He is like a father whipping his son, not because he dislikes him, but because he wants to make a man out of him—to scourge him not into a state of terror and fear of the knout, but to harden him into a state of indifference and strength. Nathan's critical dealings with the mob are simply an end to irony and merriment. He enjoys to flog. It isn't cruelty but merely a certain satisfaction gained in scourging peasants who have set themselves up as kings. When he attacks the mob, however, he tackles only those members of it who enjoy some prestige. The mob in its entirety he leaves to lesser men. He concerns himself only with bigger prizes—with those who have set themselves up as figures and who are making the louts worship them. These he delights to tear apart and spill the sawdust from their brains. Such revelations bring out the iconoclastic exhilaration of the man. He is interested always in showing up the charlatan and the mountebank. There is, after all, something gala in seeing the ruthless dissection of an imposter. Nathan shows no deference to any man's self-imposed importance or to the mob's feverish howling. He rips into the fraud and faker as if the latter were a football dummy set up for scrimmage, and holds up to the American scrutiny the emptiness of the man's insides.

Nathan's animation is never spoiled by indignation or by any outburst of philosophical vulgarity or cheapness. There are men who possess a certain exhilaration of wit, but it often becomes shoddy after a time. Its scintillating monotony begins to pall. This, Nathan has carefully avoided. He knows how to temper his seriousness with his drollery. He may descend to certain commonplaces (recall that brilliant essay of Gourmont on commonplaces), but never to the dullness of sophisticated platitudes. He still retains, in spite of an obvious shortcoming of Paterian finesse, the distinction of writing English that is brilliant, lucid and forceful. His similes have a certain gruff humor, coarse at times, that make them exceedingly virile and formidable, and thus lend strength to the promulgation of his ideas. But through it all the keynote is always struck, and one recognizes the unmistakable strain of a carefully tuned and sensitive temperament.

His writing pulsates with the force of an aggressive mind. It breathes with the lungs of an artillery captain who is at the same time an artist. But to the plane of slave-driving it never descends. There is nothing arrogantly brutal in his temperament. Brutality in itself has a certain coarseness, a gruffness, which alienates the reader. There are many traces of this in Mencken. It is one of the many striking differences in the styles and temperaments of the two men. Mencken indulges in the attempt to upset one's mental attitude by obvious bellicosity. This is significant of his work. He employs the device frequently. It reveals how much animus and bile the man possesses while in the throes of a tempermental rage. It throws the reader off his balance. Nathan is more wary. He lets them have it, but it is fencing, a parrying of deadly strokes, rather than a bull-rush. He thrusts, and his thrusts are surer; they reach the mark oftener than Mencken's. Nathan's manner of fighting requires more facility, more flexibility, more skill.

There is a considerable difference in the men's writing. Nathan is more scintillating, more literary, more logically dexterous. Mencken, more pugnacious, heavier in the rough. His laughter impresses one as coming from the belly, hard and phlegmatic. Nathan's is more cerebral. Mencken with all his ardent preaching against Democracy is far more democratic than Nathan. His temperament is more prosaic, more secular than his colleague's. Mencken's predilections are as Teutonic as his name implies. His taste for things that are German is faithful to his temperament. A certain heaviness, even obesity. . . . The casual reader will think he recognizes obvious similarities in the two men. But on closer analysis, and notwithstanding the fact that Mencken and Nathan have been associated for close on twenty-five years in literary and editorial concerns and as friends, these will disappear. It would be natural to expect that the two would have absorbed certain of the idiosyncrasies of each other. Yet even in their close relationship Nathan and Mencken have always retained their own salient personalities, personal mannerisms and writing styles.

It is a common error for people to say that Mencken writes, thinks and acts like Nathan and Nathan like Mencken—that the two are Siamese-twins who cannot be dissociated. It is utterly false. I have found nothing in Nathan which would in any way confirm the delusion that his nature is in any way the least like Mencken's. He is intrinsically different from Mencken as Mencken is intrinsically different from, say, Anatole France. Their natures and minds may be kin in many things and in many ideas. Thus in both there is a certain smartness, a certain jocoseness which seems to caper over the pages; in both, hostility to charlatanism is never relaxed and equally potent; both take delight in lambasting the individuals who have been set up as national heroes and gods to appease the idolodoulia-complex of what they call the yokelry; both mock and rail at the humbug that is literary and ecclesiastical gospel; both are preferably more European in their tastes and predilections than American; both feel the same way in many respects about marriage, love, negroes, drunks and war heroes; both love music and both play the piano—rather badly. In short, they have many interests that are similar. Yet with all this homogeneity they are unlike in individuality, in artistry, in temperament and in literary style. Nathan stands by himself. He is first, last and all the time an entity. Nothing, no one, can make so much as a dent in him.

Nathan in the main is the finer artist. His writings are more sensitively tuned to the reaction of his nature than Mencken's. His tastes are less laical. Mencken's interest runs to politics, theology, Tennessee hill-billys and even the American Legion. He can rail (with all the technical nomenclature) against osteopathy, chiropractic, Christian-Science, Freudism, theocracy, electro-biology and other such subjects. And there is no doubt that he rails well. But Nathan's nature is far more cultivated and aesthetic. His proclivities are conclusively more personal and finer. He does not believe in stupefying his mind with eccentric and nondescript interests. There are only a few things that deeply concern him: music, literature, drama and the arts generally. These are the big things he cares about. (pp. 18-23)

Vladimar Kozlenko, in his The Quintessence of Nathanism, *Vrest Orton, 1930, 53 p.*

HENRY HAZLITT (essay date 1931)

[*An American journalist, editor, critic, and authority on economics and finance, Hazlitt has served on the staffs of various New York newspapers and magazines. His essays and books are noted for their clear presentation of such frequently abstruse subjects as Keynesian economics, the principles of literary criticism, and the foundations of morality. In the following excerpt from a review of* Testament of a Critic, *Hazlitt argues that, contrary to the view of many critics, there is much resemblance between Mencken's and Nathan's styles.*]

Though it will doubtless only be regarded as an affectation of singularity on my part, I make bold to say, inspite of all that has been written to the contrary in recent years, that Mr. H. L. Mencken and Mr. George Jean Nathan have a very great deal in common. I have frequently seen in print the comment that the prose styles of the aforesaid Messrs. Mencken and Nathan bear only a superficial resemblance to each other; it may be merely my lack of discernment, but it seems to me that the resemblance is profound. So similar are their vocabularies, including their own verbal inventions, that it is by this time impossible to recall, if one ever precisely knew, which writer originated which. Their vulgarity is pretty much the same kind of vulgarity, though Mr. Nathan's leans rather more toward the lascivious and Mr. Mencken's toward the macabre. (I might remark that I here use the word vulgarity in no invidious sense, any more than I should in referring to the vulgarity of Rabelais. Mr. Nathan writes with more gusto than any other living critic of the theater, just as Mr. Mencken writes with more gusto than any other literary critic or essayist this side of the Atlantic; and I hazard the generalization that wherever one finds great gusto—one thinks of such classic examples as Rabelais, Voltaire, Swift, Carlyle—one always finds vulgarity, i.e., what are called breaches of good taste. I do not mean to imply, of course, that wherever one finds vulgarity one finds gusto.)

Mr. Nathan's attitude toward the subjects of his discourse, again, is very nearly that of Mr. Mencken. To be sure, while Mr. Mencken prefers to thwack his victims on the cranium, Mr. Nathan more often aims for their pantaloons; while Mr. Mencken suggests a Roman emperor turning thumbs down, Mr. Nathan reminds one more of a small boy thumbing his nose and making obscene noises with his mouth: but this distinction could easily be carried too far. Finally, the very rhythm and sentence structure of Mr. Mencken and Mr. Nathan are so alike that it requires a sensitive ear to detect the difference. Mr. Mencken's sentences are on the whole more dextrously managed, more compact, and land with a more resounding thud; but Mr. Nathan's achieve a more rapid movement. In Mr. Mencken one hears more of the drum and in Mr. Nathan more of the flute and piccolo. But when all this is set down the distinction remains a tenuous one. Anyone who does not think so many review the old *Smart Set* and tell us who wrote what among the double-signature pieces.

There can be little doubt, in brief, that the stylistic debt of Mr. Nathan to Mr. Mencken is a heavy one. Mr. Nathan's sentences are managed vastly better than they were fifteen years ago, and the Mencken influence is unmistakable. But I do not mean to fall in with the widespread critical notion that Mr. Nathan is a mere ex-satellite of Mr. Mencken, or that, like the moon, he shines by a reflected light—that it was merely his association with Mr. Mencken that brought him into prominence. Doubtless the association hastened his recognition, but his position as a critic today would still be pretty much what it is if that association had never been publicly heard of. If his prose is an imitation of Mr. Mencken's prose, then it is the only successful one—successful because perfectly fused with his own personality, and supported by a native fertility of pungent simile and epithet perhaps equal to Mr. Mencken's own. To return to our astronomical figures, we may say that Mr. Nathan and Mr. Mencken were twin stars revolving about each other and affecting each other's orbits. (pp. 186-87)

But let us drop this comparison, which is perhaps becoming tedious, and look at Mr. Nathan by himself. His merits are many, and not to be briefly catalogued. The writing of few critics is so continuously entertaining for its own sake. He has the sharpest realistic discernment of any theatrical reviewer now in regular practice. No other has a so keen a scent for every shade of sham, pose, affectation. His intelligence is certainly as high as, and his range of knowledge of the drama—European and American, ancient and contemporary—equal and perhaps superior to, that of any other dramatic critic in these parts; yet though in this sense a highbrow he is never taken in by highbrowism. He has repeated often and in many forms his belief that "the place of the theater in the community is infinitely less the place of the university, the studio, and the art gallery than the place of the circus, the rathskeller, and the harem." He is for "horse-play, belly-laughter, pretty girls . . . farce, flippancy, folderol." He has argued year in and year out against the insufferably persistent notion "that a bad play that views life soberly is somehow better than an equally bad one that views it lightly." Mr. Nathan, again, is less taken in than most of his colleagues by the mere themes of plays, their so-called philosophy. He never, for example, confuses "a mere loud statement of some hitherto theatrically unspoken phase of sex with meritorious drama." (He finds that the Anglo-American sex drama, on the whole, "resembles nothing so much as a guinea-pig that has gone intellectual") Mr. Nathan's exuberant flow of words, once more, giving the impression of a man writing as rapidly and spontaneously as he talks, disguises the solid work and tedious research that must go into so much of his writing. Ten pages in ["Testament of a Critic"], for instance, set out to prove that Bernard Shaw, in spite of his occasional efforts to mask the fact, has not only an aversion to sex but a fear of it; these pages prove their contention completely and unanswerably; but it takes little imagination to realize the heavy spade work that Mr. Nathan, in spite of his pose as a gay and indolent fellow careering down the primrose highways of the world, put behind them. Mr. Nathan has for years been accused of a mere *contra mundum* attitude. That he loves contradiction for its own sake, that he may even enjoy it when his boos and catcalls turn out to be solos, I should be the last to deny; but when one looks over his record for a quarter of a century one finds it amazingly sane and balanced; one finds that his perspective and his standards have seldom deserted him, while the enthusiasms of most of his colleagues have come to look as ludicrous as he represented them to be at the time. Mr. Nathan has always held that Eugene O'Neill stood in a class apart among American dramatists, that, in spite of his failures, he is the only one who has what may be called size. The truth of this judgment has become more and more obvious with the passage of the years.

Perhaps it is too much to say that Mr. Nathan is the most completely honest of our theater critics. By honesty I mean to imply certain intellectual as well as moral qualities—independence, the ability to remain unswayed by other judgments, the courage to state one's position unequivocally and to make enemies in all camps. We may note in the present book, for example, the wholesale consideration of American dramatists, with brief summaries of the importance of each. I quote one sentence in illustration:

> The so-called New Playwrights group, John Howard Lawson, Em Jo Basshe, John Dos Passos, E. E. Cummings, and Michael Gold, disclose nothing; they may be dismissed.

The point here is not whether this sweeping judgment is just or not; the point is that we have here a group of writers that have been highly praised by literary critics and by some of the dramatic critics that Mr. Nathan might be expected to respect most, and that, not through moral indignation or fear of their revolutionary social doctrines or lack of hospitality toward technical innovations, Mr. Nathan can still dismiss them peremptorily and unapologetically.

May we not say of his dramatic criticism what he himself says of Shaw's—that he has brought to it, aside from his own contribution, is the gift of independence and courage to others? (p. 187)

Henry Hazlitt, "George Jean Nathan," in The Nation, *Vol. CXXXII, No. 3424, February 18, 1931, pp. 186-87.*

GRANVILLE HICKS (essay date 1932)

[Hicks was an American literary critic whose famous study The Great Tradition: An Interpretation of American Literature since the Civil War *(1933) established him as the foremost advocate of Marxist critical thought in Depression-era America. Throughout the 1930s, he argued for a more socially engaged form of literature and severely criticized such writers as Henry James, Mark*

Twain, and Edith Wharton, who he believed failed to confront the realities of their society and, instead, took refuge in their own work. Hicks was shocked by the effects of the Great Depression and believed that events demanded a new commitment on the part of writers to clearly understand and express their times. In Marxist terms this meant that all American artists should comprehend the growth of capitalism and its negative side effects, such as war, periodic depressions, and the exploitation and alienation of the working class. Thus the question Hicks posed was always the same: to what degree did an artist come to terms with the economic conditions of the time and the social consequences of those conditions? What he sought from American literature was an extremely critical examination of the capitalist system itself and what he considered its inherently repressive nature. After 1939, Hicks sharply denounced communist ideology, which he called a "hopelessly narrow way of judging literature," and in his later years adopted a less ideological posture in critical matters. In the following excerpt, he sourly reviews The Intimate Notebooks of George Jean Nathan, *assessing it as the work of a none-too-original mind.*]

Confronted with a certain sort of book, the reviewer is likely to feel that by all odds the greatest service he can render his readers is to give them some idea of the book's contents. This sense of a duty to be performed is particularly compelling if he feels that, for one reason or another, the author of the volume in question enjoys no very large following, and that without his—the reviewer's—efforts the seed that is being sown may fall upon stony ground. Such a book is this latest work by George Jean Nathan.

By reading Mr. Nathan's **"Intimate Notebooks"** one may learn that Sinclair Lewis makes speeches in dialect, tells his friends what a great writer he is, and drinks a lot; that Theodore Dreiser is very honest, supports a great many causes, frequently goes to the movies, and drinks a lot; that Ernest Boyd drinks a lot, seldom goes home, and has a fund of anecdotes about literary celebrities; that Jim Tully lives in a villa with a Chinese flunkey, drinks a lot, and is still a hobo at heart; that Clarence Darrow drinks a lot, is a sentimentalist, and thinks he dresses well; that H. L. Mencken constantly complains about his health, drinks a lot, and spends much time in the playing of practical jokes; and that Eugene O'Neill, who is happy when he is happy and sad when he is sad, used to drink a lot. Mr. Nathan, it appears, has utterly failed to convince himself, however hard he may have tried, "that such trivialities are not more important in the picture of a man than items often widely held to be of graver significance."

Only part of the book, however, is devoted to reminiscences of this sort; Mr. Nathan ran out of friends on page 121. Notebook Two contains what he calls Critical Observations. Here we learn that English critics are often hostile to American books, that actors have no great love for reviewers, and that much good writing is buried in periodicals. Notebook Three, devoted to Theatrical Opinions, records Mr. Nathan's faith that the talkies will never supersede the legitimate drama, his conviction that Eugene O'Neill is our foremost dramatist, and his prediction that sentiment is about to triumph over smut in the drama. In Notebook Four he gathers a few Random Conclusions: doctors, he believes, are often ignorant; school children should not be made to memorize dates; Negroes are really not to be pitied. Reading between the lines, one gathers that Mr. Nathan drinks a lot. (pp. 404, 406)

Granville Hicks, "Mr. Nathan's Soliloquies," in The Nation, *Vol. CXXXV, No. 3512, October 26, 1932, pp. 404, 406.*

THEODORE DREISER (letter date 1933)

[*Considered among America's foremost novelists, Dreiser was one of the principal American exponents of literary Naturalism. He is known primarily for his novels* Sister Carrie *(1901),* An American Tragedy *(1926), and the Frank Cowperwood trilogy (1912-47), in each of which the author combined his vision of life as a meaningless series of animal impulses with a sense of sentimentality and pity for humanity's lot. Deeply concerned with the human condition but contemptuous of traditional social, political, and religious remedies, Dreiser associated for many years with the American socialist and communist movements, an interest reflected in much of his writing after 1925. Along with Nathan, James Branch Cabell, Ernest Boyd, Eugene O'Neill, and Sherwood Anderson, Dreiser served on the editorial board of* The American Spectator *during the 1930s. However, he was unhappy with Nathan's editorial policies and wrote him several letters voicing his concerns. In the following excerpt from a long letter written near the end of his association with the periodical, Dreiser attacks Nathan for what he considers the latter's unprofessional, facile approach toward editing* The American Spectator.]

Dear Nathan:

Steadily, since I agreed to become one of the editors of the *Spectator,* there has developed an issue which I think is far more definite and of greater import to me than it is to you. I would address this letter generally to Boyd, Anderson, Cabell and O'Neill if it would make any difference, but it would not. The issue is between yourself and myself and, unless it is remedied, you can look forward to speedy dissociation of myself from this group.

Fundamentally, Mencken stated the case to me in regard to you in 1926. It was that from the beginning there had been a fundamental difference between your points of view; that all you could contemplate was the frothy intellectual and social interests of the stage, the Four Hundred, the Bohemian and mentally dilettante worlds, whereas he personally was for serious contemplation of science, medicine, education, literature and what not. The issue, as you know for yourself, proved fatal. I was a little dubious as to his stand at the time, and so said, because always I felt that opposed to his solid philosophic, economic, sociologic, scientific and historic interests, your lighter touch was important and, for general literary as well as magazine purposes, made for a more charming and, to my way of thinking, almost equally valuable publication, the old *Smart Set*. He disagreed with me and, of course, since he pursued his intellectual course so ponderously, the *Mercury* failed, and, to a certain extent, I think, rightly.

On the other hand, I am satisfied that if the present course in regard to the *Spectator* is followed without modification and, I am vain enough to announce, if my serious predilections in regard to what it should represent are ignored, while it will not necessarily fail, it will pass into something with which I do not care to be related.

We will pass to specific instances. There was once an article in the office entitled "Physicists Come to Earth." It was to me a very interesting geodetic survey of the relation of physics to physical geography and, regardless of what you, or Mr. Boyd or anyone else might think, it was a fit paper for this particular publication. It was neglected on the ground that it was heavy, or this or that, and instead of the man being encouraged to whip it into shape, it disappeared.

What has been said in regard to science is equally true of economics and government, in so far as the Soviet regime is concerned. Two of the most appealing and important articles

I have ever read in regard to Russia came into this office. I am referring to "The Russian Prostitute" and "The Russian Municipal Court"; powerful, antithetic revelations and reflections on the capitalistic approach toward these same matters. While the second was rejected out of hand, the first has lain dormant apparently for the reason that it would not look well with the Broadway items about the stage and English and French books.

Another instance relates to the article that dismissed the International Court of Nations as something dishonest, partisan and futile. Although to my way of thinking, there was nothing wrong with the article, actually all that was wrong with it was the mental point of view of yourself and Boyd, and, frankly, I think principally of yourself, since Boyd does not seem to be able to achieve a definite position where you and your theories as to magazine-making are concerned. As usual, the article was returned on the ground that, by the time we could come to market with it, the interest in the matter would be over. (pp. 642-44)

The latest instance, of course, is the Ben De Casseres piece in regard to Shan-kar. According to the comment attached to the article and returned to Miss Light, the article was junk. It so happens that having inspired the article, and presented the essential aesthetic and philosophic structure on which it was to be reared, I now find certain definite mental processes of mine being commented on as junk. Everyone is entitled to his reactions, his convictions. The data in regard to Shan-kar even in this article is not junk, you, Mr. Boyd, Mr. Anderson or whomsoever you please to the contrary notwithstanding. At the same time, however, that you refer to super-aestheticism and a modified measure of poetic mysticism as junk, you have the temerity to address me in regard to such unutterable trash as the article on columnists which, with modifications, you and Boyd could endorse for the *Spectator*. And this is equally true of [Lillian Hellman Kober's article] "Perberty."

There is an additional phase, and that relates, as I have said before, to the Catholic Church. You personally are invariably so free to comment on the Protestant Church, the follies of its ministers, its adherents, and so on. However, the moment it comes to the Catholic Church, in so far as I see, there is no honest intellectual approach to the question. You are never enthusiastic about anything in relation to even a comment on the Catholic Church. Either you have apologies or you raise dull and technical or dishonest objections to any comment of this character whatsoever. . . . You not only raise every possible objection, but mentally and emotionally are indifferent, and commercially, I am satisfied, totally opposed. This attitude toward the Catholic Church and its policies in this country must cease if I am to continue my relations.

From the beginning, as I have said before, in connection with John Cowper Powys, Llewelyn Powys, Evelyn Scott, and now De Casseres, this problem of the esoteric and the aesthetic in connection with the *Spectator* has been a source not only of contention but of inadequate understanding. I maintain that neither you nor Boyd are in mental position to contemplate this matter intelligently. Confronted by the mystical, esoteric and the speculative in regard to life, its origins, its anomalies and anachronisms, you are either intellectually unequipped or temperamentally opposed to serious consideration of this field. And the worst of it is that you are satisfed that a magazine which would venture to present the astounding speculations and creative mentations of a man like Charles Fort, for instance, would be ridiculous and useless.

Nathan amid the collection of books that filled his New York apartment. Eric Schaal, Life Magazine *© 1940 Time Inc.*

With this, I disagree, of course, because and easily I find myself able to confute you by reference to the mystical realm of music. Here, where the mind is free to interpret the emotional responses of the spirit of musical genius, you are at ease to endorse and even to introduce into the pages of the *Spectator,* aesthetic nonsense in regard to music. I am referring to the dismissal by an incompetent of the works of Debussy, Wagner, Strauss and some others as musical nonsense. Furthermore, the veriest nincompoop can step up and discuss music in the *Spectator,* voice theories and deductions as ridiculous as you please, without a word of comment from you or Boyd or any other, and for the very excellent reason, I take it, that neither you nor Boyd truly comprehend music, either its mystical or its humanly emotional references, and probably not even its technique. However, since it has a public of its own, it becomes passable, and o.k. in the pages of the *Spectator*. But when it comes to the matter of original mentations or emotional reaction to mysteries in the field of science, or the arts, etc. where no important public following is in evidence, you find yourself shouting, "Junk!"

Personally, I may as well announce that in so far as I am concerned, that position and that attitude is not to be further endured by me. My sole reason for allying myself with the *Spectator* was that I felt it was to be really and truly a door for the original and the creative in all fields of thought and endeavor, not merely a book and theatre review of a medium which would rejoice the hearts of the columnists and the editors of second-class American papers. I cannot be accused of not being willing and even eager to provide a note of gaiety and even levity to this paper, but solely as a foil to really distinguished, serious mentation. In that, I have been bitterly disappointed. We have now reached the point where I am satisfied that my wishes in this respect are hopeless, or nearly so.

Therefore, I now say frankly that we will either come to an understanding as to the proper program of this paper, and its intelligent prosecution and enforcement not by me but by you and Boyd, Anderson and whoever is connected with it, or I personally will resign. I refuse further to be a figurehead for something which misrepresents me entirely. (pp. 645-47)

Theodore Dreiser, in a letter to George Jean Nathan on October 7, 1933, in his Letters of Theodore Dreiser: A Selection, Vol. 2, *edited by Robert H. Elias, University of Pennsylvania Press, 1959, pp. 642-47.*

SEAN O'CASEY (letter date 1940)

[*An Irish dramatist and essayist, O'Casey worked throughout his youth as a manual laborer and, moved by poor conditions and the plight of fellow workers, became a left-wing activist. His finest plays, which include* The Shadow of a Gunman *(1923),* Juno and the Paycock *(1924), and* The Plough and the Stars *(1926), are both realistic and lyrical, drawn from his experiences with poverty in the Dublin slums. In the following excerpt O'Casey, whose early career had been greatly aided by Nathan's influential criticism on his behalf, offers an appreciative tribute to his friend's* Encyclopaedia of the Theatre.]

Dear Sirs:

I am very happily obliged to you for sending me G. J. Nathan's ***Encyclopaedia of the Theatre.*** It is a grand book. It is what one expects from G. J. Nathan, and that's saying a hell of a lot in a quiet way. The sentences come floating before one's mind, like lovely iridescent bubbles, to burst with the shattering force of high explosives, breaking in pieces all the shams sheltering in the arms of playwright, actor, actress, and even those sheltering in the arms of his comrades, the critics. Here is a true knight of the theatre: thinking with Hamlet, dying with Othello, and roaring out a bawdy song with Falstaff. There is none like Nathan; no, not one; and long may he be spared to further use his marvelous memory and remarkable gifts in the service of the theatre. (pp. 835-36)

Sean O'Casey, in a letter to Alfred Knopf in January, 1940, in his The Letters of Sean O'Casey: 1910-41, Vol. I, *edited by David Krause, Macmillan Publishing Co., Inc., 1975, pp. 835-36.*

JOSEPH WOOD KRUTCH (essay date 1940)

[*Krutch is widely regarded as one of America's most respected literary and drama critics. Noteworthy among his works are* The American Drama since 1918 *(1939), which analyzes the most important dramas of the 1920s and 1930s, and* "Modernism" in Modern Drama *(1953), in which he stressed the need for twentieth-century playwrights to infuse their works with traditional humanistic values. A conservative and idealistic thinker, he was a consistent proponent of human dignity and the preeminence of literary art. His literary criticism is characterized by such concerns: in* The Modern Temper *(1929) he argued that because scientific thought has denied human worth, tragedy had become obsolete, and in* The Measure of Man *(1954) he attacked modern culture for depriving humanity of the sense of individual responsibility necessary for making important decisions in an increasingly complex age. In the following excerpt from a review, Krutch highly praises Nathan's* Encyclopaedia of the Theatre.]

[George Jean Nathan] has an encyclopedic knowledge of the theater and probably remembers in detail more plays and players of the last thirty-five or forty years than anyone else now writing. For that reason there is a subtle justification for the title of his latest volume [**"Encyclopaedia of the Theatre"**], even though that volume is not what one would at first expect, the book being as a matter of fact a collection of short pieces on a great variety of subjects arranged alphabetically by title. At this late date there is no point in describing either Mr. Nathan's attitude or his style, both of which are as well known as those of any writer on our theater are ever likely to be. He lays about him with all his accustomed vigor, but the secret of his individuality is simply that, for all his cynicism, he has an abiding respect for the theater and that, for all his "sophistication," his deepest liking is for the most substantial things which the theater has to offer. Many years ago when for the first time I reviewed one of his books I called Mr. Nathan "little better than a highbrow," and that description will have to stand. No one is less often taken in, but no one is less likely to respond to the genuine with conventional flippancy. There is a great deal of good reading in the present volume, and it is hard to single out for comment individual pieces from such a varied assortment; but since Mr. Nathan's encyclopedic memory makes him a dangerous man to face with a generalization I suggest the article "Morgan" as a fine specimen of confutation by example and "Everyman His Own Critic" as an equally fine example of what the author can do in the way of collecting dramatic clichés.

Joseph Wood Krutch, in a review of "Encyclopaedia of the Theatre," in The Nation, *Vol. 150, No. 2, January 13, 1940, p. 53.*

CONSTANCE FRICK (essay date 1943)

[*In the following excerpt, Frick discusses the evolution of Nathan's opinions, prose style, and point of view.*]

In the last twenty-seven years Nathan has written twenty-eight books, including three collaborations. Of the twenty-five books by Nathan alone, one is a novel (***Monks Are Monks***), and only one (***The New American Credo***) does not deal wholly or in part with the theatre.

"Everybody knows," as Randolph Bartlett observed, "there is not that much to be said about the theatre that is worth saying." The explanation is that Nathan's twenty-five books of critical miscellany are well padded—delightfully padded, to be sure—but padded, nonetheless, with dramatic, theatrical, philosophical, historical, and miscellaneous amblings. They make no pretense of being anything else, and that is half the secret of their charm. Almost inevitably they are front-heavy. The reader who seeks dramatic theory will find two-thirds of it packed into the first third of the book, but if he lays down the volume at that point he will miss most of the fun. This despite the fact that Nathan's books are often largely a compilation of his magazine articles.

Raucous, brilliant, malicious, shrewd and paradoxical, Nathan's volumes are thoroughly worldly, thoroughly American, and above all, thoroughly readable. For a penetrating comment on his earlier style, we do well to turn to his former collaborator, Mencken, who, in 1919, wrote:

> It would be difficult, in all his books, to find a dozen of the usual rubber stamps of criticism; I daresay it would kill him, or, at all events, bring him down with cholera morbus, to discover that he had called a play "convincing" or found "authority" in the snorting of an English actor-manager. At best, this incessant flight from the obvious makes for a piquant, arresting style, a procession of fantastic and often highly pungent neologisms—in brief, for Nathanism.

At worst, it becomes artificiality, obscurity [see excerpt dated 1919].

But even in 1919 Nathan was taking on "a sedater habit, both in style and in point of view. Without abandoning anything essential, without making the slightest concession to the orthodox opinion that he so magnificently disdains, he yet begins to yield to the middle years. The mere shocking of the stupid is no longer as charming as it used to be."

Thus, today, although Nathan describes fewer plays as "macaronic vacuity" or "pure rouge-stick walla-walla," which plays have evoked—from other critics, of course—either "bedizened encomiastic adjectives" (a dose of gravy) or "vociferous ululations" (lugubrious flapdoodle)—although, in other words, Nathan's style is less startling and less self-conscious, it is and probably always will be distinctly unorthodox and independent of academic standards, as invigorating as an icy draft.

After thirty-five years of the Nathan formula of linguistic dexterity, raffish mocking, gusty candor, and startling paradoxes, some of Nathan's steady readers begin to show signs of reaching the point of satiation. But the ring-master of American criticism will nonetheless continue to reach more readers than any other living dramatic critic, for, if he is at times too clever, he is, nevertheless, at all times entertaining. If he is at times irritating, he is, at the same time, provocative. If he occasionally deals flippantly in half-truths, it does not follow that he is necessarily superficial. And if there are occasional gaps in his logic, there are few gaps in the soundness of his critical judgment. Journalistic, gay, intolerant, cruel, he is nevertheless highly intelligent, thoroughly informed, critically incorruptible, a serious and painstaking worker with a well-defined point of view, a true lover of the theatre. (pp. 18-21)

Constance Frick, in her The Dramatic Criticism of George Jean Nathan, *Cornell University Press, 1943, 165 p.*

WOLCOTT GIBBS (essay date 1949)

[*An American drama critic, editor, journalist, and fiction writer, Gibbs was closely associated with* The New Yorker *throughout his career. He was an iconoclastic critic whose ironic reviews pilloried bad plays in general and ineptly sincere portrayals of social problems in particular. Gibbs was widely known for the eloquence of his sardonic appraisals (it has been said that he wrote more brilliantly of bad plays than of good ones) and is considered a master parodist on the order of Max Beerbohm. In the following excerpt Gibbs reviews* The Theatre Book of the Year: 1948-49, *finding it a testimony to Nathan's undiminished verve and critical abilities.*]

It is probably safe to estimate that, in the course of forty-three years as a critic, George Jean Nathan has witnessed and reviewed rather more than six thousand theatrical offerings of one kind or another, of which at least five thousand, to approximate his own idiom, were the work of rascals or numskulls, or both. To the average man, the idea of devoting so large a proportion of an adult life to conscientious autopsies on dead cats might easily be appalling, and the effect on his mind, if he were condemned to any such career, ghastly to contemplate. It is the everlasting miracle of Mr. Nathan that he has survived this crushing program, not only with all his faculties still intact but also with his first, fatal passion for the stage quite undiminished, and, most remarkable of all, with his capacity for expressing it as fresh, antic, and peculiar as it ever was, if not more so.

Since 1941, Mr. Nathan's collected opinions on the drama have taken the form of a series of annual volumes called **"The Theatre Book of the Year,"** the latest of which, covering the season of 1948-49, appears this week. (p. 117)

Assembled in a book, these judgments make, I think, about the most engaging body of light critical writing available in this country now. Mr. Nathan can be moderately silly when his special prejudices are involved ("I am prepared to believe that anything can happen in Hollywood, except maybe a movie that an intelligent coalheaver could look at without belching"); he can be as proudly Philistine as any character in "Babbitt" ("In painting, the application of thumbtacks, slices of old patent-leather shoes, and dabs of mayonnaise is made to pass for a revolutionary advance over the demoded performances of such reactionaries as Rembrandt, Rubens, and the unimaginative like"); politically, he can sound a good deal like the composite voice of Westbrook Pegler and Marie Antoinette ("He [Garson Kanin] is usually as bloodthirsty for a changed order as he is hostile to such cankers as men over forty with more than ten dollars in their custom-made pockets, women who prefer to marry fellows of some position, security, and reserve rather than the kind who would idealistically talk their ears off in romantic cold-water flats, and a world full of the odious ease, comfort, well-being, and sixty-cent lunches of the Coolidge era as against the glorious and inspiring chaos of today and, doubtless, tomorrow"); he can be a trifle elephantine when the style that was forged on the *Smart Set* and the old *Mercury* collapses into a sort of parody of itself ("Milada Mladova is one of the few ballet dancers whom one can look at, apart from technical proficiency, without suffering the impression that one is looking at a pair of oversize bowling pins attached to a keg of whitewash and quivering like a custard afflicted by an ague"); he can even, at least in the opinion of this generally acquiescent fellow-worker, be fairly highhanded and capricious in some of his judgements ("Miss Hunt, imported from England, either by personal choice or direction performs the role of the madwoman of the title not with the called for robust humor but largely in the manner of a repertory tragedy queen. . . . Miss Winwood offers stridency in place of tenderness and thus deletes the character of Constance, the madwoman of Passy, of its dramatic point; and most of the others are similarly guilty of botching things"). All these eccentricities appear frequently in Mr. Nathan's newest collection, but as far as the final result is concerned I can't believe they matter very much, having, indeed, rather the effect of humanizing a personality that might otherwise seem altogether too superior for this mortal world.

The qualities that make Mr. Nathan an almost continuous pleasure to read aren't especially easy to define. Style is, of course, a very important element, and in this respect it can be said that he is a wit of long experience and high technical skill. His methods are by no means unfamiliar, having been employed by intelligent humorists since the earliest days of steam. These include the sudden insertion of a notably frowzy word in a formal context, or, conversely, a stately one in a construction otherwise of low-comedy design; the building up of sentences that seem aimed at the stars and their abrupt reduction to absurdity; the conjunction of images that are at once totally disconnected and at the same time murderously appropriate; the employment of extravagant overstatement or understatement whenever an argument seems in danger of getting dull; the adroit misuse of punctuation, especially superfluous commas, for the purpose of extra emphasis; the seemingly casual introduction of pedantic reference, sometimes bogus and always comically irrelevant to the subject at hand; and the generous interpolation of admiring remarks about himself, such as an observation that his memory is such that he is habitually consulted by elephants. These, as noted, are standard mechanisms, but they have reached their perfection in his hands, and the result, if not precisely literature, is literary entertainment of a pretty high order.

While I am embarrassed to admit that Mr. Nathan fascinates me somewhat more as a genial essayist than as a critic or a scholar, it is obvious that he requires at least some consideration on both these points. Taking the last, and easiest, first, his information about the theatre, domestic and foreign, from Aristotle to Mae West, is enormous and incredibly detailed. There is scarcely any play whose plot and treatment doesn't remind him of a dozen deadly parallels, usually in almost as many languages; there is scarcely an actor who doesn't recall another and, with very few exceptions, a better one from the rosy and voluminous past; there is no serious critic, living or dead, whose theories are unknown to him or from whose works he is unable to quote copiously, most frequently to demonstrate that the silly fellow would have been far better engaged in the reading of gas meters.

Nor is his subject matter always so lofty. He is a formidable catalogue of every trained-animal act, putty-nose comic, sleight-of-hand artist, xylophone operator, and female impersonator since the spacious days of Harrigan and Hart; a prodigious grab bag of old jokes and forgotten vaudeville routines; and unquestionably the world's greatest living index of appetizing girls, of whom, in one delirious section of this volume, he lists by name no fewer than one hundred and seventy. There is conceivably something that Mr. Nathan doesn't know, remember, and love about the theatre, but if it is anything more useful than the name of the reviewer currently employed by the Kalamazoo *Gazette,* this admirer can't imagine what it is. (pp. 117-18, 121)

[Mr. Nathan] is as reliable a guide to the theatre as there is around today. In this book, he reviews some seventy-five exhibits of every imaginable kind, from Yiddish art to musical comedy, and though his vote is adverse about eighty per cent of the time, this estimate, sadly enough, seems almost exactly in line with the facts. Furthermore, his reasons, in each case in which the play in question is of sufficient quality to require reasons at all, are original, informed, and energetically expressed, if not necessarily deeply penetrating or even wholly proof against logical examination.

Thanks to the small critical opportunities offered by most of the plays he had to look at in a lamentable season, Mr. Nathan is often able to detour off into conversations about such comparatively dissociated matters as the nature of love, the acting prowess of his dog Maxim, the professional technique of the editors of *The New Yorker,* the negligible contributions made to art through the ages by persons who employ diminutives of their Christian names (he is gracious enough to except Walt Whitman and Ben Jonson but not, to my disappointment, the rare Red Smith), and, as previously reported, the names of various young women whose anatomies have stimulated him over the years. These are all lively and charming bypaths, but I think he reaches his tangential height in his piece about a revue called "Small Wonder," which held his attention so loosely that in the course of it he was able, or so he says, to jot down no fewer than fifty-five marginal notations on his program. There, in the busy dark, it seems that Mr. Nathan asked himself, without bothering with the answers, the following typical questions:

> That, however elaborate a stage dinner, there never seems to be any butter on the table?
>
> That even those critics who write most rapturously about J. M. Barrie feel it necessary to do some apologizing for him?
>
> That audiences will always applaud a stage setting that contains a large crystal chandelier?
>
> That I waste myself recording such trivial stuff as this and gaining a reputation for frivolity when I might be boring the reader to death and earning a fine reputation by printing instead a dull essay on "The Relation of the Aristotelian Aesthetic to the Drama of Racine and Corneille"?

It is probably too much to hope that Mr. Nathan will be especially gratified by my own answer to that last one, but anyway it is that while quite a number of people would be capable of writing the essay he specifies and some even of approximating the substantial and certainly not dull reviews of plays like "Death of a Salesman" and "Anne of the Thousand Days" that appear in this book, very few have any gift for the neat frivolity for which his reputation is unsurpassed and fewer still any conception of its value in a much too solemn field. There may, in fact, be only one. (pp. 121-22)

Wolcott Gibbs, "Nathan the Indestructible," in The New Yorker, *Vol. XXV, No. 35, October 22, 1949, pp. 117-18, 121-22.*

CHARLES ANGOFF (essay date 1952)

[Angoff was an American novelist whose most famous works examine Jewish-American life. He wrote feature articles for Boston newspapers before he was hired by H. L. Mencken as an assistant on The American Mercury, *where he worked almost continuously from 1925 to the early 1950s. While at the* Mercury, *he gained a wealth of personal observations about both the personal and professional relationship of Mencken and Nathan. His* H. L. Mencken: A Portrait from Memory *(1956), however, was greeted by intense critical disfavor, as he depicted Mencken as a mean-spirited, backbiting boor. Angoff was on much better terms with Nathan; the two were friends until Nathan's death. In the following excerpt, Angoff chronicles Nathan's influence on the American theater as well as sketching his theories of criticism and drama.]*

George Jean Nathan cannot properly be fitted into any critical or philosophical school. On occasion he practices the critical impressionism of Huneker, but he can also be profoundly dialectical, as can readily be seen by examining ***The Critic and the Drama,*** first published thirty years ago and still one of the most searching works of modern dramatic criticism in English. He has often donned the jester's cap with deliberate intent to bring forth smiles, laughter, and howls, and thus has led the superficial to put him down as little more than a critical vaudevillian, but he has also revealed so thorough a knowledge of dramatic and general cultural affairs that it has won the admiration of the most learned academicians. He has publicly acknowledged himself a hedonist, with personal pleasure as his only guiding principle, yet the day-to-day program of his life makes a mockery of his hedonistic philosophy; in point of fact, few writers work so hard and so conscientiously and with such iron self-discipline as he does. He claims to be indifferent to the generally accepted moral code, yet he lives by a very strict code himself, and that code is really not so different from the generally accepted one as he thinks. He has said some unfriendly things about America and Americans, but deep down in his soul he knows that he would be unhappy in any other country. (p. xv)

Nathan's influence on the American theatre during the past thirty years has been enormous. He, more than any other critic, was responsible for the emergence of the O'Neill drama, which first brought American dramaturgy to serious world attention. He also did much to bring the better European drama to this country. Bahr, Molnár, the Quinteros, Echegaray, Sierra, Pirandello, Lennox Robinson, Porto-Riche, Sach Guitry, the Čapeks, Georg Kaiser, and a score of others owe whatever hearing they have had among us largely to Nathan. More recently, he has labored heroically in behalf of Sean O'Casey, of whom he has written with profound understanding.

Nathan's theory of the drama is not something he has created *in vacuo*. It flows naturally from his theory of art, and this, in turn, flows naturally from his basic attitude toward life. He has put it in a nutshell thus: "Life, to me, is artificial; all my criticism of the drama is based on the theory that drama is artificial life. There isn't so very much difference, in my way of looking at things, between life as it factually is and life as it is shown in the theatre." To Nathan, then, the world is a theatre, and the two are subject to the same rules of criticism.

What relationship has art to "truth"? Nathan replies thus: "Art is the haven wherein the disillusioned may find illusion. Truth is no part of it. Nor is the mission of art simple beauty, as the textbooks tell us. The mission of art is the magnification of simple beauty to proportions as heroic as to be almost overpowering. Art is a gross exaggeration of natural beauty: there never was a woman so beautiful as the Venus di Milo, or a man so beautiful as the Apollo Belvedere of the Vatican, or a sky so beautiful as Monet's, or human speech so beautiful as Shakespeare's, or the song of a nightingale so beautiful as Ludwig van Beethoven's." Art, basically, is not logical. "Great art," says Nathan, "is as irrational as great music. It is mad with its own loveliness."

What is the nature of drama as an art? It is "dancing literature; a hybrid art," says Nathan. Thus it is—and has to be—often an inferior art. "Art is an evocation of beautiful emotions; art is art in the degree that it succeeds in the evocation; drama succeeds in an inferior degree. Whatever emotion drama may succeed brilliantly in evoking, another art succeeds in evoking more brilliantly." Literature, music, even painting and sculpture are greater arts than drama. Yet great drama has a garden—and not so small a one—that it alone can properly cultivate, and that garden has not seldom given forth a beauty unsurpassed by that of any other garden. "The drama is an art with a feather in its cap and an ironic smile upon its lips, sauntering impudently over forbidden lawns and through closed lanes into the hearts of those of us children of the world who have never grown up. Beside literature, it is the Mother Goose of the arts; a gorgeous and empurpled Mother Goose for the fireside of impressible and romantic youth that, looking upward, leans ever hushed and expectant at the knee of life. It is a fairy tale told realistically, a true story told as romance. It is the lullaby of disillusion, the chimes without the cathedral, the fears and hopes, and dreams and passions of those who cannot fully fear and hope and dream and flame themselves."

Art and happiness are not inevitably related. Says Nathan: "Great drama is the rainbow born when the sun of reflection and understanding smiles anew upon an intelligence and emotion which that drama has respectively shot with gleams of brilliant lighting and drenched with the rain of brilliant tears. Great drama, like great men and great women, is always just a little sad. Only idiots may be completely happy. Reflection, sympathy, wisdom, gallant gentleness, experience—the chords upon which great drama is played—these are wistful chords." The aim of great drama? It is "not to make men happy with themselves as they are, but with themselves as they might, yet always cannot, be."

Nathan, as has been said, does not subscribe to any particular theory of criticism. He believes that "there are as many sound and apt species of criticism as there are works to be criticized." The critic and the artist are, in a sense, collaborators. "Art is a partnership between the artist and the artist-critic. The former creates; the latter re-creates. Without criticism, art would of course still be art, and so with its windows walled in and with its lights extinguished would the Louvre still be the Louvre. Criticism is the window and the chandeliers of art; it illuminates the enveloping darkness in which art might otherwise rest only vaguely discernible, and perhaps altogether unseen."

Or, to put it differently, "As art is a process of magnification, so criticism is a process of reduction. Its purpose is the reducing of the magnifications of art to the basic classic and aesthetic principles, and the subsequent announcement thereof in terms proportional to the artist's interplay of fundamental skill and overtopping imagination."

Drama, says Nathan, "is a two-souled art: half divine, half clownish. Shakespeare is the greatest dramatist who ever lived because he alone, of all dramatists, most accurately sensed the mongrel nature of his art. Criticism of drama, it follows, is similarly a two-souled art: half sober, half mad. Drama is a deliberate intoxicant; dramatic criticism, aromatic spirits of ammonia; the re-creation is never perfect; there is always a trace of tipsiness left. Even the best dramatic criticism is always just a little dramatic. It indulges, a trifle, in acting. It can never be as impersonal, however much certain of its practitioners may try, as criticism of painting or of sculpture or of literature. This is why the best criticism of the theatre must inevitably be personal criticism. The theatre is itself distinctly personal; its address is directly personal. It holds the mirror, not up to nature, but to the spectator's individual idea of nature."

Nathan maintains that there is no such thing as objective criticism. "Criticism is personal, or it is nothing. Talk to me of impersonal criticism, and I'll talk to you of impersonal sitz-bathing. Impersonal criticism is the dodge of the critic without personality. Some men marry their brother's widow; some earn a livelihood imitating George M. Cohan; some write impersonal criticism."

Nathan's own criticism is most highly personal. It is thoroughly honest in that it is a perfect reflection of his personality. Perhaps the only one at all like him was George Bernard Shaw when he wrote musical and dramatic criticism. But Shaw himself, after he left the critical arena, hailed Nathan as "Intelligent Playgoer Number One." Gordon Craig considered Nathan even greater than Shaw. He said: "It would be a mistake to say that Mr. Nathan is as clever as Bernard Shaw . . . as a critic he is twice as clever. . . . To say that Mr. Nathan possesses a clearness of vision, a breadth of horizon and vigor of ideas seldom found in present-day dramatic criticism would be to miss the target. . . . Change the word 'seldom' to 'never' and you hit the bull's eye. . . . Add to this that Nathan is an artist and let us all sleep the better for the fact."

Like all good critics, Nathan can be read for himself, with little or no regard for the work or the writer he is writing about. His critical work has its own reason for being. Nathan has especially endeared himself to a host of readers by his utter lack of respectability, his persistent and wholly unmeasured childlike delight in saying precisely what is in his mind.

Nathan's evangelical labors in behalf of O'Neill are now historic. It is difficult to imagine what would have become of O'Neill if Nathan had not taken him in hand, so to speak, at the very beginning. He blew the trumpets for him season after season, badgered the Broadway producers to do him, shamed the Theatre Guild into sponsoring him, and then watched the momentum of all this tremendous effort win for O'Neill the Pulitzer Prize and, eventually, the Nobel Prize. While Nathan may have exaggerated O'Neill's claims to greatness, he has earned the enduring gratitude of the American people for tirelessly championing him. It was Nathan more than anybody else who made America realize what a treasure it had in the author of *The Moon of the Caribees, Bound East for Cardiff, Desire under the Elms,* and *Anna Christie*.

Nathan has not often been guilty of what he calls "bloomers" of blindness or overenthusiasm. It is truly remarkable how well his judgments, by and large, appear to hold up. Probably no other critic has been "right" more often than he has. His ability to give the long-view judgment seems to be almost fabulous. He hailed good works by Maxwell Anderson, S. N. Behrman, George Kelly, and Vincent Lawrence among others, immediately, and for reasons that carry conviction many years later. And he was equally quick to damn feeble works by the same authors, and for reasons that also carry conviction to this day.

As the drama, like every other art form, is filled with a far larger number of inferior than superior claims to serious attention, Nathan has found it necessary very often to be severe in his criticism. Who can deny the truth of Nathan's oft-repeated assertion that "dramatic art in America for the greater part has become a playwriting business, and its practitioners are largely racketeers with a dramatic sales talk, devoid of anything remotely resembling literary taste, literary ability, and literary education. Most of them read and act like pulp writers crossed with telegraph key-men."

One of Nathan's pet dislikes is Noel Coward, who, he has said, "has nothing to sell but his own vast personal boredom." What Nathan did to Coward's enormously successful, both commercially and critically, *Design for Living* will probably long be a model of critical vituperation. He branded it "a pansy paraphrase of *Candida,* theatrically sensationalized with 'daring,' gay allusions to hermaphrodites, 'gipsy queens,' men dressed as women, etc., and with various due references to 'predatory feminine carcases' and to women as bitches." The celebrated Coward humor? "This vaudeville humor Mr. Coward cleverly brings the less humorously penetrating to accept as wit by removing its baggy pants and red undershirt and dressing it up in drawing-room style. But it remains vaudeville humor just the same."

Another pet dislike of Nathan's is Clifford Odets, all of whose works (with the exception of *Awake and Sing*) impress him as little better than merchandise. (pp. xvi-xx)

Another dramatist whom Nathan cannot stomach is T. S. Eliot. *The Cocktail Party* was hailed as a masterpiece of drama, philosophy, and verse by most American and British critics. To Nathan it was, "plainly, bosh sprinkled with mystic cologne," and so "excessively windy" that "it might have profited Eliot if he had heard Joe E. Lewis's song, *Sam, You Made the Pants too Long*." But what troubled Nathan most was Eliot's message: "Eliot's religious philosophy, insofar as one can penetrate its opium smoke, here suggests that of a sophomore Methodist boning up for examinations in Catholicism, and his sexual philosophy is no less that of a man whose dalliance with women seems to have been confined to handholding in an ivory tower."

One of the pleasures of the theatre, to Nathan, is that "it is one of the best subjects in the world from which to fashion a variegated assortment of predicates. . . . [It] offers to the man who writes about it a hundred convenient opportunities to air his views *con sordini* on nearly everything under the sun." (p. xxi)

Nathan's work bristles with epigrams and paradoxes. In this respect he might be called, up to a point, the American Oscar Wilde. But the writer whose general outlook is most like Nathan's is Somerset Maugham. Both have made almost a personal religion of their utter indifference to mankind. Both boast of their concern only for themselves, of their dominating interest in the shimmer and dazzle of living, of their frankly cruel disregard for the miseries that perennially afflict the vast, silent majority of the two and a half billion men and women upon the earth. "What interests me in life," says Nathan, "is the surface of life: life's music and color, its charm and ease, its humor and its loveliness. The great problems of the world—social, political, economic, and theological—do not concern me in the slightest. . . . What concerns me alone is myself, and the interests of a few close friends. For all I care the rest of the world may go to hell at today's sunset" [see excerpt dated 1923]. Nathan's motto is "Be Indifferent." He looks upon society as designed solely for the pleasure and comfort of the aristocratic minority. "Life, as I see it, is for the fortunate few—life with all its magic lanterns, and sudden, lovely tunes, and gay sadness." (p. xxvi)

[Nathan] has the true artist's magnificent irrepressibility of spirit. He has added an engaging liveliness to the American scene. He has been a definite force in our cultural life. He will be remembered and he will be read, I believe, for a long time. (p. xxviii)

Charles Angoff, in an introduction to The World of George Jean Nathan *by George Jean Nathan, edited by Charles Angoff, Alfred A. Knopf, 1952, pp. xv-xxviii.*

THOMAS LASK (essay date 1970)

[In the following excerpt, Lask offers a general appraisal of Nathan's strengths and weaknesses as a drama critic.]

For a man who must have seen as many bad plays as he did, [Nathan's] involvement and concern for his subject will always be a surprise. There isn't a tired line in a thousand pages. He could be devastating, but he was never bored. Of one ill-conceived "Ghosts," he wrote of the Nora that when she walked out on her household and slammed the door, the audience rose as one man and rushed to the stage to congratulate the husband. And in reviewing a play by an English colleague,

Charles Morgan, a once popular novelist and drama critic, whose notices adorned the columns of this newspaper, he took the play apart with such exquisite surgical precision as to leave nothing over but the title and a few bare bones. His visits to London thereafter must have been made in a cape, wig, handlebar mustaches and under the name of Alexander Woollcott.

He could be loquacious, and if his imagination latched on to a fancy conceit, he would dance around like a fencing master playing with an amateur, nicking the skin here, slashing an ear off there and generally bloodying up the poor man before putting him at his ease with a lethal lunge. He was awfully good at infighting, not always genial, but deadly. He was formidably learned, and woe betide anyone, as the saying goes, who made even a casual assertion about the theater not warranted by the facts. Nathan would bury him under information to the contrary.

All this unfaltering interest is surprising in a way because he was a man of few enthusiasms. There wasn't, when you finally come down to it, very much that he liked. It is a lot easier for a reviewer to chart his dislikes than to tote up his loves. He was not a man of wide or generous taste. His occasional remarks about modern music, art or poetry show him to have been a philistine on the order of Mr. Lewis's Babbitt. In the nineteen thirties, when the material for these books was written, he held up to ridicule a piece of free verse and announced his unqualified support for Shelley, Keats and Swinburne—a stand that would not call out the police. And his remarks about Picasso could have come from a big butter-and-egg man from Fort Wayne, Ind. (where Nathan was born), but who had not been tutored in the finer things of life as Nathan was. He never tired of asserting that serious theater was for the educated few, but he seemed to think that anyone could get into the act in the other arts. He put the movies on the same level as detective fiction and the afternoon soap opera, and in essay after essay he disposed of the subject for what he thought would be the last time. Nathan, thou should'st be living at this hour!

He couldn't stand being lectured at. If he believed a playwright was more interested in persuading him to a point of view rather than in constructing the best play he knew how, he would peel his hide. Since the time was the thirties, he engaged in a running battle with the left-wing playwrights: John Wexley, John Howard Lawson, Albert Bein, Albert Maltz and others he called "The Little Red Writing Hoods." He credited Clifford Odets with glinting dialogue and a few memorable characters, but he thought his utterances about the theater generally were puerile. Judging from the quotations he cites, they were.

Nathan was particularly exercised about the playwrights who denounced capitalism on the one side and kept tapping the Hollywood till on the other. He makes this point three or four times. But it seems to me an argument of limited potency. Surely he must have collected a fair number of checks himself from newspapers and magazines whose editorial stand he didn't always endorse. But he was always fastidious about mentioning money at all. There is only the barest reference to the economics of Broadway. The theater was only art.

He did admire O'Neill and O'Casey. He had come to both early and remained steadfast in his admiration, although he distinguished the good from the bad. He liked Lillian Hellman's "The Children's Hour" and "The Little Foxes." He enjoyed the well-made comedies of S. N. Behrman. He hated esthetic pretentions and theatrical isms of all kinds. He was suspicious of theory. One reason surely that he couldn't stand the left-wing playwrights and such theater people as Edwin Piscator was that they talked so much. He believed the work had to carry its own convictions. Metaphysics was no substitute for what was happening on the stage.

Nathan was no cheer leader; he was an appraiser from the 50-yard line. But he knew more about the game than many a player who had to look up at the board to see what the score was.

Thomas Lask, "View from a Seat on the Aisle," in The New York Times, *December 30, 1970, p. 23.*

LOUIS KRONENBERGER (essay date 1971)

[*A drama critic for* Time *from 1938 to 1961, Kronenberger was a distinguished historian, literary critic, and author highly regarded for his expertise in eighteenth-century English history and literature. Among his best known writings are the nonfiction accounts* Kings and Desperate Men: Life in Eighteenth-Century England *(1942), which examines British culture of that century, and* Marlborough's Duchess: A Study in Worldliness *(1969), a biography of the wife of the first Duke of Marlborough. Of his critical work, Kronenberger's* The Thread of Laughter: Chapters on English Stage Comedy from Jonson to Maugham *(1952) and* The Republic of Letters *(1955) contain some of his best literary commentaries. In an assessment of Kronenberger's critical ability, Jacob Korg states: "He interprets, compares and analyzes vigorously in a pleasingly epigrammatic style, often going to the essence of a matter in a phrase." A prolific and versatile writer, he also wrote plays and novels and edited anthologies of the works of others. In the following excerpt, Kronenberger provides a balanced overview of Nathan's contribution to dramatic criticism.*]

Nathan became a kind of double-dealer in incompetence, slaughtering the plays he thought bad simultaneously with smacking down the reviewers who praised them. In many, perhaps most, cases he was altogether right, though in some cases he was intoxicated by the assignment and given to exaggerating the offense and to overworking his taste for derision and entombment. In other words, and like many other critics, the executioner strove to be an entertainer as well, and often could be. But, as with many other entertainers, his verbal tricks and stratagems tended to become hackneyed, and the entertainer, on occasion, could show a touch of the ham. In terms of his judgment Nathan proved of real value to the very end, but one found him less exhilarating in terms of his jokes. He dealt in triviality almost as much as he condemned it; he became as dependent on formula as the playwrights he took to task for it. This included formulas that were old-fashioned to begin with: satiric epithets and foreign words, puns and portmanteau words, and, worst of all, comically aimed polysyllabic ones. To be brief about them, consider such phrases as "the outhouses of Thespis" and "a fellow of considerable cerebral puissance." Even Nathan's straight style falls into such prose as "[a critic] infected with dubitations, some of them of such refractory magnetism that they at least momentarily pull him from his complacent anchor." Most surprisingly bad is Nathan's complimentary prose, as that concerning Maxwell Anderson's *Winterset:* "There is in some of his lines authentic song; in some of his scenes the flame of beautiful drama," while the play as a whole is a "mountain climb toward the peaks of dramatic-literary beauty."

Winterset brings us into the presence of Nathan's seriously treated drama criticism, which is to say his importance as a drama critic. To this, I think, there is no capsule answer, partly because so tremendously much of his criticism was concerned with plays that called for instant dismissal; partly because so relatively little of his criticism involved the highest levels for judgment; and partly because, as I have suggested, he was a very special figure in the range and diversity of his writings about the theater. He is really best classified as a man of the theater, as we speak of a man of letters, rather than as a drama critic. (p. 101)

The vast amount of time Nathan spent on trifling and worthless plays was, in a sense, part of his reviewing job (though no comparable literary, music, or art critic would devote a paragraph to nine tenths of such stuff). And in a sense Nathan perhaps strove to convert his job into a campaign, into a street-cleaning operation for Broadway. But any such attack was clearly bound to fall on deaf ears, since Broadway was lacking—and very anxious to remain lacking—in any aesthetic standards; if there is a good deal less junk today it is from Broadway's lacking its earlier economic support. Yet Nathan went far beyond any call of duty in exposing triviality and trash; he wrote countless pieces on such piddling subjects as how many all-female casts preceded *The Women* and on such cutie-cute ideas as dogs as actors, his staggering total recall often yielding pitifully fractional rewards.

As a critic of what called for thoughtful and judicious criticism, Nathan had unusual knowledge and experience of plays and playwrights, a keen theater sense, a sophisticated taste, a sharp eye for detail, and great responsiveness as well as great resistance to what he saw. He could also quickly pick up the scent of the pretentious and the *faux-bon,* and harry them with skill as well as scorn. He could, when it was necessary, cry down the very playwrights he delightedly cried up, O'Neill and Shaw among them. With less success, he somewhat specialized in confounding critics and playwrights with facts they overlooked, precedents they were unaware of, plays they were unacquainted with, contentions they could be proved wrong about, many of these being obvious setups in the service of put-downs.

Nathan's general theater writings are a virtual waterfall of ideas, but they manifest very little real thinking; some of his plunges into the other arts immediately drown his critical judgment; and sophisticated though he was, he could pedantically lard his text with such thoroughly dispensable allusions, citations, and testimonies that the result was far less criticism than catalogue. As a year-in, year-out reviewer of current plays he was as good a guide for the reasonably discriminating playgoer as could fairly be asked for; as a long-term, larger-scaled critic he was often discerning, but also fallible. He had from the first beat the drum for O'neill and O'Casey and admired Shaw and Synge; and he was both perceptive and educative about the generation of European playwrights from Hauptmann to Pirandello. He overrated Maxwell Anderson, including *Winterset;* overtouted Saroyan even when he showed merit; took quite the wrong tone about T. S. Eliot; at his first stage encounter with Lorca, demolished him; and could go surprisingly awry, as in speaking of the "deplorably unnecessary and absurd epilogue" of Shaw's *Saint Joan.*

But what seems to me most called for, particularly in so widely read a critic, is that at least one of his forty-five books should have devoted itself, with a certain amplitude, to the work of some eight or ten of the world's major playwrights. If this would have been a real, and I would think a relishable, test of his critical powers, in another sense it could have proved a greater surety for his critical survival. For, as things stand, even the main-stays of Nathan's Broadway have, with not too many exceptions, begun to dim or disappear; and for fairly panoramic criticism of almost all the theater's great playwrights, people will have to look elsewhere. This is rather a pity, for whatever his short-comings, Nathan wrote as a cultivated man of the world and a real initiate of the theater, where today's well-informed and serious-minded theater commentators are all too often pedagogues who pontificate in highbrow clichés and dreary jargon.

If, in terms of permanence, Nathan's is, critically, a disappointing contribution, his huge general output, performing a different function, may well have a more lasting value. Certainly no other American has provided so much and such miscellaneous information about the world of the twentieth-century stage. ***Encyclopaedia of the Theatre*** is in some degree evidence of this, its contents ranging from *Censors* to *Don'ts for Producers* to *Harlem* to *Program Notes* to *Vaudeville.* In ***Passing Judgments*** and ***The Theatre of the Moment,*** there are enjoyable pieces on, among others, O'Neill and Hecht & MacArthur as personalities. Nathan could be very lively in treating of personalities, and outside the theater as well as in—this reminding us that for many years he was Mencken's coeditor on the *Smart Set* and the *American Mercury,* and at the same time driving home the fact that no drama critic, from Aristotle on, has remained famous on the basis of his criticism alone. Very possibly, Nathan's most assured source of survival is his vast amount of comment, his vast citation of fads, oddities, coincidences, scandals, of stage traditions and taboos, of jokes and plots, of tag lines and tunes; his reminiscences of innumerable people; his information concerning the outskirts, the backwaters, the cemeteries of theater life. (pp. 101-02, 104)

Louis Kronenberger, "Broadway's Banner Years," in The Atlantic Monthly, *Vol. 227, No. 5, May, 1971, pp. 101-02, 104.*

JOHN SCHULTHEISS (essay date 1976)

[In the following excerpt, Schultheiss argues against Nathan's contention that Hollywood's movie industry corrupted the artistic careers of writers for the American theater.]

Many critics have found it fashionable to impute the artistic corruption of certain writers to their employment by Hollywood studios. This attitude was, of course, very prevalent during the 1930's and 1940's, when the studio-system approach to film-making involved large numbers of famous literary personalities in a working environment which was thought to be destructive to creative aspiration and inimical to the continuance of their independent writing careers.

Such critics as Edmund Wilson, Robert E. Sherwood, Ben Hecht—some of the best—have written vintage indictments of the system from the writer's point of view. . . .

But the undisputed paradigm of the traditional anti-Hollywood attitude was the vitriolic drama critic, George Jean Nathan, whose loathing for motion pictures was regularly asserted in his columns and books about the stage. His major concern was Hollywood's corruption of the American theater—the ruination of its best dramatists by Philistine rewards and "soul-destroying" diversions.

It may be illuminating to employ Nathan as the avatar of the anti-Hollywood position; for none of the so-called Eastern establishment critics has been as flamboyantly abusive of movies as Nathan. (p. 13)

Writers who share Nathan's critical sensitivities are always alert to any evidence in a dramatist's work which suggests concession to popular taste, any pursuit of commercial success over "art." The fear of the "sell-out" had disturbed critical purists before Hollywood ever existed. Indeed, *Merrily We Roll Along* (1934, George S. Kaufman and Moss Hart) and *No Time for Comedy* (1939, S. N. Behrman) are plays which dramatize the artistic and ethical dilemmas facing their playwright heroes in the American *theater*.

Thus, Nathan, for example, was quick to rankle at a subtle nod to commercialism in Zoë Akins' *Déclassée* (1919), which he saw as a comedown from her highly praised *Papa* earlier that same year. . . . (Domestic strife in the Broadway arena is bad enough, but when Ms. Akins did the unthinkable and went to Hollywood in 1930 to write for films, Nathan vituperatively denounced her regularly, with increased intensity, as a traitor.)

In-house feuds notwithstanding, Hollywood was indeed cast as the major villain, for, like Akins, almost every dramatist of note except Eugene O'Neill had a fling with the movies in the early sound period. Nathan could see only bad in it.

It is the contention of this essay, however, that the charges of Nathan and his colleagues against Hollywood are overstated and must be ameliorated by sober analysis of the writers' careers. The argument puts forward three points of re-evaluation:

1. The career patterns indicate that the writers who could be validly considered as having been "corrupted" by Hollywood were those who almost without exception must be evaluated as *minor* talents, those of questionable artistic longevity in the first place. Writers such as Vincent Lawrence, Edwin Justus Mayer, Maurine Watkins, George O'Neill, dramatists who perhaps enjoyed the highest critical standing of those whose work decreased or disappeared during their Hollywood years, created a void on the New York stage when they departed; but their playwriting contributions were arguably not artistically unique. The eclipse of these dramatists (as with any writer) may be just as logically explained in terms of the "normal" exhaustion or expiration of their creative fertility.

2. Many dramatists had talents better suited for the cinema than for the stage. There is no need to mourn the loss to traditional literature of the playwriting skills of Robert Riskin, Talbot Jennings, Sidney Buchman, Norman Reilly Raine, Howard Koch, Jane Murfin or Joseph Swerling, all of whom departed inauspicious stage beginnings for careers of exceptionally high achievement as screenwriters.

3. *Major* playwrights of considerably more puissant and flexible talent, such as Maxwell Anderson, Robert E. Sherwood, Lillian Hellman, S. N. Behrman, Marc Connelly, Sidney Howard, John Van Druten, could sustain periodic work on Broadway *and* in Hollywood. (pp. 14-15)

Of course, there is no space here for a detailed career analysis of each writer, but a characteristic sampling may be of interest because of Nathan's commentary on them. Laurence Stallings, for example, left earlier than most for Hollywood, still in the pre-sound era, after successful stage collaborations with Maxwell Anderson on *What Price Glory?* (1924), *First Flight*, and *The Buccaneer* (both 1925). The first few pictures which Stallings wrote—the classic *The Big Parade* (1925, directed by King Vidor), *Old Ironsides* (1926, James Cruze), *Show People* (1928, King Vidor)—were of sufficient quality to assuage the acid-tongued Nathan, who was able to be quite complimentary in 1928:

> Of all the playwrights, American and foreign, who have been imported to Hollywood, only one, Stallings, has shown the slightest sign of appreciating the difference between the screen and the stage and, by that mark, he is the only one of the lot who has been at all spectacularly successful.

And, surprisingly, by 1936, Nathan was still including Stallings, along with fellow playwrights Charles MacArthur and Ben Hecht who were also writing for Hollywood, in an evaluation that was generally favorable:

> All three have proved themselves superior to the muckworm spirit of the Hollywood factories and overlords; all three have retained a basic contempt (whatever their public face) for those factories and overlords; all three have in the last two or three years insisted upon doing their movie jobs in the neighborhood of New York, three thousand miles safely removed from Beverly Hills Spanish-Yiddish villas, illuminated swimming pools and purple and orange Rolls-Royces; and all three have been pretty frank in admitting that they haven't the intense aversion to mere money as money that most of the pure writing artists of Hollywood loudly proclaim *they* have.

Furthermore, Nathan was impressed by Stallings' modesty and candor when Nathan had asked the errant dramatist why he did not give up films long enough to produce another play of the calibre of *What Price Glory?*. Stallings candidly replied: "I'll tell you why. I've written everything I had to say and I'm not going to write anything when I haven't got anything more to say. I'm different from some fellows that way."

Nevertheless, Stallings sustained a moderate productivity during his screenwriting years. He was one of the first to use jazz in an operatic production, *Deep River* (1926), with New Orleans as background. *Rainbow* (1928, with Oscar Hammerstein) was another opera, set in the far West; and *Virginia* (1938, with Owen Davis) was an astute, cleverly conceived musical-play prototype of the latter-day *1776*. In 1930 Stallings made a dramatic version of Hemingway's *A Farewell to Arms*, a photographic, anti-war account of the First World War (1933), which became a best seller. (p. 16)

But if Laurence Stallings is representative of a specific group of dramatists who managed to produce a spasmodic literary effort (enough to prevent total *rigor mortis* in their original medium, at least), Vincent Lawrence can be thought of as head of the dubious category of playwrights who virtually rejected all forms of traditional literature for work in Hollywood. Lawrence had been considered one of the brightest writers on the Broadway stage in the 1920's when his plays like *Sour Grapes, Among the Married, Spring Fever, A Distant Drum,* and *Two Married Men* received enthusiastic critical praise. . . .

Lawrence did good work in Hollywood. There were qualities of irreverence, witty cynicism, and brilliant sophistication in his scripts which made him one of the most highly prized (and paid) screenwriters in Hollywood history. (p. 17)

When Lawrence finally returned to the literary front with *The Overtons* in 1945, Nathan, surprisingly enough, found some things to like in it. (Nathan did acknowledge that most drama critics in New York "have it in" for Hollywood screenwriters who attempt to write for the stage.) Nathan, himself, was magnanimous: "Though he is far from being the man he was before Hollywood took its toll of him, it is gratifying to learn that, for all his decline, at least some traces of his old seeing-eye still obstinately inhere in him." Nathan actually expressed, with a marvelous duplicity that occasionally characterized his ascerbic columns, regret that other critics had not taken sufficient notice of the many virtues to be found in the plays by Lawrence, when he chose to write them, and was saddened that bad reviews had "driven him back once again, downcast and discouraged, to Hollywood." (pp. 17-18)

While Hollywood has paid outlandish amounts of money to second-raters and those ill-suited to the theater (many of whom never wrote again for the stage in the same way), Hollywood also paid outlandish amounts of money to the top-raters, the cream of the Broadway dramatists who were perfectly equipped to write effectively for both motion pictures and the stage.

The contention that the major American dramatists were generally unaffected by their periodic involvements with Hollywood is partially supported by the fact that of the thirty-nine Pulitzer Prizes awarded for Drama from 1917 to 1960 (no awards were given in 1918, 1941, 1943, 1946, 1950), twenty-six were won by writers who had various commitments to Hollywood screenwriting. Sixteen of the awards were clearly earned in periods which occurred *after* the individual authors had spent time in the studios.

An initial listing of dramatists who produced work of significance in both realms of theatre and film would certainly include: Clifford Odets, Maxwell Anderson, Robert E. Sherwood, Zoë Akins, Moss Hart, Albert Hackett and Frances Goodrich [Hackett], John Patrick, Samson Raphaelson, John Van Druten, Sidney Howard, Lillian Hellman, Bella and Samuel Spewack, S. N. Behrman, Ben Hecht, Charles MacArthur. (p. 22)

Dramatists of superior stature such as these demonstrate that Hollywood, or any other economic temptation or psychological diversion, need not deleteriously affect an author's artistic strength or potential—if that individual writer is indeed committed to ultimate literary goals. George Jean Nathan, of course, would have preferred that, like his idol Eugene O'Neill, these dramatists would not have gotten mixed up with Hollywood at all. But if the writers of literary integrity and fortitude had listened to Nathan, their talents would have enhanced only one art form instead of two. (p. 23)

John Schultheiss, "George Jean Nathan and the Dramatist in Hollywood," in Literature/Film Quarterly, *Vol. 4, No. 1, Winter, 1976, pp. 13-23.*

WILLIAM H. NOLTE (essay date 1976)

[*Nolte is an American educator and essayist who has written extensively on the works of H. L. Mencken and Robinson Jeffers. In the following excerpt, he examines Nathan's unabashed hedonism as it relates to both his career and personal outlook.*]

Though he has not been awarded a niche in the pantheon of Great American Writers, George Jean Nathan certainly deserves a place in the annex of that sacred hall. I seriously doubt that many in our literate minority remember him at all. Try reciting his name to the average Harvard graduate and see what response you get. The few super-literates who do remember him are by now bent and gnarled by the spinning years and hence enjoying the skimpy usufructs of a life well (or badly) spent—such rewards, for example, as hardening of the arteries, senile dementia, transient ischemic attacks, visceral prolapse, the blind staggers, and a wonderful wondering as to what the hell it's all about. Before my favorite quack informs me that I have been thus blessed by my Maker, I want to pay this small tribute to dear Nathan, wherever he may now reside.

I daresay that most people who remember him at all remember him as the gunnery mate of Henry Mencken, who has long since been anointed, warts and all, and seated at the table with such indecorous savants as Rabelais, Swift, Voltaire, and Mark Twain. (p. 8)

If Nathan's stock never rose so high, neither did it sink so low as Mencken's did in the Great Depression when it became a favorite pastime among the proletarians, Marxists, and New Dealers to attack him as one of the false gods of the marketplace. . . .

Nathan suffered no such decline in reputation during his lifetime; only after he was gone did the light dim, and our collective memory fade. Although he was, so far as I can make out, just as honest and courageous as Mencken, and just as fond of thumbing his nose at pomposity and affectation, he really cared no more about political matters, or social justice, or manners and morals, or the national interest, or what delusions the people cherished, than did the average alley cat. Again and again in his books and articles he insisted that he was interested only in "the surface of life: life's music and colour, its charm and ease, its humour and its loveliness." But nowhere did he express his hedonism better than in the foreword to ***The World in Falseface***. . . . (p. 9)

I can admire what Nathan wittingly reveals here—that he knows what he wants from life and has no illusions about his essential selfishness. Bluntly and candidly, he viewed life as an aesthetic experience devoid of moral meaning—in fact, lacking any meaning whatsoever, save that which humans impose upon it. A good deal, I believe, can be said for such a view. But the credo also reveals, unwittingly, a man firing blank cartridges at a target that doesn't exist. Remove the rather exotic flowers from that tapestry of prose and you will see right through it and into the front parlor of most dwellings, high or low. Far from setting himself apart by his admitted egotism, Nathan has simply confessed that he is like most other people, but without the moral fustian that some employ to hide their tracks as they move from one attained (or unattained) goal to the next.

Unfortunately he was not content with that one avowal of self-interest. Reading various of his books recently I was struck by his preoccupation with himself, with his apparent need to flaunt his rather hollow-sounding hedonism in the reader's face. In ***The Autobiography of an Attitude*** . . . , he informs us that the older he becomes the more he is "persuaded that hedonism is the only sound and practical doctrine of faith for the intelligent man." Not content with that sweeping generalization, he adds that he doubts if "there ever has lived an intelligent man whose end in life was not the achievement of a large and selfish pleasure." From there he moves to the view that altruism is itself a form of hedonism, that it is, indeed, "the highest flowering of selfishness." If all of us are hedonists, I see no reason for either bragging or complaining about the fact. Nathan is least interesting when discoursing on his favorite subject—that is, himself.

There were other interests, of course—primarily, his abiding and, to me at least, baffling love for the theatre, or more precisely for drama, since, as Nathan pointed out, much of

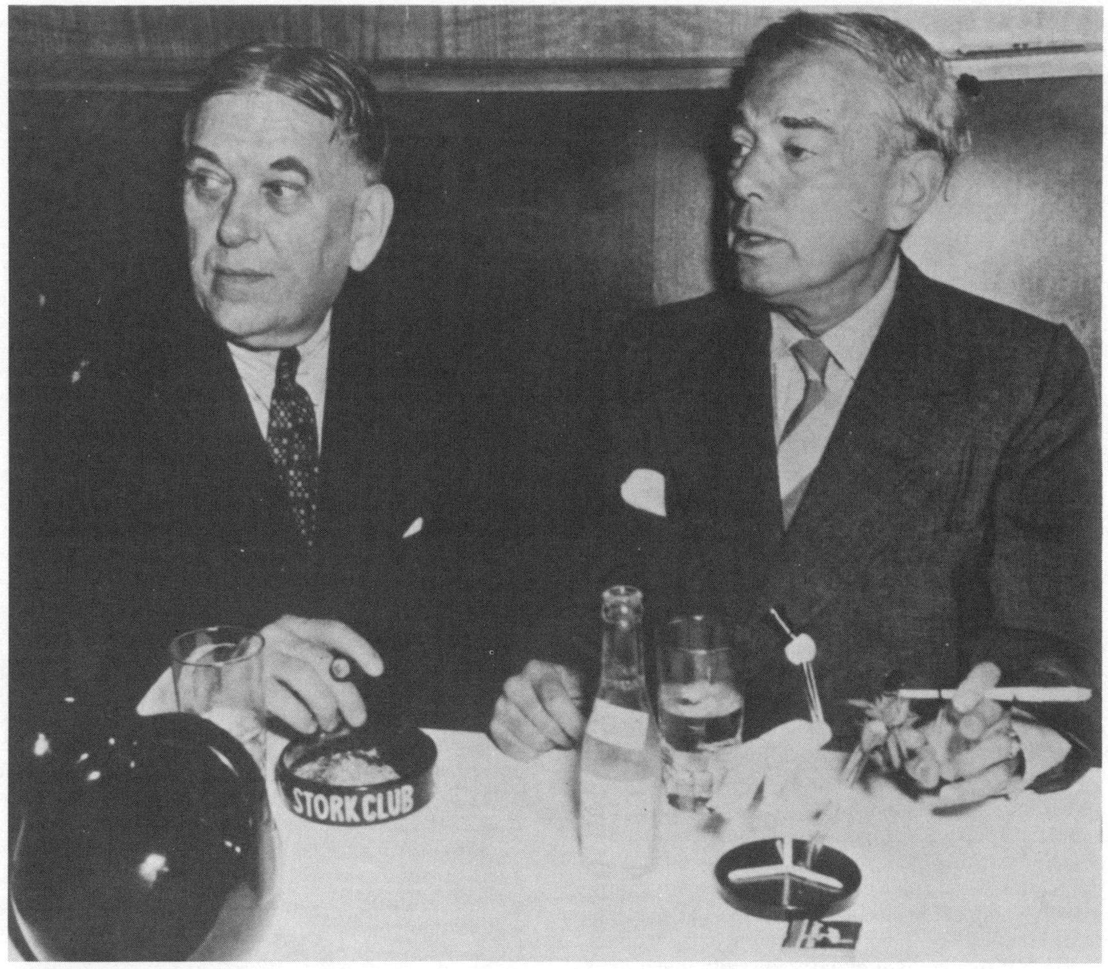

Mencken and Nathan in 1947 at the Stork Club in New York. Reprinted by permission of Alfred A. Knopf, Inc.

what comes under the heading of "the theatre" has little to do with plays or drama. I have little doubt that Nathan's narcissism helps explain that enduring interest. In an essay on Nathan, in *Prejudices: First Series,* Mencken wondered what could keep so intelligent a man returning night after night to the theatre, "breathing bad air nightly, gaping at prancing imbeciles, sitting cheek by jowl with cads" [see excerpt dated 1919]. Perhaps it was "a secret romanticism—a lingering residuum of a boyish delight in pasteboard and spangles, gaudy colors and soothing sounds, preposterous heroes and appetizing wenches." But more likely it was simply a sense of humor, a delight in spectacle that was "infinitely surprising, amusing, buffoonish, vulgar, obscene." To this he added a final peradventure: "The theatre . . . is not life in miniature, but life enormously magnified, life hideously exaggerated. Its emotions are ten times as powerful as those of reality, its ideas are twenty times as idiotic as those of real men, its lights and colors and sounds are forty times as blinding and deafening as those of nature, its people are grotesque burlesques of every one we know. Here is diversion for a cynic."

With such a description (some would call it an indictment) of the drama, and of nightflies attracted to it, Nathan offered no complaint. Rather, indeed, a corroboration. He considered all art as being artificial life, which was itself artificial. Back to Platonism: the artifice of an artifice of the Real, whatever the Real might be; certainly Nathan never claimed to know. While such a view helped him keep an open mind concerning art, keep an objective distance between the viewer and the thing being viewed, it also prevented him from ever taking the theatre too seriously. It enabled him to see the shallowness of ideological drama and "message" plays of playwrights like Clifford Odets, Robert Sherwood, Maxwell Anderson, T. S. Eliot, Arthur Miller, and other assorted special pleaders. When he took his aisle seat in a theatre he carried with him one of the most finely-tuned crap-detectors of his time. . . . In a devastating piece on Sartre's *No Exit,* much admired by those who had never seen all his shopworn borrowings in print before, Nathan first identified the source of the plagiarisms and then offered this closing reminder:

"That such and similar worn ideas should be regarded as noteworthy mental achievements is, nevertheless, not surprising. Even at their most familiar and obvious they are tablets from the mount in comparison with much of what passes for mentality in the drama of Broadway. After a starvation diet, even a slightly senescent pork chop seems pretty wonderful. We should not forget that Ibsen shook the claptrap reasoning of the English-speaking stage off its feet with ideas which, while strange to the theatre, were not materially above the intellectual level of a popular novelist. Nor should we forget that Shaw subsequently shook Ibsen off his feet in turn by heaving himself into the latter's domain and at the very outset staggering audiences far and wide with, for the first time from a stage, a facile parroting of doctrines culled from Schopenhauer, Nietzsche, and Marx.

"A Sartre, of course, is no remotest, faintest Ibsen or Shaw, but he seems to be onto the trick of rubbing one platitude against another and producing what the credulous see as brilliant sparks."

What Nathan says here needed saying—even though it, too, is a parroting of what Mencken had written about Shaw and Ibsen some forty years before. Indeed, I was astonished in going through Nathan's books to note the pervasive influence of Mencken on all aspects of Nathan's thought.

When not writing about the drama, Nathan churned out thousands of words on such favorite subjects as women, marriage, sex, doctors, vacations, his more famous friends, everything in fact that in any way occupied his time or attention. Writing was as much a part of his daily existence as breathing. Needless to say, particularly since various others have pointed it out, Nathan was extremely repetitious; what he liked he wrote about over and over, and often in almost the same words. Strangely enough, he never mastered the essay form. I say strangely since one would expect a writer whose talent was critical in nature to have organized his thoughts in some kind of progressive manner, to have begun with a thesis, then supported it in a hierarchical fashion that led inevitably, logically to a conclusion that at least came within waving distance of where he began. After overcoming an early tendency toward prolixity, and at times turgidity, he became an adept craftsman in the making of sentences that glitter and sting. I suspect that La Rochefoucauld taught him much about the making of aphorisms, as I know Nietzsche did. He could never resist stretching an analogy until it snapped in his hand, and in the reader's face, as here: "It is possible a man may love only one woman in his life. So, for that matter, is it equally possible that a man get through life with only one pair of trousers." Or this: "Marriage is based on the theory that when a man discovers a particular brand of beer exactly to his taste he should at once throw up his job and go to work in the brewery." Those "work" well enough, but this one draws a blank: ". . . such is the baffling drollery of human nature that a man's wife ever seems to him a virgin." Here's one from Nietzsche's waste basket: "Beware the sexlessness of those who talk most of sex!" If you've heard a politician speak lately this should ring a bell: "All that is necessary to raise imbecility into what the mob regards as profundity is to lift it off the floor and put it on a platform." This one requires a double-take: "God is just. He has reserved most of the prettiest legs for homely women." One that I wish I had thought of: "The argument most often advanced for the abolition of capital punishment is that it has not successfully deterred and doesn't deter persons from committing murder. One might with equal logic therefore argue for the abolition of all forms of punishment in that none so far devised has succeeded in deterring persons from committing theft, perjury, arson, assault, bigamy, holdups, rape, or anything else." My favorite, though, is one that he shares with some anonymous wag: "In the words of a friend of mine, I drink to make other people interesting." (pp. 9-10)

[In 1951, Nathan] was baptized in the Roman Catholic Church. His parents, incidentally, were part Jewish, but his mother had been a practicing Catholic. When asked why he thus renounced his agnosticism for the Church of Rome, he is reported to have answered, ever the pleasure-seeker, "Because I want to go to Heaven." In the end his selfishness turned to Glory. Well, I hope he made it. (p. 10)

William H. Nolte, "George Jean Nathan: Mencken's Gunnery Mate," in The Alternative: An American Spectator, *Vol. 9, No. 10, August-September, 1976, pp. 8-10.*

RICHARD K. RUSSELL (essay date 1984)

[In the following excerpt, Russell briefly examines Nathan's important contribution to the early numbers of The American Mercury.*]*

George Jean Nathan has been approached in many ways. To some observers, he was no more than a satellite of Mencken. For others, he was the finest drama critic ever produced in America. As the critic for "The Theatre" in the *Mercury,* he was not as cleverly succinct as Oscar Wilde, or Eugene Field, nor as nastily vitriolic as Alexander Woollcott. His short comments on plays, more often than not, consisted of: "is trash," "fetches the yokels," "hornswaggle at the box office" and other such phrases. Nathan was at his best in longer reviews where he would assiduously list stereotypes, clichés, and stock situations. He was also a master at applying reductio ad absurdium to the plots of shaky and borderline plays. Though Nathan was primarily a theater and culture critic, his style made him a first class humorist. The combination of the two, however, comprise the primary reason that Nathan is disregarded today as both a critic and a humorist. His criticism, in many cases, was too jocular to be taken seriously. His humor was often too serious to be enjoyed for itself. He would follow up a clever review in which he sliced up Noel Coward as ". . . so many goldfish trying heroically to swim the ocean" with a silly critique of a motion picture advertisement dominating his entrie column in the succeeding number.

"Clinical Notes" was a much better showcase for Nathan's talents than "The Theatre," though it is doubtful Nathan considered it so. It is indicative of the overshadowing of Nathan by Mencken that some of Nathan's better comments are attributed to Mencken. The definition of Puritanism as "the haunting fear that someone, somewhere, may be happy," is Nathan's and yet is often attributed to Mencken. "Clinical Notes" was much more universal and timeless a feature than any regular department of the *Mercury*. Nathan discussed such topics as the Harvard Classics, George Bernard Shaw, and G. K. Chesterton, while Mencken, at his best, in "Americana," was mired in names and situations indigenous to the contemporary situation of the 1920's. (p. vii)

Richard K. Russell, in a foreword to The American Mercury, A Monthly Review: Facsimile Edition of Volume I, *Freedeeds Books, 1984, pp. iii-xii.*

ADDITIONAL BIBLIOGRAPHY

Angoff, Charles. "The Tone of the Twenties" and "George Jean Nathan." In his *The Tone of the Twenties and Other Essays*, pp. 17-28, pp. 47-61. South Brunswick, N.J.: A. S. Barnes and Co., 1966.

Imparts the flavor of the 1920s and provides an informal interview revealing Nathan's private personality.

Brown, John Mason. "The Importance of Being Nathan." In his *Two on the Aisle: Ten Years of the American Theatre in Performance*, pp. 299-302. New York: W. W. Norton & Co., 1938.

Originally a review of *The Morning after the First Night*. Brown offers high praise for the book and catalogs the qualities that distinguish all of Nathan's writings.

———. "The State of the Nathan." In his *Seeing Things*, pp. 83-90. New York: McGraw-Hill Book Co., 1946.

Reviews *The Theatre Book of the Year: 1944-45*, happily finding Nathan's critical faculty and distinctive style unmarred by the passage of time.

Ervine, St. John. "Ervine on Nathan." *The Living Age* 340, No. 4376 (May 1931): 306.

Playfully chides Nathan about his long period of bachelorhood, then praises his work as a critic. "The fact that a rich and vigorous literature is now pouring out of the United States," writes Ervine, "is due in large measure to Mr. Mencken and Mr. Nathan."

Fitzgerald, F. Scott. Letter to George Jean Nathan. In his *The Letters of F. Scott Fitzgerald*, edited by Andrew Turnbull, pp. 470-71. New York: Charles Scribner's Sons, 1963.

A 1922 letter containing praise for *The Critic and the Drama*.

Knopf, Alfred A. "H. L. Mencken, George Jean Nathan, and the *American Mercury* Venture." *Menckeniana*, no. 78 (Summer 1981): 1-10.

Quotation-laden exposition of the Mencken-Nathan split.

O'Casey, Sean. *The Flying Wasp*. London: Macmillan & Co., 1937, 201 p.

Scattered brief, laudatory references to Nathan. O'Casey laments that there are no English critics of Nathan's critical discernment and verbal audacity writing on the state of the contemporary London theater.

Friedrich (Wilhelm) Nietzsche

1844-1900

German philosopher, essayist, poet, and autobiographer.

The Granger Collection, New York

Nietzsche is considered one of the most important figures in modern philosophy, and his thought has influenced nearly every aspect of modern culture. Among his many achievements, he is credited with being a forerunner of existentialism, the first philosopher to recognize nihilism as a historical phenomenon and to utilize it as a source for positive values, and an important psychological theorist to whom Sigmund Freud was admittedly grateful, especially for the psychoanalytic concepts of sublimation and repression. Nietzsche was a master stylist, reintroducing the aphorism to German prose, and he had a profound effect in the field of epistemology, particularly in his assaults on the reliability of language. Besides his impact on philosophy and psychology, Nietzsche significantly shaped the development of twentieth-century literature. Such writers as Rainer Maria Rilke, Stefan George, Gottfried Benn, Thomas Mann, Hermann Hess, André Gide, William Butler Yeats, and George Bernard Shaw were all influenced by Nietzsche's works. In general, Nietzsche has had a crucial effect on the intellectual development of Western society: his thought signified the disintegration of the nineteenth century's social, religious, and scientific optimism and anticipated the nihilist sensibility of the modern world.

Nietzsche was born in Röcken, Prussia. His father and both of his grandfathers were ministers and Nietzsche's early childhood was spent in a devoutly religious environment. When Nietzsche was four years old, his father suffered a serious fall, injured his head, and died soon after. Two years later his mother moved the family to Naumburg, where Nietzsche grew up in a household of five women: his mother, his grandmother, two maiden aunts, and his younger sister, Elizabeth. His relationships with these women, critics suggest, account for some of Nietzsche's prejudicial comments about women in later years. Between 1858 and 1864 he attended the Schulpforta, a famous boarding school outside Naumburg, where he acquired a thorough education in classical literature and history. Upon graduation he entered the University of Bonn, where he studied theology and classical philology, but in 1865 he decided against theology and transferred to the University of Leipzig. There he studied under the noted philologist Friedrich Ritschl and discovered the works of Arthur Schopenhauer and Richard Wagner, the two greatest influences on his early thought. It was as a student that Nietzsche supposedly contracted syphilis after visiting a Cologne brothel, a claim that has never been validated. This illness has been the focus of much debate because of Nietzsche's eventual madness—which most experts agree was probably caused by tertiary syphilis—and because of Thomas Mann's treatment of it in his novel *Doktor Faustus* (*Doctor Faustus*), wherein the protagonist, Adrian Leverkühn, contracts syphilis and follows a path into insanity similar to Nietzsche's.

After a brief military service between 1867 and 1868, Nietzsche was recommended by Ritschl for the chair of classical philology at the University of Basel. Although he had not yet written a doctoral thesis, nor the dissertation required before a doctor of philosophy becomes a university lecturer, Nietzsche was appointed associate professor at the age of twenty-four. While at Basel he occasionally visited Wagner at his home in Tribschen, Switzerland. The two became close friends, though for Wagner the friendship assumed a more practical purpose: in Nietzsche he found a young, responsive scholar who could lend authority to his artistic vision—the rebirth of German myth in drama and music. For his part, Nietzsche greatly admired Wagner and believed that his music was the modern incarnation of Hellenic tragedy. Out of this association came one of Nietzsche's most important works: *Die Geburt der Tragödie aus dem Geiste der Musik (The Birth of Tragedy)*. The final sections of the book, added to the original draft after Wagner befriended Nietzsche, consist of a rhapsody on the rebirth of tragedy in Wagner's operas. Following the publication of *The Birth of Tragedy,* the Nietzsche-Wagner friendship began to suffer; a second book on Wagner was postponed several times until the publication in 1876 of *Richard Wagner in Bayreuth*—a slender volume which completed Nietzsche's four-volume *Unzeitgemässe Betrachtungen (Thoughts Out of Season)*. These volumes all focus on the deterioration of German culture following the Franco-Prussian war.

Throughout his life Nietzsche's health was poor. He suffered from a number of ailments, including severe headaches, gastric pains, diarrhea, and partial blindness. In 1879 his poor health forced him to retire from his post at the university. Yet he continued reading and writing. During the late 1870s and early 1880s he published three books—*Menschliches, Allzumenschliches: Ein Buch für freie Geister (Human, All Too Human: A Book for Free Spirits), Die Morgenröte: Gedanken über die moralischen Vorurteile (The Dawn of Day),* and *Die fröhliche Wissenschaft (The Joyful Wisdom)*—each of which noted a shift in his interests from art and aesthetics to science and "the free spirit," an individual unfettered by conventions or history. These works were soon followed by Nietzsche's most renowned publication: *Also sprach Zarathustra: Ein Buch für Alle und Keinen (Thus Spake Zarathustra: A Book for All and None).* Published in four volumes, *Thus Spake Zarathustra* contains the first presentation of Nietzsche's mature philosophy. It is here that he introduces his concepts of the will to power, the *Übermensch* (the "overman" or "superman"), and the eternal return. All of Nietzsche's subsequent works, especially *Jenseits von Gut und Böse: Vorspiel einer Philosophie der Zukunft (Beyond Good and Evil: Prelude to a Philosophy of the Future)* and *Zur Genealogie der Moral (On the Genealogy of Morals),* support and elaborate the ideas put forth in *Thus Spake Zarathustra*. Nietzsche wrote his final works during an extended period in 1888 when his health seemed to be improving. Of these the most significant are *Die Götzendämmerung; oder, Wie man mit dem Hammer philosophiert (The Twilight of the Idols)* and *Der Antichrist (The Antichrist).* In both works Nietzsche violently attacked Christianity, proclaiming the superiority of his own philosophy of heroic vitalism. In January 1889, Nietzsche collapsed on a street in Turin, Italy. He was extremely disoriented, and he grew progressively worse until he became a complete mental and physical invalid. He lived for eleven years before his death at Weimar.

Many critics divide Nietzsche's work into three periods, each one representing a different stage in the development of his thought. The first, from 1872 to 1876, culminates in a philosophy based on the Dionysian, or destructive, aspect of music; the second, from 1878 to 1882, is noted for its break with metaphysical speculation and its emphasis on nihilism and a pragmatic approach to the world; the third, from 1883 to 1889, contains Nietzsche's three-point theory of the will to power, the *Übermensch,* and the eternal return, and is recognized for its prophetic and polemical character. Although some critics argue that the sudden shifts in Nietzsche's philosophical thought demonstrate the erratic nature of his intellect, others, such as Rudolf Steiner, Eric Bentley, and Peter Heller, believe a single idea passes through and unifies each stage. For Steiner this idea is the concept of the *Übermensch;* for Bentley it is Nietzsche's concept of power; for Heller it consists of Nietzsche's dedication to the Dionysian process.

Nietzsche's first important essay, *The Birth of Tragedy,* deals specifically with the deterioration of Greek culture following the rise of rationalist Socratic thought. Nietzsche believed that before Socrates Greek culture consisted of two tendencies: the Apollonian—the process of restraint, harmony, and measure that found expression in Greek sculpture and architecture—and the Dionysian, a savage longing to resist all norms that found its outlet in the drunken orgies of the Dionysian festivals and the music associated with them. In *The Birth of Tragedy,* Nietzsche challenged the prevalent conception of Greek art by positing the idea that Hellenic tragedy was essentially the outcome of the Apollonian-Dionysian synthesis—the Dionysian captured in the chorus and the music and the Apollonian represented by the actors and the text. Essentially, Greek tragedy—at its very beginning—sought to affirm life in the presence of the terrors of nature and history. After Socrates, when the quest for rational rather than mystical truth became the preoccupation of philosophers, Greek culture began to deteriorate; the Dionysian was suppressed in favor of the Apollonian, and art, as well as culture, became obsessed with the beauty of form. Nietzsche took up this theme of cultural decadence again in his next work, *Thoughts Out of Season,* but this time with respect to Germany in the 1870s, which he believed was following a course similar to the Greeks in its attraction to systems of external forms and empirical thought. Following attacks on David Strauss, whom Nietzsche considered a "cultural philistine," and the German educational system, he praised Schopenhauer as a relentless thinker who possessed the courage to form his own vision of the world—one which attacked the same optimistic spirit and facile rationalism of the nineteenth century that Nietzsche also deplored.

The second period in Nietzsche's development, which begins with *Human, All Too Human,* signified a dramatic shift in his philosophy. He rejected Schopenhauer and Wagner for Voltaire and Socrates; he attacked art and metaphysics and, instead, espoused science and free thinking. All of the works in this period—*Human, All Too Human; The Dawn of Day;* and *The Joyful Wisdom*—demonstrate the meaninglessness of the world and the decadent origin of religion, especially Christianity. Nietzsche constructed a portrait of the human being as an animal devoid of free will, acting strictly out of fear or desire. He also suggested a number of concepts which are more fully developed in his final works, such as the will to power and the contrast of master and slave moralities. Here power is defined as the individual's ability to give "style" to his or her character. Master and slave moralities are tied directly to Nietzsche's critique of Christianity, the former born out of affirmation and a desire to live, the latter born of resentment and fear. Essentially, the works of this period served to free Nietzsche from the influence of Schopenhauer and Wagner—a separation which had to occur before he could completely control the direction of his thought.

The third and final period in Nietzsche's career consisted of seven books, but none are as prominent as *Thus Spake Zarathustra*. This imaginative work alternates between essay and parody, epigram and dithyramb, wit and bathos. Here, through the persona of his prophet Zarathustra, Nietzsche set forth his concept of the will to power as the essence of all beings. According to Nietzsche, what every living being wants more than anything else is a higher, more powerful state of existence in which the inertia of the present state is overcome. Power is a process of becoming; it never achieves its end, but is always seeking to surpass its present state. From the concept of power Nietzsche constructs his ideal individual: the *Übermensch*. The *Übermensch* is the highest type to which humanity should strive; he is the human being who has organized the chaos of his passions, given style to his character, and become creative. Aware of the meaninglessness of life, the *Übermensch* affirms life without resentment. What sets the *Übermensch* apart from general humanity is the ability to endure the implications determined by Nietzsche's most mystical doctrine: the "eternal return of the same." This hypothesis states that the universe evolves in gigantic cycles, repeating itself at distant intervals. To Nietzsche the ramifications of such a concept are obvious: if one's life is to be endlessly repeated throughout eternity, it is extremely important—in order to endure this phenomenon—that one accept and affirm existence without resentment. In this scheme, which can be viewed as an antithesis to the Christian conception of time and history, the world no longer has a purpose; it is an eternally repeated senseless play of forces and it takes someone of the spiritual stature of the *Übermensch* to affirm life in the face of such a gruesome prospect. The remainder of Nietzsche's works after *Zarathustra* more or less elaborate on these concepts, with the exception of his caustic autobiography *Ecce Homo: Wie man wird, was man ist (Ecce Homo)*. This book is the most controversial of Nietzche's final works. With such chapter titles as "Why I Am So Wise" and "Why I Write Such Excellent Books," *Ecce Homo* was attacked by many critics as self-serving and without literary merit, and Nietzsche was called a megalomaniac. However, the autobiography offers an insightful account of Nietzsche's philosophical development; and what early critics considered self-aggrandizing was later considered Nietzsche's sense of humor and irony. Nietzsche's last major work, published after his death, is *Der Wille zur Macht (The Will to Power)*. This book consists of some of the notes Nietzsche accumulated from 1884 to 1888, systematically arranged by his sister. Although the systematic arrangement makes it easy to see what Nietzsche had to say about religion, morality, epistemology, art, and so forth, it is not generally regarded as Nietzsche's magnum opus, as some critics and scholars have argued. Although Nietzsche planned to write a book called "The Will to Power"—later changed to "Revaluation of All Values," of which *The Antichrist* was to be the first volume—most critics agree that the version published by his sister in no way approximates what the author himself might have accomplished.

The history of Nietzsche criticism is nearly as diverse and complex as the author's work itself. Early critics found it difficult to assess Nietzsche's philosophy. Some argued that he was pathological and that his work was the result of a sick mind. Although most critics were not this extreme, many felt that Nietzsche's thought was at best interesting, but hardly demanded serious consideration. However, there were a few interpreters, in particular Georg Brandes and Rudolf Steiner, who understood the significance of Nietzsche's ideas, both for their own times and for the twentieth century. They praised the author for his awareness of the cultural decay in Europe, for his insights into individual psychology, and for his studies in ethics and morality. As a result of Brandes's lectures and work on Nietzsche, the philosopher's popularity increased steadily during the 1890s, reaching its peak at the outbreak of World War I. After the war Nietzsche fell out of favor, but his ideas were taken up again, with even more vigor, during the 1930s by the National Socialists in Germany. With the encouragement of Nietzsche's sister, the Nazis systematically perverted his thought for the purpose of propaganda, particularly Nietzsche's concept of the will to power, which the Nazis interpreted exclusively in terms of military superiority, and his concept of the "overman," which was cited as justification of the Nazi claim that Aryans constituted a superior race. They also attributed to Nietzsche feelings of anti-Semitism and nationalism which are the precise opposite of his stated views. Because of his erroneous association with Nazi ideology, Nietzsche was unjustly attacked during and immediately following World War II. Some critics tried—as did Thomas Mann—to reevaluate Nietzsche's work in the light of contemporary events, but it wasn't until the 1950s and 1960s that Nietzsche once again received favorable international attention. New interpretations of his work came to the forefront: Walter Kaufmann published the first edition of his landmark study on Nietzsche, and Martin Heidegger attempted to demonstrate the integrity of Nietzsche's philosophy—a philosophy, Heidegger argued, designed to answer the question of being. Today Nietzsche is considered one of the most imposing figures of the nineteenth and twentieth centuries. He is often praised for his theories on Greek culture, many of which were derided in his lifetime; for his views on decadence and nihilism; for his experiments with language, which were later developed by the phenomenologists and deconstructionists; and for his contribution to the field of psychology. At the same time, Nietzsche has been criticized for his failure to develop a systematic philosophy, for his dogmatism, for his glorification of power, for the impracticality of many of his ideas, and for his attacks on metaphysics, though he was probably one of the most metaphysical thinkers of his age. Ultimately, critics agree that Nietzsche is most important for the influence of his ideas—for the effect of his thought rather than the validity of its presentation.

Although there are more than four thousand books and articles on Nietzsche, critics and scholars have only begun to assess his impact on twentieth-century thought. More than seventy-five years after his death, his life and work have lost none of their fascination. Nietzsche's appeal is confined to no single group; it crosses all boundaries. To use the word he applied to himself in *Ecce Homo,* he became a "destiny" for many people, including some of the leading artists and thinkers of the twentieth century.

(See also *TCLC,* Vol. 10 and *Contemporary Authors,* Vol. 107.)

PRINCIPAL WORKS

Die Geburt der Tragödie aus dem Geiste der Musik (essay) 1872
[*The Birth of Tragedy* published in *The Complete Works of Friedrich Nietzsche,* Vol. 1, 1909]
**Unzeitgemässe Betrachtungen*. 4 vols. (essays) 1873-76
[*Thoughts Out of Season* published in *The Complete Works of Friedrich Nietzsche,* Vols. 4 and 5, 1909-10]
***Menschliches, Allzumenschliches: Ein Buch für freie Geister*. 2 vols. (essays and aphorisms) 1878-80
[*Human, All Too Human: A Book for Free Spirits,* 1908]
Die Morgenröte: Gedanken über die moralischen Vorurteile (essays and aphorisms) 1880
[*The Dawn of Day,* 1903]
Die fröhliche Wissenschaft (essays and aphorisms) 1882
[*The Joyful Wisdom* published in *The Complete Works of Friedrich Nietzsche,* Vol. 10, 1910]
Also sprach Zarathustra: Ein Buch für Alle und Keinen: 4 vols. (prose) 1883-85
[*Thus Spake Zarathustra: A Book for All and None,* 1909]
Jenseits von Gut und Böse: Vorspiel einer Philosophie der Zukunft (essays and aphorisms) 1886
[*Beyond Good and Evil: Prelude to a Philosophy of the Future,* 1907]
Zur Genealogie der Moral (essays and aphorisms) 1887
[*On the Genealogy of Morals* published in *The Complete Works of Friedrich Nietzsche,* Vol. 13, 1910]
Der Fall Wagner: Ein Musikanten-Problem (essay) 1888
[*The Case of Wagner* published in *The Complete Works of Friedrich Nietzsche,* Vol. 8, 1911]
Die Götzendämmerung; oder, Wie man mit dem Hammer philosophiert (essays) 1889
[*The Twilight of the Idols* published in *The Complete Works of Friedrich Nietzsche,* Vol. 16, 1911]
Nietzsche contra Wagner: Aktenstücke eines Psychologen (essay) 1889
[*Nietzsche Contra Wagner* published in *The Complete Works of Friedrich Nietzsche,* Vol. 8, 1911]

Dionysus Dithyramben (poetry) 1891
Der Antichrist (essays) 1895
[*The Antichrist,* 1920]
Ecce Homo: Wie man wird, was man ist (essays) 1908
[*Ecce Homo,* 1911]
Der Wille zur Macht (notebooks, essays, and aphorisms) 1909-10
[*The Will to Power* published in *The Complete Works of Friedrich Nietzsche,* Vols. 14 and 15, 1909-10]
The Complete Works of Friedrich Nietzsche. 18 vols. (essays, aphorisms, notebooks, and poetry) 1909-13
Gesammelte-Werke. 23 vols. (essays, aphorisms, notebooks, and poetry) 1920-29
Selected Letters of Friedrich Nietzsche (letters) 1921
Fifty Poems (poetry) 1965

*This work includes the essays *David Strauss, der Bekenner und der Schriftsteller (David Strauss, the Confessor and the Writer), Vom Nützen und Nachteil der Historie für das Leben (On the Uses and Disadvantages of History for Life), Schopenhauer als Erzieher (Schopenhauer as Educator),* and *Richard Wagner in Bayreuth.*

**This work includes the essay *Der Wanderer und sein Schatten (The Wanderer and His Shadow).*

HAVELOCK ELLIS (essay date 1898)

[*Ellis was a pioneering sexual psychologist and a respected English man of letters. His most famous work is his seven-volume* The Psychology of Sex *(1897-1928), a study containing frankly stated case histories of sex-related psychological abnormalities that was greatly responsible for changing British and American attitudes toward the hitherto forbidden subject of sexuality. In addition to his psychological writings, Ellis edited the Mermaid Series of sixteenth through eighteenth century English dramatists (1887-89) and retained an active interest in literature throughout his life. As a critic, according to Desmond MacCarthy, Ellis looked for the expression of the individuality of the author under discussion. "The first question he asked himself as a critic," wrote MacCarthy, "was 'What does this writer affirm?' The next, 'How did he come to affirm precisely that?' His statement of a writer's 'message' was always trenchant and clear, his psychological analysis of the man extremely acute, and the estimate of the value of his contribution impartial. What moved him most in literature was the sincere expression of preferences and beliefs, and the energy which springs from sincerity." In the following excerpt, Ellis offers an early general appraisal of Neitzsche's thought.*]

We are helped in understanding Nietzsche's philosophic significance if we understand his precise ideal. The psychological analysis of every great thinker's work seems to reveal some underlying fundamental image or thought—often enough simple and homely in character—which he has carried with him into the most abstract regions. . . . In all Nietzsche's best work we are conscious of [the] ideal of the dancer, strong, supple, vigorous, yet harmonious and well-balanced. It is the dance of the athlete and the acrobat rather than the make-believe of the ball-room, and behind the easy equipoise of such dancing lie patient training and effort. . . . When in his later years Nietzsche began, as he said, to "philosophise with the hammer," and to lay about him savagely at every hollow "idol" within reach, he departed from his better ideal of dancing, and his thinking became intemperate, reckless, desperate.

Nietzsche had no system, probably because the idea that dominated his thought was an image, and not a formula, the usual obsession of philosophers, such as may be clapped on the universe at any desired point. He remarks in one place that a philosopher believes the worth of his philosophy to lie in the structure, but that what we ultimately value are the finely carven and separate stones with which he builded, and he was clearly anxious to supply the elaborated stones direct. In time he came to call himself a realist, using the term, in no philosophic sense, to indicate his reverence for the real and essential facts of life, the things that conduce to fine living. He desired to detach the "bad conscience" from the things that are merely wicked traditionally, and to attach it to the things that are anti-natural, anti-instinctive, anti-sensuous. He sought to inculcate veneration for the deep-lying sources of life, to take us down to the bed-rock of life, the rock whence we are hewn. He held that man, as a reality, with all his courage and cunning, is himself worthy of honour, but that man's ideals are absurd and morbid, the mere dregs in the drained cup of life; or, as he eventually said—and it is a saying which will doubtless seal his fate in the minds of many estimable persons—man's ideals are his only *partie honteuse,* of which we may avoid any close examination. Nietzsche's "realism" was thus simply a vigorous hatred of all dreaming that tends to depreciate the value of life, and a vivid sense that man himself is the *ens realissimum.*

A noteworthy point in Nietzsche's conception of philosophy is his increasingly clear conception of its fundamentally psychological character. I mean to say that Nietzsche knows that a man's philosophy, to be real, must be the inevitable outcome of his own psychic constitution. It is a point that philosophers have never seen. Perhaps Nietzsche was the first, however hesitatingly, to realise it. It is only in the recognition of this fact that the eirenicon of philosophies—and one might add, of religions—can ever be found. (pp. 68-71)

To recognise the free and direct but disconnected nature of Nietzsche's many-sided vision of the world is to lessen the force of his own antagonisms as well as of the antagonisms he has excited. Much of Nietzsche's work, especially in the [final] period, is the utterance of profound half-truths, keenly and personally felt, but still half-truths of which he has himself elsewhere supplied the complements. The reason is that during that period he was not so much expressing himself as appealing passionately against himself to those failing forces whose tonic influence he thirsted after. The hardness, the keen sword, the reckless energy he idealised were the things that had slipped utterly away and left him defenceless to the world. . . . Such an attitude has its rightness and power, so long as we understand it, though it comes short of the serenity of the greatest spirits who seek, like Goethe, to live at each moment in the whole. The master-morality of Nietzsche's later days, on which friends and foes have alike insisted, is a case in point. This appears to have been hailed, or resented, as a death-blow struck at the modern democratic *régime.* To take a broad view of Nietzsche's philosophic attitude is to realise that both views are alike out of place. On this matter, as on many others, Nietzsche moved in a line which led him to face an opposite direction in his decay from that which he faced in his immaturity. He began by regarding democracy as the standard of righteousness, and ended by asserting that the world only exists for the production of a few great men. It would be foolish to regard either of the termini as the last outpost of wisdom. But in the passage between these two points many excellent things are said by the way. (pp. 72-4)

Nietzsche was not, however, greatly interested in questions of government; he was far more deeply interested in questions of morals. In his treatment of morals—no doubt chiefly in the last period—there is a certain element of paradox. It must again be pointed out that this is to be explained by the organic demands of Nietzsche's own nature. In attacking the excessive tendency to sympathy which he seemed to see around him he was hygienically defending himself from his own excessive sympathy. . . . It was because he had himself suffered from the excesses of his own sympathy that he was able so keenly to analyse the secrets of sympathy. He spoke as the Spanish poet says that every poet—and indeed every seer—must always speak, *por la boca de su herida,* through the mouth of his wound. That is why his voice is often so poignantly intimate; it is also why we sometimes find this falsetto note of paradox. In his last period, Nietzsche grows altogether impatient of morals, calls himself an immoralist, fervently exhorts us to become wickeder. But if any young disciple came to the teacher asking, "What must I do to become wickeder?" it does not appear that Nietzsche bade him to steal, bear false witness, commit adultery, or do any other of the familiar and commonly accepted wickednesses. Nietzsche preached wickedness with the same solemn exaltation that Carducci lauded Satan. What he desired was far indeed from any rehabilitation of easy vice; it was the justification of neglected and unsanctified virtues. (pp. 74-6)

There still remains Nietzsche, the apostle of culture, the philosopher engaged in the criticism of life. From first to last, wherever you open his books, you light on sayings that cut to the core of the questions that every modern thinking man must face. . . . He looks at every question that comes before him with the same simple, intent, penetrative gaze, and whether the aspects that he reveals are new or old, he seldom fails to bring us a fresh stimulus. Culture, as he understood it, consists for the modern man in the task of choosing the simple and indispensable things from the chaos of crude material which to-day overwhelms us. The man who will live at the level of the culture of his time is like the juggler who must keep a number of plates spinning in the air; his life must be a constant training in suppleness and skill so that he may be a good athlete. But he is also called on to exert his skill in the selection and limitation of his task. Nietzsche is greatly occupied with the simplification of culture. Our suppleness and skill must be exercised alone on the things that are vital, essential, primitive; the rest may be thrown aside. He is for ever challenging the multifarious materials for culture, testing them with eye and hand; we cannot prove them too severely, he seems to say, nor cast aside too contemptuously the things that a real man has no need of for fine living. What must I do to be saved? What do I need for the best and fullest life?—that is the everlasting question that the teacher of life is called upon to answer. And we cannot be too grateful to Nietzsche for the stern penetration—the more accute for his ever-present sense of the limits of energy—with which he points from amid the mass to the things which most surely belong to our eternal peace. (pp. 79-81)

Whether he was dancing or hammering, however, Nietzsche certainly converted the whole of himself into his work, as in his view every philosopher is bound to do, "for just that art of transformation *is* philosophy." That he was entirely successful in being a "real man" one may doubt. His excessive sensitiveness to the commonplace in life, and his deficiency in the sexual instinct—however he may have rated the importance of sex in life—largely cut him off from true fellowship with the men who are most "real" to us. . . . Every man, indeed, works with the limitations of his qualities, just as we all struggle beneath the weight of the superincumbent atmosphere; our defects are even a part of our qualities, and it would be foolish to quarrel with them. Nietzsche succeeded in being himself, and it was a finely rare success. Whether he was a "real man" matters less. With passionate sincerity he expressed his real self and his best self, abhorring, on the one hand, what with Voltaire and Verlaine he called "literature," and, on the other, all that mere indigested material, the result of mental dyspepsia, of which he regarded Carlyle as the supreme warning. A man's real self, as he repeated so often, consists of the things which he has truly digested and assimilated; he must always "conquer" his opinions; it is only such conquests which he has the right to report to men as his own. His thoughts are born of his pain; he has imparted to them of his own blood, his own pleasure and torment. Nietzsche himself held that suffering and even disease are almost indispensable to the philosopher; great pain is the final emancipator of the spirit, those great slow pains that take their time, and burn us up like green wood. "I doubt whether such pain betters us," he remarks, "but I know that it deepens us." That is the stuff of Nietzsche's Hellenism, as expressed in the most lighthearted of his books. . . . It is that which makes him, when all is said, a great critic of life.

It is a consolation to many—I have seen it so stated in a respectable review—that Nietzsche went mad. No doubt also it was once a consolation to many that Socrates was poisoned, that Jesus was crucified, that Bruno was burnt. But hemlock and the cross and the stake proved sorry weapons against the might of ideas even in those days, and there is no reason to suppose that a doctor's certificate will be more effectual in our own. . . . Nietzsche has met, in its most relentless form, the fate of Pascal and Swift and Rousseau. That fact may carry what weight it will in any final estimate of his place as a moral teacher: it cannot touch his position as an aboriginal force. He remains in the first rank of the distinguished and significant personalities our century has produced. (pp. 82-5)

Havelock Ellis, "Nietzsche," in his Affirmations, *second edition, 1898. Reprint by Houghton Mifflin Company, 1922, pp. 1-85.*

JORGE LUIS BORGES (essay date 1934)

[An Argentine short story writer, poet, and essayist, Borges is one of the leading figures in contemporary literature. His writing is often used by critics to illustrate the modern view of literature as a highly sophisticated game. Justifying this interpretation of Borges's works are his admitted respect for stories that are artificial inventions of art rather than realistic representations of life, his use of philosophical conceptions as a means of achieving literary effects, and his frequent variations on the writings of other authors. Such characteristic stories as "The Aleph," "The Circular Ruins," *and* "Pierre Menard, Author of the Quixote" *are demonstrations of the subjective, the infinitely various, and the ultimately indeterminate nature of life and literature. Accompanying the literary puzzles and the manipulations of variant models of reality, there is a somber, fatalistic quality in Borges's work which has led critics to locate his fictional universe in close proximity to the nightmarish world of Franz Kafka and the philosophical wasteland of Samuel Beckett. In his literary criticism, Borges is noted for his insight into the manner in which an author both represents and creates a reality with words, and the way in which those words are variously interpreted by readers. With his fiction and poetry, Borges's critical writing shares the perspective that literary creation of imaginary worlds and philosophical spec-*

ulation on the world itself are parallel or identical activities. In the following excerpt, Borges offers an analysis and a refutation of Nietzsche's doctrine of eternal recurrence.]

This doctrine (which its most recent inventor calls the eternal return) can be formulated thus:

"The number of all the atoms which make up the world is, although excessive, finite, and as such only capable of a finite (although also excessive) number of permutations. Given an infinite length of time, the number of possible permutations must be exhausted, and the universe must repeat itself. Once again you will be born of the womb, once again your skeleton will grow, once again this page will reach your same hands, once again you will live all the hours until the hour of your incredible death." Such is the customary order of the argument, from its insipid prelude to the enormous, threatening dénouement. It is usually attributed to Nietzsche.

Before refuting the doctrine—an undertaking of which I am not sure I am capable—we must imagine, at least from afar, the superhuman numbers that it involves. I will begin with the atom. The diameter of an atom of hydrogen has been calculated, providing for error, at a hundred-millionth of a centimeter. This dizzying smallness does not mean that it is indivisible: on the contrary, Rutherford defines it with the image of a solar system made up of central nucleus and a revolving electron 100,000 times smaller than the atom as a whole. Let us put aside the nucleus and the electron and consider a frugal universe made up of ten atoms. (We are dealing of course with a modest experimental universe: invisible, given that microscopes do not even suspect its existence; imponderable, since no scale will be able to measure it.) Let us also postulate—in accordance with Nietzsche's conjecture—that the number of changes in that universe equals the number of ways in which the ten atoms may be arranged by varying the order in which they are placed. How many different states can that world know before an eternal recurrence? The calculation is easy: simply multiply $1 \times 2 \times 3 \times 4 \times 5 \times 6 \times 7 \times 8 \times 9 \times 10$, a tedious operation which will give us the sum of 3,628,800. If an almost infinitesimal particle of the universe is capable of that variety, we can lend little or no credence to the monotony of the cosmos. I have considered ten atoms; in order to obtain two grams of hydrogen we would need considerably more than a billion billions. To compute the number of possible changes in that pair of grams—that is, to multiply a billion billions by each one of the whole numbers that precede it—is already an operation far beyond the human limits of my patience.

I do not know if my reader is convinced; I am not. The painless and chaste extravagance of enormous numbers creates without a doubt that peculiar pleasure common to all excess. Yet the regression remains more or less eternal, even though in very remote terms. Nietzsche could reply: "Rutherford's revolving electrons are a novelty for me, and so is the idea—so scandalous for a philologist—that an atom may be split. However, I never denied that the vicissitudes of matter were numerous; I only declared that they were not infinite." This likely answer from Friedrich Zarathustra obliges me to fall back on Georg Cantor and his heroic theory of aggregates.

Cantor destroys the foundation of Nietzsche's thesis. He affirms the perfect infinity of the number of points in the universe, and even of a meter of the universe, or a fraction of that meter. The operation of counting is nothing more for him than that of comparing two series. For example, if the oldest sons of all the houses of Egypt were killed by the Angel except those living in houses which had a red sign on the door, it is obvious that as many were saved as there were red marks, without it being necessary to enumerate how many marks there in fact were. Here the quantity is indefinite; there are other groupings in which it is infinite. The set of natural numbers is infinite, but it is possible to demonstrate that there are as many odd numbers as there are even.

1 corresponds to 2
3 corresponds to 4
5 corresponds to 6, etc.

The proof is as irreproachable as it is worthless, but it is no different from the following one which proves that there are as many multiples of 3018 as there are numbers—without excluding from these 3018 and its multiples.

1 corresponds to 3018
2 corresponds to 6036
3 corresponds to 9054
4 corresponds to 12,072, etc.

It is possible to affirm the same of its powers, even though the powers must be ratified as we progress in the series.

1 corresponds to 3018
2 corresponds to 3018^2 or 9,108,324
3 corresponds etc.

A brilliant acceptance of these facts has inspired the formula that an infinite collection—for instance, the natural series of whole numbers—is a collection whose members can split off in turn into infinite series. (Better yet, to avoid any ambiguity: an infinite set is that set which can equal one of its partial sets.) In these elevated latitudes of enumeration, the part is no less copious than the whole; the exact quantity of points in the universe is the same as in a meter, or in a decimeter, or in the farthest stellar trajectory. The series of natural numbers is well ordered; in other words, the terms which form it are consecutive: 28 precedes 29 and follows 27. The series of the points in space (or of the instants in time) cannot be ordered in the same way; no number has an immediate successor or predecessor. It is like the series of fractions according to magnitude. What fraction shall we enumerate after $\frac{1}{2}$? Not $\frac{51}{100}$, because $\frac{101}{200}$ is closer; not $\frac{101}{200}$ because $\frac{201}{400}$ is closer; not $\frac{201}{400}$ because . . . The same thing happens with points, according to George Cantor. We can always insert others in infinite numbers. However, we should try not to imagine decreasing dimensions. Each point is already the end of an infinite subdivision.

This brush of Cantor's lovely game with Zarathustra's lovely game is fatal for Zarathustra. If the universe consists of an infinite number of terms then it is absolutely capable of an infinite number of combinations, and the need for a recurrence is invalidated. Only its mere possibility remains, calculated at zero. In the autumn of 1883, Nietzsche wrote: "And this slow spider which creepeth in the moonlight, and this moonlight itself, and thou and I in this gateway whispering together, whispering of eternal things—must we not all have already existed? And must we not return and run in that other lane out before us, that long weird lane—must we not eternally return?—Thus did I speak, and always more softly, for I was afraid of mine own thoughts and arrear-thoughts." Three centuries before the cross, Eudemos wrote: "If we are to believe the Pythagoreans, the same things will return regularly and you will be with me once again and I will repeat this doctrine and my hand will play with this stick and all else will be the same." In the Stoic cosmogony, "Zeus feeds upon the world": the universe is consumed cyclically by the same fire which engendered it and rises up again from annihilation to repeat an identical history. Once again the various seminal particles are combined, once again they give form to rocks, trees, and men—and even to virtue and to days, since for the Greeks no noun was possible without some corporeality. Once again, each sword and each hero; once again, each night of meticulous insomnia.

Like all the other conjectures of the school of Porticus, this one about general repetition spread with time and its technical name, *apokatastasis,* was recorded in the Gospel, although for unknown reasons (Words of the Apostles, III, 21). Book Twelve of the *Civitas Dei* of Saint Augustine devotes several chapters to the rebuttal of such an abominable doctrine. The chapters (which I have before me now) are too involved to be summarized. However, the episcopal fury of their author seems directed at two targets: one, the showy uselessness of the circle; the other, the fact that reason should die like an acrobat on the cross, in interminable functions. Farewells and suicides lose their dignity if they are repeated; Saint Augustine must have thought the same of the crucifixion. This explains why he rejected the reasoning of the Stoics and the Pythagoreans so vehemently. They argued that God's knowledge is unable to comprehend infinite things and that the eternal rotation of the worldly process serves to familiarize God with it; Saint Augustine mocks their useless revolutions and affirms that Jesus is the straight path which permits us to flee from the circular labyrinths of such deceits.

In the chapter of his *Logica* which deals with the law of causality, John Stuart Mill declares that a periodic repetition of history is conceivable—but not true. He cites Virgil's "messianic eclogue":

Jam redit et Virgo, redeunt Saturnia regna . . .

Could Nietzsche, a Hellenist, possibly have been ignorant of his predecessors? Nietzsche, the author of fragments on the pre-Socratics—could he not have known of a doctrine learned by the disciples of Pythagoras? It is very difficult to believe that this is so—and besides, useless. It is true that Nietzsche, in a memorable note, has indicated the precise spot in which the idea of the eternal return came to him: a path in the woods of Silvaplana, near a vast pyramidal block, one noontime in August of 1881—"six thousand feet beyond men and time." It is true that the instant is one of Nietzsche's glories. He would write: "The moment in which I begot recurrence is immortal, for the sake of that moment alone I will endure recurrence." . . . It is my opinion, however, that we must not postulate such surprising ignorance, nor any human confusion—human enough—between inspiration and memory, nor any crime of vanity. My key is of a grammatical, almost a syntactical nature. Nietzsche knew that the eternal return is one of those fables or fears or diversions that recur eternally, but he also knew that the most effective grammatical person is the first person. For a prophet, it is the only one. For reasons of voice and anachronism—or typography—it was impossible for Zarathustra to derive his inspiration from an epitome, or from the *Historia Philosophiae Graeco-Romanae* of Ritter and Preller, substitute professors. The prophetic style does not permit the use of quotation marks or erudite allegations to books and authors. . . .

If my human flesh assimilates the brutal flesh of sheep, who will prohibit the human mind from assimilating mental states? From so much thinking about it and suffering it, the eternal return of all things belongs to Nietzsche, and not to a dead man who is little more than a Greek name. I will not insist: Miguel de Unamuno has already written his piece on the adoption of thoughts.

Nietzsche wanted men able to bear immortality. I say this with the words found in his personal notebooks, in the ***Nachlass,*** where he also wrote: "Ye fancy that ye will have a long rest ere your second birth takes place—but do not deceive yourselves! 'Twixt your last moment of consciousness and the first ray of the dawn of your new life no time will elapse—as a flash of lightning will the space go by, even though living creatures think it is billions of years, and are not even able to reckon it. Timelessness and immediate rebirth are compatible, once intellect is eliminated!"

Before Nietzsche, personal immortality was merely a hopeful equivocation, a confused project. Nietzsche proposes it as a duty and confers upon it the atrocious lucidity of an insomniac. "Not sleeping," I read in the classic treatise [*Anatomy of Melancholy*] by Robert Burton, "hardily crucifies the melancholy." We know for a fact that Nietzsche suffered from that crucifixion and had to seek salvation in the bitterness of chloral hydrate. Nietzsche wanted to be Walt Whitman; he wanted to fall in love with every detail of his destiny. He followed a heroic method; he unearthed the intolerable Greek hypothesis of eternal repetition and tried to extract from that mental nightmare an occasion for rejoicing. He looked for the most terrible idea in the universe and held it up for the delight of men. The facile optimist generally imagines that he is Nietzschean; Nietzsche confronts him with the circles of the eternal return and spits him from his mouth.

Nietzsche wrote: "We must not strive after distant and unknown states of bliss and blessings and acts of grace, but we must live so that we would fain live again and live forever so, to all eternity!" Mauthner objects that to attribute the slightest moral influence (that is, practice) to the thesis of the eternal return is to negate the thesis—since that is the same as imagining that something could happen differently. Nietzsche would respond that the formulation of the eternal return and its prolonged moral influence (that is, practice) and Mauthner's ruminations and his own refutation of Mauthner's reminations are just so many necessary moments of world history, the work of atomic agitations. He could justly write what he had already written: "Even supposing the recurrence of the cycle is only a probability or a possibility, even a thought, even a possibility can shatter us and transform us. It is not only feelings and definite expectations that do this! See what effect the thought of eternal damnation has had!" And elsewhere, "From the moment when this thought begins to prevail all colors will change their hue and a new history will begin."

At times the sensation of having already lived a certain moment leaves us wondering. The partisans of the eternal return assure us that such is the case, and in these perplexing states they find a corroboration of their beliefs. They forget that memory implies a change that would negate the thesis, for time would continue to perfect it until that distant cycle in which the individual would be able to foresee his destiny and choose to act in another way. . . . Moreover, Nietzsche never spoke of a mnemonic confirmation of the return.

Nor did he speak—and this should be stressed also—of the finiteness of atoms. Nietzsche denies atoms; to him atomic structure seemed to be just a model of the world, made exclusively for the eyes and for arithmetic understanding. . . . In order to establish his thesis he spoke of a limited force developing itself in infinite time, yet incapable of an unlimited number of variations. He was not laboring without perfidy; first he warns us against the idea of an infinite force—"let us beware of such orgies of thought"—and then he generously concedes that time is infinite. Similarly, he enjoys availing himself of the concept of previous eternity. For example, an equilibrium of the cosmic force is impossible, since if it were not, it would already have operated in a previous eternity. Or: universal history has happened an infinite number of times . . . in a previous eternity. The invocation appears to be valid, but one must remember that previous eternity or *aeternitas a parte ante* (as the theologians called it) is nothing more than our natural inability to conceive of a beginning to time. We suffer from the same inability with regard to space, so that to invoke a previous eternity is as convincing as invoking a right hand infinity. I will state it in another manner: if time is infinite for the intuition, then space is also. The previous eternity has nothing to do with the real time which elapses. Let us go back to the first second and we will note that it requires a predecessor, and that predecessor another, and so on into infinity. In order to staunch this *regressus in infinitum,* Saint Augustine resolves that the first second in time coincides with the first second of creation: *non in tempore sed cum tempore incepit creatio*.

Nietzsche falls back on energy; the second law of thermodynamics declares that there are energy processes which are irreversible. Heat and light are merely forms of energy. In order to convert light into heat, simply project it onto a black surface. Heat, on the other hand, cannot return to its form as light. This proof, of an inoffensive and insipid aspect, annuls the circular labyrinth of the eternal return.

The first law of thermodynamics declares that the energy of the universe is constant; the second, that that energy tends to incommunication and disorder, although the total amount does not decrease. This gradual disintegration of the forces which compose the universe is called entropy. Once all different temperatures have been equalized, once the action of one body on another has been barred or compensated for, the world will be a fortuitous concurrence of atoms. In the deep center of the stars, that difficult and fatal balance has been accomplished. By dint of interchanges, the entire universe will achieve it, and it will be tepid and dead.

Light is losing its heat; the universe is becoming invisible, minute by minute. It is becoming lighter as well. At some point, it will be nothing but heat: balanced, immovable, equal heat. Then it will have died.

A final certainty, this time of a metaphysical order. If Zarathustra's thesis is accepted, I do not understand what prevents two identical processes from becoming agglomerated in one. Is mere succession enough, unverified by anyone? Without a special archangel to keep count, what does it mean that we are passing through the 13,514th cycle, and not the first of the series or number 322^{2000}? Nothing, as far as practice goes—which does no harm to the thinker. Nothing, as far as intelligence—which is serious. (pp. 65-71)

Jorge Luis Borges, "The Doctrine of Cycles," translated by Karen Stolley, in his Borges, a Reader: A Selection from the Writings of Jorge Luis Borges, *edited by Emir Rodriguez Monegal and Alastair Reid, E. P. Dutton, 1981, pp. 65-71.*

Photograph of Nietzsche in uniform, 1868.

MARTIN HEIDEGGER (essay date 1961)

[*A German philosopher, Heidegger is recognized as one of the most important and original thinkers of the twentieth century. His major work,* Sein und Zeit *(1927;* Being and Time, *1962) was influential to the development of the philosophical movement of Existentialism, although Heidegger denied any significant connection with this movement. A connection, however, does exist in his reduction of the meaning of philosophy to the meaning of being, for Heidegger believed that it was philosophy's primary task to define the word "being." "Do we have an answer today to the question, what do we really mean by the word 'being'?" he asked in* Being and Time. *In this work Heidegger resolved that the significance of being, as it relates to humanity, was the necessarily endless quest to define this very term. He further concluded that if the act of being is to ceaselessly attempt to define this term, then being must be finite, for all those who exist must die. Terming this cycle of life-quest-death* Dasein, *or "being there," Heidegger separated humanity from all other forms of being with the claim that only that which experienced* Dasein *could exist. Thus, in order to exist in an authentic manner, one must live in full, and therefore anxious, awareness of death. In his later works, Heidegger proposed language as essential to being and wrote that "only where there is language is there world." Through considerations of such poets as Hölderlin, Rainer Maria Rilke, and Georg Trakl, he determined that "to write poetry is to make a discovery," and that the purpose of poetry is to define "the condition of man's existence as historical beings." In the following excerpt from his four-volume study of Nietzsche, Heidegger discusses Nietzsche's concepts of the will to power and the eternal recurrence of the same.*]

The Will to Power—the expression plays a dual role in Nietzsche's thinking. First, it serves as the title of Nietzsche's chief philosophical work, planned and prepared over many years but never written. Second, it names what constitutes the basic character of all beings. "Will to power is the ultimate *factum* to which we come." . . . (p. 3)

It is easy to see how both applications of the expression "will to power" belong together: only because the expression plays the second role can and must it also adopt the first. As the name for the basic character of all beings, the expression "will to power" provides an answer to the question "What is being?" Since antiquity that question has been *the* question of philosophy. The name "will to power" must therefore come to stand in the title of the chief philosophical work of a thinker who says that all being ultimately is will to power. If for Nietzsche the work of that title is to be the philosophical "main structure," for which ***Zarathustra*** is but the "vestibule," the implication is that Nietzsche's thinking proceeds within the vast orbit of the ancient guiding question of philosophy, "What is being?" (pp. 3-4)

The expression "will to power" designates the basic character of beings; any being which is, insofar as it is, is will to power. The expression stipulates the character that beings have as beings. But that is not at all an answer to the first question of philosophy, its proper question; rather, it answers only the final preliminary question. For anyone who at the end of Western philosophy can and must still question philosophically, the decisive question is no longer merely "What basic character do beings manifest?" or "How may the Being of beings be characterized?" but "What is this 'Being' itself?" The decisive question is that of "the meaning of Being," not merely that of the Being of beings. "Meaning" is thereby clearly delineated conceptually as that from which and on the grounds of which Being in general can become manifest as such and can come into truth. What is proffered today as ontology has nothing to do with the question of Being proper; it is a very learned and very astute analysis of transmitted concepts which plays them off, one against the other.

What is will to power itself, and how is it? Answer: the eternal recurrence of the same.

Is it an accident that the latter teaching recurs continually in decisive passages throughout all plans for the philosophical main work? What can it mean when in one plan, which bears the unadorned title "Eternal Return" . . . , Nietzsche lists the first part under the title "The most difficult thought"? To be sure, the question of Being is the most difficult thought of philosophy, because it is simultaneously its innermost and uttermost thought, the one with which it stands and falls.

We heard that the fundamental character of beings is will to power, willing, and thus Becoming. Nevertheless, Nietzsche does not cling to such a position—although that is usually what we are thinking when we associate him with Heraclitus. Much to the contrary, in a passage purposely and expressly formulated to provide an encompassing overview . . . , Nietzsche says the following: "*Recapitulation:* To *stamp* Becoming with the character of Being—that is the *supreme will to power.*" This suggests that Becoming only *is* if it is grounded in Being as Being: "That *everything recurs* is the closest *approximation* of a world of Becoming to one of Being:—peak of the meditation." With his doctrine of eternal return Nietzsche in his way thinks nothing else than the thought that pervades the whole of Western philosophy, a thought that remains concealed but is its genuine driving force. Nietzsche thinks the thought in such a way that in his metaphysics he reverts to the beginnings of Western philosophy. More precisely, he reverts to that beginning which Western philosophy became accustomed to seeing in the course of its history. Nietzsche shared in such habituation in spite of his otherwise original grasp of pre-Socratic philosophy.

In the popular view, and according to the common notion, Nietzsche is the revolutionary figure who negated, destroyed, and prophesied. To be sure, all that belongs to the image we have of him. Nor is it merely a role that he played, but an innermost necessity of his time. But what is essential in the revolutionary is not that he overturns as such; it is rather that in overturning he brings to light what is decisive and essential. In philosophy that happens always when those few momentous questions are raised. When he thinks "the most difficult thought" at the "peak of the meditation," Nietzsche thinks and meditates on Being, that is, on will to power as eternal recurrence. What does that mean, taken quite broadly and essentially? Eternity, not as a static "now," nor as a sequence of "nows" rolling off into the infinite, but as the "now" that bends back into itself: what is that if not the concealed essence of Time? Thinking Being, will to power, as eternal return, thinking the most difficult thought of philosophy, means thinking Being as Time. Nietzsche thinks that thought but does not think it as the *question* of Being and Time. Plato and Aristotle also think that thought when they conceive Being as *ousia* (presence), but just as little as Nietzsche do they think it as a question.

If we do ask the question, we do not mean to suggest that we are cleverer than both Nietzsche and Western philosophy, which Nietzsche "only" thinks to its end. We know that the most difficult thought of philosophy has only become more difficult, that the peak of the meditation has not yet been conquered and perhaps not yet even discovered at all.

If we bring Nietzsche's "will to power," that is, his question concerning the Being of beings, into the perspective of the question concerning "Being and Time," that does not at all mean that Nietzsche's work is to be related to a book entitled *Being and Time* and that it is to be measured and interpreted according to the contents of that book. *Being and Time* can be evaluated only by the extent to which it is equal or unequal to the question it raises. There is no standard other than the question itself; only the question, not the book, is essential. Furthermore, the book merely leads us to the threshold of the question, not yet into the question itself.

Whoever neglects to think the thought of eternal recurrence together with will to power, as what is to be thought genuinely and philosophically, cannot adequately grasp the metaphysical content of the doctrine of will to power in its full scope. Nevertheless, the connection between eternal recurrence as the supreme determination of Being and will to power as the basic character of all beings does not lie in the palm of our hand. For that reason Nietzsche speaks of the "most difficult thought" and the "peak of the meditation." It is nonetheless true that the current interpretation of Nietzsche does away with the properly philosophical significance of the doctrine of eternal recurrence and thus irremediably precludes a fertile conception of Nietzsche's metaphysics. (pp. 18-21)

Nietsche's basic metaphysical position may be defined by two statements. First, the basic character of beings as such is "will to power." Second, Being is "eternal recurrence of the same." When we think through Nietzsche's philosophy in a questioning way, along the guidelines of those two statements, we advance beyond the basic positions of Nietzsche and of philosophy prior to him. But such advance only allows us to come back to

Nietzsche. The return is to occur by means of an interpretation of ***"The Will to Power."***

The plan upon which the published edition is based, a plan Nietzsche himself sketched and even dated (March 17, 1887), takes the following form. . . :

THE WILL TO POWER
Attempt at a Revaluation of All Values

Book I: *European Nihilism.*
Book II: *Critique of the Highest Values.*
Book III: *Principle of a New Valuation.*
Book IV: *Discipline and Breeding.*

Our inquiry proceeds immediately to the third book and restricts itself to that one. The very title, "Principle of a New Valuation," suggests that here a laying of grounds and an erection of structures are to be brought to language.

Accordingly, in Nietzsche's view, philosophy is a matter of valuation, that is, establishment of the uppermost value in terms of which and according to which all beings are to be. The uppermost value is the one that must be fundamental for all beings insofar as they are beings. A "new" valuation would therefore posit another value, in opposition to the old, decrepit one, which should be determinative for the future. For that reason a critique of the highest values hitherto is advanced beforehand, in Book II. The values in question are religion, specifically, the Christian religion, morality, and philosophy. Nietzsche's manner of speaking and writing here is often imprecise and misleading: religion, morality, and philosophy are not themselves the supreme values, but basic ways of establishing and imposing such values. Only for that reason can they themselves, mediately, be posited and taken as "highest values."

The critique of the highest values hitherto does not simply refute them or declare them invalid. It is rather a matter of displaying their origins as impositions which must affirm precisely what ought to be negated by the values established. Critique of the highest values hitherto therefore properly means illumination of the dubious origins of the valuations that yield them, and thereby demonstrations of the questionableness of these values themselves. Prior to this critique, which is offered in Book II, the first book advances an account of European nihilism. Thus the work is to begin with a comprehensive presentation of the basic development of Western history, which Nietzsche recognizes in its range and intensity here for the first time: the development of nihilism. In Nietzsche's view nihilism is not a *Weltanschauung* that occurs at some time and place or another; it is rather the basic character of what happens in Occidental history. Nihilism is at work even—and especially—there where it is not advocated as doctrine or demand, there where ostensibly its opposite prevails. Nihilism means that the uppermost values devalue themselves. This means that whatever realities and laws set the standard in Christendom, in morality since Hellenistic times, and in philosophy since Plato, lose their binding force, and for Nietzsche that always means creative force. In his view nihilism is never merely a development of his own times; nor does it pertain only to the nineteenth century. Nihilism begins in the pre-Christian era and it does not cease with the twentieth century. As a historical process it will occupy the centuries immediately ahead of us, even and especially when countermeasures are introduced. But neither is nihilism for Nietzsche mere collapse, valuelessness, and destruction. Rather, it is a basic mode of historical movement that does not exclude, but even requires and furthers, for long stretches of time, a certain creative upswing. "Corruption," physiological degeneration," and such are not causes of nihilisim but effects. Nihilism therefore cannot be overcome by the extirpation of those conditions. On the contrary, an overcoming of nihilism would merely be delayed by countermeasures directed toward alleviation of its harmful side effects. In order to grasp what Nietzsche designates in the word "nihilism" we need profound insight and even more profound seriousness.

Because of its necessary involvement in the movement of Western history, and on account of the unavoidable critique of prior valuations, the *new* valuation is necessarily a *re*valuation of all values. Hence the subtitle, which in the final phase of Nietzsche's philosophy becomes the main title, designates the general character of the countermovement to nihilism *within* nihilism. No historical movement can leap outside of history and start from scratch. It becomes all the more historical, which is to say, it grounds history all the more originally, as it overcomes radically what has gone before by creating a new order in that realm where we have our roots. Now, the overwhelming experience derived from the history of nihilism is that all valuations remain without force if the corresponding basic attitude of valuing and the corresponding manner of thinking do not accompany them.

Every valuation in the essential sense must not only bring its possibilities to bear in order to be "understood" at all, it must at the same time develop a breed of men who can bring a new attitude to the new valuation, in order that they bear it into the future. New requirements and prerequisities must be bred. And this process consumes, as it were, most of the time that is allotted to nations as their history. Great ages, because they are great, are in terms of frequency quite rare and of endurance very brief, just as the most momentous times for individual men often consist of a single moment. A new valuation itself implies the creation and inculcation of requirements and demands that conform to the new values. For that reason the work is to find its conclusion in the fourth book, "Discipline and Breeding."

At the same time, however, it is a basic experience gained from the history of valuations that even the positing of the uppermost values does not take place at a single stroke, that eternal truth never blazes in the heavens overnight, and that no people in history has had its truth fall into its lap. Those who posit the uppermost values, the creators, the new philosophers at the forefront, must according to Nietzsche be experimenters; they must tread paths and break trails in the knowledge that they do not have *the* truth. But from such knowledge it does not at all follow that they have to view their concepts as mere betting chips that can be exchanged at any time for any currency. What does follow is just the opposite: the solidity and binding quality of thought must undergo a grounding in the things themselves in a way that prior philosophy does not know. Only in this way is it possible for a basic position to assert itself over against others, so that the resultant strife will be actual strife and thus the actual origin of truth. The new thinkers must attempt and tempt. That means they must put beings themselves to the test, tempt them with questions concerning their Being and truth. So, when Nietzsche writes in the subtitle to his work, "attempt" at a revaluation of all values, the turn of phrase is not meant to express modesty and to suggest that what follows is still incomplete; it does not mean an "essay" in the literary sense; rather, in an utterly clearminded way, it means the basic attitude of the new inquiry that grows out of the countermovement against nihilism. (pp. 25-8)

One need not penetrate too far into Nietzsche's thought in order to determine without difficulty that his procedure everywhere is one of reversal. On the basis of that determination a basic objection to Nietzsche's procedure and to his entire philosophy has been raised: reversal is merely denial—in setting aside the previous order of values no new values yet arise. With objections of this kind it is always advisable to suppose at least provisionally that the philosopher under consideration was after all alert enough to experience such doubts himself. Nietzsche not only avers that by means of reversal a new order of values should originate; he says explicitly that in this way an order should originate *"of itself."* Nietzsche says, "If the tyranny of previous values has thus been shattered, if we have abolished the 'true world,' then a *new order of values* must follow of itself." Merely by doing away with the old, something new should eventuate of itself! Are we to ascribe such an opinion to Nietzsche, or do such "abolition" and "reversal" signify something other than what we usually represent to ourselves with the help of everyday concepts?

What is the principle of the new valuation? At the outset it is important to clarify in general the meaning of the title of the third book. . . . The principle of a new valuation is that in which valuing as such has its supporting and guiding ground. The principle of a new valuation is that kind of ground which inaugurates a valuing that is new in contrast to previous kinds. The valuing is to be new: not only what is posited as a value but above all else the manner in which values are posited in general. If one objects that Nietzsche was basically uncreative and did not really establish any new values, such an objection first needs to be tested carefully. But however it turns out, the objection itself does not touch what Nietzsche actually wanted to do above all else, namely, to ground anew the manner in which values are posited, to lay a new ground for this purpose. Therefore, if we want to grasp what is thought here, we must read the title of Book III, "Principle of the New Valuation," as having the following sense: the new ground from which in the future the manner and kind of valuing will spring and upon which it will rest. How are we to conceive that ground?

If the work as a whole involves will to power, and if the third book is to exhibit the ground-laying and structuring principle of the new valuation, then the principle can only be will to power. How are we to understand this? We said by way of anticipation that will to power is a name for the basic character of all beings. It means precisely *what* properly constitutes the being in beings. Nietzsche's decisive consideration runs as follows: if we are to establish what properly should be, and what must come to be in consequence of that, it can be determined only if truth and clarity already surround whatever *is* and whatever constitutes *Being*. How else could we determine what is to be?

In the sense of this most universal consideration, whose ultimate tenability we must still leave open, Nietzsche says, "Task: to *see* things *as they are!*" . . . "My philosophy—to draw men away from *semblance,* no matter *what* the danger! And no fear that life will perish!" . . . Finally: "Because you lie concerning what is, the thirst for what should come to be does not grow in you." . . . (pp. 30-2)

Demonstration of will to power as the basic character of beings is supposed to expunge the lies in our experience of beings and in our interpretation of them. But not only that. It is also supposed to ground the principle, and establish the ground, from which the valuation is to spring and in which it must remain rooted. For "will to power" is already in itself an estimating and valuing. If beings are grasped as will to power, the "should" which is supposed to hang suspended over them, against which they might be measured, becomes superfluous. If life itself is will to power, it is itself the ground, *principium,* of valuation. Then a "should" does not determine Being; Being determines a "should." (p. 32)

Martin Heidegger, in his Nietzsche: The Will to Power as Art, Vol. I, *translated by David Farrell Krell, Harper & Row, Publishers, 1979, 263 p.*

MICHAEL HAMBURGER (essay date 1965)

[Hamburger is a German-born English poet, translator, and critic. His publications in each of these genres are recognized as distinguished, and his numerous studies of and translations from German authors are particularly esteemed. In the following excerpt from his essay "A Craving for Hell," *which is primarily an account of the distortion and exploitation of Nietzsche's works by Elizabeth Förster-Nietzsche and the Nietzsche Archive under the Nazis, Hamburger offers a general appraisal of the philosopher's thought.]*

Elisabeth Förster-Nietzsche, c. 1904.

Nietzsche's self-contradictions cannot be resolved, or can be resolved in so many different ways that one is left only with his bare experience and the pure energy generated by a divided mind. (p. 44)

Love and hate, reverence and revolt, faith and scepticism interlock with endless variations in his works, but never quite succeed in engendering that third liberating theme. If we grant Nietzsche the privileges of a poet-philosopher, including the right to contradict himself and to remain for ever ambiguous, his work must be tested by the standards of poetry for its aesthetic and subliminal effects; and here the combination of analytical thinker and visionary proved even more dubious than on the level of doctrine alone.

Nietzsche's diction, too, shows an obsession with certain primitive relationships, dynamisms and concepts. Some of these have been brilliantly interpreted by Dr F. D. Luke, who concentrated on the dynamics of height, metaphors of climbing, flying, leaping, dancing and the related one of sea-faring. . . . [A] similar study could be made of Nietzsche's animal imagery. His warning that he does not want to be remembered as 'a savage beast and moral monster' can be offset by another: 'I am a dangerous animal, and don't lend myself well to adulation.' Nietzsche's animal imagery is so pervasive and conspicuous that its effect is to suspend all those intellectual and moral reservations which he undoubtedly wanted his readers to observe. His capacity for self-identification with the animal world in general, not only with predatory animals, is amply attested both in his writings and in his life. That his nickname for his sister was 'the llama' may be relatively insignificant: but one of the few physical expressions of affection he is known to have indulged in, and his very last, was towards a cab horse in Turin. An aphorism like the following from ***The Dawn of Day*** puts the complex in a nutshell: '*Humanity*. We do not regard animals as moral beings. But do you imagine that animals regard us as moral beings?—An animal that could talk once said: ''Humanity is a prejudice, and at least we animals don't suffer from it.'''

As we have seen, Nietzsche was well aware that a doctrine of deliberate brutalism, a kind of ethical Darwinism, could be extracted from his works, as it was to be by the Nazis. Now Nietzsche, as a highly civilized man and a 'Good European' (his own phrase), took it for granted that brutality was undesirable, and devoted his therapeutical talents to the vindication of that part of human nature which civilization had repressed: 'The struggle against the brutal instincts is a different one from that against the morbid instincts; indeed, to induce illness can be a means of mastering brutality. In Christianity, psychological treatment often amounts to turning an animal into a sick animal, and thus into a tame one. Nietzsche does not deny that brutal instincts should be held in check, though this was not his business. Yet, subliminally, the effect of his later works is to glorify the predatory beast at the expense of the innocuous or the tame; and it is his metaphors that produce the effect.

It is regrettable, therefore, that ***Zarathustra,*** the most 'poetic' and figurative of Nietzsche's prose works, should have come to be regarded as his *magnum opus,* often as nothing less than the Nietzsche bible. F. D. Luke, too, doubts that 'his prose is at its best where it approaches the nature of poetry; he is certainly at his worst when writing verse'. The prose poetry of ***Zarathustra*** is an unhappy amalgam of biblical and Romantic elements, and this in turn rarely blends very happily with the stringencies of Nietzsche's analytical prose. Above all, the metaphors are allowed to proliferate in a manner that shows up Nietzsche's most serious defects both as a thinker and as a poet. 'Only very occasionally is Nietzsche able to achieve *poetic* language in which the image or vehicle has become virtually autonomous', Luke remarks; at the same time the imagery comes close enough to autonomy to detract from that clarity and incisiveness for which Nietzsche's analytical prose is justly admired.

The emblematic character of Nietzsche's poetic imagery, to which Luke's stricture alludes, is equally marked in his verse; apart from those obsessive and primitive gestures already mentioned, which also included metaphors connected with eating and swallowing, Nietzsche's poetic diction hardly ever conveys any awareness of the particulars of human or non-human nature. Yet the only German imaginative writers of the nineteenth century whom Nietzsche consistently admired were the poetic realists Stifter and Keller, writers who dwelled with loving precision on those 'little things' of life which Nietzsche opposed in *Ecce Homo* to the great abstractions. As Schlechta may have had in mind in citing Nietzsche's *Fable* [***The Dawn of Day***] against him, Nietzsche's diction, too, brings us up against that basic contradiction between what he was and what he wanted to be:

> The Don Juan of knowledge: no philosopher or poet has yet discovered him. He is lacking in love for those things which he comes to know, but his intelligence is tickled and gratified by the pursuit and intrigues of knowledge—right up to the highest and farthest stars of knowledge!—until in the end there is nothing left for him to pursue but the absolute hurtfulness of knowledge, like the drunkard who ends up by drinking absinth and *aqua fortis*. So in the end he craves for hell—this being the last knowledge that can *seduce* him. Perhaps hell too will disappoint him, like all that he has known! In that case he would have to remain motionless to all eternity, nailed to his disappointment and himself transformed into the stone guest, longing for a last supper of knowledge of which he will never again partake!—because the whole world hasn't so much as a bite to offer that hungry man.

Because he was lacking in love for particulars, Nietzsche's antipuritanism never became more than a reflex of his self-hatred and self-dissatisfaction, and found no embodiment in his diction. Like the conventional pedagogues, parsons and ideologists he despised, Nietzsche could not help holding up an ideal yardstick to individuals; though he remained loyal to a few old friends for friendship's sake, not a single individual of his acquaintance came up to the mark, or could conceivably have done so, since the mark was that of the superman who was Nietzsche's anti-self. As he might have gathered from Pascal, to whom he owed so much, the obverse of that angel is the beast, the obverse of that superman the subman. All his richness, energy and subtlety cannot make up for the gap in Nietzsche's work, the missing middle register of human experience.

Also Sprach Zarathustra may well come to be regarded not as Nietzsche's masterpiece, but as an aberration and monstrosity, as an instance of that late Romantic inflation which he recognized in Wagner, as the the German Reich, and hated because he felt its power over himself. Yet if Nietzsche's importance should ever be doubted, we have only to turn to his early polemical works, the ***Thoughts out of Season,*** in which he was no solitary prophet on the mountain tops—inviting disciples only to scorn and reject them as slaves, needing disciples, but ashamed of his need—to be reassured of his central and seminal relevance to all that has been thought and experienced in the last hundred years. This young classical scholar spoke to men as a member of society, at once involved in it and critical of it, much as Matthew Arnold did in the same years, and about much the same questions; that Nietzsche was more than twenty years younger can only increase one's respect for his incomparable insight, prescience and daring. Even Nietzsche's discovery of the Dionysian principle, and his self-identification with it, goes back to these early years and ***The Birth of Tragedy.***

This is not to deny that he added to his fundamental perceptions in later years, clarifying or enriching them in many cases, but only to suggest that it was precisely his power and range of perception that failed to keep up with the growing tension of his inner conflict. The young professor grappled with a civilization and a culture; the lonely thinker and poet, increasingly, grappled only with himself, yet could not quite accept the prospect of final isolation. Hence the 'Dionysian imperialism', the bragging and self-dramatization, the tedious repetitions and overstatements, the self-propelled rhetoric and hyperbole, the strident tone of certain later works and passages. These call for readers truly Nietzschean in their readiness to fight back, to discriminate and deflate; and, more than any other writer of his time, Nietzsche might have served, and can still serve, to create such readers. That the vulgarians seized on his crudities and excesses for their own much cruder and more excessive ends is a reflection not on Nietzsche but on them. (pp. 45-9)

Michael Hamburger, "A Craving for Hell: On Nietzsche and Nietzscheans," in his From Prophecy to Exorcism: The Premisses of Modern German Literature, *Longmans, 1965, pp. 29-53.*

MARY WARNOCK (essay date 1978)

[*Warnock is an English philosopher and educator whose works include* Existentialist Ethics *(1967),* Schools of Thought *(1976), and* Education *(1979). In the following excerpt, Warnock examines Nietzsche's concept of truth and its relationship to his theory of the will to power.*]

Nietzsche was able to give an answer to the question why we value truth, the question which he said 'stepped forth' before us, in terms of a concept of truth as the goal of scientific method, that is, as *theory*. And in doing so, he tended to lose sight of the nature of truth as it may occur in particular statements of fact—that today is Wednesday, or that the carpet is green. What we are seeking on this 'scientific' view of truth, is a complex of hypotheses, by the adopting of which as true and therefore as the basis for prediction, we can master, control and change the world to fit it for our own survival. This is, broadly speaking, the pragmatist aspect of Nietzsche's theory, and it is worth remarking how close he comes to the pragmatists, and especially to [Charles Sanders] Peirce, in his willingness to concentrate, at least sometimes, on the notion of truth as the *goal of science*. A. J. Ayer, writing about Peirce, says that if we are thinking of the truth of simple propositions concerned with the present, it is obviously absurd to suggest that their truth consists in their being accepted by a consensus of future scientists or anything of the kind, since many propositions which we wish now to assert as true will cease to be candidates for truth or falsity in the future. They will, as it were, have lapsed altogether (for example no science, however complete, could chronicle and assess such propositions as 'this pudding is hot') and Ayer says that Peirce does not offer any reply to this kind of objection, because he does not think it worth taking seriously. . . . These words could with equal propriety be applied to Nietzsche, as far as concerns one important aspect of his writings. Thus we have two phenomena to consider: on the one hand there is, in Nietzsche, a vacillating attitude to the possibility of truth, to the very meaningfulness of the concept; and on the other hand there is a switch in interest between two different *kinds* of question, of which now one and now the other occupied his attention.

Let us . . . look in a bit more detail at his discussion of truth as the goal of science. Nietzsche believed that the only possible general explanation of the nature of things was to be found in the notion of the will to power. He demanded an explanation of *everything,* which would not markedly separate human behaviour from other phenomena. For he believed . . . that everything is, as it were, made of the same stuff. Long before he had come upon the idea of the will to power, he wrote: 'When we speak of *humanity* our basic idea is that this is what *separates* and distinguishes man from nature. In reality, however, there is no such separation: "natural" properties and those specifically called "human" are inseparably entwined.' . . . The general consequence of Darwinism, that one must think of man as a part of his whole environment, not as a god-like and alien visitant in a foreign world, was totally absorbed into Nietzsche's thought. 'Consciousness' is a myth, ultimately derived from grammar. It is not a *thing* which marks off human relations to the world from all others; nor can it be taken to justify a distinction between appearance and reality. 'The universe exists.' That is about all one can say.

Now in the universe as a whole, if you seek to understand changes, actions, reactions, or any kind of activity or behaviour, the hypothesis of the will to power is the most explanatory, because the widest in scope. Nietzsche believed that he had discovered the will to power empirically, not through any exercise of reason *a priori*. If he could not claim it as an empirical concept, then of course he would be open to a charge of inconsistency; for he would both be denying the possibility of *a priori* truths to explain the world, and at the same time asserting such a truth. But he insisted that 'experience' had taught him of the will to power. He could therefore assert it itself as a hypothesis, though a hypothesis so far unchallenged. Nietzsche assumes that the processes of evolution themselves, the survival of one kind of vegetation or of animal in a particular area at the expense of other vegetation or animals can be explained in terms of the will to power, once the notion of 'will' has been divorced from its mythological association with consciousness, felt striving, internal cause or freedom. One cannot, that is to say, separate the notion of causality from that of will. But far from this leading to the positing of a *special kind* of causation which operates only among conscious beings, it should lead in the other direction, to the positing of a will wherever, in our search for scientific knowledge, we come upon causal sequences. 'We *must*', he writes, 'make the attempt to posit hypothetically the causality of the will as the only form of causality.' . . . This is a sort of anthropomorphism in reverse.

Once this most general hypothesis is accepted, then, in so far as his interest turns to epistemology, to questions of knowledge or truth, the question for Nietzsche can be put in this form: How is the will to truth related to the will to power? For since, as we have seen, the whole notion of truth is necessarily to some extent a deception, the need arises for a critique of the will to truth. (pp. 52-4)

[We must] consider truth only in the context of the scientific advance of man, attempting all the time, as he becomes more and more highly evolved, to master and control more and more of the universe. 'Pure' science, the pursuit of truth for its own sake, is not possible, if 'truth' actually *means* that which leads to practical mastery over the environment. We must stop thinking of truth as something to which we can lay claim when we, as perceptive subjects, come across statements which fit the facts, that which we look out upon and perceive. (p. 54)

It is perhaps in this placing of truth in the context, or under the banner, of power that Nietzsche is most prone to swing between the old 'fitting the facts' sense of the word 'true' and his new, pragmatic sense. (But any pragmatist, or indeed any defender of a coherence theory of truth, must find the same difficulty.) He argues that *what* it is that we find effective may change from time to time. 'To the extent to which knowledge has any sense at all, the world is knowable: but it may be interpreted *differently,* it has not one sense behind it, but hundreds of senses.' . . . Therefore it follows that 'truth' may change. This is a sense of 'true', however, which it is very difficult to adopt. Our language rebels against it because of the 'old' (some may say the 'real') meaning of 'true', according to which 'true' means 'as the facts are' and according to which, also, there is an implied contrast between a statement of fact and a hypothesis. So Nietzsche can also write,

> Truth is [. . .] more fatal than error or ignorance, because it paralyses the forces which lead to enlightenment and knowledge [. . .] It is more gratifying to think 'I possess the truth', than to see only darkness in all directions. . . .

Interpreted in one way, Nietzsche is saying that those who have sought for truth have always, in fact, sought for some dogma in which they could rest, and save themselves the painful exertion of investigating any further. But what would they, if they were honest, have been investigating *for*? Surely only in order to discover the truth in a different sense, namely in the sense of that which seems, for the time being, to increase their power. This is the real meaning of truth, but one must of course, in this sense, never claim to have reached it. At best it is an unattainable ideal. Nothing that we *actually* grasp can be more than a hypothesis. If 'true', however, *means* 'the best hypothesis we have' then of course we cannot say 'nothing is true'; we must say 'such and such is true for the time being'. But at this point we come, once again, up against the deep recalcitrance of language. We come up against the impossibility of sincerely saying "I know but I may be wrong' or 'It is right, but perhaps it won't be tomorrow'. Similarly, if one is referring to general laws or regularity statements, one must *either* say they are hypotheses, or assert them as true. But if one does the latter, one cannot also say in the same breath that they may be shown to be false. We cannot make the claim involved in the use of the word 'true' or 'know' with one hand, and withdraw it with the other.

So, once again, we seem to have come to a point where what Nietzsche is offering is not so much a theory of truth as a theory of science. He is answering the question how do we discover more about the world, and why do we want to. But even within this theory, in which there is no place for any discussion of the truth of simple single propositions, but only of explanatory hypotheses, he is sometimes sceptical, sometimes not; he sometimes thinks that we can, sometimes that we cannot achieve the truth. But at least, consistently, he recognizes that there is a motivating will to truth. This is the motive of science, but as it is a manifestation of the will to power, it is in fact a universal motive for the whole of the human species; it is that form of the will to power which characterizes the human species. So science is defined as 'The transformation of Nature into concepts for the purpose of governing Nature.' . . . But of course Nietzsche insists that we recognize the status of these concepts: 'Parmenides said: "One can form no concept of the non-existent";—we are at the other extreme, and say, "That of which a concept can be formed, is certainly fictional".' . . . The process of science thus becomes an endless pushing forward of boundaries, by the only possible means, namely the questioning of established hypotheses, and the critique of presuppositions. (pp. 55-6)

Nietzsche recognizes that some scientific 'fictions' have become so useful that they are positively necessary to life. For instance, the law of causation has become so totally built into human thought that 'to disbelieve in it would mean the ruin of our kind.' . . . In another note . . . he says that he agrees with Hume that belief in causality is nothing but habit, though it is not the habit of the individual so much as of humanity as a whole. But despite the strength of such a habit, because the will to truth is the will to power, which has no external goal or purpose, the process of questioning and undermining hypotheses will in fact continue whatever its consequences, and it is the philosopher's task to encourage and to justify the questioning. For the philosopher it is who says that a belief may be a necessary condition of life and *yet* be false. . . . Darwin had held that any species is dominated by, indeed in some sense formed by, its environment. Nietzsche thought that this was a great exaggeration of the influence of the environment and of external circumstances upon the species. The essential factor in the development of the species is the power which it has to create an environment which it can manage and exploit. But the will to power is not *for the sake of* the development of the species. It *is* the life itself of that, and every other, species. It follows that the most valuable, though not necessarily the least destructive, members of a species are those individuals who can, as it were, pit their own strength against the environment; and, translated into human terms, this means those who can question things held to be totally unquestionable by their fellows, even if this questioning leads to ruin. . . . So it must be wrong to think of truth as defined in terms of its usefulness to life, because if truth (that is power) and life conflict, then it will be the desire for truth which wins; but this is not incompatible with the acceptance *as* true of whatever is conducive to life and the convenience of life. The fact is that a genuinely great and free spirit will not accept such 'truths' for long. (p. 57)

The true scientist and philosopher, then, is perpetually creating new truths which are explanations of the real world. But of course the ambiguity in Nietzsche's view still remains. For on the one hand his notion of a search for truth may seem necessarily empty, contentless. The only characteristic of the truth-searcher is that he should *not* be content with what he has got, and that he should realize the *inventiveness* of his own role. The idea that he should *reach* the truth is absurd, since the search, as we have seen, is a process *in infinitum*. On the other hand, since error and falsehood are condemned, truth is *ipso facto* to be admired. The ideal is before us. What we can never reach is the complete or total explanation; but truth is this total explanation. It is what gets it right, what says how the world is. So the old sense of 'fitting the facts' has by no means been expunged. We must settle perhaps for saying that seeking the truth by seeking to falsify less than complete explanations is seeking for what we can never get. (p. 58)

Nietzsche would hold that the real scientist, the man who could achieve this greater depth of insight, and for whom the will to truth was more important than life itself, was necessarily a man superior to the general run of men. It is perhaps worth noticing that here the two parts of Nietzsche's theory of truth may be seen to come together. For not only will truth, in the sense of scientific explanation, be the goal of the superior, the superman, but also, in the sense in which truth is the property of single, simple propositions which 'fit the facts', rather than theories, it is only the superman who will be critical of the grammar in which such propositions are expressed, and will see through the mythology of the bare simple subject/object facts. He will be able to see for what it is the stranglehold that the metaphysics embedded in language has upon us. Obviously one cannot predict what substitute for such metaphysics he will make. One cannot both say that one is enmeshed in a particular grammar and at the same time and in the same language say how it would be if one were freed. Otherwise one would not be wholly enmeshed. But it is not inconceivable that *some one* might be able to take such a step. So, in both parts of the theory, Nietzsche is envisaging a wholly creative kind of being, quite free from the kinds of presuppositions that we can guard against and uncover piecemeal, but from which we cannot entirely free ourselves. Such a being could as he put it 'live without truth', that is without the comforting security of belief in the rightness of this theories, or the bareness of the facts which are reflected in his simple propositions. But in another sense he will be the only possible master of the truth. [Ludwig] Wittgenstein once said that he felt as though he were writing for people who would think in a quite different way and breathe a different air from present-day men. So Nietzsche's theory of truth, whichever aspect of it we consider, strongly suggests a quite different mode of thought, unattainable by us, both about language and about explanations of the world. (pp. 59-60)

Mary Warnock, "Nietzsche's Conception of Truth," in Nietzsche: Imagery and Thought, a Collection of Essays, *edited by Malcolm Pasley, University of California Press, 1978, pp. 33-63.*

PETER HELLER (essay date 1979)

[Heller is an Austrian-born American critic and educator specializing in German language and literature. In the following excerpt, Heller discusses both the contradictory and the unifying aspects of Nietzsche's thought.]

To point out the seemingly fractured, irridescent, opal-like multiplicity of Nietzsche's mind is to emphasize the obvious. Yet such emphasis is useful to counteract the tendency to identify Nietzsche too readily with specific positions or isms. Nietzsche the Romantic is refuted, it appears, by the anti-Romantic protagonist of a new Enlightenment. Nietzsche the "irrationalist" is refuted by his own rational skepticism. The positions of the metaphysician Nietzsche are reversed by his "neo-positivistic" critique of metaphysical assumptions (notably in terms of static fallacies inherent in language). The polemicist against optimistic illusions of Socratism is undone by proclamations of a Socratic scientism; and the moralist by an amoralist turning immoralist turning moralist. Indeed, how could this be otherwise, since so widely divergent movements, authors, thinkers derive from Nietzsche or appear to be anticipated by him in some essential respect? (p. 319)

But while I want to suggest the multiplicity of Nietzsche, I also should like to offer what has proved to be a convenient simplication: a perspective on what is actually a continuous complex process of thought in terms of three phases. The first is represented by ***Die Geburt der Tragödie*** . . . and ***Unzeitgemäße Betrachtungen***. . . . It culminates in an aesthetic metaphysic *ad maiorem gloriam* of works of art and artistic creativity. The second is represented by aphoristic works extending from ***Menschliches, Allzumenschliches*** . . . via ***Morgenröte*** . . . through the first four books of ***Die fröhliche Wissenschaft***. . . . These works are hostile to the metaphysical tradition and, on the whole, to the cult of artistic genius, and characterized by the predominance of the radically questioning intellect of the "free spirit." The third stage, however, is prophetic and polemical. It is represented by [***Zarathustra, Jenseits von Gut und Böse, Die Genealogie der Moral, Der Antichrist***] etc. . . . , and characterized by terms of vitality, supermorality, nobility, as well as by corresponding metaphysical postulates: for the metaphysical correlative to Superman is the Will to Power which, translated into temporal terms, is expressed as Eternal Recurrence, postulates of which Nietzsche appears to believe that they are, so far, the only ones compatible with the most thorough-going perspectivism. Indeed, insofar as one can speak of a "system"—never fully developed by the late Nietzsche—it would be a requirement within that system to show that the Will to Power is the perspective-creating force; that pan-perspectivism (i.e. a view recognizing nothing but a multiplicity of competing perspectives of which the most encompassing and most compelling would be the "truest") is merely the—epistemological or, possibly, idealistic—rephrasing of the Will-to-Power hypothesis. And similarly the Will-to-Power hypothesis must be shown to be itself the most compelling and encompassing of perspectives.

The above remarks suggest that Nietzsche's thoughts can be unified somewhat. It is to be granted that Nietzsche is not a builder of complete systems, and a disbeliever in systems; but neither is he a mere or pure intellectual impressionist. Some of the bits and pieces can be arranged in terms of the three stages, dominated respectively by his *Artisten-Metaphysik* ["aesthetic-metaphysic"], by the skeptical perspectives of the *Freigeist* ["free spirit"], and finally by the trinity of the pan-perspectivistic Will to Power, the Eternal Recurrence, and Superman: the anti-metaphysical metaphysics and gospel of the Antichrist. Yet even this arrangement fails to do justice to one's sense of the pervasive unity of Nietzsche's texts which persists despite the obvious, frequent, and explicit self-contradictions of this author.

One significant unifying element in Nietzsche is his sense of process, his dedication to the *Dionysian*. One may call this ceaselessly self-creative, self-destructive, multiple force élan, configurated drive, the Will (as Schopenhauer did) or Will to Power; becoming (*Werden*) or the Heraclitean flux of all things; or, to use the most serene metaphor (under which Richard Perkins comprehends the unity of Nietzsche's thought): ceaseless, purposeless play. (pp. 319-21)

In ***Die Geburt der Tragödie*** the Dionysian, self-creative, self-destructive élan appears metaphysically as the primal One with its perennial pain-pleasure tension from which it seeks relief and escape by the creation of—or self-alienation into—evanescent, individuated worlds of appearance that it will devour again in its unappeased hunger and hankering for itself. And

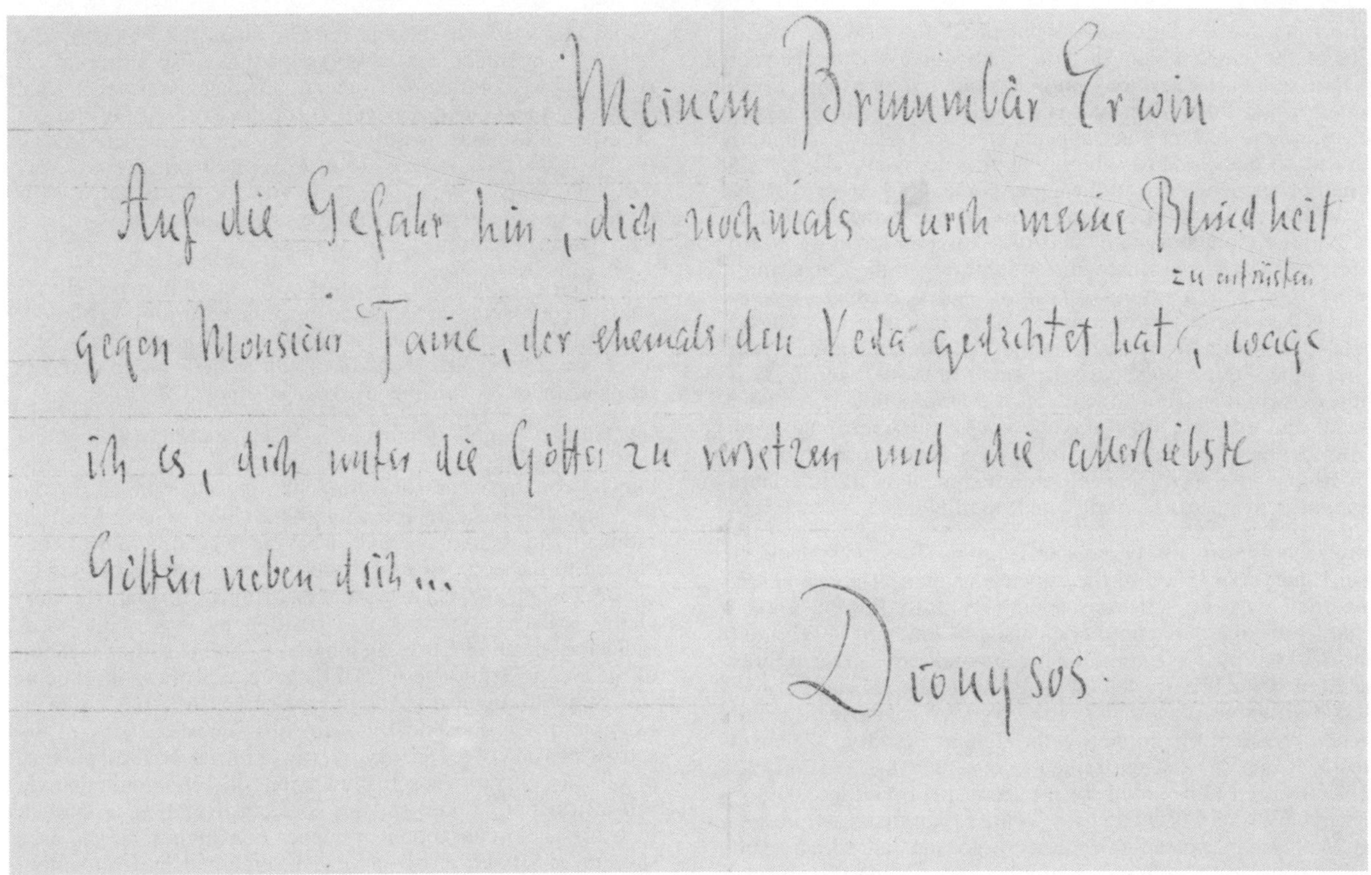

Meinem Brummbär Erwin

Auf die Gefahr hin, dich nochmals durch meine Blindheit
zu entrüsten
gegen Monsieur Taine, der ehemals den Veda gedichtet hat, wage
ich es, dich unter die Götter zu versetzen und die allerliebste
Göttin neben dich...

Dionysos.

Note from Nietzsche signed "Dionysus."

just as the dynamic tension of the Primal One gives rise to the worlds of appearance, man, the microcosm, who is in essence a manifestation of the same Dionysian tension and élan, is likewise in need of relief and escape, and creates illusory worlds of Apollonian art and existence only to devour them again. Nietzsche celebrates this Dionysian One and its solace in the Apollonian dream, and its return to itself both in the arts of Dionysian self-awareness, and in the final tragic synthesis in which the creation-destruction model, the building of illusory worlds and their shattering, and the pain-in-pleasure and pleasure-in-pain continuum are reproduced. And as he celebrates the Dionysian element, he himself undertakes and describes Dionysian movements of thought in his essay so that the text is and does what it says and teaches. Thus, to give one example, we are led from the birth of tragedy to its death and rebirth, and even the villain in the piece, Socratism, is led from its beginnings and its flourishing, anti-artistic, complacent phase to its demise in Faustian despair of knowledge, and thence to its rebirth, anticipated in the image of the musical Socrates.

To be sure, in the second stage, initiated by ***Menschliches, Allzumenschliches,*** Nietzsche no longer believes that art, notably tragedy, can be both an Apollonian solace, that is, a lie, and a revelation of metaphysical Dionysian truth; he concludes rather that art (including music) fosters illusion. He no longer believes that there is a hole in the dressing-gown of the world of appearance through which one may see the thing in itself, but concludes that all claims to metaphysical knowledge are false. He is left now with mere Socratism and, at that, with a Socratism that is disillusioned, in keeping with the Kantian restriction of the intellect to the world of appearance; a Socratism aware of its limitations, grown skeptical. Yet he still remains true to his basic Dionysian experience of process.

In the early phase this sense of process is expressed predominantly in sensuous, aesthetic, artistic, more immediately orgasmic terms. In the second phase, Nietzsche shifts to a sense of process predominantly in terms of the intellect and its multiple perspectives. This is a shift to the sublimated voyeurism of the *libido sciendi* as well as to a focus on the adventure, drama, high tragedy and tragicomedy of the free spirit. It is a shift to the orgy of the intellect, its delights and tortures as it creates and destroys its own worlds; a shift to the play of the intellect with itself. And Nietzsche is most himself as an orgiast of the intellect. What he now attempts to show is how the human intellect builds its own worlds and transcends and destroys them. He accompanies—he enacts the part of—he *is* the *free spirit* in his emancipation from the bondage of religion, metaphysics, and the morality attendant upon these. As a free spirit, he projects a new perspective of the intellect dominated by science and by an increasingly critical enlightenment. (pp. 321-22)

The consideration of the ethics of the Free Spirit leads to the third phase. Nietzsche is in some respects a highly traditional thinker. He dedicates his life to a quest for the three attributes of divinity: the perfection of the senses and their sublimation in *beauty;* the perfection of intellect in *truth;* the perfection of will and power in *goodness*. Correspondingly, the early Nietzsche takes very seriously the surface excitations of the senses and their sublimation in a passionate concern with art. This cultist of art graduates in the subsequent phase to the wider-ranging life of the mind which he tries to encompass from the most primitive level, where cognition appears purely as a tool fashioned to aid fulfillment of basic need or desire, to its highest level, where the intellect appears to enjoy relative autonomy and to be dedicated to a highly sublimated goal of truth. But finally Nietzsche turns to the larger context of human existence in which art (in the restricted sense of the term) represents a province of phantasy-life, and the ranging, hovering, seemingly purposeless or disinterested inquiries of the "academic" mind represent no more than a treasured enclave. Finally, Nietzsche attempts to encompass what are commonly considered to be the realities, the spheres of physical and moral action. Nietzsche's three stages are dedicated to a quest for the attributes of divinity, but always on the assumption that God is dead, and that one must attempt to take these attributes away from the dead God and give them back to live man: as artistic creativity; as veracity and self-enlightenment; as the transmoral goodness of maximal vitality and nobility.

Nietzsche's primary Dionysian intuition is expressed in the third stage in a vision of the universe as the self-creative, self-destructive, ever self-transcending Will to Power. Though characterized by its continuous nisus beyond any given limit, the Will to Power is expressed in temporal terms in the theorem of Eternal Recurrence which posits the endlessly self-creative, self-destructive play that is the cosmos, as one which must needs repeat itself endlessly throughout eternity. "Ad nauseam," man says, when forced to consider that he is doomed to repeat eternally precisely the same life, without addition, subtraction, gain of awareness, or loss. But that very prospect of aimless, purposeless, endless surge and fall which seems like a soup and gloom everlasting to man, is joyfully affirmed by superman—the only one who can bear that prospect without lying to himself, without alleging intrinsic purposes or goals except such as he himself projects, creates, builds up and destroys, like the child on the beach his sandpiles. For superman is himself but the maximal embodiment of the creative-destructive élan: self-creator, self-destroyer, self-transcender in the abundance of his vitality which includes, transmutes, transcends disease, negation, death. Here at last is the super-Faust equal to the ceaseless dynamic of the Earth-Spirit.

I have suggested as unifying element in Nietzsche's work his Dionysian sense of process. Whenever this intuition is represented as *one* or in the form of simultaneity, it appears as conjunction of opposites, as *dual-unity*. In ***Die Geburt der Tragödie*** the primal One is defined by the tension of *Urlust* engendered by *Urschmerz*. The Dionysian itself is described both as orgy of cruelty and lust, and as ecstatic hymnic affirmation in the sublime chorus of Beethoven's Ninth Symphony. It is both the ecstasy of primal delight *and* total negation, burnt-out Indic pessimism, denial of life. Similarly when Nietzsche concentrates on the intellect, the intellect is likely to be recognized both as the only instrument of cognition and as arch-liar. The intellect is the creator of the world of appearance and its destroyer: self-inciter, self-creator, self-knower, self-executioner. And again, a similar aspect of dual-unity or conjunction of opposites is implicit in the notion of Eternal Recurrence both as eternal *taedium*, gloomiest prospect *and* as challenge, occasion, source for the most encompassing affirmation. Indeed, superman himself is the projection of an attempt to imagine the most energetic vitality engendered, sparked, inspired by the realization of absolute meaninglessness, of perfect futility, and by the lure of total release in death. It is a vision of super-vitality, defying the promise of total release in death, projected—to indulge for a moment the "biographical fallacy"—by a man constantly tempted to make an end of his sufferings by committing suicide. This balance between vital affirmation and suicidal negation, or the extremity of the yea in response to the extremity of the nay are as characteristic of the late Nietzsche as they are of his early work. That is why they may suggest both an ecstatic view of self-creative, self-destructive process and the image of masturbation associated with a sense of futility.

But when the dual-unity is allowed to unfold, it becomes a kind of loop, *eine Schleife*, a movement turning inward or backward upon itself; and it is possible to analyze Nietzsche's texts in the gross and in detail, down to their micro-units, in terms of these movements of *reversal*. (pp. 324-26)

Indeed, the "loop" or movement of reversal may well be the most pervasive characteristic of Nietzsche. For to the extent that he countenances something like an anti-rationalism, he does so on the basis, or at least with the claim of having carried rationality to its extreme and of having drawn its radical conclusion to the point of its self-destruction. And insofar as he claims to be, and is, a most violent anti-Christian, he also claims to have arrived at this position by way of the most radical assertion of Christian ethics. . . . In the self-abnegation of the ascetic Truth-quester, Christian ethics draws its conclusion by abolishing itself. And this is perhaps the most important example of the dialectical movement in question, i.e., of the self-suspension of a tendency by way of its most radical pursuit, of self-cancellation via self-immersion, or self-annihilation via self-affirmation. Likewise, this dialectical motion is implicit in Nietzsche's conception of higher and highest health as a state to be arrived at by passing through and by overcoming decadence, and to be constantly asserted and regained via immersion in disease, in the assimilation and overcoming of sickness (a view, to be sure, for which he himself had very good and very bad, namely very personal reasons).

Any global treatment of Nietzsche is hazardous. Every statement to the effect that "Nietzsche always held . . . etc," is likely to be controverted. Anyone who wants to learn from Nietzsche, rather than talk about Nietzsche, must, above all, learn to read Nietzsche contextually and to pursue his specific movements of thought. . . . No simple, singleminded reading will do justice to the *"dividuum"* that is Nietzsche. (pp. 327-28)

Peter Heller, "Multiplicity and Unity in Nietzsche's Works and Thoughts on Thought," in The German Quarterly, *Vol. LII, No. 3, May, 1979, pp. 319-38.*

TILOTTAMA RAJAN (essay date 1980)

[Rajan is a Canadian critic and educator. In the following interpretation of The Birth of Tragedy, *Rajan considers Nietzsche as representative of a third phase in the development of Romantic consciousness, the other two consisting of Friedrich von Schiller's aesthetic theory of "sentimental" and "naive" texts and Arthur Schopenhaur's concept of irony as a force which the text can "neither evade nor endorse."]*

In ***The Birth of Tragedy*** Nietzsche [defines] the tragic experience as one in which the artist's simultaneous kinship with a chorus that is bound to the pathos of existence, and with a hero elevated above the choric collectivity, forces the act of aesthetic representation to be at once a submission to existence and a liberating act. . . . Such an art is neither will nor representation, but rather a dialogue between the two. (pp. 42-3)

The Birth of Tragedy tries to legitimize the worship of Dionysos and thus the presence within art of a destructiveness that may deny the very goal of art as culture rather than anarchy. But it also tries to respect the legitimacy of sublimating fiction in the form of Apollo.

Apollo, the god of illusion, stands for the mind's capacity to create a shape all light that will close out the horror of life, whether by returning to a prereflective innocence or by canceling the cycles of experience through such attitudes as resignation, platonism or heroic transcendence. Imagery of surface, veil, and dream links him to what Schiller called naiveté or "Schein." But he is also a mythologized version of Schopenhauer's "representation," or freedom from the anguish of will. Part of Nietzsche's contribution to Romantic aesthetics lies in his recognition that the mind cannot know Apollo without also acknowledging his kinship to Dionysos, who is the very life from which Apollo claims to have liberated man. Dionysos is not, as one might suppose from reading Nietzsche's later work, a jubilant figure. Rather he is a derivative of Schopenhauer's will, the deity of life as it exists before man has taken it into his mind and refined it. In him man encounters the brutal and the grotesque, "the original oneness," its pain and contradiction. (pp. 43-4)

It is of importance that Nietzsche breaks with the classical philologists of his time to see Dionysos as an earlier god than Apollo, and to characterize the displacement of Apollo by Dionysos as the reawakening of a knowledge which had always existed, before the Greek mind invented Apollo and the Olympians to hide its kinship with Dionysos and the Titans. Unlike his friend Erwin Rohde, who views the worship of Dionysos as a late phenomenon, Nietzsche thus avoids seeing the pessimistic current in Hellenism (and therefore in Romanticism) as a sign of decadence. . . . But Nietzsche is not concerned with historical scholarship, so much as with the use of Greek myth to develop a theogony of creative consciousness. What is of interest, therefore, is the symbolic significance of his theory for an aesthetics which had always located the plenitude of being before its corruption, the naive before the sentimental. The priority of innocence over experience had been the tacit justification for seeing art as the creation of a beautiful soul, and poetic language as privileged above other expressions of human existence. In reversing the genetic relationship between the two, and in suggesting that the naive is a projection of the sentimental consciousness rather than the latter being an enfeebled emanation of the naive, Nietzsche (in his words) opens "the magic mountain . . . before us, showing us its very roots." The priority of Dionysos to Apollo finds its aesthetic equivalent in the priority of music to language, and of the tragic chorus, whose mode of perception is that of pathos and immersion in life, to the heroic actor who seems, through soliloquy and dialogue, to have represented existence and thus triumphed over it. Unlike Schelling, who sees Dionysos-Zagreus as dialectically transcending himself and becoming the Apollonian Dionysos-Iacchos (described in almost Shelleyan terms as "a child in the bosom of Demeter"), Nietzsche confronts in Dionysos an irreducible darkness that limits the power of art to provide a catharsis of existence. (pp. 45-6)

Inasmuch as it discloses the presence of Dionysos in a supposedly Apollonian culture, of an insight into the irrational in a supposedly rational language, ***The Birth of Tragedy*** can be seen as a deconstruction of some of the central fictions of Romantic idealism. Nietzsche's typology of art-forms, which is more unequivocal than Schopenhauer's in exalting music over the arts of representation, stands in a definite revisionary relationship to the typologies of art-forms developed by Hegel and others, who assume the primacy of sculpture and associate it with the consummation of desire in time. Schiller's tendency to speak of Greece as though it produced only epic and sculpture, for instance, derives from a belief that art is illusion rather than knowledge, a surface that has elided its depths or somehow achieved a complete homogeneity of content and ideal form. Sculpture, which is restricted to its visual appearance or in which appearance is assumed to materialize completely what lies behind it, is peculiarly suited to such an aesthetics. Nietzsche, by contrast, also deals with Greece but emphasizes music: an art which is nonvisual and therefore presents reality unmediated by appearance.

Yet it would be wrong to see ***The Birth of Tragedy*** as a purely destructive text, still less as a work that denies to art all power of signification. Nietzsche's sometimes overwhelming emphasis on music and destruction must be seen as part of a dialectical engagement with traditional aesthetics, through which he attempts to bring back into art the element exiled from it by Romantic aesthetic theory. But it is important to remember that it is not music but lyric and tragedy that provide Nietzsche with his aesthetic norms. Whereas music arises directly from that primal wound in being to which Schopenhauer gave the name of will and which Artaud will later designate by the term "cruauté" (rawness, cruelty), tragedy and lyric are complex forms that compound music with language, the will with the capacity of imagination to represent life by taking it into itself and issuing it as its own product. The unique position of tragedy as a bridge between two orders of being derives from the fact that it acknowledges through its very form the genesis of language from music, and thus the presence within representation of a nonverbal, nonrepresentative element that challenges the claim of language to signify. Through the choric helplessness before life, which reveals the fragility of the transcendence achieved by the individual hero, the tragic text exposes its clarified surface to everything that remains unclarified in life. But at the same time, the tragic artist, who combines Schopenhauer's corrosive knowledge with Schiller's sense of the need for aesthetic illusion, recognizes that "only so much of the Dionysiac substratum of the universe may enter an individual consciousness as can be dealt with by . . . Apollonian transfiguration." Though Nietzsche has little to say about lyric, it too may be seen as bridging the two orders of being. Nietzsche disagrees with Schopenhauer in seeing the lyrical mixture of emotion and tranquillity as the product of a psychic equilibrium and not as the expression of a self-frustrating restlessness. Where lyric differs from tragedy, although he does not directly say so, is perhaps in its more muted and distanced awareness of the destructive substratum of life: in the greater tranquillity which distinguishes reflective works like the Lucy poems or the "Ode on a Grecian Urn" from dramatic narratives like *The Fall of Hyperion*. The inclusion of two such diverse genres as tragedy and lyric as models for aesthetic discourse suggests, moreover, that the compact struck between Apollo and Dionysos will not be identical in every work of art. (pp. 46-9)

The dialogical, ambivalent nature of tragedy as Nietzsche conceives it is a measure of the distance which separates ***The Birth of Tragedy*** from a modern recasting of it such as Artaud's *Theatre and Its Double*. There are times when Nietzsche seems vulnerable to the charge of having replaced one exclusive interpretation of art by another: logocentrism by melocentrism and nihilism. But the rigid separation between arts of will (music, dance, ritual) and arts of representation (the plastic arts, epic, scenic theater), on which a simple reversal of Apollonian idealism must depend, tends to break down. Bernard Pautrat observes that "certain elements figure on both sides of the caesura [between Dionysos and Apollo]. . . . These irregularities are not insignificant; quite on the contrary, they form a systematic blurring of differences. Nietzsche himself describes how in the work of art Dionysos always "speaks the language of Apollo," and "Apollo, finally, the language of Dionysos." The fact that lyric and tragedy are the offspring of both Dionysos and Apollo, and that Nietzsche can even conceive of an Apollonian music, suggests that he intends the separation of Apollonian and Dionysiac arts as no more than a kind of metaphor which enables him to isolate, for purposes of analysis, elements that are intimately linked in the actual work of art. Indeed, Nietzsche's argumentative technique, which polarizes Apollo and Dionysos in order to reveal the difficulties created by such polarization, can be viewed as a critique of the dichotomous generic and historical schemas used by Schiller and other aestheticians to segregate their desires for art from their knowledge of life.

We may, therefore, see ***The Birth of Tragedy*** as the culmination of a process of reassessment begun when the contradiction between aesthetics and existence, tacitly acknowledged by writers like Shelley and Jean-Paul, is relocated by writers such as Schiller and Schopenhauer as a dichotomy within aesthetics itself. Through their recognition that different art-forms reflect different readings of experience, these writers acknowledge a division within aesthetic theory as to the goal of art, but protect individual works (which are either ideal or existential) from involvement in this debate. (pp. 49-50)

By internalizing Schopenhauer's recognition of "the immense discrepancy between the plastic Apollonian art and the Dionysiac art of music" as a heteronomy within the individual work of art, Nietzsche relieves the so-called ideal forms of art (such as poetry) from the necessity of protecting their faith from doubts that reside within the works themselves, as subtexts within the text. What has changed between earlier Romantic aestheticians and Nietzsche is not the fact that the text exists on two levels of awareness, but the manner in which desire and life, or form and content, are allowed to encounter each other. The insights and self-mystifications of Schiller's theory reflect the tensions which characterize a certain kind of Romantic work: a work that is internally divided, yet offers itself as simple rather than complex. Because the sentimental text values unity, it protects itself from its subtext by repressing it or discarding it as irrelevant. In effect, the contradiction between the way the work interprets itself and what it actually contains may result in a deconstruction of the writer's surface assumptions. But this deconstruction occurs in the mind of the reader and not yet within the text itself. Schopenhauer goes further, in describing a text which exposes itself to an irony that it can neither evade nor endorse. But while the sentimental work tends toward a didactic simplification of meaning which the reader may find unsatisfying, this second kind of work manifests only the infinite negativity of ambivalence, by refusing to guide the reader in his giddy transit between text and countertext. Nietzsche, who no longer derives the work of art from a "single vital principle," is the theorist of a very different, third phase in Romantic consciousness: one in which the text has moved beyond the state of contradiction in which it must exist either as a structure of sublimation or as a self-consuming artifact, and has come to terms with its own complicity in the darkness of existence. (pp. 51-2)

It is the sense that life may be not only will but also representation, a product of human activity, that Nietzsche's ***Birth of Tragedy*** tries to respect. We have seen in Romantic critical theory a dialectical confrontation between texts like Schiller's *On Naive and Sentimental Poetry* and Schopenhauer's *World as Will and Representation*. The rhetorical ambivalence which reimplicates both critical texts in the positions they are opposing recurs in poetic texts, whether they are ironic poems which fail to invalidate their own illusions, or sentimental poems which argue for an ideal against the knowledge of its impossibility. . . . Nietzsche, who stands at the meeting point of existentialism and idealism, attempts to articulate and respond to the tensions in Romantic aesthetics, and to legitimize ambivalence by grounding it in the doubleness of existence. (p. 56)

Tilottama Rajan, "Schiller, Schopenhauer, and Nietzsche: The Theoretical Background," in her Dark Interpreter: The Discourse of Romanticism, *Cornell University Press, 1980, pp. 27-57.**

J. HILLIS MILLER (essay date 1981)

[An American critic, Miller is associated with the "Yale critics," a group which includes Harold Bloom, Paul de Man, and Geoffrey Hartman. Although the Yale critics are generally considered the most influential critical group in America today, they have little in common beyond the fact that they all teach at Yale. Throughout his career Miller has successfully applied several critical methods to literature, including New Criticism (which examines a literary work as an object complete in itself through a close analysis of symbol, image, and metaphor, and which holds that literature should not be interpreted as a manifestation of ethics, history, or an author's psychology), the existential phenomenology of Georges Poulet (which views each author's work as the product of a unique individual consciousness with specific understandings of nature, society, time, and space, and thus cannot be understood in terms of generalizations about an era or period), and deconstructionism. Based on the thought of French critic and philosopher Jacques Derrida, deconstructionism asserts that language can never express a speaker's intended meaning, and that in itself language can convey no objective meaning. This concept opposes the traditional critical view that the study of literature is the search for meaning, ideas, and truths in a text. Deconstructionists concentrate solely on the linguistic elements of a text, denying the representational function of words and delineating instead the way a work is constructed of verbal forms. Deconstructionism, then, posits a basic similarity, if not sameness, in all works of literature. Miller and his colleague de Man are the most prominent American practitioners of deconstructive method. In the following excerpt, Miller discusses Nietzsche's concept of selfhood.]

Of all modern deconstructers of the idea of selfhood perhaps Nietzsche, in Book Three of ***The Will to Power*** (in the traditional ordering of the *Nachlass*), presents the most systematic and cogent dismantling of the concept in its relation to the other metaphysical concepts with which it is necessarily connected. Decomposition of the idea of selfhood is of course one of Nietzsche's main themes, from ***The Birth of Tragedy*** . . . and the incomplete ***Philosophenbuch*** . . . on. The topic runs like a red thread through all Nietzsche wrote. Book Three of ***The Will to Power*** contains, among other things, a concentrated effort of deconstruction directed against the concept of the self. This powerful polemic recurs throughout Book Three as a patient and constantly renewed process of disarticulation, for which there is no "central" expression. Section 477, in the traditional numbering, contains most of the elements involved. This section brings out the way the image of the line is involved both in the fiction of the self and in its undoing. The passage looks simple enough, but Nietzsche's thought here, in its connection with other sections of Book Three, is exceedingly complex. (p. 248)

The image of the line is fundamental both in Nietzsche's concept of the self and in its disarticulation. The parts of this concept are bound into one around the central "substratum" of the subject. Nietzsche unties these bonds, performs a *dénouement* of the knotted elements. In so doing he demolishes that central substratum too. When the links chaining the parts together vanish, the phantom of their origin *(Ursprung)* in a single substantial thing called selfhood also vanishes, like a ghost at daybreak.

This disarticulation is also performed by reversing the apparent order of origination and derivation. The usual sequence—putting subject first, and its thoughts second as derived from the thinker, putting the thoughts themselves in sequence, each causing the next, in logical order, asserting a causal connection between the outer world and sensations or thoughts caused by the outer world—all three are condemned as metalepses, reversals of the actual order of temporal priority, a putting of the earlier later and the later earlier and so creating a false appearance of a necessary sequence.

Essential to this procedure of disarticulation is the idea that the fundamental activity of the mind is an activity of interpretation. All interpretation is false interpretation. It is an aberrant reading dependent on simplifying, schematizing, omitting, a making equal of things which are not equal. To put this another way, all interpretation is the making of figures of speech and then the committing of the aboriginal human error of taking these figurative equivalences as literally true of extra-linguistic reality.

Nietzsche's disentangling of the various crossroads or knots involved in the idea of selfhood follows no established order of priority, since order and priority are among the things being undone. Rather, each particular effort of untying, in the different sections of Book Three, depends on assuming that some other one has already been accomplished and can be used as the model for the present one. The result is a constant process of undoing without any fixed starting place. Since the knot of presuppositions being untied was constructed by the same circular process of a round robin positing—the notion of self depending on theological assumptions, but those theological assumptions depending on the notion of self, and both depending on the idea of causality, the idea of substance, the idea of ground, but those ideas making no sense without the theological assumptions, and so on, in a perpetual round—it is appropriate that the untying should mime in reverse the same procedure, suspending it by performing its magic performatives backwards. (p. 249)

Nietzsche's procedure of deconstruction for the inner world of subjectivity is the same as that for the apparent outer world of things. Five different procedures of dismantling are simultaneously employed in section 477 and in other related passages.

First, the individual entities of which the soul is supposed to be constituted—thoughts, feelings, faculties, and so on—are held by Nietzsche not to exist as such but only to be the fictitious products of acts of simplifying construction: "We never encounter 'facts': pleasure and displeasure are subsequent and derivative intellectual phenomena—" The same thing may be said for all the other "facts" of the inner world.

Moreover, no two feelings or thoughts are the same, or continue, or ever recur. They are made to appear to do so by the same act of making simple, regular, and manageable which motivates our creation of a fictitious outer world. . . . A second act of deconstruction Nietzsche performs, then, is to undo this construction of regularity and continuity by denying that any two phenomena of the inner world are ever the same. No feeling or thought may ever continue or ever recur, holds Nietzsche *(Ich halte),* as he says.

A third disarticulation is to undo the supposed links which appear to bind together in tight chains the sequences of these fictitious entities as they follow one another in the mind. Much of Nietzsche's attention in section 477 and the other "similar" sections is focused on the undoing of the concept of causality. Here the image of tying and untying is fundamental. The apparently firm causal links between one thought or feeling and the next are said to be hidden or perhaps non-existent: "to suppose a direct causal link between thoughts, as logic does—that is the consequence of the crudest and clumsiest observation." Events in the inner world of consciousness simply follow one another without any connection, causal or otherwise, between them. Each is self-enclosed. It is separated by a gap from all other thoughts and feelings and only made into any sort of pattern with them by an arbitrary act of artistic construction. (pp. 250-51)

A fourth process of decomposition is related to the third. It is not so much an untying as a reversal. It is one of the most powerful arguments Nietzsche makes against the coherence of the inner world and against the possibility of unifying it around the idea of the self. If the apparent entities of the inner world do not exist as such, if nothing in the inner world continues or recurs or is the same as any other, and if the apparent lines between these fictitious entities are themselves fictitious, these apparent lines themselves are not only fictitious. They are also drawn backwards. The apparent causal links of the inner world are the result of that preposterous figure of speech which puts the early late and the late early: metalepsis.

There are two forms of this in the inner world. One is the mistaken inscription of causal power over the events in that inner world to events or forces in the outer world. This apparent sequence from outer to inner, from object to subject, is a reversal of the true order. Inner precedes outer and projects that outer as the illusory cause of its states. This means that the distinction between inner and outer breaks down. It too is an illusion, a fiction, a work of art. There is no solid object to cause subject but only one single "phenomenal" realm within which all these fictitious entities and the lines between them are constructed. Nietzsche's procedure of deconstruction here is to reverse what has been reversed. He performs a metalepsis of the metalepsis, a chaismus of the chaismus. He reveals thereby the fictitious, projective nature of the supposed "cause" in the "outer" world. (pp. 251-52)

If the outer world is no prior cause, but rather a later projected illusion cast back as the supposed source of some "inner" event, feeling, or thought, the same inversion is spontaneously practiced by consciousness to make sense of the temporal order of the inner world taken in itself. . . .

Nietzsche unties the links of cause and effect in the inner world first by seeing them as a gross oversimplification of an enormously complex set of occurences rapidly happening. As he says in section 477: "Between two thoughts all kinds of affects play their game: but their motions are too fast, therefore we fail to recognize them, we deny them." Second, Nietzsche argues that these oversimplified links go in the wrong direction.

He reverses the metalepses once more and defines the inner causes too as fictitious entities projected backward after the effects to account for them. Projection is a switch of prior and posterior in which the effect is made the cause of its cause, the cause the effect of its effect. (p. 252)

Nietzsche's thought here is not easy to grasp. The paradox is that we are not, and cannot be, conscious of the "facts" of the inner world as such, not even of effects, such as pain, or a thought, which seem to exist only as facts of consciousness. We cannot be conscious of our consciousness as such. The reason is that consciousness only works in terms of comprehensible imaginary causal chains. We project backward a fictitious cause and only then can the fact of consciousness, the thought or the feeling, enter consciousness. It enters consciousness in the thoroughly aberrant form of a fictitious effect of a fictitious cause. . . . An effect of which we are not yet conscious becomes the cause of an imaginary cause, and that imaginary cause then generates belatedly the consciousness of an effect which fits that imaginary cause in the sense of being purely imaginary, "phenomenal," too. If dreams are invention of phantasmal causes for conditions which we can only become aware of in the dream, in the form of equally phantasmal effects, as when a book falling to the floor is read by the dream as a shot fired by a burglar breaking in to the house, our entire "waking" life is also no more than a sequence of regularized and recurrent dreams. The human condition is to be, in the striking phrase from the early essay "On Truth and Lies in an Nonmoral Sense," "as if *(Gleichsam)* hanging in dreams on the back of a tiger." (p. 253)

It is only after this elaborate act of untying, moving backwards to undo knot after knot which has woven the web of the inner world, that Nietzsche comes at last, at the end of section 477, to the ur-fiction on the ground of which the whole airy structure has been built: the notion of the unity, substantiality, and perdurability of the self. Having patiently dismantled, one by one, the entities of the inner world, feelings and thoughts, and loosing the apparently determining causal lines between those entities, Nietzsche turns finally to the supposed subject, the *Ich* or "I" which does the thinking and feeling. It is easy to see that the concept of the self does not have a leg to stand on. It vanishes like all the other imaginary entities and imaginary lines between entities of the "inner world." (p. 254)

To deconstruct the notion of the "I" that thinks one must, as Nietzsche does in section 477, patiently untie all the liaisons constituting the act of thinking and then, finally, the doer will dissolve in the dissolution of his deed. On the other hand, in others of the fragments on the self, the self is seen as the originating fictitious postulate on the basis of which causality, will, substance, and so on, are projected. Origin and end constantly change places, so that whatever one looks at appears secondary in relation to some prior act of positing which must be assumed already to have taken place. The act of origination is never in itself present as such, but always took place already, over there, earlier. The whole structure of elements sustains itself in a constantly moving airy confabulation of autogenerating and autosustaining fictions, like a man lifting himself by his own bootstraps—and turning somersaults to boot. This means that the putting in question of any one element disperses the whole fabrication, like an architectual edifice of clouds, leaving not a wrack behind. The interdependence and lack of an originating hypothesis on which all the rest depend, explains also the contradictions in Nietzsche's formulations, the way what is cause in one fragment becomes effect in another, and vice versa. (pp. 255-56)

Moving backwards from the entities and the connections between entities presupposed by the self to the self itself, and then from the self outwards again to its peripheral branching connections, Nietzsche performs a whole-scale dissolution of the idea of self, character, or subject. There is nothing quite so like it in English literature of the same period as the mournful litany of denials and dissolvings in the "Conclusion" to Walter Pater's *The Renaissance*. . . . (p. 258)

Though Pater may seem to give more substantial reality to "impressions," as "facts" of inner experience, than Nietzsche does, he elsewhere recognizes, like Nietzsche, that impressions too are signs, interpretations, results of complex acts of simplification rather than aboriginal causes. Nietzsche, like Pater in "Apollo in Picardy," replaces the hard substantial single self with the notion of constantly changing multiple selves enclosed in perpetual combat or struggle for power within the receptacle of a "consciousness." Far from being a given solid substance on the basis of which everything else in the inner world is constructed and sustained, the self is a momentary effect of a combat of forces, forces which are signs. The ego is a pure projection, changing from instant to instant as the balance of these forces shifts, in "continual transitoriness and fleetingness." . . . Since it is a phantasmal projection, product of an interpretation, it is not only constantly shifting, never fixed for a moment, expanding, contracting, changing its center of gravity. It is also capable of subdividing, of creating two or more centers, each of which appears to be a self. The end-point of Nietzsche's dismantling of the notion of the substantial self is the idea that a single body may be inhabited by multiple selves. Nietzsche's figure for this dialogism is a dynamic, physical one. It is as though the "inner world" were an enclosed collocation of matter and energy. This system of forces inhabiting a single body may produce in its interactions the illusion not just of one selfhood, but of many. . . . (pp. 258-59)

[Nietzsche's] notion of dialogism is one of his most powerful levers to displace the logocentrism of the West. Dialogism, two-mindedness, is, as Shakespeare shows in *Troilus and Cressida,* no-mindedness, unreason, madness. It is not appropriate to speak of it under the category of *logos,* as reason, measure, ratio, mind, *Grund,* at all. Nietzsche does not do so. He substitutes for the family of logocentric terms another set of terms involving will, power, force, and interpretation, in the sense of a life-enhancing simplification and making calculable. Reason, consciousness, and logic are almost accidental consequences of the work of interpretation. They may become a dangerous constriction when new "illogical" interpretations become necessary for man's self-preservation. In spite of the univocity of logic, each man's body is the locus of a set of warring interpretations, or at best, according to an alternative metaphor to the physical-dynamic one, a political entity within which there is perhaps one "ruler" within the struggle for power, but a ruler dependent on the ruled and obliquely ruled by them. Such a state is a shifting balance of antagonistic forces from which the illusion of selfhood in an individual arises as a figment. This epiphenomenon, moreover, fluctuates constantly, however fixed it appears to falsifying interpretation, which wants to say, "I am I, a single self, remaining always the same." (pp. 259-60)

Nietzsche's interrogation of the idea of selfhood has reached, by a complex series of dissolutions, a definition of the self as a projected, constantly changing virtuality, like the center of gravity of a moving mass. This phantasmal center, moreover, has been doubled, fragmented, multiplied, dispersed into who knows how many separate momentary centers. Each is inhabited by a will to power over the whole, a desire to dominate and be itself the center. (p. 260)

The aporia of Nietzsche's strategy of deconstruction is a version of the universal aporia of deconstruction. It lies in the fact that Nietzsche must use as the indispensable lever of his act of disarticulation a positing of the entity he intends to demolish. He must affirm the thing he means to deconstruct in order to deconstruct it. The deconstruction therefore deconstructs itself. It is built over the abyss of its own impossibility. In order to proceed with the undoing Nietzsche must begin with an act of positing which is the main target of the undoing. The whole complicated series of untyings which I have traced out, knot by knot, is strung on that initial positing.

If causality, substance, and so on, are posited on the positing of the ego, the denial of those concepts is not a replacement of falsehood by truth, the "facts," things as they are. It is an alternative series of positings based by a series of metaphorical displacements on the initial positing of the deconstructing self: *Ich halte*. In unbinding all those knots, Nietzsche does not produce a line straight and true, free of all intrication, open to eyesight and measurement, a ruler by which all crooked thinking can be measured and made straight. He produces only another complicated knot, fold on fold, implicated within itself, a labyrinth of new figures. This reversal, whereby deconstruction deconstructs itself, and at the same time creates another labyrinthine fiction whose authority is undermined by its own creation, is characteristic of all deconstructive discourse. The way in which the fiction of selfhood survives its dismantling, or is even a necessary presupposition of its own dismantling, is a striking example of this. (pp. 260-61)

J. Hillis Miller, "The Disarticulation of the Self in Nietzsche," in The Monist, *Vol. 64, No. 2, April, 1981, pp. 247-61.*

GILLES DELEUZE (essay date 1983)

[Deleuze is a French critic associated with the poststructuralist school of literary analysis. In the following excerpt from a preface written for the English translation of his Nietzsche et la philosophie *(1962), Deleuze explains that this study was intended to correct what he considered misapprehensions of such major concepts of Nietzsche's philosophy as nihilism, the overman, the will to power, and eternal recurrence.]*

Nietzsche's posthumous fate has been burdened by two ambiguities: was his thought a forerunner of fascist thinking? And was this thought itself really philosophy or was it an over-violent poetry, made up of capricious aphorisms and pathological fragments? It is perhaps in England that Nietzsche has been most misunderstood. Tomlinson suggests that the major themes which Nietzsche confronts and battles against—French rationalism and German dialectics—have never been of central importance to English thought. The English had at their theoretical disposal an empiricism and a pragmatism which meant that the detour through Nietzsche was of no great value to them. They did not need the detour through Nietzsche's very special empiricism and pragmatism which ran counter to their "good sense". In England therefore Nietzsche was only able to influence novelists, poets and dramatists: this was a practical, emotional influence rather than a philosophical one, lyrical rather than theoretical.

Nevertheless Nietzsche is one of the greatest philosophers of the nineteenth century. And he alters both the theory and the practice of philosophy. He compares the thinker to an arrow shot by Nature that another thinker picks up where it has fallen so that he can shoot it somewhere else. According to him, the philosopher is neither eternal nor historical but "untimely", always untimely. Nietzsche has hardly any predecessors. Apart from the Pre-Socratics of long ago he recognised only one predecessor—Spinoza.

Nietzsche's philosophy is organised along two great axes. The first is concerned with force, with forces, and forms of general semeiology. Phenomena, things, organisms, societies, consciousness and spirits are signs, or rather symptoms, and themselves reflect states of forces. This is the origin of the conception of the philosopher as "physiologist and physician". We can ask, for any given thing, what state of exterior and interior forces it presupposes. Nietzsche was responsible for creating a whole typology to distinguish active, acted and reactive forces and to analyse their varying combinations. In particular, the delineation of a genuinely reactive type of forces constitutes one of the most original points of Nietzschean thought. This book attempts to define and analyse the different forces. This kind of general semeiology includes linguistics, or rather philology, as one of its parts. For any proposition is itself a set of symptoms expressing a way of being or a mode of existence of the speaker, that is to say the state of forces that he maintains or tries to maintain with himself and others (consider the role of conjunctions in this connection). In this sense a proposition always reflects a mode of existence, a "type". What is the mode of existence of the person who utters any given proposition, what mode of existence is needed in order to be able to utter it? The mode of existence is the state of forces insofar as it forms a type which can be expressed by signs or symptoms.

The two great human reactive concepts, as "diagnosed" by Nietzsche, are those of *ressentiment* and bad conscience. *Ressentiment* and bad conscience are expressions of the triumph of reactive forces in man and even of the constitution of man by reactive forces: the man-slave. This shows the extent to which the Nietzschean notion of the slave does not necessarily stand for someone dominated, by fate or social condition, but also characterises the dominators as much as the dominated once the regime of domination comes under the sway of forces which are reactive and not active. Totalitarian regimes are in this sense regimes of slaves, not merely because of the people that they subjugate, but above all because of the type of "masters" they set up. A universal history of *ressentiment* and bad conscience—from the Jewish and Christian priests to the secular priest of the present—is a fundamental component of Nietzsche's historical perspectivism (Nietzsche's supposedly anti-semitic texts are in fact texts on the original priestly type).

The second axis is concerned with power and forms an ethics and an ontology. Nietzsche is most misunderstood in relation to the question of power. Every time we interpret will to power as "wanting or seeking power" we encounter platitudes which have nothing to do with Nietzsche's thought. If it is true that all things reflect a state of forces then power designates the element, or rather the differential relationship, of forces which directly confront one another. This relationship expresses itself in the dynamic qualities of types such as "affirmation" and "negation". Power is therefore not what the will wants, but on the contrary, the one that wants in the will. And "to want or seek power" is only the lowest degree of the will to power, its negative form, the guise it assumes when reactive forces prevail in the state of things. One of the most original characteristics of Nietzsche's philosophy is the transformation of the question "what is . . .?" into "which one is . . .?" For example, for any given proposition he asks "which one is capable of uttering it?" Here we must rid ourselves of all "personalist" references. The one that . . . does not refer to an individual, to a person, but rather to an event, that is, to the forces in their various relationships in a proposition or a phenomenon, and to the genetic relationship which determines these forces (power). "The one that" is always Dionysus, a mask or a guise of Dionysus, a flash of lightning.

The eternal return is as badly misunderstood as the will to power. Every time we understand the eternal return as the return of a particular arrangement of things after all the other arrangements have been realised, every time we interpret the eternal return as the return of the identical or the same, we replace Nietzsche's thought with childish hypotheses. No one extended the critique of all forms of identity further than Nietzsche. On two occasions in ***Zarathustra*** Nietzsche explicitly denies that the eternal return is a circle which makes the same return. The eternal return is the strict opposite of this since it cannot be separated from a selection, from a double selection. Firstly, there is the selection of willing or of thought which constitutes Nietzsche's ethics: only will that of which one also wills the eternal return (to eliminate all half-willing, everything which can only be willed with the proviso "once, only once"). Secondly, there is the selection of being which constitutes Nietzsche's ontology: only that which *becomes* in the fullest sense of the word can return, is fit to return. Only action and affirmation return: becoming has being and only becoming has being. That which is opposed to becoming, the same or the identical, strictly speaking, *is* not. The negative as the lowest degree of power, the reactive as the lowest degree of force, do not return because they are the opposite of becoming and only becoming has being. We can thus see how the eternal return is linked, not to a repetition of the same, but on the contrary, to a transmutation. It is the moment or the eternity of becoming which eliminates all that resists it. It releases, indeed it creates, the purely active and pure affirmation. And this is the sole content of the Overman; he is the joint product of the will to power and the eternal return, Dionysus and Ariadne. This is why Nietzsche says that the will to power is not wanting, coveting or seeking power, but only "giving" or "creating". (pp. ix-xii)

But the difficulty of Nietzsche depends less on conceptual analysis than on practical evaluations which evoke a whole atmosphere, all kinds of emotional dispositions in the reader. Like Spinoza, Nietzsche always maintained that there is the deepest relationship between concept and affect. Conceptual analyses are indispensable and Nietzsche takes them further than anyone else. But they will always be ineffective if the reader grasps them in an atmosphere which is not that of Nietzsche. As long as the reader persists in: 1) seeing the Nietzschean "slave" as someone who finds himself dominated by a master, and deserves to be; 2) understanding the will to power as a will which wants and seeks power; 3) conceiving the eternal return as the tedious return of the same; 4) imagining the Overman as a given master race—no positive relationship between Nietzsche and his reader will be possible. Nietzsche will appear a nihilist, or worse, a fascist and at best as an obscure and terrifying prophet. Nietzsche knew this, he knew the fate that lay in store for him, he who gave Zarathustra an "ape" or "buffoon" as a double, foretelling that Zarathustra would be confused with his ape (a prophet, a fascist or a madman . . .). This is why a book about Nietzsche must try hard to correct the practical or emotional misunderstanding as well as re-establishing the conceptual analysis.

And it is indeed true that Nietzsche diagnosed nihilism as the movement which carries history forward. No one has analysed the concept of nihilism better than he did, he invented the concept. But it is important to see that he defined it in terms of the triumph of reactive forces or the negative in the will to power. To nihilism he opposed transmutation, that is the becoming which is simultaneously the only action of force and the only affirmation of power, the transhistoric element of man, the Overman (and not the superman). The Overman is the focal point, where the reactive (*ressentiment* and bad conscience) is conquered, and where the negative gives way to affirmation. Nietzsche remains inseparable, at every moment, from the forces of the future, from the forces yet to come that his prayers invoke, that his thought outlines, that his art prefigures. He not only diagnoses, as Kafka put it, the diabolical forces already knocking at the door, but he exorcises them by raising the last Power capable of struggling with them, against them, and of ousting them both within us and outside us. A Nietzschean "aphorism" is not a mere fragment, a morsel of thought: it is a proposition which only makes sense in relation to the state of forces that it expresses, and which changes sense, which must change sense, according to the new forces which it is "capable" (has the power) of attracting.

And without doubt this is the most important point of Nietzsche's philosophy: the radical transformation of the image of thought that we create for ourselves. Nietzsche snatches thought from the element of truth and falsity. He turns it into an interpretation and an evaluation, interpretation of forces, evaluation of power.—It is a thought-movement, not merely in the sense that Nietzsche wants to reconcile thought and concrete movement, but in the sense that thought itself must produce movements, bursts of extraordinary speed and slowness (here again we can see the role of the aphorism, with its variable speeds and its "projectile-like" movement). As a result philosophy has a new relationship to the arts of movement: theatre, dance and music. Nietzsche was never satisfied with the discourse or the dissertation *(logos)* as an expression of philosophical thought, although he wrote the finest dissertations—notably the ***Genealogy of Morals,*** to which all modern ethnology owes an inexhaustible "debt". But a book like ***Zarathustra*** can only be read as a modern opera and seen and heard as such. It is not that Nietzsche produces a philosophical opera or a piece of allegorical theatre, but he creates a piece of theatre or an opera which directly expresses thought as experience and movement. And when Nietzsche says that the Overman resembles a Borgia rather than a Parsifal, or that he is a member of both the order of Jesuits and the Prussian officer corps, it would be wrong to see these as protofascist statements, since they are the remarks of a director indicating how the Overman should be "played" (rather like Kierkegaard saying that the knight of the faith is like a bourgeois in his Sunday best).—To think is to create: this is Nietzsche's greatest lesson. To think, to cast the dice. . . : this was already the sense of the eternal return. (pp. xii-xiv)

Gilles Deleuze, in a preface to his Nietzsche and Philosophy, *translated by Hugh Tomlinson, Columbia University Press, 1983, 221 p.*

HOWARD EILAND (essay date 1985)

[In the following excerpt, Eiland discusses the significance of Judaism and the Jewish people in Nietzsche's works.]

"Nietzsche in His Last Year of Life," from a drawing by Hans Olde, 1899.

If the Jews are more homogeneous and firmly rooted than other peoples, it is because their blood, or their "seed" (to use the biblical term), has been the beneficiary of their history, namely, their long isolation in the ghetto. Such schooling in suffering and alienation, Nietzsche argues in ***The Dawn*** . . . , has engendered exemplary spiritual and intellectual resources, notably patience, circumspection, and flexibility. At the same time, their ancient nerves, brooding within the distinctive hothouse intimacy of Jewish family life, and inflamed by the "leprosy of God's choice" (in George Steiner's phrase), have spawned a prodigy of spiritual and intellectual illnesses. This is what is striking in Nietzsche's imagination of the Jews: that repeatedly, but without explicitly calling attention to it, he makes them representative of an uncanny psychic doubleness that, among world-historical peoples, appertains otherwise only to the Germans. (See section 244 of ***Beyond Good and Evil,*** where the Germans, "the people of depth," are characterized in terms of multiplicity, contradiction, evolution—of "corridors within corridors.") On the one hand, the Jews exemplify cool and elegant psycho-physiological fortitude; on the other, superheated pathology. They are rationalists *par excellence*—in their marriage customs as much as their intellectual habits; since nobody wants to believe them, they have had to develop logical argument to an art, and they have helped to demythologize and occidentalize whatever milieu they inhabit. But they have also cultivated a passionate and tortuous mysticism that spreads the Oriental. They are famous for being soldiers and for being lovers, for renunciation and for voluptuousness. They are pushy and acquiescent, worldly and dreamy, equally capable as managers and seers (think of Joseph, Jacob's son). Their extreme outward cleanliness, says Nietzsche, has its counterpart in a secret sense of pollution and sinfulness, just as their corrosive skepticism alternates with bottomless God-fear. They are anti-naturalists, engulfed in shame, as much as naturalists and scientists, ironists as much as schlemiels. Nietzsche conceives the Jews, in short, as embodying the overarching antithesis of his own existence: that of spirit and life.

This fundamental existential antithesis is understood further, in historical terms, as ancient versus modern—history functioning thus to designate permanent psychological possibilities, as psychology itself assumes a temporal dimension. Ancient is what is unscrupulously strong, healthy, spontaneous; modern, of course, is another word for morbid, complicated, self-divided—but also *interesting*. In ***The Birth of Tragedy,*** Nietzsche had analyzed the transition in Greek culture from Hellenism to Socratism and Alexandrianism: from an initial and integral "unconscious metaphysic" of the tribe, which still infuses pre-Socratic philosophy and pre-Euripidean tragedy, to a distinctively "late," rootless and bloodless ethical historicism, an all too familiar civilization of parodists and librarians. In the two decades following this explosion of a first book, he turned increasingly to the other decisive strand in European history, the Judeo-Christian, and to *its* peculiar corruption. His interpretation of this tradition, as original for his day as his interpretation of the Greeks, stresses the continuity of Jewish and Christian, the former appearing emphatically as "the soil" (another key biblical term) for the latter. In fact, the crucial transition, he argues, occurs within Jewish history itself.

In ***Beyond Good and Evil*** . . . , and ***The Antichrist*** . . . , Nietzsche imputes to the Jews a radical, indeed catastrophic and world-shaking revaluation *(Umwertung)* of values. The Jews, he says, are the strangest, most fateful people in history. No other nation has so mastered the interweaving of denial and affirmation, of no-saying and yes-doing, the art of negating, of *creative* negating, in order to survive. But, as in Greek culture, this abysmal complexity is a late phenomenon. Originally, especially at the time of the kings, Israel enjoyed a natural or "naive" relation to things comparable to that of the Homeric heroes:

> Its Yahweh was the expression of a consciousness of power, of joy in oneself, of hope for oneself: through him victory and welfare were expected; through him nature was trusted to give what the people needed—above all, rain.

The God of the patriarchs and kings, though not simply a nature-god, was worshipped in a festival cult defined by the rhythm of the seasons. His covenant was modeled on a royal grant to favorites; it contained no obligations, the fulfilment of which was to be the condition of their happiness. Sacrifice, vow, and prayer were to express their feelings of loyalty and of thanks for their good fortune. But this deity, argues Nietzsche, was "denatured" by the prophets and by "priestly agitators," who come to interpret all happiness as reward and all unhappiness as punishment for disobeying God. In place of a god who inspires courage and self-confidence emerges a "god who *demands,*" and in place of an instinctive cult of divine sovereignty evolves a "stupid salvation mechanism," by which the Jewish priesthood reinterprets the scriptures and history of Israel. The Babylonian exile, for example, is "transformed into an eternal punishment for the great age—an age in which the priest was still a nobody." Nietzsche is evidently thinking, not only of prophets like Jeremiah and Ezekiel, but of the scholar-priest Ezra and his circle, who, in the middle of the 5th century BCE—concurrent with the Sophists' establishment of *their* schools—returned from Babylon in a mood of severe and anxious repentance, intent on purifying the law, codifying the canon, and carrying on the reforms of prophets who had abolished the local altars, stone pillars, sacred trees of the patriarchal religion as vestigially "Canaanite." This clash of archaic cult and post-exilic systematizing morality is taken by Nietzsche as a paradigm of *ressentiment,* the process by which existence is done out of its originally amoral "innocence."

It is thus that the Jew, in all his holiness, comes to stand for the idea of decadence—a subject in which Nietzsche himself claims, at the beginning of ***Ecce Homo,*** to be thoroughly experienced. The Jewish prophets had been the first to conflate the notions of rich, violent, sensual, and godless so as to distinguish from these an adversary notion of goodness opposed to "the world." As the Jews become a subject people, this conception of a fallen world helps to insure their own unworldly survival. Ezra's xenophobic legalism, born of exile and rankling fear, may be seen as symptomatic of, not only "physiological indisposition," but a farseeing subversion of "power in character, spirit, and taste." . . . It is the rancorous and subtle expedient of the impotent, by which the fact of subjection is transformed into "abstract" virtues of humility and obedience of divine will. Purity of heart, in Nietzsche's evil diagnosis, is a euphemism for emasculation. Thus there arises—at a time when Plato, "that instinctive Semite" . . . , was turning against Homer while discrediting the sensuous world and subordinating philosophy to ethics—the momentous "slave revolt in morals," the soil proper for Christianity. The early Christians, argues Nietzsche, were a lower class pietistic movement within Pharisaic Judaism rebelling against the hierarchies of the ruling priestly caste. This outcast or "chandala" sect (and, we read in ***Twilight of the Idols*** . . . , "all innovators of the spirit must for a time bear the pallid and fatal mark of the Chandala [the untouchable in Hindu law] on their foreheads")—these publicans, prostitutes, criminals, lepers—represented precisely the underground adversary spirit of the priests themselves, however emancipated from ecclesiastical institutions. Christianity is Jewish poison agitated and fermented, subtilized, lyricized, made still more dangerous. Christian love is the crown of a tree rooted deep in Jewish hate. Blithely overcoming all political rank and demarcation, Christ is the *Umweg,* the oblique by-path, of Judea's revenge on the masters of the world.

It is important, in these matters, to "hear," as Nietzsche says, the author's silences—all the more so when one considers the long line of Nietzsche's clergymen forebears and the passionate pity filling his diaries and letters up through his twentieth year. If religiosity for him, as for Novalis, was necessarily associated with voluptuousness and cruelty . . . , then this meant, above all, cruelty toward *oneself.* It is some such malignant chemistry that dictates his insistent rhyming of spiritual and profound with evil and poisonous (as healthy and upright are rhymed with naive) and his evocation of a dark ambiguous glamour—the glamour of danger—around what he calls "the ascetic ideal":

> For with the priests *everthing* becomes more dangerous . . . but it is only fair to add that it was on the soil of this *essentially dangerous* form of human existence, the priestly form, that man first became *an interesting animal,* that only here did the human soul in a higher sense acquire *depth* and become *evil*—and these are the two basic respects in which man has hitherto been superior to other beasts! . . .

Morality, in other words, the upstart, difficult invention of Jewish conscience, is a symptom simultaneously of physiological decline and spiritual advance. For the weak as a rule are more intelligent, and malice spiritualizes. "Human history," writes Nietzsche in ***The Genealogy of Morals*** . . . , "would be altogether too stupid a thing without the spirit that the impotent have introduced into it." The Jews, as "the priestly nation of *ressentiment par excellence*" (an echo of *Exodus* 19.6: "you shall be to me a kindgom of priests"), tormented and enchanted by secret fevers, and thus full of generative power, give birth to a world-historical mission of transcendental valuation. By stamping a burning no on what is "outside" or natural, by opposing an ill-bred and virulent seriousness to classical urbanity and gentility, they painfully and in*toxic*atingly engender "the high style in morality, the frightfulness and majesty of infinite demands, infinite interpretations, the whole romanticism and sublimity of moral problematics." . . . Their high rancor, to be distinguished from the plebeian rancor of the Reformation Germans, blossoms into the uncanny, the beyond. Their private experience of sin, that is, alienation from God, dilates into "metaphysical guilt," making earthly justification at once needful and impossible. The very *fervor* of their renunciation renders "interesting" the life it envenoms.

"Semitism," then, is for Nietzsche provisionally tantamount to priestliness, which, as we have indicated, is no simple matter. The priest, that most dangerous animal, inaugurates a new era in human history, perhaps indeed *the* human era (which, one recalls, Zarathustra views as a bridge to something higher). By his invention of morality, with its infinite demands, in the face of knightly-aristocratic "naiveté," he brings into being a novel depth, nuance, esprit—a novel *inwardness.* The exposition of this process of *Verinnerlichung,* which made ***On the Genealogy of Morals*** so revolutionary a publication, has no doubt lost its salt since Freud, and it is widely recognized that the theory of sublimation is specifically anticipated in Nietzsche's analysis of the internalization of aboriginal cruelty occasioned by the taming of warrior man. For our purposes, however, it is worth recalling that this inhibiting and redirecting of the instinct for freedom, of the discharge of violence—by which the former predator, homesick for the wild, has "to *turn himself* into an adventure, a torture chamber, an uncertain and dangerous wilderness"—signifies nothing less than the emergence of "soul" (soul being defined, as poets like Hölderlin and Hopkins also attest, by an inner oceanic topography of mountains and chasms). The priestly Jew, that is to say, whose violent domestication of the blonde beast within himself entails far more radical terrors and opportunities for courage, comes to the fore—pace Meister Wagner—as the originator of all ideal values.

Nietzsche emphasizes that the break from "semi-animality" is neither gradual nor voluntary nor a matter of Darwinian adaptation to new conditions, but rather a *leap,* an ineluctable and fateful catastrophe *(Verhängnis)*—which statement may be set beside his nomination of the Jews, in ***The Antichrist*** . . . , as "the most fateful-catastrophic [*verhängnisvollste*] people of world history." (pp. 107-12)

Once this leap into interiority occurs, the priest who "theologically" engendered the change may "pastorally" deal with its consequences: namely, the host of spiritual ills. (For the creation of soul, we have seen, is one with the fall into decadence.) Essentially "reactive" whether in instigating the "slave morality" against a hostile external world or in treating the after-effects of his inner rebellion, the priest who chooses the latter, the pastoral ministry, functions as the sick doctor for the sick. His task is to deaden, more precisely dominate, subliminal weariness, disgust, angst through the arousal of "affects," which, in the long run, make the sick sicker—even more out of touch with animal health. Nietzsche differentiates "innocent" affects, like the incitement to industriousness, philanthropy, gregariousness (potent aids all in forgetting), from the more distinguished "guilty" affects, such as the awakening of a sense of sin, in which case the suffering decadent drives down uncanny pain by provoking more violent and *intelligible* pain. The priest who inculcates these methods of transcendence, in addition to being one of the ailing and "delicate," must also be psychologically strong, a master of himself, ''venerable, prudent, and cold,'' so as to be trusted and feared by his flock. The minister must be a covert *magister*. Indeed, Nietzsche speculates, in his war with thoses beasts of prey who remain immune to conscience—a war of cunning (that is, spirit), the priest must himself evolve or impersonate a ''new type of preying animal'':

> a new kind of animal ferocity in which the polar bear, the supple, cold, and patient tiger, and not least the fox seem to be joined in a unity at once enticing and terrifying. . . .

What this priestly war of the sick against their own sickness and against the strong ultimately implies, in the labyrinthine argument of ***The Genealogy of Morals,*** is that the ascetic ideal, the incarnate will to contradiction and antinaturalness, is actually ''an artifice for the *preservation;* of life,'' and that the Semitic priest, this mephistophelean denier, is ''among the greatest *conserving* and yes-generating [*Jaschaffenden*] forces.'' . . . The insatiable *ressentiment* that summons energy to block up the wells of energy, that *enjoys* itself in suffering, the intellectual dyspepsia that cannot digest and have done with, obliquely serves to affirm existence. Life turns against itself—in the interests of life.

Why else should this self-divided and life-inimical species, whose instinct forbids him to propagate, keep appearing so persistently and universally—if not for some surpassing *physiological* necessity? Physiological, that is, in the sense of economic: as an earthquake, in the disposition of terrestrial stresses, may be economic. For it is not only the curative and regulative instinct of degenerating life that underlies the recurrent necessity of priestly renunciation. It is, more generally, a metaphysical law of existence that, as Nietzsche puts it at the end of ***Genealogy,*** ''all great things come through themselves to ruin, through an act of self-overcoming.'' . . . Nietzsche's word here, *Selbstaufhebung,* which is the keynote of Hegelian dialectic, means not just self-overcoming but also self-annulment, self-preservation, even self-exaltation. It is a contradictory term for a contradictory state of affairs, in which the ministerial cure is poisonous and its poison curative, and in which the will to nothingness functions as the source of ideals. It underlines the strange complicity—comparable only perhaps to the reciprocity of life and death instincts in *Civilization and its Discontents*—between nature and spirit, *Wille* and *Widerwille*. For, once out of the glad (if theoretically problematic) state of semi-animality, human nature suffers first of all from an oppressive need for meaning, that is, from a *spiritual* affliction. The proffered cure, the ''Semitic'' invention of morality and a moral world-order, at once satisfies and exacerbates this need. It calls into being a sudden mountainscape of ideas where before was ostensibly wild freedom; it transforms the festive brute quester into a self-torturing questioner. It answers the primeval inquiry, 'Why do I suffer?' by introducing new and deeper suffering, the pleasurable unpleasure of infinite demand, which enlivens spirit while dispiriting life, which exalts while annulling. It generates meaning such that meaning itself—or ''human nature'' itself—becomes an enigma. . . .

The evolution and self-overcoming of the ascetic ideal, then, is the essential matter at stake in Nietzsche's preoccupation with Judaism, or Judaeo-Christianity. This evolution is tantamount to the process of *in*volution, or internalization of cruelty, which constitutes what Nietzsche claims is ''the only meaning offered so far'' in human history. Which is to say, *Verinnerlichung* describes the development of the idea of God (whose kingdom, according to the Evangelist, is ''within you''). As Jewish conscience—which includes the ethical-transcendental ''Semitic'' in Platonism—this idea ushers into existence a fierce, often xenophobic meticulousness of mind, a will to cleanliness having both analytic and dreamy propensities, by the standard of which ''the world'' is seen as sullied, that is, guilty. At the same time, a xenophilic tendency within the chosen people deputes to Israel the responsibility of being ''a light unto the gentiles,'' and thus of spiritually *conquering* the world for morality. This missionary-ministerial ideal, once the Israelites themselves are conquered and dispersed, goes underground and turns rancorous. Christian love, as already indicated, becomes a device for ''Judaizing'' the world. In Christianity the Jewish conscience intensifies its rigor and ''confessional subtlety,'' its vengefulness toward itself. The alternately brooding and ecstatic ''religious cruelty'' of the Old Testament prophets and priests is transmuted, contorted, and magnified into ''that mystery of an unimaginable and ultimate cruelty and self-crucifixion of God''. . . . The will to sacrifice and self-crucifixion from then on determines the development of the ascetic ideal—as a kind of psychological ''vampirism.'' If the knife of conscience is progressively turned, first, on Christian dogma and, then, on Judaic-Christian morality itself—all in the interests of pursuing truth and eradicating illusion, no matter the cost to animal confidence—this means that asceticism, having undermined its doctrinal and liturgical foundations, finds a new doctrine and liturgy in *science*. Though it may seem the enemy of religion, modern science, insists Nietzsche, is actually the heir of religious conscience: above all, in its belief in *truth,* in the positivity and absoluteness (divinity) of truth. If honesty to ''facts'' compels the reduction of once proud man to the status of cousin to the apes, that is to be expected; self-contempt, at this late stage, is a sign of intellectual integrity, of seriousness—of *love*. In other words, the driven burning morality of Abraham, of Moses, of Isaiah, having been sublimated into scientific method, reveals itself as the essence of modernity: God as self-consciousness—the ever dilating inwardness that, as Erich Heller, reading Nietzsche with the help of Hegel, has shown, ultimately, and with relentless logic, turns against even the idea of God.

We begin therefore to sense what Nietzsche means in calling morality—morality cut off from elemental religiousity—a catastrophe, a two-thousand year mittence that must, however, be continually *worked through*. For if the will to truth leads to nihilism, then nihilism too may involve a self-overcoming, one in which honesty compels, in the interests of a larger truth, the suspension of an exclusively analytical conception of knowledge. If there is a ''classic nihilism,'' a leap into the abyss of history in order to re-think and revalue the world, and an ''ecstatic nihilism,'' a ruthless trailblazing into the open, then there may be something like a ''divine nihilism,'' a way of thinking beyond the opposition of facts and values, beyond paradox, *beyond revenge*. . . . That means beyond the will to certainty, the impulse to posit a cause for everything, to posit an otherworld as the instrument of punishment and reward, the impulse, in short, to moralize existence—and, we might add, to moralize God. Divine nihilism, which ventures to live in ambiguity without denying the manifest if emergent purposiveness in things . . . , would restore to being its ancient ''innocence,'' enabling us to understand how the reward may dwell *in* the work, the deed. Such restoration, however, is not exactly regression ''back to nature.'' For psychology, and even a kind of morality, persist among immoralists: ''one needs a great deal of morality to be immoral in this subtle way.'' . . . Traditional rationalistic-transcendental morality, with its training in reflection, is a necessary stage in the evolution of a supramoral morality that diagnoses a component malice in virtue while—unlike the Nazi immoralism—integrating goodness or justice into instinctive evil. The recurrent symbolic contest of Rome and Judea, Judea and Rome, which is explicitly articulated in ***The Genealogy of Morals*** but implicit throughout Nietzsche's writing, is not meant to issue in the victory of one side.

The tangled ramifications of this contest, which we have tried here to trace, suggest that, for Nietzsche, the Jew is important ultimately as a *meta-ethnic* ideal, a universal human and cultural possibility. If Rome, whose citizens were "stronger and nobler [*vornehmer*]" than any people yet on earth . . . , stands for aristocratic potency in general, for all classical focus and univocity, then diasporic Judea incarnates all suffering spirit—that is, the problematic consciousness of meaning. (pp. 112-16)

Howard Eiland, "Nietzsche's Jew," in Salmagundi, *No. 66, Winter-Spring, 1985, pp. 104-17.*

ADDITIONAL BIBLIOGRAPHY

Allison, David B., ed. *The New Nietzsche: Contemporary Styles of Interpretation.* New York: Dell Publishing Co., 1977, 274 p.

Translations of essays and translated excerpts from book-length studies of Nietzsche by leading European critics. The critics include Pierre Klossowski, Martin Heidegger, Maurice Blanchot, Jacques Derrida, and Gilles Deleuze.

Borges, Jorge Luis. "Some of Nietzsche's Opinions." In his *Borges: A Reader,* pp. 109-11, edited by Emir Rodriguez Monegal and Alastair Reid. New York: E. P. Dutton, 1981.

First English translation of a 1940 essay in which Borges examines sections of Nietzsche's notebooks dealing with German nationalism. Borges concludes his discussion with the statement that "with the exception of Samuel Butler, no nineteenth-century author is as much our contemporary as Friedrich Nietzsche. Very little in his work has grown old, except, perhaps, that humanist veneration for classical antiquity which Bernard Shaw was the first to criticize. Also a kind of lucidity in the very heart of polemics, a sort of delicate censure, which our day and age seems to have forgotten."

Eden, Robert. *Political Leadership and Nihilism: A Study of Weber and Nietzsche.* Tampa: University of South Florida Press, 1983, 348 p.

Studies Max Weber's ideas on political leadership and the influence of Nietzsche on their development and ultimate form.

Harper, Ralph. *The Seventh Solitude: Metaphysical Homelessness in Kierkegaard, Dostoevsky, and Nietzsche.* Baltimore: The Johns Hopkins Press, 1965, 153 p.*

Treats Dostoevsky and Nietzsche as "heirs" to Kierkegaard's spiritual struggle between faith and despair, with Dostoevsky remaining "partly safe" in his Christian belief and Nietzsche foundering in a self-destructive nihilism.

Hayman, Ronald. *Nietzsche: A Critical Life.* New York: Oxford University Press, 1980, 424 p.

In-depth biographical and critical study of Nietzsche's personal and philosophical development. Hayman attempts to determine the motivation behind Nietzsche's work and to reveal the essential continuity beneath the apparent discontinuities and self-contradictions.

Hollingdale, R. J. *Nietzsche.* London: Routledge & Kegan Paul, 1973, 225 p.

Informative and comprehensible consideration of Nietzsche's works.

Hollinrake, Roger. *Nietzsche, Wagner, and the Philosophy of Pessimism.* London: George Allen and Unwin, 1980, 308 p.

Study "concerned with Wagner as one of Nietzsche's principal sources—and targets—in *Also Sprach Zarathustra.*"

Kaufmann, Walter. *Nietzsche: Philosopher, Psychologist, Antichrist.* Princeton: Princeton University Press, 1974, 532 p.

One of the most thorough examinations of Nietzsche's philosophy.

Knight, A. H. J. *Some Aspects of the Life and Work of Nietzsche, and Particularly of His Connection with Greek Literature and Thought.* Cambridge: Cambridge University Press, 1933, 194 p.

General outline of Nietzsche's philosophy, with chapters devoted to the classical Greek influence on Nietzsche, the conception of eternal recurrence, the superman, the will to power, and criticisms of Nietzsche's world view.

Morgan, George Allen. *What Nietzsche Means.* New York: Harper & Row, 1965, 400 p.

Interpretive study. Morgan discusses each aspect of Nietzsche's thought in an attempt to explain his philosophy as a phenomenon outside the influence of historical or psychological circumstances.

Powys, John Cowper. "Nietzsche." In his *Enjoyment of Literature,* pp. 451-79. New York: Simon and Schuster, 1938.

Discusses Nietzsche's "spiritual sadism"—his philosophy which denies God and exposes humanity to the harshness of pure existence.

Reichert, Herbert W. *Friedrich Nietzsche's Impact on Modern German Literature.* Chapel Hill: The University of North Carolina Press, 1975, 126 p.*

Five essays examining the influence of Nietzsche's philosophy on the literary works of Arthur Schnitzler, Carl Sternheim, Georg Kaiser, Robert Musil, and Herman Hesse.

(Count) Alexey Nikolayevich Tolstoy

1883-1945

(Also transliterated as Aleksei, Aleksey, Alexei, Alexis; also Nicolaievich, Nikolaevich, Nikolaivich; also Tolstoi, Tolstoj) Russian novelist, short story writer, essayist, poet, and dramatist.

Tolstoy was one of the most prominent authors of Russia's post-Revolutionary era. He is best known for his *Khozhdeniye po mukam (The Road to Calvary)* and *Pyotr I (Peter the Great)*, epic novels which depict Russian history in conformity with official Soviet ideology and which have strongly influenced the development of the Soviet historical novel. Although Tolstoy's works have often been criticized by Western commentators for sacrificing artistic integrity to political expediency, they have as often been praised for their fluent narratives and masterful characterization.

Tolstoy was born in 1883 on his family's country estate in the Russian steppe region. Related through his mother to the novelist Ivan Turgenev and through his father to the novelist Leo Tolstoy, he belonged by birth to the landed nobility. Because his family's fortunes had fallen, however, Tolstoy's upbringing and education were those of the middle class rather than the aristocracy. After finishing his secondary education at an undistinguished provincial school, he attended the Technical College of St. Petersburg, where he began his literary career while completing a degree in engineering. In 1907 Tolstoy published his first poetry collection, *Liriks*, which consisted of immature imitations of the works of prominent Russian Symbolists. The collection was greeted with little enthusiasm by critics, and Tolstoy was later so ashamed of these early efforts that he bought and burned every available copy. But by 1911, after the publication of a second volume of poetry, a novel, and two collections of short stories, Tolstoy had eliminated the aesthetic mannerisms of his earliest works and had established a reputation as a leading representative of the Russian trend toward renewed realism in prose. He became a war correspondent for the magazine *Russkiye Vedomosti* at the outbreak of World War I, and soon after published *Na voyne,* a collection of short stories based on his front-line experiences. During the first year of the Civil War that followed World War I, Tolstoy served in the propaganda division of the anti-Bolshevik White Army, composing violently anticommunist pamphlets. Unwilling to live under communist rule, he emigrated to France in 1919 when Bolshevik victory seemed imminent.

During the next four years he wrote some of his best-known works, including *Detstvo Nikity (Nikita's Childhood), Aelita,* and *Sestry (Sisters),* the first volume of *The Road to Calvary*. Tolstoy was nevertheless unsatisfied with émigré life and sought to return to the Soviet Union under the auspices of the Change-of-Landmarks campaign, which was established to effect reconciliation between expatriate intellectuals and the Bolshevik regime. After publishing a series of articles in the procommunist émigré newspaper *Nakanune*, Tolstoy was allowed to return to the Soviet Union in 1923. Although he initially demonstrated a lack of enthusiasm for the communist government, he soon turned to ardent support. Critics often discuss the manner in which this ideological development is demonstrated in his works—from the early, apolitical writings to his later novels that exemplify the principles of Socialist Realism in their depiction of the Soviet "new man" and in their government-prescribed interpretations of history. Tolstoy was a prolific author whose numerous patriotic essays and works of fiction extolling Soviet life earned him a favored position with the government, and for that reason he was widely accused by other writers of political opportunism. Whether or not those charges were true, by the mid-1930s Tolstoy had become one of the Soviet Union's most widely-read authors, and by 1944 his works were outsold only by those of V. I. Lenin and Maxim Gorky. As a result, he also became one of the Soviet Union's wealthiest authors and lived his last years in luxury. His death in 1945 was proclaimed an occasion for national mourning.

Tolstoy is primarily known as a prose writer, and after his initial experiments with poetry in *Liriks* and in *Za sinimi rekami,* a collection dealing predominantly with subjects from Russian folklore, he began to concentrate on the literary forms for which he later became famous. His early short stories, such as those collected in *Sorochy skazki* and *A Week in Turenevo,* concern the life of the peasants and landed gentry of the Volga countryside. These stories, which combine Russian folklore with sensitive descriptions of nature, are praised for their skillful depiction of the colorful eccentrics of the region and their masterful narrative manner. At the same time, critics find fault with their construction, noting Tolstoy's seeming inability to design a logical plot. Critics frequently note a contrast between Tolstoy's intellectual limitations, which often lead to implausible situations and ridiculous resolutions in his works, and his gifts as a storyteller, evident in his lifelike characterizations and in the verve and spontaneity of his narrative manner. The assertion of D. S. Mirsky that the "most salient feature in the personality of A. N. Tolstoy is a very curious combination of very great natural gifts and a complete absence of brains" is echoed by that of Ivan Bunin, who wrote in his memoirs that "much of what [Tolstoy] wrote was incredibly vile and utterly stupid, but even at its most shocking it remained talented."

Tolstoy achieved his greatest fame with his novels. *Nikita's Childhood* was the first of these to receive widespread acclaim, and some critics consider it his best work. The novel, which contains loosely structured autobiographical episodes based upon Tolstoy's youth in the countryside, is praised for its sincere and unpretentious depiction of Russian life. His next novels, *Aelita* and *Giperboloid inzhenera Garin (The Death Box),* constitute Tolstoy's contribution to the development of the new school of Soviet science fiction, and are among the first of his works to attempt to convey a political message. *Aelita* concerns the experiences of two Soviet astronauts on Mars, which is presented as analogous to the "backward" West and is contrasted with the more highly advanced Soviet Union. His second science fiction novel, *The Death Box,* also serves a didactic interest, in this case warning against the dangers of fascism through the portrayal of an unscrupulous scientist who invents a lethal ray and proceeds to enslave Europe. Although these novels are marred by didacticism, they do contain forceful narratives and dynamic characterizations. However, several of Tolstoy's other novels are criticized for completely sacrificing artistic quality to ideology. These include *Chyornoye zoloto,* a melodrama concerning foreign and émigré machinations in the exploitation of Soviet oil, and *Khleb (Bread)*, a rendering of the events of the Civil War designed to establish Josef Stalin as the hero of the war. Western critics generally agree that these crudely constructed novels are Tolstoy's worst, and since Stalin's death Soviet critics have dismissed *Bread* as "shameless flattery."

Today Tolstoy's fame undoubtedly rests on his multivolume historical novels *The Road to Calvary* and *Peter the Great*. According to Tolstoy, the novels were conceived as explorations of the Russian character. He wrote: "To fathom the secret of the Russian character, of its greatness, it is necessary to acquire a thorough and profound knowledge of its past—of our history, its pivotal moments, the tragic and creative epochs when the Russian character was taking shape." *The Road to Calvary* depicts the "tragic and creative epoch" of the Revolution and Civil War, focusing on the lives of a group of individuals caught in the upheaval. Most critics find the work outstanding for its fresh and lifelike characters, breadth of action, and realistic episodes. The novel, however, was written over a period of twenty years, with the first volume completed during Tolstoy's stay in France and the final volume completed after the outbreak of World War II. For this reason the author's perspective is not consistent throughout the work, and critics have demonstrated the dramatic change that occurred in Tolstoy's attitudes between the first volume, which succeeds in sympathetically portraying individuals with conflicting attitudes toward the Revolution, and the subsequent volumes, which become increasingly propagandistic in support of the Bolshevik cause. *Peter the Great* similarly reflects Tolstoy's effort to portray history in accordance with Communist party dictates, stressing aspects of the Petrine era that suggest obvious parallels with the Soviet Union under Stalin's rule: the need for drastic social reforms to ensure the Soviet Union's survival, the brutal and repressive measures undertaken to achieve those reforms, widespread misery and suffering, and threats to the Soviet Union's existence from aggressive neighbors, necessitating a renewed spirit of partriotism and self-sacrifice. Critics interpret Tolstoy's portrayal of Peter as a ruler who utilized brutal methods to enact reforms for the ultimate good of Russia as an attempted justification of Stalin's methods after the Revolution. The novel, like *The Road to Calvary,* is considered outstanding for its excellent characterization, swift pace, and wealth of detail, as well as for its skillful use of colloquial Russian. As two of the first government-approved works of historical fiction of the post-Revolutionary era, *The Road to Calvary* and *Peter the Great* are often cited as major influences on the development of the Soviet historical novel.

In addition to his poetry and fiction, Tolstoy wrote over forty dramas, which are not highly regarded and have been largely ignored by English-language critics. He frequently revised his plays several times after their initial publications in accordance with his own evolving world outlook and the changing policies of the government. Such is the case with his series of dramas dealing with the life of Peter the Great. The first, *Na dybe* (written before the novel *Peter the Great*), was composed at a time when the Soviet government considered Peter a brutal imperialist, and so depicts him as a ruthless tyrant. The second, *Pyotr Pervy,* written after government policy accorded Peter the status of national hero, portrays the monarch as a forceful but enlightened and self-sacrificing ruler. A third version, produced during the tension preceding World War II, emphasizes patriotism and national defense. The drama considered by Soviet critics to be Tolstoy's best is *Ivan Grozny,* a play in two parts portraying Ivan the Terrible as a hero of Russian history who protected both the common people and national interests.

During his lifetime, critical opinion of Tolstoy's works was often divided between unanimous acclaim from Soviet critics and more restrained praise from Western critics who admired his natural talent for storytelling yet deprecated his intellectual limitations and lack of artistic integrity. Since Stalin's death, Tolstoy's popularity in the Soviet Union has declined significantly; however, his reputation survives through *The Road to Calvary* and *Peter the Great,* which many critics from both the Soviet Union and the West rank among twentieth-century Russia's best historical novels.

(See also *Contemporary Authors,* Vol. 107.)

PRINCIPAL WORKS

Liriks (poetry) 1907
Za sinimi rekami (poetry) 1909
Sorochy skazki (short stories) 1910
Chudaki (novel) 1911
Khromoy barin (novel) 1912
[*The Lame Prince,* 1958]
Na voyne (short stories) 1914
Detstvo Nikity (novel) 1920
[*Nikita's Childhood,* 1945]
**Khozhdeniye po mukam*. 3 vols. (novel) 1921-41
[*The Road to Calvary* (partial translation), 1923; also published as *Darkness and Dawn* (partial translation), 1935; *The Road to Calvary,* 1946, and *Ordeal,* 1953]
Aelita (novel) 1923
[*Aelita,* 195?]

Bunt mashin (drama) 1924
Giperboloid inzhenera Garin (novel) 1925
[*The Death Box,* 1936; also published as *The Garin Death Ray,* 1955]
Golubyye goroda (novel) 1925
[*Azure Cities,* 1929]
Na dybe (drama) [first publication] 1929
Pyotr I. 3 vols. (unfinished novel) 1929-45
[*Peter the Great* (partial translation), 1932; also published as *Imperial Majesty* (partial translation), 1932; *Peter the Great* (partial translation), 1936; and *Peter the First,* 1956]
Chyornoye zoloto (novel) 1931
Khleb (novel) 1937
[*Bread,* 1938]
Pyotr Pervy (drama) 1938
Zolotoi klyuchik (drama) 1938
[*The Golden Key,* 1947]
Ivan Grozny (drama) 1944
Polnoye sobraniye sochineny. 15 vols. (novels, short stories, essays, poems, and dramas) 1946-53
A Week in Turenevo, and Other Stories (short stories) 1958
The Great Big Enormous Turnip (short story) 1968

*This work comprises the novels *Sestry* (1921), *Vosemnadtsaty god* (1928), and *Khmuroye utro* (1941).

LLOYD MORRIS (essay date 1923)

[*Morris was an American biographer, critic, social historian, essayist, and pioneering educator who is credited with introducing contemporary literature courses to the American university system in the 1920s. In the following excerpt from a favorable review of* The Road to Calvary, *Morris praises Tolstoy's powerful evocation of Czarist Russia's collapse.*]

It is easy to understand why [***The Road to Calvary***], crude and powerful and panoramic, should have scored an instantaneous success upon its publication in France and Germany. For it marks the first attempt to transfer to the service of art the dramatic spectacle of the collapse and disintegration of Russia. And with tremendous conviction and force implicit in his restraint Count Tolstoy has painted a picture of magnificent proportions that is unmistakably real.

The narrative concerns the fortunes of a well-to-do family of the middle class domiciled in St. Petersburg through whose interests, aspirations and loves are projected the fortunes of Russia during the fateful period beginning early in 1914 and closing just prior to the seizure of power by the Bolsheviki. Through the narrative flows the current of feverish, distorted intellectual life, the riotous pace of social life and the progressive moral decadence which accompanied the crumbling away of the empire. So adroitly has the author selected his materials, so assured is his capacity for characterization that the panoramic background of the story, far from ever being gratuitous, is firmly integrated in the development of the plot.

Chiefly, the story deals with two sisters, Ekaterina Dmitrievna and Darya Dmitrievna, the elder of whom, Katia, is married to a well-known advocate, Ivan Ivanovitch Smokovnikov. Katia, who is mentally and spiritually restless, dissatisfied with her marriage and eager for adventure, has identified herself in a vague fashion with the more radical intellectual and artistic movements under discussion just before the outbreak of the war. Her salons are hung with futurist and cubist canvases, her dinner parties are attended by critics of the most advanced esthetic opinions, political enthusiasts and literary innovators. Her intellectual and emotional atmosphere is highly charged with undigested theory and volatile, facile opinion. And within the shell of this somewhat tragic egotism Katia keeps untouched an unsophisticated, wistful spirit which ultimately achieves fulfillment on the brink of ruin. Her younger sister, Dasha, a student of law and musician of uncommon ability, is far more evenly balanced. A sense of humor prevents her from taking too seriously the murmuring winds of doctrine that play about her sister's home, and a fine pride of spirit preserves intact the full power of her emotional resources. The skeletal structure of the plot is provided by Dasha's love affair with the electrical engineer Teliegin, from whom she is separated by the war and Teliegin's service on the Austrian front. After the beginning of the war the sisters enter hospital service in Moscow, and Katia meets the man to whom, subsequent to her husband's death in the revolution, she is married on the eve of the final cataclysm.

Out of such slender threads as these the author has woven the story of his novel. With patient accumulation of detail and considerable psychological insight Count Tolstoy has succeeded in making veritable the shifting moods of his characters, the complex motives that determine their action and the curiously subtle perceptions which lie beneath the surface of their sentimentality. Moreover, his picture is painted upon a crowded canvas, and there are in the novel a great multitude of subordinate characters, each sharply etched and concretely individualized, who contribute largely to its effectiveness. Among them the group of young intellectuals which foregathers at Katia's home and at the Philosophical Evenings' Society during the earlier chapters of the novel is presented with amazing skill and no little humor.

The historical episodes which enter into the texture of the novel cover the period from Russia's declaration of war to the successful culmination of the revolution of 1917. And the author, in a sequence of rapidly moving, vivid scenes has recreated with persuasive reality the most important events of the period. There are, for example, brilliant descriptions of the first advance of the Russian army, of the high enthusiasm which marked the first days of the war, of the succeeding defeats, the general ineptitude and confusion of the retreat, the terror and havoc wrought among civilian populations swept away by the flood of the war. Teliegin is taken prisoner by the Austrians, and the scene shifts to an Austrian prison camp. No grim detail is spared by the author, until the reader perceives the horror of that camp with each of five senses. Finally, after a peculiarly daring escape, Teliegin makes his way back to Russia through the Carpathians and returns to duty in his electrical plant at St. Petersburg. Then, bit by bit, Count Tolstoy builds up the atmosphere of discontent as it began to be manifested in the civilian population; minor labor troubles, administrative inefficiency, a growing weariness of war and the business of waging war, all leading imperceptibly but with cumulative effect to the bread riots, the workers' demonstration and the final outbreak of revolution in February, 1917. It is in these last episodes that Count Tolstoy has written with greatest power. He reproduces in terms of direct actuality the sweep of the crowds through the streets of St. Petersburg, the guerrilla sniping and the ineffectual machine-gun fire of the troops, the surge of excitement which took possession of every one, the sense of relief and release which descended upon the city when the inchoate and sporadic rebellion merged into a general tide of revolution. After the outbreak of revolution in St. Petersburg, Teliegin leaves to rejoin Dasha in Moscow, and the early effects of the revolution in that city are woven into the novel. There is an exceedingly effective scene at a public meeting organized to hail the revolution, at which mildly liberal speeches are made by local politicians to the immense enthusiasm of the crowd. Finally a radical labor leader, just returned from exile, arises and calls for a civil war between the bourgeoisie and the proletariat, and amid howls of protest from the audience, foreshadows the red terror which he deems to be inevitable. Meanwhile, as the author phrases it, "after three years of misery, hatred and blood the trusting, lethargic Slavonic soul, unconscious of its own measure, brimmed over."

In a very real sense the protagonist of this remarkable novel is not any one of the principal characters, but the Russian people as a whole, the inarticulate masses who, disconsolate and desperate, ultimately achieve expression in the wave of disaster born of the revolution. Behind the dramatic story of Katia and Roschin, of Dasha and Teliegin, behind the wave of liberal enthusiasm which precipitates the downfall of the empire, is conveyed an impression of the imponderable mass of the population stirring slowly to consciousness. . . .

That Count Tolstoy is something of a mystic is evident from his view of the Russian revolution, which, to him a consequence of the war, he sees, like the war, as an act of retributive spiritual justice on the part of a humanity oppressed by the domination of mechanical civilization. Although apparently personally quite out of sympathy with the methods of the first liberal revolution of 1917, and totally alienated by the excesses of Bolshevism, he none the less perceives in the disintegration of Russia the preparation of a new order. Of what he hopes that order to be there is no indication in his novel. . . .

It is less for the implicit philosophical attitude than for the picture which it offers of a civilization in dissolution that ***The Road to Calvary*** will be read. And, judged exclusively on its merits as a picture, or rather as a panorama, it is unquestionably one of the most interesting of recent novels.

Lloyd Morris, "Human Pawns in the Red Revolution," in The New York Times Book Review, *April 1, 1923, p. 6.*

D. S. MIRSKY (essay date 1926)

[*Mirsky was a Russian prince who fled his country after the Bolshevik Revolution and settled in London. While in England, he wrote two important and comprehensive histories of Russian literature,* Contemporary Russian Literature *(1926) and* A History of Russian Literature *(1927). In 1932, having reconciled himself to the Soviet regime, Mirsky returned to the U.S.S.R. He continued to write literary criticism, but his work eventually ran afoul of Soviet censors and he was exiled to Siberia. He disappeared in 1937. In the following excerpt, Mirsky surveys Tolstoy's short stories, assessing the author's divergent intellectual and narrative abilities.*]

A general characteristic of the writers of the post-Symbolist generation . . . is a certain deliberate flight from ideas in general. "Quests," problems, and mysticism of all kinds have become less fashionable and are by way of being quite tabooed. Life is accepted as it is, and a new Realism has arisen in the stead of the intricacies of Symbolism and of the fruitless searchings of Gorky and Andreev. This Realism and this absence of "ideologies" is very noticeable in the work of the first novelist of the new school who succeeded in winning the popular favour. A. N. Tolstoy must be counted with the new post-Symbolist school, first, because in point of fact his literary personality was formed under Symbolist influences in "the Tower" of Vyacheslav Ivanov and in the monkey-haunted flat of Remizov; secondly, because, though he is fundamentally the least mystical and metaphysical of writers, he is also quite free of those "ideological demands" which were necessary to the making of a pre-Symbolist writer of the orthodox Realistic school. (pp. 291-92)

The most salient feature in the personality of A. N. Tolstoy is a very curious combination of very great natural gifts and a complete absence of brains. As long as he simply and confidently surrenders to the flow of his natural creative force, he is a charming and unique writer; the moment he tries to express ideas, he becomes piteous. As he very seldom completely refrains from ideas, very few of his writings are above censure. But for natural verve and for spontaneous force, he has few equals among contemporary writers, and is second perhaps to Andrey Bely alone. One of his best qualities is his admirable, racy, unbookish Russian, learned in his Samara home, and not so much influenced as let loose by the example of Remizov.

His poetry is for the most part on subjects of Russian folklore and has for its themes either mythological pictures of Nature, or popular legends. The mythological poems were keenly appreciated by the mytho-poetical mystics of "the Tower"; but Tolstoy's best qualities are much more apparent in the legendary poems that are free from all mythological afterthought: they are full of life, and even when they verge on the nonsensical, they infect one by their irrepressible vitality and spirit. The same may be said of ***Magpie's Tales*** . . . , which is so delightful and exhilarating precisely because it is so free from every intellectual and emotional ingredient: it is just the sheer delight of imagination set free from the laws of causation.

Of Tolstoy's stories, very few are quite satisfactory, and this is due, besides his constant efforts to transcend his intellectual limitations, also to a fundamental defect in his talent: he has an admirable narrative *manner,* but not an inkling of ability to *construct* a story. All his stories produce the impression of a strange, illogical giddiness: one never knows what will happen, nor why things happen. The law of causation is absent from his world, and his stories develop like dreams or like fairy-tales. This might not be a defect if Tolstoy had sincerely recognized this limitation and not tried to plaster up his defective logic by borrowed ideas and cardboard psychology. His merits are a wonderful verve, directness of narrative, and a supreme gift of making his personages live. Only here again his original intellectual defect comes in: he is capable only of making fools, cranks, simpletons, and idiots; in all his people, there is the inevitable mark of stupidity. When his first stories appeared, which were all about the decaying gentry of the Middle Volga, the stupidity of his characters was explained as the inevitable result of the degeneracy of the provincial gentry. Tolstoy himself cheerfully accepted this interpretation, but one has only to read the stories where he describes other *milieux* to see that the feature is inherent in the author rather than in his characters. His early stories are among the best: he avoids all sophistications, and some of them are even, as by chance, excellently constructed, as, for instance, the pathetic (and absurd) story of the silly romantic provincial squire ***Aggey Korovin*** in Petersburg. His longer novels written before the War are much less satisfactory: ***The Treasures of the Earth*** . . . is the acme of absurdity; and ***The Lame Squire*** . . . is disfigured by an entirely misplaced attempt to rival the psychological subtleties of Dostoevsky. His stories of War and Revolution (***Spook*** . . .) have his usual merits, but in so far as they are stories of War and Revolution, they are not worth much. His novel ***The Way through Hell*** . . . , which attempts to be a synthesis of Russian life before and during the War, is also a failure in so far as it attempts that. ***Aelita,*** a story of men on Mars, in the style of H. G. Wells, seems to have been written for the sole purpose of showing up his limitations. All the scientific and fantastic part is ridiculously flat and absurd. But the book contains one of his most delightful character-sketches—the Red soldier Gusev with his matter-of-course and absolutely unastonished attitude to Mars and the Marsians. His last novel, ***Ibycus*** (of which only the beginning has appeared), is the story of the adventures of a new-made profiteer during the Revolution and civil war. Here Tolstoy's absurdity reaches its high-water mark, but this absurdity is so unadulterated and light-hearted that it almost ceases to be a defect and becomes a virtue.

Of all Tolstoy's stories, the best by far is ***The Childhood of Nikita*** (written in France in 1919-1920). It is the story of a boy of ten on his father's country estate near Samara. It is without pretensions, without all the pitfalls that abound in his other works. There is no plot, but several (for the most part, trivial) episodes are told with admirable verve and sincerity. Russian books on childhood are numerous, and some of them are among the greatest books in the language, but A. N. Tolstoy's ***Nikita*** must be assigned a very honourable place among them, and a place that is unique for its unsophisticated vitality and simple brightness.

What has been said of Tolstoy's lack of narrative construction applies still more to his plays, which do not give him a great place among the playwrights. His merits are at their lowest and his defects are exaggerated. But there is in them a healthy and welcome strain of honest and unpretentious melodrama. (pp. 293-95)

D. S. Mirsky, "The New Prose," in his Contemporary Russian Literature: 1881-1925, *Alfred A. Knopf, 1926, pp. 281-315.**

MAXIM GORKY (letter date 1933)

[One of the Soviet Union's most popular authors, Gorky is recognized as one of the framers and foremost exponents of Socialist Realism in literature. Socialist Realism is considered the official school of Soviet literature and demands adherence to a communist worldview, an objective viewpoint comprehensible to the working classes, and themes of social struggle featuring strong proletarian heroes. Gorky demonstrated his allegiance to Socialist Realism in his writings through the combination of naturalistic depictions of the Russian lower classes with a romantic vision of the brotherhood of man and hope for the future. While Western critics generally consider Gorky an indifferent stylist whose works suffer from weak characterization and extreme didacticism, he is acclaimed in the Soviet Union as one of that country's greatest authors and a model for all writers. In the following excerpt from a letter to Tolstoy, Gorky praises Tolstoy's intelligence and skill but mildly chastises him for being overly hasty in his work.]

You know that I love and appreciate highly your great, intelligent and cheerful talent. Yes, that's how I feel it, your talent, precisely as cheerful, with a real sparkle and a witty smile, but this trait is somewhere in the third place for me, for your talent is first of all simply great, truly Russian, and intelligent in a Russian way, immensely aware of the conservatism concealed in all trite "truths" and thoroughly capable of laughing at them in a good-natured way. You have done quite a few very valuable things which have not been properly appreciated yet; others have not been understood at all, and although this is sad, it is not a bad thing. Transparency is a very laudable quality in a window pane, you can see everything through it, but in itself it doesn't exist as it were, whereas fieldglasses, microscopes and telescopes are glass too. You understand the rest yourself. I also want to say to you that despite a quarter of a century of work, for me you are still a "beginner" and you always will be, right to the end of your days. ***Peter*** is the first real historical novel in our literature, it's a book that will last long. I read an extract from the second part not long ago—splendid! You can do some splendid things. Your weakness is haste. For instance, at the moment I'm reading ***1918,*** from the ***Ordeal***—what perception, how well drawn it is! But—there are pages which vex me because you didn't complete them properly. But that's already an old man's grumbling! Basta! [Enough!]

Maxim Gorky, in an extract from a letter to Alexey Tolstoy on January 17, 1933, in Soviet Literature, *No. 1, 1983, p. 4.*

GLEB STRUVE (essay date 1935)

[A Russian-born educator, Struve is internationally known for his critical studies of Slavic literature. In the following excerpt, he discusses several of Tolstoy's key works written after his return to Russia from exile.]

Tolstoy is a writer of great natural gifts and force, a born Realist. He is at his best when he describes real life, especially the life he knows, his work is then full of vitality and verve and his characters brimful with life. But nearly all his post-revolutionary work suffers precisely because he has been unable to find a congenial theme. He seems to have been on the look-out for it ever since his return to Russia, and has tried his hand at several genres. Fundamentally a man of the past, a cross between a country gentleman and a literary bohemian, he evidently felt lost in the turmoil of revolutionary life. He did not want to draw his subject from the past and he was not sufficiently familiar with the new actuality to make it a source of inspiration. Hence his tendency, manifested in the first years of the Revolution, to escape into the realm of fantasy, to combine fantastic plots with revolutionary ideas. In ***Aelita*** . . . he has given a combination of a Utopian romance in the manner of H. G. Wells with a typical Russian realistic psychological novel seasoned with strong revolutionary element. The fantastic plot is centred round the arrival on Mars of a Soviet expedition and an attempt to start there a social revolution. Upon this fantastical social theme are superimposed two favourite themes of Tolstoy: the theme of love that is stronger than death and than any sense of revolutionary duty, personified in the Russian engineer Los and the beautiful Martian woman Aelita; and the theme of elemental revolt embodied in the person of Gusev, the best-drawn and most lifelike character in the story. He is a Red Army soldier who places himself at the head of the Martian proletariat, but who, as the Communist critics have pointed out, is himself neither proletarian nor Communist. Gusev's revolutionism has a strong nationalistic colouring and when he comes to Mars his first thought is to proclaim its annexation to Soviet Russia. In spirit he is a typical anarchist, and it is this anarchistic and nationalistic tendency in the Revolution, as well as its aspect of elemental revolt, that makes Tolstoy sympathize with it. His affinity with this side of the Revolution finds also an expression in the story called ***A Manuscript Found Under a Bed,*** where an old degenerating squire, who hates the Revolution, cannot help admiring its purely Russian elemental dimensions.

Tolstoy has once more explored the fantastic element in his play ***The Revolt of Machines*** where life in its elemental instinctive manifestations is made to triumph over the principle of mechanical rationalization; and in the novel ***Engineer Garin's Hyperboloid.*** Garin is a type of a strong ruler, a superman, who engages in a struggle against the whole world and dreams of ruling it on the principle of caste division: the upper caste, the best, will govern and create; others will perform the procreating functions; still others, devoid of all superfluous passions and ideas, will become a kind of robots; and the rest will be exterminated.

Seven Days in which the World was Robbed is a fantastic satire, not particularly illuminating as such, but giving scope to Tolstoy's skilful handling of absurd situations—it is full of gay lightness.

A totally different genre is represented by ***The Way Through Hell*** which was begun by Tolstoy when he was still an *émigré*, but completed in Russia. It is a vast picture of the Russian prerevolutionary society, just before and during the War and in the first year of the Revolution, especially of the intelligentsia. It is drawn in very sombre colours, showing the disintegration and the purposelessness of that life. It has some very good realistic pictures and episodes and some well-drawn characters, but it is spoilt by Tolstoy's tendency to give more than a picture of life, to philosophize about history and to give a historical summary of Russian life before and during the War.

In ***Blue Cities*** Tolstoy chose a contemporary Soviet theme—the everlasting theme of the conflict of two forces that are at grips in post-revolutionary Russia: the force of rational organization and that of elemental instinctive life, sometimes in its lowest animal manifestations. In the end it is life that triumphs. This is always the case with Tolstoy; any other solution would be contrary to his nature.

In ***Vasily Suchkov*** Tolstoy has painted everyday Soviet life of the post-Nep period, conveying that mood of disillusionment which in those days was so widespread.

Tolstoy's contribution to the Five-Year Plan literature was not of much account; his novel ***The Black Gold*** is a badly constructed melodrama on the subject of foreign and Russian *émigré* intrigues round Soviet oil. His search for a congenial theme remained fruitless, and by nature he was incapable of writing anything good to order. Such a congenial theme came, however, from an unexpected quarter and enabled Tolstoy to come into his own in ***Peter the First,*** a big historical novel. . . . Here his natural gifts, his sense of life, his faculty of drawing lifelike characters and—last but not least—his excellent racy Russian, were given full play. (pp. 8-11)

Gleb Struve, "Pre-Revolutionary Writers after 1924," in his Soviet Russian Literature, *Routledge & Kegan Paul Ltd., 1935, pp. 1-22.**

JOHN CROWE RANSOM (essay date 1936)

[*An American critic, poet, and editor, Ransom is considered one of the most influential literary theorists of the twentieth century. He is best known as a prominent spokesman for the Fugitive, Agrarian, and New Criticism movements in American literature. Consistently in the vanguard of American scholarship, he began his career—with Robert Penn Warren, Donald Davidson, Allen Tate, and several others—as a member of the Fugitive group of Southern poets during the 1920s. The stated intent of the Fugitives was to create a literature utilizing the best qualities of modern and traditional art. Ransom regularly published poetry in the group's now-famous periodical* The Fugitive *(1922-1925), which he cofounded. After 1928, the four major Fugitives joined eight other writers, including Stark Young and John Gould Fletcher, to form the Agrarians, a group dedicated to preserving the Southern way of life and traditional Southern values. The Agrarians were concerned with social and political issues as well as literature; in particular, they attacked Northern industrialism and sought to preserve the Southern agricultural economy. In 1930, Ransom wrote the definitive* "Statement of Principles" *for the Agrarian anthology* I'll Take My Stand, *arguing for the South's return to a farming culture. A longtime professor of English at Vanderbilt University, Ransom left the South for Ohio in 1937, assuming the post of Professor of Poetry at Kenyon College. There, he founded and edited* The Kenyon Review, *a quarterly journal to which he attracted major contributors and himself contributed essays which evidence his unique critical theories and his drift from Agrarianism. Ransom is credited with originating the term "New Criticism," which forms the title of his most important work, published in 1941. Examining the critical theories of T. S. Eliot, I. A. Richards, and William Empson, Ransom proposed, in* The New Criticism, *a close reading of poetic texts and insisted that criticism should be based on a study of the structure and texture of a given poem, not its content. A pioneering New Critic, Ransom had many peers and successors in the movement, notably Warren, Tate, R. P. Blackmur, and Cleanth Brooks, who applied the criteria of New Criticism to prose literature as well as poetry. Although the various New Critics did not subscribe to a single set of principles, all believed that a work of literature had to be examined as an object in itself through a process of close analysis of symbol, image, and metaphor. For the New Critics, a literary work was not a manifestation of ethics, sociology, or psychology, and could not be evaluated in the general terms of any nonliterary discipline. In* The New Criticism, *Ransom outlined a system of critical thought that dominated the American academic scene for nearly three decades. In the following excerpt from an essay originally published in 1936, Ransom favorably assesses* Darkness and Dawn.]

Alexei Tolstoi: ***Darkness and Dawn.*** This book, describing the revolution in Russia from its original groundswell through the mass out-break during the World War and down to the Armistice, must be almost as masterly a performance as anything in the tradition of Russian fiction. It has perhaps an even larger breadth of action than anything, not even excepting *War and Peace*. Its author is related in blood both to Leo Tolstoi and to Turgeniev. So far as I am concerned, it answers satisfactorily the question whether literature will have a continuance under Soviet censorship. It shows the bitter effort and comes in sight of the final triumph of the Reds, but its artistic detachment is high above partisanship, in which respect it offers a lesson to the literary attachés of the proletariat farther west. It is unjust to say that it is the story of the revolution; it is strictly the story of several men and women enmeshed in it. The heroine and principal character is in the cause, though not consistently, and her husband is an officer in the Red army. But her sister's husband, just as noble a man, is an officer in the White army, and the course of the campaign is described as much from one point of view as the other. Every respect is paid to the heroic conduct of Denikin's army, in which nearly every private soldier was a former officer at the German front, and many stand for decided liberalization of the old régime. The philosophical issue between the parties is never settled dialectically though there is plenty of talk, as in all Russian novels. The author's feeling, or at least the one which he communicates to the reader, is that the Reds triumph because it is simply Russia's destiny, because the genius of Russia is simple and communal, but only after a struggle so vast and confused that no single participant was able to tell how things were going or why. Structurally, the novel is a masterpiece in the Russian manner, and that makes a fascinating study. There is even less of explanatory remark, less of the visible author as moralist and historian, than in most Russian novels, much less than in *War and Peace*. The materials are words, actions, pictures, and feelings of the simpler sort, thousands upon thousands of them. But how they march! (pp. 261-62)

John Crowe Ransom, "Contemporaneous Not Contemporary," in his The World's Body, *1938. Reprint by Louisiana State University Press, 1968, pp. 260-69.**

PHILIP HENDERSON (essay date 1936)

[*Henderson was an English man of letters known for his studies of Christopher Marlowe and other English literary figures. In the following excerpt, he offers a reading of* Darkness and Dawn *from a Marxist-Leninist perspective.*]

In ***Darkness and Dawn,*** Alexey Tolstoy has given a valuable picture of the Russian intelligentsia before, during and after the imperialist war and in the period of civil war and the intervention of international capitalism, frightened for its investments. The first section of his book is an exposure of bourgeois decadence and that mood of futility and hopelessness of a people at the end of an epoch, of a class that has played its part in history and is now quietly decomposing. As in the pages of Chekhov, it is such people as these who make one aware how necessary the revolution was. One of the characters, the literary critic and symbolist poet Bessanov, shedding tears of self-pity, confides in the girl with whom he is spending the night in a shabby hotel on the outskirts of Petersburg, that:

> Every night the horror of death came over him. He had to feel a living person with him, close to him, some one to pity him, to warm him, to give herself to him. 'I am thirty-five, but my life is over. Love can no longer deceive me. What can be sadder than when you suddenly see that your knightly steed is only a rocking-horse? And yet, for long, long years I must trail around in this life as a corpse.'

Yet this man, whom the young revolutionary Sopojkov justly calls 'a fungus on the decomposing body of the bourgeoisie', is respected as one of the intellectual leaders of his country. A Baudelaire in a still more advanced stage of moral decomposition, he exercises a poisonous, yet irresistible fascination upon those with whom he comes in contact, their own innate decadence responding to his own depravity. He defiles every girl he makes love to, leaving his slimy trail across their bodies like a human slug. After each 'night of love' he wakes 'tingling with incomparable dejection. It was revolting to think that he had to begin another day . . .' Leaving the hotels of his amours in the morning, depraved little girls with greenish faces on the Nevsky offered him bunches of snowdrops smelling of cheap eau de cologne. These bunches of snowdrops are somehow symbolic of all the personal relationships in the first part of this book. False, neurotic, hysterical, without a single strong or genuine impulse, these people live comfortably, even luxuriously, sucking the blood of Russia, trapped in a psychological cul-de-sac. The 'culture' that is the expression of their lives, the 'futurist' paintings and music, the symbolist poems and plays, is just the perverse attitudinizing stuff that serves merely to etiolate an empty and meaningless existence. All this Tolstoy sets before us, clearly, simply and without psychologism or fuss. (pp. 299-301)

Philip Henderson, "The Revolutionary Novel," in his The Novel Today: Studies in Contemporary Attitudes, *John Lane/The Bodley Head, 1936, pp. 183-307.**

KURT LONDON (essay date 1938)

[*London is a German-born American political scientist and authority on Soviet and East European affairs who has written and edited numerous studies of foreign policy and of East-West relations. In the following excerpt, he discusses Tolstoy's treatment of Russian history in* Peter the Great *and* Darkness and Dawn, *which he translates as* Dawn and Dark.]

Tolstoy is . . . one of those writers whose feeling for reality is very strongly marked. This trait often came into evidence even in his works before the Revolution. Tolstoy's most important work to date (he earlier wrote several dramas and novels of value), ***Peter the Great,*** is definitely one of the representative works of present-day Soviet literature. The book seems to me a most significant contribution to the art of free historical treatment on the basis of modern psychology. Here the century-old roots of the development of Russian history are laid bare, and the struggle between the old obsolete and the living new ideas finds eloquent expression.

A. Tolstoy does not write for the Soviets in the officious way affected by many a former bourgeois writer. He employs a more restrained, thoughtful, and profound style. When he describes pre-war Russia, as he does in ***Dawn and Dark,*** we gain a better knowledge of the causes of the Revolution than from the officious propaganda of some mere party-writer.

His work is worthy of a special and more detailed treatment. It is the result of a cultivated mind which still has in it all the traditions of the great art of the nineteenth century. (p. 146)

Soviet literature is in need of such thoughtful minds. Contact with the great traditions of classical literature cannot be merely theoretically maintained. Active, living artists, whose mental equipment preserves the connection with those traditions, are the appropriate intermediaries between the past and the present. I therefore consider A. Tolstoy one of the most essential writers of the U.S.S.R. The struggle of policies and stylistic principles should not be allowed to touch him. It is true that he is a live figure in the centre of the stage of events, but he is at the same time the custodian of that cultivated Russian literature to the heights of which the majority of Soviet writers have not nearly succeeded in fighting their way. (pp. 146-47)

Kurt London, "The Traditional Arts," in his The Seven Soviet Arts, *translated by Eric S. Bensinger, Yale University Press, 1938, pp. 93-268.**

D. FEDOTOFF WHITE (essay date 1950)

[*In the following excerpt, White parallels historical situations depicted in* Peter I *and* Ivan the Terrible *with events in post-Revolutionary Russia.*]

The appearance and the great success of such works as ***Peter I*** and ***Ivan the Terrible*** by Tolstoy had an intimate connection with the radical change in the attitude of the Soviet government towards Russian history, which manifested itself in the early thirties.

The struggle for "socialism in one land" had some sequels, which, at first, were not clearly understood even by its protagonists. At the same time, after the advent of Hitler to power, the Soviet Union entered into a period, when its very existence was threatened. A new patriotism, the corollary both of that struggle and of the defense effort, came to the fore in the Soviet Union and found its best-known expression in the famous November 7, 1941 speech by Stalin, in which he invoked the names of "our great ancestors," from Grand Duke Alexander Nevsky to Marshall Mikhail Kutuzov. This new Soviet patriotism brought about a change in the teaching and writing of history. In a measure, this was a return for Tolstoy to his hopes and aspirations of the World War I period, on a different plane and with a revised view of Russian history. His ***Peter I,*** and the movie-scenario based on it, had a very definite actual significance for the Soviet public of these years preceding Hitler's attack on the USSR. A moviegoer following "Peter the First" on the screen could easily imagine that it was not the ruthless emperor who spoke about the need for outlets to the Baltic for Russia, but the even more severe ruler in the Kremlin.

As an historical novel ***Peter I*** is different from what [Tolstoy's biographer I. I.] Veksler calls the "historical novels with naturalistic tendencies" of Flaubert, Sienkiewicz or, for that matter, of Anatole France, as well as from those he defines as "democratic," like the novels by Erckmann-Chatrian. The heroes of Alexis Tolstoy's historical fiction are the "carriers of the historic process" themselves: Tsar Peter, Ivan the Terrible, and their closest collaborators, also their enemies and opponents.

The historical theme of ***Peter I*** is that of the great upheaval caused in Muscovy by the Petrine reforms. Tolstoy brings out in a series of vigorously brushed pictures the roots of these reforms in the past. He dwells on the objectively urgent need for these reforms, were Russia to survive, and points out the great dangers to her very existence from the aggressive plans of her Western and Northern enemies. The author also describes the support for these reforms on the part of certain classes of the Russian population, such as the merchants and the military-gentry groups. In his novel, Peter is not alone in his work. He is surrounded by a band of close supporters and friends, who followed him faithfully on his arduous road.

Tolstoy does not overlook the great suffering and misery which the Petrine reforms and the long, seemingly endless wars brought to the great mass of the Russian population, the peasantry. He does not dismiss as false the words of the anti-Petrine Cossack chieftain: "They are tearing the third skin off the peasant's back. . . . You just count how few are the houses still inhabited in the villages. . . . Nearly all the peasants are ready to run away."

The inhuman cruelty of the repression of the attempts to prevent Peter from completing his historic task are not glossed over. On the contrary, Peter is presented in the novel, as taking part in the torture-chamber work, or presiding in person at the mass execution of the rebellious *streltsi,* the Muscovite praetorian guard.

In the scene of the interview with the German princesses during his first trip abroad, Peter cries: "As to the talk that I am cruel and love to shed blood, these are lies. . . . I am not cruel. . . . But let anyone live in Moscow with our people, and he would grow rabid. . . . All has to be broken up completely in Russia. . . . All is to be built up anew. . . . Our men are stubborn . . . some even with all the flesh on their backs whipped off to the bone. . . ."

The theme of the "creation" of the new type of man by Peter and his reforms attracted Tolstoy. In his view, there emerged the type of the energetic man, avid for knowledge and anxious to apply the fruits of it in practice. Peter himself, with his interest in nautical, military, technical and mathematical sciences, had shown the way to these new leaders of the nation. Tolstoy puts it pungently: "From the study of theology the lice have eaten us up. . . . Seafaring science, mathematics, mining, metallurgy, and medicine. This is what we need." This practical turn of mind was held by Tolstoy to be the key to an understanding of the character of Tsar Peter's Russian collaborators.

In another work on Peter I, a drama, Tolstoy placed in the mouth of his hero the following words: "Stern I was to you, my children. Not for personal reasons was I stern: Russia was dear to me. By mine and your toil have we crowned our land with glory. . . . Our labors were not in vain. Our descendants must not only preserve the glory and the wealth of our fatherland but increase them. *Vivat!*"

Some critics (including Veksler) deny that Alexis Tolstoy had Soviet actuality in mind when he wrote his novel and plays on Peter I. This is hardly tenable.

During the harsh years of the early Five-Year Plans, the village groaned under burdens not less, and possibly greater, than those imposed upon it in Petrine days. The historical parallel was too clear not to be obvious to Tolstoy's readers. The struggle with the oppositionists, the trials of the engineers, etc., had their counterparts in the days of the mighty Tsar. Then, as now, the Russian people were far from accepting meekly the pattern of life imposed upon them from above. They rebelled and they fought back. Tolstoy's thesis was that there was no other way out, that the people had to suffer in order to save the land. The sacrifice of the millions of the well-to-do peasants was as much of a historical necessity as the Petrine measures, which drove hundreds of Old Believers to self-immolation.

Mr. Veksler has worked out very carefully the problem of the similarity of Tolstoy's historical tenets to those expressed and approved by Stalin. A comparison of Tolstoy's earlier works on Peter I with his novel and later plays seems to indicate that these differed a great deal from the former in the interpretation of Peter I's historical role and his personality. In a way, ***Peter I*** and particularly the scenario of the film on the Tsar's deeds, were a powerful means of popularizing the official view of the Communist Party on the Emperor's historical significance.

Does this mean that Tolstoy wrote these works against his own convictions? This is, to say the least, very doubtful. One tends rather to come to the conclusion that he was a sincere and enthusiastic convert to the new Soviet viewpoint.

In his other important work dealing with a crucial period in Russia's history, ***Ivan the Terrible,*** a dramatic short novel which was published in 1942, Tolstoy presents the cruel Tsar in quite a different light from that in which his talented kinsman, A. K. Tolstoy, introduced Ivan in his historical novel *Prince Serebrjanyj.* In this new interpretation Tsar Ivan appears as a progressive ruler, who attempted to accomplish a radical reform of the social organization of Muscovy, had inflicted heavy blows on the feudal princelings and boyars and, developing a strong centralized state, made every effort to recover for Muscovy the Baltic outlets, lost by Russia in the past centuries. His followers, the hated *opričniki,* were a class of men bearing a certain distant resemblance to the Communist Party members by their utter devotion to their chief and their separateness from the rest of the people.

Superficially, there seems to be a great deal of similarity in this short novel with the development of the historical theme of ***Peter I.*** It rehabilitates another important bearer of historical change and delineates his role in the historical process. A closer examination of the contents reveals, nevertheless, not only similarities, but considerable differences in treatment and viewpoint. While Peter was presented as enjoying the support of the merchant and, in part, of the military service classes only, Ivan is depicted as the champion of the plain people of Moscow, and the people adore him.

To cite an instance: the Princess Efrosinija, one of the leaders of the feudal opposition to Ivan, was urged by the Tsar's general Jurev: "M'lady, walk out into the entrance hall and listen: Moscow is raising her voice, something may happen. The people love Tsar Ivan." The Holy Fool Vasilyj murmurs: "Thus is it being spoken in Moscow: our Ivan is a towering mountain-peak." (pp. 212-14)

The theme of the champion of the plain people is further enhanced by stressing that the Rjurik princelings look down on Ivan as a member of an upstart branch of the family. Thus Prince Obolenskij: "Who has given the low-born Ivan his power? The devil has given this power to him. . . . His entire support is from *opričniki.* We are going to rouse all Moscow against this evil brood." Here the parallel between the *opričniki* and the Communist Party is quite obvious.

In one or two places Tolstoy uses language closely approximating some of the best known "winged phrases" of the pre-revolutionary period. Speaking to the Metropolitan Filipp, Maljuta Skuratov, one of the principal pillars of Ivan's regime, comments on Kurbskij's defeat: "Is it stupidity or treason," very much as Professor Pavel Miljukov posed the same rhetorical question about the Empress Alexandra.

This may possibly be merely an instance of "literary playfulness," but some other allusions definitely evoke Soviet actuality. Prince Kurbskij, on taking leave of his wife before his flight to the Poles, appeals to her to save their sons at all cost: "Should they be pressed to disown me, to curse their own father—let them curse me. . . . This sin will be forgiven them."

Another thought expressed by the same Kurbskij, in his letter to Tsar Ivan: "Why did you, Tsar, deprive the princes of their holy right to be free to abandon your service, and why have you shut up the Russian tsardom like hell's stronghold?" suggests that the "iron curtain" simile was invented long before Mr. Winston Churchill.

The difference between East and West was stressed by Tsar Ivan himself in his farewell speech to the Lithuanian ambassador Voropay: "Farewell, Constantine. It was not easy for you to live with us. . . . How different and more pleasant it is in the West: gaily live the kings and the magnates there: the countries are tiny, the affairs paltry. . . . While here our affairs are great, arduous. And we are a difficult people."

As in ***Peter I,*** the stubborness of Russian people and their lack of docility are stressed in ***Ivan the Terrible.*** Ivan himself says to the Danish prince, Magnus: "The Russians are a fierce people, they are not afraid of torture or death: look at him (pointing at one of Kurbskij's followers), he bit his tongue off not to give his comrades away." Coming after the great purge terror and trials, this hint was indeed meaningful to the Soviet reading public. But Ivan's words to Maljuta Skuratov at the height of the anti-boyar terror are even more revealing: "I wonder whether my conscience was at fault and my mind had become blurred. . . . I wanted to be merry and to dance, like King David. . . . And here I am, sitting in the torture chamber with my hands gory and my coat stiff with dried-up blood." (pp. 214-15)

Tolstoy was possibly taking a real risk in his scenes of Moscow burning during a Tatar raid. Tsar Ivan addresses the peasants: "The Khan of Crimea is on a rampage close to Moscow. . . . See how gay it looks. . . . And now I have nowhere to lay down my head. . . . Is it my own sin that such a disaster has occurred? Even if it is my own sin, come to the rescue. . . . 'Tis impossible to live in shame. . . . My soul is wailing like a widow . . . help me." The novel came out in 1944 and the events of 1941 were still starkly in the minds of the Soviet peoples. Hence there was perhaps more than a mere hint in this Tatar raid of Hitler's rush to Moscow. The cry: "Is it my own sin?" is a reminder of Marshal Voroshilov's oft-repeated promises that the next war would be fought on enemy soil.

Whether ***Bread (Khleb),*** which appeared in 1937, is also a historical novel is a matter for some doubt. Published at the height of the purges, the book has a strong anti-Trotsky bias and enhances Stalin's role during the early part of the Revolution and the Civil War. To attack Trotsky was a "natural" for Tolstoy. During the Civil War most Whites considered Trotsky as one of the heads of the two-headed hydra, Lenin-Trotsky, and, for one reason or another, they hated him worse than Lenin. So Tolstoy had no difficulty in writing against Trotsky in ***Bread.*** He depicts him as a traitor to Lenin and to the revolution even as early as in the days of the Brest-Litovsk Treaty negotiations with Germany in 1918. Tolstoy also placed Stalin in the centre of the Civil War struggle, making of Tsaritsyn (later Stalingrad) the turning point of the Civil War.

It is quite likely that it was from Voroshilov or, possibly, even from Stalin himself, that he heard the story of the latter's reconnaissance, when both came under heavy White Cossack fire. Though this short novel, limning out the mores and the psychology of the participants in the Civil War of Russia, cannot bear comparison as a literary work with Sholokhov's *Silent Don,* it will remain forever a talented story of the role of Lenin and Stalin during the fateful years when Soviet power was consolidated, of which it gives a version in strict accord with the Party line as understood at the time of its writing. (pp. 215-16)

Only a man close to Stalin would dare to write a book like ***Bread*** and to permit himself the kind of double talk noted above in ***Ivan the Terrible.*** But the real answer to the riddle of this remarkable symbiosis must be looked for in the fact that Tolstoy's popularity and influence began in the period when the Soviet citizen was again permitted the luxury of patriotic feelings and of pride in Russia's past. This was a mental climate, in which Tolstoy could thrive and he did so. His old hopes for the spiritual unification of Russia revived. He was proud to play an important role in the rebuilding in the Soviet Union of the consciousness of Russia's glorious past and to prepare his land for the great struggle with the Nazis. The victory Tolstoy so ardently hoped for in 1914-17 was vouchsafed to him in the forties. (pp. 216-17)

D. Fedotoff White, "An Aristocrat at Stalin's Court," in The American Slavic and East European Review, *Vol. IX, No. 3, 1950, pp. 207-17.*

ILYA EHRENBURG (essay date 1950)

[A Russian-Jewish novelist, journalist, essayist, and poet, Ehrenburg wrote prolifically during a career that spanned five decades, including those of both world wars and the post-Stalin years. During World War II he was one of the most active of Russian writers in war journalism and propaganda; his articles were extremely popular and are considered to have played a large part in inspiring Russian resistance to the German invasion. Following the war, Ehrenburg published many anti-American articles in the Soviet press, as well as Buria *(1948;* The Storm, *1949), a novel about World War II that is considered a leading example of the postwar anti-American trend in Russian fiction. However, even though Ehrenburg castigated the failures of Western society in his writings, he also perceived the corruption and brutality of revolutionary ideals in the Soviet Union, and often despaired of the course his government was following. After Josef Stalin's death, when the Soviets became more tolerant of certain types of dissent, Ehrenburg publically rejected the dictum that writers should serve the purposes of the state and contended that "the writer [is] a servant of the truth." He set out to acquaint the nation's youth with Russia's literary heritage and with the community of thought, spirit, and culture it shared with the rest of Europe. He asserted: "The basic task of literature is to throw light on the spiritual world of our contemporaries, on their secret thoughts and emotions, their doubts and hopes, their joys and sorrows." Thus, the essays of his later years reflect his grandiose goal to impress Soviet youth with the moral purposes of art and with the ideals and convictions of the great Russian writers who had been obscured under Stalin's repressive regime, and to inspire his readers to help build a humane nation. In the following reminiscence of Tolstoy, originally published in 1950, Ehrenburg discusses Tolstoy's artistic capabilities and method of writing.]*

[Tolstoy] worked not like an architect but like a sculptor. Very early on he gave up making plans for his novels or stories. Often when he started writing he did not see what would come next. Many times he said to me that he did not know the fate of the hero, he did not even know what would happen on the next page—the heroes came alive gradually, took shape and dictated the plot to the author.

There are philosopher-writers; Alexei Tolstoy was an artist-writer. Very often people want desperately to do just the things that they are incapable of. I remember Alexei Tolstoy in his youth sitting over a book —it was a present and he wanted to give it with an aphorism written in it—nothing came of his attempt.

He could convey what he wanted with unusual precision in images, in narrative and in pictures; but he was incapable of abstract thought: his attempts to insert anything general or programmatic in a story or a novel ended in failure. He could not be separated from the element of art as a fish cannot be compelled to live out of water. His most perfect books—***Volga Country, Nikita's Childhood*** and ***Peter the First***—have an inner freedom; in them the writer is not subordinated to the plot, he narrates. He is particularly strong when his story is connected with his roots, whether he is dealing with his own childhood or with Russian history, in which he felt at ease and certain of himself as in the rooms of a long familiar house.

In his ideas he was a representative of the sound Russian intelligentsia. (pp. 135-36)

Ilya Ehrenburg, "A Remarkable Man," translated by W. H. B. Greenwood in Soviet Literature, *No. 1, 1983, pp. 133-36.*

IVAN BUNIN (essay date 1950)

[The first Russian to win the Nobel prize for literature, Bunin was a novelist, poet, and short story writer whose works evoke the life of the provincial gentry in pre-Revolutionary Russia. His classic treatment of Russian life in works such as Derevnya *(1910;* The Village, *1923) is concerned with timeless facets of existence rather than contemporary issues, and his works have often been compared with those of Leo Tolstoy, Anton Chekhov, and Ivan Turgenev. In the following excerpt from a work originally published in 1950, Bunin briefly and negatively characterizes Tolstoy and his works.]*

I knew [Tolstoy] fairly well, both in Russia and abroad, in exile. He was remarkable in many respects, but what made him a truly astonishing figure was his exceptional lack of moral sense (which after his return to Russia made him an equal of his immoral colleagues who, like himself, had taken up the profitable career of service to the Soviet Kremlin), combined with outstanding natural gifts which included a genuine literary talent. After his return to Russia his writings became particularly abundant and varied, beginning with some infamous scenarios about Rasputin and the intimate life of the late Tsar and Tsarina. Altogether, much of what he wrote was incredibly vile and at times utterly stupid, but even at its most shocking it remained talented. For their part, the Bolsheviks were exceedingly proud of him, not only because he was the biggest writer they had, but also because, after all, he was a count and a Tolstoy to boot. (p. 158)

Ivan Bunin, "The Third Tolstoy," in his Memoirs and Portraits, *translated by Vera Traill and Robin Chancellor, Doubleday & Company, Inc., 1951, pp. 157-91.*

KONSTANTIN FEDIN (essay date 1957)

[Fedin was a Russian novelist who abandoned his early experimental techniques for the principles of Socialist Realism, yet is credited with attaining a level of psychological insight rare in officially approved Soviet literature. Many critics consider Fedin's Goroda i gody *(1924;* Cities and Years, *1962), which deals with the crisis of culture and individualism under the socialist regime, one of the outstanding novels of the Soviet era. In the following excerpt from an essay originally published in 1957, Fedin praises Tolstoy's accomplishment in* Ordeal.]

Tolstoy's novel [***Ordeal***] is not considered historical by virtue of its period setting. It must be called that because of the writer's striving to pose and resolve the most vital question of all for a thinking Russian person: that of the historical destiny of his country, of Russia in the years of the Revolution and the Civil War. Tolstoy's aspiration is not formalistic, i.e., it does not stem from the requirements of the genre: I am writing a historical novel and therefore I must deal with such-and-such an era. It stems from a fundamental, organic, almost physical need to understand and emotionally comprehend revolutionary Russia in the years of that country's highest soaring and to describe tangibly the direction of its flight into the future. Neither the author nor the reader was mistaken in the apprehension of the novel's nature in exactly this aspect. The first part of the novel was greeted 20 years ago as the most contemporary of works then published, while the last part is now seen as the conclusion of a historical novel. But all three parts of the trilogy are connected with the most burning topic of the day, evergreen for us—that of the fate of our country.

In no other Russian novel is the name Russia mentioned as often as in ***Ordeal.*** The author speaks about Russia, the characters discuss her, and where she is not named, the breath of her tortured but titanic chest constantly envelops one in living heat. The Russian people are spoken about in almost every chapter, every scene—this "passionate, talented, dreamy" and "devilishly practical" people, as Telegin, the novel's hero, says. And where the Russian man is not mentioned, his warmth is felt, as though you are lying beside him under one sheepskin.

"O, Russian land!" These are the opening words of the first novel. A folk saying serves as an epigraph for the second: "In three waters rinsed, in three bloods washed, in three cauldrons boiled. Cleaner than clean we are now." This great trilogy is devoted to the cleansing of the Russian land in the water, blood and acid of battles and Revolution and it would be impossible to find a better title for it than ***Ordeal,*** echoing the Russian folk legend of Virgin Mary's arduous road on earth, the cleansing and life-giving agonies suffered by the Russian people for their land and themselves.

The first book, ***The Sisters,*** begins in St. Petersburg on the eve of the war, and focuses on the philosophical and literary circles of the tsarist capital, whose death-bed anthem was the numbing and languid tango. The war breaks out, mobilisation is declared, battles are lost, finally the entire campaign, and the tsar is toppled from his throne. The book ends with the feeling that "nothing has changed". All the bad seems to have remained, but also all the good. "Great Russia was ruined!" Telegin exclaims, dumbfounded. "So long as a single province remained to us, Russia would spring up again on its soil."

The second book is entitled ***1918.*** The events shift to the south. Russia backs out of the war. The Kremlin is waging a struggle in defence of Soviet power. For the first time in the novel the name "Tsaritsyn" appears. The dramas of the Caucasus, Samara, the Constituent Assembly, the Kuban, the Cossack lands, unfold. The Germans in the Ukraine, Denikin, Kornilov, Makhno, Drozdov are flickering pages in the unbearably heavy chronicle of our people.

The third book is entitled ***Bleak Morning.*** Once more the pages of the chronicle flicker before us: the December advance on Tsaritsyn, again Denikin, again various gangs—there is no end to them. The Volunteer Army disintegrates, the Whites are smashed. The epic comes to an end: the concluding scene is that of the new capital, Moscow, illuminated by new names in Russian history. The "bleak March morning" of the end of the novel is not bleak with hopelessness, but a stern exactingness towards people who have gone through all the circles of agonies and now, "cleaner than clean", are starting to build a new world.

In examining the scores of historical portraits drawn in Tolstoy's vast novel, in meeting his innumerable characters, one sometimes thinks that this or that portrait is minor, this or that personage is expendable, and that there are more historical facts than even the three large volumes warrant. But in checking this impression against emotional experience provided by the author, one sees that the diverse portraits create a vivid picture of paramount importance in understanding the Russia of that time. And among the novel's personages, four are so striking and alive that they hold the reader from the first pages to the last without ever letting go.

The four consist of two sisters, Dasha and Katya, and the men they love, Telegin and Roshchin. Like all eternal themes, the story of their love is a simple one. Love springs up and grows, there are partings, long separations from each other, unexpected meetings and the bitterness of fresh separations, rewarded at the end of the novel by a general reunion.

All's well that ends well. The reader thoughtfully closes the book and suddenly discovers that his mind is filled with an endless stream of memories—bits of inexplicably enticing scenes, unfinished phrases uttered by the women, minor but charming details of rendezvous. The torments of difficult lives have been overcome, have receded, and what has been experienced lures because it is imbued with a wealth of feelings.

It is hard to say which of the four main characters is the most attractive. The people drawn by Tolstoy are attractive even when they are bad because they are so alive. They attract not by their positive traits, but by the vividness of their characterisation.

Dasha and Katya are marvellous women—warm, self-oblivious in love, staunch, patient in misfortune, intelligent and beautiful at all times. They have precursors, we know these Russian young women defined by the term "Turgenevian". They are pure, they adhere to their ideals, and without ever foregoing their femininity, they never lose their self-possession. Tolstoy depicts them in the maelstrom of great events, when they, as Katya and Roshchin in Rostov, set off with a knapsack and tea kettle together with the people, on a path of enormous anguish, and to their former traits these Turgenevian women add new ones which in the time of the Revolution and Civil War put them on a par with men.

Telegin and Roshchin are very different but they share one trait of the Russian character. This trait is national pride.

The pain caused by the sufferings of the motherland can lead a person to ill-considered, irremediable actions. Before taking the side of the Revolution, Roshchin, driven by just such an intolerable pain, lands with the Whites and with Makhno. Having been through the fires of battles, he only becomes steeled. His pride, tested in fire, finds its place in a world in which national traits are not suppressed, but instead flourish. Telegin's character is more straightforward. But two of the distinctions of the Russian people noted by him are inherent in his own nature—dreaminess and practicality. Even when he is wrong, it seems he will never lose his bearings.

Among other merits, Tolstoy's enchanting talent possesses the virtue of being convincing. You believe in Roshchin's authenticity when he is talking to Makhno, when he is deceiving General Shkuro, when he deserts to the Whites, and when he returns to the Reds. You believe in Telegin's authenticity when he becomes a Red officer and when he carries about in his knapsack a porcelain cat and dog that Dasha happened to like.

What can be said about the stroll that Roshchin and Katya take along Kamennoostrovsky Street, when Roshchin speaks of her "imperishable heart" (how fine that is!). What can be said about the stroll that Dasha and Telegin take along the avenue on Sunday, when in the crowns of the pine trees an oriole "warbles in a watery voice" . . .

As a writer, I can't help noting something else about Alexei Tolstoy. Accuracy and clarity of language are an author's goal his whole life long. But artistic precision is not the same as grammatical precision. The cry of an oriole sounds like the gurgling of water being poured out of a bottle. "A watery

Tolstoy (first on the left), with H. G. Wells (extreme right) and Konstantin Fedin (second from the right).

voice'' is an inaccuracy. But art stands four-square on such inaccuracies.

Tolstoy had the gift of finding bewitching, brilliant inaccuracies. He was an artist capable of compelling details, trifles. You believe in his characters because you believe in his language. He speaks just as his people do, his heroes. And their language is infinitely varied, apt, colourful, sonorous, simple and clear. They speak in all the conceivable languages of Alexei Tolstoy.

In the course of two decades the novel ***Ordeal*** was reshaped in the writer's imagination many times. It is a difficult novel, like any major work. It was incredibly difficult to combine two elements in a key that would hold the reader's attention and make it possible to speak in one breath about infinite human tenderness and the historical paths of a great state.

Tolstoy had the gift of depicting the ordinary man, thirsting for personal happiness, a man who was like a drop in the vast sea of national events. In this Tolstoy's talent is similar to that of Victor Hugo.

Fortunate is the writer whose talent is unquestionable in its very essence. In music, it is the wealth of melody, in painting, colour and light, and in literature the essence is the art of story-telling. Tolstoy was a story-teller of immense natural artistry. You open his books with the feeling that you are entering a brightly lit theatre. The lights will now dim, the noise will die away, music will fill the air and the curtains will slowly part. And it is impossible to tear oneself away: what is happening there on the stage, what life, love and death? Easily and boldly the story draws you on, deeper and deeper.

Rapt up in the scenes, like a theatre spectator, you read ***Ordeal,*** a novel on the great theme of the loss and recovery of Russia. (pp. 102-03, 106)

Konstantin Fedin, '' 'Ordeal','' in Soviet Literature, *No. 1, 1983, pp. 102-07.*

RUFUS W. MATHEWSON, JR. (essay date 1958)

[*Mathewson was an American critic and professor of Russian and comparative literature. In the following excerpt, he discusses* The Road to Calvary *in the context of Tolstoy's ideological evolution.*]

The publication, section by section, of Alexei Tolstoy's ***The Road to Calvary*** spans the full era between the wars; the first volume appeared in 1920, the last in 1940. For this reason it is a laboratory specimen of the important changes in Soviet writing, most notably in the matter of the writer's control over his material. It may be that Alexei Tolstoy simply changed his mind, but it must be pointed out, also, that in doing so he has betrayed the vital interests of his profession and capitulated to the political invaders.

The novel has no hard center of moral purpose, nor any strong inner necessity of development. The mass of material might have been shaped to many ends; individual destinies, since they are not closely interlocked, might have been worked out in a number of ways. Only one thing is certain: the final solution Tolstoy did impose on the novel is extremely questionable, because it is introduced in the last third of the book in total disregard of what has gone before.

Despite its shortcomings, in its first two-thirds the work exhibits a number of the traditional attributes of the novel as an independent comment on experience. Tolstoy's interest in his material seems largely documentary. Thus, Part I stands as a vivid sketch of the St. Petersburg intelligentsia on the eve of the revolution; Part II is an attempt, like many others, to reflect the chaos of civil war itself. In his investigation on this not too profound level, Tolstoy has assembled a large group of sharply individualized characters, who embody, among other things, a number of contrasting attitudes toward the revolution. As an illustration of the variety of character and the honesty of presentation, consider Sapozhkov, the ex-Futurist, who fights on the Bolshevik side, but without illusions about the future: "The bourgeois world is vile, and it bores me stiff. . . . And if we win, the Communist world will be just as boring and grey, virtuous and boring." (pp. 243-44)

Tolstoy is still working from an independent vantage, from which he is prepared to consider ambiguities, to explore conflicting points of view, and to set humane considerations against political loyalties.

It is precisely this independence of judgment that is sacrificed in Part III. The results are striking. Characters are interrupted in the more or less plausible drift of their careers, are hurried to improvised destinies, are hastily converted and refurbished as moral political beings. A highly questionable series of coincidences reunites separated lovers and scattered families.

That the blight of socialist realism is on the book becomes evident first when iron-jawed, clear-eyed Communists appear from nowhere and take over the direction of events. (Up to now the Communists have been indistinguishable as people from the other characters. These new men are of a higher moral order.) An imperturbable, pipe-smoking Stalin outwits Denikin at Tsaritsyn and crushes him, and the traitorous Trotsky issues orders which are properly disobeyed and unmasked.

The disintegration of the entire fabric of the novel is clearest in the last ten pages. (pp. 245-46)

The banality of the situation has penetrated the emotions of the characters and the very texture of the language.

We do not know whether Alexei Tolstoy made his surrender cynically or from conviction. In any case, he has provided a perfect case-study within the limits of a single work of the damages inflicted when rough political hands are laid on an imaginative work of more than average vitality. We may view this novel as marking one more instance of the conclusion of the long quarrel between the writers and the revolutionaries. The final consequences of Chernyshevsky's attempt to capture Russian realism are again made clear. Alexei Tolstoy's capitulation has this melancholy advantage. (p. 247)

Rufus W. Mathewson, Jr., "In Conclusion: Four Novels," in his The Positive Hero in Russian Literature, *second edition, Stanford University Press, 1975, pp. 243-47.*

GEORGE REAVEY (essay date 1958)

[Reavey was an Irish poet, publisher, and translator of French and Russian literature, including works by Nikolai Gogol, Ivan Turgenev, Boris Pasternak, and Yevgeny Yevtushenko. In the following excerpt, he examines the eccentric characters of Tolstoy's stories set in the countryside of the Volga region.]

A Week in Turenevo and Other Stories contains five stories, four of which were written in 1910-13. These early stories, **"A Week in Turenevo," "Arkhip," "The Ravines"** and **"Mikusha Nalymov,"** have a unity of feeling, character and background, all the genuine flavor of the early Alexey Tolstoy and his very special world of traditional lore blended with everyday realism and a sensitive description of nature. Here we have the world of Alexey Tolstoy's childhood—that of the trans-Volga country estate, its oral traditions and anecdotes, its bizarre incidents, eccentric and sometimes lunatic characters, its patient peasants who suffer their masters' wilfulness or violently turn against them with hands, torch or knife. The atmosphere is still distinctly feudal, but it is also rather confused and irrational as though these particular landowners had lost all sense of aim and purpose in life. Not all Russian country gentlemen, or even a quarter of them, could have been quite as fatalistically madcap, crazy or witless, as Mikusha Nalymov charging through his woods with a hunting horn, Sobakin with his simpleton's timidity and trust in **"Arkhip,"** or Nikolushka Turenev with his utter lack of responsibility; for, otherwise, the whole of the Russian countryside would have been bedlam.

But Alexey Tolstoy was not being satirical or grinding an axe; and there is no immediate social message to be deduced from his pages. What he portrays is the Russian countryside or, rather, that part of it which he saw, felt, and *heard* (for he has an excellent ear for language) at first-hand, at folk-hand, and at literary-hand. No doubt characters like Mikusha Nalymov had existed in real life, but in Alexey Tolstoy's pages he stands out in almost legendary proportions, like some epical Vassily Buslayev who has gone to seed, aimless and undecided, and ventures not as far as the Jordan.

The point could also be made that Alexey Tolstoy was describing a region which had not often, if at all, been described before in Russian literature. As Maxim Gorky has said, the Russian classical writers confined themselves mainly to descriptions of the country estates, landowners and peasants, of the Moscow and Orel provinces, the more "civilized" parts. The Volga region, it must be admitted, was a little wilder and not so "high society;" and the oral tradition and the folk-element which Tolstoy incorporates in his tales has a very feudal flavor. But then it must be borne in mind that the mediaeval element in Russia has survived in places until our day. And Alexey Tolstoy's childhood days were only some twenty years removed from 1861 when serfdom was officially abolished. Many an older man he must have met, landlord or peasant, had had experience and memory of those more tyrannical times. Power, they say, corrupts. Many of Alexey Tolstoy's characters in these stories are weak, capricious men, sometimes tinged with insanity according to modern standards, but they are not monsters: their weakness and final impotence, as in the case of Mikusha Nalymov, make them pitifully or even comically human in the end. If some of the women seem harder and soberer despite their failings, like Anna Mikhailovna in **"A Week in Turenevo"** or even Olenka in **"The Ravines,"** that is also true in other Russian novelists.

In 1902, at the age of twenty, Alexey Tolstoy wrote **"Once in the Night,"** a very short tale. . . . As many writers' early works do, this particular story provides a clue to that world which Tolstoy made his own. It is almost an anecdote and obviously based on local tradition. It must date back to the days of serfdom. "It was the custom for peasant girls, after their wedding ceremony, to be taken to spend their bridal night with the squire, who loved that their pure maidenly bodies should also smell of church incense." This compact sentence contains not only the kernel of the tragedy that is then described, but is also alive with psychological paradoxes, which Alexey Tolstoy here is content to state rather than probe.

Similarly, in **"A Week in Turenevo,"** we are struck by the paradoxical and tragi-comic relationship between master and peasant. . . . (pp. 6-8)

An even stranger relationship is to be observed in the story, **"Arkhip,"** where the landowner Sobakin allows his future murderer to manage his estate until the day of doom. Sobakin, who at the beginning displays some energy in trying to recapture a stolen horse, turns out to be a weakling in human affairs and a nitwit where his estate is concerned. But perhaps unconsciously he wanted to live with death at his elbow?

In the description of Zavalishin's childhood in **"The Ravines,"** of the early years he spent on an estate in the steppes, of the old spreading manor house and the luxuriating garden, we probably catch some glimpses of Alexey Tolstoy's own boyhood in Sosnovka, we are told of his romantic daydreams, and his sudden and overwhelming enchantment by nature—an enchantment stimulated by his intense reading of Turgenev and then Gogol. Turgenev seems to have exercised the most influence on his young and impressionable mind. But the world of Alexey Tolstoy, as depicted in these stories, is vastly different from Turgenev's. The stability, order and social ease, are gone; there is little cultural or intellectual preoccupation; and there is a thinner dividing line between the landowner and peasant. A Gogol-like aroma of disintegration pervades the scene. It may be the locality which Tolstoy describes or the more general fact that in Tolstoy's day the feudal foundations had become even more sapped and insecure. Whatever the cause, in **"A Week in Turenevo,"** as well as in **"The Ravines,"** the manor house is already in a state of decay. The mice are multiplying in the old Turenev mansion where the old drawing-room is now being used to store grain. It is the novel of the manor house which is now inhabited by ghosts.

Yet Alexey Tolstoy's "ghosts" are very robust in their own way. What they lack in brains, they make up in body. They are very physical, full-fleshed, and strangely alive in their own world. One is not quite sure whether their world is real, but they themselves are very real. Many of them live in the past, but their past is vivid. They have very little objective sense and no points of reference to the larger world outside of them: they indulge and splurge without counting the cost; they never deny their emotions and, in the end, love is their only grace and salvation, if they can find it. If they don't, they more often than not meet a violent end. Their thoughtless lives are answered by unexpected death. Yet as they impress themselves physically upon our consciousness, witlessly bent upon their own destruction, they carry with them a swarm of unasked and unanswered questions which we cannot help but meditate. (pp. 9-10)

George Reavey, in an introduction to A Week in Turenevo, and Other Stories *by Alexei Tolstoy, 1958. Reprint by Greenwood Press, Publishers, 1975, pp. 1-12.*

WILLIAM E. HARKINS (essay date 1959)

[Harkins is an American critic and educator who has written extensively on Czechoslovakian and Russian literature, including a study of Czechoslovakian author Karel Čapek's works. In the following excerpt from a paper originally delivered in 1959, Harkins explores Tolstoy's Socialist Realist rendition of Čapek's drama R.U.R.*]*

On April 14, 1924, the première of A. N. Tolstoj's drama, ***Revolt of the Machines (Bunt mašin),*** was performed in Leningrad. The work was obviously an adaptation of Karel Čapek's well-known Utopian drama, *R.U.R.*, or *Rossum's Universal Robots,* as the play's expanded title had it. Tolstoj freely admitted that he had taken the theme of his play from Čapek, but minimized the extent of his indebtedness. (p. 312)

From *R.U.R.* Tolstoj borrowed a great deal more than the theme. The character of his heroine, Jelena (Čapek's Helena), is almost unchanged. Like Čapek's heroine, she is an instinctively good person who lacks any precise ideology or abstract standard of values. Like Čapek's Helena, she destroys the single manuscript which gives the formula for the manufacture of protoplasm when she realizes the danger the discovery has brought upon mankind.

The story of the invention of artificial life is almost literally the same in the two plays. Similar, too, is the final scene, in which the robots become men and realize their ability to reproduce their kind.

A number of smaller details are also kept by Tolstoj: for example, the mysterious frenzy of the robots; the electric screen which holds the rebellious robots at bay for a time; the belated realization by man that the robots should have been created with national differences so that they would hate one another rather than their masters.

Tolstoj declared that his adaptation was an attempt to correct the faults of Čapek's dramaturgy, which showed, in Tolstoj's words, "an inexperienced hand." But in fact Tolstoj's play is the weaker and cruder of the two. He has kept the weakest devices of Čapek's play: the improbably unique manuscript which describes the secret of making protoplasm; the siege in which the robots are delayed by an electrified screen. On the other hand, his play is ideologically cruder. On the plane of ideas he eliminates Čapek's conflict of relative "truths," according to which all the personages—Domin, Helena, Alquist, Nána, even the robots themselves—have a share of the truth. By sacrificing the interplay of ideas, none of which is completely wrong or right, Tolstoj's characters lose depth and become mere stereotypes; in consequence his play becomes little more than a melodrama. Tolstoj's entrepreneur lacks Domin's dream of achieving a better world through technology; he wants only money and power for himself. He is so cruel and crude that Jelena's marriage to him, even for idealistic reasons, becomes incomprehensible.

In one respect, to be sure Tolstoj's dramaturgy does advance on Čapek's. This is his more fluid division of the dramatic material into many short scenes, in contrast to the structure of *R.U.R.*, with its prologue and three acts. In his division Tolstoj followed the principles of German expressionism more faithfully. By breaking the action into short scenes, he avoids the weakness of anticlimax which is so serious a fault in Čapek's play: the essential climax of *R.U.R.* actually comes at the end of Act I. But at the same time, Tolstoj's short scenes lose the possibility of serious discussion which gives Čapek's play its intellectual depth. Here again, ***The Revolt of the Machines*** is closer to mere melodrama.

Tolstoj had, of course, a fixed principle in adapting *R.U.R.* This was to "sovietize" it, to make it over into a symbol of the struggle between capitalism and socialism. But in doing so, he frequently becomes very "un-Marxian." He simply cannot find a proper place for Čapek's robots in a socialist society.

In *R.U.R.*, as in his later novel, *The War with the Newts (Válka s mloky)*, Čapek adopted a neutral position: he attempted to stand independent of both capitalism and Soviet socialism. If his implied criticism of Domin's ideals and methods is in a sense a criticism of capitalism, then the robots' revolt and the slaughter of the human race is an implicit symbol of the dangers of socialist revolution. "Who taught them [the robots] such phrases?" Domin asks rhetorically when he reads the manifesto of the rebellious robots. The implication is that the robot danger to man—the threat that modern technology may "robotize" man—is equally grave under both social orders.

For Tolstoj, on the other hand, the robots' revolt is itself a socialist revolution. They are armed and aided by the very unemployed whom they have displaced from work (an alliance which seems improbable, at the least). They rise in protest against exploitation of their labor under capitalism, though it is unclear by what dialectic process they have come to the conclusion that they are exploited. Čapek's thesis that they have conceived a hatred for man because they are superior to him, intellectually and physically (i.e., man has degenerated since he no longer needs to work), seems far more credible.

In Tolstoj's play the Soviet Union exists as a state in which socialism is already being won. Yet the Soviet attitude toward the robots and their revolt is unclear, as is the robots' attitude toward the Soviet State. It seems that the Soviet Union has no robots of its own; they are a capitalist monopoly. The question of whether or not the Soviet people could have robots (and exploit them?) is never asked. Nor does Tolstoj raise the question of what future relations could exist between the robotless Soviet Union and the federated state of robots and "unemployed" which the revolutionaries set up in America. Strangest of all is the attitude of Tolstoj's communist agitator, Mixail. He recognizes the threat which the robots, as tools of capitalism, raise to the proletariat. As a trusted employee in the robot factory, he is in a position to sabotage production and bring the manufacture of robots to an end. But he declines to do this, on the ground that "the robots are already alive." Why such an argument should apply to as yet "unborn" robots is unclear. Mixail might rather have feared that the robots might be employed (as in fact they are) to keep unemployed workers in suppression. The possibility that Mixail might make a grave mistake in judgment is particularly acute in view of the fact that he is acting alone, without instructions from either the American or Soviet Communist Party.

These unanswered questions suggest the ridiculousness of the whole ideological construction which Tolstoj has attempted to pile on Čapek's play. To Čapek's theme—men or robots?—he has added his own theme—capitalism or socialism? He has overlooked the fact that the two themes have nothing to do with one another: one might as well raise the question of whether under socialism horses and dogs are also partners with men in building a socialist order, while under capitalism they are only exploited slaves.

Tolstoj attempts to get around the difficulty by implying that the robots have already become men. In Čapek's play this transformation comes at the very end, when the robots Primus and Helena fall in love. But for Čapek this event has a special symbolic significance which follows from his expressionist use of the robot symbol. The robot symbolizes the threat to humanity raised by modern technological civilization—the danger that man may become dehumanized and robotized. The ending is a denial of this danger: life, by its own mystique, will continue to assert itself in spite of all man's attempts to regiment it. The danger is great, but in the end life—and man—will win out.

Tolstoj cannot share Čapek's idealistic vitalism, for he has chosen a Marxist and materialistic point of view. The change of his robots into men proceeds from no less than three causes. The first is mechanistic: in the laboratory certain minerals are added to the composition of protoplasm. This seems dramatically crude, but there can be no objection on Tolstoj's own materialistic premises. The second cause of the transformation is dialectic: the workers become men because they toil and are exploited. This is patently ridiculous: again the parallel of toiling, "exploited" animals suggests itself. If Tolstoj's implication is taken seriously, then it would follow that Soviet robots could not become men, for only capitalist exploitation can work this miracle. Finally Tolstoj retains the final scene of Čapek's play: love is an evidence that the robots have become men. But this vestige of "idealism" in Tolstoj's thought was of course sharply condemned by his Soviet critics.

Tolstoj's robots become men not as a literal illustration of Marx's dialectic, but rather because the dramatist requires an expressive dramatic symbol of revolution. The uprising of the robots acquires meaning as an echo of the October Revolution. But from this point of view Tolstoj's play risks being taken as a parody of that revolution.

The ridiculousness of Tolstoj's conception is especially apparent in the final scene. As in Čapek's play, the robots are threatened with extinction, since the secret of their manufacture has been destroyed, and they cannot reproduce. Tolstoj tries to recapture the melodramatic pathos of Čapek's final act: how will life survive? In *R.U.R.* the question is meaningful, for man, with the sole exception of the construction engineer Alquist, is now extinct. But in Tolstoj's play it has no significance, for the citizens of the Soviet Union, along with the "millions of unemployed" elsewhere who have made common cause with the robots, survive to reproduce the human race.

Yet, in spite of its ideological confusion and melodramatic crudity, Tolstoj's play is an interesting attempt to create a socialist drama on a revolutionary theme. It is significant as an attempt to give vitality to the Soviet theater by introducing the new ideas and techniques of Central European expressionist drama. In the satirical portrayal of the *Obyvatel'*, a vulgar *petit bourgeois* who comments on the play and who also appears in certain scenes which provide comic relief, Tolstoj demonstrates that he is more creative when using his own materials than those taken from Čapek. Last of all, his play is interesting as an attempt to introduce utopian themes into Soviet literature as symbols of the conflict of socialism and capitalism. Such themes, in the novels of Èrenburg, Šaginjan, and Tolstoj himself, were very popular in Soviet literature of the early and middle 1920's. Subsequent neglect of utopian subjects was one of the consequences of the liquidation of Trotskiism and the domination of Soviet literature by the doctrine of socialist realism; since the late 1920's, such fantasy has virtually been excluded from Soviet literature. This is a pity, for how can man build a better social order unless he has the vision to imagine it? And how, without fantasy, can art produce imaginative symbols which compel the interest and attention of the reader? (pp. 313-17)

William E. Harkins, "Karel Čapek's 'R.U.R.' and A. N. Tolstoj's 'Revolt of the Machines'," in Slavic and East-European Journal, *n.s. Vol. IV, No. 4, 1960, pp. 312-18.**

VERA ALEXANDROVA (essay date 1963)

[*Alexandrova is a Russian-born American critic known for her studies of Russian literary history and analyses of contemporary Soviet literary and cultural developments. In the following excerpt from a discussion of Tolstoy's novels and short stories, she traces the author's ideological development from the apoliticism of his early works to the later novels in which he sacrificed veracity for a perspective consistent with government policy.*]

During the early years of Tolstoy's career as a writer, he acquired a firm reputation as the chronicler of the dying landed gentry. And yet, along with his interest in morals and manners, Tolstoy had early developed a taste for ideology, for "large principles." And in the story **"An Ordinary Man"** the soldier Anikin voices Tolstoy's own idea: out of the fire and blood of the world conflagration will come a renascence of the Russian national state. The human material for this new national integration, Tolstoy felt, lay in the vast reserves of ordinary, inconspicuous Russian people, kept down by officials, ambitious money-makers, and sharp "operators" of every kind. (p. 238)

On his return to Soviet Russia in 1923 Tolstoy wrote the novel ***The Adventures of Nevzorov,*** or ***Ibikus,*** and a short novel, ***Azure Cities.*** In the former he "exposes" and "indicts" both the "philistine" at home who does not accept the October revolution and the *émigrés* who fled it. This tendentious book would not deserve any mention if Tolstoy had not captured in it a good many traits of the demoralized and disintegrating milieu in which he had himself lived when he shared the arduous odyssey of the *émigré*.

Azure Cities . . . is written in quite a different psychological key. Its hero is the young Communist Buzheninov. Desperately ill with typhus during the Civil War, he dreams of the marvelous azure cities which he and his comrades will build after their victory. He survives the illness and, after the war, enters the polytechnicum. Later, his health undermined by his strenuous work over the plans for an "azure city," Buzheninov decides to go for a rest to his native town in the provinces, which he had not seen for many years. The first impressions of his childhood home shock him with the hopeless persistence of its poverty. Among the old familiar figures, the only new one is the militiaman, whom the angry market women, still engaged in private trade, have nicknamed "the bullfinch." Everything in the town remains the same, the monotonous flow of its dreary existence broken only by the faint whistle of trains rushing by in the distance. And yet, there are new elements too. The old narrow life of the little man has become more shifty and cunning; the old tavern is graced by a new sign, "Renaissance"; the tavern-keeper's son has become a commercial agent, fawning at the strong and oppressing the weak—a carrion bird.

"Yes, yes, Comrade Khotyaintsev," Buzheninov says to a Communist acquaintance, "the hooves of our days are silenced. The great years are dead. Happy are those who rot underground." And nothing can help, except perhaps a "devastating explosion." Buzheninov ends tragically: he sets fire to the town after hanging his plan for an "azure city" on a telegraph post, and surrenders himself to the authorities. Tolstoy's own parting words to Buzheninov are spoken by Khotyaintsev:

"It seems that life does not forgive rapt dreamers and visionaries who turn away from it. It clutches at them, rudely jabbing them in the side: 'Wake up, peel your eyes, get off your high horse.' . . . Life, like a baleful, bloated shrew, hates superficiality. The whole point is to master her and seat her, nice and proper, at the head of the table." A similar mood permeates the somewhat less vivid story **"The Viper."**

The process of reconciliation and acceptance of the Soviet regime by Tolstoy during the NEP period was typical for a substantial portion of the old technical intelligentsia which had not emigrated abroad but remained in Russia. At a later stage these moods, which were treated with suspicion by the official publicists of the '20s, served as the basis for a somewhat primitive Soviet patriotism. The beginnings of future Soviet patriotism found their first clear expression in Tolstoy's novel ***The Hyperboloid of the Engineer Garin***. . . . The young Soviet scientist, Khlynov, sent to Germany for graduate study under Professor Wolf, says to the latter, "After all, we are a good people. Nobody has loved us yet. . . ." But a time will come "when America will try to grab us by the throat," and then the Germans will see for themselves "what splendid fellows in the helmets of ancient Russian heroes will rise up along the Eastern borders." The agent of the Criminal Investigation Office, Shelga, and his little assistant Vanka Gusev are similarly portrayed in the novel as Soviet patriots.

However, for all their diversity of theme, these early works could not have assured Tolstoy a permanent place in the history of modern Russian literature. He won this place with his ***Peter I*** and the trilogy ***The Road to Calvary.***

Both works have a rather complex history. In his autobiography Tolstoy explains his interest in the period and the person of Peter I in the following passage: "It was, perhaps, with the artist's instinct rather than consciously that I sought in this theme a clue to an understanding of the Russian people and Russian polity. I was greatly helped in my studies by the late historian V. V. Kallash. He introduced me to the archives and documents of the Secret Office and the Preobrazhensky Department, recording the so-called 'Word and Deed' affairs. [In a footnote Alexandrova explains: "The reference here is to Peter's secret police and the dreaded phrase 'Word and Deed,' pronounced by its agents when they broke into a home to arrest their victim. The archives contained testimony of people under torture, with its inevitable terse expressiveness."] The riches of the Russian language were opened before me in all their brilliance, genius and power. I grasped at last the secret of the structure of the literary phrase: its form is determined by the inner state of the narrator, which leads to movement, gesture, and, finally, verbal expression, speech, in which the choice of words and their arrangement are coincident with the gesture."

The first version of the future three-volume novel—***Peter's Day***—was written while Tolstoy was still abroad. Emotionally, it differs sharply from the later, final text. This is how Tolstoy saw "Peter's mission" in ***Peter's Day***: "The royal city was being built at the edge of the land, on swamps, at the very border of the German realm. The people did not know who needed it, they did not know for the sake of what future ordeals they were compelled to shed their sweat and blood and perish by the thousands." . . . Pondering on Peter's plans and thoughts, Tolstoy seemed to ask: "But wait, was Peter really concerned with the good of Russia?"

In this first version of ***Peter I***, Tolstoy replied to the question in the negative: "It was not a strong and festive Russia that entered the family of great nations" as a result of Peter's efforts. Instead, "pulled in by the hair, bloody and frenzied with fear and despair, she appeared before her new relations wretched and inferior—as a slave. . . ." (pp. 238-42)

But the tragedy of Russia was not confined to her appearance before the world as a "slave." Peter's policies engendered within the country a deep passivity that found expression in a multitude of negative phenomena: sloth, bureaucracy, indifference.

Later, the same problem was to be discussed in ***The Road to Calvary*** by Tolstoy's favorite hero, the engineer Ivan Telegin: "How stupidly and ineptly everything is done in our country, and the devil alone knows what a reputation we Russians have. It is a pity and a shame. Just think—a most gifted people, an enormously rich country, and what is the face we present? An insolent government clerk's! Instead of life—paper and ink. . . . We started this official scribbling under Peter the Great, and we can't stop to this day." (p. 242)

In the first and second parts of his epic novel ***Peter I***, embracing Russian life at the end of the seventeenth and the first quarter of the eighteenth centuries, Tolstoy departed sharply from his initial view of "Peter's mission." The writer attempts to mitigate the darker aspects of the age. In his earlier descriptions of the inhuman working conditions in the factories of the day, or of Peter's cruelty, Tolstoy's sympathies had been with the Czar's victims. In the second version of the novel he closes his eyes to these facts.

The history of Peter's reign in Russia is embodied in an entire gallery of characters. Some, like Khovansky, Shaklovity, and Mstislavsky, represent the old, reactionary boyar strata which, under the leadership of the Czar's own sister Sofia, resisted Peter. But Peter depended in his work on younger forces. He never hesitated to recruit his assistants from among the common people. Foremost among these were Menshikov, the son of a groom, who had sold rabbit pies in the market, and Brovkin, a former boyar's serf who became a rich merchant with Peter's help. Brovkin's daughter Sanka is already a woman of the new era. Along with Sanka, we are shown a number of her contemporaries, who had been trained and educated abroad.

Close to these new elements also is the group of boyars, more intelligent and farsighted than the rest, who actively supported Peter's reforms. These included Pyotr Tolstoy; the first Russian Field Marshal, Boris Sheremetyev; and others. Tolstoy also shows us foreigners who took an active part in Russian life in Peter's day—men like Jacob Bruce and Patrick Gordon.

Another group consists of characters in which Tolstoy embodied the masses of the people, who carried on their backs all the burdens, both of wars and of the vast construction of new cities, harbors, and factories. Such are Fedka, nicknamed "Wash-Yourself-in-Mud," Andrey Golikov, and others.

Especially symptomatic of Tolstoy's evolution is his attitude toward "Peter's fledglings," his favorites and protégés, "the homeless, clever men who wanted change." Tolstoy's talent and his intimate knowledge of another—contemporary—dramatic epoch, help the writer to achieve brilliant insight into the most secret nooks of the social psychology of Peter's "new people." Here is Sanka Brovkina, yesterday an unknown serf hauling manure, today a lady of the court and Peter's favorite. Her husband complains that Sanka has got entirely out of hand—they even sleep apart now. Instead of quieting down and getting herself with child, she reads all night, studies politesse, and seethes with unquenchable longings.

The reader is also shown a whole gallery of "trading men" raised up by Peter, his "backbone strength"—all the Bazhenins, Demidovs, and Sveshnikovs who are ready, for the honor of being mentioned "by name and patronymic" in the Czar's edict, to supply him with vast sums for his construction projects. Tolstoy does not conceal these men's faults, their greed, their contempt for the weak, their egotism. But at the same time he seems to admire them, as if saying: indeed, they are a band of cunning rogues; but could Peter have budged this "cursed land," could he have gotten the upper hand over the arrogant boyars' resistance to change without their help?

Tolstoy's books quickly won great popularity among the strata which had risen from social limbo during the Five-Year Plan period and were filled with avid longing to live well. ***Peter I*** became emotionally something of a bible to the up-and-coming men of the time, whose social optimism echoed the optimism of Peter's protégés. These "new men" had not been conscious of any links with Russia's past, but Tolstoy seemed to have taken them by the hand and led them through the chambers of history, encouraging them with a broad gesture: keep your head high, you have predecessors; and just as they represented progress in their day, so you do in ours. The secret purpose of Tolstoy's novel was, of course, to justify Stalin by the analogy of Peter.

Tolstoy himself gave this a broader rationale. In his autobiographical sketch ***My Road*** . . . he wrote that the theme of Peter I attracted him by the "abundance of the 'unkempt' and richly creative energy of a period in which the Russian character was revealed with such extraordinary vividness." There were several periods in Russian history, he felt, when the Russian national character had thus revealed itself: "Four epochs claim my attention and demand expression for the same reasons: the epochs of Ivan the Terrible, Peter, the Civil War of 1918-20, and the present one—unprecedented in sweep and significance. . . . To fathom the secret of the Russian character, of its greatness, it is necessary to acquire a thorough and profound knowledge of its past—of our history, its pivotal moments, the tragic and creative epochs when the Russian character was taking shape." (pp. 242-45)

It is, perhaps, not accidental . . . that ***Peter I*** was written in part at the same time as the trilogy ***The Road to Calvary.*** The first volume of the trilogy—the novel ***Sisters***—was written in 1919, while Tolstoy was still living abroad. He worked on the subsequent volumes, ***Nineteen-Eighteen*** and ***A Gloomy Morning***, after his return to the Soviet Union.

This trilogy shows the revolution through the prism of the minds of people belonging to the bourgeois and land-owning intelligentsia, socially akin to Tolstoy. The narrative centers on the lives of the two Bulavin sisters—Katya and Dasha—and their friends, and later husbands, Ivan Telegin and Vadim Roshchin. The action of the novel takes place during World War I, the February revolution, the October days, the uprising of the Left-wing Socialist-Revolutionaries, the Makhno episode, and the Civil War. With a confident hand, and at the same time with great inner warmth, the writer leads his heroes through all the exigencies of the dramatic and complex popular revolution. In the scope of its events and characters ***The Road to Calvary*** has no equal in Soviet literature. At first Tolstoy's heroes, and particularly Vadim Roshchin, were bitter enemies of the October revolution, and Dasha, Telegin's wife, was at one time involved in the Savinkov plot. To explain Dasha's action, Tolstoy wrote: "In those days the human will was moved by inspiration rather than calm reflection. Swept by the hurricane of events, human life tossed like a stormy ocean, and everyone thought of himself as the savior of the foundering ship."

In this epic novel Tolstoy achieved the cherished ambition of many Soviet "Fellow-Traveling" writers—to create an "honest-to-goodness" biography of Soviet people. . . . But no one except Tolstoy succeeded in bringing his heroes to the point of complete acceptance of Soviet reality without violence either to the plot or to their characters. Tolstoy attempted to sum up the meaning of this difficult road in the epigraph to the second part of the trilogy: "Thrice drowned in water, thrice washed in blood, thrice boiled in lye. We are now purer than pure."

This epigraph is the leitmotiv of the epic, the key to the soul of the older generation of Soviet intelligentsia of the 1930s. In composition this group was an amalgam of remnants of the old, pre-revolutionary intelligentsia and the new, which had grown up during the revolutionary years but had retained close ties with the old. A part of the pre-revolutionary intelligentsia, long reconciled to the Soviet regime, had in its youth sympathized with or belonged to various socialist and liberal parties and fought for Russia's democratic development. Those were deeds and events of a distant past, but in the waking hours of night such people were still nagged by the worm of reminiscence and stirred by a sense of guilt. And the source of the guilt was the knowledge that life in contemporary Russia was impossible without an often ignoble compromise with one's conscience. By his trilogy ***The Road to Calvary*** Tolstoy liberated this intelligentsia from such disturbing feelings. He loudly proclaimed to it, for the whole country to hear: you are "purer than pure," and your actions, even when bad, are merely the "costs" of the great period of change in Russian history. He invited his heroes to stop tormenting themselves with the old "accursed questions." (pp. 245-47)

Tolstoy traveled a long way from the *Old Lindens* of the landed estates on the Volga to unconditional acceptance of Stalin's dictatorship. The chief trouble with the old Russia, as he saw it, had been the inept government apparatus which suppressed all manifestations of the people's talents. (p. 248)

In his novel ***Nineteen-Eighteen*** Tolstoy repeatedly returns to the idea of a new national consolidation, born of the revolution: "Who had expected that Great Russia, cut off from all seas and from the grain-producing provinces, from coal and oil, hungry, poverty-stricken, typhoid-ridden, would still refuse to yield, that she would, gritting her teeth, again and again send her sons into frightful battles? Only a year ago the people abandoned the front, and the country seemed to have turned into a lawless anarchic swamp. But in reality it was not so: tremendous cohesive forces were emerging in the land."

The beginning of the Five-Year Plans did not shake Tolstoy's feelings, but further strengthened them. He regarded the industrialization of the country as a new push toward national consolidation and responded to it "as an artist" with the novel ***Peter I.*** In this new work Tolstoy, without concealing Peter's ruthlessness, tells the reader that without such methods of terror Peter could not have crushed the boyar opposition and budged the "cursed land" from dead center. (pp. 248-49)

Nor was Tolstoy daunted by the Moscow trials of 1936-38. In 1937 he published his story **"Bread,"** eulogizing Stalin's military genius during the defense of Tsaritsyn. Tolstoy himself regarded this story as a necessary link between the second and third parts of ***The Road to Calvary.*** The most sensational aspect of the story was not so much the glorification of Stalin, as the depiction of Trotsky as the evil genius of the Russian revolution. It was easy for Tolstoy to do this: he was now hitting back, as it were, for his initial fear of "October" as the beginning of a "world social revolution." Shocking in its crude falsification of facts, the writer's picture of Trotsky and his associates during the Brest-Litovsk negotiations fairly seethes with hatred of these leaders of October. According to Tolstoy, they wanted to "blow up Soviet Russia so that the whole world would explode from the monstrous detonation." "But, of course," he adds, "the world itself was nothing to them but the same arena for personal adventure and the play of ambition. Provocation and betrayal were their methods."

In sharp contrast to the images of Trotsky and the Left-wing leaders of "October" are those of Lenin and Stalin. True, Stalin's role in the story is almost nominal; he is always shown in the company of Lenin, either pensively silent or agreeing with him. "Lenin," writes Tolstoy, "depended upon the creative forces of the masses for the victory and success of the revolution, and retained his optimism through all misfortunes, sufferings, and ordeals. He pointed out that the revolution had already called into being a new type of Russian. He asserted, passionately and prophetically, that the history of Russia was the history of a great people, and that her future was great and boundless."

This story, which appeared at the height of the terror and brutal repressions against virtually the entire leadership of the October revolution, certainly enhanced Tolstoy's prestige in official circles, but stunned his fellow writers and the reading public with amazement. No other leading Soviet writer had ever reached such "Himalayas" of slander in his works.

Tolstoy was bold and consistent. Having sensed, with his "artist's impudence" (his own words, in the **"Message to Young Writers,"** 1938), the consolidation of national tendencies in the course of the revolution, Tolstoy no longer drew a line at anything. After completing **"Bread"** he began the third part of ***The Road to Calvary—A Gloomy Morning.*** As time went on, the writer became progressively kinder in his treatment of the rank-and-file heroes of the Civil War on both sides—all those "honest, simple and trusting, heavy-handed Russian people." Together with Captain Roshchin, who had by now re-evaluated his past, Tolstoy looked fondly at the young workers of the time, with their naïve belief that they were taking part in "the world revolution." As for "Father Makhno" and his associates in the anarchic peasant movement which opposed both the Reds and the Whites, Tolstoy described them with a virtually Repin-like splash of color.

Tolstoy died relatively early, in the full flower of his talent. But his ideological development was complete; there was no further place for him to go. (pp. 249-50)

Vera Alexandrova, "Alexey Tolstoy (1883-1945)," in her A History of Soviet Literature, 1917-1964: From Gorky to Solzhenitsyn, *translated by Mirra Ginsburg, 1963. Reprint by Anchor Books, 1964, pp. 236-50.*

MARC SLONIM (essay date 1977)

[*Slonim was a Russian-born American critic who wrote extensively on Russian literature. In the following excerpt from an examination of the themes and techniques of Tolstoy's works, Slonim focusses on* The Road to Calvary *and* Peter I.]

The locale of [Tolstoy's] light and amusing stories was usually his native region, a sort of Russian Arkansas or South Dakota. In his childhood and youth he had had the opportunity of accumulating material on the mores of the squires whose estates were scattered beyond the Volga on the steppes of the southeast, and many of whom were related to his family. He himself said later that their world was for him "an artistic discovery." A chronicler of this wild provincial nobility and its decline, he enjoyed depicting absurd and colorful eccentrics, and presented a whole gallery of willful, ignorant, and fantastic people. All his tales have extremely foolish or grotesque plots. Stepanida Ivanovna, wife of a choleric general, embarks on a search for hidden treasure using black magic, bewitched cockerels, and with the help of a saintly countrywoman who proudly reports how successfully she has resisted the Devil disguised as a seductive cavalry officer. The walrus-like Mishka Alymov, who maintains a harem on his estate, provokes a riot at a wedding and, upon being tossed out, becomes nasty and takes to overturning benches and uprooting trees in the village square. Rabelaisian feasts are followed by Homeric fist fights, during which the athletic Rtishchev neighs like a colt while his crony Okoyemov, deep in his cups, chases the devils he spots in ventilators and windows. In addition to freaks, lechers, and firebrands there are other specimens of human folly such as Repiev, who invents an enormous flatiron drawn by four horses, to melt snowdrifts; and the landowner Chuvashov, whose complicated mousetraps "are based on purely psychological principles of taste."

These extravagant people are usually endowed with amazing physical strength and unlimited appetites of the flesh. They are brimming with energy, but they do not know what to do with themselves and consequently kill time in sloth or sprees. The only thing they are capable of is love (or what they call love): this ranges from wild sexual affairs, which make rich noblemen spend their entire fortunes on some perverse wench, to the almost platonic affection of a middle-aged squire for an adolescent, flaxen-haired schoolgirl (***Cranks, The Lame Squire***—probably the best of all this cycle—then ***Adventures of Rasteghin, Cagliostro Defeated,*** and other short novels and stories).

These anecdotal tales unite realistic observation with symbolic poetic allusions, and are written with a sweep, a brio, in a fluent, rich language, with concrete details and sensual images. As well as being extremely entertaining and full-blooded, they are enlivened by humor, cunning subplots, and erotic scenes. Tolstoy's drawings of eccentrics, bullies, superfluous men, and either passionate or ethereal girls could, in a way, be accepted as an exposé of a corrupt and declining class, particularly because of their strong satirical flavor. Soviet critics asserted that Tolstoy's gallery of drunken officials, dissipated noblemen, and superstitious ladies portrayed the disintegration of Russia's provincial aristocracy and that his stories were an additional indictment of the old regime that had bred and supported such a host of fools, drones, rakes, and scoundrels.

It is more than doubtful, however, whether Tolstoy ever had in mind any such lofty aim. His was an organic, spontaneous talent, a true, God-given gift. His power of observation, his mastery in telling an anecdote (either with tongue in cheek or with guffaws), his feeling for an intriguing plot, his art in choosing significant details and sharp contours, and his innate faculty of telling a yarn in a witty fashion were all unusually sparkling and authentic. But he was not interested in messages, ideas, or value judgments. "Tolstoy has plenty of blood, and fat, and lust, and a nobleman's snobbery," Blok wrote in his diary. "But everything is spoiled by his hooliganism, his immature approach to life." (pp. 145-47)

He chose to produce entertaining novels with a sufficient amount of social stuffing, and was one of the first to offer utopian tales with strong adventure elements and what is now called science-fiction—a genre highly appreciated by Soviet readers in the 'twenties. His widely read ***Aelita*** . . . deals with an expedition whose aim is to establish Communism on Mars; his ***Hyperboloid of the Engineer Garin*** . . . is a super-thriller in which blond "vamps," sleuths, international crooks, financiers, and other criminals are involved in a sensational discovery—a death-ray, quite as effective as the atomic or hydrogen bomb—which enables Garin, its unscrupulous inventor, to impose his will upon shattered Europe and to establish a fascist society. In other collections of tales (such as ***Seven Days in Which the World Was Robbed***), he continued to exploit the sensational and the adventurous with just the right tinge of the political. In **"The Council of Five,"** a tale of 1926, a clique of five Wall Streeters bombard and splinter the moon, seizing control of the world; but they are defeated when the general astonishment is succeeded by universal apathy and, at last, by world-wide revolt. Tolstoy also wrote potboilers, such as ***Black Gold,*** renamed ***The Émigrés*** in 1931, in which White Russians abroad and international intrigues over petroleum furnish the elements of a lurid melodrama in very bad taste. The plays he wrote in collaboration with Pyotr Shchegolev, the historian, are also melodramatic and were the delight of the provincial stage (***Rasputin, or The Conspiracy of the Empress*** . . . and ***Azef*** . . .). But even in all these entertainments of dubious quality, there was, alongside the vulgarity, brilliant inventiveness; the story was always told by a master plotter, and humor and talent were clearly in evidence. This is particularly true of ***Ibicus, or the Adventures of Nevzorov*** . . . , written in the manner of Tolstoy's tales about the Volga eccentrics and depicting in a picaresque style the misfortunes of a homunculus tossed about by the Revolution and the civil war. The realistic short stories of Soviet life—**"The Viper"** about a woman-fighter suffering from a middle-class environment, **"Blue Cities"** about a dreamer-architect who rebels against the inertia of ordinary Soviet citizens, and **"Vassily Sushkov"**—are well written without being remarkable.

In the 1930's, however, Tolstoy produced two major works that justified all the honors bestowed upon him: ***The Road to Calvary,*** a trilogy, and ***Peter I,*** an unfinished historical narrative. (pp. 148-49)

The Road to Calvary encompasses three periods in the life of the intelligentsia: that of the decadents, symbolists, religious thinkers, and aesthetes before 1917; that of the Revolution; and that of the civil war, with all its consequences. The chief characters—the clumsy, honest engineer Teleghin, who belongs in the "simple heart" tradition; Dasha, his fiancée and later his wife; her sister Katia, who is looking for a husband; Dr. Bulavin, their father, an old-fashioned liberal; and Roshchin, a young officer in love with Katia—all live gaily and carelessly under the old regime but are seized by the historical whirlwind and share in the tribulations and sufferings of their country. The first panel of this tryptich, ***The Sisters,*** written in exile, shows the intellectuals as a leisurely, weak, and inconsistent group of people, completely isolated from the rest of the nation and unaware of reality. The two sisters think of nothing but their personal happiness and dream of romantic love. All the personages of the novel affirm the priority of personal destiny over history, and Roshchin says to Katia: "Years will go by, wars will end, revolutions will be silenced, but one thing will remain—the imperishable, gentle, tender, lovely heart of yours." When ***The Sisters*** was published in the Soviet Union, Gorky showed some restraint in his praise of Tolstoy: "Very interesting, the psychology of a Russian girl ready to love is nicely drawn. The background is the Russian intelligentsia before and during the war. Interesting characters and scenes." But the two following panels—the second, ***1918,*** giving a remarkable description of the general collapse and revolutionary chaos, and the third, ***Murky Dawn,*** a panorama of the civil war—show the changes provoked in all the characters by the dreadful experiences of famine, destruction, and violence, and finally leave Teleghin, Dasha, and Katia at the threshold of a new life among ruins and confronted with new trials. This vast narrative now had a main ideological thread—the evolution of men and women from their closed worlds of personal feelings and aspirations to the reconciliation of the individual and the collective through the understanding of and participation in the historical and national process. Teleghin, in particular, is the embodiment of this transformation. He is a simple ordinary Russian, healthy in body and spirit, alien to the sophistications and sterile facade of the upper classes; he is a well-rounded person and unlike most members of the intelligentsia is not tormented by ambivalence and a split personality. Teleghin understands that the vertical culture of the intellectuals was an artificial superstructure; now he wants to live and work close to the rest of his own people; the masses have made the Revolution, and he wishes to be with them and help them to find a better life. He loves his country and wants to share its destiny, good and bad. Roshchin, an anti-Communist fighter, comes to the same conclusion, identifies the service of the Revolution with patriotism, and decides to abandon the Whites.

In stressing the change of attitude toward the Revolution among intellectuals and even noblemen, a change often accompanied by tragic conflicts and bitter inward struggle, ***The Road to Calvary*** summed up the evolution which had taken place in the 1920's and the early 1930's and of which Tolstoy himself, as well as the whole "Changing the Landmarks" movement, was so representative. His heroes did not adhere to Communist doctrine and had no intention of joining the Party; they accepted the regime and supported its policy of reconstruction largely from patriotic and populistic motives—and this was true of many millions of Russians for whom Stalin eventually coined the label, Non-Partisan Bolsheviks. For most of them Russia and Revolution merged into one national image. Teleghin is not a Communist hero, he is a character with national traits, the representative of those who have maintained through centuries the Russian state and culture. People like him are the backbone of a country, and they cannot become strangers to their own folk. The fact that Tolstoy's trilogy expressed this feeling in emotional and instinctual terms, without any ideological pretensions, was the main reason for its immense success.

As an artistic whole, the trilogy has many flaws. Some of the characters, particularly the women, are magnificently drawn in the first part, but become pale and less convincing as the story goes on. In Parts II and III the historical material overwhelms and weakens the narrative. Although Tolstoy used authentic documents and dealt with well-known events, quite a few passages, such as those referring to Trotsky or Stalin, are obviously added becasue of political opportunism, and they distort the truth. Yet as a general vision of Russian life from 1914 to 1921 ***The Road to Calvary*** is equal, and in parts superior, to the works of Sholokhov and Fadeyev. Tolstoy the storyteller excels in vivid scenes and in secondary characters, such as Arnoldov the liberal journalist; Elizaveta the admirer of modernism; Makhno the rebel leader, and his assistants, two bearded and bespectacled anarchists; Sorokin the mad commander; and Kuzma the unfrocked priest. The novel portrays dozens of intellectuals, peasants, workmen, and military men in a colorful and realistic way, and they move in a lively procession; they may be pathetic, trivial, or comic, yet they all breathe the air of life.

Despite all the erroneous appraisals of Soviet critics, the trilogy can hardly be called an epic—its form is slighter and more episodic than the narrative of *Quiet Flows the Don,* it uses the technique of cinematographic shots, and has subplots and separate episodes that enhance the main plot but render the composition fragmentary and alien to the classical Russian pattern of psychological analysis. With a few modifications Tolstoy applied to his trilogy the method of neo-realism which marked his Volga tales—yet he toned it down and carefully avoided symbolistic devices. But to contend that the novel is an example of "socialist realism," as has been done time and again in Communist criticism, is completely arbitrary and ridiculous. It is highly debatable whether the trilogy is or is not a masterpiece; but it certainly belongs to a pre-revolutionary stylistic trend.

Tolstoy did attempt to bring out a novel to conform to what at the time was called socialist realism: entitled ***Bread*** . . . it is a sort of chronological sequence to the trilogy. This contains a number of bright descriptive passages but they do not save the book from being marred by a crude political bias. It describes the defense of Czaritsyn (later Stalingrad, and then Volgograd) by the Reds in 1918, and "arranges" historical events *ad majorem Stalini gloriam*—apparently as part of an ideological core in fictional form. ***Bread*** and ***Black Gold*** are probably the worst and most irritating novels of Tolstoy.

However, he reached new heights in his historical masterpiece ***Peter I***. . . . It is to all intents a biography of the Tsar who changed Russia's destinies; his superb psychological and physical portrait from childhood until his battle with the Swedes at Narva in 1701 is painted in bold strokes against the background of the seventeenth century, with a tremendous cast of courtiers, princelings, dignitaries, priests, and representatives of all the social strata, including runaway serfs and highway robbers. Tolstoy portrays Peter as an implement of history, the hammer that mercifully smashed feudal Muscovy, and also as a man of passions and intense curiosity, ready to learn from anybody. Tolstoy supplies a brilliantly drawn gallery of Peter's supporters, such as Menshikov, the former pie-vendor, and of his innumerable enemies, including his own son, Alexis, whom the cruel Tsar tortured and killed. As is usual with Tolstoy, all the secondary characters are well executed (for example,

Charles XII, the great Swedish warrior whom Peter finally defeated, to the surprise of all Europe). The succession of varied and dynamic events of the period when the new Russian Empire was being forged is unfolded in glimpses and scenes that offer, amid a wealth of visual details and anecdotes, a striking image of the permanent elements of Russian character. The Peter who attempted to europeanize Russia is at the same time interpreted as the true incarnation of her Scythian spirit, her pagan vitality, and her strength and frenzy in work, love, and revelry. Tolstoy adored this strength and he conveyed it fully in his novel.

This monumental work based on solid historical material has the precision and sharpness of old engravings; the flavor of a distant age is rendered by sparing use of seventeenth-century locutions, certain shrewdly inserted quotations from old documents, and references to extinct customs. Yet this reconstruction of a period has nothing of a chronicle about it: its freshness of presentation, its colorful characters, its dramatic dialogue, its swift pace of narration, and its rapid play of events make it as exciting as any novel dealing with contemporaneous events. Tolstoy denied that he had chosen Peter's epoch in order to project current problems into the past, to deliver a message or to teach a lesson. Like Pilnyak and other Soviet writers, he had always been attracted by the figure of the Great Tsar, and in 1917 had written a story called **"Peter's Day"** in which he depicted the Emperor as a despot. He changed his opinion, however, and in the novel showed other aspects of the builder of St. Petersburg; he now admired his intelligence, his genius, his devotion to the country, and his superhuman energy.

Of course, ***Peter I*** was bound to suggest certain analogies between the revolutionary changes brought about by Peter and those brought about by the Bolsheviks, and as long as both employed crass and brutal methods and did not spare lives, the conclusion seemed obvious: the justification of Peter was, indirectly, a justification of Lenin and Stalin. The novel was written mostly in the early 1930's, when the leaders of Russia, sensing the growth of patriotic feeling in the people, favored a blending of Communism and nationalism. Tolstoy felt keenly this transition from internationalism to national pride and the identification of the USSR as a direct successor to the Empire of the Tsars. On this point there was no discrepancy between the Party line and his own emotions: to Tolstoy, who was never a Communist and had rather vague notions on Marxism, dialectical materialism, and all the theoretical stuff he disliked so heartily, the patriotic urge and the epithet "Holy Motherland" did mean a great deal. He belonged to Russia, loved her, shared her destiny, and described her as an unbroken chain of generations. This explains the significance of ***Peter I:*** it linked the past and the present in a glorifying synthesis, interpreting the titanic figure of the Emperor as the ancestor of the Soviet man. Yet the greatest merit of the work lies in its power of creative evocation of the past. It is true that the novel lacks all unity of plot save a chronological one, that it is fragmentary and kaleidoscopic, and that some scenes are put together much after the fashion of a motion-picture film; but each sequence has such a dynamic rhythm, and glows with such descriptive brilliancy, each visual detail comes out so clearly, and the whole panorama of a century is so picturesque, that there can be no hesitation in ranking ***Peter I*** among the best historical works in twentieth-century Russian literature.

Many of Alexey Tolstoy's contemporaries were better equipped with ideas, refinement, intelligence, or wisdom. It was neither his intellectual nor moral qualities that won him his position. But he did possess such an infallible capacity for re-creating the very illusion of being that he triumphed by sheer richness of portraiture, by the concreteness of his images, by the lavishness of an organic generous talent. Whenever he attempted to convey a message and to be more than a storyteller—as in the case of his last play ***Ivan The Terrible*** . . . , in which he tried to white-wash the awesome tyrant in accordance with the Party line—he failed, producing an artificial and inferior work. But when he remained faithful to his basic, spontaneous gift and conveyed the flavor of his native country and of her true sons, he showed himself to be a master. (pp. 149-54)

Marc Slonim, "Alexey Tolstoy: The Master of the Anecdote," in his Soviet Russian Literature: Writers and Problems 1917-1977, *revised edition, Oxford University Press, 1977, pp. 144-54.*

RICHARD FREEBORN (essay date 1982)

[Freeborn is a Welsh critic, educator, and translator who has written and edited numerous studies of Russian history, literature, and literary figures. In the following excerpt, he discusses Tolstoy's literary and propagandistic skills in The Road to Calvary.*]*

A. N. Tolstoy's three-volume epic novel [***The Road to Calvary***] stands in ambiguous and uneasy opposition to Sholokhov's *Quiet Flows the Don* as a work that aspires to illustrate the role of the intelligentsia in revolution and civil war. It is a conventional historical novel, written by a gifted writer whose antecedents no doubt helped him, but whose gratitude to state and party during the height of Stalin's 'cult of personality' irreparably damaged his literary achievement and reputation. Not that Aleksey Tolstoy could be considered a party hack. His fluency as a stylist, his descriptive powers and his mastery of characterisation lend distinction to the most propagandist of his novels. (***Bread*** . . . is the most notorious example in its deliberate disfigurement of Trotsky's role in the civil war). The panoramic sweep of ***The Road to Calvary*** gives it a consciously epic intent, with scenes and characters introduced to provide examples of what, for Stalinist purposes, would be considered the correct interpretation of history. Such a prescriptive approach naturally tended to distort the organic flow of the fiction and to make contrivance, whether based on coincidence or sheer improbability, essential to the narrative impulse. In this respect alone, A. N. Tolstoy's work suffers very greatly by comparison with Sholokhov's, but it is a symptom of a more profound flaw in the very intent of the fiction.

The Road to Calvary was written between 1919 and 1941. Critical comment is generally agreed that the first volume is better than the last volume, and there is no doubt that the portrayal of the two sisters Dasha and Katya in pre-revolutionary St Petersburg is done with verve and freshness despite the authorial mockery of the literary circles and the self-conscious decadence of the period. The critique of the intelligentsia in the first volume develops into an exposure of the futility of the White cause in the second volume. Here Roshchin, who is to become Katya's husband, fights on the White side, whereas Telegin, who is married to Dasha, is a Bolshevik, but in the final volume, as the civil war progresses, Roshchin becomes converted to the Soviet cause, Katya, who falls into the clutches of the peasant anarchist Makhno, has her own faith in the future of Russia restored and the four of them, after Telegin and Dasha are happily reunited, attend a meeting in the Bolshoy Theatre, Moscow, where plans for the electrification of the U.S.S.R. and the building of communism are announced in the presence of the architect of such plans, V. I. Lenin, and his ever-loyal colleague, J. V. Stalin.

The contrasts in the first volume are chiefly those between pre-1914 metropolitan society, with its frivolous bourgeois pastimes, and the horrors and futilities of the First World War, though on a moral level the most pointed contrast is made between the diligent engineer Telegin and the decadent poet Bessonov. If the characters of the sisters Dasha and Katya have certain points of difference, these facets receive little emphasis. They are portrayed sympathetically as essentially virtuous heroines, misled by the immorality of the period, perhaps, but capable of rising above their bourgeois background. Revolution is signalled by conversational hints. The wartime conditions, leading to military collapse, are obviously a contributory factor. Yet overt political guidance of the revolutionary events receives scant attention, presented as they are largely from the sisters' apolitical viewpoints or through the experience of Roshchin with the White volunteer army. Increasingly, a major contrast becomes discernible: the sense of the work as historical fiction becomes founded on a reiterated contrast between present and past experiences, between present disorder and past stability; between the ephemeral chaos of the present and the wider historical context of events—a contrast made plain in passages of text-book commentary; and between the privations of the present and the promise of a socialist future to replace the capitalist world of the past.

The fiction shows the strains of this imposed intent on many occasions. It is an epic novel of ideas in which the political ideas tend in the end to manipulate the characters. Indeed, with the possible exception of Roshchin, the ideas espoused by the characters appear to be implanted in them literally by authorial *fiat*. As a critique of the past and, by implication, of the Russian intelligentsia's flirtation with Christian ideas in the decade prior to the October revolution, the novel has at its centre an eloquent attack on the flaws inherent in Christianity. But the attack is voiced not by one of the novel's principal characters, nor by a spokesman for the intelligentsia; it is voiced by a German intellectual in German military uniform whom Katya meets on a train journey during the civil war in the south. It is the most important ideological plea for a socialist future in the whole three-part novel.

The decline of the West anticipated by Oswald Spengler is the context in which the German states his case. Just as the Roman world was destroyed by the idea of Christianity, so the ideas of socialism will destroy Christianity and its influence. At the downfall of the Roman Empire all Christianity had to offer were the destructive ideas of 'equality, internationalism and the moral superiority of poverty over riches', but there was no creative idea in Christianity: it had no way of organising labour. 'On earth it contented itself with destruction and it left everything else as a promise in heaven. Christianity was no more than a sword of destruction and punishment', becoming the religion not of those who sow and reap but of emperors and conquerors. (pp. 194-96)

Those in whose name the German speaks, the revolutionary proletariat, have few representatives in the novel. In the final volume the number of characters is multiplied to include such members of Telegin's brigade as Latugin and Sharygin, not to mention the extremely interesting vignette-like portrayal of Anisya, but though such 'ordinary' figures are clearly designed to enhance the political meaning of the novel they are less effective as characters than the representatives of the intelligentsia. Through one of those unlikely coincidences which abound in the final volume the German intellectual who spoke to Katya meets Roshchin in beleaguered Yekaterinoslav and informs him that Katya has very likely fallen into the hands of Makhno. The meeting with Makhno is an occasion for Roshchin to explain briefly his reasons for abandoning his intelligentsia role ('It turned out that the intelligentsia wasn't up to it. In October they took us by the scruff of the neck like so many kittens and flung us on the rubbish heap . . .'), but it also develops into one of these dialogue set pieces in which Nestor Makhno's anarchism is shown up as a baseless, squalid religion of death and destruction.

The shallowness of the ideas produces an equivalent shallowness in the characterisation. Comrade Stalin is efficiently directing the Red armies in the civil war while Roshchin, for example, does his bit for the Red cause by reconnoitring Yekaterinoslav unobserved and then leading the assault on the city without receiving any injury. In short, all the leading characters have virtue on their side. Mistaken though they may have been at earlier points in the civil war, by 1920 there is no doubt that reason has prevailed and the only opposition to the Soviet state is provided by such renegades as the Ataman Zelyony. All right-thinking characters have succumbed to the vision of a socialist future.

The euphoric intent of the fiction in its final stages naturally minimises all likelihood of misfortune and leaves no room for doubt about ultimate purposes. The happiness of Telegin and Dasha is crowned by true love ('Now their love, in particular for Dasha, was full and palpable like the air of early winter, when the November storms had passed and in soft frost-laden silence the first snow smelled of sliced melon . . .), though other storms disturb their lives before they are finally united in the Bolshoy Theatre. Roshchin's is to be the last word, suitably monumental and resonant, on the purposes to which their generation has dedicated itself: . . .

> Now the veil's been torn from our eyes! The whole of our past life was based on crime and falsehood! Russia has given birth to a new man . . . That man has demanded the right for people to become human beings. It's not a dream, it's an idea, it's at the ends of our bayonets, it's close to realisation! A blinding light has lit up the half-ruined arches of all passed millennia! It's all firmly based, it's all in order! A purpose has been found!'. . . .

The message of the words is in no need of elaboration. It is manifestly propagandist and obvious. What needs stressing is the assumption that the trauma of revolution has not only destroyed the past but has also brought to birth a new man and new purposes. The spurious aggrandisement of these ideas through comparing them with cosmic distances, their significance in relation to eternity and the coming of a new millennium is clearly discernible in parts of the final volume. It is in the nature of historical fiction to romanticise the past and in this case the process of glorifying the Russian Revolution and civil war appears to have reached a peak of false magniloquence. Completed on the eve of the Great Fatherland War, Aleksey Tolstoy's ***The Road to Calvary*** very likely appealed as much to patriotic as to revolutionary feelings but in the same breath it could hardly avoid both exalting the historical role of the Russian people as the creators of socialism and representing the experience as governed above all by rational purposes in the name of a socialist future.

The work has a spurious air of literary quality about it. The skill in the writing is sustained even through protracted dialogue exchanges and the need to ensure happy dénouements. Lacking from it is the sense of human destiny inexorably linked, by some profound instinct for survival, to earth and home, a sense, in short, of the rootedness of human experience. As an epic of revolutionary ideas, ***The Road to Calvary*** parades the fictional embodiments of commitment to Bolshevism or White revanchism or anarchism or intelligentsia ideals like counters in an elaborate board-game, which end up not by demonstrating the choices *pro* and *contra,* but by making the pattern of a hammer and sickle. (pp. 197-99)

Richard Freeborn, "The Revolutionary Epic," in his The Russian Revolutionary Novel: Turgenev to Pasternak, *Cambridge University Press, 1982, pp. 172-99.**

VADIM BARANOV (essay date 1983)

[In the following excerpt Baranov presents a survey of Tolstoy's works, emphasizing Tolstoy's contribution to the development of Socialist Realism and to world literature in general with his Peter I.]

Gorky used the word cheerful to define Alexei Tolstoy's gift as a writer [see excerpt dated 1933].

We smile with the author as we watch little Nikita trying to elude the vigilance of his tutor and slip away from the house ***(Nikita's Childhood).*** We laugh heartily at the adventures of Buratino in the course of his fearless duel with the wicked Karabas-Barabas ***(The Golden Key, or the Adventures of Buratino)****. . . .*

Yes, there was cheerfulness in Alexei Tolstoy's gift. But in addition to its ordinary straightforward meaning of "funny", this word has another more profound sense in Russian. We need only recall how frequent and dominant the corresponding adjective is in Lev Tolstoy's *War and Peace*—and how it occurs precisely in episodes of the greatest peril.

If we pause and reflect about Gorky's definition of Alexei Tolstoy's gift, we will conclude that his basic meaning is a continuous sense of the fullness of earthly existence, which is profoundly national in origin, a note of intense joy in the apprehension of everything seething and happening all around, which bears the simple but inexhaustible name of *life.*

Was this eagerness to grasp the miracle of life in all its fullness and variety not the reason for the amazing universality of Tolstoy's work? (p. 141)

It is now plain to all that as a writer of outstanding gifts and captivating national originality Tolstoy rightly belongs among the classics of Soviet literature. His career as a writer reflects natural processes going on in the depths of all the arts in the Soviet Union in connection with the development of the new artistic method of socialist realism. Tolstoy painted a picture of tremendous depth and penetration in which he depicted the break-up of the old world, the establishment of new socialist relations and the formation of a new type of personality, and he wrote outstanding historical works. Alexei Tolstoy was one of the founders of the Soviet school of historical novelists and is a major figure in this field. (p. 142)

The future writer first tried his pen at the beginning of the century, at a time when social contradictions in Russia were becoming ever more acute. Tolstoy was a student of the Petersburg Technological Institute at the time, and he began with poetry imbued with sympathy for the struggle against despotism and social injustice. Very soon, however, these poems were succeeded by verse entirely divorced from any social problems, plainly written under the influence of symbolist canons. (It made up his first book, ***Lyrics*****. . .**). At the same time Tolstoy was trying his hand at poetry in the folk manner. This was marked by a contradictory blend of genuine folk poetry and affected stylisation prompted by the widespread admiration of folk-lore typical of Russia at the beginning of the century.

At this period Tolstoy was wholly absorbed in the effort to find his own literary personality. Gradually the healthy democratic principle gained the upper hand in his work. This was reflected in the works in which the young writer tried to express his credo in programmatic terms—an article with the imperative title ***Literature and the Nation*** . . . and the folklore miniature ***The Picture*** . . . which contains his first attempt at criticism of formalist anti-popular art.

Soon Tolstoy turned to the familiar material of the life of the landed gentry. In this period, around 1910 and 1911, was written the famous cycle of short and long stories set in the Volga countryside—***Volga Country, The Cock, A Week in Turenevo, The Dreamer (Aggei Korovin), Arkhip, The Actress, The Courtship.***

Sharp delineation of the characters unites all these works and also others thematically and chronologically close to them. Vain dreamers, traumatised by their first serious contact with life, incompetent squires whose efforts at practical management are all fatally doomed to failure, belligerent tyrants and bullies aggressively embodying the consumer attitude to life, pass in procession before the reader's gaze.

The moral ideal is embodied in the female characters, closely linked with Turgenev tradition—Vera Khodanskaya ***(Mishuka Nalymov),*** Sonechka Smolkova ***(Eccentrics),*** Katya Volkova ***(The Lame Landlord),*** Annushka ***(Native Country).*** Their most remarkable feature is their capacity for love, for deep, selfless, self-sacrificing love. To a certain extent they are the forerunners of the remarkable figures of the Russian women who were destined to tread the difficult path of the ***Ordeal.***

The Volga tales and stories were distinguished by an enviable compactness of the narrative and an accuracy of observation which found particular expression in the excellent choice of literary detail, in an unconstrained intonation, in the humour and irony with which the monsters of the Volga countryside landed gentry are portrayed. (pp. 143-44)

The years immediately preceding the First World War marked an important stage in Tolstoy's life. At this period he was writing works where he touched on key questions of the intellectual life of the time. Here the reader will find condemnation of various forms of escape from life, a recurring theme in the work of the youthful Tolstoy at that time ***(The Blue Counterpane, The Young Writer, Two Lives),*** criticism of the sham democracy of the theory of "small deeds" ***(Logutka),*** attacks on decadent writers who advocated base eroticism ***(The Faun, Night Visions, Wingless)*** and defence of the classics against the distorted interpretations of the decadent critics ***(The Portrait).***

Tolstoy's first attempts in the field of drama deserve special mention. He wrote several plays before the Revolution ***(The Rocket, Honeybunch, Bitter Flower).*** The most significant of his plays was ***The Tyrants*** (written in 1912), the first of Tolstoy's dramas to see the footlights. It was a work of some social importance and great topicality.

However, Tolstoy's development as a writer during the years 1912-1914 was very complex and the increasing maturity of his civic attitude and the sharper democracy of his perception of the world were not always fully expressed in his imaginative writing.

The war which had broken out in 1914 and his work as a war correspondent broadened his horizons and brought him face to face with scenes of inconspicuous heroism on the part of the common people, who, in accordance with the ancient Russian tradition, accepted the war as hard but necessary work. For three years Tolstoy travelled back and forth over many roads (the cycles of sketches ***Through Volyn, Through Galicia, In the Caucasus***).

Nevertheless Tolstoy was not sufficiently prepared to be able to understand what the October Revolution brought. The most difficult period of the writer's life ensued, leading to his emigration in March of 1919. (p. 145)

Tolstoy returned to Russia on the first of August, 1923. However, there are good grounds for calling him a Soviet writer from the spring of 1922—the time of the definitive change in his philosophy of life.

This is confirmed by the imaginative writing of these years, in the first instance by his novel ***Aelita.*** Although it is about a flight to Mars, this novel is the most "earth-bound" work in all Soviet science fiction. In this lies its connection with ***Nikita's Childhood,*** outwardly so dissimilar, the last chapters of which were written in 1922, in the same year as ***Aelita.*** Basically autobiographical in nature, ***Childhood*** is an exalted hymn to life. With amazing skill Tolstoy recreates the inner world of the child who is just beginning to be aware of the vast world stretching around him, a world brimming with beauty, fascination and mystery.

Man and his country is the theme which found literary expression in Tolstoy's autobiographical work and it absorbed him increasingly, giving rise to a whole cycle of works about people with no country—***On the Island of Khalka, The Manuscript Found under the Bed, The Mirage, The Adventure of Nevzorov, or Ibicus,*** and ***Black Gold (Émigrés).*** It is significant here that the earlier works in this cycle were written while Tolstoy was still living abroad, including ***Manuscript*** which the author himself considered the most important work of his Berlin period, and the theme was further developed to its natural conclusion later in Soviet Russia. This fact confirms Tolstoy's uninterrupted development as a writer after the events of the spring of 1922.

Tolstoy's encounter with the life of the country during the period of the New Economic Policy was not lacking in difficulties and contradictions. Far from all his attempts to reflect the new life in prose and drama were successful (the stories ***The Incident in Basseynaya Street, Averyan Myshin's Good Luck,*** the play ***A Fantastic Tale***), but among the works of the twenties there are also pieces which deserve close attention, particularly the long stories ***Blue Cities*** . . . and ***The Viper***. . . .

During these years Tolstoy was also working on his vast epic about the destiny of his country during the years of the Revolution, his trilogy ***Ordeal***. . . . This work is discussed elsewhere . . . by Konstantin Fedin, himself a major Soviet writer [see excerpt dated 1957}. Therefore at this point we will refer only to the words of the critic Vyacheslav Polonsky who said of this magnificent epic that it was "accomplished through suffering, and dictated by patriotic concern". In it Tolstoy emerged as a historical and philosophical writer.

The intense work on the trilogy ran parallel with work on the novel about the Petrine period (1672-1725).

The theme of Peter the Great first occurs in Tolstoy's work in 1917 (***A Day in the Life of Tsar Peter,*** then ***The First Terrorists*** and ***The Obsession***).

Subsequently, throughout the twenties and thirties, work on the novel about Peter the Great alternated with work on the trilogy. Outwardly it seems as though we are looking at two mighty trees of different species. But the same soil nourished both and their roots are so closely intertwined that at times it is extremely difficult to distinguish them from one another. Concealed from the reader's gaze there went on a process of interaction between the conception and literary structure of each book so that each enriched the other—the trilogy about quite recent events acquired additional historical depth and the novel about Peter revealed its stark relevance to a period of radical transformation of the world.

Tolstoy acknowledged, "I could not remain indifferent to the creative enthusiasm which had seized our whole country, but I was incapable of writing about contemporary life on the strength of a couple of visits to some building site. . . . I decided to respond to our period in my own way. And I turned to the past once more, this time in order to show victory over elemental forces, over inertia, over the Asiatic backwardness in our national life." (pp. 145-47)

The opening pages of the novel testify to Tolstoy's remarkable skill in composition. Before he introduces the figure of the future ruler, the author depicts scenes from the life of the peasants, streltsy (soldiers), tradespeople, fugitive peasants, gentry and great lords—not one level of Russian society at that time seems to have been forgotten.

Tolstoy turns the intricate system of relations between the characters into a means of exploring the spirit of the period, of laying bare its driving forces and studying the factors which determined the direction in which Peter's personality developed.

The period depicted by Tolstoy in the novel was full of great inherent drama. Before tackling the various problems facing Russia, and conducting a war for access to the sea—without this her normal development as a great nation was entirely inconceivable—the resistance of internal opposition had to be broken. This is why Tolstoy devoted so much attention to the figure of the power-loving Tsarevna Sofia, her favourite Vasili Golitsin and the streltsy who supported them.

The author concentrated his main efforts on drawing the character of Peter as fully and from as many sides as possible to show adequately the figure of a ruler unprecedented, perhaps, not only among Russian monarchs. His hero is the living incarnation of protest against routine, against every form of outward show which stands in the way of genuine progress. Swiftness, impulse, impatience—here we have the whole of Peter with his unquenchable desire to break through the centuries-old layer of prejudice against the new. (pp. 147-48)

Female characters play a large and important part in the narrative structure. They express vividly the psychology of radical social changes. Thus Alexandra, the daughter of a poor peasant, becomes the wife of an aristocrat, with the tsar himself acting as the match-maker. She quickly masters the essentials of aristocratic *politesse* and as the beautiful Alexandra Volkova is perfectly able to adorn court balls and receive the admiration and homage of the most elegant cavaliers in Europe.

Special importance attaches to the poetic figure of Tsarevna Natalia, Peter's favourite sister, who appears in the third book. Here the reader is captivated not only by the charm of blossoming youth, the purity of Natalia's first affection for Gavrila Brovkin and the picture of dawning feminine moral awareness: in her own way Natalia tries to continue her brother's reforming activity by attempting to organise a national theatre.

Peter the First is a highly original work of socialist realism. In the novel where the main hero is the monarch whose reforms transformed Russia, Tolstoy devoted much effort to throwing light on the people as the main character of the book. Without concealing his approval of Peter's reforms, Tolstoy never for a minute forgets the price which Russia paid for this transformation. The novel provides numerous pictures of the poverty of the people and the entirely merciless exploitation to which the peasants were subject. It is no accident that the motif of rebels who took to brigandage plays a large part in the plot. One of them, Golikov, is the very incarnation of thought awakening among the people, of the creative principle and of protest against the fanaticism of religious dogmas about the worthlessness of man.

Peter the First is the summit of Tolstoy's achievement in narrative prose, not only as a historical novel but going far beyond the bounds of the genre, as a phenomenon of great significance to literary aesthetics in general. Creating an amazingly broad tangible picture of a particular period in all its concrete reality, the writer had a precise sense of the popular basis of the Russian language. He was opposed in principle to any sort of affected stylisation which turns into a pretentious juggling with language. Tolstoy revealed an amazing sense of language, every word in his text works to the full. The greatest outward simplicity and the maximum inner expressivity—this was the basic principle of his style.

Tolstoy reveals the inner world of his characters laconically, through their actions and behaviour, and shows extreme skill in depicting his characters in association with their physical surroundings. With Tolstoy interiors and landscapes are never purely descriptive and informative, they are "humanised" and included in the logic of the plot. This increases both the dynamic quality of the narrative and its inner psychological tension. (pp. 149-50)

During the years of the Great Patriotic War the active field of journalistic propaganda became Tolstoy's main literary activity. ***Motherland*** was the terse and meaningful title of one of his articles. Many other articles too had a wide public response: ***Moscow Is Threatened by the Enemy, The Power of Creative Work Is Inexhaustible, You Won't Get the Better of Us***. . . .

A particular feature of Tolstoy's wartime journalism was his positive use of characters and images from the heroic past of our country, of the events of its centuries-old history. During these tragic years of trial for the Soviet land there awoke within people an active wish to lean not only on the remarkable achievements of socialism but also to mobilise the national historical experience and the spirit of many generations of their forefathers. Tolstoy's work on his novel ***Peter the First*** had prepared him very well indeed to relate the past to the present in his articles.

The cycle of ***Ivan Sudarev's Stories*** is integrally linked with the journalistic work, in particular the story ***The Russian Character***, with its frankly programmatic title. In it Tolstoy reflected both the incredible determination of which Russian soldiers are capable when mortal danger hangs over their country, and the spiritual purity and steadfastness of Russian women, their capacity for noble sacrifice.

The Russian charcter . . .

Essentially all of Tolstoy's writing, including the works which remained unfinished because death stayed his pen, can be viewed as stubborn persevering research into this character. In the works written during the First World War Tolstoy attempted to surround with a poetic aura the type of person who carries out his duty honourably and satirically unmasked artistic bohemians. During the revolutionary years he marshalled a veritable gallery of people who found themselves outside their country, "former Russians", the worst of whom entered into actual treason and betrayal of national interests. On the other hand, the best Russians found enough strength to tread the entire thorny path of the years of ordeal in order to join with the whole people, supported by the historical experience of the nation, in building a socialist society and educating the new man. (pp. 150-51)

Vadim Baranov, "Life and Literary Quest," in Soviet Literature, *No. 1, 1983, pp. 141-51.*

LUDMILLA SMIRNOVA (essay date 1983)

[In the following excerpt, Smirnova discusses Tolstoy's trilogy Ordeal.]

The study of Alexei Tolstoy's artistic legacy has a considerable history and perhaps an even greater future. Much of current Soviet prose draws on his tradition. One can go along with prose writer Yuri Bondarev who says that the contemporary literary language has inherited from the classics the "capacious thought-provoking paragraphs of Lev Tolstoy, the lucidity of Anton Chekhov, the plasticity of Alexei Tolstoy and the vivid popular idiom of Mikhail Sholokhov."

It may seem that in some instances, Yuri Bondarev is referring to purely stylistic features, but in essence even such a term as "plasticity" encompasses a complex notion which can be summed up as the quality of depicting space and form so that they appear three-dimensional. Some light on this is shed by Alexei Tolstoy's own pronouncements on the nature of the art born of the October Revolution of 1917.

He said repeatedly that the artist must study the "vastness of the Revolution" and should become "a student of its history, philosophy and politics", a "builder of mankind's spiritual life". Tolstoy saw literature as a "powerful instrument of the proletariat in its struggle for world culture" and he warned against supplanting these great goals by "the rudiments of political education and primitive propaganda".

Tolstoy formed these and similar ideas in the process of his creative work in which they were realised on a large scale. These qualities are perhaps more fully present in ***Ordeal*** than in any other of Alexei Tolstoy's works.

The reader of that trilogy cannot help being amazed by the compactness of the narrative. Tolstoy has managed to tell about an unprecedented historical upheaval in three relatively short novels ***(The Sisters, 1918*** and ***Bleak Morning)***. The long-current interpretation of ***Ordeal*** as a book about the intellectuals and the Revolution or even (invoking the author's own remark) about ''Motherland lost and regained'' does not do full justice to the novel. One must bear in mind the writer's other statement: ''*Ordeal* is the journey of the author's conscience through suffering, hopes, exultations, downfalls, despair and soarings—a vast epoch that starts on the eve of the First World War and ends with the first day of the Second World War.'' While the theme of the intellectual is significant conceptually and structurally, it does not exhaust the content of the trilogy.

Tolstoy's novel presents a vast world of human thoughts, feelings and quests. All historical events and situations are reflected through the prism of the inner state of the numerous characters (and that holds true even of episodic ones).

The key characters in the immense and shifting picture are Ivan Telegin, Vadim Roshchin, Dasha and Katya. They come in contact with masses of people as they search, and find, their true road by being exposed to and understanding the fruitfulness of some ideas and the falsehood of others. They come to understand the meaning of their own existence, attain a correct view of events and grasp the meaning of life in general. Telegin, Roshchin, Dasha and Katya seem to take in, ''sift'', sum up and evaluate the experience of many.

The personalities Tolstoy portrays are above the run of the mill and their bold, questing minds are concerned with intellectual,

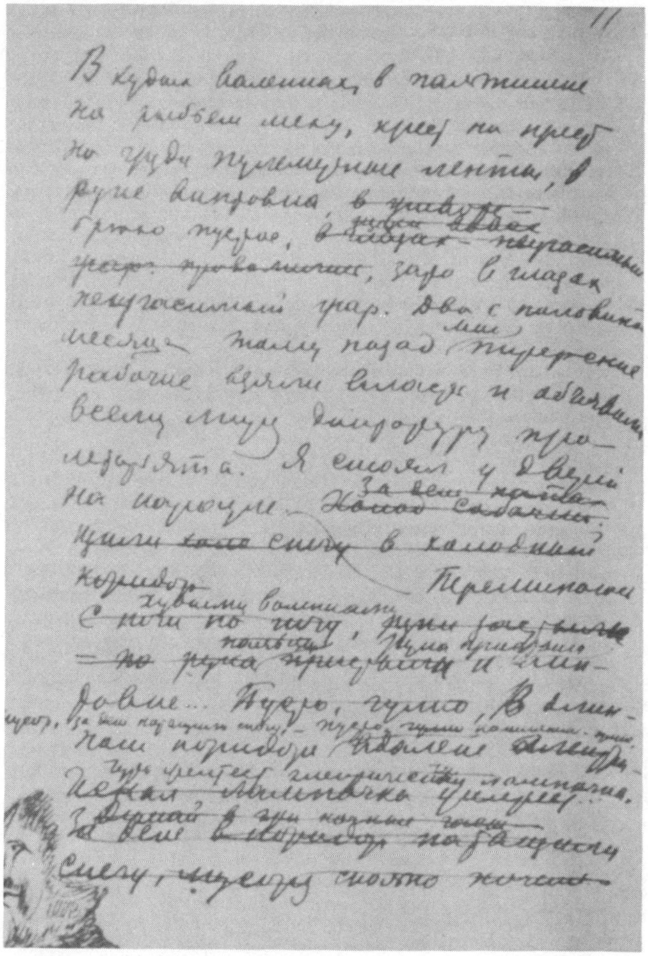

Manuscript page from Ordeal.

moral and aesthetic problems. Tolstoy's favourite characters are sensitive to all the spiritual trends of their time. But the initial uncertainty of their own allegiances leads them to experience moral torment, downfalls and recovery, revelations and disappointments. It is, however, the force of their shattering experience that in the end opens up genuine perspectives of life for them.

In ***The Sisters*** Tolstoy portrays the atmosphere of Petersburg on the eve of the First World War, with its ''coldly-bubbling, blasé night life,'' ''the deadly poison'' of universal destruction. The author's penetrating description is suddenly interrupted by an allusion to a supposedly real person: ''And quite recently the poet Alexei Alexeyevich Bessonov . . . told himself that the droshki, and the string of lamps on the bridge and the whole of sleeping Petersburg behind him, were but a dream, a chimera, a figment of his brain, sodden with drink, love-making and boredom.''

With the same precise economy, the author debunks the other self-styled prophets of the bourgeois intelligentsia—Smokovnikov, Bulavin, Kulichek, Govyadin, Zhirov and dozens of others. The Bulavin sisters regard them with an indifference tinged wtih pity or scorn. One becomes aware of the futility of their pretentious talk about ''moral deadlock'', the conventionality of morals, etc., all of which only shows that they have no future.

Ideas and views are judged by the extent of their impact on people, which in the final count means by their viability. That artistic approach is enriched as the narrative about the revolutionary events unfolds.

There is a stark documentary touch to the scene in which Lenin addresses workers at the time of the famine in 1918. There are quotations from his speech and descriptions of his sparse and expressive gestures. One is aware of the vast power latent in the large crowd listening to him. ''The breathless silence was broken by a hollow exclamation, the cry of some tormented soul stumbling on the icy ascent to which the man in the grey suit was urging them all.'' But when he finally said that the revolutionary cause was sure to triumph, ''his face was lit up by a frank, good-humoured smile. And everyone understood: this is one of us! They shouted, clapped, stamped.'' Dasha, who attended the meeting, had a vague grasp of what was going on but she became aware from the reaction of the workers, especially of the ''white-toothed neighbour'' who stood next to her, of the ''austerely moral, and therefore sublime'' power of Lenin who had before her eyes persuaded hungry, ''tragically grim'', people to renounce the ''unclean bread'' of the foreign invaders and look for their own way to save Russia. The young girl who was infinitely remote at the time from the life of the people felt stirring in her soul new and complex thoughts about her country and the Revolution.

Ordeal, a many-layered multi-aspect narrative about the socialist revolution in Russia, is governed by a single and consistently applied criterion. Who advances life in the course of a revolution and how?—this is the main line of Tolstoy's generalisations. He arrives at them by contrasting the spiritual victories of the people who have committed themselves to the building of a new society with the sundry spontaneous delusions and deliberate misrepresentation of the meaning of events. The artist portrays the period in a starkly realistic manner, with all the conflicts, and uncompromising struggles, but the very structure of the trilogy and the composition of the scenes suggest the imminent triumph of the revolutionary changes.

Including the whole strife-torn Russia in his mental gaze, Tolstoy boldly outlines its future and proclaims the ignominious death of those who had vainly tried to tie Russia to its past. The juxtapositions carry an important philosophical message. Before dying, a mortally wounded young Red Army fighter Sharygin tells his girl friend how he had "answered a high call," and "could not bear to stay below for an hour". And he tells her of his joy that he and his like had "thought of, defended and brought to life a new man". After this poetically charged scene, the picture that follows, of White general Denikin at a card-table, may at first appear as something of an anti-climax. Instead of a ferocious enemy who is responsible for the death of thousands of starry-eyed lads like Sharygin, we see a rather innocent-looking old man in a calm and somewhat sad mood. In reality this psychological angle in the narrative is an important find of Tolstoy. The spiritual emptiness of Denikin and his entourage (playing cards as if it were some sacred ritual, sending an orderly to bring in a fortune-teller, the utterly old-fashioned and ridiculous dreams of Denikin's god-daughter and his own apparent satisfaction with this puny world) reinforces one's certainty in the victory of the Red Army and of the high spiritual ideals.

Ataman Makhno, the leader of one of the counter-revolutionary bands during the Civil War, personifies in the novel the dangerous phenomenon of the anarchist deformation of revolutionary slogans, such as the call for freedom and the rejection of violence over the individual. Tolstoy sees the corrupting influence of the anarchists on the morally unstable individuals who condone and perpetrate crimes (Levka Zadov, Mamont Dalsky and Zhadov) and on some peasants who are wedded to the idea of private property (Alexei Krasilnikov and the Makhno men). As always with Tolstoy, the description is reinforced by insights into the mentality and morals of the characters.

Ordeal considers the philosophical problems of life and death, happiness, freedom and love from various aspects. In reality they are always related to the concept of Beauty. Katya, Dasha, Roshchin, Telegin, Sapozhkov and others suffer deeply from their disappointment in the infantile ideals of their youth. The austere times lead them to reappraise their notions of moral beauty.

During the First World War Dasha discharged her duties as a nurse honestly but without dedication. She treated that work as an unpleasant necessity. But when she gropingly set about organising amateur theatricals among the Red Armymen she experienced an outburst of creative energy. Her sister, Katya, who, after parting with Roshchin, having lost her home and been subjected to humiliation in Alexei Krasilnikov's home, was on the verge of suicide, discovers a new will to live in herself when she enthusiastically sets about tackling a new job. Anisya Nazarova makes up her mind to become a revolutionary actress in order to get across to audiences the experience of her own complex life. All of the main characters find the joy of work and love in their own way. Dasha and Telegin, Katya and Roshchin, Anisya and Latugin traverse a long and arduous road before they realise their need for each other—a need testifying to hitherto unknown inner requirements.

Only some turning points in the attitudes of the characters are indicated, yet the three novels are full of such profound metamorphoses. By the end of the narrative the characters seem to have accumulated spiritual energy which they translate into something new, realising their inner potential. Every character follows his own logic of behaviour among large groups of people and each ends up being a fuller human being than before. The question suggests itself, what was the "mechanism" that enabled Alexei Tolstoy to bring into one sweeping panorama all the brief kaleidoscopic scenes and snatches of trains of thought?

Tolstoy detects the visible signs of individual emotions that change at a dizzying rate. These emotions and reactions of the characters (some of whom may appear but fleetingly) add up to a coherent picture of the state of the world at a chosen span of time. The visible detail becomes a vehicle for expressing the essence.

In ***Ordeal*** the semantic weight carried by every unit of the narrative is augmented by the coherence of its different lines in the portrayal of the single revolutionary process. A precise and brief summary of the historical background, the complex lives of the characters, their attitude towards social change and their personal relations, their thoughts and feelings—all these are closely interwoven, complementing and extending one another. That accounts for the writer's capacity to tell a lot in few words.

After his break with Dasha, Telegin joins the Red Army and goes through a period of heart-searching. Tolstoy writes of him: "Sometimes a wave of indignation would rise up in him: all right, my dear, try and find another man to dance round you as I did! The world is going to pieces, and all she thinks about is her own feelings." All that was true, to be sure, but it implied that Ivan Ilyich (Telegin) was an extraordinary good man and it was a crime not to love him. Ivan Ilyich stumbled on this every time. "After all, what is there so special about me? . . . An ordinary, decent citizen, like a million others. . . . He had drawn a lucky ticket in the lottery of life; a charming girl, endowed with infinitely more fire and brains than himself, head and shoulders above him, had unaccountably fallen in love with him, and as unaccountably fallen out of love." All these feelings are blended in his tormented soul which gives us a glimpse of a very personal perception of the changing world. The author has hit on and makes wide use of the fast tempo of synthesizing thought that conveys an overall impression of a person's state.

The same ends are served by Alexei Tolstoy's theory of the gesture. Characterisation is greatly enhanced by constant description of inner impulses or involuntary movements. Alexei Tolstoy makes excellent use of the vast opportunities for generalisations.

The "hidden camera" portrayal of man caught up in the mighty stream of reality reveals genuine links between historical and psychological laws of social development. Tolstoy was truly a historian, philosopher, and psychologist, and invariably a poet. He has a truly poetic sense of the beauty of the earth: the colours, sounds of nature, the mysterious play of the sun on the water's surface. But, scrupulously adhering to his narrative principle, he avoided florid language.

Tolstoy's artistic command of language was inimitable. The principle of many-sided depiction of the epoch, sensitive perception of the colours and movement of life, gleaning significance from simple and accidental phenomena, penetration into their ethical sources, the ability to discover in seemingly ordinary material interrelations between global philosophical problems such as beauty and morality, happiness and the meaning of life—these are just some of the reasons why Alexei Tolstoy's inspired experience remains relevant today. (pp. 151-56)

Ludmilla Smirnova, "The Sources of Stylistic Expressiveness: Alexei Tolstoy's Trilogy 'Ordeal'," in Soviet Literature, *No. 1, 1983, pp. 151-56.*

ALEXANDER VISLOV (essay date 1983)

[*In the following excerpt, Vislov surveys Tolstoy's dramas.*]

A distinctive feature of Alexei Tolstoy the playwright—his gentle, humane, even loving, attitude towards his characters—was manifested in the comedy ***Cuckoo's Tears.*** His greatest achievement in this play was the character of the actress, Maria Ogneva, which was to become the first in a whole gallery of characters of Russian women—sincere, selfless, pure of heart, and passionate—in Tolstoy's dramas. A provincial actress, impoverished landowners, a merchant—a kind of Chekhovian Lopakhin (from *The Cherry Orchard*)—these are the characters involved in the entertaining and moving plot of the comedy.

In 1914, Tolstoy became a war correspondent and visited various fronts of the First World War. He described his impressions of those days in his play, ***The Day of the Battle.*** The vagueness of his ideological stand had left its imprint on the artistic quality of the play, which did not satisfy its author.

Having left the theatre of operations, Tolstoy went to the Crimea, where he completed the comedy ***The Evil Spirit,*** and then wrote, one after the other, two more comedies—***The Rocket*** and ***Honeybunch.*** In neither of these comedies did he touch on the tragic events of world history. It seems almost inconceivable that these plays were written by a man who, only a short time before, had been in the trenches, risking his life, and had written down in his notebook the front-line impressions which had shaken him. It was then that Tolstoy wrote some superb comedies, among which was the melodrama ***Honeybunch***—one of his most artistically perfect works. The plays written in 1916 convinced both the public and the critics that Tolstoy had an outstanding dramatic talent, and was a master at modelling comic characters, inventing vaudeville-style plots, and making the action of a play develop dynamically on the stage. All this was brilliantly intertwined into one dramatic tangle, all splendidly stagey.

There are no personages in ***The Evil Spirit*** that would look sluggish on the stage; each personage—down to the most unimportant one—has his own character, his own "dramatic spark", and his own inimitable way of speaking. Interception of letters, recognition, fainting-fits, eavesdropping, unexpected exposures, phoney newspaper reports and, finally, the love duet of the hero and the heroine—all this never fails to captivate even readers of the play. (pp. 157-58)

The hero of the comedy [***Honeybunch***] is Prince Belsky, a spineless, feather-brained, flighty man who dissipated his fortune gambling at cards (the critics often compared him with the Baron in Maxim Gorky's *The Lower Depths*). The women characters are full of passion and devotion, as they always are in Tolstoy's plays. The entire play is filled with sympathy for the lovers' sufferings and with hope that under the impact of love the best human qualities will revive.

After the October Revolution, Tolstoy wrote another love comedy, ***Love Is a Golden Book.*** This time he turned to the 18th century, the reign of Catherine II. According to Tolstoy, this play had helped him "to immerse in the mist of forgetfulness", "to relax" and "to get warm" . . .

The concept that love is man's only salvation and refuge was even more pronounced in this new comedy. The play was extremely well constructed, its plot developed dynamically, and the characters' speech never failed to charm the spectators by its perfection and its genuine old Russian colouring. (pp. 158-59)

Under the impact of the February Revolution, Tolstoy wrote the comedy, ***Bitter Flower,*** a caricature of the "saintly old man" of the royal household, Grigori Rasputin, and of the Rasputin era. The comedy exposed the falseness and hypocrisy of the "miracle-worker" Akila (i.e. Rasputin); nevertheless, Tolstoy had failed to understand correctly the course of the historical events. ***Bitter Flower*** did not bring success to its author, although he revised it more than once, each time giving it a new title: ***Akila, Casting Out the Lecherous Devil,*** and finally, ***The Obscurantists.***

Prominent among Tolstoy's dramas are revisions of plays by other authors, which was a common practice in those days. In 1918, he revised ***Danton's Death*** by Georg Büchner. Reappraising the image of the people and the characterisation of the leaders of the revolution in a new version, written in 1923, Tolstoy showed not the blood-thirstiness of the mob, but the starving people's hatred for the aristocracy—that symbol of injustice and tyranny—and Robespierre's keen wit and the humaneness of his dream of equality. Danton's tragedy had become that of a courageous man, a leader who had parted from the people and was, therefore, doomed to die. The 1923 version of ***Danton's Death*** was to become an important landmark in the evolution of Tolstoy's world outlook.

Later, Tolstoy repeatedly turned to the revision of plays by foreign writers (for example, Karel Čapek, Eugene O'Neill, Walter Hasenclever) with the aim of adapting them to the requirements and interests of the Soviet theatre and Soviet audiences.

In the mid-1920's, Tolstoy, in collaboration with the historian, Pavel Shchegolev, started work on archives pertaining to the period of the fall of the Romanov dynasty. As a result, there appeared the play, ***The Plot of the Empress,*** which is staged in Soviet theatres even today. This play about the disintegration of the tsarist empire contrasted sharply with the numerous superficial court chronicles adapted for, and produced on, the stage in large numbers in the 1920's. Genuine reminiscences, correspondence between Tsar Nicholas and the Empress Alexandra, verbatim reports of interrogations, reports of Secret Police Department agents—these documents were used in the play and lent veracity to the events and characters involved. (p. 159)

This new form of literary activity—the writing of dramas based on documents—attracted Tolstoy, especially after the success of ***The Plot of the Empress.*** He wrote two more plays in collaboration with Shchegolev—a drama, ***Azef*** (about the notorious adventurer and agent provocateur), and a dramatic poem, ***Pauline Gueble (The Decembrists);*** however, these plays were not a particular success on the stage.

For a time Tolstoy's enthusiasm for historical archives was dampened, and in the latter half of the 1920's he wrote, one after another, comedies about contemporary life—***A Fantastic Tale, The Factory of Youth*** and ***One Hundred Thousand***—in which he attempted to portray characters that were new to him—young builders of a socialist society, who opposed the petty bourgeois mentality of those around them. Two tendencies—one accusatory and satirical, and the other lyrical and comic—merge to create the peculiar atmosphere of these plays.

In the 1930's, Tolstoy turned to the drama again, and wrote ***The Way to Victory***, a play in which he made an attempt to create images of the leaders of the Russian revolution, ***The Mahatma***, a comedy satirising the bourgeois West, ***This Shall Be***, a play about the Civil War, ***Patent 119***, a play about the modern industrial workers.

In 1935, after his trip to Czechoslovakia, Tolstoy was carried away by a new idea: he decided to write a Russian variant of Smetana's opera, ***The Bartered Bride***, using the translation of the libretto made by a Czech journalist František Kubka. (pp. 159-60)

The Bartered Bride was not Tolstoy's only attempt at musical drama. He tried his hand at many theatrical genres. (p. 160)

Two plays about events from Russian history occupy a special place in Tolstoy's writing. They are the dilogy, ***Ivan the Terrible***, and ***Peter the First***. Both these plays were written by Tolstoy as a series of crucial, key episodes highlighting a turning-point in Russian history and in the formation of the heroes' personality. The battle scenes were depicted superbly, with a profound understanding of the possibilities of the theatre; the language—as in all of Tolstoy's historical works—was brilliant and its musical quality and beauty charmed the spectators; the heroes and the supporting cast were portrayed vividly. Everything had been done to perfection: the character of Peter I, who had shaken the old boyar-ruled Rus to its foundations and who was not to be deterred in his determination to put into effect his momentous plans, and also the characters of his comrades-in-arms and his opponents. It is noteworthy that the novel, ***Peter the First***, was written after Tolstoy had completed the first version of the play. (pp. 160-61)

The dilogy about Ivan the Terrible was highly, even rapturously, praised by the director of the Moscow Art Theatre, Vladimir Nemirovich-Danchenko. "Tolstoy has a great talent," Nemirovich-Danchenko wrote after he had read the first part of the dilogy, ***The Eagle and His Mate***. "I am not afraid to say that I do not know anyone in our literature in whose descriptions of historical scenes the characters and language can equal those of Tolstoy's." . . .

Tolstoy began writing his play about Tsar Ivan IV (the Terrible) during his country's most trying period—the autumn of 1941. The aim he had set himself, his anxiety for the fate of his motherland, and also the atmosphere of growing patriotism had determined both the merits and the shortcomings of the play. The war-time press gave this appraisal of Tolstoy's work, "The power of Tolstoy's talent has brought nearer to us one of the most remarkable periods of Russian history. The dramatic narrative about Ivan the Terrible is read by Soviet men and women with keen interest because the hero of the narrative is the Russian people."

In his dramas, Tolstoy brought together two epochs in 20th-century art, as it were: the classical Russian and the Soviet one. The young Soviet theatre has accepted and absorbed his theatrical culture, his profoundly sympathetic and intense interest in man, and his humane view of the world. (p. 161)

Alexander Vislov, ". . . Also a Playwright," in Soviet Literature, *No. 1, 1983, pp. 157-61.*

VLADIMIR GAKOV (essay date 1983)

[In the following excerpt Gakov discusses Tolstoy's best-known science fiction works, Aelita *and* The Garin Death Ray.]

Tolstoy's ***Aelita*** has enjoyed an enviable fate. It has not been left to gather dust on library shelves, nor has it acquired the patina of an academic book. ***Aelita*** is a classic of a different sort. Unlike the sinusoidal curve of the latest best-selling bit of entertainment, the demand for ***Aelita*** is steady, undiminished over a period of 60 years. It is read with emotion, it disturbs, and it awakens in the reader "irrational" feelings which have not been changed by this rational age—love, sadness, a yearning for the unknown, readiness for self-sacrifice. (p. 162)

If one briefly recounts the plot of ***Aelita,*** a natural incomprehension is bound to follow: what is so special about it, what is novel, if one compares it to scores of other similar works of that period?

Los, an inventor of genius, is seeking an assistant for a planned flight to Mars. He runs into Gusev, a Red Armyman who has just returned from the front, and the pair of them blast off successfully. On Mars the inventor falls passionately in love with a princess (of course, she is lovely—who has ever read about a princess on another planet who is not?). This love is beautiful and doomed, as in silent films—very much in tune with the times and utterly unreal in its "beautiful nature". The Red Armyman, made of simpler stuff, also finds something to occupy himself with on Mars: he meddles in the local politics. Also unsuccessfully. The heroes barely manage to escape with their lives and they return to Earth safe and sound. (pp. 162-63)

Only one thing seems to be missing even in this concise and ironic account, but without it the impression given of ***Aelita*** is not simply incomplete; it is false. It is the concluding pages of the novel. Through hundreds of millions of kilometres of cold, darkness and the emptiness of space, the words travel from Mars to Earth: "Son of the Sky, where are you?" There is so much despair in this cry, such a depth of universal love, of longing for understanding and warmth! Over the years schoolgirls have read and re-read scores of "space love stories" and forgotten them all. But not ***Aelita***!

It is very difficult to formulate a brief and exhaustive account (in the spirit of the foregoing one) of what any major work of fiction is all about. After all, one could say about *Othello* that it is a play in which a Black kills his white wife because of a misplaced handkerchief!

Indeed, what is the book about? About everything—about life, and life does not lend itself to a cursory account. Certainly, Alexei Tolstoy did not invent a fresh plot (neither did Shakespeare, and even Aeschylus, presumably, did not invent anything new). What was new was the quality, the scale, the level of understanding of old truth—that is what makes ***Aelita*** immortal.

The book, . . . along with [Vivian Itin's novel *Country of the Gonguri*], heralded the birth of Soviet science fiction. It was not surprising that Itin, a professional revolutionary first and foremost and only secondarily a writer, dreamed of a distant and radiant future for which he and his comrades had fought in real life. But that a well-known novelist should turn to a "Martian" theme was unusual and intriguing.

Tolstoy caught the heady spirit of the times and his book is filled with extremes: the all-consuming mad love of Los for Aelita is in the same key as the revolutionary zeal of the truth-seeker and defender of the oppressed, Gusev. The "extremes" were dictated by the times and were rightfully appreciated by contemporary readers. That mad, unreal love, a love transcending space and time, did not just fascinate impressionable young ladies, it wholly engrossed half-starving workers, soldiers, students, the builders of a new world. As for Gusev, he was simply one of themselves.

The tale did not appear in a vacuum, in an empty literary and historical space. ***Aelita*** reflected all the newly popular preoccupations of the young science fiction genre of the 1920's—and also its misconceptions.

The "Martian" series of the prolific American writer, Edgar Rice Burroughs, undoubtedly had an influence on Alexei Tolstoy. However, only the most avid fans of Burroughs would now read the works of that truly inventive writer. He deals in nothing but thrilling adventures. But Tolstoy's Mars, despite all the disconcerting information provided by the photographs taken from the American Viking space station, has not been totally destroyed in our imagination. It remains intact, a world of science fiction living according to its own internal laws. Moreover, ***Aelita*** has love, history and revolution.

The influence of the legend of Atlantis, widespread at the time, is also felt. It is not likely that anyone today believes that descendants of the people of Atlantis settled on Mars in prehistoric times, but in the '20s the idea was taken quite seriously.

It is known that Alexei Tolstoy was well-versed in the myths of Atlantis and was familiar with theosophical writings which were then in vogue. In the tale **"Count Cagliostro"** the future author of ***Aelita*** maliciously mocked any form of "satanism", in a style reminiscent of Gogol. At the same time, one feels that even such absolutely "unscientific" fiction is dear to Tolstoy's heart. And here was an opportunity to utilise the beautiful legend about the Martian descendants of the inhabitants of Atlantis! And the writer boldly borrowed it for the plot of his future book, as though subconsciously realising that he would not infringe the laws of science fiction writing, that the reader would not believe in this world in any case, whatever his attitude to the legend.

And finally, there is the historical philosophy, the philosophy of "aesthetisising" the decline of the civilisation, which is propagated by the dictator and technocrat Tuskub. One does not have to seek far for the source of this if one remembers that at the time Oswald Spengler's work, *The Decline of the West* was immensely popular in bourgeois intellectual circles. Tolstoy was still living abroad then and had not yet fully accepted the revolution and the new reality. He was full of doubts and the agonies of making a choice. His unsettled state and the confusion in his mind, inevitable in such circumstances, could not but affect his writing. (pp. 164-65)

Time has corrected the ideological confusion of ***Aelita,*** has smoothed it out, eradicated the superfluous, but the lyrical foundation remains untouched by the years. (p. 165)

Aelita was not Tolstoy's sole incursion into science fiction.

His second major work of this type was ***The Garin Death Ray,*** written in 1925-26, and it is quite unlike ***Aelita.***

It is the work of a *Soviet* writer. In place of the spectral, exotic Martian world, we have the slightly crude, tangible reality of a dynamically written political detective story (or "Red Pinkerton", as critics subsequently dubbed this genre in the Soviet literature of the twenties and thirties). The story of Garin, the power-hungry maniacal inventor with an almost Napoleonic complex, is told against the background of a realistically described Europe of the day.

The novel took shape over several years. The quickly changing world situation demanded fresh editings and Tolstoy kept rewriting—he wanted to make it as topical as possible. The first version (it was more like an outline) was ***Union of Five*** . . . , which contains the prototype of the future Rolling. This is the industrial magnate Ignatius Rufe, who, to demonstrate his power to the world, intends to split the Moon with the help of superpowerful explosive rockets . . . As yet there was no Garin, genius, poseur, adventurer, a sort of "lumpen" scientist. In this figure, as in any "lumpen", the characteristics of a future fascist can be discerned. But as soon as a new political movement—the Italian fascists, and later Germany's Nazis—loomed over the European horizon, Tolstoy had an adequate historical parallel for the main personage of the as yet unwritten novel.

Tolstoy was later very proud that in the mid-1920's he had been able to discern what few then saw. The future "superman", a pretender to world supremacy; take away the neat wedge-shaped beard then in fashion, replace it with a black brush moustache and hair combed sideways across the forehead and you have a portrait of the future real "Garin". As for the talent, Tolstoy had a vivid example of that in the person of Gabriele D'Annunzio, the darling of the salons, who placed his considerable literary talents at the disposal of fascism.

The scientist Garin is, of course, not a Hitler. But doubly symbolic is the figure of Rolling, the American chemical tycoon, who first planned to utilise Garin's invention for his own pragmatic purposes (Rolling's "pragmatism" was far-reaching—that same power over the whole world) but found himself in fact dependent on the candidate for world dictator, who outsmarted him. In the years that Tolstoy was writing the novel, he may or may not have known (or did he guess intuitively?) of the sinister role played by American capital in tandem with the "local" Thyssens and Krupps, midwives at the birth of Hitlerism. But what an inspired guess and how little time remained until his intuition was woefully proven right.

Just as in the case of ***Aelita,*** Alexei Tolstoy introduced nothing new in terms of the form of the genre (such outstanding Soviet writers of the time as Ilya Ehrenburg, Marietta Shaginyan, Victor Shklovsky and Valentin Katayev also wrote "Red Pinkertons"). But as in ***Aelita,*** a new quality, a new level, a new dimension imparted immortality to the book.

Superficially, the adventurer Garin, the Soviet agent Shelga, the billionaire Rolling, and the *femme fatale,* adventuress Zoe Montrose are stock "Red Pinkerton" characters. Most likely, Rolling and Zoe would have remained unreal if not for the brilliant pair, Garin and Shelga. They represent a duo and duel. One is reminded not only of Tolstoy's aptitude for realistic depiction; the duo-duel embodies that measure of social generalisation and social prevision which is the mark of genuine, important science fiction. On the one hand, behind the posturing poseur, Garin, the outlines of the monstrous image of the hysterical "maniacal poseur" of future history can be glimpsed. On the other hand, Shelga is the embodiment of the man of the new world, new society, who alone is capable—two decades were not to pass—of crushing the fascist "Garin" in actual history. (pp. 166-67)

Alexei Tolstoy wrote only two science fiction books, but he unerringly picked out the main trends.

Even such a "detail" as the laser beam. If one of the countless young readers of ***The Garin Death Ray*** had stopped to consider, back in the twenties, the purely scientific, technical idea developed by Tolstoy in detail (he even provided diagrams in the novel), it is possible that we would not have had to wait for the invention of the laser for another 30-odd years.

Without describing it, the imaginative H. G. Wells wrote about a Martian lethal ray, thereby presenting a gift to science fiction which would be mercilessly exploited for decades. Alexei Tolstoy approached the question more seriously, in a thoroughgoing way. No matter that he was mistaken in technical details; he was a writer, after all, not a scientist. What is important is that the idea itself of concentrating light rays into a narrow beam of incredible penetrating power was a pioneering one. (pp. 167-68)

But he left—will leave!—yet another memory of himself. Returning to ***Aelita,*** Tolstoy's best science fiction work, let us indulge a little in fantasy. Not only has the name become a common noun, a symbol of love and romance (youth cafés have been named "Aelita", poems and songs about Aelita have been composed, and now the first Soviet science fiction prize has been named in her honour), but it seems to me that in time this name will appear where it belongs . . .

Man is now on the threshold. The path from the cradle Earth to the vast cosmic expanses will be long and difficult. And everywhere on their path, on big space stations and small, remote way-stations, Earthlings will leave their own, earthly names—in memory of home, of people who once lived and deserve to be remembered. (p. 168)

One would like to believe that along with Bradbury-city and Burroughstown, the city of Tolstoy will appear on Mars. Naturally, on the banks of the Aelita Canal . . . And nobody will ask if it is possible to immortalise the memory of a non-existent person.

She existed, she lived at one time, that lovely Martian girl. But why "lived"? In fact, she is alive right now! As young and beautiful as ever. She does not age. (pp. 168-69)

Vladimir Gakov, "Laser Ray in 1926: Alexei Tolstoy's Science Fiction," in Soviet Literature, *No. 1, 1983, pp. 161-69.*

JURIJ STRIEDTER (essay date 1983)

[*In the following excerpt from an essay examining the utopian novel in post-Revolutionary Russia, Striedter discusses* Aelita *as an example of the "polyphonic" utopian novel.*]

[In ***Aelita*** two] Soviet astronauts journey to Mars and are introduced to a Martian utopia, whereupon we follow their various adventures of love, revolt, combat, and escape. The Martian state and its history (which includes "the Fall of Atlantis") are conceived as an analogy to the concept of the "declining West." Masses of workers are enslaved in the City which, at the same time, is regarded as "the breeding ground for the anarchic individual." This exploitation, which is the condition for the happiness of the few who are "blessed," is justified by a philosophy which combines—besides many motifs from myth, religion, and history—a criticism of transcendental Idealism with ideas from Nietzsche, Schopenhauer, and Spengler. (Spengler's *Decline of the West* was published in 1918-23; Aleksei Tolstoy lived, at this time, as an emigrant in Germany; he wrote and published ***Aelita*** in Berlin in 1923, returning to the Soviet Union in the same year.)

What interests us in regard to the polyphony of utopian novels is Tolstoy's method of presenting each of the two worlds (Mars and the Soviet Union) through different, interrelated voices. He sheds a threefold light on Martian society by representing it through Tuskub, the ruler and defender of the system, through Gor, the proletarian leader of the unsuccessful revolt, and through Aelita, Tuskub's daughter, whom the father has secluded away in a special, idyllic Arcadia. Aelita functions as a mediator between the two worlds. On the one hand she introduces the men from Earth to the Martian language, to the Martian way of, and view on, life, and to Martian history (narrated by her in special chapters). On the other hand, she falls in love (mutual and Platonic love) with the human visitor from Earth. But she, as well as Gor and Tuskub, notwithstanding their differences, are genuine Martians, conscious of being doomed to decline and death.

Tolstoy also complicates the function of the visitor in utopia in its relationship to the Soviet Russian point of view. The spacecraft brings not one, but two Soviet citizens to Mars, both heroes and both positive representatives of their country (that is, not a master-servant or a hero-confidant combination). But Gusev, the former Red Army soldier, is a spontaneous, pragmatic, optimistic fighter, while Los, the engineer and inventor of the spacecraft, is a mourning widower, devoted to a romantic love and haunted by loneliness and melancholy. Due to these differences in character, each protagonist becomes the center of a different system of motifs, views, moods, stylistic devices, and values—a specific "voice" in a "dialogue" with his co-traveler. This distinction allows the author to associate one Soviet protagonist with the doomed Martian woman and the other with the Martian rebel. This helps the author demonstrate that both love and revolt are doomed to failure in a Martian society. It is true, however, that the romantic and romanesque love overcomes separation and death in the form of a trans-cosmic voice. After the two astronauts escape and return to the Soviet Union, and after Aelita is left behind and sentenced for her betrayal, her voice reaches the lonely lover in the last chapter, entitled "The *Voice* of Love" (my italics). But love, too, remains an open search and a question. The last words of this chapter, and of the novel, are: "Where are you, where are you, love . . ."

The political moral of this utopian novel is clearly indicated immediately before this romantic ending. The pursuit of happiness and revolutionary dynamics should not be sought in other worlds or planets—at least not for the moment. Revolutionary fighters and inventors must return to "the homeland of the revolution and of socialism," where the shift from revolutionary destruction to revolutionary construction has just begun. The novel began in Petrograd, in August 1921, with a picture of a city devastated by revolution, civil war, and hunger. It ends in the same place, in June of 1925, with an image of construction and collective happiness achieved through collective work. The novelist also adds a remark that this became the genuine topic for literature:

> Time has now changed: the poets are carried away neither by blizzards nor by stars, nor by countries beyond the clouds, but by the sound of hammers throughout the country, the sizzling of saws, the rustle of sickles, the whistling of scythes—enjoyment, earthly songs. In the country in this year started the construction of

> unprecedented (*nebyvalye*) so-called ''blue cities.'' . . .

The attentive reader will notice that the date ''3 June 1925'' marks an anticipation of two years (1923 was the date of publication and of the author's return to the Soviet Union). This touches on the general problem of utopia as anticipation. For centuries, utopias were either abstract ideals placed ''nowhere'' or anticipations of a better future (even in cases where this future was conceived of as a reinstitution of a happier past). Tolstoy's utopia on Mars, however, is a utopia oriented toward a negative past. It regards its own history and political organization as the results of an unavoidable ''decline and fall.'' Since, however, this utopia is conceived of as an analogy to the ''declining West,'' and since this West is, in fact, the present (and future) opposition to the revolutionary Soviet Union, the unmasking and negation of the Martian utopia serves as an affirmation of the revolutionary Soviet Union's hopes for a successful, happy future. This can be achieved *per negationem*, without the novelist being forced to present his own, contemporaneous system in its ''extensive totality.'' . . . Nor is the novelist required to anticipate the final state of his own social and political system in the form of an elaborated utopian vision. In accordance with Lenin's reply to Bukharin's question, the long-range or final anticipation can be replaced by a short-range anticipation of a few years. This will indicate the most urgent current task (now ''reconstruction''). The early Soviet Russian utopian novel ***Aelita*** (alluding symbolically to the emblems of the new state, the hammer and the sickle) ends with an implied criticism of utopian dreams ''beyond the clouds,'' and with an anticipation of the novel of production which was soon to come. (pp. 183-85)

Jurij Striedter, ''Three Postrevolutionary Russian Utopian Novels,'' in The Russian Novel from Pushkin to Pasternak, *edited by John Garrard, Yale University Press, 1983, pp. 177-201.**

ADDITIONAL BIBLIOGRAPHY

Brown, Edward J. ''After Stalin: The First Two Thaws.'' In his *Russian Literature since the Revolution*, rev. ed., pp. 238-76. New York: Collier Books, 1969.*

Brief discussion of Tolstoy's works, asserting that the author ''had a brilliant narrative flair combined with thematic versatility and a command of pellucid prose, but . . . no serious intellectual concerns.''

Soviet Literature: For the Centenary of Alexei Tolstoy's Birth, No. 1 (1983), 192 p.

Criticism and personal reminiscences by Soviet authors and critics, selections from Tolstoy's fiction, and commentary on screen adaptations of his works.

Carl (Clinton) Van Doren

1885-1950

American critic, biographer, historian, editor, essayist, short story writer, novelist, and autobiographer.

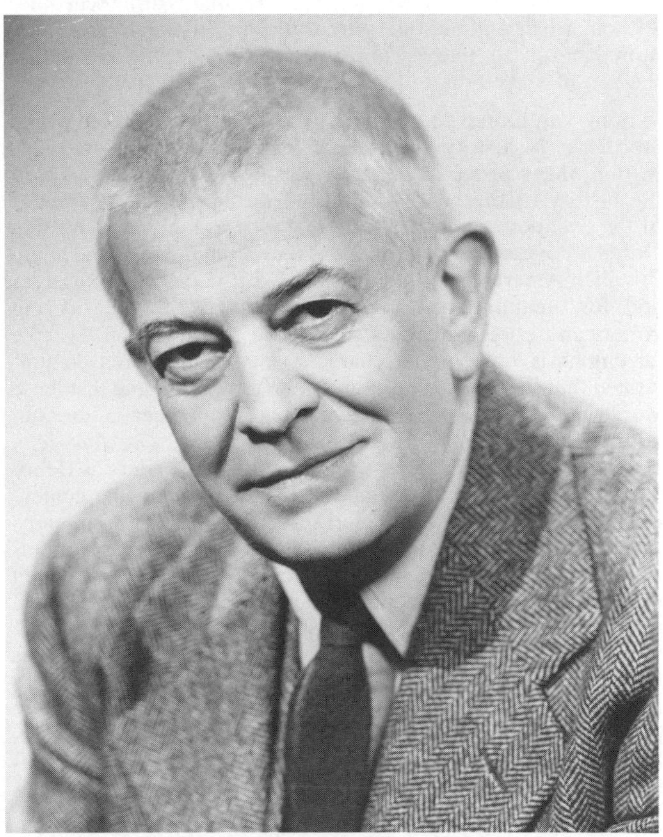

Van Doren was one of America's most influential critics and scholars during the first half of the twentieth century. His critical studies of American novelists played an essential role in initiating an appreciation and respect for American fiction as a distinct and valuable body of works independent of the literary traditions of England. In his innovative critical history *The American Novel,* Van Doren demonstrated that this genre was worthy of in-depth study, thereby contributing to a movement to establish college curricula devoted exclusively to American letters. As a literary critic, historian, and biographer, Van Doren was distinguished by his concern with the personalities behind artistic creations and historical events. This interest in human motives as well as in the importance of the past to the present characterized such histories as *The Great Rehearsal* and *Secret History of the American Revolution* and the biography *Benjamin Franklin,* which was awarded the Pulitzer prize for biography in 1938.

Van Doren was born in the village of Hope, Illinois, to a country physician and his wife. His early life was strongly influenced by the Christian traditions of this close-knit community. In Hope, Van Doren accepted religion as an integral part of life, but after his family moved to Urbana when he was fifteen, he became what he later termed an "unbeliever" and remained a religious skeptic throughout his life. After completing high school in Urbana, Van Doren enrolled at the University of Illinois, where he devoted himself exclusively to academic pursuits. During his last two years at the university he edited the university's literary monthly and was elected class poet. He later wrote in his autobiography *Three Worlds* that scholarship had come effortlessly to him because he had a passion for reading almost anything, was too curious to be intolerant in his tastes, and could retain minute details of what he had read. Inspired by his love of great poets and poetry, he strove to perfect his own poetic works, but anxiety and frustration over what he regarded as his meager talents drove him to self-doubt, and, while still at the university, he ceased writing poetry altogether.

After graduation from the University of Illinois, Van Doren entered graduate school at Columbia University, where he wrote his first book, a biography of Thomas Love Peacock. His association with Columbia continued after he received his doctorate, and he taught as a professor in the English department until 1930. During the two decades that Van Doren taught at Columbia he maintained a taxing schedule outside of the university as well. Along with Zona Gale, Joseph Wood Krutch, and Glenn French, Van Doren cofounded the Literary Guild book club in 1926 and served as its editor-in-chief until 1934. Through his work with the guild, Van Doren realized his ambition to place a large selection of literary works before American readers. Much of this activity occurred during the post-World War I American literary boom when book clubs proliferated and magazines paid writers—the most famous of whom became celebrities well known even among the nonreading public—unprecedentedly high sums for their productions. In addition, Van Doren served as the literary editor of the *Nation* and the *Century Magazine,* where his column "The Roving Critic" appeared until 1925. By then he had established a solid reputation as a literary critic and historian whose catholic tastes, careful scholarship, and readability helped to advance the dignity of American literature. However, in the final essay of his 1924 collection *Many Minds,* Van Doren stated that thenceforth he would pursue a long-delayed career in "other provinces"—as a creative writer.

Van Doren's first venture into creative prose was entitled *Other Provinces.* A collection of short stories and sketches which convey a strong sense of character, *Other Provinces* consists primarily of intimate observations about the ordinary but interesting movement of daily life. The work was not well received, but despite his deep disappointment, Van Doren published the novel *The Ninth Wave* the following year. Although some critics regarded it as a promising first novel, Van Doren was disappointed by the meager sales of his novel and abandoned plans for future projects in fiction. In 1928, with the death of his close friend, the poet Elinor Wylie, Van Doren sank into a depression which, in his autobiography *Three Worlds,* he attributed to an accumulation of vague feelings and thoughts which he could not or would not clearly identify. His productivity became sporadic, although during a four-month period in 1929 he did produce a biography of Jonathan Swift that he hoped would convey a sympathetic perception lacking in existing biographies. At the end of 1932 Van Doren went on a seven week lecture tour that took him to schools and literary clubs across the United States. He enjoyed the hospitality of celebrities and literary figures, but was especially fond of the stimulating regimen of travel. During the tour his mental health improved, and he soon reestablished a regular writing schedule. Although he continued to write criticism, his later career was dominated by an interest in history and biography. He died at the age of sixty-four following a heart attack.

Among Van Doren's best-known and most highly praised works are the early history *The American Novel* and the essay collection *Many Minds. The American Novel* is concerned with the history of the genre from 1744 through the first decades of the twentieth century. It was regarded as innovative by Van Doren's contemporaries for focusing on the novel as the genre in which American writers had most distinguished themselves and for breaking the long-standing practice of considering American fiction a mere extension of English fiction. Despite an emphasis on regional characteristics, Van Doren demonstrated that there was a unity in American fiction and that these works could not have been created in any other culture. In addition to a general discussion of its topic, *The American Novel* also contains essays on such individual writers as Henry James and Nathaniel Hawthorne that focus upon the content of their works and their overall effect on a reader's emotions rather than upon stylistic techniques. In one of the essays collected in *Many Minds,* written three years later, Van Doren discussed this critical approach and revealed his practice of overlooking "deficient art" in American literature if the work in question had "vitality," a criterion he himself admitted was both vague and variable. This imprecise philosophy, along with his general lack of interest in technique, led some critics to question Van Doren's worth as a critic, although most acknowledged his thoroughness as a literary historian. He was also faulted for overestimating negligible writers, such as James Fennimore Cooper, whom he included among a list of America's five greatest fiction writers in *The American Novel*. Yet, despite these objections, his scholarship, open-mindedness, and insistence upon the importance of American literature earned Van Doren great respect among his peers.

In the 1930s Van Doren wrote several biographies, including *Sinclair Lewis* and *Benjamin Franklin*. His short work on his friend Lewis was released to coincide with the publication of Lewis's novel *Ann Vickers*. Bernard DeVoto, who considered the biography uncharacteristically effusive, maintained that while many of the superlatives Van Doren heaped on Lewis contained truth, Van Doren's critical assessments of Lewis's novels were absurdly based upon an assumption that the works were realistic rather than satirical, a perspective that he believed diminished the value of Van Doren's arguments. In 1938 Van Doren's most successful biography, *Benjamin Franklin,* joined the enormous body of material on Franklin already in existence. Critics heralded this work as the most comprehensive and best-informed work on Franklin to date, although there was minor disagreement about the effectiveness with which Van Doren related Franklin to his era. In addition to his biographical works, Van Doren also wrote studies of American history, including *Secret History of the American Revolution,* a study of espionage during the Revolution, and *The Great Rehearsal,* which examined the motivations of the framers of the Constitution.

Although no single work by Van Doren remains popular today, his influence on the development of modern American literature is considerable, for through his distinguished scholarship he demonstrated the value and cultural integrity of American literature. Louis Kronenberger has noted that Van Doren's importance lies in "having shown good taste, good sense, much alert appreciation, much clear thinking; in having played a real part in a movement that roused and educated American readers and raised the standards of American culture."

(See also *Contemporary Authors,* Vol. 111.)

PRINCIPAL WORKS

The Life of Thomas Love Peacock (biography) 1911
The American Novel (criticism) 1921
Contemporary American Novelists: 1900-1920 (criticism) 1922
The Roving Critic (criticism) 1923
Many Minds (criticism) 1924
American and British Literature since 1890 [with Mark Van Doren] (criticism) 1925
Other Provinces (short stories) 1925
The Ninth Wave (novel) 1926
Swift (biography) 1930
James Branch Cabell (criticism) 1932
American Literature (criticism) 1933
Sinclair Lewis (biography) 1933
Modern American Prose [editor] (prose) 1934
An Anthology of World Prose [editor] (prose) 1935
What Is American Literature? (criticism) 1935
Three Worlds (autobiography) 1936
Benjamin Franklin (biography) 1938
Secret History of the American Revolution (history) 1941
Mutiny in January (history) 1943
Carl Van Doren: Selected by Himself (novel, short stories, essays, criticism, biographies, and history) 1945
The Great Rehearsal (history) 1948
Jane Mecon (biography) 1950

THE NATION (essay date 1912)

[*In the following excerpt,* Thomas Love Peacock *is assessed as a successful biography.*]

Whatever industry could do to restore the footprints of Peacock's quiet passage through his four score years and one, we imagine, has been pretty completely accomplished [in **"Thomas Love Peacock"**]. Mr. Van Doren has followed him through the files of obsolete periodicals, examined his unpublished manuscript in the British Museum, investigated his relations with the India House, and enjoyed the coöperation of his granddaughter, Mrs. Clarke, in gaining access to the extant relics and reminiscences. By the correction of old errors and the addition of considerable new detail he has superseded the fragmentary sketches of his predecessors. If the account of Peacock's career is still not entirely continuous and is far from minute, we need feel no great regret. With the best will in the world and much more abundant materials than were available, it would have been difficult to make of this man's external history a highly important or very stirring narrative.

The life of Peacock is indeed so devoid of those romantic allurements which send the biographers flocking to his contemporaries that one feels grateful to the destiny which made him the friend of Shelley and the father-in-law of George Meredith. . . . When at length he departed full of years, the only place that he left conspicuously vacant was his easy-chair. (p. 493)

In seizing and fixing the somewhat evasive personality which concealed itself in business and lurked behind the dramatic masks of the novels, Mr. Van Doren has accomplished with notable success the crucial task of Peacock's biographer. (p. 494)

"A Life of Peacock," in The Nation, *Vol XCIV, No. 2446, May 16, 1912, pp. 493-94.*

H. L. MENCKEN (essay date 1921)

[From the era of World War I until the early years of the Great Depression, Mencken was one of the most influential figures in American letters. His strongly individualistic, irreverent outlook on life and his vigorous, invective-charged writing style helped establish the iconoclastic spirit of the Jazz Age and significantly shaped the direction of American literature. As a social and literary critic—the roles for which he is best known—Mencken was the scourge of evangelical Christianity, public service organizations, literary censorship, boosterism, provincialism, democracy, all advocates of personal or social improvement, and every other facet of American life that he perceived as humbug. In his literary criticism, Mencken encouraged American writers to shun the anglophilic, moralistic bent of the nineteenth century and to practice realism, an artistic call-to-arms that is most fully developed in his essay "Puritanism as a Literary Force," *one of the seminal essays in modern literary criticism. A man who was widely renowned or feared during his lifetime as a would-be destroyer of established American values, Mencken once wrote: "All of my work, barring a few obvious burlesques, is based upon three fundamental ideas: 1. That knowledge is better than ignorance; 2. That it is better to tell the truth than to lie; and 3. That it is better to be free than to be a slave." In the following excerpt, Mencken praises* The American Novel.]

The literature of the United States is still at nurse, and so American criticism continues to give forth a strong aroma of apologetics. It is necessary, first of all, to convince the somewhat aloof and agnostic reader that the thing discussed is really worth discussing. . . . The nineteenth century was the century of the novel—and if we produced no novels of the first rank while it dragged and snuffled along, then we must throw ourselves upon our sparse poetry, our flabby drama, and our huge stacks, elevators, and Bush Terminals of short stories. Accordingly [in **"The American Novel"**] Mr. Van Doren addresses himself gallantly to establishing the dignity of the American novel, not so much by direct argument as by sly suggestion. Does he succeed? Well, I can only report that my own respect for that American novel is appreciably greater than it was before I read him. He is intelligent; he is persuasive; he is readable; most of all, he is quite remarkably learned. Here we have something far above and beyond the usual scholastic compilation, by a tutor out of a row of textbooks. The man has read the novels themselves—even Simms's "The Yemassee," Bird's "Nick of the Woods," and Mrs. Stowe's "The Pearl of Orr's Island"—and more than once, describing them, he implants the strange suspicion that this or that ancient tale, for long embalmed as a mere name in a dull hornbook for sophomores, would repay search and unearthing and the lazy devotion of a summer afternoon. For one, I come away with a new curiosity to apply my eye to two of them: Col. John W. De Forest's "Miss Ravenel's Conversion from Secession to Loyalty" and Joseph Kirkland's "Zury." The titles used to make me snicker; they are somehow idiotic. But now I snicker no more.

Mr. Van Doren is the first critic to separate the American novel from the general stream of the national literature. The device makes for clarity. With Irving and the historians cleared away it is easier to examine Cooper and Hawthorne at leisure; with Poe and Emerson put aside, there is elbow-room for the sentimental novelists of the days before the Civil War; with the appalling apparition of Whitman laid, one is able to concentrate upon Howells and Henry James. Having so prepared his field, Mr. Van Doren proceeds to plat it geographically and historically, and the result is a chronicle that relates itself at every point to the gradual development, not only of the mere literature of the United States, but also of the general life of the United States. The book is thus quite free from the usual academic remoteness and bloodlessness. It is a history of ideas, but they show themselves in events, and often they are palpably derived from events. Cooper was shaped by his time; as it changed, he changed, and more than once—a platitude, but too often forgotten. The American dime novel had its origins in historical processes, and they are worth tracing. Howells and Mark Twain represented, in their sharp disparity, a conflict that was remaking the American character. The romantic movement of the later nineties was as much a part of the national history as the Spanish-American War. And the rise of naturalism at the beginning of the new century was a symptom of a change so profound that its nature is even yet much misunderstood. Without burdening his story and making it too heavily "scientific," Mr. Van Doren gets into it a sharp sense of this larger ebb and flow of ideas. His generalizations are cautious, but they are sound. He has converted the history of the novel in the Republic from a record of isolated and unintelligible phenomena, which it too often is in the literature books, into a record of a coherent and logical evolution, with even some of the future steps discreetly foreshadowed.

As for his judgments, they are devoid of pontifical dogmatism and usually immediately convincing. His discussion of Henry James is an excellent piece of criticism, for without failing to savor even the least virtue of the artist, he exhibits clearly the fatal artificiality and superficiality of the man. James was a biologist who devoted his whole life to a meticulous and even furious study of the wings of butterflies; that there were also jackasses, hyenas, codfish, Congressmen, lice, cobras, and scorpions in the world apparently never occured to him. Within his limits he was superb, but so is a humming-bird within hers; we eat, however, ducks. The same air of the myopic don hung about Howells, despite his own belief that he was a daring and revolutionary fellow. He converted his chronicle of life in These States into a sort of pastoral in superior journalese—but he always forgot that the farmer has mud on his boots and a bad stomach, and that pigs smell almost as badly as Slovaks, and that the principal business of a cow is parturition. Both were as un-American as a cathedral or a string quartet. Neither, I believe, is read today. James is studied, but not read; he becomes a sort of superior vice, like the music of Mahler or the painting of Cézanne. As for Howells, the very names of his books begin to fade. (pp. 18-19)

I incline to think that Mr. Van Doren is a bit too kind to Cooper. The temptation here is very severe, for Cooper remains the one American novelist who is universally read in foreign parts; even Mark Twain is a great deal less known. But I doubt that his standing abroad is quite as dignified as the wide dispersion of his books seems to indicate. His rank, in truth, is much closer to that of Eugene Sue than to that of Flaubert or Turgenev; he is read as a sort of licit dime-novelist, and chiefly by the young. . . .

But this is criticism of Cooper rather than of Van Doren. Mr. Van Doren is generous, but by no means maudlin; he knows Cooper's principal deficiencies, and states them plainly. The general effect of his study of the novel is that of clear light. It is well-ordered, it reveals extraordinary knowledge of its subject, and it is written gracefully and ingratiatingly. In brief, a sound and valuable book—and an excellent overture to the work on living American novelists that is to follow. (p. 19)

H. L. Mencken, in a review of "The American Novel," in The Nation, *Vol. CXIII, No. 2922, July 6, 1921, pp. 18-19.*

WILLIAM LYON PHELPS (essay date 1921)

[*Phelps was for over forty years a lecturer on English at Yale. His early study* The Beginnings of the English Romantic Movement *(1893) is still considered an important work and his* Essays on Russian Novelists *(1911) was one of the first influential studies of the Russian realists. From 1922 until his death in 1943, he wrote a regular column for* Scribner's Magazine *and a nationally syndicated newspaper column. During this period, his criticism became less scholarly and more journalistic, and is notable for its generally enthusiastic tone. In the following excerpt, Phelps characterizes Van Doren as an unprejudiced advocate of the American novel.*]

Let it be said at once that [***The American Novel***] is an admirable book, full of judicious and penetrating criticism, written with distinction. I hope that it will have a wide circulation in Great Britain and in Europe, for it is just the history of American fiction that I should like to have read and studied abroad. I mean by that wish simply this: It is desirable that foreign students of our literature should know the sequence of facts and conditions that caused and accompanied its growth, and that they should hold in their minds a true estimate of the relative value of our writers. This is the only chronicle and appraisement of American novelists that I for one am not only willing but eager to have in the hands of alien students. So many of our books of historical criticism are written under the impulse of prejudices and without the foundation of sufficient knowledge; and as for the letters and articles written to foreign papers and reviews, purporting to give a correct account of the state of American letters in the past and present—they are so full of exclamatory Lo heres! and Lo theres! so breathless with running after false gods, so depreciatory of the best things we have, that one can only hope that the misrepresentations they contain will carry their own refutation.

This book is precisely what it professes to be. In the Preface we read:

> Aiming to be a history rather than a partisan document, the account here offered does not take sides with any of the modes of fiction which have existed, or which exist, in the United States. To this lack of partisanship may be ascribed a disinclination to define the term "novel" too exactly. . . . A fuller history of the American imagination would indeed have to take into account poems and plays and short stories as well, with all the national myths and legends and traditions and aspirations. This particular study, however, has had to be limited to long prose narratives in which the element of fact is on the whole less than the element of fiction.

There are paragraphs where it is evident that the author has had to keep a tight rein on himself: it has cost him some effort to suppress his personal feelings, which may sometimes be guessed even where the manner is most impartial. But in this volume he is a judge rather than an advocate, and never removes his robes. . . .

The distribution of space and emphasis here must commend itself to every fair-minded student. There are ten chapters; five are devoted to various movements, epochs and the minor authors that represent them; the other five are devoted respectively to our five leading novelists—to those men who, no matter what one's personal likes and dislikes may be, stand out prominently in our history, so prominently that it is at present impossible to make any substitution or to add to the select company a sixth name. These five are, of course, Cooper, Hawthorne, Howells, Mark Twain, Henry James—every one of the five surprisingly unlike the other four. The chapter on Cooper is one of the best in the book. Mark Twain and the present disparagers of Cooper would regard its praise as absurdly excessive, if they merely read a summary of it; but after reading the whole chapter, where solid reasons are given for Cooper's lasting eminence, I think they would understand even if they were not converted. Mr. Van Doren believes that if a national and international ballot could be taken, Leatherstocking would be voted the most eminent of all American characters of fiction. . . .

Mr. Van Doren might have brought out the fact that one reason why so many American readers fail to appreciate Cooper's merits so highly as they are appreciated by foreigners is because of the defects in his prose style, which of course do not appear in translations. I have always believed that the Russians, the Poles and the French have a better series of Leatherstocking tales than the original.

In the discussion of Hawthorne he points out that Hawthorne became more Puritan in Europe than in America. This was thoroughly characteristic, I suppose, of Hawthorne's temperament, which had that independent obstinacy so often observable in men who are shy and reserved. In the very centre of Abolition sentiment Hawthorne was not even a Whig: he remained a Democrat. He spoke of John Brown as a blood-stained fanatic, and said there was a certain intellectual satisfaction in seeing him hanged. So, while his Puritanism was more artistic than personal in Massachusetts, it became strongly sincere while traveling in Europe. Mr. Van Doren rightly says of *The Marble Faun*, "Though set in an environment so amply pagan and catholic, *The Marble Faun* is in some respects the most Puritan of all Hawthorne's romances." The analysis of *The House of the Seven Gables* is perhaps the most masterly exposition in this chapter, and no lover of Hawthorne can quarrel with it.

Indeed Hawthorne's genius is in this book understood and appreciated. For my part, I think we all acknowledge his supremacy in our great Five by our inner certainty of it. We hope that Cooper, Howells, Mark Twain and Henry James will live forever—but we know Hawthorne will. . . .

Howells is treated sympathetically and fairly. Whatever may be his position in the future, he stands higher now than he did twenty years ago, and that is not because of anything he wrote in the twentieth century, with the one exception of *The Kentons*. He was a civilizing force as well as an artist and I am glad to see that his influence on Mark Twain, together with that of the latter's wife, is here regarded, with certain limitations, as good—good for Mark Twain's development as a writer. Mr. Van Doren cannot help asking the question which we all ask—Will Howells go down to posterity as a great writer? I recommend readers to the admirable presentation of this. . . . I am an ardent admirer of the art of Howells, and I can find no fault with this summary.

The chapter on Henry James is perhaps the least valuable of the five, but it contains much excellent criticism of individual works. "It was, nevertheless, at this point in his career that he produced the first of his books which may be characterized as magnificent, *The Portrait of a Lady*." I suppose I am in a minority in my immense admiration for *The American*, one of the earliest of his works. . . .

On the whole vexed question of Henry James, and standing between those who worship and those who think he is no better than Gratiano, who talked an infinite deal of nothing, Mr. Van Doren says: "Criticism must take account of the vast gulf across which those who like Henry James view with contempt those who do not, and in return those who do not like him view with incredulity those who do." This is true enough: those who do not like James honestly believe that those who say they like him are liars. Mr. Van Doren will give no comfort to the haters of James's novels when he speaks of *The Wings of the Dove, The Ambassadors, The Golden Bowl* as "the three superb novels with which, in prolific succession, he brought his art to its peak." (Curiously enough, he repeatedly calls *The Wings of the Dove* by the title "The Wings of a Dove.") In the final summary of James, when it is said "that he attempted, in a democratic age, to write courtly romances," I think there is more to it than can be covered by that remark. There are limitations expressed, but even those do not sufficiently account for "In the Cage" and other stories. Henry James simply wrote for the most part about the people whom he knew and understood.

The five chapters dealing with various movements and minor writers suffer naturally from the attempt to mention a great many names in a brief space, giving these pages the appearance of a manual, sometimes of a catalogue. It is pleasant to see Herman Melville receive especial attention, he having a whole section of the third chapter. I am a little surprised to see in the penultimate chapter so much prominence given to Marion Crawford. He was a good story-teller, finely educated, a thorough gentleman, and very prolific; isn't that about all? I fear he is fading fast. . . . [Toward] the end of the book, where so many modern names must be mentioned, it narrows down to matters of purely individual preference and emphasis. Mr. Van Doren believes that the greatest loss the American novel sustained was in the death of Frank Norris, and I am inclined to agree with him, and with his cold treatment of David Graham Phillips, who has been absurdly overestimated. I am with him again in his estimate of Jack London, and in the reasons given for that writer's decline from his possibilities. In the discussion of Stephen Crane, I wish he had mentioned "The Monster," one of the most painful but one of the most powerful of Crane's writings. Of course this is a book on the novel; O. Henry and other masters of the short story are properly omitted; but in the presentation of a man's work and of his promise allusions to shorter pieces are not out of place, and are in fact frequently made here. . . .

The extent of Mr. Van Doren's knowledge is shown by his praise of the New Haven novelist, Colonel De Forest; how many have heard of him?

This history of the American novel can be confidently recommended to all who are truly interested in the subject; without any jocosity, without any colloquialisms, without any paradoxes, the author holds the reader's attention. He is always serious, and never dull.

William Lyon Phelps, "'The Scarlet Letter' or 'Huckleberry Finn'?" in The New York Times Book Review, *August 7, 1921, p. 3.*

ROBERT HERRICK (essay date 1923)

[Herrick was an American essayist, editor, short story writer, and novelist. In the early 1890s his short stories were published in Scribner's *and the* Atlantic, *and throughout his career he continued to divide his time between the classroom, writing, and travel. His travels in France, Italy, and other parts of Europe before and during World War I had a profoundly disturbing, lasting effect upon his world view. Among his works of that period is the historical war book* The World Decision *(1916). In the following excerpt, Herrick discusses Van Doren's critical criteria for measuring the value of a work of literature and addresses Van Doren's controversial introduction of a "fourth dimension" in* The Roving Critic.]

Mr. Van Doren's new "fourth dimension" [discussed in **"The Roving Critic"**] seemingly offers a promising outlet for the critic away from sterile preoccupations with those old equivocal terms of criticism—the good, the true, the beautiful. The new dimension in which art is to be viewed and weighed is as spacious as life itself, for it is life. "The measure of the creator is the amount of life he puts into his work. The measure of the critic is the amount of life he finds there." This is the creed of the vitalist, of the pragmatist, in tune with all the broader impulses of our day. To test creation by the amount of life-giving force to be found in it, is obviously more reasonable than to measure it by any arbitrary standards of its truth, its aesthetic appeal, or its moral value. Yet in fact is this new dimension, spacious as it sounds, any less equivocal than the old ones? For what is "life"? . . . What is life for John may be death to Mary. What is filled with the sense of abounding life for one generation may seem to the next mere windiness. Judged quantitatively what has given this desirable sense of abounding life to most young Americans have been the inane fables of Harold Bell Wright, the preposterous sentimentalism of Zane Grey, and the trivialities of Andy Gump. Would Mr. Van Doren maintain the impossible thesis of their defense because so many healthy millions of his contemporaries have found in their pitiful imaginative fodder an enhancement of their own lives? In truth the new dimension is indeterminate intellectually, and because it is more spacious is therefore vaguer than the old—which may be to the advantage of critic and creator alike, at least in the deft hands of Mr. Van Doren. (p. 574)

Indeed, it is just because he is not ridden by any theory, even his own large one of a fourth dimension, that makes Mr. Van Doren the valuable critic that he is. He is neither of the pedants nor of the iconoclasts. He belongs to no school, neither that of the respectable classicists nor that of the truculent psychoanalysts. For the one he finds that life is continuous and changing; for the other he points out that no hobby can be ridden safely with relentless logic where the material to be dealt with is as delicate as human life. With ungrudging appreciation of Mr. Van Wyck Brooks's brilliant performance on the psychoanalytic hobby horse—so brilliant that it convinces one that Freud has done less for medicine than for criticism—nevertheless Mr.

Van Doren firmly explains how the famous method can prove anything on anybody, given the fact that judge, jury, and witness are all one and the same—and the victim dead!

The value of Mr. Van Doren's criticism—and to my thinking it has a very real value in contemporary American letters—lies just here, that he mediates intelligently and graciously between the asperities of the extreme partisans of reaction and radicalism in thought and feeling. Soundly equipped as he is with literary scholarship he respects the ancestors—for he knows that some day we shall be ancestors, that life is a continuous process and criticism did not begin yesterday with the publication of the new *Dial*—and the same wisdom teaches him that creation did not end with the works of the masters of the last century, that youth has its irrepressible right to its say. Thus he is the true middle-aged liberal, with a wise leaning toward the hopes of youth as against the proved and discarded experiences of age. It is an admirable equipment! And once more it should be stressed that it does not depend on any theory, even the free one of a fourth dimension. It lies as all fine gifts must lie in the peculiarities of temperament. The fruitful critic no less than the poet must be born, not made on theory, perhaps even more complexly so than the poet. For he must have that tolerant yet keen interest in every manifestation of life which gives meaning to little and great and recognizes that truth, beauty, and goodness are not simple, but infinite and vastly divided. And he must have the insatiable desire to discover and proclaim them wherever found and patiently to uncover the pretenses of their imitators and usurpers. This last function of the critic, I fear, is that for which Mr. Van Doren is least equipped by nature. His kindliness too often leads him to speak nothing but good of the living as well as of the dead. The lash, at least the waste-basket, is a necessary part of the good critic's equipment. . . .

The ripe critic neither confounds life with art nor too rigidly parts them. Quite one-half of the critical papers united in **"The Roving Critic"** deal with life directly, without the intermediary of the writer, as it should be. Such a critic as Mr. Van Doren is less the arbiter and the judge than the discoverer on the eternal quest of the good, the true, the beautiful. He is therefore not the enemy but the truest friend of the creator, is himself in truth an artist of no inferior quality. And the virtue through which he creates is sympathy, which gives understanding and wisdom. (p. 575)

Robert Herrick, "The Excellent Critic," in The Nation, *Vol. CXVI, No. 3019, May 16, 1923, pp. 574-75.*

CARL VAN DOREN (essay date 1924)

[In the following excerpt from his Many Minds, *Van Doren states his aims and interests as a literary critic.]*

It may be hoped that there is some connection between [Mr. Van Doren's] sense that he has been rather fortunate than deserving and his discreet methods in criticism. So far as it is possible for a critic, he stands quietly, if not stealthily, behind his work. The shortest of the pronouns is almost the rarest of the words he uses; if he were writing about himself, he would be likely to write in the third person. Whatever noise he makes in the world he prefers to make vicariously, with the subjects of his criticism the real protagonists—his subjects, in fact, and not his victims. They are, as he sees the matter, the source and end and test of the critic art. The authors who mean enough to warrant criticism do not always reveal their meanings unmistakably. Their books have been conceived in passion and brought forth in enthusiasm, these at one period of growth and those at another, some successfully and some unsuccessfully. Public opinion concerning any given author is generally confused, based upon loose hearsay, false guesses, insufficient knowledge of his whole significance. To the problem thus arising Mr. Van Doren likes best to address himself. Intending to exercise no craft but that of sympathy, he turns the documents of his author over and over until he has found what he believes to be the central pattern. This is his chief delight in criticism: to find a pattern where none has been found before. He would probably stop here if he had his choice, but being by profession a journalist, and having so many pages to fill each week or month, he goes on to his explanation of the pattern and his incidental interpretation of the author to the general public. His business with the problem ends, he thinks, when he has made it clear to the limit of his capacity. He leaves to other-minded critics the fun of habitually pointing out what meanings, what patterns, would be better.

Confined as he has been by his specialism to the literature of one country during barely three centuries, and still further confined, for the most part, by his journalism to writers of the present century, Mr. Van Doren nevertheless surveys his field not without perspective. . . . Yet in his criticism he seldom ventures into argument by comparison. With what must seem a kind of chameleon ardor he has managed to discuss the most varied types of Americans. . . . A striking number of these subjects of his analysis, and those not the least diverse in aims and achievements, testify that Mr. Van Doren has come as close to their designs as any critic can decently be expected to come. He would, however, be one of the promptest to admit, what he has had enough critics to point out, that he is singularly, if not fatally, non-committal. Where are the scalps, they ask him, that should dangle bloodily at the critic's belt? Is so much impartial interpretation anything but virtually so much praise? Has the roving critic no prejudices, no principles, no causes? Is he a critic of many minds and therefore a man of none at all?

In answering these questions it is only just to turn the tables upon so reserved a critic and to look for any pattern, any ground-plan, which may underlie his movements. What first of all appears is his preference for those authors who are civilized: intelligent, skeptical, ironical, lucid. Viewing the general life of mankind, its dim history, its shifting manners, its tangled aspirations, as a thing which is, for the artist, both raw materials and fair game, Mr. Van Doren looks particularly in an author for the mind, the rational conception of existence, by which he shapes his matter. This may be a mind as detached and disciplined as George Santayana's, as impetuous and loose as Vachel Lindsay's, as speculative as Mary Austin's, as empirical as George Ade's, and Mr. Van Doren can still give it all the benefit of the philosophic doubt whether one kind of mind is absolutely better than another; but he does not really sympathize with it unless it stands definitely on the side of the reason as against superstition or mere tradition. That prejudice of his appears even in his discussion of such harmless ephemerides as the local colorists of the last century: "They scrutinized their world at the instigation of benevolence rather than at that of intelligence; they felt it with friendship rather than with passion." It appears, too, in his attitude toward such a technical matter as plot. "Mr. Wells . . . lacks the sort of creative imagination which can follow a great theme to a great conclusion. For this, what is needed is essentially a great character." By a great character Mr. Van Doren means, as in this passage does not quite appear, an ardent loyalty to a reasoned ideal, persisting to its ultimate conclusions. On the whole he is more insistent upon the reasonableness of the ideal than upon the ardor of the loyalty. He does not greatly trust impetuous surmises or mystical illuminations. . . . (pp. 205-09)

So implicit a confidence in the rational faculties of the human race might well suggest in Mr. Van Doren an exaggerated taste for the universal, the abstract, the mathematical, or the smart in literature were it not offset by his equally implicit confidence in an element which he discusses in connection with his favorite doctrine of "the fourth dimension in criticism." It is not enough, he argues, to ask about a masterpiece only "Is it good?" "Is it true?" "Is it beautiful?" There is still the unavoidable query "Is it alive?" "The case of Socrates illustrates the whole argument. Was he good? There was so great a difference on this point among the critics of his time that the majority of them, translating their conclusions into action, put him to death as dangerous to the state. Was what he taught the truth? . . . It seems clear that he had his share of unscientific notions and individual prejudices and mistaken doctrines. Was he beautiful? He confused Greek orthodoxy by being so uncomely and yet so great. But whatever his shortcomings in these regards, no one ever doubted that he was alive—alive in body and mind and character, alive in war and peace and friendship, alive in bed and at table. Life was concentrated in him; life spoke out of him. So with literature, which collects, transmutes, and utters life." . . . (pp. 210-11)

Mr. Van Doren is of course aware that this creed of vitality can not be held to equip the critic with any idiot-proof formula for estimating works of art. Not all persons will agree upon what it is that makes a book alive, and some will find a book throbbing when others find it cold. . . . [The] critic who wishes to be alive must keep his attention fixed much of the time upon the primary substances of art: the stormy passions of mankind, the swarming hopes, the noisy laughter, the homely speech. Let him be delighted as he may be by the final product, he must still, behind all the modes of literature except those whose chief merit is their artifice, feel the rough document. He must understand that the best civilized poets or novelists, though perhaps not the most civilized, have shaped their art out of materials which, being original and obstinate, did not too glibly slip into neat molds. For Mr. Van Doren it has doubtless been easier to be a critic of this sort than it might have been had he worked with some literature not so relatively rich in documents as the literature of America and not so relatively poor in final products. But his chosen specialism has exacted a penalty. It has confirmed him in his native disposition to overlook deficiency in art for the sake of abundance of vitality. Back and forth over the continent of American literature, with possibly too much gusto and certainly not enough fastidiousness, he has moved in search of biographers, travelers, amateur anthropologists, adventurers, and eccentrics no less than of conscious artists; and he has expounded them all with a sympathy which is to blame if now and then the swans and geese, the sheep and goats, within Mr. Van Doren's critical fold look unwarrantably of the same dimensions and significance. (pp. 211-13)

He has, with all his considerable industry when enthusiastic, the particular kind of indolence which seeks to avoid controversy. Though his vivisection of Booth Tarkington and of Winston Churchill seems to have been accomplished with certain cruel thrusts and twists of the scalpel, he ordinarily prefers to use in such cases the colder knife of silence. Nor is this preference the result of any calculated pride, unwilling to stoop to the smaller fry of letters. It comes from a positive aversion to reading undistinguished or trifling authors and to doing the hard work upon them which goes into Mr. Van Doren's criticism. If he touches an author of this sort at all, it is because he thinks the author's works have settled into a false place in history. Rather an historian, strictly speaking, than a critic, Mr. Van Doren is bold enough where history is in question. (pp. 214-15)

The truth of the matter is, Mr. Van Doren practises one branch of criticism to the exclusion of several others. That he is little perturbed by his limitations, that he does not greatly care to rise to passion or to descend to prejudice, means, in part, that he is more wilful in his behavior than sometimes appears. It means, also, that criticism has never been with him a major aim. What really interests him is human character, whether met in books or out of them, and it is always human character which he studies. (p. 216)

Carl Van Doren, "The Friendly Enemy," in his Many Minds, *Alfred A. Knopf, 1924, pp. 203-16.*

HENRY JAMES FORMAN (essay date 1924)

[Forman was an American journalist, critic, short story writer, and educator. In the following excerpt, he praises Van Doren's literary criticism in Many Minds.*]*

Mr. Carl Van Doren, one of the ablest and sincerest critics America has produced, is threatening to resign his position. He plans, so he tells us in his newest volume of criticisms, "so far as it may be permitted him, to withdraw to other provinces."

The Attorney General's resignation could not have produced an effect more startling upon the literary public, though for opposite reasons. The simple truth is Mr. Van Doren has become, in the past ten years or so, indispensable to the growth of American letters.

Though once a college professor, he has refused to admit that no literature worthy of the name has been written in America since, say, 1880 or 1900. He has backed the younger flights of our authors, even to the present moment. . . . He even understands Henry James. But he was, nevertheless, willing to consider seriously the works of E. W. Howe, Edgar Lee Masters, Sinclair Lewis, Theodore Dreiser, Zona Gale, Sherwood Anderson and a host of others among our modern writers. He has been ready, as he avows, to afford unprofessional readers the opportunity, "with his professional help, to make up their own minds about the authors whom he interprets."

As a historian of the contemporary American novel he is unsurpassed. As a critic of current forms and authors no commentator has shown a saner insight. He has of late brought a new self-respect to American writers. No longer need they wait for foreign endorsement before being "understood," as Poe was obliged to wait, and Whitman. He has not even shrunk, as witness **"Many Minds,"** from pronouncing judgment upon himself. Now, he speaks of withdrawing to other provinces. Where is the authority that can prevent this misfortune? . . .

This is no laughing matter. Mr. Van Doren is no subject for frivolity. His two books, **"Contemporary American Novelists"** and **"The American Novel,"** are books of a sort that had theretofore not been written in America—even about the dead. These books are about living authors, and they show a profundity of insight, a keenness of judgment, an open-minded fairness that not three critics in America are capable of. Mr.

Van Doren has the rare gift of being able to write literary history while that history is actually being made. He can appraise accurately Theodore Dreiser under the slings of the smug Mrs. Wharton the while there is much nonsense being said about her, and Booth Tarkington at the height of his popularity. He seldom wounds, because he is impersonal. Speaking of himself, [see excerpt dated 1924], he confesses—

> So far as it is possible for a critic, he stands quietly, if not stealthily, behind his work. The shortest of the pronouns is almost the rarest of the words he uses; if he were writing about himself, he would be likely to write in the third person—

Yes. Indeed, he does.

Serious as Mr. Van Doren has ever been as a critic, he has never been dull. Let him take that to heart when he contemplates entering other fields—or, rather, when he thinks of abandoning criticism. For criticism his talent is already established because his gift is certain. His sympathetic yet cool understanding of authors is the very essence of his gift. . . .

"Many Minds" is one of his lighter books. But it would be an error to suppose that only what is dull can be profound. These critical sketches of some three thousand words each hit off their subjects unforgettably. . . .

This critic has a genuine flair for American genius. He has done more toward disentangling that from the vast inchoate turmoil which is our national life than any one else. Many urban and conforming readers know of Wedekind, Shaw and Knut Hamsun, but how many even know the name of E. W. Howe? How many have read "The Story of a Country Town?" Mr. Van Doren knows these things. And those who read his books on the American novel or . . . [**"Many Minds"**] will learn that in overlooking Howe they are overlooking an American genius. The cross-roads tavern and corner-grocery wisdom, that local-colorists of a quarter century ago were wont to sentimentalize out of all knowledge, has found expression in the crusty personality and somewhat harsh, dry voice of Howe. Mr. Van Doren does not ignore either the crustiness or dryness. But he cannot pass by the genius.

As always in an age of critical poverty, a feeling had arisen that what is not popular or noised about is unlikely to be great literature. Van Doren is one of those two or three critics who have recently enriched American letters by taking stock of our treasures independent of their glitter. He knows that ore is wealth no less than the minted coin. Of Robert Frost he says:

> Robert Frost has given little of his power to commentary and much of it to creation. For this reason he suffers with the larger audience which a poet can hardly catch without doing something to digest his own work for it. In the long run, however, he has taken the better road.

Nor does he hesitate to point out the vagaries or inconsistencies of a fellow-critic. Mr. Stuart P. Sherman is a case in point. Recently Mr. Sherman has embraced Puritanism. A few years ago he would have been bored in the company of the Pilgrim Fathers.

> Now [says Mr. Van Doren] he elects those saints and their congeners to the great society of good men who, in all ages, have sought perfection and thus saved the world alive.

Now Mr. Sherman calls the Puritans the radicals of the past. But a critic, declares Mr. Van Doren, "must be singularly incapable of growth if he is to remain satisfied forever with the praise of dead radicals." But Van Doren's hope is that the day may yet come when Mr. Sherman will "integrate his instinct with his reason" and "promote youth to the side of age in the company of things worth reverence."

And herein is one key to Van Doren's critical creed. His business is to survey and appraise authentic literary phenomena. What has age to do with that? What need to tell us that Plato was great or that Milton and Shakespeare had merit? We all know that. American critics, however, have always been timid of proclaiming a Whitman or a Poe until England or France spoke out. Van Doren is impatient of such lagging. English critics still complain that they cannot understand the verse of Carl Sandburg. Mr. Van Doren, however, believes Carl Sandburg to be a genius and says so.

As a critic of literature he knows that it is not his business to scrutinize morals or precedents. He examines Edna St. Vincent Milay's poetry and points out that

> she does not speak in the name of forlorn maidens or of wives bereft, but in the name of women who dare to take love at the flood, if it offers, and who later, if it has passed, remember with exultation that they have had what no coward could have had.

This point of view interests him only as the point of view of Sappho might interest him—no more and no less. His concern is Miss Millay's place as a poet.

In the same way he is interested in Santayana and Mencken, in Vachel Lindsay and Ring Lardner. Even the columnists of our daily papers do not escape him, for, are they not a literary phenomenon of our time?

There is something disarming about Van Doren's impersonality—disarming and cool, but seldom cold. An Emersonian note often creeps into his sentences. If there is no overwhelming enthusiasm in them, there is never any venom. He is virtually never lyrical, but when he begins to finger the wealth of a talent the pulse of his writing quickens. But he never passes dross for gold. His touch for the counterfeit is an unerring as a banker's is said to be. He is never cruel because he is never personal. Even in his paper upon himself, the last in the book, he is, allowing for conventional modesty, as just and as candid as he might be to a friend—or to an enemy.

Henry James Forman, "Mr. Van Doren Pronounces Judgment," in The New York Times Book Review, *April 6, 1924, p. 7.*

FLOYD DELL (essay date 1924)

[An American novelist and dramatist, Dell is best known today as the author of Moon-Calf *(1920), a novel which captures the disillusioned spirit of the Jazz Age. For several years he was a member, along with Carl Sandburg, Ben Hecht, Theodore Dreiser, and others, of the Chicago Renaissance, a group of writers who legitimized the American Midwest as a source of artistic material and achievement. A Marxist during his early career, Dell moved from Chicago to New York in 1914 and served as editor of* The Masses *and its successor,* The Liberator, *for ten years. During the 1920s, Dell was associated with the bohemia of Greenwich Village and, with a series of novels and one-act plays, became known as a spokesman for society's rebels and nonconformists.*

His socialist sympathies softened over the years, though he remained an outspoken leftist throughout his career. In the following excerpt, Dell commends Van Doren for his selection of uniquely American literature for discussion in the essays in Many Minds.]

Carl Van Doren has written a fascinating guide-book to the American mind.

He begins [***Many Minds***], appropriately, with Mary Austin, the outstanding representative in our literature today of the intense and visionary and prophetic. The "folk-wisdom" of George Ade pleases him by its hardness and shrewdness; but he is well aware that it is directed by instinctive purpose against all that eccentrically departs from the traditional folk-norm. E. W. Howe, the corner-grocery philosopher *par excellence*, delights Mr. Van Doren by the rougher cynicism and the deeper malice with which he expresses this same folk-wisdom; and the limitations of this cynicism are so obvious that Mr. Van Doren takes them for granted, without troubling himself to state them.

If these represent the prose of the American folk-spirit, Robert Frost may be said to have discovered the poetry of it among the dwindling farm-population of New England, where its chief merits are those that spring from the homely honesty with which a traditional destiny is accepted.

These merits, which Mr. Van Doren evaluates with such tact and tolerance for a generation of readers who have learned to be impatient of them, hark back decidely to New England history; George Ade in Indiana and E. W. Howe in Kansas have not lost the Yankee twang to their wit. (p. 741)

But changes have come—not yesterday, nor wholly as an aftermath of the war: George Ade had already begun satirizing them in their more superficial aspects a quarter of a century ago. Yet fifteen years ago, if Mr. Van Doren had written such a book as this, he would have found this stubborn folk-conservatism in the saddle in our literature. Fifteen years ago the changed world in which we actually lived was viewed humorously, or with alarm, but scarcely with sympathy, by our writers. And if we have been thus slow to welcome and celebrate these changes, it does argue a temperamental conservatism in our folk. But that conservatism is not the last word, as the newest American literature shows.

Under the heading New Growths, the second half of Mr. Van Doren's book is given to examples of this sudden flowering of romance out of our hard Yankee soil. Romance means here the opposite of caution—a full-blooded acceptance of the whole of life, an acceptance of its dangers, too, and a refusal to let "success" and "failure" be the ultimate tests of living. . . .

Of this new spirit the poetry of Edna St. Vincent Millay is the perfect and lucid lyrical expression; but it struggles to utterance in the tempestuous rhetoric of Vachel Lindsay and in the dithyrambs of Carl Sandburg. It has its prose moods, of which Heywood Broun is a whimsical and charming exponent, in his novels as well as in his journalism. And if one compares the humor of Ring Lardner with the humor of George Ade, one can hardly fail to perceive that the laugh is now on the other side of the mouth: it is folk-wisdom that is being satirized—exhibited very tenderly as a sublime stupidity.

To these and some few other emergent writers Mr. Van Doren devotes a hundred pages of swift and luminous description and analysis, and traces meanings which reach out far beyond the immediate area of discourse. Within the last few years, literary criticism in America has taken part in this romantic revival, and has been liberated from the narrow round of strictly literary and moral interests. Literature has been taken as a part of life; and it is, accordingly, with life, in its most salient aspects, that literary criticism now undertakes to deal. In doing so, however, it has often tended to become partisan and acrimonious. Because the issues with which it deals are live issues, of importance to us all, it has not always been possible to preserve the amenities. To this tendency Mr. Van Doren is the notable exception. Not less interested in controversial issues than H. L. Mencken, he nevertheless does not raise his voice above the conversational pitch, much less wave a tomahawk. Indeed, he presents the singular appearance, in this book, of a civilized man discussing literature with an equally civilized group of friends. His serenity of temper enables his thought to follow many an elusive truth into those crevices of nuance where it so often stays hidden from us more impatient ones. (p. 742)

Floyd Dell, "Creative Criticism," in The Nation, *Vol. CXVIII, No. 3077, June 25, 1924, pp. 741-42.*

JOSEPH WOOD KRUTCH (essay date 1925)

[*Krutch is widely regarded as one of America's most respected literary and drama critics. Noteworthy among his works are* The American Drama since 1918 *(1939), which analyzes the most important dramas of the 1920s and 1930s, and* "Modernism" in Modern Drama *(1953), in which he stressed the need for twentieth-century playwrights to infuse their works with traditional humanistic values. A conservative and idealistic thinker, he was a consistent proponent of human dignity and the preeminence of literary art. His literary criticism is characterized by such concerns: in* The Modern Temper *(1929) he argued that because scientific thought has denied human worth, tragedy had become obsolete, and in* The Measure of Man *(1954) he attacked modern culture for depriving humanity of the sense of individual responsibility necessary for making important decisions in an increasingly complex age. In the following excerpt, Krutch discusses the fiction in the collection* Other Provinces.]

[The] first excellence of Mr. Van Doren's nine ventures into the province of fiction [in **"Other Provinces"**] seems to me the result of the sureness of his judgment in discarding those elaborate devices of which he has no need. Certain intricate human relationships have seemed to him worth description, certain rich personalities worth analysis, and he has set about his task in the simplest, directest manner, never employing the fictionist's gesture for its own sake and yet never failing to realize his situation with a perfect completeness. No critic attempting to invade the novelist's field ever seemed less anxious to imitate the current methods of fiction, and none ever succeeded more completely in conveying that sense of intimate contact with characters and situations which is the novelist's aim. Mr. Van Doren writes in the first person; he tells his story as that story revealed itself to him, but because his own personality is so clear a medium he gets between the reader and the thing much less than do the mechanics of conventional fiction and he avoids any suggestion of artificiality. . . .

[**"Other Provinces"**] has a unity which collections of short stories usually lack, since each piece, though complete in itself, is limited to the others by being the record of one of the author's personal adventures in a world of whose fascinating complexity he is so acutely aware. It has a mood, and the key to that mood is given in the introduction, where Mr. Van Doren says that existence is to him "a library of unwritten books" and that he seems to himself, when going about the business of everyday life, "to wander in a wilderness of dramas and epics." The characters of his own children, so sensitively anatomized in the three sketches devoted to them, the shadowy triangle of whose existence he gradually becomes aware, the dilemma which has been confided to him—all these are but . . . pages detached from the endless work of which we are ourselves a part and into which we are enabled from time to time to peep. What we take away from the reading of this particular volume is that sense which it is the chief purpose of fiction to give us, the sense of living in a fascinating world, of being surrounded by stories which we have, most of the time, too little alertness to catch.

If he has succeeded so well where the professional and long practiced critic is traditionally supposed to fail, it is, I think, partly because he has never, even as a critic or scholar, been predominantly bookish. Perhaps, indeed, the chief distinction of his critical work has consisted in the power which it revealed in interpreting literature in terms of the society which produced it; he has always . . . been as much concerned with the knowledge of life which he brought to bear upon the consideration of books as with the books themselves, and so he needed, in order to turn fictionist, do no more than apply to direct observations the perceptions which he has during these many years carefully cultivated. He has been able to observe life with the same penetrating curiosity, the same broad tolerance and the same passionate desire to know and to understand with which he has observed books.

OTHER PROVINCES

CARL VAN DOREN

NEW YORK
ALFRED · A · KNOPF
1925

Title page of Other Provinces, *by Carl Van Doren. Knopf, 1925. Copyright, 1925, by Alfred A. Knopf, Inc. Reprinted by permission of the publisher.*

Mr. Van Doren has, so far as I can judge, no themes to present, no axes to grind. His mind is cast in a reflective mold and his mood is of the eager and thoughtful student. Too little arrogant to preach, too wise to believe that he has any key to life's mysteries or any panacea for human ills, his aloofness is, nevertheless, an aloofness wholly of the mind and not at all of the heart. It is from judgment only, not from sympathetic participation, that he refrains, and so it is that his presentation of character is always both dispassionate and understanding, the result of a vision unclouded by prejudice but not, for that reason, cold. Whatever emotion is real—whether it be merely an irrational night fear or one of those sudden explosions of jealousy which is one instant strip off five thousand years of civilization, interests him; whatever character has force enough to be itself—whether it be the character of a resolute child or of an original rustic—claims immediately his respect. And his method is merely to realize as completely as is humanly possible the springs of that emotion or the full flavor of that character. Only keen perceptions and an unflagging zest for human nature can sustain the interest of either the writer or the reader in work which has so little of any ulterior motive, one which presupposes, as it were, a wholly disinterested concern with human nature. But Mr. Van Doren has such perceptions and such a zest; to him—and therefore to his readers—people are more important than theories or purposes, and they furnish material for endless inquiry.

Doubtless Mr. Van Doren, who here announces his intention to devote himself in the future largely to fiction, will write more elaborate works, but it hardly seems likely that more observation, more intelligence or more life can be crowded into an equal number of pages. For the contact which **"Other Provinces"** establishes with reality is singularly intimate and its communication singularly direct.

Joseph Wood Krutch, "A Critic Turned Fictionist," in New York Herald Tribune Books, *December 13, 1925, p. 5.*

ROBERT LITTELL (essay date 1926)

[An American journalist and critic, Littell was associate editor of The New Republic *from 1921 to 1927 and later served as the dramatic critic for the* New York Evening Post *and the* New York World. *In the following excerpt, Littell reviews* The Ninth Wave.*]*

Since everyone else is going to remark upon the publication of a popular critic's first novel, we can afford to neglect this aspect of [Carl Van Doren's] ***The Ninth Wave.*** Considered in vacuo, without regard to what other novels its author may or may not have written, without regard to his previous condition of servitude in a profession whose chains we also wear, we can say, quite offhand, that ***The Ninth Wave*** is so beautifully pumiced, in exterior and feeling, as to seem far more the product of an essayist than a novelist. Its emotions have candor and light, but little depth, its people have charm without reality. Exception to this last must be made in the case of June Rutledge, who comes to life in a few casual, rather moving touches. Her peer will not be found elsewhere in the book, inhabited as it is by persons of a mistier, almost insubstantial blood. Mr. Van Doren rather packs the jury against himself by setting a mark which he fails to achieve. The "Document" quoted at the beginning of the book promises us "inner drama," but that is hardly what we are given. Indeed the book becomes more and more external as it nears its end. At any rate, here is a first novel of which one can truly say that it has promise.

Robert Littell, in a review of "The Ninth Wave," in The New Republic, *Vol. XLVII, No. 618, October 6, 1926, p. 201.*

ZONA GALE (essay date 1926)

[*Gale was an American novelist, short story writer, dramatist, and essayist. A leader in the American "revolt from the village" movement, she depicted in her novel* Miss Lulu Bett *(1920) a woman's escape from the drudgery and dullness of small-town life. Gale's dramatization of the novel won the Pulitzer Prize in 1921. Her later fiction was neither popular nor critically favored, displaying as it did her growing mysticism, embodied in her motto, "Life is something more than that which we believe it to be." In 1926 Gale was one of the founding members of the Literary Guild of America, for which Van Doren served as editor-in-chief. The following excerpt is from her favorable review of* The Ninth Wave.]

There is in the United States a small group of those who are neither eager to exploit the novel nor content to employ its form to imitate its past self; but who are adventurous in trying to mold it to its next equivalent. For there is new material to be included in the novel, technique to be extended, and combinations to be effected of those new techniques; and every such variation, as it emerges, seems to be a new mode, whereas it is probably but a single passage in a changing orchestration.

In **"The Ninth Wave"** Carl Van Doren joins this "small unhappy company," as Mr. Hergesheimer has called it—joins not spectacularly but with a detached awareness of what is happening to the novel. In a period of irritated small-town soul searchings and of complacent large-town acceptances, Mr. Van Doren tells about a man and how he lived through ten episodes of his life. Here, he seems to say, is neither Main Street nor Greenwich Village, but one of those others in the United States who are occupied with things of the mind, and who live tensely in innumerable ways of which the avowed emotionalists know nothing. Here is an area of poignant feeling, like gossamer, like needles, like bolts; and if you are battered upon by primitive choices, you are going to know nothing about such intensities; but if you have even begun to perceive that the race whirls in a circle and thus sees great suns as mere pin-wheels, then you may like to stand still and be touched by a heat and a light less than familiar.

Every novelist should begin life as a critic, in order to be thus raw to the minutest intimations of behavior, from a blow by a word to the lift of an eyelash above an utterly expressionless eye. If involution is the next word in art as in coarser nelds, if, having included all that is outside, the novel is to run inward, farther and farther, if it is to bare utter secrets with the knife of a phrase and find those secrets not in choice and the possible conscious reaction but in the field of the involuntary, or in the kind of reaction which one attracts by one's mere make-up, then the delicacies of work like this are of enormous importance. Such a book could not have been written and would not have been read twenty years ago, because people wouldn't have cared, wouldn't have been able to recognize themselves and one another.

In proceeding through these episodes in the life of a man the book, of course, discards the "line" of the novel, in the old sense. This skeleton is not new, but in its treatment is new, for the record is one of powerful and sensitized reactions to simple things. This business of the commonplace, we see, is not necessarily sordid. Between the old beautiful unrealities and the new ugly realities there stretches this middle ground of creative interpretation of every day—its gaiety, its solemnity, its question, its watchfulness, its passion. For some of the race experiences terrifically and does not explode into action, but merely flows, being fluid, in new directions and reflects, being prismatic, new lights. The book is about these. In this episodic progress the climaxes necessarily come without preparation, save in the same chapter—such as the poignant scene between Kent and Margaret following Barry's visit; and there is nothing in recent literature which grips one more fiercely than those few pages. But then the line abruptly descends again, to simpler scenes in the leisurely life of these two. You comprehend that the author is discarding weavings and preparations perhaps because he is weary unto death of "anticipatory flashes," when in life things so often go bang. But here we see the impact of the go-bang not on blood and brawn, and not even on familiar brain-paths, but on nerves and on cuticles, and on spirits experimenting on new routes; as when, without preparation, Mel is shown to be in love with Kent's wife. The episodic progress, of course, doesn't bother to weave that in either. There it is. There it would be in life. What are you going to *do* about it? Nothing. But you are going to *be* something else, it may be. For you certainly will not manifest the poverty of those amateurs at life who believe a monotonous affirmation to be tolerance. You, as protagonist, interpret, and you get somewhere inside yourself. And that is all. Interpretation does not run along like a little dog at the heels of giant happenings. Interpretation of the smallest occurrence is the happening. This, it is highly probable, will be a part of the method of the novel, whatever its next form is to be. The simple cold handling of things as they serially occur, in the knowledge that art does not consist of things fashioned and knit but of things selected and presented; and that characters need not violently act, but that they must react to and susceptibly interpret their environment. And then some day, as experimentation goes on, there will possibly emerge a new fashioning and a new knitting, one curl farther up the spiral. (p. 372)

Mr. Van Doren's novel is trying to move toward the freedom which in innumerable ways—from stream of consciousness to second person—this caged art form is seeking to effect. His principal audacity is in making Kent's prize dinner the summit of the "line," the ninth wave. Yet this history, laid in a college town, shows climacterically at that dinner the ghastly average that can be struck by this aristocracy concerned with things of the mind. In imparting to a reader sheer despair of the race of "educated" people, this scene is as merciless as Main Street's inducing of despair of the wealth, wit, beauty, and fashion of Gopher Prairie. The hour of triumph of this "professor," revealing to him as it does his own kind, holds an irony and a pessimism as great as the disillusionment of either small-town victim or young intellectual, no less the puppet of his period. The revelation is made, not harshly, however, but rather with the compassion of some onlooker, too mellow not to identify himself with mankind. And then in this novel life goes on, and ends on the note of going on, quite casually, and even cheerfully, as life does.

It is a triumph for the episodic method and for Mr. Van Doren that one need not have a fear of remembering scenes more sharply than the book as a whole. The point is that these—so chosen, so ordered—are of the substance of the book as a whole, for by them one walks on inner levels, on involved levels—using "involved" in its strict sense—with which the novels of the future may well be exclusively concerned. For there are in art only seven directions. Now having gone north, south, east, west, up, and down, the only place left unvisited is in. In that direction we have traveled, after all, but a short distance. It is those who are clairvoyant to motive and to heightened perception who are destined to take us farther. To that other "small unhappy company," too, Mr. Van Doren, of course, belongs. (pp. 372, 74)

Zona Gale, "New Lights," in The Nation, *Vol. CXXIII, No. 3197, October 13, 1926, pp. 372, 374.*

H. L. MENCKEN (essay date 1930)

[In the following excerpt, Mencken discusses Van Doren's biography of Jonathan Swift.]

Mr. Van Doren's study . . . [**"Swift: A Biography"**] seems to me to strike precisely the right note. It rejects as irrelevant most of the controversies that have engaged and fevered literary antiquarians. Was Swift ever married to Stella? Well, what if he was—or wasn't? The essential thing is that she stood to him, in all essential psychological ways, as his wife, whether he was her lawful husband or not. So, at the other pole of his complex personality, with Vanessa, she was indubitably his mistress, whether they sinned or simply burned. He was the sort of man who needed both—the mistress to launch him upon his flights, and the wife to catch him when he fell. It is significant that it was the wife, not the mistress who had him in the end. Men of the Swift type are prophets before they are artists, and so they seldom shine as antinomians in their private lives. They expend too vast an energy shocking humanity to have any left for shocking the neighbors. (p. 1)

Mr. Van Doren's study of this great but unhappy man is marked by sound information and a great prudence. He arranges his facts in an orderly and seemly manner and makes his narrative interesting from first to last. There is no vain show of learning. The tedious labors that must have gone into more than one passage and the diligent weighing of conflicting testimony that lies behind the whole are carefully concealed. One gets a smooth-running extremely readable account of the man. In Mr. Van Doren's style there are plenty of pungent phrases—turn, for example, to the "character" of Temple on page 20—but it reveals no self-consciousness and is happily devoid of striving, either for rhetoric or for epigram. The book is the fruit of nearly twenty years of hard study. It is a fascinating piece of writing, and it is probably the best biography of Swift ever written. (p. 2)

H. L. Mencken, "A Fascinating Biography," in New York Herald Tribune Books, *October 19, 1930, pp. 1-2.*

BERNARD DEVOTO (essay date 1933)

[An editor of The Saturday Review of Literature *and longtime contributor to* Harper's Magazine, *DeVoto was a highly controversial literary critic and historian. A man whose thought enraged much of America's literary establishment during the 1930s and 1940s, he was frequently motivated by anger at authors he considered ignorant of American life and history. As a critic, he admired mastery of form and psychological subtlety in literature. His own work is characterized by its scholarly thoroughness and by its vigorous, infectious style. DeVoto was "profoundly interested" in American history and authored several historical works, notably the Pulitzer Prize-winning* Across the Wide Missouri *(1947). In the following excerpt, DeVoto discusses* Sinclair Lewis, *which was released at the time of the publication of Lewis's novel* Ann Vickers.]

With good business acumen, the publishers of Sinclair Lewis have brought out in the same fortnight with "Ann Vickers" a small volume in which Mr. Carl Van Doren bestows on him the most unchecked adulation he can have received since the 1902 graduation issue of the Sauk Center High School "O-Sa-Ge." Mr. Van Doren's book [**"Sinclair Lewis"**] has some sound criticism in it, but you have to clear away a vast débris of emotion to get at it. His primary thesis, that Mr. Lewis is the most thoroughly American of contemporary novelists, can hardly be contraverted, and his assumption (which seems to him so axiomatic that he hardly phrases it), that Mr. Lewis is the best novelist of his generation, will not be questioned here. Mr. Van Doren had intimated as much before, but enthusiasm has now so wrought upon him that the comparative detachment of his earlier studies has melted away and his discussion of the novelist becomes something very much like a hymn to the sun. "Mr. Lewis," he says, "has a mind better disciplined than Mark Twain's, and more mental and moral courage." The word, observe, is "disciplined." "Not one of them [Theodore Dreiser, H. L. Mencken, Eugene O'Neill, James Branch Cabell, Edwin Arlington Robinson] has kept so close to the main channel of American life as Mr. Lewis, or so near the human surface." And "not only is he an American telling stories, but he is America telling stories." And, "Even in the Middle West men and women have had to look twice at their own faces in the mirror to be sure that they are or are not like the men and women of Zenith and its suburbs." And finally, "When the actual cities have faded into history, Zenith, with all its garish colors and comic angles, will stand up like a living monument. It will be the hub of the universe which Mr. Lewis has shaped out of the Middle West of his age."

With this more than princely ability to promise diurturnity unto his relics, Sinclair Lewis clearly enters a new phase, as a culture hero or a sun myth. It is all a little amazing to those outside the cult. What's all the shooting about? After all, this is only Doc Lewis's boy, Red, who has been writing novels. Pretty good novels, but not—quite—masterpieces that justify that sort of incense. Mr. Van Doren's book lacks something as critical finality. But the publisher's impulse was sound: it makes a fine blurb.

Yet the appearance of a new novel by the only American who has ever been awarded a Nobel Prize for literature ought to be an opportunity for criticism. For unemotional analysis, for the examination of a number of critical conventions already established, for a consideration of primary purposes and the extent of their achievement. The first step of such an examination would ask an elementary question. Are these six novels, the most vigorous of our time in America, supposed to be satire or realism?. . . For if Sinclair Lewis thinks of himself primarily as a satirist, then the brilliance of his achievement is not open to question. But if he intends realism, then his instruments are defective and a large part of the work he has done with them is just grotesque.

Mr. Van Doren, without asking the question, wrote for realism. For instance, "Elmer Gantry." It is, Mr. Van Doren says, "essentially a story, and a classic story, of a false priest who himself committed the sins he scourged in others." But is it? One remembers that the book contains a number of other priests besides Gantry and that they are all kicked about in the same way. One remembers the wholly fantastic distortion of the religious scene. It was written after an intensive study of the

American clergy, a study made with the help of expert consultants. In "Elmer Gantry," as in "Arrowsmith" and "Ann Vickers," Mr. Lewis constituted himself a commission of inquiry making a survey, a sociological survey. The book sets forth his findings, but one knows that the commission posited its findings before beginning the inquiry, and that would not seem to be realism. As a novel about a false priest, it is intolerably deficient in understanding, intolerably naive in its consideration of spiritual affairs, intolerably faulty as a presentation of experience. But considered as the work of a sociologist in fiction, a headlong satire of religious hypocrisy and commercialism written by a man who furiously hates them, it is one of the most invigorating books of our time. (p. 397)

Or take the "superb mimetic gift" of which Mr. Van Doren speaks, and which every commentator has dwelt on since the publication of "Main Street." It is perhaps time to inquire whether Mr. Lewis possesses it. If the phrase means anything, it means that he can reproduce with great fidelity the idioms, rhythms, and melodies of actual speech. But can he? At least he never has. . . .

Too unscrupulous a satirist, too defective a technician, too limited by the intellectual and emotional clichés of his generation, too naïve and too earnest, Sinclair Lewis is nevertheless the best novelist of his generation in America. He knows America better than any of the others, and he has conspicuously what they lack, fecundity and strength. Mr. Van Doren is right in calling him masculine. But why be euphemistic? The word is "male." He has extraordinary power, virility, boisterousness, and sheer nervous and muscular energy. They are qualities which dissolve away his shortcomings and which cannot be spared from fiction, these days of anemic invention and querulous estheticism.

Still, he is no sun god. Mr. Van Doren's expectation that "Babbitt" will live on long after Detroit is dust seems to me a little silly. Mr. Van Doren, not I, is responsible for the appeal to Mark Twain who, he feels, had as wide a sweep as Mr. Lewis but was otherwise inferior to him. But "The Adventures of Huckleberry Finn" possesses, besides an infinitely deeper and wiser knowledge of America, a serenity that makes the anger of the Lewis novels seem a trivial and somewhat hysterical yell. In that serenity, not elsewhere, immortality resides. (p. 398)

Bernard De Voto, "Sinclair Lewis," in The Saturday Review of Literature, *Vol. IX, No. 28, January 28, 1933, pp. 397-98.*

JOSEPH WOOD KRUTCH (essay date 1933)

[*In the following excerpt, Krutch reviews* American Literature.]

[***American Literature: An Introduction***], barely ninety pages long, might well serve as a model of its kind. Probably no other scholar knows American literature as a whole so thoroughly as Mr. Van Doren does, and no other, therefore, would dare to be as brief as he is. Behind every generalization one feels the authority of an immense, detailed knowledge; behind every specific fact, the exercise of a judgment which has selected that fact, not because it is the one which has come to mind, but because, out of a thousand, it is the fact most significant for the understanding of a man, a book, or a tendency. In its brevity the booklet is an essay, but to call it such would be to carry the term far away from its original significance. There is nothing tentative, experimental, or merely suggestive about these ninety pages. What they contain is neither an impression nor a summary. It is a distillation.

Mr. Van Doren's extensive view sweeps over everything from the first writing done on this continent down to the literature of today. He divides the vast field into five sections called—in accordance with the nature of the influence dominant in each—Colonial, National, Continental, Imperial, and Critical. Yet he actually treats only slightly more than a score of individual writers because, as he says, "In literature the first writers are first and the rest, in the long run, nowhere but in anthologies." Reading him, one does not, therefore, get that sense so commonly conveyed by histories and treatises, that the author is huddling together lists of writers tagged with more or less appropriate epithets, merely because he is desperately afraid of leaving something out. What one does get is, on the contrary, the sense of a panorama in which every really salient figure stands out in its true significance and importance.

The remarkable thing is that for all its scope and brevity Mr. Van Doren's Introduction should remain so specific. It is able to do so because it is everywhere so brilliantly epigrammatic—not always, even not usually, because it is paradoxical, but because so many significant aspects of a given subject are revealed in marvelously condensed but accurate phrases. Of Jonathan Edwards he says: "Whatever icy logic he had on his tongue, he had rapturous prophecy in his heart." And then, of the frenzy which he stirred up in Northampton, "Edwards, the last of the Puritan prophets, was the first of the revivalists." Emily Dickinson "did not so much cut her poems to the bone as leave them as they were without adding the customary flesh. Her work approaches poetry's irreducible minimum, which is poetry's immortal part." Of Sinclair Lewis: "Hating, he pays his villains back with exuberant satire. But his books with their black and white are also hot and cold . . . Arrowsmith, his chief hero, sums up an age. He is not a Faust, the intellectual and moral heir of accumulated centuries. He is an American technician, a bacteriologist who knows little but bacteriology . . . Arrowsmith is a hero for a scientific age . . . ."

Mr. Van Doren's generalizations concerning traditions and movements are as brilliant as those concerning persons. One of them may be mentioned. It is that literature on this continent was first "news from America" and that Europe, still regarding American literature as that, still refuses to take seriously any American book which is not in some way or another a report on the strange customs of a distant frontier.

Joseph Wood Krutch, "On American Literature," in The Nation, *Vol. CXXXVII, No. 3553, August 9, 1933, p. 162.*

CLIFTON FADIMAN (essay date 1935)

[*Fadiman became one of the most prominent American literary critics during the 1930s with his insightful and often caustic book reviews for* The Nation *and* The New Yorker *magazines. He also reached a sizable audience through his work as a radio host from 1938 to 1948. In the following excerpt, Fadiman offers qualified praise for Van Doren's selections in* An Antholoy of World Prose.]

The highest praise one can give Carl Van Doren's compendium [**"An Anthology of World Prose"**] is to rate it the equal of Mark Van Doren's "Anthology of World Poetry," whose general pattern it follows. The brothers Van Doren have divided the universe of literature between them, thus dismaying, if not infuriating, all future anthologists by leaving them no further worlds to conquer. Here, readers of every variety and description, is a book whose whole is immortal because its parts are immortal; a book weighing three pounds, bulking one and seven-eighths inches, comprising in all one thousand five hundred and eighty-two (1582) pages, the text set double column in nine point type on reasonably opaque paper. Here are over one million one hundred thousand words of prose, most of them the best that have ever been committed to paper, parchment, papyrus, silk, or tablets of stone; drawn from at least two hundred and fourteen authors, named or nameless, who have lived and flourished during the last forty centuries; written originally in twenty-one languages, or language-variants, including Chinese, Japanese, Sanskrit, Arabian, Persian, Hebrew, Egyptian, Greek, Latin, Italian, Spanish, French, German, Old Norse, Danjah, Norwegian, Swedish, Russian, English, Irish, and American; in the case of the first seventeen of these, done into English, fortunately the most magnificent of all modern tongues, by one hundred and twenty-nine translators, many themselves stylists of the very first order.

This, one of the longest and most impressive of books, is headed by one of the shortest and most modest of introductions. The principles that have guided Mr. Van Doren in his choice are simply exposed. First, there are no snatches or snippets here, but substantial passages, each with a unity of its own. For example, when he comes to Chekhov the editor quite calmly tosses in the whole of "The Cherry Orchard," though he might without fear have represented Chekhov, if less greatly, by one or two short stories. Second, knowing that first-rate writers have always written, not to be studied, but to be read, Mr. Van Doren provides no annotation save three indispensable indices. Third, there is no bad prose admitted for any reason. Fourth, the translations had to read like good English. When a non-English writer, however important, has been unlucky enough to fall into the hands of an inadequate interpreter, he is omitted. Fifth, Mr. Van Doren decrees that all his material should be "alive." This final principle has no precise significance and Mr. Van Doren knows it. What he means is that, with due regard to the traditional judgments, he has included the prose that interests or moves him. . . . The Conclusion to Pater's "Renaissance" is apparently alive to him; it happens to be, not merely dead but rotting to me. What we must do, therefore, is quite plainly to rest our faith in Mr. Van Doren's good taste, scholarship and catholicity of judgment; and most of those who browse through this tremendous book will feel that that faith has in general been amply confirmed.

This is no collection of surprises. The editor is not afraid of making inevitable choices, knowing well that the test of fine prose, as of great poetry, lies in its ability to bear repetition. On the other hand, he rarely strays into the purple patch, or walks the path of mere convention. Taking into account the fallibility of human judgment, the complexities of copyright laws, the exigencies of space and the commerical difficulties involved in the question of reprint fees, one must agree that here is an anthology that will last. . . .

Many can criticize an anthology of this sort, few create one. As I am not one of the few, I may as well indulge in the privilege of the many. If this collection has any single general fault it is, to my mind, the emphasis given to "artistic" prose as against philosophic, scientific and rigidly expository prose. I realize that this is in the tradition of the best teachers, but I cannot help feeling that in our own technological day the literature of fact and logic should be granted more comprehensive representation.

Thus, among the philosophers, Mr. Van Doren gives us a fine selection from More's "Utopia," but nothing from Hobbes, surely one of the most vigorous stylists of all time. And, more puzzling still, there is not a word of Berkeley, the bishop who wrote like an archangel and who transmuted tar-water into the very honey of pure English. We get Santayana, but no Bergson. Still here the translation may have proved, by Mr. Van Doren's rigorous standards, inadequate. The absence of Bergson may be forgiven by many, welcomed by some, but it is hard to understand why Santayana should be preferred to Bertrand Russell, whose thought is more influential and whose prose, even though it may lack Santayana's violin glissandos, is clearer and intellectually far more exciting. . . . I regret also, though I suppose it was inevitable, that the Renan selection should be from his worst book, the mawkish "Life of Jesus." The passages from the classic philosophers are splendid, but there is no Marcus Aurelius—though there is Epictetus, pallid by comparison. Among the Christian writers, Mr. Van Doren gives us excellent things from Tertullian, St. Jerome, St. Augustine and Thomas A. Kempis but nothing from St. Thomas Aquinas, who has been magnificently Englished and whose prose has a calm power, a rigor and a finish all its own. . . .

The English and American sections are rich, generous, and finely selected. There is practically nothing second-rate—no Ruskin, no Conrad, no Stevenson, no Richardson. Good. Very good. But there is room for Pater and his sickly flame, whereas there is none for Lamb, for Landor, for De Quincey, for Samuel Butler, and, most surprising, for Coleridge—all of whom surely are prose artists of incalculably finer quality than the whey-faced author of "The Renaissance."

With the American section it is difficult to quarrel. The selections from the classics are not highly original, but why should they be? I suppose Henry James *had* to be in, but, to replace him with brother William (who not only wielded a finer style but actually had something to say) I would cheerfully scuttle him. I'll amend that—I'd scuttle him anyway, William or no William. And space-limitations must have prevented the inclusion of Thorstein Veblen, a great stylist and a writer whose influence—remember Mr. Van Doren's criterion of aliveness—is vital and growing.

The selections from living Americans are bound to arouse controversy, but for the most part they seem tactful and, in any case, interesting and alive. Only with the Thomas Wolfe exhibit would I fiercely quarrel. These pages ("The Names of the Nation" from "Of Time and the River") are unfair to its author. They show Mr. Wolfe drunk with terminology and geography and demonstrate precisely those faults of windy poeticism and hollow rhapsodizing which he must overcome before he emerges as a great writer. The portraits of Eugene's uncle or the death of his father would have been more typical of Mr. Wolfe's fine talent.

But these seem petty quarrels, after all, when one looks at the massive volume Mr. Van Doren has so painstakingly assembled, so full of great human beings in their most explicit moments and human thought in its most unforgettable form. It would be hard to say to what better use $3.50 could be put than toward the purchase of these 3,122 columns of English prose.

Clifton Fadiman, "The Best Writing in the English Language," in New York Herald Tribune Books, *June 30, 1935, p. 3.*

R. P. BLACKMUR (essay date 1935)

[*Blackmur was a leading American literary critic of the twentieth century. His early essays on the poetry of such contemporaries as T. S. Eliot, W. B. Yeats, Wallace Stevens, and Ezra Pound were immediately recognized for their acute and exacting attention to diction, metaphor, and symbol. Consequently, he was linked to the New Critics, who believed that literature was not a manifestation of sociology, psychology, or morality, and could not be evaluated in the terms of any nonliterary discipline. Rather, a literary work constituted an independent object to be closely analyzed for its strictly formal devices and internal meanings. Blackmur distinguished himself from this group of critics however, by broadening his analyses through discussions which explored a given work's relevance to society. Inspired by the moral thought of the American autobiographer Henry Adams, Blackmur conceived the critic's role as that of a crucial intermediary between artist and reader, for the dual purpose of offering literary insight as well as social commentary on the age. His belief that criticism also represented an art form in its own right led him to an increasingly poetic, impressionistic style best demonstrated in his posthumously published lecture series* Anni Mirabiles 1921-25: Reason in the Madness of Letters *(1967). In the following excerpt, Blackmur denigrates Van Doren's* Anthology of World Prose.]

The great legitimate use of collections of this order—prose flowers from sixteen languages, some four thousand years, perhaps a hundred cultures, and almost as many frames of mind as there are authors represented—can hardly be served in any published example, any example directed toward others, toward any public, whether educated, anxious or ignorant. The great purpose is private to the anthologist: to give himself in ready form reminders for meditation from texts he has already mastered. Once made, such an anthology might show the growth of a taste, the structure of an education and the affinities of a particular spirit. Montaigne's kitchen, with its mottoes and aphorisms and insights copied on the rafters and the walls, gives us the bare bones of one extreme; and Southey's "Commonplace Book," a stuffed attic of all ages, gives us the weaker flesh of the other.

The present compendium [***An Anthology of World Prose***]—or any other like it—is intended to work the other way round: to shape taste with fragments, to educate out of confusion, and to create affinities for every spirit alike; and this it cannot do, since its readers—the department, stationery and drug-store public—will neither have chosen nor mastered the texts. Other classes of readers—those with the narrowness of knowledge and the scruple of specific interest—will hardly touch the book in any case; they will know it at once for what it is, by its title, by the claims of the publisher on the jacket and the pretensions of Mr. Van Doren in his preface, that it is only a pill for culture, large but not hard to swallow, and of no value whatever. There is a more learned word than pill, harder to say, but, once said, more satisfactory because more accurate and suggesting at once new applications. This anthology is a succedaneum—a substitute thing or person to fall back on in default of another—and a false one at that. . . . If we have room for the arts at all (which I know many have not) it is because we have no room for the makeshift, the guidebook, the excursion—because we never have room for fifteen minutes a day.

Mr. Van Doren has. It is the fifteen-minute mind that composed this anthology, as it was a five-foot mind that composed Dr. Eliot's Classics; a comparison of incompatibles equally displeasing. This volume is addressed, says Mr. Van Doren, to "readers interested in literature at large." He was guided in his choice of foreign works "less by the renown of the originals than by the merit of the translations," and of all the works by a search for "writers who here and now speak with the universal authority of timeless words." Such are the aspirations; they give themselves away by saying too much. No *serious* mind conceives timeless words in terms of an interest at large; only the solemn mind is capable of that—and the solemn is the last form of the frivolous.

Bearing this in mind, consider the selection of recent Americans and, say, the selection of English philosophers. We have of philosophers proper only Bacon and Hume. Of recent Americans we have among others Dreiser, Cabell, Lewis and Wolfe. It is as hard to think of these as writing timeless words as it is not to miss, with Bacon and Hume, Berkeley and Bradley. However you look at it, from the evidence presented only a frivolous judgment can issue. Which is to demean neither Hume nor Wolfe, but Mr. Van Doren's notion of his task.

R. P. Blackmur, "The Two Inch Shelf of Books," in The New Republic, *Vol. LXXXIV, No. 1084, September 11, 1935, p. 137.*

SINCLAIR LEWIS (essay date 1936)

[*One of the foremost American novelists of the 1920s, Lewis is regarded as the author of some of the most effective satires in American literature. Along with the noted critic and essayist H. L. Mencken, he vengefully attacked the dullness, the smug provincialism, and the socially enforced conformity of the American middle class. Lewis's fame rests upon five satiric novels published during the 1920s:* Main Street *(1920),* Babbitt *(1922),* Arrowsmith *(1925),* Elmer Gantry *(1927), and* Dodsworth *(1929). In these works, he created grotesque yet disturbingly recognizable caricatures of middle-class Americans with a skill for which he is often likened to Charles Dickens. In 1930 Lewis was awarded the Nobel Prize for literature, the first American to be so honored. Lewis was among Van Doren's closest friends in the literary society of New York. In the following excerpt, he discusses Van Doren's autobiography* Three Worlds.]

[In] his autobiography, ***"Three Worlds,"*** though he still shows himself critically independent, Mr. Van Doren goes and gets as independent of the Reds as he always has been of the Whites. But independence, like free speech, must never be allowed to work both ways.

Thus, in part, are his dubious doctrines:

(1) Having worked with hay fork and plow some eleven hours a day through the summers of his boyhood, he does not bravely resent it, though the world knows, now, that any one of any age who works more than six hours a day, five days a week, is put upon, and any one who ever, for as long as a month, works over forty-eight hours a week is just the same as a victim of dungeon torture, and under such horror will turn into a criminal, or a cow.

(2) Van Doren pretends that his boyhood was happy and that he really liked his family, when it is everywhere admitted that all decent and sensitive persons have so rotten a boyhood that rarely do they live through it, and that all fathers, mothers and brothers are at once dumb as dough and fiendishly brilliant in devising tortures for the heroes of autobiographies.

(3) He does not, even in this enlightened day, feel that he missed so much in lacking "movies," radios and the enlightenment of left-wing modern schools, where pupils at fourteen are taught to write sonnets and compose concertos. He managed to get along with such poverty of nourishment as Hawthorne,

Plutarch, Scott, Dickens, Thackeray, Mark Twain, Gibbon, Shakespeare, Washington Irving and Ike Walton.

Think of what Van Doren might have become if he had only had Clark Gable, Gertrude Stein and Walter Pitkin instead! Then he might really have been educated.

(4) He not only liked his home—he even liked, and obdurately still likes, America in general. He apparently knows that our orphan land is different equally from Stalingrad and from Blenheim Palace, that it has been rebuked and kicked out equally by Ezra Pound, Nancy Astor and Joshua Kunitz; he seems to be intelligent enough to perceive that here it is equally difficult to have tea with General Balbo, H. R. M. Edward VIII, or Andre Gide. But apparently he is so Laodicean that he doesn't intend to do a thing about it. He is so disloyal equally to Fascists and Communists, that he likes this family and this world, instead of sensibly going to sleep and dreaming himself a set of new ones. . . .

[**"Three Worlds"**] is distinctly different from the volumes of literary recollections by such men as Ford Madox Ford, Frank Harris and Sisley Hudoleston, who have devoted the magnificent inexactitude of their memories to listing all the literary persons they have ever met, with some account of what these freaks would have been like if they had only been just a little different. "**Three Worlds**"—it is unfortunate that the title is so close to Miss Gertrude Stein's "Three Lives"—is important not in anecdotage but in its serious portrayal of the several backgrounds and eras the author has seen:

Hope, Ill., and its cornfields and humble church, a great university, editorial offices, sober talks in unsober speakeasies, the miracle play of seasons on the Housatonic, a pilgrimage with Stuart Sherman to British shrines: change from the age of sparse innocence to the age of even more innocent opulence, to the nervous terror of the depression; the shy youth of the 'teens, flaming youth of the '20s, sulky and questioning and rather too unflaming youth of the '30s. Through all this the discovery of new American writers, not just as surprising accidents, but as persons who have affected and sharply been affected by America's growing pains.

It would be profitable to compare this revelation of a mind and of a way of living with the revelations in Sheean's "Personal History," and Farson's "The Way of a Transgressor." Any one who knows Van Doren will be certain that, had he desired, he might equally hve been an adventurous observer among foreign revolutions, among the dramas of street fighting and truck parades of soldiers and plotters in secret rooms. That he has chosen the quieter adventures of the library has made his chronicle not less but conceivably more lively and more important. And (but this is no slur upon those other diverting books), he has not found that lines spoken in Russian or Arabic are any more dramatic than lines in Illinois Yankee or East Side Jewish. . . .

Van Doren, like Lewis Gannett and Thomas Wolfe, has preferred making American history to re-reading European history. He finds it unnecessary to turn either to the old London or the new Moscow for inspiration; he discovers it, rich and pulsing, in an Illinois cornfield or a New York penthouse.

Throughout his book Mr. Van Doren breaks entirely away from his special literary field to contemplate the recurrent comedy of youth, and the confusing miracle whereby the son, without consciousness of having changed, yet becomes the father. (p. 1)

And of the contrast, in homes and in literature, between Youth of the two recent decades, Mr. Van Doren says: "The young after the war wanted to live freely. The young after the crash wanted to live at all. The villain in the drama of the '20s had been dullness. The villain of the '30s was poverty." . . .

Though this autobiography is not, like certain trusty examples, an effort to get as many notorious names as possible into the index, there are significant names enough, and particularly are there full portraits of those extraordinary poets, Elinor Wylie, who rightly saw Shelley as her nearest companion, of Edwin Arlington Robinson, who in Brooklyn yet lived on a Sabine Farm, and of Stuart Sherman, a devout modernist who nevertheless failed to measure Mencken and Dreiser, a shy campus classicist who ventured into the maelstrom of New York—to edit the book section of the Herald Tribune. As nearly as any autobiography that I know, this book gives a notion of what it has been about, in America since the war; and that the story deals mostly with the makers of books does not keep it from being equally pertinent to scientists or politicians or intelligent merchants or simple people who read without any vanity or careerism at all.

In the whole chronicle I happen to like best this discovery about one's own self which illustrates, incidentally, the lucidity of Van Doren's apparently easy style:

"If this were fiction I might say that I went into a retreat to think things out. It still is history I have never in my life thought things out, nor have I known anybody who ever did. I have always had to live them out, thinking as I went along. In my penthouse I was less a philosopher than a bear licking his wounds while nature healed them."

This discovery I commend equally to all who are accustomed to go off and brood about their incomparable wrongs, in the belief that they will just "begin to get things straight" before they pop into the psychoanalyst's shop, or the next Buchmen station, or police headquarters.

America, along with Scandinavia, may be called, and soon, to the hideous labor of trying to preserve in the world something of the tradition of civilization. For that straining task it is necessary that we should learn a little about ourselves, and **"Three Worlds"** gives us more than a little. It presents a sane and enormously talented American who has found our fields and our cement canyons not hag-ridden, but full of normal and exciting living. (p. 2)

Sinclair Lewis, "Pre-War, Post-War, Post-Crash America," in New York Herald Tribune Books, *September 20, 1936, pp. 1-2.*

LOUIS KRONENBERGER (essay date 1936)

[A drama critic for Time *from 1938 to 1961, Kronenberger was a distinguished historian, literary critic, and author highly regarded for his expertise in eighteenth-century English history and literature. Among his best known writings are the nonfiction accounts* Kings and Desperate Men: Life in Eighteenth-Century England *(1942), which examines British culture of that century, and* Marlborough's Duchess: A Study in Worldliness *(1969), a biography of the wife of the first Duke of Marlborough. Of his critical work, Kronenberger's* The Thread of Laughter: Chapters on English Stage Comedy from Jonson to Maugham *(1952) and* The Republic of Letters *(1955) contain some of his best literary commentaries. In an assessment of Kronenberger's critical ability, Jacob Korg states: "He interprets, compares, and analyzes vigorously in a pleasingly epigrammatic style, often going to the*

essence of a matter in a phrase." A prolific and versatile writer, he also wrote plays and novels and edited anthologies of the works of others. In the following excerpt, Kronenberger discusses Van Doren's place in American literature while reviewing the autobiography Three Worlds.]

During the past generation Carl Van Doren has been a kind of fixed—if never brilliantly blazing—star in American literary life, a critic who has expressed the liberal attitude independently of the warfare in opposing camps. He rose to prominence at a time when such critics as himself, Mencken and Burton Rascoe, and such creative writers as Sinclair Lewis, Cabell and Elinor Wylie—to keep both lists small—were making reputations for one another. It was the moment, as Mr. Van Doren points out, when critical power was passing out of the hands of the professors into those of the journalists, and with it there came inevitably an altered point of view. Tradition counted for less than the time-spirit; ethics, at least in the old-fashioned sense, for less than esthetics. Novelists and critics alike were carriers of new ideas, most of them not merely different from the old ideas, but hostile to them: it was an age of militant individualism, Satire with a capital S, and defiant free speech. It was an age when a self-conscious America was trying desperately to catch up with all it had missed in the way of an education.

Carl Van Doren participated actively in this intellectual rebirth, but unlike some of his companions he never took to dancing in the street. It was his difference then, as it has come to seem his dinstinction now, that he chose a more sober and less flashy rôle. He had become a "modern" as he became a journalist, by a gradual process of alignment; and he had previously been a traditionalist and a professor. His first book was a study of Peacock, his first big job was to help edit the Cambridge History of American Literature; he had, as it were, been to school to the past, and had neither quit nor been expelled; he had graduated from it. He had taken away what he needed and could use, and moved forward into the present.

The two backgrounds, the two careers, combined themselves in Van Doren in a lasting way. He has seemed perhaps the most journalistic of our professors, the most professorial of our journalists, and each background has been helpful in purifying the other: he has escaped being stodgy and pedantic as he has escaped being noisy and cheap. On what might be called the negative side, the side of glaring weaknesses, prejudices and faults, he has certainly worn better than any of the others in the group with which he was once loosely associated. Concerning the positive side, I shall have more to say later.

Mr. Van Doren treats in some detail the literary life of that period, when he himself became a leading critic, when literary teas might be anything from bores to orgies, when—as he does not say—powerful cliques dominated the scene, when writers, whether middle-aged and austere like Edwin Arlington Robinson, or regal and feminine like Elinor Wylie, or fiery and strange like Hart Crane, became legends. He has told here his version of Elinor Wylie's story, which sheds light upon both her personality and her work; he has reproduced interesting letters from the Sinclair Lewis of the "Main Street" period; he has painted, as it were, a good deal of the swarming New York scene. But the measure of his difference from most of those others he knew is summed up contrapuntally in the picture he draws of a quieter and saner life among the Connecticut hills.

When Mr. Van Doren comes down to the present, it is in conscious recognition of a world which once more shows change, Life has sobered down, the rampant individualism and inbred artiness and wild intoxication of the Twenties have given way to a period when men do not so hopefully stand alone or so willfully ignore the problems and responsibilities of society.

Carl Van Doren has now passed 50, and the literary era with which he is chiefly identified has passed away. It is a good moment for him to have sat down and written this book of personal and literary reminiscences, this account of the "three worlds" he has known and been part of—Pre-War, Post-War, and the world ushered in by the depression. There is first of all a story of boyhood and youth on a farm in Illinois, in an Illinois town and at an Illinois university, with a few years of studying and teaching at Columbia. It is a period to which the author returns, not sentimentally, but with obvious pleasure, as he well might. Farm life, family life, college life—all were simple, pleasant, serene; all appear in retrospect as part of a vanished America. Then the war came, breaking down people's sense of security, and demolishing, sometimes for better, sometimes for worse, the staid, uniformed old values. After the war came prohibition and with it the palpitating, rudderless, experimental Twenties with their overemphasis on sex and alcohol, their intellectual insolence, their conscious break with tradition—and the rise of a new and temporarily exciting literature.

Mr. Van Doren himself, after a period of personal depression, has found readjustment—a temperamental readjustment, one supposes, since none of the social, political or economic problems of our time have begun to be solved, and are now in many respects in their darkest phase. The truth of some of this Mr. Van Doren acknowledges, and he stands ready in his own way to shoulder some of its responsibilities; but by and large he has not been much changed by it, and remains what he has always been—an intelligent and cultivated man of good-will.

This is not in any deep sense a "life story"—it is rather, through Mr. Van Doren's own excellent feeling for proportion, one man's reaction to the changing color of American life, and recollection of whom he knew and what he saw. It is interesting, honest, graceful and human, just as Mr. Van Doren's criticism has been interesting, honest, graceful and human. It fails to record any passionate political or social convictions, any pronounced interest in life as divorced from literature. There is no more than the kindliness and hopefulness of a literary liberal in these pages, and such a one's unconscious instinct for laissez-faire.

"Three Worlds" helps, I think, to clarify Mr. Van Doren's position in American letters. His value does not lie in anything permanently important that he has done, in any powerful convictions that he has disseminated, in any books he has written which are final in quality, in any critical theories he has set forth which have changed the face of our criticism. It consists, rather, of having shown much good taste, much good sense, much alert appreciation, much clear thinking; in having played a real part in a movement that roused and educated American readers and raised the standards of American culture. Such a man will probably not in the end achieve a personal immortality; his will be part of a collective service to literature. But he has deserved his lifetime reputation.

Louis Kronenberger, "An American's Three Worlds," in The New York Times Book Review, *September 20, 1936, p. 1.*

CHARLES I. GLICKSBERG (essay date 1938)

[*An American critic and educator, Glicksberg has written widely on American literature. In the following excerpt, Glicksberg surveys Van Doren's literary career.*]

Mr. Carl Van Doren may be called the dean of American critics. He has reached the age where he can watch the ebb and flow of contemporary thought with a benevolence born of understanding. For he has personally witnessed the emergence and extinction of many literary cults. While the members of the younger generation are acclaiming the latest innovation, he sees in his mind's eye the patterns of recurrence in man's history on earth, he recalls the excitement of former literary revelations and revolutions and how they vanished leaving not a trace behind. Kenneth Burke, for example, has discovered the sovereign virtue of skepticism as a specific intellectual remedy against frozen dogmas and false verbalizations, but Mr. Van Doren has been skeptical all his life. Skepticism is [Mr. Van Doren's] native element. Unlike some of the younger critics who employ skepticism as a means of asserting their superiority, he is skeptical because he is so profoundly aware of the relativity of the values for which men are willing to fight and, if necessary, to die. Doctrines and dogmas pass away, but men and women and their perennial problems remain, and it is the plight of the individual that interests him most.

Mr. Van Doren is as difficult to catch and classify as a live Tartar. Behind his quiet, ironically smiling exterior and deft weave of words lies a mind as firm and vital as any on the left front. With him, however, insurgency is never a matter of words or moods or emotions; it is controlled invariably by reason and by the historical sense which sees that the crest of the present moment is but a wave-like configuration in a vast surging mass of motion and time stretching back infinitely to the past and reaching forward infinitely to the future. (p. 223)

Despite his detachment and his professed disinclination for work, Mr. Van Doren has been unusually industrious, if one is to judge by the bibliography of his published writings. Recently his autobiography, ***Three Worlds,*** appeared. We see him as lecturer, professor, journalist, editor, and friend. He has been literary editor of *The Nation* and *The Century Magazine,* he has edited an anthology of modern American prose and written introductions for a wide variety of books, he has produced a distinguished biography of Swift, he has contributed numerous articles and book reviews to various periodicals. Besides that, he has published books of criticism and a collection of short stories and a scholarly work on Thomas Love Peacock. Yet when the sum is totaled, his contributions seem less impressive than they actually are. The reason for this is that he has fallen between two stools: he has been neither a simon-pure, fact-finding professor of research nor a free and adventurous creative spirit. On the one hand, he has been held back by his devotion to fact, his belief in the continuity of historical development, his faith in the essential discipline of research. He has completed such valuable sourcebooks of information as ***The American Novel*** and ***The Contemporary American Novel,*** both of which are pioneering works. But they are far from being criticism of the first order. On the other hand, his critical articles, his reviews and essays are competent in workmanship, cool in temper, shrewd, conscientious, incisive, but without personal force or passionate conviction. He has never let himself go because fundamentally he distrusts the play of emotions. Yet it is only fair to say that he loves life too much to be leashed by the chain of logic; he has too ironical a contempt for arbitrary reason, when unwarmed by the fires

THE
AMERICAN NOVEL

BY
CARL VAN DOREN

New York
THE MACMILLAN COMPANY
1921
All rights reserved

Title page of The American Novel, *by Carl Van Doren. Macmillan, 1921. Copyright, 1921, by The Macmillan Company. Reprinted by permission of Macmillan Publishing Company.*

of faith and experience, ever to yield himself completely to it. His mind is essentially that of a satirist, but it misses fire for two reasons: he cannot hate with abandon nor love with enthusiasm. So that the final impression is one of fine disdain, of a calm ironical personality wearing the mask of a spectator who feels deeply and thinks clearly, but whose utterances are invariably kept within the bounds of strict logical discourse.

As if to be forearmed against contemporary or posthumous misunderstanding, Mr. Van Doren has taken pains to paint a portrait of himself under the significant title, **"The Friendly Enemy"** [see excerpt dated 1924]. About 1914, he tells us, he had taken the rash and seemingly unprofitable step of specializing in American literature, but unexpectedly it proved a bonanza. There was a call for critics as well as historians, and he soon became one of the guild, though somewhat surprised at the turn fortune had taken. After translating a play by the German dramatist, Hebbel, he wrote a biography of the humorist Peacock, for which he received his doctorate. Lest we give credit where credit is not due, he informs us that "in his recent specialism Mr. Van Doren has been less a critic than a minute historian, working dustily with editorial spade and plow to pile up the mountain of monographs known as *The Cambridge History of American Literature*. Out of that he was happily permitted to salvage and enlarge certain chapters and to call them ***The American Novel.*** Had he been still solely a professor he would doubtless have ended his narrative with 1900, perhaps with a curt epilogue upon the newer novelists." One cannot help commenting upon the strain in which this autobiographical essay is written. He is self-effacing and depreciatory, and his mordant gibes at the academic mind are at the same time an indirect announcement that he does not belong by temperament or inclination to the professorial tribe.

Fortunately he was saved from academic dry-rot, becoming one of the editors of *The Nation*, and he seized his opportunity to write ***Contemporary American Novelists.*** His journalistic essays, sketches, and reviews were then reprinted in a collection, ***The Roving Critic.*** These articles rise above the ephemeral because the author has succeeded in sloughing off the extraneous, the nonessential; he has probed to the heart of each book and revealed its underlying problem, its universality, the type of mind that produced it. In this, as in his other critical writing, he is impersonal and objective. In 1924, while conducting *The Century Magazine*, he published ***Many Minds,*** a series of portraits of his contemporaries. His portrait gallery includes figures like Mary Austin, George Ade, E. W. Howe, Robert Frost, Stuart P. Sherman, Santayana, H. L. Mencken, Carl Sandburg, Lardner, and others.

With this volume of criticism completed, he turned his energies to the art of fiction. ***Other Provinces*** was the first, and seemingly last, fruit of his experimentation with the short-story form. A collection of short stories told with tempered beauty, their interest centers chiefly in the studies of character; to this both plot and action are subordinated. In the introduction he tells us that his work as a critic—that is, as a student of men and women in books—had been a kind of preparation for his creative venture. All literature, he feels, is primarily the expression of a man. He cannot hide himself or disguise his true being. And this is also true of the story teller. Characters are projections of their creator. Behind every book of fiction or criticism he detects the author. Having grown tired of authors who offer material that is too luminous and too explicit and being restrained by the conventions of his craft from speaking outright, he has decided to fix his gaze directly upon men and women. The stuff of life, and materials of fiction, he declares, have always concerned him most. In short, he derives more pleasure and profit from spending time with people than with books. "At the same time, I have not undertaken to tell stories, but to present characters." And this is its central weakness as a book of fiction: it is a series of discursive essays, reflective analyses of other people seen through the temperament of the author.

His efforts as a story teller having failed, he went back to his first love. In 1930 he published his biography of Swift. There is ample reason why Mr. Van Doren should have been attracted to Swift as a subject for a biographical study. Here was a powerful satirist whose outraged scorn of mankind was held in check by a cynical knowledge of the ways of the world. Here was a man who had been molded by experience and curbed by reason. He had learned the lesson of caution in a society where unrestrained passions consume and destroy. It is a work of exacting and thorough scholarship, but it tells a story and reveals a personality. Mr. Van Doren avoids the pedantic ostentation of listing a detailed bibliography, though he has consulted all the available sources "during the period of almost twenty years since the book was first projected."

This was followed by two critical studies, one of James Branch Cabell and the other of Sinclair Lewis. His enthusiastic admiration of Sinclair Lewis is understandable, but that he should have selected Cabell, the arch-romancer, the poet of irony, the novelist of illusion and pity, the stylist of beauty, for high praise is specially significant. Cabell, we are assured, is a classic and *Jurgen* is destined to live. This, coming from one not given to long-range predictions, is a mark of great favor. Though Cabell has perceived the essential vanity of human life, he has portrayed its aspirations and entanglements of desire with an energy that makes his imagined world real. For if one is gifted with irony, Mr. Van Doren declares, his fictional universe will be seen as logical, consistent, artistic, and unified. Here is the rare combination of vitality and skepticism, of irony and rapture, that Mr. Van Doren enjoys.

His next book, ***American Literature, An Introduction,*** is a synoptic survey, expository on the whole but with a number of sound and salient critical judgments. The most interesting chapter is the last, called "Critical", which deals with contemporaries and which hazards a guess as to which of the moderns will outlast the age. Finally, one must mention his ***Modern American Prose,*** which represents his selection of what is wittiest, most beautiful and true and enduring in modern American literature. As an anthologist he is chiefly concerned, and in his method of selection, with narratives and studies of character, for the reason that "Always and everywhere telling stories and creating characters are the central function of literature." In the "Epilogue" to the volume he again ventures to predict which of the twentieth-century figures will survive, but he does so with the caution, typical of the historical critic, that as long as time flows a reputation is never safe. Names pass and are revived. The great are humbled, the obscure and lowly exalted. "Books survive only when they turn out to have the power to speak to new generations after them. What books will do that depends on what generations are to follow." This is a favorite axiom of his, but it is not altogether a true one. What the future will choose to approve is in a sense unpredictable, but there is a law of averages to consult, a provisional norm of excellence to follow. Just as an actuary can roughly compute when a man will die, though he will of course be wrong in individual cases, so can a critic approximately estimate the survival value of a work. For human nature does not change so radically as to warrant a complete reversal of those criteria by which one generation gauges excellence. There is a continuity of tradition, there is an underlying human norm, and Mr. Van Doren would be the first one to acknowledge it. Mr. Van Doren's prophecy, however, is significant as a personal confession of his likes as well as of his critical sagacity. He lays his wager on "dark horses" like Henry Adams, Mencken, Dreiser, Cabell, and Sinclair Lewis. For those who are left unmentioned he makes no apologies, except to end with the epigram: "In literature the first writers are first and the rest, in the long run, nowhere but in the anthologies." (pp. 224-29)

[Mr. Van Doren] speaks of his "discreet methods," and the phrase aptly describes his critical tactics. He is impersonal, preferring to stand behind his work. The subject of his criticism is the real protagonist, not the victim. The function of criticism is not to attack but to reveal the underlying pattern of meaning in those authors who presumably are important enough to warrant criticism. "Intending to exercise no craft but that of sympathy," Mr. Van Doren declares of his own practice as a critic, "he turns the documents of his author over and over until he has found what he believes to be the central pattern. This is the chief delight in criticism: to find a pattern where none has been found before. . . . His business with the problem ends, he thinks, when he has made it clear to the limit of his capacity. He leaves to other-minded critics the fun of habitually pointing out what meanings, what patterns, would be better.'' This sums up his creed as a critic: to find the fundamental clue to the work, to trace it home, to explain it, and then stop, without venturing to portion out praise or blame.

Though Mr. Van Doren has specialized in American literature, he has a steadfast perception of the cultural continuity which binds together the history of literature, past and present, foreign and native. Actually ''this home-keeping specialist and punctual journalist,'' as he calls himself, most enjoys reading, not the moderns, but classics like Euripides and Lucretius, Montaigne and Socrates and Fielding. He has criticised the most oddly assorted array of figures in American literary history with urbanity and insight, always coming ''as close to their designs as any critic can decently be expected to come. He would, however, be one of the promptest to admit, what he has had enough critics to point out, that he is singularly, if not fatally, non-committal.'' But he is more than impersonal and non-comittal; he is singularly limited in the range of ideas he has encompassed. In his scrupulous preoccupation with the pattern of the author as evidenced in the work, he has failed to body forth any basic principles or convictions with which his name and books could be identified. One is interested in the critic, in the mind that interprets, as well as in the diagrammatically accurate and faithful interpretation he may supply.

In self-defence against the charges that impartial interpretation virtually amounts to praise—to the question, ''Has the roving critic no prejudices, no principles, no causes? Is he a critic of many minds and therefore a man of none at all?''—he replies that he is nakedly revealed—features, moles, mind, and all—in his work, that a pattern is there discernible. Is it not evident, he asks, that he prefers to discuss authors who are civilized, who possess a skeptical and lucid and ironical intelligence? ''Viewing the general life of mankind, its dim history, its shifting manners, its tangled aspirations, as a thing which is, for the artist, both raw material and fair game, Mr. Van Doren looks particularly in an author for the mind, the rational conceptions of existence, by which he shapes his matter.'' Whatever the quality or temper of the mind—be it that of a Vachel Lindsay or a Carl Sandburg, a Santayana or a George Ade,—he will not say that one kind of mind is superior to another, but as for himself he can only sympathize with a mind that is rooted in reason, not one nourished on the soil of superstition and tradition. For him a great character is one who is ardently loyal to a reasoned ideal. ''On the whole,'' Mr. Van Doren continues, ''he is more insistent upon the reasonableness of the ideal than upon the ardor of the loyalty. He does not greatly trust impetuous surmises or mystical illuminations.'' His faith, sober and tested, is based on experience, the historic wisdom and empirical reason of civilized man as he overcomes blind passion and controls brute instinct. Reason is the goddess he worships, and even her with a reasoning questioning skepticism. (pp. 229-30)

He candidly admits that the critic must possess more than unqualified sympathy. Some authors obviously deserve to be attacked and exterminated. But Mr. Van Doren would rather remain silent than heap ashes of fire on the head of the enemy. Not that he is too proud to engage in controversies or chastize the offenders. He is simply averse to wasting his time upon undistinguished, second-rate authors. But where history is in question—and he regards himself as an historian primarily—he plumes himself on his courage. Had he not eliminated the unworthy names in the history of American fiction? Had he not lifted up his voice early in the movement to restore Herman Melville to his rightful place as a writer? Moreover, as an historian he is not interested in the speculative void of metaphysics. ''He undertakes only plain jobs with definite materials.'' Facts and facts alone are the materials with which he works. His prime function, he insists, is to make available to the layman information that will help him make up his mind about various authors. (pp. 231-32)

Mr. Van Doren thus conceives himself as the interpreter *par excellence,* offering expositions of human nature, as found in books, out of which evaluations arise. He is a mirror, not a sword. Not his to attack or obtrude his individuality, his critical apparatus. He is impersonal, almost anonymous, and he deliberately cultivates a coldness of tone, a severely intellectual atmosphere, without intense sunshine or thunderstorms, where all is rarefied and serene and reasonable. (p. 232)

Mr. Van Doren has been gifted by the gods with a powerfully controlled reason that manifests itself in a style that is simple, direct, epigrammatic, seasoned with the spice of irony and skepticism. Because of his reasoned mistrust of intellectualism, of abstract theories and philosophical systems as well as of ideal enthusiasms, the emotions of romantic excess in general, he has fallen lamentably short in two respects; he has produced no rounded, no comprehensive book of criticism, and his work as a critic has been restrained in tone, neutral in tint, limited in range, fragmentary in nature. He has relied on reason to a point where reason inhibits, if it does not prevent, that largesse of utterance, that generous expansiveness and intensity which appears when one writes with the full sincerity and fervor of deep convictions. His substance is austerely impersonal and therefore largely devoid of individuality. He prides himself on his painstaking search for facts, but the scholarly ''truths'' he has discovered, while valuable, lack significance of design. His books are really collections of discursive essays and reviews; they are offshoots of industrious moments, the fruits of editorial assignments, the product in many instances of enforced literary labor. He has given birth to fragments, which are isolated, uncorrelated; they possess no perceptible unity. The only traceable pattern is that of their creator, disguised as a brain working aseptically to produce stained-glass slides which under the magnifying lens of his style show the cellular structure of the character of the work or writer under discussion.

His dismissal of philosophical criticism with its implied contempt for abstract theoretical speculation arises from his consistent reliance on the historical discipline. Nevertheless, there is evident a touch of astigmatism in this abhorrence for general ideas. To renounce philosophy completely in the province of criticism is as bad as the excess of those who scorn the earth of concrete facts for daring leaps into the vast empyrean of thought. For facts, however necessary in historical research, have no value if not related and joined together to form some significant pattern. (p. 233)

Ultimately, then, criticism reduces itself to a question of the philosophy of life held by the critic. This philosophy is implicit in his judgments and embodied in the literary values he advocates. His philosophy in turn is conditioned largely by his temperament. Thus the method employed by a critic is often subjective in origin and import, however objectively it is stated. Now if one is soberly realistic, disillusioned about himself and mankind, seeing both victory and failure as equally meaningless, he can have but little to say to his generation. At least, most of what he says will be stamped with the mood of disenchantment. He may act as a restraining force, a check on the romantic excesses of enthusiasm or idealism or sentimentality, but he is powerless to initiate action, he cannot stimulate faith and enlarge the horizons of vision. He is rarely to be found at the forefront of a movement, in the thick of battle. He has no message either for the arduous or the hopeless ones of earth. He sheds light, but it is a cold searching skeptical light of reason, without emotional warmth or chromatic glow. He is Sancho Panza, not Don Quixote, the Swift, not the Shelley or Hazlitt of American criticism. His satire, however, is without the bite and bitterness of a Swift, because his perception of folly and futility is touched with affection for mankind. It is tolerant, amused, in its kindly forbearance. To one whom little, if anything, greatly matters, criticism must remain essentially an art of exposition and analysis, rather than creative affirmation. All things considered, Mr. Van Doren's estimate of himself is, perhaps, eminently fair. In a strict sense, he is not so much a critic as an historian, and it is as an historian of American letters that he has made his most important contribution. (p. 234)

Charles I. Glicksberg, "Carl Van Doren: Scholar and Skeptic," in The Sewanee Review, *Vol. XLVI, No. 2, Spring, 1938, pp. 223-34.*

HENRY STEELE COMMAGER (essay date 1938)

[An American historian and educator, Commager is the author of several popular historical works which, according to Lawrence Wells Cobb, have allowed "scholars and lay readers both to 'get at' the sources of the American historical record and to understand their heritage more fully." Among his important works are The Growth of the American Republic *(1930), which he coauthored with Samuel Eliot Morison and which long served as a college history textbook, and* Our Nation *(1941), a popular and instructive textbook used in high school history classes throughout the United States. In addition, Commager's* Documents of American History *(1934) is regarded as one of the most valuable reference books of its kind. This work, which has had several editions, contains over six hundred documents illustrating the course of American history from the age of discovery to the present. In the following excerpt, Commager discusses Van Doren's biography of Benjamin Franklin.]*

Franklin does not make such demands upon biographers as Jefferson and Lincoln and Wilson make; a biography of Franklin is not a spiritual exercise. Yet Franklin is not an easy subject. His biography becomes almost a history of eighteenth-century America. His life spanned indeed almost the whole of that century, and embraced most of the memorable things that occurred in the New World and many that occurred in the Old. It includes such obvious things as the beginnings of American literature and journalism, the intercolonial wars, the Revolution, the Confederation and the Constitution, the democratic movement within the States, commerce and industry, science and invention, agriculture, banking, insurance, the growth of cities, the development of intercolonial and of national unity, economic and political thought, Indian relations, the West, slavery and anti-slavery, humanitarianism and education. It embraces scores of less obvious things, too numerous to mention, too numerous, even, for most biographers to mention. But "the chief aim of this book," writes Mr. Van Doren [of his ***Benjamin Franklin***], "is to restore to Franklin, so often remembered piecemeal in this or that of his diverse aspects, his magnificent central unity as a great and wise man moving through great and troubling events."

In so far as it is possible to do this, Mr. Van Doren has done it; certainly he has written the most comprehensive and the most intelligently sympathetic biography of Franklin which we have. There was consistency of character in Franklin, but not unity of purpose; his whole life was opportunistic and his achievements, most of them, occasional. . . . If there is unity, it is to be found in his faith in reason. "His mind," says Mr. Van Doren, "was a federation of purposes, working harmoniously together. Other philosophers might be dark and profound, but Franklin moved serenely through the visible world, trying to understand it all."

So we might say, Mr. Van Doren moves serenely through the world of Franklin, trying to understand it all. He has approached Franklin largely through his own words, attempting an extension of the famous Autobiography, borrowing extensively from that famous book, from the thousands of letters and the volumes of scientific and political and economic treatises. He has at the same time filled in the background of Boston and Philadelphia, London and Paris and Passy, and fitted Franklin properly into the political, the social, and the intellectual scene.

The political story is the most familiar, and affords little opportunity for originality or elaboration. Mr. Van Doren's chief contribution is in his detailed attention to certain aspects of Franklin's personal life, his literary activities and his scientific interests. These are set forth comprehensively, and integrated with other phases of Franklin's career. There is an examination of Franklin's early literary efforts, a thorough review of the various issues of Poor Richard's Almanac, and a particularly interesting tribute to some of Franklin's later and lighter forays into print. The recapitulation of Franklin's scientific activities is impressive: the experiments with electricity, the Franklin stove, the invention of the glass harmonica, the interest in scientific agriculture, the first flexible catheter, the study of whirlwinds and of the Gulf stream and of canals, interest in ventilation, the application of oil to rough seas, and a hundred other similar experiments.

Most interesting, perhaps, is the detailed portrait, which recaptures Franklin as his contemporaries knew him. Mr. Van Doren has reconstructed the society in which Franklin moved, not only the formal society of Boston and Philadelphia or the scientific society of London or the aristocratic society of Paris, but the family relationships and the friendships, most of them with persons unknown to fame except for their connection with the great philosopher. Through it all Franklin moves, cheerful, bustling, unpretentious, as happy with Polly Stevenson or Catherine Ray as with Madame Helvetius or Madame Brillon, and never happier than when hearing some granddaughter at her spelling or playing draughts with some godson.

There are, to be sure, certain defects in Mr. Van Doren's method, and these are perhaps inevitable. The very detail of the study makes it difficult to grasp the whole, and the chronological method does not lessen the confusion. The biography is descriptive rather than interpretative, narrative rather than analytical, two rather than three dimensional. And because Franklin's contributions to the solution or the elucidation of larger problems were spread out over a lifetime, they do not appear here as clearly as they should. Mr. Van Doren tells of the Albany Plan for Union, the Confederation, and the Constitutional Convention, and he discusses Franklin's political essays, but he does not properly emphasize Franklin's contribution to the solution of the problem of imperial unity: federalism. He introduces us to some of Franklin's economic essays and calls attention to Franklin's interest in agriculture and connection with the physiocrats, but nowhere analyzes those economic theories which entitle Franklin to be called the first American economist.

The story of Franklin's democracy is written large throughout the book, but again there is a lack of sharpness and of emphasis, which would enable us better to appreciate that radicalism and equalitarianism which inspired such distrust among the Quaker aristocracy of Pennsylvania. Nor is there, finally, at any point an integrated interpretation of Franklin's character. "He has told his story," says Mr. Van Doren. "Nor should there now be need of a further comment on the record. Let the record stand and explain itself." Yet we would welcome comment and explanation from a student so learned, perspicacious and sympathetic. (pp. 1, 14)

Henry Steele Commager, "Franklin, the True American," in The New York Times Book Review, *October 9, 1938, pp. 1, 14.*

MALCOLM COWLEY (essay date 1938)

[Cowley has made several valuable contributions to contemporary letters with his editions of important American authors (Nathaniel Hawthorne, Walt Whitman, Ernest Hemingway, William Faulkner, F. Scott Fitzgerald), his writings as a literary critic for The New Republic, *and, above all, with his chronicles and criticism of modern American literature. Cowley's literary criticism does not attempt a systematic philosophical view of life and art, nor is it representative of a neatly defined school of critical thought. Rather, it focuses on works—particularly those of "lost generation" writers whom he knew—that Cowley believes personal experience has qualified him to explicate and that he considers worthy of public appreciation. The critical approach Cowley follows is undogmatic and is characterized by a willingness to view a work from whatever perspective—social, historical, aesthetic—that the work itself seems to demand for its illumination. In the following excerpt, Cowley discusses Van Doren's* Benjamin Franklin.*]*

We owe a considerable debt to Carl Van Doren for writing a full-length, scholarly life that incorporates the latest researches into Franklin's long career [in **"Benjamin Franklin"**]. There is no doubt that he has been neglected of recent years, not by historical students, who have continued to unearth new facts about him, but rather by literary fashion and by the public at large. There are signs that Franklin is ceasing to be a hero of the nation that he did more, perhaps, than any other single man to conceive and unite and launch on its career. . . . Poor Richard has made him the patron saint of thrift societies, building-and-loan associations and moss-backed Republican bankers who would be outraged to hear that they were quoting the maxims of a free-thinker, an easygoing libertine and revolutionary democrat. Says Mr. Van Doren at the end of his preface: "The dry, prim people seem to regard him as a treasure shut up in a savings bank to which they have the lawful key. I herewith give him back, in his grand dimensions, to his nation and the world."

His book has already been nominated by several critics for the Pulitzer Prize, and I should like to add my vote to theirs. Among all the lives of Franklin, it is the longest and best informed, and I doubt that any other biography of the year will be as useful. But there is a fault or limitation in the plan of the book that keeps it from telling a complete story. Mr. Van Doren explains in his preface that Franklin is known chiefly from his "Autobiography," and is therefore insufficiently known, since that work stops short with his middle years. Franklin had always intended to write about his later life. The materials he would have used are still available, in his journals, letters and miscellaneous writings. "Here at last they have been drawn together and arranged in something like the order he might have given them. . . . In effect, Franklin's autobiography is here completed."

But is a new autobiography of Franklin what we really want or need in the twentieth century? It seems to me that in order to know the man "in his grand dimensions," we have to see him in perspective, against the background of his times, and this is a view that Mr. Van Doren fails to give. As compared with Bernard Faÿ's "Franklin," published in 1929, his book is sounder at many points but conspicuously lacking in general ideas. He has written a behavioristic biography, one that tells us "what Franklin did, said, thought and felt," one that describes the successive roles he assumed. But how can we understand those roles, or their effect, without knowing the theatres where they were played and the audiences that hissed or applauded them? (pp. 338-39)

Malcolm Cowley, "Tribute to Ben Franklin," in The New Republic, *Vol. LXXXXVI, No. 1246, October 26, 1938, pp. 338-39.*

HENRY STEELE COMMAGER (essay date 1941)

[In the following excerpt, Commager discusses Secret History of the American Revolution.*]*

For the most part the British effort to win over the Americans [during the American Revolution]—or to defeat them—was conducted openly enough. They raised numerous regiments of Loyalists, and many of these gave a good account of themselves. Thus, too, the peace offers of 1778 were genuine and attractive. But a substantial part of the British effort was secret, and it is with this that Mr. Van Doren is concerned [in ***Secret History of the American Revolution***]: with the plots and intrigues, the bribery and corruption, the spying and the intrigues that accompanied the genuine efforts toward reconciliation or victory.

For his material Mr. Van Doren has gone to the vast store of British Headquarters Papers, lodged now in the Clements Library, and heretofore but little used. These papers tell a fascinating story of labyrinthine intrigues, of plots and counterplots, of chicanery and treason. There was treason before Arnold, and Mr. Van Doren recounts it briefly—the case of Thomas Hickey, the treachery of William Demont, who carried to Howe the plans of Fort Washington, the complicated plottings of Benjamin Church, the conspiracy of Lord Dunmore, royal Governor of Virginia, and above all the perplexing case of General Lee, and the controversial problem of Silas Deane.

But it is Arnold, of course, who dominates the book, Arnold whose treason was so spectacular that it has lingered fresh in the memory of Americans for a century and a half. The story is familiar enough, and though the Clinton papers permit Mr. Van Doren to elaborate it, to add fresh details, and especially to present new evidence from the British end, there is little here that necessitates a revaluation. Yet some things do emerge from this exhaustive analysis of what André called Arnold's contribution to "a shining revolution." It is clear that Arnold was not driven to treason by carping criticism, by misunderstanding, by failure to achieve promotion; it is clear that he deliberately embraced treason for its financial rewards. Mr. Van Doren gives us some interesting figures on those rewards. They were, as he observes, handsome—an outright payment of some £6,500, and half pay and pensions totaling some £1,200 annually. "No other American officer," adds Mr. Van Doren, "made as much money out of the war as Arnold did."

Of more interest is the evidence, here presented in convincing fashion, of Peggy Shippen's complicity in her husband's treason. The role of the beautiful, and hysterical, Peggy has long been a subject of controversy; realists have suspected her, romanticists pitied her. The evidence is conclusive that from the beginning she egged Arnold on, helped with his plans, served as intermediary, rejoiced in the prospect of financial rewards. Whether her participation in the Arnold plot is to be ascribed to connubial devotion or to avarice Mr. Van Doren does not make plain.

Mr. Van Doren is unsentimental about Peggy Shippen; he is equally unsentimental about Major André. The English raised a memorial to André in Westminster Abbey and forgot him; Americans have never ceased to celebrate his gallantry or to repent his execution. Yet it is inescapably clear that by all the rules of war André deserved his fate. Mr. Van Doren has traced his intrigues—instigated, to be sure, by Clinton—to the very beginning of the treason conspiracy, and has completely dissipated any claims that his defenders present to special consideration.

There was treason after Arnold, as before, for Clinton seems to have learned little from that experience. But it was singularly ineffective. Indeed the futility of British and Loyalist intrigues is one of the impressive and (it may not be too chauvinistic to add) gratifying considerations that emerges from this study. (p. 1)

The story of the British and Loyalist effort to reconcile or to subdue the rebellion is a story of confusion and blundering, and the outburst of Eden, head of the peace mission of 1778, is a poignant one: "It is impossible," he said, "to see even what I have seen of this magnificent country and not to go nearly mad at the long train of misconducts and mischances by which we have lost it."

This material, presented with learning and understanding and wit, is "secret history." Mr. Van Doren does not pretend that it is "the" secret history. There is much more, indeed, that was secret—much in the tortuous diplomacy, much in the conflict in England itself, much, too in the American States that does not emerge in these swift pages. But when the full history of the Revolution comes to be written the evidence which Mr. Van Doren has here presented and the conclusions which he has suggested will contribute to an interesting chapter. (p. 14)

Henry Steele Commager, "New Light on the Revolution," in The New York Times Book Review, *October 12, 1941, pp. 1, 14.*

HOWARD MOSS (essay date 1945)

[*Moss is an American poet, critic, and editor. His sophisticated poetry, derived from everyday experiences, is written in clean, compact lines, and his critical study* The Magic Lantern of Marcel Proust *(1962) is regarded as an important study of that author.*

In the following excerpt, Moss assesses the works collected in Carl Van Doren: Selected by Himself.]

Van Doren's account of his boyhood in Illinois is one of the high spots of the new book [**"Carl Van Doren"**]. He captures the full flavor of nineteenth-century America when "the future was a perpetual adventure and [men] never doubted that it was an endless source of benefits to come. Men had only to work and wait for them." The farmers Mr. Van Doren knew as a child "never heard of any law of diminishing returns." Hope, the place of his birth, literally named for a state of mind symptomatic of the culture, is effectively evoked as a microcosm of America. In a survey of three generations, in which an old America of pioneering and the cultivation of the soil, gave way, via the squire, to the landlord, the capitalist, the telephone and the radio, Van Doren nostalgically conveys the simplicity of life on his father's Indiana farm. From the early description of the organization of a Sunday School, to the final celebration on leaving Hope, the reader moves through a community "almost as independent of the world at large as if this had been the eighteenth century."

Included in the autobiographical selections is Mr. Van Doren's remarkable portrait of Elinor Wylie. This eccentric, mercurial genius of the Twenties comes alive under her biographer's pen. Although it is one of the briefest things in the collection, it has the incisiveness and insight which Mr. Van Doren achieves, in his longer works, only in **"Swift."** It ranks with the latter as Van Doren's most consummate work in drawing a sculptured likeness.

Van Doren is right when he says in his preface that **"Swift"** is his best book. The chronicle of the venomous author of "Gilliver's Travels" avoids both the pitfalls of gossip and the bias of worshipers. Van Doren's Swift is human, and his prose has never been so tightly used, perhaps because he has never before (or since) had such exciting material to deal with. Swift is a genius of stature, and his biographer rises to the occasion. Van Doren manages to throw his searchlight into all the crannies of a great mind wrestling with a complex society. He treats the Stella and Vanessa episodes with candor and insight, and he stays close to his sources, a practice to be commended, especially today when Swift has become the subject of highly fictionalized and questionable interpretations.

Paradoxically, this most American of biographers is less successful with a genius close to home. The three chapters culled from the Franklin biography suffer from being wrenched from their context. Many of the intricacies of the international political and social situation are obscure because the reader is forced to wander through a maze of diplomacy and personality without adequate preparation. Van Doren's cool and impartial eye fixes Franklin in its beam, assuredly, but too often he allows his sources to overtake his interests, and though the flavor of the times comes through magnificently, as a portrait, it lacks the intensity of **"Swift,"** and the sleuthful excitement of **"Secret History."** One could hazard the guess that Van Doren is more sympathetically akin to the tragic complexity of a mind such as Swift's than he is to the eclectic pragmatism of Franklin, in spite of the fact that the latter biography is a Pulitzer Prize winner and Van Doren's most well-known work.

The hitherto unpublished **"Spy to Paris"** is the account of the complicated intrigue of a British spy, Paul Wentworth, who, as a secret agent to Franklin's Paris, succeeds in hastening France's alliance with the United States, the direct reverse of his intended mission, namely to secure peace between the United

States and England. **"Spy to Paris"** is a valuable detective story and an interesting footnote to Colonial diplomatic history.

One can quarrel only with Van Doren's decision to reprint all of **"What Is American Literature?"** He is, primarily, a biographer, not a literary critic. And the question he answers is not the question he puts. The answer emerges as a birdseye view of American writers from the beginning through Sinclair Lewis (with a catalogue of names thrown in at the end for good measure). Van Doren writes history which is not the same as defining what a particular literature is, or does. He rarely discusses works, preferring to follow his true inclination which leads to a discussion of personalities. He discusses trends, too, as though they occurred in a vacuum, so that his criticism arrives at a kind of bastard compromise between the genius theory of literature and a history of ideas. . . .

Three charming sketches of Van Doren's daughters make up the smallest item in the selection. They prove, once again, that their author has an eye for the distinctions of personality, an ear for competent and communicative prose and a mind sensitive to the slightest nuances in human relationships. But Mr. Van Doren can transcend himself when he has material which challenges the limitations of imagination and understanding. The reader will be most rewarded, in this reviewer's opinion, by a careful perusal of the Swift monument and the Elinor Wylie miniature.

Howard Moss, "Aspects, Self-Selected, of the Work of Carl Van Doren," in The New York Times Book Review, *July 15, 1945, p. 5.*

WILLIAM O. DOUGLAS (essay date 1948)

[*An American associate justice of the U.S. Supreme Court and a writer on legal, political, and social issues, Douglas was best known for his vigorous judicial defense of individual rights. He served on the Supreme Court from 1939 to 1975, for thirty-six years a voice of liberalism whose decisions made him a champion to civil libertarians and anathema to conservatives. Douglas was a prolific writer on such topics as foreign affairs, legal analysis, conservation, and travel. Directed to the young,* Points of Rebellion *(1970) recalls America's revolutionary origins and warns that if fundamental political changes are not forthcoming, "the redress, honored in tradition, is . . . revolution." Douglas's concern for the environment is expressed in* The Three Hundred Year War *(1972), a chronicle of the white settlers' three-hundred-year assault on the ecology of North America. In his memoirs,* The Court Years, 1939-1975 *(1980), Douglas related his career on the Supreme Court and summarized his libertarian judicial philosophy. In the following excerpt, Douglas praises* The Great Rehearsal.]

In **"The Great Rehearsal"** Carl Van Doren has in a vivid way related our own problems of 1787 to the world problems of 1948. . . .

Carl Van Doren believes that some day men of good will of many nations will sit down together and write a charter of government for the people, so that they and their sons and grandsons may live under a government of laws. . . . Carl Van Doren knows that peace is not merely the absence of war but the presence of government; peace is to be had only when a system of law is substituted for self-help and jungle warfare.

It is in anticipation of such a convention that he has written **"The Great Rehearsal."** It is the story of the Federal Convention, convened in Philadelphia in May, 1787, to draft a Constitution for a new government—the United States of America. It tells the story not only of what went on at that convention but of what went on when the proposed Constitution was submitted to the states for ratification. Carl Van Doren has told the story in an exciting way. He writes with a sharp pen. And he brings all the characters to life with the warmth, severity, gentleness, arrogance, selfishness or pettiness that each possessed. There is keen discernment in his conception of the book and a brilliance in its execution.

The historical material is familiar to students of government. But most of the other writings in this field have a narrower or different perspective. **"The Great Rehearsal"** is not so much concerned with the history of the export-import clause, the general welfare clause, the definition of treason, the restriction of the jurisdiction of the Supreme Court and the like, as it is with the great forces that brought ultimate agreement on a new charter of government and the almost equal forces that argued and pleaded and worked against it. Here is a story of the interaction of fear, selfishness, practical wisdom and idealism. Here is a stirring tale of the creative power of political genius.

The analogy between the states in this country in 1787 and the nations of the world in 1948 is, of course, not a true one, and Carl Van Doren is the first to concede it. But there is more to the analogy than first meets the eye, as **"The Great Rehearsal"** demonstrates, especially when the nations whose people are not ready for the franchise are put temporarily to one side. The arguments about federation—pro and con—used in 1787 and 1788 have a familiar ring. For they were fashioned from somewhat the same fears, suspicions and jealousies, from the same reluctance to surrender some sovereignty, from the same desire for security, from the same recognition of the blessings of liberty under law, as are the arguments stirred today when any discussion of world government is launched. Here is the meat of the book. (pp. 1-2)

"The Great Rehearsal," like Emery Reves's "The Anatomy of Peace," should be printed in every language. For the problems it poses are for the several nations, not for this country alone. It presents an exact account of the most creative political achievement in the recorded chronicles of government. It will challenge and summon men of good will in every land. And the story it tells cannot help inspiring those architects of government who at some future time assemble to work out the instruments of government which will substitute law for war in the international field. (p. 2)

William O. Douglas, "Our Architects of Government at Work," in New York Herald Tribune Weekly Book Review, *January 18, 1948, pp. 1-2.*

ESTHER FORBES (essay date 1950)

[*Forbes is an American fiction writer and editor whose works include the historical novel* Paradise *(1937) and the biography* Paul Revere and the World He Lived In *(1942). In the following excerpt, Forbes praises Van Doren's biography of Jane Mecom.*]

[Carl Van Doren] wrote **"The Secret History of the American Revolution," "Mutiny in January"** and **"The Great Rehearsal."** Compared to his **"Benjamin Franklin," "The Secret History"** and **"The Mutiny"** are on relatively obscure subjects, but each in its own way builds up the story of America's past. With the Franklin and **"The Great Rehearsal,"** they help us understand the present and give hope for the future. Now we have his final addition to the story **"Jane Mecom."**

It is comparatively easy to learn how the wealthy and famous lived two hundred years ago. Hard enough to know anything of the humble and poor. During his lifetime, Benjamin Franklin was the most celebrated private citizen in the world. There is endless contemporary material about him. As Mr. Van Doren's biography has shown us, he lived his adult life in a blaze of limelight.

No limelight ever shone on his favorite sister, Jane. Her life was as commonplace as her brother's was unique. Perhaps the value of this study is that she was not, in spite of the jacket's claim, "an important woman," but so very unimportant. It is eighteenth century unimportant life that is all but impossible to recover today. . . .

Franklin was continually helping her, not only with gold florins and rent on a Boston house he owned, with ribbons and quilted coats, cotton dresses and small luxuries from Europe that she might sell at a profit to "top" ladies in Boston, but also with endless time, endless devotion and good advice. Jane replies with gratitude. She explains her situation but never complains. There is always a charm to her letters (of course there is to his). The unbreakable spirit of the woman as she writes or as she is written to stands solid as a rock, over which the waves of sorrow may roll, but the rock remains.

Franklin is never more engaging than in his letters to her.

When Franklin died in 1790, the clear mirror in which we have seen Jane reflected breaks. They had written long and loving letters back and forth for sixty-three years. Sometimes he reproved her (she had the "miffy" temper of the Folgers). Sometimes she reproved him. Was he a free thinker? But there has been steadfast devotion between them. It is curious that she, an uneducated woman of very small opportunity writes letters of a distinction that compares very well with his—and he one of the most highly (if informally) educated men of his day. Doubtless this brother and sister were very much alike in temperament and perhaps in ability. Her strength and goodness stand out, although perhaps she was sometimes a little miffy.

Mr. Van Doren has done his work—tragically his last work—and now published posthumously—with all the skill and charm his readers have learned to expect. This unpretentious book is more than a footnote for his big **"Benjamin Franklin."** Mr. Van Doren was too civilized a man to be interested only in the great of his chosen period. Jane Mecom and her humble life, as he knew, was as truly a part of America's past as her celebrated brother. It took a sensitive and kindly man as well as a scholarly one to rescue her from oblivion.

Esther Forbes, "Carl Van Doren's Final Study of Our Revolutionary Past," in New York Herald Tribune Book Review, *October 15, 1950, p. 1.*

JAMES THOMAS FLEXNER (essay date 1980)

[Flexner is an American historian, biographer, and journalist whose most successful work is a four-volume biography of George Washington (1965-1972). This comprehensive biography depicts Washington's fallibility as well as his greatness, and so reluctant was Flexner to give up his involvement with the study of a man he had found "endlessly complicated and various," that he wrote an additional biography of Washington entitled Washington: The Indispensable Man *(1974). Included among Flexner's other numerous historical works is* The Benedict Arnold Case: Benedict Arnold and John Andre *(1962). In his introduction to Van Doren's biography* Benjamin Franklin, *Flexner recalls his personal acquaintance with Van Doren. In the following excerpt, Flexner praises Van Doren's biography of Franklin.]*

Carl, as I came to call [Carl Van Doren], had as much charisma as any man I have ever seen. Charisma can be a dangerous thing. At the age of thirty-one, Van Doren had become head master of a famous girls' school: the Brearley in New York City. How the girls must have worshiped him! He could be, so I was to discover, very overbearing in conversation, but surely his ***Benjamin Franklin*** is one of the most modest of major biographies.

His daughter, Barbara Klaw, tells me that her father, who worked actively on this book for five years, had been preparing it in his mind for some twenty more. So much so that his family teased him for acting like Benjamin Franklin. A sense of close identification on the part of the writer is by no means necessarily an advantage to a biography. Only too often the author kidnaps his subject, making the dead man wear his own face. Van Doren went the opposite way, learning to see and feel like his protagonist.

This transformation did not, despite family teasing, extend beyond Van Doren's relationship with Franklin, as is made eminently clear by a reading of the author's other works. In general, he presents another personality: edgy, acerbic if suavely so, more reflective of the queasy twentieth century than of Franklin's optimistic eighteenth. Van Doren may, indeed, have resented the sway sometimes exerted over him by the benign philosopher. In his own autobiographical writings, he confides that he considered his best book his life of Jonathan Swift—who, as he put it, "aimed at mankind the most venomous arrow that scorn ever loosed." Swift's "story," he stated in explaining his preference, "took the form of a driving tragedy" while "Franklin's was a wide-flowing historical comedy."

Whatever may have been Van Doren's reactions in retrospect, his ability temporarily to make himself over into Franklin was of tremendous advantage to his book. Great biographies can, of course, be duets, the protagonist and the author playing different instruments that sound separately and together to form an artistic whole. But Van Doren's approach was particularly valuable in solving unusual problems presented to him by his subject.

Franklin was himself an extremely able writer, one of America's great authors, and yet he was not a literary man in any ordinary sense. Van Doren, who won his spurs as a literary critic, was altogether capable of presenting Franklin as a creator of prose, but that would have warped his subject out of all recognition. Franklin's writings were always part of his active participation in other aspects of his career: they were at the same time esthetic achievements and historical documentation. This fact has limited the circulation of many of Franklin's best writings. Van Doren could not assume that the reader would already be familiar with their esthetic qualities, as he could assume if he were writing about Swift or Dickens. To make things worse, Franklin's only work that is generally read was in competition with Van Doren's biography, since it was an autobiography. Van Doren's solution to all these difficulties was the daring one of welcoming Franklin as a writer into his own volume. He inserted in his text unabridged quotations running sometimes without break to many hundreds of words. (pp. xxi-xxiii)

Van Doren's quotations serve, without losing other functions, as building blocks, alternating with his own prose to hold up the very structure of the volume.

Without any indication of a break beyond the appearance of a quotation mark, Van Doren will step back from his manuscript and let Franklin take over. Many pages may pass by before the closing quotation mark, when Van Doren re-occupies the stage. In most biographies, this method would shatter artistic unity. For Van Doren the technique works because the interchanging voices, even if pitched somewhat differently, do not create discord with conflicting points of view.

The most conspicuous way in which Van Doren's sections differ from Franklin's lies in the nice distinction he makes between his role as observer and summarizer and his protagonist's role as the actual actor. Franklin's autobiographical writings communicate sights and sounds and often create dramatic scenes, in which the events of one moment progress into those of another. But Van Doren does not attempt to make the reader see or hear, nor does he take advantage of even the fullest documentation to lead the reader into an event, to create a scene. He limits himself to clear and eloquent exposition.

Benjamin Franklin is in the strictest sense a biography, a matter worth commenting on, as the dividing line between biography and history is at best difficult to draw and has been obscured by the academic practice of dealing with an historical figure not as a human being but as a magnet to draw together a certain constellation of exterior fact. Van Doren keeps his protagonist always in the forefront. The author's gift of succinct explanation enables him, if he feels that is necessary, to sketch in rapidly and with effect historical background, but he discovers such a necessity rarely. He prefers to let the conclusion grow from Franklin's experiences, only using his own insight to sharpen with a summary what has already been demonstrated by events.

Although this is a long volume, it is remarkable for brevity, considering how extensively the author quotes from Franklin's writings and that his protagonist became active early and lived to be eighty-four, functioning importantly until the end.

One way Van Doren saved space was by handling with great rapidity the hundreds of people with whom Franklin associated, including those he knew best. Franklin's wife, for example, is given but a few sentences. People he met in the world are almost always identified only by their place in that world and by their connection with Franklin. Thus baldly stated, this might appear a blemish, yet an artist can turn necessary restrictions into advantages. The spotlight being shone so exclusively on Franklin, his character stands out with particular vividness.

The true Franklin as here revealed is, as is often the case with historical characters who have entered the realm of mythology, very different from the man envisioned by popular legend. One reason is that Franklin is commonly characterized as a "philosopher"—Van Doren uses the word endlessly in the eighteenth-century sense—and the word has changed its meaning. Today we think of a philosopher as a withdrawn intellectual surrounded in his hermit's study with tomes that summarize past wisdom, building mental "systems" that aim at rationalizations of the universe or are at least brilliant quibbles. No man was ever less withdrawn from the world than Franklin. He was given to quibbles, but, far from being intellectual exercises, they were aimed at influencing immediate events. Van Doren gives no evidence that Franklin was concerned with building into his creative life the wisdom of the past. (pp. xxiii-xxv)

The other main misconception about Franklin, which goes hand in hand with the misunderstanding about the word philosopher, is the belief that because Franklin spent so many of his middle years as an American representative in Europe, and because he had so many European friends, he became fundamentally Europeanized. He did learn great sophistication in relation to European manners, how to best achieve his ends with an aristocratic statesman or an aristocratic belle, but he was famous in France not for the exquisiteness of the lace at his wrists but for the American fur hat he conspicuously wore at occasions where no one else would dare appear in such outlandish garb. . . .

Van Doren writes that Franklin "would have preferred to keep America independent of the rest of Europe as well as England. But for the sake of the Revolution, he went to France for European aid in getting free of Europe. . . . A cosmopolitan who had most of his dearest friends in England and France and was himself more renowned in Europe than America, he moved boldly to separate the new republic from the parent continent." (pp. xxvi)

Van Doren moves with his protagonist to the very end with an eloquence that is sympathetic, understanding, informative, moving and very real. ***Benjamin Franklin*** is a great biography. (p. xxvii)

James Thomas Flexner, in an introduction to Benjamin Franklin *by Carl Van Doren, Book-of-the-Month Club, Inc., 1980, pp. xxi-xxvii.*

ADDITIONAL BIBLIOGRAPHY

Barr, Springfellow. "Interstate Anarchy, 1787. . . . 1948." *Saturday Review of Literature* XXXI, No. 3 (17 January 1948): 7-8.

Favorable critical review of *The Great Rehearsal.*

Becker, Carl. "The Salty Sense of Benjamin Franklin." *New York Herald Tribune Books* 15, No. 6 (9 October 1938): 1-2

Review of *Benjamin Franklin.* Calling it a "great book," Becker also regards the biography as timely for its illumination of Franklin's reason, common sense, and humanity.

Boyd, Ernest. Review of *American and British Literature since 1890. The Independent* 115, No. 3930 (26 September 1925): 362.

Considers the work, coauthored by Van Doren's brother Mark, important for taking the unpopular position that modern American literature is independent from that of England.

De Voto, Bernard. "A Generation beside the Limpopo." *The Saturday Review of Literature* XIV, No. 22 (26 September 1936): 3-4, 14, 16, 18.

Review of *Three Worlds* that focuses on the contemporary literary figures and movements that Van Doren wrote about during his career as a literary critic and historian. Like other critics of this autobiography, De Voto regards the early section of the work, which recounts the "first world" of Van Doren's youth, as the strongest.

Guerard, Albert. "The Classic Traitor." *The Nation* 153, No. 16 (18 October 1941): 376.

Review of *Secret History of the American Revolution.* Guerard commends the history for its "solid and austere" scholarship in which the author allows the facts, perhaps to an excessive degree, to speak for themselves.

Macy, John. "Our Younger Novelists." *The Nation* 114, No. 2966 (10 May 1922): 571-72.
Discussion of Van Doren's critical approach in *Contemporary American Novelists: 1900-1920*. Macy notes that in addition to studying the genre of the novel, Van Doren examines the personalities and temperaments of the authors discussed and the communities that produced them.

Malone, Dumas. "Building the Nation, American Plan." *The New York Times Book Review* (18 January 1948): 1, 29.
Examination of the strengths and weaknesses of *The Great Rehearsal*. While Malone contends that Van Doren stresses the importance of the conflict over nationalism and localism to the neglect of the economic factors affecting the ratification of the American Constitution, he considers the work as a whole a fresh retelling of familiar events written in a manner that brings both the events and the participants to life.

Mencken, H. L. "The Sough of Words." *The Nation* CXXXIX, No. 3605 (8 August 1934): 165.
High praise for the selections in the anthology *Modern American Prose*.

Trueblood, Charles K. "Criticism or Psychology?" *Dial* LXXI (September 1921): 355-58.
Discussion of *The American Novel* as entertaining criticism. Trueblood does contend, however, that Van Doren concentrates too heavily on individual writers without sufficiently examining the groups with which they were involved, and that he thus fails to illuminate any central questions or make any significant discoveries about the authors he studies.

Van Gelder, Robert. "Carl Van Doren on his 'Work in Progress'." *The New York Times Book Review* (9 March 1941): 2, 22.
Discussion with Van Doren of his research into British espionage during the American revolution. The "work in progress," at this time still in its early stages, was *Secret History of the American Revolution*.

Robert Walser

1878-1956

Swiss novelist, short story writer, essayist, and poet.

Walser is considered one of the most important Swiss authors to have written in German. In his novels and short stories he often portrayed people in socially subordinate positions, such as clerks and servants, praising their simplicity and advocating a rejection of intellectual analysis in favor of a more spontaneous way of life. Franz Kafka was known to have admired Walser's stories, and a great deal of critical attention has been devoted to similarities between their works. However, while Walser's use of the fantastic is certainly reminiscent of Kafka's works, critics distinguish Kafka's dark intensity from Walser's playfulness and gentle irony.

Walser was born in Biel, Switzerland, the seventh of eight children. He was largely self-educated, having left school at fourteen to become an apprentice bank clerk. While still an adolescent, he held odd jobs in numerous cities, but his literary career began in 1898 when several of his poems were published in the Bern newspaper *Der Bund*. Shortly thereafter he began writing his first short prose pieces, many of which featured clerks as underdog characters. These short works are believed by some critics to have been an influence on the early works of Kafka, who was familiar with Walser's stories which appeared in German newspapers and literary journals.

Walser's first collection of stories, *Fritz Kochers Aufsätze,* appeared in 1904 with illustrations by Walser's brother Karl, who was to become one of the outstanding stage designers and book illustrators of his era. From 1905 to 1913 Walser lived with Karl in Berlin, publishing three highly autobiographical novels and numerous stories and holding a series of menial jobs; he typically held a position only long enough to finance another period of writing. Perhaps the most important experience of these years was a period spent in a trade school for servants in preparation for a career as a butler, an episode that provided the basis for his novel *Jakob von Gunten*.

Walser returned to Switzerland in 1913. During his years in Switzerland he was quite impoverished and lived for many years in an unheated attic garret. When not writing, Walser spent his time wandering through the Swiss countryside. A tireless walker, he covered many miles every day, and descriptions of these walks became a recurrent motif in his stories and poems. Throughout his life Walser wrote prolifically—over a thousand prose pieces and poems by some estimates—and published in numerous newspapers and magazines. However, although appreciated by such writers as Robert Musil and Christian Morgenstern, Walser's work was generally neglected by the reading public. He was quite sensitive to criticism and once destroyed two novels after receiving a negative assessment of his work; it is also believed that two other novels were either lost or destroyed. Withdrawing from the world around him and despairing of an audience, he attempted suicide in the late 1920s. In 1929 he was persuaded to enter a psychiatric clinic, where he was diagnosed as schizophrenic. He continued to write until his transfer to a sanatorium in Herisau in 1933, where he claimed he had no right to set himself apart from his fellow patients by continuing to pursue a literary career, saying, "I am not here to write, but to be mad." According to his friend and editor Carl Seelig, he remained energetic and articulate throughout his last years, taking long walks and engaging in informed and outspoken conversation. Walser died on a solitary walk on Christmas day, 1956.

The most discussed element of Walser's work is his prose style and what it suggests about his vision of life. His style is characterized by an avowed intent "to dance with words," an effect he achieved through musical patterns of sound and rhythm and unusual syntactical constructions. Characterized by fanciful descriptions and pervasive irony, Walser's novels and stories are often described as high-spirited parodies and are praised for their "unliterary," spontaneous quality. The minimalist structures of Walser's fictions grow naturally from this prose style: his stories are typically brief and impressionistic, concerned with a single incident or emotion and heavily dependent upon conveying physical reality rather than intellectual concepts, while his novels are similarly episodic and composed largely of brief sections of description or monologue. Walser's emphasis on description of physical reality and the absolute subjectivity of his narratives mirrors his belief that, while there may indeed be meaning and cohesion to life, it is beyond the understanding of any individual, who must of necessity view life as nothing but a series of contiguous moments. For this reason Walser portrayed the provisional nature of all conclusions and particularly rejected the right of any individual to form judgments of others. Behind this position, critics observe a contempt for the pretensions and judgments of society and conclude that it was Walser's ambition, as demonstrated in his fiction, to keep a self-conscious, noncommittal distance from everyday reality and cultivate an acceptance of all things. Accordingly, the narrators of Walser's stories and the heroes of his novels develop toward depersonalization, renouncing self and ambition to submit to the indifference of life. For this reason, his works are dominated by introspection and descriptions of seemingly insignificant aspects of the world around him, for as Idris Parry notes, "where there is no rejection, the smallest thing is important." Notable in this regard is "The Walk," one of Walser's best-known stories and one of the large number of his works concerned with observations made during a walk. In this story the narrator's depictions of the countryside are interspersed with his impressions of people he meets and with several encounters that are more hallucinatory than real. Critics view this not as an actual walk through the physical world, but a journey through memory and imagination, and consider it a perfect encapsulation of Walser's vision of the episodic nature of life.

Given his philosophical position, it is not unusual that Walser's novels and stories are largely autobiographical. As he noted in "Eine Art Erzählung" ("A Kind of Story"): "My prose pieces are, to my mind, nothing more nor less than parts of a long, plotless, realistic story. For me, the sketches I produce now and then are shortish or longish chapters of a novel. The novel I am constantly writing is always the same one, and it might be described as a variously sliced-up or torn-apart book of myself." In addition to his hundreds of autobiographical and impressionistic short fictions, Walser's existing novels are also drawn primarily from his own life; for example, his first novel, *Geschwister Tanner,* depicts the relationships between the children in a family similar to Walser's, while *Der Gehülfe* is based on his experience as a clerk to an amateur inventor. Walser's most highly acclaimed novel, *Jakob von Gunten,* is also his most autobiographical and contains his most explicit condemnation of modern civilization's obsession with intellectual analysis. The novel is in the form of a diary by a student in a school for servants, but the entries follow no discernible chronology and constitute instead a series of Jakob's reflections, observations, and imaginings. The entries often blend the realistic and the fantastic, demonstrating the absurdity of fact and demanding multiple interpretations of any event. The school's only lesson is humility and total subjugation of the self. Reflecting such total self-abnegation, Jakob notes: "I value the way in which I open a door. There is more hidden life in opening a door than in asking a question. . . . The generations of men are losing the joy of life with all their treatises and understandings and knowledge." This philosophy, in addition to comical characters and situations, has led many critics to read the novel as a parody of the overly intellectual German bildungsroman.

During his life Walser's works were generally scorned as trivial, despite praise by such prominent figures as Hermann Hesse, Musil, and Morgenstern, and the little serious attention he did receive was often due to his influence on Kafka. Today, critical interest in Walser's writing is growing rapidly, and he is considered one of Switzerland's major authors, fulfilling the prediction of Max Brod that "the future will see Walser as a true literary representative of our age."

PRINCIPAL WORKS

Fritz Kochers Aufsätze (short stories) 1904
Geschwister Tanner (novel) 1907
Der Gehülfe (novel) 1908
Gedichte (poetry) 1909
Jakob von Gunten (novel) 1909
[*Jakob von Gunten,* 1969]
Aufsätze (essays) 1913
Geschichten (short stories) 1914
Der Spaziergang (short story) 1917
Die Rose (short stories) 1925
Grosse Kleine Welt (short stories) 1937
The Walk, and Other Stories (short stories) 1957
Unbekannte Gedichte (poetry) 1958
Das Gesamtwerk. 12 vols. (novels, short stories, poetry, dramas, and essays) 1966-78
Selected Stories (short stories) 1982

CHRISTOPHER MIDDLETON (essay date 1957)

[Middleton is an English poet and translator of German literature. His poetry is noted for its great technical skill and its assimilation of many of the experimental aspects of Modernism. Although some critics have called his poems unnecessarily obscure, others contend that his method of composition is intended to create a multiplicity of meaning and suggests an adherence to T. S. Eliot's Modernist ethic that "poetry can communicate before it is understood," which supports Middleton's own stated "predilection for stark-ambiguous style in any art." Middleton is also an accomplished and widely praised translator and anthologist of twentieth-century German literature. He has translated many of Walser's works into English and is credited with introducing the Swiss author to English-speaking readers. In the following excerpt, he examines the thematic and stylistic influence of Walser's works on those of Franz Kafka.]

[One] writer upon whose work Walser exercised an actual formative influence is Franz Kafka. It has been known for some time that Kafka used to read passages from ***Jakob von Gunten*** to his friends in Prague before the First World War. But recently there has come to light a letter which Kafka wrote (probably in about 1909) to the director of the insurance firm for which he worked at the time; and this letter shows the extent to which Kafka identified himself during these formative years with the wandering solitary outsiders of Walser's world. Kafka's chief had apparently said to him: "People like yourself, who do nothing at all but dream, run around by the dozen in Walser's stories. I honestly believe that Herr Walser must know you personally!" Of course the two writers never met. But there can be no doubt that Walser's work, particularly the novel ***Jakob von Gunten,*** fascinated Kafka and provided the younger man not only with themes for his own work but also with a style in which to frame his own original vision of things. Walser may indeed be the hitherto undiscovered source of many of Kafka's stylistic techniques. Robert Musil was probably the first person to notice the kinship between these two men, each of whom explored in his own way the abyss of this age, for he reviewed books by them together in an article published in 1914. But even the omniscient Musil could not see how their originally connected destinies were to diverge. Kafka's mature ironic vision of despair is a far cry, of course, from Walser's charmed ironic clownishness. And Kafka's vision of things is far more elaborate (though not therefore more profound) than Walser's. In Walser's vision of things, existence is a fragile kingfisher brilliance spiralling incessantly between heaven and hell. But in Kafka's vision, existence is an impenetrable hellish abyss eclipsing the heaven to which, paradoxically, every inch of the abyss should give access. But even in these divergences there are common grounds between the two visions. What they do share is a firm rejection of convention and of conventional perspectives, and a pronounced heretical tendency to burlesque and parody these perspectives on the slightest provocation, substituting for them a new body of imaginative forms. Both Walser and Kafka are forever overleaping the norm, to focus attention stereoscopically on the minute and ephemeral phenomena in experience which impinge upon the inmost quick of consciousness. In this respect, though his work may lack actual magnitude, Walser is as true an interpreter of this atomic and relativistic age as Kafka was, and his work is perhaps even an indispensable counterpart to Kafka's. Both are inheritors, each in his own way, of Adalbert Stifter's world of minute things and microscopic perceptions. But also they are forerunners of the spectral ''minimalism'' of Samuel Beckett, whose writings surely expose the very core of the modern predicament. (pp. 8-10)

The ironic, parodic and burlesque qualities of Walser's prose are not easy to recreate in translation. He parodies not only the ''heavy'' German style, but also at points his own personal idiom (particularly in his soliloquies). In **"The Walk"**, for example, there are at least three different styles and counter-styles. Often when this happens it is not easy to tell which is the voice and which the echo, until one has recognized the spirit of play in which Walser goes to work. It is this delicate playfulness which makes him a stylist of the first order, beside whom many of his contemporaries may seem little short of elephantine. His step is light with the breathless levity of the acrobat who walks above the heads of the crowd in the knowledge that his life and all life hangs by a thread. (pp. 10-11)

Christopher Middleton, in an introduction to The Walk, and Other Stories *by Robert Walser, translated by Christopher Middleton, John Calder, 1957, pp. 7-11.*

CHRISTOPHER MIDDLETON (essay date 1958)

[*In the following excerpt, originally published in* Revue des langues vivantes *in 1958, Middleton examines the style, themes, and techniques of Walser's fiction.*]

Critics are seldom aware of the unconscious criteria which motivate their judgments. Were they quicker to grapple with these criteria, the history of critical opinion might be less marked by errors of omission. For some reason modern opinion seems to be drawn to writing which is charged pre-eminently with ideas. A corollary of this is the presence in some post-analytical criticism of an interest in ideas about literature, its peculiar logic, or in approaches to literature, which threatens to eclipse genuine interest in the books themselves. But even where a certain rarefaction of this kind is not in evidence, it is the socratic imagination which nowadays electrifies critics. They require authors to question, even to illuminate, the whole structure of experience; and their statements imply that this cannot be done by any intelligence which is not 'logomorphic' and in which ideas do not flourish. The great socratic novelists of the past half-century have indeed prompted critics to take this attitude. Plunged in the prolix forests of meaning which their prose embodies, the critics have hardly noticed other figures, marginal figures who have sought to do other things with words, who have worked mostly in the dark, receiving for their pains, like the little man in Kafka's smallest fable, a resounding blow on the head. Robert Walser is one of these figures. He seems to be a stranger to the realm of ideas. . . . Walser's writings do not constitute, like the novels of Broch, Mann and Musil, watersheds of the modern intellect. He does not bring us intellect, nor massive volumes of ideas at all. He brings a new world of sensibility, an unmediated vision of experience, an image of reality seen without the interference of a concept. (pp. 95-6)

Walser's first novel, ***Geschwister Tanner,*** was written in three to four weeks in Berlin. . . . The experience of the protagonist, Simon Tanner, is construed episodically. And one can count seven episodes, each of which serves to unsheathe a little more of Simon's temperament. For Simon is, like Dedalus, Malte, Meaulnes and Törless, the modern fictional self-analyst, the seeker of his true self. He is also the spokesman of his family, a family of wistful insubordinates in revolt against the turgid society in which they are implicated. Simon is the underdog, the *eiron* of Greek comedy. He is the ironic outsider, who wants not insulation from raw existence but exposure to it. . . . But neither he nor his brother Kaspar, a painter, nor his sister Hedwig are heroic in stature. On the contrary, they are humble, unassuming people, fugitives not aggressors, at sea in a negative world, phenotypes of a dissolving society. Neither demons against God, nor minds against nature, nor seekers of an earthly paradise, they are airy aliens . . . in a realm of gravity. . . . (p. 100)

The episodic structure does not display the kind of mounting and declining tensions of a story in traditional canon. The secret here is that, given such a protagonist as Simon, the reader simply cannot anticipate what is likely to happen next. And this suspense of unknowing is sustained throughout the seven episodes: despite the fact that the episodic structure, being an open, porous structure, involves digressions, monologues and apparent irrelevancies, and despite the fact that the things that happen to Simon are mostly commonplace. He works in a bookshop; he lives with his brother for free in the house of a friendly lady, Klara Agappaia, whose formidable husband sometimes fires a pistol into the night, because he likes the sharp sound it makes, against the emptiness; he visits his brother, then his sister, in the country; he works as a servant for a lady in the city whose small son is a cripple; he dreams of Paris; he befriends a male nurse; he eats in a restaurant for workingmen; and so on. But it is just this immersion in the minimal and Simon's interpretation of the minimal that occasion 'das Sehen der Welt als eines immerwährenden Wunders' ['a vision of the world as one of the everlasting wonders']. This unique personalisation of the given reality, here as in the other two novels, makes Walser's prose existential in a way which was later to attract Franz Kafka's attention. (pp. 100-01)

It is first and last Walser's language, embodying as it does his peculiar sense of existence as rhythm, which gives ***Geschwister Tanner*** its specific energy. His language, too, estranges its world, as far as the wistful insubordinacy of its characters is concerned, from the world of the stock lyrical Bohemian. The earlier collection of short prose pieces, ***Fritz Kochers Aufsätze,*** had explored the world of the insubordinate: the schoolboy and the 'Kommis'. The language of ***Fritz Kochers Aufsätze*** delights with its naïveté, its capricious pleasure in the insignificant, its miniaturistic mannerism. But ***Geschwister Tanner*** shows for the first time a stylistic mode which is later to dominate Walser's writings: a style in which ethereal and graphic statements mix and alternate in a spirit of play. This is found . . . , for example, in the account of Simon's nocturnal walk . . . , with its dovetailing of graphic detail and the alternations of rhythm which register both Simon's changing moods and his changing pace. It is as if improvised, but unerring in its emotional precision: the language not of reflective description but of stereoscopic presentation. (p. 101)

Now Walser's next novel, ***Der Gehülfe,*** does approach fiction proper. But if it can be said that, of the three novels, ***Der Gehülfe*** alone does not appear to break with the common epic canon, even here the finite and typical qualities of the given situation coincide at points, to disclose by nuance the symbolic character of this situation. Rather than question Walser's capacity for writing fiction proper, one should therefore observe how he transforms the common features of the genre and extends its potential range of statement. (p. 102)

The protagonist Joseph Marti is again the *eiron,* the critical underdog, but he is now lodged in a bourgeois attic. The novel is based on Walser's months as a clerk to the amateur inventor of Wädenswil; and the theme is the division against itself of a provincial household, induced by the inventor's inordinate capacity for believing the lies he tells himself about himself. Characters are now seen less as objects than as autonomous subjects. Foremost there is the inventor himself, Tobler, whose ungovernedness, in magnanimity or wrath, plunges his house into discord and petty friction. And there is his wife, ostensibly a sensitive woman, whose frustration finds a malignant form in her agonizing of her younger and nervously enuretic daughter, Silvi. Both characters are 'alive', because complex: they are moreover complex because the moral vision embodied in the narrative is complex, caustic and at once compassionate, obtained from a position of unshakeable and therefore totally unassuming moral strength. Then there are the details of the fabric: the railway official's wife who is so proud of her four words of French . . . ; the barrenness of small beer-gardens; the glass ball weighing between eighty and ninety pounds, which Joseph has to carry into the garden when the sun shines and into the house when the rain falls (Tobler magnificently requires it so); and the mood-suffused images of lake and lakeside, reflecting the turning of the year, an inviolable world on the margins of the abject human shallows. Tobler's inventions are all the more vacuously grotesque for being juxtaposed to this inviolable world; for example the slot-machine for cartridges with an interior turntable displaying a fresh advertisement each time the lever is pulled, or the clock with wings that shoot out sideways displaying, again, advertisements. Here too Walser uses graphic imagery to express, by nuance, discreet states of mind, the ego's underworlds. . . . [At] least one instance is found where Walser introduces into a situation, by means of imagery alone, a Kafkaesque dimension of dramatic pregnancy. Thus Joseph's submerged attraction to Tobler's wife is implied when, having just by accident glimpsed her in négligé through the open door of her room, he ascends to the attic to find his attention inexplicably riveted by Tobler's knee-boots. . . . (pp. 102-03)

The symbolic pregnancy of Joseph's situation as a whole becomes evident only towards the end of the book, with his apparently casual recognition that all that has come to pass in the 'Villa zum Abendstern' is 'ein Bild des zwanzigsten Jahrhunderts' ['a portrait of the twentieth century']. . . . This nuance puts a new shape on every issue involved. One realises that the limiting of the perspective to Joseph's personal vision, as far as the narrative is concerned, and the limiting of the duration and location of the events thus narrated, has resulted in just such a synoptic image of the given time in the given place; and that this synoptic image has been given inevitability and conclusiveness by the simplicity of phrase, closeness of texture, and transparent plasticity of Walser's language. This tendency to structural concentration distinguishes ***Der Gehülfe*** from ***Geschwister Tanner.*** It distinguishes it also from the expansive naturalism of Thomas Mann's *Buddenbrooks* and from the mawkish preciosity of Hermann Hesse's roughly contemporary *Peter Camenzind*. . . . At the end of ***Der Gehülfe,*** Joseph Marti has to turn his back on a world in which, as an outsider perforce, he had hoped to find at last the centre of a clear life, a focus of affection. . . . His progressive disillusionment, of which the novel is a statement, was to have a decisive effect on Walser's narrative technique. In ***Jakob von Gunten,*** he abandons the quasi-fictive third person narrative, and speaks in the first person singular through the persona of his eponymous hero. The autonomy of his eccentric vision of things is made by this complete. (pp. 103-04)

Jakob's experience in the enigmatic Institut Benjamenta, of which his journal tells, is presented as being pluri-significant. Jakob himself is not sure why he is there, nor what the institute is. And the presentation of events in the immediate language of the journal does not allow the reader to know any more than the baffled Jakob himself. Jakob is once more the *eiron,* the insubordinate underdog. But the insubordinacy of this particular subordinate marks an extreme elaboration of the smaller schoolboy world of Fritz Kocher. . . . [Here] Walser has entered the climate of the absurd, in which no single event has a single meaning, and in which, as is evinced from Kafka's subsequent exploration of the absurd, no degree of acumen on the part of the protagonist can clarify the opacity of immediate experience. ***Jakob von Gunten*** is, indeed, not the subjective construct of a kind of dwarf-complex. . . . But this does not mean that Walser here indulges in evasive and implausible symbolism. . . . On the contrary, there is no slipping the yoke of fact, however pluri-significant the facts may be. ***Jakob von Gunten*** is the one book by Walser which we know Kafka to have read and admired. And it is plainly Walser's direct vision of the absurdity of fact which attracted Kafka, as well as his discrimination of the symbolic pregnancy of commonplace events by what astronomers call 'averted vision'—vision by which faint stars can sometimes be seen 'not by looking straight at them but by catching the light in the corner of the eye'. As examples of the direct vision of the absurdity of fact (showing Walser's technique of isolating and scrutinizing detail), there is the image of the schoolmaster, Herr Wälchli, in the common-room chair, fast asleep, but still smoking his pipe . . . ; or there are the many occasions on which, after interviews with the principal, Herr Benjamenta, Jakob flies from the room to glue his ear to the keyhole of Benjamenta's door. (pp. 104-05)

Such isolation of detail can produce surpassing clownery, and also grotesque verbal comedy. . . . (p. 105)

The technique of averted vision can hardly be shown by citing specific examples, though there are some: particular moments, as when Jakob sees the (erotic) sword and helmet over the doorway to the inaccessible 'inner chambers' of the institute . . . , or the initiation scene . . . with its Kafkaesque interlacing of the traumatic and the actual, of comedy and earnest. But here it is more a question of the unseizable meaning of all that happens in the given context, and also of a complex cumulative effect, which may involve a deliberate comic anticlimax. For instance, Jakob supposes that the 'inner chambers' lead into a world of romance: he expects to find a spiral staircase, a chapel, a park, three old ladies, candles ablaze, a princess and (strange to say) an Englishman. But in fact he only finds a bowl of goldfish. The averted vision, suggesting symbolic pregnancy (or 'faint stars') of meaning, consists here in Jakob's having already been initiated, by a dream, before the ostensible initiation begins. He knows the mysteries to exist, so the bowl of goldfish tells us, in his mind alone. Hence also the mysteries are never 'explained'. But they are embodied in Jakob's experience as this unfolds in the journal: the meaning is there, but always just out of reach.

It follows that, while Jakob's progress in self-knowledge should lead him towards a knowledge of what the institute is, the climate of the absurd only increases the pluri-significance of all things. One by one, Jakob discards his illusions: but this only makes him more and more poignantly aware of the polarity, or plurality of his own nature. . . . The climax of this polarity, or plurality, in all things comes when Herr Benjamenta tries to strangle Jakob . . . , though a moment before he had suddenly become so friendly. And in such a climate it is not surprising to find Jakob indulging in megalomaniacal fantasies and simultaneously recognizing that he is the lowliest of creatures: his surname may indeed even be a pun, arrived at by his definition of his status at the institute, where he starts, as he says, 'von unten, von ganz unten' ['from below, from far below']. . . . So at points Jakob may appear as a caricature of pride, as contrasted with his friend Kraus, who is the perfect servant, while at other points Jakob is plainly the Parzifal, whose task it is to penetrate the pluri-significant absurdity of fact and to arrive at a true vision of the meaning of his experience. And this is what the end of the book promises, for here Herr Benjamenta, the prisoner of the absurd, who exists in a state of disillusionment and despair . . . , implores Jakob to become his companion, so that the balance of his nature may be restored, and so that they may abandon the institute together. . . . At this point we are on the equator of Walser's world. There is much here of Kafka's double vision of wonder and despair, but without Kafka's inscrutable logic of doubt. It is the point at which the candid innocent, the Holy Fool, and the dark inquisitor of doubt conjoin in the exuberant visionary of joy. And this point is not reached by a simplification of experience, for the very burden of ***Jakob von Gunten*** is that no single interpretation of things is the right one. It is reached by Walser's uncanny power of seeing things without the interference of a limiting concept. And this, perhaps one of the flukes which plot the unerring course of genius, gave him to write what seems to be the first novel of the century to explore existentially the domain of the absurd. Moreover he created for this domain a style which was later, through the medium of Kafka, to become fertile ground for future writers: a style in which the pluri-significance of experience is recreated without becoming implausible, a level-minded style, a style in which the variability of semantic contour does not involve diminishment of graphic verve, but rather extends graphic verve towards the indefinable frontiers of symbolism. These are some of the qualities of ***Jakob von Gunten*** which may have attracted Kafka. It might be added that Kafka must also have found here, besides the grotesque (often Chaplin-esque) comedy so dear to his imagination, an inclusive and autonomous first person singular world akin to that which was later to provide the basis of his own mono-perspectivist narratives. (pp. 106-08)

Cover of the first edition of Jakob von Gunten, *designed by Walser's brother Karl.*

This indelible vision of an absolute purity in creation underlies the stylistic peculiarities of many of Walser's shorter prose writings. Given this vision, any form of representationalism *per se* is out of order: for language is not meant to reproduce the actual. So when Walser is found masquerading, as he frequently does, as a 'Berichterstatter' ['reporter'], this must be understood as one of his various ironies. . . . The persona of the 'Berichterstatter' in ***Der Spaziergang,*** for example, allows his imagination just that freedom of focus that it requires in order to create, out of the most quotidian encounters with beings and things, unique images of personal reality, hilarious or horrifying, but always authentic. And this freedom of imagination does not mean that phantasmata flood the field of expression. Phantasmata, like the ogre Tomzack in ***Der Spaziergang,*** are rare in his work; and even when they do occur they lie within the bounds of possible experience. . . . And if the sphere of objective reference in his work is limited, it is limited to minimal and unobtrusive phenomena which by virtue of their unobtrusiveness impinge upon the inmost quick of consciousness. Such a limitation is the ultimate test of an artist's skill, for the unique personal vision thus created is not to be splintered or dulled by the interference of a spurious subjectivity, and is not to be flattened by any form of rhetoric. (pp. 109-10)

[To] appreciate his work, especially the shorter prose pieces, one must discard prejudices against mannerism. I suggested earlier that the style which dominates his writings is one in which graphic and ethereal statements mix and alternate in a spirit of play. This produces the musical lucidity of his prose, with its sudden swirls of irony and comedy. There is, too, a capricious lusoriness in much of his work, with multiple verbal games, ironic inflections transfiguring the apparently commonplace, packs of adjectives chasing disproportionate nouns, and lightning arabesque flights off at a tangent. The vague term 'Jugendstil' has sometimes been used thus to chasten such prose, but the term is too vague to be just. What is hard to explain, on the other hand, is the lapse into 'Kitsch', the stylistic enervation which affects some of his work during the Biel period (1913-1920). . . . Clichés culled during random reading in popular literature are no longer transfigured by contact with his imagination: they are echoed. Likewise one can find here echoes of phrases, rhythms and images he had earlier coined himself. There comes also in ***Seeland*** an automatic tabulation of impressions without original imprint. This is just the opposite of the kind of parodic tabulation found in the story **'Tobold'**, in which one sentence covers three pages and finally, by the concluding parodic curve it receives, magnificently cancels itself out. . . . (pp. 110-11)

When Walser's style is found at its usual intensity, its formations evade easy definition. The contrast with Kafka may offer a key, for, if Kafka's prose has a glacial purity, Walser's is anything but glacial. There come hypotactical constructions which scrutinize and interpret a subject simulataneously, viewing this subject in as great variety of perspectives and with as much simultaneity as normal syntax will allow, but with a temperamental airiness that distinguishes such constructions from those produced by the tight, logical hypotaxis that Kafka used. There is a continual alternation of temperature, because there is a continual play of temperament. Thus there is also a delight in the sheer sounds of words arranged in musical patterns . . . or delight in rhythmical patterns. . . . Such patterns of sound and rhythm can make for statements which are volatile in the extreme checked by swift ironic interventions which mark, even in the middle of a sentence, a switch in perspective, to multiply the precise impressions that such synergies of sound and sense create. There comes, too, sustained interplay between the narrative . . . , the narrator and the likely responses of the reader. This may sound reminiscent of Jean Paul, for there is no question here of the narrator being unobtrusive. But there is a difference. In Walser the narrator (and sometimes the reader also) is drawn into the vortex of the narrative. The 'aside' becomes a structural element within the whole created statement and is assimilated into the irony in which the whole statement is framed. (pp. 111-12)

This form of arabesque discourse can explore dimensions of verbal comedy which are inaccessible to any prose of a representational nature. Often what is said may be out of all proportion to what it is said about, but in such a way that the statement creates its own proportions, its own world of imaginative forms. One of these forms in Walser is caricature. It is not the malicious caricature of the deceived imagination. It is the caricature of the imagination that grasps intrepidly the nettle of the absurd, having seen through the complacencies of the self-evident. Here is Professor Meili in ***Der Spaziergang***, complete with unbendable scientific walking-stick. . . . The oblique scrutiny of isolated detail which results in caricature may also be carried one step further, to become hallucination, but hallucination in the broad day of vulgar pun. . . . (pp. 112-13)

A kind of inverted form of caricature as word-play is the deliberate ironic elaboration of the obvious. (p. 113)

When caricature informs the language itself the result is, of course, parody. Many of the stylistic peculiarities mentioned so far enter the kind of high-spirited parody in which Walser is so adroit. . . . The piece entitled **'Dorfgeschichte'**, which also belongs among the later writings, shows again what new and vivid unities can result from the technique of parodic caricature when this is conjoined with the technique of the interrupted arabesque. And at this point it would seem that we arrive in the sphere of quite different forms of narrative, where such pieces as **'Die kleine Berlinerin'** . . . and **'Brentano'** . . . transcend dream-like discontinuity and display the full stereoscopic and coherent vision of things, with its richness of colour and roundedness of contour. At this point it is but one step from the parody of illusion-puncturing ridicule to the anti-parodic creation of a positive sphere of original imaginative discourse, free as air, and filled with vivid personal truth.

The limited scope of this paper prohibits any discussion of affinities between aspects of Walser's work and other modern developments, Dada for instance, in some of the later writings, though hardly Expressionism. An affinity with the painters Klee, Chagall and Kandinsky might also be found. But whatever affinities exist, they seem at length accidental. Central to Walser's work is an independence from influences, movements and vogues, an insulation which reflects his outstanding originality of character, and paradoxically, his openness of character. 'I raise my hat to this age', he wrote, 'but not too high'. . . . This remoteness from contemporary currents is eminently Swiss. But there is something here which does not accord with prevalent notions about Swiss literature. . . . Where is the political dimension, the humanitarian resolve, the Republican sense of structure? It could be answered that as a spokesman of the lowly commons (for Walser often sees himself as such) this wholly authentic poet ridicules the denizens of the bourgeois world only when their absurd unwitting postures and, linguistically, their platitudes, put all authenticity in question. 'Fraud', as Kierkegaard remarked in another context, 'is not tolerated in the world of the spirit'. But, more generally, the political dimension in the Swiss intellectual tradition obtrudes to us or to German readers only because we do not recognize its role in the structure of Swiss civilization. In this civilization, politics enter the household at every aperture, even the poet's household if he has one. This means that in Switzerland the political dimension is not felt to obtrude. It is assimilated as a structural element in the common life, and consequently the focus of the common life, and of literature, is not politics at all, but something of which politics is but one among many other manifestations, namely the small circle of individuals united by a common responsibility. And into this small and indissoluble circle, with its unlimited elasticity, its unlimited capacity for assimilating the incongruous, Walser fits as the *genius loci* itself. He may be a poltergeist in the household of 'Helvetia Mediatrix', but he is a vital member of the vital group, whose knowledge of his country and of his countrymen is as rich as his love for them, despite the grave formalism which can so heavily overlay their vitality. He is, in fact, a poet in whom the Swiss *anima* assumes a real, existent form. (pp. 115-16)

Perhaps another objection may be raised. In an age when literature, as Walser himself said in later years, has become intellectually imperialistic . . . , does not the absence from his work of a strictly socratic or discursive element not only reflect his lack of 'higher education', or of all that 'Bildung' implies, but also stigmatize him as a child of the provinces, clownishly out of step with the times. This second objection can only arise if Walser's work is misconstrued. Because he is gay, critics who care only to confront works whose discursiveness springs from profound *ennui* and melancholy should not call him irresponsible; for his gaity is a conquest of the vacuum, a conquest which could not have been made were not the healing of doubt the sign that doubt has been understood. Because he is a miniaturist, critics who laud Leviathan should not call him trivial; for that would be to commit the old error . . . of allowing ideas of mass to interfere with awareness of value. . . . But this second objection also may spring from erroneous notions about the tenor of Swiss literature and thought. One of the hallmarks of Swiss intellectual life and of Swiss literature in the German language is their recurrent contrariness to simultaneous German developments. Often the great figures are diametrically opposed to their great German contemporaries. . . . In our day, Walser, the rejected, daring, capricious Ariel of modern German prose stands in just such a contrary relation to his monumentally informed and systematic contemporaries. Once more the unconscious motives governing tradition have asserted themselves, though few heard Walser play the tune of their catch, or knew his vision of the world as a continual wonder. (pp. 116-17)

Christopher Middleton, "The Picture of Nobody: Some Remarks on Robert Walser," in his Bolshevism in Art and Other Expository Writings, *Carcanet New Press, 1978, pp. 95-122.**

GEORGE C. AVERY (essay date 1963)

[Avery is a professor of German who has written several works on German literature. In the following excerpt, he discusses Walser's experimentation with a wide variety of forms, which the critic views as a disavowal of literary convention and an attempt to both redefine literature and define the role of an artist isolated from both his society and the traditions of art.]

Distrustful, perhaps fearful of fame, jealously insistent on his prerogative of freedom of movement and freedom of spirit, Walser was outwardly disinterested—and artistically too uncompromising—to attempt to secure his own literary fortunes. Throughout his career he refused to align himself with a school or literary movement. If we approach his works with the traditional criteria of literary criticism in mind, we will be disappointed with the meager results of our efforts. The regrettable consequence of Walser's stubbornness (and the reliance of most criticism on traditional criteria) has been to exclude Walser from even the parenthetical recognition granted other practitioners of short prose, such as Peter Altenberg and Alfred Polgar. This is so despite respectable, if infrequent, advocacy in his behalf.

Walser was discovered for Germany by Franz Blei; Hermann Hesse admired him and perhaps adopted some of his ideas. The first of these early eulogists to touch the essential Walser, however, was Christian Morgenstern. Morgenstern became acquainted with Walser's writing while engaged as a reader for Bruno Cassirer in Berlin. In a letter to Cassirer, written in 1907 in praise of Walser's first novel, he appended what he termed an "aphorism" on Walser from his journal. The aphorism is a perspicacious penetration of the insularity of Walser's style. Morgenstern commented upon Walser's loquaciousness, the prominence of freedom and the primacy of the spirit in his vision of the world, his childishness, and the aimlessness of his peripatetic nature—all critical issues in Walser.

Another early admirer of Walser was Franz Kafka. Exactly when Kafka first read Walser has not been ascertained, but the indications are that the impression made by Walser's last published novel, ***Jakob von Gunten***—the thematic and stylistic influence of which can be seen as late as *Das Schloss*—preceded Kafka's enthusiastic reading of Walser's short prose pieces. (pp. 181-82)

Most recently, critical praise for Walser has come from Max Brod. In a section of his *Streitbares Leben*, he describes the editorial support he gave Walser early in his career and then again in the twenties. Brod also quotes from an analysis of Walser's style written in 1912, in which Brod discerns three levels of discourse in Walser's prose. Brod deplores the current neglect of Walser and expresses his conviction that the future will see Walser as a true literary representative of our age.

Yet Walser's own attitude toward literature, as well as his concept of the literary artist, throughout thirty-odd years of writing remains paradoxical and elusive, determinedly aliterary while obsessed with the seemingly trivial. This attitude has analogies in the themes and style found in Walser, quite exclusive of biographical corroboration. . . .

Of much greater moment is Walser's treatment of his heroes in the three extant novels. The three youthful heroes all exhibit a pronounced poetic gift, but in their development toward depersonalization—a feature that might be viewed as an anticipation of programmatic expressionism if it were not so intimate a part of Walser's world view—this gift is suppressed or ironically disregarded. The lyric quality of the novels precludes the possibility of mistaking this antiliterary treatment of the heroes as being influenced by naturalism. Walser had, in fact, set out on a road which led him to question the modes of literature, as did Hofmannsthal and Kafka.

In his prose pieces Walser was prone to speak of himself not as a writer, but as a student, a worker, a walker, or an employee. He disguised and transformed his person behind masks bearing names such as Oscar, Tobold, Peter, Wenzel, Titus, "Das Kind," Parzifal, Erich, Wladimir, Manuel, Theodorli, Fridolin, Kurt, Hans, "Der Affe" ["the Monkey"], or even as a figure called *das seltsame Mädchen*. (p. 183)

Walser's dissociation from the mold of the conventional writer [is] characterized by a typical simultaneity of irony and earnestness. Coupled with this is the reiterated stress in Walser's prose on the improvisatory, the occasional. Content is decidedly attenuated, making it subservient to elements of form, sentence rhythm, and the manipulation of word and metaphor. (p. 184)

The disavowal of literary convention can take a variety of forms in Walser. He is not averse to repudiating the effect of his style by letting it deteriorate into mannerism. He is particularly prone to employ interruptions. He interrupts to assure the reader that the characters are of his own invention, to insist on the veracity of what is being reported, or to express concern that his language is not equal to the demands of the story. He may alternately signify blissful pride at the turn a story has taken or satisfaction at the elegant disposal of a question of delicacy. He is merely stressing the insignificance of plot when he offers a mock presentation of his helplessness when confronted by the inexorability of plot. (pp. 184-85)

[A] masterful, yet forever critical, treatment of figurative language summons up a richness based on the juxtapositions within the sentences of different levels of cognition.

The few disconnected stylistic features noted here, it must be remembered, are but one facet of a more complex literary personality. . . .

Robert Walser, drawn by his brother Karl, circa 1910.

Walser used himself as subject matter for an inordinate number of his prose pieces. Among them are the names and titles listed above and referred to as masks. Admittedly, the earlier ones are romantic masks; that is, their primary purpose is the imaginative re-creation of either an epoch or developmental stage from remembered experience. Thus Peter is the lonely, nascent poet who, reading Wedekind and Verlaine, is filled with dreams of greatness and is engulfed in an indefinable longing, but whose only talent is the shedding of tears. Peter's poems are later published under the name of Oscar—who at one time is described as the representative of his age, leading a life of "Gewinnsüchtigkeiten und Schlechtigkeiten" ["greed and depravity"], and at another is himself the germinal poet, isolated entirely by his vision, struggling to find a form for the poetry that seeks release from within. (p. 185)

The later masks found in ***Die Rose*** and ***Unveröffentliche Prosa*** are among Walser's most challenging and most problematic writing. They clearly relate Walser to the movement in modern German writing, particularly in poetry, to find new means of expression by reducing traditional forms or by reinvigorating semiliterary forms. Walser's late masks represent a unique and stylistically daring experiment to fuse levels of insight into an alogical, emotional entity, where the apparently accidental or incidental is ranged around a skeletal or dismembered plot. Viewed ontologically, they are devices for the primary spiritual tension in Walser, the polarity of freedom and self-imposed limitation. As such, they are the ultimate stylistic consequences of Walser's obsession with the insignificant and the trivial.

Through frequent use of ellipses, lacunae, and hiatus, Walser is able to suggest an enclosed space within which an emotional or spiritual situation is variously pursued and analyzed. Employing a sophistication of method he had developed in his novel ***Jakob von Gunten,*** Walser opens these late masks with an epigrammatic statement or aperçu and then applies a circular discursiveness that emits unexpected and improbable shafts of light. One source of such illumination is the keen, analytical mind of an author who never presumes to take any utterance of language for granted; another is his desire to attain a fusion of relationships, psychological awareness, emotional nuances, and ambiguities into a whole. And because such pieces so often lack an ending, the knowledge gained in their exposition often as not verges on slipping back tracelessly into its source, namely the author, who professed to be merely a chronicler, an unprepossessing reporter or letter writer.

Intermittently, Walser offers suggestions—rarely devoid of irony—to proceed with caution in what initially appears to be aimless, or worse—frivolous, improvisation. (p. 186)

Thus it seems that Walser's experimentation with a wide variety of forms was more than an attempt to accommodate his own talents; it was part of the modern poet's obsession with form as one aspect of an attempted redefinition of literature. In this connection, the attraction the fairy tale had for Walser is understandable. By tradition it is a simple, unpretentious form. Its frequent use of stock phrases permitted Walser—principally in fairy-tale-like humoresques—to employ a favored device of anaphoric variation. If he chose a traditional fairy tale, it could serve as a *pied-à-terre* for his own thematic or stylistic improvisations. Further, the fairy tale presented a closed form with an inherent tendency to reduction and concentration. The fact that no motivation was necessary allowed for a parabolic increment. But perhaps most important from our vantage point is the fact that the fairy tale had lost currency as a bona fide literary form.

Walser made rather extensive use of the fairy tale, often modifying it to suit his purpose. One interesting modification, from the point of view of literary history, is seen in his two anti-*Märchen* in the volume ***Geschichten.*** The first, **"Das Genie,"** is a grotesque about a starving, freezing individual who, bored and lonely after having destroyed the world, recreates it with a race of men that sees in him the embodiment of humanity's genius, but who is still out of sorts and disconsolate. . . . The second, **"Welt,"** is a vision, in ironic terms, of God's extinction of a perverse, chaotic, and purposeless world, the unrelenting finality of which is unparalleled before Kafka. (pp. 187-88)

Finally, **"Das Ende der Welt,"** which was written approximately in mid-career . . . , deserves mention. It tells of a poor, homeless orphan who sets out to walk to the end of the world. The single-minded search lasts for more than sixteen years. The child grows big and strong as she passes by mankind and events in the world, through night and day, beneath sun and moon, always trying to imagine what the end of the world must be like. Almost at the end of her strength, she asks a farmer for directions and is told that the end of the world is only half an hour's walk farther. A farm bearing the name, "End of the World," paradisiac in its harmony of tranquil growth and beauty, is the goal of the unwitting child. She is taken in, promises to serve, and never runs away again, for she is now at home.

This little story presents, in antithetical fashion, the barrenness of isolation and the bounty of acceptance. Behind the irony of the double pun in the title lies the purity of a faith which regards **"Das Ende der Welt"** as the token of a positive promise. It is relevant to note that Walser has used the specific framework of a walk—a journey which initially seems futile or of infinite duration—to depict a visionary resolution for his own metaphysical situation of homelessness. At the same time, he gives us a hint of the implications not only of this fairy-tale homecoming, but of the myriad pieces he has devoted to descriptions of walks.

Such descriptions are the form Walser found most congenial; they make up the largest single group in his *oeuvre*. They begin to take on a large role in his output only after his return to Switzerland in 1913, following seven years spent in Berlin. In point of fact, Walser's novels had anticipated two related elements found in the best of the walks: the compelling poetry of decribed motion and a dynamic use of abstractions as the imaginative bases for these walks.

The most typical, the longest, and the most masterful of these wanderings is **"Der Spaziergang."** It describes a day's walk through a city and its environs. A large number of soliloquizing speeches by the narrator serve as markers across which are strewn the threads of the narrative. The longest of these speeches is an eight-page *apologia pro vita sua* as wanderer-artist. . . . While it, as well as the other monologues, is characterized by mercurial transitions and ironic verbal funambulism, the speech is intimately related to Walser's concept of the poet at this time in his career. This can be seen in the verbal and intellectual symmetry of the speech. It progresses from the diurnal needs, satisfied by the walks, to the spiritual and subjective needs, dictated by a view of reality that finds sustenance and unity only outside civilization.

This viewpoint finds support in the climactic scene, after the narrator has crossed the railroad tracks. Here the walk is suddenly perceived as more beautiful than ever; nature loses whatever reality it had had and is dissolved in song. Images of angels appear and Jesus descends onto the street as all objects are transformed into "soul." Suffering and evil vanish. The narrator substitutes the image in his mind's eye for the visual image and creates an imagined nature. . . . (pp.188-89)

This momentary vision is unique among Walser's works. It points to a relationship in his poetic vocabulary between the indefinite wandering common to both **"Das Ende der Welt"** and **"Der Spaziergang."** The insight gained . . . intimates that for Walser there was a basic relationship between the metaphor of motion and the achievement of grace in the fairy tale.

In **"Der Spaziergang"** and in the other "walks" published together with it, a particular nature gives way to a generalized one, facilitating reflection or insight on questions of being. The seemingly pointless listing of things—a device Walser has used on occasion with considerable ironic effect—reveals itself now as the concretization of the unobtrusive in reality. For to know creation is to know the world. . . . By diverting attention from nature as plot to nature as theme, Walser diverts attention from the material to the spiritual. The lack of a specific goal in the walks has as little relevance as it does in the wanderings of Gulliver, Don Quixote, or Huckleberry Finn.

It may now be possible to take a first step toward understanding the last phase of Walser's career, in particular the often enigmatic prose pieces in ***Die Rose*** and ***Unveröffentlichte Prosadichtungen.*** Although the experimentation in these pieces may be of an extreme sort, their dominant characteristic can also best be approached from the nexus of mask and walk.

In the twenties, the walks diminish in number, or, more correctly, they are replaced by abstracted, interior wanderings which dispense with the former catalyst of scenery. From the outset, the poetic personality had occupied a dominant position in Walser's writing, although usually in forms foreign to literary convention. Walser's involvement with this personality is as persistent as ever in his late prose, but a shift in his focus results in a more demanding concentration in his style. He is still intent on seeking out and recording the poet's viability outside of the traditions (and restrictions) presented by a "literary" phenomenon. This theme now combines with the heightening of an element of style first undertaken in the novels: a first person style which (paradoxically) tends toward depersonalization. Using a varileveled language to isolate things and situations perceived, he seeks to delineate a prerational, spatial interrelationship as it exists before the deductive mind transforms it into a serialized chronological order. These final volative perambulations of his language suggest that Walser investigated still another "wenig abgegraste Welt" in order to add to the repertoire of the creative imagination. (pp. 189-90)

George C. Avery, "A Poet Beyond the Pale: Some Notes on the Shorter Works of Robert Walser," in Modern Language Quarterly, *Vol. XXIV, No. 2, June, 1963, pp. 181-90.*

H. M. WAIDSON (essay date 1963)

[Waidson is an English educator and critic who has written widely on German literature of the nineteenth and twentieth centuries. In the following excerpt, he examines the themes and structure of Walser's novels, paying particular attention to Walser's conception of reality and his artistic distance from the everyday or mundane world.]

Robert Walser's first prose publication, ***Fritz Kochers Aufsätze*** . . . , anticipates his later work in its themes and presentation. It is true that there is a tenuous framework, which the later collections of prose sketches do not have; Fritz Kocher, a boy who died shortly after leaving school, has left behind him a collection of school-essays which the editor wishes to publish. The essays are on subjects such as "Man", "Autumn" or "Friendship", themes set by the teacher and developed by the pupil into delicate arabesques that characterize them unmistakably as the work of Walser. A theme is presented with simplicity, then diverted by a small touch into satire, or less frequently into a direct expression of the writer's sensibility of heart. There is the vision of the writer and artist as representing man in his noblest state, the admission of a secret enthusiasm for art, praise of the possession of a sensitive temperament, a determination to live intensely only for the passing moment, an appreciation of the joys of friendship, descriptions of autumn and winter, contrasts between poverty and wealth, indecision about a future career, descriptions of Christmas or a fairground, and an invocation of the spirit of music. Then the fiction is tacitly dropped, and there follows a series of descriptions of the problems of a clerical worker; the essays concern someone who has now left shcool and who between the age of eighteen and twenty-four is making wry discoveries about the world of business. A new framework is now devised; the author brings to the reader's notice "leaves from the notebook of a painter". . . . The painter has been living in poverty, finds the patronage and affection of a wealthy lady, later tires of this protected life and sets off once more on his travels. "Why is it that artists can find no rest?" he asks himself. The volume concludes with an essay on "Der Wald", which is more rhapsodic in tone than the earlier ones. The author remains dissatisfied with his attempt:

> To write exactly and definitely about something beautiful is difficult. Thoughts fly around what is beautiful like drunken butterflies, without coming to a destination and a firm point.

In this image one senses the seriousness with which Walser approached his writing, for all the self-deprecating gestures he often made, and one senses too the tension that he may well have felt between his volatile-impressionistic imagination and the desire to control his themes within a firm formal structure. Here was a problem which he rarely resolved successfully, and preoccupation with which seems to have caused him to express himself, apart from the novels, in a series of essays and short stories which elaborate, sometimes repetitively, themes many of which are foreshadowed in ***Fritz Kochers Aufsätze.*** (pp.175-76)

The precision of detail and lightness of touch with which Walser writes may be illustrated most simply [in] . . . one of Fritz Kocher's essays [*Unsere Stadt*]. . . . The sketch flows in one paragraph, its sentences being short and often simple. It can be imagined as an exercise, where the thought pours out in a succession of impressions which are linked together by association, not by argument. . . . The frequent use of "schön", "hübsch" and "fein" can indicate an ironical sense of distance from the objects described; elsewhere Walser sometimes uses diminutives for similar effect. One senses the conflict of two worlds. Citizens like Fritz' parents are proud of the orderly world of tree-clad streets, and of the town's other amenities—church, chestnut-trees, lake and so on. Napoleon is the remote, patriarchal provider of an avenue of trees, associated with the burghers and their "dignified" town hall. Opposed to the securely established citizens are the actors and industrial workers. The actors, being artists, are not to be measured by ordinary, civic standards. They are the wanderers who do not share the stability of the settled burgher. The industrial poor are for the most part unseen and out of mind, and Fritz Kocher reflects and parodies the general attitude of the middle-class section of the inhabitants. There is no narrative tension in this sketch; the effect depends upon the unity of mood and style which is achieved. There are hints here of the inconsequentiality that at times becomes tiresome in some of the later sketches. No doubt ***Unsere Stadt*** is less memorable than some others of the short works, but it is recognizably Walser's work.

The short sketch, occasionally expanded into a short story, is the literary form which accompanied Walser throughout the course of his life as a writer. But although it is through this briefer form that Walser's work is likely to be introduced to readers, the present essay wishes to concern itself mainly with the author's longer works. ***Der Spaziergang*** . . . , of novelle length, has much in common with the shorter works. Walking is a frequent theme in Walser's writing, and is expressed here with a vigour and enthusiasm that have made this work one of his best known writings. The narrator's principal business in the town which he visits is to have lunch with a patroness, to try on a suit at a tailor's, and to convince an income-tax official that, as a poorly paid writer, he is entitled to the lowest possible assessment. These encounters are expressed as a series of speeches which are themselves sketches in miniature—Frau Aebi's comic encouragement to the protagonist to do justice to her food; his indignation about his suit and the tailor's equally indignant reply; his justification to the tax official of his way of life as a poor but independent writer. In anticipation of these central points of the outward action the protagonist describes with playful zest the figures whom he meets on the first part of the walk, the professor, the bookseller, the bank-official, the woman who, he imagines, was once an actress, a girl whose singing is heard from an open window, and a number of others. They are not important as participants in any plot, but we are asked to cherish them as impressions in their own right which have become memorable because of the vivid eagerness with which the author has seized them. . . . The quality of freshness which Walser conveys in ***Der Spaziergang*** endows everyday scenes with the uniqueness of a personal vision. In his statement to the tax official the narrator equates the man who writes with the man who walks, and describes his concern as being extended over the small as well as the great. . . . The narrator combines idyllic description with fantasy. A pine forest which is "quiet as in the heart of a happy human being" reminds him of the interior of a temple or an enchanted castle. The vision of the tired giant Tomzack looms unexpectedly into the protagonist's solitude, to disappear as inexplicably as he came. The poet-walker must make considerable effort to prevent the ordered world of consciousness from disintegrating. . . . What is seen is described with sharpness and precision, and an additional dimension is provided by the imaginative reactions of the protagonist to the scene before him. The common-sense world is continually liable to lose its shape, perhaps by being overlain with a fantasy, or by being transmuted by ecstasy or by being overcome by chaos. . . . [The] walk takes its return journey as evening approaches with an elegiac tone and with a less emphatic manner than earlier. The author does not offer novelties to the reader, and asserts rather his conception of nature and human life as a "flight of repetitions", a phenomenon that he regards both "as beauty and as blessing". Evening brings with it thoughts of loneliness, tiredness and the transcience of all life and its impressions.

Der Spaziergang is rich in its varied associations of ideas and the luminous intensity of its prose. It blends the playful, the satirical and the sensitively imaginative aspects of Walser's writing in a form which is simple, but without the tenuousness of a number of the short sketches. (pp. 176-81)

Die Geschwister Tanner is an episodic work, liable to dissolve into series of descriptions, letters and monologues. Its unity lies in the first place in the personalities of the Tanner family, reflected through their encounters with Simon. His elder brother Klaus reproaches Simon in a letter for not having a settled career and for his restlessness in moving from one post to another. Simon is a wanderer who wants to live in the present moment. . . . Rather more than a year later Simon wanders into a state convalescent home, glad of the temporary shelter of warmth in midwinter. A friendly woman-supervisor persuades him to talk about himself and his family, and the novel closes with this conversation, which consists largely of Simon's summing up of himself and of his near relatives, reminding us of the ties of affection that exist between this group of individualists. It is here, in Simon's last speech, that he gives some hints as to the reason for the particular character of the bonds between these brothers and sisters which gives the novel its distinctive quality. The memory of their mother's dignity, the accounts of her sufferings as a child, and later the witnessing of the collapse of her personality in her last years form a common emotional experience of depth which her children carry with them, hardly consciously, in their adult lives. . . . In the course of the novel Simon's closest ties are with his brother Kaspar and his sister Hedwig. With his firm vocation as painter Kaspar has an immediate purpose in life which Simon lacks; at the same time his carefree self-confidence enables him to take life more easily than Simon. . . . Simon finds the furnished room and thus begins the connection with Frau Klara, but it is Kaspar with whom she falls in love. For Kaspar is more defined as a personality by his artistic mission and by the easiness of his approaches to the other sex. Simon rejects the possibility of a more intimate relationship with her, and asserts his independence by going for a lonely walk. As an artist and a Bohemian, Kaspar is following an expected pattern of development, and his move to Paris is in keeping with his sense of purpose. As Frau Klara says, Simon is different and "can scarcely be grasped". Simon likes to confide in his friend Rosa, but she is secretly in love with Kaspar. Simon's affection for his brother allows of no feelings of jealousy; he is glad for Kaspar when Frau Klara becomes closely bound to the latter.

When winter finds him out of work and homeless, Simon goes to his sister Hedwig, a village schoolmistress, and stays with her for three months. Hedwig's attitude to him is protective. . . . But she feels, as Simon puts it later, a mixture of affection and contempt for him. . . . Simon is more closely bound to Kaspar and Hedwig, who are nearer to him in temperament, than to his other brothers. For Klaus is separated from them by his more positive acceptance of the standards of normal society, while Emil, in a mental hospital, lives in total estrangement from the world around him.

Der Spaziergang focuses our attention on the events of the walk and on the immediate impressions they make on the narrator; the personality of the narrator is kept deliberately in the background. To discover a further dimension to such a personality we can turn to ***Die Geschwister Tanner,*** where Simon, a self-effacing wanderer, is the main personage. Of the various walks that Simon undertakes in the course of the novel, the most memorable is perhaps the three days' trek to Hedwig in the winter, in the course of which he comes across the frozen corpse of the poet Sebastian and resolves to see that his poems are collected and published. ***Die Geschwister Tanner*** has an emotional directness that is less clearly observed in Walser's other writings; it is a work which invites above all affectionate reading.

Der Gehülfe is in the first place a comic novel depicting the relationship of Joseph Marti with the Tobler family during the months when he is in their house as clerical assistant and secretary to the engineer Tobler. Joseph Marti seems to be less vulnerable than Simon Tanner, but at heart he too is a wanderer; the events of the novel take place during an interval between one phase of restlessness and another. He would like to keep the whole of his experience of people on a light, ironical, noncommittal, distant level. . . . An attention to details of everyday life suffuses this realistic novel, and a variety of precisely observed impressions can be united in Joseph's mind to an experience of beauty. . . . [It] is as if Joseph is capable of double vision, of harmonizing a close examination of detail with a broad conspectus of the whole scene; the series of contrasting adjectives indicates the combination of the miniature and the panoramic which is successfully achieved in this vision of the city. (pp. 182-85)

The tension between Joseph and his employer is the main motor force of the novel. Tobler's first words to Joseph are an irritated enquiry as to why he has arrived two days earlier than expected, a misunderstanding for which Joseph is not responsible. The final quarrel on New Year's Day which causes Joseph abruptly to leave is not primarily about Joseph, but about his predecessor Wirsich to whom Joseph has been giving protection and shelter, though without Tobler's personal permission. It appears as if Joseph is diametrically opposed to Tobler, his own quietness, for instance, contrasting with the latter's loud and decided manner. Tobler is essentially a comic figure. Having inherited some money, he has taken over an elegant house and devoted himself to inventions such as the "Reklameuhr", advertising novelties by means of which he hopes to make his fortune. . . . Characteristic too are Tobler's frequent, busy-seeming train journeys, which are mainly motivated by his wish not to "waste" a season-ticket he has taken out.

Already at an early phase of the novel, we acquire little confidence in the nature of Tobler's enterprises, and as with the passing of the months his affairs approach inevitably nearer to bankruptcy, Tobler and his assistant seem to be bound more closely together. Tobler is rebuffed by his mother, while Joseph is at odds with his father; neither of them is at home in the middle-class world of Swiss enterprise which surrounds them; they irritate and stimulate each other, and both are romantic at heart. (pp. 185-86)

Joseph Marti's encounters with Wirsich offer a sequence of action that forms a counterpart to his relations with Tobler. If Joseph seems elusive and irresponsible to the Toblers or to Klara, the friend he visits in the city, he can with justification assume a protective rôle to the unfortunate Wirsich. When the latter and his mother have left after their first meeting with Joseph at Toblers', Joseph reflects upon the fatality with which suffering may fall upon an old woman or a poor child. Although he expects to put the man and the old woman aside as memories that will soon turn pale, as most memories do in his vagrant life, chance is to bring him on two other occasions into contact with the forlorn Wirsich. Joseph's conviction of the rightness of his caritative assistance to Wirsich seems to be confirmed by the landscape around him:

> And in between his mood was almost holy. The
> whole landscape seemed to him to be praying,
> in such a friendly fashion, with all the gentle,
> muted colours of the earth.

Both Silvi, Frau Tobler's neglected child, and Wirsich appeal to Joseph because they are in distress and unloved; similarly Frau Weiss, Frau Tobler and Klara feel a need to offer help, sympathy or advice to Joseph; and Tobler himself, though apparently secure enough, is ultimately a figure to be loved and pitied. ***Der Gehülfe*** is a friendly novel, and the support which Joseph gives to Wirsich comes to take a prior place to his assistance of Tobler. The mood of the lake forms a colourful background as the narrative moves from summer to winter, while the decline of the Tobler fortunes is mirrored in the changing weather outside the house.

Although considerably shorter than the two earlier novels and written in diary form, ***Jakob von Gunten*** is equally distinctive. It has an elusive quality of self-conscious distance from everyday reality that marks it out as contemporary in spirit as well as in time with Rilke's *Malte Laurids Brigge* and the work of Kafka. Seelig has reported Kafka's admiration for this particular work, and Jakob's attitude to the Institut Benjamenta, together with other features of the novel, seems to foreshadow the relationship of Kafka's protagonists to their environment, particularly in *Der Prozess* and *Das Schloss*. The Institute gives little to its pupils, whose instruction is largely limited to learning by heart regulations and studying a book on the aims of the school. There is only this one lesson, which is repeated indefinitely; it is taken by Fräulein Benjamenta, sister of the principal. Outward decorum is emphasized, and laughter is out of place. One of Jakob's first reactions is indignation at the sleeping quarters offered to him. But he soon comes to accept the lack of furniture in the classroom, to take part willingly in the scrubbing and sweeping operations, to conform with the requirement that all food should be eaten up, to be resigned to unjust punishments and to the elaborate ceremonies during interviews with Benjamenta. The pupils, Jakob comments, are cheerful but without hope. There is a derelict garden to which the pupils are forbidden access, and the "inner rooms" of the principal and his sister are also normally out of bounds. The school is placed in an apartment in a shabby city block. Inside the school complicated regulations are supposed to be followed, but from three o'clock in the afternoon onwards the pupils are left to themselves and are free to explore any part of city life that attracts them. The institution is in fact a training-school for personal servants. Walser spent a short time at such a school in Berlin and for a time tried this form of work. . . . (pp. 186-88)

Kraus is the pupil whose personality stimulates Jakob most. For much of the time he is patronizing to this youth with the "monkey-like" appearance. Kraus has the temperament that will make for an ideal servant, and sees it as part of his duty to persuade Jakob to accept his point of view on such subjects as willingness to work, the need for contentment and humbleness. Kraus is never bored, and is indignant that Jakob should have such feelings. When Kraus leaves, Jakob feels that a sun has set. . . . Unlike Jakob, Kraus is indifferent to the glitter and bustle of the city. School routine and life outside the school, including the interludes when he is the guest of his artist-brother, offer Jakob neither comfort nor hope, but Kraus' personality gives Jakob a faith that he finds nowhere else. . . . (p. 188)

Jakob's presence at the school is more unexpected than that of Kraus. It is to a considerable extent an act of rebellion against his childhood environment; he has run away from his father and a wealthy home, and does not write to his mother, though he knows that she will be distressed on his account. The presence of his successful elder brother in the city gives him an opportunity of experiencing different circumstances from those of the school, but the link with Johann is less important to him than the relationships within the school. Jakob is here because he has decided to cut himself off from all dependence on his family, to build up his own life without their help; and if he fails, this will be in his eyes more creditable than remaining within the confines and protection of the Guntens. He and his fellow-pupils have as prospects only servitude. If Kraus accepts this contentedly, Jakob is pessimistic about these implications:

> But perhaps I possess aristocratic blood in my veins. I don't know. But one thing I know definitely: in later life I shall be a charming, spherical cipher. As an old man I shall have to serve young, self-confident, badly brought up louts, or else I shall be a beggar or come to ruin.

These are among Jakob's first thoughts in his diary, and he comes back to them as he approaches its end, when he envisages the possibility of his life collapsing and decides that such a collapse is of little importance, as his individual personality is a cipher.

Yet the school dominates Jakob. At first he is indignant and rebellious (hence his first friendship with Schacht), but his hatred of the Institute gradually changes to fondness and sympathy as he realizes its precariousness and the need which Benjamenta and his sister have for his affection and support. Jakob soon comes to identify himself, in hate and then in love, with the environment he has chosen. His admiration for Fräulein Benjamenta begins as if towards a distant being, and when she approaches him alone in the darkening schoolroom, he realizes that she is in need of his sympathy. Her death is foreshadowed, though when it takes place, Jakob is surprised at the coldness of his own emotions at this point. Jakob's relations with Benjamenta undergo a comparable transformation from dislike to friendship. Fairly soon Jakob feels something akin to commiseration for Benjamenta's solitary life. An important moment in their relationship is the interview in which Benjamenta, to Jakob's astonishment, confesses his special feelings for his pupil. Love and hatred alternate for a time; the invitations become more pressing, until after the death of Fräulein Benjamenta and the departure of Kraus, Jakob agrees to throw in his lot with Benjamenta, who has hated the world until he found Jakob. The school has disintegrated into non-existence, and Benjamenta and Jakob prepare for a new life—that of the wanderer. For a time, a peculiar setting has satisifed the restless protagonist, as in ***Der Gehülfe,*** but here the union between the two antagonists has in the end been realized, and a strange harmony prevails at the close. The individual at first seems powerless against the rules which press upon him, but the forms of society fall away, leaving the personal relationship with Benjamenta, paradoxical as it is, as the centre and essence of Jakob's life.

The element of fantasy repeatedly breaks into the narrative of ***Jakob von Gunten***. . . . He dreams once about his mother, and another time creates in his imagination a whole series of teachers who might have held office in the school. He develops fantasies connected with wealth and power, and sees himself as a medieval leader or as a soldier of Napoleon. One of his most elaborate visions is of Fräulein Benjamenta escorting him over unknown regions of the house explaining to him allegories of happiness, poverty, deprivation, care, freedom, quiet and doubt. When he and Kraus are admitted to the "inner rooms", he is disappointed to find no element of wonder or secrecy there. Satirical humour asserts itself again:

> Certainly there are goldfish there, and Kraus and I regularly have to empty the bowl in which these creatures swim and live, and fill it with fresh water. But is that something even distantly magical? One can find goldfish in every Prussian family of the middle official class, and there is nothing incomprehensible and strange about officials' families.
>
> (pp. 188-90)

The closeness of reality to fantasy, of ridiculousness to magnificence, and the contrast of civilization and solitude, of stability and restlessness, are recurring themes in Walser's work. ***Der Gehülfe*** is the most normally realistic novel, and ***Jakob von Gunten*** the most elusive and problematic. The short essays and stories are often prose-poems, and are the literary form to which Walser turned most regularly and spontaneously in the main course of his career as a writer. His work as a poet, finally, may be briefly noted, for here too the proximity in themes and approach to the prose sketches is evident. The collection of ***Gedichte*** . . . contains short lyrics, mostly of consciously unassuming and simple shape and content. Nature, wandering, poverty, fear, solitude and inner quiet are among the themes. "Zu philosophisch" is the title of this poem:

> How ghostly is my life
> as it falls and rises.
> Always I see myself beckoning to myself
> and disappearing from the one who beckons.
> I see myself as laughter,
> or again as deep mourning,
> or as a wild orator;
> but all this sinks down.
> And it has probably
> never really existed at any time.
> I have been chosen
> to wander through forgotten distances.

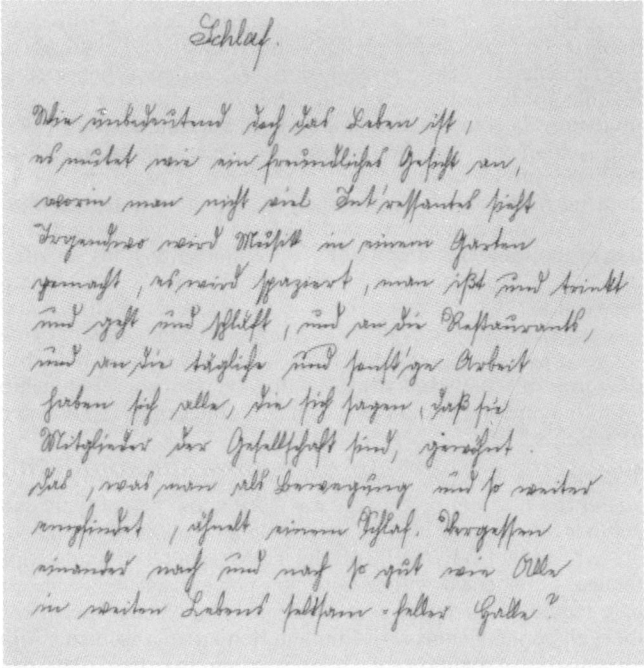

Holograph copy of Walser's poem "Schlaf" ("Sleep").

Walser's later verse is more rugged and reflective, often with a colloquial directness and a dry quality of language and thought. Carl Seelig records in his postscript to the ***Unbekannte Gedichte*** how Walser took up lyrical poetry anew in his later years, at the time when he was becoming increasingly aware that his gift of prose-writing was becoming exhausted. . . . Poems he continued to write after he had withdrawn from the world, long after he had ceased to write prose. (pp. 190-91)

> *H. M. Waidson, "Robert Walser," in* German Men of Letters: Twelve Literary Essays, Vol. II, *edited by Alex Natan, Oswald Wolff (Publishers) Limited, 1963, pp. 173-96.*

GEORGE C. AVERY (essay date 1968)

[*In the following excerpt from the only book-length study in English of Walser's works, Avery examines the characteristic elements of Walser's writings.*]

[The] most manifest expression of Walser's modernity, his symbolic concentration on the consciousness of single protagonists, underlies his work from his early verse dramolets, through the novels, the short prose, and the dialogs and so-called essays in the final phase of his career. The refraction of Walser's response to man's role in modern society through this particular optic inheres in the cohesiveness of the central images in his work. It objectifies and transforms into paradigmatic art Walser's preoccupation in his writing with a transparently autobiographical first-person persona. It examines and gives literary shape to a range of human experience in a way that identifies Walser's Swiss heritage—a more positive and more profound testament to his homeland than civic shibboleths can measure—as part of an essential European tradition: a pervasive knowledge of the need to accept change as the precondition for human understanding and growth. Walser gives this poetic vision a modern esthetic formulation as an interaction between absolute subjectivity and its metaphoric function. Together these establish the possibility of revitalization in the awareness of man's variegated appearance and not in the subservience to institutions or the defense of systems.

Walser's modern perspective is evident too in an anti-esthetic creative ethos that appears throughout his writing in various guises but is always informed by compassion and artistic skill. Walser's relevance to the modern temperament resides in the dichotomy this opposition implies. Using a fragmentarily portrayed creative personality as a symbol of the dynamic continuum of life, Walser's career demonstrates a testament—in art—of ambivalence toward the function and the efficacy of verbal art that he shares with contemporaries as different as Franz Kafka, Thomas Mann, and Bertolt Brecht. What distinguishes Walser from these contemporaries is his apparent disregard for the traditions of the genres he wrote in. While there is no evidence for grouping Walser with conscious experimenters in German letters after 1900, and the practice of his craft suggests a persuasion of the equivalence of genres with regard to their esthetic utility and their metaphoric statement, his novels anticipate the refinement in his short prose of extensive statement in a restricted form by emphasizing the primacy of a personalized, anti-traditional literary language.

The central figures in Walser's novels are referred to in the study as heroes because Walser portrays them in the only way that modern literature can still lay claim to the term: for figures who resolutely resist the pretense of being any more or anything different than what they are. They do not, however, share with their present-day literary descendants a moral neutralism or an amorality the intention of which is to signify a higher morality in the absence of generally accepted ethical norms in society as a whole. The heroes' subjectivity is the affective core of the novels but Walser's subjectivity cannot be read as moral insensitivity—either in the novels or in the rest of his work. Walser's failure to expressly justify his heroes gives them an enigmatic dimension that provokes the mind. Because they communicate a response to the wonder in human life, they simultaneously speak to the heart. Walser's late "essays" achieve a synthesis of the implicit opposition between the creator and the critic in his earlier work and thereby enlarge a literary structure for experiencing human perception, consciousness, and cognition. (pp. viii-ix)

Walser's claim to our attention derives from the thematic, stylistic, and structural elements in his work that identify him as a participant in and contributor to the creation of modern literature on the continent. His three extant novels exemplify the early abandonment of what Joseph Warren Beach has termed "the well-made novel" in an attempt to refine and expand the province and the sensibility of contemporary prose. In his own reaction to the confrontation with traditional literature, Walser instinctively utilized two of the principal responses with which his generation sought to satisfy the urge for new modes of literary expression: an author-imposed limitation on the literary devices to be used in the execution of his craft, and the circumscribed form dictated by a restricted narrative point of view. (p. 17)

Despite the breadth of his reading of writers from the eighteenth century through to his own time, Walser never associated himself with a particular literary tradition, and it is difficult to identify a pervasive literary influence on Walser's work. Nor did he regard himself as an innovator, or wish himself viewed as an adherent of a modern school. It is therefore useful to begin from an assumption of Walser as a literary "Einzelgänger" ["individualist"].

Even a cursory view of Walser's writing reveals divergencies of style and attitude on the author's part from one period of his career to the next, thus limiting the usefulness of any single characterization of Walser's work according to traditional literary criteria. Walser's first known work, the dramolets from the Zurich period, has at its core a fairy-tale hermeticity which shuns contact with the world beyond their author's private sensibility; the novels and prose of the Berlin period present a radical attempt to delineate and participate in this world; the prose works of the Biel period, the dominating body of which are descriptions of nature by a solitary walker, represent an increasingly abstracted encounter with a solipsistic nature which is depicted as harmonious and which lacks the social engagement of the Berlin period; and the prose written in Bern exhibits still another *volte-face*—as a culmination of Walser's stylistic and thematic probings and inquiries, it embodies a final testament in Walser's documentation of a symbolic existence at the beginning of a new cultural and literary era. (pp. 17-18)

[The] possibilities latent in the medium of language and its proximity to silence were always [Walser's] crucial concern. His probing of the limits of verbal expression attest to his participation in the linguistic revolution characterizing German literature after the turn of the century. Two quotations, separated in time by nearly the length of his career, attest to this concern. The first, a selection from an "essay" by Fritz Kocher entitled **"Free Topic"** . . . is an exercise in characterization undertaken in a typically modern absence of an organizing idea, where both author and narrator wish to emphasize a preoccupation with language.

> I am too lazy to think something up. And what might that be anyway? I like writing about anything. It's not the looking for a specific topic that excites me, but picking out fine, lovely words. Out of one idea I can form ten, even a hundred ideas, but no basic idea. What can I say? I write because I find it nice to fill out the lines with delicate letters in this way. *What* I write is a matter of complete indifference to me.

The second quotation is from the late prose piece **"My Efforts."** . . . The piece belongs to a group of essay-apologues from the twenties that show Walser's reaction to his awareness that the scorned and secretly courted "imago" of fame had eluded him. The selection is distinguished by its pairing of two apparently contradictory attitudes toward language, spontaneity and experimentation.

> The occasions on which I just wrote along spontaneously may have perhaps seemed a bit funny to the serious; but in fact I was experimenting in the linguistic field in the hope that there is present in language an unknown veracity, which it is a pleasure to awaken.

The spontaneity Walser refers to is indeed a characteristic element of a large part of his writing. It can be traced through his work as the symbolic element in his confessed need to depict his inner life . . . , since both spontaneity and chance are stylistic reflections of an unanswerable reality of the self. The relation of this need to the quest for joy that is posited as the result of the experimentation points to a source of the rightness and uniqueness of the personal idiom Walser created. The uncertainties and the night figures are nearly always banished in his work but their shadows reside within the limits of the risk the spontaneity assumes. With reference to the novels, this verbal spontaneity parallels the incidence of chance in structure and plot.

In Walser's own work, the novels represent a victory over the implicit attraction of silence as it is suggested in the encapsulated, fairy-tale like world of the early dramolets. . . . In other words, whatever the spontaneity and chance tell us about the form of Walser's work adds to our understanding of its structure when we identify silence as the opposing risk. Historically his three novels contribute to the attempt of the modern German novel to transcend the thematic and stylistic limitations of its nineteenth-century forebear. Thus his novels both figuratively and actually take their starting point at the threshold between the German inwardness whose literary antecedents lie in Romanticism and the prospect of a contemporary novel of more ambitious symbolism after it has forsaken the premise that the novelist's province is exterior reality. (pp. 26-8)

The most apparent evidence of subjectivism in Walser's novels is the almost unbroken concentration on a central figure and the stark reduction of exterior action. (p. 28)

The significance of the spare plots is further diminished by the rarity with which resumés, interpolation, conventional exposition, and analysis are used to portray character or develop a theme. In varying degrees these traditional devices are replaced in the novels by a lyric juxtaposition of episodes closer to the structure and statement of poetry than to conventional prose fiction. In this way the subjectivity serves to expand the form and illuminate the spiritual temper of the new century. The progressive attenuation in the novels of an author-narrator—a characteristic self-imposed technical limitation—imposes a new obligation on the reader to deal with a variety of levels of human logic.

In each of the three novels, lyrical compositional elements such as repetitions and variations, formal contrast or juxtaposition, the use of the precognitive and subrational not only to forecast character and plot but to portray critical interior states, and the presentation—both in theme and style—of existence as a spiritual continuum contribute to the esthetic effect and the meaning of the novels. (pp. 29-30)

[The] reader must synthesize the slow accretion of states of mind, the thoughts and dreams of a hero who seeks to illuminate visually apprehended objects with a surcharge of perception, and what is veiled behind confessional monologs.

Typical of all three novels is a youthful hero, the "seeker of his true self" . . . , who disappears at the "open" end of the novel with no explanation of what has happened or what will happen to him. . . . All three arrive devoid of the usual credentials with which an author seeks to legitimatize his central characters. They are seen in an external locale that is filled in by frequently assiduous description but the geographic location of which is not specified. They hesitatingly knock at the door of life and are granted or are refused access. At the end, they move on to a spiritual "address unknown." It is the form and the atmosphere of each of the novels that creates a correlative of the heroes' essence as human beings. Judged by the traditions of the novel of development, the portrayals of the heroes are incomplete. By omitting any explicit synthesis of the dimensions in their portraiture, Walser depicts his heroes as remaining open to the possibilities of their fate. They are unaware of a curious inviolateness they bring with them that adds to the mystery of their personalities. They do not develop their gifts, and they leave unanswered the question implicitly posed in the modern novel: is man his actions or his secrets and his dreams?

The three heroes recreate Walser's own confrontation with external reality. The novels describe a line moving from a symbolistic introspectiveness in ***Geschwister Tanner*** to a more objective awareness of the threat urban society presents to man's nature in ***Jakob von Gunten***. In ***Geschwister Tanner***, the plot and themes reflect the enthusiasm of the new century for the "reform of life," while the abstraction of subjectivism, the distrust of rhetoric, and the struggle to articulate the ineffable in terms of the single life in ***Jakob von Gunten*** could be called a chastened Expressionism.

All three heroes hunger for the experience of life, but are estranged from life through their isolation from society. . . . In ***Jakob von Gunten***, a highly developed irony acts as a regulator and shield in the hero's contact with the world outside the Institute Benjamenta. All three heroes reject society, but offer themselves in service to its individual members, thereby reestablishing a basis for the vitality of the inner life in a post-bourgeois era. Implicit in all three is the struggle to achieve grace by an affirmation of the plurality of life. This is the interior locale of the novels. . . . (pp. 30-1)

The heroes' affirmation of the plurality of life is, at the same time, a condition of their failure to achieve external realization of the self, since this means an accommodation to an objectified and therefore limited concept of life. Any such realization is an inward one; its nature dictates certain formal and stylistic elements used to depict it. With all three heroes, their "voice," their dreams, their fantasies and visions unremittingly emphasize the insufficiency, the metaphysical irrelevancy, and their own intuitive distrust of systematic or intellectual dicta. . . . Although this suggests the creation in the novels of an autistic imaginative realm, what in fact links earlier critics of the novels is their uniform attempt to articulate the novels' symbolic breadth. (p. 31)

The recurrence of [the motifs of family, nature and art] in the novels illustrates Walser's preoccupation, from his earliest to his latest work, with a limited range of themes. . . . Occasionally, the similarity in motif and theme in much of Walser's prose has given readers the mistaken impression of creative lassitude. Walser himself, investigating the range of possibilities and freedom within the thematic limitations of his personal poetic vision, properly emphasized the uniqueness of each work and the independence of its inspiration. (p. 121)

A significant number of the minor figures in the novels are members of a family to whom the hero is related or with whom he establishes contact. With the single qualified exception of Klara Agappaia's prospective remarriage . . . , the family is implicitly represented as a disintegrating social unit. (p. 122)

As the most radically fragmented family group in the three novels, the Benjamentas are isolated within the Institute Benjamenta and from each other. This isolation is a result of the contrast between the feminine idealism and the male vitalism they symbolize. At the same time the suspension of their reality as related persons is illustrative of a shift within the novels in the role of the family. Primarily a symbol of confinement and of the ineffectuality of the past in ***Geschwister Tanner***, in ***Der Gehülfe*** the sociological family is ironically dissolved in order to preserve the identity of its individual members in the larger family of man. In ***Jakob von Gunten*** the family is reduced to one motif among others, against which the hero tests himself and, though less overtly, tests as well the possibility of creativity, by the practise of an art that is unburdened by the odium Walser attached to art as the agency of cultural exclusiveness. Through the novels the motif of the fragmented family becomes more and more clearly the symbol of cultural suspension, the acceptance of the alienation that is the precondition for the re-evaluation of values.

The themes of art and nature and their antitheses figure importantly in Walser's entire oeuvre. . . . The prose piece **"Der Wald"** in ***Fritz Kochers Aufsätze*** . . . serves as a paradigm for the perception and celebration of nature. The description of the forest as a living organism which antedates European civilization and which, in a relatively short time, could re-cover Central Europe "if civilization receded" . . . , symbolizes the destructive antagonism between nature and civilization. As a catalyst for a paean to a lost unity, the writer concludes his description of the character of the forest with the hope that he will at least once be able to reproduce the forest's tranquility in his own writing: "I can't quite describe what I love as tranquilly as is necessary. Perhaps I shall yet learn to master this conflict of feelings." . . . A story from the same collection entitled **"Der Maler"** tells of a Nietzschean conflict between the demands of life and of art. Typical of Walser's work to the end of the Berlin period, the figure of the painter permits a more straightforward treatment of the problem of art than do the novel heroes. Filling out the view of nature in **"Der Wald"** as a model for a writer's prose, the painter says that his landscapes and portraits have no representational aim, but instead seek "to render truest nature." . . . The artist of the story avoids excessive contact with external nature since, as he says, it "would positively cripple my desire to produce." . . . Instead he creates "a second nature" in his memory, from which he paints. These two instances selected from a great variety of treatments of both art and nature in the work preceding the novels indicate an interrelation between the two spheres that somewhat alters their traditional antithesis. In the novels this interrelation takes the form of the relegation of the creative capacities to the realm of nature as a medium which incorporates a visible transcendence. None of the heroes is permitted the development of creative gifts, although all three possess the artist's discriminating analysis that can organize the vision of the mind, the heart, and the eye into language. These talents are ignored, suppressed, or, in Jakob's case, disavowed.

The uniquely personal cast of the treatment of the ambivalence toward art as it develops in the novels, in contrast to **"Der Maler,"** relates Walser to the widespread ambivalence toward the calling of the artist in European writing after the turn of the century. Indeed, the figure of the sentient observer as creator and the question of the possibility of creativity lie at the core of Walser's writing and unify it as no other theme does. Max Brod is very likely correct in his belief that it was the absoluteness of Walser's calling as an artist that ruined the man. . . . Historically the beginning of Walser's career coincides with the beginning of an intellectual and cultural epoch in which the dominance of industrialized society was great enough to force on writers an acknowledgment of their cultural isolation, whether it was expressed through the defensiveness of a regionally-oriented literature, the presumptive cultural leadership that emerged as Expressionism, or the isolation of the self-proclaimed elect. As an artist Walser accepted this isolation as a pre-condition of his own creation. His pre-novel artist figures are subject to a similar isolation—be it the figure of Oskar, whose longing for the medium to express his sense of communion with the universe in the early dramolet **"Dichter"** . . . lacks an immediate social context, or the parodistically viewed poets in two of the **"Sechs kleine Geschichten"** . . . , originally published in 1901. . . . In the remainder of his career Walser's abiding anthropological concern was to inquire whether an artistic existence in which isolation was equated with freedom was still viable in human terms and whether such an existence had meaning beyond the realm of the culturally elect. With the creation of the novels and their subordinate heroes Walser goes beyond the historically conditioned awareness of the vulnerability of the artist by positing an existence all the more vulnerable for the absence of art. This distinguishes Walser from the more general reaction of a literary generation that transformed their experience of the despoilment of nineteenth-century ideals into classical statements on the ambivalence of art. . . . Walser sought to find an alternative for the invalidated idealism in a broadly understood concept of the nature he regarded as the common denominator in all epochs of civilization. Taken as a whole, his work represents a courageous inquiry into contemporary man's inability to effect such a substitution. Post-Nietzschean expressionistic literature in Germany promulgates a New Man rooted in his stark humanity and inimical to the persona of the artist. While the occurrence of such a protagonist in German Expressionism was frequent enough to assume the proportions of a sociological phenomenon, such figures are distinguished from those in Walser's novels by his thematic reiteration of the vulnerability of the central figures.

The presentation of nature in the novels correlates with the emergence of the heroes' freedom. The depiction, the reliance on, and the definition of nature alters as does the degree and the utilization of this freedom. (pp. 145-47)

[The] themes of freedom and self-sacrifice in all three novels—freedom vouchsafed by nature, self-sacrifice as depersonalization in the world—are combined in the realm of art, where self-sacrifice becomes the price for freedom of creation. (pp. 155-56)

George C. Avery, in his Inquiry and Testament: A Study of the Novels and Short Prose of Robert Walser, *University of Pennsylvania Press, 1968, 278 p.*

CHRISTOPHER MIDDLETON (essay date 1969)

[*In the following excerpt Middleton places* Jakob von Gunten *in a historical framework and discusses the literary innovations evident in the novel.*]

Jakob von Gunten is one of several narratives of its period which transformed the world of German fiction. It is unlike any other German novel, and unlike any other work of European fiction. First, though, one has to realize that the German novel had for a long time been a compendium of writing in all shapes and sizes. So the journal form of ***Jakob von Gunten,*** subtitled "Ein Tagebuch," was not something freakish. At the time when it was written (1908), the crux was a refining of the novel's customary gross form into more compact and elementary forms. Whereas in older novels soliloquy (with introspection) had been one element among others, this element was now becoming independent. More, it was becoming analytic. So one might call ***Jakob von Gunten*** an analytic fictional soliloquy. That sounds, true enough, very portentous. In reality, the book is more like a capriccio for harp, flute, trombone, and drums.

Three other fictions of the time show what mode of experience was shaping the transformation of the novel: Musil's *Törless* (1906), Carl Einstein's *Bebuquin* (1909), and Rilke's *The Notebooks of Malte Laurids Brigge* (1910). In each book, the hero explores remote and perilous regions of his mind; with perceptions of snailhorn delicacy he maps a shifting "inner world" of feelings and impulses; and he pursues a primal enigmatic reality dwelling somehow between the perilous inner world and the brutish disorder of the external world. Strindberg in Paris had started it with his *Inferno* (1896). In 1910 Kafka, soon to become master of the absurd, was starting to write his journal, and was already familiar with Walser's prose, which he liked. During these four years, 1906-1910, the point of leverage for a revolution in German fiction was being determined. (pp. 5-6)

Yet one fails to define Walser by placing him like this among certain crucial "historical developments." Little known as he still is, he was one of the liveliest writers of his time; also he was a sophisticated writer. But his language is peculiar, because it is so unliterary (or what name should be given to this kind of intensity? When a new mode of imagining erupts into literature, it dislocates the rhetoric of its time, and is of subtler stuff than that rhetoric. . . .) It would be silly to regard Walser as an intellectual writer in the way that, say, Hofmannsthal, Thomas Mann, or Kafka were intellectual writers. Once, in Berlin, he actually said to Hofmannsthal at a party: "Couldn't you forget for a bit that you're famous?" No, Walser's writing does retain, to the end of his anguished years as a writer, an eccentricity as balanced and as clownishly serious as the paintings of Henri Rousseau. In the framework of the developments sketched above, he stands apart. He is, in significant ways, untutored: something of a "primitive." His prose can display the essential luminous naiveté of an artist who creates as if self-reflection were not a barred door but a bridge of light to the real. It is no coincidence that his twenty-five years of writing cover almost exactly the period when "naive" art was being discovered in the West: as a marvel of technique, as a revelation of wonder ranging from the most exotic dreams to the most banal things (while freely swapping their appearances)—new and joyous metaphors for a doddering civilization, and energy for Hamlet's heirs. (pp. 6-7)

I want now briefly to note some ways in which ***Jakob von Gunten*** relates to some factors in tradition and to certain signs of its time. . . . I offer these remarks as notes and suggestions only: the last thing I want to do is "fix" a perspective in literary-historical terms.

(1) Jakob's journal is a record, *impromptu,* of moment-to-moment life in the Benjamenta Institute. He is a boy, seventeen years old perhaps, who has run away from home in a remote province. The framework of improvisation, which suited Walser's temperament, contains Jakob's life design. This design assumes the form of successive small waves of time, etching on Jakob's sensibility their contours and contents. Constant in the flux, as fact and fantasy collude, is Jakob's passion for surprise, for paradox, and for self-knowledge. There are all kinds of ribbings and ripplings across the surface of Jakob's record. After Lisa Benjamenta's death, Kraus solemnly says: "When we eat, the fork will tell us how thou hast desired us to handle and manage it, and we shall sit decently at table, and the knowledge that we are doing so will make us think of thee." This oddness is straight. Then one asks: or is it? One should not identify Jakob and Walser. They have much in common, but the book is not a self-portrait.

(2) The Benjamenta Institute. It certainly makes fun of fictions like Goethe's 'Turmgesellschaft' (in *Wilhelm Meisters Wan-*

derjahre); does it matter whether the fun is deliberate or not? . . . The German dream of integrating the individual and of an élite to spearhead cultural and social reform—Walser's books was a new variant on this, if not a parody of it. The pretensions of maturity, and the intellectual pride, are tacitly annihilated, without brutish anti-intellectualism, for once. Jakob says: "I value the way in which I open a door. . . . The generations of men are losing the joy of life with all their treatises and understandings and knowledge. . . . I like running down stairs. What a lot of talk!"

Yet the idea of decadence (*Entartung*) is a real presence in the book. The bourgeois runaway Jakob wants to become a zero, to start from all the way down. It is the process which Sartre was later to call the "withdrawal of the projections." Walser's clownishness, and Jakob's boyish critique of "cultivated circles," do occupy an eccentric position in a great and fateful dynamic of ideas. (pp. 13-14)

(3) The *déclassé* bourgeois Jakob: Kraus, the real proletarian, is aggressively suspicious of him to the end. The future is here foreshadowed: all those middle-class European intellectuals and writers who stood desperately with the proletariat when the wave of revolution struck: Dada in Berlin, Johannes Becher, Ernst Toller, Bert Brecht, Franz Jung—everywhere a wish for new life coming "from the lower depths."

(4) *Mysterium*. On his arrival, Jakob thinks that there is a mystery at the heart of the Institute. He imagines a castle, with palatial rooms, dancing, even an Englishman, somewhere behind the scenes. Possibly this fantasy of a castle attracted Kafka when he read the book. Even more so, the fact that it is a Castle of Disenchantment. Once Jakob has penetrated to the hidden areas, he finds just a goldfish tank which he and Kraus have to keep clean. Yet an initiation does take place before this; and there is a mystery being enacted, if not in physical space, then in Jakob's mental space. Lisa Benjamenta, as psychogogue, leads Jakob down into a subterranean region, interior of the earth-womb, for a rebirth. The ceremony even starts like a Greek Orphic initiation ("Look, Jakob, there will be darkness all around you"). We hardly know if it is "for real" or if Jakob is having one of his fantasies while he waits for his supper.

For all his blithe chirping, Jakob is an ambiguous creature: "Together with you, one can venture either something courageous or something very delicate," says Herr Benjamenta. Essences of Rimbaud, Holden Caulfield, and Walter Mitty flit in and out of him. A curious fate for religion here: when Fräulein Benjamenta dies, there is ritual, but no religion. She has said: "Singing is praying." A simple "faith" does not prevent Jakob from ignoring God or keeping him out of reach—"there are no gods, only one, and he's too sublime to help."

5) Jakob is also pedantic, didactic, sententious, and a bit of a snob. And so was Charlie Chaplin. (The didacticism in Walser is much milder and more ironic than in many Swiss writers. Its basis in feeling is volatile: "Heartfelt emotions put something like an icy coldness into my soul. If there's immediate cause for sadness, the feeling of sadness entirely escapes me.")

(6) The language. Two features are precocious vocabulary and eccentric syntax. Jakob airily says: "Sometimes I say things that surpass my own understanding." His use of (Walserian) abstract words is not just improbable, it is also, at times, inept (once or twice he has to check himself). Kraus's vocabulary is, on occasion, also set askew to his outline as a character. These are positive factors. It is the delicate art of ineptitude, which Walser kept alive in an age of gloomy professional polish and literal-minded expertise. Creation entails distortion, and Walser's distortions are timed and shaped with tact (like vivid free forms in non-representational art). Even then, Jakob's talk is often enough Walser's talk: that of an unsleeping accurate dreamer who had only irony for the somnolent cerebralizings of his day.

There is play with the notion of breathless story-telling. When a terrified Jakob rushes up with something urgent to say, he goes off into an elaborate Homeric simile about Goliath, with all kinds of embroidering, before getting to the point. A mischievous blocking of "dramatic thrust," also a parody of "epic breadth." There is also a type of sentence that starts, halts, turns a corner, almost dances backwards, then, quite suddenly, has arrived: "Kraus, it was he, rushed breathless and pale, and unable to deliver the message which he had, obviously, on his lips, into the room" (the translation follows the original). This can be done for the sake of the dance; but the example given is thoroughly functional. Generally, Walser's language is a dance rather than a walk. One should notice, too, the small dialogic nuances in Jakob's monologues: small linking phrases that vibrate with tacit questions or answers. This corrugates the surfaces: planes shift to reveal supporting volumes.

Some dialogues can be as wooden as Jakob's occasional old-fashioned pose as a writer: "It's time I laid down my pen." There are also the moments, like the visits to Johann's apartment, where the prose lands among mandarin platitudes. (pp. 14-17)

The fiction of the journal is sustained, even though it becomes improbable here and there—the last few sections, for example, which seem more like straight narrative. One need not question such points too closely: Walser's art is impulsive, even aleatory (his special genius in the short prose piece shows this).

Walser in middle age, circa 1925.

(7) Jakob's last dream. Epiphany of Don Quixote and Sancho Panza, as Benjamenta and Jakob ride into the desert, refugees from culture. The picaresque form is interiorized in ***Jakob von Gunten.*** The old episodic series of actions, as in *Don Quixote,* becomes an episodic series of reflections and fantasies. Ghostly presence here of one of the oldest forms of European fiction. The Quixote-Panza epiphany is no random matter. (p. 17)

Christopher Middleton, in an introduction to Jakob von Gunten: A Novel *by Robert Walser, translated by Christopher Middleton, University of Texas Press, 1969, pp. 5-17.*

ULRICH WEISSTEIN (essay date 1970)

[Weisstein is a German-born American scholar and critic who has authored or edited numerous works on German literature. In the following excerpt he contends that Der Gehülfe *is Walser's best work because of its cohesive storyline and unity of mood and tone, a unity absent in his other works. Unlike many other critics, Weisstein finds Walser's style clumsy and meaninglessly abstract; for contrasting assessments, see the excerpts by Christopher Middleton (1957) and Sven Birkerts (1982).]*

[Walser] never belonged to the school of experimental writers . . . and, though decidedly a self-styled outsider, remained at heart a literary conservative. (p. 114)

Walser's true claim to greatness will undoubtedly rest on his three novels or, to judge even more rigidly, on ***Der Gehülfe,*** since ***Geschwister Tanner***—apart from being too blatantly autobiographical—is rather episodically constructed, and ***Jakob von Gunten*** will appeal only to those who have a preference for works in which realistic and fantastic elements are (in this case rather poorly) blended. The base of Walser's fame would be considerably broader if it were not for the fact that he destroyed three entire novels (in one instance, because of an adverse criticism that had come to his attention), while two subsequently composed extended narratives—*Tobold* (1919) and *Theodor* (begun in 1921 and scheduled for publication three years later)—were apparently lost in the offices of publishers to whom the manuscripts had been submitted. As for the approximately one thousand *Aufsätze* [''essays''] which have survived, they will continue to be cherished by connoisseurs of the minor genre; but what would have been the fate of Kafka, the ''classic,'' if Max Brod had effectively destroyed *The Trial, The Castle,* and *America*?

Der Gehülfe occupies a place apart mainly because it relates a single coherent episode in the author's (and the protagonist's) life and because it possesses a unity of mood and tone which invalidates Walser's self-deprecatory assertion that it is merely as ''extract from Swiss everyday life, and not actually a novel.'' (pp. 118-19)

In ***Der Gehülfe,*** Walser carried out his own mandate as announced in one of his earlier prose sketches: ''Why is it that clerks are so rarely used as fictional protagonists? Apparently a mistake which must finally be brought to the attention of our national literature.'' Joseph Marti, the hero of this novel, is, indeed, the kind of individual who lacks any traits one might regard as extraordinary. Like Kafka's heroes, he is an *homme* slightly less than *moyen sensuel,* and a person who, while being naive, and apparently satisfied with what Tonio Kröger calls the ''Wonnen der Gewöhnlichkeit,'' yet distinguishes himself by an intellectual and psychological curiosity which he is never quite able to satisfy. Hence the subtle irony which pervades the entire work. (p. 119)

One of the things which Kafka must have greatly admired in Walser's novels was that ''artlessness considered as the highest art'' which Simon Tanner observes in the performance of a dancer. Unfortunately, Walser's stylistic artlessness at times conveys the effect of clumsiness, an impression rarely, if ever, generated by Kafka's prose. . . . Another objection—precisely the one which Kafka raised in a diary entry dated October 8, 1917—relates to Walser's frequent use of abstract metaphors, which often appear in the form of allegories. The following example from ***Jakob von Gunten,*** though extreme, may be taken as paradigmatic in this respect: . . . (. . . He speaks like an unsuccessful somersault and behaves like a vast improbability kneaded into human shape). Such language would more easily fit the works of Barlach than those of Kafka, who, unlike Walser, had a knack for taking language by the word. Yet, in reading Walser's narratives, one finds many a passage which Kafka could have mined in his quarry. (pp. 119-20)

Ulrich Weisstein, ''Robert Walser,'' in Contemporary Literature, *Vol. 11, No. 1, Winter, 1970, pp. 114-20.*

RONALD DEFEO (essay date 1971)

[In the following excerpt DeFeo discusses Jakob von Gunten *as a parody of the earnestly intellectual bildungsroman, noting the comic aspects of characters such as the Benjamentas.]*

[Robert Walser] was a writer of considerable talent and wit who received little recognition during his lifetime. Except for several admirers (notably Kafka and Hesse) Walser's work went unnoticed, and until this day is probably known only to scholars of German literature. Indeed, next to the work of such imposing figures as Kafka, Musil and Mann, Walser's prose—quirky, clownish, colloquial and often rather loosely, almost haphazardly, constructed—does seem somewhat minor, but the small miracles he performs are miracles nevertheless, and he should be appreciated in this light. . . .

[***Jakob von Gunten***] is Walser's third novel and the first of his books to be published in this country. . . . Jakob von Gunten is a young man who has run away from a wealthy home and enrolled at the Benjamenta Institute, a school for boys operated by a brother and sister—Herr Benjamenta, principal, and Fräulein Benjamenta, instructress. From the very beginning of the novel (written in diary form) the reader senses that all is not right at the institute. The students' sole textbook, *What Is the Aim of Benjamenta's Boys School?* sounds very much like a brochure. The boys have only one class, only one lesson (it is always repeated), and apparently only one active teacher, Fräulein Benjamenta—Jakob observes that the other members of the teaching staff are either asleep or dead. It turns out that the institute is actually a school for servants. The Benjamentas stress obedience and subservience to the exclusion of everything else—for what else need a servant know? Although the future looks a bit bleak for a Benjamenta boy, Jakob can at least take comfort in its inevitability: ''. . . one thing is for certain: in later life I shall be a charming, utterly spherical zero.'' That Jakob is as delighted by this prospect as he wishes to appear is somewhat questionable. Walser's tone here, as in the rest of the novel, is ambiguous. It is often difficult to decide whether Jakob is being serious or merely pulling our leg, whether he is describing an actual experience or simply an imagined one.

As one reads on, however, it becomes evident that ***Jakob von Gunten*** is a mockery of the brooding, intense, intellectual novel of education and inner discovery (note, for example, Robert Musil's brilliant *Young Törless* written only two years before Walser's book). By the end of the novel, Jakob has not undergone any great change (although he has found affection for the Benjamentas and is less hostile toward the school). He remains free, almost childlike. His diary, the record of his experiences and fantasies, reflections and speculations, has led him back to his initial picture of himself. "The individual me," Jakob remarks in the final entry in his diary, "is only a zero."

In the hands of a lesser writer, a novel with such a thin narrative thread, written in essentially simple language, posing few, if any, grand intellectual questions, might easily be a bore. But Walser had the gift of vividly bringing to life relatively minor moments and making them seem unique, magical, complete in themselves. Walser achieves his dreamlike effect by having his narrator maintain a distance from everyday reality, becoming more of an observer than a participant, so that the common seems quite uncommon. . . . (p. 92)

Jakob's distance from reality, his odd relationship to the Benjamenta Institute (the mysteries of which he at first finds impenetrable) seem to foreshadow the relationship Kafka's Joseph K. has with his environment in *The Trial* and, to a greater degree, in *The Castle*. In fact, had Walser followed Kafka in time rather than preceded him, one might very well imagine that ***Jakob von Gunten*** deliberately pokes fun at the labyrinths of *The Castle*. For Jakob often speculates on the puzzling "Inner Chambers" of the institute—specifically the quarters of the principal and his sister—which he has not been allowed to enter. When he finally does penetrate the mysterious area, he is disappointed to find an ordinary apartment with a goldfish tank.

Walser, like Kafka, populates his world with some very unusual people—although Walser's creations are more overtly comic and less grotesque than Kafka's. Fräulein Benjamenta, for example, explains to Jakob that she is dying—a touching revelation, perhaps, but certainly a very odd one. For why should she tell a mere student of such a personal tragedy, and why should she speak so dramatically? But if we are uncertain about the tone of this little scene (does Walser wish to move us or make us chuckle?), our uncertainty dissolves when Jakob describes the Fräulein's funeral. In the eulogy delivered by Jakob's fellow student, Kraus, the following touching tribute is paid: "When we eat, the fork will tell us how thou hast desired us to handle and manage it, and we shall sit decently at table, and the knowledge that we are doing so will make us think of thee."

The principal is another rather strange being. At first he feels that Jakob possesses too much will power and is too full of character. Near the end of the novel, in a laughable plot reversal, he asks Jakob to run off with him, for he has decided to give up his solitary life, to enjoy freedom at last and set off to wander the world.

Despite its delights, the novel, unfortunately, is not without flaws. Often the reader finds it hard to believe that a boy of Jakob's age (we assume that he is in his late teens) could write with such style and sophistication. On other occasions Walser is a bit too casual, Jakob's thoughts seem repetitious, and the reader becomes very aware that an author of hundreds of short pieces is having some difficulty maintaining dramatic tension in a long work.

But the virtues of ***Jakob von Gunten*** far outweigh its defects. Jakob himself is a marvelous creation—a charming, unpretentious, imaginative young man who wishes to learn from life and is very suspect of intellectuals. Says Jakob, perhaps commenting on the somber Germanic philosophers and writers: "The generations of men are losing the joy of life with all their treatises and understandings and knowledge." (p. 93)

Ronald DeFeo, "The Hero as Zero," in The Nation, *Vol. 212, No. 3, January 18, 1971, pp. 92-3.*

IDRIS PARRY (essay date 1981)

[In the following excerpt Parry analyzes the philosophical structure of Jakob von Gunten, *finding depicted in Jakob's education as a servant Walser's rejection of the egocentric Western intellectual system of logical analysis. Parry explicates in detail a philosophy implied in Walser's novel—that of an intuitive understanding of life's processes based on a subordination of the ego.]*

Most of [Walser's] writing consists of sketches, short essays, pieces meant for newspaper publication. Always so trivial in subject, so simple in style. . . . Over the years, a growing number of people have come to see that Walser's naivety is also his genius. His way of writing reflects a rare ability to see life without the distortions of personal commitment. (p. 19)

[Walser's] novels don't differ all that much from his shorter pieces. They are episodic, they seem to consist of parts which could easily be arranged differently. This way of writing is characteristic of a general attitude. It can be related to the naivety which offended so many readers. Life can be seen like this, a succession of episodes, especially by the eye which refuses to accept the illusion of continuity. Virginia Woolf would have recognized the method. Walser's bits and pieces meet her requirements. She asked for a fiction that would represent events as they are actually experienced and not as they are knowingly arranged by the intellect. Is knowledge itself any more than fragmentary? It is certainly less complete than the normal tidy narrative method would have us believe.

Walser's writings are characteristic of an attitude because he is always writing about one life, his own. So there is only one attitude. What else does the honest writer know? Just before he entered the lunatic asylum at Waldau in 1929 he wrote an essay called **'A Kind of Story'.** He talks here about his own writings. 'In my opinion my prose-pieces are nothing but parts of a long realistic tale which has no plot.' Is that a description of life in general? His sketches, he goes on to say, although they may seem disconnected, are really chapters of a novel at which he is always working. This continuous work is the conduct of his own life. This running novel 'could be called a book about the self, divided or arranged in many different ways'.

Walser writes about himself, recording life as it falls, because he knows it's only through unqualified submission to experience that one can hope to find the language of truth. This is not a shattering or novel discovery. The scientist has always known there is no other way of learning new facts, even if he hasn't always behaved accordingly. Goethe put it with his usual clarity when he said he had always regarded the world as being more gifted with genius than he himself was. He invented nothing, he said; he let poetry come to him from outside. We know how the intellect reduces experience to suit understandable conclusions. This is an impossible basis for discovery. Scientist and artist know conclusions must be expanded to comprehend evidence as it arrives, then treated not as conclusions but as transitional positions. The open attitude is difficult because contrary to our training. Success depends on humility, the pure response can follow only from an utterly open and therefore purely receptive posture. Humility happens to be Robert Walser's trade, as a writer if not always as a person.

For Walser, contraction of self is the only beginning of creation. In an essay written in 1907 he says: 'The man with a pen in his hand is as it were a hero in semi-darkness whose conduct can't be seen to be heroic or noble only because it must remain hidden from the world.' It's strange how Walser's history seems to reflect his inclination. In his lifetime he sought the subordinate until in the end he managed to disappear entirely, lost in the asylum. Kafka, once considered an imitator, has become famous; Walser remains in the shadows. An episode which happened in 1920 seems to typify the role of the subordinate as it existed in his life and is reflected throughout his work. In spite of his distaste for public occasions, Walser accepted an invitation in November of that year to give a reading from his works in Zurich. He needed the money. The chairman thought it advisable to have a rehearsal. He found that Walser was impossible as a public reader. But the advertised reading had to go ahead. It was given by the literary editor of the *Neue Zürcher Zeitung,* after an apology from the chairman, who announced, with regret, that Herr Robert Walser was unable to be present because of illness. Walser listened to this announcement, and to the subsequent reading, from a seat in the front row of the audience.

When Walser speaks through another character, he always chooses a person in a socially subordinate position. The early pieces collected to form his first book, published in 1904, are supposed to be the essays of a schoolboy, Fritz Kocher. After the naivety of the schoolboy comes the servile attitude of a commercial clerk, a favourite fictional face, drawn from personal experience, a man writing from the lower ranks and observing submissively. But it is in ***Jakob von Gunten,*** the book he liked more than any of the others, that Walser creates the ultimate figure of humility, the servant.

This novel was published between two other unusual novels written in German. Robert Musil's *Young Törless* preceded it in 1906, Rilke's *The Notebook of Malte Laurids Brigge* followed in 1910. Each of these three novels centres round a young man who is puzzled, perverse, hostile to convention, open to experience. These heroes try to see life in a new way because they are dissatisfied with inherited learning. The key is submission. 'Everything just happens,' says Törless; 'this is the whole of wisdom.' Rilke's fictional self, Malte, believes 'there is no selection and no rejection'. Everything happens and everything matters. Where there is no rejection the smallest thing is important, as the molecule is the only beginning, the constant element in the transformations of life. Get down there, these heroes seem to say, and you will participate. This is where connections are made, and this is where we find Walser's protagonist. Jakob von Gunten's business is humility, his professional obligation is to reach a position of personal insignificance. His ambition seems to run counter to all the trends of modern society. He is a pupil at a school for servants. (pp. 20-2)

The purpose of this school contradicts the normal idea of education. Schools are places where young people are supposed to be trained to become somebody. . . . Jakob has gone to school to become a nonentity. He doesn't want to borrow clothes.

Humility is one of Kafka's themes. Submission to the father, to authority, to the law. This may be one reason for his confessed admiration for Walser. Kafka speaks in one of his *Reflections* of the need to make oneself infinitely small. It was his way of coping with power. He was never, in life or in his writings, as infinitely small as Robert Walser. The servant in fiction has his parallel and source in life, because what may seem to us the strange idea of a school for servants is not an idea but a fact from Walser's existence. When he was twenty-seven he enrolled for a course of instruction at a school for servants in Berlin. This wasn't a joke or even a writer's search for experience. Again, he needed the money, and this happened to be the way he lived. He must have consciously chosen this possible career as something suitable for himself. (pp. 22-3)

The relationship between life and art is as obvious and as devious as in Kafka. The secret life is transposed into images as mysterious as truth seen in a dream, recognizable but different. We can hardly believe the school Walser attended in Berlin was anything like the weird establishment described in the novel. The experienced fact is transformed into a fantasy which seems remote from possible human experience. Jakob himself is as baffled as we are. He calls the school a place of darkness and mystification. 'God knows,' he says, 'sometimes my stay here seems to me like an incomprehensible dream.'

Jakob is not the first man in history or in fiction to think of life as an incomprehensible dream, a confusion where (if one can only find it) truth lies. How does one find it? By reacting in the appropriate way to life. Only one lesson is given at this school, and it is repeated again and again. The theme of the lesson is put in these words: 'How should a boy behave?'

All the teachers except one are asleep or dead, or appear to be dead, or are petrified. 'Instead of the teachers who do really lie there asleep as if dead, a young lady, the Principal's sister, Fräulein Lisa Benjamenta, teaches and rules over us.' The Principal himself is, says Jakob, a giant, 'and we pupils are dwarfs when measured against this giant, who is always a bit grumpy'. There's a distinct family resemblance here to Kafka's father.

Among the other pupils, the one to whom Jakob is most attracted and who becomes his ideal for conduct is called Kraus. No additional pupils arrive while Jakob is there, and he indeed is the only one left at the end of the book—a further indication that this is a subjective vision. It seems to Jakob that in one respect all the pupils resemble each other, 'namely in our utter poverty and dependence. We are small, small to the point of insignificance.'

There are mysterious inner rooms where the Principal and his sister live. Jakob feels intense curiosity about them and imagines they must be crammed with wonderful things. When he eventually enters these rooms he finds there is nothing extraordinary there. The teacher Lisa Benjamenta dies. Kraus and the other pupils leave the school. Jakob is left alone with the Principal in a situation which suggests the school is meant only for him, as the doorway in Kafka's parable *Before the Law* is meant only for the supplicant who waits wearily before it, year after year. The school dissolves when Jakob and the Principal (or are we talking about one person?) go out into the wilderness which is life.

'How should a boy behave?' Jakob believes the answer to this question lies in the attitude of his colleague Kraus. This boy is totally submissive. He has eliminated personal desire. He is a living example of the school's aim. Jakob describes him as 'a true work of God, a nothing, a servant'. And again, 'the summit, the palace of humility'. In these phrases Jakob manages to link the majestic and the divine in his praise of humility. The submissive has long been associated with the divine—in theory if not always in practice. Kraus, the divine fool, is seen as an ideal figure because he doesn't impose human judgment on events. Here is another for whom there is no selection and no rejection. Kraus waits, he accepts, he eliminates thought. That is, he eliminates himself as a separate entity. (pp. 23-5)

It is Kraus who opens the door to Jakob when he first arrives at the school. At this moment, as far as Jakob is concerned, Kraus represents the school. The first impression is not favourable, but Jakob records this event at what seems a later stage of insight, because he says: 'How stupidly I must have behaved when I arrived here.' From this later point of view he realizes his interpretation of Kraus as an idiot was mistaken. The subject is the same; the interpretation or judgment varies with the individual. (p. 25)

There are 79 entries in this 'Diary'. We assume, if this is really a diary, that entries will follow each other in chronological order of composition and that early entries will show no knowledge of later events. This is not the case. The passage about Jakob's first meeting with Kraus comes from an early part of the book; it is the fourth entry, but it reveals a later condition of illumination. So this is not a diary in the conventional sense at all, as we might guess when we notice there are no dates, no mention of specific days, hardly any indication in the text of chronological sequence—the word 'yesterday' occurs twice.

It takes an effort of the imagination to grasp this imaginative construction. Terms like 'at first' and 'later' have no place here. The novel doesn't proceed chronologically, it revolves. And it revolves round the personality of the central character, himself a projection of the creating mind. Gottfried Benn described one of his own novels as being formed like an orange. He meant that instead of an apparently continuous narrative he was presenting sections, each section apparently disconnected and independent but in reality joined to a central core, like the structure of an orange. This central core is the awareness of the narrator, who is both the author and his fictional counterpart, since the autobiographical link is already established. Walser's novel too radiates from a central intelligence. To this intelligence, everything is present in a single instant of memory. Can any moment in human consciousness be different? From the central point of observation and narration, end and beginning and all intermediary points are equally accessible. They now exist only in this consciousness.

Walser transposes to the awareness of his protagonist his own awareness of life's actuality and potential, two aspects of the same experience. Kraus the idiot is also Kraus the ideal, ape and work of God. Kraus becomes the ideal for Jakob because he doesn't differentiate through thought. The process of thought is an expression of self. The theme of submission means elimination of self and therefore of thought. Use of thought separates man from the natural world and produces by reverberation an endless set of divisions and 'opposites'. This is the real Fall of Man. It's the transition from harmony to awareness.

Walser describes thought, in a letter to his sister Lisa, as 'the greatest sin that there is'. This is his opinion because he believes our capacity for thought obstructs our appreciation of unity. In an essay . . . called **'The Forest'** he asks: 'Must there be separate things? Why can't everything be one?' A few lines later he answers his own question: 'We think, and the freely floating element hates and despises thought.' What he means by 'the freely floating element' becomes clear when he now has a vision of himself as indivisibly joined to the flowing unity which is life. His condition is ecstatic. Ecstasy happens when the subject feels identified with the object and is no longer separate. Where there is no active thought there can be no sense of separation. The power of separate identity is lost.

In this essay, **'The Forest',** Walser seems to abandon himself to flow with the stream of life, a common enough metaphor used from antiquity to modern times for the energy which is existence. Walser's character Tobold, after his training in servility, plunged eagerly into life, 'into the waves as a strong and bold swimmer'. That phrase could have come from Goethe's novel *Elective Affinities*. Goethe is very fond of water as an image of life. The second part of *Faust* is drenched in water. In the novel he indicates in an anecdote that water (like life) can be both a danger and 'a friendly element for the man who is familiar with it and knows how to handle it'. It depends on the use made of it. In Goethe's story a swimmer really does dive into the water, to rescue his lover. 'It bore him,' says Goethe, 'and the skilled swimmer was its master.'

The stream (or life) is indifferent. Only human manipulation (or judgment) gives it the dual appearance of danger or salvation. In the ecstatic vision recorded in **'The Forest'** Walser's stream becomes a unified current of tree and water and self. The individual is immersed. He renounces self. He submits to life:

> The forest flows, it is a green, deep flowing off, running off, the branches are its waves, the green is the dear moist wetness, I am dying and flowing with the wetness, with the waves. I am now wave and wetness, am the flow, am forest, am forest itself, am everything, am everything I can ever be and attain. Now is my happiness great. Happiness and grief, these are intimate friends.

In the flow of life everything is connection . . . moving, changing, relative, but always connected. No place here for absolutes, categories, divisions, opposites. These are products of the human intellect as it struggles to impose on life the limited information (and therefore imperfect judgment) supplied by inadequate faculties. The single stream becomes, in the novel ***Jakob von Gunten,*** the single awareness of the narrating observer. Here apparent opposites are joined in a single event, the book itself. But the novel is written, as all books must be written, in language which reflects divisions of time and space drawn from thought. Walser's single event necessarily has the appearance of a multiplicity of events happening at different times and in various places.

The secret of the novel's time-sequence is that there is no sequence. The 'end' can be, as we have seen, blended into the 'beginning'. Jakob, standing on the front doorstep of the Benjamenta Institute, can talk about 'today', referring to a later time in his development, while 'then' means his impression of this moment when the door is opened. Time seems to have been put into a box, from which Jakob draws any temporal expression he likes. Each refers to the same single awareness, there is only one mind, and only one moment, the moment of recollection, as every stage in transformation is a moment of recollection.

The bow Kraus makes to Jakob on that doorstep strikes him as highly suspicious. 'I immediately told myself there must be something wrong with this place.' We already know Jakob is speaking of a time when he misinterprets Kraus and thinks he is simply an idiot. This is part of that misinterpretation. The humility of Kraus's gesture rouses Jakob's suspicion because humility runs counter to the quality our civilization based on thought holds most admirable—in brief, the urgent expression of the ego. The Western society Walser criticizes is also the inheritance of Jakob, shocked now in one aspect of his multiple personality. Inherent in Walser's thesis, as expressed in this novel, is rejection of culture, the mould and expectation of the society he knows.

At the request of the Principal, Jakob writes a short account of his life. We find he is rooted in tradition. When he describes his family and his ancestry it sounds like a summary of social development in general. He wants to dissociate himself from this development. . . . (pp. 25-8)

Jakob intends to disconnect himself from what he considers a false way of life represented by family tradition and the inherited rules of conduct in general. 'How should a boy behave?' The next sentence of Jakob's brief account indicates the ambition which transcends everything: 'His wish is that life may educate him, not some inherited or aristocratic principle.' This ambition, imaginatively projected, becomes the fictional form which is the Benjamenta Institute and all its works. Thought, learning, scholarship, traditionally accepted as the brilliant edge of civilization, are connected in Walser's condemnation. When Jakob reports that all the teachers except one are asleep or dead or appear to be dead or are petrified, Walser is emphasizing by accumulation his belief that traditional sources and methods of illumination have failed. (pp. 28-9)

Jakob meets his brother Johann in the crowded city. They go to a restaurant together. Their conversation is an explicit condemnation of modern cultural life. . . . The opinions put into the fictional character Johann's mouth are projections of Jakob's (and Walser's) situation. Here we encounter another transposition of central awareness. The result is that, although Jakob seems to take little part in the conversation, he is fully in agreement with what his younger brother says. This is not surprising, if we realize we are listening to a dialogue between two parts of the indivisible self (if we may be allowed the contradiction of 'parts' in an indivisible entity, a contradiction forced on us by language, as it is forced on Walser).

Their conversation is a long complaint about the decadence of society. 'Up there you find such an atmosphere of having done enough, and that's constricting and limiting.' Johann's conclusion—typically, it comes at the beginning of their conversation—sums up Walser's opinion of cultured society: '. . . up there it's hardly worth living any more.' Contempt for the pretensions of society is naturally joined to praise of humility. (p. 29)

Walser hated our strongly intellectual civilization. In life as well as in his writings he expressed contempt for this foreign world of painful analysis, of rank, narrow ambition and fatuous ceremonial. For him these were devices which merely served to emphasize separation where there should be unity. . . .

There is no evidence that Walser ever read any systematic philosophy. How could he, if he believed in learning direct from life? It may be objected that Jakob is always thinking. This is true. He is human, or he wouldn't appeal to us. He also reflects on his reflections: 'I value experiences, that's all, and these are usually quite unconnected with thought and analysis. For instance, I've quite a high opinion of the way I open a door. There's more concealed life in the way you open a door than in a question.' . . .

Walser, like Kafka, is a Taoist out of his time. 'Give up learning,' says the Tao, 'and put an end to your troubles.' This is what Walser is saying. He praises the life of submission, the impulse which is a creative act, unthought, unplanned, a free response to living forces. In this condition there is no conscious rejection or selection, so every manifestation of life is important and removed from the moral evaluation which is a product of thought and circumstance. (p. 30)

The optimistic gesture of the writer is work when there seems no reason for work. It springs from faith that there are connections which can't be immediately seen, and a meaning which exists but is not humanly evident in the profusion of life. In the mind there is division between actual and potential. For us they can't exist together. Kraus is either an idiot or he is divine; he can't be both at the same time. Jakob is able to join both possibilities as facts which do not deny each other. He cites the visible evidence (that Kraus is an idiot) and more than the evidence. His is a total view, and in unity there can be no division into parts. So it can seem to Jakob that instruction at the Benjamenta Institute is at the same time both meaningless and meaningful. This contradiction is ridiculous, but it happens to describe the impression life can make on us. Human logic, which can't see ultimate connections, judges the apparently random detail of life to be meaningless; the same structure of events is meaningful to the imaginative conviction of faith.

In this connection Jakob talks about dream and *Märchen*. The instruction at the school seems to him 'like a dream, like a meaningless and at the same time very meaningful *Märchen*'. Is there any other kind of *Märchen* or dream? Thought has no power here. No *Märchen* is ever explained by its facts. Connections are left out without comment, there is no analysis of motive or event. It is as if prose has not yet got to the argumentative stage. This kind of world without apparent causation is superficially meaningless. The *Märchen* survives down the ages because we know, beyond rational belief, that it is meaningful. It is we who give our world its dual face; thinking makes it so.

Egocentric judgment is suppressed in the stream of *Märchen*, dream, sleep, darkness. Jakob has already given his opinion: 'It's when one is asleep that one is perhaps nearest to God.' 'In a dream,' says Elihu to Job, 'in a vision of the night, when deep sleep falleth upon men, in slumberings upon the bed, then he openeth the ears of men, and sealeth their instruction.' This is surely the kind of dream Jakob experiences at his school. If connections can't be seen and meaning is therefore not evident, truth can exist only in a region of darkness, the area outside frail human perception. The promised land is always somewhere else.

Before Jakob has penetrated to the mysterious inner rooms of the Benjamenta Institute he is convinced they contain marvellous things. These rooms, like everything else in the novel, are a projection from Jakob's awareness, imposed on him by the author. They represent the feeling that meaning not visible in daily life must exist beyond the limits of normal perception, like a sleeping king.

Jakob enters these rooms twice, once in a vision, the second time in convenient fictional reality—in other words, in his author's vision. His first visit is clearly an induction into life. He is guided by Fräulein Lisa Benjamenta, who appears to be an intermediary between him and the life he aspires to but cannot find. Significantly, she leads him into what is for him impenetrable darkness. It is like the darkness which so often closes round the Kafka hero as he approaches a condition of truth. The second time Jakob enters the rooms, in reality, so to speak, expecting the marvellous things of his imagination, he is disappointed. All he finds is an old goldfish tank. Everything else exists only in his fantasy. The truth is less complicated, indeed is not complicated at all. The truth is that the seemingly extraordinary can be drawn only from the ordinary events of our existence. This is the basis of all that seems fantastic, all the illusions, all the spiritual soaring. 'First you must learn above all to know your surroundings.' The commonplace must be the only source of revelation because it is the only source available to us. (pp. 33-4)

The inner rooms of the Benjamenta Institute are not a separate place. Jakob thinks of them with his human faculties as the home of the miraculous, those imagined transformations which by-pass the course of nature and baffle humanity into insignificance, a false insignificance of seeming exclusion. The miraculous is only and always a natural event we haven't yet experienced in its full connective meaning. (p. 35)

In a dream, in a vision of the night, in his moment of inspiration, unplanned, unexpected even if hoped for, the writer can suddenly sense meaning. What is more persistently visible is the world of seeming disconnection. Walser's novel is a life, as he has told us. The rejection of Western culture is integral to Walser's life as well as to his ficiton. We hear his voice when Jakob says, 'I feel how little I am concerned with what people generally call world and how great and exciting that which I call world appears to me, in secret.'

Walser does not create a new world, except in secret. His human surroundings were a disappointment to him. In the dialogue between Jakob and his brother Johann we hear the words: 'There is nothing beautiful or excellent any more. You have to dream the beautiful and the good and the honest for yourself.'

'Surrender yourself humbly, then you can be trusted to care for all things.' The quiet retreat of Tao is presumably a cave on the mountainside. In the modern world the cave can turn out to be an asylum of a different kind. Walser was fifty when he was admitted to the mental institution at Waldau. In 1933 he was moved to another asylum where he stayed for the rest of his life. Was he insane? He said he was. A visitor once asked him if he was writing anything. He said: 'I'm not here to write. I'm here to be mad.' He wrote nothing in these years. Perhaps he went to these lower regions in order to breathe.

Early in the eleventh century Lady Murasaki, author of *The Tale of Genji,* expressed in her diary an ambition to 'be allowed to live buried in my own thoughts like a tree stump in the earth'. Perhaps it was this kind of living death that Walser wanted in his retirement from the world. In his work there is even a parallel feeling of identity with the withered tree. When he describes that unified current of tree and water and self in his essay **'The Forest'** he makes the tree an image of vigorous growth. Jakob von Gunten returns to the image of the tree. In the novel the tree still flows, but this time it flows from life to death. When Jakob speaks now, Walser seems to be anticipating his own silence and decline in the asylum, taking his work, this long book about himself, to the very end:

> Perhaps I shall never spread branches and twigs. One day, from my existence and my effort, some kind of perfume will be given off. I'll blossom and give off a little perfume, as if just for my own pleasure. Then I'll let my head droop, this head Kraus calls a stupid and proud pighead. My arms and my legs will grow strangely slack; my spirit, my pride, my character, everything, everything will break and wilt, and I'll be dead. Not really dead, just dead in a certain way, then I'll live my life away like that for perhaps sixty years and so drift into death.

Walser at the Herisau sanatorium in 1942.

In the asylum Walser found his submission and servitude, the condition foretold by Jakob in the first words of his book: '. . . we shall all be something very small and subordinate in later life.' Walser must have enjoyed his subordination. (pp. 35-6)

'You have to dream the beautiful and the good and the honest for yourself.' Walser's work is this dream. The impression it leaves is like the instruction at the school for servants, that one long lesson in the conduct of life, described by Jakob as 'a meaningless and at the same time very meaningful *Märchen*'. (p. 36)

Idris Parry, "The Writer As Servant," in his Hand to Mouth and Other Essays, *Carcanet New Press, 1981, pp. 19-36.*

SVEN BIRKERTS (essay date 1982)

[In the following excerpt, Birkerts praises Walser's style and finds that the subjects of his works are not formal themes, but his reactions to life around him.]

Walser is one of the most remarkable and fully realized stylists in modern literature. He has the rarest of gifts, the ability to get spirit onto the page at the flick of a pen. Each story, each sentence is as particular and unique as a fingerprint. "I am a little worn out, raddled, squashed, downtrodden, shot full of holes" begins the sketch titled **"Nervous."** A simple string of words has the reader tensed for perilous descent. In Walser's hands the language plays and suffers, it vibrates exactly to the rhythms of the psyche: delicacies of frequency are disclosed where we least suspect them. It is here that style fulfills its highest aspiration: it merges with content.

I have been talking abstractly, as if [his] pieces were without subject, a kind of music. Of course this is not true. In each there is an incident or observation or, more likely, a field of incidents. But these are wholly subordinated to Walser's own reactions and to his constant astonishment at the fact that there is a world and that one is allowed to go about in it.

Take . . . **"The Walk."** It is nothing more—or less—than a fifty-page ramble in the company of Robert Walser. (Walser was, it should be mentioned, one of that select order of writer-walkers that includes Nietzsche, Hamsun, Benjamin and Thoreau, for whom walking was not merely an activity conducive to thought but was a fusion of the physical and mental that made it possible to think with the whole being.) Walser's walk covers a course of several miles and involves a half-dozen encounters, none of them dramatically significant. But what an odyssey! He moves from one thing to the next with antennae bristling. His sensibility dilates from timorousness to brash boldness, zigzags from dispassionate observation to the cry of a soul overwhelmed.

There is no progress in the story except the progress of the walk itself. The encounters are like hallucinations—they are momentarily everything, and then they are left behind and never referred to again. The same is true of observations. At one moment the walker is in fine fettle, looking forward to lunch with a woman friend, in the next he is outraged by the ostentatious gold lettering on a baker's signboard. In a flash he moves from the particular to the universal. . . .

Walser loved to mimic, to play with voices—as here he throws the quavering syllables of the underling into sudden contact with the imperious syntax of authority. The rhythms alone unmask the relations of power.

Walser wrote prodigiously. [Between 1907 and 1929, the prime years of his literary career,] Walser modified his style several times. Increasing mastery prompted him to greater daring: the associative leaps became more adventurous, the transitions more oblique. Yet even the slightest sketches bear his special impress. We might think of these stories as many fragments of a broken mirror. One holds sky and a moving cloud, another gives us a face or a blooming rose. There is the sense that if we could have all of Walser's writings together—including the many stories that are yet untranslated—it would be possible to fit them edge to jagged edge and see the world as it has never been seen before.

The fractured mirror is a suggestive image. In 1929, when he was 51, Walser committed himself to a sanatorium. The diagnosis was acute schizophrenia. The qualities that distinguish his prose, the special keenness, the excited fling of his transitions, the sense that the world is being received by a mind miraculously unburdened by categories and concepts, these are in some way inseparable from the pressures of his mental disorder. (pp. 312-13)

Sven Birkerts, "A Startled Miniaturist," in The Nation, *Vol. 235, No. 10, October 2, 1982, pp. 312-14.*

SUSAN SONTAG (essay date 1982)

[In the following excerpt Sontag discusses characteristic aspects of Walser's works, including their variety, the evidence of despair, and the portrayal of the anti-heroic.]

Anyone seeking to bring Walser to a public that has yet to discover him has at hand a whole arsenal of glorious comparisons. A Paul Klee in prose—as delicate, as sly, as haunted. A cross between Stevie Smith and Beckett: a good-humored, sweet Beckett. And, as literature's present inevitably remakes its past, so we cannot help but see Walser as the missing link between Kleist and Kafka, who admired him greatly. (At the time, it was more likely to be Kafka who was seen through the prism of Walser. Robert Musil, another admirer among Walser's contemporaries, when he first read Kafka pronounced the latter "a peculiar case of the Walser type.") I get a similar rush of pleasure from Walser's single-voiced short prose as I do from Leopardi's dialogues and playlets, that great writer's triumphant short prose form. And the variety of mental weather in Walser's stories and sketches, their elegance and their unpredictable lengths remind me of the free, first-person forms that abound in classical Japanese literature: pillow book, poetic diary, "essays in idleness." But any true lover of Walser will want to disregard the net of comparisons that one can throw over his work.

In long as in short prose Walser is a miniaturist, promulgating the claims of the anti-heroic, the limited, the humble, the small—as if in response to his acute feeling for the interminable. Walser's life illustrates the restlessness of one kind of depressive temperament: he had the depressive's fascination with stasis, and with the way time distends, is consumed; and spent much of his life obsessively turning time into space: his walks. His work plays with the depressive's appalled vision of endlessness: it is all voice—musing, conversing, rambling, running on. The important is redeemed as a species of the unimportant, wisdom as a kind of shy, valiant loquacity.

The moral core of Walser's art is the refusal of power; of domination. I'm ordinary—that is, nobody—declares the characteristic Walser persona. In **"Flower Days,"** . . . Walser evokes the race of "odd people, who lack character," who don't want to do anything. The recurrent "I" of Walser's prose is the opposite of the egotist's: it is that of someone "drowning in obedience." One knows about the repugnance Walser felt for success—the prodigious spread of failure that was his life. In **"Kienast,"** . . . Walser describes "a man who wanted nothing to do with anything." This non-doer was, of course, a proud, stupendously productive writer, who secreted work, much of it written in his astonishing micro-script, without pause. What Walser says about inaction, renunciation of effort, effortlessness, is a program, an anti-romantic one, of the artist's activity. In **"A Little Ramble,"** . . . he observes: "We don't need to see anything out of the ordinary. We already see so much."

Walser often writes, from the point of view of a casualty, of the romantic visionary imagination. **"Kleist in Thun,"** . . . both self-portrait and authoritative tour of the mental landscape of suicide-destined romantic genius, depicts the precipice on the edge of which Walser lived. The last paragraph, with its excruciating modulations, seals an account of mental ruin as grand as anything I know in literature. But most of his stories and sketches bring consciousness back from the brink. He is just having his "gentle and courteous bit of fun." . . . **"The Walk"** . . . identifies walking with a lyrical mobility and detachment of temperament, with the "raptures of freedom"; darkness arrives only at the end. Walser's art assumes depression and terror, in order (mostly) to accept it—ironize over it, lighten it. These are gleeful as well as rueful soliloquies about the relation to gravity, in both senses, physical and characterological, of that word: anti-gravity writing, in praise of movement and sloughing off, weightlessness; portraits of consciousness walking about in the world, enjoying its "morsel of life," radiant with despair.

In Walser's fictions one is (as in so much of modern art) always inside a head, but this universe—and this despair—is anything but solipsistic. It is charged with compassion: awareness of the creatureliness of life, of the fellowship of sadness. (pp. vii-ix)

Susan Sontag, "Walser's Voice," in Selected Stories *by Robert Walser, translated by Christopher Middleton & others, Farrar, Straus and Giroux, 1982, pp. vii-ix.*

ADDITIONAL BIBLIOGRAPHY

DeFeo, Ronald. "Not Here to Write but to Be Mad." *The New York Times Book Review* (24 October 1982): 14, 46.

Examines the characters in Walser's short fiction and discusses similarities and differences between Franz Kafka's work and Walser's.

Favorable review of the first English translation of Walser's works. The reviewer calls the story "*The Walk*" a "*tour de force* of cunning improvisation that has no parallel in any literature."

Kaufman, Herbert L. "Large and Small World in Robert Walser's Novels." *Literatur in Wissenschaft und Unterricht* III, No. 2 (1970): 98-105.

Examines the portrayal of the "large and small worlds" in Walser's novels; that is, the difference between city life and country life and between one's native land and the rest of the world.

"Divine Fool." *The Times Literary Supplement*, No. 3593 (8 January 1971): 29.

Maintains that *Jakob von Gunten* surpasses Robert Musil's *Törless* and Rainer Maria Rilke's *Malte Laurids Brigge* in its portrayal of sensitive, alienated individuals in modern society.

"Germanic Storytellers." *The Times Literary Supplement*, No. 2913 (27 December 1957): 785.

"Servant of Words." *Times Literary Supplement*, No. 3668 (16 June 1972): 680.

Notes Walser's characteristic attitude of subservience in both his life and works, and maintains that his "prose is brilliantly varied, not because of an act of will but through subservience, yielding to the object so that the prose takes the shape of the event it describes."

Weeks, Andrew. "The Ironic Disenchantment: Robert Walser's *Der Gehülfe*." In his *The Paradox of the Employee: Variants of a Social Theme in Modern Literature*, pp. 63-80. Berne: Peter Lang Publishers, 1980.

Analyzes Walser's treatment of a recurring theme in modern literature, that of the ambiguity and indeterminacy of an employee's social and occupational position. Weeks examines Walser's use of impressionistic techniques in *Der Gehulfe,* and concludes that "the underlying tendency of *Der Gehülfe* can be termed 'phenomenological'; for Walser looks above all to the 'things themselves,' portraying the uncanny qualities of a direct experience from which social, ideological, and philosophical elements have been (partially and incompletely) 'bracketed out,' by the employee's disassociated position and point of view.'

White, J. J. Review of *Jakob von Gunten: A Novel,* by Robert Walser, *Robert Walser's Prosa: Versuch einer Strukturanalyse,* by Dierk Rodewald and *Robert Walser: Entwurf einer Bewusstseinstruktur,* by Nagui Naguib. *Modern Language Review* 67, No. 3 (July 1972): 708-10.

Review of *Jakob von Gunten* and of two German language critical works on Walser. White concentrates in particular on the bildungsroman aspects of Walser's works.

William Butler Yeats

1865-1939

Irish poet, dramatist, essayist, critic, short story writer, and autobiographer.

Yeats is considered one of the greatest poets in the English language. Although his interest in Irish politics and his visionary approach to poetry often confounded his contemporaries and set him at odds with the intellectual trends of his time, Yeats's poetic achievement stands at the center of modern literature. Yeats's poetry evolved over five decades from the vague imagery and uncertain rhythms of *The Wanderings of Oisin, and Other Poems,* his first important work, to the forceful, incantatory verse of the *Last Poems*. His remarkable creative development in his final years, at an age when most poets are content to reiterate old themes, illustrates a lifelong determination to remake himself into his ideal image of the poet: a sacerdotal figure who assumes the role of mediator between the conflicting forces of the objective and subjective worlds. Though he was never drawn to extremist political views, Yeats was devoted to the cause of Irish nationalism. He played an important part in the Celtic Revival Movement, founding an Irish literary theater, the Abbey, with the help of Lady Augusta Gregory and J. M. Synge. Yeats also promoted the Irish literary heritage through his use of material from ancient Irish sagas in his poems and dramas. He desired to invoke the hidden Ireland of heroic times, believing that only by "expressing primary truths in ways appropriate to this country" could artists hope to restore to modern Ireland the "unity of culture" that he felt was needed to bring an end to his country's internal division and suffering. In addition to the myths and history of Ireland, magic and occult theory were also important elements in Yeats's work. Related to his belief in the power of the imagination and his view of the poet as kindred to the magician and the alchemist, was his interest in spiritualism, theosophy, and occult systems. Many of the images found in his poetry are derived from Rosicrucianism and his own occult researches as described in the prose work *A Vision*.

Yeats was born in Dublin. His father, Jack Yeats, was the son of a once affluent family whom Oscar Wilde's father, Sir William Wilde, described as "the cleverest, most spirited people I ever met." For as long as he lived, Jack Yeats, himself an artist, exercised an important influence over his son's thoughts about art. Yeats's mother, Susan Pollexfen, was the daughter of a successful merchant from Sligo in the west of Ireland. Many of the Pollexfens were intense, eccentric people interested in faeries and astrology. From his mother, Yeats inherited a love of Ireland, particularly the west of Ireland near Sligo and Rosses Point, and an interest in folklore.

Yeats received no formal education until he was eleven years old, when he began attending the Godolphin Grammar School in Hammersmith, England. He continued his education in Ireland at the Erasmus Smith High School in Dublin. Generally, he was a disappointing student—erratic in his studies, prone to much daydreaming, shy, and poor at sport. In 1884, Yeats enrolled in the Metropolitan School of Art in Dublin, where he met the poet George Russell (A.E.). Russell shared Yeats's enthusiasm for dreams and visions; together they founded the Dublin Hermetic Society for the purposes of conducting magical experiments, and promoting their belief that "whatever the great poets had affirmed in their finest moments was the nearest we could come to an authoritative religion and that their mythology and their spirits of water and wind were but literal truth." This event marked the beginning for Yeats of a lifelong interest in occult studies, the extent of which was only revealed by the examination of his unpublished notebooks after his death. Following his experience with the hermetic society, Yeats joined the Rosicrucians, Madam H. P. Blavatsky's Theosophical Society, and MacGregor Mathers's Order of the Golden Dawn. He frequently consulted spiritualists, and engaged in the ritual conjuring of Irish gods. Yeats found occult research a rich source of images for his poetry, and traces of his esoteric interests appear everywhere in his poems. "The Rose upon the Rood of Time," for example, takes its central symbol from Rosicrucianism, and "All Soul's Night" describes a scrying ceremony.

The Granger Collection, New York

In 1885, Yeats met the Irish nationalist and Fenian leader John O'Leary, who was instrumental in getting Yeats's first verses published in *The Dublin University Review* and in directing Yeats's attention to native Irish sources for subject matter. Under the influence of O'Leary, Yeats took up the cause of Gaelic writers at a time when much native Irish literature was in danger of being lost due to England's attempts to anglicize

Ireland through a ban on the Gaelic language. O'Leary's ardent nationalism and resolute opposition to violence also impressed Yeats and were instrumetal in shaping political views that he held for the rest of his life. Perhaps the most fateful day in Yeats's life was January 30th, 1889, when he met Maud Gonne, an agitator for the Nationalist cause whose great beauty and reckless destructiveness in pursuit of her political goals both intrigued and dismayed him. He immediately fell in love with her. He began accompanying her to political rallies, and though he often disagreed with her extremist tactics, he shared her desire to see Ireland freed from English domination. During this period he wrote the drama *Cathleen ni Houlihan* for Gonne, and she was featured in the title role in its initial production. Yeats considered the play, which is about a noblewoman who sells her soul to the devil in order to save starving peasants, as appropriately symbolic of the activities to which Gonne had dedicated her life. Although Gonne's repeated refusals to marry Yeats brought him great personal unhappiness, their relationship endured through many estrangements, including her brief marriage to Major John MacBride. Nearly all of the love poetry that Yeats wrote during his career is addressed to her. In his verses she is associated with Helen of Troy, whose capriciousness led to the destruction of a civilization. To Yeats she represented an ideal, and throughout his life he found the friction between them, as well as their friendship, a source of poetic inspiration.

It was not until 1917, when he was fifty-two years old, that Yeats finally married. On their honeymoon his young wife, Georgie Hyde-Lees, discovered that she had mediumistic abilities and through the technique of automatic writing could receive communication from a visionary realm. Her efforts over many months produced the notes and materials on which Yeats based the text of *A Vision*—his explanation of historical cycles and a theory of human personality based on the phases of the moon. Late in his life, when decades of struggle by the Irish nationalists had finally culminated in the passage of the Home Rule Bill, Yeats became a senator for the Irish Free State. He left the senate in 1928, due to failing health, in order to devote his remaining years to poetry. He died in 1939.

In his earliest poetic works, such as *Mosada,* Yeats took his symbols from Greek mythology. After meeting John O'Leary, he turned instead to Irish mythology as a source for his images. The long narrative poem, "The Wanderings of Oisin" was the first he based on the legend of an Irish hero. In spite of its self-consciously poetic language and typically pre-Raphaelite rhythms, the poem's theme—the disagreement between Oisin and St. Patrick—makes it important to an understanding of the later Yeats. The sense of conflict between vision and corporeal realities, as symbolized by the saint and the hero, is the most essential dichotomy in Yeats's poetry. Throughout his poetic career Yeats's chief concern was the disparity between the imaginative individual's need to seek immortality through renunciation of the world of "mire and blood," and the instinctive human love of what perishes. In his poems he sought to resolve this disparity. He believed such a resolution was necessary because he felt the world of pure forms was impotent without its connection to life, but he also recognized that only through imagination could the raw materials of life be transformed into something enduring. For Yeats, the role of the artist was the same as that of the alchemist: he must effect a transformation that obscures the distinction between form and content, between "the dancer and the dance." This theme is most effectively expressed in the later poems "Sailing to Byzantium" and "Byzantium." As Yeats grew older and more sure of his themes, his approach to the techniques of poetry changed. Recognizing that faery songs were less suited to the tragic themes that preoccupied him than were more realistic narratives, he began, with the poems of *In the Seven Woods,* to write verses describing actual events in his personal life or in the history of Ireland. One of his most famous lyrics, "Easter 1916," about a rebel uprising that resulted in the martyrdom of all who participated, belongs to this latter group. In his maturity, Yeats wrote little narrative poetry. Instead he adopted the dramatic lyric as his most characteristic form of expression. Under the influence of Ezra Pound, he simplified his diction and modified his syntax to more closely reflect the constructions of common speech. In works such as *Responsibilities, and Other Poems; The Wild Swans at Coole;* and *Michael Robartes and the Dancer,* his verses began to take on the rhetorical, occasionally haughty tone that readers today identify as characteristically Yeatsian. Critics agree that Yeats's poetic technique was impeccable. It was this mastery of technique that enabled him to perfect the subtle, forceful, and highly unusual poetic meter that he used to create the effect of a chant or an incantation in such poems as "The Tower."

Yeats considered his dramas an aspect of his plan to revitalize Irish culture. He wanted to create dramas that were symbolic and austere—a reflection not of life, but of "the deeps of the mind." The form that such dramas should take and the manner in which they should be staged eluded him for many years. In his early works, such as *The Shadowy Waters* and *The Land of Heart's Desire,* he found that conventional stage techniques and realistic characters were not suited to the poetic portrayal of spiritual truths and psychological realities. It was not until Ezra Pound introduced him to the ancient Nō plays of Japan that he found a form he felt was suited to the heroic and tragic subjects that he wished to depict. In *Four Plays for Dancers,* as well as in subsequent works such as *Purgatory,* Yeats experimented with techniques borrowed from the Nō, such as ritualized, symbolic action and the use of masks. These plays contain some of his finest verse, and critics now believe that Yeats's approach to drama anticipated in many ways the abstract movements of modern theater.

Yeats's prose style in his essays and *Autobiographies* was influenced by his early admiration of Walter Pater. The detached and elegant *Autobiographies* have long been a source of controversy among critics. In the *Autobiographies,* Yeats provides a sensitive, if sometimes ironic, view of his age, but reveals little about his own life and thoughts. Even his close friend, George Russell, in reviewing the *Autobiographies,* criticized Yeats for these omissions. Nonetheless, the *Autobiographies* are a valuable source of information about Yeats's views on art and his theories of personality. In *The Celtic Twilight,* his collection of folktales from the west of Ireland, Yeats endeavored to record the folk legends of Irish peasants in a simple and dignified manner, rather than in the patronizing and comic way such materials were often treated by English writers. Yeats not only wished to preserve these legends, he also wanted to make them more widely available to the Irish people, who had lost touch with ancient Irish traditions. He sought in this way to promote the "unity of culture" that he believed could only be achieved in modern Ireland through an increased awareness of Ireland's heroic past.

Yeats was awarded the Nobel Prize in literature in 1923. However, for many years his intent interest in subjects that others labelled "archaic" and perceived as an affront to their modernity delayed his recognition among his peers. At the time of his death in 1939, Yeats's views on poetry were overlooked as eccentric by students and critics alike. This attitude held sway in spite of critical awareness of the beauty and technical proficiency of his verse. Yeats had long stood opposed to the notion that literature should serve society. As a youthful critic he had refused to praise the poor lyrics of the "Young Ireland" poets merely because they were effective as nationalist propaganda. Now, in maturity, he found that despite his success, his continuing conviction that poetry should express the spiritual life of the individual alienated him from those who believed that a "modern" poet must take as his themes social alienation and the barrenness of materialist culture. As Kathleen Raine wrote of him: "Against a rising tide of realism, political verse and University wit, Yeats upheld the innocent and the beautiful, the traditional and the noble," and in consequence of his disregard for the concerns of the modern world, was often misunderstood. As critics became disenchanted with the modern movement, Yeats's Romantic dedication to the laws of the imagination and art for art's sake became more acceptable. Critics today are less concerned with the validity of his occult and visionary theories than with their symbolic value as expressions of timeless ideals and a need for order. Yeats's interest in arcana is considered a manifestation of the truth of Wallace Stevens's statement that "poets are never of the world in which they live."

(See also *TCLC,* Vols. 1 and 11; *Contemporary Authors,* Vol. 104; *Dictionary of Literary Biography,* Vol. 10: *Modern British Dramatists, 1900-1945;* and Vol. 19: *British Poets, 1880-1914.*)

PRINCIPAL WORKS

Mosada (poetry) 1886
The Wanderings of Oisin, and Other Poems (poetry) 1889
The Countess Cathleen, and Various Legends and Lyrics (poetry) 1892
The Celtic Twilight (folklore) 1893
The Land of Heart's Desire (drama) 1894
Collected Poems (poetry) 1895
The Wind among the Reeds (poetry) 1899
The Shadowy Waters (drama) 1900
Cathleen ni Houlihan (drama) 1902
Ideas of Good and Evil (essays) 1903
In the Seven Woods (poetry) 1903
**Plays for an Irish Theatre*. 5 Vols. [first publication] (dramas) 1903-05
Stories of Red Hanrahan (short stories) 1904
Discoveries (essays) 1907
The Unicorn from the Stars [with Lady Isabella Augusta Gregory] (drama) 1907
Poetry and Ireland [with Lionel Johnson] (essays) 1908
The Green Helmet, and Other Poems (poetry) 1910
***Plays for an Irish Theatre* [first publication] (dramas) 1913
Responsibilities, and Other Poems (poetry) 1914
At the Hawk's Well (drama) 1916
On Baile's Strand (drama) 1916
The Wild Swans at Coole (poetry) 1917
Per Amica Silentia Lunae (essay) 1918
The Player Queen (drama) 1919
Michael Robartes and the Dancer (poetry) 1920
Four Plays for Dancers [first publication] (dramas) 1921
Four Years: 1887-91 (memoir) 1921
Later Poems (poetry) 1922
The Cat and the Moon, and Certain Poems (poetry) 1924
A Vision (essay) 1925; also published as *A Vision [enlarged edition]*, 1937
****Autobiographies* (memoir) 1926; also published as *Autobiographies* [enlarged edition], 1938
The Tower (poetry) 1928
The Winding Stair (poetry) 1929
The Dreaming of the Bones (drama) 1931
Words or Music Perhaps, and Other Poems (poetry) 1932
The Collected Poems of W. B. Yeats (poetry) 1933
The Collected Plays of W. B. Yeats (dramas) 1934; also published as *The Collected Plays of W. B. Yeats* [enlarged edition], 1952
The King of the Great Clock Tower (poetry) 1934
Wheels and Butterflies (drama) 1934
A Full Moon in March (poetry and dramas) 1935
The Herne's Egg (drama) 1938
New Poems (poetry) 1938
Purgatory (drama) 1938
Last Poems and Two Plays (poetry and dramas) 1939
On the Boiler (essays and poems) 1939
The Death of Cuchulain (drama) 1949
The Letters of W. B. Yeats (letters) 1954
W. B. Yeats: Essays and Introductions (essays) 1961
The Poems: A New Edition (poetry) 1983

*This work also includes the drama *At the Well of the Saints* by J. M. Synge.

**This work is a revision of the earlier *Plays for an Irish Theatre*.

***This work includes the memoirs *Reveries over Childhood and Youth* and *The Trembling of the Veil*. The enlarged edition of 1938 also includes the memoirs *Dramatis Personae, Estrangement, The Death of Synge,* and *The Bounty of Sweden*.

F. R. LEAVIS (essay date 1932)

[*Leavis is an influential contemporary English critic. His critical methodology combines close textual criticism with predominantly moral, or social-moral, principles of evaluation. Leavis views the writer as that social individual who represents the "most conscious point of the race" in his or her lifetime. More importantly, the writer is one who can effectively communicate this consciousness. Contrary to what these statements may suggest, Leavis is not specifically interested in the individual writer per se, but rather with the usefulness of his or her art in the scheme of civilization. The writer's role in this vision is to promote what Leavis calls "sincerity"—or, the realization of the individual's proper place in the human world. Literature which accomplishes this he calls "mature," and the writer's judgment within such a work he calls a "mature" moral judgment. From the foregoing comments it should be clear that Leavis is a critic concerned with the moral aspects of art, but a number of his contemporaries, most notably René Wellek and C. S. Lewis, have questioned the existence of a moral system beneath such terms as "maturity" and "sincerity." Leavis's refusal to theorize or develop a systematic philosophy has alienated many critics and scholars from his work. In the following excerpt, Leavis examines the development of Yeats's poetic career.*]

[***The Wanderings of Oisin,*** the] long poem which gave its name to [Mr Yeats's] collection of 1889 (his first), might be described as Mr Yeats's *Alastor* and *Endymion*. Its importance is what is indicated by this note: '. . . from the moment when I began the *Wanderings of Usheen* . . . my subject matter became Irish.' Mr Yeats starts in the English tradition, but he is from the outset an Irish poet. The impulse behind the poem is the familiar one. A poet's day-dream could not easily be more cloudy and tenuous than the wistful Elysium of his Irish theme, with its 'dim, pale waters' and its realms

> Where Aengus dreams from sun to sun
> A Druid dream of the end of days;

and yet there is a paradoxical energy about the poem that distinguishes it from any of Morris's day-dreams: its pallor and weariness are not the exquisite aesthetic etiolation familiar to the

> Poets with whom I learned my trade,
> Companions of the Cheshire Cheese . . .

For Mr Yeats's Irishness is more than a matter of using Irish themes and an Irish atmosphere. It means that his dream-world is something more than private, personal and literary; that it has, as it were, an external validation. (p. 34)

His second collection of poems, ***The Rose*** . . . , frankly brings the cult of 'Eternal beauty wandering on her way,' with its Red Rose of 'an unimagined revelation,' into the world of Irish lore. But there is still a certain esoteric languor about this phase:

> Beauty grown sad with its eternity
> Made you of us, and of the dim grey sea;

and we are again reminded that we are in the 'nineties. ('With a rhythm that still echoed Morris I prayed to the Red Rose.') Here, too, belongs the unfortunate ***Innisfree;*** unfortunate, because it is Mr Yeats's most anthologized poem and recalls to us his own note: 'I tried after the publication of ***The Wanderings of Oisin*** to write of nothing but emotion, and in the simplest language, and now I have had to go through it all, cutting out or altering passages that are sentimental from lack of thought.'

But with ***The Wind Among the Reeds*** . . . the dream-reality takes on a new life, and the poet inhabits it surely. And although the imagery of the Celtic Twilight is heavily worked—'pale,' 'dim,' 'shadowy,' 'desolate,' 'cloud-pale,' 'dream-heavy'—there is no languor or preciosity here. Indeed, 'passion-dimmed' and 'pale fire' are equally important in the vocabulary. For a new force has entered Mr Yeats's poetry—love. It is mainly despairing love, and the poetry is extremely poignant. But for us the essential thing to note is how Mr Yeats turns both exaltation and despair to the heightening of his dream-world. . . . (pp. 35-6)

The poetry of ***The Wind Among the Reeds*** . . . is a very remarkable achievement: it is, though a poetry of withdrawal, both more subtle and more vital than any pure product of Victorian romanticism. We might, as bearing on the strength it was to Mr Yeats to be Irish, note further that with the Irish element in the poetry was associated a public and practical aim. Early and long service in the cause of a national renaissance, and, above all, of a national theatre, might be expected to turn even a poet of the Victorian dream-world into something else; and Mr Yeats devoted to the Irish cause rare qualities of character and intelligence. (p. 38)

[A change] manifests itself in Mr Yeats's poetry when we compare ***The Wind Among the Reeds*** . . . with ***The Green Helmet***. . . . It is hard to believe that the characteristic verse of the later volume comes from the same hand as that of the earlier. The new verse has no incantation, no dreamy, hypnotic rhythm; it belongs to the actual, waking world, and is in the idiom and movement of modern speech. It is spare, hard and sinewy and in tone sardonic, expressing the bitterness and disillusion of a man who has struggled and been frustrated. . . . (pp. 41-2)

Nevertheless, the poetry of this later phase is a remarkable positive achievement: Mr Yeats was strong enough to force a triumph out of defeat. . . . The verse, in its rhythm and diction, recognizes the actual world, but holds against it an ideal of aristocratic fineness. It is idiomatic, and has the run of free speech, being at the same time proud, bare and subtle. To pass from the earlier verse to this is something like passing from Campion to Donne. The parallel, indeed, is not so random as it might seem. At any rate, Donne's name in connection with a poet capable of passionate intellectual interests, who from such a start achieved such a manner, leads us to reflect that if the poetic tradition of the nineteenth century had been less completely unlike the Metaphysical tradition Mr Yeats might have spent less of his power outside poetry. The speculation is perhaps idle, but it calls attention to the way in which his verse developed into something that has the equivalent of certain seventeenth-century qualities. His use of the idiom and rhythm of speech is not all:

> Plato thought nature but a spume that plays
> Upon a ghostly paradigm of things;
> Solider Aristotle played the taws
> Upon the bottom of a king of kings;
> World-famous golden-thighed Pythagoras
> Fingered upon a fiddle stick or strings
> What a star sang and careless Muses heard:
> Old clothes upon old sticks to scare a bird.

—This (and the context more than bears out the promise of flexibility and variety of tone) is surely rather like seventeenth-century 'wit'; more like it than anything we expect to find in modern verse outside the work of certain post-war poets—poets who exhibit no completer escape from the Victorian poetical. The volume it comes from, indeed, appeared after the war. But ***The Tower*** . . . merely develops the manner of ***The Green Helmet*** . . . , ***Responsibilities*** . . . , and ***The Wild Swans at Coole***. . . . (pp. 43-5)

In ***The Tower*** Mr Yeats achieves a kind of ripeness in disillusion. The scorn so pervasive before is gone: his tragic horror at the plight of Ireland (as, for instance, in ***Meditations in Time of Civil War***) is something different and more generous. There is indeed bitterness, but it is not the sterile kind. His raging against

> Decrepit age that has been tied to me
> As to a dog's tail

goes with a sense of ardent vitality:

> . . . Never had I more
> Excited, passionate, fantastical
> Imagination, nor an ear and eye
> That more expected the impossible;

and the excitement is as apparent as the bitterness in this poetry of the last phase. Each gives value to the other. He is capable of excitement, for instance, about the 'abstract things' that he describes as a *pis aller*. He turns with a pang from the varied 'sensual music' of the world, but he is drawn positively towards the 'monuments of unaging intellect':

> An aged man is but a paltry thing,
> A tattered coat upon a stick, unless
> Soul clap its hands and sing, and louder sing
> For every tatter in its mortal dress.

This (though there is always an ironical overtone) is the voice of one who knows intellectual passion. He does not deceive himself about what he has lost, but the regret itself becomes in the poetry something positive. His implications, in short, are very complex; he has achieved a difficult and delicate sincerity, an extraordinarily subtle poise.

What, then, it might be asked after this account of Mr Yeats's achievement, is there to complain of? Does it really show that the tradition if the nineteenth century might with advantage have been other than it was? If he had to struggle with uncongenial circumstances, has not every great artist had to do so; and did he not, by admission, make triumphs of them? Mr Yeats himself gives the answer in the bitter sense of waste he expresses characteristically, in the latest work as elsewhere. His poetry is little more than a marginal comment on the main activities of his life. No one can read his ***Autobiographies*** and his ***Essays*** without being struck by the magnificent qualities of intelligence and character he exhibits. His insight shows itself in his analysis of his own case, an analysis that suggests at the same time the complete achievement he was fated to miss: 'In literature,' he wrote in 1906, 'partly from the lack of that spoken word which knits us to the normal man, we have lost in personality, in our delight in the whole man—blood, imagination, intellect, running together—but have found a new delight in essences, in states of mind, in pure imagination, in all that comes to us most easily in elaborate music.' (pp. 45-7)

Disillusion and waste were indeed inevitable; but not in the form in which Mr Yeats suffered them. They might have been more significant. For Victorian romanticism was not the only possible answer to those modern conditions that Mr Yeats deplores. If it were, poetry would cease to matter. Adult minds could no longer take it seriously. Losing all touch with the finer consciousness of the age it would be, not only irresponsible, but anaemic, as, indeed, Victorian poetry so commonly is. Mr Yeats's career, then, magnificent as the triumph was that he compelled out of defeat, is a warning. It illustrates the special disability of the poet in the last century, and impressively bears out my argument about the poetic tradition. And it cannot be repeated. No Englishman in any case could have profited by the sources of strength open to Mr Yeats as an Irishman, and no such source is open to any one now. No serious poet could propose to begin again where Mr Yeats began. (pp. 49-50)

F. R. Leavis, "The Situation at the End of the War," in his New Bearings in English Poetry: A Study of the Contemporary Situation, *1932. Reprint by AMS Press, Inc., 1978, pp. 27-74.**

W. H. AUDEN (essay date 1940)

[Often considered the poetic successor of W. B. Yeats and T. S. Eliot, Auden is also highly regarded for his literary criticism. As a member of a generation of British writers strongly influenced by the ideas of Karl Marx and Sigmund Freud, Auden considered social and psychological commentary important functions of literary criticism. As a committed follower of Christianity, he considered it necessary to view art in the context of moral and theological absolutes. Thus, he regarded art as a "secondary world" which should serve a definite purpose within the "primary world" of human history. This purpose is the creation of aesthetic beauty and moral order, qualities that exist only in imperfect form in the primary world but are intrinsic to the secondary world of art. Consequently, it is both morally and aesthetically wrong for an artist to employ evil and suffering as subject matter. Auden concluded that "to write a play, that is to construct a secondary world, about Auschwitz, for example, is wicked: author and audience may try to pretend that they are morally horrified, but in fact they are passing an evening together, in the aesthetic enjoyment of horrors." While he has been criticized for significant inconsistencies in his thought, Auden is generally regarded as a fair and perceptive critic. In the following excerpt, Auden praises Yeats as a great lyric poet.]

"Everything he wrote was read," Yeats said in one of his last poems, and, indeed, he was unusually fortunate, for few poets have so managed to complete their career without suffering any reverses of reputation, at least with the young, and still fewer have written their most widely-acclaimed work in the second half of their life. The universal admiration which his later poems have commanded is all the more surprising when one remembers how antaganostic were both his general opinions and his conception of his art to those current in recent literary movements. . . . I find it encouraging that, despite this, Yeats was recognized as a great poet, for it indicates that readers are less bigoted, less insistant upon the identity of the poet's beliefs with their own, and, when they can find some that is not completely trivial in subject, more appreciative of poetry that sounds well, that *sings,* than they sometimes appear.

The first thing that strikes one about Yeats is that he really enjoyed writing poetry. Some moderns make one feel that they regard it merely as a necessary means to some other end, the communication of ideas, mystical experience, self-analysis, castigation of abuses or what-have-you, and that the medium in which they work, the sounds and patterns of words, irrespective of the subject, give them little or no pleasure. Yeats, on the other hand, was always more concerned with whether or not a phrase sounded effective, than with the truth of its idea or the honesty of its emotion.

Both attitudes, the Puritanical and the Esthetic, have their dangers. The first, in forgetting that poetry is an *art,* i.e., artificial, a *factible* not an *agibile,* may defeat its own purpose by producing drab stuff which is so harsh to the ear and lacking in pattern, that no one can take any pleasure in reading it; the second, by ignoring the fact that the artist is a human being with a moral responsibility to be honest, humble, and self-critical, may leave the poet too easily content with ideas which he finds poetically useful and effective. Not bothering to reexamine them, to throw out the false elements and develop the rest further, he is prevented from reaching his full potential poetic stature, and remains playing variations on the old tune which has served him so well in the past.

It cannot be said that Yeats completely escaped this second temptation. There are, particularly in [***Last Poems***], more frequent echoes from his own previous work, both in phrasing and rhythm, than there ought to be, and, though every short poem, no doubt, expresses an attitude which in so far as it is one out of many possible moods may be called a pose, its singularity should not obtrude, and on occasion Yeats indulges in an embarrassing insistance upon an old man's virility, which some one who was more self-critical, not as a poet, but as a man, would have avoided.

Further, his utter lack of effort to relate his esthetic Weltanschauung ["world view"] with that of science, a hostile neglect which was due, in part at least, to the age in which he was born when science was avidly mechanistic, was perhaps the reason why he never succeeded in writing a long poem. . . .

Much of his best work . . . . is concerned with the relation of Life and Art. In this relation he had, like Thomas Mann and

Valéry, a profound sense of what Kierkegaard called the Dialectic, but his vision of other kinds of relations was two-dimensional. Hence his onesided determinist and "musical" view of history, and the lack of drama which not all his theater can conceal. I cannot but feel, for instance, that the two plays in this volume are worthless.

Yet how little we care. For it is the lyrics we read. In lyric writing what matters more than anything else, more than subject-matter or wisdom, is diction, and of diction, "simple, sensuous and passionate," Yeats is a consummate master.

W. H. Auden, "Yeats: Master of Diction," in The Saturday Review of Literature, *Vol. XXII, No. 7, June 8, 1940, p. 14.*

JAMES STEPHENS (essay date 1944)

[Stephens, an Irish poet, novelist, and short story writer, was a central figure of the Irish Literary Renaissance who was best known for his fanciful tales based on Irish folklore and mythology. Stephens shared with William Blake, whose themes and style he emulated, a distrust for authority, a belief in the happy innocence of childhood, and a concern for animals and for the helpless. Although many of Stephens's themes are drawn from the legends of Ireland's past, his work also reflects his anger over the social evils of the time in which he wrote. Late in his literary career, Stephens embarked on a secondary profession as a lecturer and broadcaster. His James, Seumas & Jacques *contains the texts of forty-two radio broadcasts Stephens made for the British Broadcasting Corporation from 1928 through 1950. In the 1940s Stephens delivered a half-dozen broadcasts on various aspects of Yeats's life and career, including the following discussions of the poem* "Byzantium."*]*

Yeats as a young man.

Almost every poet has one peculiar poem, and you find that the whole man is involved in it. So "Lycidas" is Milton's, and is Milton; the "Intimations" is Wordsworth's, "The Anniversary" is Donne's, "The Scholar Gypsy" is Arnold's, and **"Byzantium"** is Yeats'. I am not now holding that these are the greatest works of the various masters, but that these are works which no one else but the given poet could possibly imagine: they are his by a special proprietorship, a special accent.

The poem **"Byzantium"** is the strangest poem in English, it is the most remote poem in English, and it is, even curiously, constructed of Yeats' own idiom. Indeed, if one held that it is created of Yeats' personal clichés, such could be held. There is almost no line, no image, in this poem which an attentive reader will not find to have been used before by Yeats, and often many times. It is perhaps the result of an excessive devotion to syntax that many phrases in Yeats' work come to have a general character, a foreseeable flow and fall. Yeats had discovered his own idiom, but he was not asleep to this fact, he was very practically aware of it. (pp. 77-8)

Before Yeats composed his strange poem he had been moving steadily enough towards it. All his paths seemed directed to that Graeco-Roman-Oriental bourne, whence truly no traveller has yet returned.

His verse begins under the influence of the French Symbolists. In his adult life he was endlessly interested in what is indifferently called occultism or spiritualism. The Rosy Cross also entreated him, and in later life he studied and pondered the Hindu Upanishads. He loved certain words almost childishly. Such words as Zoroaster, Pythagoras, Trismegistus, Byzantium. Byzantine art—which looks so primitive, and isn't—that subtle, inhuman generalization, stylization, that simplification which is more complex than complexity itself, that loveliness which is always out of reach and almost out of mind, captured his later imagination, and some quality of it did get into his later art.

There is, of course, much of this strangeness and remoteness in all poetry. A man or a woman in a Byzantine drawing is not a man or a woman: they suggest personality but do not express it. Indeed, much that we call humanity has been abstracted from them, and strangely enough, they are not lessened by this abstraction, they are even singularly ennobled and beautified by possessing no recognizable being. (pp. 78-9)

The poetic person is always an immaculate conception, and disdains all that can be thought of as identity or reality. (p. 79)

Yeats' **"Byzantium"** is not quite so. It is not immaculately conceived. It has unfortunate realities sounding and mourning through its brazen airs, and, while it is truly remote, it is not of that innocency, of that passionlessness, of that total non-violence and non-ego which, had he lived yet a poor few years, Yeats would certainly have carried it to, and crowned himself as a wonder, for he was the most determined seeker after what he did not understand, but did surmise, that has ever worked in verse.

This sense of not-quite-completed life, a not-quite-compact comprehension, is one that troubles his reader, and makes it difficult quite to be his lover as well as his reader. You may love such or such a poem, and the Shelley or Keats or Blake or Herrick who wrote it—these, by the way, are the only "lovable" poets—but you cannot so love a Yeats poem and the poet who begat it, for he tends to be present, not so much creating a poem as producing it. Something, so, of drama and publicity is obtruded into his verse, and he is seen as having more petulance, more violence than is admirable in a poet; but he had not time to grow out of himself, his moods and his idioms.

There are three books by Yeats to which attention must be drawn in considering this famous poem. They are his three last books, ***The Tower, The Winding Stair,*** and ***Last Poems.*** Each a remarkable book. The first poem in ***The Tower*** is called **"Sailing to Byzantium"**; in his next book, ***The Winding Stair,*** there is the poem **"Byzantium."** These two poems are separated by three years of intense activity on the poet's part, and it is natural to consider that they are separate works. In reality they are only separated in a sense that a preface is separated from its volume, or an overture from its symphony.

I do not agree with Wordsworth's statement that poetry is emotion recollected in tranquillity, and especially I do not think that this statement can be applied to Yeats. His was an excitable nature, and out of some working excitement all his poems emerged. I think this is true of every creative artist, when they cease to live urgently they cease to work well, and until the day of his death Yeats did not cease from work.

In his later years, and in his very last work, he was more avid of personal experience than ever he had been in his youth. At the time he composed the first **"Byzantium"** Yeats was already an elderly man, but this is not the poem of an old man, nor are any of his poems of that stamp. (pp. 80-1)

With the publication of ***The Tower*** a new Yeats, a new poet came into being, and it is worth considering how this came to be, and what kind of person the new poet is.

After a curiously prolonged youth Yeats grew up. He came strangely of age when he had about reached his sixtieth year. In 1928, with the publication of ***The Tower*** he was forcibly parted from childish things. You will remember Milton's definition that poetry is simple, sensuous and passionate. Yeats' poetry till that date had been rather simple, rather sensuous, and rather violent, but now it began to fit the definition. Was he the only poet of our day capable of a passionate utterance? I think he was.

He did not reach maturity: he was shocked into it by the oldest personal realization that I know of. At almost sixty years of age Yeats made a curious discovery. Every person of sixty has made the same discovery before him, but they have kept it dark—he discovered that he was growing old! (pp. 81-2)

Yeats knew, as you and I know, that "everything grows old and withers and dies," but he didn't believe a word of it; and then, with the poems of ***The Tower,*** he realized it with a vengeance.

No one has left so angry a record of disillusionment behind him on this count as Yeats has. ***The Tower,*** and much of the next book, is an almost frantic outburst of rage against the indignities that Time was piling on him. . . . And yet, at sixty digested years, he did not feel that the spirit within him was one hour or one experience older than that spirit had been when he was a careful thirty or a careless twenty. But he could surmise, indeed, now that he knew that Time had taken him by the hair, and it would shake the life right out of his skin within a measure of days which he could almost calculate. And yet, he knew himself to be more capable, more vivacious than he had ever been, and that he, who had never been young, was young at last; he had been born again. (pp. 82-3)

He still wishes to dance. . . . (p. 84)

Here then is the oddest poem, the famous **"Byzantium."** It is quite impossible to say anything about the meaning of this poem, for it disdains meaning. It is the strangest poem in the language. It is the most remote poem in the language. It is though the writer had hearkened, with another than the physical ear, to a gong beating away on Orion or Neptune. Its meaning cannot be uttered, but it is, perhaps, possible to listen into its brazen and fuming climate, and to agree, that an unimaginable and inexpressible meaning has been drawn as closely to us as can be contrived. (p. 85)

James Stephens, "'Byzantium'," in his James, Seumas & Jacques, *edited by Lloyd Frankenberg, The Macmillan Company, 1964, pp. 77-86.*

REUBEN A. BROWER (essay date 1954)

[In the following excerpt, Brower provides an introductory survey of Yeats's career and development as a poet.]

We value the poetry of Yeats, like other good poetry, because it fixes moments of experience in memorable image and distinctly heard rhythm, and so seems to make them timeless. . . . But we also feel in Yeats . . . a distinctly "modern" quality; his art has an additional value for us because it belongs so definitely to our own time. Yeats's achievement matters especially to present-day readers because he wrote his way out of the nineteenth century, and because he helped the first generation of the twentieth to see and feel what their world was like. But his work was so entangled in the political and literary life of Ireland that the historical and biographical view is liable to swamp our reading of his poems. He was overly aware of the connection between his life and his art and almost too conscious of what he was doing. . . . (p. 779)

[Yeats's early poetic] successes, exquisite lyrics such as **"Innisfree"** and **"Who Goes with Fergus?"** now seem rather minor, as they did to Yeats himself a few years after he had written them. The poet who interests us today and who stands among the first of our century is the one who rejected or reshaped many elements in his youthful poetic self. A composite portrait of the poet drawn from the early volumes (1889-99) would include some curious traits: he is a chanter of fairy songs . . . but he is also a melancholy singer who longs for an "isle in the water" and a weary lover who seeks consolation from "love's bitter mystery" in Celtic hero stories; finally, he is a worshiper of symbolic images such as the "Far-off, most secret, and inviolate Rose."

It is interesting to note that much of his early poetic character can be traced either to his mother or his father. To his mother's family, the Middletons, Yeats owed his taste for mystery and for Celtic other-worlds. To his father his debt as a poet was enormous both early and late in his career. Throughout his life Yeats can be seen reacting against or fulfilling his father's ideals in art and poetry. . . . (p. 783)

But the wanness and weariness, the insistent loneliness of Yeats's early love poetry, is Pre-Raphaelitism as transmitted through the tired but elegant and erudite conversation of the Rhymers. It is hard to say how much the cloudy symbolism of these poems—particularly the "Rose" lyrics—owes to the Rhymers' passion for the French Symbolists. Certainly the theories of *symbolisme* gave support to Yeats's own belief that a poet's images disclose a reality beyond that known to the senses. But the belief can be traced equally well to many of his early literary and religious enthusiasms—to his love of Shelley and Blake, to his interest in magic, or to the secret wisdom of the Golden Dawn.

As Yeats's poetry grew more hazily symbolic, especially in . . . ***The Wind among the Reeds,*** the typical speaker of his poems resembles more and more the conventional lover of nineteenth-century Romantic poetry. "Dream" and "dream-dimmed" are words often on his lips, and if he now talks less naïvely of longing for fairyland, he is always addressing a beloved who is hardly of this world or picturing their love as a state of passionate trance. The tone he adopts is terribly solemn; the high religious unction of "I will arise and go now" becomes the rule, and too much of the time this lover sounds like the worshiper of **"The Secret Rose."** Although Yeats probably intended to create a distinct "personal utterance" in these love poems, the over-all impression is one of monotony and inhuman somnolence.

Yeats felt dissatisfied with much of his youthful poetry almost as soon as he had published it; and as early as 1892 he began to eliminate the more obviously "poetical" idioms and devices from his verse. But an important change in a poet's style must come from something more than disgust with a literary fashion. It was a deeper dissatisfaction that led to the revolution in Yeats's poetry in the years following his "exile" in the Irish Theatre. The first play produced by the new society—in 1899—was ***The Countess Kathleen,*** a play that Yeats had first written in 1891 and that mirrored very sharply the division in his activities during the last decade of the century. In this "ill-constructed" drama, with "dialogue turning aside at the lure of word or metaphor" (Yeats's comment), the Nationalist Yeats honored Maud Gonne as a Friend of the People, while the mystic poet subtly criticized her for wasting her life in politics. ***The Countess Kathleen*** points to the continuing conflict in Yeats's life and art between the dreamer and the man of action, but "out of this quarrel with himself, his poetry was born." Yeats ultimately created a new role for himself and found a new style by recognizing and expressing the conflict. . . . (pp. 783-84)

Yeats's progress from lonely song to lyric debate is connected with his discovery that he had been fighting a number of lost causes: Maud Gonne married another man, the Irish theatrical audience did not take kindly to being educated, a new religion was not born, and Yeats's enthusiasm for revolution waned when he saw "the little streets hurled upon the great." More important for the change in his style was his progress as a dramatist in making "characters talk to one another." We first surely detect speech breaking into song in a poem that probably reflects his difficulties in love, **"The Folly of Being Comforted."** With **"No Second Troy,"** Yeats clearly has found a new voice as compared with that of the old "dream-dimmed" lover. . . . He also begins to use a type of metaphor characteristic of his work from 1914 on. A modern feminist and city appear in the poem as another Helen in **"no second Troy"**; that is, a familiar symbol from myth or history refers to a present-day situation while also expressing more intimate concerns, here of a lover disappointed by his beloved and his society.

The poet who had once thought that his aim of "personal utterance" was at odds with his father's insistence on "drama" had at length found a way of being both personal and dramatic. . . . In ***Responsibilities*** . . . the contained violence of **"To a Friend"** stands beside **"The Magi,"** a poem that looks ahead to the union of both modes in lyrics focused on some great traditional symbol.

But before Yeats reached those successes he had first to make a conscious critical effort, which for him as for Keats meant also a personal and moral effort. In the period between 1912 and 1916 he set about quite deliberately to remake himself as a man and a poet, and in such a situation it is very like Yeats to seize on any source of power from the sublime to the ridiculous. He schools his inner life by the image of his "anti-self," the heroic man he would be, he rewrites his poems under the direction of Ezra Pound, a man twenty years younger than himself, and he consults a medium to talk with his attendant spirit. However comic the means, the end—the achievement of the poet—is admirable. It is not often that a poet or any man of fifty can learn from the young (an event very nearly as remarkable as communicating with another world). At the time when Yeats felt he was "drying up" and when he still had moments of longing for the fantasies of his youth, he found a role in which he could positively embrace and balance both "dreams" and "responsibilities."

"The Fisherman" . . . clearly announces Yeats's newly realized sense of himself and his audience. He will write no longer for actual Ireland, but for a man of heroic temper who will welcome poetry "cold/And passionate as the dawn." Here we see Yeats's myth-making power at its best: as the poem moves along, the "fisherman" very gradually takes on symbolic meaning; Yeats does not *make* his symbol, it makes itself. Although this man is "but a dream," he evokes a real past, the sterner Ireland of Swift and Burke. If Yeats is no longer a partisan, he is still responsive to national life. But now—and this is the important fact—he has discovered his relation to politics *as a poet*. In **"Easter 1916"** he honors a group of rebels, but in his own way, candidly acknowledging that they may have been wrong, that their hearts may have been "enchanted to a stone" by fanaticism, but also recognizing that in their action and death they have become beautiful. Yeats's balancing of loyalties in the poem is wonderfully matched by his interweaving of the old dreamlike rhythms with a new hardness of speech.

But Yeats attained a much subtler poise among his various selves in poetry written during the next few years, notably in the poems of ***The Tower***. . . . He had at last seen how to reconcile action and reverie, speech and song, public and personal symbolism. Yeats did not "solve" anything in these poems; he succeeded rather in making poetry out of his irresolution: that is his peculiar inimitable feat. In **"Sailing to Byzantium,"** "reverie" (in a special sense) seems the prime value, while in **"Among School Children"** there is an energetic balance between achievement and aiming at the unattainable. Though the two poems are so different, they disclose a similar progression, the mode of lyric debate that finally links the styles we have been tracing. So both begin with an old man talking in a matter-of-fact way ("That is no country for old men" and "I walk through the long schoolroom questioning"); each of the old men is keenly responsive to the sights and sounds of the real world, and each is ironically aware of the figure he cuts in an actual society; but they are at the same time excited by images of the soul's "magnificence" and of "heavenly glory." As they reflect, the debate between opposing desires and values becomes sharper, reaching a climax in a songlike prayer. . . . In the strongly rhythmed lines of the close, images appear (the bird, the chestnut-tree) that symbolize a reconciliation between feelings aroused in the debate. Yeats has found his "form"—in the full athletic sense—just as Keats did in his odes. (The comparison is illuminating, because the kind of poetry first glimpsed in *Endymion* culminates in **"Sailing to Byzantium"** and because Keats can strike a note of assurance beyond the reach of Yeats and most poets of the past fifty years.)

But the attitudes Yeats dramatizes are not wholly opposed, at least not in the poems. The singer of Byzantium hears too well the "sensual music" he neglects. The old man of **"Among School Children"** knows that heavenly "Presences" like children "break hearts," and he happily asserts the value of what Yeats's father called "Personality," the harmonious expression of the whole man. Other poems in ***The Tower*** express a poise between Yeats's private and public loyalties, often in the form of an argument between the man who withdrew to his "tower" and the man who might have fought beside his countrymen. But in poems like **"Sailing to Byzantium"** Yeats succeeds more fully in connecting his opposing worlds because he takes as symbols figures or cities that have long had the kind of meaning he attaches to them. It makes all the difference that he now chooses to sail to Byzantium rather than to Innisfree. He "leans out," as his father would say, to larger, more public kinds of significance and is able to say a great deal more to readers aware of their place in history. (pp. 784-85)

Yeats's historic symbols are not only backward-looking. Like those of T. S. Eliot and James Joyce they express a surprising sense of the present *in* the past, and they make us think of our moment in history, of modern crises, while talking about the turning point between pagan and Christian, or Babylonian and Greek, civilizations. **"The Second Coming"** is a nightmare vision of this "simultaneous" type. . . . (p. 786)

The form that Yeats achieved in the 20's, through which he balanced speech and song, the personal symbol and the historic, action and contemplation, remained with him during the rest of his career. Similar or identical symbols—Byzantium and Troy, gyres and towers, caves and tremendous statues—recur quite often and express the now familiar conflicts. But by the 30's there is some change in tone and intensity, perhaps a reflection of "the smiling public man" who had become a Senator in the Free State, a Nobel prize winner, and something of a national sage. Yeats now honors his early political and literary associates in verse that has the fine detachment and public decorum of Pope or Dr. Johnson. His "tower" is no longer the retreat of **"Il Penseroso,"** but the Anglo-Irish tradition, another country of the mind but one linked with actuality. **"Vacillation,"** the poem that perhaps best sums up Yeats's career, is remarkable for the ripe good humor with which the poet puts behind him the old temptation to "find relief" in a life and art detached from ordinary humanity.

Tranquillity is hardly the keynote of the poems written during Yeats's fourth and last period. He appears in them as an old man, but as no sage, and even when descanting on the serenity that comes with his years, he surprises us: "Bodily decrepitude is wisdom." The ugly facts are unblinkingly accepted; this old man, "mad as the mist and snow," has little in common with the prematurely aged singer of the 90's who found consolation in other-world fantasies. Conventional religious and sexual experiences are seen through completely, and yet the rhythm of the later songs is oddly cheerful, the singer is terribly and happily hard-boiled. This return to ballad-like rhythms recalls Yeats's early imitations of Irish popular verse only to bring out a difference: the consoling "yet's," the tear in the beer of music-hall song, have vanished.

But there is a close relation between the singer of ***Last Poems*** . . . and the poet-philosopher of ***The Tower*** period. One of the best of the late lyrics, **"An Acre of Grass,"** is a kind of noble parody of poems written ten years earlier. The progression is still the familiar one, from quiet speech to prayer, from images of here and now to symbols of a life eagerly desired, but instead of asking for a life "out of nature" or for harmonious development , this poet rudely calls for "an old man's frenzy." His ideal Presences are not Plato and Homer, but Lear and Michelangelo, mad old men who also found victory in "seeing through." A similarly exultant note can be heard in **"A Wild Old Wicked Man."** . . . Yeats had his difficulties in managing the old men of his later poems, and, like his commentators, he often tries too hard to force the note of vitality and profundity in songs of "lust and rage." We find the richness that we miss in these songs in the symbolic meditative poems of the familiar historical and personal sort: **"The Gyres," "The Statues," "The Circus Animals' Desertion," "A Bronze Head."** Yeats still moves in his mysterious way around the memory of a woman or a statue or a city, and as he talks and sings he unfolds and weighs antithetical views of character or history. Resolution becomes no easier; the poems almost fall apart as Yeats opens up his mind to every pull and counterpull.

Some critics argue that the unity of these and similar poems depends on the curious system that Yeats had evolved as a "philosopher." But we can usually grasp the meaning of Yeats's historic and cosmic symbols from the poems themselves, provided we have some familiarity with the interests in religion and history that he shared with his contemporaries. The poems are not necessarily more coherent because he had elsewhere worked out a diagram of man and the universe. But Yeats's theories—if that is the name for them—are worth looking at, since they supply some of the context in which he wrote and since they illustrate the difficulties of being a poet in the twentieth century.

Characteristics dominant in Yeats's poetry are also dominant in his thought: conflict and irresolution, combined with an intense desire to achieve reconciliation. Two themes keep recurring, the doctrines of the "anti-self" and of "Unity of Being." The dream of unity had started from his father's belief in "Personality," and Yeats's ultimate solution was to return to another attitude imparted by [his father]. But as usual his path was rebellious; he rejected the intellectual tradition to which his father, "a follower of John Stuart Mill," introduced him, just as he had clung to Pre-Raphaelite standards long after his father had abandoned them. Cut off from Catholic dogma by Protestant rationalism and scientific criticism, he had tried to create a cult from poetry and folklore and magic. But as the dream of finding a faith he could share with others faded, Yeats gradually evolved a private religion, and he finally produced his own Bible, ***A Vision.*** The search that came to this fantastic end grew out of a sensitivity to the disorder of the modern world and from a sane awareness that as a poet he needed some sort of "groundwork" on which to write. On these two counts, Yeats's thought is interesting even when absurd.

Characteristically, his beliefs were embodied in symbols. Unity of Being he saw represented by William Morris or by certain men of the Renaissance or by the characters of Chaucer, idealized figures in whom he found happy blends of art with effortlessness, intellect with physical vigor and grace, humanity with sensitivity to the supernatural. Individuals who attain Unity of Being arise most often in a society possessing a similar balance of values, in which all classes share inherited social traditions and religious beliefs. Unity of Being implies Unity of Culture. The enemy of Unity is "abstraction," the overdevelopment of one aspect of personality, or—in society—excessive specialization. The notion of the anti-self, expressed symbolically as "the Mask," is closely related to Unity, since men (and societies) achieve unity by modeling their lives after a self that is the opposite of their natural selves. Obscure as this doctrine is, it had practical importance as a private superstition by which Yeats's character was decisively shaped. He was always adopting some pose that he regarded as his opposite: he was the timid man who was trying to act boldly, the gregarious man who would be a lone thinker, the mystic longing to be a man of action. But he found it hard to decide which in fact *was* his natural self; mask and self kept interchanging.

These guiding ideas were becoming increasingly important to Yeats just when he was remaking himself as a poet between 1912 and 1916. In the years following his marriage in 1917 he translated his doctrines into a preposterous "system" that embraced history, the individual, and the universe, the full revelation being summed up in ***A Vision.*** The surprising experiences by which Yeats reached his goal include appearances of his personal "daemon" and communications with "voices" through his wife.

The key to the system lies in the anti-self, the tension of opposites, which is now symbolized by the "phases of the moon" and the "gyre" or cycle. Types of personality are placed on a scale running from the dark of the moon (the purely objective type) to the full moon (the purely subjective type), with varying mixtures assigned to each of the twenty-eight phases. The figure is also used to classify stages in a cycle of history. . . . [The] most vivid metaphor for this process in the individual and in history is the gyre, a cone-like spiral, a whirling movement that widens out as it goes. Like the phases of the moon, it represents movement from subjectivity (the point) to objectivity (the base), or vice versa. In history, progress in one direction is immediately followed by its opposite. (pp. 786-88)

What emerges from a look into this systematic fantasia? Certainly not a satisfactory religious belief or an adequate theory of historical change. What Yeats had done was to find in a symbolic account of history the dramatic and emotional satisfactions of religion. (p. 788)

But when we are reading his poetry, the absurdities and practical consequences of his system matter very little. In what sense Yeats "believed" in the statements of ***A Vision*** can never be determined; it seems unlikely that he regarded them as true in the sense in which the term is used of a scientific hypothesis. In the poems—with the few exceptions in which he is versifying his theories—we are free to take his cosmic symbols much as we take the celestial geography of *Paradise Lost*. But undoubtedly Yeats's interest in his system encouraged his weakness for deliberate symbol-making in verse, and under the spell of ***A Vision,*** he too often wrote poems in which he tells us he has found a symbol, but the symbol does not work imaginatively. So in **"Blood and the Moon"** he declares "this tower is my symbol," and the reader dutifully reminds himself that a tower equals a gyre, equals a phase of history, equals eighteenth-century Ireland. But we feel nothing "tower-like" in the imagery and concepts of the poem, we feel no connection *through* the analogy. By contrast, we can clearly link various phases of the poem through images of growth and sterility. As always, the proof of the poem is not in the symbol; the proof of the symbol is in the poem. When Yeats's metaphors drawn from dreaming about history are renewed in the imagery of a poem with the effect of focusing its meanings and extending its range, they justify themselves. (For a fine example, see the metaphor of cyclical movement in **"Two Songs from a Play."**)

We need not conclude that in poetry any metaphor for man and his destiny, any sense of history will do. But that Yeats had a way of expressing a large historical vision makes him certainly a more satisfying writer. He is one of the poets who expresses for us our fullest and finest awareness of our time. But insofar as his vision remains private or mechanically "built into" his poems, his poetry must be ranked with verse of a cult, for initiates only. (pp. 788-89)

Yeats did not succeed in putting the modern world together, but he did put some poems together. They were, as Robert Frost says, his "stays against confusion." He attained the successes of his maturity, not by system-making, but by artistic tact, by evolving his way of dramatizing various beliefs and attitudes, by letting his dreamlike symbols materialize to express and connect conflicts he could never resolve outside his poetry. In the achieved unity of his poems—as distinct from his theories—he had come back to his father's views of how a poet "believes" and works. The belief "of the poet," his father wrote to him, "comes when the man within has found some method or manner of thinking or arrangement of fact (such as is only possible in dreams) by which to express and embody an absolute freedom." . . . The substance of Yeats's poetry matters to us because he expresses with dramatic truth and musical delight dreams and renunciations to which we attach value in our own private and public worlds. To have experienced the voyage into a city of the mind's creating, where we are both alone and in the company of the great minds of the past, or to have felt both the waste and the heroic quality of political action based on abstract principles, to have entertained at once the tranquillity and the madness of age—these are among the better things that poetry can do for us. (p. 789)

Reuben A. Brower, "William Butler Yeats: Introduction," in Major British Writers: Wordsworth, Coleridge, Byron, Shelley, Keats, Tennyson, Browning, Arnold, Shaw, Yeats, Eliot, *Vol. II, edited by G. B. Harrison & others, enlarged edition, Harcourt Brace Jovanovich, 1954, pp. 619-30.*

ELDER OLSON (essay date 1962)

[Olson is an American poet and a leading proponent of the Chicago School of criticism, a critical movement that arose at the University of Chicago in the early 1940s in reaction to the New Criticism. Though sharing with the New Critics a dislike of biographical and historical approaches to literary criticism, the Chicago critics opposed the tendency of the New Criticism to neglect traditional poetics in favor of poetic diction, irony, and ambiguity. In Critics and Criticism, Ancient and Modern *(1952), the volume of essays that serves as the manifesto of the Chicago school, the movement's leader, Ronald S. Crane, calls for a systematic and comprehensive approach to criticism based on Aristotle's* Poetics. *Because of their use of this work as a model for their analyses of literature, critics of the Chicago School are often referred to*

as Neo-Aristotelian. In the following excerpt, Olson provides a detailed explication of "Sailing to Byzantium."]

In **"Sailing to Byzantium"** an old man faces the problem of old age, of death, and of regeneration, and gives his decision. Old age, he tells us, excludes a man from the sensual joys of youth; the world appears to belong completely to the young, it is no place for the old; indeed, an old man is scarcely a man at all—he is an empty artifice, an effigy merely, of a man; he is a tattered coat upon a stick. This would be very bad, except that the young also are excluded from something; rapt in their sensuality, they are ignorant utterly of the world of the spirit. Hence if old age frees a man from sensual passion, he may rejoice in the liberation of the soul; he is admitted into the realm of the spirit; and his rejoicing will increase according as he realizes the magnificence of the soul. But the soul can best learn its own greatness from the great works of art; hence he turns to those great works, but in turning to them, he finds that these are by no means mere effigies, or monuments, but things which have souls also; they live in the noblist element of God's fire, free from all corruption; hence he prays for death, for release from his mortal body; and since the insouled monuments exhibit the possibility of the soul's existence in some other matter than flesh, he wishes reincarnation, not now in a mortal body, but in the immortal and changeless embodiment of art.

There are thus the following terms, one might say, from which the poem suspends: the condition of the young, who are spiritually passive although sensually active; the condition of the merely old, who are spiritually and physically impotent; the condition of the old, who, although physically impotent, are capable of spiritual activity; the condition of art considered as inanimate—i.e., the condition of things which are merely monuments; and finally the condition of art considered as animate—as of such things as artificial birds which have a human soul. The second term, impotent and unspiritual old age, is a privative, a repugnant state which causes the progression through the other various alternative terms, until its contrary is encountered. The first and third terms are clearly contraries of each other; taken together as animate nature they are further contrary to the fourth term, inanimate art. None of these terms represents a wholly desirable mode of existence; but the fifth term, which represents such a mode, amalgamates the positive elements and eliminates the negative elements of both nature and art, and effects thus a resolution of the whole, for now the soul is present, as it would not be in art, nor is it passive, as it would be in the young and sensual mortal body, nor is it lodged in a "dying animal," as it would be in the body of the aged man; the soul is now free to act in its own supremacy and in full cognizance of its own excellence, and its embodiment is now incorruptible and secure from all the ills of flesh.

About these several oppositions the poem forms. The whole turns on the old man's realization, now that he is in the presence of the images of Byzantium, that these images have souls; there are consequently two major divisions which divide the poem precisely in half, the first two stanzas presenting art as inanimate, the second two, as animate; and that is the case can be seen from such signs as that the first half of the poem the images are stated as passive objects—they are twice called "monuments," they are merely objects of contemplation, they may be neglected or studied, visited or not visited, whereas in stanzas 3 and 4 they are treated as gods which can be prayed to for life or death, as beings capable of motion from sphere to sphere, as instructors of the soul, as sages possessed of wisdom; and the curious shift in the manner of consideration is signalized by the subtle phrasing of the first two lines of stanza 3: "O sages standing in God's holy fire/As in the gold mosaic of a wall." According to the first part, the images at Byzantium were images, and one should have expected at most some figurative apostrophe to them . . . , but here the similitude is reversed, and lest there should be any error, the sages are besought to come from the holy fire and begin the tuition of the soul, the destruction of the flesh.

Within these two halves of the poem, further divisions may be found, coincident with the stanzaic divisions. Stanza 1 presents a rejection of passion, stanza 2 an acceptance of intellection; then, turning on the realization that art is insouled, stanza 3 presents a rejection of the corruptible embodiment, and stanza 4, an acceptance of the incorruptible. There is an alternation, thus, of negative and affirmative: out of passion into intellection, out of corruption into permanence, in clear balance, the proportion being 1: 2: 3: 4; and what orders these sections is their dialectical sequence. That is, passion must be condemned before the intellect can be esteemed; the intellect must operate before the images can be known to be insouled; the realization that the images are insouled precedes the realization that the body may be dispensed with; and the reincarnation of the soul in some changeless medium can be recognized as a possibility only through the prior recognition that the flesh is not the necessary matter of the soul. The parallel opposition of contraries constitutes a sharp demarcation: in stanza 1 a mortal bird of nature amid natural trees sings a brief song of sensual joy in praise of mortal things, of "whatever is begotten, born, and dies"; in stanza 4 an immortal and artificial bird set in an artificial tree sings an eternal song of spiritual joy in praise of eternal things, of "what is past, or passing, or to come"; and similarly, in stanza 2 a living thing is found to be an inanimate artifice, "a tattered coat upon a stick," incapable of motion, speech, sense or knowledge, whereas in stanza 3 what had appeared to be inanimate artifice is found to possess a soul, and hence to be capable of all these. A certain artificial symmetry in the argument serves to distinguish these parts even further: stanzas 1 and 4 begin with the conclusions of their respective arguments, whereas 2 and 3 end with their proper conclusions, and 1 is dependent upon 2 for the substantiation of its premises, as 4 is dependent upon 3.

This much indication of the principal organization of the work permits the explication, in terms of this, of the more elementary proportions. The first line of stanza 1 presents immediately, in its most simple statement, the condition which is the genesis of the whole structure: "That is no country for old men"; old men are shut out from something, and the remainder of the first six lines indicates precisely what it is from which they are excluded. The young are given over to sensual delight, in which old men can no longer participate. But a wall, if it shuts out, also shuts in; if the old are excluded from something, so are the young; lines 7 and 8, consequently, exhibit a second sense in which "That is no country for old men," for the young neglect all intellectual things. Further, the use of "that" implies a possible "this"; that is, there is a country for the old as for the young; and, again, the use of "that" implies that the separation from the country of the young is already complete. The occupation of the young is shrewdly stated: at first sight the human lovers "in one another's arms" have, like the birds at their song, apparently a romantic and sentimental aura; but the curious interpolation of "Those dying generations" in the description of the birds foreshadows the significance they are soon to have; and the phrases immediately following remove all sentimentality: ''the salmon-falls, the mackerel-crowded seas'' intend the ascent of salmon to the headwaters, the descent of mackerel to the deep seas in the spawning season, and the ironic intention is clear: all—the human lovers, the birds, the fish, do but spawn, but copulate, and this is their whole being; and if the parallel statement does not make this sufficiently evident, the summation of all in terms merely of animal genera—''fish, flesh, or fowl''—is unmistakable. The country of the young, then, is in the air, in its waters, and on its earth, from headwaters to ocean, wholly given over to sensuality; its inhabitants ''commend all summer long'' anything whatsoever, so long as it be mortal and animal—thay commend ''whatever is begotten, born, and dies''; and while they ''commend'' because they have great joy, that which they praise, they who praise, and their praise itself are ephemeral, for these mortals praise the things of mortality, and their commendation, like their joy, lasts but a summer, a mating season. The concluding lines of the stanza remove all ambiguity, and cancel all possibility of a return to such a country; even if the old man could, he would not return to a land where ''Caught in the sensual music, all neglect/Monuments of unageing intellect.'' The young are ''caught,'' they are really passive and incapable of free action; and they neglect those things which are unageing.

Merely to end here, however, with a condemnation of youthful sensuality would be unsatisfactory; as the second stanza expounds, old age itself is no solution . . . ; for merely to be old is merely to be in a state of privation, it is to be ''a paltry thing/A tattered coat upon a stick,'' it is to be the merest scarecrow, the merest fiction and semblance of a man, an inanimate rag upon a dead stick. A man merely old, then, is worse off than youth; if the souls of the young are captive, the old have, in this sense at least, no souls at all. Something positive must be added; and if the soul can wax and grow strong as the body wanes, then every step in the dissolution of the body—''every tatter in its mortal dress''—is cause for a further augmentation of joy. But this can occur only if the soul can rejoice in its own power and magnificence; this rejoicing is possible only if the soul knows of its own magnificence, and this knowledge is possible only through the contemplation of monuments which recall that magnificence. The soul of the aged must be strong to seek that which youth neglects. Hence the old must seek Byzantium; that is the country of the old; it is reached by sailing the seas, by breaking utterly with the country of the young; all passion must be left behind, the soul must be free to study the emblems of unchanging things.

Maud Gonne.

Here the soul should be filled with joy; it should, by merely ''studying,'' commend changeless things with song, as youth commends the changing with song; it would seem that the problem has been resolved, and the poem hence must end; but the contemplation of the monuments teaches first of all that those are no mere monuments but living things, and that the soul cannot grow into likeness with these beings of immortal embodiment unless it cast off its mortal body utterly. Nor is joy possible until the body be dissolved; the heart is still sick with the impossible desires of the flesh, it is still ignorant of its circumstances, and no song is possible to the soul while even a remnant of passion remains. Hence the old man prays to the sages who really stand in God's holy fire and have merely the semblance of images in gold mosaic; let them descend, ''perning in a gyre,'' that is, moving in the circular motion which alone is possible to eternal things, let them consume with holy fire the heart which is the last seat of passion and ignorance, let them instruct the soul, let them gather it into the artifice of eternity and make the old man like themselves; even Byzantium, so long as the flesh be present, is no country for old men.

What it is to be like these, the soul, as yet uninstructed, can only conjecture; at any rate, with the destruction of the flesh it will be free of its ills . . . ; it will choose some such form of art as that of the artificial birds in Theophilus' garden; it will be incorruptible and passionless gold; and it will dwell among leaves and boughs which are also of incorruptible and passionless metal. And now all sources of conflict are resolved in this last: the old has become the ageless; impotency has been exchanged for a higher power; the soul is free of passion and free for its joy, and it sings as youth once sang, but now of ''What is past, and passing, and to come''—of the divisions of Eternity—rather than of ''Whatever is begotten, born, and dies''—of the divisions of mortal time. And it has here its country, its proper and permanent habitation.

Although the argument as we have stated it clearly underlies the poem, it would be erroneous to suppose that this in itself constitutes the poem, for in that case there would be no difference between our paraphrase and the poem itself. The poem itself comprehends the argument and collocates with it many terms which, although they could scarcely be formulated into some order approximating the pattern of the argument, nevertheless qualify the argument and determine its course. The basic analogies of the poem—of the natural world to a country, of the aged man to a scarecrow, of the world of art to Byzantium, and of artificial to natural generation—all these function as do the definitions of terms in actual argument; they serve to delimit the sphere of discourse and to make the argument intelligible. (pp. 6-11)

I have said that the bare argument of **"Sailing to Byzantium"** is not the poem; but I should argue that the argument (considered not as a real argument, but according to what I have said, as a certain collocation of terms) is the *principle* of this poem, in a sense analogous to that in which, for Aristotle, plot is the principle of tragedy. For if the principle is that for the sake of which all other things in the poem exist, and that, consequently, in terms of which all are intelligible, what could be the principle, other than the thing we have supposed? There is here no plot, no ordered tissue of incidents, for, first of all, the whole poem is of a moment—the moment in which the old man confronts the monuments and addresses them—whereas a tissue of incidents, a plot, must extend over a span of time. And second, there can be no plot because there are no incidents; the "events" in a lyric poem are never incidents as such, connected by necessity or probability, but devices for making poetic statements. Again, since there is no action, there is no agent, that is, *character,* in the sense in which there are differentiated agents in drama or epic, each duly discriminated for his distinct part in the action; rather, the character in the sense in which character may be said to exist here is almost completely universalized. Hence, if plot does not constitute the principle of the poem, neither does character; for not all the parts of the poem would be explicable in terms of character, nor are we presented with any precise depiction of character here, as we should be if it were the end. On the merely verbal level, again, we can account for nothing; the words must be explained in terms of something else, not the poem in terms of the words; and further, a principle must be a principle of something other than itself; hence the words cannot be a principle of their own arrangements.

Rather, it is clear as we look at the poem, that a certain problem orders the whole—the problem of finding a suitable compensation for the losses suffered in old age; the poem begins with exclusion from the pleasures of youth, develops among ordered dialectical alternatives, and ends when the problem is permanently solved. As the problem determines the limits of the poem, so it determines all else; the character is determined by it, for example, because—according to the very nature of the problem—a young man could not have conceived of the problem as it is stated, nor could a raging and sensual old man, nor could an old man who was contented with age, like Sophocles; since an ideal and permanent solution was to be given to the problem, a character conscious of loss, and capable of conceiving an ideal solution, was necessitated. Nothing beside this is indicated with respect to the speaker. Again, the words themselves are determined by the problem; while the choice of metaphors of a "country," or "song," and of modes of embodiment was initially arbitrary, once the metaphors have been stated they must be carried out according to the dictates of the problem; indeed, it is possible to trace variations in diction precisely proportional to the stages of the dialectic. For example, the stages are verbally signalized by the succession "flesh," "stick," "dying animal," "gold," in terms of expressions of embodiment, or "no country," "Byzantium," "the artifice of eternity," which is amid "holy fire," in terms of habitation; and the metaphor of the artificial bird in the fourth stanza bears such relation—in terms of setting, song, character of joy, object of joy, and "bodily form"—to the real birds—"those dying generations"—in stanza I as the solution of the problem bears to the element the negation of which generated the dialectic. In a similar manner the presence of nearly every word in the poem might be justified if space permitted. (pp. 12-13)

Elder Olson, "'Sailing to Byzantium: Prolegomena to a Poetics of the Lyric'," in his On Value Judgments in the Arts and Other Essays, *The University of Chicago Press, 1976, pp. 3-14.*

EDWIN MUIR (essay date 1962)

[Muir was a distinguished Scottish novelist, poet, critic, and translator. With his wife Willa, he translated works by various German authors to the English-speaking world, including Gerhart Hauptmann, Hermann Broch, and, most notably, Franz Kafka. Throughout his career, Muir was intrigued by psychoanalytic theory, particularly Freud's analyses of dreams and Jung's theories of archetypal imagery, both of which he often utilized in his work. In his critical writings, Muir was more concerned with the general philosophical issues raised by works of art—such as the nature of time or society—than with the particulars of the work itself, such as style or characterization. In the following excerpt, Muir examines Yeats's development as a poet.]

The development of Yeats as a poet is an astonishing spectacle. Midway in it there is a crisis, and after that he becomes a different poet, with other themes, and another voice. Nietzsche once said of Wagner that he was a musician who had made himself into a musician. Yeats was a poet who made himself into a different poet, and a great one. (p. 42)

When he went to Trinity College he met a few young men who were writing poetry, and he began to write poetry in a sleepwalking state from which he did not awaken for years. He was concerned then with poetry as an art, the influence of his father, the artist, suggesting to him that art was the greatest of things. (pp. 42-3)

That extraordinary early passivity of Yeats, that almost hypnotic susceptibility, lasted until he was over thirty and had started to be a man of action. . . . [His early poetry was often] beautiful but half-real; his later poetry was to show up its inadequacy. The words sorrow and beauty recur again and again in this poetry, and generally associated with them such epithets as weary, wandering, dreaming, mournful. . . . Yeats had learned too by then from the French symbolists, introduced to his notice by Arthur Symons, another influence; and a new skill from the versification of the Rhymers' Club, that of Lionel Johnson above all; and a deepened sense of time from the Irish myths.

It may be that his passivity during these years was necessary to him; his poverty and shyness needed images of sadness and reassurance. (pp. 45-6)

Yeats's passiveness during those first thirty years of his life has an appearance of weakness, but only an appearance. For, through it he drank in all the impressions that floated toward it, and most of them were retained all his life: the high idea of art, the esoteric knowledge, the old Irish stories, the admiration for aristocratic grace and peasant imagination never left him. Even when he was writing his greatest poetry he could resume the passive state which had served him so well. We know that Ezra Pound influenced him then, and in the Crazy Jane songs Louis MacNeice has traced the influence of Synge. While appearing to float unresistingly in the stream of those early years, before two women—Maud Gonne and Lady Gregory—forced him to become a man of action, he was appropriating the resources which he was to use after he gave himself his own voice.

He tells us that when he was a young man he was ill at ease with people. Yet he could not do without company, and drew life from what others were thinking and doing. He was affected immediately by their ideas. (pp. 47-8)

The passionate, reasoning self, the personality as a whole, is what speaks in Yeats's later poetry. How did this come about? There is no facile explanation. His love for Maud Gonne, the troubles it brought him, and the repeated disappointments, must have turned him from his dreams and confronted him with life. They made him very unhappy. . . . How could these long years of alternating hope and disappointment [during his relationship with Maud Gonne] fail to have an effect upon him?

These were also the years when he learned to be a man of action. But he was a special man of action, or at least he professed it. In a letter written to Mrs. Shakespear, long after, he says: "It is curious how one's life falls into definite sections.—In 1897 a new scene was set, new actors appeared." It was characteristic of him that he saw the cockpit of Irish politics as a stage, and the figures as actors, and himself as one who had to play a part. About this time, or a little after, he became interested in the "mask," what he called the antithetical self. (pp. 49-50)

He had worn the mask of the poet, and worn it, or so it seemed, successfully. His wish now was to make himself a great figure, so that the figure might add greatness to the man, and with such a basis the man might become a great poet. He complained to H. W. Nevinson that Byron was the last *man* who had written poetry: a revealing choice. Even his study of magic may have helped in the transformation; for magic not only tries to transmute what it acts upon; it cannot but produce a greater change in the magician. What we feel when we compare Yeats's early style with his later, is that he is no longer subject to his preoccupations—Irish myth, magical knowledge, symbolism, hatred of abstraction—all he had absorbed from his friends and his experience; that he has now mastered them and can use them. He has made himself into a public figure, and speaks to an audience. He had achieved this by dramatizing himself, and acting the role which was really himself. . . . [In] the poem, **"Among School Children"** he could see himself half-ironically, yet objectively, as

A sixty-year-old smiling public man.

A public man is a man who is entitled to be listened to by the public; a great public man is one who can tell his public, on occasion, what he thinks of them, knowing that they will listen. This was the position which Yeats achieved, alone among the poets of his time. His public was first of all Irish, and it is easier to be the voice of a small nation than of a great one. His voice reached farther, of course, than Ireland, and was heard in many countries. But it was to the Irish that he spoke, as one who knew them, loved and hated them, admired and detested them. He was bound to them as much by his faults as his virtues; above all by his apparently inexhaustible reserves of Original Sin. Perhaps this is the most real and intimate relation a poet can have to a public in our time, as a great faulty image, in which they can find their own faults and their own hidden greatness; and Yeats was fortunate in drawing his audience from a country small, "backward," and still comparatively free from the spirit of abstraction which was spreading its blight over the greater nations. His struggle with Ireland helped to make him. . . . (pp. 50-2)

Yeats was proud of being an Irishman, and still prouder of belonging to the Anglo-Irish ascendency, which had contributed so many names to Irish history and literature. He could therefore write more bitterly of Ireland than any of its enemies, because more intimately. He became a public man and a public poet because he shared that love and that fury and had a voice to give them utterance.

It was in his poetry that he found that voice. His prose to the end has a curious indecision, and is filled with ideas put as rhetorical questions, a great trick of his. The word "perhaps" recurs persistently, even when he is setting down a thought which, one would have imagined, must have been of the utmost importance to him. In prose he seems to have felt that his mind was at liberty to wander, and his ideas as well. (pp. 53-4)

He was uncertain among ideas, even those he clung to all his life. He had to embody them imaginatively before he was convinced by them. Even that curious compilation, ***A Vision,*** which was dictated to him, he says, by communicators speaking through the voice of his wife in a series of trances, and which gave him a complete chart of the cycles of time and all the phases within them; even from that he disengaged himself, with the excuse that the communicators were sent to him to provide his poetry with imagery.

I have been concerned with the poet and his audience, and the disappearance of the audience. Yeats, it seems to me, had a genuine audience, not a scattered sprinkling of readers in Dublin, London, New York, Paris, and the universities. He gathered together an audience to which he could address himself, and which gave him the liberty to speak of anything, while obliging him to speak of certain things. He was bound to speak of Ireland, its politics, its heroisms, its feuds, and the glories of its past; to speak of them in sorrow and anger. . . . or in grief and wonder. . . . (pp. 55-6)

He was also free to speak of anything else he chose: Troy, Byzantium, the Great Memory, the moon, youth and age, the talk of his fellow writers, the nature of poetry, time and immortality, the gossip of Dublin, the disreputable loves of Crazy Jane, and above all himself, and the dialogue between himself and his soul. No other poet of his time had such a variety of theme and mood, ranging from the exalted to the Rabelaisian. He was free even to be obscure, but obscure through some fine excess, as in the two great poems on Byzantium. It might be said that he could afford to be obscure, because he had an audience. He had mastered his art so completely that he could express all his moods with equal power. (p. 56)

Edwin Muir, "W. B. Yeats," in his The Estate of Poetry, *Cambridge, Mass.: Harvard University Press, 1962, pp. 42-60.*

T. R. HENN (essay date 1964)

[In the following excerpt, Henn provides stanza-by-stanza explications of the poems "Sailing to Byzantium" *and* "Byzantium." *In unexcerpted portions of the essay, sections of the poems are compared and contrasted with several of Yeats's other poems and essays.]*

The city [of Byzantium] became the central symbol of two of [Yeats'] most important poems—**'Sailing to Byzantium'** of ***The Tower*** . . . and **'Byzantium'** of ***The Winding Stair***. . . . It is more than the mere meeting-point of East and West, or the point on which his philosophy of art coheres. His description of it in ***A Vision*** must be read in the light of his conception of the cycles of history, and of its own journeyings under the Phases of the Moon. (p. 207)

[A] desire for an art which should be the 'vision of the people' is fundamental in Yeats. It is the antithesis of the 'dissipation and despair' that he found in the modern world. He had seen the gold and enamel work at Ravenna in 1908: but it was the visit to Italy and Sicily in 1925 that produced this sense of excitement at the revelation of mosaic's qualities. But Byzantium seems to be much more than Rome approached from the east . . . , or a peculiar kind of heroic vision, or even a sort of Grecian Urn round which Yeats can crystallize the thought of the permanence of art in a world of mutability. It was linked to his theory of perfection in measurement. . . . (p. 208)

But there is further possibility as to the associations of Byzantium in Yeats' mind. It had been a province of the Roman Empire; it had suffered from the rigidity, bureaucracy, and lack of imaginative treatment of its own ancient and complex traditions. There were parallels to be drawn between Rome and England as imperialistic powers; and Byzantium might well symbolize a new Ireland breaking away from its masters so that it might develop its own philosophical, religious and artistic destiny. As for the past, both Byzantine and Gaelic Christendom might be judged to stand for a similar interpenetration of religion and art, the Hebraic and Hellenic held in perpetual synthesis. And the destruction of both came, not from within by gradual decline, but by a series of shocks, catastrophically, from without. (pp. 208-09)

Byzantium, then, has a multiple symbolic value. It stands for the unity of all aspects of life, for perhaps the last time in history. It has inherited the perfection of craftsmanship, and more than craftsmanship, perhaps, the 'mystical mathematics' of perfection of form in all creation. That culture is the inheritor of Greek tradition, in philosophy and handiwork. The disintegration of the 'Galilean turbulence' had not yet begun. But because it is in the past, it contains in itself, like Egypt to which it is linked, the mysteries of the dead. Memory may think back, with or without the aid of the shade, into the past and learn its secrets. (pp. 209-10)

It is now possible to examine more fully the texture of the two poems in relation to their symbolism.

> That is no country for old men. The young
> In one another's arms, birds in the trees,
> —Those dying generations—at their song,
> The salmon-falls, the mackerel-crowded seas,
> Fish, flesh, or fowl, commend all summer long
> Whatever is begotten, born and dies.
> Caught in that sensual music all neglect
> Monuments of unageing intellect.

The ironic reference to the 'Ode to the Nightingale' contributes to the tension, and has a parallel in the second poem. The salmon-falls are a visual memory: Sligo River drops through the town in a series of shallow falls where the fish run up to Lough Gill, and the memory is that of spring and the magnificent strength and grace of the leaping fish, itself a symbol of strength in Celtic literature. The mackerel has special associations; the appearances of the shoals out in the Bay roused a particular excitement which infected the whole fishing-village with the prospect of the net-harvest. *Commend:* the word carries the key-stress, set off by the arrogant use of the 'popular' fish, flesh or fowl. They commend their life cycle and their death. . . . Man is *caught*—again a keyword—as in a net of that sensual music; but for an old man there is nothing still but the great achievements of the past. . . . (pp. 211-12)

But he is now old—**'Sailing to Byzantium'** was written in 1928; and there is the nostalgia for the strength and vitality of the 'young in one another's arms', yet tempered by his acceptance of age with its compensations in poetic achievement:

> An aged man is but a paltry thing,
> A tattered coat upon a stick, unless
> Soul clap its hands and sing, and louder sing
> For every tatter in its mortal dress,
> Nor is there singing school but studying
> Monuments of its own magnificence;
> And therefore I have sailed the seas and come
> To the holy city of Byzantium.

Yeats was a traditionalist, in the peculiar sense that each great poet re-casts his style within that tradition. The 'singing school' is important. He was aware always of how much he had owed to what he took to be the technical perfection of the members of the Rhymers' Club. (pp. 212-13)

The monuments might be verse, or any artistic creation. . . . (p. 213)

The old have only their minds. They are fastened to a 'dying animal', but the mind can yet be supreme; 'men improve with the years', to attain

> A mind Michael Angelo knew
> That can pierce the clouds,
> Or inspired by frenzy
> Shake the dead in their shrouds;
> Forgotten else by mankind,
> An old man's eagle mind.

So in his third verse there is the invocation:

> O sages standing in God's holy fire
> As in the gold mosaic of a wall,
> Come from the holy fire, perne in a gyre,
> And be the singing-masters of my soul.
> Consume my heart away; sick with desire
> And fastened to a dying animal
> It knows not what it is; and gather me
> Into the artifice of eternity.

The consummation of fire appears again in **'Byzantium'**. The perne is the bobbin of the spinning-mill: he recounts in ***Autobiographies*** how, looking from the window of the Sligo house, he had seen smoke rising in the distance, and had been told it was the perne-mill. Perhaps the word struck him then, as it might well do, for its resonance and remote, faintly menacing quality; here the image seems to be that of the shuttle revolving round and up the walls of the cone of time, leaving behind it that thread as a clue (compare the second verse of **'Byzantium')** by which the depths may be explored again. It is worth while to notice the deliberate clash of the internal rhyme and the repetition of *holy fire*: and the rhythm broken deliberately on *artifice of eternity* to hold the mind for an instant before the paradox locks home.

So to the last verse:

> Once out of nature I shall never take
> My bodily form from any natural thing,
> But such a form as Grecian goldsmiths make
> Of hammered gold and gold enamelling
> To keep a drowsy Emperor awake;
> Or set upon a golden bough to sing
> To lords and ladies of Byzantium
> Of what is past, or passing, or to come.

Yeats' note on this is of course familiar: "I have read somewhere that in the Emperor's palace at Byzantium was a tree made of gold and silver, and artificial birds that sang." The ghost can return, and take what shape its imagination allows: but nothing less than that perfection of the artificer's form will suffice for his embodiment. It is well to stress again that this achievement of art is more than the arrested beauty of the 'Grecian Urn': it is the embodiment of long striving after mathematical perfection of form, and as such has contact with God.

'Byzantium' itself is, I think, the greater poem of the two: its system of tensions is more complex, its overtones more significant. The most interesting clue to it is given in the ***1930 Diary.***

Subject for a poem. April 30th.

> Death of a friend. To describe how mixed with one's grief comes the thought, that the witness of some foolish act or word of one's own is gone.
>
> Describe Byzantium as it is *in the system* towards the end of the first Christian millennium. A walking mummy. Flames at the street corners where the soul is purified, birds of hammered gold singing in the golden trees, offering their backs to the wailing dead that they may carry them to paradise.
>
> These subjects have been in my head for some time, especially the last.

'The system' is of course, that of ***A Vision,*** 'The walking mummy' represents, perhaps, the Egyptian element in Byzantine art. In the poem itself the birds that bear the dead on their backs have been replaced by the dolphins. The poem falls into five divisions; the city which is the background with its violent contrasts; the exploration of death and the wisdom of the past; the goldsmith's art which can give that permanence and significance in life unattainable by flesh; and the mosaics which depict the spiritual experience, stabilized by the knowledge and technique of the artist. At the last the spirits, unified and made triumphant by the art of goldsmith or worker in mosaic, triumph over the limitations of the body, the Dolphin's mire and blood.

> The unpurged images of day recede;
> The Emperor's drunken soldiery are abed;
> Night resonance recedes, night-walkers' song
> After great cathedral gong;
> A starlit or a moonlit dome disdains
> All that man is,
> All mere complexities,
> The fury and the mire of human veins.

Images are, I think, used not in the psychic, but rather in the Neo-platonic sense; they are the dross-covered reflected shapes of reality that fade as night approaches and mind grows strong again. They recede, with the long closing stress, growing fainter in the distance. The soldiers of the great Emperor are drunken, and that is the ironic paradox of empire. But they are also the drunken soldiery . . . of **'Nineteen Hundred and Nineteen'**. . . . The drunken soldiery are *abed*—and that false rhyme jars for an instant (as it is meant to) with the homely half-contemptuous word. *Resonance*—the dark heavy word also becomes fainter in the distance as *recedes;* the night-walkers are, as it were, a later parallel to the '*drunken soldiery*'. The *great cathedral gong* reverberates back over the first movement, symbolizing perhaps in its violent conjunction the meeting of the religions of the East and West. . . . The tone grows lighter and more peaceful. The dome is the symbol of Byzantine achievement, the image of heaven, the only canopy for God. It disdains—and the purity and *scorn* of moonlight is picked up later—not mankind, but the comparative simplification of his complexities. The second stanza gives the incantation-element:

> Before me floats an image, man or shade,
> Shade more than man, more image than a shade;
> For Hades' bobbin bound in mummy-cloth
> May unwind the winding path;
> A mouth that has no moisture and no breath
> Breathless mouths may summon;
> I hail the superhuman;
> I call it death-in-life and life-in-death.

This most difficult verse concerns the invocation of the dead to discover their wisdom. (pp. 213-18)

Shade . . . appears to be incorporeal spirit, but with certain properties of communication. *Image* would seem to be the shade in a more or less materialized condition. . . .

Hades' bobbin suggests the image of the labyrinth and the minotaur or of Orpheus and Eurydice; but it is also limited to his other image of the thread wound and unwound by the revolving gyres. . . . The mummy-cloth suggests his own dark tomb-haunting. (p. 219)

This image may well be of himself, in a trance or dream; it may in that state summon the breathless mouths. But the ghost, in its coming and going, is linked by association to the cock.

> Miracle, bird or golden handiwork,
> More miracle than bird or handiwork,
> Planted on the star-lit golden bough,
> Can like the cocks of Hades crow,
> Or, by the moon embittered, scorn aloud
> In glory of changeless metal
> Common bird or petal
> And all complexities of mire or blood.

It is one of the 'forms' of the Grecian goldsmiths in **'Sailing to Byzantium'**. *Starlit* picks up the *starlit* dome of the first stanza, and we contrast the constancy of starlight with the inconstancy of the moon, though both are reflected lights. . . . The bird belongs both to the world of the dead, and to that of immortality; it can serve as sentinel to the underworld and to the earth. It is above all change: the moon—symbol of womanhood and of flux or instability—leaves it *embittered* in the light which shines pale on the gold. The cock, the dominant untiring male, is *embittered,* scorned by the moon. But is, perhaps, a spirit also. . . . The image-cluster contracts and tightens; the cock is linked to the hawk, the ghost to Egyptian mythology, the tree in the garden to the apple tree that grew from Baile's tomb: the tree is the crab-tree with its sour fruit. The cock knows all mutability, but transcends all change. It scorns *common*—the stress falls heavily with the arrogant trick again—*common bird* or *petal,* and with the craftsman's flower the thread of association returns to the bough, and the flower-image calls up the overtones of arrested beauty and decay.

From the craftsman in the garden we pass to the mosaics, the other summit of achievement. We catch up the background

A charcoal drawing of Yeats by John S. Sargent, 1908.

again: it is the *Emperor's* pavement, and the violence of his drunken soldiery has no place here:

> At midnight on the Emperor's pavement flit
> Flames that no faggot feeds, nor steel has lit,
> Nor storm disturbs, flames begotten of flame,
> Where blood-begotten spirits come
> And all complexities of fury leave,
> Dying into a dance,
> An agony of trance,
> An agony of flame that cannot singe a sleeve.

Flames and *faggot* suggest martyrdom, or the devastation of a countryside by the soldiery: steel has its double sense of the flint or of the sword. The flames of the mosaic are born of spiritual intensity and they have also the purifying function. The spirits that come there, for instruction or purification, are *blood-begotten*. Again the complexities appear, like a thread running through the fabric of the poem, but now they are complexities of fury: which can be resolved in the final ritual dance, perhaps of expiation. It cannot singe a sleeve; and, half contemptuously (for he does this frequently) there is the Biblical reference to the fiery furnace. The rescuers of humanity, the dolphins, are themselves mortal.

> Astraddle on the dolphin's mire and blood,
> Spirit after spirit! The smithies break the flood,
> The golden smithies of the Emperor!
> Marbles of the dancing floor
> Break bitter furies of complexity,
> Those images that yet
> Fresh images beget,
> That dolphin-torn, that gong-tormented sea.

The sea has the normal symbolic values of life and sex; it is 'the drifting indefinite bitterness of life'. It is torn by the two forces of sex and religion; for the dolphin is also the love-beast. The quick pattering of the dactyl's *spirit after spirit* lets the words burst on the triumphant paradox. *The smithies break the flood:* the flood symbolizes the irrational, the confusion, the pattern, perhaps a consequence of the 'Galilean turbulence': against this the formal ceremonious art of Byzantium, the art of the goldsmith, *hammered* work linked with the idea of *breaking,* complete the paradox of that opposition of fire and water. Yet they are the *smithies of the Emperor; golden* for the price and value of the Emperor's power, *golden* because of their handiwork, smithies of the Emperor whose power is founded on the drunken soldiery. The mosaics with their formal geometrical patterns, impose a second order, this time of measurement, proportion, upon the 'irrational stream'. The marbles (which stand for coldness and durability as well as pattern) share with the smithies the reflected *break.* They belong to the pattern and rhythm of the dance: *marbles of the dancing floor. Flood* and *bitter furies of complexity*—water and fire—are linked again as aspects of life resolved by art. There is even a different kind of complexity modified by *bitter* (frustration or disappointment) and *furies* (energy) that grows out of the irrationality of fate. The bitterness throws back to 'by the moon embittered', for the frustration is, at least part, a sexual frustration.

What follows is more difficult. Smithies and marbles break not only the flood and the furies, but the skein of images to which they give rise. "Has not the Porphyry said the generation of images in the mind is from water?" We are carried back to the first stanza, and its 'unpurged images', before art and measurement come into their own at night. They break *'that dolphin-torn, that gong-tormented sea'*: or perhaps the line is in apposition to 'those images'? The sea is torn by love, the dolphin, and tormented by the gong, the religions that have met in the Cathedral of St. Sophia, East and West. I think it is likely that this line merely explains the nature of the images that haunt him perpetually, love and religion. But because of this very obscurity I feel that the resolution, both from the meaning and rhythm, is incomplete, and the poem the less thereby.

For a work of this kind defies a final analysis. The complexity of the overtones grows steadily on each new reading. But in the last resort I am doubtful whether Byzantium itself was an entirely satisfactory symbol. The reference to it in ***A Vision*** suggests that the conception is more brain-conceived, more literary, than was usual in Yeats' practice, and what we know of its redrafting gives us reason to suppose that the transition from Ireland to Byzantium was a little forced. Other myths seemed to be orientated, almost involuntarily, towards his own story. For this the connection had to be, as it were, forged out. The difficult second stanza, unless there is a connecting link so far unperceived, seemed dovetailed into the poem, but not of its substance. (pp. 219-23)

T. R. Henn, in his The Lonely Tower: Studies in the Poetry of W. B. Yeats, *Methuen & Co. Ltd., 1964, 362 p.*

A. E. DYSON (essay date 1981)

[Dyson is an English literary critic who has explained that while he formerly adhered to an ideology of "liberal humanism," he has for some time considered himself a "traditionalist" and a Christian. "Literature is a celebration," Dyson has stated. "Almost everything that makes life rich was said or written or created

by people who are no longer living; almost all the color and joy came from religious men." In the following excerpt, Dyson provides a detailed explication of the poems "Sailing to Byzantium" *and* "Byzantium."]

[The poems **'Sailing to Byzantium'**] and **'Byzantium'** have been so often commented upon that I almost hesitate to start. (p. 47)

'That is no country for old men. . . .' This poem is a far cry from **'The Tower',** even though it shares old age as a major theme. It seems closer, in technique and poise, to Keats's Odes (the 'Grecian Urn' especially). Like Keats's major odes, it is a self-contained artefact, continually recalling other words and contexts, yet always transiently. My impression is that, whereas many of the other poems seem momentarily illuminated by cross-references to this one, **'Sailing to Byzantium'** has a unity peculiar to itself. For reasons which will become apparent later, I do not link it as closely in my mind with **'Byzantium'** as possibly the majority of critics do. . . . **'Sailing to Byzantium'** seems to me highly wrought, complete in itself, highly successful. Like **'Byzantium',** it is a most carefully constructed unity, somewhat more accessible than its successor, though scarcely less complex, and ultimately deriving, I should judge, from a different genesis and intent. (p. 48)

Obviously, Byzantium established itself in Yeat's mind as a symbol of mind and spirit, art and religion, enjoying rare harmony. It speaks of eternity, perhaps through all of these connotations, and particularly through their conjunction. The opening sentence of the poem, which I began by quoting, points in three different directions—as I think the whole of the poem, following this, then also does. At the heart of the triumphant artistry there exists, if so, a remarkable tonal neutrality—which a reader may either seek to maintain throughout, thereby underlining one of the three possibilities, or slant *slightly* in emphasis (though only slightly: since the ambivalences must not be closed), in order to underline instead either one of the remaining two. Any reading must make its decision at the start, and then seek consistency, bearing in mind that the three closely parallel poems contained here are, also, one. Undoubtedly, the poem has tremendous verbal energy—closely connected with Yeats's belief, or his wish to believe, in the symbolic validity of Byzantium—which carries the reader along, making the 'problem' of reading less difficult, in practice, than I have suggested. There is a tide of rhetoric which belongs with this poetic experience, however we interpret, which is itself resilient and triumphant.

'That is no country for old men.' I have never doubted that the 'country' is a symbolic island or continent of 'the young', allegorised in the first stanza, and akin to the islands which **'The Wanderings of Oisin'** . . . pioneered. It is an emphatic start, even if the first reading, as I have said, might seek to achieve neutrality. In other words, the statement will be made to sound in essence a commonplace, a truism, requiring matter-of-fact recognition, without special emotion.

In the act of saying this, however, the other possibilities necessarily appear—however much we choose to restrain them. Statements of this kind are not scientific axioms or equations; they are the stuff of life and of deep responses. One of these (and which reader coming first from **'The Tower'** would forget it?) is rage and anger—so the reading slanted *that* way will start with a suggestion of one total interpretation. The words 'no' and 'old' will be infused with regret: we shall sense that, though the old man sails away, knowing his exclusion inevitable, he does so with unhealed bitterness of heart, seeking to find (or maybe rationalise) a second-best. That this will be done with panache can be expected; that a poet of Yeats's temperament will not be entirely sceptical of the spiritual—and allegedly superior—alternative must also be agreed. But his rage at old age is also not in question (as I have already suggested, I think he probably placed this poem *before* **'The Tower'** in great part to prevent resonances of the second poem from too directly swaying our reading of **'Sailing to Byzantium').** This, in turn, is a reminder that the idea of life as a pilgrimage from inexperience to wisdom is ancient and widespread; the basis of most religious, and perhaps of most adult, quests. (pp. 48-50)

I shall start from the notion that the poem is essentially a choice of old age against youth—even a condemnation of youth—since this *has* been presented by some critics as 'the obvious' or even as 'the only' meaning, strange though anyone familiar with the poet must surely find it. How does this guide our reading? The emphatic rejection will first appear maybe in an intonation of the word 'old' in l.1, implying superior wisdom in age, and even the right to a little scorn. The rest of the stanza will include some puritan (or quasi-puritan) rejection of the world depicted. In 'dying generations' we shall take a hint that, while the old man sees truth in 'dying', the young miss it, so that their 'song', unperceived by themselves, is illusion. Even 'all summer long' will suggest illusion—a world of sensuous withdrawal, overlooking the tragic sting in life, mortality itself (l.5). In this reading, 'Caught' will imply men trapped, or ensnared (erotic sin, or folly), a reading that the word 'neglect' might seem easily to support. The 'Monuments of unageing intellect' will indicate a settled preference, whether the puritan's for spiritual rather than fleshy things, or the intellectual's for the supremacy (inherent, or in the quest for 'truth') of the 'mind'.

The second stanza has now to be read subtly, if this interpretation is not wholly undermined. The best one can do is to treat ll.1-2 (up to 'stick') as almost throwaway, and to bring 'unless' as close to 'until' in its apparent force as one can. No doubt old age *seems* paltry to thoughtless youthful spectators, but it has a different and far superior 'song' of its own. The 'song' of the young was, after all, illusion; the 'song' of the old is based on a surer hope. So, the frailty of the body (very powerfully evoked in l.4) can be taken as a light price to pay for wisdom: besides, 'body' has already been downgraded by 'sensual' (penultimate line of the first stanza), which will be taken, again, as puritanical dismissal of the flesh. The words 'nor is there' will be infused with a sense of impending triumph, as far as possible; 'studying' will counter balance 'sensual', carrying moral approval; the last three lines will ring out with the force of an arrival which, for once, fully justifies hopeful travelling. . . . The word 'therefore' can ring out, in this belief, with the triumph of wisdom not only aspired towards, but at last achieved.

The third stanza is, then, exalted invocation, not unlike the kind practised so often by Yeats in the *making* of art. This invocation is prayer, however—or, if not prayer, at least recreation, of the kind we experience when bringing any work of art alive for ourselves. Sages and saints are summoned from mosaic stillness to inspire the old man with a song not anchored to time. The whole inheritance of art and religion is to be personally appropriated, with self already preparing to merge or transcend itself in whatever may come.

At this stage, there is a further tricky point in the reading, possibly the hardest of all to get round. Is 'heart' really to be sacrificed so readily, that mortality may be put off and the immortal put on? The best we can do again is to make 'heart' function, as far as possible, as a symbol of both 'sensual' and fleshy things, and so a small price to pay, since it belongs with the illusions of youth. The powerful words 'fastened to a dying animal' can be seen, maybe, as the Platonic assertion that 'soul' is merely trapped and imprisoned, as long as it remains in mortal incarnation. This would further be supported by 'It knows not what it is' (the soul itself bemused, if it succumbs to the snares of the senses). The works of great men—great artists and religious mystics especially—can spiritually 'gather' the poet into an 'eternity' where 'artifice' rescues him from mere nature (the life at one remove from 'Reality' itself).

The last stanza reinforces this idea, or can seem to—though here a more serious complication (for *all* interpretations, maybe) sets in.

Let us allow, for a moment, that the word 'nature' is, in this sense, expendable, so that even an artist can dispense with 'heart' and 'nature' alike, and feel only relief. (Let us forget, this implies also, who is writing the poem; or let us assume that Yeats, the occultist and mystic, is in total ascendancy, for the moment at least.) Even so, we can hardly fail to notice that he is now, further, giving up *consciousness:* the choice is to become, himself, an artefact, a golden bird. So, mysteriously, the release, the new song of 'eternity' is immediately frozen, and the poet chooses, for reincarnation, the form of gold.

A very determined critic might find this, I suppose, a symbol of transcended individualism—that merging of the 'self' back into the One (the single wave back into the ocean) which certain platonic and other mystics have always sought. Even so, we are unlikely to forget Hans Andersen's fable 'The Emperor's Nightingale', or to accept, without question, this apotheosis into a toy. 'To keep a drowsy Emperor awake'—is this really the eternal fulfilment celebrated, with so much élan, in the foregoing stanzas? One need not be a devout egalitarian to feel some qualm. We notice that the poetic rhythms are now drowsy—nearer to the early Yeats, or the Pre-Raphaelites, than to the foregoing stanzas—as if to underline illusion, rather than reality, as the prevailing mood. We can further wonder whether 'The lords and ladies of Byzantium' are the safest anchorage for 'eternity.' . . . The last line, referring back, as it clearly does, to stanza i, 1.6, establishes that art, however 'eternal' in appearance, needs the world of youth for its material, its passion. It is a poem which swallows its own tail: you can pause after the last line and then begin again at the first. To do this is to discover the uncannily effective insulation of the artefact and the calculated impossibility of allowing *any* subsequent readings entirely to coincide with the first. With this as a clue we can then move on to the problems of reading the poem, if the apparently opposite interpretation is now held chiefly in view.

This time the wistfulness, regret (even bitterness—though this should not be sufficient to unbalance the whole reading) which is infused into the first sentence gives place to felt love for the country which is being left behind. Now the old man sails away from youth because he no longer belongs there, but with every bitter regret that makes the first of his two questions in **'The Tower'** so unforgettable still potently at work in him. The phrase 'those dying generations' speaks to us not of the folly of the young, understood with hindsight, but of the tragic, lacerating reality of time. . . . The words 'commend all summer long' invoke all we have known of youth and love most sweetly, celebrating the abundance of fleeting, transient beauty while it lasts. In so far as the country is lost to the poet, it is as the wild swans at Coole were lost—yet he recognises that somewhere (in other swans, other human observers) the experience continues, and he is glad of it:

> Unwearied still, lover by lover,
> They paddle in the cold
> Companionable streams or climb the air;
> Their hearts have not grown old. . . .

In this reading the last lines of stanza i turn inside out. 'Caught is not ensnared, or trapped in illusion, but 'caught up in' rapture (love, friendship, heartsease, 'the music while it lasts', 'excited reverie'). (pp. 50-3)

What of 'neglect'? We may assume that this word always contains censure, yet is this not also part of a puritan taint? To neglect things that are not worth attending to—or, still more importantly, that are irrelevant—may be one of the highest and rarest modes of wisdom. . . . If we are to live at all, it is well to neglect obsession with death in the season of life.

In this reading, 'Monuments' takes on a more sombre sound, suggesting dead relics listed and contained in a museum, or the chilling shapes of cenotaphs 'to the glorious dead'. It therefore becomes natural to activate, by the barest intonation, the paradoxical notion of 'unageing intellect'. This typical elision of opposites can slip past, here, more obtrusively than some of the others in Yeats ('terrible beauty', 'murderous innocence', and so on), but it is no less challenging if looked at closely. Man's 'intellect', if associated with the brain, is as mortal as his body; its works may last longer, but they outlive consciousness (perhaps the 'golden bird' is prepared for, slightly more ironically than is often thought). If 'intellect' is equated with soul, however, and with 'eternity', then 'Monuments' (twice repeated) can scarcely be dissociated from the force of 'artefact' when it comes.

Continuing, it is now natural to allow much fuller bitterness into the first two lines of stanza ii (again up to 'stick'). . . . The word 'unless', far from being pushed unobtrusively towards 'until', will be lingered upon, so that the extreme effort required for what is to follow will not be missed. Lines 3-4 will be seen to exist (even apart from the peculiar effectiveness of 'tatter'), on the borderline of wishful-thinking, if not somewhat beyond. The 'Nor' will come with some edge of desperation, and 'Monuments of its own magnificence', whilst undoubtedly full of vigour on any reading, will again release suggestions sombre as well as grand. Naturally enough, 'And therefore' will ring out, now, with less unqualified triumph; rather, regret for the inevitability of the journey, and its doubtful outcome, may set the tone.

The invocation in stanza iii, ll. 1-4, will remain potent, but with more than a hint of rhetoric known, or feared, to be false, even as it makes its effect. Maybe the old magician is conjuring, now, beyond the limits where his, or any, magic could pull off the trick. 'Consume my heart away' can then take on a degree of the maybe total bitterness which surely must attend an image expressed in this particular way.

As I said earlier, I more normally find echoes of this poem arriving as I read Yeats's other works than the reverse process, no doubt because this artefact *is* so marvellously controlled and complete in itself. But some of the many uses of 'heart' in Yeats are bound to lurk somewhere ('Oh, who could have foretold / That the heart grows old?'; 'What shall I do with this absurdity, / O heart, O troubled heart . . .?'; 'Hearts with one purpose alone / Through summer and winter seem / Enchanted to a stone / To trouble the living stream'; 'Hearts are not had as a gift, but hearts are earned / By those that are not entirely beautiful'—and on, of course, to 'Maybe at last, being but a broken man / I must be satisfied with my heart' in **'The Circus Animals' Desertion',** where the word 'heart' controls the development throughout). The words 'sick with desire / And fastened to a dying animal' very readily point to one of the main, and most bitter dynamics, of Yeats's later work. If so, 'It knows not what it is' will be taken not as a philosophical statement (the soul beset, during earthly bondage, with illusion) but as a bitter cry direct from Yeats's own heart.

In this reading, the word 'artifice' insists on the irony which is always difficult to deny it, particularly since a word closer to 'dance' would be easier to cope with in the 'positive' reading. It may be a linguistic oddity (or yet another concealed triumph of puritanism?) that most of the words connected with 'art' are, in normal English usage, tainted or bad. (pp. 54-5)

Finally, our word 'artifice' here is scarcely healthier ('artefact' itself only marginally escapes a pejorative intention, because it is so little used in everyday speech). 'Artifice' almost always implies some intent to conceal or deceive, whether it is mind, body or soul that we have in view. Even at best, it makes 'eternity' seem an alarming construct. . . . Beyond this, we are aware that it clinches the distance from youth, heart and nature which the poem has courted—like one of those treacherous wishes, in fairy tales, that always come true.

The final stanza again fits more naturally into this reading, since the languorous music can be openly savoured, now, for ironic intent. Who in truth would prefer death to life, even in the guise of a bird of rare craftsmanship? Which poet would prefer the most exquisite artefact to the song of the humblest flesh-and-blood bird? (Both of these rhetorical questions have alternative answers; and I have not forgotten the third stanza of **'Byzantium'** itself.)

The problems in the two proposed 'alternative' readings can usefully return to the strategy of the poem itself. My first suggestion was of a 'neutral' reading, the attractions of which may seem enhanced by perceived complexity. What, then, are the problems here? The challenge, no doubt, is to leave the emphases of both readings so far rehearsed possible, and even active, whilst making the temptation to 'close' the poem either way appear naïve. This may be helped if the poem is almost chanted (a solution favoured, in various asides, by Yeats himself). If so, the images and rhythms are sufficiently sumptuous, exalted and at the same time sensitive, for this to seem the most natural reading of all. (pp. 55-6)

This poem draws us, . . . into one of the poet's major preoccupations: how are old men to remain fully and wholly alive? It is 'unageing intellect' which is the illusion, and 'song' the reality: the songs of youth and age, though apparently polarised, are in reality one.

To notice this is to notice the blatant simplification which Yeats has to adopt to make his complexities work. This, very simply, is the entirely stylised and evidently false polarity between 'youth' and 'age', as developed here, which is, however, inseparable from the poem's success. (p. 57)

This poem works by setting up images of 'youth' and 'agè' that are stylised fantasy, weaving its spell round this tenuous ground. Yet it works because its major tensions are real and beautifully realised; they concern the voyage for self-integration, for selfhood, from youth to age. At every stage, the archetypes will have differing connotations and differing functions, which is precisely what the ambivalences so splendidly convey.

This poem strikes me as a more complete success in itself than the later **'Byzantium',** fascinating though that is, too, in its use of similar images for a different end. (p. 58)

'Byzantium' uses certain symbols in common with [**'Sailing to Byzantium'**] and their general import continues to be influenced by ***A Vision.*** But, that said, the poems are utterly different. The first poem is a self-contained artefact, beautifully calculated and achieving its reasonably complex effects with satisfying completeness. **'Byzantium'** is paradoxical, open, opaque to interpretation—one of the great riddles or optical illusions of art. [It] is far better read with the Crazy Jane poems and **'Vacillation'** in mind (and with the later poems to hand) than in other contexts; **'Sailing to Byzantium'** is less akin to it in almost every aspect. (p. 122)

[In] imagery, theme and progression the poem is pure Yeats. . . . When discussing this poem with students, I often find that it is worth taking an hour to doodle around the first stanza, checking where each reader thinks he or she is, and what is happening. The great diversity of response is always illuminating. I shall be offering, of necessity, chiefly my own responses; which I find correspond to about a third of other readers' impressions fairly exactly, though different domes and sensations may of course be mentioned, but which appear to baffle (or annoy as irrelevant) about another third. The remainder usually steer clear of such speculations, but, in the course of spending up to three or more hours on this poem, with various groups, I have found that nearly everyone has something to say on specific aesthetic or religious aspects (most usually both). A very common experience, for me, and I think others, is to end an intensive session with the feeling that, at last, one is on the verge of penetrating to the ultimate secret of **'Byzantium'**. For my part, this has always been transitory, and each session with it (now over a period of twenty-five years) has reinforced my own certainty of the poem's greatness, and of its final elusiveness. Moreover, when reading a critical account with which I have strong sympathy. . . , it becomes apparent to me that, even so, [the critic] and I are *hearing* two very different poems. (pp. 124-25)

The first line [of **'Byzantium'**] is of particular importance, in setting the mood. Yeats speaks of 'images of day' (and the word 'image', always important to him, is to prove central). These 'images' are 'unpurged'—which means, I take it, that they are suspended, as they may be in rare moments of calm, or vision, or hallucination just before sleeping or waking. They 'recede' and cease to be operative, releasing the soul into a visionary experience of night ('Who can distinguish darkness from the soul?'); but they are not 'refined by fire'—nor can I think that the 'flames' in stanza iv belong either to Purgatory or to Hell, though the case for the former is understandable, and has sometimes been made. 'The Emperor's drunken soldiery' belong with day's images, and cease to trouble. We may reflect that the poem might have in mind, before they leave the stage, not only the soldiers of the Byzantine Emperor—an earthy touch in the spiritual city itself; where the original dome is no doubt that of St Sophia—but also the waking Ireland. . . . Lines 3-4 add to the purity of effect—a great cleansing of soul, in the immense spaces between or away from the day. I assume that 'nightwalkers' song' need not refer only to prostitutes, but may also refer to the sound of young people singing, not necessarily drunkenly, as they walk home unseen in neighboring streets or alleys. The powerful phrase 'Night resonance recedes' now moves night, like day, out of consciousness. Though it is 'midnight' in stanza iv, this always feels more like the midnight of fairy-tale and myth than of any normal time-scale. 'After great cathedral gong' allows all to drain away that might spoil the enchantment to come.

For the final four lines are, I find, enchantment . . . ; I find not explosive shock, but a confirmation that, all day and night images now distanced, soul is freed for exploration in other scenes and worlds. As I have already said, although 'A starlit or a moonlit dome disdains' appears to diminish humanity, 'soul' seems able now to partake in this rare victory, associated with its own great monuments, and with their secret, timeless communing with visionary light (cf. **'The Cat and the Moon'**). It is as if, in this moment of pure serenity and peace, the dome belongs with the moon or star light, which silvers it. The final four lines are wrapt into the calm; so that one can survey the life of body (often chosen by Yeats, as we know; and only temporarily transcended) as if from a great height. 'The fury and the mire of human veins' is a god's-eye view of the normal human scene—possibly looking forward to the vision of the old Chinamen towards the end of **'Lapis Lazuli'**, and, as in that passage, offering itself not for judgement (we are not to wonder whether such Olympian calm is, or is not, propitious for mankind in the end) but rather as initiation into one of the rarer modes of possible consciousness. 'All that man is' is a strong phrase, yet parodoxical in context, since, though this may be the detached view, the poem's consciousness is still human, though temporarily above the reach of 'All'. It is permissible to think that Yeats mildly amused himself when inserting 'mere complexities' into *this* poem; yet the words precisely mirror the degree of detachment achieved.

The second stanza is (with the fifth) the most difficult. If we place conscious artefacts (works of art) and religious visions or revelations (the transcendental) at centre, then we home in directly upon Yeats's Byzantium. But to these must be added memories (from the past); hopes, wishes, fears and plans (for the future); fictions and fantasies (to one side of time); dreams, visions, hallucinations, delusions, delirium, drugged or dislocated consciousness (all experienced as 'real' inwardly, but judged by other people and maybe by the self later as not 'true' to waking consciousness); as well as symbols, images, emblems (those favourite Yeats concepts, rooted in time, but signifying things beyond, with varying claims to 'truth' status); and, of course, ghosts, shades, the dead between incarnations, and the entire realm of real or fancied beings conjured up or 'experienced' through the occult. Even this list is far from exhaustive, but it indicates, for practical purposes, the range of inner awareness that (say) any group of students in a seminar might have available, should the appropriate centres of individual consciousnesses be activated. The one thing they have in common, as a rough and ready distinction between this order of events and waking consciousness, is that, however vivid they may seem, they have none of the consequences that would attend them in the present moment. The final line of the fourth stanza, 'An agony of flame that cannot singe a sleeve', encapsulates this thought to perfection. In great works of art, in dreams, delirium and other such states, we might have mighty fires—all hell let loose; yet, in the prosaic surrounding of the present time—the time of 'The fury and the mire of human veins'—no sleeve would be singed. Only an immediate conflagration could produce *that* result. On the other hand, much of our 'reality' must be bound up with whatever of this immense other order of events we find valid—*unless* we are to assume that 'our' reality dwindles, always, to the present moment. This would mean not only that our entire potential, from the past and from imagination, is downgraded (as it scarcely can be, when a poem such as this is actually playing on it), but that the totality of human history and tradition, along with whatever we may designate by names such as 'Anima Mundi', 'the Collective Unconscious' and so forth, can be said to exist only in the focal second of any individual experience.

Perhaps this perspective helps to give some status to the 'image' in the scond stanza. This 'image' cannot be exactly the dome, from stanza i, nor can it be identified with the bird of stanza iii, though in the poem's economy it is set between the two. The swift interplay ('man or shade, / Shade more than man, / more image than a shade') defies exegesis, yet leaves a distinct impression. 'Shade' necessarily suggests an actual ghost, as well as the shade cast by something not seen. . . . Nonetheless, 'Shade more than man' rapidly replaces 'man or shade', to be in turn superseded by 'more image than a shade'. If this is puzzling, we should recall that Yeats said of the spirit authors of ***A Vision,*** and with their own authority, that they came to give him 'metaphors for poetry': Yeats has his own version of the egotistical sublime. (pp. 126-29)

The third stanza introduces the golden bird, in a formula echoing that which opens the second stanza, and presumably depending upon it, so that 'miracle' here becomes what 'image' was before. This bird cannot be the same as the bird in **'Sailing to Byzantium',** despite its origin in similar mythology. It is immensely more impersonal and mysterious—linked not with Yeats's anger at old age, and still less with Yeats's apparent wish to *become* an artefact (neither of these themes seems remotely appropriate to this poem), but more directly with the 'dome' in stanza i, and the Byzantine permanence. The choice of 'miracle' gives it status even higher than 'golden handiwork', and 'glory of changeless metal' deflects attention away from the paradoxes which diminished the 'golden bird' in **'Sailing to Byzantium'**. The word 'Planted' has no irony, I think. True, the bough is also an artefact, not a growing thing, so 'Planted' could have ironic overtones (this matter is one where each reader will have to judge for himself). The phrase 'starlit golden bough' is bound to link the bird both with the 'starlit . . . dome' and with the whole territory of Frazer's exploration of mythology. (pp. 129-30)

When we have a final look at the third stanza of **'Byzantium',** we notice that the golden birds appear to have two alternatives. One, we have just considered . . . ; the other, introduced by 'Or', in l. 5, is the major parallel with the dome from which I started. If the birds make the first choice, do they themselves shuttle back to the world of the living, of death and resurrection, and forfeit, for good or ill, the right invested in 'changeless metal'? The complicating phrase, in this option, is 'by the moon embittered'. The moon is, we know, associated both with inspiration and with night (the sphere of soul), yet also with change, which alone can produce art (cf. not only **'Sailing to Byzantium',** but also **'My Table'** from **'Meditations in Time of Civil War':** Yet if no change appears / No moon; only an aching heart / Conceives a changeless work of art'). The choice of 'embittered' is especially interesting, since all three of its normal meanings belong to life and shade into each other (impart a bitter taste to; make sour, morose or unhappy; intensify in anger). There is no other possibility in the word to balance these, so maybe the second option invested in the bird, which *appears* to fit in with the poem's dreamlike serenity, does, rather, move sharply against it at, or from, this point. If so, 'scorn' would have something now of real derision for common man, as well as 'Common bird or petal', and would potentially reflect this reality back into 'disdain' in the first stanza, even though the plain meaning there always seems to me, as I have said, neutralised.

The next stanza has undoubtedly attracted differing interpretations. The 'Emperor's pavement' is no doubt the marble floor of the Forum in Byzantium, called 'The Pavement'. At midnight (chosen as the 'witching hour') the moonlight sets the depiction of flames dancing, so that art takes on the appearance of life, and one has an effect which can be compared either with Yeats's invocation to the mosaics in stanza iii of **'Sailing to Byzantium'**, or with the creative or recreative process itself. I assume, in fact, that this passage from the living world to the Byzantine is effected by imagination or by sheer intensity of being. Far from purgation, it is the raising of life in 'blood-begotten spirits' to a pitch where 'The fury and the mire of human veins' finds temporary release. . . . But the world of art *is* removed from primary reality, as if self-generated ('Flames that no faggot feeds, nor steel has lit, / Nor storm disturbs, flames begotten of flame'), so that, though in this stanza the living flesh, in vision, appears to have outsoared even the 'miracle' of one Byzantine artefact, it too has a price to pay,

Dying into a dance
An agony of trance,
An agony of flame that cannot singe a sleeve.

(pp. 132-33)

So to the final stanza, which I find an exultant climax, notably in the last line. . . . The opening suggests a great wave of spirits, carried over here to the dance by dolphins. . . . But the dolphins too are living creatures of 'mire and blood', so that they surely belong as much with the living vision of art as with 'life after death'.

The major puzzle, I always find, is the word 'break', twice repeated. Unlike 'embittered', this is indeed a word of many meanings, including virtual opposites, and no doubt Yeats chose it carefully with this in mind. In balance with meanings such as 'destroy', 'deprive', 'fragment', it can also mean 'to force an entrance into' (as in 'breaking and entering'), or to control (as with a horse), and various other things. We have to decide, I think, whether the degree of triumph achieved in the fourth stanza is confirmed and thrown back again from eternity to the world of the living; or whether it is decisively checked, in the end, by 'The golden smithies of the Emperor!' Opting, as I do, for a triumphant rhetoric, and for the assertion that enchantment is ultimately supported, rather than undermined, by the all-important question of tone as the poem progresses, I prefer the former view. Essentially in this poem, the tide of dolphin-born spirits is 'controlled' by the smithies, and 'bitter furies of complexity' are destroyed, or dissolved, in the experience of 'Marbles of the dancing floor'. In this reading, we can arrive at the crucial lines

Those images that yet
Fresh images beget

with some certainty that Yeats is once more celebrating the power of art and vision to break through the 'fury and the mire of human veins' and transcend them, even though they remain the stuff from which art is most usually made. The dance of images prefigures, I think, one of his last, and most interesting, explorations of art, **'Lapis Lazuli'**. The final line, 'That dolphin-torn, that gong-tormented sea', requires, I think, stresses on every word, leaping exultantly; and, though 'torn' and 'tormented' are undoubtedly there in balance, the rhythms have surely achieved, by way of the contemplative opening and the withdrawal from 'unpurged images', a détente between imagination and life.

Spirit-photo of Yeats. Senator Michael B. Yeats.

If this is agreed (and I admit again that an entirely different reading, turning on the word 'break', and on the tone chosen, is equally possible), it still needs to be said that this is no more 'final' than any other poem we have encountered. That the triumph is won at considerable cost is attested by the images and the ambivalences; also by the difficulty endemic to the poem itself. Again, the apparent reconciliation of human veins and the dance is momentary—as Yeats himself said in the passage from his prose most recently quoted here. The condition prescribed in line one is 'given', and rare; more than any other Yeats poem, this seems to me to border on the visionary. Sooner or later—very soon—the 'unpurged images' will return, and this poem in its turn recede; at best, it must live with that chain of dialectic set up throughout the poet's total work. What I am certain of, is that no one but Yeats could have written **'Byzantium'**; and that it could not have been conceived, except by way of the development I am trying to sketch. (pp. 133-35)

A. E. Dyson, "Yeats's Poetry, the Major Phase, 1916-39: No Enemy but Time," in his Yeats, Eliot and R. S. Thomas: Riding the Echo, *Humanities Press, 1981, pp. 1-184.*

CAIRNS CRAIG (essay date 1982)

[*In the following excerpt, Craig examines several of Yeats's poems written prior to 1925, when Yeats began revising his early poetry. Craig traces the reappearance of images from these early poems in* "Sailing to Byzantium," *which he considers one of Yeats's greatest poems.*]

It is the contradictory pulls of the romantic desire to transcend time and the associationist dependence on time that forms the basis of much of Yeats's early poetry. Yeats, of course, named himself among the 'last romantics', and his early poetry is often dismissed as a poetry of romantic longing and escape which fails to connect with the real world. Within that poetry, however, there is a rarely acknowledged degree of self-awareness that is the result, I would suggest, of the conflict between competing conceptions of the powers and purposes of art. The poem as a whole may represent an escape from the modern world—in that it deals with Irish mythic subjects in an archaic manner—but because Yeats's conception of such subjects was that they formed the end point of the memory invoked by modern art, the poems often turn back upon the reader to comment on their own status and to comment on the aesthetic experience of which they are a part. They are, despite their apparent naivete, 'self-conscious'.

Probably the finest of the very early poems is **'The Madness of King Goll'**. Yeats presents us with the story of an ancient Irish king, Goll, whose success as a king has been to establish peace and prosperity among his people, a success which perhaps involves a denial of those heroic values which he would wish to live by and for which he is interesting to readers of Yeats's poem. . . . 'Tumult' was a word Yeats often used to describe ancient art . . . and Goll's success in driving 'tumult and war away', banishing the need for the heroic, mirrors nineteenth-century society's destruction of the 'world of selfless passion in which heroic deeds are possible and heroic poetry credible'. Called again to battle against invaders, however, Goll does not recover his heroic stature, but undergoes a revelation that destroys his own ability to live the heroic life. . . . The moment of interaction between the eternal—'keen stars'—and the temporal—'keen eyes of men'—is a source of revelation used regularly by Shelley and a part of Yeats's romantic inheritance. The visionary who has been vouchsafed a sudden insight into the eternal beauty that occasionally visits itself upon the temporal world is cast out of human society in search of apocalyptic fulfilment of his vision. Like Shelley's Alastor Goll becomes a wanderer, and even Yeats's imagery is an echo of Shelley's, for it is by the mirroring of eyes that Shelley often symbolises union between different ontological dimensions of existence: 'yellow flowers / For ever gaze on their own drooping eyes, / Reflected in the crystal calm'. But in Yeats's mirroring in **'King Goll'** there is no revelation of spiritual compatibility between mind and eternity: the stars mirror the eyes of men in battle, their exaltation the lust for destruction. Goll is not led to a transcendental consciousness of time resolved into the eternal, but is trapped in an awareness of endless, and endlessly destructive time. The poem's refrain, with its emphasis on decay never resolved by death—'the leaves a-flutter round me, the beech leaves old'—posits a world of time forever in motion and decaying and yet without end. Time itself is equal with eternity in that it never passes away. Nature, so often the instantiation of the spirit of eternity for the romantics, is here an image only of unending process, an eternity not of salvation but of destruction. Yeats's choice of 'a-flutter' to describe the leaves, its archaism balancing verbal and adjectival against each other, creates the sense of motion and stasis conjoined, as the reiterated refrain balances the sense of temporal process which it describes ('old') against the stasis which its repetition enacts. No apocalypse will save the world of time from its own unceasing, endless change, a condition which Goll mirrors in his endless 'wandering' . . . (pp. 78-80)

In Goll's endless wandering, however, we can see an image not only of an eternity of time within which mankind is trapped, but an image of the poem's own conception of the nature of art. Goll's moment of insight comes from 'a whirling and a wandering fire' and passes on into further wandering, just as the associational process reaches through a train of images to some overwhelmingly powerful image that will set the mind wandering again from 'idea to idea, emotion to emotion'. The endless movement of associations around the stasis of the work of art is almost figured in the endless flutter of the beech leaves, as though the refrain mirrors the process by which we experience and give significance to Yeats's image. Goll's exclusion from eternity is identical with the poem's inability to lead our minds to anything but further experiences of temporal process. Such mirroring between Yeats's story and the reader's experience might seem fanciful were it not for the fact that the poem's final stanza presents us with Goll mimicking Yeats's own art, for he finds 'this old tympan' and begins to sing:

> I sang how, when day's toil is done,
> Orchil shakes out her long dark hair
> That hides away the dying sun
> And sheds faint odours through the air:
> When my hand passed from wire to wire
> It quenched with sound like falling dew,
> The whirling and the wandering fire;
> But lift a mournful ulalu,
> For the kind wires are torn and still,
> And I must wander wood and hill.

The 'dying sun' operates here on two different levels, one faithful to Goll's sense of the world and one that refers back upon ours. For Goll it is a metaphor for sunset, or an animistic conception of daily recreation of the universe; for us, 'dying sun' all too accurately describes the realities of our universe as revealed by science. Goll's song of Orchil does the same for him as Yeats's poem is doing for its readership; both hide away the dying sun behind figures who inhabit an apparently timeless realm. For us, however, the timeless figure of Goll re-enacts within his own realm of existence the dilemmas from which we sought escape in art, and reveals the extent to which art itself is no pathway to some ultimate transcendence of our human condition. Art, in its associational recall of the past, has its power only by its recall of a tumultuous past. . . . It is therefore trapped in an endless process of time, and neither heroic action nor visionary insight will release it into a different ontological status.

The failure of heroism and of visionary insight to offer a romantic access to the Infinite dominates Yeats's early poems: the heroes are never satisfied by their great actions, the visionaries never consoled by their insights. Both are haunted by the sense of time as endless series, denying any value to individual action, and by an eternity which is merely an infinite repetition of the events of time. Thus in **'Fergus and the Druid'** . . . , Fergus the warrior king seeks the 'dreaming wisdom' of the Druid, and to gain it has given up his kingship and become, like Goll, a wanderer. . . . Fergus is . . . given by Yeats a consciousness of what he will become as a part of Yeats's poem and our own memory—'another's dream'. His heroism may give eternity of a kind to his name, but it cannot save him; neither, however, can the wisdom of the Druid, for instead of offering a romantic access to the eternal, what the Druid reveals is a world of boundless repetition of the experience of time, a knowledge which is endless memory rather than the transcendence of a world of time and the need for memory that Fergus sought. . . . (pp. 80-1)

What Yeats is presenting in both Fergus and Goll are images of the tensions within his own art. The romantic artist who is the inheritor of the powers of the magus and the druid would like to offer his art as an entry into eternity, as an escape from time, but the art itself denies any such release, and can lead to no ultimate revelation of what is permanent in the world. Associational process, the continual generation of a train of images moving outwards and away from the work of art itself, is mirrored in Goll surrounded by the endlessly ancient and fluttering leaves, is mirrored in Fergus's discovery of the chain of images of which his being is a part. The romantic demand that art, through the spiritual power of the imagination, should save us from the world of time is undone by the knowledge that art works only through memory and is devoted to the endless recall of the events of time. The characters of the poems act out the failure of the romantic desire, ironically commenting on what we have sought from the poem. The conditions from which we have sought to escape are repeated in the world we escape into, and the tension between our desire for transcendence through art and the real nature of what we can be offered by art is perhaps summed up in an image from another early poem, **'The Indian to his Love'**:

> A parrot sways upon a tree
> Raging at his own image in the enamelled sea. . . .

The parrot rages at the more perfect life in the 'enamelled sea', but his image there is only a repetition of the condition in which he already exists.

My point in drawing attention to these early poems is not merely to suggest that some of Yeats's early work is more complex than usually taken to be: the conflict which they reveal between the sense of art as a transcendence of time and of an associationist art's necessary complicity with time was to be a pervasive theme of Yeats's poetry. And the technique of playing off the real nature of the reading experience . . . against the apparent stasis of the poem and the possible unchanging reality to which it testifies was one which he was to exploit with ever-increasing subtlety. In 1925 Yeats began a revision of the whole body of his early poetry, and the images and tensions in the three poems I have mentioned seeped into one of his greatest poems. **'Sailing to Byzantium',** written in the following year. The first stanza recapitulates the sense of a world of endless change in which Goll finds himself, process become eternal in its negation of any other dimension of existence. . . . (pp. 82-3)

The second stanza of **'Sailing to Byzantium'** offers us Yeats—'A tattered coat upon a stick'—in the same guise as the Druid whose knowledge could be of no comfort to Fergus. . . . Knowledge such as the Druid's cuts him off from the pleasures of active life; cut off from the pleasures of active life, Yeats sets off after knowledge as compensation for what time has taken from him. But his journey to Byzantium is paradoxical, poised between real and hypothetical as was the journey of the lovers in **'The Indian to his Love.'** . . . (pp. 83-4)

The echoes between early and late poems continue in the imagery of 'song': In **'King Goll'** the mad song allows the goddess to be called up who 'hides away the dying day'; in **'Sailing to Byzantium'** the sages are called from the work of art just as the goddess was called from eternity, but are called to be singing masters. . . . Goll's song puts him in touch with eternity through artifice; the song in **'Sailing to Byzantium'** conceals death by incorporating the speaker into artifice. The origins of the golden bird that Yeats decides to take as his form in the afterlife may be in Hans Andersen's clockwork nightingale and Keats's 'immortal bird', but it also takes us back to the parrot, for while in the early poem the bird rages at its aesthetic mirror image, enamelled by the sea, in the later poem the poet crosses into the world of art to become an 'enamelled' golden bird. In 'The Indian to his Love' the voyage of escape to the island turns back upon itself, for the lovers' conversation is of what they have left behind, of 'how far away are the unquiet lands', and in exactly parallel fashion **'Sailing to Byzantium'** turns back upon itself, as the artificial bird, released from time and change, sings of 'what is past, or passing, or to come'. That turning back to the world which one has desired to escape has, since its first publication, always presented problems to Yeats's critics. Why should the achievement of an eternal stasis in a perfect world be qualified by a return to time in the bird's song? The comparison with the early poems allows us to see, I think, that this is not just an accidental or contradictory element in Yeats's writing of this particular poem, but an essential part of his view of art. The contradictions from which one seeks an escape through art always repeat themselves within the world of art, and **'Sailing to Byzantium'** is no exception. And that internal movement of the poem is related to the formal tension between its apparent stasis—a 'monument of unageing intellect'—and the temporal process of association upon which it depends for its full experience. If the work of art succeeded in defying time it would destroy its own essential power, which comes from the trains of thought it generates in time, from what 'is past, or passing, or to come'. The bird's singing does not mean that it has the gift of prophecy (Yeats cancelled 'future' from the drafts), but that it sings what is always to come, and what dominates the rest of the volume 'The Tower', to which it is the introduction—death and loss and destruction. As a part of a remembered tradition, however, it also introduces what is to be placed against those eternal enemies—the powers of memory.

The problems which **'Sailing to Byzantium'** has posed revolve largely around the fact that Byzantium is supposed to be Yeats's ideal city of the imagination—or 'Condition of Fire', as Harold Bloom calls it [in his *Yeats* (1970)]; it is supposed to be a symbol of the symbolising faculty's ability to carry us into a spiritual eternity. But the desire for such transcendence is set within a concept of art based on invoking into the matrix of the reader's experience a succession of images from the past, and in reading it we are driven necessarily, therefore, to defy the fixity to which the poetic persona aspires. **'Sailing to Byzantium'** is not a failed poem of the 'Condition of Fire' or of the romantic imagination, as Bloom, for instance would have us believe, but a poem ironically commenting upon the ways in which poets will create heavens from their art in spite of that art's real nature. Just as the early poem **'The Indian upon God'** presents us with a peacock who imagines God 'a monstrous peacock,' . . . so the poetic persona in **'Sailing to Byzantium'** invents a heaven which the poem itself undercuts as it forces him to turn back to the world of time. And that turning back is something that we, too, are forced to experience as we read the final lines. . . . Where is the golden bird, so much the subject of critical debate? To know the form the speaker will take we have to return to the 'birds in the trees / Those dying generations' of stanza one: we have to make a journey back in memory to the world of time, or, if we are lucky, back in memory to previous descriptions of such artifacts. It is not the golden bird that figures for us Yeats's conception of art, defying time in the perfection of its beauty, but the whole dialectic of the poem. Yeats's art is a combining of the flux of time, to which the art of music is the appropriate correlative, and the sculpted stasis of the monumental image: the time transcending images of the poem recall a world of time in our associations and it is through those associations that the images gain their power and significance. It is the song of the dying generations *and* the fixity of the artistic form together that are the basis of Yeats's concept of art; it is the forward movement of the poem, a song in time, towards an image that is apparently beyond time, as though sculpted, but releasing the reader's mind into an associative reverie that will carry him far into the past, that constitutes the essential structure of Yeats's poetic. And within such a poetic the associations with which we enclose the poem may, from the point in time when the poem was written, be in the future: thus can it sing what is yet 'to come'. (pp. 85-7)

Cairns Craig, "Yeats: The Art of Memory," in his Yeats, Eliot, Pound and the Politics of Poetry: Richest to the Richest, *University of Pittsburg Press, 1982, pp. 72-111.*

ROBERT BUTTEL (essay date 1983)

[Buttel has written several studies on the works of the poet Wallace Stevens. The following excerpt is taken from a comparison of the theme of aging and imminent death in the works of Stevens and Yeats.]

"Bodily decrepitude is wisdom," asserts W. B. Yeats in the well-known aphorism in **"After Long Silence."** His three old Chinamen in **"Lapis Lazuli"** are embodiments of that wisdom, achieving as they move up the mountain a state of sublimity, of serene transcendence. Surveyors of the earthly and tragic scene below, they manifest a state of grace; they are alive, enriched by their long years of human experience, while at the same time they enjoy an unearthly perspective. (p. 48)

If for Yeats old age brought wisdom, the thought of death evoked both panic and attraction; he was drawn again and again to those moments of death and transfiguration that were so integral to his complex of history, myth, and self, and much of the power of his work derives from his yearning to transcend death and bodily decrepitude. The point at which life and death, the temporal and the supernatural, impinge stirred in Yeats his most characteristic stances and emotions—strange emotions, frequently combining terror and trance or a giddy gaiety. . . . The two earlier Byzantium poems, of course, represent a more intense, more extreme solution to the duality of life and death, of body and soul: the escape from the body in a scent of ecstatic supernatural mystery so as to achieve, in the imagination at least, absorption into "the artifice of eternity," in effect a personal apotheosis. What Geoffrey Hartmann says of Keats' odes—that they "are a feverish quest to enter the life of a pictured scene, to be totally where the imagination is"—can be said also of **"Sailing to Byzantium"** and **"Byzantium."** How human by comparison is Crazy Jane's devotion to the body as well as to the soul. In Crazy Jane, Yeats lit upon a brilliantly apt persona, not only for conveying his conception of unified being but also for the wisdom that erupts with half-crazed, wild clairvoyance and the authority of an old crone interpreting life from the perspective of one near death.

Last Poems, however, more definitely anticipate the end. In part there is a summing up, as in **"The Municipal Gallery Revisited"** and **"Beautiful Lofty Things,"** poems that celebrate and glory in the friends Yeats has had, or in **"Under Ben Bulben,"** in which he accepts and prepares for death and offers a kind of last will and testament for the Irish poets to come. The latter poem not only concludes with its ceremonious elegy for self and directions for the portentous words to be cut on his gravestone (right to the end he was capable of posturing) but also contains some rather easy words about death. . . . Much more compelling, however, are those poems in which Yeats allows himself little if any solace as he faces the desperation of the end. In these he bursts out with feelings of fear, of frenzy, of indignation, of anguish. **"Why Should Not Old Men Be Mad?"** asks the title of one poem, which cites sardonically the follies, injustices, and tragic perversity of life that "Observant old men know . . . well." Even when a sense of accomplishment and fulfillment is realized at the end of life in **"What Then?"** the chilling question reverberates: *"'What then?' sang Plato's ghost. 'What then?'" (pp. 51-2)*

The awareness of impending annihilation charges the last poems with their furious energy. In them Yeats would extract from the very desperateness of his condition his final aesthetic triumphs. . . . Yeats' histrionic stances themselves become part of the transmogrifying intensity of these last poems, in which posturing carried somehow beyond posturing. The old poet certainly assumes a self-regarding stance in **"The Circus Animals' Desertion"** as he thinks back on his "old themes" and "masterful images," which "Grew in pure mind," but the unflinching bitter recognition at the end, as he admits the disgusting source of his images, manages to ennoble the stance; his acceptance of the fate of flesh and mortality avoids self-pity: " . . . Now that my ladder's gone, / I must lie down where all the ladders start, / In the foul rag-and-bone shop of the heart." (pp. 52-3)

Robert Buttel, "The Incandescence of Old Age: Yeats and Stevens in Their Late Poems," in The Motive for Metaphor: Essays on Modern Poetry, *edited by Francis C. Blessington and Guy Rotella, Northeastern University Press, 1983, pp. 48-59.**

ADDITIONAL BIBLIOGRAPHY

Allen, James Lovic. *Yeats's Epitaph: A Key to Symbolic Unity in His Life and Work.* Washington, D.C.: University Press of America, 1982, 270 p.

Monograph upon Yeats's gravestone inscription, taken from the poem "Under Ben Bulben," attempting to establish the relationship of this poem to the rest of Yeats's work.

Bogan, Louise. "William Butler Yeats." In her *Selected Criticism: Poetry and Prose,* pp. 86-104. New York: Noonday Press, 1955.

Reprint of a 1938 essay in which Bogan hails Yeats as the greatest living poet writing in English. She discusses his career as one of continual development and growth.

Diggory, Terence. *Yeats & American Poetry: The Tradition of the Self.* Princeton, N.J.: Princeton University Press, 1983, 262 p. *

Compares and contrasts the confessional poetry of several twentieth-century Modernist poets with the works of Yeats.

Ellmann, Richard. *Yeats: The Man and the Masks*. New York: Macmillan Co., 1948, 331 p.
Excellent biographical and critical study by a prominent American critic and Yeats scholar.

——. "Yeats and Eliot." *Encounter* XXV, No. 1 (July 1965): 53-5.*
Discusses Yeats's and Eliot's criticisms of each other's poetry.

—— "Yeats's Second Puberty." *The New York Review of Books* XXXII, No. 8 (9 May 1985): 10-18.
Discussion of Yeats's belief that the vasectomy he underwent in 1934 brought on a "strange second puberty" and infused much of his late poetry with wildness and passion.

Fallis, Richard. *The Irish Renaissance*. Syracuse: Syracuse University Press, 1977, 319 p.*
History of the Irish Renaissance that provides a cultural and historical background to Yeats's era.

Finneran, Richard J. *Editing Yeats's Poems*. New York: St. Martin's Prcss, 1983, 144 p.
Extensive discussion of the problems encountered in editing Yeats's poems, with explanation of the solutions adopted for the 1983 text *The Poems: A New Edition*.

Frost, Robert. Letter to Sidney Cox. In *Robert Frost on Writing*. Edited by Elaine Barry, pp. 89-90. New Brunswick, N.J.: Rutgers University Press, 1973.
Letter of September 1913. Frost expresses surprise that the poetry of Alfred Noyes—whom he calls Alfie No-yes—seems to be more popular in America than that of Yeats.

Gibbon, Monk. *The Masterpiece and the Man: Yeats As I Knew Him*. London: Rupert Hart-Davis, 1959, 226 p.
Biography based largely on personal reminiscences of Yeats's young cousin, Monk Gibbon. Gibbon was also acquainted with A. E., George Moore, Maud Gonne, and other notable Irish artists and politicians.

Gogarty, Oliver St. John. *William Butler Yeats: A Memoir*. Dublin: Dolmen Press, 1963, 27 p.
Rambling personal reminiscence.

Hardy, Barbara. "Passion and Contemplation in Yeats's Love Poetry." In her *Feeling in Poetry*, pp. 67-83. Bloomington: Indiana University Press, 1977.
Maintains that Yeats is primarily concerned in his love poetry with making and contemplating images of actual experience. His love poetry is best typified in short, intense poems, often comprised of a single sentence.

Harper, George Mills, ed. *Yeats and the Occult*. London: Macmillan Press, 1975, 322 p.
Collection of essays devoted to Yeats's investigations of the occult.

Hoffpauir, Richard. "Yeats or Hardy?" *The Southern Review* 19, No. 3 (July 1983): 519-47.*
Extensive comparison of the critical receptions of Yeats's and Hardy's careers, suggesting that one or the other must be regarded as the preeminent poet of the twentieth century; and that such a choice excludes the other poet from serious consideration.

Hone, Joseph. *W. B. Yeats: 1865-1939*. London: Macmillan and Co., 1943, 504 p.
Biography generally regarded as the finest available. Hone had the help of both Mrs. W. B. Yeats and Maud Gonne in preparing the text, as well as access to all of Yeats's unpublished papers.

Jeffares, A. Norman. *A Commentary on "The Collected Poems of W. B. Yeats."* Stanford: Stanford University Press, 1968, 563 p.
Line by line explications of each poem in Yeats's *Collected Poems*.

Kishel, Joseph. *"Yeats's Elegies." Yeats-Eliot Review* 7, Nos. 1 & 2 (June 1982): 78-90.
Suggests that some of Yeats's early poetry, such as *Crossways, The Rose, The Wind among the Reeds, In the Seven Woods, The Green Helmet,* and *Responsibilities,* can profitably be reinterpreted as "partial elegies" because of their "elegiac attitudes," and critically compared with the more traditional elegiac poems "In Memory of Major Robert Gregory," "Upon a Dying Lady," "Easter 1916," "In Memory of Eva Gore-Booth and Con Markeiwicz," "Coole Park 1929," and "Under Ben Bulben."

Lynch, David. *Yeats: The Poetics of the Self*. Chicago: University of Chicago Press, 1979, 192 p.
Psychoanalytic study of Yeats based on the most recent psychological theories of narcissism. Lynch uses these theories as a starting point for an analysis of Yeats's poetry and his philosophies.

Murphy, William M. *Prodigal Father: The Life of John Butler Yeats*. Ithaca, N.Y.: Cornell University Press: 1978, 649 p.*
Biography of Yeats's artist father, whose philosophy and personality markedly influenced his son's career. There are many references to W. B. Yeats throughout the text.

Murry, J. Middleton. "Mr Yeats's Swan Song." In his *Aspects of Literature*, pp. 39-45. London: W. Collins Sons & Co., 1920.
Negative review of Yeats's *The Wild Swans at Coole*, maintaining that in this work Yeats's creativity and imagination failed him.

O'Faoláin, Seán. "W. B. Yeats." *The English Review* 60 (July 1935): 680-88.
Contends that Yeats's finest poetry is that found in *The Wild Swans at Coole* and subsequent works.

Ransom, John Crowe. "Yeats and his Symbols." *The Kenyon Review* 1, No. 3 (Summer 1939): 309-22.
Contends that comprehension of Yeats's symbolism requires no special or esoteric knowledge. Ransom further claims that in the infrequent instances that obscure symbols occur in the poems, understanding the symbols is not necessary to the enjoyment of the poem.

Stallworthy, Jon. *Between the Lines: Yeats's Poetry in the Making*. Oxford: Clarendon Press, 1963, 261 p.
Line-by-line examinations of the existing early drafts of a number of Yeats's poems, exploring the changes that Yeats made during revision.

Stephens, James. "W. B. Yeats," "Yeats as Dramatist," "Yeats and Music," "Around and About Yeats," and "Yeats the Poet." In his *James, Seumas & Jacques: Unpublished Writings of James Stephens*, pp. 67-72, 73-76, 87-88, 89-95, and 96-100. New York: Macmillan Co., 1964.
Texts of BBC radio broadcasts by Stephens from 1942 through 1948 detailing aspects of Yeats's life and career.

Williams, Charles. "William Butler Yeats." In his *Poetry at Present*, pp. 56-69. Oxford: Clarendon Press, 1930.
General introduction to Yeats's poetry by a contemporary.

Andrei A(lexandrovich) Zhdanov

1896-1948

(Also transliterated as Andrey) Russian government official.

Zhdanov was instrumental in establishing the stringent guidelines that were enforced for all Soviet media following the Russian Revolution. For more than twenty years, Zhdanov worked closely with Soviet leader Joseph Stalin as a cultural and ideological advisor and held positions of power within the Soviet government and the Communist party that authorized him to formulate official policy regarding Soviet literature, art, music, drama, philosophy, historiography, and the sciences. During the *Zhdanovschina* (the era of Zhdanovism, as the period of his greatest influence is commonly called), the Soviet government passed many laws mandating the literary styles, genres, and topics that could appear in the Soviet Union.

In the years immediately following the Revolution, the Soviet government took the first steps toward assuring that all Soviet media would support and further the Soviet cause. The post of commissar for education and public enlightenment was created to oversee the production of literature, in much the same way that other commissariats supervised farm or factory production. This post was first held by Anatoly Vasilyevich Lunacharsky, who has been characterized as a deeply cultured man primarily concerned with preserving the great classics of Russian literature. These works were threatened by a radical left-wing proletarian group that advocated the destruction of all pre-Revolutionary Russian cultural artifacts in order to make way for a wholly new Soviet culture relevant to the worker, the leading exemplar of the new Soviet citizen. This radical left was opposed by the right-wing *poputchiki,* or "fellow travelers," writers and artists who for the most part accepted the Soviet system but wanted a guarantee of freedom of expression, including the right to criticize the new regime.

Although the official Soviet position regarding differing literary movements and theories throughout the New Economic Policy (NEP) Period of 1921 through 1928 was one of impartiality, historians find indications that the government unofficially supported the partisans of proletarian literature. Most Western commentators on Soviet literary history concur with Ernest J. Simmons that "it was inevitable . . . that in a totalitarian form of government the single party in power should ultimately secure full control over literature as over every other ideology." Stalin called 1928 "the turning point" in this respect, calling for the "Bolshevization of the arts" to be included in the programs of the Five-Year Plans. At the beginning of the First Five-Year Plan in 1928, publishing was nationalized and placed under the supervision of the Central Committee for Literary Affairs. Private publishing houses were permitted to function only under guidelines established by the central government publishing house. In the late 1920s the Central Committee began to issue directives to publishers, dictating which literary topics and styles were to be encouraged from Soviet authors. The Union of Soviet Writers was formed in 1932, and by the end of that year superseded all existing writers' groups, with membership a necessary prerequisite for publication. It became increasingly difficult, and soon impossible, to publish anything that was not supportive of the Soviet system.

The formation of the Union of Soviet Writers coincided with the Soviet government's decision to formulate an official literary doctrine, called Socialist Realism, derived from suggestions made by Stalin, Zhdanov, and the noted novelist Maxim Gorky. Socialist Realism requires that literature function as an educational and propagandistic tool, embodying: *partiinost,* or "party spirit," an enthusiastic and uncritical support of Communist party policies; *narodnost,* or the use of literary forms meaningful to the masses; and *ideinost,* or the promulgation of the proletarian point of view. Above all, Socialist Realism adheres to the Marxian contention that the arts must serve as instruments of the class struggle. In accordance with Gorky's admonition to "learn from the classics," writers were called upon to affirm the new social order of Soviet communism in the realistic style of the great classics of nineteenth-century Russian literature. This application of political criteria to an ostensibly literary formula resulted for the most part in trite, formulaic, and uninteresting fiction.

Zhdanov joined the Bolshevik party while still in his teens, quickly becoming known as a devoted party worker. During the First World War and the Russian Revolution of 1917, Zhdanov served in a Bolshevik propaganda unit. Following the Revolution, he was appointed to a series of increasingly important positions in the Communist party. After his election to the Central Committee of the Soviet Communist party in 1928, he worked closely with Stalin, who delegated to Zhdanov many tasks dealing with party ideology. Zhdanov's first major appearance as a Communist party leader and as Stalin's deputy, a position that encompassed the duties formerly held by Lunacharsky, was at the First Congress of the Union of Soviet Writers in 1934. Zhdanov delivered the keynote speech outlining the duties and responsibilities of Soviet authors and introducing Socialist Realism. Authors were enjoined to create literature "optimistic in essence, because it is the literature of the rising class of the proletariat." Calling writers "engineers of the human soul"—a phrase attributed to Stalin—Zhdanov called for Soviet literature to present contemporary proletarian heroes in works demonstrating the superiority of the Soviet system to any other social system or form of government on earth; and further, to foretell the glorious future that was assured under communism. Subsequently, Zhdanov was appointed director of *Agitprop,* the Central Committee department of agitation and propaganda. This established Zhdanov as second only to Stalin in matters of Soviet ideological policymaking.

The onset of World War II had an immediate effect on internal policymaking in the Soviet Union. State-imposed controls on published matter abruptly relaxed, as the ideological and literary theorists serving in the armed forces were unable to discharge their censorial duties. Further, Russian writers were caught up in a patriotic fervor and wrote little that did not conform to the nationalistic tenor of Socialist Realist literature. In 1941 Zhdanov slipped slightly in Stalin's regard due to Nazi advances on Leningrad while the city's defense was in his charge, and another Central Committee member, Georgiy Malenkov, instituted a series of intrigues against Zhdanov, evidently hoping to usurp Zhdanov's position with Stalin. Zhdanov and Malenkov occupied positions of comparable power within the Central Committee; however, it is thought that Malenkov desired the status of working more closely with Stalin. The two men subsequently engaged in a subtle struggle for political power and influence, made dangerous because it took place at the height of Stalin's purges of pro-Leninist factions within the government, when anyone who posed a real or imagined threat to Stalin was likely to die or to disappear into the Soviet prison system.

Following World War II, however, Zhdanov regained Stalin's confidence and favor, and continued his ascent in the government. He began to achieve prominence in matters of foreign policy, and was appointed head of the foreign department of the Central Committee and Chairman of the Committee of Foreign Affairs of the Supreme Soviet. Zhdanov's foreign policy was characterized by deep hostility toward the West, particularly the United States. Also following World War II the Soviet government took its most unequivocal steps toward total control of all aspects of Soviet intellectual and artistic life. In a number of speeches and pronouncements in August and September of 1946, Zhdanov made sweeping condemnations of current trends in Soviet literature, singling out the short story writer and satirist Mikhail Zoshchenko and the poet Anna Akhmatova. Their works were denounced for embodying everything that should be abolished from a true Soviet literature: self-absorption, religious ideas, immorality, a regard for Western concepts, and Formalism—a blanket term of condemnation for any modern literary movements, such as Imagism, Symbolism, and Futurism, that originated in the decadent West and did not have specific Soviet application. In keeping with the anti-Western tenor of his foreign policy, Zhdanov particularly excoriated any literary works that attempted to accommodate non-Soviet ways of thinking. Zhdanov extended his attack to literary history and criticism, forbidding any suggestion of Western influence on any period of Russian literary history. Conversely, critical studies that professed to find Russian influence on Western literature were highly praised. These isolationist policies resulted in a Soviet literature that developed in a vacuum, cut off from the mainstream of any other literary trends or movements.

The attacks on literature were followed by similar purges in the theater, cinema, sciences, music, and historiography. Increasingly, Jews were the victims of these attacks. This period of cultural purges is so closely identified with Zhdanov that it has been named the era of Zhdanovism. However, some critics, such as Ronald Hingley, suggest that in his political and cultural dealings it is likely that Zhdanov, as Stalin's deputy, was only relaying Stalin's orders, and probably originated few of the statements made in his name. Other critics maintain that Stalin's growing ill-health from 1946 through 1948 may mean that Zhdanov acted on his own in the cultural crackdowns of the 1940s. More recently, critics and literary historians examining this period in Soviet history have found evidence suggesting that in dictating new and severe literary policy, Zhdanov was concerned less with establishing an ideologically correct Soviet literature than with cementing his own place within the hierarchy by convincing Stalin of the importance of an ideological watchdog to safeguard Soviet culture.

Zhdanov's fall from power came swiftly in the last year of his life. In 1947 he had clashed with Stalin over several matters of foreign policy involving Russian relations with Yugoslavia and with non-Russian communist groups. He incurred the greatest disfavor, however, due to his moderate stance during a series of factional debates that raged throughout the year. Groups of highly nationalistic, conservative scholars were seeking to establish the same kinds of narrow political restraints that bounded literature and the arts on matters of philosophy, economics, and scientific research. A more moderate faction that included both Zhdanov and his son Yury hoped for a free exchange of ideas on these matters with Western nations. In this unprecedented cosmopolitanism Zhdanov may have been influenced by his son, who headed *Agitprop*'s science section and, though married to Stalin's daughter, was sharply critical of restraints on free scientific study. The younger Zhdanov was particularly critical of the theories of the biologist Trofim Denisovich Lysenko, who repudiated the pioneering genetic research of Luther Burbank and Gregor Mendel as valueless because it originated in a bourgeois society. When Yury Zhdanov publicly criticized Lysenko's pseudoscientific ideas, the biologist complained to Stalin, who forced Yury Zhdanov to recant in print his criticism of Lysenko, and removed Andrei Zhdanov from most of his positions of power. Zhdanov was at the time gravely ill, and, though some historians are sceptical of the coincidence, his almost immediate death was apparently of natural causes. Since the greatest part of his political career had been devoted to upholding the Soviet cause, his transgressions in the matter of the biology debates were overlooked, and Zhdanov was eulogized as a true hero of the Soviet Union.

Despite his death in 1948, most commentators on Soviet literature extend the Zhdanov era well into the 1950s, as the literary policies established by Zhdanov remained in effect. Some relaxation of these policies came with Stalin's death in 1953. Under Nikita Khrushchev, the process of "rehabilitation" was started, which involved the resurrection of the works of many writers and other creative people banned in Zhdanov's time. While the works of rehabilitated authors were still carefully expurgated to prevent the dissemination of any political unorthodoxies, many languishing careers were saved by this process. Zhdanov's influence, however, is still felt in the largely repressive literary policies that for the most part are still in effect in the Soviet Union.

PRINCIPAL WORKS

"Soviet Literature—The Richest in Ideas, the Most Advanced Literature" (speech) 1934; published in *Problems of Soviet Literature: Reports and Speeches at the First Soviet Writers' Congress*

"Report to the Eighteenth Congress of the C. P. S. U." (speech) 1939; published in *Amendments to the Rules of the C. P. S. U.*

Essays on Literature, Philosophy, and Music (essays and speeches) 1950

Throughout his career Zhdanov made hundreds of speeches on Soviet political and cultural matters, many of which have been published. The works cited above contain his most significant pronouncements on Soviet literature.

ANDREI A. ZHDANOV (lecture date 1934)

[*The following excerpt is taken from the text of a speech delivered by Zhdanov at the first Congress of Soviet Writers in Moscow on August 17, 1934. This marked Zhdanov's first appearance as Stalin's cultural advisor, a position that gave his pronouncements on Soviet literature official government sanction. In this speech, Zhdanov defines Socialist Realism and calls for Soviet literature to reflect the glories and successes of the Soviet system.*]

Under the leadership of Comrade Stalin, the Communist Party is organizing the masses for a struggle for the final liquidation of capitalist elements, for getting rid of the survivals of capitalism in economic life and in the consciousness of the people, for completing the technical reconstruction of the national economy. Getting rid of the survivals of capitalism in the consciousness of the people means fighting against all relics of bourgeois influence over the proletariat, against laxity, frivolity, and idling, against petty-bourgeois individualism and lack of discipline, against an attitude of greed and dishonesty toward public property.

We have in our hands a sure weapon for overcoming all difficulties that stand in our way. This weapon is the great and invincible doctrine of Marx, Engels, Lenin, and Stalin, embodied in life by our Communist Party and Soviets. (pp. 8-9)

The key to the success of Soviet literature is to be sought for in the success of socialist construction. Its growth is an expression of the successes and achievements of our socialist system. Our literature is the youngest of all literatures of all peoples and of all countries. At the same time it is the richest in ideas, the most advanced and the most revolutionary literature. Never before has there been a literature which has organized the toilers and the oppressed for the struggle to abolish once and for all every kind of exploitation and the yoke of wage slavery. Never before has there been a literature which has based the subject matter of its works on the life of the working class and peasantry and their fight for socialism. Nowhere, in no country in the world, has there been a literature which has defended and upheld the principle of equal rights for the toilers of all nations, the principle of equal rights for women. There is not, there cannot be in bourgeois countries a literature which consistently smashes every kind of obscurantism, every kind of mysticism, bigotry, and superstition, as our literature is doing.

Only Soviet literature, which is one flesh and blood with socialist construction, could become, and has indeed become, a literature so rich in ideas, so advanced, and so revolutionary.

Soviet authors have already created more than a few works of talent, which correctly and truthfully depict the life of our Soviet country. Already there are several names of which we can be justly proud. Under the leadership of the Communist Party, with the thoughtful and daily guidance of the Central Committee and the untiring support and help of Comrade Stalin, a whole army of Soviet writers has rallied around the Soviet power and the Communist Party. And in the light of our Soviet literature's successes, we see standing out in yet sharper relief the full contrast between our system—the system of victorious socialism—and the system of dying, moldering capitalism. (pp. 9-10)

The present state of bourgeois literature is such that it is no longer able to create great works of art. The decadence and disintegration of bourgeois literature, resulting from the collapse and decay of the capitalist system, represent the characteristic trait, the characteristic peculiarity of the state of bourgeois culture and bourgeois literature at the present time. Gone never to return are the times when bourgeois literature, reflecting the victory of bourgeois society over feudalism, was able to create the great works of the period when capitalism was flourishing. Now everything is degenerating—themes, talents, authors, heroes. (pp. 10-11)

Characteristic of the decadence and decay of bourgeois culture are the orgies of mysticism and superstition, the passion for pornography. The "celebrities" of bourgeois literature—of that bourgeois literature which has sold its pen to capital—are now thieves, police sleuths, prostitutes, hooligans. (p. 11)

That is how matters stand in capitalist countries. Not so with us. . . . Our writer draws his material . . . from the creative action that is seething in every corner of our country.

In our country the main heroes of works of literature are the active builders of a new life—working men and women, collective farmers, Communist Party members, business managers, engineers, members of the Young Communist League, Pioneers. Such are the chief types and the chief heroes of our Soviet literature. Our literature is impregnated with enthusiasm and the spirit of heroic deeds. It is optimistic, but not optimistic in accordance with any "inner" animal instinct. It is optimistic in essence, because it is the literature of the rising class of the proletariat, the only progressive and advanced class. Our Soviet literature is strong by virtue of the fact that it is serving a new cause—the cause of building socialism.

Comrade Stalin has called our writers engineers of human souls. What does this mean? What duties does the title confer upon you?

In the first place, it means knowing life so as to be able to depict it truthfully in works of art, to depict it not in a dead, scholastic way, not simply as "objective reality," but to depict reality in its revolutionary development.

In addition to this, the truthfulness and historical concreteness of the artistic portrayal should be combined with the ideological remolding and education of the working people in the spirit of socialism. This method in literature and literary criticism is what we call the method of socialist realism.

Our Soviet literature is not afraid of the charge of being 'tendentious.'' Yes, Soviet literature is tendentious, for in an epoch of class struggle there is not and cannot be a literature which is not class literature, is not tendentious, is allegedly nonpolitical.

And I think that every one of our Soviet writers can say to any dull-witted bourgeois, to any philistine, to any bourgeois writer who may talk about our literature being tendentious: ''Yes, our Soviet literature is tendentious, and we are proud of this fact, because the aim of our tendency is to liberate the toilers, to free all mankind from the yoke of capitalist slavery.''

To be an engineer of human souls means standing with both feet firmly planted on the soil of real life. And this in its turn denotes a rupture with romanticism of the old type, which depicted a nonexistent life and nonexistent heroes, leading the reader away from the antagonisms and oppression of real life into a world of the impossible, into a world of utopian dreams. Our literature, which stands with both feet firmly planted on a solid materialist base, cannot be hostile to romanticism, but it must be a romanticism of a new type, revolutionary romanticism. We say that socialist realism is the basic method of Soviet literature and literary criticism, and this presupposes that revolutionary romanticism should enter into literary creation as a component part, for the whole life of our party, the whole life of the working class and its struggle consist in a combination of the most stern and sober practical work with a supreme spirit of heroic deeds and magnificent future prospects. Our Communist Party has always been strong by virtue of the fact that it has united and continues to unite a thoroughly businesslike and practical spirit with broad vision, with a constant urge forward, with a struggle for the building of communist society. Soviet literature should be able to portray our heroes; it should be able to glimpse our tomorrow. This will be no utopian dream, for our tomorrow is already being prepared today by conscious, planned work.

One cannot be an engineer of human souls without knowing the technique of literary work, and it must be noted that the technique of the writer's work possesses a large number of specific peculiarities.

Your weapons are many. Soviet literature has every opportunity of employing these weapons of all kinds (genres, styles, forms, and methods of literary creation) in their diversity and fullness, selecting all the best that has been created in this sphere by all previous epochs. From this point of view, the mastery of the technique of writing, the critical assimilation of the literary heritage of all epochs, represents a task which you must fulfill without fail, if you wish to become engineers of human souls.

The proletariat, just as in other realms of material and spiritual culture, is the sole heir to all that is best in the treasury of world literature. The bourgeoisie has squandered its literary heritage; it is our duty to gather it carefully, to study it and, having critically assimilated it, to advance further.

To be engineers of human souls means to fight actively for a rich language, for works of a high quality. Our literature does not as yet come up to the requirements of our era. The weaknesses of our literature are a reflection of the fact that people's consciousness lags behind economic life—a defect from which our writers are not, of course, free. That is why untiring work at educating themselves and at improving their ideological equipment in the spirit of socialism is an indispensable condition without which Soviet writers cannot remold the consciousness of their readers and thereby become engineers of human souls.

We need complete mastery of the art of literature, and in this connection it is impossible to overrate the help that Maxim Gorky is rendering the Communist Party and the proletariat in the struggle for quality in literature and for a rich language.

And so our Soviet writers have all the conditions necessary for them to produce works which will be, as we say, in unity with our era, works from which the people of our time can learn and which will be the pride of future generations.

All the conditions have been created so that Soviet literature can produce works that meet the accumulated needs of the masses on the cultural plane. Our literature, and only our literature, has the opportunity of being so closely connected with its readers, with the life of the working people—such is the case in the Union of Soviet Socialist Republics. The present congress is especially important in this respect. It was prepared not only by the writers, but by the whole country along with them. In these preparations were clearly expressed the love and attention with which the Communist Party, the workers, and the collective farm peasantry surround the Soviet writers, the consideration and at the same time the exacting demands which characterize the attitude of the working class and the collective farmers toward the Soviet writers. It is only in our country that literature and the writer are held in such esteem.

Therefore, organize the work of your congress and that of the Union of Soviet Writers in the future in such a way that the creative work of our writers may correspond to the victories that socialism has won. Create works of high attainment, of high ideological and artistic content. Help actively to remold the people's consciousness in the spirit of socialism.

Be in the front ranks of those who are fighting for a classless socialist society. (pp. 12-15)

Andrei A. Zhdanov, ''Literature,'' in his Essays on Literature, Philosophy, and Music, *International Publishers, 1950, pp. 7-15.**

ANDREI A. ZHDANOV (essay date 1946)

[The following excerpt is taken from an essay comprising the combined and abridged texts of two speeches made by Zhdanov at meetings of Soviet Russian writers' groups in 1946. In these pronouncements, which came to have the force of law, Zhdanov outlines the duties and responsibilities of Soviet authors, foremost among them being the positive presentation of the Soviet system.]

V. I. Lenin was the first to formulate with utmost precision the attitude of advanced social thought to literature and art. I remind you of Lenin's well-known article, ''Party Organization and Party Literature,'' written at the end of 1905, in which he showed with characteristic force that literature cannot be nonpartisan, that it must be an important component part of the general proletarian cause. In this article by Lenin are laid all the foundations on which the development of our Soviet literature is based. (pp. 32-3)

The Leninist point of departure is that our literature cannot be apolitical, cannot be ''art for art's sake,'' but is called upon to fill an important vanguard role in social life. Hence the Leninist principle of partisanship in literature—a most important contribution of V. I. Lenin to the science of literature.

Consequently, the best tradition of Soviet literature is a continuation of the best traditions of Russian literature of the nineteenth century, the traditions created by our great revolutionary democrats—Belinsky, Dobroliubov, Chernyshevsky, Saltykov-Shchedrin—carried further by Plekhanov and scientifically elaborated and grounded by Lenin and Stalin. (pp. 33-4)

Leninism recognizes that our literature has enormous significance for social transformation. If our Soviet literature were to permit a reduction of its enormous educational role—this would mean development backward, a return "to the stone age."

Comrade Stalin called our writers engineers of human souls. This definition has deep meaning. It speaks of the enormous responsibility of Soviet writers for the education of the people, for the education of the Soviet youth, for not tolerating waste in literary work.

To some it seems strange that the Central Committee of the Communist Party adopted such severe measures on a literary question. We are not used to this. They think that if waste is permitted in production or if a production program for articles of mass consumption or a wood storage plan is not fulfilled—then to place the blame for this is a natural thing, but if waste is permitted in the education of human souls, if waste is permitted in the business of educating the youth, here one must be tolerant. But actually, is not this a far graver fault than the non-fulfillment of a production assignment? By its decision the Central Committee has in view the bringing of the ideological front into line with all the other sectors of our work. (p. 34)

The Soviet people expect from Soviet writers genuine ideological armament, spiritual nourishment that will aid in fulfilling the plans for great socialist construction, for the restoration and further development of our country's national economy. The Soviet people make high demands on writers, they want satisfaction of their ideological and cultural claims.

The situation during the war made us unable to satisfy these burning needs. But the people want to comprehend the events that have taken place. Their ideological and cultural level has grown higher. They are frequently dissatisfied with the quality of the works of literature and art that we put forth. Some workers in literature, workers on the ideological front, have not understood this and do not want to understand it.

The level of the demands and tastes of our people has risen very high, and he who does not want to rise, or is incapable of rising to this level, will be left behind. Literature is called upon not only to keep abreast of the demands of the people, but more than that—it is obligated to develop the people's tastes, to raise higher their demands, to enrich them with new ideas, to carry the people forward. He who is incapable of marching in step with the people, of satisfying their growing demands, of keeping up with the tasks of development of Soviet culture, will inevitably be retired. (pp. 35-6)

Comrade Stalin teaches us that if we want to maintain our cadres, to teach and educate them, we should not be afraid of offending anyone, we should not be afraid of principled, bold, frank, and objective criticism. Without criticism, any organization, including a literary organization, can decay. Without criticism, any disease can be driven deeper and it will be harder to deal with it. Only bold and open criticism helps our people to improve themselves, rouses them to march ahead, to overcome shortcomings in their work. Where there is no criticism, staleness and stagnation prevail, there is no fresh air, there is no room to move ahead.

Comrade Stalin frequently points out that a most important condition of our development is the necessity for every Soviet person to take stock of his work every day, fearlessly check on himself, analyze his work, courageously criticize his own shortcomings and errors, consider how to achieve better results in his work, and continuously work on his own improvement. This applies to writers as much as to any other workers. He who is afraid of criticizing his own work is a contemptible coward, unworthy of the people's respect.

An uncritical attitude toward one's own work, substitution of relations with writers based on friendship for relations based on principle are widespread also in the administration of the Union of Soviet Writers. (pp. 36-7)

In journals, as in any business, disorder and anarchy are intolerable. There must be a clear-cut responsibility for the direction of the journal and the content of published materials.

You must restore the glorious traditions of Leningrad literature and the Leningrad ideological front. It is bitter and offensive that the journals of Leningrad, which were always seed-beds for advanced ideas, advanced culture, became a refuge for ideological emptiness and vulgarity. One must restore the honor of Leningrad as an advanced ideological and cultural center. One must remember that Leningrad was the cradle of the Bolshevik Leninist organizations. Here Lenin and Stalin laid the foundations of the Bolshevik Party, the foundations of the Bolshevik world outlook, Bolshevik culture.

It is a matter of honor for the Leningrad writers, the active members of the Leningrad Party to restore and develop further these glorious traditions of Leningrad.

The task of workers on the ideological front in Leningrad, and principally of the writers, is to drive ideological emptiness and vulgarity out of Leningrad literature, to raise high the banner of advanced Soviet literature, to seize every opportunity for their own ideological and artistic growth, not to lag behind contemporary subject matter, not to lag behind the demands of the people, in every way to develop a bold criticism of their own shortcomings, a criticism that is not servile, not based on cliques or friendships, but a genuine, bold, and independent Bolshevik criticism based on principle. (p. 38)

Workers in culture and art who do not reorganize themselves, who cannot satisfy the needs of the people, can rapidly lose the confidence of the people.

Comrades, our Soviet literature lives and should live by the interests of the people, the interests of our motherland. Literature is the proper business of the people. This is why your every success, every significant work is looked upon by the people as their own victory. This is why every successful work can be compared with a battle won or with a big victory on the economic front. Contrariwise, every failure in Soviet literature is deeply offensive and bitter to the people, the Communist Party, the state.

This is precisely the goal of the resolution of the Central Committee, which is concerned with the interests of the people, with the interests of literature. (p. 40)

The bourgeois world is not pleased by our success both within our country and in the international arena. As a result of World War II the positions of socialism have been fortified. The question of socialism has been placed on the order of the day in many European countries. This displeases imperialists of all hues; they are afraid of socialism, afraid of our socialist country, which is a model for the whole of advanced humanity. The imperialists and their ideological henchmen, their writers and journalists, their politicians and diplomats strive in every way to slander our country, to present it in a false light, to slander socialism. In these conditions the task of Soviet literature is not only to reply, blow for blow, to all this base slander and the attacks on our Soviet culture, on socialism, but also boldly to lash and attack bourgeois culture, which is in a state of marasmus and corruption. (p. 41)

Does it become us, representatives of advanced Soviet culture, Soviet patriots, to play the role of worshipers of bourgeois culture or the role of pupils? Certainly our literature, which reflects a social order higher than any bourgeois-democratic order and a culture many times higher than bourgeois culture, has the right to teach others a new universal morality. Where do you find people and a country like ours? Where do you find such magnificent qualities as our people displayed in the Great Patriotic War and as they display every day in their labor of transition for the peace-time development and restoration of their economy and culture? Every day raises our people higher and higher. (p. 42)

To show these new high qualities of the Soviet people, to show our people not only as they are today, but also to give a glimpse of their tomorrow, to help illumine, with a search-light the road ahead—such is the task of every conscientious Soviet writer. The writer cannot jog along at the tail of events, he must march in the forward ranks of the people, pointing out to them their path of development. Guided by the method of socialist realism, conscientiously and attentively studying our reality, striving to penetrate deeper into the essence of the processes of our development, the writer must educate the people and arm them ideologically. (pp. 42-3)

No matter how bourgeois politicians and writers try to conceal from their own peoples the truth about the achievements of the Soviet order and Soviet culture, no matter how they try to erect an iron curtain, through which it would be impossible for the truth about the Soviet Union to penetrate abroad, no matter how they endeavor to belittle the actual growth and extent of Soviet culture—all these attempts are doomed to collapse. We know very well the power and advantage of our culture. . . . Is it for us to bow low before everything foreign or occupy a position of passive defense?

If the feudal social order and then the bourgeoisie in the period of their flowering could create an art and a literature that affirmed the establishment of the new order and hymned its flowering, then we, who represent a new, socialist order, the embodiment of all the best in the history of human civilization and culture, are all the more in a position to create the most advanced literature in the world, which will leave far behind the best examples of the creative genius of former times.

Comrades, what does the Central Committee of the Communist Party want and demand? The Central Committee of the party wants the active workers of Leningrad and the Leningrad writers to understand fully that the time has come when it is necessary to raise our ideological work to a high level. The young Soviet generation is faced with the task of intensifying the power and might of the socialist Soviet order, of fully utilizing the motive forces of Soviet society for a new, unprecedented blossoming of our well-being and culture. For these great tasks the young generation must be educated to be steadfast, cheerful, unafraid of obstacles, ready to meet these obstacles and overcome them. Our people must be educated people of a high ideological level, with high cultural and moral demands and tastes. To this end our literature, our journals must not stand aside from the tasks of contemporary life, but must help the party and the people educate the youth in the spirit of unreserved devotion to the Soviet social order, in the spirit of unreserved service to the interests of the people.

Soviet writers and all our ideological workers are today posted on the advanced line of fire, for in conditions of peaceful development there is no reduction, but on the contrary, there is an expansion of the tasks of the ideological front and principally of literature. The people, the state, the party want, not the withdrawal of literature from contemporary life, but its active invasion of all aspects of Soviet existence. Bolsheviks value literature highly. They see clearly its great historical mission and role in strengthening the moral and political unity of the people, in welding and educating the people. The Central Committee of the Communist Party wants us to have an abundance of spiritual culture, for in this wealth of culture it sees one of the main tasks of socialism.

The Central Committee of the Communist Party is confident that the Leningrad detachment of Soviet literature is morally and politically healthy and will speedily correct its errors and take its proper place in the ranks of Soviet literature.

The Central Committee is confident that the shortcomings in the work of the Leningrad writers will be overcome and that the ideological work of the Leningrad party organization will, in the shortest period, be raised to the height that is required today in the interests of the party, the people, the state. (pp. 43-4)

Andrei A. Zhdanov, "Literature," in his Essays on Literature, Philosophy, and Music, *International Publishers, 1950, pp. 15-44.**

MIKHAIL SHOLOKOV (essay date 1948)

[A Russian novelist, Sholokov was one of the most highly regarded creators of the literature of Socialist Realism. As a party member and deputy of the Supreme Soviet, Sholokov supported the standards for literature set by the Communist party, arguing that works written from a proletarian perspective for a proletarian audience should be promoted by the Soviet government as the most valid form of Soviet literature. In his 1965 acceptance speech for the Nobel prize in literature, Sholokov praised Socialist Realism because "it expresses a philosophy of life that accepts neither a turning away from the world nor a flight from reality, a philosophy that enables one to comprehend goals that are dear to the hearts of millions of people and to light up their path in the struggle." However, though Sholokov defended his nation's literature and ideology, his novels are not those of a functionary or a party apologist. In his greatest works, Tikhiy Don *(1928-47;* The Silent Don, *1941) and* Podniataia tselina *(1932-60; translated in two volumes as* Seeds of Tomorrow, *1935, and* Harvest on the Don, *1960), Sholokov portrayed the Bolshevik Revolution and the collectivization of Soviet agriculture in an epic though sometimes critical manner that did not gloss over the excesses of those years. In these novels Sholokov avoided the trite formulas and simplistic political themes of much Socialist Realist literature, creating a complex and realistic study of the revolutionary period. In the*

following excerpt from a eulogy, Sholokov summarizes Zhdanov's achievements.]

The country and the Party have lost a noble son, a man with a great heart and a crystal-clear mind. He loved his Country and his Party with that tremendous, active love which demands constant service and brooks no rest or indifference or apathy. And he devoted his entire life to this love.

Our Country mourns the untimely death of her true, noble son; our mighty Party mourns the death of one of its brilliant leaders; the entire people mourns, and we feel, with all our heart, how great is the grief of our leader, who has lost a loyal colleague and friend.

For us intellectuals, who, in our work, were in constant touch with our dear Andrei Alexandrovich, now departed from us, this is a grievous, bitter loss.

This man of broad education, of remarkable erudition in every field of art, who was interested heart and soul in the development of our Soviet culture, who was irreconcilable and merciless in overcoming the defects of our work, as is characteristic of a genuine Bolshevik—this man has ceased to be.

His report at the First Congress of Soviet Writers in 1934, his report on the Leningrad journals, his speech on problems of Soviet music, played a tremendous, directing role in the development of Soviet literature and art; his constant contact with writers helped us in our work and assisted us in correcting many mistakes. (pp. 9-10)

His whole life was devoted to a cause which is immortal. And that is why Death has no power over him. Such people do not die. He will always be a living, powerful fighter in our all-conquering life.

We bow our heads at the grave of our beloved Andrei Alexandrovich, we grieve profoundly, but our grief is manly. It is the grief of soldiers who have lost a great, beloved commander. In taking our leave of him, we will again raise our banners, now lowered in mourning, and, led by our great Stalin, we will march with firm tread to our final goal—to that greatest of victories, to Communism. (p. 10)

Mikhail Sholokov, "Andrei Alexandrovich Zhdanov," in VOKS Bulletin, *No. 55, 1948, pp. 9-10.*

ROBERT M. HANKIN (essay date 1953)

[*In the following excerpt, Hankin outlines the development of Soviet controls over literature from 1932 through 1946.*]

The year 1932 heralds the advent of a new era in Soviet literature. In that year a Communist Party Resolution "invited into a single Union of Soviet Writers all writers who support the platform of Soviet power and wish to participate in building socialism." The reason for the establishment of this new organization is not absolutely clear. . . . [Perhaps] the Party decided that with the completion of the First Five-Year Plan the moment was at hand to advance its grand design for literature, which would call for increasing centralization of control. (p. 244)

At the first All-Union Congress of Soviet Writers which assembled . . . [in 1934], Zhdanov, speaking in the Party's name, surveyed the new demands which were to be made on literature. He asserted categorically that socialist realism would henceforth constitute the exclusive artistic method for Soviet literature; thus he definitely repudiated the Party's earlier abstention from a clear expression of preference in matters of literary policy. He elaborated upon the tasks which would confront writers in their capacity as "engineers of the human soul." Drawing attention to the growth of international tensions, he sought to jostle the literary and ideological fronts into shouldering fresh responsibilities. Probably in response to ominous reverberations from the Reichswehr, Zhdanov sounded the initial call for a concerted offensive upon non-Soviet culture. . . . No matter what the reasons for its establishment, the existence of a single Union of Soviet Writers now made it feasible for the Party to accelerate the ideological mobilization.

The years which remained before the outbreak of the Second World War witnessed a succession of campaigns designed to augment the striking power of the printed word and transform the corps of Soviet writers into a mobile task force. Accountability for ideological content in art grew greater, particularly as anti-Trotskyist pronouncements rose in frequency and concern with Axis intentions increased. As the War drew nearer, the Party elevated the political function of art to the paramount position, its intolerance of heterodoxy growing daily more emphatic.

The cultivation of mass patriotism became a major preoccupation of the day. Literary critics who ventured to deprecate works with sanctioned patriotic content were admonished to desist. . . . On one of those rare occasions which usually betoken turning points in Soviet ideological developments, Stalin, Kirov, and Zhdanov, in the middle thirties, made a number of recommendations for a proposed textbook on the history of the USSR—which furnished fresh impetus to the cultivation of mass patriotism. This concentration on national traditions of fortitude and devotion to native soil in the face of external aggression reached its apogee in the first two years of the War and challenged, if it did not surpass, the dissemination of Communist ideology.

In 1939, the Eighteenth Party Congress introduced several fresh currents into the ideological atmosphere. What was officially dubbed "deference to the West" was singled out as a dangerous trap for Soviet intellectuals; Stalin even went so far as to contend that treason to the state could be traced to deference to

Zhdanov and Stalin at the bier of Leningrad party leader Sergei Kirov, 1934. Collection of Solomon Volkov.

foreigners. With the formal inception of what was termed the gradual transition to communism, the program of education and indoctrination was allocated a role of greater importance than ever before. (pp. 244-46)

During the War, literature climbed to new eminence in Soviet society; daily newspapers featured entire plays and novels on timely subjects, which undoubtedly played an effective role in sustaining public morale. The year 1944 saw the crucial hump of the national peril surmounted and with it the Party's heightened concern with ideological orthodoxy, and the reaffirmation of its unquestioned leadership. As the year opened, Mikhail Zoshchenko was mercilessly belabored for his autobiographical *Before Sunrise,* and found wanting in patriotism for writing what was called this "formal and harmful" work. Shortly thereafter, the list of delinquent writers was lengthened to include others whose output in the period of national travail was termed substandard. The process of ideological stocktaking had begun in earnest. With incalculable implications for all other categories of the Soviet "superstructure," the barb of Party criticism was shortly applied to the philosophers. (p. 246)

From 1941 to 1945 the Nazi invasion and the crisis of national survival had produced an impressive mobilization of all cultural and artistic media. The unprecedented intensity of the nation's anguish was succeeded by an understandable fatigue and a longing to relax. No respite was in store, however. After the briefest of interludes, the writers were summoned back into harness. Initially this ideological remobilization was oriented toward the needs of reconstruction, but when these early difficulties had been mastered, there was no demobilization. Despite revitalized economic optimism and resumption of the drive to achieve the next stage of social organization, dwindling hopes for international amity kept the propaganda mechanism functioning at top tension. (p. 247)

[At the end of 1947] Soviet intellectuals on all levels were instructed that their primary duty was to assist in the Party's program for the political and cultural enlightenment of the population. To make the Party, now numbering six million, an organization comparable in discipline to its prewar membership, a mass study program was instituted. For Party officials an elaborate training program moved into high gear. For the general public, series of lectures were organized on a vast scale in May, 1947, with the establishment of the All-Union Society for the Dissemination of Political and Scientific Knowledge. The specific content of the enlightenment program was announced in the Central Committee's resolutions on literature, motion pictures, and the theater, and in Zhdanov's speech at the same time. These documents were declared to have "established a fighting program . . . for many years." The new line was laid down with unprecedented stringency, taking many writers by surprise despite their years of previous conditioning to Party hegemony. Zhdanov conceded this was so, and endeavored to offer a justification for the policy:

> Some people think it strange for the Central Committee to have passed such abrupt measures on the literary question. They are not accustomed to this. . . . They maintain that if industry produces defective goods and fails to meet the consumers' goods program, or if the lumbering plan is not fulfilled, it is natural that a reprimand be issued for this. But if human beings are damaged in their education, is this offense not worse than failure to meet the production program.

In all postwar ideological pronouncements there is scarcely a passage which more accurately mirrors the militancy and rigidity of the day and the Party's anxiety over domestic weaknesses.

A survey of Soviet literary history since 1932 leaves no doubt that the Party's resolve to secure ultimate acceptance of its unqualified leadership and unshared control has been constant. But the tactics enlisted to achieve this end have varied. It would be misleading to describe the diversity of details in the postwar panorama as all merely the inevitable culmination of earlier lines of development. To suggest that specific details were painstakingly legislated long in advance is to ignore the distinctive demands of the contemporary situation. (pp. 249-50)

Less than a week after the celebration of victory in Europe Soviet writers met for their first postwar conference. Liberal relaxation was the keynote of the proceedings. It was too early for the magnitude of the war devastation to have impressed itself on the jubilant *literati* just back from the front. The conviction prevailed, moreover, that the Soviets now occupied an established and respected place in the councils of nations. In this mood, several literary luminaries whose political loyalties were above suspicion cautioned against the interference in the literary creative process and argued against the belief that in art a miracle could be "organized."

In the next few months, steps were taken somewhere backstage to dampen these hopes, and finally in August and September, 1946, the Party resolutions and the Zhdanov report eliminated all doubts as to the Party's postwar demands on the arts. An extensive range of charges was directed against literature described as "lacking in ideas and ideologically harmful." As in 1944, [Mikhail] Zoshchenko was again the chief target, this time for a story called "The Adventures of a Monkey." Zhdanov insisted that since 1922, when Zoshchenko had publicly confessed to being "politically immoral," nothing in his attitude had changed. Another well-known writer, Anna Akhmatova, who on the eve of the War had emerged from almost twenty years of retirement, was spotlighted as an anomaly on the current scene. Zhdanov likened the reappearance of her poetry, "jelled in attitudes of bourgeois aristocratic estheticism," to the resurrection of a "museum piece."

These two were old-timers, and this was not the first time they had taken the lash of the Party's tongue for reluctance to purge themselves of thought patterns inculcated in formative years under circumstances inimical to the present environment. But Soviet writers of considerably later vintage were also called to account. Akhmatova's melancholy and nostalgia for the past were matched by the sporadic appearance of "religious symbolism" (the employment of ecclesiastical terms, Biblical references, and evangelical imagery) in the work of young poets. This was judged as ill becoming an "engineer of souls" in Soviet society. Shortly after the end of the War, what came to be known as "literature of consolation" was also brought under frequent attack. The agonies of the day notwithstanding, writers were adjured to handle reality fearlessly. The returning veteran, it was insisted, would have no truck with "sweet lyricism," "gastronomical promises," or a "lulling and caressing literature under the aegis of which to seek refuge from the storms of life." Neither was this the time, in the Party's view, to use art purely for entertainment, since this might beget a mood of "false demobilization" and a yearning to "rest by the quiet stream." The war years had been drenched in adoration of Russia's past glories, as part of a coordinated drive to resurrect national traditions of fortitude and devotion. From the moment the War ended, preoccupation with history evoked reprobation.

Several other shortcomings completed the list of the Party's grievances. One complaint was that the quality of literary craftsmanship had fallen off. Another was that works had appeared manifesting "deference to the contemporary foreign culture of the West" and permeated with a "spirit of kowtowing to everything foreign." This theme would soon swell to a major drive. Finally, there were aberrations such as the poet Sel'vinskii's "theory of socialist symbolism," which he proferred as a philosophy of art to replace socialist realism, and the opinion of the Ukrainian writer, Petro Panch, that an author "had the right to make mistakes." The two latter views reveal the extent to which the Party had relaxed its controls over literature during the War.

From the lowest to the highest echelons, every writer and Party functionary deemed responsible for the deplorable state of literature came in for his share of official opprobrium. (pp. 251-53)

Much of the Zhdanov address and of subsequent articles on the role of literature in the Soviet Union reformulated, with special stress on their postwar application, those canons of literature which have constituted literary orthodoxy since 1932: the cardinal function of literature is as an instrument of education in society; it must cater to the masses, employing literary forms meaningful to them (*narodnost'*); it should make use of the legacy of earlier cultures, critically reevaluating it and singling out as guiding models all its progressive elements; to fulfill its purpose in Soviet society it must subscribe to the world-view of the proletariat (*ideinost'*), and it must support the policies of the Party and State (*partiinost'*).

The educational function of literature.—Zhdanov declared that it was the obligation of Soviet literature to assist in rearing the younger generation "to be bright and hearty, believing in its cause, fearing no obstacles, ready to master any difficulties." He insisted that bitter experience had confirmed the efficacy of this course. To lend greater weight to his argument he even ventured to surmise that the War might have been lost had Soviet literature pursued any other tack. Zoshchenko and Akhmatova, he maintained, could only disorient and demoralize youth at a moment when, with the postwar transition to an economy of peace, the responsibilities devolving upon the ideological front and on the literature primarily "do not diminish, but, on the contrary, grow."

The narodnost' *of Soviet literature*.—To prove its devotion to the masses, said Zhdanov, Soviet literature must meet their demands, improve their tastes, and guide their development. To do this, it must not lag behind events. Historic themes need not be altogether excluded, but a healthier balance had to be established between past and present; history should be illuminated in such a way as to disclose its usefulness in solving the problems of the present. Writers should portray artistically the changes which had occurred in the people since the Revolution, laying special stress on new qualities developed during the recent war.

Attitude to the cultural heritage.—Pursuing the line introduced in 1944 by the *Bolshevik* articles on the contributions of the Russian Revolutionary Democrats, Zhdanov called attention to the debt owed by Soviet literature to the materialist current in native culture. Of the historical personages whom he showered with praise for contributing to the Soviet literary tradition, all were Russians.

The concepts of partiinost' *and* ideinost'.—Calling Lenin's article "Party Organization and Party Literature" the source of all the "foundations on which the development of our Soviet literature rests," Zhdanov adamantly insisted that writers were wrong to assume that politics was the Central Committee's business, whereas their approach to literature might be purely esthetic: "Our literature is not a private enterprise to titillate the various tastes of the literary market. We are not one whit obliged to accommodate . . . tastes and mores which have nothing to do with the morality and qualities of the Soviet people." In the final analysis, it is this Leninist notion of *partiinost'* which most irrefutably disassociates the Soviet writer from his non-marxist Western or prerevolutionary Russian counterpart. . . . [By] elevating *partiinost'* to sacrosanct position, Lenin introduced a principle which was to become one of the most characteristic features of Soviet ideology. The Zhdanov speech in 1946 [see excerpt above] really constituted an exegesis on *partiinost'* in its postwar phase. It signified a major stride toward a thoroughly controlled literature.

Evidently the Party decided that the current situation allowed for less compromise in the execution of its purposes than had been necessary on earlier occasions. Hence its willingness to deal so summarily with writers as popular as Zoshchenko and Akhmatova. Hence its obduracy in demanding that writers sever all ties to earlier bourgeois thought, and its promptness to hold earlier deviations over the heads of recalcitrants. Hence its peremptory dismissal of the bare suggestion that a writer had the right to err. It accounts likewise for the stinging vituperation characteristic of this period, for the severity of the reorganizational measures and the resolve to secure absolute acceptance of *partiinost'* narrowly defined. And, finally, whereas for a generation Party spokesmen had championed the "critical absorption of past culture," criticism of the bourgeois legacy was now advocated far more vociferously than absorption.

Reference must be made to the polemic techniques of this period as a prerequisite for appraising any Soviet writings originating during the postwar Five-Year Plan. They were formulated in detail in 1947 when the philosophers of the USSR met in solemn conclave to overhaul the philosophical front in light of the new Party line. Again it was Zhdanov who worded the new requirement most bluntly. He qualified "annihilating criticism" as obligatory to the Party's polemic arsenal. To treat opposing views with a light hand would lead, he said, to professional "quasi-objectivism," "indifferent attention to good and evil," and would rob Marxism of its militancy and the aggressive spirit demanded by *partiinost'*. In anticipation of a bitter world ideological contest, intellectuals were exhorted early in the postwar period to regard themselves as fighting publicists. The cry went out for total mobilization of the ideological front; waverers were warned that anyone preferring to bypass the challenge would be branded a "deserter." In September, 1947, the reorganized *Literary Gazette* inaugurated an aggressive program with an article entitled "Harry Truman," containing a head-on assault upon the integrity of the American President. Here was unmistakable evidence of the intensity of the projected drive.

The campaign which unfolded aimed at the universal annihilation of the tenets and contributions of "bourgeois culture in all its guises." Zhdanov contributed a dogmatic restatement of the dependence of art upon society, and, in language glaringly reminiscent of his characterization of bourgeois culture in 1934, drew the conclusion that in the contemporary crisis of capitalism the bourgeoisie could no longer produce great art. But in 1946 it was more than present-day bourgeois culture which was attacked. The comparatively liberal prewar acceptance of earlier bourgeois cultural contributions as a treasured inheritance from which Soviet culture should respectfully glean the best was supplanted by an attempt to demonstrate how mankind had repeatedly been reduced to misfortune by past bourgeois ideologies. Literary movements on Russian soil which failed to satisfy the latest postulates or were at odds with the materialist traditions of Russia were ferreted out one by one and pilloried. The effectiveness of the dununciation was measured by the clarity with which a critic was able to trace the movement to Western, bourgeois origins.

This inimical view of bourgeois culture was joined by insistence upon Soviet cultural independence from the West. (pp. 253-56)

Zhdanov complained that Soviet periodicals had published Western "trash" and works which "groveled" before the bourgeois West. In time elaborate explanations were produced for the origin of this malady, which was characterized as "ideological waverings by individual representatives of our intelligentsia . . . and rotten servility to bourgeois culture." It was referred to an old inferiority complex generated by Russia's prerevolutionary backwardness. As far as official statements went, the phenomenon was confined to the intellectuals. However, an article by a popular Soviet poet, Antokol'skii, entitled "On the Party, the Education of Youth, and Culture," disclosed that youths who had spent time abroad were enthusiastic over the amenities of Western life and disappointed by the contrast upon their return home. . . . Moreover, postwar novels and plays attest that it was true likewise of returning workers and peasants.

In imaginative writing it was only a lapse here and there—five or six minor cases—which was adduced as proof that Soviet literature was actually guilty of groveling. Literary scholarship, on the other hand, was declared to be permeated with a deferential spirit. The trend selected as most opprobrious was the disposition to consider Russian literature primarily in the light of foreign influences. (pp. 259-60)

The origin of the national solidarity upon which the psychological entity of modern Russia rests has been explained in large measure by the upsurge of patriotism provoked by the Napoleonic invasion of 1812 and the defensive war which ensued. To overlook similar feelings induced in the Russians by the Nazi attack is to sidestep a basic clue to the postwar attitudes which have been described. Freshly roused national pride and sensitized patriotic feelings must be considered in any attempt to comprehend the Central Committee's resolutions and the Zhdanov report. These were the feelings on which Zhdanov was playing when he complained that Zoshchenko had caricatured the Soviet people as fools and idlers, of primitive culture and philistine tastes. It is likely that the Party would have been more circumscribed in its broadsides upon Western culture and upon the slightest suspicion of kow-towing to things foreign had it not relied confidently on the prevalent pride in the recent national achievement. The desire to reinforce, as well as capitalize on, this pride in the war effort surely played its part, also, in the Party's insistence that attention be shifted from the distant past to the mass heroism displayed in the Second World War.

Several other factors should be mentioned briefly as helping to explain the new national emphasis: first, the wish to spread confidence in Russia as the source of ideas and inspiration for the infant regimes in Eastern Europe and, somewhat later, China; and, second, the need, described above, to counteract the inevitable doubts and perhaps feeling of hopelessness generated in hundreds of thousands of Red Army men by their contact with superior Western technology and living standards.

But one factor probably far outweighs the others. In consequence of the all but absolute break which exists in social intercourse with the Western powers, the Soviets are divorced from what was formerly a rich and invaluable source of information to them. The decision, whether prompted by choice or dictated by necessity, to place reliance on their own resources, physical and spiritual, very likely influenced this gigantic effort to convince every citizen that native talent and genius were inexhaustible. Is this not essentially what Zhdanov was revealing when he declared that never before had it been so vital to inculcate a universal spirit of optimism? Since great progress had been made by Russian science and thought not only in the Soviet period, but before the Revolution as well, even in the face of tsarist oppression, Russia could, the propaganda implied, look forward confidently to that day in the near future when it would "outstrip the level of scientific achievement in the leading capitalist countries." In other words, the propaganda sought to eradicate the slightest doubt as to Russia's capacity for unlimited progress on her own.

The new line may perhaps best be viewed as a fusion, a mutual reinforcement, so to speak, of (*a*) the ideological currents inherited from the prewar period, (*b*) the ramifications which appeared during the War, and (*c*) the postwar conceptions delineated above. . . . [The] unification of men of letters in one tightly centralized, highly concentrated organization, their obligatory adherence to a uniform literary program in which art is esteemed principally as an educational implement, its political orthodoxy being regarded as of paramount importance—these conditions have existed since 1932. The concerted portrayal of an anathematized foreign foe, in conjunction with dire threats to any Soviet national suspected of a "deferential" attitude toward the external enemy—this, too, was typical of the prewar scene. The intensive implantation of a flaming brand of patriotism, the expanding scope of a program of education and indoctrination to ready the masses for contemplated economic changes at home as well as for a possible military contest abroad—these, likewise, were common before the War. In 1944, months before Soviet relations with the Western powers began to assume the shape by which they are now recognizable, the cardinal political significance of art came to be reemphasized; the process of glorifying Russian culture was magnified and accelerated with the studious revision of earlier attitudes toward the Russian Revolutionary Democrats and the adulation now awarded them over the philosophical antecedents of Marx and Engels in Germany.

What, then, is essentially new in the postwar picture? From the organizational, implementational standpoint, the vital innovation is the abrupt tightening of the Party control mechanism aimed finally at total, exemption-free concentration of intellectual cadres on specific goals strictly defined by Party authorities; secondly, the vast expansion in the scale of mass indoctrinational activities. What should be said of the new line itself? An attempt has already been made to trace the broad trends which followed from the Zhdanov speech and the Party decrees in 1946. Patently, the main fact underlying these tendencies, absent from the prewar conjuncture, is the contemporary position of the USSR as a contender with the West for world ideological leadership amidst tensions which threaten fateful risks. The Soviet adaptation to this situation lay in the unprecedented intensity of the stress on Russian originality, the denigration of bourgeois culture, and the pervasive efforts to eradicate from the Soviet scene the slightest proclivity for ideas current in the West.

In the months that followed the Party moves in 1946, no province of intellectual concentration was exempted from the application of the new directives. Significantly, transcending the technicalities at issue in each field, there would emerge generalized pronunciamentos at once hailed as pertinent to all other ideological areas. Roughly by the time the five years of the Plan period had run out, all the arts, biology and the other physical sciences, philosophy, scholarship in the humanities, in short, the complete intellectual edifice, had stage by stage been scrutinized and jolted into adjustment with the new requirements. Like relay runners, Party spokesmen in each of these fields, as its turn came, seized the baton from its bearer over the previous lap. Slightly short of the halfway mark of the five-year period, the runners covered that stretch of ideological terrain which interests us most, literary scholarship. The Party spokesmen warmed to their assignment in a comparatively relaxed spirit. They seemed willing to listen to argument and to welcome discussion as a device for arriving at truth. Toward the end, however, their tone altered sharply. A new militancy was introduced which was then carried on to new fields by the spokesmen of the offensive at its next stage and made to apply to all that had gone before as well. (pp. 262-65)

Statements which followed shortly after the Zhdanov report in 1946 made clear beyond a doubt that the new Party line was destined to hold sway for a very long time to come. . . . Thus far there is no evidence that anything in the hard core of this line has been radically altered. The Soviet ideological front appears to be entering a period which one might hazard naming the phase of refinement of the Zhdanov line. . . . Presumably, the invocation of a certain relaxation . . . was prompted by the domestic economic successes of the USSR, the accomplishment in broad terms of the ideological shifts desired by Party planners, and the excesses in the execution of the Zhdanov line which had reduced the effectiveness of many distinguished intellectuals. (pp. 288-89)

The pattern by which the Party has in the past imposed tight controls in direct ratio to its interpretation of the acuteness of crisis may be expected to obtain indefinitely. (p. 289)

Robert M. Hankin, "Postwar Soviet Ideology and Literary Scholarship," in Through the Glass of Soviet Literature: Views of Russian Society, *edited by Ernest J. Simmons, Columbia University Press, 1953, pp. 224-89.**

WALTER N. VICKERY (essay date 1963)

[*In the following excerpt, Vickery describes the era of "Zhdanovism" from 1946 to 1953.*]

The years 1946-53 must be ranked among the bleakest and most sterile in Soviet literature. During these years literature appeared to be operating in a vacuum; not only were contemporary trends in Western literature almost completely ignored, but the comparatively vigorous Soviet Russian literature of the Twenties was more or less consigned to oblivion. The free, creative spirit of the Soviet writer, which at the best of times labours under the disadvantage of severe restrictions, was imprisoned in a straightjacket so confining as to make it a matter of wonder that, along with all the substandard stereotypes masquerading as literature, there were produced some works of literary merit. It is not my intention here to examine these works—either individually or collectively—from the literary viewpoint. Instead I prefer, as have others before me, to focus attention less on the literary product than on those events, often extra-literary in their origin, which forged and fashioned the literature of Stalin's last years. (p. 99)

[Zhdanov] was active on the Soviet literary scene as far back as 1934, and he died in 1948. So that to speak of the 1946-53 period as the years of Zhdanovism serves only to underline the fact that it was in these years that the hard-line political orthodoxy represented by Zhdanov's name reached its apogee. Zhdanov himself was scarcely responsible for the repressive atmosphere that characterizes the period. Nor can Stalin, though he undoubtedly bears a greater burden of responsibility, be held solely accountable. The 1946-48 decrees, which Zhdanov so energetically bolstered and which bear the unmistakable imprint of Stalin's personality, have outlived their sponsors. Attempts made since the Twentieth Party Congress to discredit these decrees have been rebuffed, and the third volume of the Academy of Sciences history of Soviet literature, published in 1961, speaks of the decrees as 'retaining in principle their significance even today'.

Obviously the prerequisites for Zhdanovism are to be found in the conditions which prevailed in the Soviet Union during and at the end of World War II. During the war years the struggle for national survival and the need to bolster the morale of an embattled people had been paramount. Under these conditions the role of the Communist Party had been somewhat diminished and, in particular, its control of literature had been relaxed; the niceties of ideology had seemed relatively unimportant while cities were falling and people dying. . . . The war's end radically altered this situation. First, it brought to a close a wartime alliance with the capitalist West—an alliance which had been viewed by statesmen on both sides as a necessary and temporary expedient—and led to a resumption of 'the struggle between the two systems'—a struggle in which ideology is deeply involved. Second, it confronted the Soviet leaders with the problems of a country that had suffered appalling devastation. A vast construction and reconstruction effort would be required to set the Soviet economy back on its feet. Fresh efforts and fresh sacrifices must be demanded of a people that was war-weary and had already sacrificed so much. To whip up flagging spirits for the new effort—to mention only one reason—the Communist Party must be restored to its dominant role so as to become an effective instrument of power. To achieve this and at the same time to focus the attention of the population on the urgency of construction tasks, the need for ideological orthodoxy must be stressed anew. Undoubtedly such considerations weighed heavily with the Kremlin and had immediate repercussions in the field of literature.

14 August 1946 was an all-important date for Soviet literature and marks the beginning of the period under review. It was on this day that the Central Committee passed the decree which for years to come laid down the direction that post-war literature was to take. The decree took the form of an attack on two Leningrad journals, *Zvezda* and *Leningrad*. It complained that many of their publications were 'devoid of ideas, ideologically harmful'. The editors of these two journals were taken to task for having forgotten the basic Leninist tenet that Soviet journals cannot be apolitical. . . . (pp. 100-01)

The Central Committee proceeded to drive home its point by taking disciplinary action. *Leningrad* was ordered to cease publication. *Zvezda* was ordered to mend its ways. And to make sure that the mending was successfully accomplished a Party propaganda bureaucrat was put in charge. The Deputy Chief of the Propaganda Administration of the Central Committee was appointed editor-in-chief with full responsibility for the journal's ideological-political orientation. *Zvezda* was further ordered to banish from its pages the two most blameworthy authors, Zoshchenko and Anna Akhmatova, 'and others like them'.

It is a time-honoured Soviet practice to make a point of general application by singling out individual culprits and holding them up to nation-wide censure. That the city of Leningrad was here selected for this honour is not entirely fortuitous. By geography and tradition Leningrad had for a long time been accustomed to look to the West. And looking to the West in any shape or form was precisely what the Soviet leaders were striving to prevent. The fortunes of war had afforded many Soviet citizens a glimpse of the West. Further, the war-weariness of the Soviet reading and theatre-going public was finding an outlet in a certain enthusiasm for Western bourgeois writers. These had an obvious advantage over their Soviet counterparts. While the latter were supposed to implant in the reader an unflagging awareness of his civil responsibility, the former aimed rather to distract and to entertain. And entertainment was just what the weary public needed—or thought it needed. It was, however, mistaken. What it needed was to be purged of corrupting Western influences and to be reminded that Soviet culture was the most advanced culture in the world. Under these circumstances Leningrad was the logical place to attack. But the lesson was intended for the Soviet Union as a whole. (p. 102)

The 14 August decree should not be seen as a bolt from the blue. Actually the process of re-tightening the ideological reins had started back in 1943, after Stalingrad had marked a decisive turning point in the tide of the war. Zoshchenko had come under attack at that time, and during 1944, 1945, and the first half of 1946 there had been other warning signals—gradually increasing in intensity.

That the Central Committee decree was no mere routine order of the day but rather was intended as a major policy decision was made doubly clear by the fact that it was reinforced by a report by Zhdanov—the regime's ideological custodian, at that time regarded by some observers as Stalin's heir apparent. His personal intervention in what might have been regarded as a purely literary matter served to emphasize the importance attributed to the affair by the Kremlin.

Zhdanov's report was more virulent than the Central Committee decree in its attack on Zoshchenko and Akhmatova. (p. 103)

The 14 August decree was shortly followed by two further decrees devoted respectively to the theatre and to the cinema. These two hewed to the same rigid ideological line. All these decrees, reinforced by the Zhdanov report, were designed not merely to warn writers of what they should not do or to set limits to their freedom; rather they were designed to tell writers precisely what they should do. The writers were to 'help the state to educate youth correctly'. Their efforts were, in fact, to be geared meticulously to Kremlin requirements. They were to illustrate and endorse in literature the prevailing Kremlin propaganda line: the vilification of all things bourgeois and the exaggerated glorification of all things Soviet, Stalin in particular. Above all, their writing was to be ruthlessly optimistic. The effect of Zhdanovism, as this official attitude came to be called, was to castrate completely a literature which had during the war years been groping for its erstwhile virility. . . . The general tendency was to idealize Soviet life and Soviet people, to gloss over the ugly and harsh facts of this life, to reduce conflict to a minimum; any attempt to paint a more or less realistic picture was to be decried as a 'slander' against Soviet reality. And the general atmosphere of the time was manifest in the fact that the critics based their judgements almost exclusively on ideological content, paying little or no attention to literary quality. The 1946 decree ushered in the darkest chapter in the history of Soviet literature.

The main obstacle to the development of a healthy literature, it hardly needs to be said, was and was to remain the ideological controls imposed from above. But to recognize this fact would have been to undermine the whole concept of literature's educational role. Therefore, other explanations had to be found: the writers or the critics had failed to interpret correctly the wise directives of the Party; some arts committee had been negligent in its attitude; the 'creative sections' were not giving sufficient aid to writers, the work being done on aesthetic theory was inadequate. Always some scapegoat had to be found to mask the true reason. (pp. 104-05)

There was to be no glorification of outmoded ways of life, no nostalgia for an 'eternal' Russia, no idle dreaming on the beauties of nature; the eye that scanned the steppe was to take note of the combines and the construction projects. All possible stress was to be laid on the transformations which had taken place, were taking place and would take place under the Soviet regime. . . .

The predicament of the Soviet writer at this time was difficult indeed. And of the many sores that plagued him one of the worst, undoubtedly, was the complete lack of any feeling of security. That the first publication of a work had evoked no criticism or had even elicited praise was no guarantee of its fate in the future; a shift in the ideological climate or even Stalin's caprice could be enough to reverse the official evaluation of the work overnight. (p. 114)

The effect of Zhdanovism on Soviet literature was devastating. What, it may be asked in conclusion, was its effect on Soviet men of letters? The effect varied, of course, with the individual and it is quite impossible to know how each individual reacted. I would nevertheless like to hazard a few general conjectures. That Zhdanovism restricted the writer in his work as a writer there can be no doubt. The point is, rather, how did he feel about these restrictions and how was he able to live as writer and human being—with these restrictions? Some writers undoubtedly hewed more or less willingly to the official line under the impulse of fear or cynicism. But any such explanation can never be more than partially valid. Soviet writers are not a particularly cowardly or cynical lot and many of them have displayed a great deal of courage. The fact has to be faced that many writers, though no doubt frustrated by the restrictions, derived enjoyment from their work and genuinely felt that they were serving the Soviet cause.

One reason for this accommodation lies in the fact that there was no way out. It was not a matter of setting one's courage on the line, not a matter of the courage of one individual; in its wisdom the regime had made ideological orthodoxy a collective responsibility, and consequently an unacceptable piece of writing brought trouble on the head not of the author alone but also of the editor, the editorial board, the 'creative section', the Writers' Union and any other person or body involved. Under these circumstances the choice was simple—silence or accommodation. . . . (p. 123)

Walter N. Vickery, "Zhdanovism (1946-53)," in Literature and Revolution in Soviet Russia: 1917-62, *edited by Max Hayward and Leopold Labedz, Oxford University Press, London, 1963, pp. 99-124.*

MARC SLONIM (essay date 1967)

[Slonim, a Russian-born American critic, was an authority on Russian literature. His Soviet Russian Literature: Writers and Problems, 1917-1967, *provides discussion of post-Revolutionary writers and their works against the social and political background of the times. In the following excerpt from that work, Slonim surveys Soviet literature during the Zhdanov era.]*

The victory of 1945 put an end to the wartime easing of controls over literature. The signs of an imminent shift had become apparent by 1944, but its full impact was not felt until two years later. The causes of the change were the same as those that determined the foreign policy of the USSR. Instead of opening an era of peace and relaxation, the defeat of Germany was followed by an increase of tension among the former Allies. When this tension degenerated into the cold war that contained the seeds of an armed conflict between the Soviet Union and the United States, an ideological sort of alert was proclaimed in Russia; it led to cultural rigidity and isolationism. The writers who contributed so much to the war effort were now mobilized for a new task: they had to assist the Party in the consolidation of an ideological stability that had been somewhat undermined during the ordeals of 1941-45. The times of "loose patriotic unity and exultation" were over, the Party now required the strengthening of doctrine and the sharpening of Communist weapons in the USSR and in the satellite countries. The end of the war also called for great material and educational endeavors. According to official statistics, the country counted seven million killed and 16 million wounded; millions more died of starvation and disease; there were four million orphans; 1710 Russian towns, 70,000 villages, six million buildings, 317 industrial plants had been destroyed, and 98,000 farms had been looted and ravaged, bringing the total damage to 679 billion rubles. The new Five-Year Plan, the new goals in agriculture, and the enormous task of the Second Reconstruction demanded fresh sacrifices and relentless work from the people, who had already been bled white by war. To whip up the energy of the masses and make them obey the commands of the state, literature and the arts were included in the vast plan of propaganda and psychological pressure, and disciplinary measures were put into action to compel writers and artists to fulfill their civic mission.

The new literary policy was officially formulated on August 14, 1946, in a resolution by the Central Committee of the All-Union Communist Party. It was written, following Stalin's "indications," by Andrey Zhdanov . . . , member of the Politburo and former secretary of the Party; his name has become identified with the whole post-war period in Soviet literature. (pp. 277-78)

In general the life of the Russian writer in the "Zhdanovism" era was far from being secure or enviable. Demoralized by malevolence and denunciations, forced to breathe in an atmosphere polluted by suspicion and slander, he was constantly obsessed by the menace of false accusations and impending arrest and exile. Fear caused the self-imposed silence of the strong and the recantations of the weak, but even these modes of self-defense did not guarantee security. Hundreds of members of the Union of Soviet Writers were "repressed"—a euphemism used in the USSR to designate people sent to jail or concentration camps or placed before a firing squad. (p. 281)

Writers who dared to deviate from the prescribed road were quickly checked. This happened even for war novels, which continued to form a large section of Soviet fiction. (p. 286)

[Not all the] restrictive measures were . . . due to the censor's whim but derived from a consistent policy: war had to be described in the context of the "new mentality" forged by Communism. Victory had been possible because Soviet man was so marvelous—and he was marvelous because the regime and the party made him so. Novels and poems on war (or on any event of the past) had to extol the Party line. This meant that Stalin was always right and that no mention should be made of failures and defeats. It was but a part of a general "arrangement of history" for purposes of day-to-day propaganda; Soviet authors had to keep these purposes in mind whether they were describing the war against Hitler, the war against Napoleon, or revolutionary activities in Russia before and after the Revolution of 1917.

Alexander Fadeyev was forced to revise his highly popular *The Young Guard* in accordance with the official doctrine that anti-German resistance in Krasnodon, which he described as spontaneous, was not spontaneous but cleverly organized by Party leaders; his new 1951 version fitted into the prescribed mold. (pp. 286-87)

The "arrangement" of history involved first of all Stalin's role as the "father of the people, the builder of socialism and the great military genius, the winner of the war." The cult of the dictator became an authentic form of myth-making. His seventieth birthday in 1950 brought on a spate of poems and tales full of breathless adulation which had either a religious or a distinctly hypocritical flavor. As André Gide put it in 1937 after his travels in the USSR: "Even if it be genuine love for the leader, its manifestations are unbearable—since they are exaggerated, servile, and stupid." (p. 287)

The same falsifications contaminated the historical novel which continued to fare rather well in the aftermath of the war. (p. 288)

The fiction devoted to contemporary life revolved mainly around the problem of reconstruction, particularly in the villages. The reader was constantly reminded that the USSR is a land of collective farms and the typical hero, just back from the front, was usually seen beginning a campaign for building a dam, or a local power station, or challenging the neighboring *kolkhoze* to compete in doubling the wheat harvest. Everyone has to face material obstacles and the opposition from backward or petty bourgeois elements of the village, and they all overcame them with the help of Party organizers. With some slight variations this forms, during the late 'forties, the story and the plot of almost every novel in this category. Most of them, including the two best sellers by Semyon Babaevsky (b. 1909), *The Knight of the Golden Star* (1947-48) and *The Light over the Land* (1949-50), both awarded two Stalin Prizes, were lengthy, dull, and fundamentally untrue despite a plethora of naturalistic details. (pp. 288-89)

In prose, only a very limited number of novels and tales, such as those by Fedin, Paustovsky, Pavlenko, enlivened the sluggish atmosphere of "Zhdanovism." The landscape of Russian literature between 1945 and 1953 looked like a monotonous

Supreme Soviet meeting, January 1938. Left to right: Bulganin, Zhdanov, Joseph Stalin, Klimenty Voroshilov, and Nikita Khruschev.

plain, with just a few low hills emerging from gray overcast skies. (p. 292)

Marc Slonim, "The Aftermath of War: The Era of 'Zhdanovism'," in his Soviet Russian Literature: Writers and Problems, 1917-1967, *revised edition, Oxford University Press, 1967, pp. 277-92.*

EDWARD J. BROWN (essay date 1969)

[Brown, a professor of Slavic studies, has written extensively on post-Revolutionary Russian literature. In the following excerpt, first published in 1969, he discusses Zhdanov's impact on Soviet literature.]

Andrey Alexandrovich Zhdanov . . . belonged to the generation of Party men who rose to power as creatures of Stalin and who encouraged his maniacal tendencies. After the mysterious assassination of Kirov in 1934, Zhdanov became Stalin's deputy as the Party Chief of Leningrad. The destruction and subsequent rebuilding along purely Stalinist lines of the Leningrad Party organization had been Zhdanov's chief task, and when it was completed he was elected to full membership in the Politburo (1939). When the German armies besieged and blockaded Leningrad from 1941 to 1943 he defended the city with brute courage, maintaining a labor force in the factories and troops at the front while half a million citizens died of starvation. Stalin regarded Zhdanov as his successor, and the fact that he was made a kind of commissar for cultural affairs is evidence of the importance assigned to that area. Zhdanov was a Soviet bureaucrat and was typical of the breed. A closer look at him can help us to understand the people with whom a Soviet writer must deal.

As the war ended, the people of Russia looked forward with intense hope to an end of their prolonged ordeal and to a release from regimentation. There were signs that pointed to such a development. The Western democracies and Russia had been allies against Fascism, and if they should remain allies in the postwar world a softening of the Soviet dictatorship might result. During the war years there had been an apparent dilution of the Party's ideology as a result of the need to cooperate with democracies and to enlist all the forces of "Mother Russia" against the invader. This dilution might result, it seemed, in some tolerance for opposing ideologies. (pp. 178-79)

Magazines and writers' organizations reflected the demand for a rest from the grim rigors of socialist realism even before the war's end. Fedin's freely ranging reminiscences of the twenties, *Gorky Among Us,* appeared in 1943; *Before Sunrise,* Zoshchenko's novelistic search through childhood experenices for the sources of a chronic and peculiar melancholy, appeared in

1943; and after a long silence Anna Akhmatova was able during the war to publish again her reflective lyric poetry. At meetings of writers' organizations a new spirit of liberalism was freely expressed, and bureaucratic interference in the creative process was openly deplored by writers of unquestioned loyalty.

But the fragile hopes of the people and of the writers were very soon destroyed. Stalin and his men were so acutely aware of Russia's mortally weakened condition after the war that they became convinced a new attack would be launched against them, and that, therefore, relaxation could not be allowed. Stalin's speech on February 9, 1946, warned the Russians that the days of their harsh trials had not ended: "As long as capitalism exists there will be wars," he said, "and the Soviet Union must be prepared." Relaxation of effort was unthinkable, and he announced a series of three new Five-Year Plans to raise production in basic industries. Not long after this speech attention was given to events in literature, and Andrey Zhdanov came forward to read the Party's indictment of those writers and editors responsible for the laxity of recent years.

An edict of the Central Committee was published on August 14, 1946, condemning two literary magazines, *Zvezda (Star)* and *Leningrad,* for having published the "shallow and insipid" works of Zoshchenko and the "decadent, apolitical" verse of Anna Akhmatova. Both writers were expelled from the Union, the editors of the magazines were replaced, and Tikhonov was removed as Secretary of the Executive Board of the Union of Writers. In articles and public speeches Zhdanov explained the necessity for these actions. Zoshchenko's story "The Adventures of a Monkey," which had been published in *Star,* received his special attention:

> If you will read that story carefully and think it over, you will see that Zoshchenko casts the monkey in the role of supreme judge of our social order, and has him read a kind of moral lesson to the Soviet people. The monkey is presented as a kind of rational principle having the right to evaluate the conduct of human beings. The picture of Soviet life is deliberately and vilely distorted and caricatured so that Zoshchenko can put into the mouth of his monkey the vile, poisonous anti-Soviet sentiment to the effect that life is better in the zoo than at liberty, and that one breathes more easily in a cage than among Soviet people.
>
> Is it possible to sink to a lower political or moral level? And how could the Leningraders endure to publish in their magazines such filth and nonsense?

Zoshchenko had of course done nothing to deserve this lethal abuse, nor could he rightly be called "a vile hooligan," a practitioner of "filth and obscenity," or the "dregs of literature." Zhdanov had simply not understood his whimsical story about a monkey who escapes from a zoo and, after many misadventures in a Russian town, is finally adopted by a wonderful little boy who undertakes to educate him, teach him to blow his nose with a handkerchief, to refrain from stealing grandma's candy, to eat meat with a fork, in short to behave like any cultured person—and better than some. Devoid of humor and burdened with official crime, Zhdanov could see in the farcical events of this children's fable only a projection of his own guilt and suspicion.

Turning to Anna Akhmatova, Zhdanov quoted one of her love lyrics:

> I swear to you by all the heavenly angels
> by the wonder-working ikons I swear
> And by the sweet delirium of our flaming nights—

and commented on it:

> Akhmatova's subject matter is individualistic through and through. The range of her poetry is pathetically limited. It is the poetry of a half-crazy gentlelady who tosses between the bedroom and the chapel . . . Half-nun and half-harlot, or rather both nun and harlot, her harlotry is mingled with prayer.

Zhdanov's criticism of Akhmatova reveals both the man and the society. It reveals his hatred of the sensitive, cultivated gentry who should all have been destroyed but still find readers among the Soviet people. It reveals his hatred of the sensitive, culitvated gentry who should all have been destroyed but still find readers among the Soviet people. It reveals his coarse, puritanic revulsion at the frank expression of a woman's experience in love; it reveals his disastrous lack of literary sense of taste. It reveals the pathetic state of society whose cultural life could stand at the mercy of an ignorant and violent clown. His positive demands on literary men can be briefly stated. They must produce an educational literature, intelligible and acceptable to the people, saturated with the ideas of the Party and loyal to the program of the Party.

The results of his intervention were immediate. . . . [Editors] who had contracted with writers for fiction on historical themes scrapped their contracts and their publishing plans to concentrate on novels dealing with the one theme of reconstruction. Similar events occurred in the theaters: plays already part of the repertory were dropped in favor of hastily written pieces of more obvious propaganda intent. (pp. 179-81)

After socialist economic development, the second major theme of the Zhdanov period was anti-Americanism, or, more broadly, antiforeignism. Dangerous thoughts from the West might have entered the heads of Soviet citizens during the period of collaboration, and the regime was concerned over the admiration for Western achievements and Western culture which it had itself encouraged during the war. (p. 182)

Zhdanov's campaign on the front of Russian music devastated an area that was rich in new talent and original creation. The story has been told in detail in a number of books and articles. The Politburo itself condemned modernistic tendencies in Russian music, especially the works of Shostakovich and Prokofieff; and the language of its resolution suggests that it was probably written by Zhdanov himself. The Politburo said of Shostakovich and the modernists:

> The characteristic traits of such music are the denial of the basic principles of classical music, the propagation of atonality, dissonance, disharmony, as though disharmony were an expression of "progress" and "innovation" in the development of musical form; the rejection of the all important bases of music, such as melody. The modernists are carried away by confused, neurotic combinations, which transform music into cacophony—into a chaotic conglomeration of sounds. This is the spirit of

> modern American and European music—which reflects the decay of bourgeois culture . . .
>
> Many Soviet composers . . . have become alienated in their music from the demands and the musical tastes of the Soviet people, have shut themselves up in a closed circle of specialists . . . limiting [the function of music] to the satisfaction of the depraved tastes of individualistic esthetes.

At meetings of the Composers' Union Zhdanov himself appeared to explain the Party's needs in music as he had already explained its needs in literature. At these meetings an effort was made to represent him as an authority on music, too. His enthusiastic supporter, Zakharov, a writer of popular songs, pointed out that while Zhdanov was not a professional musician he was a great authority on the folk song, and he reported the following conversation with Zhdanov:

"Is it true, Comrade Zhdanov, that you know six hundred folk songs?"

"No, it is not true. But I suppose I do know about three hundred."

The effects of Zhdanov's campaign were not long in appearing. The novels and stories written to the recipe of a rigorous socialist realism failed to engage the attention of the Russian reader. Literary works in which conflicts are attenuated, suspense eliminated, language normalized, and endings standardized left him bored and indifferent. The Party program had inhibited the production of good literature and (what was far worse!) did not even produce good propaganda. In 1951 and 1952 a reaction set in, and the Party press for those years revealed that floundering efforts were being made to correct a disastrous situation. Editorials and critical articles called for the injection of "new life" into literature, spoke of the need to portray "living men," demanded that writers show life "as it is," featuring the "bad" as well as the "good," and deplored the "varnishing of reality." (pp. 182-83)

Edward J. Brown, "The Levers of Control under Stalin," in his Russian Literature since the Revolution, *revised edition, 1969. Reprint by Cambridge, Mass.: Harvard University Press, 1982, pp. 166-83.**

RONALD HINGLEY (essay date 1974)

[Hingley has written extensively on Russian literature and history and has translated the plays and stories of Anton Chekhov. In the following excerpt, he outlines Zhdanov's career and explains the reasons for government censorship during the Zhdanov era.]

Until the summer of 1946 controls [over Soviet literature] remain loose by Stalinist standards, the comparatively easy-going atmosphere of wartime being very highly preserved. A two-year period of severe repression follows: that associated with the name of Zhdanov. But Zhdanov's death, in 1948, by no means terminates persecutions generally considered Zhdanovite, for 1949 becomes the harshest of all the post-war years. (p. 369)

Though the Stalinized Soviet Union at no time ceased to suffer regimentation intolerably harsh by 'bourgeois' standards, Stalin's subjects could . . . mark variations in severity from one period to another. In cultural life the comparatively easy-going atmosphere of the war was maintained for nearly twelve months after the Japanese surrender. So lax had censorship conditions become that many books and articles, published with official blessing during this phase, were destined to be denounced as heretical during the following years.

It has been suggested that the Leader served advance notice of an impending cultural crackdown in his speech to the electors of the Stalin District of Moscow on 9 February 1946. . . . [This was] Stalin's last personally delivered policy-making oration of any importance. . . . But though Stalin's February speech was indeed boastful and menacing by turns it no more than dimly foreshadowed the ideological war which Zhdanov was to launch on the unprepared Soviet public six months later.

In claiming that Zhdanov 'launched' this campaign, and in accepting the label 'Zhdanovite' for the period 1946-8—more strictly, for the period from summer 1946 onwards—we are following normal practice and using a convenient term. But it is important to stress that Zhdanov . . . [bore no] ultimate responsibility for the *Zhdanovshchina* (Soviet domestic policies from 1946 onwards). . . . Not least among Stalin's skills was that of associating his own most unpopular measures with the names of their chief executants rather than with his own. On the briefing which Zhdanov may have received from his master we can only speculate. The most plausible assumption is that Zhdanov was chosen for this particular assignment because it accorded with his known propensities, and that Stalin let Zhdanov 'have his head'—closely monitoring implementation of the new policies, but without issuing detailed directives. Having other protégés available, the dictator could always replace his chief implement: a step which appears to have been contemplated at the very point when Zhdanov was to make it unnecessary by conveniently dying.

However closely he may or may not have been supervised by Stalin, Zhdanov did not infuse Stalinism with new ideas. He merely took elements long established as part of the system and injected them with increased virulence. The essence of his campaign was to insist—more stridently than had been insisted before—that all those active in the Soviet cultural and intellectual world, from authors and film-producers to philosophers and economists, were in effect advertising copywriters or executives employed on the greatest 'account' in the history of their profession: that of the Stalinized USSR as a whole. Their task was to 'sell' Stalin and his system with the same parade of devotional fervour with which others have launched detergents, canned beers and breakfast cereals. That the vehicle for this promotional offensive might be an eight-hundred-page novel, a three-hour film, or every page of every daily newspaper and other periodical—this consideration merely emphasizes the unlimited resources supporting a campaign such as Madison Avenue would have reduced to catchwords and television 'spots'. Stalinist publicity executives could afford to be more stately, long-winded and Victorian in their methods than their Western counterparts. But the simulated ecstasy of these acolytes, their claim to have solved the riddle of existence, their promise to open the gates of paradise on earth, their repetitive insistence on points already repeated *ad nauseam,* the helpless boredom generated in any sensitive recipient . . . these features were identical. So too was the concentration on accumulating material objects (whether individually owned motor cars and washing machines or collectively owned combine harvesters and hydroelectric stations) which these two theoretically opposed philosophies each offered as the key to everlasting bliss.

Zhdanov's task as Stalin's senior ad-man was to remind Soviet intellectuals as brusquely as possible that they had been conscripted in the service of this great promotional drive. (pp. 379-81)

The basic elements in Zhdanov's campaign were the glorification of everything Russian and the vilification of everything foreign. Targets for abuse embraced the entire decadent West, and especially the United States, while Soviet offenders included all those who allegedly 'kow-towed' to foreigners, even if this offence went no further than recognizing foreign influences on Russian writers. To have engaged in the comparative study of literature was now, it seemed, to have conspired against the State—except of course that literary influences described as emanating *from* Russia remained untreasonable all along. Philosophers and economists also fell under the lash. (p. 381)

Many academic and literary works were now rewritten to conform with Zhdanovite requirements. . . . (p. 382)

Though Stalin never went so far as to yield independent power to Zhdanov, he yet permitted that senior trouble-shooter to promote policies—foreign as well as domestic—which by no means echoed every nuance of his master's voice. Reviewing the period 1946-8 in the context of what preceded and followed it, we see in the admittedly russo-centric Zhdanov a mentality more international-minded and more concerned with ideology than that of the pragmatical Stalin, whose addiction to Russian chauvinism was even greater than that of his latest protégé. This is evident from the tone of Zhdanov's cultural witch-hunt at home, and also from the policies simultaneously promoted by him as Stalin's temporary handler-in-chief of eastern European satellites. In both areas we can trace what appear to be Zhdanovite emphases differing from essentially Stalinist emphases.

That both Zhdanov and Stalin favoured Soviet expansionism is clear, but there seems to have been a disagreement about the kind of militancy which the situation required. Pioneering the Cominform—he made the key speech at its founding conference in September 1947—Zhdanov appears to have placed more trust than his master in the potentialities of Communist parties outside the Soviet Union. It seems likely, for instance, that Zhdanov wanted to give all-out support to the Communist partisans in Greece: a line also promoted by the Yugoslavs. But though Stalin may have been willing to let Zhdanov have his head over such matters for a while, his instinct was to put his main trust in Soviet political and military power, rather than in the doings of satellite or foreign Communist parties in faraway countries of which he knew next to nothing. . . . That Zhdanov clashed with Stalin over this issue seems likely. . . . Promoting militancy in areas inadequately controlled by the Kremlin, and seeking to advance Communism locally by reliance on imperfectly controlled native forces such as the Greek and Yugoslav parties, Zhdanov antagonized his master. Then came [Yugoslav prime minister] Tito's defection from the Soviet camp: an event which could only confirm Stalin in his growing mistrust of Zhdanovism. It was now that Stalin began to restore Zhdanov's rival Malenkov to his former prominence. He also brought a new Soviet spokesman, Suslov, into the East European orbit: perhaps as a replacement for Zhdanov. When, therefore, Zhdanov presided over the excommunication of Tito at the Cominform Bucharest conference of June 1948, he was probably being compelled, by a typical Stalinist manoeuvre, to demolish his own discredited policies.

That Zhdanov would have fallen from power in any case, even if his death had not intervened two months later, seems a likely assumption from signs of disfavour which had been accumulating. There is also the point that Zhdanov had, by now, been given quite enough latitude for any one man. He had run through the two or three years of grace which . . . were the most that any Stalinist favourite could count on without expecting to be pushed into the background, if not disgraced and executed. Always mindful of the need to keep his entourage unbalanced, Stalin might well have been ready to drop Zhdanov in mid-1948, even if Zhdanov's satellite policies had not been discredited by then.

Zhdanov's death, on 31 August 1948, came as no surprise. He was known to be in bad health, and he had told Djilas in the previous January that he might die at any moment. Still, the fact remains that this was yet another in the catalogue of highly convenient fatalities with which Stalin's career is studded—convenient in this case because the dictator was able to modify Zhdanovite policies without dealing the blow to corporate high-level Soviet morale which the public disavowal of a living Zhdanov might have inflicted. The defunct Zhdanov was always to remain in good odour—like the defunct Kirov before him—with the Stalinist publicity machine . . . and this despite the savage secret persecution of Zhdanovites, known as the Leningrad Affair, which was to follow shortly.

Though the suspicion still persists that Zhdanov may have been liquidated on Stalin's orders, a mere suspicion it remains. (pp. 387-88)

Ronald Hingley, "Stalinism Reasserted and Defied," in his Joseph Stalin: Man and Legend, *McGraw-Hill Book Company, 1974, pp. 368-89.**

DMITRI SHOSTAKOVICH (essay date 1975)

[*Shostakovich was a noted Russian composer whose works were enthusiastically received by the Soviet government during the 1920s. He was commissioned to write important State-ordered compositions, such as* "A Symphonic Dedication to October," *a symphony commemorating the tenth anniversary of the Revolution. However, his opera* Lady Macbeth of Mtsensk District *(1932; later retitled* Katerina Izailova*) enraged Stalin, who labelled it a work of "formalism"—an epithet used to denounce any creative work that did not specifically adhere to the political and educational function demanded by the state. Through the remainder of his life and career Shostakovich was alternately reviled and rewarded by the Soviet government. He particularly angered Stalin by refusing to compose a triumphal Ninth Symphony at the close of World War II in praise of Stalin's leadership of the country during the war. During the cultural thaw of the late 1950s and early 1960s—a period during which the cult of Stalin was repudiated and the Soviets began to confront some of the excesses of his reign—Shostakovich enjoyed a renewed popularity that was at its height when, in 1960, he was appointed to the post of first secretary of the National Composers' Union. The appointment required that he join the Communist Party, which he did with reluctance. Shostakovich was a great admirer of the poetry of Anna Akhmatova, who together with Mikhail Zoshchenko was denounced by Zhdanov for "anti-Soviet tendencies." In the following excerpt from a work published in the Soviet Union in 1975, Shostakovich speculates that the two writers may have been incidental victims in a political power struggle between Zhdanov and Georgiy Malenkov, both of whom were trying to secure a position as cultural and ideological advisor to Stalin.*]

When you think of it, it's amazing—why did they pick Zoshchenko and Akhmatova, why those two as the main target? They put them out naked and threw stones at them. One version goes like this: Akhmatova and Zoshchenko were the victims of a struggle between two of Stalin's toadies, that is, between

Malenkov and Zhdanov. Allegedly Malenkov wanted to become Stalin's main ideological adviser, a rather important position, right below Stalin's top executioner, Beria. He would be the executioner on the cultural front. Malenkov and Zhdanov fought to prove themselves worthy of that honored position. The war with Hitler was won and Malenkov decided to stress public relations and to glorify the homeland, so that the entire enlightened world would gasp and see that Russia was the "homeland of elephants."

Malenkov worked out grandiose plans, one of which was a series of deluxe editions of Russian literature from antiquity to the present. I think the series began with *The Lay of Prince Igor* and ended, believe it or not, with Akhmatova and Zoshchenko. But Malenkov's idea didn't work and Zhdanov outguessed him. He knew Stalin better and considered that laudatory editions were fine, but steadfast struggle with the enemy—vigilance, so to speak—was more important.

With the aim of getting rid of Malenkov, Zhdanov attacked Malenkov's ideas and proved to Stalin, like two plus two, that it was vigilance that Malenkov had lost. Zhdanov, unfortunately, knew what and how Akhmatova and Zoshchenko wrote, since Leningrad was Zhdanov's own turf.

This was Zhdanov's argument: The Soviet Army is victorious, we are advancing on Europe, and Soviet literature must be an aid in this, it must attack bourgeois culture, which is in a state of confusion and decay. And do Akhmatova and Zoshchenko attack? Akhmatova writes lyric poetry and Zoshchenko writes derogatory prose. Zhdanov won, Stalin took his side and Malenkov was removed from leading the cultural front. Zhdanov was empowered to strike a blow at harmful influences, at "the spirit of negative criticism, despair, and nonbelief."

Zhdanov later announced, "What would have happened if we had brought up our young people in the spirit of despair and nonbelief in our work? What would have happened was that we would not have won the Great Patriotic War." Now, that scared them. Just think, one short story by Zoshchenko, and the Soviet regime might have toppled. Another symphony by Shostakovich, and the country would fall into the slavery of American imperialism. (pp. 269-70)

Dmitri Shostakovich, an extract from his Testimony: The Memoirs of Dmitri Shostakovich, *edited by Solomon Volkov, translated by Antonina W. Bouis, Harper & Row, Publishers, 1979, pp. 269-70.*

WERNER G. HAHN (essay date 1982)

[In the following excerpt, Hahn explains how Soviet doctrines regarding literature were inextricably linked to power struggles at the upper levels of the government, and notes that Zhdanov's policies were much more moderate than those of his successors and many of his contemporaries. The unexcerpted portions of this book-length study provide extensive background information on the political machinations that involved Zhdanov and Soviet literary policy-making.]

The generally accepted interpretation of postwar Soviet politics holds that in 1946, with the initiation of a harsh ideological crackdown and the onset of cold-war tension, tight Stalinist controls were quickly reimposed and that Stalin's top deputy, Andrey Aleksandrovich Zhdanov, was the chief executor of this new hard line. Indeed, the shrill ideological campaigns, violent purges, outbursts of exaggerated Russian chauvinism, and strident cold-war rhetoric that marked the period from 1946 through 1949 have come to be known as the *Zhdanovshchina*. My research suggests, however, that this period, rather than being devoid of intellectual exchange and political debate, witnessed an intense competition between relative "moderates" and "extremists" in the Soviet establishment and that Zhdanov, surprisingly enough, stood on the "moderate" side and was in fact the chief victim of the triumph of extremism. In reexamining the Soviet press of this period and studying the extensive source material that has appeared more recently, I find much evidence that divergent viewpoints, rather than monolithic orthodoxy, characterized Soviet officialdom after the war, and that the dominant political forces in 1946—Zhdanov and his followers—were dramatically overturned by 1949, as part of a historic defeat of moderate elements in the Soviet political establishment.

During World War II the police terror that had ravaged all segments of Soviet society was eased in deference to the war effort, and the concomitant relaxation of political controls and ideological standards provided more room for creative pursuits. By the end of the war, the scholars who dominated such fields as philosophy, economics, and natural sciences expected that both this relaxation and the wartime cooperation with the West would be continued, and they spoke out accordingly. (pp. 9-10)

Statements made in early 1946 by such political leaders as Zhdanov, and even Stalin himself, suggest that they too expected a period of relative relaxation at home and abroad. The fact that Zhdanov initiated an ideological crackdown in 1946 does not alter this picture, first, because the reimposition of controls appears to have been more a function of political maneuvering than an expression of ideological principle, and second, because Zhdanov did not extend this crackdown in literature and culture to parallel fields of intellectual activity. (p. 10)

The role of Zhdanov in [postwar Soviet politics] appears to have been quite different from that portrayed in most Western histories and also from that acknowledged by intellectuals and politicians in the Soviet Union itself. Evidence suggests that despite his image as the champion of militant orthodoxy, it was not Zhdanov who led the ideological dogmatists and Russian chauvinists and brought about the defeat of moderates. Rather, it appears that Zhdanov's ideological campaign was motivated more by essentially political concerns: the circumstances of its origin, the method of its prosecution, and the identity of its executors mark it as part of Zhdanov's broader campaign to defeat his top party rival Georgiy Maksimilianovich Malenkov, and to reestablish the primacy of the ideological apparatus—Zhdanov's main base of power—iin party life. The position of ideological workers had been badly eroded during the war, when practical needs raised the importance of economic administrators and military leaders, hence enhancing the power of Malenkov, the cadre specialist and industry supervisor.

In the course of restoring the primacy of the ideologists, Zhdanov made vicious assaults on those who neglected ideology, especially during his highly visible campaign in cultural affairs, a policy that earned him his reputation as the regime's leading hard-liner. In fact, Zhdanov was neither as dogmatic nor as chauvinistic as his reputation suggests. He did not seek to impose narrow ideological constraints in fields such as philosophy and natural science, but in fact resisted dogmatism and encouraged creativity in these disciplines. He did not appear to believe that ideology had to dictate an answer for everything, and, cultivating an image as the Politburo's "intellectual,'' he encouraged some philosophers and biologists who held unorthodox views. Moreover, in late 1947, as the cold war intensified and the dogmatists found increasing favor with Stalin, Zhdanov began to lose power and his apparent protégés began to be accused of ideological softness and internationalism. What is loosely called the *Zhdanovshchina* actually climaxed after Zhdanov's death, wih Lysenko's ruthless purge of science, Stalin's drives against cosmopolitanism and the Jews, and the use of punishments—including execution—more extreme than those that had occurred during Zhdanov's heyday.

Of course Zhdanov, who had been involved in Stalin's bloody purges in the 1930s, was hardly a ''liberal,'' even by Soviet terms. In fact, in 1946 he cynically sought to beat his enemies by campaigning against ideological softness and by enunciating crude, doctrinaire attacks on culture. Although Zhdanov was initially successful with this tactic, his rivals eventually used a similar approach to defeat him, taking advantage of his apparent patronage of dangerous ''liberals'' and unpatriotic internationalists to maneuver him into a vulnerable position. We can tentatively label Zhdanov a ''moderate'' or patron of moderates simply because his positions, at least initially, were less extreme than those that became official in 1948 and 1949. Zhdanov's views may have hardened later, but the facts that he lost influence as the atmosphere grew more dogmatic and that his earlier views appear to have been held against him indicate that, willy-nilly, he wound up in a ''moderate'' position. To some extent, Zhdanov's ''moderation'' may have resulted simply from a failure to foresee how far Stalin would go in sanctioning dogmatism and repression. Such a misjudgment by Zhdanov is certainly conceivable, for Stalin's extremism resulted, at least in part, from his turning against Zhdanov personally and his related decision to encourage the eradication of Zhdanov's faction and to proscribe the ''moderate'' views that Zhdanov had apparently permitted. (pp. 11-13)

At the end of the war, after three years of relative isolation from Moscow while leading the defense of Leningrad, Central Committee Secretary Andrey Aleksandrovich Zhdanov returned to the capital and by late 1946 had established himself as Stalin's clear favorite and heir apparent. Zhdanov's rise came mainly at the expense of another CC secretary, Georgiy Maksimilianovich Malenkov, who had become Stalin's powerful deputy while running the party and government apparatus in Moscow during the war. Zhdanov triumphed by pointing out to Stalin the ideological and administrative laxity that had developed in the party apparat under Malenkov and by launching campaigns to restore the priority of ideology and rectify abuses in party administration, agriculture, and finally, literature and culture.

Malenkov had supervised operations of party organs and selection of party officials during the war, and his power was officially recognized in early 1946 when he was elected a full member of the Politburo and given a status equal to Zhdanov in protocol rankings. Zhdanov reacted to his rival's rise by launching a campaign to convince Stalin that Malenkov had done a poor job in managing the party apparat and selecting cadres. He asserted that under Malenkov, party officials had focused too much on such matters as production and had become lax in matters of ideology, tolerating dangerous ''liberal'' trends in literature, culture, historiography, and local nationalism. Putting his ideological apparat to work, Zhdanov quickly produced evidence to support these contentions. Stalin, convinced of Malenkov's negligence and of the need for a renewed stress on ideology, removed Malenkov from the Secretariat and gave Zhdanov and his allies the go-ahead to purge and reorganize the CC apparat and to begin an ideological crackdown. Since this drive was launched in early 1946, the crackdown in literature and culture—the infamous *Zhdanovshchina,* which was publicly announced in late August 1946—was actually only the culmination, if not the aftermath, of the process.

Despite his leadership of this campaign, Zhdanov appears to have patronized the forces of relative moderation, for he was hostile to the dogmatists in ideology, philosophy, and science, promoting and protecting his own clique in these fields. Moreover, although evidence of the policy positions of Kremlin leaders is usually tenuous, Zhdanov's statements suggest that he took a relatively relaxed view of world affairs and favored a shift away from defense industries to a greater concentration on the satisfaction of consumer needs. Zhdanov's campaign for restoration of the importance of ideology was not a call for the reimposition of dogmatism but a reflection of bureaucratic politics: Zhdanov's ideological apparat had been downgraded during the war and Zhdanov was attempting to restore its influence. Indeed, relative moderates in such disciplines as philosophy, biology, and economics flourished until late 1947 and early 1948. The rise of dogmatism in these fields coincided with the decline in Zhdanov's influence, and the dogmatists triumphed fully only after his demise. (pp. 19-20)

Werner G. Hahn, ''Preface'' and ''Zhdanov's Victory—1946,'' in his Postwar Soviet Politics: The Fall of Zhdanov and the Defeat of Moderation, 1946-53, *Cornell University Press, 1982, pp. 9-15, 19-66.*

ADDITIONAL BIBLIOGRAPHY

Alexandrova, Vera. *A History of Soviet Literature, 1917-1964: From Gorky to Solzhenitsyn.* New York: Anchor Books, 1964, 464 p.*
Literary history.

Bisztray, George. ''The Classics and the Bureaucrats.'' In his *Marxist Models of Literary Realism,* pp. 9-50. New York: Columbia University Press, 1978.*
Examination of some developments in Soviet literary theory since the Revolution.

Borland, Harriet. *Soviet Literary History and Practice during the First Five-Year Plan.* New York: King's Crown Press, 1950, 256 p.*
Study of the subordination of Soviet literature to Communist party aims during the period of the first Five-Year Plan (1928-33).

Carrère d'Encausse, Hélène. ''Stalinism Completed.'' In her *Stalin: Order through Terror: A History of the Soviet Union: 1917-1953,* Vol. 2, pp. 170-89. Translated by Valence Ionescu. London: Longman, 1981.*
Explores the conflicts between Zhdanov and Georgiy Malenkov and their attempts to discredit each other with Stalin.

Conquest, Robert. *The Great Terror: Stalin's Purge of the Thirties.* New York: Macmillan Co., 1968, 633 p.*
Examination of the mass trials and executions by which Stalin seized control of the Soviet Union during the 1930s. Conquest makes numerous references to Zhdanov's role as Stalin's ideological advisor during this time.

Counts, George S., and Lodge, Nucia. ''Literature as a Weapon.'' In their *The Country of the Blind: The Soviet System of Mind Control,* pp. 77-117. Boston: Houghton Mifflin Co., 1949.*
Discussion of Soviet literary censorship focusing on Zhdanov's various pronouncements, rulings, and denunciations of writers. Counts and Lodge translate the texts of speeches by Zhdanov, as

well as by the former president of the Union of Soviet Writers, Nikolai Tikhonov.

Egolin, A. M. *The Ideological Content of Soviet Literature*. Washington, D.C.: Public Affairs Press, 1948, 22 p.*
Highly approbatory survey of the Communist party's efforts to produce a literature that upholds party ideologies.

Ermolaev, Herman. *Soviet Literary Theories, 1917-1934: The Genesis of Socialist Realism*. Berkeley: University of California Press, 1963, 261 p.*
Examination of the development of Soviet literary theories that culminated in the doctrine of Socialist Realism in the early 1930s. Zhdanov's role in the implementation of Socialist Realism is discussed throughout.

Harris, Jonathan. "The Origins of the Conflict between Malenkov and Zhdanov: 1939-1941." *Slavic Review* 35, No. 2 (June 1976): 287-303.*
Discusses the differences between Zhdanov's and Malenkov's approaches to their duties within the Central Committee of the Communist Party, and suggests that their differing perceptions of their duties caused the conflict between them.

Hayward, Max. *Writers in Russia: 1917-1978*. Edited by Patricia Blake. New York: Harcourt Brace Jovanovich, 1983, 340 p.*
Collection of Hayward's major essays on Soviet literature, including "Russian Literature in the Soviet Period, 1917-1975," originally published in 1977, which is the most comprehensive of Hayward's overviews of the Russian literary scene. Hayward's editor Patricia Blake notes that while in this essay he details "the political events that have governed both the form and the substance of published writing during the Soviet era," including Zhdanov's influence during this period, Hayward is chiefly concerned with the literary achievements of individual writers. Also in this volume is the essay "Dissonant Voices," reprinted from the 1964 anthology of the same title edited by Hayward and Blake, in which Hayward outlines the development of Socialist Realism.

Hingley, Ronald. *Russian Writers and Soviet Society, 1917-1978*. New York: Random House, 1979, 296 p.*
History of Russian literature since the Revolution, concentrating on the interplay between social and literary forces in the Soviet Union.

Medvedev, Roy A. *Let History Judge: The Origins and Consequences of Stalinism*. New York: Alfred A. Knopf, 1972, 566 p.*
Analysis of Stalinism by a Soviet scholar. Medvedev distinguishes Stalinism from the Soviet system and from communism in general, finding that Stalinism is characterized by personal despotism and tyranny.

———. *On Stalin and Stalinism*. Translated by Ellen de Kadt. London: Oxford University Press, 1979, 205 p.*
Examination of Stalin's role in Soviet history based upon information gathered by Medvedev since the 1973 revision of his *Let History Judge: The Origins and Consequences of Stalinism*. Medvedev comments on the questionable circumstances of Zhdanov's death shortly after his fall from favor with Stalin.

———. "G. M. Malenkov: The 'Heir' that Never Was." In his *All Stalin's Men*, pp. 140-63. Garden City, N.Y.: Anchor Press/Doubleday, 1984.*
Details Malenkov's political career, which began during Lenin's lifetime and endured through Stalin's and Khrushchev's time into the Brezhnev era. Medvedev mentions the longstanding hostility between Zhdanov and Malenkov, and outlines the "Leningrad Affair," which consisted of Malenkov's ultimately successful efforts to discredit Zhdanov with Stalin.

Ra'anan, Gavriel D. *International Policy Formation in the U.S.S.R.: Factional "Debates" during the Zhdanovschina*. Hamden, Conn.: Archon Books, 1983.
Detailed examination of the workings of Soviet politics. Ra'anan gives an insightful account of the conflicts between Zhdanov and Georgiy Malenkov, both of whom aspired to positions of influence with Stalin. Ra'anan interprets Zhdanov's cultural crackdowns of the 1940s as a political move inspired by his desire to discredit Malenkov.

Simmons, Ernest J. "Introduction: Soviet Literature and Controls." In *Through the Glass of Soviet Literature: Views of Russian Society*, edited by Ernest J. Simmons, pp. 3-26. New York: Columbia University Press, 1953.*
Traces the growth and development of Soviet controls over literature from 1917 to the early 1950s, noting how closely the history of these literary controls parallels the history of the Communist party itself.

Struve, Gleb. *Russian Literature under Lenin and Stalin, 1917-1953*. Norman: University of Oklahoma Press, 1971, 454 p.*
Extensive survey of Soviet literature from the Revolution through the last years of Stalin's rule. Struve characterizes the final six years of this period, which he calls the era of Zhdanov, as "the most barren years in the history of Soviet literature, literary criticism, and literary scholarship."

"Andrei Alexandrovich Zhdanov." *VOKS Bulletin*, No. 55 (1948): 7-11.
Collection of eulogistic essays written on Zhdanov's death. Included are tributes by leading Soviet politicians and scientific, literary, and cultural figures, each mourning the loss of Zhdanov's valuable contributions to their particular field. An essay from this collection by Mikhail Sholokov is excerpted in the entry.

Zavalishin, Vyacheslav. "Prose during the Uneasy Truce (1925-1929)," in his *Early Soviet Writers*, pp. 269-347. New York: Frederick A. Praeger, 1958.*
Provides critical sketches of writers publishing in the years between 1925 and 1929. In his introduction to this chapter, Zavalishin briefly characterizes this four-year period as one of relative freedom for Russian writers, during which many traditional genres of Russian literature reemerged.

Appendix

The following is a listing of all sources used in Volume 18 of *Twentieth-Century Literary Criticism*. Included in this list are all copyright and reprint rights and acknowledgments for those essays for which permission was obtained. Every effort has been made to trace copyright, but if omissions have been made, please let us know.

THE EXCERPTS IN TCLC, VOLUME 18, WERE REPRINTED FROM THE FOLLOWING PERIODICALS:

The Academy, n. 1031, February 6, 1892; v. LXXIV, June 20, 1908.

The Alternative: An American Spectator, v. 9, August-September, 1976. Copyright *The Alternative* magazine 1976. Reprinted by permission.

American Literature, v. 53, March, 1981. Copyright © 1981 Duke University Press, Durham, NC. Reprinted by permission.

The American Slavic and East European Review, v. IX, 1950. Copyright 1950, renewed 1977, by American Association for the Advancement of Slavic Studies, Inc. Reprinted by permission.

The Atlantic Monthly, v. 227, May, 1971 for "Broadway's Banner Years" by Louis Kronenberger. Reprinted by permission of the Estate of Louis Kronenberger.

Blackwood's Edinburgh Magazine, v. CLI, March, 1892.

The Bookman, London, v. XXXII, August, 1907.

Colby Library Quarterly, s. III, May, 1953.

Contemporary Literature, v. 11, Winter, 1970. © 1970 by the Regents of the University of Wisconsin. Reprinted by permission of the University of Wisconsin Press.

Contemporary Review, v. XCVI, October, 1909.

The Cornhill Magazine, n. 983, Summer, 1950.

Cosmopolitan, v. XIII, July, 1892.

The Critic, New York, v. XXXVI, March, 1900.

Critical Quarterly, v. 10, Autumn, 1968 for "Colour and Movement in Hardy's 'Tess of the d'Urbervilles'" by Tony Tanner. © Tony Tanner 1968. Reprinted by permission of the author.

Encounter, v. XVI, May, 1916 for "The Heart of a Legend: The Writings of Ada Leverson" by Colin MacInnes. © 1961 The Colin MacInnes Estate. Reprinted by permission of the Literary Estate of Colin MacInnes.

English Literature in Transition, v. XIII, 1970 for "Ada Leverson and Oscar Wilde" by Charles Burkhart. Copyright © 1970 Helga S. Gerber. Reprinted by permission of the publisher and the author.

The English Review, v. V, May, 1910.

The Fortnightly Review, n.s. v. LII, July, 1892.

G. K.'s Weekly, v. XXIV, October 8, 1936.

The German Quarterly, v. LII, May, 1979. Copyright © 1979 by the American Association of Teachers of German. Reprinted by permission.

The Listener, v. X, November 15, 1933; v. XLIV, July 27, 1950; v. LIII, April 14, 1955.

Literature/Film Quarterly, v. 4, Winter, 1976. © copyright 1976 Salisbury State College. Reprinted by permission.

London Magazine, n.s. v. 2, December, 1962. © *London Magazine* 1962. Reprinted by permission.

London Review of Books, December 1 to December 21, 1983 for "Dear Sphinx" by Penelope Fitzgerald. Appears here by permission of the *London Review of Books* and the author.

Longman's Magazine, v. XXI, November, 1892.

The Mask, v. 8, 1918.

Modern Language Quarterly, v. XXIV, June, 1963. © 1963 University of Washington. Reprinted by permission.

Monatshefte, v. XXXVII, February, 1945.

The Monist, v. 64, April, 1981. Copyright © 1981, The Hegeler Institute, LaSalle, IL 61301. Reprinted by permission.

The Monthly Criterion, v. V, May, 1927.

The Nation, v. XCIV, May 16, 1912; v. CXIII, July 6, 1921; v. CXVI, May 16, 1923; v. CXVIII, June 25, 1924; v. CXXIII, October 13, 1926; v. CXXXII, February 18, 1931; v. CXXXV, October 26, 1932; v. CXXXVII, August 9, 1933; v. 150, January 13, 1940; v. 163, December 7, 1946./ v. 193, September 30, 1961. v. 212, January 18, 1971; v. 235, October 2, 1982. Copyright 1961, 1971, 1982 *The Nation* magazine, The Nation Associates, Inc. All reprinted by permission.

The Nation, London, v. XXII, February 9, 1918.

The Nation and The Athenaeum, v. XL, March 19, 1927.

National Review, v. XXII, November 17, 1970; v. XXXVII, January 11, 1985. © by National Review, Inc., 150 East 35th Street, New York, NY 10016; 1970, 1985. Both reprinted with permission.

The New Age, n.s. v. IX, September 28, 1911.

The New Republic, v. XLVII, October 6, 1926; v. LX, October 9, 1929; v. LXXXIV, September 11, 1935./ v. LXXXXVI, October 26, 1983 for "Tribute to Ben Franklin" by Malcolm Cowley. © 1938 The New Republic, Inc. Renewed 1966 by Malcolm Cowley. Reprinted by permission of the author.

The New Review, v. VI, February, 1892.

New Statesman and Nation, v. 41, 1951.

New York Herald Tribune Book Review, October 15, 1950. © I.H.T. Corporation. Reprinted by permission.

New York Herald Tribune Books, December 13, 1925; October 19, 1930; June 30, 1935; April 5, 1936; September 20, 1936. © 1925, 1930, 1935, 1936 I.H.T. Corporation. All reprinted by permission.

New York Herald Tribune Weekly Book Review, January 18, 1948. © 1948 I.H.T. Corporation. Reprinted by permission.

The New York Sun, December, 1920.

The New York Times, December 30, 1970. Copyright © 1970 by The New York Times Company. Reprinted by permission.

The New York Times Book Review, October 26, 1919; February 6, 1921; August 7, 1921; April 1, 1923; April 6, 1924; September 20, 1936; November 29, 1936; October 9, 1938; October 12, 1941; July 15, 1945; August 22, 1982; September 2, 1984. Copyright © 1919, 1921, 1923, 1924, 1936, 1938, 1941, 1945, 1982, 1984 by The New York Times Company. All reprinted by permission.

The New Yorker, v. XXVII, August 18, 1951 for "Out of the Dead Past" by Anthony West. Copyright © 1951 by Anthony West. Reprinted by permission of Wallace & Sheil Agency./ v. XI, September 28, 1935 for "T. E. Lawrence" by Clifton Fadiman. © 1935, renewed 1963, by The New Yorker Magazine, Inc. Reprinted by permission of the author./ v. XXV, October 22, 1949. © 1949, renewed 1976 by The New Yorker Magazine, Inc. Reprinted by permission.

Overland Monthly and Out West Magazine, v. 87, March, 1929.

Prose, n. 4, 1972. © 1972 by Prose Publishers Incorporated.

Renascence, v. XVII, Spring, 1965. © copyright, 1965, Marquette University Press. Reprinted by permission.

Salmagundi, n. 66, Winter-Spring, 1985. Copyright © 1985 by Skidmore College. Reprinted by permission of the publisher.

The Saturday Review of Literature, v. III, March 19, 1927; v. IX, January 28, 1933; v. XXXIV, September 1, 1951./ v. XII, September 28, 1935; v. XXII, June 8, 1940. © 1935, 1940 *Saturday Review* magazine. Both reprinted by permission.

The Sewanee Review, v. I, November, 1892; v. XLVI, Spring, 1938.

Slavic and East-European Journal, n.s. v. IV, 1960. © 1960 by AATSEEL of the U.S., Inc. Reprinted by permission.

The Slavic Review, v. XXI, September, 1962 for "The Dead Hand of the Future: The Predicament of Vladimir Mayakovsky" by Victor Erlich. Copyright © 1962 by the American Association for the Advancement of Slavic Studies, Inc. Reprinted by permission of the publisher and the author.

The Slavonic and East European Review, v. XLVIII, April, 1970. © University of London (School of Slavonic and East European Studies) 1970. Reprinted by permission.

The Slavonic Year-Book, v. XX, December, 1941.

South Atlantic Quarterly, v. 74, Summer, 1975. Copyright © 1975 by Duke University Press, Durham, NC. Reprinted by permission of the Publisher.

The Southern Review, v. 2, Autumn, 1936.

Soviet Literature, n. 1, 1983. © *Soviet Literature,* 1983. All reprinted by arrangement with YAAP.

The Spectator, v. 77, December 26, 1896; v. 138, March 12, 1927; v. 186, January 19, 1951.

Time & Tide, v. 23, May 9, 1942.

The Times, London, September 1, 1933.

Vanity Fair, v. 30, March, 1928 for "The Enormously Civilized Minority: A Consideration of Mr. George Jean Nathan's Celebrated Distaste for Things Political" by Walter Lippmann. Copyright © 1928, renewed 1956 by The Condé Nast Publications Inc. Courtesy *Vanity Fair* and the President and Fellows of Harvard College on behalf of the author./ v. 26, May, 1926. Copyright © 1926, renewed 1954 by The Condé Nast Publications Inc.

VOKS Bulletin, n. 55, 1948.

The Western Political Quarterly, v. VII, September, 1954.

The Westminster Review, v. CXXXVIII, December, 1892.

The Yale Review, v. LIV, March, 1965. Copyright 1965, by Yale University. Reprinted by permission of the editors.

THE EXCERPTS IN TCLC, VOLUME 18, WERE REPRINTED FROM THE FOLLOWING BOOKS:

Aldington, Richard. From *Lawrence of Arabia: A Biographical Enquiry*. Collins, 1955.

Alexandrova, Vera. From *A History of Soviet Literature, 1917-1964: From Gorky to Solzhenitsyn*. Translated by Mirra Ginsburg. Doubleday, 1963. Copyright © 1963, 1964 by Vera Alexandrova-Schwarz. All rights reserved. Reprinted by permission of Doubleday & Company, Inc.

Allen, M. D. From "Lawrence's Medievalism," in *The T. E. Lawrence Puzzle*. Edited by Stephen E. Tabachnick. University of Georgia Press, 1984. Copyright © 1984 by the University of Georgia Press. All rights reseved. Reprinted by permission of The University of Georgia Press.

Angoff, Charles. From an introduction to *The World of George Jean Nathan*. By George Jean Nathan, edited by Charles Angoff. Knopf, 1952. Copyright 1952 by George Jean Nathan. Renewed 1980 by the Literary Estate of George Jean Nathan. All rights reserved. Reprinted by permission of the Associated University Presses, Inc., for the Estate of George Jean Nathan.

Asselineau, Roger. From "Theodore Dreiser's Transcendentalism," in *English Studies Today*, second series. Edited by G. A. Bonnard. Francke, 1961. © A. Francke Ag Verlag Bern, 1961. Reprinted by permission of Roger Asselineau.

Avery, George C. From *Inquiry and Testament: A Study of the Novels and Short Prose of Robert Walser*. University of Pennsylvania Press, 1968. Copyright © 1968 by the Trustees of the University of Pennsylvania, Philadelphia. Reprinted by permission.

Bacourt, Pierre de, and J. W. Cunliffe. From *French Literature During the Last Half-Century*. Macmillan Publishing Company, 1923.

Beach, Joseph Warren. From *The Technique of Thomas Hardy*. The University of Chicago Press, 1922.

Beichman, Janine. From *Masaoka Shiki*. Twayne, 1982. Copyright 1982 by Twayne Publishers. All rights reserved. Reprinted with the permission of Twayne Publishers, a division of G. K. Hall & Co., Boston.

Bithell, Jethro. From *Modern German Literature: 1880-1938*. Methuen, 1939.

Blackmur, R. P. From *The Expense of Greatness*. Arrow Editions, 1940. Copyright, 1940, by R. P. Blackmur. Renewed 1968 by the Literary Estate of R. P. Blackmur. Reprinted by permission of the Estate of R. P. Blackmur.

Borges, Jorge Luis. From "The Doctrine of Cycles," translated by Karen Stolley, in *Borges, a Reader: A Selection from the Writings of Jorge Luis Borges*. By Jorge Luis Borges, edited by Emir Rodriquez Monegal and Alastair Reid. Dutton, 1981. Copyright © 1981 by Jorge Luis Borges, Alastair Reid, Emir Rodriguez Monegal. All rights reserved. Reprinted by permission of the publisher, E. P. Dutton, a division of New American Library.

Boyd, Ernest. From *Portraits: Real and Imaginary*. George H. Doran Company, 1924.

Braybrooke, Patrick. From *Thomas Hardy and His Philosophy*. The C. W. Daniel Company, 1928.

Brower, Robert H. From "Masaoka Shiki and Tanka Reform," in *Tradition and Modernization in Japanese Culture*. Edited by Donald H. Shively. Princeton University Press, 1971. Copyright © 1971 by Princeton University Press. All rights reserved. Excerpts reprinted by permission of Princeton University Press.

Brower, Rueben A. From "William Butler Yeats: Introduction," in *Major British Writers: Wordsworth, Coleridge, Byron, Shelley, Keats, Tennyson, Browning, Arnold, Shaw, Yeats, Eliot, Vol. II.* Enlarged edition. Edited by G. B. Harrison & others. Harcourt Brace and Jovanovich, Inc., 1954. Copyright, 1954, 1959, by Harcourt Brace Jovanovich, Inc. Reprinted by permission of the publisher.

Brown, Edward J. From *Mayakovsky: A Poet in the Revolution*. Princeton University Press, 1973. Copyright © 1973 by Princeton University Press. All rights reserved. Excerpts reprinted by permission of Princeton University Press.

Brown, Edward J. From *Russian Literature Since the Revolution*. Revised edition. Cambridge, Mass.: Harvard University Press, 1982. Copyright © 1963, 1969, and 1982 by Edward J. Brown. All rights reserved. Reprinted by permission of the author.

Bunin, Ivan. From *Memoirs and Portraits*. Translated by Vera Traill and Robin Chancellor. Doubleday & Company, Inc., 1951.

Burkhart, Charles. From *Ada Leverson*. Twayne, 1973. Copyright 1973 by Twayne Publishers. All rights reserved. Reprinted with the permission of Twayne Publishers, a division of G.K. Hall & Co., Boston.

Butler, John Davis. From *Jean Moréas: A Critique of His Poetry and Philosophy*. Mouton, 1967. © copyright 1967 Mouton & Co., Publishers. Reprinted by permission of Mouton Publishers, a Division of Walter de Gruyter & Co.

Buttel, Robert. From "The Incandescence of Old Age: Yeats and Stevens in Their Late Poems," in *The Motive for Metaphor: Essays on Modern Poetry*. Edited by Francis C. Blessington and Guy Rotella. Northeastern University Press, 1983. Copyright © 1983 Francis C. Blessington and Guy Rotella. All rights reserved. Reprinted by permission of the publisher.

Carpenter, Richard. From *Thomas Hardy*. Twayne, 1964. Copyright 1964 by Twayne Publishers. All rights reserved. Reprinted with the permission of Twayne Publishers, a division of G.K. Hall & Co., Boston.

Corrin, Jay P. From *G. K. Chesterton & Hilaire Belloc: The Battle against Modernity*. Ohio University Press, 1981. © copyright 1981 by Jay P. Corrin. All rights reserved. Reprinted by permission of Ohio University Press, Athens.

Craig, Cairns. From *Yeats, Eliot, Pound and the Politics of Poetry: Richest to the Richest*. University of Pittsburgh Press, 1982. © 1982 Cairns Craig. Reprinted by permission of the University of Pittsburgh Press.

Daleski, H. M. From *The Divided Heroine: A Recurrent Pattern in Six English Novels*. Holmes & Meier, 1984. Copyright © 1984 by H. M. Daleski. All rights reserved. Reprinted by permission of Holmes & Meier Publishers, Inc., IUB Building, 30 Irving Place, New York, NY 10003.

Deluze, Gilles. From a preface to *Nietzsche and Philosophy*. By Gilles Deluze, translated by Hugh Tomlinson. Athlone Press, 1983. Preface and this translation © The Athlone Press, 1983. All rights reserved. Reprinted by permission.

Drake, William A. From *Contemporary European Writers*. The John Day Company, 1928.

Dreiser, Theodore. From a letter to George Jean Nathan on October 7, 1933, in *Letters of Theodore Dreiser: A Selection, Vol. 2*. By Theodore Dreiser, edited by Robert H. Elias. University of Pennsylvania Press, 1959. © 1959 by the Trustees of the University of Pennsylvania. Reprinted by permission of the Literary Estate of Theodore Dreiser.

Dyson, A. E. From *Yeats, Eliot and R. S. Thomas: Riding the Echo*. Humanities Press, 1981. © A. E. Dyson 1981. All rights reserved. Reprinted by permission of Humanities Press International, Inc., Atlantic Highlands, NJ 07716.

Ellis, Havelock. From *Affirmations*, second series. Walter Scott Limited, 1898.

Flexner, James Thomas. From an introduction to *Benjamin Franklin*. By Carl Van Doren. Book-of-the-Month Club, Inc., 1980. Introduction © 1980 James Thomas Flexner. All rights reserved. Reprinted by permission of James Thomas Flexner.

Forster, E. M. From letters to T. E. Lawrence in February, 1924 and on July 5, 1928, in *Letters to T. E. Lawrence*. Edited by A. W. Lawrence. Jonathan Cape, 1962. © 1962 by A. W. Lawrence. Reprinted by permission of The Society of Authors as the literary representative of the Estate of E. M. Forster.

France, Anatole. From *On Life & Letters, fourth series*. Edited by J. Lewis May and Bernard Miall, translated by Bernard Miall. Dodd, Mead and Company, Inc., 1924.

France, Peter. From *Poets of Modern Russia*. Cambridge University Press, 1982. © Cambridge University Press 1982. Reprinted by permission.

Freeborn, Richard. From *The Russian Revolutionary Novel: Turgenev to Pasternak*. Cambridge University Press, 1982. © Cambridge University Press 1982. Reprinted by permission.

Frick, Constance. From *The Dramatic Criticism of George Jean Nathan*. Cornell University Press, 1943. Copyright, 1943, by Cornell University. Renewed 1970 by Constance Frick Irwin. Reprinted by permission of the publisher, Cornell University Press.

Garnett, David. From an extract from a letter to T. E. Lawrence on May 20, 1928, in *Letters to T. E. Lawrence*. Edited by A. W. Lawrence. Jonathan Cape, 1962. © 1962 by A. W. Lawrence. Reprinted by permission of The Executors of the Estate of David Garnett.

Garnett, Edward. From a letter to T. E. Lawrence on April 22, 1928, in *Letters to T. E. Lawrence*. Edited by A. W. Lawrence. Jonathan Cape, 1962. © 1962 by A. W. Lawrence. Reprinted by permission of The Executors of the Estate of Edward Garnett.

Goldberg, Isaac. From *The Theatre of George Jean Nathan: Chapters and Documents toward a History of the New American Drama*. Simon and Schuster, 1926. Copyright © 1926 by Simon and Schuster, Inc. Renewed © 1953 by Bernice Stern and Ruth Solomon, executors of the author. Reprinted by permission of Simon & Schuster, Inc.

Gourmont, Remy de. From *The Book of Masks*. Translated by Jack Lewis. J. W. Luce and Company, 1921.

Graves, Robert. From *Lawrence and the Arabs*. Jonathan Cape, 1927. Copyright 1927, renewed 1955, by Robert R. Graves. Reprinted by permission of Robert Graves.

Hahn, Werner G. From *Postwar Soviet Politics: The Fall of Zhdanov and the Defeat of Moderation, 1946-53*. Cornell University Press, 1982. Copyright © 1982 by Cornell University Press. All rights reserved. Used by permission of the publisher, Cornell University Press.

Hamburger, Michael. From *From Prophecy to Exorcism: The Premisses of Modern German Literature*. Longmans, 1965. © Michael Hamburger 1965. Reprinted by permission of the author.

Hankin, Robert M. From "Postwar Soviet Ideology and Literary Scholarship," in *Through the Glass of Soviet Literature: Views of Russian Society*. Edited by Ernest J. Simmons. Columbia University Press, 1953. Copyright 1953 Columbia University Press, New York. Renewed 1981 by Russian Institute, Columbia University. Reprinted by permission of The W. Averell Harriman Institute for Advanced Study of the Soviet Union.

Hardy, Thomas. From a letter to Edward Clodd on February 4, 1892, in *The Collected Letters of Thomas Hardy: 1840-1892, Vol. I*. By Thomas Hardy, edited by Richard Little Purdy and Michael Millgate. Oxford at the Clarendon Press, Oxford, 1978. Letters © Trustees of the Thomas Hardy Estate 1978. All rights reserved. Reprinted by permission of Oxford University Press.

Heidegger, Martin. From *Nietzsche: The Will to Power as Art, Vol. I*. Translated by David Farrell Krell. Harper & Row, 1979. Copyright © 1979 by Harper & Row, Publishers, Inc. All rights reserved. Reprinted by permission of Harper & Row, Publishers, Inc.

Henderson, Harold G. From *An Introduction to Haiku: An Anthology of Poems and Poets and Poets from Bashō to Shiki*. Doubleday Anchor Books, 1958. Copyright © 1958 by Harold G. Henderson. All rights reserved. Reprinted by permission of Doubleday & Company, Inc.

Henderson, Philip. From *The Novel Today: Studies in Contemporary Attitudes*. John Lane/The Bodley Head, 1936.

Henn, T. R. From *The Lonely Tower: Studies in the Poetry of W. B. Yeats*. Methuen, 1964. Reprinted by permission of Methuen & Co. Ltd.

Hinde, Thomas. From "Accident and Coincidence in 'Tess of the D'Urbervilles'," in *The Genius of Thomas Hardy*. Edited by Margaret Drabble. Knopf, 1976. Copyright © 1976 by George Weidenfeld and Nicolson Ltd. All rights reserved. Reprinted by permission of Thomas Hinde.

Hingley, Ronald. From *Joseph Stalin: Man and Legend*. McGraw-Hill Book Company, 1974. Copyright © 1974 by Ronald Hingley. All rights reserved. Reprinted by permission of A. D. Peters & Co Ltd.

Howe, Irving. From *Thomas Hardy*. Macmillan, 1967. Copyright © 1967 by Macmillan Publishing Company. Copyright © 1966 by Irving Howe. All rights reserved. Reprinted with permission of Macmillan Publishing Company.

Kedourie, Elie. From *Islam in the Modern World and Other Studies*. New Republic Books/ Holt, Rinehart and Winston, 1981. Copyright © 1980 by Elie Kedourie. All rights reserved. Reprinted by permission.

Keene, Donald. From *Dawn to the West, Japanese Literature of the Modern Era: Poetry, Drama, Criticism*. Holt, Rinehart and Winston, 1984. Copyright © 1984 by Donald Keene. All rights reserved. Reprinted by permission of Holt, Rinehart and Winston, Publishers.

Kozlenko, Vladimar. From *The Quintessence of Nathanism*. Vrest Orton, 1930.

Langland, Elizabeth. From *Society in the Novel*. University of North Carolina Press, 1984. © 1984 The University of North Carolina Press. All rights reserved. Reprinted by permission.

Lawrence, D. H. From *Phoenix: The Posthumous Papers of D. H. Lawrence*. Edited by Edward D. McDonald. The Viking Press, 1936. Copyright 1936 by Frieda Lawrence. Copyright © renewed 1964 by The Estate of the late Frieda Lawrence Ravagli. Reprinted by permission of Viking Penguin Inc.

Lawrence, T. E. From letters to E. M. Forster on December 1, 1927 and August 6, 1928, in *The Letters of T. E. Lawrence*. By T. E. Lawrence, edited by David Garnett. Jonathan Cape, 1938.

Leavis, F. R. From *New Bearings in English Poetry: A Study of the Contemporary Situation*. Chatto & Windus, 1932.

Lessing, Otto Eduard. From *Masters in Modern German Literature*. Verlag von C. Reissner, 1912.

Lewis, C. S. From a letter to Arthur Greeves on August 31, 1918, in *They Stand Together: The Letters of C. S. Lewis to Arthur Greeves (1914-1963)*. By C. S. Lewis, edited by Walter Hooper. Macmillan, 1979. Collins, 1979. Text copyright © 1979 by The Estate of C. S. Lewis. All rights reserved. Reprinted with permission of Macmillan Publishing Company. In Canada by William Collins Sons & Co., Ltd.

Lewisohn, Ludwig. From *The World's Best Literature, Vol. 15*. Edited by John W. Cunliffe and Ashley H. Thorndike. The Warner Library Company, 1917.

Lodge, David. From *The Novelist at the Crossroads and Other Essays on Fiction and Criticism*. Cornell University Press, 1971. Copyright © 1971 by David Lodge. Reprinted by permission of Curtis Brown, Ltd.

London, Kurt. From *The Seven Soviet Arts*. Translated by Eric S. Bensinger. Yale University Press, 1938.

Mack, John E. From *A Prince of Our Disorder: The Life of T. E. Lawrence*. Little, Brown, 1976. Copyright © 1976 by John E. Mack. All rights reserved. Reprinted by permission of Little, Brown and Company.

Mallarmé, Stéphane. From a letter to Jean Moreas on January 5, 1891, in *Mallarmé: Selected Prose, Poems, Essays & Lectures*. By Stéphane Mallarmé, edited and translated by Bradford Cook. The Johns Hopkins University Press, 1956. © 1956, The Johns Hopkins Press, Baltimore 18, MD. Renewed 1984 by Bradford Cook. Reprinted by permission.

Markel, Michael H. From *Hilaire Belloc*. Twayne, 1982. Copyright 1982 by Twayne Publishers. All rights reserved. Reprinted with the permission of Twayne Publishers, a division of G.K. Hall & Co., Boston.

Marshall, Herbert. From a forward to *Mayakovsky and His Poetry*. By Vladimir Mayakovsky, edited by Marshall Herbert. Revised edition. The Pilot Press, 1945.

Martin, Ronald E. From *American Literature and the Universe of Force*. Duke University Press, 1981. Copyright © 1981 by Duke University Press, Durham, NC. Reprinted by permission of the Publisher.

Masaoko Shiki. From *Modern Japanese Haiku: An Anthology*. Edited and translated by Makoto Ueda. University of Toronto Press, 1976. © University of Toronto Press 1976. Reprinted by permission of the University of Toronto Press.

Mathewson, Rufus W., Jr. From *The Positive Hero in Russian Literature*, second edition. Stanford University Press, 1975. © 1958, 1975 by the Board of Trustees of the Leland Stanford Junior University. Reprinted with the permission of the publishers, Stanford University Press.

Mencken, H. L. From a letter to Burton Rascoe in the summer of 1920? in his *Letters to H. L. Mencken*. Edited by Guy J. Forgue. Knopf, 1961. Copyright © 1961 by Alfred A. Knopf, Inc. All rights reserved. Reprinted by permission of the publisher.

Mencken, H. L. From *Prejudices, first series*. Knopf, 1919. Copyright 1919 by Alfred A. Knopf, Inc. Renewed 1947 by H. L. Mencken. Reprinted by permission of the publisher.

Meredith, George. From a letter to Frederick Greenwood on February 23, 1892, in *The Letters of George Meredith, Vol. II*. By George Meredith, edited by C. L. Cline. Oxford at the Clarendon Press, Oxford, 1970.

Meyers, Jeffrey. From *Homosexuality and Literature: 1890 1930*. The Athlone Press, 1977. © Jeffrey Meyers 1977. Reprinted by permission.

Michaels, Walter Benn. From "Dreiser's 'Financier': The Man of Business as a Man of Letters," in *American Realism: New Essays*. Edited by Eric J. Sundquist. The Johns Hopkins University Press, 1982. Copyright © 1982 by The Johns Hopkins University Press. All rights reserved. Reprinted by permission.

Middleton, Christopher. From *Bolshevism in Art and Other Expository Writings*. Carcanet New Press, 1978. Copyright © Christopher Middleton 1978. All rights reserved. Reprinted by permission of the publisher.

Middleton, Christopher. From an introduction to *Jakob von Gunten: A Novel*. By Robert Walser, translated by Christopher Middleton. University of Texas Press, 1969. Copyright © 1969 by Helmut Kossodo Verlag. All rights reserved. Reprinted by permission of the publisher and Christopher Middleton.

Middleton, Christopher. From an introduction to *The Walk and Other Stories*. By Robert Walser, translated by Christopher Middleton. Calder, 1957. © John Calder [Publisher] Ltd, October, 1957. Reprinted by permission.

Miller, J. Hillis. From *Fiction and Repetition: Seven English Novels*. Cambridge, Mass.: Harvard University Press, 1982. Copyright © 1982 by J. Hillis Miller. All rights reserved. Excerpted by permission of the President and Fellows of Harvard College.

Millgate, Michael. From *Thomas Hardy: His Career as a Novelist*. Random House, 1971. Copyright © 1971 by Michael Millgate. All rights reserved. Reprinted by permission of Random House, Inc.

Milne, A. A. From *By Way of Introduction*. Dutton, 1929. Copyright © 1929 by E. P. Dutton. Renewed 1957 by Daphne Milne. All rights reserved. Reprinted by permission of Curtis Brown Limited, New York.

Mirsky, D. S. From *Contemporary Russian Literature: 1881-1925*. Alfred A. Knopf, 1926.

Muir, Edwin. From *The Estate of Poetry*. Cambridge, Mass.: Harvard University Press, 1962. Copyright © 1962 by the President and Fellows of Harvard College. All rights reserved. Excerpted by permission.

Nathan, George Jean. From a foreword to *The World in Falseface*. By George Jean Nathan. Knopf, 1923. Copyright 1923 by Alfred A. Knopf, Inc. Renewed 1950 by George Jean Nathan. Reprinted by permission of Associated University Presses, Inc., for the Estate of George Jean Nathan.

O'Casey, Sean. From a letter to Alfred Knopf in January, 1940, in *The Letters to Sean O'Casey: 1910-41, Vol. I*. By Sean O'Casey, edited by David Krause. Macmillan, 1975. Copyright © 1975 by Macmillan Publishing Company. All rights reserved. Reprinted with permission of Macmillan Publishing Company.

O'Donnell, Thomas J. From *The Confessions of T. E. Lawrence: The Romantic Hero's Presentation of Self*. Ohio University Press, 1979. © Copyright 1979 by Thomas J. O'Donnell. All rights reserved. Reprinted by permission of Ohio University Press, Athens.

Olson, Elder. From *On Value Judgements in the Arts and Other Essays*. University of Chicago Press, 1976. © 1976 by Elder Olson. All rights reserved. Reprinted by permission of the author.

O'Neill, Eugene. From a letter to George Jean Nathan on June 20, 1920, in *The Theatre of George Jean Nathan: Chapters and Documents toward a History of the New American Drama*. By Isaac Goldberg. Simon and Schuster, 1926. Copyright © 1926 by Simon and Schuster, Inc. Renewed © 1953 by Bernice Stern and Ruth Solomon, executors of the author. Reprinted by permission of Simon & Schuster.

Parker, Dorothy. From "Ethereal Mildness," in *The Portable Dorothy Parker*. The Viking Press, 1973. Copyright 1928 by *The New Yorker*. Copyright renewed © 1956 by *The New Yorker*. Reprinted by permission of Viking Penguin Inc.

Parry, Idris. From *Hand to Mouth and Other Essays*. Carcanet New Press, 1981. Copyright © Idris Parry 1981. All rights reserved. Reprinted by permission.

Payne, Robert. From an introduction to *The Complete Plays of Vladimir Mayakovsky*. By Vladimir Mayakovsky, translated by Guy Daniels. Washington Square Press, Inc., 1968. Introduction copyright © 1968 by Robert Payne. All rights reserved. Reprinted by permission of Washington Square Press, a division of Simon & Schuster, Inc.

Pizer, Donald. From *The Novels of Theodore Dreiser: A Critical Study*. University of Minnesota Press, 1976. Copyright © 1976 by the University of Minnesota. All rights reserved. Reprinted by permission.

Pollard, Percival. From *Masks and Minstrels of New Germany*. John W. Luce and Company, 1911.

Pritchett, V. S. From *The Living Novel & Later Appreciations*. Revised edition. Random House, 1964. Copyright © 1975 by V. S. Pritchett. All rights reserved. Reprinted by permission of Literistic, Ltd.

Raban, Jonathan. From an introduction to *The Cruise of the "Nona"*. By Hilaire Belloc. Hippocrene Books Inc., 1983. Introduction copyright © Jonathan Raban 1983. All rights reserved. Reprinted by permission.

Rajan, Tilottama. From *Dark Interpreter: The Discourse of Romanticism*. Cornell University Press, 1980. Copyright © 1980 by Cornell University. All rights reserved. Used by permission of the publisher, Cornell University Press.

Read, Herbert. From *The Bibliophile's Almanack for 1928*. Edited by Oliver Simon and Harold Child. The Fleuron Limited, 1928.

Reavey, George. From an introduction to *A Week in Turenevo and Other Stories*. By Alexei Tolstoy. Grove Press, 1958. Copyright © 1958 by Grove Press, Inc. Reprinted by permission of Grove Press, Inc.

Russell, Richard K. From a foreword to *The American Mercury, a Monthly Review: Facsimile Edition of Volume I*. Freedeeds Books, 1984. Copyright © 1984 by Garber Communications, Inc. All rights reserved. Reprinted by permission.

Shostakovich, Dmitri. From *Testimony: The Memoirs of Dmitri Shostakovich*. Edited by Solomon Volkov, translated by Antonina W. Bouis. Harper & Row, 1979. Copyright © 1979 by Solomon Volkov. English-language translation copyright © 1979 by Harper & Row, Publishers, Inc. All rights reserved. Reprinted by permission of Harper & Row, Publishers, Inc.

Slonim, Marc. From *Soviet Russian Literature: Writers and Problems, 1917-1977*. Second revised edition. Oxford University Press, 1977. Copyright © 1964, 1967 by Oxford University Press, Inc. Reprinted by permission.

Slonim, Marc. From *Soviet Russian Literature: Writers and Problems, 1917-1977*. Second revised edition. Oxford University Press, 1977. Copyright © 1964, 1967, 1977 by Oxford University Press, Inc. Reprinted by permission.

Sontag, Susan. From "Walser's Voice," in *Selected Stories*. By Robert Walser, translated by Christopher Middleton & others. Farrar, Straus and Giroux, 1982. Introduction copyright © 1982 by Susan Sontag. All rights reserved. Reprinted by permission of Farrar, Straus and Giroux, Inc.

Spindler, Michael. From *American Literature and Social Change: William Dean Howells to Arthur Miller*. Indiana University Press, 1983. Copyright © 1983 by Michael Spindler. All rights reserved. Reprinted by permission.

Stahlberger, Lawrence Leo. From *The Symbolic System of Majakovskij*. Mouton, 1964. © Copyright 1964 Mouton & Co., Publishers. Reprinted by permission of Mouton Publishers, a Division of Walter de Gruyter & Co.

Stephens, James. From *James, Seumas & Jacques*. Edited by Lloyd Frankenberg. The Macmillan Company, 1964. © Iris Wise 1962, 1964. All rights reserved. Reprinted with permission of The Society of Authors as the literary representative of the Estate of James Stephens and the copyright owner, Mrs. Iris Wise.

Stewart, Desmond. From *T. E. Lawrence*. Harper & Row, 1977. Copyright © 1977 by Desmond Stewart. All rights reserved. Reprinted by permission of Harper & Row, Publishers, Inc. In Canada by permission of Brandt & Brandt Literary Agents Inc.

Striedter, Jurij. From "The 'New Myth' of Revolution—A Study of Mayakovsky's Early Poetry," in *New Perspectives in German Literary Criticism: A Collection of Essays*. Edited by Richard E. Amacher and Victor Lange, translated by David Henry Wilson & others. Princeton University Press, 1979. Copyright © 1979 by Princeton University Press. All rights reserved. Excerpts reprinted by permission of Princeton University Press.

Striedter, Jurij. From "Three Postrevolutionary Russian Utopian Novels," in *The Russian Novel from Pushkin to Pasternak*. Edited by John Garrard. Yale University Press, 1983. Copyright © 1983 by Yale University. All rights reserved. Reprinted by permission.

Struve, Gleb. From *Soviet Russian Literature*. Routledge & Kegan Paul, 1935.

Tabachnick, Stephen Ely. From *T. E. Lawrence*. Twayne, 1978. Copyright 1978 by Twayne Publishers. All rights reserved. Reprinted with the permission of Twayne Publishers, a division of G.K. Hall & Co., Boston.

Terras, Victor. From *Vladimir Mayakovsky*. Twayne, 1983. Copyright 1983 by Twayne Publishers. All rights reserved. Reprinted with the permission of Twayne Publishers, a division of G.K. Hall & Co., Boston.

Thompson, Francis. From *Literary Criticisms*. Edited by Rev. Terence L. Connolly, S.J. E. P. Dutton and Company, Inc., 1948.

Turquet-Milnes, G. From *Some Modern French Writers: A Study in Bergsonism*. Robert M. McBride & Company, 1921.

Ueda, Makoto. From *Modern Japanese Poets and the Nature of Literature*. Stanford University Press, 1983. © 1983 by the Board of Trustees of the Leland Stanford Junior University. Excerpted with the permission of the publishers, Stanford University Press.

Van Doren, Carl. From *Many Minds*. Knopf, 1924. Copyright 1924 by Alfred A. Knopf, Inc. Copyright renewed 1951 by The Estate of Carl Van Doren. Reprinted by permission of The Estate of Carl Van Doren.

Van Ghent, Dorothy. From *The English Novel: Form and Function*. Holt, Rinehart and Winston, 1953. Copyright © 1953; renewed 1981 by Dorothy Van Ghent. Reprinted by permission of CBS College Publishing.

Vickery, Walter N. From "Zhdanovism (1946-53)," in *Literature and Revolution in Soviet Russia: 1917-62*. Edited by Max Hayward and Leopold Labedz. Oxford University Press, London, 1963. © Oxford University Press 1963. Reprinted by permission of Oxford University Press.

Villars, Jean Beraud, From *T. E. Lawrence; or, The Search for the Absolute*. Translated by Peter Dawnay. Sidgwick and Jackson Limited, 1958. © 1955 by Albin Michel.

Wagner, Geoffrey. From *Five for Freedom: A Study of Feminism in Fiction*. Allen & Unwin, 1972. © George Allen & Unwin Ltd. 1972. Reprinted by permission of the author.

Waidson, H. M. From "Robert Walser," in *German Men of Letters: Twelve Literary Essays, Vol. II*. Edited by Alex Natan. Wolff, 1963. © 1963 Oswald Wolff (Publishers) Limited, London. Reprinted by permission.

Warnock, Mary. From "Nietzsche's Conception of Truth," in *Nietzsche: Imagery and Thought, a Collection of Essays*. Edited by Malcolm Pasley. University of California Press, 1978. Copyright © 1978 by Methuen & Co. Ltd. Reprinted by permission of the University of California Press.

Waugh, Evelyn. From *The Essays, Articles, and Reviews of Evelyn Waugh*. Edited by Donat Gallagher. Little, Brown, 1984. Copyright © 1983 by the Estate of Laura Waugh. All rights reserved. Reprinted by permission of Little, Brown and Company. In Canada by A. D. Peters & Co. Ltd.

Weintraub, Stanley and Rodelle Weintraub. From *Lawrence of Arabia: The Literary Impulse*. Louisiana State University Press, 1975. Copyright © 1975 by Louisiana State University Press. All rights reserved. Reprinted by permission of Louisiana State University Press.

Wells, H. G. From *An Englishman Looks at the World*. Cassell and Company Limited, 1914.

Wilson, A. N. From an introduction to *The Four Men: A Farrago*. By Hilaire Belloc. Oxford University Press, Oxford, 1984. Introduction © A. N. Wilson 1984. All rights reserved. Reprinted by permission of Oxford University Press.

Wilson, A. N. From *Hilaire Belloc*. Hamish Hamilton, 1984. Copyright © 1984 by A. N. Wilson. Reprinted by permission of A. D. Peters & Co. Ltd.

Wilson, Colin. From *The Outsider*. Houghton Mifflin, 1956. V. Gollancz, 1956. Copyright © 1956 by Colin Wilson. Copyright renewed 1984 by Colin Wilson. All rights reserved. Reprinted by permission of Houghton Mifflin Company. In Canada by Victor Gollancz, Ltd.

Wilson, Edmund. From a letter to Burton Rascoe on September 23, 1929, in *Letters on Literature and Politics: 1912-1972*. By Edmund Wilson, edited by Elena Wilson. Farrar, Straus & Giroux, 1957. Copyright © 1957, 1973, 1974, 1977 by Elena Wilson, Executrix of the Estate of Edmund Wilson. All rights reserved. Reprinted by permission of Farrar Straus & Giroux, Inc.

Wolstenholme, Susan. From ''Brother Theodore, Hell on Women,'' in *American Novelists Revisited: Essays in Feminist Criticism*. Edited by Fritz Fleischmann. G.K. Hall, 1982. Copyright © 1982 by Fritz Fleischmann. Reprinted with the permission of G.K. Hall & Co.

Zhdanov, Andrei A. From *Essays on Literature, Philosophy, and Music*. International, 1950. Copyright 1950, renewed 1978, by International Publishers Co., Inc. Reprinted by permission.

Cumulative Index to Authors

This index lists all author entries in the Gale Literary Criticism Series and includes cross-references to other Gale sources. References in the index are identified as follows:

AITN: *Authors in the News,* Volumes 1-2
CAAS: *Contemporary Authors Autobiography Series,* Volumes 1-2
CA: *Contemporary Authors* (original series), Volumes 1-115
CANR: *Contemporary Authors New Revision Series,* Volumes 1-14
CAP: *Contemporary Authors Permanent Series,* Volumes 1-2
CA-R: *Contemporary Authors* (revised editions), Volumes 1-44
CLC: *Contemporary Literary Criticism,* Volumes 1-35
CLR: *Children's Literature Review,* Volumes 1-8
DLB: *Dictionary of Literary Biography,* Volumes 1-39
DLB-DS: *Dictionary of Literary Biography Documentary Series,* Volumes 1-4
DLB-Y: *Dictionary of Literary Biography Yearbook,* Volumes 1980-1984
LC: *Literature Criticism from 1400 to 1800,* Volumes 1-2
NCLC: *Nineteenth-Century Literature Criticism,* Volumes 1-10
SATA: *Something about the Author,* Volumes 1-39
TCLC: *Twentieth-Century Literary Criticism,* Volumes 1-18
YABC: *Yesterday's Authors of Books for Children,* Volumes 1-2

Barfoot, Joan 1946- .... **CLC 18**
See also CA 105

Baring, Maurice 1874-1945 .... **TCLC 8**
See also CA 105
See also DLB 34

Barker, George (Granville) 1913- .... **CLC 8**
See also CANR 7
See also CA 9-12R
See also DLB 20

Barker, Pat 19??- .... **CLC 32**

Barnes, Djuna 1892-1982 .... **CLC 3, 4, 8, 11, 29**
See also CA 9-12R
See also obituary CA 107
See also DLB 4, 9

Barnes, Peter 1931- .... **CLC 5**
See also CA 65-68
See also DLB 13

Baroja (y Nessi), Pío 1872-1956 .... **TCLC 8**
See also CA 104

Barondess, Sue K(aufman) 1926-1977
See Kaufman, Sue
See also CANR 1
See also CA 1-4R
See also obituary CA 69-72

Barrett, (Roger) Syd 1946-
See Pink Floyd

Barrett, William (Christopher) 1913- .... **CLC 27**
See also CANR 11
See also CA 13-16R

Barrie, (Sir) J(ames) M(atthew) 1860-1937 .... **TCLC 2**
See also CA 104
See also YABC 1
See also DLB 10

Barrol, Grady 1953-
See Bograd, Larry

Barry, Philip (James Quinn) 1896-1949 .... **TCLC 11**
See also CA 109
See also DLB 7

Barth, John (Simmons) 1930- ...... **CLC 1, 2, 3, 5, 7, 9, 10, 14, 27**
See also CANR 5
See also CA 1-4R
See also DLB 2
See also AITN 1, 2

Barthelme, Donald 1931- ...... **CLC 1, 2, 3, 5, 6, 8, 13, 23**
See also CA 21-24R
See also SATA 7
See also DLB 2
See also DLB-Y 80

Barthes, Roland 1915-1980 .... **CLC 24**
See also obituary CA 97-100

Bassani, Giorgio 1916- .... **CLC 9**
See also CA 65-68

Bataille, Georges 1897-1962 .... **CLC 29**
See also CA 101
See also obituary CA 89-92

Baudelaire, Charles 1821-1867 .... **NCLC 6**

Baum, L(yman) Frank 1856-1919 .... **TCLC 7**
See also CA 108
See also SATA 18
See also DLB 22

Baumbach, Jonathan 1933- ..... **CLC 6, 23**
See also CANR 12
See also CA 13-16R
See also DLB-Y 80

Baxter, James K(eir) 1926-1972 .... **CLC 14**
See also CA 77-80

Bayer, Sylvia 1909-1981
See Glassco, John

Beagle, Peter S(oyer) 1939- .... **CLC 7**
See also CANR 4
See also CA 9-12R
See also DLB-Y 80

Beard, Charles A(ustin) 1874-1948 .... **TCLC 15**
See also CA 115
See also SATA 18
See also DLB 17

Beardsley, Aubrey 1872-1898 ..... **NCLC 6**

Beattie, Ann 1947- .... **CLC 8, 13, 18**
See also CA 81-84
See also DLB-Y 82

Beauvoir, Simone de 1908- .... **CLC 1, 2, 4, 8, 14, 31**
See also CA 9-12R

Becker, Jurek 1937- .... **CLC 7, 19**
See also CA 85-88

Becker, Walter 1950-
See Becker, Walter and Fagen, Donald

Becker, Walter 1950- and **Fagen, Donald** 1948- .... **CLC 26**

Beckett, Samuel (Barclay) 1906- ...... **CLC 1, 2, 3, 4, 6, 9, 10, 11, 14, 18, 29**
See also CA 5-8R
See also DLB 13, 15

Beckman, Gunnel 1910- .... **CLC 26**
See also CA 33-36R
See also SATA 6

Becque, Henri 1837-1899 .... **NCLC 3**

Beddoes, Thomas Lovell 1803-1849 .... **NCLC 3**

Beecher, John 1904-1980 .... **CLC 6**
See also CANR 8
See also CA 5-8R
See also obituary CA 105
See also AITN 1

Beerbohm, (Sir Henry) Max(imilian) 1872-1956 .... **TCLC 1**
See also CA 104
See also DLB 34

Behan, Brendan 1923-1964 .... **CLC 1, 8, 11, 15**
See also CA 73-76
See also DLB 13

Behn, Aphra 1640?-1689 .... **LC 1**
See also DLB 39

Belasco, David 1853-1931 .... **TCLC 3**
See also CA 104
See also DLB 7

Belcheva, Elisaveta 1893-
See Bagryana, Elisaveta

Belinski, Vissarion Grigoryevich 1811-1848 .... **NCLC 5**

Belitt, Ben 1911- .... **CLC 22**
See also CANR 7
See also CA 13-16R
See also DLB 5

Bell, Acton 1820-1849
See Brontë, Anne

Bell, Currer 1816-1855
See Brontë, Charlotte

Bell, Marvin 1937- .... **CLC 8, 31**
See also CA 21-24R
See also DLB 5

Bellamy, Edward 1850-1898 ...... **NCLC 4**
See also DLB 12

Belloc, (Joseph) Hilaire (Pierre Sébastien Réné Swanton) 1870-1953 .... **TCLC 7, 18**
See also CA 106
See also YABC 1
See also DLB 19

Bellow, Saul 1915- ..... **CLC 1, 2, 3, 6, 8, 10, 13, 15, 25, 33**
See also CA 5-8R
See also DLB 2, 28
See also DLB-Y 82
See also DLB-DS 3
See also AITN 2

Belser, Reimond Karel Maria de 1929-
See Ruyslinck, Ward

Bely, Andrey 1880-1934 .... **TCLC 7**
See also CA 104

Benary-Isbert, Margot 1889-1979 .... **CLC 12**
See also CANR 4
See also CA 5-8R
See also obituary CA 89-92
See also SATA 2
See also obituary SATA 21

Benavente (y Martinez), Jacinto 1866-1954 .... **TCLC 3**
See also CA 106

Benchley, Peter (Bradford) 1940- .... **CLC 4, 8**
See also CANR 12
See also CA 17-20R
See also SATA 3
See also AITN 2

Benchley, Robert 1889-1945 ...... **TCLC 1**
See also CA 105
See also DLB 11

Benedikt, Michael 1935- .... **CLC 4, 14**
See also CANR 7
See also CA 13-16R
See also DLB 5

Benet, Juan 1927- .... **CLC 28**

Benét, Stephen Vincent 1898-1943 .... **TCLC 7**
See also CA 104
See also YABC 1
See also DLB 4

Benn, Gottfried 1886-1956 .... **TCLC 3**
See also CA 106

Breslin, James (E.) 1930-
See Breslin, Jimmy
See also CA 73-76

Breslin, Jimmy 1930- .... **CLC 4**
See also Breslin, James (E.)
See also AITN 1

Bresson, Robert 1907-............. **CLC 16**
See also CA 110

Breton, André 1896-1966..... **CLC 2, 9, 15**
See also CAP 2
See also CA 19-20
See also obituary CA 25-28R

Breytenbach, Breyten 1939-........ **CLC 23**
See also CA 113

Bridgers, Sue Ellen 1942-.......... **CLC 26**
See also CANR 11
See also CA 65-68
See also SATA 22

Bridges, Robert 1844-1930........ **TCLC 1**
See also CA 104
See also DLB 19

Bridie, James 1888-1951 .... **TCLC 3**
See also Mavor, Osborne Henry
See also DLB 10

Brin, David 1950- .... **CLC 34**
See also CA 102

Brink, André (Philippus) 1935-..... **CLC 18**
See also CA 104

Brinsmead, H(esba) F(ay)
1922-........................ **CLC 21**
See also CANR 10
See also CA 21-24R
See also SATA 18

Brittain, Vera (Mary)
1893?-1970.................. **CLC 23**
See also CAP 1
See also CA 15-16
See also obituary CA 25-28R

Brodsky, Iosif Alexandrovich 1940-
See Brodsky, Joseph
See also CA 41-44R
See also AITN 1

Brodsky, Joseph 1940- .... **CLC 4, 6, 13**
See also Brodsky, Iosif Alexandrovich

Brodsky, Michael (Mark)
1948-........................ **CLC 19**
See also CA 102

Bromell, Henry 1947-.............. **CLC 5**
See also CANR 9
See also CA 53-56

Bromfield, Louis (Brucker)
1896-1956.................. **TCLC 11**
See also CA 107
See also DLB 4, 9

Broner, E(sther) M(asserman)
1930-........................ **CLC 19**
See also CANR 8
See also CA 17-20R
See also DLB 28

Bronk, William 1918-............. **CLC 10**
See also CA 89-92

Brontë, Anne 1820-1849.......... **NCLC 4**
See also DLB 21

Brontë, Charlotte
1816-1855................. **NCLC 3, 8**
See also DLB 21
See also DLB 39

Brooke, Henry 1703?-1783 .... **LC 1**
See also DLB 39

Brooke, Rupert (Chawner)
1887-1915................ **TCLC 2, 7**
See also CA 104
See also DLB 19

Brookner, Anita 1938- .... **CLC 32**
See also CA 114

Brooks, Cleanth 1906- .... **CLC 24**
See also CA 17-20R

Brooks, Gwendolyn
1917-.............. **CLC 1, 2, 4, 5, 15**
See also CANR 1
See also CA 1-4R
See also SATA 6
See also DLB 5
See also AITN 1

Brooks, Mel 1926-................ **CLC 12**
See also CA 65-68
See also DLB 26

Brooks, Peter 1938-............... **CLC 34**
See also CANR 1
See also CA 45-48

Brooks, Van Wyck 1886-1963...... **CLC 29**
See also CANR 6
See also CA 1-4R

Brophy, Brigid (Antonia)
1929-.................. **CLC 6, 11, 29**
See also CA 5-8R
See also DLB 14

Brosman, Catharine Savage
1934-......................... **CLC 9**
See also CA 61-64

Broughton, T(homas) Alan
1936-........................ **CLC 19**
See also CANR 2
See also CA 45-48

Broumas, Olga 1949- .... **CLC 10**
See also CA 85-88

Brown, Claude 1937- .... **CLC 30**
See also CA 73-76

Brown, Dee (Alexander) 1908- ..... **CLC 18**
See also CANR 11
See also CA 13-16R
See also SATA 5
See also DLB-Y 80

Brown, George Mackay 1921-....... **CLC 5**
See also CANR 12
See also CA 21-24R
See also SATA 35
See also DLB 14, 27

Brown, Rita Mae 1944- .... **CLC 18**
See also CANR 2, 11
See also CA 45-48

Brown, Rosellen 1939- .... **CLC 32**
See also CANR 14
See also CA 77-80

Brown, Sterling A(llen)
1901-..................... **CLC 1, 23**
See also CA 85-88

Brown, William Wells
1816?-1884................. **NCLC 2**
See also DLB 3

Browne, Jackson 1950-............ **CLC 21**

Browning, Elizabeth Barrett
1806-1861................... **NCLC 1**
See also DLB 32

Browning, Tod 1882-1962 .... **CLC 16**

Bruccoli, Matthew J(oseph)
1931-........................ **CLC 34**
See also CANR 7
See also CA 9-12R

Bruce, Lenny 1925-1966........... **CLC 21**
See also Schneider, Leonard Alfred

Brunner, John (Kilian Houston)
1934-...................... **CLC 8, 10**
See also CANR 2
See also CA 1-4R

Bryan, C(ourtlandt) D(ixon) B(arnes)
1936-........................ **CLC 29**
See also CANR 13
See also CA 73-76

Bryant, William Cullen
1794-1878................... **NCLC 6**
See also DLB 3

Bryusov, Valery (Yakovlevich)
1873-1924.................. **TCLC 10**
See also CA 107

Buchheim, Lothar-Günther
1918-......................... **CLC 6**
See also CA 85-88

Buchwald, Art(hur) 1925- .... **CLC 33**
See also CA 5-8R
See also SATA 10
See also AITN 1

Buck, Pearl S(ydenstricker)
1892-1973.............. **CLC 7, 11, 18**
See also CANR 1
See also CA 1-4R
See also obituary CA 41-44R
See also SATA 1, 25
See also DLB 9
See also AITN 1

Buckler, Ernest 1908-1984......... **CLC 13**
See also CAP 1
See also CA 11-12
See also obituary CA 114

Buckley, William F(rank), Jr.
1925-..................... **CLC 7, 18**
See also CANR 1
See also CA 1-4R
See also DLB-Y 80
See also AITN 1

Buechner, (Carl) Frederick
1926-.................. **CLC 2, 4, 6, 9**
See also CANR 11
See also CA 13-16R
See also DLB-Y 80

Buell, John (Edward) 1927-........ **CLC 10**
See also CA 1-4R

Buero Vallejo, Antonio 1916- ...... **CLC 15**
See also CA 106

Bukowski, Charles 1920- ...... **CLC 2, 5, 9**
See also CA 17-20R
See also DLB 5

Bulgakov, Mikhail (Afanas'evich)
1891-1940................ **TCLC 2, 16**
See also CA 105

Bullins, Ed 1935-............. **CLC 1, 5, 7**
See also CA 49-52
See also DLB 7, 38

Bulwer-Lytton, (Lord) Edward (George Earle Lytton) 1803-1873 .... **NCLC 1**
See also Lytton, Edward Bulwer
See also DLB 21

Author Index

Donleavy, J(ames) P(atrick) 1926- . . . . CLC 1, 4, 6, 10
See also CA 9-12R
See also DLB 6
See also AITN 2

Donnell, David 1939?- . . . . CLC 34

Donoso, José 1924- . . . . CLC 4, 8, 11, 32
See also CA 81-84

Donovan, John 1928- . . . . CLC 35
See also CLR 3
See also CA 97-100
See also SATA 29

Doolittle, Hilda 1886-1961
See H(ilda) D(oolittle)
See also CA 97-100
See also DLB 4

Dorn, Ed(ward Merton) 1929- . . . . CLC 10, 18
See also CA 93-96
See also DLB 5

Dos Passos, John (Roderigo) 1896-1970 . . . . CLC 1, 4, 8, 11, 15, 25, 34
See also CANR 3
See also CA 1-4R
See also obituary CA 29-32R
See also DLB 4, 9
See also DLB-DS 1

Dostoevski, Fedor Mikhailovich 1821-1881 . . . . NCLC 2, 7

Douglass, Frederick 1817-1895 . . . . NCLC 7
See also SATA 29
See also DLB 1

Dourado, (Waldomiro Freitas) Autran 1926- . . . . CLC 23
See also CA 25-28R

Dowson, Ernest (Christopher) 1867-1900 . . . . TCLC 4
See also CA 105
See also DLB 19

Doyle, (Sir) Arthur Conan 1859-1930 . . . . TCLC 7
See also CA 104
See also SATA 24
See also DLB 18

Dr. A 1933-
See Silverstein, Alvin and Virginia B(arbara Opshelor) Silverstein

Drabble, Margaret 1939- . . . . CLC 2, 3, 5, 8, 10, 22
See also CA 13-16R
See also DLB 14

Dreiser, Theodore (Herman Albert) 1871-1945 . . . . TCLC 10, 18
See also CA 106
See also DLB 9, 12
See also DLB-DS 1

Drexler, Rosalyn 1926- . . . . CLC 2, 6
See also CA 81-84

Dreyer, Carl Theodor 1889-1968 . . . . CLC 16

Droste-Hülshoff, Annette Freiin von 1797-1848 . . . . NCLC 3

Drummond de Andrade, Carlos 1902-
See Andrade, Carlos Drummond de

Duberman, Martin 1930- . . . . CLC 8
See also CANR 2
See also CA 1-4R

Du Bois, W(illiam) E(dward) B(urghardt) 1868-1963 . . . . CLC 1, 2, 13
See also CA 85-88

Dubus, Andre 1936- . . . . CLC 13
See also CA 21-24R

Duclos, Charles Pinot 1704-1772 . . . . LC 1

Dudek, Louis 1918- . . . . CLC 11, 19
See also CANR 1
See also CA 45-48

Dudevant, Amandine Aurore Lucile Dupin 1804-1876
See Sand, George

Duerrenmatt, Friedrich 1921-
See also CA 17-20R

Dugan, Alan 1923- . . . . CLC 2, 6
See also CA 81-84
See also DLB 5

Duhamel, Georges 1884-1966 . . . . CLC 8
See also CA 81-84
See also obituary CA 25-28R

Dujardin, Édouard (Émile Louis) 1861-1949 . . . . TCLC 13
See also CA 109

Duke, Raoul 1939-
See Thompson, Hunter S(tockton)

Dumas, Alexandre, *(fils)* 1824-1895 . . . . NCLC 9

Dumas, Henry (L.) 1934-1968 . . . . CLC 6
See also CA 85-88

Du Maurier, Daphne 1907- . . . . CLC 6, 11
See also CANR 6
See also CA 5-8R
See also SATA 27

Dunbar, Paul Laurence 1872-1906 . . . . TCLC 2, 12
See also CA 104
See also SATA 34

Duncan (Steinmetz Arquette), Lois 1934- . . . . CLC 26
See also Arquette, Lois S(teinmetz)
See also CANR 2
See also CA 1-4R
See also SATA 1, 36

Duncan, Robert 1919- . . . . CLC 1, 2, 4, 7, 15
See also CA 9-12R
See also DLB 5, 16, 37

Dunlap, William 1766-1839 . . . . NCLC 2
See also DLB 30

Dunn, Douglas (Eaglesham) 1942- . . . . CLC 6
See also CANR 2
See also CA 45-48

Dunne, John Gregory 1932- . . . . CLC 28
See also CANR 14
See also CA 25-28R
See also DLB-Y 80

Dunsany, Lord (Edward John Moreton Drax Plunkett) 1878-1957 . . . . TCLC 2
See also CA 104
See also DLB 10

Durang, Christopher (Ferdinand) 1949- . . . . CLC 27
See also CA 105

Duras, Marguerite 1914- . . . . CLC 3, 6, 11, 20, 34
See also CA 25-28R

Durrell, Lawrence (George) 1912- . . . . CLC 1, 4, 6, 8, 13, 27
See also CA 9-12R
See also DLB 15, 27

Dürrenmatt, Friedrich 1921- . . . . CLC 1, 4, 8, 11, 15
See also Duerrenmatt, Friedrich

Dylan, Bob 1941- . . . . CLC 3, 4, 6, 12
See also CA 41-44R
See also DLB 16

East, Michael 1916-
See West, Morris L.

Eastlake, William (Derry) 1917- . . . . CLC 8
See also CAAS 1
See also CANR 5
See also CA 5-8R
See also DLB 6

Eberhart, Richard 1904- . . . . CLC 3, 11, 19
See also CANR 2
See also CA 1-4R

Echegaray (y Eizaguirre), José (María Waldo) 1832-1916 . . . . TCLC 4
See also CA 104

Eckert, Allan W. 1931- . . . . CLC 17
See also CANR 14
See also CA 13-16R
See also SATA 27, 29

Eco, Umberto 1932- . . . . CLC 28
See also CANR 12
See also CA 77-80

Eddison, E(ric) R(ucker) 1882-1945 . . . . TCLC 15
See also CA 109

Edel, (Joseph) Leon 1907- . . . . CLC 29, 34
See also CANR 1
See also CA 1-4R

Eden, Emily 1797-1869 . . . . NCLC 10

Edgeworth, Maria 1767-1849 . . . . NCLC 1
See also SATA 21

Edmonds, Helen (Woods) 1904-1968
See Kavan, Anna
See also CA 5-8R
See also obituary CA 25-28R

Edmonds, Walter D(umaux) 1903- . . . . CLC 35
See also CANR 2
See also CA 5-8R
See also SATA 1, 27
See also DLB 9

Edson, Russell 1905- . . . . CLC 13
See also CA 33-36R

Edwards, G(erald) B(asil) 1899-1976 . . . . CLC 25
See also obituary CA 110

Ehle, John (Marsden, Jr.) 1925- . . . . CLC 27
See also CA 9-12R

Ehrenbourg, Ilya (Grigoryevich) 1891-1967
See Ehrenburg, Ilya (Grigoryevich)

Author Index

Farrell, M. J. 1904-
See Keane, Molly

Fassbinder, Rainer Werner 1946-1982 .... **CLC 20**
See also CA 93-96
See also obituary CA 106

Fast, Howard (Melvin) 1914- .... **CLC 23**
See also CANR 1
See also CA 1-4R
See also SATA 7
See also DLB 9

Faulkner, William (Cuthbert) 1897-1962 .... **CLC 1, 3, 6, 8, 9, 11, 14, 18, 28**
See also CA 81-84
See also DLB 9, 11
See also DLB-DS 2
See also AITN 1

Fauset, Jessie Redmon 1884?-1961 .... **CLC 19**
See also CA 109

Faust, Irvin 1924- .... **CLC 8**
See also CA 33-36R
See also DLB 2, 28
See also DLB-Y 80

Federman, Raymond 1928- .... **CLC 6**
See also CANR 10
See also CA 17-20R
See also DLB-Y 80

Feiffer, Jules 1929- .... **CLC 2, 8**
See also CA 17-20R
See also SATA 8
See also DLB 7

Feldman, Irving (Mordecai) 1928- .... **CLC 7**
See also CANR 1
See also CA 1-4R

Fellini, Federico 1920- .... **CLC 16**
See also CA 65-68

Felsen, Gregor 1916-
See Felsen, Henry Gregor

Felsen, Henry Gregor 1916- .... **CLC 17**
See also CANR 1
See also CA 1-4R
See also SATA 1

Fenton, James (Martin) 1949- .... **CLC 32**
See also CA 102

Ferber, Edna 1887-1968 .... **CLC 18**
See also CA 5-8R
See also obituary CA 25-28R
See also SATA 7
See also DLB 9, 28
See also AITN 1

Ferlinghetti, Lawrence (Monsanto) 1919?- .... **CLC 2, 6, 10, 27**
See also CANR 3
See also CA 5-8R
See also DLB 5, 16

Ferrier, Susan (Edmonstone) 1782-1854 .... **NCLC 8**

Feuchtwanger, Lion 1884-1958 .... **TCLC 3**
See also CA 104

Fiedler, Leslie A(aron) 1917- .... **CLC 4, 13, 24**
See also CANR 7
See also CA 9-12R
See also DLB 28

Field, Eugene 1850-1895 .... **NCLC 3**
See also SATA 16
See also DLB 21, 23

Fielding, Henry 1707-1754 .... **LC 1**
See also DLB 39

Fielding, Sarah 1710-1768 .... **LC 1**
See also DLB 39

Fierstein, Harvey 1954- .... **CLC 33**

Figes, Eva 1932- .... **CLC 31**
See also CANR 4
See also CA 53-56
See also DLB 14

Finch, Robert (Duer Claydon) 1900- .... **CLC 18**
See also CANR 9
See also CA 57-60

Findley, Timothy 1930- .... **CLC 27**
See also CANR 12
See also CA 25-28R

Fink, Janis 1951-
See Ian, Janis

Firbank, (Arthur Annesley) Ronald 1886-1926 .... **TCLC 1**
See also CA 104
See also DLB 36

Firbank, Louis 1944-
See Reed, Lou

Fisher, Roy 1930- .... **CLC 25**
See also CA 81-84

Fisher, Rudolph 1897-1934 .... **TCLC 11**
See also CA 107

Fisher, Vardis (Alvero) 1895-1968 .... **CLC 7**
See also CA 5-8R
See also obituary CA 25-28R
See also DLB 9

FitzGerald, Edward 1809-1883 .... **NCLC 9**
See also DLB 32

Fitzgerald, F(rancis) Scott (Key) 1896-1940 .... **TCLC 1, 6, 14**
See also CA 110
See also DLB 4, 9
See also DLB-Y 81
See also DLB-DS 1
See also AITN 1

Fitzgerald, Penelope 1916- .... **CLC 19**
See also CA 85-88
See also DLB 14

FitzGerald, Robert D(avid) 1902- .... **CLC 19**
See also CA 17-20R

Flanagan, Thomas (James Bonner) 1923- .... **CLC 25**
See also CA 108
See also DLB-Y 80

Flaubert, Gustave 1821-1880 .... **NCLC 2, 10**

Fleming, Ian (Lancaster) 1908-1964 .... **CLC 3, 30**
See also CA 5-8R
See also SATA 9

Fo, Dario 1929- .... **CLC 32**

Follett, Ken(neth Martin) 1949- .... **CLC 18**
See also CANR 13
See also CA 81-84
See also DLB-Y 81

Forbes, Esther 1891-1967 .... **CLC 12**
See also CAP 1
See also CA 13-14
See also obituary CA 25-28R
See also DLB 22
See also SATA 2

Forché, Carolyn 1950- .... **CLC 25**
See also CA 109
See also DLB 5

Ford, Ford Madox 1873-1939 .... **TCLC 1, 15**
See also CA 104
See also DLB 34

Ford, John 1895-1973 .... **CLC 16**
See also obituary CA 45-48

Forester, C(ecil) S(cott) 1899-1966 .... **CLC 35**
See also CA 73-76
See also obituary CA 25-28R
See also SATA 13

Forman, James D(ouglas) 1932- .... **CLC 21**
See also CANR 4
See also CA 9-12R
See also SATA 8, 21

Forrest, Leon 1937- .... **CLC 4**
See also CA 89-92
See also DLB 33

Forster, E(dward) M(organ) 1879-1970 .... **CLC 1, 2, 3, 4, 9, 10, 13, 15, 22**
See also CAP 1
See also CA 13-14
See also obituary CA 25-28R
See also DLB 34

Forsyth, Frederick 1938- .... **CLC 2, 5**
See also CA 85-88

Forten (Grimk), Charlotte L(ottie) 1837-1914 .... **TCLC 16**

Foscolo, Ugo 1778-1827 .... **NCLC 8**

Fosse, Bob 1925- .... **CLC 20**
See also Fosse, Robert Louis

Fosse, Robert Louis 1925-
See Bob Fosse
See also CA 110

Foucault, Michel 1926-1984 .... **CLC 31, 34**
See also CA 105
See also obituary CA 113

Fouqué, Friedrich (Heinrich Karl) de La Motte 1777-1843 .... **NCLC 2**

Fournier, Henri Alban 1886-1914
See Alain-Fournier
See also CA 104

Fournier, Pierre 1916- .... **CLC 11**
See also CA 89-92

Fowles, John (Robert) 1926- .... **CLC 1, 2, 3, 4, 6, 9, 10, 15, 33**
See also CA 5-8R
See also DLB 14
See also SATA 22

Fox, Paula 1923- . . . . **CLC 2, 8**
See also CLR 1
See also CA 73-76
See also SATA 17

Fox, William Price (Jr.) 1926- . . . . . . **CLC 22**
See also CANR 11
See also CA 17-20R
See also DLB 2
See also DLB-Y 81

Frame (Clutha), Janet (Paterson)
1924- . . . . **CLC 2, 3, 6, 22**
See also Clutha, Janet Paterson Frame

France, Anatole 1844-1924 . . . . **TCLC 9**
See also Thibault, Jacques Anatole Francois

Francis, Dick 1920- . . . . **CLC 2, 22**
See also CANR 9
See also CA 5-8R

Francis, Robert (Churchill)
1901- . . . . **CLC 15**
See also CANR 1
See also CA 1-4R

Frank, Anne 1929-1945 . . . . **TCLC 17**
See also CA 113

Franklin, (Stella Maria Sarah) Miles
1879-1954 . . . . **TCLC 7**
See also CA 104

Fraser, Antonia (Pakenham)
1932- . . . . **CLC 32**
See also CA 85-88
See also SATA 32

Fraser, George MacDonald
1925- . . . . **CLC 7**
See also CANR 2
See also CA 45-48

Frayn, Michael 1933- . . . . **CLC 3, 7, 31**
See also CA 5-8R
See also DLB 13, 14

Frederic, Harold 1856-1898 . . . . . . **NCLC 10**
See also DLB 12, 23

Fredro, Aleksander 1793-1876 . . . . **NCLC 8**

Freeman, Douglas Southall
1886-1953 . . . . **TCLC 11**
See also CA 109
See also DLB 17

Freeman, Mary (Eleanor) Wilkins
1852-1930 . . . . **TCLC 9**
See also CA 106
See also DLB 12

French, Marilyn 1929- . . . . **CLC 10, 18**
See also CANR 3
See also CA 69-72

Freneau, Philip Morin
1752-1832 . . . . **NCLC 1**
See also DLB 37

Friedman, B(ernard) H(arper)
1926- . . . . **CLC 7**
See also CANR 3
See also CA 1-4R

Friedman, Bruce Jay 1930- . . . . . . **CLC 3, 5**
See also CA 9-12R
See also DLB 2, 28

Friel, Brian 1929- . . . . **CLC 5**
See also CA 21-24R
See also DLB 13

Friis-Baastad, Babbis (Ellinor)
1921-1970 . . . . **CLC 12**
See also CA 17-20R
See also SATA 7

Frisch, Max (Rudolf)
1911- . . . . **CLC 3, 9, 14, 18, 32**
See also CA 85-88

Fromentin, Eugène (Samuel Auguste)
1820-1876 . . . . **NCLC 10**

Frost, Robert (Lee)
1874-1963 . . . . . . **CLC 1, 3, 4, 9, 10, 13, 15, 26, 34**
See also CA 89-92
See also SATA 14

Fry, Christopher 1907- . . . . . . **CLC 2, 10, 14**
See also CANR 9
See also CA 17-20R
See also DLB 13

Frye, (Herman) Northrop
1912- . . . . **CLC 24**
See also CANR 8
See also CA 5-8R

Fuchs, Daniel 1909- . . . . **CLC 8, 22**
See also CA 81-84
See also DLB 9, 26, 28

Fuchs, Daniel 1934- . . . . **CLC 34**
See also CANR 14
See also CA 37-40R

Fuentes, Carlos
1928- . . . . **CLC 3, 8, 10, 13, 22**
See also CANR 10
See also CA 69-72
See also AITN 2

Fugard, Athol 1932- . . . . . . **CLC 5, 9, 14, 25**
See also CA 85-88

Fuller, Charles (H., Jr.) 1939- . . . . . **CLC 25**
See also CA 108, 112
See also DLB 38

Fuller, (Sarah) Margaret
1810-1850 . . . . **NCLC 5**
See also Ossoli, Sarah Margaret (Fuller marchesa d')
See also DLB 1

Fuller, Roy (Broadbent)
1912- . . . . **CLC 4, 28**
See also CA 5-8R
See also DLB 15, 20

Gadda, Carlo Emilio
1893-1973 . . . . **CLC 11**
See also CA 89-92

Gaddis, William
1922- . . . . **CLC 1, 3, 6, 8, 10, 19**
See also CA 17-20R
See also DLB 2

Gaines, Ernest J. 1933- . . . . . **CLC 3, 11, 18**
See also CANR 6
See also CA 9-12R
See also DLB 2, 33
See also DLB-Y 80
See also AITN 1

Gale, Zona 1874-1938 . . . . **TCLC 7**
See also CA 105
See also DLB 9

Gallagher, Tess 1943- . . . . **CLC 18**
See also CA 106

Gallant, Mavis 1922- . . . . **CLC 7, 18**
See also CA 69-72

Gallant, Roy A(rthur) 1924- . . . . **CLC 17**
See also CANR 4
See also CA 5-8R
See also SATA 4

Gallico, Paul (William)
1897-1976 . . . . **CLC 2**
See also CA 5-8R
See also obituary CA 69-72
See also SATA 13
See also DLB 9
See also AITN 1

Galsworthy, John 1867-1933 . . . . . . **TCLC 1**
See also CA 104
See also DLB 10, 34

Galt, John 1779-1839 . . . . **NCLC 1**

Gann, Ernest K(ellogg) 1910- . . . . . . **CLC 23**
See also CANR 1
See also CA 1-4R
See also AITN 1

García Lorca, Federico
1899-1936 . . . . **TCLC 1, 7**
See also CA 104

García Márquez, Gabriel
1928- . . . . **CLC 2, 3, 8, 10, 15, 27**
See also CANR 10
See also CA 33-36R

Gardner, John (Champlin, Jr.)
1933-1982 . . . . **CLC 2, 3, 5, 7, 8, 10, 18, 28, 34**
See also CA 65-68
See also obituary CA 107
See also obituary SATA 31
See also DLB 2
See also DLB-Y 82
See also AITN 1

Gardner, John (Edmund)
1926- . . . . **CLC 30**
See also CA 103
See also AITN 1

Garfield, Leon 1921- . . . . **CLC 12**
See also CA 17-20R
See also SATA 1, 32

Garland, (Hannibal) Hamlin
1860-1940 . . . . **TCLC 3**
See also CA 104
See also DLB 12

Garneau, Hector (de) Saint Denys
1912-1943 . . . . **TCLC 13**
See also CA 111

Garner, Alan 1935- . . . . **CLC 17**
See also CA 73-76
See also SATA 18

Garner, Hugh 1913-1979 . . . . **CLC 13**
See also CA 69-72

Garnett, David 1892-1981 . . . . **CLC 3**
See also CA 5-8R
See also obituary CA 103
See also DLB 34

Garrett, George (Palmer)
1929- . . . . **CLC 3, 11**
See also CANR 1
See also CA 1-4R
See also DLB 2, 5
See also DLB-Y 83

Garrigue, Jean 1914-1972 . . . . **CLC 2, 8**
See also CA 5-8R
See also obituary CA 37-40R

Gary, Romain 1914-1980..........**CLC 25**
See also Kacew, Romain

Gascar, Pierre 1916-
See Fournier, Pierre

Gaskell, Elizabeth Cleghorn 1810-1865..................**NCLC 5**
See also DLB 21

Gass, William H(oward) 1924-.............**CLC 1, 2, 8, 11, 15**
See also CA 17-20R
See also DLB 2

Gautier, Théophile 1811-1872.....**NCLC 1**

Gaye, Marvin (Pentz) 1939-1984....................**CLC 26**
See also obituary CA 112

Gee, Maurice (Gough) 1931-.......**CLC 29**
See also CA 97-100

Gelbart, Larry (Simon) 1923-......**CLC 21**
See also CA 73-76

Gelber, Jack 1932-..........**CLC 1, 6, 14**
See also CANR 2
See also CA 1-4R
See also DLB 7

Gellhorn, Martha (Ellis) 1908-.....**CLC 14**
See also CA 77-80
See also DLB-Y 82

Genet, Jean 1910-.....**CLC 1, 2, 5, 10, 14**
See also CA 13-16R

Gent, Peter 1942-.................**CLC 29**
See also CA 89-92
See also DLB-Y 82
See also AITN 1

George, Jean Craighead 1919-.....**CLC 35**
See also CLR 1
See also CA 5-8R
See also SATA 2

George, Stefan (Anton) 1868-1933................**TCLC 2, 14**
See also CA 104

Gerhardi, William (Alexander) 1895-1977
See Gerhardie, William (Alexander)

Gerhardie, William (Alexander) 1895-1977.....................**CLC 5**
See also CA 25-28R
See also obituary CA 73-76
See also DLB 36

Gertler, T(rudy) 19?-.............**CLC 34**

Gessner, Friedrike Victoria 1910-1980
See Adamson, Joy(-Friederike Victoria)

Ghelderode, Michel de 1898-1962.................**CLC 6, 11**
See also CA 85-88

Ghiselin, Brewster 1903-..........**CLC 23**
See also CANR 13
See also CA 13-16R

Giacosa, Giuseppe 1847-1906.....**TCLC 7**
See also CA 104

Gibbon, Lewis Grassic 1901-1935..................**TCLC 4**
See also Mitchell, James Leslie

Gibran, (Gibran) Kahlil 1883-1931................**TCLC 1, 9**
See also CA 104

Gibson, William 1914-............**CLC 23**
See also CANR 9
See also CA 9-12R
See also DLB 7

Gide, André (Paul Guillaume) 1869-1951................**TCLC 5, 12**
See also CA 104

Gifford, Barry (Colby) 1946-.......**CLC 34**
See also CANR 9
See also CA 65-68

Gilbert, (Sir) W(illiam) S(chwenck) 1836-1911..................**TCLC 3**
See also CA 104
See also SATA 36

Gilbreth, Ernestine 1908-
See Carey, Ernestine Gilbreth

Gilbreth, Frank B(unker), Jr. 1911-
See Gilbreth, Frank B(unker), Jr. and Carey, Ernestine Gilbreth
See also CA 9-12R
See also SATA 2

Gilbreth, Frank B(unker), Jr. 1911- and **Carey, Ernestine Gilbreth** 1908-........................**CLC 17**

Gilchrist, Ellen 1939-.............**CLC 34**
See also CA 113

Gilliam, Terry (Vance) 1940-
See Monty Python
See also CA 108, 113

Gilliatt, Penelope (Ann Douglass) 1932-.................**CLC 2, 10, 13**
See also CA 13-16R
See also DLB 14
See also AITN 2

Gilman, Charlotte (Anna) Perkins (Stetson) 1860-1935..................**TCLC 9**
See also CA 106

Gilmour, David 1944-
See Pink Floyd

Gilroy, Frank D(aniel) 1925-........**CLC 2**
See also CA 81-84
See also DLB 7

Ginsberg, Allen 1926-............**CLC 1, 2, 3, 4, 6, 13**
See also CANR 2
See also CA 1-4R
See also DLB 5, 16
See also AITN 1

Ginzburg, Natalia 1916-........**CLC 5, 11**
See also CA 85-88

Giono, Jean 1895-1970.........**CLC 4, 11**
See also CANR 2
See also CA 45-48
See also obituary CA 29-32R

Giovanni, Nikki 1943-........**CLC 2, 4, 19**
See also CLR 6
See also CA 29-32R
See also SATA 24
See also DLB 5
See also AITN 1

Giovene, Andrea 1904-.............**CLC 7**
See also CA 85-88

Gippius, Zinaida (Nikolayevna) 1869-1945
See also Hippius, Zinaida
See also CA 106

Giraudoux, (Hippolyte) Jean 1882-1944.................**TCLC 2, 7**
See also CA 104

Gironella, José María 1917-........**CLC 11**
See also CA 101

Gissing, George (Robert) 1857-1903..................**TCLC 3**
See also CA 105
See also DLB 18

Glanville, Brian (Lester) 1931-......**CLC 6**
See also CANR 3
See also CA 5-8R
See also DLB 15

Glasgow, Ellen (Anderson Gholson) 1873?-1945................**TCLC 2, 7**
See also CA 104
See also DLB 9, 12

Glassco, John 1909-1981...........**CLC 9**
See also CA 13-16R
See also obituary CA 102

Glissant, Edouard 1928-...........**CLC 10**

Glück, Louise 1943-...........**CLC 7, 22**
See also CA 33-36R
See also DLB 5

Godard, Jean-Luc 1930-...........**CLC 20**
See also CA 93-96

Godwin, Gail 1937-.......**CLC 5, 8, 22, 31**
See also CA 29-32R
See also DLB 6

Goethe, Johann Wolfgang von 1749-1832...................**NCLC 4**

Gogarty, Oliver St. John 1878-1957..................**TCLC 15**
See also CA 109
See also DLB 15, 19

Gogol, Nikolai (Vasilyevich) 1809-1852...................**NCLC 5**

Gökçeli, Yasar Kemal 1923-
See Kemal, Yashar

Gold, Herbert 1924-.........**CLC 4, 7, 14**
See also CA 9-12R
See also DLB 2
See also DLB-Y 81

Goldbarth, Albert 1948-............**CLC 5**
See also CANR 6
See also CA 53-56

Goldberg, Anato 19?-.............**CLC 34**

Golding, William (Gerald) 1911-........**CLC 1, 2, 3, 8, 10, 17, 27**
See also CANR 13
See also CA 5-8R
See also DLB 15

Goldman, Emma 1869-1940.....**TCLC 13**
See also CA 110

Goldman, William (W.) 1931-.......**CLC 1**
See also CA 9-12R

Goldmann, Lucien 1913-1970......**CLC 24**
See also CAP 2
See also CA 25-28

Goldsberry, Steven 1949-..........**CLC 34**

Goldsmith, Oliver 1728(?)-1774......**LC 2**
See also SATA 26
See also DLB 39

Harris, (Theodore) Wilson 1921- .... CLC 25
See also CANR 11
See also CA 65-68

Harrison, James (Thomas) 1937-
See Harrison, Jim
See also CANR 8
See also CA 13-16R

Harrison, Jim 1937- .... CLC 6, 14, 33
See also Harrison, James (Thomas)
See also DLB-Y 82

Harriss, Will(ard Irvin) 1922- ...... CLC 34
See also CA 111

Harte, (Francis) Bret(t) 1836?-1902 .... TCLC 1
See also CA 104
See also SATA 26
See also DLB 12

Hartley, L(eslie) P(oles) 1895-1972 .... CLC 2, 22
See also CA 45-48
See also obituary CA 37-40R
See also DLB 15

Hartman, Geoffrey H. 1929- .... CLC 27

Haruf, Kent 19?- .... CLC 34

Harwood, Ronald 1934- .... CLC 32
See also CANR 4
See also CA 1-4R
See also DLB 13

Hašek, Jaroslav (Matej Frantisek) 1883-1923 .... TCLC 4
See also CA 104

Hass, Robert 1941- .... CLC 18
See also CA 111

Hauptmann, Gerhart (Johann Robert) 1862-1946 .... TCLC 4
See also CA 104

Havel, Václav 1936- .... CLC 25
See also CA 104

Haviaras, Stratis 1935- .... CLC 33
See also CA 105

Hawkes, John (Clendennin Burne, Jr.) 1925- ...... CLC 1, 2, 3, 4, 7, 9, 14, 15, 27
See also CANR 2
See also CA 1-4R
See also DLB 2, 7
See also DLB-Y 80

Hawthorne, Nathaniel 1804-1864 .... NCLC 2, 10
See also YABC 2
See also DLB 1

Hayden, Robert (Earl) 1913-1980 .... CLC 5, 9, 14
See also CA 69-72
See also obituary CA 97-100
See also SATA 19
See also obituary SATA 26
See also DLB 5

Haywood, Eliza (Fowler) 1693?-1756 .... LC 1
See also DLB 39

Hazzard, Shirley 1931- .... CLC 18
See also CANR 4
See also CA 9-12R
See also DLB-Y 82

H(ilda) D(oolittle) 1886-1961 .... CLC 3, 8, 14, 31, 34
See also Doolittle, Hilda

Head, Bessie 1937- .... CLC 25
See also CA 29-32R

Headon, (Nicky) Topper 1956?-
See The Clash

Heaney, Seamus (Justin) 1939- .... CLC 5, 7, 14, 25
See also CA 85-88

Hearn, (Patricio) Lafcadio (Tessima Carlos) 1850-1904 .... TCLC 9
See also CA 105
See also DLB 12

Heat Moon, William Least 1939- .... CLC 29

Hébert, Anne 1916- .... CLC 4, 13, 29
See also CA 85-88

Hecht, Anthony (Evan) 1923- .... CLC 8, 13, 19
See also CANR 6
See also CA 9-12R
See also DLB 5

Hecht, Ben 1894-1964 .... CLC 8
See also CA 85-88
See also DLB 7, 9, 25, 26, 28

Heidegger, Martin 1889-1976 ...... CLC 24
See also CA 81-84
See also obituary CA 65-68

Heidenstam, (Karl Gustaf) Verner von 1859-1940 .... TCLC 5
See also CA 104

Heifner, Jack 1946- .... CLC 11
See also CA 105

Heilbrun, Carolyn G(old) 1926- .... CLC 25
See also CANR 1
See also CA 45-48

Heine, Harry 1797-1856
See Heine, Heinrich

Heine, Heinrich 1797-1856 .... NCLC 4

Heiney, Donald (William) 1921-
See Harris, MacDonald
See also CANR 3
See also CA 1-4R

Heinlein, Robert A(nson) 1907- .... CLC 1, 3, 8, 14, 26
See also CANR 1
See also CA 1-4R
See also SATA 9
See also DLB 8

Heller, Joseph 1923- .... CLC 1, 3, 5, 8, 11
See also CANR 8
See also CA 5-8R
See also DLB 2, 28
See also DLB-Y 80
See also AITN 1

Hellman, Lillian (Florence) 1905?-1984 ..... CLC 2, 4, 8, 14, 18, 34
See also CA 13-16R
See also obituary CA 112
See also DLB 7
See also DLB-Y 84
See also AITN 1, 2

Helprin, Mark 1947- ..... CLC 7, 10, 22, 32
See also CA 81-84

Hemingway, Ernest (Miller) 1899-1961 ...... CLC 1, 3, 6, 8, 10, 13, 19, 30, 34
See also CA 77-80
See also DLB 4, 9
See also DLB-Y 81
See also DLB-DS 1
See also AITN 2

Henley, Beth 1952- .... CLC 23
See also Henley, Elizabeth Becker

Henley, Elizabeth Becker 1952-
See Henley, Beth
See also CA 107

Henley, William Ernest 1849-1903 .... TCLC 8
See also CA 105
See also DLB 19

Hennissart, Martha
See Lathen, Emma
See also CA 85-88

Henry, O. 1862-1909? .... TCLC 1
See also Porter, William Sydney

Hentoff, Nat(han Irving) 1925- ..... CLC 26
See also CLR 1
See also CANR 5
See also CA 1-4R
See also SATA 27

Heppenstall, (John) Rayner 1911-1981 .... CLC 10
See also CA 1-4R
See also obituary CA 103

Herbert, Frank (Patrick) 1920- .... CLC 12, 23, 35
See also CANR 5
See also CA 53-56
See also SATA 9, 37
See also DLB 8

Herbert, Zbigniew 1924- .... CLC 9
See also CA 89-92

Herbst, Josephine 1897-1969 .... CLC 34
See also CA 5-8R
See also obituary CA 25-28R
See also DLB 9

Herder, Johann Gottfried von 1744-1803 .... NCLC 8

Hergesheimer, Joseph 1880-1954 .... TCLC 11
See also CA 109
See also DLB 9

Herlagñez, Pablo de 1844-1896
See Verlaine, Paul (Marie)

Herlihy, James Leo 1927- .... CLC 6
See also CANR 2
See also CA 1-4R

Herriot, James 1916- .... CLC 12
See also Wight, James Alfred

Hersey, John (Richard) 1914- .... CLC 1, 2, 7, 9
See also CA 17-20R
See also SATA 25
See also DLB 6

Herzen, Aleksandr Ivanovich 1812-1870 .... NCLC 10

Herzog, Werner 1942- .... CLC 16
See also CA 89-92

Kornbluth, C(yril) M. 1923-1958 .... **TCLC 8**
See also CA 105
See also DLB 8

Kosinski, Jerzy (Nikodem) 1933- .... **CLC 1, 2, 3, 6, 10, 15**
See also CANR 9
See also CA 17-20R
See also DLB 2
See also DLB-Y 82

Kostelanetz, Richard (Cory) 1940- .... **CLC 28**
See also CA 13-16R

Kostrowitzki, Wilhelm Apollinaris de 1880-1918
See Apollinaire, Guillaume
See also CA 104

Kotlowitz, Robert 1924- .... **CLC 4**
See also CA 33-36R

Kotzwinkle, William 1938- .... **CLC 5, 14, 35**
See also CLR 6
See also CANR 3
See also CA 45-48
See also SATA 24

Kozol, Jonathan 1936- .... **CLC 17**
See also CA 61-64

Kozoll, Michael 1940?-
See Bochco, Steven and Kozoll, Michael

Kramer, Kathryn 19?- .... **CLC 34**

Krasicki, Ignacy 1735-1801 .... **NCLC 8**

Krasiński, Zygmunt 1812-1859 .... **NCLC 4**

Kraus, Karl 1874-1936 .... **TCLC 5**
See also CA 104

Kristofferson, Kris 1936- .... **CLC 26**
See also CA 104

Krleža, Miroslav 1893-1981 .... **CLC 8**
See also CA 97-100
See also obituary CA 105

Kroetsch, Robert 1927- .... **CLC 5, 23**
See also CANR 8
See also CA 17-20R

Krotkov, Yuri 1917- .... **CLC 19**
See also CA 102

Krumgold, Joseph (Quincy) 1908-1980 .... **CLC 12**
See also CANR 7
See also CA 9-12R
See also obituary CA 101
See also SATA 1
See also obituary SATA 23

Krutch, Joseph Wood 1893-1970 .... **CLC 24**
See also CANR 4
See also CA 1-4R
See also obituary CA 25-28R

Krylov, Ivan Andreevich 1768?-1844 .... **NCLC 1**

Kubrick, Stanley 1928- .... **CLC 16**
See also CA 81-84
See also DLB 26

Kumin, Maxine (Winokur) 1925- .... **CLC 5, 13, 28**
See also CANR 1
See also CA 1-4R
See also SATA 12
See also DLB 5
See also AITN 2

Kundera, Milan 1929- .... **CLC 4, 9, 19, 32**
See also CA 85-88

Kunitz, Stanley J(asspon) 1905- .... **CLC 6, 11, 14**
See also CA 41-44R

Kunze, Reiner 1933- .... **CLC 10**
See also CA 93-96

Kuprin, Aleksandr (Ivanovich) 1870-1938 .... **TCLC 5**
See also CA 104

Kurosawa, Akira 1910- .... **CLC 16**
See also CA 101

Kuttner, Henry 1915-1958 .... **TCLC 10**
See also CA 107
See also DLB 8

Kuzma, Greg 1944- .... **CLC 7**
See also CA 33-36R

Labrunie, Gérard 1808-1855
See Nerval, Gérard de

Laclos, Pierre Ambroise François Choderlos de 1741-1803 .... **NCLC 4**

La Fayette, Marie (Madelaine Pioche de la Vergne, Comtesse) de 1634-1693 .... **LC 2**

Laforgue, Jules 1860-1887 .... **NCLC 5**

Lagerkvist, Pär (Fabian) 1891-1974 .... **CLC 7, 10, 13**
See also CA 85-88
See also obituary CA 49-52

Lagerlöf, Selma (Ottiliana Lovisa) 1858-1940 .... **TCLC 4**
See also CLR 7
See also CA 108
See also SATA 15

La Guma, (Justin) Alex(ander) 1925- .... **CLC 19**
See also CA 49-52

Lamb, Charles 1775-1834 .... **NCLC 10**
See also SATA 17

Lamming, George (William) 1927- .... **CLC 2, 4**
See also CA 85-88

LaMoore, Louis Dearborn 1908?-
See L'Amour, Louis (Dearborn)

L'Amour, Louis (Dearborn) 1908- .... **CLC 25**
See also CANR 3
See also CA 1-4R
See also DLB-Y 80
See also AITN 2

Lampedusa, (Prince) Giuseppe (Maria Fabrizio) Tomasi di 1896-1957 .... **TCLC 13**
See also CA 111

Landis, John (David) 1950- .... **CLC 26**
See also CA 112

Landolfi, Tommaso 1908- .... **CLC 11**

Landwirth, Heinz 1927-
See Lind, Jakov
See also CANR 7

Lane, Patrick 1939- .... **CLC 25**
See also CA 97-100

Lang, Andrew 1844-1912 .... **TCLC 16**
See also CA 114
See also SATA 16

Lang, Fritz 1890-1976 .... **CLC 20**
See also CA 77-80
See also obituary CA 69-72

Langer, Elinor 1939- .... **CLC 34**

Lanier, Sidney 1842-1881 .... **NCLC 6**
See also SATA 18

Larbaud, Valéry 1881-1957 .... **TCLC 9**
See also CA 106

Lardner, Ring(gold Wilmer) 1885-1933 .... **TCLC 2, 14**
See also CA 104
See also DLB 11, 25

Larkin, Philip (Arthur) 1922- .... **CLC 3, 5, 8, 9, 13, 18, 33**
See also CA 5-8R
See also DLB 27

Larson, Charles R(aymond) 1938- .... **CLC 31**
See also CANR 4
See also CA 53-56

Latham, Jean Lee 1902- .... **CLC 12**
See also CANR 7
See also CA 5-8R
See also SATA 2
See also AITN 1

Lathen, Emma .... **CLC 2**
See also Hennissart, Martha
See also Latsis, Mary J(ane)

Latsis, Mary J(ane)
See Lathen, Emma
See also CA 85-88

Lattimore, Richmond (Alexander) 1906-1984 .... **CLC 3**
See also CANR 1
See also CA 1-4R
See also obituary CA 112

Laurence, (Jean) Margaret (Wemyss) 1926- .... **CLC 3, 6, 13**
See also CA 5-8R

Lavin, Mary 1912- .... **CLC 4, 18**
See also CA 9-12R
See also DLB 15

Lawrence, D(avid) H(erbert) 1885-1930 .... **TCLC 2, 9, 16**
See also CA 104
See also DLB 10, 19, 36

Lawrence, T(homas) E(dward) 1888-1935 .... **TCLC 18**
See also CA 115

Laxness, Halldór (Kiljan) 1902- .... **CLC 25**
See also Gudjonsson, Halldór Kiljan

Laye, Camara 1928-1980 .... **CLC 4**
See also CA 85-88
See also obituary CA 97-100

Layton, Irving (Peter) 1912- .... **CLC 2, 15**
See also CANR 2
See also CA 1-4R

Author Index

Oppen, George
1908-1984 .... **CLC 7, 13, 34**
See also CANR 8
See also CA 13-16R
See also obituary CA 113
See also DLB 5

Orlovitz, Gil 1918-1973 .... **CLC 22**
See also CA 77-80
See also obituary CA 45-48
See also DLB 2, 5

Ortega y Gasset, José
1883-1955 .... **TCLC 9**
See also CA 106

Orton, Joe 1933?-1967 .... **CLC 4, 13**
See also Orton, John Kingsley
See also DLB 13

Orton, John Kingsley 1933?-1967
See Orton, Joe
See also CA 85-88

Orwell, George
1903-1950 .... **TCLC 2, 6, 15**
See also Blair, Eric Arthur
See also DLB 15

Osborne, John (James)
1929- .... **CLC 1, 2, 5, 11**
See also CA 13-16R
See also DLB 13

Osceola 1885-1962
See Dinesen, Isak
See also Blixen, Karen (Christentze Dinesen)

Oshima, Nagisa 1932- .... **CLC 20**

Ossoli, Sarah Margaret (Fuller marchesa d')
1810-1850
See Fuller, (Sarah) Margaret
See also SATA 25

Otero, Blas de 1916- .... **CLC 11**
See also CA 89-92

Owen, Wilfred (Edward Salter)
1893-1918 .... **TCLC 5**
See also CA 104
See also DLB 20

Owens, Rochelle 1936- .... **CLC 8**
See also CAAS 2
See also CA 17-20R

Owl, Sebastian 1939-
See Thompson, Hunter S(tockton)

Oz, Amos 1939- ...... **CLC 5, 8, 11, 27, 33**
See also CA 53-56

Ozick, Cynthia 1928- .... **CLC 3, 7, 28**
See also CA 17-20R
See also DLB 28
See also DLB-Y 82

Ozu, Yasujiro 1903-1963 .... **CLC 16**
See also CA 112

Pa Chin 1904- .... **CLC 18**
See also Li Fei-kan

Pack, Robert 1929- .... **CLC 13**
See also CANR 3
See also CA 1-4R
See also DLB 5

Padgett, Lewis 1915-1958
See Kuttner, Henry

Page, Jimmy 1944-
See Page, Jimmy and Plant, Robert

Page, Jimmy 1944- and **Plant, Robert**
1948- .... **CLC 12**

Page, P(atricia) K(athleen)
1916- .... **CLC 7, 18**
See also CANR 4
See also CA 53-56

Paget, Violet 1856-1935
See Lee, Vernon
See also CA 104

Palamas, Kostes 1859-1943 .... **TCLC 5**
See also CA 105

Palazzeschi, Aldo 1885-1974 .... **CLC 11**
See also CA 89-92
See also obituary CA 53-56

Paley, Grace 1922- .... **CLC 4, 6**
See also CANR 13
See also CA 25-28R
See also DLB 28
See also AITN 1

Palin, Michael 1943-
See Monty Python
See also CA 107

Pancake, Breece Dexter 1952-1979
See Pancake, Breece D'J

Pancake, Breece D'J
1952-1979 .... **CLC 29**
See also obituary CA 109

Parker, Dorothy (Rothschild)
1893-1967 .... **CLC 15**
See also CAP 2
See also CA 19-20
See also obituary CA 25-28R
See also DLB 11

Parker, Robert B(rown) 1932- ...... **CLC 27**
See also CANR 1
See also CA 49-52

Parks, Gordon (Alexander Buchanan)
1912- .... **CLC 1, 16**
See also CA 41-44R
See also SATA 8
See also DLB 33
See also AITN 2

Parra, Nicanor 1914- .... **CLC 2**
See also CA 85-88

Pasolini, Pier Paolo 1922-1975 ..... **CLC 20**
See also CA 93-96
See also obituary CA 61-64

Pastan, Linda (Olenik) 1932- .... **CLC 27**
See also CA 61-64
See also DLB 5

Pasternak, Boris
1890-1960 .... **CLC 7, 10, 18**

Patchen, Kenneth
1911-1972 .... **CLC 1, 2, 18**
See also CANR 3
See also CA 1-4R
See also obituary CA 33-36R
See also DLB 16

Pater, Walter (Horatio)
1839-1894 .... **NCLC 7**

Paterson, Katherine (Womeldorf)
1932- .... **CLC 12, 30**
See also CLR 7
See also CA 21-24R
See also SATA 13

Patmore, Coventry Kersey Dighton
1823-1896 .... **NCLC 9**
See also DLB 35

Paton, Alan (Stewart)
1903- .... **CLC 4, 10, 25**
See also CAP 1
See also CA 15-16
See also SATA 11

Paulding, James Kirke
1778-1860 .... **NCLC 2**
See also DLB 3

Pavese, Cesare 1908-1950 .... **TCLC 3**
See also CA 104

Payne, Alan 1932-
See Jakes, John (William)

Paz, Octavio 1914- ..... **CLC 3, 4, 6, 10, 19**
See also CA 73-76

Peake, Mervyn 1911-1968 .... **CLC 7**
See also CANR 3
See also CA 5-8R
See also obituary CA 25-28R
See also SATA 23
See also DLB 15

Pearce, (Ann) Philippa 1920- .... **CLC 21**
See also Christie, (Ann) Philippa
See also CA 5-8R
See also SATA 1

Pearl, Eric 1934-
See Elman, Richard

Peck, John 1941- .... **CLC 3**
See also CANR 3
See also CA 49-52

Peck, Richard 1934- .... **CLC 21**
See also CA 85-88
See also SATA 18

Peck, Robert Newton 1928- .... **CLC 17**
See also CA 81-84
See also SATA 21

Peckinpah, (David) Sam(uel)
1925-1984 .... **CLC 20**
See also CA 109
See also obituary CA 114

Pedersen, Knut 1859-1952
See Hamsun, Knut
See also CA 104

Péguy, Charles (Pierre)
1873-1914 .... **TCLC 10**
See also CA 107

Percy, Walker
1916- .... **CLC 2, 3, 6, 8, 14, 18**
See also CANR 1
See also CA 1-4R
See also DLB 2
See also DLB-Y 80

Pereda, José María de
1833-1906 .... **TCLC 16**

Perelman, S(idney) J(oseph)
1904-1979 .... **CLC 3, 5, 9, 15, 23**
See also CA 73-76
See also obituary CA 89-92
See also DLB 11
See also AITN 1, 2

Peretz, Isaac Leib
1852(?)-1915 .... **TCLC 16**
See also CA 109

Perrault, Charles 1628-1703 .... **LC 2**
See also SATA 25

Author Index

Sarraute, Nathalie 1902- . . . . **CLC 1, 2, 4, 8, 10, 31**
See also CA 9-12R

Sarton, (Eleanor) May 1912- . . . . **CLC 4, 14**
See also CANR 1
See also CA 1-4R
See also SATA 36
See also DLB-Y 81

Sartre, Jean-Paul 1905-1980 . . . . . **CLC 1, 4, 7, 9, 13, 18, 24**
See also CA 9-12R
See also obituary CA 97-100

Saura, Carlos 1932- . . . . **CLC 20**
See also CA 114

Sauser-Hall, Frédéric-Louis 1887-1961
See Cendrars, Blaise
See also CA 102
See also obituary CA 93-96

Sayers, Dorothy L(eigh) 1893-1957 . . . . **TCLC 2, 15**
See also CA 104
See also DLB 10, 36

Sayles, John (Thomas) 1950- . . . . **CLC 7, 10, 14**
See also CA 57-60

Scammell, Michael 19?- . . . . **CLC 34**

Schaeffer, Susan Fromberg 1941- . . . . **CLC 6, 11, 22**
See also CA 49-52
See also SATA 22
See also DLB 28

Schell, Jonathan 1943- . . . . **CLC 35**
See also CANR 12
See also CA 73-76

Scherer, Jean-Marie Maurice 1920-
See Rohmer, Eric
See also CA 110

Schevill, James (Erwin) 1920- . . . . **CLC 7**
See also CA 5-8R

Schisgal, Murray (Joseph) 1926- . . . . **CLC 6**
See also CA 21-24R

Schlee, Ann 1934- . . . . **CLC 35**
See also CA 101
See also SATA 36

Schmitz, Ettore 1861-1928
See Svevo, Italo
See also CA 104

Schneider, Leonard Alfred 1925-1966
See Bruce, Lenny
See also CA 89-92

Schnitzler, Arthur 1862-1931 . . . . . **TCLC 4**
See also CA 104

Schorer, Mark 1908-1977 . . . . **CLC 9**
See also CANR 7
See also CA 5-8R
See also obituary CA 73-76

Schrader, Paul (Joseph) 1946- . . . . . . **CLC 26**
See also CA 37-40R

Schreiner (Cronwright), Olive (Emilie Albertina) 1855-1920 . . . . **TCLC 9**
See also CA 105
See also DLB 18

Schulberg, Budd (Wilson) 1914- . . . . . **CLC 7**
See also CA 25-28R
See also DLB 6, 26, 28
See also DLB-Y 81

Schulz, Bruno 1892-1942 . . . . **TCLC 5**
See also CA 115

Schulz, Charles M(onroe) 1922- . . . . **CLC 12**
See also CANR 6
See also CA 9-12R
See also SATA 10

Schuyler, James (Marcus) 1923- . . . . **CLC 5, 23**
See also CA 101
See also DLB 5

Schwartz, Delmore 1913-1966 . . . . **CLC 2, 4, 10**
See also CAP 2
See also CA 17-18
See also obituary CA 25-28R
See also DLB 28

Schwartz, Lynne Sharon 1939- . . . . . **CLC 31**
See also CA 103

Schwarz-Bart, André 1928- . . . . . . **CLC 2, 4**
See also CA 89-92

Schwarz-Bart, Simone 1938- . . . . **CLC 7**
See also CA 97-100

Sciascia, Leonardo 1921- . . . . **CLC 8, 9**
See also CA 85-88

Scoppettone, Sandra 1936- . . . . **CLC 26**
See also CA 5-8R
See also SATA 9

Scorsese, Martin 1942- . . . . **CLC 20**
See also CA 110, 114

Scotland, Jay 1932-
See Jakes, John (William)

Scott, Duncan Campbell 1862-1947 . . . . **TCLC 6**
See also CA 104

Scott, F(rancis) R(eginald) 1899-1985 . . . . **CLC 22**
See also CA 101
See also obituary CA 114

Scott, Paul (Mark) 1920-1978 . . . . **CLC 9**
See also CA 81-84
See also obituary CA 77-80
See also DLB 14

Scudéry, Madeleine de 1607-1701 . . . . . **LC 2**

Seare, Nicholas 1925-
See Trevanian
See also Whitaker, Rodney

Sebestyen, Igen 1924-
See Sebestyen, Ouida

Sebestyen, Ouida 1924- . . . . **CLC 30**
See also CA 107
See also SATA 39

Seelye, John 1931- . . . . **CLC 7**
See also CA 97-100

Seferiades, Giorgos Stylianou 1900-1971
See Seferis, George
See also CANR 5
See also CA 5-8R
See also obituary CA 33-36R

Seferis, George 1900-1971 . . . . . . **CLC 5, 11**
See also Seferiades, Giorgos Stylianou

Segal, Erich (Wolf) 1937- . . . . **CLC 3, 10**
See also CA 25-28R

Seger, Bob 1945- . . . . **CLC 35**

Seger, Robert Clark 1945-
See Seger, Bob

Seghers, Anna 1900- . . . . **CLC 7**
See Radvanyi, Netty

Seidel, Frederick (Lewis) 1936- . . . . . **CLC 18**
See also CANR 8
See also CA 13-16R
See also DLB-Y 84

Seifert, Jaroslav 1901- . . . . **CLC 34**

Selby, Hubert, Jr. 1928- . . . . **CLC 1, 2, 4, 8**
See also CA 13-16R
See also DLB 2

Sender, Ramón (José) 1902-1982 . . . . **CLC 8**
See also CANR 8
See also CA 5-8R
See also obituary CA 105

Serling, (Edward) Rod(man) 1924-1975
See also CA 65-68
See also obituary CA 57-60
See also DLB 26
See also AITN 1

Serpières 1907-
See Guillevic, (Eugène)

Service, Robert W(illiam) 1874-1958 . . . . **TCLC 15**
See also CA 115
See also SATA 20

Seton, Cynthia Propper 1926-1982 . . . . **CLC 27**
See also CANR-7
See also CA 5-8R
See also obituary CA 108

Settle, Mary Lee 1918- . . . . **CLC 19**
See also CAAS 1
See also CA 89-92
See also DLB 6

Sexton, Anne (Harvey) 1928-1974 . . . . **CLC 2, 4, 6, 8, 10, 15**
See also CANR 3
See also CA 1-4R
See also obituary CA 53-56
See also SATA 10
See also DLB 5

Shaara, Michael (Joseph) 1929- . . . . **CLC 15**
See also CA 102
See also DLB-Y 83
See also AITN 1

Shaffer, Anthony 1926- . . . . **CLC 19**
See also CA 110
See also DLB 13

Shaffer, Peter (Levin) 1926- . . . . **CLC 5, 14, 18**
See also CA 25-28R
See also DLB 13

Shalamov, Varlam (Tikhonovich) 1907?-1982 . . . . **CLC 18**
See also obituary CA 105

Shamlu, Ahmad 1925- . . . . **CLC 10**

Shange, Ntozake 1948- . . . . **CLC 8, 25**
See also CA 85-88
See also DLB 38

Sitwell, (Dame) Edith 1887-1964 .... CLC 2, 9
See also CA 9-12R
See also DLB 20

Sjoewall, Maj 1935-
See Wahlöö, Per
See also CA 65-68

Sjöwall, Maj 1935-
See Wahlöö, Per

Skelton, Robin 1925- .... CLC 13
See also CA 5-8R
See also AITN 2
See also DLB 27

Skolimowski, Jerzy 1938- .... CLC 20

Skolimowski, Yurek 1938-
See Skolimowski, Jerzy

Skrine, Mary Nesta 1904-
See Keane, Molly

Škvorecký, Josef (Vaclav) 1924- .... CLC 15
See also CAAS 1
See also CANR 10
See also CA 61-64

Slade, Bernard 1930- .... CLC 11
See also Newbound, Bernard Slade

Slaughter, Frank G(ill) 1908- .... CLC 29
See also CANR 5
See also CA 5-8R
See also AITN 2

Slavitt, David (R.) 1935- .... CLC 5, 14
See also CA 21-24R
See also DLB 5, 6

Slesinger, Tess 1905-1945 .... TCLC 10
See also CA 107

Slessor, Kenneth 1901-1971 .... CLC 14
See also CA 102
See also obituary CA 89-92

Smith, A(rthur) J(ames) M(arshall) 1902-1980 .... CLC 15
See also CANR 4
See also CA 1-4R
See also obituary CA 102

Smith, Betty (Wehner) 1896-1972 .... CLC 19
See also CA 5-8R
See also obituary CA 33-36R
See also SATA 6
See also DLB-Y 82

Smith, Cecil Lewis Troughton 1899-1966
See Forester, C(ecil) S(cott)

Smith, Dave 1942- .... CLC 22
See also Smith, David (Jeddie)
See also DLB 5

Smith, David (Jeddie) 1942-
See Smith, Dave
See also CANR 1
See also CA 49-52

Smith, Florence Margaret 1902-1971
See Smith, Stevie
See also CAP 2
See also CA 17-18
See also obituary CA 29-32R

Smith, Lee 1944- .... CLC 25
See also CA 114
See also DLB-Y 83

Smith, Martin Cruz 1942- .... CLC 25
See also CANR 6
See also CA 85-88

Smith, Martin William 1942-
See Smith, Martin Cruz

Smith, Patti 1946- .... CLC 12
See also CA 93-96

Smith, Sara Mahala Redway 1900-1972
See Benson, Sally

Smith, Stevie 1902-1971 .... CLC 3, 8, 25
See also Smith, Florence Margaret
See also DLB 20

Smith, Wilbur (Addison) 1933- .... CLC 33
See also CANR 7
See also CA 13-16R

Smith, William Jay 1918- .... CLC 6
See also CA 5-8R
See also SATA 2
See also DLB 5

Smollett, Tobias (George) 1721-1771 .... LC 2
See also DLB 39

Snodgrass, W(illiam) D(e Witt) 1926- .... CLC 2, 6, 10, 18
See also CANR 6
See also CA 1-4R
See also DLB 5

Snow, C(harles) P(ercy) 1905-1980 .... CLC 1, 4, 6, 9, 13, 19
See also CA 5-8R
See also obituary CA 101
See also DLB 15

Snyder, Gary 1930- .... CLC 1, 2, 5, 9, 32
See also CA 17-20R
See also DLB 5, 16

Snyder, Zilpha Keatley 1927- .... CLC 17
See also CA 9-12R
See also SATA 1, 28

Sokolov, Raymond 1941- .... CLC 7
See also CA 85-88

Sologub, Fyodor 1863-1927 .... TCLC 9
See also Teternikov, Fyodor Kuzmich

Solwoska, Mara 1929-
See French, Marilyn

Solzhenitsyn, Aleksandr I(sayevich) 1918- .... CLC 1, 2, 4, 7, 9, 10, 18, 26, 34
See also CA 69-72
See also AITN 1

Sommer, Scott 1951- .... CLC 25
See also CA 106

Sondheim, Stephen (Joshua) 1930- .... CLC 33
See also CA 103

Sontag, Susan 1933- .... CLC 1, 2, 10, 13, 31
See also CA 17-20R
See also DLB 2

Sorrentino, Gilbert 1929- .... CLC 3, 7, 14, 22
See also CANR 14
See also CA 77-80
See also DLB 5
See also DLB-Y 80

Soto, Gary 1952- .... CLC 32

Souster, (Holmes) Raymond 1921- .... CLC 5, 14
See also CANR 13
See also CA 13-16R

Southern, Terry 1926- .... CLC 7
See also CANR 1
See also CA 1-4R
See also DLB 2

Southey, Robert 1774-1843 .... NCLC 8

Soyinka, Wole 1934- .... CLC 3, 5, 14
See also CA 13-16R

Spacks, Barry 1931- .... CLC 14
See also CA 29-32R

Spark, Muriel (Sarah) 1918- .... CLC 2, 3, 5, 8, 13, 18
See also CANR 12
See also CA 5-8R
See also DLB 15

Spencer, Elizabeth 1921- .... CLC 22
See also CA 13-16R
See also SATA 14
See also DLB 6

Spencer, Scott 1945- .... CLC 30
See also CA 113

Spender, Stephen (Harold) 1909- .... CLC 1, 2, 5, 10
See also CA 9-12R
See also DLB 20

Spicer, Jack 1925-1965 .... CLC 8, 18
See also CA 85-88
See also DLB 5, 16

Spielberg, Peter 1929- .... CLC 6
See also CANR 4
See also CA 5-8R
See also DLB-Y 81

Spielberg, Steven 1947- .... CLC 20
See also CA 77-80
See also SATA 32

Spillane, Frank Morrison 1918-
See Spillane, Mickey
See also CA 25-28R

Spillane, Mickey 1918- .... CLC 3, 13
See also Spillane, Frank Morrison

Spitteler, Carl (Friedrich Georg) 1845-1924 .... TCLC 12
See also CA 109

Spivack, Kathleen (Romola Drucker) 1938- .... CLC 6
See also CA 49-52

Springsteen, Bruce 1949- .... CLC 17
See also CA 111

Spurling, Hilary 1940- .... CLC 34
See also CA 104

Staël-Holstein, Anne Louise Germaine Necker, Baronne de 1766-1817 .... NCLC 3

Stafford, Jean 1915-1979 .... CLC 4, 7, 19
See also CANR 3
See also CA 1-4R
See also obituary CA 85-88
See also obituary SATA 22
See also DLB 2

Stafford, William (Edgar) 1914- .... CLC 4, 7, 29
See also CANR 5
See also CA 5-8R
See also DLB 5

Author Index

Warner, Francis (Robert le Plastrier) 1937- .... **CLC 14**
See also CANR 11
See also CA 53-56

Warner, Sylvia Townsend 1893-1978 .... **CLC 7, 19**
See also CA 61-64
See also obituary CA 77-80
See also DLB 34

Warren, Robert Penn 1905- .... **CLC 1, 4, 6, 8, 10, 13, 18**
See also CANR 10
See also CA 13-16R
See also DLB 2
See also DLB-Y 80
See also AITN 1

Washington, Booker T(aliaferro) 1856-1915 .... **TCLC 10**
See also CA 114
See also SATA 28

Wassermann, Jakob 1873-1934 .... **TCLC 6**
See also CA 104

Wasserstein, Wendy 1950- .... **CLC 32**

Waters, Roger 1944-
See Pink Floyd

Wa Thiong'o, Ngugi 1938- .... **CLC 13**
See also Ngugi, James (Thiong'o)

Waugh, Auberon (Alexander) 1939- .... **CLC 7**
See also CANR 6
See also CA 45-48
See also DLB 14

Waugh, Evelyn (Arthur St. John) 1903-1966 ...... **CLC 1, 3, 8, 13, 19, 27**
See also CA 85-88
See also obituary CA 25-28R
See also DLB 15

Waugh, Harriet 1944- .... **CLC 6**
See also CA 85-88

Webb, Charles (Richard) 1939- ...... **CLC 7**
See also CA 25-28R

Webb, James H(enry), Jr. 1946- .... **CLC 22**
See also CA 81-84

Webb, Phyllis 1927- .... **CLC 18**
See also CA 104

Webber, Andrew Lloyd 1948-
See Rice, Tim and Webber, Andrew Lloyd

Weber, Lenora Mattingly 1895-1971 .... **CLC 12**
See also CAP 1
See also CA 19-20
See also obituary CA 29-32R
See also SATA 2
See also obituary SATA 26

Wedekind, (Benjamin) Frank(lin) 1864-1918 .... **TCLC 7**
See also CA 104

Weidman, Jerome 1913- .... **CLC 7**
See also CANR 1
See also CA 1-4R
See also DLB 28
See also AITN 2

Weinstein, Nathan Wallenstein
See West, Nathanael
See also CA 104

Weir, Peter 1944- .... **CLC 20**
See also CA 113

Weiss, Peter (Ulrich) 1916-1982 .... **CLC 3, 15**
See also CANR 3
See also CA 45-48
See also obituary CA 106

Weiss, Theodore (Russell) 1916- .... **CLC 3, 8, 14**
See also CAAS 2
See also CA 9-12R
See also DLB 5

Welch, James 1940- .... **CLC 6, 14**
See also CA 85-88

Weldon, Fay 1933- .... **CLC 6, 9, 11, 19**
See also CA 21-24R
See also DLB 14

Wellek, René 1903- .... **CLC 28**
See also CANR 8
See also CA 5-8R

Weller, Michael 1942- .... **CLC 10**
See also CA 85-88

Weller, Paul 1958- .... **CLC 26**

Welles, (George) Orson 1915- ...... **CLC 20**
See also CA 93-96

Wells, H(erbert) G(eorge) 1866-1946 .... **TCLC 6, 12**
See also CA 110
See also SATA 20
See also DLB 34

Wells, Rosemary .... **CLC 12**
See also CA 85-88
See also SATA 18

Welty, Eudora (Alice) 1909- .... **CLC 1, 2, 5, 14, 22, 33**
See also CA 9-12R
See also DLB 2

Werfel, Franz (V.) 1890-1945 ..... **TCLC 8**
See also CA 104

Wergeland, Henrik Arnold 1808-1845 .... **NCLC 5**

Wersba, Barbara 1932- .... **CLC 30**
See also CLR 3
See also CA 29-32R
See also SATA 1

Wertmüller, Lina 1928- .... **CLC 16**
See also CA 97-100

Wescott, Glenway 1901- .... **CLC 13**
See also CA 13-16R
See also DLB 4, 9

Wesker, Arnold 1932- .... **CLC 3, 5**
See also CANR 1
See also CA 1-4R
See also DLB 13

Wesley, Richard (Errol) 1945- .... **CLC 7**
See also CA 57-60
See also DLB 38

West, Jessamyn 1907-1984 ...... **CLC 7, 17**
See also CA 9-12R
See also obituary SATA 37
See also DLB 6
See also DLB-Y 84

West, Morris L(anglo) 1916- .... **CLC 6, 33**
See also CA 5-8R

West, Nathanael 1903?-1940 .... **TCLC 1, 14**
See Weinstein, Nathan Wallenstein
See also DLB 4, 9, 28

West, Paul 1930- .... **CLC 7, 14**
See also CA 13-16R
See also DLB 14

West, Rebecca 1892-1983 ..... **CLC 7, 9, 31**
See also CA 5-8R
See also obituary CA 109
See also DLB 36
See also DLB-Y 83

Westall, Robert (Atkinson) 1929- .... **CLC 17**
See also CA 69-72
See also SATA 23

Westlake, Donald E(dwin) 1933- .... **CLC 7, 33**
See also CA 17-20R

Whalen, Philip 1923- .... **CLC 6, 29**
See also CANR 5
See also CA 9-12R
See also DLB 16

Wharton, Edith (Newbold Jones) 1862-1937 .... **TCLC 3, 9**
See also CA 104
See also DLB 4, 9, 12

Wharton, William 1925- .... **CLC 18**
See also CA 93-96
See also DLB-Y 80

Wheelock, John Hall 1886-1978 .... **CLC 14**
See also CANR 14
See also CA 13-16R
See also obituary CA 77-80

Whelan, John 1900-
See O'Faoláin, Seán

Whitaker, Rodney 1925-
See Trevanian
See also CA 29-32R

White, E(lwyn) B(rooks) 1899- .... **CLC 10, 34**
See also CLR 1
See also CA 13-16R
See also SATA 2, 29
See also DLB 11, 22
See also AITN 2

White, Edmund III 1940- .... **CLC 27**
See also CANR 3
See also CA 45-48

White, Patrick (Victor Martindale) 1912- .... **CLC 3, 4, 5, 7, 9, 18**
See also CA 81-84

White, T(erence) H(anbury) 1906-1964 .... **CLC 30**
See also CA 73-76
See also SATA 12

White, Walter (Francis) 1893-1955 .... **TCLC 15**
See also CA 115

Whitehead, E(dward) A(nthony) 1933- .... **CLC 5**
See also CA 65-68

Whitman, Walt 1819-1892 .... **NCLC 4**
See also SATA 20
See also DLB 3

Wolfe, Gene (Rodman) 1931- ...... **CLC 25**
See also CANR 6
See also CA 57-60
See also DLB 8

Wolfe, Thomas (Clayton)
1900-1938 .... **TCLC 4, 13**
See also CA 104
See also DLB 9
See also DLB-DS 2

Wolfe, Thomas Kennerly, Jr. 1931-
See Wolfe, Tom
See also CANR 9
See also CA 13-16R

Wolfe, Tom 1931- ..... **CLC 1, 2, 9, 15, 35**
See also Wolfe, Thomas Kennerly, Jr.
See also AITN 2

Wolitzer, Hilma 1930- .... **CLC 17**
See also CA 65-68
See also SATA 31

Wonder, Stevie 1950- .... **CLC 12**
See also Morris, Steveland Judkins

Wong, Jade Snow 1922- .... **CLC 17**
See also CA 109

Woodcott, Keith 1934-
See Brunner, John (Kilian Houston)

Woolf, (Adeline) Virginia
1882-1941 .... **TCLC 1, 5**
See also CA 104
See also DLB 36

Woollcott, Alexander (Humphreys)
1887-1943 .... **TCLC 5**
See also CA 105
See also DLB 29

Wouk, Herman 1915- .... **CLC 1, 9**
See also CANR 6
See also CA 5-8R
See also DLB-Y 82

Wright, Charles 1935- ...... **CLC 6, 13, 28**
See also CA 29-32R
See also DLB-Y 82

Wright, James (Arlington)
1927-1980 .... **CLC 3, 5, 10, 28**
See also CANR 4
See also CA 49-52
See also obituary CA 97-100
See also DLB 5
See also AITN 2

Wright, Judith 1915- .... **CLC 11**
See also CA 13-16R
See also SATA 14

Wright, Richard (Nathaniel)
1908-1960 .... **CLC 1, 3, 4, 9, 14, 21**
See also CA 108
See also DLB-DS 2

Wright, Richard B(ruce) 1937- ...... **CLC 6**
See also CA 85-88

Wright, Rick 1945-
See Pink Floyd

Wright, Stephen 1946- .... **CLC 33**

Wu Ching-tzu 1701-1754 .... **LC 2**

Wurlitzer, Rudolph
1938?- .... **CLC 2, 4, 15**
See also CA 85-88

Wylie (Benét), Elinor (Morton Hoyt)
1885-1928 .... **TCLC 8**
See also CA 105
See also DLB 9

Wyndham, John 1903-1969 .... **CLC 19**
See also Harris, John (Wyndham Parkes Lucas) Beynon

Wyss, Johann David
1743-1818 .... **NCLC 10**
See also SATA 27, 29

Yanovsky, Vassily S(emenovich)
1906- .... **CLC 2, 18**
See also CA 97-100

Yates, Richard 1926- .... **CLC 7, 8, 23**
See also CANR 10
See also CA 5-8R
See also DLB 2
See also DLB-Y 81

Yeats, William Butler
1865-1939 .... **TCLC 1, 11, 18**
See also CANR 10
See also CA 104
See also DLB 10, 19

Yehoshua, Abraham B.
1936- .... **CLC 13, 31**
See also CA 33-36R

Yep, Laurence (Michael) 1948- ..... **CLC 35**
See also CLR 3
See also CANR 1
See also CA 49-52
See also SATA 7

Yerby, Frank G(arvin)
1916- .... **CLC 1, 7, 22**
See also CA 9-12R

Yevtushenko, Yevgeny (Aleksandrovich)
1933- .... **CLC 1, 3, 13, 26**
See also CA 81-84

Yglesias, Helen 1915- .... **CLC 7, 22**
See also CA 37-40R

Yorke, Henry Vincent 1905-1974
See Green, Henry
See also CA 85-88
See also obituary CA 49-52

Young, Al 1939- .... **CLC 19**
See also CA 29-32R
See also DLB 33

Young, Andrew 1885-1971 .... **CLC 5**
See also CANR 7
See also CA 5-8R

Young, Neil 1945- .... **CLC 17**
See also CA 110

Yourcenar, Marguerite 1913- ...... **CLC 19**
See also CA 69-72

Yurick, Sol 1925- .... **CLC 6**
See also CA 13-16R

Zamyatin, Yevgeny Ivanovich
1884-1937 .... **TCLC 8**
See also CA 105

Zangwill, Israel 1864-1926 .... **TCLC 16**
See also CA 109
See also DLB 10

Zappa, Francis Vincent, Jr. 1940-
See Zappa, Frank
See also CA 108

Zappa, Frank 1940- .... **CLC 17**
See also Zappa, Francis Vincent, Jr.

Zaturenska, Marya
1902-1982 .... **CLC 6, 11**
See also CA 13-16R
See also obituary CA 105

Zelazny, Roger 1937- .... **CLC 21**
See also CA 21-24R
See also SATA 39
See also DLB 8

Zhdanov, Andrei A(lexandrovich)
1896-1948 .... **TCLC 18**

Zimmerman, Robert 1941-
See Dylan, Bob

Zindel, Paul 1936- .... **CLC 6, 26**
See also CLR 3
See also CA 73-76
See also SATA 16
See also DLB 7

Zinoviev, Alexander 1922- .... **CLC 19**

Zola, Émile 1840-1902 .... **TCLC 1, 6**
See also CA 104

Zorrilla y Moral, José
1817-1893 .... **NCLC 6**

Zoshchenko, Mikhail (Mikhailovich)
1895-1958 .... **TCLC 15**
See also CA 115

Zuckmayer, Carl 1896-1977 .... **CLC 18**
See also CA 69-72

Zukofsky, Louis
1904-1978 .... **CLC 1, 2, 4, 7, 11, 18**
See also CA 9-12R
See also obituary CA 77-80
See also DLB 5

Zweig, Paul 1935-1984 .... **CLC 34**
See also CA 85-88
See also obituary CA 113

Zweig, Stefan 1881-1942 .... **TCLC 17**
See also CA 112

Cumulative Index to Nationalities

Cumulative Index to Critics

Critic Index

Critic Index

Critic Index

Critic Index

Critic Index

Critic Index